Hellenic Studies 37

HIPPOTA NESTOR

Other Titles in the Hellenic Studies Series

http://chs.harvard.edu

HIPPOTA NESTOR

DOUGLAS FRAME

CENTER FOR HELLENIC STUDIES
Trustees for Harvard University
Washington, DC
Distributed by Harvard University Press
Cambridge, Massachusetts, and London, England
2009

Hippota Nestor
  by Douglas Frame
Copyright © 2009 Center for Hellenic Studies, Trustees for Harvard University
All Rights Reserved.
Published by Center for Hellenic Studies, Trustees for Harvard University,
  Washington, DC
Distributed by Harvard University Press, Cambridge, Massachusetts,
  and London, England
Production: Nancy Kotary
Cover Design and Illustration: Joni Godlove

EDITORIAL TEAM:
Senior Advisers: W. Robert Connor, Gloria Ferrari Pinney, Albert Henrichs,
  James O'Donnell, Bernd Seidensticker
Editorial Board: Gregory Nagy (Editor-in-Chief), Christopher Blackwell,
  Casey Dué (Executive Editor), Mary Ebbott (Executive Editor),
  Scott Johnston, Olga Levaniouk, Anne Mahoney, Leonard Muellner
Production Manager for Publications: Jill Curry Robbins
Web Producer: Mark Tomasko

Fourth corrected printing, December 2014.

LIBRARY OF CONGRESS CATALOGING-IN-PUBLICATION DATA

Frame, Douglas, 1942–
Hippota Nestor / by Douglas Frame.
    p. cm. -- (Hellenic studies ; 37)
  Includes bibliographical references and indexes.
  ISBN 978-0-674-03290-3
  1. Homer--Characters--Nestor. 2. Epic poetry, Greek--History and criticism.
    3. Trojan War--Literature and the war. 4. Nestor (Greek mythology) 5.
    Homer. Odyssey. 6. Homer. Iliad. I. Title.
  PA4037.F5685 2009
  883'.01--dc20
                        2009035103

To the memory of John H. Finley, Jr.,
an inspiring teacher and friend

τοῦ καὶ ἀπὸ γλώσσης μέλιτος γλυκίων ῥέεν αὐδή

CONTENTS

Contents

Acknowledgments

This study has been supported by a number of sources in the course of its progress. Since 2000 I have had the good fortune to work for the Center for Hellenic Studies, and one of the benefits of this has been to bring to a close work that began several decades earlier. Before the CHS the New York Public Library was a crucial resource for many years, and before that a Mellon Fellowship at Columbia University gave rise to what is now Part 5 of the study. The heart of the study goes back a decade earlier, to the early 1970s, when a leave from Wellesley College and a grant from the National Endowment for the Humanities allowed me to follow up immediately on an unexpected insight into a problem that had concerned me previously, and to work out my basic argument. I could not foresee then how long it would take to elaborate this argument satisfactorily.

Among those who have read all or parts of this study I wish to thank in particular Anthony Snodgrass, who read an early draft of the entire study, and who responded generously and helpfully on many points. Gloria Ferrari also reacted to an early draft, and her reserve with regard to Part 3 is not out of place; there will be others who hesitate at that part of the argument, and I respect her position fully. I am grateful for advice, which I have sometimes followed and sometimes not, to several people who read some or all of Parts 1 and 2: Anna Bonifazi, Joel Christensen, Martine Cuypers, Casey Dué, Mary Ebbott, Peter Jackson, Olga Levaniouk, and Donna Wilson. To my old Homeric colleagues, Gregory Nagy and Leonard Muellner, I owe a great deal for their interest and support over the years. Their suggestions, and those of Mary Ebbott and Casey Dué, have improved my translations of Homeric passages. It has been a great pleasure to collaborate with all four in recent years.

I have had considerable help producing a simultaneous print and electronic publication. I wish to thank Emily Collinson, Christopher Dadian, Jeremy Lin, and Leonard Muellner in particular. I am grateful to Jill Curry Robbins for preparing the maps and figures, and to Erika Bainbridge and

Acknowledgments

Temple Wright for their support in the CHS library. Caitlin Frame, who helped with the manuscript at an early stage, has my lasting gratitude and affection. The many others who have contributed with information or insights along the way I cannot acknowledge by name, except in my own mind.

INTRODUCTION

Nestor, the subject of this book, figured in my earlier book, *The Myth of Return in Early Greek Epic*, which had largely to do with the Greek word *nóstos*, "return." The name Nestor contains the verbal root of *nóstos*, namely **nes-*, and a chapter of my earlier book was devoted to the Homeric figure. The present book builds on that chapter, and on a second chapter of the same book, which dealt with comparative evidence in Vedic Sanskrit. Vedic has a cognate of the Greek name *Néstōr* which goes to the heart of the Indo-European twin myth, and this cognate is relevant to Nestor as an epic figure. The cognate is the name *Nā́satyā*, which belongs to the twin gods of the Vedic pantheon. In my earlier work I did not pursue the consequences of this comparison between the names *Néstōr* and *Nā́satyā*, although I had become well aware of them, because I knew that the subject required a longer study. I now present that study, which is organized into five parts as described below.

In Part 1 the Greek-Vedic comparison in question is introduced in Chapter 1, and the evidence for each side of the comparison is laid out separately in Chapter 2, on Greek, and Chapter 3, on Vedic. Nestor's epithet *hippóta*, "the horseman," is part of the comparison, and this accounts for the book's title, *Hippota Nestor*, "the horseman Nestor."[1] The Vedic twins are also called "horsemen"; this is the meaning of their second and more common name, *Aśvínā*. There is thus a double comparison between the *Aśvínā Nā́satyā* in Vedic and *hippóta Néstōr* in Greek. To interpret this double comparison, and to reconstruct Nestor's myth, the Greek Dioskouroi are also taken into account. The basic myth of this paradigmatic pair of Indo-European twins completes the picture for both Vedic and Greek.

---

1 Nestor's full Homeric title is *Gerḗnios hippóta Néstōr*, "the Gerenian horseman Nestor," which occurs twenty-one times in the *Iliad* and ten times in the *Odyssey*. The phrase *hippóta Néstōr* by itself occurs only once, in *Iliad* 9.52. For the epithet *Gerḗnios*, the meaning of which is not certain, see n1.6 and n4.189 below.

In Part 2 Nestor's Homeric role is interpreted in the light of his reconstructed myth. Nestor's myth is a variant of the Indo-European twin myth, and it is the key to his role in both the *Iliad* and the *Odyssey*. But his myth is never fully disclosed in the *Iliad* and the *Odyssey*; instead it is presented ironically, and this irony must be understood in order to uncover his myth. In the *Iliad* two of Nestor's stories about his youth concern his twin myth, and both occur in the context of the story of Patroclus. Nestor tells the first of these stories to Patroclus himself in *Iliad* 11, when he instigates Patroclus to take Achilles' place in battle; he tells the second story in *Iliad* 23, when Patroclus has died as a result of Nestor's advice, and Nestor accepts an honorary prize from Achilles at Patroclus's funeral. Chapters 4 and 5 are devoted to these two pivotal stories in the *Iliad*. Chapters 6 and 7 are concerned with Nestor's role in the *Odyssey*. In Chapter 6 Nestor's role in the *nóstos* of Odysseus is examined, and Nestor's own account, in *Odyssey* 3, of his last parting from Odysseus is shown to be highly ironical; a significant foreshadowing of what took place on that fateful occasion is also seen to exist in an episode in *Iliad* 8. The Phaeacians are the subject of Chapter 7, in which Alcinous, the Phaeacian king, is the main focus. From every significant point of view Alcinous is cast as a second Nestor, deliberately duplicating the Pylian king; the two have not only the same twin myth, but also genealogies which mirror each other point for point. When Odysseus tells the story of his adventures to his Phaeacian audience, his account includes a catalogue of heroines whom he met in the underworld. This catalogue, in *Odyssey* 11, contains Nestor's genealogy, and the focus of the catalogue can be shown to be Nestor's twin myth. Internal and external evidence shows that there were two different versions of the catalogue at different stages in Homeric tradition. Distinguishing an earlier Ionian version from a later Athenian version allows Nestor's twin myth to stand out clearly and distinctly in the earlier Ionian version. In *Odyssey* 11 Alcinous listens to this catalogue as it is delivered, and the underlying issue in the episode is his relationship to Nestor; Nestor's name means "homebringer," but it is Alcinous, and not Nestor, who brings Odysseus home.

In Part 3 the Phaeacians are investigated further. In Chapter 8 Arete and Nausicaa, the Phaeacian queen and princess, are both viewed in relation to the goddess Athena, who on the one hand is the Olympian daughter of Zeus, and on the other hand is the ancient city goddess of Athens. A case is made that Nausicaa evokes the Olympian daughter of Zeus, and that Arete evokes an earlier form of the city goddess of Athens than has otherwise been preserved. In Chapter 9 I reconstruct forward from this ancient form of the city goddess of Athens, posited on the basis of the Phaeacian queen, to Athena's known historical cult. The key issue is the primitive relationship of the city goddess of Athens to the figure Erechtheus, a relationship that is evoked in a well-known passage of *Odyssey* 7. A case is made that the relationship presupposed by *Odyssey* 7 was radically altered later, in the time of Solon, when both Erechtheus and the city goddess Athena were transformed into their known historical forms. I argue that the Athenian festival of the Skira was the context in which these transformations were realized.

Part 4 considers Nestor's relevance to a key question in Homeric studies: the circumstances of the composition of the Homeric poems. The view that the poems were composed in Ionia in the late eighth and early seventh centuries BC is accepted, and the circumstances are pursued. The key to these circumstances is the tradition that Nestor was one of twelve sons of Neleus; this tradition was an alternative to Nestor's twin myth, and in my view it arose as a reflection of the Ionian dodecapolis, a well-defined union of twelve cities. Neleus, the founder of Pylos, was the clan ancestor of the kings of Miletus, and I argue that the Neleids of Miletus were instrumental in the development of the Ionian dodecapolis. The myth of Neleus's twelve sons, representing the dodecapolis in a symbolic way, was paralleled by another similar myth, which pretended to historicity as well, namely the myth of Kodrid founders. In this myth Miletus was founded from Athens by a second Neleus, a descendant of Pylian Neleus, and a son of the Athenian king Kodros. This myth too was extended from Miletus to other cities of the dodecapolis, where a Kodrid founder became the mark of Panionic status. I argue that in the Homeric poems the Ionians of the dodecapolis are represented by the Phaeacians, whose king and queen, Alcinous and Arete, are linked with Pylos and Athens through their relationships to Nestor and Athena respectively. The Phaeacians thus embody the two stages of the Neleids' past, as this past was symbolically extended to other Panionians. The Phaeacians, who are Odysseus's audience when he tells his adventures in the *Odyssey*, represent the Homeric audience, and thus by implication the Homeric audience was Panionic; the festival of the Panionia, celebrated by the cites of the dodecapolis, is therefore the likely context in which the Homeric poems were expanded to the form in which we have them. An analysis of the poems' basic structure reveals that there are twelve units of four books each in the two poems taken together, and this structure would be well accounted for by the poems' formation at a twelve-city festival. The early history of this festival at Panionion on Cape Mycale is investigated on the basis of literary and archaeological evidence. An argument is made that the last Neleid king of Miletus, a figure named Leodamas, was closely associated with the creation

of the Homeric poems. In the organization of Part 4, Chapter 10 deals with
the Kodrid myth, both as it is embodied in the Phaeacians in the *Odyssey*, and
as it occurred historically in the cities of the Ionian dodecapolis. Chapter 11
then focuses on the Panionia as the likely occasion for the composition of the
Iliad and the *Odyssey*.

Part 5 returns to the story that Nestor tells Patroclus in *Iliad* 11, as
previously interpreted in Part 2. The gist of this story is that Nestor in his
youth took the place of his warrior brother Periklymenos, who had died in
battle, and became the champion of Pylos himself, and that he thereby won
the title *hippóta*, "the horseman." This is Nestor's variant of the twin myth,
and the myth, as Nestor tells it in the *Iliad*, is relevant to Patroclus, who at
Nestor's urging will take Achilles' place in battle. Nestor's story, as a para-
digm for Patroclus, is simple and schematic, but there were two versions of
this story, and our text of *Iliad* 11 contains the more complicated version.
This fact, which is the starting point for Chapter 12, was recognized by the
Swiss scholar Cantieni, who showed that passages of detailed geography in
Nestor's story were added secondarily to it, and need only be removed to
recover the simpler earlier version. In support of this conclusion, with which
my analysis of Nestor's twin myth is in complete agreement, an indirect
argument is developed that has to do with the location of Nestor's city Pylos.
In the earlier version of Nestor's story in Iliad 11 the location of Pylos was
vague and unrealistic, but in the passages of detailed geography in this story
Pylos is in a very definite place, namely in the historical region of Triphylia.
I argue that these passages were not added until the fifth century BC, under
circumstances that evoked the heroic conflict in Nestor's story between
the cities of Pylos and Elis. What in particular may have motivated this late
editorial intervention makes an interesting story in itself, and it is the last
subject considered in the book, in Chapter 14. But there is an earlier stage to
the argument. In Chapter 13 a case is made that when the Pythian section of
the *Homeric Hymn to Apollo* was composed, in the late seventh or early sixth
century BC, not long before the First Sacred War, the passages of detailed
geography in Nestor's story did not yet exist. The reason for this is that the
Hymn to Apollo locates Pylos in Elis, north of Triphylia, and it does so on the
basis of the Homeric text. The *Hymn to Apollo* reinterprets the Homeric text in
a minimalist way to achieve its end, but it could not have done so if Nestor's
story in *Iliad* 11 contained massive evidence for Triphylia as the location of
Nestor's city. Why the *Hymn to Apollo* wished to locate Nestor's city in Elis is
a separate question, which is also addressed; the answer, it is argued, is that
the Pythian section of the *Hymn to Apollo* reflects Spartan interests after the

Second Messenian War, when Pylians still surviving in Messenia were finally driven from the Peloponnesus. The Homeric text was vague enough as to the location of Nestor's city for Spartans to claim that when the coast of Messenia was cleared of its inhabitants this had nothing to do with Nestor's Homeric city; Nestor's famous city was not in Messenia, but in Elis, according to the Spartan reinterpretation of the Homeric text.

As is evident from the summary above, the argumentation in this study is complex, and the subject matter involves new interpretations in a number of areas. In the main body of the text I have tried to limit discussions to what is essential for the argument to proceed, so that it is not weighed down by secondary matters. As a result the footnotes carry a larger burden than would otherwise have been the case. When discussions in the footnotes also became too complex, I have relegated part of the discussion to a series of Endnotes. I would like to think that the entire study can be read as presented, with secondary material supporting primary material, and tertiary material supporting secondary material, and, indeed, I have worked to make it so. On the other hand I do not think that it is advisable to try to take everything on board at once. There is enough complexity in the main body of the text to deal with that alone at first; that is where the *logos* of the study is to be found, and that is what matters in the first instance. It remains to say a word about the numbering of footnotes and Endnotes. The main divisions of the study are the five Parts described above, each of which was developed separately, and the footnotes and Endnotes are therefore numbered by Part. The same is true of the paragraph numbers in the main body of the text.

Part 1.

NESTOR'S INDO-EUROPEAN BACKGROUND

Chapter 1.

THE PROBLEM

§1.1 There is a discrepancy between the *Iliad* and the *Odyssey* as to the number of sons that Nestor's father Neleus is said to have had: twelve sons in the *Iliad* versus three sons in the *Odyssey*. In the *Iliad* Nestor himself says that he was one of twelve sons of Neleus when he tells how the other eleven sons all perished in Heracles' attack on Pylos, leaving Nestor alone to deal with Pylos's hostile neighbors (*Iliad* 11.689–693):

> ὡς ἡμεῖς παῦροι κεκακωμένοι ἐν Πύλῳ ἦμεν·
> ἐλθὼν γάρ ῥ' ἐκάκωσε βίη Ἡρακληείη
> τῶν προτέρων ἐτέων, κατὰ δ' ἔκταθεν ὅσσοι ἄριστοι·
> δώδεκα γὰρ Νηλῆος ἀμύμονος υἱέες ἦμεν·
> τῶν οἶος λιπόμην, οἱ δ' ἄλλοι πάντες ὄλοντο.

> Few of us were left in Pylos and we were badly off,
> for mighty Heracles had come and hurt us badly
> in earlier years; all the best men had been killed.
> Twelve sons of faultless Neleus we had been,
> but of those only I was left; the others had all perished.

In the *Odyssey* Nestor's mother Chloris, whom Odysseus meets in the underworld, is said to have borne Neleus three sons, Nestor, Chromios, and Periklymenos, and also a daughter Pero (*Odyssey* 11.285–287):

> ἡ δὲ Πύλου βασίλευε, τέκεν δέ οἱ ἀγλαὰ τέκνα,
> Νέστορά τε Χρομίον τε Περικλύμενόν τ' ἀγέρωχον.
> τοῖσι δ' ἐπ' ἰφθίμην Πηρὼ τέκε, θαῦμα βροτοῖσι.

She reigned over Pylos and bore him splendid children,
Nestor and Chromios and proud Periklymenos.
After them she bore steadfast Pero, a wonder to mortals.

§1.2 The discrepancy between the twelve sons of Neleus in the *Iliad*
and the three sons of Chloris and Neleus in the *Odyssey* provided an argu-
ment for the ancient *khōrízontes*, "separatists," who held that the *Iliad* and the
Odyssey were by different poets.[1] The irony of this is that Nestor himself is to
a remarkable extent the same figure in both poems; he thus weighs far more
heavily for the opposite view, that the two poems are related.[2] But the fact

---

1 Scholia to *Iliad* 11.692.
2 An example of this is the motif of Nestor's three-generation lifespan, which occurs in both
   poems. In the *Iliad* this motif occurs as soon as Nestor is introduced, when he intervenes in
   the quarrel between Achilles and Agamemnon (*Iliad* 1.247–253):

   τοῖσι δὲ Νέστωρ
   ἡδυεπὴς ἀνόρουσε λιγὺς Πυλίων ἀγορητής,
   τοῦ καὶ ἀπὸ γλώσσης μέλιτος γλυκίων ῥέεν αὐδή·
   τῷ δ' ἤδη δύο μὲν γενεαὶ μερόπων ἀνθρώπων
   ἐφθίαθ', οἳ οἱ πρόσθεν ἅμα τράφεν ἠδ' ἐγένοντο
   ἐν Πύλῳ ἠγαθέῃ, μετὰ δὲ τριτάτοισιν ἄνασσεν·
   ὅ σφιν ἐὺ φρονέων ἀγορήσατο καὶ μετέειπεν.

         Nestor stood up between them,
   the sweet-spoken clear-voiced speaker of the Pylians,
   whose voice flowed from his tongue sweeter than honey.
   For him two generations of mortal men had already
   perished, those who were born and raised with him earlier
   in holy Pylos, and he ruled among the third generation;
   being well disposed to them he spoke in the assembly and addressed them.

   In the *Odyssey* the motif is not used to introduce Nestor at his first appearance, but is
   uttered at a later point by Telemachus, who proposes to Athena/Mentor to ask Nestor
   about a new subject (*Odyssey* 3.243–246):

   νῦν δ' ἐθέλω ἔπος ἄλλο μεταλλῆσαι καὶ ἐρέσθαι
   Νέστορ', ἐπεὶ περίοιδε δίκας ἠδὲ φρόνιν ἄλλων·
   τρὶς γὰρ δή μίν φασιν ἀνάξασθαι γένε' ἀνδρῶν,
   ὥς τέ μοι ἀθάνατος ἰνδάλλεται εἰσοράασθαι.

   But now I wish to inquire and ask about another story
   from Nestor, since he beyond others knows justice and wisdom;
   for they say that he has ruled during three generations of men,
   and so to me he seems like an immortal when I look at him.

   The motif is the same in the two poems, but what makes the poems seem related is not
   only this, but also the way in which the motif is deployed in the *Odyssey*. Nestor does not
   need to be reintroduced in the *Odyssey* because he has already been introduced in the *Iliad*,

remains that the *Iliad* and the *Odyssey* differ on a point that is not at all trivial. The separatists had good reason to draw attention to the different number of Neleus's sons in the *Iliad* and the *Odyssey*, and the discrepancy has not yet been satisfactorily explained.[3]

§1.3 To explain the discrepancy the key point to recognize is that, however many brothers Nestor was said to have had, only one of them had a real epic tradition, namely Periklymenos; the other sons of Neleus, whether ten in the *Iliad* or one in the *Odyssey*, are shadows by comparison with Nestor and Periklymenos, the two who alone count. Periklymenos, who is named in *Odyssey* 11 (his only Homeric occurrence), was the great opponent of Heracles when Pylos was sacked. While he is not named in *Iliad* 11, the story of Heracles' sack centered on him, as we know from Hesiod and later sources. In Hesiod Periklymenos is more than a great warrior; he is a shape-shifter who uses his exotic skill to frustrate Heracles until finally Athena points him out in the form of a bee and Heracles shoots him.[4] We do not know whether Periklymenos had the same exotic ability in Homeric tradition or was perhaps

---

and that introduction is now assumed. Thus the motif of his three-generation lifespan is presented almost parenthetically by another figure, who implies that the motif is well known by using the word *phasín*, "they say"; to the Homeric audience, I suggest, the word *phasín* would bring to mind the poet's own authoritative statement in the *Iliad*. Regarding the relationship between the two poems more generally, it is the *Odyssey's* awareness of the *Iliad*, as in the present case, that is to me of primary significance. But the *Odyssey* rarely shows its awareness of the *Iliad* in such a positive way; it does so more tellingly in a negative way, by not repeating episodes from the *Iliad* in its reminiscences of the Trojan war (this complementary distribution of thematic material was observed by D. B. Monro and is aptly referred to as "Monro's Law"). The implication of such a complementary distribution of thematic material is that the *Iliad* and the *Odyssey* were meant to be experienced together as one composite, unified work. What this means for the genesis of the two poems is a question to which I will return later in this study. The issue, however, is not only whether the *Odyssey* is aware of the *Iliad*, but whether the *Iliad* is also aware of the *Odyssey*. If the latter proposition can be demonstrated it has clear implications for the genesis of the two poems.

3 Aristarchus (scholia to *Iliad* 11.692) argued that, just as Priam is said to have had nineteen of his fifty sons "from one womb" and the rest by other women (*Iliad* 24.495–497), a wife other than Chloris could have borne Neleus nine more sons. But the two cases are different. In order to have fifty sons Priam had to have them by more than one woman, whereas Neleus did not have to have more than one wife to have his twelve sons. More importantly, there was no tradition for any wife of Neleus but Chloris as far as we know, and as far as Aristarchus knew. The uncertainty was not about the mother of Neleus's sons, but their number.

4 Hesiod fr. 33 MW; cf. "Apollodorus" 1.9.9.

a more conventional warrior.[5] What the Hesiodic fragments do make clear, however, is that Periklymenos alone stood in Heracles' way in his attack on Pylos, for the other sons of Neleus fell as one when Periklymenos was slain, only Nestor escaping this fate; the point is clear despite the fragmentary nature of the text (Hesiod fr. 35.2–9 MW):

ὄφρα μὲν οὖν ἔζ]ωε Περικλύ[μ]ενος θε[ο]ειδής,
οὐκ ἐδύναντο Πύ]λον πραθέειν μάλα περ μεμαῶτες·
ἀλλ' ὅτε δὴ θανάτο]ιο Π[ε]ρικλύμενον λάβε μοῖρα,
ἐξαλάπαξε Πύλοιο πόλιν Διὸς ἄ[λ]κιμο[ς] υἱός,
κτεῖνε δὲ Νηλῆος ταλα]σίφρονος υἱέας ἐσθλούς,
ἕνδεκα, δωδέκατος δὲ Γερ]ήνιος ἱππότα Νέστωρ
ξεῖνος ἐὼν ἐτύχησε παρ' ἱ]πποδάμοισι Γερηνοῖς·
οὕτω δ' ἐξέφυγεν θάνατο]ν καὶ κῆ[ρ]α μέλαιναν.

While godlike Periklymenos still lived,
they could not destroy Pylos, eager though they were.
But when the destiny of death took Periklymenos,
the mighty son of Zeus sacked the city of Pylos
and killed stout-hearted Neleus's brave sons,
eleven of them, but the twelfth, the Gerenian horseman Nestor,
happened to be a guest among the horse-breaking Gerenians;
and so he escaped death and black doom.[6]

---

5 The battle with Heracles is Periklymenos's only distinctive myth in extant sources. He was one of the Argonauts according to Pindar, who addresses him with a conventional warrior's epithet in this context (*Periklúmen' eurubía*, "Periklymenos, with far-reaching might," *Pythian* 4.175).

6 Hesiod explains Nestor's survival of Heracles' attack by his timely absence from Pylos "among the horsebreaking Gerenians" (*par' hippodámoisi Gerēnoîs*, fr. 35.8 MW). This is evidently a Hesiodic invention based on Nestor's Homeric epithet "the Gerenian horseman" (*Gerēnios hippóta*); Gerenians are otherwise unknown in early sources. According to later sources a town of Gerenia bordered Phērai on the Messenian Gulf (Strabo 8.4.4, Pausanias 3.26.8; cf. Kiechle 1960:61); here there was a temple of Asklepios (Strabo 8.4.4) and the Homeric hero Makhaon, a son of Asklepios (Pausanias 3.26.9, 4.3.9), and also a tomb of Makhaon (Pausanias 3.26.9, 4.3.2). According to Pausanias 3.26.8 Gerenia was once the Homeric town of Enope (*Iliad* 9.150, 292), a view also reported by Strabo 8.4.5. It seems to have been well recognized that the town of Gerenia was not of Homeric vintage but a latter-day invention (for Makhaon's presence in Gerenia cf. n2.20 below). What the real meaning of Nestor's Homeric epithet *Gerēnios* was we do not know (but see n4.189 for a strong possibility).

§1.4 Hesiod names all twelve sons of Neleus in typical catalogue fashion when Chloris, their mother, is first introduced in the *Catalogue of Women*. Only Periklymenos, who is named last, receives individual attention. His skill as a shape-shifter and his death at the hands of Heracles are the subject of the passage that follows his name. Although the Hesiodic list is fragmentary, it has been restored from "Apollodorus" 1.9.9, containing a complete list of Neleus's sons; "Apollodorus's" source was doubtless this very passage of Hesiod (Hesiod fr. 33a.8–15 MW):

ἣ δέ οἱ ἐν μ]εγάροισιν ἐγείνατο φαίδιμα τέκ[να,

Εὐαγόρην τ]ε καὶ Ἀντιμένην καὶ Ἀλάστορα [δῖον

Ταῦρόν τ' Ἀσ]τέριόν τε Πυλάονά τε μεγάθυμ[ον

Δηίμαχόν τε] καὶ Εὐρύβιον κλειτόν τ' Ἐπίλαον

Νέστορά τε Χ]ρομίον τε Περικλύμενόν τ' ἀγέρωχον,

ὄλβιον, ὧι πόρε δῶρα Ποσειδάων ἐνοσίχθων

παντοῖ', ἄλλοτε μὲν γὰρ ἐν ὀρνίθεσσι φάνεσκεν

αἰετός....

And she bore him splendid children in his halls,
Euagoras and Antimenes and shining Alastor
and Tauros and Asterios and great-hearted Pylaon
and Deïmakhos and Eurybios and famed Epilaos
and Nestor and Chromios and proud Periklymenos,
the fortunate one, to whom Poseidon the earthshaker gave gifts
of all sorts, for sometimes among birds he took shape
as an eagle....

The restored line that ends the Hesiodic list, containing the names Nestor, Chromios, and Periklymenos, is identical with *Odyssey* 11.286, and evidently depends on it. The three previous lines, containing nine further names, were most likely a Hesiodic invention. The third of these three lines, containing the names Deimakhos, Eurybios, and Epilaos, seems to have been used in another Hesiodic catalogue for three of the children of Lysidike, a daughter of Pelops:[7] the three names thus have a generic rather than a specific quality. Of the six names in the first two lines of the catalogue Alastor and Pylaon are

---

7 Hesiod fr. 193.15 MW (the beginning and the end of the line have been lost): Δηΐμαχόν] τε καὶ Εὐρύβιον κλειτόν τ' Ἐ[πίλαον, "Deïmakhos] and Eurybios and famed E[pilaos."

aptly chosen for sons of Neleus, Pylaon because it evokes the city of Pylos, and Alastor because one of Nestor's Pylian captains in *Iliad* 4.295 has this name. But apart from Nestor and Periklymenos none of the sons of Neleus is anything more than a name, and in Homer only Chromios among the other ten sons has even a name. His name, moreover, seems almost deliberately chosen to show the lack of substance of its bearer. Six different figures in Homer apart from Nestor's brother are called Chromios, and they too are all little more than a name, occurring only in catalogues or pairs of names.[8] Oddly enough, in "Apollodorus" 1.9.9, which seems to contain Hesiod's list of the twelve sons of Neleus, Chromios alone of the twelve sons does not occur; his name has been replaced by an equimetrical Phrasios. Since there seems to be no doubt about the name Chromios in the Hesiodic fragment,[9] the names Chromios and Phrasios must have been variants in Hesiodic tradition. One can only speculate that the name Chromios, despite its Homeric authority, was felt to be colorless and was therefore rivaled by the more expressive name Phrasios.[10] If Homeric authority for the name Chromios was disregarded in this way, the name itself looks tenuous at best. We return to the point that apart from Nestor and Periklymenos none of the sons of Neleus had a real tradition or even a fixed name. A completely different list of the twelve sons

---

8 All six are in the *Iliad*, five of them Trojans or Trojan allies, to wit: one of two sons of Priam slain on a single chariot by Diomedes (5.160); one of seven Lycians slain by Odysseus (5.677); one of nine Trojans shot by Teucer (8.275); one of ten Mysian allies urged on by Hector (17.218); one of two warriors accompanying Hector and Aeneas in a futile attempt to capture Achilles' horses (17.494 and 534). The remaining figure named Chromios is one of five Pylians around whom Nestor arranges his forces (4.295). The fact that this figure is a Pylian like the son of Neleus in *Odyssey* 11.286 is interesting, but it hardly gives greater subtance to the son of Neleus. Indeed the line naming Chromios as one of Nestor's captains is itself formulaic; compare the line in question, 4.295: ἀμφὶ μέγαν Πελάγοντα Ἀλάστορά τε Χρομίον τε, "around great Pelagon and Alastor and Chromios," with 5.677, naming three of seven Lycians slain by Odysseus: ἔνθ' ὅ γε Κοίρανον εἶλεν Ἀλάστορά τε Χρομίον τε, "then he slew Koiranos and Alastor and Chromios." Two of the Iliadic lines with the name Chromios are very close in form to *Odyssey* 11.286, namely 8.275: Δαίτορά τε Χρομίον τε καὶ ἀντίθεον Λυκοφόντην, "Daitor and Chromios and godlike Lykophontes," and 17.218: Φόρκυν τε Χρομίον τε καὶ Ἔννομον οἰωνιστήν, "Phorkys and Chromios and the augur Ennomos." A comparison of these lines with *Odyssey* 11.286: Νέστορά τε Χρομίον τε Περικλύμενόν τ' ἀγέρωχον, "Nestor and Chromios and proud Periklymenos," shows how easily the name Chromios might have suggested itself in all three lines.
9 The editors of the fragment indicate that only the name's initial letter is missing.
10 The name *Phrásios*, derived from the verb *phrázō*, "point out, advise," is appropriate to the counselor Nestor, hence to a supposed brother.

of Neleus is in fact found in the scholia to *Iliad* 11.692: the only names that this list has in common with the Hesiodic list are Nestor and Periklymenos.[11]

§1.5 The main thesis that I wish to propose and develop in the study to follow is that Nestor's origins are to be found not in Homeric epic, nor in Bronze Age Pylos, nor anywhere else in Greek tradition, but earlier, in the Indo-European twin myth. My reason for thinking this is a comparison between Nestor and the twin gods of the *Rig-Veda* based on Nestor's name and one of the two names of the Vedic twins. This name is *Nā́satyā*, and I studied it in full in my previous work, *The Myth of Return in Early Greek Epic*.[12] I studied the name *Néstōr* in the same work, and it might be asked why there should be more to say about either name now. Here I need to say something about the chronology of my earlier work, which began as a doctoral dissertation,[13] but incorporated a new discussion of the Vedic twins when it was published. Although my revised study of the Vedic twins had important implications for Nestor, I was not able to consider them in the framework of my original study. It is for that reason that I return to the question now.

§1.6 The comparison with the Vedic twins involves not just Nestor's name, but also his epithet *hippóta*, "the horseman." The Vedic twins are also called "horsemen," *Aśvínā*, and it is their two names together, *Aśvínā Nā́satyā*, that are a comparison for *hippóta Néstōr*. I was struck by this double comparison in my original study of the Vedic twins, but I did not see how it could be relevant to the problem of Nestor's mythic origins.[14] The difference between a pair of twins and a solitary figure seemed to outweigh any etymological connection between them. I also pointed out that in both parts of the comparison there are common roots but differences of word formation. In the two words for "horseman," the common root is Indo-European **ekwos*, "horse," giving Greek *híppos* and Sanskrit *aśva-*, but the nouns *hippóta* and *Aśvínā* are formed differently: *hippóta* is formed with an exclusively Greek

---

11 The origin of this list is not known. Three of the twelve names are non-Homeric: *Lusímakhos*, *Lusíppos*, and *Agēsílaos* (the last must have had the form *Agēsíleōs* if it occurred in a hexameter source, but this is uncertain). The other seven names, in addition to Nestor and Periklymenos, are *Peisístratos*, *Álkimos*, *Hupsḗnōr*, *Pulaiménēs*, *Hippokóōn*, *Peisḗnōr*, *Hippólokhos*. For the sake of comparison Hesiod's ten names are again: *Euagórēs*, *Antiménēs*, *Alástōr*, *Taûros*, *Astérios*, *Puláōn*, *Dēḯmakhos*, *Eurúbios*, *Epílaos*, *Khrómios*. Cantieni 1942:58 aptly calls the ten brothers besides Nestor and Periklymenos "Füllfiguren," whose names accordingly vary.
12 Frame 1978:134–152.
13 Frame 1971.
14 Frame 1971:159–160.

suffix and *Aśvin-* is formed with a highly characteristic Sanskrit suffix.[15] In the names *Néstōr* and *Nā́satyā* the common element is Indo-European **nes-*, a verbal root whose meaning was the focus of my earlier study. I will return to this root shortly, and also to the different processes of word formation in the two names. But it is clear from the start that *Néstōr*, with the agent suffix *-tōr*, was formed differently from *Nā́satyā*.

§1.7 What changed my mind about the significance of the etymological comparison was the work of the Swedish scholar Stig Wikander on distinctions between the two Vedic twins as reflected in Sanskrit epic.[16] It became clear to me after reading Wikander's study that the twins' two names, *Aśvínā* and *Nā́satyā*, each originally designated a different twin, and the significance of this for Nestor struck me immediately: the "horseman Nestor" combines the characteristics of both twins, and this is the essence of his myth. Nestor becomes a "horseman" in order to take the place of a twin brother. This is the point of the story that Nestor tells Patroclus in *Iliad* 11, and Periklymenos is thus an essential part of this story. Nestor and Periklymenos are twin figures, but they are twins who separate.

§1.8 This is the main thesis of the study to follow, and it will require the full length of the study to make the case for it. One of the most intriguing aspects of Nestor's myth, which will emerge more and more clearly as I proceed, and which for now I can simply state, is that his myth, though

---

15 *Hippóta* contains the specifically Greek suffix *-tēs* (< *-tās*); the nominative in *-ta*, found in this and a few other Homeric epithets of gods and heroes (*mētíeta Zeús*, "deviser Zeus," *nephelēgeréta Zeús*, "cloud-gatherer Zeus," etc.), is perhaps a frozen vocative (Risch 1954, 1974:37); for various attempts to explain the *-ta* suffix as an original nominative see the convenient summary and further analysis in Moreschini 1984, esp. 341–342. In Risch's view the noun *hippóta* may be old but need not be identical with Latin *eques, -itis*; in general Risch considers denominatives in *-tēs* (like *hippóta*) to be secondary to deverbatives, hence relatively recent (Risch 1974:35). Sanskrit *aśvín-* is formed with the suffix *-in-*, which in this zero-grade form is found widely in Sanskrit and less widely in Avestan, but seems not to occur with any certainty outside of Indo-Iranian (cf. Wackernagel-Debrunner 1957:349–350); elsewhere the full-grade and lengthened-grade of the suffix are found (Latin *seneciō*, Greek *malakíōn*, etc.). Sanskrit denominatives formed with *-in-* (like *aśvín-* from *áśva-*) are considered primary to deverbatives by Wackernagel-Debrunner 1957:348; the meaning of the suffix in denominatives is "provided with, possessed of," as in *parṇín-*, "provided with wings, winged," *rathín-*, "provided with a chariot, chariot-possessing," and *aśvín-*, "provided with horses, horse-possessing" (see Wackernagel-Debrunner 1957:348).

16 Wikander 1957. I became aware of Wikander's work in 1973 by reading Dumézil 1968. My own previous work led me to modify Wikander's study in one crucial point (see §1.50–§1.54 and n1.143 below). I could only suggest the importance of Wikander's work for Nestor in a footnote at the end of my study of the Vedic twins (Frame 1978:152n72).

known to the Homeric poets, was never fully divulged by them. One element or another of the myth was always withheld. Thus in *Iliad* 11, where Periklymenos is an essential part of the story, Periklymenos is not named. Nestor speaks instead of the twelve sons of Neleus. It was in fact the rival tradition of the twelve sons of Neleus that accounts for the twin myth's always remaining partially hidden. Nestor was not just one of two brothers, however deep the roots for this tradition went; he was also one of twelve. But then what accounts for the tradition that he was one of twelve? In comparison with the Indo-European twin myth, this tradition was very recent indeed if it had to do, as I will argue that it did, with the twelve cities of the Ionian dodecapolis. This idea, which was proposed by Georg Busolt more than a hundred years ago, and has since been repeated by others, has never been fully accepted, or even fully explained.[17] The key to this tradition, I believe, is the ruling family of Miletus, the Neleids, for only they claimed descent from Neleus, and only they had a name that meant "descendants of Neleus." Among Neleus's sons the ancestor claimed by the Neleids, significantly, was Periklymenos, one of the original pair of brothers.[18] If the twelve sons of Neleus represented the twelve cities of the dodecapolis, it is not because each of the cities claimed a different son as ancestor[19]—we have already seen that the twelve sons are not individuals but a group—but because the Neleids of Miletus extended their own origins to the entire dodecapolis, at least in terms of this myth. It must have been the Neleids themselves who promoted a new version of Neleus's offspring, in which there were not just two sons, but twelve. This in turn makes the Neleids prime movers in the creation of Panionism, and in the foundation of the Panionia, the common festival of the twelve cities. The actual origins of the Ionians were very diverse, as Herodotus in particular pointed out;[20] hence a common myth was needed to

17 Busolt 1885:220n1 = 1893:317n4; cf. Momigliano 1932:277; Lenschau 1944: 235, *RE* 'Iones' 1876; Càssola 1957:89.
18 Hellanicus *FGrHist* 323a F 23. See below for the Neleids of Miletus.
19 Momigliano (n1.17 above) thought that this was originally the case. Busolt's idea, which Busolt did not elaborate, was criticized as a "sehr vage Vermutung" by Toepffer 1889:237n2. It is interesting to note that Busolt, who in his second edition of 1893 reacted to Toepffer's criticism on other points, did not change his mind on this point (see n1.17 above). The idea that the twelve sons of Neleus represented the dodecapolis is undeniably vague, and it is a mistake to imagine that it was ever intended to be otherwise.
20 Herodotus 1.146.1. Sakellariou 1958 exhaustively investigates the Ionians' diverse origins as reflected in the traditions and institutions of the individual cities. Cf. also Vanschoonwinkel 1991:367–404 and n1.56 below.

unify them, and the Neleids seem to have provided one by giving twelve sons to their own ancestor Neleus.[21]

§1.9 We will return to the Neleids of Miletus, the formation of the Ionian dodecapolis, and the foundation of the Panionia, for all three have an important bearing on the genesis of the Homeric poems. But these matters too will take time to develop, and we are not ready for them yet. We began with the discrepancy between the *Iliad* and the *Odyssey* regarding the number of Neleus's sons: twelve in the *Iliad* versus three in the *Odyssey*. The twelve sons, then, are to be taken as a relatively recent tradition having to do with the Ionian dodecapolis. Another tradition for just two sons, Nestor and Periklymenos, went back much further, to the Indo-European twin myth. This myth is never fully acknowledged by the Homeric poets, as we have just seen in *Iliad* 11, where the number of sons is twelve and Periklymenos is not named. The same holds for *Odyssey* 11, where Periklymenos is named, but

---

21 A later myth, first attested by Herodotus 1.145, was that the Ionians of the dodecapolis came from the twelve cities of Achaea in the Peloponnesus; for this tradition cf. EN4.2 (end). We do not know when the Ionian league of twelve cities began, but a simile in *Iliad* 20 seems to show that the Panionia, the league's common festival, already existed in the Homeric era; Busolt 1885 (n1.17 above) cited this simile together with the twelve sons of Neleus in *Iliad* 11 as evidence for the early existence of the dodecapolis. The cult celebrated at the Panionia was dedicated to Poseidon Helikonios (Herodotus 1.148.1), and the Homeric simile evokes the bellowing of a bull sacrificed to this god (*Iliad* 20.403–405):

αὐτὰρ ὃ θυμὸν ἄϊσθε καὶ ἤρυγεν, ὡς ὅτε ταῦρος
ἤρυγεν ἑλκόμενος Ἑλικώνιον ἀμφὶ ἄνακτα
κούρων ἑλκόντων· γάνυται δέ τε τοῖς ἐνοσίχθων.

But he breathed forth his spirt and bellowed, as when a bull
bellows as it is dragged around the altar of the Helikonian lord;
youths drag him, and the earth-shaker is gladdened by them.

Strabo 8.7.2 records the ancient view that this simile alludes to the Panionia. There were, however, cults of Poseidon Helikonios elsewhere: in Miletus (Pausanias 7.24.5, scholia to *Iliad* 20.404); in colonies of Miletus (Sinope and Tomi, see Nilsson 1906:78–79); in other Ionian cities, namely Samos (Köhler 1885), Teos (Pausanias 7.24.5), and probably Thebes on Mykale (there is a temple of Poseidon there, *Inschriften von Priene* [Hiller 1906] 364 line 3); also in Athens (Kleidemos *FGrHist* 323 F 1). Cf. Busolt 1893:317n4 and Peter Hommel in Kleiner et al. 1967:56. The simile in *Iliad* 20 could allude to any of these cults then in existence. It would seem more likely, however, that the simile evoked a shared experience of the Homeric audience. As Wilamowitz 1906/1971:46/137 suggests, the cults in individual Ionian cities may have been branches of the Panionian cult. See Part 4 below for other evidence for the date of the league and festival; an early date is supported by the literary historical record, but not as yet by the archaeological evidence at Panionion on Cape Mykale, the site of the festival (cf. Jeffery 1976:209). See Part 4 below also for the Panionia as the likely occasion for the genesis of the Homeric poems.

not as one of a pair of brothers; here he is one of three brothers. The point seems to be that if Nestor and Periklymenos are twins in their old myth, they are now also part of a larger group. Chromios has been added to the pair of brothers to make that point. Thus what looks like a discrepancy is instead a partial reconciliation of an older tradition to a newer one. Both poems had to reconcile the two traditions in one way or another.[22]

§1.10 Before we turn to the comparison between Nestor and the Vedic twins, and seek to trace Nestor's ultimate origins to the Indo-European twin myth, we should note that Nestor's family, beginning with his father Neleus, has twins in it already. Neleus had a twin brother Pelias, from whom he separated. Neleus left Pelias behind in Thessaly when he went to found Pylos in the Peloponnesus. This myth is referred to in the same catalogue of heroines in *Odyssey* 11 that features Nestor and his two brothers. The mother of Neleus and Pelias was Tyro, and she is the first heroine to speak to Odysseus in the underworld (*Odyssey* 11.235–259). Tyro married Kretheus, to whom she bore three sons, but first she bore twin sons to the god Poseidon: Pelias, who lived in Iolkos, and Neleus, who lived in Pylos (*Odyssey* 11.254–257):

ἡ δ' ὑποκυσαμένη Πελίην τέκε καὶ Νηλῆα,

τὼ κρατερὼ θεράποντε Διὸς μεγάλοιο γενέσθην

ἀμφοτέρω· Πελίης μὲν ἐν εὐρυχόρῳ Ἰαολκῷ

ναῖε πολύρρηνος, ὁ δ' ἄρ' ἐν Πύλῳ ἠμαθόεντι.

And she conceived and bore Pelias and Neleus,
who became strong servants of great Zeus,
both of them; Pelias in spacious Iolkos
had his home, owning many sheep, the other one in sandy Pylos.[23]

If Nestor truly became *hippóta Néstōr* by separating from his brother and taking his brother's place as a warrior, it is not without significance that his father Neleus was a twin who likewise separated from his brother. Nestor and

---

22 In Nestor's twin myth he survived one brother, but in the new myth he survives many brothers, and this naturally makes him the youngest of the group (implicitly so in his story in *Iliad* 11, explicitly so after Homer). This too is at odds with his twin myth.

23 The phrase *theráponte Diós*, "servants of Zeus," in *Odyssey* 11.255, implies that Pelias and Neleus were both kings; Pelias succeeded Kretheus as king of Iolkos, and Neleus went to the western Peloponnesus ("Apollodorus" 1.9.9, 1.9.11, cf. 1.9.16). The *Odyssey* does not specifically call Neleus the founder of Pylos, but later tradition does so (Hesiod fr. 33a.5 MW, Diodorus Siculus 4.68.6).

Periklymenos are not called twins, but they follow the pattern of a pair of twins a generation before them.

§1.11 There is a second pair of brothers in Nestor's extended family, Melampus and Bias, who are not called twins, but who have the attributes of twins.[24] Melampus and Bias are first of all Nestor's cousins in that they are sons of Amythaon, one of the three sons of Tyro and Kretheus; they also successfully woo Nestor's sister Pero. Both of these connections to Nestor come up in the catalogue of heroines. Amythaon, the father of Melampus and Bias, is named in the same passage as Nestor's father Neleus; after Tyro bore the twins Pelias and Neleus to Poseidon she bore Amythaon and two other sons to her husband Kretheus (*Odyssey* 11.258–259):

τοὺς δ' ἑτέρους Κρηθῆϊ τέκεν βασίλεια γυναικῶν,
Αἴσονά τ' ἠδὲ Φέρητ' Ἀμυθάονά θ' ἱππιοχάρμην.

The queen among women bore her other sons to Kretheus,
Aison and Pheres and the chariot-fighter Amythaon.

The wooing of Pero by Melampus and Bias is alluded to in the same passage that names Nestor and his two brothers. Pero, who was born last after her brothers, was wooed by all her neighbors, but Neleus set as her brideprice the retrieval of the cattle of Iphiklos. Melampus is not named in this passage but is referred to as the "faultless prophet" who alone undertook to retrieve the cattle. His story is told more fully in *Odyssey* 15.225–238 in the genealogy of Melampus's descendant, the seer Theoklymenos. Melampus wooed Pero on behalf of his brother Bias, but he was imprisoned for a year before he succeeded in winning the cattle of Iphiklos.[25] Unlike Nestor and Neleus, who separated from their twin brothers, Melampus and Bias remained together, not only in Pylos, where they wooed Pero, but also in Argos, where they went from Pylos.[26] This second set of twin figures, and their association with

---

24 Cf. Ward 1968:3 for twin figures who are not explicitly called twins.
25 A detail found in *Odyssey* 11 but not mentioned in *Odyssey* 15 is Melampus's use of prophecy to win the cattle of Iphiklos (*thésphata pánt' eipónta*, "after he spoke all the prophecies," 11.297; cf. "Apollodorus" 1.9.12). See below on Agamemnon and Menelaus for the motif of one brother wooing for the other.
26 In Argos Melampus healed the daughters of Proitos of madness in return for two thirds of Proitos's kingdom, a third for himself and a third for his brother Bias ("Apollodorus" 2.2.2, cf. 1.9.12). In *Odyssey* 15.238–242 only Melampus is mentioned as having moved from Pylos to Argos, but the passage traces the ancestry of Theoklymenos, a descendant of Melampus, and there is thus no need to mention Bias, who is not in Theoklymenos's direct line.

Nestor's sister Pero, is no less important than the pair Neleus and Pelias for the underlying myth of Nestor and Periklymenos.

§1.12 In the two chapters that follow I will review my earlier work on the names *Néstōr* in Greek and *Nā́satyā* in Vedic. In what I previously said about Nestor and his name there are points of detail and emphasis to be changed, but overall the basis on which I will build is in place. I have nothing to change in what I previously said about the name *Nā́satyā*, but there is still more to say about the Indo-European origins of what I believe I have shown is the meaning of this name in Vedic. The point of the Vedic comparison for Nestor is that it puts him in the context of the Indo-European twin myth, and the Greek Dioskouroi are essential to establishing the basic features of this myth. The Dioskouroi already played a large part in my previous study of the *Nā́satyā*, but there are further points of comparison to be pursued between the Vedic and Greek twins to establish the Indo-European form of their myth. Nestor too will contribute to an understanding of the Indo-European myth, both in the direct comparison between his name and the name of the Vedic twins, and in the discussion of his Homeric role, which will be pursued in Part 2 of this study. But the immediate issue, on which all else depends, is the linguistic comparison between *Néstōr* on the one hand and *Nā́satyā* on the other.

Chapter 2.

GREEK

§1.13 As an agent noun with the suffix *-tōr* Nestor's name belongs to a class of Greek names that are particularly clear in meaning. The suffix *-tor* was inherited from Indo-European (compare Greek *dótōr*, Sanskrit *dā́tar-*, Latin *dator*, "giver"), but Greek is unusual in using this agent suffix to form names as well as common nouns.[27] Eighteen names in *-tōr* occur in Homer, and all but one contain the root of a Greek verb.[28] Four of these names are paralleled by Homeric common nouns: *Amúntōr* (*amúntōr*, "defender"), *Kalḗtōr* (*kalḗtōr*, "crier"), *Mḗstōr* (*mḗstōr*, "counselor"), *Epístōr* (*epiístōr*, "one who knows, knower").[29] Others are paralleled by common nouns in later Greek.[30]

---

27 Benveniste 1948:54 cites parallels only in Avestan (four examples); Heubeck 1957:29n6 (= 1984:474n6) cites parallels in Illyrian; Neumann 1988:8, 14 cites parallels in Phrygian (three examples).

28 Only *Alástōr* (from the verbal adjective *álastos*) does not contain the root of a verb. Besides *Néstōr*, the other sixteen names (and related verbs) are: *Áktōr* (*ágō*, "lead"), *Aléktōr* (*aléxō*, "ward off"), *Amúntōr* (*amúnō*, "defend"), *Daítōr* (*daíomai/daínumi*, "divide/feast"), *Damástōr*, in *Damastorídēs* (*damázō*, "tame"), *Dmḗtōr* (*dámnēmi*, "tame"), *Hḗktōr* (*ékhō*, "hold, protect"), *Epístōr* (*oîda*, "know"), *Kalḗtōr* (*kaléō*, "call"), *Kástōr* (*kaínumi*, perf. *kékasmai*, "excel"), *Mástōr/Mastorídēs* (*maíomai*, "search"), *Méntōr* (*mémona*, "be eager," see below in text), *Mḗstōr* (*mḗdomai*, "plan"), *Onḗtōr* (*onínēmi*, "help"), *Sténtōr* (*sténō*, "roar"), *Théstōr*, in *Thestorídēs* (*théssasthai*, "ask in prayer"). *Philḗtōr* is a further example if it is from *philéō*, "love," but it may be a compound of *phílos* "dear," and *êtor*, "heart" (cf. Risch 1974:63).

29 The name *Epístōr*, if from *epí* and root **wid-* like *epiístōr*, differs from the common noun in ignoring ϝ and eliding the final vowel of *epí*; *h-* from ϝ is also absent (cf. *hístōr*).

30 Later Greek has examples of *áktōr*, "leader" (Aeschylus), *(sun)daítōr*, "(fellow) feaster" (Aeschylus), perhaps *onḗtōr*, "helper" (conjecture in Pindar, otherwise the name of a plaster). Common nouns with the agent suffix *-tēr* parallel two further Homeric names in *-tōr*: *dmētḗr*, "tamer" (*Homeric Hymn* 22.5), paralleling *Dmḗtōr*, and *mastḗr*, "searcher" (Sophocles, Euripides), paralleling *Mástōr*. The suffix *-tēr*, unlike *-tōr*, was not used to form names; cf. Benveniste 1948:54.

§1.14 The meanings of the names in -tōr, being particularly clear, are sometimes evoked by the Homeric poets, and this, I will argue, is especially the case with Nestor's name. But this is not obviously the case with Nestor's name, and I wish to consider only the obvious cases for now. The names in question are *Sténtōr*, *Théstōr* (in the patronymic *Thestorídēs*), *Héktōr*, and *Méntōr*, of which the first two are relatively minor in significance for the poems, and the last two relatively important. *Sténtōr* is the name of the brazen-voiced hero whose likeness Hera assumes to shout to the Achaean army (*Iliad* 5.785); he appears nowhere else in the *Iliad*, and his name, from the verb *sténō*, "roar," matches his one and only attribute.[31] Muted by comparison, but also apparently intentional, is the evocation of the meaning of *Théstōr*, "he who asks for in prayer," in the patronymic *Thestorídēs* of the seer Calchas, whose calling is evidently responsible for his patronymic.[32] The name *Héktōr*, from the verb *ékhō*, "hold, protect," is taken by the Homeric poets in the sense of "protector," which is Hector's role in relation to his city and people.[33] This meaning of his name is alluded to in Andromache's lament for Hector, in which she foresees the destruction of her city now that her husband, who "protected" (*ékhes*) its women and children, is dead (*Iliad* 24.729–30):

ἦ γὰρ ὄλωλας ἐπίσκοπος, ὅς τέ μιν αὐτὴν
ῥύσκευ, ἔχες δ' ἀλόχους κεδνὰς καὶ νήπια τέκνα.

For indeed you, who were its guardian, have perished,
    you who kept
the city itself safe and protected its good wives and infant children.[34]

---

31 The verb *sténō* is used of the roaring of the sea in *Iliad* 23.230: *ho d' éstenen oídmati thúōn*, "it roared, seething with the swell." The English adjective "stentorian," deriving from Stentor's role in *Iliad* 5.785, perhaps makes the evocation of Stentor's name in this line seem more familiar that it would otherwise be.

32 For the root of *Théstōr* from *théssasthai*, "ask in prayer," cf. also compounds in -*thestos* (*polú-thestos*, "much prayed for," and *apó-thestos*, "prayed away, despised").

33 "Hector Protector" is a familiar phrase in English from a nursery rhyme.

34 Note that *rhúskeu*, "you protected," glosses the next word *ékhes* in the particular sense required for *ékhes*; the poet clearly strives to evoke the meaning of Hector's name. There are two other instances in which the meaning of Hector's name seems to be evoked. In *Iliad* 5.473–474 Sarpedon reminds Hector of his boast to "protect" (*hexémen*) the city by himself: φῆς που ἄτερ λαῶν πόλιν ἑξέμεν ἠδ' ἐπικούρων / οἶος, "you once said that you would protect the city without your warriors and allies, / alone." According to *Iliad* 6.403 the Trojans called Hector's son *Astúanax*, "ruler of the city," because "Hector alone protected Ilion" (οἶος γὰρ ἐρύετο Ἴλιον Ἕκτωρ). O'Hara 1996:10 discusses word play with Hector's name in the *Iliad*, but he omits *Iliad* 24.730 (in the text above).

§1.15 The name *Méntōr*, like the name *Sténtōr*, belongs to a figure whose likeness a god assumes. Mentor is the aged Ithacan in whose likeness Athena appears in the *Odyssey* on two occasions, first when she accompanies Telemachus to Pylos to meet Nestor, and again when she encourages Odysseus before the final battle with the suitors.[35] The *Odyssey* connects the name with the root **men-* of the noun *ménos*, "spirit," and the verb *mémona*, "be eager"; the *Odyssey* also suggests a connection with the enlarged form of the root (**mn-ā < *mn-eə₂*) of the verb *mimnḗskō*, "remind" (aorist *émnēsa*)/ *mimnḗskomai*, "remember" (perfect *mémnēmai*).[36] The name *Méntōr* contains the simple form of the root, and I therefore take it to mean "he who instills *ménos*," "he who incites." The intransitive perfect form with the simple root, *mémona*, "be eager," implies a transitive present form **ménō*, "make eager, incite," on the pattern of such pairs as perfect *diéphthora*, "be ruined"/ present *diaphtheírō*, "destroy," or perfect *pépoitha*, "be persuaded, put trust in"/ present *peíthō*, "persuade." The verb **ménō*, "make eager, incite," has a virtual existence in the name *Méntōr*, and in the equivalent name, *Méntēs*. The latter name belongs to a Taphian trader in whose likeness Athena first appears to Telemachus before she appears to him as Mentor. The two names, *Méntēs* and *Méntōr*, which differ only in their use of different agent suffixes, focus attention on the root **men-* in defining Athena's role in relation to Telemachus. Athena's purpose in visiting Telemachus is to stir him up, as she herself announces to the rest of the gods in *Odyssey* 1.88–89:

αὐτὰρ ἐγὼν Ἰθάκηνδε ἐλεύσομαι, ὄφρα οἱ υἱὸν
μᾶλλον ἐποτρύνω καί οἱ μένος ἐν φρεσὶ θείω.

But I will go to Ithaca so that I may stir up
his son the more and put incitement in his heart.

In this passage the verb *epotrúnō*, "stir up," corresponds exactly to what the names *Méntēs* and *Méntōr* signify, and the phrase *ménos en phresì theíō* suggests the actual derivation of these two names.[37] After her appearance

---

35 The latter episode is *Odyssey* 22.205–240.

36 The enlarged form of the root is rare outside Greek: Greek *mémona*, "I am eager," and Latin *memini*, "I remember," are formal equivalents, having the simple form of the root, but the meaning of the Latin verb corresponds with that of the enlarged root in Greek. Presumably Latin *memini* preserves the Indo-European meaning of the simple root, which in Greek was taken over by the enlarged root.

37 The verb *epotrúnō* in this passage stands in for the virtual verb **ménō* implied by the names *Méntēs* and *Méntōr*; cf. the following two Homeric passages in which the verb *otrúnō* functions as the transitive counterpart to intransitive *mémona*: in *Iliad* 5.482 Sarpedon speaks

as Mentes Athena flies off and the poet comments on the effect of her visit on Telemachus: she has accomplished her purpose, which was to put "spirit" (*ménos*) in his heart; at the same time she has also "reminded" (*hupémnēsen*) Telemachus of his father (*Odyssey* 1.319–322):

ἡ μὲν ἄρ' ὣς εἰποῦσ' ἀπέβη γλαυκῶπις Ἀθήνη,
ὄρνις δ' ὣς ἀνόπαια διέπτατο· τῷ δ' ἐνὶ θυμῷ
θῆκε μένος καὶ θάρσος, ὑπέμνησέν τέ ἑ πατρὸς
μᾶλλον ἔτ' ἢ τὸ πάροιθεν.

So speaking grey-eyed Athena departed,
and like a bird she flew away on high; into his heart
she put incitement and boldness, and she reminded him of his
    father
even more than before.

As Mentes Athena has not only incited Telemachus, but also reminded him of his father, and the two notions are closely linked in the passage above, such that the name *Méntēs*, "inciter," is also felt to mean "reminder." When the figure Mentor enters the story his name too evokes both notions, but the notion of "reminding" is emphasized. The aged figure Mentor appears in his own right just long enough to demonstrate this meaning of his name: in the assembly called by Telemachus, he reminds the Ithacans of Odysseus, their absent king, whom no one "remembers" (*Odyssey* 2.230–233):

μή τις ἔτι πρόφρων ἀγανὸς καὶ ἤπιος ἔστω
σκηπτοῦχος βασιλεύς, μηδὲ φρεσὶν αἴσιμα εἰδώς,
ἀλλ' αἰεὶ χαλεπός τ' εἴη καὶ αἴσυλα ῥέζοι,
ὡς οὔ τις μέμνηται Ὀδυσσῆος θείοιο.

---

of his willing contribution to the war despite the fact that he is only an ally of the Trojans: ἀλλὰ καὶ ὣς Λυκίους ὀτρύνω καὶ μέμον' αὐτὸς / ἀνδρὶ μαχήσασθαι, "but even so I stir up the Lycians and am myself stirred up / to fight man to man"; in *Iliad* 4.73 Zeus stirs up an already eager Athena: ὣς εἰπὼν ὄτρυνε πάρος μεμαυῖαν Ἀθήνην, "so saying he stirred up Athena, who was stirred up already." The verb *otrúnō* also has a close connection to the noun *ménos* in Homer in the phrase *ótrune ménos*, "he/she stirred up the *ménos* of," as in the repeated line: ὣς εἰπὼν ὄτρυνε μένος καὶ θυμὸν ἑκάστου. For the close relationship between the noun *ménos* and the verb *mémona*, note *Iliad* 5.135–136, where Diomedes is described as "already eager," καὶ πρὶν...*memaós*, when "three times the *ménos* seized" him, τρὶς τόσσον ἕλεν *ménos*.

May no scepter-bearing king any longer
be truly gentle and kind, or mindful in his heart of what is due,
but may he always be harsh and do what is unjust,
<u>since no one remembers godlike Odysseus</u>.

When Athena assumes Mentor's likeness and accompanies Telemachus to Pylos, she too acts to "remind" Telemachus of his father, for the very purpose of his journey is to learn about Odysseus. She first appears to Telemachus as Mentor shortly before they take ship together for Pylos, and she picks up where the real Mentor left off in the Ithacan assembly, by reminding Telemachus of his father. She does so with a variation of the *ménos* theme, reminding Telemachus of his father's *ménos*, and suggesting that this very *ménos* has been instilled into Telemachus himself (*Odyssey* 2.270–272):

Τηλέμαχ', οὐδ' ὄπιθεν κακὸς ἔσσεαι οὐδ' ἀνοήμων·
εἰ δή τοι σοῦ πατρὸς ἐνέστακται <u>μένος</u> ἠΰ,
οἷος κεῖνος ἔην τελέσαι ἔργον τε ἔπος τε.

Telemachus, you won't turn out to be cowardly or foolish
if indeed your father's brave <u>spirit</u> has been bred into you,
such a man was he to carry out both deed and word.

In this passage the ideas of "inciting" and "reminding" are fused, and the word *ménos* is the passage's focal point. In Pylos Telemachus is afraid to approach Nestor and address him since he has no experience in such speech-making; Athena, as Mentor, ironically tells him that he will think of some things himself, and that "a god" will suggest other things to him (*Odyssey* 3.26–28):

Τηλέμαχ', ἄλλα μὲν αὐτὸς ἐνὶ φρεσὶ σῇσι νοήσεις,
ἄλλα δὲ καὶ δαίμων ὑποθήσεται· οὐ γὰρ ὀΐω
οὔ σε θεῶν ἀέκητι γενέσθαι τε τραφέμεν τε.

Telemachus, some things you yourself will think of in your mind,
and other things a god will prompt; for I do not think
that you were born and raised against the gods' will.

Here there is no form related to the name *Méntōr*, but the verb *hupothḗsetai*, "will put in mind," seems to reflect Athena's role with respect to Telemachus

27

in a more general way, for she herself is the "god" who is there at his side, disguised as *Méntōr*, to remind and incite him.[38]

§1.16 Like *Sténtōr*, *Méntōr* is an assumed name, chosen to describe a particular role, and its significance is ever present while that role continues.[39] The name *Néstōr*, by contrast, does not designate a role, but the entire identity of an epic hero, and its significance therefore cannot continuously be evoked. But the one Homeric episode in which the meaning of Nestor's name does seem present throughout is the very episode in which Athena first disguises herself as Mentor. Telemachus visits Nestor to find out about his father's *nóstos*, "return home," and *nóstos* has the same verbal root as the name *Néstōr*. It is the root **nes-* of the verb *néomai*, "return home," and of the related noun *nóstos*. It is significant that it is Nestor who tells Telemachus the basic story of the Achaeans' *nóstos* from Troy, for his name uniquely qualifies him to tell this story.[40] But Nestor's name does not have the intransitive sense "he who returns" that would correspond to the meaning of the middle

---

38 In *Odyssey* 12.37–38 Circe tells Odysseus to listen to what she tells him about his journey home, and then adds that when the time comes "the god himself will *remind* you" (*mnḗsei dé se kaì theòs autós*). This is a more explicit case of "reminding" than the passage with *hupothḗsetai* in *Odyssey* 3, but it is not dissimilar.

39 The name is also significant when Athena, as Mentor, incites Odysseus before the final battle with the suitors. Note in particular her address to Odysseus in *Odyssey* 22.226–235, where the two nouns *ménos* and *alkḗ* at the beginning of her speech (οὐκέτι σοί γ᾽, Ὀδυσεῦ, μένος ἔμπεδον οὐδέ τις ἀλκή, "your *ménos* is no longer firm, and you have no *alkḗ*") are picked up at the end of her speech in the name *Méntōr* and the patronymic *Alkimídēs* that now occurs for the first and only time (*Odyssey* 22.233–235):

ἀλλ᾽ ἄγε δεῦρο, πέπον, παρ᾽ ἔμ᾽ ἵστασο καὶ ἴδε ἔργον,
ὄφρ᾽ εἰδῇς, οἷός τοι ἐν ἀνδράσι δυσμενέεσσι
Μέντωρ Ἀλκιμίδης εὐεργεσίας ἀποτίνειν.

But come here, good friend, stand next to me, and see my deeds,
so that you may know what Mentor Alkimides is like
to repay good deeds in the midst of hostile men.

The currency of the English and French word "mentor," meaning "wise and trusted counselor," is derived less from the *Odyssey* than from a late seventeenth-century romance, the *Télémaque* of the Archbishop Fénelon, in which Mentor's role as "counselor" is prominent (*OED* s.v. "mentor"); Greek *Méntōr* does not mean "counselor," but "inciter," and by extension "reminder." Formally it is possible that *Méntōr* derives from *ménō*, "await, withstand," but this is clearly not how the *Odyssey* understands the name. For consideration of the name *Menélaos*, which is usually derived from the verb *ménō*, "await, withstand," see Part 2 below.

40 In *Odyssey* 1.326–327 the bard Phemios is represented as singing the "Achaeans' grim return" (*Akhaiôn nóston...lugrón*) to the suitors, but it is Nestor who delivers the actual substance of this song in *Odyssey* 3. For Nestor's role as narrator of the Achaeans' *nóstoi* in *Odyssey* 3, cf. Marks 2008, ch. 5.

verb *néomai*: the name *Néstōr* has a transitive sense, "he who brings back." This makes his name significant for Odysseus in particular, about whom Telemachus has come to ask. Odysseus did not return home after the war, and Nestor, "he who brings home," has more to do with this than he explicitly says. This is of course not *communis opinio* in the history of Homeric criticism, for the meaning of the name Nestor seems to have been forgotten completely in the post-Homeric period, and certainly for us today the name Nestor, in contrast to the names Mentor, Stentor, and even Hector, has no intrinsic meaning whatever.[41] Nevertheless I think that it can be shown that the name *Néstōr* had as clear a meaning for the Homeric poets as did the name *Méntōr*, and that it was no less important than the name *Méntōr* in the development of the story of the *Odyssey*. I will go even further and suggest that the choice of the name *Méntōr* for the disguised Athena in the journey of Telemachus to Pylos was in large part conditioned by the name *Néstōr* in the same episode.

§1.17 It is plain enough that the verbal root in the name *Néstōr* is **nes-*, but the key point, that the name means "he who brings back" and not "he who returns," was not suggested until relatively recently. As far as was known previously the Greek root **nes-* had only the intransitive meaning "return" of the middle verb *néomai* and the related noun *nóstos*. The new evidence for an active, transitive meaning of the root has to do with Nestor's father, Neleus, and the family that claimed descent from him, the Neleids of Miletus. The name of this family, *Nēleîdai*, is in fact ambiguous, for the family claimed descent not only from Nestor's father, the founder of Pylos, but also from a second Neleus in the same line, the founder of Miletus.[42] This second Neleus was said to be a direct descendant of the first, and he must have been as important a figure to the Neleids as their earlier ancestor, for it was he, the founder of Miletus, who legitimated their rule in their own city. The name of this second founder, although it is given as *Nēleús* in most sources, was in fact not the same as the name of the first founder: Herodotus preserves the true form of his name, which was *Neíleōs*.[43] The two names appear to be dialectal

---

41 Apart from designating the Homeric hero, the name's only wider use is as a type of wisdom and, more often, as a metonymy for old age. Nestor is found as a symbol of "overliving" (living too long) in Propertius 2.13.46–50 and Juvenal 10.246–255; there were presumably earlier instances of this in Greek tradition (cf. §2.71 below on *Odyssey* 3.108–112).

42 Hellanicus F 23 (cf. n1.18 above).

43 Herodotus 9.97: the passage concerns a temple of Eleusinian Demeter established on Cape Mykale by Philistos, a supposed follower of *Neíleōs*, the founder of Miletus (τῇ Δήμητρος Ἐλευσινίης [ἐστὶ] ἱρόν, τὸ Φίλιστος ὁ Πασικλέος ἱδρύσατο Νείλεῳ τῷ Κόδρου ἐπισπόμενος ἐπὶ Μιλήτου κτιστύν, "there is a temple there of Eleusinian Demeter, which Philistos the son of Pasikles founded when he followed Neileos the son of Kodros for the foundation of

variants, *Nēleús* an Aeolic form, *Neíleōs* the Ionic form.[44] We would expect the rulers of Miletus to have used the Ionic form of their own name (*Neileîdai*), and thus to have called themselves descendants of their own city's founder. But just as this founder's name is leveled out in most of our sources, so too the distinction in the family's name.[45]

§1.18 Unlike the form *Nēleús*, the form *Neíleōs* has a clear etymology. The second half of the name is Ionic *leōs*, Homeric *laós*, "warfolk," and the name is of the same type as e.g. Homeric *Agé-laos* (Ionic *Agé-leōs*), "he who leads the warfolk." The first part of the name *Agélaos* is a transitive verb (*Agé-* from *ágō*, "lead")[46]; so too is the first part of the name *Neíleōs*: *Nei-* is to be reconstructed as **Nese-*, from an active verb **néō*, "bring back," corresponding to the middle verb *néomai*, "return."[47] Here, then, in the name *Neíleōs*, "he who leads the warfolk home," is the root **nes-* with an active meaning. This in effect was the Neleids' name too, insofar as they were "descendants of *Neíleōs*." Nestor, who was the epic hero of the Neleids, had a closely related name: "he who brings home."

§1.19 We can take this argument back a stage further to Mycenaean Greek, for the name *Neíleōs* occurs in its Mycenaean form on a Linear-B tablet

Miletus"); see §4.14 below for the same name *Neíleōs* on a sixth-century BC Samian inscription; cf. also Callimachus fr. 191.76–77 Pfeiffer (*Iambus* 1), where Thales' alleged dedication of a gold cup to Apollo at Didyma reads in part τῷ μεδεῦντι Νείλεω δήμου, "to the lord of the people of Neileos" (see Martin 1993:113 on the relationship to Thales of this dedication, written by Callimachus). Pausanias uses a hybrid form *Neileús* of the founder of Miletus; this form also appears in Milesian territory on a second-century AD inscription from Didyma (Fontenrose 1988:197 no. 23 line 8). The grammarian Herodian similarly distinguishes between the name of Nestor's father *Nēleús* on the one hand, and the forms *Neíleōs* and *Neileús* (which are interchangeable) on the other hand (*Grammatici Graeci*, vol. 3.2, p. 450.23–26 Lentz). But Hellanicus, the Marmor Parium, Strabo, and others call the founder of Miletus *Nēleús*.

44 Wackernagel 1891 cols. 6–7 first suggested this on the basis of the correspondence between *Nei-* and *Nē-* in the first part of the two names, which is like the correspondence between e.g. Ionic *keînos* and Aeolic *kênos* ("that one"); he did not address the difference in the second part of the names.

45 There is one important exception: a local inscription of the first century BC (Collitz-Bechtel 1884–1915 no. 5501) has the phrase *patrias Neileidōn*, "of the lineage (*patriá*) of the *Neileîdai*." The inscription records an official of the deme Teichioussai, fifteen miles south of Miletus (cf. n4.172 below). Outside its local context the family's name would have been influenced by the Homeric patronymic *Nēlēiádēs*. Herodian, who preserves the name *Neíleōs*, preserves the associated patronymic *Neileídēs* as well (*Grammatici Graeci*, vol. 3.1, p. 67.11, vol. 3.2, pp. 435.26, 513.16 Lentz).

46 For the first element in these compounds as an old third-person singular verb see Watkins 1970:94–96.

47 **Nese-* became *Nei-* by loss of intervocalic *-s-* (already in Mycenaean, cf. n1.49 below) and subsequent (Ionic) contraction of the two vowels to secondary long *e*, represented as *-ei-*.

from Pylos.[48] The Linear-B form of the name is *ne-e-ra-wo*, which is to be interpreted as *Nehe-lawos*.[49] The context of this name on the tablet makes it clear that it does not belong to a king, much less to the Neleids' original ancestor, but to a person of modest rank.[50] But the very occurrence of the name on a Pylos tablet is important for the name of the Neleids' original ancestor. We know this ancestor as *Nēleús* from his earliest occurrence in Greek in the Homeric poems, but in the Bronze Age his name was most probably *Nehelawos*. We need to consider how and why this name took two different forms in later Greek. We have already seen that the Ionian rulers of Miletus preserved the name in its Ionic form, *Neíleōs*, but that they no longer used this Ionic form of their original ancestor; they used it of the founder of their own city. The name of their original ancestor became the Aeolic form *Nēleús*, which was no longer clear in meaning.[51] The tradition was that this ancestor came from

48 It was the discovery of the Linear-B name that actually led to the interpretation of the Ionic form *Neíleōs*; I have reversed this order in my discussion of the Ionic and Mycenaean forms to emphasize the role of the Neleids of Miletus, which I believe is of primary importance.

49 PY Fn 79.5; see Mühlestein 1965:157n14 for the wide agreement on the interpretation of this name (Ventris and Chadwick, Palmer, Heubeck); cf. Frame 1978:82–83. There are grounds for thinking that intervocalic *-h-* from intervocalic *-s-* was still retained in Mycenaean pronunciation (thus *Nehe-* from *Nese-*), but the feature was not normally noted in Linear-B spelling (hence *ne-e-*); cf. Palmer 1963:44. It should also be emphasized that the second half of the name, *ra-wo*, interpreted as *lawos*, "warfolk," is not isolated, but is paralleled in the name *a-ke-ra-wo*, which is interpreted as *Age-lawos*, "he who leads the warfolk" (or possibly *Arkhe-lawos*, "he who rules the warfolk"); see Ventris and Chadwick 1973:529 for occurrences of this name; see Chadwick and Baumbach 1963:216–217 for other evidence of *laós* as the first element in Mycenaean compounds.

50 The name, which is in the dative, belongs to the recipient of an allotment of grain and olives. Sergent 1982:25, arguing that there was a noble *génos* of Neleids in Pylos, proposes that this could be a "retired" official of royal rank.

51 The vowel contraction that gave *-ei-* in Ionic would have given *-ē-* in Aeolic (as in Ionic *keînos* vs. Aeolic *kênos*; cf. n1.44 above). Why the second half of the name, *-laos*, "warfolk," became *-leús*, with the purely grammatical suffix *-eús*, is a problem; L. R. Palmer's view that the name in *-leús* is a "short-form" of the name in *-laos* is the simplest and probably the best solution (Palmer 1956:9, 1963:80); for a less likely explanation by Marcello Durante see n1.54 below. For the actual process that gives the "short-form" in question, see Fick-Bechtel 1894:15–21, 373–377: names with two stems keep the entire first stem but only the beginning of the second stem, to which a new "pet-name ending" ("kosende Endung") is added, as in e.g. *Eurustheús* from *Euru-sthénēs*, *Menestheús* from *Mene-sthénēs* (Fick-Bechtel 374; cf. also von Kamptz 1982:62, 125, 195, 209); in line with this pattern the name *Nēleús* keeps the full (Aeolic) form of the first element, *Nē-*, but only the beginning of the second element (the *l-* of *-laos*). This etymology of *Nēleús* is accepted by e.g. Ruijgh 1988:164 (cf. also Ruijgh 1985:174 and 1967:369–370). The etymology is not accepted by e.g. Heubeck 1987, who regards *Nēleús* as similar in formation to *Pēleús*, *Perseús*, *Tudeús*, *Atreús*, etc., and who regards the patronymic *Nēlēïádēs* as similar in formation to *Pēlēïádēs*, *Persēïádēs*, etc. Heubeck's view certainly has prima facie plausibilty, given the series of close formal parallels. But just as *Nēleús* can be explained apart from

31

Iolkos in Thessaly, an Aeolic-speaking area in historical times. The tradition
for Neleus's foundation of Pylos seems to reflect a real movement of settlers
from Thessaly to the Peloponnesus in the Bronze Age, and we may therefore
believe that the Neleids themselves came originally from Iolkos as their tradi-
tion said.[52] The name of their ancestor even seems to have left a trace close to
their place of origin in the derivative form *Nḗleia*, the name of a small town
near Iolkos.[53] It makes sense that the Neleids' earliest ancestor was called by
the Aeolic form of his name in Homer, for he was associated with an area that
in Homeric times preserved relics of his name in its Aeolic form.[54]

---

other bisyllabic names in *-eús*, so too the patronymic *Nēlēiádēs* can be explained on its own.
The regular patronymic suffix in Homer is *-ídēs*, of which there are more than 30 examples
after a second-declension name like *Nehelāwos* (*Priamídēs, Dardanídēs, Aiakídēs, Aiolídēs*, etc.).
The ending *-iádēs* most likely developed from *-ídēs* when added to second-declension names in
-ios by dissimilation of the vowel (e.g. **Asklēpiídēs > Asklēpiádēs* in the patronymic of *Asklḗpios*)
and was extended for metrical reasons to names in which a long syllable precedes the suffix
(e.g. **Laertídēs > Laertiádēs* in the patronymic from *Laértēs*; see Risch 1974:148–149). The patro-
nymics *Pēlēiádēs, Persēiádēs*, etc., adduced by Heubeck are explained by the presence of such
a long syllable before the suffix (original forms **Pēlēw-ídēs, *Persēw-ídēs*, etc.) and so too is
the hypothetical form **Nehelāw-iádēs* (original form **Nehelāwídēs*). For the patronymic suffix
-iádēs added to a second-declension name like *Nehelāwos*, there are admittedly not as many
parallels as there are for names in *-eús*, but there is one, namely *Arētiádēs*, the patronymic of
Árētos. As regards *Nēleús*, there are no other "short-forms" in *-leús* from compounds in *-laos*
to compare with it, so that it too is admittedly isolated among names in *-eús* (cf. Mühlestein
1965:164n48 for this point). For the anomalous patronymic *Lampetídēs* from the name *Lámpos*
in *Iliad* 15.526, cf. n1.212 below and EN1.4 to n1.212.

52 Cf. Nilsson 1932:86, 143–144; Wilamowitz 2006:351–354.

53 Strabo 9.5.15 (form *Nēlía* in the manuscripts corrected to *Nḗleia* by Meineke); for the loca-
tion, cf. Stählin *RE* 'Neleia' 2268–2269. For the relationship between the forms *Nēleús* and
Nḗleia (*Nēleús* is the founding form, *Nḗleia* the founded form) cf. the pairs *basileús* and *basí-
leia*, "king" and "queen," *hiereús* and *hiéreia*, "priest" and "priestess," and see Chantraine
1933:103. For other evidence of the name *Nēleús* in Thessaly, see Sakellariou 1958:52 (a cult
of Aphrodite *Nēleía* in Magnesia, a fountain named *Nḗleia* in Hestiaiotis); cf. also von Kamptz
1982:125, who cites the similarly formed place-names *Pḗleia, Túdeia*, from *Pēleús, Tudeús*
(both places are, like *Nḗleia*, in southern Thessaly; cf. Fick 1897:208, 1911:149–151, 1914:73).

54 By "Homeric times" I mean the period in which the *Iliad* and the *Odyssey* were composed
on a monumental scale substantially as they exist today; in Part 4 below I define this
period as the late eighth and early seventh centuries BC; cf. also n2.16 and n2.173 below.
Durante 1967:35–41 has pointed out an important difference between the name *Nēleús* on
the one hand and both the patronymic *Nēlēiádēs* and the patronymic adjective *Nēlḗios* on
the other hand. The difference is one of rhythm and it suggests that while the patronymics
are deeply traditional in Homeric epic, the name *Nēleús* is not. All three forms contract the
first two syllables of the underlying form *Nehelawos* (*Nehe- > Nē-*), but the rhythm of the two
patronymics, which excludes their first syllable from the first syllable of a foot, allows this
syllable to be resolved into two short syllables in all cases (only in the late form *Nēleídao* in
Iliad 23.652 is the first syllable first in a foot and therefore unresolvable). The name *Nēleús*,
by contrast, has its first syllable first in a foot in seven of eleven Homeric occurrences.
Durante concluded from this that the name behind the patronymic (originally *Nehelawos*)

§1.20 I have already suggested that the Neleids of Miletus gave the inherited form of their original ancestor's name to a secondary ancestor because it was more important to them to be known as the descendants of their own city's founder than it was to be called descendants of the founder of Pylos. It was probably when the myth of the foundation of Miletus came into being, and the supposed founder of Miletus was called *Neíleōs*, that the name of the Neleids' original ancestor was shifted to its Aeolic form in Homeric epic.[55] There was a further reason to use the Aeolic form of this figure's name if, as the father of twelve sons, he was meant to be, in the symbolic sense discussed earlier, the ancestor of the entire Ionian dodecapolis. The cities of the dodecapolis had very diverse origins, as previously noted, but one area of origin that many of them had in common was Thessaly.[56] The founder

---

had been forgotten, and that the Homeric poets invented the name *Nēleús* as a back formation from the adjective *Nēléïos* on the model of such Homeric pairs as *Odusseús:Odussḗïos*. I was initially attracted to this idea (cf. Frame 1978:97), but I now reject it for two reasons: first, the Thessalian place-name *Nēleia* indicates that *Nēleús* was the true Aeolic form of this hero's name (*Nēleia* is derived from *Nēleús* and not the reverse, *pace* Sakellariou 1958:51n1; see n1.53 above); secondly, the Neleids of Miletus demonstrably did not forget the original form of their original ancestor's name (*Neíleōs* < *Nehelawos*), but applied it to a more recent ancestor. The significance of Durante's observation is that the use of the Aeolic form of the name Neleus in epic is not as old as the use of the patronymic, and this I think is certainly true. I surmise that in pre-Homeric epic the form of the name was non-Aeolic *Neélaos* < *Nehelawos* (by way of example note that in *Odyssey* 11.254, telling how Tyro gave birth to twin sons, the line-end Πελίην τέκε καὶ Νηλῆα can be recast as Πελίην τέκε καὶ Νεέλαον). When epic replaced *Neélaos* with *Nēleús*, the change from *Nee-* to *Nē-* in the patronymics followed automatically.

55 See n1.54 above for the name *Nēleús* as relatively recent in epic. For Neileos and Neleus as distinct figures by the late eighth or early seventh century BC, cf. Herda 1998:16; Erika Simon (*LIMC* 'Neleus' 728) also stresses that both figures must have had hero cults.

56 Cf. n1.20 above. Högemann 2001:61 succinctly sketches an Ionian migration that took place over considerable time in impoverished circumstances and had no single point of origin, although Boeotia and Thessaly stand out; leadership, on the other hand, fell to Ionic speakers from Euboea and Attica: "The 'Ionian colonization' was not a one-time enterprise, but a process that demonstrably began in the Protogeometric period (about 900 BC), as in Miletus, and came to an end only in the Homeric period. The 'colonization' also did not leave from a single city or region, not from Pylos, and not from Achaea or Athens, but the immigrants came from many regions of an impoverished and backward Greece, above all from Boeotia and Thessaly, and thus from the northern Mycenaean world; those who set the tone, however, were the Ionic speaking inhabitants of Euboea and Attica" ("Die 'Ionische Kolonisation' war...kein punktuelles Unternehmen, sondern ein Prozess, der in protogeometrischer Zeit (vor 900) nachweisbar begann, so in Milet, und erst in homerischer Zeit zum Abschluss kam. Die 'Kolonisation' nahm auch nicht von einer eizigen Stadt/Landschaft ihren Ausgang, nicht von Pylos, nicht von Achaia oder Athen, sondern aus vielen Gegenden des verarmten und zurückgefallenen Griechenland kamen die Einwanderer, vor allem aber aus Boiotien und Thessalien, also aus der nordmykenischen Welt; tonangebend wurden aber die ionischsprachigen Bewohner Euboias und Attikas").

of Pylos came from Thessaly, and this connection would be emphasized by using the Aeolic form of his name. By the same token, the direct relationship of the Neleids of Miletus to this figure would be played down by not using their own inherited form of this ancestor's name, *Neíleōs*, in epic. If it was the Neleids who promoted the myth of the twelve sons of Neleus in order to fashion Panionism in their own image, but who at the same time did not wish to seem to do so overtly, such a distancing from themselves would have been welcome: while they alone were descendants of Athenian *Neíleōs*, they and all other Panionians were descendants of Thessalian *Nēleús*.

§1.21 We need to look now at the myth of the foundation of Miletus, which literally duplicates the myth of the foundation of Pylos. The fact that there are two eponymous ancestors of the Neleid family is connected with the duplication of this myth. *Nēleús*, the founder of Pylos, was a twin who separated from his brother in order to found a new city; Pelias, who stayed behind, inherited his father's kingdom, and both brothers thus became kings.[57] *Neíleōs*, the founder of Miletus, was the son of the Athenian king Kodros.[58] He too had a brother from whom he separated when he left Athens to found Miletus. *Médōn*, the brother who stayed behind, not only inherited the kingdom of Athens from his father, but himself began a line of rulers named after him (the *Medontídai*).[59] Neileos and Medon, even though they are not called twins, are twin figures, cut from the same mold as Neleus

---

57 Pelias inherited the kingdom of Iolkos from his stepfather Kretheus (see n1.23 above). When Pelias was killed by Medea, Akastos, the son of Pelias, inherited the kingdom and exiled Jason and Medea to Corinth (Jason was the grandson of Kretheus through Aison); cf. "Apollodorus" 1.9.27.

58 Kodros himself was the son of Melanthos, a refugee from Pylos who went to Athens at the time of the Dorian invasion (the return of the Herakleidai) and won the kingship there by prevailing as the Athenians' champion in a border war with the Boeotians; Melanthos was the fourth descendant of Periklymenos, the son of Neleus. Kodros was famous for his sacrificial death, by which he prevented the Dorians from conquering Athens (Hellanicus *FGrHist* 323a F 23; cf. Herodotus 5.76, who connects the Dorian invasion of Attica in which Kodros fell with the Dorian foundation of Megara).

59 The line of Medontidai was the subject of much historical reconstruction by Atthidographers (see n4.150 below). The line must have ended by 683/2 BC, when the list of annual archons (who replaced the former rulers) begins. The last Medontid ruler was said to be Hippomenes, who was connected with a place-name, *Par' híppon kaì kórēn*, "By the horse and the maiden," in Athens, and who was said to have been the last of his line to rule because of his cruelty (cf. n4.151 and n4.152 below). There followed (according to the Atthidographers) a succession of lifelong archons and ten-year archons, until the annual archonship was instituted in 683/2 BC. There is inscriptional evidence for the name *Medontídai* in Athens, but the question is whether it refers to a phratry or a *génos* (see n4.150 and EN4.10 below).

and Pelias, and also modeled on this pair to a large extent.[60] We know that the name Neileos was transferred from the old myth to the new. It is interesting that Pero, the daughter of Neleus who was wooed by all her neighbors in Pylos, is also duplicated in the new myth, in which Neileos has a daughter named Peiro. But the myth itself has been perverted, for instead of being wooed by many suitors, Peiro alienates potential suitors by seeking to satisfy her sexual appetites in a novel and indecent way.[61]

60 Twin figures do not have to be called twins, as pointed out earlier (cf. Ward 1968:3, cited n1.24 above). Of the two sons of Kodros Hellanicus *FGrHist* 323a F 23 calls Medon the older (*presbúteros*) and Neleus (*sic*) the younger (*neóteros*); even between twins one is of course older and the other younger, but that issue is not raised. Pausanias 7.2.1 calls Medon and Neileus the eldest sons of Kodros (*presbútatoi tôn Kódrou paídōn*), setting them off as a pair without calling them twins (see below for further sons of Kodros). As is natural in the myth of twins who separate, Neleus and Pelias are said to have quarreled before they parted ("Apollodorus" 1.9.9); this motif is found again in the myth of Neileos and Medon, who, according to Pausanias 7.2.1, quarreled about the kingship because Medon, the elder, was lame in one foot and Neileus did not wish to be ruled by him; when the Delphic oracle chose Medon, Neileus left Athens and founded Miletus. In addition to Medon and Neileos, his oldest sons, Kodros was given other sons. The additional "sons of Kodros" (*Kodrídai*) were said to have founded a number of the other cities of the dodecapolis besides Miletus. The addition of these Kodrids to the basic set of twins is to be explained in the same way as the tradition for the twelve sons of Neleus, which was grafted onto an earlier twin myth: both have to do with the formation of the dodecapolis, and the leading role of the Neleids of Miletus in that formation. The myth of Kodrid founders was coeval with the myth of the twelve sons of Neleus (see discussion §4.1–§4.10 below); they were parallel myths meant to address the same issue from different perspectives and for different purposes.

61 The bizarre myth of Peiro, also called Elegeis, is found in two entries of the *Etymologicum Magnum*. Under "*Elegēís*" this is said to be the name of the daughter of Neleus, the leader of the Ionian colonization of Caria, whose proper name is Peiro. The name Elegeis is connected with a verb *elegaínein*, glossed as *akolastaínein*, "be licentious," and the comment is added: "for this reason (*dió*) none of the Athenians wished to marry her." Another entry, "*aselgaínein*," says that the verb in question means properly "have unnatural intercourse with women," but is also used of any sort of lewd behavior (*akolastaínein*). The verb *aselgaínein* is equated with the verb *elegaínein*, which is said to come from Elegeis, the name of the Attic woman who first invented the particular perversion. The entry concludes: "Elegeis, the daughter of Neleus, was dissolute (*ásōtos*); her father heard her beating her genitals and shouting: 'Seek, seek a big man...who will take you to Miletus, a woe for the Carians' " (ἧς καὶ ὁ πατὴρ ἤκουσεν ἐπικροτούσης τὸ αἰδοῖον καὶ βοώσης, Δίζεο δίζεο δὴ μέγαν ἄνδρα ἀ[...] ὅς σ' ἐπὶ Μίλητον κατάξει πήματα Καρσί [Gaisford ad loc. emends the two verses, both of which are corrupt, as follows: Δίζεο δίζεο δὴ μέγαν ἄνδρα ἀπόπροθι πάτρης / ὅστ' ἐπὶ Μίλητόν σε κατάξει πήματα Καρσί]). The vocalism of the name *Peiró* should be noted since it parallels that of Ionic *Neíleōs*, and the two names are thus distinguished from the names *Pēró* and *Nēleús* in the same way. Peiro would thus seem to be the Ionic equivalent of an Aeolic Pero. With regard to the perversion of the old myth of Pero in the new myth of Peiro, see Part 4 below for a possible context, namely the rivalry of Ephesus with Miletus for leadership of the dodecapolis. If Ephesus perverted Miletus's foundation myth, it would not be the only such instance (see §4.10–§4.11 below). I would suggest Pherekydes

§1.22 We return now to the name *Néstōr*, which, according to the argument, has the same transitive root **nes-* as Mycenaean *Nehelawos* and Ionic *Neíleōs*. In the aftermath of the discovery of the Bronze Age city of Pylos in 1939 and the decipherment of the Linear-B tablets in 1952, belief in a historical king Nestor was high, and the pair of names *Néstōr* and *Nehelawos* was taken as a good example of the custom, inherited from Indo-European, of giving a son a name that repeated part of the father's name.[62] I am skeptical about a historical king Nestor, although I think that the possibility that there was such a king must always be granted.[63] In any case I am more interested in the Indo-European origins of the Homeric figure, who stood in close relation to the Neleid rulers of Miletus, but not as their ancestor. He was their epic hero, and his name related to their name, not on the level of history, but on the level of myth. In Homer the name *Nēleús* has no connection with the name *Néstōr*, for the Aeolic form *Nēleús* has lost its connection with the root **nes-*.[64] But what of the name *Neíleōs*, which does not occur in Homer, but which must have been in existence during the Homeric era,

───────────

as the source of the Peiro myth rather than the *Ionica* of Panyassis, which Robertson 1988:244–245 proposes (see §4.10 below). Robertson, on the other hand, seems to me right to connect the Elegeis myth with a rite of Demeter in Eleusis other than the Mysteries (see n1.43 above for the foundation of a cult of Eleusinian Demeter on Cape Mykale by Philistos, a follower of Neileos in the colonization of Miletus, Herodotus 9.97).

62 Durante 1967:36 cites as examples the philosopher *Sōkrátēs*, the son of *Sōphronískos*, and the orator *Lukoûrgos*, the son of *Lukóphrōn*.

63 Just as the idea arose that Plato was flat-headed because his name is connected with the adjective *platús*, "flat" (Diogenes Laertius 3.4), one could argue that a real king Nestor was made in epic to act in terms of the Indo-European twin myth because of his name. I repeat that I am skeptical of this.

64 In Homer the name *Nēleús* may have been connected by paronomasia with the adjective *nēleḗs*, "pitiless," as it was in later antiquity (cf. "Herodian" *Epimerismoi* p. 92.4 Boissonade): according to *Odyssey* 15 Neleus held the property of Melampus for a year while Melampus won Pero for Bias, and Melampus, upon his return, somehow repaid this "wicked deed" (*etísato érgon aeikés*); does this story perhaps present Neleus as "pitiless"? A modern line of scholarship has accepted the etymology of *Nēleús* as "the pitiless one" and interpreted the figure as originally a god of the underworld like Hades, who is described in Hesiod *Theogony* 456 as *nēleès êtor ékhōn*, "having a pitiless heart" (a similar phrase is used of Achilles in *Iliad* 9.497). This line of interpretation starts from the premise that Pylos was not originally a city, but an entrance to the underworld (see e.g. Wilamowitz 1931:337–338, and, with bibliography, Sakellariou 1958:50–51, Càssola 1957:92). Although I do not think that "pitiless" is the original meaning of the name *Nēleús*, there certainly was an ancient current of thought that already in Homer equated Pylos with the "gates" (*púlai*) of Hades, for Heracles is said to have wounded Hades "in Pylos among the corpses" (*en Púlōi en nekúessi*) in *Iliad* 5.397. It has been pointed out that already in the Linear-B texts from Pylos there is a considerable number of names having a connection with Hades (Mühlestein 1965:164n49).

as it was before and after it?[65] Was the meaning of this name still under-stood by the family that had inherited it as part of their own name? The answer to this is, I think, that if they still understood Nestor's name, then they must have understood their own name as well; to put it more simply, if they understood that *Néstōr* contains the transitive root **nes-*, they would have understood that *Neíleōs* does too.

§1.23 The question of whether the name Nestor was still understood in the Homeric poems is in any case the central one for us, and for this ques-tion a cardinal piece of evidence is still to be considered. In my earlier study I argued in detail that the hypothetical active verb **néō*, "bring home," which is presupposed by the name *Neíleōs*, actually occurs in Homer, but disguised as something else. The verb, I think, occurs in *Odyssey* 18, in a speech of Penelope to the suitors, in which Penelope recalls Odysseus's farewell speech to her twenty years before. When Odysseus left for Troy he told Penelope to remarry whom she chose when their son had grown if he himself did not return. Odysseus starts his farewell speech by saying that he does not think that all the Achaeans will return safely from Troy because the Trojans are formidable foes in all the pursuits of war. He uses the verb *aponéomai*, a compound of *néomai*, to express the idea that some may not "return" (*Odyssey* 18.259–260):

ὦ γύναι, οὐ γὰρ ὀΐω ἐϋκνήμιδας Ἀχαιοὺς
ἐκ Τροίης εὖ πάντας ἀπήμονας <u>ἀπονέεσθαι</u>.

Woman, I do not think that the well-greaved Achaeans
will all <u>return home</u> safe and unharmed from Troy.

After listing the Trojans' strengths in war (*Odyssey* 18.261–264) Odysseus reverts to his main thought, namely that he himself may not return, and he expresses this thought as follows (*Odyssey* 18.265):

τῶ οὐκ οἶδ', ἤ κέν μ' <u>ἀνέσει</u> θεός, ἤ κεν ἁλώω.

Therefore I do not know if a god will <u>*anései*</u> me, or I will die.

---

65 The meaning of Ionic *Neíleōs* (< Mycenaean *Nehelawos*) could, I think, have remained alive in the Homeric period. The pattern of names like *Agéleōs* (*Odyssey* 22.131, 247) would still have been perceptible in *Neíleōs/*Neélaos* (cf. n1.54 above for a presumed name **Neélaos* in pre-Homeric epic, and note that in Homer there is still an equivalence between -*ei*- and -*ee*- in pairs like contracted ἐφίλ<u>ει</u> and uncontracted φιλ<u>έε</u>σθε; cf. Chantraine 1958:39). See below for the crucial question whether the verbal element in *Neíleōs/*Neélaos*, like the verbal element in *Agéleōs*, retained its meaning in the Homeric period (for *Agéleōs* as a "significant name" in the *Odyssey* see Haubold 2000:123–124).

The verb *anései* in this line is unintelligible;[66] I have therefore proposed that the phrase *m' anései* masks an original phrase *me nései*, in which *nései* is the future of the verb *néō*. The restored line is thus:

τῷ οὐκ οἶδ', ἤ κέν με <u>νέσει</u> θεός, ἤ κεν ἀλώω.

Therefore I do not know if a god will <u>bring</u> me <u>back</u>, or I will die.

The verb *nései*, "bring home," thus picks up the verb *aponéesthai*, "return home," in the opening of Odysseus's speech. It is the active form of the middle verb.

§1.24 While *nései* seems clearly right as the form originally intended in *Odyssey* 18.265, the problem remains of determining when it was replaced by the form *anései*. In my previous study I argued that the Homeric poets themselves no longer knew a transitive verb *néō*, and that they therefore changed a traditional phrase (*me nései*) in a traditional line in order to make sense of it.[67] I have changed my mind about this, and I am now convinced that the change did not take place until the post-Homeric period, whether in oral or written tradition or both. But I did not change my mind on this point until I became convinced that the Homeric poets still understood the name *Néstōr* as "he who brings home": if they understood the name *Néstōr* they must also have understood the verb *nései*. The poets' understanding of the verb and their understanding of the name are inseparable issues and we must leave this matter to one side until we consider the relevant parts of Nestor's Homeric role. The key to his role is his connection with the Indo-European twin myth, and we will continue with the examination of his name in order to place him in the context of this myth.

§1.25 A key question affecting the interpretation of Nestor's name is the meaning of the root **nes-* in early Greek, whether used transitively in the verb **néō* and the name *Néstōr*, or intransitively in the verb *néomai* and the noun *nóstos*. The basic intransitive notion is "return safely," and the basic transitive

---

66 The form *anései* can only be the future of a compound verb from the root **sed-* of Greek *hízō*, "to seat," and *hézomai*, "to sit," but the meaning of the compound verb, which is found only in a few aorist forms in Homer, is "to set upon," as in *Iliad* 13.657: *es díphron d' anésantes*, "setting (a wounded warrior) upon a chariot," and this meaning is wholly inappropriate in *Odyssey* 18.265. The form *anései* must have been understood as the future of the verb *aníēmi*, which means "release" (as in *ánesán te púlas*, "and they opened the gates," in *Iliad* 21.537) and is thus vaguely appropriate in *Odyssey* 18.265 ("I do not know whether the god will *release* me or I shall die"), but the future of *aníēmi* is always *anḗsei*, with a long vowel, and thus cannot have been what was originally intended in this verse. Cf. Frame 1978:99–102.

67 See n1.66 above, and Frame 1978:102.

notion is "bring back safely," but there were two different contexts in which forms from the root *nes- were used, and which affected their meanings. Both contexts, moreover, seem to go back to Indo-European. The first context, which survived in Homeric *nóstos*, is a "safe return *home*." This meaning of the root *nes- is what is also to be assumed in the Mycenaean name *Nehelawos*, hence "he who brings the warfolk safely *home*." While the notion of a "return *home*" is not found in the main Indo-European cognates of Greek *néomai*, this context was nevertheless old if the Sanskrit and Iranian neuter noun *astam*, "home," contains a zero-grade of the root *nes- (original form*ṇstam*).[68] But even in Greek a "safe return *home*" was probably not originally implicit in the verb *néomai* itself: it should be noted that in the Homeric formula *oíkónde néesthai*, "to return home," the context of a return *home* is specified by the word *oíkónde*.[69]

§1.26 The second context of the root *nes- is what we will be concerned with in the Indo-European twin myth and in the Vedic form of that myth. This is also the context to which the name *Néstōr* originally belonged insofar as Nestor too has to do with the Indo-European twin myth. This context of the root *nes- was a "return *from death to life*," and this meaning of the Greek verb *néomai*, although it did not survive into the Homeric era, nevertheless left clear traces in the traditional diction of Homeric epic. The crucial form for this context of early Greek *néomai* is a root aorist participle with zero-grade of the root *nes, namely *ásmenos*, to be reconstructed as *ṇs-menos*.[70]

---

68 Greek *néomai* has an exact cognate in the Sanskrit middle verb *násate*, "approach, resort to, join," in which the context of a "safe return *home*" seems no longer present. Both Greek and Sanskrit also have reduplicated verbs from the root *nes-: Greek *nís(s)omai*, "go," Sanskrit *nímsate*, "kiss"; the Sanskrit meaning "kiss" looks like a further development from the meanings "approach, resort to, join" of *násate*. For *astam*, "home," reconstructed as*ṇs-tam* (root*nes- of *násate*), see Mayrhofer 1956–1980 s.v. This form indicates that the context "return *home*" can be reconstructed for Sanskrit *násate* in line with Greek *néomai*; cf. Benveniste's reconstruction of the meaning of the IE root *nes- as "revenir à un état familier" (Benveniste 1966:172).

69 Note also *oíkade...neómetha* in *Iliad* 2.236, 16.205. The verb's second context (see below in text) must also be specified in Greek; Durante 1976:80 points out that in both Greek and Sanskrit verbs have a large range of meaning that must be specified in context, and that this characteristic distinguishes the two languages. See §1.27 below on Germanic, where, in the case of the cognate verb, one context is generalized to the exclusion of the other.

70 See Frame 1978:6–24 for a full discussion of this form and its place in the formulaic diction of Homeric epic. The root aorist found in Greek *ásmenos* has a Vedic correspondence in the first person plural optative *[sam-]nasīmahi*, *RV* 2.16.8; see García Ramón 2004:34, 43. García Ramón argues that in *Iliad* 2.629 and *Odyssey* 15.254 the sigmatic aorist ἀπενάσσατο, which in these lines must mean "went away," is from *néomai* and not from *naíō*, "dwell," (*nas- for *as- from the zero-grade of the root would be accounted for by analogy with the syllabification of present *néomai*, the same explanation as for Vedic *[sam-]nasīmahi* in relation to

This participle became detached from the paradigm of *néomai* in pre-Homeric Greek and survived as an adjective meaning "happy" in Homeric and later Greek.[71] But in the *Odyssey* the word still functions as a participle in a highly traditional two-line refrain following three deadly encounters that Odysseus undergoes during his *nóstos*.[72] The crucial phrase in this refrain is *ásmenoi ek thanátoio*, "having returned from death":

ἔνθεν δὲ προτέρω πλέομεν ἀκαχήμενοι ἦτορ,
ἄσμενοι ἐκ θανάτοιο, φίλους ὀλέσαντες ἑταίρους.

From there we sailed onward grieving at heart,
having returned from death, having lost dear companions.

When this refrain was first composed it was evidently used of successive encounters in which there was a literal passage through death by the hero and a progressive loss of companions. Even in our *Odyssey* a sense remains in several of the hero's adventures that the encounter is with death itself, explicitly so in the journey to the underworld in *Odyssey* 11.[73] The context in which a literal "return from death" seems to have originated is solar myth, and there are still overt instances of such a solar context in the *Odyssey*:[74] Circe, who acts as the threshold to the underworld, sending the hero there and receiving him back again, is the daughter of the sun god Helios (*Odyssey* 10.138);[75] Helios himself destroys all of Odysseus's remaining companions for

---

present *násate*), and he argues further, pp. 42–43, that in Greek the root aorist (*ἄστο) was replaced by this sigmatic aorist ([ἀπε-]νάσσατο). If this argument is correct the participle *ásmenoi* no longer belonged to a paradigm in Homeric Greek. For further reasons to think that this was the case see below.

71 See Frame 1978:24–28 for a discussion of the semantic development.
72 The Ciconians, *Odyssey* 9.62–63, Cyclops, *Odyssey* 9.565–566, and Laestrygonians, *Odyssey* 10.133–134.
73 Circe, who sends Odysseus and his companions to the underworld and receives them back, calls them *disthanées*, "dying twice" (*Odyssey* 12.22).
74 In my earlier study I used Mircea Eliade's *Patterns in Comparative Religion* for a cross-cultural perspective on solar myth (Frame 1978:22, 32 for quotations of Eliade 1958). The key point is that the sun in setting is thought to pass through death without actually dying, unlike the moon, which in waxing and waning is actually thought to die.
75 Circe is associated with both west and east (sunset and sunrise) and thus both ushers the hero into and receives him back from the underworld. In *Odyssey* 12.1–4, when Odysseus returns from the underworld, Circe's association with the dawn is highlighted; on the other hand, Hesiod *Theogony* 1011–1016, locates Circe in the west among the Etruscans. In *Odyssey* 10.190–192, when Odysseus first arrives in Circe's land, the confusion between east and west is itself highlighted. See Frame 1978:47–53 for a discussion of Circe, especially p. 50 for the suggestion that the name *Kírkē* means "circle, ring," with reference to the movement of the sun.

eating his sacred cattle, but Odysseus is able to return from Helios's island unharmed. The Cyclops episode, although not overtly a solar myth, combines all the features of a "return from death" in a solar context. The one-eyed giant embodies the destructive aspect of solar myth associated with sunset, and his sheep are analogous to the sacred cattle of Helios.[76] Most importantly, his cave is a place of death through which the hero passes unharmed, but from which not all his companions return.

§1.27 Just as the phrase *oîkónde néesthai*, "to return home," specifies one context of the root **nes-* by the word *oîkónde*, so the phrase *ásmenoi ek thanátoio*, "having returned from death," specifies a different context by the words *ek thanátoio*. These two contexts may be distinguished as "sacred" and "secular" insofar as solar myth justifies the term "sacred," and the term "secular" expresses a contrast with this. The sacred context was inherited from Indo-European on the evidence of Germanic, where the root **nes-* is widely attested. Modern German *genesen*, "get well," which is composed of a perfective element *ge-* and the root **nes-*, shows clearly that the underlying notion of "return" in the Germanic root is a "return to life."[77] In Germanic the sacred context, "return to life," seems to have been generalized to the exclusion of a secular context, "return home." This was the opposite of what happened in Greek, where the secular context survived, but the sacred context can be seen in the process of dying out within epic tradition. The latter development is clear from the form *ásmenos* itself, which the Homeric poets no longer understood as a verb but as an adjective meaning

---

76 For the destructive aspect of solar myth, see Eliade 1958:136–137. In the *Odyssey* Helios has both cattle and sheep (*Odyssey* 12.127–130); for the sheep of Helios, cf. also *Homeric Hymn to Apollo* 411–413 and the story of Euenios in Herodotus 9.93–94 (both discussed in Frame 1978:43–44, 46–47).

77 The meaning of the Germanic root **nes-* is reconstructed as "return to life" ("zum Leben zurückkehren") by Feist 1939 s.v. *ganisan*. Gothic *ganisan*, "be saved," is the equivalent of modern German *genesen*. The contexts of the Gothic verb, which is used to translate Greek *sṓzesthai*, include recovery from illness, which was generalized in the case of modern German *genesen*, "get well"; cf. *Mark* 5:23, ἵνα σωθῇ καὶ ζήσῃ, *ei ganisai jah libai* ("that she may get well and live"). In addition to an intransitive verb from the root **nes-* (Gothic *ganisan*, modern German *genesen*), Germanic had a causative verb found in all three branches of Germanic, including Gothic *nasjan*, "save," Old English *nerian*, "save," and modern German *nähren*, "feed"; the underlying notion in the causative verb is "bring back to life." See Frame 1978:126–132 for a full discussion of the Germanic evidence, including Nordic forms of the causative verb. For solar myth as the context of the meaning "return to life" of the IE root **nes-*, the main comparison with Greek is Vedic (see below on the Vedic twins) rather than Germanic (but see Frame 1978:129–130 for a suggestive context of Old English *nerian*, "save," in *Beowulf* 569ff.).

"happy."[78] This semantic change made the syntax of the traditional refrain highly irregular, for the phrase *ásmenoi ek thanátoio*, taken to mean "happy from death," now stood alone without a verb. A verb was in fact added in the only occurrence of the phrase outside the traditional refrain, in *Iliad* 20.350: *phúgen ásmenos ek thanátoio*, "he <u>has escaped</u> happily from death."[79] The syntax of the phrase *ásmenos ek thanátoio* has been regularized in this verse, but what was once, in the traditional refrain, a "return" from death, has now become a "happy escape" from death. A similar process of reinterpretation occurs in the actual episodes followed by the traditional refrain when the refrain in each case is adapted to the particular episode. In the traditional refrain, as originally intended, the "return from death" of Odysseus and some of his companions is contrasted with the loss of other companions. In the adaptations of the refrain the loss of companions remains essentially the same (in two of the episodes it is expressed by the same verb *óllumi* as in the refrain). But what was once a "return from death" has now become an "escape from death," as expressed by the phrase *phúgomen thánaton* or by the verb *phúge* alone. The Ciconian episode, in which the adaptation of the refrain immediately precedes the refrain itself, shows these features clearly (*Odyssey* 9.60–61):

> ἓξ δ' ἀφ' ἑκάστης νηὸς ἐϋκνήμιδες ἑταῖροι
> <u>ὤλονθ'</u>· οἱ δ' ἄλλοι <u>φύγομεν θάνατόν</u> τε μόρον τε.

> Six well-greaved companions from each ship
> <u>were lost</u>; but the rest of us <u>escaped death</u> and doom.

In the Laestrygonian episode only Odysseus's ship escapes from the Laestrygonian harbor; all the other ships are destroyed inside it. In the adaptation of the refrain, which again occurs immediately before the refrain itself, the phrase "happily escaped" (*aspasíōs...phúge*) is used of Odysseus's ship, and the verb "were lost" (*ólonto*) is used of all the other ships (*Odyssey* 10.131–132):

---

78 Thus *Iliad* 14.108: *emoì dé ken asménōi eíē*, "it would be pleasing to me," "I would be happy with that." For the semantic development from "having returned" to "happy" of Homeric *ásmenos* see Frame 1978:24–28: instances in which classical Greek *ásmenos*, "happy," occurs in the context of a "return to the light" (e.g. Herodotus 8.14.1, Plato *Cratylus* 418c, Euripides *Heracles* 524) still suggest the semantic connection; Greek *pháos*, "light," has the metaphorical meanings "deliverance" and "happiness" (see LSJ s.v.; Tarrant 1960:182), which are also taken into account (cf. Euripides *Bacchae* 608–609 and *Ion* 1437–1439, where *pháos* in this metaphorical use is collocated with forms of *ásmenos*).

79 In this line Achilles refers to Aeneas, who through Aphrodite's help *has escaped* him.

ἀσπασίως δ' ἐς πόντον ἐπηρεφέας <u>φύγε</u> πέτρας
νηῦς ἐμή· αὐτὰρ αἱ ἄλλαι ἀολλέες αὐτόθ' <u>ὄλοντο</u>.

<u>Happily</u> my ship <u>escaped</u> from the overhanging rocks
into the sea; but the other ships <u>perished</u> there together.

The phrase *aspasíōs...phúge* in this passage reinterprets the phrase *ásmenoi ek thanátoio* in the traditional refrain as "happy from death" (the word *aspasíōs* makes that very clear), and it changes what was once a "return from death" into a "happy escape."[80]

§1.28 The phrase *ásmenoi ek thanátoio* in the traditional refrain opens a window onto an earlier stage of Greek epic when a *nóstos* was not only a "return home," but also a "return to life." The traditional refrain is not the only relic in the *Odyssey* of this earlier stage of the *nóstos* theme. A second highly traditional line again juxtaposes the verb *néomai*, used of the hero, with the loss of companions. The line occurs in the prophecy of Teiresias to Odysseus in the underworld (*Odyssey* 11.114):

ὀψὲ κακῶς νεῖαι, ὀλέσας ἄπο πάντας ἑταίρους.

You will return late and in bad condition, having lost all your companions.

The contrast between the "return" of the hero on the one hand and the loss of companions on the other hand is the same as in the traditional refrain,

---

80 In the Cyclops episode, which is more complex than the Ciconian and Laestrygonian episodes, the adaptation of the refrain occurs a hundred lines before the refrain itself; whereas the refrain concludes the entire episode (*Odyssey* 9.565–566), the adaptation of the refrain occurs when Odysseus and his companions escape from the Cyclops's cave and return to their ship, where the companions who await them then grieve for those lost in the cave (*Odyssey* 9.466–467):

ἀσπάσιοι δὲ φίλοισ' ἑτάροισι φάνημεν,
οἳ φύγομεν θάνατον· τοὺς δὲ στενάχοντο γοῶντες.

We were a welcome sight to our dear companions,
those of us who escaped death; the others they groaned and wept for.

The contrast between those who returned and those who were lost is again clear. The verb *óllumi* is not used in this case of those who were lost, but is merely implied. As in the other two episodes, what was once a "return from death" in the traditional refrain has in the adaptation become an "escape from death" (*thánaton phúgomen*). The adjective *aspásioi* is again used in connection with those who escaped, although more loosely than in the Laestrygonian episode. It is again the phrase "having returned from death," now understood as "happy from death," that seems to have called forth the adjective *aspásioi*, "welcome," in this looser adaptation of the traditional refrain.

except that the reference is now to the future, when the hero will return alone and all his companions will be lost. The singular participle *olésas*, "having lost," corresponds to the plural participle *olésantes* in the refrain, and the second person singular verb *neîai*, "you will return," corresponds to the plural participle *ásmenoi*, "having returned," in the refrain. If we take into account the context of prophecy in the underworld, the meaning of the form *neîai* is not only "you will return home," but also, implicitly, "you will return from death." The purpose of Odysseus's journey to the underworld is to learn about his *nóstos* from Teiresias,[81] and it is in this line that Teiresias reveals what the final outcome of Odysseus's *nóstos* will be. It is a deeply traditional line to judge by its correspondence with the refrain, and this gives it the appropriate weight to be the ultimate object of Odysseus's journey to the underworld. It is not just the line itself, but also the context of prophecy in the underworld that seems to be traditional. The same line is later repeated by Circe, who gives Odysseus more immediate advice for his *nóstos*, but this second occurrence seems to be an extension of the line's primary occurrence in the prophecy of Teiresias.[82] The verb *neîai* itself in this line of course no longer meant "you will return to life" to the Homeric poets, but simply "you will return home"; adaptations of the line elsewhere in the *Odyssey* leave no doubt about this.[83] But the correspondence with the traditional refrain

81 *Odyssey* 10.492, 538–540.
82 Not all Homeric manuscripts include this line and the one before it in Circe's speech. Of the hardships that await Odysseus on his *nóstos* Teiresias speaks only of the cattle of Helios (*Odyssey* 11.104–115). Circe, after hearing from Odysseus what he learned in the underworld (*Odyssey* 12.35), tells him what he will encounter on the way to the cattle of Helios (*Odyssey* 12.39–126); she ends by repeating verbatim what Teiresias said about the cattle, that if he harms them, he will lose his companions and ship, and that if he manages to escape himself, he will return home late and in evil condition (*Odyssey* 12.139–141):

εἰ δέ κε σίνηαι, τότε τοι τεκμαίρομ' ὄλεθρον
[νηΐ τε καὶ ἑτάροισ'. αὐτὸς δ' εἴ πέρ κεν ἀλύξῃς,
ὀψὲ κακῶς νεῖαι, ὀλέσας ἄπο πάντας ἑταίρους.]

But if you should harm them I foresee destruction
[for your ship and companions; if you yourself should escape,
you will return late and in bad condition, having lost all your companions.]

83 There are three adaptations of the line, in *Odyssey* 2.174, 9.534, and 13.340. In each case Odysseus's ultimate loss of all his companions is expressed with the same phrase (ὀλέσας ἄπο πάντας ἑταίρους, 9.534, 13.340; ὀλέσαντ' ἄπο πάντας ἑταίρους, 2.174); the idea that Odysseus will himself "return" also remains constant, but with more variety of expression, and without the implication of a "return to life" of Teiresias's prophecy. When Athena meets with Odysseus soon after his arrival on the shores of Ithaca, she says that she knew all along that he would "return home" (ᾔδε', ὃ νοστήσεις, ὀλέσας ἄπο πάντας ἑταίρους,

indicates that the original notion in the verb *neîai*, as in the phrase *ásmenoi ek thanátoio*, was a "return from death."

§1.29 There is a third line that seems to have been inherited from an earlier stage of the *nóstos* tradition in Greek epic, namely the reconstructed form of the line *Odyssey* 18.265, in which the active verb *néō* occurs:

τῷ οὐκ οἶδ᾽, ἤ κέν με νέσει θεός, ἤ κεν ἀλώω.

Therefore I do not know if a god will bring me back, or I will die.

This line parallels the traditional refrain (with *ásmenoi*) and the traditional prophecy (with *neîai*) in presenting a contrast between two fates: a "return" on the one hand and destruction on the other hand. In this case it is not a contrast between the hero and his companions, but the hero's own fate that is in the balance. Just as the intransitive verb *néomai* earlier meant "return from death" in a sacred context, so the verb *nései* in *Odyssey* 18.265 in all likelihood once meant more than simply "bring home." In its present context,

---

Odyssey 13.340), as he has now done. Reaching "home" is made entirely explicit when the Cyclops curses the fleeing Odysseus, praying to Poseidon that if Odysseus is fated "to see his dear ones and reach his well-built home and his fatherland" (*Odyssey* 9.532–533), "may he come late and in evil condition" (ὀψὲ κακῶς ἔλθοι, ὀλέσας ἄπο πάντας ἑταίρους, *Odyssey* 9.534). In *Odyssey* 2 the prophet Halitherses recalls to the suitors that he once foretold that Odysseus, who was about to leave for Troy, would "come home" (οἴκαδ᾽ ἐλεύσεσθαι) in the twentieth year unrecognized by all, having suffered many woes and having lost all his companions" (*Odyssey* 2.174–176):

φῆν κακὰ πολλὰ παθόντ᾽, ὀλέσαντ᾽ ἄπο πάντας ἑταίρους,
ἄγνωστον πάντεσσιν ἐεικοστῷ ἐνιαυτῷ
οἴκαδ᾽ ἐλεύσεσθαι.

I declared that he would come home
having suffered many evils, having lost all his companions,
unrecognized by all, in the twentieth year.

Here the three words ὀψὲ κακῶς νεῖαι, "you will return late and in bad condition," of Teiresias's prophecy are each elaborated and expanded upon: *opsé*, "late," is specified as *eeikostôi eniautôi*, "in the twentieth year," *kakôs*, "in bad condition," is expanded into *kakà pollà pathónt'*, "having suffered many evils," and *neîai*, "you will return," is recast as *oíkad' eleúsesthai*, "he would come home." Halitherses' speech retains the context of prophecy of Teiresias's speech, but like the other two adaptations of Teiresias's speech this one lacks the implication of a "return to life." See Frame 1978:13–15 for a detailed analysis of the relationship between the single line of Teiresias's prophecy and its three adaptations. I emphasize that only the traditional line with the phrase *opsè kakôs neîai* exactly fills one line: the adaptation in *Odyssey* 13.340 is shorter than a full line (the phrase ἤδε᾽, ὅ, "I knew that...," occupies the beginning of the line); the adaptation in *Odyssey* 2.174–176 is expanded into two and a half lines; and the adaptation in *Odyssey* 9.534 (with the verb *élthoi*, "may he come," for the traditional *neîai*, "you will return") depends on the two previous lines for the sense of coming "home" in the Cyclops's curse.

Odysseus's farewell speech to Penelope, the verb *nései* relates specifically to Odysseus's "return home."[84] But there were doubtless other contexts besides a farewell speech in which the hero faced the uncertainty of his own "return."[85] I therefore prefer not to define the traditional context of this line more narrowly than by what can be inferred from the line itself.

§1.30 There is indirect evidence that the phrase *me nései* in this line once meant "will bring me back to life" if we consider closely the alternative fate, *ê ken halóō*, "or I shall perish." The verb *halônai*, "to die," actually means "to be caught"; the meaning "to die" arose from the phrase *thanátōi...halônai*, "to be caught by death," through an ellipsis of the word *thanátōi*, "by death."[86] But without the word *thanátōi* the meaning "to die" of *halônai* does not make sense, for "to be caught," or "to be captured," is not the same as "to die." The question then is, how did the ellipsis of *thanátōi* arise in the first place, and the answer, I think, lies in *Odyssey* 18.265, where the two alternatives, "whether the god will bring me back (from death), or I shall be caught," express exactly the two possible fates of the hero who seeks a *nóstos* in the original sense. If he succeeds, he will have a safe passage through death; if he fails, he will be caught (by death).[87] Odysseus's ability to enter and return from the Cyclops's

---

84 As we have seen, this verb answers to the verb *aponéesthai*, "return home," earlier in Odysseus's speech.

85 For one such context see below on *Odyssey* 15.300, an adaptation of the traditional line *Odyssey* 18.265.

86 The full phrase *thanátōi...halônai*, "to be caught by death," occurs three times in Homer, twice in the line: νῦν δέ με λευγαλέῳ θανάτῳ εἵμαρτο ἁλῶναι, "but I was fated now to be caught by a wretched death" (*Odyssey* 5.312 = *Iliad* 21.281), once in the line: νῦν δ' ἄρα σ' οἰκτίστῳ θανάτῳ εἵμαρτο ἁλῶναι, "but you were fated now to be caught by a most pitiable death" (*Odyssey* 24.34); cf. Frame 1978:104.

87 See §1.26 and n1.74 above for the hero's safe passage through death in the context of solar myth. For the notion of being "caught" by death, cf. Hesiod *Theogony* 765–766, where *Thánatos*, "death," is depicted as "seizing" and "holding" its victims: ἔχει δ' ὃν πρῶτα λάβῃσιν / ἀνθρώπων, "he holds whomever of men he first seizes." For the verb *halônai*, "be caught," in the context of a "return from death" there is a striking piece of evidence in Pindar *Pythian* 3.56–57, where Asklepios is criticized for an unholy deed, namely "bringing back from death a man already caught": ἄνδρ' ἐκ θανάτου κομίσαι / ἤδη ἁλωκότα. The perfect participle *halōkóta* is ambiguous, for it could mean "having died" in accord with the elliptical usage of *halônai*, "to die," in Homer. But Pindar may well have in mind the literal meaning of *halōkóta*, "having been caught," for in this passage the ellipsis of "by death" is exactly the same as in *Odyssey* 18.265; the only difference is that what is implicit in the verb *nései* in Homer (namely a return from death) is explicit in the phrase *ek thanátou komísai*, "bring back from death," in Pindar. The passages of Hesiod and Pindar are discussed in Frame 1978:105n43 and 108–109.

cave, in contrast to what befalls six of his companions, well illustrates the difference in question.[88]

§1.31 As in the case of the other two traditional lines, the line with *nései* was adapted elsewhere in Homer. In *Odyssey* 15.300 Telemachus, who has set sail for home from Pylos, is described as "pondering whether he would escape death or perish":

ὁρμαίνων, ἤ κεν θάνατον φύγοι ἤ κεν ἀλοίη.

Pondering whether he would escape death or die.

The similarity between this line and *Odyssey* 18.265 is clear: uncertainty is expressed in the first foot and a half of each line, followed by two alternative fates. The second alternative, as expressed by the verb *halônai*, is virtually the same in the two lines. But for the first alternative the phrase *ế kén me nései theós*, "whether the god will *bring me back*," has been replaced by the phrase *ế ken thánaton phúgoi*, "whether he would *escape death*." This adaptation is like those of the traditional refrain in which the phrase *thánaton phúgomen* (*phúgomen thánaton*), "we escaped death," reinterprets the phrase *ásmenoi ek thanátoio*, "having returned from death," of the refrain. The parallelism between the two adaptations is complete if the line with the phrase *me nései* was also highly traditional, and if the phrase itself originally meant "will bring me back from death."[89]

88 The case for the semantic development "to die" of the verb *halônai* is presented in more detail in Frame 1978:103–109. The case includes consideration of the meaning "to kill" of Homeric *hairéō*, "to seize," as in the formulaic phrase *hélen ándra(s)* (in six of seven occurrences of this phrase *hélen* means "killed"; it means "seized" only in *Odyssey* 24.441: *táphos d' hélen ándra hékaston*, "amazement seized each man"). Cf. also *Iliad* 11.738 (quoted n1.93 below) where *hélon*, "I killed," contrasts with *kómissa*, "I took." The verbs *hairéō* and *halískomai* (aorist *halônai*) are an antithetical pair (cf. their meanings "convict" and "be convicted" in Attic legal usage); the artificial meaning "to die" of *halônai*, I suggest, gave rise to the corresponding artificial meaning "to kill" of *hairéō*, which is again limited to the Homeric *Kunstsprache* in Greek. If the meaning "kill" of *hairéō*, in line with the meaning "be killed" of *halískomai*, is to be laid ultimately to the account of the line containing the phrase *me nései*, "will bring me back to life," it is a further sign of how traditional this line was.

89 In *Odyssey* 18.265, as previously discussed, the two alternatives, "whether the god will bring me back (from death) or I shall be caught (by death)," make perfect sense with this literal interpretation of the verb *halônai*, "be caught." But in the adaptation of this line in *Odyssey* 15.300 the alternatives are no longer clear. The alternatives in this line are "to escape death" or "to be caught," and it is not clear, in spite of the close proximity of the word *thánaton*, whether "to be caught" means to be caught "by death" (i.e. "to die"), or to be caught by the human agents in the situation, namely the evil-minded suitors. It is only the fact that the meaning "to die" of *halônai* had established itself in the Homeric *Kunstsprache* that makes it certain that "to die" is meant in *Odyssey* 15.300. I take this as a further sign that *Odyssey* 15.300 is the adaptation and *Odyssey* 18.265 is the highly traditional model,

§1.32 By indirect means we arrive at a conclusion for the active verb *nései* that is consistent with what we previously concluded for the middle verb *néomai* and the noun *nóstos*. When the line that is now found at *Odyssey* 18.265 first originated, the verb *nései* meant to "bring back to life," but by the Homeric era this meaning had been lost, and in *Odyssey* 18.265 the meaning was rather to "bring home." The relevance of this to the name *Néstōr* is clear. In the Homeric era the meaning of the name, in line with the verb *nései*, was "he who brings home," but in the not too distant past of Greek epic tradition his name must have meant "he who brings back to life." In my previous study, as I have said, I did not believe that the Homeric poets still knew the verb *nései* in *Odyssey* 18.265, for I believed that it was they who at some point in the tradition changed this verb to the form *anései*. I therefore did not imagine that Nestor's name still had any meaning for the Homeric poets, and I considered only the earlier meaning of his name, "he who brings back to life." I have changed my mind about the synchronic meaning of Nestor's name for the Homeric poets, and I will address this issue in Part 2 when we consider Nestor's role in the *nóstos* of the Achaeans acccording to his own account in *Odyssey* 3. But I have not changed my earlier view concerning the diachronic meaning of Nestor's name, namely that this meaning, "he who brings back to life," is relevant to the earliest level of his epic tradition, and in particular to the story that he tells about his own youth in *Iliad* 11.[90] There is a sense in this story that Nestor, the sole survivor among Neleus's sons of Heracles' sack of Pylos, brings his city back to life. The Pylians in the aftermath of Heracles' attack are described as *paûroi kekakōménoi*, "few and in bad condition," and therefore prey to their hostile neighbors to the north, the Epeians, who are identified in the story with the historical Eleians. Nestor carried out a cattle raid against these neighbors, and the booty that he brought home was distributed among the Pylians, to whom it was owed, for the Pylians had been too weak to protect their own cattle, and had lost this chief means of life to the Epeians (*Iliad* 11.688–689):

πολέσιν γὰρ Ἐπειοὶ χρεῖος ὄφειλον,

ὡς ἡμεῖς παῦροι κεκακωμένοι ἐν Πύλῳ ἦμεν.

---

and that the verb *nései* of the model originally meant "will bring back *from death*." It is not clear what the wording of the first foot and a half of this traditional line was, other than that uncertainty was expressed; the phrase *tôi ouk oîd'* in 18.265 could have been the model for *hormaínōn* in 15.300, but this was not necessarily the case.

90 Frame 1978:94–95.

For the Epeians owed a debt to many,
since few of us were left in Pylos and we were badly off.

By his cattle raid Nestor brought his people back from virtual (if not actual) extinction, and it was the cattle raid that particularly interested me in the interpretation of Nestor's name and Nestor's myth. I was convinced, as I have said, that solar myth was the original context of the *nóstos* tradition that underlies the *Odyssey*, and this context is still very clear from the poem itself.[91] Cattle, which represent sustenance and life, are a repeated feature in the various forms of the *nóstos* myth in the *Odyssey*, and they are the central feature of the solar myth at its most literal in the poem, the myth of the cattle of Helios. It was therefore very significant to me that Nestor's cattle raid also seems to have a close connection with solar myth. The Epeian king Augeias, "the shining one," and his daughter Agamede, a specialist in drugs, look like local forms of Helios, the sun god, and his granddaughter Medeia, likewise a specialist in drugs.[92] Augeias and his daughter do not play a prominent role in Nestor's story, but they are still there in the background.[93] In post-Homeric tradition Augeias himself was famous for his cattle, as in the myth of the cleaning of his stables by Heracles, and this further connects him with Helios and his cattle.[94] There are other traces of Nestor's association with

---

91 Cf. §1.26 above.

92 The names *Agamḗdē* and *Mḗdeia*, both containing the root of the verb *mḗdomai*, "plan, devise," are themselves closely related. The name *Augeías* is from *augḗ*, "bright light, radiance," as in the frequent Homeric formula *hup' augàs ēelíoio*, "under the rays of the sun" (cf. Frame 1978:88–89). In post-Homeric tradition Augeias is called the son of Helios; this makes Agamede, like Medeia, a granddaughter of Helios.

93 In the battle following Nestor's cattle raid Nestor immediately slays the leader of the Epeian horsemen, Moulios, who is the husband of Agamede, and it is here that Agamede's knowledge of drugs is described (*Iliad* 11.738–741):

πρῶτος ἐγὼν ἕλον ἄνδρα, κόμισσα δὲ μώνυχας ἵππους,
Μούλιον αἰχμητήν· γαμβρὸς δ' ἦν Αὐγείαο,
πρεσβυτάτην δὲ θύγατρ' εἶχε ξανθὴν Ἀγαμήδην,
ἣ τόσα φάρμακα ᾔδη ὅσα τρέφει εὐρεῖα χθών.

I was the first to slay a man, and I took his solid-hoofed horses,
the spearman Moulios; he was the son-in-law of Augeias
and had his oldest daughter, golden-haired Agamede,
who knew as many drugs as the wide earth grows.

In *Iliad* 11.698–702 Augeias deprives Neleus of the horses and chariot sent to Elis to compete for prizes; for this episode see below §5.45–§5.46.

94 The cattle of Augeias are closely equated with the cattle of Helios in Theocritus 25.118–121, 129–131 (see Frame 1978:89–90).

both cattle and solar myth in his traditions.⁹⁵ I pointed these connections out in my previous study, but I had nothing more to say about the exact nature of Nestor's myth.⁹⁶ I have since become convinced that Nestor's story in *Iliad* 11 provides the key to his myth once his connection with the Indo-European twin myth is made clear. We will start with his story in *Iliad* 11 when we turn to the interpretation of Nestor's Homeric role in Part 2 below.

§1.33 There is another issue that significantly affects the interpretation of the name *Néstōr*, and that is also central to Nestor's connection with the Indo-European twin myth: the etymology of Greek *nóos*, "mind." The etymology of *nóos* (contracted form *noûs*) has long been debated, and in my earlier study of the *nóstos* theme I was much concerned with this issue.⁹⁷ The form of *nóos* is clear: it is a verbal noun containing the o-grade of a verbal root, like *lógos*, "word," related to *légō*, "say," *phóros*, "tribute," related to *phérō*, "bear," *phóbos*, "panic flight," related to *phébomai*, "flee in panic." But in *nóos* the verbal root is no longer clear because the final consonant of the root was lost between vowels. In Greek three consonants were lost between vowels, -u̯-, -i̯-, and -s-, and roots ending with each of these consonants have been proposed for the etymology of *nóos*. A root **neu̯-* has been made unlikely for *nóos* by the Mycenaean Greek form *wi-pi-no-o*, interpreted as the personal name *Wiphinoos*, the equivalent of later Greek *Iphínoos*.⁹⁸ If the second element of this compound has to do with the noun *nóos*, *nóos* did not originally have a -u̯-, for Mycenaean Greek still preserves this consonant (noted as -w-) between vowels.⁹⁹ If the root **neu̯-* is thus excluded, the formal question is all

---
95 Nestor's other story of his exploits among the Epeians concerns his participation in the funeral games at Bouprasion of a figure named *Amarunkeús* (*Iliad* 23.629–642); the name of this Epeian figure is related to the verb *amarússō*, "sparkle, shine," and it thus indicates as much as does the name *Augeías* a context of solar myth. The report in Pausanias 4.36.2–3 of a cave near the Messenian city of Pylos in which the cattle of Neleus and Nestor were said to have been stabled is also suggestive of solar myth; cf. the sheep stabled in the Cyclops's cave; the sheep of Helios stabled in a cave in Apollonia in the story of Euenios (Herodotus 9.93–94); and the sacred sheep of Helios on Cape Tainaron, where an entrance to the underworld was said to be (see Frame 1978:43–44, 46–47, 90–93).
96 Frame 1978:113–115.
97 The title of my Ph.D. dissertation was *The Origins of Greek* ΝΟΥΣ (Frame 1971); cf. §1.5 above.
98 KN V 962; Ventris and Chadwick 1973:591.
99 Mycenaean Greek preserves original -w- in all positions (note the initial consonant of *Wiphinoos*, lost in classical Greek *Iphínoos*).

but settled: since there is no known Greek root *neį-,[100] the root *nes- is the only likely possibility, and nóos can thus be reconstructed as *nosos.[101]

§1.34 For the semantics of Greek nóos the essential fact is the close connection that the word has with the faculty of vision.[102] This connection is particularly clear in the denominative verb noéō, "perceive";[103] noéō is derived directly from nóos, and a similar meaning defines the essence of this action noun: nóos is a "perceiving." But this meaning derives in turn from the action expressed by the noun's verbal root. This action, I believe, was a "bringing back to the light" in the context of solar myth.[104] The derivational sequence was thus: néō, "bring back to life and light" > nóos, a "bringing back to life and light" = a "perceiving" > noéō, "perceive."[105]

---

100 Sanskrit has a root *neį- in the verb náyati, "lead" and the noun naya-. The noun, whose meanings include "behavior" and "worldly wisdom," has been proposed as an exact comparison for Greek nóos, "mind," but the absence of the root in Greek and the large semantic gap between the Greek and Sanskrit nouns make this comparison unlikely.

101 Intervocalic -s- was lost in Greek before the Mycenaean stage; at this stage -h- was still present in pronunciation but not normally noted in the writing system (thus ne-e-ra-wo = Nehelawos < *Neselawos). Intervocalic -y- was also lost before the Mycenaean stage. I must point out that for now I have ignored the possibility that the second element of the name Wiphinoos has no relation to the noun nóos. The name has been convincingly interpreted as containing a verbal element -noos from the root *nes- and thus as meaning "bringing back by his force" (see Mühlestein 1965:157; as a parallel for the o-grade of -noos Mühlestein cites Hippóthoos, in which -thoos contains the root of théō, "run" [IE *dheų-]; cf. also the Homeric epithet laossóos, "inciting the warfolk," related to seúō, "incite" [IE *kįeų-]; for the derivation of the epithet see Frisk 1960–1972, Chantraine 1999, s.v. σεύομαι). The question is whether this verbal element is related to the noun nóos. I am convinced that it is, but the derivation of nóos from *nes- has not yet been established (see §1.38–§1.41 below for a correction of my own earlier argument), and new attempts continue to be made to connect nóos with the root *neų- of Greek neúō, "nod" (Krischer 1984, Heubeck 1987:236–238); these attempts, as I hope to show, are illusory and should be abandoned.

102 See Frame 1978:28–31 (with references to Snell 1931:77, von Fritz 1943:88 and 1945:223; cf. n1.105 below).

103 The phrase oxù nóēse, "he/she perceived sharply," which occurs eight times in the Iliad (six times in the conditional clause ei mè ár' oxù nóēse, "if he/she had not perceived sharply"), is used when someone sees a danger and acts to avert it.

104 Specifically in the context of the Indo-European twin myth (see Chapter 3 below). For "intelligence" as an important aspect of solar myth, cf. Eliade 1958:124, 150-151 on the role of rationality and a rational elite in the further evolution of solar myth where it occurs; cf. also Frame 1978:32.

105 For nóos as a "perceiving" that is equivalent to a "bringing back to life and light," cf. von Fritz 1943:89, who describes noeîn in contrast to vision as a "truer recognition which... penetrates below the visible surface to the real essence of the contemplated object," and 1945:224, where he refers to a "νόος which penetrates beyond the surface appearance [and] discovers the real truth about the matter"; Snell 1931:77 earlier wrote: "Noeîv stands...in close relation to the organ of the eye. But in the word the function of the eye (seeing) appears as separated from the organ. Noeîv is a 'seeing,' but a 'mental' seeing" ("Das voeîv

§1.35 Nestor's name, with the original meaning "he who brings back to life and light," makes him the virtual personification of *nóos* if this noun originally meant a "bringing back to life and light." Nestor is of course one of the two counselors on whom the Achaeans at Troy rely, and it is not surprising that he, like the other principal counselor, Odysseus, is renowned for his intelligence. But for Nestor this reputation is particularly associated with the noun *nóos*. Some of the Homeric passages that bear this out can only be considered in the context of particular episodes, and we will postpone these until later.[106] For now there are two passages in which Nestor's association with *nóos* is little short of a theme in its own right and thus detachable from its immediate context.[107] The first passage is in *Iliad* 9, when Nestor urges Agamemnon to send an embassy to appease Achilles, reminding him that he took Achilles' war prize in the first place against Nestor's advice. Nestor introduces his counsel by insisting heavily on the words *nóos* and *noéō*, both of which he uses in close relation to himself (*Iliad* 9.103–108):

> steht...in naher Beziehung zum Organ des Auges. Nur dass die Funktion des Auges (das Sehen) in dem Wort erscheint als abgelöst von dem Organ. Das νοεῖν ist ein 'Sehen,' aber ein 'geistiges' Sehen"). Snell and von Fritz have been criticized for identifying *nóos* too closely with sense perception, and for excluding mental reflection from the semantics of the Homeric word (cf. Lesher 1981:9–20 and 1994:1–10). I agree that mental reflection takes place in Homer and that it should not be divorced from the semantics of Homeric vocabulary. My interest is in etymology, which is different from synchronic meaning, but which can still have an unusual relevance in a conservative medium like Homeric epic. As will be argued in Part 2 below, the reconstructed meaning of *nóos* as a "bringing back to life and light" has such heightened relevance for key episodes in Nestor's Homeric role. For the formal pattern of the proposed sequence *néō* > *nóos* > *noéō*, cf. such parallels as *phérō* > *phóros* > *phoréō* and *phébomai* > *phóbos* > *phobéō* (unless *phoréō* and *phobéō* are deverbative rather than denominative verbs: Chantraine 1961:240 considers it impossible to determine whether *phoréō* is an iterative from *phérō* or a denominative from *phóros*; Frisk thinks that *phobéō* was originally causative but later functioned as a denominative; Chantraine 1961:240 also entertains this possibility). For Ruijgh's suggestion to compare *noéō* directly with the Gothic causative *nasjan*, see Frame 1978:30n27. This is a formal possibility, but there is no reason to abandon the usual interpretation of *noéō* as a denominative from *nóos*; Chantraine 1999 s.v. νόος points out that the meaning of *noéō* corresponds exactly to that of *nóos*.

106 See below §2.48–§2.52 and §2.68–§2.70.
107 Both passages are discussed in Frame 1978:84–85; a third less distinctive passage may also be mentioned: in *Iliad* 4 Nestor concludes his tactical instructions to his Pylian warriors as follows (*Iliad* 4.308–309):

> ὧδε καὶ οἱ πρότεροι πόλεας καὶ τείχε' ἐπόρθεον
> τόνδε <u>νόον</u> καὶ θυμὸν ἐνὶ στήθεσσιν ἔχοντες.

> Thus did earlier men sack cities and walls,
> with this <u>mind</u> and spirit in their breasts.

αὐτὰρ ἐγὼν ἐρέω ὥς μοι δοκεῖ εἶναι ἄριστα.
οὐ γάρ τις <u>νόον</u> ἄλλος ἀμείνονα τοῦδε <u>νοήσει</u>
οἷον ἐγὼ <u>νοέω</u> ἠμὲν πάλαι ἠδ᾽ ἔτι καὶ νῦν—
ἐξ ἔτι τοῦ ὅτε διογενὲς Βρισηΐδα κούρην
χωομένου Ἀχιλῆος ἔβης κλισίηθεν ἀπούρας
οὔ τι καθ᾽ ἡμέτερόν γε <u>νόον</u>.

But I will speak as seems best to me.
For no one <u>will think of</u> a better <u>plan</u> than this one
that <u>I am thinking of</u>, both long ago and to this very moment,
ever since the time when you, Zeus-born one, went and took
the maiden Briseis from the tent of furious Achilles,
not at all according to my <u>advice</u>.

Nestor tells Agamemnon that no one will devise a better plan than his, and he bases his claim, with due respect to Agamemnon, on the fact that he had been right in the first place, when Agamemnon ignored him. But the way that Nestor expresses this conveys another message, equally clear, which might be put as follows: "I, and no one else, am the man of *nóos*, both now, when you finally must heed me, and formerly too, when you made a mistake by not heeding me."[108]

§1.36 The passage in *Iliad* 9 insists on the relevance of *nóos* to Nestor through the repetition of the noun and the denominative verb *noéō*; another passage is eloquently brief and pointed. Nestor is again the speaker when, returning from his meeting with Patroclus in *Iliad* 11, he encounters the Achaean leaders in full retreat and advises them to take counsel; he expresses this advice as follows (*Iliad* 14.61–62):

ἡμεῖς δὲ φραζώμεθ᾽ ὅπως ἔσται τάδε ἔργα
<u>εἴ τι νόος ῥέξει</u>.

Let us consider how these matters will be,
<u>if mind will accomplish anything</u>.

---

108 The second line in the above passage (*Iliad* 9.104) is similar to another line, *Iliad* 7.358 and 12.232: οἶσθα καὶ ἄλλον <u>μῦθον</u> ἀμείνονα τοῦδε νοῆσαι, "You know how to think of another <u>word</u> better than this one." This line is used when one speaker rejects another speaker's proposal: in *Iliad* 7 Paris rejects Antenor's proposal to return Helen to the Atreidai; in *Iliad* 12 Hector rejects Polydamas's exhortation not to attack the Achaean ships. The change from *mûthos* to *nóos* in *Iliad* 9 in what amounts to Nestor's definition of his own role is highly instructive.

Nestor here seems to act almost as the symbol of wise counsel, for after he calls on the leaders to deliberate, he leaves it to one of them (Diomedes) to propose the plan that is actually put into effect (the wounded champions urge on their followers from behind the lines). Since Nestor's role is raised to a symbolic level in this episode, so too is his statement. When he says, "let us take thought how these matters will be, if *nóos* will accomplish anything," *nóos*, as subject of the active verb *rhéxei*, is strongly personified: *nóos* is equated with Nestor himself in this passage, and this is entirely appropriate if in some sense they are one and the same thing—that is, if Nestor is indeed the personification of *nóos*.

§1.37 Another name that is relevant to the etymology of *nóos* is *Alkínoos*, a close equivalent in both form and meaning of *Iphínoos*/Mycenaean *Wiphinoos*. Alcinous, as king of the Phaeacians in the *Odyssey*, has the particular function of bringing Odysseus home to Ithaca.[109] This final stage in Odysseus's *nóstos* is presented poetically as a "return to life" in that Odysseus aboard the Phaeacian ship sinks into a deep sleep "most like death" (*thanátōi ánkhista eoikṓs, Odyssey* 13.80); his arrival in Ithaka, where he awakens, is thus simultaneously a "return home" and a "return to life." In line with Alcinous's function in the *Odyssey* his name, like the name *Iphínoos*, has been interpreted as "he who brings home with his might": in both names the second part of the name is not the verbal noun *nóos*, originally a "bringing back to life and light," but a verbal adjective meaning "bringing back."[110] Alcinous, who as king of the Phaeacians brings Odysseus back to life and light, at least metaphorically, at the end of his *nóstos*, acts out the etymology of *nóos*, with which the second part of his name is closely related but not identical.[111]

---

109 The relationship between Nestor, who does not bring Odysseus home, and Alcinous, who does, is an important issue to be considered later (see Part 2, Chapter 7 below).

110 See Mühlestein 1965:158, who interprets Homeric *Alkínoos* (like Mycenaean *Wiphinoos*, cf. n1.101 above) as containing the root **nes-*; Mühlestein notes the possibility that the noun *nóos* also contains the root **nes-* (he cites the agreement of Alfred Heubeck and Ernst Risch on this point, 158n18), but he does not pursue the issue, which the formal evidence cannot resolve. Whatever etymological relationship there may be between such apparently similar Homeric forms as *Alkínoos*, "he who brings home with his might," and *ankhínoos*, "close-minded, shrewd," the two forms are of course semantically quite distinct. The question is whether the noun "mind" contained in *ankhínoos* is also perceived in *Alkínoos*, and this depends on whether the noun still has any verbal force.

111 He acts this out from a distance, to be sure: the sailors who take Odysseus home are his proxies. The Phaeacian ships, like the Phaeacian king, have a connection with *nóos*, being called "quick as an arrow or a *thought* (*nóēma*)": τῶν νέες ὠκεῖαι ὡς εἰ πτερὸν ἠὲ νόημα (*Odyssey* 7.36).

§1.38 Nestor and Alcinous are both keys to the etymology of Greek *nóos*, "mind." I considered both figures in my previous study from the standpoint of *nóos*, and I will return to both of them from the same standpoint in Part 2 below. In my previous study I also devoted much attention to a third figure in relation to the etymology of *nóos*, namely Odysseus. Odysseus and Nestor are the two counselors on whom the Achaeans at Troy rely, and Odysseus like Nestor is characterized by his intelligence. In addition Odysseus is the hero who "returns," and it is his *nóstos* in the *Odyssey* that reveals that a "return home" was in origin a "return to life." Odysseus's famous intelligence figures prominently in his return in the *Odyssey*, and this suggested to me that the two things, his return and his intelligence, are connected in the word *nóos*. Hence I reconstructed the original meaning of *nóos* as "return to life and light," with the middle (intransitive) meaning "return" of the root **nes-*. In fact I did not distinguish sharply between the active and the middle meaning of the root **nes-*, but used both meanings in different parts of my argument to reconstruct the original meaning of *nóos*. This was a methodological problem that I did not fully recognize, for, as I now see more clearly, the noun should have had only one meaning or the other, and not both at once. I remain convinced that there is a deep connection between the return and the intelligence of Odysseus, but I no longer think that the noun *nóos* meant "return." The keys to *nóos* are the names *Néstōr* and *Alkínoos*, which have the active sense of the root **nes-*, "bring back." The connection between Odysseus's return and his intelligence is, I think, at least one step removed from the etymology of the noun *nóos*.[112]

§1.39 A number of arguments that I made in my previous study make better sense if they are modified in light of what I have just said. First, the names *Alkínoos* and *Wiphínoos*, interpreted with an active sense of the root **nes-* as "he who brings back with his might" and "he who brings back with

---

112 From a formal standpoint *nóos* could be not only a *nomen actionis* but also a *nomen rei actae*: cf. the noun *gónos* (root **gen-*), which means both a "begetting" (*nomen actionis*) and "that which is begotten, offspring" (*nomen rei actae*); on this analogy *nóos* could mean both a "bringing back" and "that which is brought back" (cf. Frame 1978:28n26). For the possible relevance of this to Odysseus I think of the reciprocal relationship between Alcinous ("he who brings back") and Odysseus in Odysseus's return home. However this may be, the role of intelligence in solar myth (cf. n1.104 above) remains in my view a dominant factor in the tradition behind Odysseus's return. Sisyphus, who literally returns from death by his wits (*Theognis* 702–712), provides a striking parallel to Odysseus for the connection between intelligence and return (see Frame 1978:36–37). Other attempts to derive *nóos* from the IE root **nes-* in an intransitive sense have been made by Frei 1968 (cf. Frame 1978:33n32) and (following Frei) Létoublon 1985:175–176. An exception in this regard is Ruijgh's reconstruction of a transitive meaning (see n1.105 above).

his force" respectively, imply an active sense of the root in the noun *nóos* as
well: a noun identical in form with the second part of these names would
not be expected to contrast with them in meaning by having a middle sense
of the root; since the forms are identical, the meanings should be parallel.
Secondly, there is a problem in reconstructing the same original meaning,
"return to life and light," for two different nouns, *nóstos* and *nóos*: why would
there have been two nouns with the same meaning, and, if there were, why
did they develop such different meanings as "return home" on the one hand
and "mind" on the other? The two nouns must have had distinct meanings
from the beginning, and this was the case if *nóos* had the active sense and
nóstos the middle sense of the root **nes-*.[113] Finally, there is Odysseus, whose
characteristic intelligence is not *nóos*, as it is for Nestor, but *mêtis*, "shrewd-
ness," as in his particularized epithet, *polúmētis*, "having many shrewd coun-
sels." This is not a clearcut issue, for common nouns like *nóos* and *mêtis* may
be characteristic of certain figures, but their use is of course not restricted
to these figures. Thus the word *nóos* and its derivatives are used more than
once of Odysseus (in e.g. *Iliad* 10.247, *Odyssey* 1.66, and *Odyssey* 10.329); *nóos*
is even used of Odysseus in connection with his escape from the Cyclops's
cave, when he himself later recalls that escape to encourage his men (*Odyssey*
12.211–212):

> ἀλλὰ καὶ ἔνθεν ἐμῇ ἀρετῇ βουλῇ τε <u>νόῳ</u> τε
> ἐκφύγομεν.

> But even from that place, by means of my valor, plan, and
> > <u>intelligence,</u>
> we escaped.

To take the reverse case we have a very striking and memorable use of the
word *mêtis* in Nestor's speech of advice to his son Antilochus before the
chariot race in the funeral games of Patroclus (*Iliad* 23.313–318):

> ἀλλ' ἄγε δὴ σὺ φίλος <u>μῆτιν</u> ἐμβάλλεο θυμῷ
> παντοίην, ἵνα μή σε παρεκπροφύγῃσιν ἄεθλα.
> <u>μήτι</u> τοι δρυτόμος μέγ' ἀμείνων ἠὲ βίηφι·

---

113 Létoublon 1985:176 suggests that the noun *nóstos* was not created until the noun *nóos* had
lost its connection with the verb *néomai*; this possibility would in fact allow both nouns
to contain the root **nes-* in an intransitive sense. But, as I will argue in Part 2 below, the
Homeric noun *nóos* still has a connection with the root **nes-* in a transitive sense (the name
Néstōr is the key to this connection).

μήτι δ' αὖτε κυβερνήτης ἐνὶ οἴνοπι πόντῳ
νῆα θοὴν ἰθύνει ἐρεχθομένην ἀνέμοισι·
μήτι δ' ἡνίοχος περιγίγνεται ἡνιόχοιο.

But come, dear son, and put into your mind <u>intelligent schemes</u>
of all sorts so that the prizes do not escape you.
<u>By intelligence</u> the woodcutter is much better than by strength;
<u>by intelligence</u>, moreover, a helmsman on the wine-dark sea
holds his swift ship on course when it is battered by the winds;
and <u>by intelligence</u> charioteer surpasses charioteer.

If Nestor is indeed the personification of *nóos*, we shall certainly want to
know why in this passage he repeats the word *mêtis*, the characteristic
quality of Odysseus, with as much insistence as when he repeats the words
nóos and *noéō* in his speech to Agamemnon in *Iliad* 9.[114] But the fact remains
that *mêtis* is the quality that particularly characterizes Odysseus. It comes
to the fore especially in the "return" from the Cyclops's cave, the episode
which, after the Nekyia, captures most the sense of a "return from death" in
the *nóstos* of Odysseus. Even the name *Oûtis*, "no one," with which Odysseus
tricks Polyphemos, is turned into *mêtis* by way of the phrase *mḗ tis*, "no one,"
which the other Cyclopes utter at the moment of the ruse's success (*Odyssey*
9.410): εἰ μὲν δὴ μή τίς σε βιάζεται οἶον ἐόντα, "if <u>no one</u> is overpowering
you, alone as you are." A few lines later Odysseus makes the connection
with *mêtis* overt when he says (*Odyssey* 9.414): ὡς ὄνομ' ἐξαπάτησεν ἐμὸν
καὶ μῆτις ἀμύμων, "thus my name and faultless <u>mêtis</u> deceived him." Later,
on the night before he kills the suitors, Odysseus steels himself by remem-
bering how he took courage in the Cyclops's cave, until *mêtis* led him
out (*Odyssey* 20.20–21): σὺ δ' ἐτόλμας, ὄφρα σε μῆτις / ἐξάγαγ' ἐξ ἄντροιο
ὀϊόμενον θανέεσθαι, "you took courage until <u>mêtis</u> led you out of the cave,
thinking that you were going to die."

§1.40 I discussed these passages concerning Odysseus's *mêtis* in my
previous study, where I argued that the word *mêtis* and other similarly
descriptive vocabulary, including the word *boulḗ*, "counsel," had replaced the
word *nóos* in the old connection between *nóos* and *nóstos*.[115] My assumption
was that the Homeric poets were only dimly aware of that primitive etymo-
logical connection, and that they therefore transformed it with a new and

114 For this passage see below §2.49 and §2.51 and n2.57 and n2.63.
115 Frame 1978:69–73.

more highly charged vocabulary. I now think that the original meaning of *nóos* was not as dim to the Homeric poets as such an arbitrary process of transformation would imply. But to see the live poetic connection one must look in the right place, and that place is not in the return of Odysseus. Odysseus uses *mêtis* to escape from the Cyclops's cave, not because of anything having to do with *nóos*, but because *mêtis* is his characteristic quality. The key to *nóos* is Nestor, and the question how far the Homeric poets still understood the original meaning of *nóos* belongs with the question how far they still understood the original meaning of *Néstōr* and of *nóstos*.[116] All of these questions should be kept open and considered carefully when we examine Nestor's Homeric role.

§1.41 Since I have rejected in the preceding pages arguments that I considered carefully in my previous study, I should clearly state that I only changed my mind on such a basic question as the etymology of *nóos* after I realized the significance of the Sanskrit evidence for this etymology. It was the same evidence that simultaneously changed my view of Nestor. Indeed the Greek name *Néstōr* and the Greek noun *nóos* become inseparable parts of one and the same problem when they are viewed in the light of the Vedic name *Nā́satyā*.

---

116 I have been careful to distinguish at each step of the argument what the Homeric poets still knew from what was embedded in traditional epic diction. The Homeric poets no longer knew the sacred meaning "return to life" of the root **nes-*, but traditional epic diction preserved traces of this meaning. This is clearest in the case of the verb *néomai* because of its root aorist participle *ásmenos* and the formulaic usage of this participle. The same distinction between a sacred and a secular context of the root **nes-* applies to the noun *nóstos*, the verb *néō (nései)*, and the noun *nóos*. For none of these forms is there a surface meaning "return to life"/"bring back to life" of the root **nes-* still present. But while a sharp distinction between a sacred and a secular context can be made at the lexical level of these forms from **nes-*, the distinction was probably far less sharp at the thematic level. By this I mean simply that a *nóstos*, while its meaning at the lexical level in the *Odyssey* was a "return home," must have kept strong associations of a "return to life" at the thematic level because of the episodes that compose this *nóstos*, including a journey to the underworld, the return from the Cyclops's cave, and the cattle of the sun. How far the same was true of the verb *néō*, the name *Néstōr*, and the noun *nóos* cannot be decided in the abstract but only in the context of actual episodes; the issue will return in Part 2 below.

Chapter 3.

Vedic

§1.42 The twin gods of the *Rig-Veda* have two dual names: they are not only *Aśvínā*, "horse-possessors," a name that occurs 398 times in the *Rig-Veda*, but also *Nā́satyā*, a name that occurs 99 times in the *Rig-Veda*.[117] The name *Nā́satyā* is old. It has an exact cognate in Avestan *Nā́ŋhaiθya*, the name of a demon in the Zoroastrian religious system.[118] The Iranian singular suggests that in Common Indo-Iranian the twins' dual name also occurred in the singular to name one twin in opposition to the other.[119] It would have been this twin that was demonized by the Zoroastrian religious reform.[120] The name *Nā́satyā* also occurs in Mitanni, the branch of Indic that became separated from the main branch of Indic and settled in northwest Mesopotamia, and was transformed through contact with native Hurrian speakers. Among the Indic elements preserved in Mitanni are the names of certain gods, and in particular the name *Nasattiia(nna)*, which occurs beside Mitanni equivalents of the Vedic gods Mitra, Varuṇa, and Indra, and which must designate the same twin gods as Vedic *Nā́satyā*.[121]

---

117 The 99 occurrences of the dual include a single instance of the compound name *Indranā́satyā* ("Indra and the *Nā́satyā*"). In addition to the 99 occurrences of the dual there is one occurrence of a singular *Nā́satya-* (RV 4.3.6; see n1.207 below).

118 The name occurs twice in the *Avesta* (*Vīdēvdāt* 10.9 and 19.43).

119 For dual forms like Homeric *Aíante* as originally meaning "Ajax and his brother" ("elliptic duals"), see Wackernagel 1877.

120 For discussion of the Iranian demon see Frame 1978:169–170 (with bibliography); cf. also §1.67 below.

121 The name occurs on a treaty in the fourteenth century BC between the Mitanni king Matiwāza and the Hittite king Suppiluliuma; for the Mitanni evidence, see Mayrhofer 1966:14–15, Burrow 1973:27–30. The same group of gods found in Mitanni is found (with the addition of the war god Vāyu) in two hymns of the *Rig-Veda*; these gods have been inter-

§1.43 We do not know whether the twins' old name *Nāsatyā* still had a
clear meaning in the *Rig-Veda*. In the post-Vedic period it did not. Various
interpretations of the name were then current, all based on folk etymolo-
gies.[122] Although the etymology of *Nāsatyā* has yet to be established with
certainty, the prevailing modern view is to derive the form from the root
*nes-. The Vedic twins have the characteristic functions of "saving" and
"healing" distressed mortals, and this has suggested a connection with the
Gothic verb *nasjan*, "save" and "heal," which contains this root.[123] The under-

---

preted by Dumézil as the Indic representatives of what he calls the three "functions" of
Indo-European ideology: priestly magic and authority (Mitra and Varuṇa), war (Indra and
Vāyu), and agricultural production and fertility (the twin gods). In India the three functions
of Indo-European ideology became rigidified as three castes: brahmans (priests), kṣatriyas
(warriors), and vaiśyas (agricultural producers). Hence the gods of the three functions are
also gods of these three castes, and the twins in particular are the vaiśya gods.

122 One of these, deriving the name from *na-a-satya*, "not-un-true," may have originated
already in the Vedic period. Although this derivation is first found in Pāṇini, the name's
metrical pattern in the *Rig-Veda* may already have suggested it (see §1.68 below). There
are good formal and semantic reasons for rejecting this derivation: *na-* instead of *an-* for
"not" in such a compound would be highly unusual, and the meaning "not untrue" (or
"not unreal") is too abstract and undistinctive to be old; cf. Lommel 1951:29. A different
derivation, *nāsā-tya*, "nose-born," is given by Yāska (*Nirukta* 6.13) and this too, although
it has been defended in modern times (Lommel 1951:29–31), must be rejected. The story
on which it is based is found in the *Bṛhaddevatā* 6.162–6.167.7 to *RV* 10.17.1–2: the twins'
mother Saraṇyū conceived them when she and her husband Vivasvat, in the form of
horses, attempted to mate; the seed of Vivasvat fell on the ground and Saraṇyū breathed it
in through her nostrils. This myth, which has a close parallel in the Purāṇas (see Lommel
1951:30), cannot have to do with the original meaning of the name *Nāsatyā*. The decisive
objection, which will be argued in detail below, is that *Nāsatyā* was originally singular and
designated one twin in opposition to the other. The interpretation "nose-born," which
must concern both twins equally, is thus to be rejected. Another derivation, *nā* (i.e. *nar* =
netar-) + *satya*, "true leaders," is clearly impossible (Böhtlingk and Roth 1855–1875, who
cite all three etymologies, do not give the source for this one).

123 The basic evidence for the existence of the root **nes-* in Sanskrit is the middle verb *násate*,
"approach, resort to, join," an exact cognate of Greek *néomai*; for the meanings of the
Sanskrit verb, which have developed too far to shed light on the original Indo-European
verb, see n1.68 above. For Gothic *nasjan*, "save, heal," see n1.77 above. The comparison
of Gothic *nasjan* with Vedic *Nāsatyā* was first suggested by Brunnhofer 1892:99 (cited by
Güntert 1923:259 and Lommel 1951:29). The problem has been to explain the morphology
of *Nāsatyā*. Güntert proposed the most widely accepted solution (Debrunner accepts it
[Wackernagel-Debrunner 1957:939], and Mayrhofer, to whom a derivation from **nes-*
seems likely, regards Güntert's solution as the best [Mayrhofer 1956–1980 s.v.; 1986ff. s.v.]).
Güntert began with the Indo-Iranian ancestor of Sanskrit *násate*, to which he ascribed
the meaning "hasten to safety" on the basis of the Germanic evidence. He then posited a
nominal derivative **nasati-*, "salvation through hastening to the rescue," on the parallel
of *vasati-*, "dwelling," from *vásati*, "to dwell." The name *Nāsatyā* would then be derived
from **nasati-* just as the name *āditya-* (used of a particular group of gods) is derived from
the abstract noun *áditi-* ("unboundedness"). Güntert's solution is possible, but the hypo-

lying meaning of Gothic *nasjan*, as earlier discussed, is "bring back to life."[124] A similar implication of the name *Nā́satyā* is indicated by the twins' rescue myths, in several of which they are said to bring mortals "back to life." The mortal Rebha was bound, stabbed, and cast into the waters for nine days and ten nights before being saved by the twins; *RV* 10.39.9 says that he was "dead" (*mamr̥vā́ṃsam*) when the twins "raised (him) up" (*úd airayatam*).[125] Bhujyu was saved after his father or evil companions abandoned him at sea; *RV* 1.119.4 refers to the twins as "bringing (Bhujyu) home from the dead ancestors" (*niváhantā pitŕ̥bhya ā́*).[126] Little is known of Śyāva, to whom there are only two references in the *Rig-Veda*.[127] But one of these, *RV* 1.117.24, says that he was "split in three" (*trídhā...víkastam*) when the twins "raised him up to live" (*új jīvása airayatam*).

§1.44 The Vedic twins not only "bring back to life," they also "bring back to the light," and this is equally significant for the meaning of their name *Nā́satyā*. To Bhujyu, who was "cast forth on the unsupporting darkness" (*anārambhaṇé támasi práviddham*, 1.182.6), the twins gave "light-bringing help" (*svàrvatīr...ūtī́r*, 1.119.8). Rebha they "raised up to see the sun" (*úd... aírayataṃ svàr dr̥śé*, 1.112.5),[128] as they did Vandana as well (ibid.). Vandana, who was buried in a pit when he disintegrated with old age, is the object of a pair of similes that strikingly connect the ideas of "returning from death" and "returning from darkness" in a solar context: *RV* 1.117.5 says that the twins restored Vandana "like one who had fallen asleep in the womb of the

---

thetical abstract noun **nasati-* is weak. One would expect **nasti-* in view of Gothic *ga-nists*, "salvation," or even **asti-* on the basis of Indo-Iranian *astam*, "home" (for Gothic *ganists*, see Frame 1978:128). In addition the names *Nā́satya-* and *Ā́ditya-*, which have the same metrical shape, are treated differently in Vedic verse with regard to metrical resolutions, and this makes it doubtful that the two were created through the same process of word formation (see §1.68 below). I have proposed a different solution for the formation of *Nā́satyā*, which assumes that the name, in line with Avestan *Nā̊ŋhaiθya*, was originally singular. I will return to the question of word formation at the end of this discussion, once it is clear that the name *Nā́satyā* had to do with distinctions between the twins, and that it properly named one twin in opposition to the other.

124 n1.77 and §1.27 above.
125 Cf. also *RV* 1.117.4, another reference to the myth of Rebha: "you two, by your miraculous powers, put him back together again when he had come apart" (*sáṃ táṃ riṇītho víprutaṃ dáṃsobhir*). For other references to this myth see Geldner 1951–1957 on *RV* 1.116.24.
126 Geldner takes *pitŕ̥bhya ā́* as "to his parents," but the *Rig-Veda* always uses the dual when the meaning is "parents," and the case ending (ablative) is against the meaning "to." For other references to the myth of Bhujyu, see Geldner on *RV* 1.116.3–5.
127 *RV* 1.117.24 and 10.65.12.
128 Rebha, who was bound, stabbed, and cast into the waters for ten nights and nine days, is evidently conceived as having been saved by the twins at dawn on the tenth day.

death goddess" (*suṣupvā́ṃsaṃ ná nírṛter upásthe*)[129] and "like the sun dwelling in darkness" (*sū́ryaṃ ná...támasi kṣiyántam*).

§1.45 A solar context marks the twins' cult as well as their myths. They are invoked at dawn, the time of their principal sacrifice, and they have a close connection with Uṣas, the dawn goddess. Uṣas is bidden to awaken them (8.9.17), they follow her in their chariot (8.5.2, etc.), she is born when they hitch their steeds (10.39.12), and their chariot is once said to arrive before her (1.34.10). By their invocation at dawn the twins are closely associated with a "return from darkness" in cult as well as myth. In three hymns the poet marks the time of invocation with the phrase "we have reached the other shore of this darkness" (*átāriṣma támasas pārám asyá*).[130] In another hymn the poet prays for "sustenance (*íṣam*) that will deliver us across the darkness" (*yā́ naḥ pī́parad...támas tiráḥ*, 1.46.6). The twins are called "darkness slayers" (*tamohánā*, 3.39.3), and their horses and chariot are described as "uncovering the covered darkness" (*aporṇuvántas táma ā́ párīvṛtam*, 4.45.2). One hymn invokes the twins as "you who have made light for mankind" (*yā́v... jyótir jánāya cakráthuḥ*, 1.92.17).[131]

§1.46 In the *Rig-Veda* the twins are viewed as an identical pair almost without exception. Their names and epithets are thus virtually always in the dual. But there were distinctions between the twins which both the *Rig-Veda*, in one exceptional verse, and Sanskrit epic, in an indirect form, have preserved. These distinctions can be correlated with a distinction between the two names *Nā́satyā* and *Aśvínā* as they are used in the *Rig-Veda*. This is of great importance for the twins' two names, for they are thus seen to contrast with one another, each properly designating a different twin.[132]

§1.47 RV 1.181.4, the only verse of the *Rig-Veda* that explicitly contrasts the two twins, says that they were "born here and there" (*ihéha jātā́*)[133] and that each was the son of a different father: one is called the son of *Súmakha*, the other the son of *Dyaús*. *Dyaús* is the Indo-European sky god, cognate with Greek *Zeús*; *Súmakha* is otherwise unknown. The twin who is said to be the

---

129 Vedic *nírṛti-* can be either the goddess or the concept of "destruction" or "dissolution," and it is not clear which is meant in this verse. The related verbal adjective *nírṛta-* is applied to Vandana in 1.119.7: "Vandana, who was decomposed by old age (*nírṛtaṃ jaraṇyáyā*), you miracle-workers put back together again (*sám invathaḥ*) as craftsmen do a chariot."

130 *RV* 1.183.6, 1.184.6, and 7.73.1. The same phrase occurs in *RV* 1.92.6 to Uṣas.

131 See §1.55 below for the twins' close connection with a female figure called alternatively *Sūryā́* (the feminized form of *sū́rya*, "sun") and *duhitā́ sū́ryasya*, "daughter of the sun."

132 They are "elliptic duals" (cf. n1.119 above).

133 Cf. *RV* 5.73.4, which says that the twins were "born differently" (*nā́nā jātā́u*) but does not elaborate further.

son of *Súmakha* has the epithets *jiṣṇú*, "conquering," and *sūrí*, "lordly," characterizing him as a warrior. The name of this twin's father, *Súmakha*, most likely means "good warrior," and so interpreted it reinforces this twin's own characterization as a warrior. The other twin has the less distinctive epithet *subhága*, "bountiful."[134]

§1.48 The opposition between the two twins revealed by this single verse of the *Rig-Veda* is confirmed indirectly by Sanskrit epic.[135] The heroes of the *Mahābhārata* are the five Pāṇḍavas, "sons of Pāṇḍu," who in addition to being the sons of the mortal Pāṇḍu are the sons of different gods. The two youngest brothers are the twins Nakula and Sahadeva, and they are the sons of the twin gods. All of the Pāṇḍavas are characterized in terms of their divine fathers, who as a group represent a highly archaic religious structure.[136] The Pāṇḍavas, who reembody this structure, reveal archaic features of their fathers that even the *Rig-Veda* does not attest. In particular the twins Nakula and Sahadeva preserve old oppositions between their fathers that confirm and go beyond what is found in RV 1.181.4. As a survey of their characteristic epithets shows, Nakula is consistently portrayed as "warlike," whereas Sahadeva is portrayed as uniquely "intelligent." Sahadeva's distinctive epithets are "wise" (*vidvān*, 17.2.54), "intelligent" (*prājña*, 17.2.56), "endowed with understanding" (*buddhimān*, 14.72.2103), "learned" (*paṇḍita*, 2.63.2155), "clever" (*matimān*, 3.269.15710), "acute" (*nipuṇa*, 5.49.1838), and "clairvoyant" (*cakṣuṣin*, 6.75.3282). Nakula's distinctive epithets, on the other hand, are "skillful in all forms of war" (*sarvayuddhaviśārada*, 7.165.7364), "good in

---

134 The meaning of the Vedic noun *makháḥ* in the name *Súmakha* is difficult to determine on its own and more than one etymology is possible; see Mayrhofer 1956–1980 s.v. For a possible connection with Greek μάχομαι see (besides Mayrhofer) Chantraine 1999 s.v. Grassmann 1873 glosses *súmakha* as "schön (kräftig) kämpfend, kampftüchtig"; cf. also Güntert 1923:257–258. The complete text of RV 1.181.4 is as follows:

ihéha jātā sám avāvaśītām / arepásā tanvā nā́mabhiḥ svaíḥ
jiṣṇúr vām anyáḥ súmakhasya sūrír / divó anyáḥ subhágaḥ putrá ūhe

Born in different places the two faultless ones agreed in body [or the two agreed in faultless body] and in their names; one of them (is considered) the conquering, lordly (son) of Sumakha, the other is considered the bountiful son of Dyaus.

135 As Wikander 1957 demonstrates.

136 The gods are those of the three Indo-European "functions," as Wikander 1947 showed; part of Wikander's article was translated from Swedish to French by Dumézil 1948:37–53. The only difference from the Vedic scheme (see n1.121 above) is that Mitra and Varuṇa, the two "first-function" gods of Vedic, have been replaced by Dharma, "moral right," in the epic scheme: Dharma is the father of Yudhiṣṭhira, the oldest of the Pāṇḍavas; Indra and Vāyu, the war gods, are the fathers of Bhīma and Arjuna, who are next in age; and the Aśvins are the fathers of Nakula and Sahadeva, the youngest of the Pāṇḍavas.

war" (*kuśalaṃ yuddhe*, 7.98.3976), and, most characteristically, "fighting in a wondrous manner" (*citrayodhin*, 1.139.5533, 5.47.1832, 5.49.1996, 5.89.3168, 8.76.3814, 9.10.477). Nakula's other epithets concern his warrior's "beauty"; he is called "beautiful" (*darśanīya*, 3.27.1020, 4.3.61, 5.49.1996), "the most beautiful in the world" (*darśanīyatamo loke*, 2.78.2625), and "the most beautiful of heroes" (*darśanīyatamo nṝṇām*, 2.75.2555).[137] Two scenes in the *Mahābhārata* underscore the contrast between Nakula's "warrior beauty" and Sahadeva's "intelligence."[138] In the great dice game, Yudhiṣṭhira, the twins' eldest brother, characterizes each of them when he puts them up as stakes: Nakula he calls "dark, young, with eyes of flame, the shoulders of a lion, and huge arms" (2.63.2152), but Sahadeva, he says, "teaches justice and has acquired a reputation in this world for being *learned*" (*paṇḍita*, 2.63.2155). Similarly, near the end of the poem, when the twins die, Yudhiṣṭhira interprets their deaths as the result of peculiar moral flaws:[139] Nakula's flaw was to think "there is no one equal to me in beauty" (*rūpeṇa matsamo nāsti kaścid iti*, 17.2.62); Sahadeva, on the other hand, "always thought that no one was as *intelligent* as himself" (*ātmanaḥ sadṛśaṃ prājñaṃ naiṣo 'manyata kañcana*, 17.2.56).[140]

§1.49 The contrast between the warrior Nakula and his brother Sahadeva confirms the contrast between the divine twins in *RV* 1.181.4, where only the

---

137 The references, which are Wikander's, are to the Bombay and the Calcutta edition of the *Mahābhārata*. Note that when the twins are characterized as a pair at their birth, both are said to possess incomparable beauty (see Dumézil 1968:56 on *Mahābhārata* 1.124.4836–4852 [critical edition 1.115]; this illustrates how the distinctive attribute of one twin is automatically shared by the other if the context does not specify distinctions between them.

138 Wikander 1957:73–74.

139 Yudhiṣṭhira interprets the deaths of Arjuna, Bhīma, and Draupadī (the Pāṇḍavas' common wife) in the same way in this episode; see Dumézil 1968:81–82 for each character's flaw as that character's essential feature.

140 Sahadeva's "intelligence" is also a marked feature in two aberrant traditions of the *Mahābhārata*, as Dumézil 1968:82–85 has shown. The first of these is the Persian account of the "Sons of Pan" (see Dumézil 1968:82–83). According to this text, each of the five sons received a particular talent as a result of his teacher's prayers; Sahadeva, "who looked for wisdom and who did not speak unless spoken to, asked for the science of the stars and a knowledge of hidden matters." The other aberrant version is that of the eighteenth-century Swiss Colonel de Polier, who studied with an Indian teacher and whose extensive notes, including a résumé of the *Mahābhārata*, were published as *La Mythologie des Indous* by his cousin, the Chanoinesse de Polier, in 1809 (see Dumézil 1968:42–43 for the nature and value of this text). In the *Mahābhārata* of the Colonel de Polier, the five Pāṇḍavas are all characterized at their births, and Sahadeva is called "the most enlightened of mortals, the most perspicacious, and the most learned in the knowledge of past, present, and future" (see Dumézil 1968:84). The fault that causes Sahadeva's death in this version is more particular than it is in the vulgate: Sahadeva did not tell his brothers that their mother Kuntī had had a son (Karṇa) by the sun god Sūrya before they were born, "although he had penetrated this mystery by means of his great intelligence" (see Dumézil 1968:85).

son of Sumakha is characterized as a warrior. The characterization of Sahadeva as uniquely "intelligent," on the other hand, goes beyond what is found in *RV* 1.181.4 and bears directly on our primary concern, namely the name *Nā́satyā* as a derivative of the IE root **nes-* and a cognate of Greek *Néstōr* and Greek *nóos*. But before we can address the name *Nā́satyā* itself, there is a second contrast between Nakula and Sahadeva which bears on both names of the divine twins, *Aśvínā* as well as *Nā́satyā*. This contrast is found in the fourth book of the *Mahābhārata*, where the twins and their three older brothers all assume different disguises to spend the last year of their thirteen-year exile at the court of king Virāṭa. The twins both disguise themselves as vaiśyas (members of the third caste), and this is itself a reflection of their fathers' archaic nature.[141] But the twins' disguise as vaiśyas also reveals a contrast between them that would not have been suspected otherwise: while Nakula disguises himself as a groom and takes charge of Virāṭa's "horses," Sahadeva speaks warmly of his preference for "cattle" and becomes Virāṭa's cowherd.[142]

§1.50 The warrior Nakula is associated with horses, as one would expect. The intelligent Sahadeva is associated with cattle, and this is a revelation. The question then is whether the contrast between horses and cattle that characterizes the epic twins also characterizes their divine fathers. The answer is that it does, for a contrast between cattle and horses is found in several of the twins' Vedic hymns, one of which is particularly significant.[143] In *RV* 2.41.7 the contrast between cattle and horses is correlated with a contrast between the twins' two names, *Nā́satyā* and *Aśvínā*: the name *Aśvínā* is associated with horses, as one would expect, and the name *Nā́satyā* is associated with cattle. The verse is divided into three segments, the first two of which articulate the

---

141 For the divine twins as the vaiśya gods see n1.121 above; for the twins' disguises at Virāṭa's court see Dumézil's translation of Wikander 1947 (Dumézil 1948:48). The disguises of all five Pāṇḍavas reflect the natures of their divine fathers, who are the gods of the three castes, brahmans, kṣatriyas (warrriors), and vaiśyas; see Dumézil 1948:48–50 and 1968:70–71 for the disguises of the three older brothers: Yudhiṣṭhira as a dice-playing brahman, Arjuna as a eunuch dancemaster, and Bhīma as a butcher. In Vedic the two war gods Indra and Vāyu represent different aspects of warfare, Indra the warrior's finesse, Vāyu (whose name means the "wind") brute force; this difference is reflected in their sons Arjuna and Bhīma, whose disguises as dance master and butcher show the difference clearly. Strictly speaking Yudhiṣṭhira does not disguise himself, for his brahman code does not allow it.

142 Wikander 1957:76. Sahadeva expresses his preference for and competence in handling cattle in 4.3.67–72 and 4.10.288–293 (English translation van Buitenen 1978:29–30, 39–40; van Buitenen follows the Poona [critical] edition of the *Mahābhārata*, in which the second passage is 4.9, not 4.10).

143 For the following analysis see Frame 1978:146–152; in it I depart from Wikander, who did not notice the evidence in question and was thus misled about the name *Nā́satyā* (cf. §1.54 below).

double opposition in question: "cattle" and "horses" are contrasted in these two segments by two neuter adjectives modifying the noun *vartís*, "path," which is in the third segment. The first segment begins with the adjective *gómad*, "rich in cattle," and ends with the vocative *Nāsatyā*, whereas the second segment begins with the adjective *áśvāvad*, "rich in horses," and ends with the vocative *Aśvinā*. The parallelism between these two segments makes it crystal clear that "cattle" are associated with the name *Nā́satyā* and "horses" with the name *Aśvínā*:

gómad ū ṣú nāsatyā / áśvāvad yātam aśvinā / vartī́ rudrā nṛpā́yyam

Quickly come (*ū ṣú...yātam*) along the path (*vartī́*) rich in cattle, you *Nā́satyā*; quickly come along the path rich in horses, you *Aśvínā*; quickly come, you *rudrā*, along the man-protecting (*nṛpā́yyam*) path (*RV* 2.41.7).[144]

§1.51 The articulation of this verse, which is masterful, is wholly designed to associate the first word, *gómad*, with the name *Nā́satyā*. This association is confirmed by another verse in the *Rig-Veda*, which likewise associates the name *Nā́satyā* with cattle in opposition to horses. This verse, *RV* 7.72.1, has two segments, and the adjectives "rich in cattle" (*gómatā*) and "rich in horses" (*áśvāvatā*) again contrast with each other in different segments of the verse (the adjectives modify the noun *ráthena*, "chariot," which is in the instrumental case). In this verse the name *Aśvínā* is omitted in the second segment concerning "horses," but "cattle" are closely associated with the name *Nā́satyā* in the first segment:

ā́ gómatā nāsatyā ráthena / áśvāvatā puruścandréṇa yātam

Come here (*ā́...yātam*) on your chariot (*ráthena*) rich in cattle, you *Nā́satyā*; come here on your chariot rich in horses and abundant with gold (*puruścandréṇa*) (*RV* 7.72.1).

144 *RV* 2.41.7 is a Gāyatrī, consisting of three eight-syllable segments. The verse's simple prose message, *ū ṣú...yātam...vartís*, "quickly come on the path," is deployed across all three segments of the verse, one word per segment (*ū ṣú*, "quickly," in the first segment functions as one word). Each segment also contains a neuter adjective modifying the noun *vartís*, "path," and a dual vocative addressed to the twins. There are thus three words in each segment, each with a separate function. The arrangement of these three words is identical in the first two segments, but in the third segment it is different: the order 1, 2, 3 of the first two segments (neuter adjective, prose message, dual vocative) becomes 2, 3, 1 in the third segment (prose message, dual vocative, neuter adjective). The different word order of the third segment puts the twins' epithet *rudrā*, "ruddy," and the neuter adjective *nṛpā́yyam*, "man-protecting," outside the double contrast of the first two segments.

The evidence of *RV* 2.41.7, which is supported by the evidence of *RV* 7.72.1, is given additional weight by another factor: *RV* 2.41.7 belongs to one of the rare Vedic hymns that present the gods of the three "functions" who are found also on the Mitanni treaty from the fourteenth century BC.[145] There is thus good reason to regard the content of *RV* 2.41.7 as highly traditional.

§1.52 On the evidence of *RV* 2.41.7 we can conclude that the name Nāsatyā properly belonged to the father of the intelligent Sahadeva, the divine twin who is called the son of *Dyaús* in *RV* 1.181.4. The name *Aśvínā*, by the same token, properly belonged to the father of the warrior Nakula, the divine twin who is called the son of *Súmakha* in *RV* 1.181.4. Next we must consider whether Sahadeva's reputation for "intelligence" also characterized the divine twin who was properly called *Nāsatyā*. The answer to this question is again yes, and the evidence is provided by the twins' Vedic epithet *dasrá*. This epithet, which is used 44 times of the twins, means "miracle-working (wundertätig)," and it relates to the twins' function as "magic healers": twice they are called *dasrā bhiṣájā(u)*, "miracle-working physicians."[146] Etymologically *dasrá* means simply "clever, skillful": these are the meanings of the exact Avestan cognate *daŋrō*, and the Vedic adjective too must have implied "intelligence."[147] What

---

145 For the Mitanni gods as the representatives of the three "functions" of Indo-European society, see n1.121 above; for a modified form of the same group of gods embedded in the structure of Sanskrit epic, see n1.136 above. This manifestly old scheme of gods is found in a few hymns of the *Rig-Veda* (see Dumézil 1947:45–56, 1968:51), among which *RV* 2.41 has a particularly clear structure. The first nine verses of *RV* 2.41 are arranged in three groups of three verses each: verses 1–3 are addressed to Indra and Vāyu, the second-function gods; verses 4–6 are addressed to Mitra and Varuṇa, the first-function gods; and verses 7–9 are addressed to the twins, the third-function gods. Our attention has been focused on the first verse of the three verses addressed to the twins, *RV* 2.41.7. The other principal text for this scheme of gods, which Dumézil also analyzes, is *RV* 1.139.1–3; Dumézil cites two further texts, *RV* 1.2 and, "with alterations," *RV* 1.23, but neither of these includes the twins.
146 *RV* 1.116.16 and 8.86.1.
147 The Indo-Iranian adjective contains the root*dŋs-, which is also found in Greek *daênai*, "learn," and *daíphrōn*, "wise [in mind], prudent" (see Mayrhofer 1956–1980 s.v. *dasráḥ*). For the connotation of intelligence of the Vedic adjective note the collocation *dasra mantumaḥ*, "you miracle-working wise one," which twice modifies the god Pūṣan (*RV* 1.42.5 and 6.56.4). This collocation corresponds to the Avestan collocation *daŋrā mantū*, "by wise resolution" (*Yasna* 46.17), and a Common Indo-Iranian origin for the phrase is thus indicated (see Schmitt 1967:160–161). Related to the Vedic adjective is the Vedic neuter noun *dáṃsaḥ*, "miraculous power, wonderful deed," to which Greek *dénea*, "counsels, plans," corresponds (see Mayrhofer 1956–1980, Frisk 1960–1972 s.vv.). The Vedic noun *dáṃsaḥ*, like the Vedic adjective *dasrá-*, is used in relation to the twins' miraculous cures, as in the myth of Rebha: "you two, by your miraculous powers (*dáṃsobhir*), put him back together again when he had come apart" (*RV* 1.117.4, quoted n1.125 above); the twins are five times called *purudáṃsaḥ*, "having many marvelous deeds." As the cognates of *dáṃsaḥ* and *dasrá-* all show, what is taken in Vedic as "miraculous" is in origin a matter of "intelligence."

associates this epithet with the twin properly called Nā́satya- is a contrast between cattle and horses in three further verses of the twins' Vedic hymns. In these verses cattle are associated with the epithet dasrā́ just as they are with the name Nā́satyā in the two verses that we have already considered. In all three verses with dasrā́ the cattle side of the opposition is expressed by the same eight-syllable segment, gómad dasrā híraṇyavat, in which the dual vocative dasrā is addressed to the twins, and the words gómad, "rich in cattle," and híraṇyavat, "rich in gold," are neuter adjectives modifying a noun which is outside the segment. The double opposition between cattle and the epithet dasrā́ on the one hand and horses and the name Aśvínā on the other hand is clearest in RV 8.22.17, a three-segment verse, in which the collocation áśvāvad aśvínā in the first segment balances the collocation gómad dasrā in the third segment; the neuter adjectives modify the noun vartís, "path," in the second segment:

> ā́ no áśvāvad aśvínā / vartír yāsiṣṭam madhupātamā narā / gómad dasrā híraṇyavat

> Come to us (ā́ no...yāsiṣṭam) along the path (vartír) rich in horses, you Aśvínā; come, you who most enjoy the sacrificial drink, you heroes (madhupātamā narā); come along the path rich in cattle, you dasrā́, rich in gold (RV 8.22.17).[148]

In the other two Vedic verses that contain the segment gómad dasrā híraṇyavat the segment pertaining to "horses" is modified, but the contrast between "horses" and "cattle" remains clear. The first of these verses, RV 1.30.17, is a Gāyatrī, with three eight-syllable segments, and the contrasting segments are the first and the third. In this verse the syntax is varied in the segment pertaining to horses so that the adjective "rich in horses" now appears in the feminine instrumental (áśvāvatyā) to agree with the noun iṣā́, "sustenance," and the segment gómad dasrā híraṇyavat is appended loosely, its two neuter accusative adjectives no longer agreeing with the noun that they modify:

> áśvināv áśvāvatyā / iṣā́ yātaṃ śávīrayā / gómad dasrā híraṇyavat

---

Geldner translates the dual vocative dasrā as "ihr Meister," which captures the basic sense of "skillful"; Gonda 1959:115 translates the epithet as "exhibiting marvellous skill."

148 In this verse the first and third segments, which have eight syllables, are parallel, and the second segment, which has twelve syllables, is not; the double contrast is articulated in the two parallel segments. The articulation of RV 2.41.7, analyzed in n1.144 above, is similar insofar as two of the verse's three segments are parallel, the third not.

Come here (*ā́..yātam*) with surpassing sustenance (*iṣā́..śávīrayā*) <u>rich in horses, you *Aśvínā*; rich in cattle, you *dasrā́*</u>, rich in gold (*RV* 1.30.17).

The traditional noun which the adjectives "rich in cattle" and "rich in horses" modified in this context was *vartís*, "path" (as in *RV* 2.41.7 and 8.22.17). This noun appears again in the final example, *RV* 1.92.16, and the neuter adjective *gómad* thus agrees with it. But in the segment pertaining to "horses" the adjective *áśvāvad* is omitted altogether, leaving only the vocative *Áśvinā* to express the contrast of "horses" to "cattle." The contrasting segments in this three-segment verse are the first and the second, which both have eight syllables, as opposed to the third segment, which has twelve syllables:

<u>*áśvinā*</u> *vartír asmád ā́* / <u>*gómad dasrā*</u> *híraṇyavat* / *arvā́g rátham̐ sámanasā ní yachatam*

Being of one mind rein in your chariot in this direction [segment 3], along the path toward us, you <u>*Aśvínā*</u> [segment 1], (which is) <u>rich in cattle, you *dasrā́*</u>, rich in gold [segment 2] (*RV* 1.92.16).

It is clear from a comparison of the three verses in which the segment *gómad dasrā híraṇyavat* occurs that this segment was itself traditional; the grammatical freedom with which the segment is used in *RV* 1.30.17 is a further sign of its traditionality. The evidence of *RV* 8.22.17, supported by the evidence of *RV* 1.30.17 and *RV* 1.92.16, leaves no doubt that in the opposition between cattle and horses in the twins' hymns the epithet *dasrā́*, like the name *Nā́satyā*, belongs on the cattle side of the opposition.[149]

149 Gonda 1959:115 argues that the twins' epithet *dasrā́* has to do with their skill as horsemen; but in ten of eleven verses that he cites to support this argument *dasrā́* occurs in the same verse with *Aśvínā*, and an opposition between these two terms (*dasrā́* and *Aśvínā*) rather than an equivalence is most likely at issue (cf. n1.151 below). Gonda draws particular attention to the epithet *híraṇyavartani-*, which occurs six times in the dual of the twins (and twice in the singular of rivers); in five of the six occurrences of the twins the collocation *dásrā (dasrā́) híraṇyavartanī* makes up an eight-syllable verse segment. Gonda (with Geldner) understands *híraṇyavartanī* to mean "having gold wheel rims," and he infers from this meaning a connection between the twins' skill as horsemen and the epithet *dasrā́*, with which *híraṇyavartanī* is collocated. While the feminine noun *vartaní* can mean "wheel rim," its more common meaning is "path," which is (as we have seen) the meaning of the closely related noun *vartís* (for *vartaní* of the twins' "path," see *RV* 4.45.3). The verse segment <u>*dásrā híraṇyavartanī*</u> cannot be separated from the verse segment *gómad* <u>*dasrā híraṇyavat*</u>, in which the two neuter adjectives, *gómad* and *híraṇyavat*, modify the noun *vartís*, "path," which is outside the verse segment itself; in *dásrā híraṇyavartanī* the noun *vartís* is simply incorporated within the verse segment through its equivalent *vartaní*. The epithet *dásrā* in this verse segment has no more to do with the twins' skill as horsemen than it does in the

§1.53 It was the father of Sahadeva, the epic "cowherd," to whom the two Vedic duals, *Nā́satyā* and *dasrā́*, properly belonged. Another of the twins' dual epithets, *divó nápātā*, "sons of Dyaús," properly belonged to this twin as well: in RV 1.181.4, where the twin gods are distinguished from each other, one is called the "son of Dyaús," the other the son of *Súmakha*. As we have seen, the son of *Súmakha* must be the father of the warrior Nakula, and the son of *Dyaús*, by default, must be the father of Sahadeva. In the dual epithet *divó nápātā*, which occurs five times of the twins, the distinctive mark of this twin is extended to both twins as a pair. This is what takes place in the case of the duals *Nā́satyā* and *dasrā́* as well.

§1.54 The relationship between the name *Nā́satyā* and the epithet *dasrā́*, which are both associated with cattle, is one of close similarity: they are isofunctional terms in hymns of the twins that contrast cattle with horses. This close relationship between the two terms seems to have given rise to the Sanskrit epic dual form *Nāsatyadasrau*, which names one of the twins *Nāsatya-* and the other *Dasra-*. Wikander takes this late form as evidence for an old opposition between the name and the epithet.[150] But, as Wikander recognizes, there is no Vedic evidence for such an opposition.[151] One could even argue that two of the four verses in the *Rig-Veda* in which both terms occur suggest the contrary, and that the epithet *dasrā́* actually serves to gloss the twins' old name *Nā́satyā*. In one such verse the twins are invoked as having restored a mortal's eyes; the mortal is Ṛjrā́śva, who was blinded by his father after he offered a hundred rams to a she-wolf: the verse in question is a Triṣṭubh whose final two eleven-syllable segments are:

tásmā akṣī́ nāsatyā vicákṣa / ā́dhattaṃ dasrā bhiṣajāv anarván

---

             verse segment with the adjective *gómad*, "rich in cattle."

150 Wikander 1957:77, 81, 84.

151 Wikander 1957:81: "pour ce qui concerne les termes *nāsatyā* et *dasrā*, on n'observe nulle part, dans les texts vediques, une relation claire entre les deux, ni d'opposition ni d'autre sort"; Wikander rightly rejects Geldner's contention that the terms *Nā́satyā* and *dasrā́*, wherever they occur in the twins' hymns, represent the result of a split dual compound containing two opposed terms; the basic problem with this argument is that the two terms *Nā́satyā* and *dasrā́* occur only rarely (four times) in the same verse. Wikander's own attempt to apply a similar argument to other epithets of the twins is interesting but does not bear on the name *Nā́satyā*; his main result is to show that, by the criterion of frequent co-occurrence in the same verse, it is the dual terms *dasrā́* and *Aśvínā* that are opposed to each other (*Aśvínā* occurs in the same verse in 24 of 44 instances of *dasrā́* in the twins' hymns; cf. Frame 1978:147, 149–150). Wikander's supposition that the Iranian figure *Nā́ŋhaiθya* was demonized because he was a warrior and a "horseman" has no positive evidence to support it (cf. Frame 1978:169–170).

To him you two <u>Nā́satyā</u>, you two <u>miracle-working physicians</u>, gave
eyes to see securely (*RV* 1.116.16cd).

In this verse the phrase *dasrā́ bhiṣájau*, "miracle-working physicians," clearly
fits the context of magic healing, and it is thus tempting to think that *Nā́satyā*
is also used to suit this context. The same is perhaps true in *RV* 1.116.10,
which concerns the aged Cyavāna, whom the twins made young again; the
name *Nā́satyā* occurs in the first half of this verse and the epithet *dasrā́* in the
second half, and both parts of the verse concern the same miraculous deed of
rejuvenation. These examples cannot be pressed;[152] nevertheless they suggest
how the epic compound *Nāsatyadasrau* may have arisen. Far from contrasting
one twin with the other, this dual seems instead to be like such dual English
expressions as "might and main," "hue and cry," and "time and tide," in which
only one of the two terms still has its own meaning, and it thus glosses the
other term, which is obsolete.[153] The relationship between *Nā́satyā* (with a
faded meaning) and *dasrā́* (with a clear meaning) is similar, particularly when
dasrā́, "miracle-working," is amplified to *dasrā́ bhiṣájau*, "miracle-working
physicians."

§1.55 We will return to the question of how far the name *Nā́satyā* had
lost its meaning in the Vedic period. The question that we must address first
is how to interpret this name as a singular belonging only to the son of *Dyaús*.
To this question the Sanskrit evidence, including the "intelligent" Sahadeva,
offers no clue, and we must make use of comparative evidence. Fortunately
there is solid comparative evidence for an Indo-European form of the twin
myth, to which we now turn. The starting point for this comparison is the
fact that in three Indo-European traditions, including Indic, there are twins
called the sons of the Indo-European sky god **Di̯ḗus*. In Vedic the twins have

---

152 In the abstract there is no way to distinguish verses in which two dual terms reinforce
each other from those in which they contrast with each other, or in which no particular
relationship may be present. For example, the duals *divó nápātā* and *Aśvínā* each properly
designate a different twin (on this there is agreement), and both terms occur in a verse,
RV 1.117.12, whose context is again a miraculous rescue: this verse says that the twins dug
up a buried mortal (perhaps Vandana) on the tenth day "like a pot of gold," and in the first
half of this verse the twins are called *divó nápātā*, in the second half *Aśvínā*.

153 "Main" and "hue" are no longer independent nouns in English ("hue" in the meaning
"color" has a separate etymology); English "tide," cognate with German "Zeit" (cf. "noon-
tide," "Yuletide," etc., for the meaning "time"), still exists as an independent noun in
English but with a new meaning. Two other examples of such phrases are "wrack and
ruin" and "part and parcel" ("parcel" still means "part" in e.g. Shakespeare *Henry IV, Part
1*, 3.2.164). Not all English "twin words" are synonyms (in the phrase "kith and kin" "kith"
means friends, not relatives). The alliteration of the English expressions (apart from "hue
and cry") does not apply to the two Sanskrit names.

the epithet *divó nápātā*, "sons of Dyaus," and in Greek they have the corresponding name *Dióskouroi*, "sons of Zeus." The correspondence between these two traditions is confirmed by Baltic, where the Latvian twins are called *Dieva dēli* and the Lithuanian twins *Dievo sunéliai*, both meaning "sons of (the sky-)god."[154] The Baltic traditions, which have survived into the modern era, attest another striking component of the Indo-European myth. The Baltic twins have a sister who corresponds to Helen, the sister of the Dioskouroi. Vedic has an equivalent figure, but she is the twins' common wife rather than their sister. The name of the Vedic figure is *Sūryā*, the feminized form of *sūrya*, the "sun," and this figure is also called *duhitā sūryasya*, "daughter of the sun." The sister of the Baltic twins is likewise called "daughter of the sun," Latvian *saules meita* and Lithuanian *saulès dukterys*. The corresponding Vedic and Baltic names insure the Indo-European origins of this female figure; they also insure a solar context for the Indo-European twin myth itself.[155] In Indo-European the "daughter of the sun" was apparently at once the sister and the common wife of the twins.[156]

---

154 Ward 1968 offers a convenient summary of the comparative evidence for the Indo-European twin myth; the main source for the Baltic twins is popular songs, Latvian *dainas* and Lithuanian *dainos* (Ward 1968:9–10).

155 The Greek Helen is called the daughter of Helios in the late first-century/early second-century AD Ptolemaios Chennos *Nova Historia* as excerpted by Photius *Bibliotheca* 190, Bekker p. 149a. See Dihle *RE* 'Ptolemaios' 1862 no. 77 for this generally unreliable source. It is possible, given the Vedic and Baltic correspondences, that even so late a source as this has preserved something old (cf. Ward 1968:11). In Helen the Indo-European female figure associated with the twins was apparently combined with a native Aegean vegetation deity; cf. *Helénē dendrîtis* in Rhodes, Pausanias 3.19.10, and a plane tree sacred to Helen in Sparta, Theocritus 18.45–48. For Helen as a vegetation deity see Nilsson 1967:315, 487; for Helen as an Indo-European figure see Clader 1976. Steets 1993 is a recent study of the Indo-European female figure. For Helen's divine status in Sparta, cf. EN1.1 to n1.181 below.

156 The Vedic *Sūryā* characteristically mounts the twins' chariot at dawn (e.g. *RV* 5.73.5, *ā́ yád vāṃ sūryā́ ráthaṃ tíṣṭhad*, "when Sūryā mounts your chariot..."); as "daughter of the sun" she mounts their chariot (*RV* 1.116.17, 1.118.5, and 6.63.5) and "chooses" their chariot (*RV* 1.117.13 and 4.43.2). The verb *avṛṇīta*, "chose," in the last two passages is significant because it reflects the twins' role as Sūryā's suitors, whom she "chose"; cf. *RV* 1.119.5, "the splendid maiden chose (*avṛṇīta*) you two as husbands," and *RV* 7.69.4, "the maid, the daughter of the sun, chose (*avṛṇīta*) the beauty of you both." The twins are called not only Sūryā's "husbands" (*páti*, *RV* 1.119.5, 4.43.6), but also her "suitors" (*varā́*, *RV* 10.85.8–9: the noun *varā́*, "suitors," contains the root of *avṛṇīta*, "chose"). There is no real evidence that the wife of the Vedic twins was also their sister. There is one reference to a sister of the twins who is said to "bring" them (*RV* 1.180.2), but the reference in this isolated text is not clear (Macdonell 1897:51 thinks that Dawn is meant; so also Geldner 1951–1957 ad loc.). The Latvian *Dieva dēli*, on the other hand, are actually said to be their sister's suitors; see Ward 1968:11 and 95n19. In Greek, where the Dioskouroi are Helen's brothers, a second pair of brothers, Agamemnon and Menelaus, are her (successful) suitors. In the Greek

§1.56 The function of the Vedic twins as "saviors" and their attribute as "horsemen," to which their names *Nā́satyā* and *Aśvínā* respectively correspond, both have Indo-European origins. The Greek Dioskouroi have the same function as "saviors" and the same attribute as "horsemen," as do the Baltic twins.[157] It is the Greek twins that matter most to us. They are famous "horsemen," who, for example, are called *takhéōn epibétores híppōn*, "mounters of swift horses (chariots)" in two Homeric hymns.[158] They are also "saviors" of mortals in distress, particularly at sea;[159] *Homeric Hymn* 33 vividly portrays one such rescue at sea, as sailors caught in a storm pray to the twins, and the twins, heeding the

myth one brother woos for the other (Agamemnon woos for Menelaus), whereas in Vedic both twins are called suitors and both are called husbands of Sūryā. This may be another case in which Vedic has lost a distinction between the twins. The Greek form of the myth appears again in the case of the brothers Melampus and Bias, who woo Nestor's sister Pero (Melampus, like Agamemnon, woos for his brother; cf. §1.11 above); both these differentiated pairs of brothers are discussed §2.102–§2.103 below.

157 For the twins as "horsemen," see Ward 1968:11–12; for their role as "saviors" and "magic healers," see Ward 1968:14–15, 18. In Baltic tradition there are scores of Latvian *dainas* in which the horses of the *Dieva dēli* are described. Although the *Dieva dēli* are not saviors of mortals in distress, they row a boat to save their sister, the "daughter of the sun," when she is drowning at sea (386–33969); another *daina* says that they appeared on horseback to save the sun when its sledge overturned (381–33912; see Ward 1968:95n19 for the standard collection of Latvian *dainas*, which he cites by page and song number). In the Baltic myth, as in the Greek myth, twin chariot drivers became twin horseback riders. The Indo-European myth of the twin horsemen has been dated to the last quarter or the end of the third millennium BC, when the horse-drawn chariot evolved in the steppes of southeastern Europe; this setting "best explains the distribution of the early chariot lore among the Aryans, Greeks and Balts" (Parpola 2004/2005:6). Cf. also Mallory 1989:136–137, 241.
158 *Homeric Hymn* 33.18 = 17.5; they are called *hippótai sophoí*, "skilled horsemen," in Alcman fr. 2 Page [PMG 2], *leukópōloi*, "having white horses," in Pindar *Pythian* 1.66; in Euripides *Helen* they are imagined as flying through the air with horses (μόλοιτέ ποθ' ἵππιον οἶμον / δι' αἰθέρος ἱέμενοι / παῖδες Τυνδαρίδαι, "may you come rushing through the air on the path for horses, you youthful sons of Tyndareus," *Helen* 1495–1497), and as "riding over the sea" (πόντον παριππεύοντε, *Helen* 1665). After the Homeric period the image doubtless changes from chariot drivers to horseback riders, but the phrase *takhéōn epibétores híppōn*, "mounters of swift horses," in the two Homeric hymns still implies chariots (cf. in *Odyssey* 18.263 the phrase *híppōn t' ōkupódōn epibétoras*, "mounters of swift-footed horses," used of the Trojans). The evidence for both Vedic twins as "horsemen" (apart from the nearly 400 occurrences of the name *Aśvínā* in the *Rig-Veda*) is summarized by Macdonell 1897:50; the twins' chariot, which is drawn by horses in RV 1.117.2, 4.45.7, etc. is drawn by birds, eagles, swans, buffaloes, and an ass in other verses, but the comparative evidence shows that horses are old in this context.
159 *Sōtḗr(es)*, "saviors," is both a literary epithet and a cult title: the epithet occurs in *Homeric Hymn* 33.6 (see below), Euripides *Helen* 1500 (*sōtḗre tâs Helénas*, "Helen's two saviors") and 1664 (also in reference to Helen), and in Theocritus 22.6; for the cult title in Attica see Aelian *Varia Historia* 4.5, *IG* II² 4796 (Roman imperial period), and cf. Furtwängler, Roscher's *Lexikon* 'Dioskuren' 1166.

prayer, fly to the rescue and calm the seas (*Homeric Hymn* 33.5–17; the excerpt begins with Leda, who gives birth to the two "saviors" of men and ships):[160]

κελαινεφέϊ Κρονίωνι
σωτῆρας τέκε παῖδας ἐπιχθονίων ἀνθρώπων
ὠκυπόρων τε νεῶν, ὅτε τε σπέρχωσιν ἄελλαι
χειμέριαι κατὰ πόντον ἀμείλιχον. οἱ δ' ἀπὸ νηῶν
εὐχόμενοι καλέουσι Διὸς κούρους μεγάλοιο
ἄρνεσσιν λευκοῖσιν ἐπ' ἀκρωτήρια βάντες
πρύμνης· τὴν δ' ἄνεμός τε μέγας καὶ κῦμα θαλάσσης
θῆκαν ὑποβρυχίην, οἱ δ' ἐξαπίνης ἐφάνησαν
ξουθῇσι πτερύγεσσι δι' αἰθέρος ἀΐξαντες,
αὐτίκα δ' ἀργαλέων ἀνέμων κατέπαυσαν ἀέλλας,
κύματα δ' ἐστόρεσαν λευκῆς ἁλὸς ἐν πελάγεσσι,
ναύταις σήματα καλὰ πόνου σφίσιν· οἱ δὲ ἰδόντες
γήθησαν, παύσαντο δ' ὀϊζυροῖο πόνοιο.

To the dark-clouded son of Cronus
she bore sons, saviors of men who dwell on earth
and of swift-sailing ships, whenever squalls rush
in storms across the pitiless deep. From ships men
call on the sons of great Zeus, praying,
climbing with white sheep onto the highest part
of the stern; and the great wind and the waves of the sea
have put the stern under water when suddenly they appear,
with rapid wings darting through the sky,
and immediately they stop the squalls of the the hard winds,
and smoothe the waves of the white sea upon the deep,
good signs for sailors and their toil; they, seeing them,
rejoice and cease from their grievous toil.

§1.57 Distinctions found between the two Vedic twins are also closely matched by the Greek twins. The basic correspondence is dual paternity. The Greek twins as a pair are called Dióskouroi, "sons of Zeus," but only Polydeuces

---

160 The electrical phenomenon known as St. Elmo's fire, which appears in ships' rigging during storms, was thought to signal the presence of the Dioskouroi.

is really the son of Zeus; Castor is the son of Tyndareus.[161] Castor is further distinguished from Polydeuces in that he alone is characterized as a "horseman" when the two are contrasted with each other; Polydeuces is instead known for his boxing skill.[162] Castor is a "warrior," and, as with the son of Sumakha in *RV* 1.181.4, this sets him apart from his brother, the son of the sky god.[163]

§1.58 There is another more basic contrast between the Greek twins: whereas Polydeuces, the son of Zeus, is immortal, Castor, the son of Tyndareus, is mortal.[164] This contrast is inherited from the twins' two fathers, for Tyndareus too is a mortal.[165] Castor, who is fated to die, is killed in a battle with the twins Idas and Lynkeus, cousins of the Dioskouroi. Polydeuces brings his brother back to life by sharing his immortality with him, and by accepting a share of his brother's mortality. Thenceforth the twins together are alive and dead on alternate days. This is the central myth of the Dioskouroi, for it explains how they were changed in mid-career from heroes to gods. It is this myth that also explains what it means for just one twin to be a "savior." When Castor is killed Polydeuces is given a choice by Zeus between sharing his immortality with his brother or becoming entirely a god himself. As Pindar tells the myth, Polydeuces "chose the life of his brother who had perished in battle" (*Nemean* 10.59):

εἵλετ' αἰῶνα φθιμένου Πολυδεύκης Κάστορος ἐν πολέμῳ.

Polydeuces chose the life of Castor, who had perished in battle.

161 Just as both twins are called *Diòs koûroi*, "sons of Zeus" (e.g. *Homeric Hymn* 33.1), both are also called *Tundarídai*, "sons of Tyndareus" (e.g. *Homeric Hymn* 17.2, 5; *Homeric Hymn* 33.2, 18; cf. *Odyssey* 11.299).

162 In epic Castor's fixed epithet is *hippódamos*, "horsebreaking"; Polydeuces, on the other hand, is *pùx agathós*, "good with his fists" (Κάστορά θ' ἱππόδαμον καὶ πὺξ ἀγαθὸν Πολυδεύκεα, *Iliad* 3.237 = *Odyssey* 11.300), *aethlophóros*, "prizewinning" (Κάστορά θ' ἱππόδαμον καὶ ἀεθλοφόρον Πολυδεύκεα, *Cypria* fr. 11.6 Allen), and *amómētos*, "blameless" (Κάστορά θ' ἱππόδαμον καὶ ἀμώμητον Πολυδεύκεα, *Homeric Hymn* 33.3).

163 Cf. "Apollodorus" 3.11.2: "Of the sons of Leda Castor practiced the arts of war, Polydeuces boxing" (τῶν δὲ ἐκ Λήδας γενομένων παίδων Κάστωρ μὲν ἤσκει τὰ κατὰ πόλεμον, Πολυδεύκης δὲ πυγμήν).

164 *Cypria* fr. 6 Allen makes this distinction explicitly:

Κάστωρ μὲν θνητός, θανάτου δέ οἱ αἶσα πέπρωται,
αὐτὰρ ὅ γ' ἀθάνατος Πολυδεύκης, ὄζος Ἄρηος.

Castor was mortal, and a fate of death was allotted to him,
but Polydeuces, scion of Ares, was immortal.

165 In Pindar *Nemean* 10.80–82 Zeus tells Polydeuces that he, Polydeuces, is his own son, but that a "hero" fathered Castor: ἐσσί μοι υἱός· τόνδε δ' ἔπειτα πόσις / σπέρμα θνατὸν ματρὶ τεᾷ πελάσαις / στάξεν ἥρως, "You are my son; but as for this one, a hero afterwards instilled his mortal seed when he approached your mother as her husband."

Pindar attenuates the force of the word *phthiménou*, "perished," in the actual
narrative, where Polydeuces finds his brother "not yet dead, but gasping for
breath."¹⁶⁶ Nevertheless it is clear that when Polydeuces "opens the eye, then
the voice" of Castor,¹⁶⁷ he brings his brother back to life in terms of the under-
lying myth.¹⁶⁸

§1.59 An originally singular form *Nā́satya-* in Indo-Iranian, interpreted
as "he who brings back to life and light," is well explained by the Greek myth.
The question is whether the Greek myth originated in Indo-European and
also survived in Indo-Iranian. *RV* 1.181.4, which attests the dual paternity of
the Vedic twins, shows that there was more to their myth than was commonly
articulated by the Vedic poets. Sumakha, the father of one of the twins, is not
called a mortal like the Greek Tyndareus, but he is known from only this one
verse of the *Rig-Veda* and he is therefore unlikely to be a god.¹⁶⁹ If Sumakha
was a mortal, presumably the twin who was his son was also mortal, as in the
Greek myth. The distinction between an immortal and a mortal twin may be
further indicated by the twins' Vedic ritual. The evidence of the *Rig-Veda* is
almost entirely for a morning ritual, which was the only important one for
these two light-bringing divinities.¹⁷⁰ But in addition to the morning ritual
there is also evidence for an evening ritual. In three hymns of the *Rig-Veda*
the two times, evening and morning, are paired and contrasted: *doṣā́...uṣási*,
8.22.14; *doṣā́m uṣásaḥ*, 10.39.1; *doṣā́ vástor*, 10.40.4.¹⁷¹ The evening/morning
contrast that characterizes the twins' ritual is likely to have characterized

166 καί νιν οὔπω τεθναότ', ἄσθματι δὲ φρίσσοντα πνοὰς ἔκιχεν, "and he found him not yet
   dead, but gasping out his halting breath," line 74.
167 ἀνὰ δ' ἔλυσεν μὲν ὀφθαλμόν, ἔπειτα δὲ φωνὰν χαλκομίτρα Κάστορος, "he opened the eye,
   and then the voice of bronze-clad Castor," line 90.
168 In "Apollodorus" 3.11.2 Castor's death is unambiguous: Idas "kills" (*kteínei*) Castor, and
   Polydeuces refuses immortality from Zeus "while Castor is a corpse" (*óntos nekroû Kástoros*);
   cf. also *Cypria* fr. 6 (quoted in n1.164 above), which speaks of the "fate of death" (*thanátou
   aîsa*) allotted to the mortal Castor.
169 While it is unlikely that a god should be named in one Vedic verse and be otherwise
   unknown, the name Sumakha, "good warrior," could conceivably be an epithet of another
   god, such as Indra. But again it seems unlikely that such a god's fame would be deliber-
   ately concealed through use of an otherwise unknown epithet. Dual paternity is a common
   feature of twin mythology and a contrast between a god and a mortal often characterizes
   the two fathers (cf. Ward 1968:3–8 on "universal Dioscurism," and p. 4 on dual paternity in
   particular). Such a contrast would seem to be the likeliest case in Vedic even apart from
   the Greek comparison.
170 See §1.44–§1.45 above for the twins' connection with dawn in myth and ritual; for ritual cf.
   also Oldenberg 1894:208, and for myth Macdonell 1897:51.
171 Cf. also *RV* 5.76.3, which bids the twins to come "day and night" (*dívā náktam*), but appar-
   ently a third time as well, namely "midday" (*madhyáṃdine*).

the twins themselves. A passage quoted by Yāska (*Nirukta* 12.2) supports this conclusion by stating that "one (of the twins) is called the son of night, the other the son of dawn."[172] In terms of solar myth, just as sunrise is associated with a "return to life," sunset is associated with "death." If the distinction between a morning and evening ritual has to do with a distinction between the twins themselves, the myth of a mortal twin who dies and is brought back to life is indicated. Whether this myth remained alive in Vedic times we have no way of knowing. The evening ritual itself seems to have been close to extinction.[173]

§1.60 The death of a mortal twin, if it was closely associated with sunset, would have been seen as a daily occurrence. This would fit with a singular name *Nā́satya-*, for the role of the immortal twin in bringing his brother back to life would also have been seen as a daily occurrence. But the identification of one twin with sunset and the other twin with sunrise separates the brothers,[174] and there is another perspective from which they remain paired, even in the alternation between life and death. This perspective survives in the Greek myth where the alternation between life and death takes place on successive days and the twins themselves are thus seen as remaining together.[175] In Pindar, who emphasizes the twins' common fate, they spend

---

172 The Vedic twins were probably also identified with the morning and evening stars; for bibliography see Ward 1968:15–18, who considers the evidence of other Indo-European twins as well.

173 One of the twins' hymns, *RV* 5.77.2, after calling for their morning sacrifice (*prātár yajadhvam*), specifically rejects the evening sacrifice, saying that it does not reach the gods (*ná sāyám asti devayā́*) and is unpleasing (*ájuṣṭam*).

174 The identification of the twins with the morning and evening stars also implies their separation.

175 The two different perspectives, though logically incompatible, probably coexisted in the Indo-European form of the myth; such a double perspective is characteristic of both the Greek and the Vedic myth. For the identification of the twins with the morning and evening stars, see Ward 1968:15–18, who regards the evidence for the Indo-European twins as "not entirely conclusive," and points out that for the Greek twins most of the evidence is late. With respect to the Greek twins, cf. Frazer 1921, vol. 2, 32n1, on "Apollodorus" 3.11.2: "It has been plausibly argued that in one of their aspects the twins were identified with the Morning and Evening Stars respectively, the immortal twin (Pollux) being conceived as the Morning Star, which is seen at dawn rising up in the sky till it is lost in the light of heaven, while the mortal twin (Castor) was identified with the Evening Star, which is seen at dusk sinking into its earthy bed.... It would seem that this view of the Spartan twins was favoured by the Spartans themselves, for after their great naval victory at Aegospotami, at which Castor and Pollux were said to have appeared visibly in or hovering over the Spartan fleet, the victors dedicated at Delphi the symbols of their divine champions in the shape of two golden stars, which shortly before the fatal Battle of Leuctra fell down and disappeared, as if to announce that the star of Sparta's fortune was about to set for ever" (see Cicero *On Divination* 1.34.75, 2.32.68 and Plutarch *Lysander* 12.1). For stars as attributes of

one day on Olympus with Zeus and the next day beneath the earth at
Therapne, their cult site near Sparta (*Nemean* 10.55–57):

μεταμειβόμενοι δ' ἐναλλὰξ ἀμέραν τὰν μὲν παρὰ πατρὶ φίλῳ
Δὶ νέμονται, τὰν δ' ὑπὸ κεύθεσι γαίας ἐν γυάλοις Θεράπνας,
πότμον ἀμπιπλάντες ὁμοῖον.

Alternating back and forth they spend one day with their father
Zeus, the next day under the depths of the earth in the hollows
      of Therapne,
both fulfilling a like fate.[176]

The death of the Dioskouroi on alternating days is only implied in Pindar. In
Odyssey 11 it is made explicit, but in this passage, in the catalogue of heroines
met by Odysseus in the underworld, the alternation between life and death
takes place entirely beneath the earth (*Odyssey* 11.298–304):

καὶ Λήδην εἶδον, τὴν Τυνδαρέου παράκοιτιν,
ἥ ῥ' ὑπὸ Τυνδαρέῳ κρατερόφρονε γείνατο παῖδε,
Κάστορά θ' ἱππόδαμον καὶ πὺξ ἀγαθὸν Πολυδεύκεα,
τοὺς ἄμφω ζωοὺς κατέχει φυσίζοος αἶα·
οἳ καὶ νέρθεν γῆς τιμὴν πρὸς Ζηνὸς ἔχοντες
ἄλλοτε μὲν ζώουσ' ἑτερήμεροι, ἄλλοτε δ' αὖτε
τεθνᾶσιν· τιμὴν δὲ λελόγχασιν ἶσα θεοῖσι.

---

the Dioskouroi in Greek iconography see Hermary *LIMC* 'Dioskouroi' nos. 232–237, 239–241,
243, 245–248; no. 232 is the Spartan dedication at Delphi after Aegospotami. For the attri-
bute in Etruscan and Roman iconography, see De Puma *LIMC* 'Dioskouroi/Tinas Cliniar' nos.
7, 23, 24, 29, 42, 43, 46, 48, 53 and Gury *LIMC* 'Dioskouroi/Castores' 631, who comments that
the star is the most systematically retained attribute of the Dioskouroi from the repub-
lican era on.

176 Cf. also *Pythian* 11.61–64:

καὶ Κάστορος βίαν,
σέ τε, ἄναξ Πολύδευκες, υἱοὶ θεῶν,
τὸ μὲν παρ' ἆμαρ ἕδραισι Θεράπνας,
τὸ δ' οἰκέοντας ἔνδον Ὀλύμπου.

And mighty Castor,
and you, lord Polydeuces, both sons of the gods,
living from day to day now in your sanctuary at Therapne,
now in Olympus.

And I saw Leda, the wife of Tyndareus,
who under Tyndareus gave birth to two strong-minded sons,
horse-breaking Castor and Polydeuces, good with his fists,
both of whom the life-giving earth holds alive;
and they, having honor from Zeus even under the ground,
are alive on alternate days, and then in turn
they are dead; and they receive honor equal to the gods.

This passage, with the phrase "under the earth," comes close to picturing the twins as heroes rather than gods.[177] Like Pindar, the passage in *Odyssey* 11 seems to have the twins' cult site at Therapne in mind;[178] hero cults are strongly localized, and that is how the twins' worship is here portrayed. The twins are in fact half heroes and half gods, and this passage emphasizes their heroic side, rooted in the earth.[179] In their career before the climactic death and return to life of Castor the twins are imagined entirely as heroes. In *Iliad* 3, when Helen looks out from the walls of Troy, she expects to see her brothers fighting with the other Achaean heroes for her return; thus they once fought for her when Theseus carried her off to Aphidna.[180] When she cannot see her

---

177 Line 304, which says that the twins obtained "honor (i.e. sacrifices) *equal to* the gods'," seems to distinguish between the twins on the one hand and the gods on the other, and this too suggests the twins' heroic as opposed to divine status (cf. Nagy 1979:118–119 for *timḗ* in relation to hero cults). Note also that the mortal Tyndareus is presented as the father of the twins in this passage (11.299). The twins' name in Sparta was *Tindarídai*, and the passage in *Odyssey* 11 seems to have this cult name in mind (for the twins' name in Sparta, see Ziehen *RE* 'Sparta [Kulte]' 1478–1479). Zeus's role as father is implied in *Odyssey* 11 (the twins live on alternate days even beneath the earth because Zeus grants them "honor," line 302), but it is not emphasized.

178 Alcman also represented the Dioskouroi as living beneath the earth at Therapne according to the scholia to Euripides *Troades* 210: οἰκητήριόν φασι τὰς Θεράπνας τῶν Διοσκούρων παρόσον ὑπὸ τὴν γῆν τῆς Θεράπνης εἶναι λέγονται ζῶντες, ὡς Ἀλκμάν φησιν, "they say that Therapnai is the dwelling place of the Diokouroi inasmuch as they are said to be alive beneath the earth of Therapne, as Alcman says" (the quotation of Alcman's verse has unfortunately not been preserved).

179 For formal differences between divine cults and hero cults, see Brelich 1958, and cf. Nagy 2005:86–89.

180 The story of Helen's earlier abduction is not told in the *Iliad*, but it is suggested by the presence of Theseus's mother Aithra as Helen's attendant in *Iliad* 3.144. With Aithra at her side Helen approaches the Trojan elders on the city walls and looks out with them at the Achaean heroes fighting to win her back; the reminder of her earlier abduction in the person of Aithra is clearly significant at this point (cf. Jenkins 1999; *Iliad* 3.144 was athetized by Aristarchus and is regarded as Athenian by some modern editors, including Kirk 1985 ad loc.). The myth of Helen's earlier abduction is attested for Alcman (scholia to *Iliad* 3.242) and Stesichorus (Pausanias 2.22.6–7), and is told at some length by Herodotus 9.73. According to Plutarch *Theseus* 31.3 and 34.1 Theseus made Aithra Helen's companion at Aphidna, and the

brothers she thinks that they either stayed home in Lacedaemon or avoid battle out of shame for her (*Iliad* 3.236–242). But in fact, the poet says, the life-giving earth held them fast in Lacedaemon (*Iliad* 3.243–244):

ὣς φάτο, τοὺς δ' ἤδη κάτεχεν φυσίζοος αἶα
ἐν Λακεδαίμονι αὖθι φίλῃ ἐν πατρίδι γαίῃ.

So she spoke, but already the life-giving earth held them there in Lacedaemon in their dear fatherland.

This passage even more than *Odyssey* 11 portrays the twins as dead heroes, buried in their homeland: the first line closely parallels *Odyssey* 11.301, except that it omits the word *zōoús,* "alive." But if the *Iliad* does not use the word *zōoús,* it also does not exclude it. Rather the two Homeric passages complement each other, the *Iliad* making explicit the location of the twins' grave in Lacedaemon, the *Odyssey* making explicit the twins' continued existence beneath the earth there. It was possible to emphasize either the mortal or the immortal side of the twins' dual nature. The *Iliad* emphasizes their mortal side more than the *Odyssey* does, and both Homeric passages emphasize their mortal side more than Pindar does. But in each case it is simply a matter of emphasis, for the twins themselves are both gods and heroes.[181]

§1.61 There is nothing comparable in the Vedic hymns, where the twins are treated entirely as gods. Thus, for example, they are invited to receive the Soma sacrifice like the other gods.[182] But in later tradition,

Dioskouroi took her as well when they rescued Helen. For other ancient references to the myth see "Apollodorus" 3.10.7 with Frazer's note (Frazer 1921, vol. 2, 25n2).

181 The Dioskouroi are referred to as "heroes" in literary sources: Pindar *Isthmian* 1.17 calls Castor and the Theban Iolaos "the mightiest chariot drivers among heroes" (κεῖνοι γὰρ ἡρώων διφρηλάται...κράτιστοι); in Theocritus 22.163 the Dioskouroi are called "distinguished among all heroes" (ὑμεῖς δ' ἐν πάντεσσι διάκριτοι ἡρώεσσι). The cult title of the Dioskouroi in Sparta, namely *ánakes,* "lords" (Doric for *ánaktes*), fits either gods or heroes (Homeric *ánax* is used of both). If the Dioskouroi were thought of as buried beneath the earth at Therapne, as Alcman and Pindar (and less specifically Homer) attest, their cult must have included the principal feature of hero cults, namely a grave (for attempts to define features of hero cults, which are not uniform, see Nagy 1979:114–117, 159–161; Snodgrass 1988; Kearns 1989:1–4). Unfortunately nothing is known of the twins' cult at Therapne, which is never again mentioned after Pindar (Pausanias says nothing of it in his remarks concerning Therapne, 3.19.9–3.20.1). The issue of a grave for the Dioskouroi at Therapne is discussed further in EN1.1.

182 As in e.g. *RV* 3.58.7, 9; 8.8.5; 8.35.7–10. In *RV* 8.35 the first three verses all end with the phrase "together with Uṣas and Sūrya drink the Soma, you Aśvins"; in the first verse various other gods are simltaneously invited (8.35.1), and in the third verse all the gods are included in the invitation with the phrase *víśvair devaís* (8.35.3).

starting with the Vedic Brāhmaṇas, there is a myth that the twins were at first excluded from the Soma sacrifice because they associated too closely with mortals. It required a special act to include them in the Soma sacrifice with the other gods. Their mythic career thus has two stages to it like that of the Dioskouroi: at first they live close to mortals and do not receive sacrifices as gods; then they are accepted among the gods.[183] In one form of the myth Viṣṇu, who represents divine sacrifice as a whole, is beheaded, and the twins, as physicians, are asked to restore his head; their reward for this cure is to receive their part of the sacrifice, which is precisely the "head."[184] The better-known form of the myth features the ascetic Cyavana, who in the *Rig-Veda* (there called Cyavāna) is the subject of one of the twins' rescue myths: he is rejuvenated by the twins in his extreme old age; one hymn says that the twins made him again the "husband of girls" (*pátim kanînām*, *RV* 1.116.10);[185] another says that the rejuvenated Cyavāna again "arouses the desire of his bride" (*RV* 5.74.5).[186] In the *Rig-Veda* the twins are the bene-

183 Dumézil has compared the initial exclusion of the twins from the Soma sacrifice in India with other Indo-European traditions, notably in Scandinavia and Ireland (also in Rome in a transposed form), where third-function gods are at first separated from first- and second-function gods, and are then integrated with these gods. In India the separation of the twins from the gods of the first and second functions is also reflected in the sons of the gods in the *Mahābhārata*, where the twins Nakula and Sahadeva have a different mother, Mādrī, from the three older Pāṇḍavas, whose mother is Kuntī (see Dumézil 1968:54–56, 69–70, 73–76). My comparison between the Indic twins and the Greek Dioskouroi does not conflict with Dumézil's interpretation of the Indic evidence, but parallels it, and also, I think, underlies it. The Indic twins, although they are gods of the third function, also comprise the first and second functions in their contrasting attributes of "intelligence" and "war" (cf. below EN1.2 to n1.190); one can make the case that the third function, comprising the other two functions, is the basic one, and that the opposition between the twins is more basic than their place in the trifunctional scheme.

184 *Śatapatha-Brāhmaṇa* 14.1.1.1–15 tells how Viṣṇu's head was cut off and became the sun when his bowstring was cut by ants (text and translation in Muir 1874, vol. 4, 124–126). The *Taittirīya-Saṃhitā* 6.4.9.1 tells how the twins replaced the head and this became their share of the sacrifice; but first the gods required the twins to be purified, saying "these two are unclean, going about as physicians among men" (*apūtau vai imau manuṣyacarau bhiṣajau*). In this text the focus is less on the twins' closeness to men than on their function as physicians, since this function is forbidden to brahmans as unclean and making one unfit to sacrifice (text and translation in Muir 1874, vol. 5, 253). The *Taittirīya-Āraṇyaka* 5.1.1–7 gives a more precise identification of the twins' libation (*āśvina graha*) with the "head" of the sacrifice in this myth (Muir 1874, vol. 4, 127–129); cf. also the *Pañcaviṃśa-Brāhmaṇa* 7.5.6 (Muir 1874, vol. 4, 129).

185 For this verse, in which the twins are invoked with the two dual vocatives Nāsatyā and dasrā, cf. §1.54 above.

186 There are nine references to the myth of Cyavāna in the *Rig-Veda*: 1.116.10, 1.117.13, 1.118.6, 5.74.5, 5.75.5, 7.68.6, 7.71.5, 10.39.4, 10.59.1. Note that I use different forms of his name to distinguish Cyavāna in the *Rig-Veda* from the Cyavana of later tradition (long versus short second vowel).

factors of the aged Cyavāna, but in the later myth Cyavana, through the power of his asceticism, is no less the benefactor of the twins, gaining their admission to the gods' sacrifice. Cyavana's bride in the later myth is called Sukanyā, and she is given to the aged ascetic to appease him when he is inadvertently offended. The twins, who try to seduce this ill-matched but faithful princess, are rejected by her, and Cyavana, whom the twins deride for his old age, tells them through Sukanyā that they are incomplete. To learn how they are incomplete he forces them to rejuvenate him, and then he tells them that the gods do not include them in their sacrifice at Kurukṣetra. The twins go to the gods and say that the gods worship with a headless sacrifice. The twins are then admitted to the sacrifice to restore its head, which is their libation. This is the version in the *Śatapatha-Brāhmaṇa* 4.1.5.1–15.[187] In the *Mahābhārata* Cyavana is a more potent figure still.[188] He defeats the twin gods in a contest for the hand of Sukanyā, although this is due more to her than to him.[189] His truly awesome deed in the epic is to force Indra, the king of the gods, to admit the twins to the gods' sacrifice despite Indra's vehement objections. Cyavana uses the power of his austerity to create the monster Māda, "intoxication," which threatens to engulf not only the gods but the entire world. The twins thus owe their

---

187 Muir 1874, vol. 5, 250–253. *Jaiminīya-Brāhmaṇa* 3.121 is similar: Cyavana rewards the twins for his rejuvenation by giving them information that leads to their inclusion in the Soma sacrifice (cf. Goldman 1977:166n11).

188 The story was a popular one in epic. It is told three times in the *Mahābhārata*: the principal text is *Mahābhārata* 3.121.22–3.124.10 (translation in Goldman 1977:50–59); the other two texts are *Mahābhārata* 13.141.16–30 and 14.9.31–36 (cf. Goldman 1977:117; Muir 1872:470–471 gives the version in Book 13).

189 When the twins fail to seduce the faithful Sukanyā, they offer to rejuvenate Cyavana provided that she then choose between him and the two of them; they then both assume the appearance of the rejuvenated Cyavana when, with the twins beside him, he steps from the pool in which he is transformed; Sukanyā uncannily still succeeds in choosing her own husband among the three identical youths (*Mahābhārata* 3.123.1–23). What seems noteworthy here is that the twins, who in the *Rig-Veda* are the successful suitors of the "daughter of the sun"—she "chooses" them (see n1.156 above)—here lose to Cyavana as suitors. It is a more subtle exaltation of the human sage over the twin gods than in the *Śatapatha-Brāhmaṇa*, where the twins are forced to rejuvenate Cyavana to learn how they are incomplete. A suggestion for this development of the myth was perhaps found in the juxtaposition of myths in RV 1.117.13:

yuváṃ cyávānam aśvinā járantam / púnar yúvānaṃ cakrathuḥ śácībhiḥ
yuvó rátham duhitā́ sū́ryasya / sahá śriyā́ nāsatyāvṛṇīta

You Aśvínā made the aged Cyavāna young again by your might;
the daughter of the sun chose your chariot with its wealth, you Nā́satyā.

inclusion in the gods' sacrifice to the spiritual power of an ascetic. This is a distinctively Indian myth.[190]

§1.62 In the Indic myth, even before the twins are admitted to the gods' sacrifice, they already have the function that characterizes them as gods in the *Rig-Veda*, namely saving and healing. Their nature is thus not fundamentally changed when they join the other gods, as it is in the Greek myth. The starting point for the Indic myth is precisely the twins' old rescue myths, one of which, the myth of Cyavana, has become the specific context for their joining the other gods. The restoration of Viṣṇu's severed head likewise derives from the twins' old function as magic healers. What underlies the same "rescuer" function in the Greek myth, namely the immortal twin's rescue of his mortal brother, has disappeared from the Indic myth. What remains that is directly comparable to the Greek myth is the notion that the twins are not fully gods in the first half of their career, that they are "incomplete." Although they are not portrayed as heroes like the Greek Dioskouroi at the same stage of their career, they are nevertheless thought of as very close to mortals. This motif, the closeness of the twins to mortals, is a constant in the various versions of the myth of their inclusion in the sacrifice. In *Śatapatha-Brāhmaṇa* 4.1.5, for example, the motif occurs twice: when the twins encounter Sukanyā and wish to seduce her, the scene is set with the words: "the Asvins wandered over this (world) performing cures" (*aśvinau ha vai idam bhiṣajyantau ceratuḥ*, 4.1.5.8); and when the twins approach the gods and ask to be admitted to the sacrifice, the gods at first refuse with the words: "we will not invite you, for you have wandered about very familiarly among men, performing cures" (*bahu manuṣyeṣu saṃsṛṣṭam acāriṣṭam bhiṣajyantau*, 4.1.5.14).[191] The original myth, in which the twins

---

190 Hostility toward the gods, as displayed by Cyavana in his confrontation with Indra, is characteristic of the myths of a particular family of priests, the Bhārgavas. They were said to be descended from a semi-mythical family of priests in the *Rig-Veda*, the Bhṛgus, and their myths, which include that of Cyavana, play a prominent part in the *Mahābhārata*. Their myths are in fact so prominent in the poem's overall structure that Bhārgavas are thought to have made a thorough revision of the great warrior epic of the Bhāratas (the *Mahābhārata*). This theory was proposed by Sukthankar 1936/1937, and the myths on which the theory is based have been further studied by Goldman 1977. Hostility toward the gods is one of the distinctive Bhārgava themes (Goldman 1977:113–128). Another is a preoccupation with violent death and a consequent return to life (Goldman 1977:75–92). These themes are discussed further in EN1.2.

191 In the *Mahābhārata* the twins are refused admission to the sacrifice by Indra until Cyavana forces him to yield. In the version in Book 3 Indra says: "Doctors, tradesmen, changing their appearance at will, wandering about in the world of mortals (*loke carantau martyānām*), how could these two be worthy of Soma?" (3.124.12). In the version in Book 13 Indra refuses

were themselves mortal until they became gods, is lost in Indic, but it is preserved by the Greek Dioskouroi.[192]

§1.63 The Greek distinction between a mortal and an immortal twin seems to have belonged to the Indo-European form of the twin myth and at some point to have been eliminated from the Indic myth. Two further features of the Indo-European myth remain to be considered, both of which are well preserved in Indic. They both concern Sahadeva, the "intelligent cowherd," who contrasts with Nakula, the "warrrior horseman," in Sanskrit epic. Both parts of this contrast, as we have found, also once characterized the twin gods in the *Rig-Veda*: an "intelligent cowherd" is indicated by the *Rig-Veda's* use of the epithet *dasrā* (and the name *Nāsatyā*) in close association with the notion of cattle; a contrasting "horseman" is indicated by the use of the name *Aśvinā* in the same contexts in close association with the notion of horses; in addition, one of the twins is specifically characterized as a "warrior" in the only verse of the *Rig-Veda* that makes explicit distinctions between the two twins (*RV* 1.181.4). For the Indo-European form of the myth we have already found a "warrior horseman" indicated by the close correspondence with Indic of the Greek Castor, who is a warrior, and who is distinguished from his brother the boxer by the epithet "horse-breaking": *Kástorá th' hippódamon kaì pùx agathòn Poludeúkea* (*Iliad* 3.237 = *Odyssey* 11.300).[193] To be

---

Cyavana's request with the words, "How can they become drinkers of Soma when they are reviled by us and do not measure up to the gods (*devair na sammitāv etau*)?" (13.141.17). In the *Taittirīya-Saṃhitā* 6.4.9.1 (cf. n1.184 above) the gods grant the twins a libation but then make them purify themselves, saying, "These two are unclean, going about as physicians among men (*apūtau vai imau manuṣyacarau bhiṣajau*)." Since in the Indic myth the twins are already magic healers before they become "complete," the gods throw up against them the charge that they are doctors as a mark of low status. This motif is secondary, having to do with a brahman prejudice, but as such it goes well with the new form of the myth.

192 Closeness to mortals is a somewhat ambiguous characteristic, for the Dioskouroi are close to mortals not only as heroes but also as gods: the twins (Vedic as well as Greek) can appear suddenly and rescue sailors at sea precisely because they are close enough at hand to be invoked in a desperate situation. But this closeness to mortals derives from the mortal side of the twins' nature even when they act as gods. We may think of the earth that "holds" the Dioskouroi once they become gods. This earth, which is the mark of the mortal part of their nature, actually holds the gods close to their mortal worshippers in Lacedaemon. The twins' closeness to mortals and their own mortality are thus intertwined, and this was presumably once also true of the Indic twins.

193 Cf. n1.162 above. In Theocritus 22 Castor alone fights the battle with Idas and Lynkeus; Polydeuces has his own episode, a boxing match. Theocritus introduces Castor's battle with a series of epithets marking him as a "warrior" and a "horseman" (22.135–136): σὲ δέ, Κάστορ, ἀείσω, / Τυνδαρίδη ταχύπωλε, δορυσσόε, χαλκεοθώρηξ, "I will sing of you, Castor, son of Tyndareus, having swift horses, spear-brandishing, with bronze breastplate" (for Castor as *khalkeothórēx*, "with bronze breastplate," cf. *khalkomítra Kástoros*, "Castor with the

considered now is whether the immortal twin was associated with "cattle" and characterized by "intelligence" in the Indo-European form of the myth. In the Greek myth these traits are not marked, but they have left clear traces nonetheless, so that the answer in both cases seems to be yes. To begin with the second trait, Polydeuces' skill as a boxer is a specialized instance of "intelligence."[194] The evidence for this does not occur until the Hellenistic poets, but there it occurs twice. Theocritus and Apollonius of Rhodes tell the same myth of a boxing match that took place during the voyage of the Argo, when Polydeuces defeated the Bebrycian giant Amykos in his own kingdom. In both versions it is the triumph of brains over brawn.[195] The myth itself was traditional, and this feature of the myth, the cleverness of Polydeuces, was very likely traditional too.[196]

§1.64 In Apollonius, when the fight is about to begin, Polydeuces is compared to the evening star, and Amykos is compared to the monstrous offspring of Typhoeus or of Earth herself (Apollonius of Rhodes 2.38–42). When the fight actually begins Amykos is compared to a wave cresting over a ship, which the ship narrowly avoids by the "skill" of the "crafty" helmsman (*hē d' hupò tutthòn / idreíēi pukinoîo kubernētễros alúskei*, 2.71–72); Amykos presses his foe relentlessly, but Polydeuces, "by his cunning" (*hền dià mễtin*,

---

bronze *mítra*," in Pindar *Nemean* 10.90, quoted above n1.167.) Even in Polydeuces' episode, when Castor calls the other Greek heroes to watch his brother's boxing match, Theocritus characterizes him as *hupeírokhos en daï Kástōr*, "Castor pre-eminent in war" (22.79).

194 One may say in general that skill with the two hands characterizes the crafts, and makes their practitioners "crafty"; for boxing as a craft, cf. Theocritus 22.67, where Amykos, the opponent of Polydeuces, calls on him to exert himself with his fists and not to spare his "skill": πὺξ διατεινάμενος σφετέρης μὴ φείδεο τέχνης.

195 There is no agreement as to which poet followed which in narrating this episode; see Köhnken 1965:84–121 and 2001, who argues for the priority of Theocritus, and Sens 1997:24–36, who argues for the priority of Apollonius. There is the same issue with respect to the treatment of the Hylas myth in both poets. Köhnken 2001:73n2 cites recent opinion on the question, which remains undecided; Hunter 1999:264–265 thinks it more likely that the two Theocritus poems, *Idylls* 13 and 22, presuppose a knowledge of Apollonius of Rhodes Books 1 and 2 than vice versa.

196 Epicharmus in the early fifth century BC wrote a comedy *Amykos*; in a fragment Castor tells Amykos not to abuse his older brother (Ἄμυκε, μὴ κύδαζέ μοι / τὸν πρεσβύτερον ἀδελφεόν, Epicharmus fr. 6 Kassel and Austin 2001), from which it is clear that Polydeuces encounters the same truculent figure as in the Hellenistic poets; the scholia to Apollonius of Rhodes 2.98–100 (see on Epicharmus fr. 7 Kassel and Austin 2001) say that in Epicharmus Polydeuces ties Amykos up, sparing his life; in Theocritus Polydeuces likewise spares Amykos, but in Apollonius he kills him. Sophocles wrote a satyr play called *Amykos*, but apart from two phrases quoted for unusual words by Athenaeus 9.400b and 3.94e (Sophocles frs. 111–112 Radt) its contents are unknown (for possible artistic representations of the play see Radt 1999:150).

2.75), avoids his opponent's onrush. "Perceiving" (noḗsas, 2.76) his opponent's
brutish fighting, both his strengths and his weaknesses, Polydeuces holds his
ground, gains the advantage, and delivers a fatal blow. In Theocritus's version
(Theocritus 22) Polydeuces gains an initial advantage by maneuvering
Amykos into the sun's glare, and the poet congratulates him for outwit-
ting the big man with his "skill" (idreíēi mégan ándra parḗluthes, ō Polúdeukes,
Theocritus 22.85). In Theocritus Amykos is compared to Tityos as he presses
in against his foe with his eyes to the ground, but Polydeuces stands firm
and pummels him on this side and that with both hands in turn (22.91–96).[197]
Amykos reels with the blows and spits blood, and his eyes are swollen shut;
Polydeuces throws feints from every direction,[198] and when he "perceives"
(enóēse, 22.103) that Amykos is baffled he knocks him to the ground. The fight
continues when Amykos gets up, and it ends when he is knocked down again
and swears to cease forcing strangers to fight with him when they enter his
kingdom.

§1.65 There is a second striking piece of evidence for the "intelligence" of
Polydeuces: Mnāsínoos is the name of his son on two works of art from the sixth
century BC. Both of the Dioskouroi had sons by the daughters of Leukippos,
and on the two works of art in question the name of Castor's son was Ánaxis or
Anaxías. Pausanias describes both works: a statue group in the temple of the
Dioskouroi in Argos (2.22.5), and a relief sculpture on a throne in the temple
of Apollo at Amyklai (3.18.13). The statue group in Argos, by the sculptors
Dipoinos and Skyllis, represented the two daughters of Leukippos, Hilaeira
and Phoibe, the two Dioskouroi, and their two sons, Ánaxis and Mnāsínous;
the throne in Amyklai, by the sculptor Bathykles, contained, among others,
mounted figures of Anaxías and Mnāsínous and mounted figures of the two
Dioskouroi. Pausanias does not match the two sons with the two fathers, or
the two fathers with the two mothers. But "Apollodorus" 3.11.2, who presents
the variant forms Anógōn and Mnēsíleōs of the sons' names, makes the affili-
ations explicit: Castor had Anogon by Hilaeira, Polydeuces had Mnesileos by
Phoibe.[199] To use the names attested by Pausanias for the Archaic period,

197 Polydeuces' skill with his fists is expressively portrayed in lines 95–96, especially in the allit-
erative second line: ἤτοι ὅγ' ἔνθα καὶ ἔνθα παριστάμενος Διὸς υἱός / ἀμφοτέρῃσιν ἄμυσσεν
ἀμοιβαδίς, "standing beside him the son of Zeus on this side and that / ripped him with
both hands in turn." See n1.194 above for skill with the hands as a token of "craftiness."
198 τὸν μὲν ἄναξ ἐτάρασσεν ἐτώσια χερσὶ προδεικνύς / πάντοθεν, "the lord (Polydeuces)
baffled him, displaying empty blows (feints) from all sides" (Theocritus 22.102–103).
199 "Apollodorus" 3.11.2: καὶ γίνεται μὲν Πολυδεύκους καὶ Φοίβης Μνησίλεως, Κάστορος δὲ καὶ
Ἰλαείρας Ἀνώγων, "and Mnesileos was born from Polydeuces and Phoibe, Anogon from
Castor and Hilaeira." Consistent with this positive information is the order of names of the

Castor's son was *Ánaxis* or *Anaxías*, and Polydeuces' son was *Mnāsínous* (i.e. *Mnāsínoos*). The name of Castor's son contains the element *anaxi-*, which occurs in such compound forms as *anaxiphórminx*, *Anaxídāmos*, *Anaxagóras*, etc.[200] The name is thus related to *ánax*, "lord, king"/*anássō*, "rule," and to *ánakes*, the cult title of the Dioskouroi in Sparta. *Mnāsínoos*, the name of Polydeuces' son, is a particular type of Greek compound named after the compound *terpsímbrotos*, "delighting mortals" (cf. the compounds with first element *anaxi-* cited above). The first element, *Mnāsí-* (Attic-Ionic *Mnēsí-*), contains the (enlarged) root *mn-ā* (<*mn-eə₂*) and means "remembering," as in the adjective *mnēsíkakos*, "remembering evil, vindictive."[201] *Mnāsínoos* has the interesting meaning "remembering *nóos*." How exactly this meaning should be construed is not clear, but the importance of the name is not its precise reference, but the connection it establishes between Polydeuces, the immortal twin, and *nóos*, "mind." For our purposes it is enough to say that the name of Polydeuces' son confirms Polydeuces' own characterization in terms of "intelligence."[202]

---

two sons (Anaxis and Mnasinoos) and two mothers (Hilaeira and Phoibe) in Pausanias's description of the statue group in Argos: μετὰ δὲ ταῦτα Διοσκούρων ναός. ἀγάλματα δὲ αὐτοί τε καὶ οἱ παῖδές εἰσιν Ἄναξις καὶ Μνασίνους, σὺν δέ σφισιν αἱ μητέρες Ἱλάειρα καὶ Φοίβη, "After these is the temple of the Dioskouroi. The statues are the Dioskouroi themselves and their sons Anaxis and Mnasinous, and with them their mothers Hilaeira and Phoibe" (Pausanias 2.22.5). The order of the names pairs Anaxis with Hilaeira and Mnasinoos with Phoibe.

200 For these *terpsímbrotos* compounds see Knecht 1946:45; Risch 1974:191–193; Chantraine 1999 s.v. *ánax*; and cf. below in text. The names *Ánaxis* and *Anaxías* appear to be "short-forms" (cf. n1.51 above on the name *Nēleús*).

201 Cf. also the related verb *mnēsikakéō*, "remember past injuries, bear a grudge." For other compounds in *mnēsí-* see Chantraine 1999 s.v. *mimnēskō*, sections 11–12; for Mycenean *Manasiweko* = *Mnāsiwergos* (later Greek *Mnēsíergos*), cf. also Bader 1965:93–94.

202 It is worth noting that in Pindar's *Nemean* 10 the verb *noéō* occurs in connection with Polydeuces' act of bringing his brother back to life; when Zeus gives Polydeuces a choice of fates, either to become entirely a god himself or to share his immortality with Castor, he expresses the second alternative with the phrase: "but if you are minded (*noeîs*) to share everything equally" (*Nemean* 10.85–88):

ει δὲ κασιγνήτου πέρι
μάρνασαι, πάντων δὲ <u>νοεῖς</u> ἀποδάσσασθαι ἴσον,
ἥμισυ μέν κε πνέοις γαίας ὑπένερθεν ἐών,
ἥμισυ δ' οὐρανοῦ ἐν χρυσέοις δόμοισιν.

But if you fight for your brother,
and <u>are minded</u> to share everything equally,
you would breathe half the time being under the ground
and half the time in the golden houses of the sky.

The poet's use of a particular word is of course less significant than the name of Polydeuces' son, attested in two separate cults of the Archaic period, but the context is still suggestive.

§1.66 The final element to be established for the Indo-European form of the twin myth is the immortal twin's association with "cattle." The Vedic twin called "son of Dyaus" has a clear association with cattle when Sanskrit epic is taken into account.[203] Greek, however, has nothing like the clear opposition of Sanskrit epic between Sahadeva the cowherd and Nakula the horseman, or the Vedic text that opposes the names *Nā́satyā* and *Aśvínā* in terms of cattle and horses (*RV* 2.41.7). The distinction between cattle and horses exists in Greek, but it is not emphasized in our sources, despite the fact that it figures in the twins' central myth. This myth actually has two episodes, the second of which is the battle between cousins in which the warrior Castor dies. In Pindar, our oldest source for the myth, all attention is focused on this second episode, except for a brief allusion to the first episode, which is a cattle raid: in the introduction to the narrative Idas is said to have wounded Castor with his spear "out of anger for some cattle" (*amphì bousín pòs kholōtheís*, *Nemean* 10.60). We cannot be certain about the specifics of this episode;[204] but the mere fact that there are two episodes, a cattle raid followed by a battle, is itself highly significant in this central myth of the Dioskouroi.[205] This much

---

203 The twins' opposition in terms of cattle and horses also seems to have been preserved in Iranian despite the absence of the twins themselves in the Zoroastrian system. Dumézil argues that the Indo-European twins were transformed into two other pairs of figures in Iranian: Old Avestan *Haurvatāt*, "Wholeness, Health," and *Amərətāt*, "Immortality" (Dumézil 1945:89–90, 91–92, 158–170, cf. 1968:88, 105); and Young Avestan *Drvāspā*, "mistress of healthy horses," and *Gə̄uš Tašan*, "builder of the cow," or *Gə̄uš Urvan*, "soul of the cow" (Dumézil 1968:88–89). The latter pair seems to preserve the old opposition.

204 "Apollodorus" 3.11.2 presents the following version: the four cousins together steal cattle from Arcadia; Idas and Lynkeus make off with all the spoil after cheating the Dioskouroi of their share; the Dioskouroi raid the cattle back again and set an ambush for their cousins; Lynkeus discovers the ambush and Castor is killed in battle. Lynkeus's role in discovering the ambush is also found in the *Cypria* and Pindar: in *Cypria* fr. 11 Allen Lynkeus looks out from Taygetos with his extraordinary eyes and sees the Dioskouroi inside a hollow oak; Pindar *Nemean* 10.61–63 follows this closely. In the *Cypria* Lynkeus appears to kill Castor, but in "Apollodorus" Idas kills Castor; Pindar leaves the point vague. The cattle raid carried out by the Dioskouroi against their cousins motivates the battle in which Castor dies, and these two episodes, the cattle raid and the battle, are the two essential parts of the myth. There was a variant tradition that the conflict between the cousins arose when the Dioskouroi carried off the daughters of Leukippos, who had been betrothed to the Apharetidai (Theocritus 22 is the earliest literary source). The relationship between the two different traditions is discussed in EN1.3.

205 Dumézil 1968:87 sees Polydeuces as differentially associated with cattle in this myth: "la seule fois que des vaches jouent un rôle dans la vie du couple, Polydeukès y triomphe et Kastôr y succombe." This formulation seems to me essentially correct, but I add the important qualification that the mortal Castor succumbs not in the cattle raid itself, but in the battle that follows: the two episodes are distinct. The cattle raid, on the other hand, should be seen as belonging primarily to the immortal twin. In *Homeric Hymn* 33, as discussed earlier,

of the Greek evidence must suffice for now to establish the association with cattle of the immortal twin in the Indo-European myth.[206]

§1.67 There is a close correspondence between Indic and Greek regarding oppositions between the two twins. The Vedic name *Nā́satyā* completes the picture of these oppositions if it indicates that in Indo-Iranian, as in Greek, an immortal twin had the function of bringing his mortal brother back to life. What precisely did the name *Nā́satyā* mean? I have proposed an etymology that presupposes that the name was originally singular like its Iranian cognate *Nā̊ŋhaiθya*.[207] The starting point for this etymology is the

---

both twins act as "saviors" of distressed sailors; it is worth noting that sheep appear in this context: as the ship sinks the sailors retreat to the highest point of the stern "with white sheep" (*árnessin leukoîsin*) and pray to the Dioskouroi, who come to the rescue (*Homeric Hymn* 33.8–12; see §1.56 above). As tokens of sustenance and life sheep are equivalent to cattle (thus the "cattle" of Helios in *Odyssey* 12 include sheep as well as cattle, and Helios likewise has sheep in the *Homeric Hymn to Apollo* 411–413; cf. Frame 1978:40–47). The connection between sheep and "salvation" in *Homeric Hymn* 33 is very striking; it recalls the Vedic association of the adjective *gómad*, "rich in cattle," with the name *Nā́satyā*, "you two saviors." A final point about the two distinct episodes in the central myth of the Dioskouroi: Theocritus 22 also devotes distinct episodes to the two twins, but in such a way that Castor does not participate in Polydeuces' episode (the boxing match) and (more striking from the standpoint of tradition) Polydeuces does not participate in Castor's episode (the battle against Idas and Lynkeus, which Castor now fights—and wins!—on his own); furthermore, the two episodes in Theocritus are unconnected, in contrast to the central myth of the Dioskouroi. Theocritus manipulates the twins' tradition to his own ends, but by having a pair of episodes, one for each twin, he still recaptures an essential feature of their central myth.

206 A myth consisting of two episodes, a cattle raid followed by a battle, is also central to Nestor's version of the twin myth (see §2.1–§2.5 below); Nestor, no less than the Dioskouroi, constitutes the Greek comparison to the Indic twins and allows a reconstruction of essential features of the Indo-European twin myth. Cattle raiding is sometimes seen as the primary Indo-European form of warfare (e.g. Lincoln 1976 and 1981), but this blurs the distinction between cattle and horses made clear by the Indo-European twin myth; cf. n2.7 below on Nestor's cattle raid.

207 Frame 1978:135–137. For the Iranian demon *Nā̊ŋhaiθya* as deriving from an Indo-Iranian immortal twin (and as attesting an old use of the singular form of the name) see above §1.42 and n1.120. The Vedic name *Nā́satyā* itself occurs in the singular in *RV* 4.3.6; it is modified here by the epithet *párijman*, "traversing," which elsewhere in the *Rig-Veda* is used of the twins as a pair and of their chariot. There is a metrical problem in the verse (it is a syllable short) making this evidence for the singular uncertain. The metrical problem is eliminated by changing the singular *nā́satyāya* to the dual *nā́satyābhyām* and by taking the epithet *párijmane* with the god Vāta in the previous segment of the verse (Vāta has this epithet elsewhere in the *Rig-Veda*; see Geldner 1951–1957 ad loc.). A better solution, proposed by Karl Hoffmann in Schindler 1972:15, is to change the dative *kṣé*, "to the earth," to *yakṣé*, an infinitive from *yakṣ-*, "appear," in the sequence *párijmane nā́satyāya <ya>kṣé*: the verse will then say "What do you want to say, Agni (*kád...agne...brávas*) to the traversing *Nā́satya-*, that he appear"; cf. Goto 1991:979.

Sanskrit cognate of Greek *néomai*, namely *násate*, "approach, resort to, join."[208]
Although the Sanskrit verb and its Greek cognate are classified as "middle
only verbs" (*media tantum*), we have already seen that Greek had an easily
reconstructed active verb *néō*, "bring back," beside the middle verb *néomai*,
"return." I believe that Indo-Iranian had the same active verb, **násati*, beside
the middle verb *násate*.[209] The active verb, in my view, is contained in the
name *Nā́satyā*, which I have proposed to derive from an archaic syntagma,
*nasati-ya, "he who brings back to life," of which the first element is the third
person singular of the verb in question and the second element is the rela-
tive pronoun *ya-*; *Nā́satyā* is then the nominalization (with *vṛddhi* length-
ening of the root vowel) of this syntagma. This proposal follows exactly
Gregory Nagy's proposal for the etymology of Old Persian *xšāyaθiya-*, "king"
(New Persian *šāh*), namely, that the underlying Iranian form **xšāyatya-* is the
nominalization (with *vṛddhi*) of an archaic syntagma **kšayati-ya* "he who has
power."[210] Nagy proposed this etymology on the basis of evidence for similar
formations in Celtic as discussed by Calvert Watkins.[211] Watkins himself, in
discussing the Celtic evidence, noted that the syntactic order of third person
verb followed by relative pronoun is well attested in Vedic. This is significant
for the proposed reconstruction of Vedic *Nā́satyā*/Avestan *Nā̊ŋhaiθya*, and of
Old Persian *xšāyaθiya-*.[212]

208 For the meanings of the Sanskrit verb, which have developed too far to shed light on the
meaning of the Indo-European middle verb, cf. n1.68 above.
209 The Indo-European middle verb is **nesetoi* (> Sanskrit *násate*, Greek *néetai*); the active
verb is **neseti* (> Sanskrit **násati*, Greek **néei*; the Greek active ending is an innovation of
obscure origin; cf. Chantraine 1961:297). I think that it is likely that the active verb existed
in Indo-European, but I do not insist on it; the correspondence between Greek and Indo-
Iranian that I propose could be due to common innovation instead of common retention.
210 Nagy 1970:43n121. The Old Persian form is a Median borrowing; for the verb in question,
cf. Old Persian *xšay-*, "rule," Avestan *xšāy-*, "have power," and Sanskrit *kṣay-*, "possess."
211 Watkins 1963:24. Old Irish has special relative forms that combine the relative pronoun
with a verb in the third singular, third plural, or first plural. The etymology of these forms,
which is no longer clear in Irish, is still clear in Gaulish *dugiiontiio*, "who serve." Thus e.g.
Old Irish *bertae*, "who carry," comes regularly from **bheronti-io*. In the Old Irish forms the
relative pronoun can also be the object of the verb; thus *bertae* is both "who carry" and
"whom they carry."
212 For the syntactic order of third person verb followed by relative pronoun, Watkins cites
e.g. *RV* 1.70.5: *dā́śad yó asmāi*, "who worships him." Nagy reports a number of parallels in
Italic and Celtic for the process of noun formation, and in Hittite for the syntactic order,
which Watkins suggested to him (Nagy 1970:43n121):

> *Lūcetius*, the name of one of the followers of Turnus: Vergil, *Aeneid* IX 570. Servius ad
> loc.: *...lingua Osca Lucetius est Iuppiter, dictus a luce.* Cf. also Gaulish *Leucetios*, epithet of the
> god of war. For references and further instances (including a possible occurrence in the
> *Carmen Saliare*), cf. J. Whatmough, *The Prae-Italic Dialects of Italy* II 197.

§1.68 The reconstruction **nasati-ya*, "he who brings back to life," is supported by the scansion of Vedic *Nā́satyā*. In 67 of 100 occurrences in the *Rig-Veda* the name has four syllables instead of three. This is in sharp contrast to the name *Ā́ditya-*, which has the same metrical shape as *Nā́satya-*, but which requires resolution of one of its syllables in only 7 of 135 occurrences. This contrast in metrical behavior casts further doubt on the proposal to derive *Nā́satya-*, like *Ā́ditya-*, from an abstract noun in *-ti-*; the difference in metrical behavior between the two names suggests that they are also derived by different processes.[213] I propose that the metrical resolution in fully two-thirds of the occurrences of *Nā́satyā* in the *Rig-Veda* has an etymological basis in the combination of third-person singular verbal ending and rela-

---

Δουκέτιος, the name of a king of the Sicels: Diodorus Siculus 11.78.5. For references and further instances, cf. again Whatmough, *PID* II 452.

Hence **leuketi-i̯o* "he who shines" and **deuketi-i̯o* "he who leads," both nominalized. There is a parallel syntagma in Hittite: e.g. in *Laws* I 25, *paprizzi kuiš* "he who defiles" (a well, in this case); also, in an Akkadian-Hittite vocabulary (*Keilschrifttexte aus Boghazköi* I 42 31), the Akkadian participle *ḫābilu* "gewalttätig" is glossed as *dammešḫiškizzi kuiš*, literally "welcher schädigt."

Nagy has subsequently (1979:198–199) suggested as a Greek parallel *Lampetíē*, the name of one of the two daughters of Helios who guard Helios's cattle in *Odyssey* 12.132: νύμφαι ἐϋπλόκαμοι, Φαέθουσά τε Λαμπετίη τε, "the fair-haired nymphs, Phaethousa and Lampetie." The names *Phaéthousa* and *Lampetíē*, both meaning "bright, shining," are feminine equivalents of masculine *Lámpos* and *Phaéthōn*, the names of the horses who bring the dawn goddess in *Odyssey* 23.246: Λάμπον καὶ Φαέθονθ᾽, οἵ τ᾽ Ἠῶ πῶλοι ἄγουσι. Reconstructed as **lampeti-yā*, *Lampetíē* means "she who shines": **lámpeti*, from the thematic verb *lámpō*, has the athematic third singular ending *-ti*, which, like the formation itself, would be an archaism; the lack of assibilation (*-ti* versus *-si*) is also an archaism (cf. the names *Ortílokhos* and *Orsílokhos* of a grandfather and grandson in *Iliad* 5.546 and 549 and see Chantraine 1933:40); **yā* in the reconstruction is the feminine relative pronoun (Greek *hḗ*). The name *Lampetíē* is discussed further in EN1.4. These possible examples are sufficient, I think, to support the process of noun formation proposed for *Nā́satya-*. The etymology is acknowledged by Mayrhofer 1986ff. s.v. *Nā́satya-*, who cites Nagy 1990:93n46 and 249n80; Nagy in both places cites Frame 1978:135–137 (cf. also Nagy1979:199n2); Frame 1978 cites Nagy 1970 for the basis of the etymology, Old Persian *xšāyaθiya-*. The proposed etymology of *Nā́satya-* occurred to Nagy and me in the late 1960s after Calvert Watkins had made Nagy's etymology of Old Persian *xšāyaθiya-* known to me in a different context. I hasten to add that for *Nā́satya-* Mayrhofer regards an etymology based on the hypothetical noun **nasati-* (see n1.123 above) as probable.

213 See n1.123 above for Güntert's derivation of *Nā́satyā* from a hypothetical abstract noun **nasati-*, parallel to the derivation of *Ā́ditya-* from *áditi-*. Other factors may also bear on the difference in metrical treatment of these two names: whereas *Nā́satyā* is dual, *Ā́ditya-* is usually plural and thus has a different metrical shape overall; I have also not excluded that the time of composition of the hymns in which the two names occur may differ. (For *áditi-*, "unboundedness," understood as "freedom from offense, innocence," and for the *Ā́ditya-s* as the "gods who uphold *áditi-*," see Brereton 1981:197 and 288–292).

tive pronoun (-ti ya-). The original scansion of the name, in other words, was
Násatiyā, and this accounts for the striking preponderence of four-syllable as
opposed to three-syllable instances of the name.[214] The additional complica-
tion, however, is that the four-syllable form of the name can also be scanned
Náasatyā, with resolution of -ā- in the initial syllable into -aa-, and it is not
easy to say which pattern of resolution, Násatiyā or Náasatyā, was actually
used. Vedic meter, which like Greek meter is based on the alternation of long
and short syllables, is a matter of rhythmical tendencies, in contrast to the
more fixed patterns of Greek meter (i.e. of Greek lyric meters, which, like
Vedic meters, have fixed syllable counts). The rhythmical patterns Násatiyā
($^-\ \check{}\ \check{}\ ^-$) and Náasatyā ($\check{}\ \check{}\ ^-\ ^-$) are each favored in different positions in the
verse, but they are not required in those positions. Thus it is possible that
only one of the two patterns was used in all 67 instances of resolution, but
which of the two patterns this would have been does not emerge.[215] A more
balanced view is that both rhythmical patterns seem to have been used in
the Rig-Veda.[216] I believe that this was in fact the case, but I would argue that

214 The form Násatiyā (four syllables) was presumably shortened to Násatyā (three syllables)
     in the natural language once the etymology was no longer transparent. This parallels the
     situation of such nominal derivatives with alternate forms in -iya and -ya in the Rig-Veda as
     e.g. ápiya vs. ápya, "watery": the forms in -iya are inherited from a stage of the language at
     which the morpheme boundary was still perceived (ap + iya) and the derivational process
     was still productive, whereas the forms in -ya belong to a later stage when the morpheme
     boundary was no longer perceived and the derivational process had ceased to be produc-
     tive (cf. Nagy 1970:7–8 and 41–42). In Násatiyā the original morpheme boundary (Násati + yā)
     is differently placed than in such nominal derivatives, but the result of the erosion of this
     boundary is the same. Avestan Nåŋhaiθya also reflects erosion of the original morpheme
     boundary, presumably by the same process as in Vedic (see Nagy 1970:41 for pairs of
     nominal derivatives in -iya and -ya in Avestan paralleling those in Vedic). Old Persian
     xšāyaθiya-, as derived by Nagy, has likewise eroded the morpheme boundary between the
     third person singular ending and the relative pronoun (-θiya < *-tya; original *-tiya would
     have remained -tiya); see Nagy 1970:43 and n121, who also points out that the Old Persian
     form is a Median borrowing since Old Persian -θiya > -šiya. Besides the evidence of the
     Rig-Veda, which is still to be discussed, the Mitanni form Nasattiya(nna) perhaps reflects an
     original rhythm Násatiyā.
215 Oldenberg 1909:17, commenting on RV 1.20.3, points out that the numerous instances
     in which a four-syllable form of the name comes immediately after the early caesura
     in trimeter (i.e. after syllable 4) favor the rhythm Náasatyā, except that this is also the
     most convenient metrical position for Násatiyā ("doch wird dies Argument [for Náasatyā]
     dadurch abgeschwächt, dass auch für Násatiyā eben dies die bequemste metrische Stellung
     war"); on the other hand, the instances in which a four-syllable form occupies syllables
     3–6 of a dimeter favor the rhythm Násatiyā; the other scattered instances of a four-syllable
     form "entscheiden nicht." In EN1.5 to n1.219 below the statistical evidence is analyzed and
     elaborated.
216 Oldenberg 1909:17 and Arnold 1905:99 both favor this view.

Nā́sati-yā́, reflecting the etymology of the name, was the original rhythm, and that this rhythm was altered as the original meaning of the name was forgotten. The new rhythm was *Nā́-asatyā́*, which reinterprets the name as the colorless (but synchronically transparent) "not untrue ones."[217] The shift from one rhythm to the other was of course gradual, hence the apparent use of both rhythms in the *Rig-Veda*. The four-syllable rhythm itself, as I have interpreted it, is a great archaism, going back to Common Indo-Iranian. It was only in poetic diction that the name still had four syllables; in the natural language the name had three syllables, and 33 (one third) of the examples of the name in the *Rig-Veda* reflect this new synchronic reality.[218] I think it is a measure of how deeply rooted the four-syllable form of the name was in the traditional diction of the *Rig-Veda* that the original number of syllables was preserved in a majority of instances even as this four-syllable form developed a new rhythm and a new meaning.[219]

§1.69 We have reconstructed the syntagma **nasati-ya*, "he who brings back to life and light," as the basis of the Common Indo-Iranian name *Nā́satya-*. There is good reason to think that this syntagma described not only a mythic act, in which an immortal twin brought his mortal brother back to life, but also a mental function.[220] The original context for the combined mythic act and mental function was the Indo-European twin myth, from which Greek *Néstōr* and Greek *nóos* (as I argue) also derive. We may ask exactly

---

217 This interpretation is first found in Pāṇini (cf. n1.122 above), but it is based, I suggest, on an actual pronunciation of the name in Vedic verse.

218 The coexistence in the *Rig-Veda* of the four- and three-syllable forms of the name has the same explanation as the coexistence of e.g. the alternative forms *ápiya* and *ápya* (see n1.214 above).

219 In EN1.5 it is argued that in RV 2.41.7, which contrasts the vocatives *Nāsatyā* and *Aśvinā* in terms of cattle and horses, the scansion *Nāsatiyā* is found, and that the influence of this archaic verse explains the other unusually frequent instances of a four-syllable form of the name in syllables 5–8 of dimeters. It is also argued that it was in syllables 5–8 of trimeters, where both scansions of the name are possible (cf. n1.215 above), that the scansion *Nāasatyā* began to replace the scansion *Nā́satiyā*, in accord with the reinterpretation of the name as the "not untrue ones."

220 The twins' epithet *dasrā́*, "miracle-working," which connects their role as "saviors" with the notion of "intelligence," is indicative of a similar semantic link in their name *Nā́satyā*; in addition the case of the epic hero Sahadeva, whose reputation for "intelligence" contrasts him with his brother Nakula, shows that the epithet *dasrā́*, with its implication of "intelligence," must also have distinguished one of the twin gods from the other. The contrast in the twins' Vedic hymns between the two dual vocatives *dasrā* and *Aśvinā*, paired with "cattle" and "horses" respectively, bears out this conclusion. The myth in which one twin is *dasrá-*, "miracle-working," in relation to the other is preserved in Greek, where Polydeuces not only brings Castor back to life, but is also characterized by "intelligence" in contrast to his brother.

what the mental function was that was represented by this myth. Since the solar context of the twin myth contrasts sunrise and sunset perhaps the basic notion was simply "consciousness" as opposed to "unconsciousness," in the daily alternation between the two.[221] "Consciousness" suits the basic myth of the Dioskouroi, in which Polydeuces "opens the eye, then the voice" of his fallen brother (ἀνὰ δ᾽ ἔλυσεν μὲν ὀφθαλμόν, ἔπειτα δὲ φωνὰν χαλκομίτρα Κάστορος, Pindar *Nemean* 10.90). In Vedic the idea that the returning light of day sets the mind in motion is present even apart from the twins' hymns,[222] and the twins themselves are twice called *dhiyaṃjinvā*, "thought-awakening," in the context of their morning ritual (*RV* 1.182.1, 8.26.6);[223] in a third verse (8.5.35) they are called by the equivalent epithet *dhījavanā*, "thought-awakening."[224] But "consciousness" is just the starting point in defining the mental function represented by the twin myth.[225] The key to the more developed mental functions represented by this myth is the Greek *Néstōr* insofar as he personifies *nóos*, "mind," in his own myths and in his role in the Homeric poems. We will consider this aspect of the Homeric figure as we examine his Homeric role in the next part of this study. We have now reached the point where the double comparison between the *Nā́satyā Aśvínā* and *hippóta Néstōr* puts the Homeric figure squarely in the frame of the Indo-European twin myth, and we must now address his myth accordingly.

---

221 For the possibility that "consciousness" is the basic underlying notion in *nóos*, cf. Frame 1978:30.

222 Note in particular the well-known "Gāyatrī," repeated daily by brahmans, which prays for the light of the sun god Savitar, who will "set our thoughts in motion" (*RV* 3.62.10):

 tát savitúr váreṇyam / bhárgo devásya dhīmahi / dhíyo yó naḥ pracodáyāt

 May we receive this choice light of the god Savitar, who will set our thoughts in motion.

223 The basic notion of the element *-jinva* (root *jinv*) is "set in rapid motion, arouse"; Geldner translates *dhiyaṃjinvā́* as "Gedankenwecker, Gedanken anregend."

224 In the verse in question (*RV* 8.5.35) the epithet *dhījavanā* occurs first in a dimeter where it is followed by a four-syllable form of the name *Nā́satyā* (see above n1.219 and EN1.5 to n1.219 for *RV* 2.41.7 as setting the rhythmical pattern for the name *Nā́satyā* in this position); the collocation of *dhījavanā* with *Nā́satyā* in this verse may be significant insofar as the name *Nā́satyā* itself still carries the meaning of the epithet *dhījavanā* (cf. §1.54 above on the the the name *Nā́satyā* as being glossed by the epithet *dasrā́*).

225 Duality is central to the twin myth in general, and to the mental function that it represents in particular. As a physical basis for duality in the mental function at issue one might consider not only the use of the two hands (see n1.194 and n1.197 above on the notion of "craftiness" associated with skillful use of the two hands), but also the functions of the two hemispheres of the brain; ancient cultures were presumably not aware of the different functions of the brain's hemispheres, but it is another (perhaps unanswerable) question whether the effects of the different functions were nevertheless experienced and given expression in the twin myth.

Endnotes, Part 1

EN1.1 (Endnote to n1.181)

If the Dioskouroi were thought of as buried beneath the earth at Therapne, their cult must, one assumes, have included the principal feature of hero cults, namely a grave. Unfortunately nothing is known of the twins' cult at Therapne, which after Pindar is never mentioned again. Bölte *RE* 'Therapne' 2365 suggests that after Pindar's time the twins' cult was moved to other locations nearer Sparta, such as the Dromos and the Phoibaion, where shrines of the Dioskouroi are attested in Pausanias 3.14.6 and 3.20.2. The main sanctuary at Therapne was the "Menelaion" (so called first by Polybius in the second century BC), where Helen and Menelaus were worshipped as gods (not as heroes) according to Isocrates 10.63. Their worship at Therapne is attested for the sixth century BC by a story in Herodotus 6.61 about Helen's cult, and by dedications to both Menelaus and Helen found in excavations of the Menelaion carried out by the British School in Athens in the 1970s (Catling 1977:36–37: there is one dedication to Menelaus, dated early fifth century; there are two dedications to Helen, not specifically dated but apparently older). Bölte *RE* 'Therapne' 2360–2362 argues that the Dioskouroi were once worshipped at the Menelaion, and he associates their burial place with the peak of the hill on which the shrine is located (*RE* 'Therapne' 2356, 2360). The British archaeologists do not discuss the Dioskouroi in their study of the shrine, which they date to the early fifth century BC (they also identify two predecessors of the shrine, which they date to c. 600 BC and c. 700 BC (Catling 1977:35–36; cf. Deoudi 1999:124–125). If the worship of the Dioskouroi did not take place at the Menelaion, there is no way of knowing where else in Therapne it might have taken place. The British excavators discovered a second hilltop shrine not far from the Menelaion, but the objects in the deposit of this shrine do not seem to concern the Dioskouroi (cf. Catling 35). The only other evidence relating to the twins' sacred space in Therapne is the word *kolōnân* in a badly preserved entry of Hesychius; it is a fragment of lyric poetry attributed to Alcman by Diehl (fr. 8) and left unattributed by Bergk (adespota fr. 74) and Page (*PMG* 983 = adespota fr. 65):

> τυίδε (τύδαι cod.)· ἐνταῦθα. Αἰολεῖς. τυδᾶν κολωνᾶν·
> Τυνδαριδᾶν κολωνᾶν.

Whatever the correct wording of the quoted phrase (Page suggests τυίδ' ἀν Τυνδαριδᾶν κολωνάν, "hither up the hill of the Tyndaridai"), the occurrence of *kolónē*, "hill, mound" in connection with the *Tundarídai* is perhaps significant in view of the word's occasional meaning "sepulchral mound, barrow" (LSJ cite Sophocles *Electra* 894; cf. also *Iliad* 2.811). There is of course no guarantee of that meaning here, especially since Therapne itself is a hill (cf. Pindar's reference to Castor as "dwelling in the high-placed seat of Therapne," Τυνδαρίδας...ὑψίπεδον Θεράπνας οἰκέων ἕδος, *Isthmian* 1.31). If we assume that a tomb played a part in the twins' cult, this may be why a tomb also plays a part in the myth of Castor's death and return to life as told by Pindar in *Nemean* 10. After Castor is killed, Polydeuces finds Idas and Lynkeus "near their father's tomb" (τοὶ δ' ἔναντα στάθεν τύμβῳ σχεδὸν πατρωΐῳ, line 66). They seize an "image of Hades, smooth stone" (ἄγαλμ' Ἀΐδα, ξεστὸν πέτρον, line 67) and hurl it at Polydeuces, but it does not hurt him. Polydeuces then kills Lynkeus with his spear and Zeus smites Idas with a thunderbolt. The significance of the tomb in this myth is two-fold: it symbolizes Polydeuces' immortality (he is not crushed by the *ágalma* of Hades), and it marks the site where Idas and Lynkeus meet their end. The latter twins' father Aphareus, a brother of Tyndareus (Stesichorus, cited by "Apollodorus" 3.10.3), was Messenian in origin, but his tomb must have been appropriated by the Spartans as a result of the Messenian Wars: Pausanias 3.11.11 reports its presence in Sparta not far from the bones of Orestes (3.11.10), which the Spartans had likewise expropriated from abroad (Herodotus 1.67–68; see Hiller von Gaertringen *RE* 'Aphareus' 2711); the Messenians, playing a similar game, claimed that Messenia was the birthplace of the Dioskouroi (Pausanias 3.26.3, 4.31.9; cf. Luraghi 2002:65). According to Pausanias 3.13.1 there was a *mnêma* (memorial) of Castor in Sparta, and over it was a sanctuary of the Dioskouroi, which was said to have been built when the pair first received divine worship forty years after their battle with Idas and Lynkeus. This *mnêma* may represent Castor's grave (cf. Kearns 1992:66), and graves of Idas and Lynkeus were also to be seen nearby; Pausanias thinks that Idas and Lynkeus must have been buried in Messenia, and that only the Messenians' long absence from their own country (after the Messenian Wars) can account for the Spartans' claim to this pair's burial place: ἔστι δὲ καὶ Κάστορος μνῆμα, ἐπὶ δὲ αὐτῷ καὶ ἱερὸν πεποίηται· τεσσαρακοστῷ γὰρ ὕστερον ἔτει τῆς μάχης τῆς πρὸς Ἴδαν καὶ Λυγκέα θεοὺς τοὺς Τυνδάρεω παῖδας καὶ οὐ πρότερον νομισθῆναί φασι. δείκνυται δὲ πρὸς τῇ Σκιάδι καὶ Ἴδα καὶ Λυγκέως τάφος. κατὰ μὲν δὴ τοῦ λόγου τὸ εἰκὸς ἐτάφησαν ἐν τῇ Μεσσηνίᾳ καὶ οὐ ταύτῃ· Μεσσηνίων δὲ αἱ συμφοραὶ καὶ ὁ χρόνος, ὅσον ἔφυγον ἐκ Πελοποννήσου, πολλὰ τῶν ἀρχαίων καὶ κατελθοῦσιν ἐποίησεν ἄγνωστα, ἅτε δὲ ἐκείνων οὐκ εἰδότων ἔστιν ἤδη τοῖς ἐθέλουσιν ἀμφισβητεῖν, "There is also a memorial of Castor, and over it a temple has been constructed. For they say that the sons of Tyndareus first came to be considered gods in the fortieth year after their battle with Idas and Lynkeus and not before. The tomb of Idas and Lynkeus is pointed out next to the Canopy [assembly place]. It is likely from the story that they were buried in Messenia and not here; but the Messenians' misfortunes and the time that has passed since they fled from the Peloponnesus have made many of the old traditions unknown to them even now that they have returned, and since they do not know it is open to those who wish to argue about them" (Pausanias 3.13.1–2).

EN1.2 (Endnote to n1.190)
Supporting the thesis of Sukthankar 1936/1937 that the Bhārgava family of priests thoroughly reshaped the *Mahābhārata* at some point in the tradition, Goldman 1977 studies the poem's distinctive Bhārgava themes, including hostility toward the gods (Goldman 1977:113–128) and a preoccupation with violent death and a subsequent return to life (Goldman 1977:75–92). The ability to bring back to life is particularly associated with Śukra, also called Uśanas Kāvya. He is not the only Bhārgava with this ability, but he alone commands the *mṛtasaṃjīvinī vidyā*, the secret spell for bringing the dead back to life (Goldman 1977:88–92). Like Cyavana, Uśanas Kāvya occurs in the *Rig-Veda*, where he is a sage. In epic he, like Cyavana, embodies the Bhārgava theme of hostility toward the gods, for he is the priest of the Asuras, the demons who war against the gods. His counterpart Bṛhaspati, the priest of the gods, specifically does not command the *mṛtasaṃjīvinī vidyā* (Goldman 1977:125–126). What the theme of bringing back to life may have to do with the twin gods one can only speculate; at any rate the family's hostility to the gods does not extend to the twins, with whom there is instead, in the case of Cyavana, a kind of well-meaning mutual rivalry. The Bhārgavas' role in shaping the *Mahābhārata* may explain a basic feature of the twins' role in the poem, namely the distinctions between them that are ignored elsewhere in Indic tradition. To the point here is another of the Bhārgava themes in the *Mahābhārata*, namely the family's highly ambivalent relations with kṣatriyas,

especially in the case of Cyavana and his line (Goldman 1977:93–112). The twins straddle the division between priests and warriors, as is still evident in the contrasting affinities of the epic twins Nakula and Sahadeva: whereas Sahadeva is often paired with the priestly Yudhiṣṭhira, Nakula is often paired with the warrior Bhīma (see Wikander 1957:75; cf. also Dumézil 1968:80). One wonders whether this distinction between the twins reflects the Bhārgava preoccupation with relations between brahmans and kṣatriyas in their own family. Was it the Bhārgava reworking of the *Mahābhārata* that brought the distinctions between the twins Nakula and Sahadeva to the fore? The distinctive Bhārgava themes of the *Mahābhārata* had an earlier history to judge by one clear case: Cyavana's power over Indra in the myth of the twins' inclusion in the Soma sacrifice has an antecedent in the *Jaiminīya-Brāhmaṇa* 3.159–161. Here Indra objects when Cyavana makes an offering of a sacrificial ladle to the twins, whereupon Vidanvat, another Bhārgava sage, objects to Indra's own ladle. A violent dispute erupts between the gods and the sages and the sages create the demon *Māda*, "intoxication," whereupon the gods are forced to yield to the sages' superiority; see Goldman 1977:166n11.

EN1.3 (Endnote to n1.204)
In a variant of the central myth of the Dioskouroi the conflict between the Dioskouroi and their cousins that leads to Castor's death arises when the Dioskouroi carry off not cattle, but the daughters of Leukippos, who are betrothed to the Apharetidai (Theocritus 22 is the earliest literary source; other sources include the scholia to *Iliad* 3.243, the scholia to Pindar *Nemean* 10.60, Tzetzes, Hyginus, Ovid; cf. Frazer 1921, vol. 2, 30n4, on "Apollodorus" 3.11.2). The daughters of Leukippos are themselves cousins of both pairs of twins, for Leukippos is the brother of Tyndareus and Aphareus. From an Indo-European standpoint the marriages of the Dioskouroi to the Leukippides are secondary to their relationship with a solitary female figure who was at once their sister and common wife (see §1.55). With this in mind we may view the theft of wives by the Dioskouroi as patterned after their theft of cattle. In literature and art the theft of wives became more popular than the theft of cattle (see Pausanias 1.18.1, 3.17.3, 3.18.11, 4.31.9 for citations of artistic representations). "Apollodorus" 3.11.2 somewhat illogically combines both variants of the myth in one version: the Dioskouroi are said to have carried off the daughters of Leukippos from Messene, and to have had sons by them, before they carry out the joint cattle raid with their cousins; the Apharetidai are simply left out of account in this version until they participate in the joint cattle raid. The Leukippides had cult associations in Sparta; they had a sanctuary

of their own and priestesses, also called *Leukippídes* (Pausanias 3.16.1). Frazer 1921 on "Apollodorus" 3.11.2 makes the case for possible theriomorphism in this cult: an obscure gloss in Hesychius s.v. *pōlía* may mean that two maiden priestesses of the Leukippides were called "colts of the Leukippides." It is possible that the Dioskouroi and their wives were themselves worshipped in the form of horses, but the only evidence is the name *Leukippídes* of the wives and the epithet *leukópōloi* of the twins. The epithet, which occurs in Pindar *Pythian* 1.66, is better taken as "owners of white horses" (cf. n1.158), but a doubt is raised by the Theban twins Amphion and Zethos, who are actually called "white colts of Zeus" in a fragment of Euripides' *Antiope* (*leukò...pōlō tò Diós*, fr. 223.127 Kannicht 2004); cf. Ward 1968:12, who cites parallels in the Latvian and Indic traditions (for Saraṇyū, who was said to have conceived the Vedic twins in the form of a horse, see n1.122).

EN1.4 (Endnote to n1.212)
The derivation of the name *Lampetíē* from a syntagma **lampeti-yā*, "she who shines," must exclude alternative explanations based on different forms from the same root. The verb *lampetáō*, "shine" (*Iliad* 1.104, *Odyssey* 4.662), is not relevant; Chantraine 1958:358 derives *lampetáō* from *lámpō*, like *eukhetáomai* from *eúkhomai*, "pray" (there is no related noun in either case; contrast *naietáō*, "dwell," from *[peri]naiétēs*, "dweller," *Iliad* 24.488); a form *Lampetíē* from the verb *lampetáō* would be unparalleled and difficult to explain. The adjective *kallilampétēs*, "beautifully shining," in the phrase *hélie kallilampétē*, Anacreon fr. 106 Page [*PMG* 451] (for the vocative *kallilampétē* instead of *kallilampéta* cf. Hipponax fr. 139 Degani and Degani ad loc.) is formed like Homeric *hupsibremétēs*, "high thundering" (agent suffix *-tēs*); this formation has no relation with the form *Lampetíē*. The adjective *khrusolámpetos*, "shining with gold" (Hipponax fr. 79.7 Degani) contains a verbal adjective in *-etos* (cf. Hawkins 2004:203 and Chantraine 1933:299–300); an identically formed masculine name *Lámpetos* seems to be implied by the Homeric patronymic *Lampetídēs* (see below). *Lampetíē* could be derived from the name *Lámpetos* through an extended form *Lampétios* (cf. *phílos* and *phílios*); a Christian-era name *Lampétios* is in fact attested (Photius *Bibliotheca* 52, Bekker p. 13); cf. also the fragmentary name *Lampeti-* in *IG* V.2.175 (Tegea, undated), perhaps representing *Lampetíōn* (Boeckh *CIG* 1512, Pape-Benseler 1911 S.V.), this also to be derived from *Lámpetos*. But if we consider earlier evidence the name *Lámpetos* itself is suspect: the Homeric patronymic *Lampetídēs* does not mean "son of *Lámpetos*," but "son of *Lámpos*," on the explicit evidence of *Iliad* 15.526: Λαμπετίδης, ὃν Λάμπος ἐγείνατο φέρτατον υἱὸν, "Lampetides, whom <u>Lampos</u>

bore as his strongest son" (cf. n1.51 end). This, I think, is clear evidence that the name *Lámpetos* did not exist in the Homeric period; the name, which occurs in a fragment of Hellenistic poetry, must be a back formation from *Lampetídēs* (it occurs in the first line of a passage from the *Foundation of Lesbos*, perhaps of Apollonius of Rhodes, which is quoted by Parthenius *Erotica Pathemata* 21: ἔνθα δὲ Πηλεΐδης κατὰ μὲν κτάνε Λάμπετον ἥρω, "then Peleus's son killed the hero Lampetos"); see Cuypers 2002/2003, whose interpretation of the fragment leaves little doubt that *Lámpetos* is derived secondarily from Homeric *Lampetídēs* (see esp. p. 129). What needs to be explained is the anomalous Homeric patronymic *Lampetídēs*. The regular patronymic from *Lámpos* would be **Lampídēs*, which does not fit the meter; the normal metrical expedient in this situation would have been **Lampiádēs* (cf. n1.51), but instead we have *Lampetídēs*. I suggest that to explain this form we need to take into account the relationship between the names *Lámpos* and *Lampetíē* as masculine and feminine equivalents (see n1.212); this would account for the anomalous patronymic by an analogy: *Lámpos* : *Lampetíē* :: *Lámpos* : *Lampetídēs*. If this is correct, it is the name *Lampetíē* that explains the name *Lámpetos/Lampétios*, and not the reverse. There is no other obvious explanation of the name *Lampetíē*. The abstract noun suffix *-tíē* survives in the Homeric noun *akomistíē*, "want of care," *Odyssey* 21.284, but in Ionic this suffix regularly becomes *-síē*, as in Homeric *huposkhesíē*, "promise," *Iliad* 13.369. Old abstract nouns with this suffix are mostly compounds, like the two forms just cited (see Chantraine 1933:83–84), although simple forms also occur, like Homeric *eiresíē*, "rowing" (see Chantraine 1933:85–86). To explain *Lampetíē* as an abstract noun meaning "shining," like *eiresíē*, "rowing," one would have to account for the lack of assibilation, which in *akomistíē* is phonetic (the few late examples cited by Chantraine 1933:83 in which *-t-* is retained in compounds are clearly not relevant).

EN1.5 (Endnote to n1.219)
Two-thirds of the examples of resolution of the name *Nā́satyā* (44 of 67) occur in syllables 5–8 of trimeters (eleven-syllable and twelve-syllable verses). Trimeters are divided into two segments by a caesura after the fourth or fifth syllable, and the two syllables after the caesura are regularly short. In the examples in question the name *Nā́satyā* follows the "early" caesura after syllable 4, and the normal rhythm in syllables 5–8 would be *Náasatyā* (˘ ˘ ‾ ‾); syllables 5–7 of the trimeter are called the "break," and the normal break after early caesura is ˘ ˘ ‾, occurring in 40 percent of trimeters in the archaic period and more frequently thereafter (Arnold 1905:183). But while the rhythm *Náasatyā* (˘ ˘ ‾ ‾) would be "normal," the rhythm *Nā́satiyā* (‾ ˘ ˘ ‾) is

by no means abnormal: a break after early caesura of the form ¯ ˘ ˘ is among
those next in frequency after the "normal" break, being one of three forms
that Arnold calls "subnormal" (there are also "occasional" and "irregular"
forms, which are still less frequent). Of the three "subnormal" forms the
pattern ¯ ˘ ¯ occurs in about one-seventh of trimeters in the archaic period;
Arnold does not give figures for the other "subnormal" patterns, ¯ ˘ ˘ and
˘ ˘ ˘, but the frequency of the pattern ¯ ˘ ˘ at least seems to be on the same
order (this is suggested by Arnold's figures for the relative frequency of trim-
eters with long versus short seventh syllable, and by the greater frequency
of ¯ ˘ ˘ vs. ˘ ˘ ˘ after early caesura, at least in certain time periods; see Arnold
1905:183–184). My interpretation of these numbers is that it was precisely
in this position (after the early caesura in trimeters) that the new rhythm
Náasatyā (˘ ˘ ¯ ¯) replaced the old rhythm *Nā́satiyā* (¯ ˘ ˘ ¯) and became
increasingly well-established. Of the remaining 23 examples of resolution
of the name in other positions in trimeters or in dimeters (eight-syllable
verses), there are seven examples in which the name occupies syllables 3–6 of
dimeters, and this position strongly favors the rhythm *Nā́satiyā* (¯ ˘ ˘ ¯). The
reason for this is that the rhythm of all Vedic verses is more fixed at the end
of the verse than at the beginning, and in dimeters in particular the cadence
(syllables 5–8) has an iambic rhythm (˘ ¯ ˘ ¯) in over 94 percent of examples
(figure calculated from Arnold's table on p. 153, which includes "rather less"
than half the dimeter verse of the *Rig-Veda* [Arnold p. 150]; my calculation
excludes Arnold's figures for trochaic Gāyatrī and epic Anuṣṭubh, which
operate on different principles and have different cadences from other dime-
ters). Just as the rhythm *Nā́satiyā* (¯ ˘ ˘ ¯) is strongly favored in syllables 3–6 of
dimeter by the heavy preponderance of an iambic cadence in this verse-form,
the rhythm *Náasatyā* (˘ ˘ ¯ ¯) is strongly disfavored in this position by the
occurrence of a long fifth syllable in less than 0.7 percent of dimeters (figure
again calculated from Arnold's table on p. 153). There is thus no reason to
think that the rhythm was anything but *Nā́satiyā* (¯ ˘ ˘ ¯) in this position. But
figures do not reveal everything. There are nine examples of resolution of
the name in syllables 5–8 of dimeter, and in this position (the cadence) both
rhythms are irregular and rare: the rhythm ˘ ˘ ¯ ¯ ("syncopated") occurs in
less than 0.3 percent of examples and the rhythm ¯ ˘ ˘ ¯ is included in "other
irregular forms" by Arnold (table on p. 153), all of which together account for
about 1 percent of examples. What is striking is the large number of exam-
ples (nine) of the four-syllable form of the name in this position where either
of the possible rhythms is irregular and rare. I hasten to point out that one
of the nine examples is *RV* 2.41.7, which I have already argued is old because

of its clear contrast between the names *Nā́satyā* and *Aśvínā* in terms of cattle and horses, and because of its context in a list of gods of the three "functions" closely resembling the similar Mitanni list. Since the rhythmical tendencies of Vedic verse become more fixed as time goes on, with fixation occurring first at the end of the verse and gradually moving toward the beginning of the verse, the cadence of *RV* 2.41.7a will not have been irregular when it was first composed if it was composed early enough (cf. Nagy 1974:30–31, 36, who compares Greek dimeters); a double short in this position looks especially old (cf. Nagy 1974:31 with n13). *RV* 2.41.7 contains another possible sign of early composition, namely a short fourth syllable, which is only a third as common as a long syllable in this position (Arnold p. 151, Nagy 1974:159; Nagy 1974:157–159 considers the increasing fixation of a long fourth syllable as a factor in the replacement of an inherited phrase *śráva[s] ákṣitam*, cognate with Greek *kléos áphthiton*, by a newer equivalent *ákṣiti śrávas* in verse-final position in dimeter). I therefore posit that *RV* 2.41.7a contained the rhythm *Nā́satiyā* (ˉ ˘ ˘ ˉ) in verse-final position, and that this traditional verse served as the model for the other eight examples of resolution of the name in this position (*RV* 5.74.2b, 8.5.32c, 8.5.35c, 8.9.9a, 8.25.10b, 8.26.2b, 8.85.1a, 8.85.9a; note that four of these eight verses contrast the duals *Nā́satyā* and *Aśvínā* in different segments of a Gāyatrī just as 2.41.7 does: these four verses are 8.5.32, 8.9.9, 8.85.1, and 8.85.9). If this argument is correct, *RV* 2.41.7, which has already been crucial to this investigation of the twins' two names *Nā́satyā* and *Aśvínā*, also supports by its rhythm the reconstruction **nasati-ya*, "he who brings back to life and light," of the first of these names. Here, with resolutions and scansion indicated, is the text of *RV* 2.41.7 (note the "regular" scansion of the second and third segments, each with iambic cadence and long fourth syllable, in contrast to the "irregular" scansion of the first segment, with non-iambic cadence and short fourth syllable):

gómad ū ṣú nāsatiyā / áśvāvad yātam aśvinā / vartī́ rudrā nṛpā́yiyam
ˉ ˘ ˉ ˘ ˉ ˘ ˘ ˉ / ˉ ˉ ˉ ˉ ˘ ˉ / ˉ ˉ ˉ ˘ ˉ ˘ ˉ

The remaining seven instances of resolution of the name *Nā́satyā* include four in syllables 1–4 of trimeter, where rhythm is freest and both scansions are equally likely, and three in unique positions, all open to either scansion (syllables 8–11 and 2–5 in trimeter and 2–5 in dimeter). It remains to point out that in Van Nooten and Holland 1994 the metrically restored text of *RV* 2.41.7 is as above.

Part 2.

NESTOR'S HOMERIC ROLE

Chapter 4.

ILIAD 11

§2.1 The basic text for Nestor's myth is his story in *Iliad* 11.670–761.[1] I have already suggested that the essence of Nestor's myth is that he is a twin who has lost his brother and who therefore must take his brother's place. What points to this is the etymological correspondence between the solitary *hippóta Néstōr* and the dual *Aśvínā Nā́satyā*, provided that the Vedic names each properly designated a different twin.[2] That point, I think, has now been established.

§2.2 For the interpretation of *Iliad* 11 the other crucial piece of evidence to emerge from the study of the Vedic twin gods is the distinction between a cattleman twin and a horseman twin. This distinction applies directly to Nestor's story when we consider its basic structure, namely its division into two distinct episodes, a cattle raid followed by a battle between horsemen. Nestor refers to both events at the start of his story (*Iliad* 11.670–672):

εἴθ' ὡς ἡβώοιμι βίη δέ μοι ἔμπεδος εἴη
ὡς ὁπότ' Ἠλείοισι καὶ ἡμῖν νεῖκος ἐτύχθη
ἀμφὶ βοηλασίῃ.

I wish I were young and the strength in me were steadfast
as when a battle between the Eleians and us came about
over a cattle raid.

---

1 For the scholarly tradition of treating this story as an independent epic lay that was inserted into the *Iliad* (the so-called "Nestoris") see Willcock 1976:132–133 and Dickson 1995:173, 206n24. With the necessary qualification that Nestor's traditions must have been oral this approach has merit in that it deals with the basic fact, namely that Nestor's traditions were very old.

2 Cf. §1.7 above.

First a cattle raid (*boēlasíē*), and then a battle (*neîkos*): this is like the basic myth of the Dioskouroi.[3] Between these two episodes, both of which focus on Nestor's deeds, is a passage explaining how the Pylians came to be victimized by their neighbors in the first place. It is here that we learn that all twelve of Neleus's sons except Nestor perished when Heracles sacked Pylos in earlier years, and that Pylos was thus left defenseless against its overbearing neighbors. Left unsaid in this crucial passage is the fact that Pylos's great defender was Nestor's brother Periklymenos, who kept Heracles at bay until finally he was vanquished and Pylos was sacked. It is Periklymenos's place that Nestor must take, and to do so he must first become a "warrior horseman." This he does in the second part of his story. Nestor's story in *Iliad* 11 is, in essence, the story of how he became *hippóta Néstōr*. It is his version of the twin myth.

§2.3 We have already considered how Nestor's cattle raid is connected with his name, "he who brings back to life."[4] That connection is confirmed by the close association of cattle with the Vedic name Nā́satyā. Cattle are the domain of the Indo-European immortal twin, who brings his mortal brother back to life; in the opposition between the twins, cattle represent sustenance and life, horses warfare and death. When Nestor carries out his cattle raid, he brings his people back from virtual extinction. Nestor's "cattle raid" (*boēlasíē, Iliad* 11.672) includes sheep, pigs, goats, and horses, all of which represent sustenance and life, even the horses, for they are mares that suckle young (*Iliad* 11.677–681):[5]

λητΐδα δ' ἐκ πεδίου συνελάσσαμεν ἤλιθα πολλὴν
πεντήκοντα βοῶν ἀγέλας, τόσα πώεα οἰῶν,
τόσσα συῶν συβόσια, τόσ' αἰπόλια πλατέ' αἰγῶν,
ἵππους δὲ ξανθὰς ἑκατὸν καὶ πεντήκοντα
πάσας θηλείας, πολλῇσι δὲ πῶλοι ὑπῆσαν.

We drove together from the plain immense spoil:
fifty herds of cattle, as many flocks of sheep,

---

3 See §1.66 above for the cattle raid followed by a battle when Castor is killed and Polydeuces brings him back to life. Cantieni 1942:27 draws attention to the unusual nature of Nestor's two-part story but does not explain it.
4 §1.32; Frame 1978:93–95.
5 Cantieni 1942:30 points out that Nestor's story pays greater attention to the spoil of the cattle raid than to the cattle raid itself; this narrative "inconcinnity" (Cantieni's term) in fact shows what the real point of Nestor's cattle raid is.

as many droves of pigs, and as many wide-ranging herds of
    goats;
also a hundred and fifty golden-haired horses,
all of them mares, many with foals underneath.

When these abundant herds and flocks are distributed to the Pylians we learn
how low the Pylians had sunk, for all of this was a "debt" (*khreîos*) owed to
them in Elis, and they themselves had been reduced to a "few badly off"
(*paûroi kekakōménoi*) survivors (*Iliad* 11.685–695):

κήρυκες δ' ἐλίγαινον ἅμ' ἠοῖ φαινομένηφι
τοὺς ἴμεν οἷσι χρεῖος ὀφείλετ' ἐν Ἤλιδι δίῃ·
οἳ δὲ συναγρόμενοι Πυλίων ἡγήτορες ἄνδρες
δαίτρευον. πολέσιν γὰρ Ἐπειοὶ χρεῖος ὄφειλον,
ὡς ἡμεῖς παῦροι κεκακωμένοι ἐν Πύλῳ ἦμεν·
ἐλθὼν γάρ ῥ' ἐκάκωσε βίη Ἡρακληείη
τῶν προτέρων ἐτέων, κατὰ δ' ἔκταθεν ὅσσοι ἄριστοι·
δώδεκα γὰρ Νηλῆος ἀμύμονος υἱέες ἦμεν·
τῶν οἶος λιπόμην, οἳ δ' ἄλλοι πάντες ὄλοντο.
ταῦθ' ὑπερηφανέοντες Ἐπειοὶ χαλκοχίτωνες
ἡμέας ὑβρίζοντες ἀτάσθαλα μηχανόωντο.

The heralds made a shrill cry when dawn appeared
for those to come to whom a <u>debt</u> was owed in shining Elis,
and the Pylians' leading men came together
and divided the spoil. For the Epeians owed a <u>debt</u> to many,
since <u>few</u> of us were left in Pylos and we were <u>badly off</u>,
for mighty Heracles had come and hurt us badly
in earlier years; all the best men had been killed.
Twelve sons of faultless Neleus we had been,
but of those only I was left; the others had all perished.
Emboldened by this the bronze-clad Epeians
treated us outrageously and devised reckless deeds.

§2.4 In the cattle raid Nestor acts out his name, "he who brings back to
life." In the battle that follows he earns his epithet, "the horseman." The focus
shifts to the battle when the Epeians attack two days after the cattle raid ("on

the third day" after by inclusive Greek reckoning); this is a force of horsemen, and their horses (*híppoi*) are mentioned at the outset (*Iliad* 11.707–709):

οἳ δὲ τρίτῳ ἤματι πάντες
ἦλθον ὁμῶς αὐτοί τε πολεῖς καὶ μώνυχες ἵπποι
πανσυδίῃ.

On the third day they all
came, both the many men themselves and the solid-hoofed <u>horses</u>,
at great speed.

The great heroes of the Epeians were the twins called the Molione, whom even Heracles could not defeat in battle; Heracles would kill them one day, but by stealth rather than might.[6] The Molione now rode with the Epeian horsemen against Pylos, but like Nestor they were still young and untested in battle (*Iliad* 11.709–710):

μετὰ δέ σφι Μολίονε θωρήσσοντο
παῖδ' ἔτ' ἐόντ', οὔ πω μάλα εἰδότε θούριδος ἀλκῆς.

And with them the two Molione armed themselves,
although they were still young, not yet knowing much of furious
warfare.

As for Nestor, his father tried to keep him away from the battle altogether because he thought him still too young for war: when Athena came by night to warn the Pylians and gather them for battle Neleus hid Nestor's horses. But Nestor went anyway, on foot, and even so he kept pace with the Pylian horsemen (*Iliad* 11.717–721):

οὐδέ με Νηλεὺς
εἴα θωρήσσεσθαι, ἀπέκρυψεν δέ μοι ἵππους·
οὐ γάρ πώ τί μ' ἔφη ἴδμεν πολεμήϊα ἔργα.
ἀλλὰ καὶ ὧς ἱππεῦσι μετέπρεπον ἡμετέροισι
καὶ πεζός περ ἐών, ἐπεὶ ὣς ἄγε νεῖκος Ἀθήνη.

Neleus did not
allow me to arm myself, but hid my horses;

6 Pindar *Olympian* 10.26–34; "Apollodorus" 2.7.2; see n2.12 below.

for he said that I did not yet know the deeds of war.
But even so I stood out among our horsemen,
although I was on foot, for so Athena led the battle.

When the two armies clashed, Nestor, still on foot, slew the leader of the enemy horsemen and seized his chariot (*Iliad* 11.737–746):

ἀλλ' ὅτε δὴ Πυλίων καὶ Ἐπειῶν ἔπλετο νεῖκος,
πρῶτος ἐγὼν ἕλον ἄνδρα, κόμισσα δὲ μώνυχας ἵππους,
Μούλιον αἰχμητήν· γαμβρὸς δ' ἦν Αὐγείαο,
πρεσβυτάτην δὲ θύγατρ' εἶχε ξανθὴν Ἀγαμήδην,
ἣ τόσα φάρμακα ᾔδη ὅσα τρέφει εὐρεῖα χθών.
τὸν μὲν ἐγὼ προσιόντα βάλον χαλκήρεϊ δουρί,
ἤριπε δ' ἐν κονίῃσιν· ἐγὼ δ' ἐς δίφρον ὀρούσας
στῆν ῥα μετὰ προμάχοισιν· ἀτὰρ μεγάθυμοι Ἐπειοὶ
ἔτρεσαν ἄλλυδις ἄλλος, ἐπεὶ ἴδον ἄνδρα πεσόντα
ἡγεμόν' ἱππήων, ὃς ἀριστεύεσκε μάχεσθαι.

But when the battle began between the Pylians and the Epeians,
I was the first to slay a man, and I took his solid-hoofed horses,
the spearman Moulios; he was the son-in-law of Augeias
and had for wife his oldest daughter, golden-haired Agamede,
who knew as many drugs as the wide earth grows.
Him I hit with my bronze-tipped spear as he advanced,
and he fell in the dust; and I, leaping onto his chariot,
stood with the front rank of fighters; and the great-hearted
        Epeians
fled in all directions when they saw that man fallen,
the leader of their horsemen, who was the best at fighting.

§2.5 Although the exciting climax of Nestor's story is yet to come, the point of his story is already clear: this is the story of how Nestor first became a horseman. When Neleus hides his horses from him Nestor is emphatically not a horseman; to participate at all he must go on foot. He is without horses until he wins them in battle, and win them he must in order to become a warrior.[7] Nestor first becomes *hippóta Néstōr* when he leaps onto his conquered

---

7 In his successful cattle raid Nestor kills the Epeian Itymoneus (*Iliad* 11.672); when Nestor comes home with the cattle Neleus rejoices in the success of his young son "going to war"

foe's chariot, and as such he immediately proves himself a match for two men at once: he single-handedly kills the double occupants of fifty chariots as he rushes forward like a dark whirlwind; he would even have killed the Epeian twins if they had not been rescued from his path by their father Poseidon (*Iliad* 11.747–752):

αὐτὰρ ἐγὼν ἐπόρουσα κελαινῇ λαίλαπι ἶσος,
πεντήκοντα δ' ἕλον δίφρους, δύο δ' ἀμφὶς ἕκαστον
φῶτες ὀδὰξ ἕλον οὖδας ἐμῷ ὑπὸ δουρὶ δαμέντες.
καί νύ κεν Ἀκτορίωνε Μολίονε παῖδ' ἀλάπαξα,
εἰ μή σφωε πατὴρ εὐρὺ κρείων ἐνοσίχθων
ἐκ πολέμου ἐσάωσε καλύψας ἠέρι πολλῇ.

But I rushed ahead like a dark whirlwind,
and I seized fifty chariots, and on either side of each two
men bit the ground with their teeth, subdued by my spear.
And I would also have destroyed the young Aktorione Molione
if their father, the wide-ruling earthshaker,
had not saved them from the battle, covering them with a great
    mist.

The Pylians drove the Epeians through the plain all the way to Bouprasion (*Iliad* 11.753–756):

ἔνθα Ζεὺς Πυλίοισι μέγα κράτος ἐγγυάλιξε·
τόφρα γὰρ οὖν ἐπόμεσθα διὰ σπιδέος πεδίοιο

(*Iliad* 11.683–684): γεγήθει δὲ φρένα Νηλεύς, / οὕνεκά μοι τύχε πολλὰ νέῳ πόλεμόνδε κιόντι. But when the Epeian horsemen attack, Neleus tries to keep Nestor at home because he thinks he does not yet know the "deeds of war" (*Iliad* 11.719): οὐ γάρ πώ τί μ' ἔφη ἴδμεν πολεμήϊα ἔργα. The cattle raid is a hostile act and it entails a violent deed (Itymoneus dies defending his flocks and herds, *Iliad* 11.674). But the cattle raid still does not establish Nestor as a warrior; to become a warrior he must become a horseman and fight in battle with other horsemen. Bader 1980:33 sees the difference between the cattle raid and the battle in Nestor's story, interpreting the battle as an initiation ritual in which Nestor becomes a warrior for the first time; for the cattle raid as something quite different, having an "economic" rather than a truly warlike aspect, cf. Bader 1980:18, 32, 44, who well notes the difference between the λαοὶ ἀγροιῶται, "rustic folk," who flee when Nestor kills Itymoneus (*Iliad* 11.676), and the Epeian horsemen who later attack Pylos (Bader 1980:37). Walcot 1979:337, on the other hand, does not see the fundamental difference between the two episodes, and therefore finds it "nonsensical" that Neleus tries to prevent Nestor from going into battle when Nestor has already proved himself in "war." Cf. n1.206 above on the Dioskouroi.

κτείνοντές τ' αὐτοὺς ἀνά τ' ἔντεα καλὰ λέγοντες,
ὄφρ' ἐπὶ Βουπρασίου πολυπύρου βήσαμεν ἵππους.

Then Zeus bestowed great power on the Pylians;
for we followed through the flat plain,
killing them and collecting their fine war gear,
until we brought our horses into Bouprasion rich in wheat.

There Nestor slew his last man and the Pylians turned back for home, hailing Zeus among gods and Nestor among men (*Iliad* 11.759–761):

ἔνθ' ἄνδρα κτείνας πύματον λίπον· αὐτὰρ Ἀχαιοὶ
ἂψ ἀπὸ Βουπρασίοιο Πύλονδ' ἔχον ὠκέας ἵππους,
πάντες δ' εὐχετόωντο θεῶν Διὶ Νέστορί τ' ἀνδρῶν.

Then I killed the last man and left him. But the Achaeans
drove their swift horses back from Bouprasion to Pylos,
and all prayed to Zeus among gods and Nestor among men.

Thus Nestor's story ends.[8]

§2.6 Nestor's most important encounter in terms of the underlying meaning of his story is the one that does not take place. The Molione, who are rescued from Nestor's path by Poseidon, are another pair of Indo-European twins with clear distinctions between them. Like the Dioskouroi they have dual paternity, being sons of a god, Poseidon, and a mortal, Aktor: their patronymic *Aktoríōne* contains their mortal father's name.[9] In the Catalogue of Ships, where two of the four leaders from Bouprasion and Elis are sons of the Molione, the Molione themselves are given individual names, Kteatos and Eurytos.[10] Pindar *Olympian* 10.26–27 calls Kteatos the son of Poseidon, and

---

8 For *Iliad* 11.757–758, which I have left out of account, see n2.16 below.
9 Their other name, *Molíone*, is obscure; Hesiod (fr. 17b MW) interprets it as a metronymic, giving the twins a mother *Molínē* (*Moliónē* is the form of her name attested by Ibycus fr. 4 Page). On the twins' name *Molíone* see Wilamowitz 2006:344–345 with Dräger's notes.
10 *Iliad* 2.620–621. Hesiod also uses these names of the Molione, whom their mother bore to Aktor and Poseidon (Hesiod fr. 17a.14–16 MW):

ἣ δ' ἄρ' ἐνὶ μεγ]άροις διδυμάονε γείνατο τέκ[νω
Ἄκτορι κυσαμ]ένη καὶ ἐρικτύπῳ̣ι ἐννοσιγαί[ωι,
ἀπλήτω, Κτέα]τό̣ν τε καὶ Εὔρυτον.

She conceived and bore twin children in her halls
to Aktor and to the loud-crashing earthshaker,
the formidable pair Kteatos and Eurytos.

Eurytos must therefore be the son of Aktor. In Homer the Molione appear again in Nestor's story in *Iliad* 23, where further distinctions between them play a crucial role.[11] Nestor must not kill the Epeian twins in his story in *Iliad* 11 because Heracles later kills them, and the tradition for that was fixed.[12] But if Nestor cannot encounter the twins in his story, why are they featured so prominently?[13] They are there because Nestor himself has a twin myth, and his virtual encounter with twins signals this myth. The Molione were invincible because they were inseparable.[14] Nestor, who lost his brother, became a

---

11 *Iliad* 23.638–642; see Chapter 5 below.
12 Cf. Cantieni 1942:76. Heracles ambushed and killed the Molione at Kleonai; apart from a brief reference in Ibycus fr. 4 Page, Pindar is the earliest source (*Olympian* 10.26–34):

> ... ἐπεὶ Ποσειδάνιον
> πέφνε Κτέατον ἀμύμονα,
> πέφνε δ' Εὔρυτον, ὡς Αὐγέαν λάτριον
> ἀέκονθ' ἑκὼν μισθὸν ὑπέρβιον
> πράσσοιτο, λόχμαισι δὲ δοκεύσαις ὑπὸ Κλεωνᾶν
>   δάμασε καὶ κείνους Ἡρακλέης ἐφ' ὁδῷ,
> ὅτι πρόσθε ποτὲ Τιρύνθιον
> ἔπερσαν αὐτῷ στρατόν
> μυχοῖς ἥμενον Ἄλιδος
> Μολίονες ὑπερφίαλοι.

> ... when he slew faultless Kteatos,
> Poseidon's son,
> and slew Eurytos too, so that he, willing, might
> exact from proud Augeias, unwilling,
> payment for his servitude; waiting for them
> in the wood beneath Kleonai
>   Heracles defeated them on the road,
> because earlier they,
> the arrogant Molione,
> had destroyed his Tirynthian army
> when it sat in the hollows of Elis.

According to "Apollodorus" 2.7.2 the Molione were on their way to compete in the Isthmian games when Heracles ambushed them.
13 Cantieni 1942:37 calls it "not quite understandable" ("nicht recht verständlich") that only the Molione are mentioned when the Epeians attack, given the fact that they have no real role in the battle.
14 The proverb *pròs dúo oudè Heraklês*, "against two not even Heracles," refers to the Epeian twins, whom even Heracles could not defeat (Eustathius 882.34 on *Iliad* 11.750). The inseparability of the Epeian twins came to be taken literally: they appear as Siamese twins first in Hesiod frs. 17a and 18 MW; see Frazer 1921 on "Apollodorus" 2.7.2 for other references. An Attic Late Geometric vase painting (c. 700 BC) represents conjoined twins mounted on a chariot who may be the Molione (see Snodgrass 1998:30–31 and figure 11), but there is no reason to believe that they are conjoined in Homer (cf. Wilamowitz 2006:347, who calls this development of their inseparability "crass").

match for the Molione when he took his brother's place as a warrior. He too now had the opposed characteristics of a pair of twins. As soon as he wins horses he defeats the double occupants of fifty chariots, and this unlikely feat shows that he has indeed become a match for two men at a time.[15] The Molione are mentioned to put Nestor's feat explicitly in the context of the twin myth. The same Nestor who carried out the cattle raid two days earlier had now become a horseman, and as such he would have defeated even the invincible Molione had he encountered them.[16]

§2.7 The aged Nestor appears as a horseman in the present action of the *Iliad* only twice: in *Iliad* 8 (we will return to this later) and in *Iliad* 11. The episode in *Iliad* 11 immediately precedes Nestor's story, and it sets the stage for what this story tells: how Nestor became a horseman in the first place. In the episode preceding the story the fighting rages around Nestor and Idomeneus, who hold their ground against Hector until Makhaon on the Greek side is wounded by an arrow of Paris.[17] Idomeneus then bids Nestor to

---

15 It is hardly possible in reality to drive a chariot and fight at the same time; this led Cantieni 1942:55 to speculate that Athena was the driver of Nestor's chariot. But this mistakes the character of Nestor's story, which is not intended to be entirely realistic; compare his conquest of fifty chariots with the largest number conquered by a single hero in the *Iliad*, namely three by Agamemnon (*Iliad* 11.93, 102, 127; cf. Dickson 1995:172). Exaggeration also characterizes the geography of Nestor's story; cf. n5.45 below.

16 The text of Nestor's account of his battle with the Epeians requires a comment here. Cantieni 1942 argues that three passages in Nestor's account are spurious, namely *Iliad* 11.711–713, 722–734, and 757–758, all of which relate to the Epeians' siege of a town on the border between Elis and Pylos in the neighborhood of the Alpheios River. I will consider these passages (together with lines 696–702 in the division of Nestor's spoil, which Cantieni likewise regards as spurious) in Part 5 below. For now I have simply left these passages out of account. I am convinced that Cantieni is correct, and I will give my reasons for this in due course. These passages are wholly alien to the purpose of Nestor's story as I interpret it, but they make a great deal of sense if they reflect the circumstances of a later day and age; see Part 5, Chapters 12 and 14 below. I should also state that I do not wish to over-simplify the long and complex history of the Homeric poems, which continued to have an oral dimension long after the Ionian phase of their development, by using a word like "spurious." I do think, however, that Nestor's role in the Homeric poems is wholly Ionian in origin, and that it has survived virtually intact from this early stage. I will therefore use the word "Homeric" to refer to this early stage of development in contrast to later developments, which were various and complex, but, I think, much smaller in scale as compared with the Ionian legacy. This is of course not a proposition to be accepted on faith, but one to be tested and modified through the analysis of texts. Although I will use the word "Homeric" to mean Ionian, and will defend this usage, I have no quarrel with a different use of the term to cover the entire history of the Homeric poems through the Hellenistic period. I think it will emerge clearly as my study proceeds why it is necessary for me to focus on the Ionian phase as essentially distinct.

17 *Iliad* 11.500–507:

take Makhaon on his chariot back to the ships, for Makhaon is a physician and as such too valuable to lose (*Iliad* 11.511–515):

ὦ Νέστορ Νηληϊάδη μέγα κῦδος Ἀχαιῶν
ἄγρει σῶν ὀχέων ἐπιβήσεο, πὰρ δὲ Μαχάων
βαινέτω, ἐς νῆας δὲ τάχιστ' ἔχε μώνυχας ἵππους·
ἰητρὸς γὰρ ἀνὴρ πολλῶν ἀντάξιος ἄλλων
ἰούς τ' ἐκτάμνειν ἐπί τ' ἤπια φάρμακα πάσσειν.

Nestor, son of Neleus, great glory of the Achaeans,
come and mount your chariot, and by your side let Makhaon
mount, and with all speed drive your solid-hoofed horses to the ships.
For a man who is a healer is worth many others,
both to cut out arrows and to apply soothing drugs.

§2.8 Makhaon is a twin. He and his brother Podaleirios are sons of Asklepios, and like Asklepios they are both physicians.[18] With this pair of

βοὴ δ' ἄσβεστος ὀρώρει
Νέστορά τ' ἀμφὶ μέγαν καὶ ἀρήϊον Ἰδομενῆα.
Ἕκτωρ μὲν μετὰ τοῖσιν ὁμίλει μέρμερα ῥέζων
ἔγχεΐ θ' ἱπποσύνῃ τε, νέων δ' ἀλάπαζε φάλαγγας·
οὐδ' ἄν πω χάζοντο κελεύθου δῖοι Ἀχαιοὶ
εἰ μὴ Ἀλέξανδρος Ἑλένης πόσις ἠϋκόμοιο
παῦσεν ἀριστεύοντα Μαχάονα ποιμένα λαῶν,
ἰῷ τριγλώχινι βαλὼν κατὰ δεξιὸν ὦμον.

An inextinguishable shout arose
around great Nestor and warlike Idomeneus.
Hector had come among them doing woeful deeds
with his spear and chariot, and was destroying ranks of young men;
but the shining Achaeans would not have yielded from his path
if Alexander, the husband of beautiful-haired Helen,
had not stopped Makhaon, shepherd of the warriors, from his valiant deeds,
hitting him in the right shoulder with a three-barbed arrow.

18 In the *Iliad* they lead the men from a region of Thessaly (*Iliad* 2.729–732):

οἳ δ' εἶχον Τρίκκην καὶ Ἰθώμην κλωμακόεσσαν,
οἵ τ' ἔχον Οἰχαλίην πόλιν Εὐρύτου Οἰχαλιῆος,
τῶν αὖθ' ἡγείσθην Ἀσκληπιοῦ δύο παῖδε
ἰητῆρ' ἀγαθὼ Ποδαλείριος ἠδὲ Μαχάων.

The men who inhabited Trikka and rugged Ithome,
and who inhabited Oikhalia, the city of Oikhalian Eurytos,
those men the two sons of Asklepios led,
the good healers, Podaleirios and Makhaon.

doctors we are again in the realm of the Indo-European twin myth (cf. the *dasrā́ bhiṣájā*, "two miracle-working physicians," of Vedic). Makhaon's name means "warrior" (from *mákhomai*, "fight") and it thus identifies him with the mortal twin of the Indo-European myth.[19] This pair of twins, moreover,

---

Messenia also claimed to be their home (see n2.20 below). In the *Iliou Persis* Poseidon rather than Asklepios is called their father (fr. 5 Allen; see n2.19 below); the dual paternity seems in line with their nature as twins, but cf. below n2.19 end.

19 A distinction in the kind of medicine practiced by the two twins is made in the *Iliou Persis*: whereas Makhaon is a surgeon, who treats bodies, Podaleirios specializes in hidden, mental diseases (scholia to *Iliad* 11.515 = *Iliou Persis* fr. 5 Allen):

αὐτὸς γάρ σφιν ἔδωκε πατὴρ κλυτὸς Ἐννοσίγαιος
ἀμφοτέροις, ἕτερον δ' ἑτέρου κυδίον' ἔθηκε·
τῷ μὲν κουφοτέρας χεῖρας πόρεν ἔκ τε βέλεμνα
σαρκὸς ἑλεῖν τμῆξαί τε καὶ ἕλκεα πάντ' ἀκέσασθαι,
τῷ δ' ἀκριβέα πάντ' ἄρ' ἐνὶ στήθεσσιν ἔθηκεν
ἄσκοπά τε γνῶναι καὶ ἀναλθέα ἰήσασθαι·
ὅς ῥα καὶ Αἴαντος πρῶτος μάθε χωομένοιο
ὄμματά τ' ἀστράπτοντα βαρυνόμενόν τε νόημα.

Their father, the famed earthshaker, himself endowed
them both, and he made each more glorious than the other;
to the one he gave more nimble hands to pull out shafts
from the flesh and make incisions and heal all wounds;
to the other he made all things clear in his breast,
to know hidden causes and to heal incurable diseases;
indeed he was the first to know that angry Ajax's
eyes were flashing and his mind oppressed.

The scholia to *Iliad* 11.515 say that in the view of some the same distinction between the twin physicians is found in Homer: ἔνιοι δέ φασιν ὡς οὐδὲ ἐπὶ πάντας τοὺς ἰατροὺς ὁ ἔπαινος οὗτός (*Iliad* 11.514–515) ἐστι κοινός, ἀλλ' ἐπὶ τὸν Μαχάονα, ὃν μόνον χειρουργεῖν τινες λέγουσι· τὸν γὰρ Ποδαλείριον διαιτᾶσθαι νόσους. καὶ τεκμήριον τούτου· Ἀγαμέμνων τρωθέντος Μενελάου οὐκ ἄμφω ἐπὶ τὴν θεραπείαν καλεῖ, ἀλλὰ τὸν Μαχάονα (cf. *Iliad* 4.193–197). τοῦτο ἔοικε καὶ Ἀρκτῖνος ἐν Ἰλίου πορθήσει νομίζειν, ἐν οἷς φησιν 'αὐτὸς γάρ σφιν ἔδωκε πατήρ...,' "Some say that this praise (*Iliad* 11.514–515) is not for all doctors in general, but for Makhaon, who alone, some say, performs surgery; for Podaleirios diagnoses diseases. And as evidence of this: when Menelaus is wounded Agamemnon does not call both of them for the treatment, but Makhaon (cf. *Iliad* 4.193–197). Arctinus also seems to believe this in the *Sack of Troy* in the lines where he says 'their father himself endowed them....' " Skill with the surgeon's knife suggests the warrior twin; skill in the diagnosis of hidden diseases suggests the twin marked by intelligence. From the Indo-European standpoint this is a secondary distinction, since in the Indo-European myth "saving" and "healing" belong wholly to the immortal twin when he is contrasted with his brother. Nevertheless the distinction still suggests the basic contrast between the twins. Melampus and Bias are in some ways a comparable pair of brothers to Podaleirios and Makhaon: Bias like Makhaon has a warrior's name (from *bíē*, "force"); Melampus like Podaleirios is the healer of mental diseases (he cures the daughters of Proitos of madness). The names "black foot" (Melampus) and "lily foot" (Podaleirios) resemble each other, but what significance this, and the contrasting colors, may have is not obvious. It is not clear whether

does not stay together; whereas Podaleirios survives the war and becomes the founder of new cities, Makhaon, according to the *Little Iliad*, dies in battle at Troy.[20] Makhaon is the counterpart to Nestor's brother Periklymenos, who likewise dies in battle. Periklymenos's death is the unspoken point of Nestor's story in *Iliad* 11; in the episode leading up to this story the overt image is of a pair of figures, one rescuing the other. Nestor and Makhaon are both twin figures, and together they present the image of a pair of twins; in their myths both of these figures become separated from their brothers, but the idea of separation is now left to one side as together they mount Nestor's chariot (*Iliad* 11.516–520):

ὣς ἔφατ᾽, οὐδ᾽ ἀπίθησε Γερήνιος ἱππότα Νέστωρ.
αὐτίκα δ᾽ ὧν ὀχέων ἐπεβήσετο, πὰρ δὲ Μαχάων
βαῖν᾽ Ἀσκληπιοῦ υἱὸς ἀμύμονος ἰητῆρος·
μάστιξεν δ᾽ ἵππους, τὼ δ᾽ οὐκ ἀέκοντε πετέσθην
νῆας ἔπι γλαφυράς· τῇ γὰρ φίλον ἔπλετο θυμῷ.

So he spoke, and the Gerenian horseman Nestor was not
unpersuaded.
He immediately mounted his chariot, and by his side Makhaon

Podaleirios and Makhaon, in addition to other contrasts between them, also have dual paternity: in *Iliad* 2 the mortal Asklepios is their father, in the *Iliou Persis* fragment quoted above Poseidon is their father, but the two fathers are nowhere directly contrasted.

20 Pausanias 3.26.9 reports that in the *Little Iliad* Eurypylos the son of Telephos kills Makhaon (in Homer the only occurrence of Eurypylos the son of Telephos is in *Odyssey* 11.519–520, where Neoptolemos is said to have killed him). Pergamum, where Telephos's traditions were important, knew the tradition for Telephos's son as the slayer of Makhaon: Pausanias 3.26.10 reports that in the temple of Asklepios at Pergamum Telephos was honored but his son was deliberatedly not mentioned because he had slain Makhaon, the son of Asklepios. The Messenians claimed that Makhaon was buried in Gerenia, the Homeric Enope (Pausanias 3.26.8–9); Nestor was supposed to have brought Makhaon's bones home with him from Troy (Pausanias 3.26.10). The tradition for Podaleirios, on the other hand, was that he was blown off course on his way from Troy and that he founded the Carian city of Syrnos (Pausanias 3.26.10; cf. "Apollodorus" *Epitome* 6.18); Podaleirios was said to have founded other cities as well (see Kenner *RE* 'Podaleirios' 1133; for city-founding as a function of twin figures acting both together and alone see n2.139 below). Messenia seems to have rivaled Thessaly as the homeland of Makhaon (at least) from a relatively early period: in the Catalogue of Ships Oichalia, the city of Eurytos, belongs to the territory of Podaleirios and Makhaon in Thessaly in one passage (*Iliad* 2.730, n2.18 above), but in another passage (*Iliad* 2.596) Oichalia is in Messenia; in the *Odyssey* Odysseus is said to have met Eurytos's son Iphitos in "Lacedaemon" (i.e. Messenia), not in Thessaly (*Odyssey* 21.11–14). Cf. Simpson and Lazenby 1970:85 and Kiechle 1960:50–51, 1959:80.

mounted, the son of the faultless healer Asklepios;
he whipped his horses, and not unwillingly they flew
toward the hollow ships; for this way was dear to them in their
spirit.

This image of the aged Nestor racing across the plain with the wounded
warrior twin Makhaon at his side sets the stage for Nestor's story, the story of
how he first became a horseman; the story of *hippóta Néstōr* is thus set in the
frame of the twin myth from the start.

§2.9 Nestor tells the story of how he first became a horseman to
Patroclus. When Nestor emerges from battle Achilles cannot see who the
wounded warrior is on Nestor's chariot, and he sends Patroclus to Nestor's
tent to find out.[21] This is a fateful moment for Patroclus, as is signaled in the

---

21 Achilles sees Nestor and calls Patroclus in *Iliad* 11.596–603:

ὣς οἳ μὲν μάρναντο δέμας πυρὸς αἰθομένοιο·
Νέστορα δ' ἐκ πολέμοιο φέρον Νηλήϊαι ἵπποι
ἱδρῶσαι, ἦγον δὲ Μαχάονα ποιμένα λαῶν.
τὸν δὲ ἰδὼν ἐνόησε ποδάρκης δῖος Ἀχιλλεύς·
ἑστήκει γὰρ ἐπὶ πρυμνῇ μεγακήτεϊ νηΐ
εἰσορόων πόνον αἰπὺν ἰῶκά τε δακρυόεσσαν.
αἶψα δ' ἑταῖρον ἑὸν Πατροκλῆα προσέειπε
φθεγξάμενος παρὰ νηός.

So they fought like blazing fire,
but the Neleian horses, sweating, brought Nestor from the battle,
and carried Makhaon, shepherd of the warriors.
Seeing him swift-footed shining Achilles took notice;
for he was standing on the stern of the deep-flanked ship
looking at the hard toil and the tear-bringing rout.
Immediately he addressed his companion Patroclus,
calling from the ship.

Achilles sends Patroclus to find out who is with Nestor, saying that Nestor's chariot passed
too quickly for him to see clearly (*Iliad* 11.611–615):

ἀλλ' ἴθι νῦν Πάτροκλε Διῒ φίλε Νέστορ' ἔρειο
ὅν τινα τοῦτον ἄγει βεβλημένον ἐκ πολέμοιο·
ἤτοι μὲν τά γ' ὄπισθε Μαχάονι πάντα ἔοικε
τῷ Ἀσκληπιάδῃ, ἀτὰρ οὐκ ἴδον ὄμματα φωτός·
ἵπποι γάρ με παρήϊξαν πρόσσω μεμαυῖαι.

But go now, Patroclus, dear to Zeus, and ask Nestor
who this is that he brings wounded from the battle;
from the back everything resembles Makhaon
the son of Asklepios, but I didn't see the man's eyes;
for the horses darted past me as they pressed on.

narrative when Patroclus first hears Achilles call him and he comes out from his tent (*Iliad* 11.603–604):

ὃ δὲ κλισίηθεν ἀκούσας
ἔκμολεν ἶσος Ἄρηϊ, κακοῦ δ' ἄρα οἱ πέλεν ἀρχή.

He heard and came out
from the tent, equal to Ares, but for him it was the beginning of
evil.

After telling his story Nestor urges Patroclus to go back to Achilles and try to persuade him to save the hard pressed Achaeans; if he cannot persuade him, then let Achilles send him into battle in his place, and let him give Patroclus his arms so the Trojans will think that he is Achilles himself (*Iliad* 11.794–803):

εἰ δέ τινα φρεσὶν ᾗσι θεοπροπίην ἀλεείνει
καί τινά οἱ πὰρ Ζηνὸς ἐπέφραδε πότνια μήτηρ,
ἀλλὰ σέ περ προέτω, ἅμα δ' ἄλλος λαὸς ἑπέσθω
Μυρμιδόνων, αἴ κέν τι φόως Δαναοῖσι γένηαι·
καί τοι τεύχεα καλὰ δότω πόλεμόνδε φέρεσθαι,
αἴ κέ σε τῷ εἴσκοντες ἀπόσχωνται πολέμοιο
Τρῶες, ἀναπνεύσωσι δ' ἀρήϊοι υἷες Ἀχαιῶν
τειρόμενοι· ὀλίγη δέ τ' ἀνάπνευσις πολέμοιο.
ῥεῖα δέ κ' ἀκμῆτες κεκμηότας ἄνδρας ἀϋτῇ
ὤσαισθε προτὶ ἄστυ νεῶν ἄπο καὶ κλισιάων.

But if he is avoiding some divine sign in his mind,
and if his revered mother has told him one from Zeus,
then let him send you forth, and let the rest of the warriors
        follow,
the Myrmidons, if you may become a light for the Danaans.
And let him give you his fine armor to carry into battle,
if the Trojans may take you for him and hold back from battle,
and the warlike sons of the Achaeans may get a breathing
        space,
being hard pressed; small is the breathing space in war.

> But being untired men yourselves you would easily push men
> worn out by battle
> toward the city away from the ships and tents.

What Nestor here urges Patroclus to do is what is in fact destined to take place. Nestor's words stir Patroclus's heart and he sets off at a run to return to Achilles (*Iliad* 11.804–805):

> ὣς φάτο, τῷ δ' ἄρα θυμὸν ἐνὶ στήθεσσιν ὄρινε,
> βῆ δὲ θέειν παρὰ νῆας ἐπ' Αἰακίδην Ἀχιλῆα.

> So he spoke, and he stirred his heart in his breast,
> and he began to run past the ships to Achilles, Aeacus's descendant.

§2.10 The point of Nestor's story is that he took the place of his brother Periklymenos as a warrior horseman. His story is thus a paradigm for Patroclus who is to take the place of his warrior companion Achilles in battle. But the point of Nestor's story, as we have seen, is disguised since Periklymenos is not named in it; his name is left unspoken and the twelve sons of Neleus are mentioned instead. Just so the relevance of Nestor's story to Patroclus is disguised. On the surface of the narrative Nestor does not relate his past behavior to Patroclus's future course of action; he contrasts it with Achilles' present behavior. When Nestor first hears why Patroclus has come to his tent, he wonders why Achilles takes pity on the Achaeans (*Iliad* 11.656–657):

> τίπτε τὰρ ὧδ' Ἀχιλεὺς ὀλοφύρεται υἷας Ἀχαιῶν,
> ὅσσοι δὴ βέλεσιν βεβλήαται;

> Why does Achilles feel this sorrow for the sons of the Achaeans
> who have been struck by weapons?

He goes on to say that in fact Achilles has no pity for the Achaeans, and asks if he is waiting for the ships to burn and the Achaeans to be killed (*Iliad* 11.664–668):

> αὐτὰρ Ἀχιλλεὺς
> ἐσθλὸς ἐὼν Δαναῶν οὐ κήδεται οὐδ' ἐλεαίρει.
> ἦ μένει εἰς ὅ κε δὴ νῆες θοαὶ ἄγχι θαλάσσης
> Ἀργείων ἀέκητι πυρὸς δηΐοιο θέρωνται,
> αὐτοί τε κτεινώμεθ' ἐπισχερώ;

But Achilles,
though he is a good warrior, does not care for or pity the Danaans.
Is he waiting for the swift ships by the sea
to be burned by blazing fire against the Argives' will,
and for us to be killed one after another?

Nestor himself no longer has the strength to save the day as he once did; he wishes he were as young and strong as he was in the conflict between Pylos and Elis, and with this he begins his story (*Iliad* 11.668–671):

οὐ γὰρ ἐμὴ ἲς
ἔσθ' οἵη πάρος ἔσκεν ἐνὶ γναμπτοῖσι μέλεσσιν.
εἴθ' ὡς ἡβώοιμι βίη δέ μοι ἔμπεδος εἴη
ὡς ὁπότ' Ἠλείοισι καὶ ἡμῖν νεῖκος ἐτύχθη.

For my strength is not
like it once was in my joints and limbs.
I wish I were young and the strength in me were steadfast
as when a battle between the Eleians and us came about.

At the end of his story Nestor contrasts his behavior even more pointedly with that of Achilles (*Iliad* 11.762–764):

ὣς ἔον, εἴ ποτ' ἔον γε, μετ' ἀνδράσιν. αὐτὰρ Ἀχιλλεὺς
οἶος τῆς ἀρετῆς ἀπονήσεται· ἦ τέ μιν οἴω
πολλὰ μετακλαύσεσθαι ἐπεί κ' ἀπὸ λαὸς ὄληται.

So I was, if ever I was, among men. But Achilles
alone will benefit from his greatness; mark me, though, I think
that he
will greatly lament it after the warriors are destroyed.

§2.11 Nestor's story purports to be relevant to Achilles' behavior, but a moment's reflection shows that such relevance is only a surface illusion: Achilles does not hear Nestor's story, and it thus cannot affect his behavior; if the purpose of Nestor's story is to change Achilles' behavior, he wastes his breath and his story is pointless.[22] If, on the other hand, the purpose of

22 This is the usual judgment, that the story is long-winded and not much to the point. That this
is not a satisfactory conclusion has been realized by some. In an important article Victoria
Pedrick carefully considers the paradigmatic purpose of Nestor's speech (Pedrick 1983; the

Nestor's story has to do with Patroclus, it has a great deal of point, but the point is disguised on the surface of the narrative. The point emerges indirectly through parallels between Nestor and Patroclus within the narrative as it develops. As we have seen, Nestor rescues the wounded Makhaon from the battlefield on his chariot. Makhaon has been wounded in the shoulder by an arrow of Paris. When Nestor and Makhaon depart for the ships the scene shifts to the other side of the battlefield, where another hero, Eurypylos, is hit in the thigh by another of Paris's arrows and he too must depart from the battlefield for the ships, but he goes on foot. When Patroclus finishes his visit to Nestor and sets off at a run for Achilles, he meets Eurypylos limping back to the ships and he stops to tend Eurypylos's wound. Nestor and Patroclus both tend to a victim of Paris's arrows, and this is a deliberately constructed parallel between them in *Iliad* 11. At the end of *Iliad* 11 Patroclus and Nestor have both tended to their patients' wounds and for the time being they both remain at their patients' sides.

---

author addresses the question from the perspective of paradigmatic speeches in general). While she does not abandon the idea that Nestor's speech is meant for Achilles, she qualifies this idea heavily in her conclusion, p. 68: "We perceive the full force of the scene when we recognize the manipulation of the paradigmatic exhortation: the example is not simply a tale carefully molded for the listener's edification. It is an aristeia meant to remind an angry hero of his responsibility and to inspire him to his own glorious performance. Ironically, the paradeigma works—on the wrong hero. Patroklos does not pass on the lesson to his friend; instead he attempts his own aristeia." Cf. also Martin 2000, who cites Pedrick (p. 54); like Pedrick, whom he quotes on this point, Martin is sensitive to the fact that irony must be at work in Nestor's story in *Iliad* 11. Cantieni, who well appreciates how carefully Nestor's story is prepared for in the narrative of the *Iliad* (Cantieni 1942:18), does not resolve its purpose: while Nestor pointedly singles out Achilles and his behavior both before his story and after it (Cantieni, pp. 10 and 22, draws attention to the anaphora *autàr Akhilleús*, "but Achilles," in *Iliad* 11.664 and 762), his story cannot be construed as a "warning speech" directed at Achilles since no such point is emphasized at the end (see Cantieni, pp. 20–21, who contrasts Phoenix's speech in *Iliad* 9 in this respect). Minchin 1990/1991 shows that Nestor's speech, when viewed in terms of effective one-on-one communication, is well suited to the situation at this crucial point in the poem; as far as Nestor's story is concerned, the rhetorical contrast in lines 762–763 between Nestor, as he once was μετ' ἀνδράσιν, "among men," and Achilles, who is now οἶος, "alone," is certainly the point on the surface of the poem (cf. Minchin 1990/1991:282). But even this fine appreciation of the speech's appropriateness does not eliminate the idea that the speech is still somehow tedious (cf. Minchen 1990/1991:285); restoring the speech's excitement is, I think, partly a matter of text (cf. n2.16 above), and partly a matter of looking deeper for the speech's purpose. Alden 2000:88–101 has gone beyond Pedrick and Martin in recognizing that Nestor's story is really aimed at Patroclus (see especially pp. 95–96, with further bibliography in 95n53); my interpretation, which proceeds along different lines from Alden's, has this central point in common with it. For other scholarship relevant to Nestor's Homeric stories and speeches see Dickson 1995:99n67 and n69.

§2.12 The parallel between Nestor and Patroclus in *Iliad* 11 is crucial for
understanding the purpose of Nestor's story, but the two are not completely
parallel. There is also an element of contrast. This can be seen in the way that they
treat their patients. Nestor, for his part, has his maidservant Hekamede prepare
a *kukeṓn*, which he and Makhaon both drink; when Patroclus arrives Nestor and
Makhaon are already enjoying a pleasant conversation (*Iliad* 11.642–644):

τὼ δ' ἐπεὶ οὖν πίνοντ' ἀφέτην πολυκαγκέα δίψαν
μύθοισιν τέρποντο πρὸς ἀλλήλους ἐνέποντες,
Πάτροκλος δὲ θύρῃσιν ἐφίστατο ἰσόθεος φώς.

After the two of them drank and slaked their parching thirst,
and were taking pleasure in words, speaking one to the other,
Patroclus stood at the door, a godlike man.

In contrast to this nearly magical cure, in which attention is devoted entirely
to Nestor's fabulous cup and the *kukeṓn* prepared in it (*Iliad* 11.628–641), while
the removal of the arrow goes unmentioned, Patroclus meets Eurypylos and
tends to him in an atmosphere of sweat and blood (*Iliad* 11.806–813):

ἀλλ' ὅτε δὴ κατὰ νῆας Ὀδυσσῆος θείοιο
ἷξε θέων Πάτροκλος, ἵνά σφ' ἀγορή τε θέμις τε
ἤην, τῇ δὴ καί σφι θεῶν ἐτετεύχατο βωμοί,
ἔνθά οἱ Εὐρύπυλος βεβλημένος ἀντεβόλησε
διογενὴς Εὐαιμονίδης κατὰ μηρὸν ὀϊστῷ
σκάζων ἐκ πολέμου· κατὰ δὲ νότιος ῥέεν <u>ἱδρὼς</u>
ὤμων καὶ κεφαλῆς, ἀπὸ δ' ἕλκεος ἀργαλέοιο
<u>αἷμα</u> μέλαν κελάρυζε· νόος γε μὲν ἔμπεδος ἦεν.

But when Patroclus came running by the ships of godlike
        Odysseus,
where the place of assembly and judgment
was, and where the altars of the gods had been built,
there the wounded Eurypylus encountered him,
the Zeus-born son of Euaimon, wounded by an arrow in the thigh,
limping out of battle; a shower of <u>sweat</u> ran down
from his shoulders and head, and from his painful wound
black <u>blood</u> gushed; his mind, however, was steady.

Eurypylos tells Patroclus of the plight of the Achaeans and asks for help getting back to his ship and removing the arrow from his thigh; Patroclus agrees despite his hurry to return to Achilles. *Iliad* 11 ends with Patroclus performing surgery on Eurypylos in his tent (*Iliad* 11.842–848):

ἦ, καὶ ὑπὸ στέρνοιο λαβὼν ἄγε ποιμένα λαῶν
ἐς κλισίην· θεράπων δὲ ἰδὼν ὑπέχευε βοείας.
ἔνθά μιν ἐκτανύσας ἐκ μηροῦ τάμνε μαχαίρῃ
ὀξὺ βέλος περιπευκές, ἀπ᾽ αὐτοῦ δ᾽ αἷμα κελαινὸν
νίζ᾽ ὕδατι λιαρῷ, ἐπὶ δὲ ῥίζαν βάλε πικρὴν
χερσὶ διατρίψας ὀδυνήφατον, ἥ οἱ ἁπάσας
ἔσχ᾽ ὀδύνας· τὸ μὲν ἕλκος ἐτέρσετο, παύσατο δ᾽ αἷμα.

He spoke, and taking hold of him under the chest he led the
    shepherd of the warriors
into his tent; his attendant saw and spread oxhides underneath.
Stretching him out there he used his knife and cut from his
    thigh
the pointed shaft, which was exceedingly sharp, and washed the
    dark blood
from him with warm water, and applied a bitter root,
pain-killing, rubbing it in his hands, and it stopped all
the pain; the wound dried and the blood stopped.

The two wounds, one in the shoulder and the other in the thigh, reinforce the element of contrast within otherwise parallel situations; Eurypylos's thigh wound is more serious than Makhaon's shoulder wound, and Eurypylos feels the full effect of his wound when he has to make his way from battle on foot. The contrast between Nestor's rescue and cure of Makhaon and Patroclus's rescue and cure of Eurypylos is reflected in other characteristics that differentiate the two figures. For Patroclus the dominant theme is pity, which is mentioned immediately when he meets Eurypylos (*Iliad* 11.814–818):

τὸν δὲ ἰδὼν <u>ᾤκτειρε</u> Μενοιτίου ἄλκιμος υἱός,
καί ῥ᾽ ὀλοφυρόμενος ἔπεα πτερόεντα προσηύδα·
"ἆ δειλοὶ Δαναῶν ἡγήτορες ἠδὲ μέδοντες
ὣς ἄρ᾽ ἐμέλλετε τῆλε φίλων καὶ πατρίδος αἴης
ἄσειν ἐν Τροίῃ ταχέας κύνας ἀργέτι δημῷ."

Seeing him Menoitios's resolute son <u>pitied</u> him,
and lamenting he spoke winged words to him:
"ah, wretched leaders and counselors of the Danaans,
like this then, far from dear ones and fatherland, you were fated
to glut the swift dogs in Troy with your shining fat."

Pity comes through again at the end when Patroclus says that he will not abandon Eurypylos however eager he is to return to Achilles with Nestor's message (*Iliad* 11.838–841):

πῶς τὰρ ἔοι τάδε ἔργα; τί ῥέξομεν Εὐρύπυλ' ἥρως;

ἔρχομαι ὄφρ' Ἀχιλῆϊ δαΐφρονι μῦθον ἐνίσπω

ὃν Νέστωρ ἐπέτελλε Γερήνιος οὖρος Ἀχαιῶν·

ἀλλ' οὐδ' ὥς περ σεῖο μεθήσω τειρομένοιο.

How is this to be? What are we to do, hero Eurypylus?
I am on my way to tell keen-spirited Achilles the words
that Gerenian Nestor, guardian of the Achaeans, commanded me to,
but even so I will not abandon you since you are hard pressed.

When Nestor cures Makhaon, on the other hand, Nestor's intelligence and his serene command of the situation are highlighted. His intelligence is conveyed only symbolically since his serving woman prepares the *kukeṓn* and he does nothing himself; but this serving woman, who is named *Hekamḗdē* ("far-counseling"), the daughter of *Arsínoos* ("sound-minded"), bespeaks Nestor's own intelligence, for she has been given as a prize to Nestor for being "best of all in counsel" (*Iliad* 11.622–627):

αὐτὰρ ἔπειτα

ἐς κλισίην ἐλθόντες ἐπὶ κλισμοῖσι κάθιζον.

τοῖσι δὲ τεῦχε κυκειῶ ἐϋπλόκαμος Ἑκαμήδη,

τὴν ἄρετ' ἐκ Τενέδοιο γέρων, ὅτε πέρσεν Ἀχιλλεύς,

θυγατέρ' <u>Ἀρσινόου</u> μεγαλήτορος, ἥν οἱ Ἀχαιοὶ

ἔξελον οὕνεκα <u>βουλῇ ἀριστεύεσκεν ἁπάντων</u>.

But then
they went into the tent and sat down on chairs.
An elixir was prepared for them by <u>Hekamede</u> with the beautiful
        tresses,

whom the old man won from Tenedos when Achilles destroyed it,
the daughter of great-hearted <u>Arsinoos</u>; her the Achaeans
picked out especially for him because <u>he was best of all in
counsel</u>.

§2.13 If Patroclus is parallel to Nestor, Achilles, who is out of action (by
his own choice, but nevertheless out of action), and whose place in battle
Patroclus must therefore take, is parallel to the unnamed Periklymenos
of Nestor's story in *Iliad* 11. It was the death of Periklymenos, Pylos's great
champion, that put Pylos at the mercy of the Epeians; just so, it is the absence
of Achilles, the Achaeans' great champion, that has put the Achaeans at the
mercy of the Trojans. To this extent Patroclus and Achilles reenact the myth
of Nestor and Periklymenos, and categories of the Indo-European twin myth
also apply to them. When Nestor finishes his story, he immediately contrasts
his behavior with that of Achilles, as we have seen. But he then goes on to
what Patroclus must do: either *rouse* Achilles to battle or *take his place*. In
terms of the Indo-European twin myth the immortal twin either brings the
mortal twin back to life, as Polydeuces does Castor, or he replaces him, as
Nestor does Periklymenos. Nestor guides Patroclus toward what he must do
by telling him to remember the words of his father Menoitios when he and
Achilles left for the war. Nestor had come to Phthia with Odysseus to recruit
Achilles and Patroclus for the war, and he thus heard the advice of Peleus
to Achilles, always to excel in war, and the advice of Menoitios to Patroclus,
which pointedly contrasted the greater status and strength of Achilles with
the greater age and wisdom of Patroclus (*Iliad* 11.786–789):

τέκνον ἐμὸν γενεῇ μὲν ὑπέρτερός ἐστιν Ἀχιλλεύς,
πρεσβύτερος δὲ σύ ἐσσι· βίῃ δ' ὅ γε πολλὸν ἀμείνων.
ἀλλ' εὖ οἱ φάσθαι πυκινὸν ἔπος ἠδ' ὑποθέσθαι
καί οἱ σημαίνειν· ὃ δὲ πείσεται εἰς ἀγαθόν περ.

My son, Achilles is higher born than you,
but you are older; in might he is much the better.
But tell him wise words and instruct him well,
and point things out to him; he will agree to what is good.

This is similar to the contrast between the Indo-European twins: the warrior-
strength of the mortal twin on the one hand, and the intelligence of the
immortal twin on the other hand. It is in his role as counselor that Patroclus,

remembering his father's words, is to try to *rouse* Achilles to reenter the war (*Iliad* 11.790–793):

ὣς ἐπέτελλ' ὃ γέρων, σὺ δὲ λήθεαι· ἀλλ' ἔτι καὶ νῦν
ταῦτ' εἴποις Ἀχιλῆϊ δαΐφρονι αἴ κε πίθηται.
τίς δ' οἶδ' εἴ κέν οἱ σὺν δαίμονι θυμὸν <u>ὀρίναις</u>
παρειπών; ἀγαθὴ δὲ παραίφασίς ἐστιν ἑταίρου.

So the old man commanded, but you have forgotten; yet even now
you might say these things to keen-spirited Achilles to see if he
    will agree.
Who knows whether with a god's help you might <u>stir</u> his heart
if you try to persuade him; a companion's persuasion is a good
    thing.

The plan that Patroclus is to try first is exactly that of the twin myth, in which the immortal twin brings the mortal warrior twin back to life, and this action is itself a mental process; for Patroclus it would be an act of persuasion. But if Patroclus fails to persuade Achilles, as he is in fact destined to do, he is to follow Nestor's own example and *take the place* of Achilles in battle (*Iliad* 11.794–803).

§2.14 It is worth looking more closely at the contrast between intelligence on the one hand and might on the other hand in the case of Patroclus and Achilles. The contrast is there, but it should not be overstated. Patroclus's superior counsel is presented as a matter of greater age rather than greater intelligence, even though good counsel remains a matter of intelligence in the end. Both Patroclus and Achilles, furthermore, are skilled physicians: when Eurypylos asks Patroclus for help he says that Patroclus got his knowledge of drugs from Achilles, whom the centaur Cheiron taught (*Iliad* 11.828–832):

ἀλλ' ἐμὲ μὲν σὺ σάωσον ἄγων ἐπὶ νῆα μέλαιναν,
μηροῦ δ' ἔκταμ' ὀϊστόν, ἀπ' αὐτοῦ δ' αἷμα κελαινὸν
νίζ' ὕδατι λιαρῷ, ἐπὶ δ' ἤπια φάρμακα πάσσε
ἐσθλά, τά σε προτί φασιν Ἀχιλλῆος δεδιδάχθαι,
ὃν Χείρων ἐδίδαξε δικαιότατος Κενταύρων.

But you, save me by bringing me to my black ship,
and cut the arrow from my thigh, and wash the dark blood

from me with warm water, and sprinkle on gentle drugs,
good ones, which they say you were taught by Achilles,
whom Cheiron, the most just of the Centaurs, taught.

Like the twins Podaleirios and Makhaon, Patroclus and Achilles both have
medical skill. It is interesting that Eurypylos immediately goes on to say that
the twin doctors are both unavailable: the wounded Makhaon needs a doctor
himself and Podaleirios still fights on the plain (*Iliad* 11.833–836):

ἰητροὶ μὲν γὰρ Ποδαλείριος ἠδὲ Μαχάων
τὸν μὲν ἐνὶ κλισίῃσιν ὀΐομαι ἕλκος ἔχοντα
χρηΐζοντα καὶ αὐτὸν ἀμύμονος ἰητῆρος
κεῖσθαι· ὃ δ’ ἐν πεδίῳ Τρώων μένει ὀξὺν Ἄρηα.

As for the healers Podaleirios and Makhaon,
I think that one of them is lying in his tent with a wound,
needing a faultless healer himself;
the other faces the Trojans' sharp warfare on the plain.

In these passages there seems to be an implicit comparison of Patroclus and
Achilles as doctors with the twin sons of Asklepios,[23] and such a comparison
makes perfect sense at this point near the end of *Iliad* 11. It reflects the way in
which Patroclus and Achilles have been cast as twins in relation to Nestor and
his myth earlier in the book. It bears emphasizing that Nestor himself is the
master doctor in this book.[24]

---

23 Cf. Kenner *RE* 'Podaleirios' 1132. Arieti 1983/1984 sees significance for *Iliad* 11, and for the
Iliad generally, in the parallel between Achilles and Makhaon as doctors, but he misreads
Iliad 4.218–219 in stating that Makhaon, like Achilles, was taught by Cheiron: the passage
says only that Cheiron gave healing drugs to Makhaon's father, Asklepios.

24 The contrast between the age and wisdom of Patroclus on the one hand and the strength
of Achilles on the other hand has a close parallel in *Iliad* 19.216–219, where Odysseus
contrasts himself with Achilles in just these terms:

ὦ Ἀχιλεῦ Πηλῆος υἱὲ μέγα φέρτατ’ Ἀχαιῶν,
κρείσσων εἰς ἐμέθεν καὶ φέρτερος οὐκ ὀλίγον περ
ἔγχει, ἐγὼ δέ κε σεῖο νοήματί γε προβαλοίμην
πολλόν, ἐπεὶ πρότερος γενόμην καὶ πλείονα οἶδα.

Achilles, Peleus's son, much the strongest of the Achaeans,
you are mightier than I am and stronger by not a little
with a spear, but in understanding I might be better than you
by much, since I was born earlier and I know more.

Here the contrast is between the main heroes of the *Iliad* and the *Odyssey*, and the twin
myth is not directly relevant.

§2.15 The carefully crafted parallelism between Nestor and Patroclus in
Iliad 11 continues when they both return to action later in the poem. In a pair
of scenes in *Iliad* 14 and *Iliad* 15 first Nestor and then Patroclus leave their
patients as they hear the din of battle coming closer because the Achaeans
are now in full retreat. Nestor leaves Makhaon in the care of Hekamede,
who will bathe his wounds, and he himself joins the retreating Achaeans for
a council. Patroclus, who has been tending Eurypylos's wounds with drugs,
leaves Eurypylos to the care of his own attendant so that he himself can
return to Achilles and urge him to fight. In his short speech to Eurypylos it
is Nestor's advice that Patroclus repeats, and the latter part of it in Nestor's
own words (*Iliad* 15.401–404):

ἀλλὰ σὲ μὲν θεράπων ποτιτερπέτω, αὐτὰρ ἔγωγε
σπεύσομαι εἰς Ἀχιλῆα, ἵν' ὀτρύνω πολεμίζειν.
τίς δ' οἶδ' εἴ κέν οἱ σὺν δαίμονι θυμὸν ὀρίνω
παρειπών; ἀγαθὴ δὲ παραίφασίς ἐστιν ἑταίρου.

Have your attendant entertain you, but I
must hurry back to Achilles to stir him up to fight.
Who knows whether with a god's help I may stir his heart
when I try to persuade him? A companion's persuasion is a good
   thing.

§2.16 The parallelism between Nestor and Patroclus reaches a climax
in *Iliad* 16, but only if we understand the point of Nestor's story in *Iliad* 11,
namely that his story tells how and why he first became a horseman. For
when Patroclus returns to Achilles and puts into effect what Nestor has
told him, he too is transformed into a horseman: now for the first time he
is called *Patróklees hippeû* and *Patróklees hippokéleuthe*, both phrases meaning
"horseman Patroclus," and he is repeatedly addressed as such until he is killed
in battle. Not until *Iliad* 16, when he takes Achilles' place, does he get these
vocative epithets, but in *Iliad* 16 they occur seven times.[25] The first occurrence
is at the beginning of Book 16, when Patroclus comes to Achilles in tears and
Achilles asks why he is weeping. In his reply Patroclus, using Nestor's words,
asks Achilles to send him into battle in his place; in the line introducing his
speech the poet for the first time addresses Patroclus as "horseman": τὸν δὲ

---

25 *Patróklees hippeû* occurs four times and *Patróklees hippokéleuthe* three times; both epithets are
   unique to Patroclus. See Bader 1980:14 for the close relationship between the terms *hippeús*
   and *hippóta* (*hippótēs*) as class designations, both originally designating the warrior class.

βαρὺ στενάχων προσέφης Πατρόκλεες ἱππεῦ, "groaning deeply you addressed him, horseman Patroclus" (*Iliad* 16.20). The second occurrence is spoken by Achilles himself after he agrees to let Patroclus go into battle in his place; when Achilles sees the Trojans setting fire to the Achaeans' ships he urges Patroclus to go: ὄρσεο διογενὲς Πατρόκλεες ἱπποκέλευθε· / λεύσσω δὴ παρὰ νηυσὶ πυρὸς δηΐοιο ἰωήν, "Rise, Zeus-born Patroclus, driver of horses. / I see the rush of destructive fire by the ships," *Iliad* 16.126–127).

§2.17 Just as Nestor, in taking his brother's place, became *hippóta Néstōr*, so Patroclus, in taking Achilles' place, becomes *Patróklees hippeû/Patróklees hippokéleuthe*.[26] Given such a particular correspondence there is every reason to believe that Nestor in his story in *Iliad* 11 provides the paradigm for Patroclus to follow, and that Patroclus in fact follows it. This must be at least part of what the poet intends to convey when he addresses Patroclus as "horseman" in *Iliad* 16. If we accept that Patroclus, who has taken Nestor's advice by replacing his companion in battle, has at the same time followed Nestor's example, as set forth in his story in *Iliad* 11, then the point of this story is confirmed: Nestor first became a horseman by replacing his brother, just as Patroclus became a horseman in replacing his companion.

§2.18 Now that we have interpreted Nestor's story in *Iliad* 11, and supported the interpretation by considering the place of this story in the larger story of the *Iliad*, it is time to face squarely the fact that both the interpretation and its support rest not on the surface of the poem, but below the surface. Thus, if the point of Nestor's story is that he takes his brother's place, and that it is the example of this deed that Patroclus follows in taking Achilles' place, Nestor's actual story does not even mention Periklymenos, but only the twelve sons of Neleus, of whom Periklymenos was one. In other words, his presence in the story is implied but not stated. Likewise, if the story is meant as a paradigm for Patroclus, Nestor does not say so, but instead presents his youthful deeds as a contrast to the behavior and attitude of Achilles. Why is this so? If we are correct in our interpretation only one explanation is possible, and that is that both the point of Nestor's story and its relevance to Patroclus have been deliberately disguised and intentionally

---

26 *Patróklees hippeû* is always the poet's own address to the hero; the three other occurrences of the phrase (and their contexts) are: *Iliad* 16.744 (Patroclus exults scornfully after killing Hector's charioteer); *Iliad* 16.812 (Euphorbos is the first to strike the disarmed Patroclus); *Iliad* 16.843 (Patroclus answers Hector's taunt before he dies). Of the two further occurrences of the phrase *Patróklees hippokéleuthe*, one, *Iliad* 16.584, is the poet's address (Patroclus angrily goes to avenge a fallen comrade); the other, *Iliad* 16.839, is spoken by Hector in a taunt (Hector imagines Achilles addressing Patroclus as *Patróklees hippokéleuthe* when he sent him into battle).

withheld. What the reason for this might be we cannot yet say, but the same phenomenon, the intentional concealing of relevance, will be evident in Nestor's role in other parts of the *Iliad* and *Odyssey*, and particularly in the episode that we will consider next, namely the chariot race in the funeral games for Patroclus.

Chapter 5.

ILIAD 23

§2.19 We have so far looked only for similarities between Nestor and Patroclus in their respective bids to become horsemen. There is also a glaring difference between the two, namely that Nestor survived his battle with the Epeians and lived to reach old age, but in his battle with the Trojans Patroclus is slain. It is thus very significant that at the funeral games for Patroclus Nestor is again on hand for the main event, the chariot race. Nestor is too old to compete in this race himself, but his son Antilochus is a contestant, and before the race begins Nestor addresses a lengthy speech to his son on tactics for rounding the turning post. In the actual race that is then described the turning post plays no role. When the race is over and the prizes have been awarded, one prize is left over, and this is awarded to Nestor by Achilles as a memorial of Patroclus, whom Nestor will never see again. This prize should have gone to Eumelos, who had the fastest horses, but who crashed in the race and finished last. Achilles awards Eumelos a special prize, leaving last prize open for Nestor. In accepting the prize from Achilles, Nestor recalls how he once competed in the funeral games for king Amarynkeus in Bouprasion. There he won all the contests but one, namely the chariot race, which he lost to the Aktorione, the Epeian twins. It has never been sufficiently appreciated how striking it is that *hippóta Néstōr* should have lost only the chariot race on this day. Bearing in mind Nestor's story in *Iliad* 11, which tells how he became a horseman for the first time, we may conclude that when he competed against the twins at Bouprasion he had not yet learned to take his brother's place, and that he had yet to become a horseman. His failure in the chariot race will

then be relevant to Patroclus, who in his bid to become a horseman brought
help to the Achaeans but himself met defeat.[27]

---

27 Amarynkeus, at whose funeral Nestor lost the chariot race, is an obscure figure. In partic-
ular his relationship to Augeias is not clear. Both these Epeian figures are connected
with solar myth by virtue of their names (see above §1.32 and n1.92, n1.94, and n1.95). In
Nestor's two stories Amarynkeus seems to precede Augeias: Augeias is king of the Epeians
in *Iliad* 11, where Nestor triumphs as a horseman; in *Iliad* 23 Amarynkeus has already
passed from the scene when Nestor loses as a horseman. In Nestor's myth, as I understand
it, it only makes sense that his loss precedes his triumph (see below); hence I suspect that
in Nestor's tradition Amarynkeus was the father of Augeias. In the Catalogue of Ships, on
the other hand, this cannot be the relationship between the two figures. In the catalogue
the Epeians, who inhabit Elis and Bouprasion, have four leaders (each apparently from a
different town, cf. n5.29 below): two of the leaders are sons of the Aktorione, another is
the son of Amarynkeus, and the fourth is the grandson of Augeias (*Iliad* 2.615–624). Here
Augeias belongs to an earlier generation than Amarynkeus, and not the reverse. The
Aktorione also seem to be in the wrong generation in the catalogue from the point of
view of Nestor's stories: if they competed as young men at the funeral of Amarynkeus,
they should not be in the same generation as Amarynkeus, as they are as the fathers of
leaders at Troy in *Iliad* 2. It is possible that the patronymic *Amarunkeḯdēs* in *Iliad* 2.622,
means "descendant of Amarynkeus" rather than "son of Amarynkeus"; this would allow
Amarynkeus himself to belong to an earlier generation. But it is also possible, and I think
more likely, that the catalogue operates outside Nestor's old traditions and has its own
agenda and sources. The catalogue, as mentioned, says that the Epeians inhabited Elis and
Bouprasion. The distinction between the two places was later seen as a matter of sepa-
rate kingdoms. Whether or not such a distinction was also part of Nestor's traditions (I
do not think that it was, but there is no way to be sure), it can easily be read back into his
traditions: in *Iliad* 23 Amarynkeus is buried in Bouprasion, so this must be his kingdom; in
Iliad 11 Augeias and Elis are both mentioned, so this must be the other kingdom. In a later
version of the myth Augeias gives Amarynkeus, whose father came from Thessaly, a share
in the rule of Elis (Pausanias 5.1.11); for further variations on the relationship between
Amarynkeus and Augeias see Swoboda *RE* 'Elis' 2376–2377; cf. also Cantieni 1942:44–45,
citing Robert 1920:16. As to the order of Nestor's stories in terms of his heroic "biography,"
the assumption is sometimes made that the order of the stories in the *Iliad* is also their
chronological order; Bader 1980:17, for example, arranges Nestor's three stories in *Iliad* 7,
11, and 23 in just this order, from youngest to oldest in terms of Nestor's age. But such an
order is by no means necessary, as Nestor's brief story in *Iliad* 1 about the war between
the Lapiths and Centaurs shows, for in this his first story Nestor is already an estab-
lished warrior. Bader's reasons for supposing that the story in *Iliad* 23 follows the story
in *Iliad* 11 chronologically are not convincing. In particular, the idea that the Molione are
still young and inexperienced in the story in *Iliad* 11 (παῖδ' ἔτ' ἐόντ', οὔ πω μάλα εἰδότε
θούριδος ἀλκῆς, *Iliad* 11.710), but had come of age in the story in *Iliad* 23 and therefore had
a better outcome against Nestor (Bader 1980:33), puts the emphasis in the wrong place: in
both stories it is Nestor's age that matters. The Molione are a constant foil to Nestor: they
are horsemen, ranked with other horsemen, in *Iliad* 11, and they are horsemen in *Iliad* 23;
Nestor, on the other hand, does not join the rank of horsemen until the battle in his story
in *Iliad* 11 begins.

§2.20 Nestor does not tell explicitly how he lost to the twins in Bouprasion. What he does say, however, indicates that the fact that they were twins was crucial to their victory (*Iliad* 23.638–642):

οἵοισίν μ' ἵπποισι παρήλασαν Ἀκτορίωνε
πλήθει πρόσθε βαλόντες ἀγασσάμενοι περὶ νίκης,
οὕνεκα δὴ τὰ μέγιστα παρ' αὐτόθι λείπετ' ἄεθλα.
οἳ δ' ἄρ' ἔσαν δίδυμοι· ὃ μὲν ἔμπεδον ἡνιόχευεν,
ἔμπεδον ἡνιόχευ', ὃ δ' ἄρα μάστιγι κέλευεν.

Only with the horses did the two Aktorione surpass me,
surging ahead because of their greater number, eager for victory
because the biggest prizes were left for that event.
They were twins, you see; the one steadfastly held the reins,
steadfastly held the reins, and the other urged on with the whip.

Nestor says that the twins drove past him because of their "number" (*plḗthei*). He then expands on this by saying that each twin had a different function in the race, for while one of them steadily held the reins, the other urged the horses on with the whip.[28] The fact that the twins have different functions clearly suggests the Indo-European twin myth, and the reason for their victory seems rooted in an opposition between their very natures.[29] But if the twins won by their greater number, we may turn this around and say that Nestor lost by the fact that he was only one against two, and this brings us straight to his variant of the twin myth. The reason that Nestor was only one was that he had lost his brother, Periklymenos. If this was the reason for his loss, then the different functions of the two twins also relate to Nestor, and we must ask which function he had and which he did not. The two functions, holding the reins and applying the whip, can be described more abstractly as "restraint" on the one hand and "incitement" on the other. In terms of the Indo-European twin myth, "incitement" suggests the immortal twin's function of "bringing back to life," and that is the function that Nestor, by his very name,

28 The noun *hēníokhos*, "charioteer," is literally "he who holds (-*okhos* from *ékhō*) the reins (*hēnía*)." The verb *hēniokheúō* means "act as *hēníokhos*," and thus "drive" a chariot, but the literal meaning "hold the reins" is still clear in both the noun and the verb. "Completely incomprehensible" ("ganz unverständlich") is Wilamowitz's comment on these lines as the explanation of the twins' victory (Wilamowitz 2006:343).

29 Both twins are horsemen, as are the two *Aśvínā*, but, as horsemen they are differentiated from each other. This is similar to the situation of the twins Podaleirios and Makhaon: they are both doctors, as are the two *Nā́satyā*, but as doctors they are differentiated from each other (see n2.19 above).

must have had. It follows that the function that he lacked was an ability to control the chariot by use of the reins; "holding the reins," in other words, must have been the function of the horseman twin, whom Nestor had not yet learned to replace. Failure to control the chariot leads to wasted motion, and this could have caused Nestor's loss to the Aktorione.[30] But there was a more particular danger for a driver who could not control his horses, and this was the turning post. In order to make the turn the driver had to slow his chariot down, and to do so he had only the reins to use. In Nestor's description of the twins' victory, the turning post as the crucial point in the race is suggested by an iconic use of language. The phrase *émpedon hēniókheuen*, "steadfastly held the reins," is repeated at the end of one line and the beginning of the next, *émpedon hēniókheu'*, and the turning post is equated poetically with the verse-end between. In the twins' race, as it is thus described, one twin steadfastly controlled the chariot going into the turn, and he still had control of the chariot coming out of the turn, and the other twin then applied the whip on the straightaway to finish the race in victory. If we now take the reason for the twins' victory and turn it around to find the reason for Nestor's defeat, we must focus on the point in the race that is emphasized in the description of their victory, and this is the turning post. If Nestor lost control of his chariot at this point in the race, there can have been only one result, and this is that he crashed and did not finish the race.[31] If the whole point of this episode is, as I take it to be, to demonstrate Nestor's lack of horsemanship, then a crash provides by far the most graphic demonstration of it, much more than, for example, a close second-place finish behind the twins. We should also bear in mind that the funeral games at Bouprasion seem to come from Nestor's own epic tradition. He was clearly the center of attention, winning every contest but one (*Iliad* 23.634–640). Thus it would seem that even in defeat he must have been the center of attention, and this he would not be if he lost a close and exciting race to the twins. They would be. The episode needs a dramatic finish from Nestor's standpoint, and this is provided by a crash.

§2.21 Now that we have interpreted Nestor's story in *Iliad* 23, we must support this interpretation by considering its wider context in the poem, beginning with the rest of the chariot race in the funeral games for Patroclus. Nestor tells his story at the end of this race in accepting the vacant last prize.

---

30 Nestor describes just such a driver in *Iliad* 23.319–321; see below for discussion of this passage.

31 A crash at the turning post must have been a regular occurrence in actual chariot races (cf. Aristophanes *Peace* 904–905 where one such is imagined). A spirit called *Taráxippos* ("disturber of horses") was supposed to make chariots crash at a particular point of the racecourse at Olympia; this was not the turning post according to Pausanias 6.20.15–19, but see Frazer 1913 on 6.20.15 for other sources (Dio Chrysostom, Tzetzes) suggesting that it was the turning post; cf. also Nagy 1983:46 (= 1990:215).

It is significant that this prize should have gone to Eumelos, who crashed in his race, but who was awarded a special prize by Achilles. Instead of Eumelos, Nestor receives this prize. He then tells his story, which shows to those who understand it that last prize is precisely what Nestor deserved, at least for his race at that earlier time and place. But he also deserves it in the present because it was he who set Patroclus on the course that led to his death, and for this disaster Nestor's crash, not his later emergence as a victorious horseman, provides the paradigm. Achilles gives last prize to Nestor as a memorial of Patroclus, whom he will never see again. By accepting it, and telling the story of his own youthful race, Nestor acknowledges his role in Patroclus's fate. But he does so only to those who know his epic traditions, for his crash is no more acknowledged on the surface of the poem than was the real relevance of his story in *Iliad* 11.

§2.22 But it is not just at the end of the episode, when Nestor receives his prize and tells his story, that his story is present in the chariot race of *Iliad* 23. His story, to those who knew it, is present from the very beginning of the episode, when Antilochus steps forward as one of the contestants, and Nestor delivers a long speech of advice to his son on tactics for rounding the turning post. In the actual race, the turning post plays no part. It is simply ignored as the description moves from the first half of the race, in which the racers are presented as an undifferentiated group in a short but vivid passage (*Iliad* 23.362–372), to the much longer second half of the race, in which the individual contests unfold and are narrated at length (*Iliad* 23.373–533).[32] Since the

---

32 At the end of the opening passage of the race, which is relatively short, the racers still have not rounded the turning post (*Iliad* 23.362–372):

οἳ δ' ἅμα πάντες ἐφ' ἵπποιιν μάστιγας ἄειραν,
πέπληγόν θ' ἱμᾶσιν, ὁμόκλησάν τ' ἐπέεσσιν
ἐσσυμένως· οἳ δ' ὦκα διέπρησσον πεδίοιο
νόσφι νεῶν ταχέως· ὑπὸ δὲ στέρνοισι κονίη
ἵστατ' ἀειρομένη ὥς τε νέφος ἠὲ θύελλα,
χαῖται δ' ἐρρώοντο μετὰ πνοιῆς ἀνέμοιο.
ἅρματα δ' ἄλλοτε μὲν χθονὶ πίλνατο πουλυβοτείρῃ,
ἄλλοτε δ' ἀΐξασκε μετήορα· τοὶ δ' ἐλατῆρες
ἕστασαν ἐν δίφροισι, πάτασσε δὲ θυμὸς ἑκάστου
νίκης ἱεμένων· κέκλοντο δὲ οἷσιν ἕκαστος
ἵπποις, οἳ δ' ἐπέτοντο κονίοντες πεδίοιο.

They all raised their whips over the horses,
and lashed them with the reins, and shouted out vehemently
with words; the horses quickly traversed the plain,
away from the ships with speed; the dust under their chests
rose and stood like a cloud or a squall,

race that actually occurs ignores the turning post, why does Nestor, immediately before the race begins, deliver a 43 line speech on tactics for rounding it (Iliad 23.306–348)?[33] Either there is no reason,[34] or this speech is meant to evoke Nestor's own race, long before, in which the turning post was decisive.

§2.23 But one would have had to know the tradition for Nestor's crash to perceive this evocation, for on the surface of the text there are few hints. Indeed, everything in the race that Nestor foresees for Antilochus, and for which he prepares him, is different from the race that we must imagine took

---

and their manes streamed in the blasts of wind.
Now the chariots neared the earth that feeds many,
now they rose up in the air; the drivers
stood in the chariots, and the heart of each beat
as they strove for victory; each called out to his
horses, and they flew over the plain raising the dust.

When the narrative continues in the next line, it emerges that the turning post has already been rounded without any direct mention of it, and the real races now begin (Iliad 23.373–375):

ἀλλ' ὅτε δὴ πύματον τέλεον δρόμον ὠκέες ἵπποι
ἂψ ἐφ' ἁλὸς πολιῆς, τότε δὴ ἀρετή γε ἑκάστου
φαίνετ', ἄφαρ δ' ἵπποισι τάθη δρόμος.

But when the swift horses were completing the end of the course
back toward the grey sea, then indeed the strength of each
showed itself, and at once the horses strained their hardest.

In Nestor's race against the twins, as he himself describes it, the turning post is represented by a pause between verses (see §2.20 above). There is something similar in the passage above (see EN5.1 below for a more detailed analysis). The two instances are not unrelated: the silence about the turning point in the chariot race for Patroclus prepares for silence about the turning point in Nestor's youthful race against the twins.

33 After Nestor finishes his speech and sits down, only one more line (the entry of Meriones as the final contestant, Iliad 23.351) intervenes before the charioteers mount their chariots, take their places according to lots, mark the turning post, and begin the race (Iliad 23.352–363). The transition from Nestor's speech to the race itself is all but immediate (Iliad 23.349–352):

ὡς εἰπὼν Νέστωρ Νηληΐος ἂψ ἐνὶ χώρῃ
ἕζετ', ἐπεὶ ᾧ παιδὶ ἑκάστου πείρατ' ἔειπε.
Μηριόνης δ' ἄρα πέμπτος ἐΰτριχας ὁπλίσαθ' ἵππους.
ἂν δ' ἔβαν ἐς δίφρους, ἐν δὲ κλήρους ἐβάλοντο....

So speaking Nestor the son of Neleus went back to his place
and sat, after he had told his son the main points of each thing.
Meriones, the fifth contestant, also harnessed his beautiful-maned horses.
Onto their chariots they went and cast their lots....

34 The usual critical judgment.

place between Nestor and the twins. To begin with, and as Nestor himself acknowledges at the outset of his speech, Antilochus is already an accomplished horseman, whom Zeus and Poseidon have taught, and who therefore needs little further instruction. In particular, he knows well how to round the turning post.[35] Antilochus is the very opposite of his father, who had not yet learned horsemanship when he raced against the twins and who, in particular, did not know how to round the turning post. We can imagine a further contrast in the horses that Antilochus uses in his race, and the horses that the young Nestor must have used. Antilochus has the slowest horses and it is for this very reason that he needs to employ the shrewd tactics that he knows already and that his father is now advising him in as well.[36] The youthful Nestor, on the other hand,

35 *Iliad* 23.306–309:

Ἀντίλοχ' ἤτοι μέν σε νέον περ ἐόντ' ἐφίλησαν
Ζεύς τε Ποσειδάων τε, καὶ ἱπποσύνας ἐδίδαξαν
παντοίας· τὼ καί σε διδασκέμεν οὔ τι μάλα χρεώ·
οἶσθα γὰρ εὖ περὶ τέρμαθ' ἑλισσέμεν.

Antilochus, young as you are, Zeus and Poseidon
have loved you and taught you all aspects
of horsemanship; therefore it is not really necessary to instruct you;
for you know well how to round the turning post.

36 In his speech Nestor tells Antilochus that he has the slowest horses (*Iliad* 23.309–312):

ἀλλά τοι ἵπποι
βάρδιστοι θείειν· τώ τ' οἴω λοίγι' ἔσεσθαι.
τῶν δ' ἵπποι μὲν ἔασιν ἀφάρτεροι, οὐδὲ μὲν αὐτοὶ
πλείονα ἴσασιν σέθεν αὐτοῦ μητίσασθαι.

But your horses
run the slowest; I think that will be trouble.
The others have faster horses, but they themselves do not
know more than you how to devise intelligent schemes.

In the race it comes out that the horses are actually Nestor's when Antilochus addresses a speech to them (Ἀντίλοχος δ' ἵπποισιν ἐκέκλετο πατρὸς ἑοῖο, "Antilochus exhorted his father's horses," *Iliad* 23.402). In his speech Antilochus threatens them that if they do not perform Nestor will kill them (*Iliad* 23.410–413):

ὧδε γὰρ ἐξερέω, καὶ μὴν τετελεσμένον ἔσται·
οὐ σφῶϊν κομιδὴ παρὰ Νέστορι ποιμένι λαῶν
ἔσσεται, αὐτίκα δ' ὔμμε κατακτενεῖ ὀξέϊ χαλκῷ,
αἴ κ' ἀποκηδήσαντε φερώμεθα χεῖρον ἄεθλον.

For I will tell you this, and it will be done:
there will be no care for you at the hands of Nestor, shepherd of the warriors,
but he will immediately kill you with the sharp bronze,
if you two flag and we carry off an inferior prize.

must be imagined as having just the opposite sort of horses in his race, if excessive speed, and the inability to control it, was his undoing.

§2.24 After Nestor points out to Antilochus the marker (a grave) that will serve as the turning post in the race, he gives detailed instructions for rounding it (*Iliad* 23.334–348). He tells his son to drive his chariot close to the grave and to lean with his body to the left as he enters the turn. As he does so, he is to whip the right-hand horse and give it free rein, but he is to have the left-hand horse come close to the turning post, so that the hub of the chariot wheel seems to reach its very edge. But he must be careful not to touch the stone of the turning post, lest he damage his horses and break his chariot. This would be a joy to the others, but a reproach to himself. Antilochus should be alert and careful at the same time, for if he pulls ahead of the others at the turning post, no one could catch him, no matter how swift his horses.

§2.25 Nestor's advice is tailored to the slow horses of Antilochus, who is to compensate for his lack of speed by turning as tightly as possible around the turning post. To do this he must achieve exactly the right balance between his horses, inciting the right-hand horse with voice and whip, while guiding the left-hand horse, presumably with the reins, as close as possible to the turning post. This balance is similar to the balance of the Epeian twins in their race against Nestor, when one twin held the reins while the other used the whip. And this was the balance that, we have inferred, Nestor himself lacked in the same race, and therefore crashed. There is thus deep irony when Nestor the old man warns his young son about the danger of a crash at the turning post, especially when he says that such a crash will be a joy to others but a shame to himself (*Iliad* 23.340–343):

λίθου δ' ἀλέασθαι ἐπαυρεῖν,
μή πως ἵππους τε τρώσῃς κατά θ' ἅρματα ἄξῃς·
χάρμα δὲ τοῖς ἄλλοισιν, ἐλεγχείη δὲ σοὶ αὐτῷ
ἔσσεται.

But avoid grazing the stone
so that you don't somehow wound your horses and break your
     chariot;
a joy for the others, but a reproach for yourself,
will come of that.

In *Iliad* 8 Nestor himself has trouble with his horses when his trace horse is shot and gets tangled in the traces; Diomedes, who rescues him, chides the old man for his slow horses (*bradées dé toi híppoi*, *Iliad* 8.104; cf. §2.76 below). It is remarkable that in *Iliad* 23 Antilochus races with his father's horses, which are old and slow like his father himself, and not with horses of his own; Nestor is as much a part of Antilochus's race as Antilochus himself (see below).

But the irony is subtle because the crash that is envisioned in Nestor's speech would result from guiding the left-hand horse too close to the turning post, and, in terms of the correct balance between the inciting of the right-hand horse and the restraining of the left-hand horse, this would mean an excessive use of restraint. But for Nestor, we have inferred, it was a lack of restraint that caused his crash.

§2.26 Thus Nestor does not really reveal himself as he once was in warning his son about the danger of a crash. The crash envisioned is one that would occur in the race of a skilled charioteer, like Antilochus, who used shrewd tactics but pressed them slightly too hard. But there is another passage in Nestor's speech of advice in which the old man does describe himself as he must once have been. In this passage he draws a contrast between a charioteer, like Antilochus, who knows how to use shrewd tactics, and who can thus compensate for slower horses, and one who recklessly relies on his horses and chariot and fails to control them. Nestor describes the latter charioteer first, after extolling the quality of shrewdness itself, which Antilochus already possesses (*Iliad* 23.319–321):[37]

ἀλλ' ὃς μέν θ' ἵπποισι καὶ ἅρμασιν οἷσι πεποιθὼς
ἀφραδέως ἐπὶ πολλὸν ἑλίσσεται ἔνθα καὶ ἔνθα,
ἵπποι δὲ πλανόωνται ἀνὰ δρόμον, οὐδὲ κατίσχει.

But the one who, trusting in his horses and chariot,
swerves widely from one side to the other without any thought,
his horses stray along the track, and he does not check them.

In the phrase *oudè katískhei*, "and he does not restrain (his horses)," Nestor, in effect, describes himself, and the irony is as heavy here as it is in the subsequent passage, where Nestor envisions an actual crash at the turning post. Here there is no talk of a crash or of the turning post. But such a crash is easily imagined in the case of the reckless charioteer, especially when the following lines, which depict the skillful charioteer, locate this charioteer's skill precisely in his ability to round the turning post (*Iliad* 23.322–323):

ὃς δέ κε κέρδεα εἰδῇ ἐλαύνων ἥσσονας ἵππους,
αἰεὶ τέρμ' ὁρόων στρέφει ἐγγύθεν....

---

37 The quality extolled is *mêtis*: see n2.57 below for more on this passage in relation to Nestor's own intrinsic quality, *nóos*.

But the one who, driving worse horses, knows all the tricks,
he, keeping his eye on the turning post, turns close to it....

If the description of the reckless charioteer is actually meant to describe the youthful Nestor, the description of the skillful charioteer is meant to describe Antilochus in the race that he is about to run. This applies not so much to his rounding of the turning post, for that is not described in the actual race, but to what follows it. The skillful charioteer, after rounding the turning post, keeps an eye on the leader, and waits for his chance to seize the lead (*Iliad* 23.323–325):

οὐδέ ἑ λήθει

ὅππως τὸ πρῶτον τανύσῃ βοέοισιν ἱμᾶσιν,

ἀλλ᾽ ἔχει ἀσφαλέως καὶ τὸν προύχοντα δοκεύει.

and it does not escape his notice
how he may first bring his horses to full speed with the oxhide reins,
but he drives steadily and keeps his eye on the leader.

In the actual race it is Antilochus who, after rounding the turning post, keeps an eye on the charioteer in front of him, namely Menelaus, and who seizes the chance to pass him when it presents itself.

§2.27 This brings us to the actual chariot race in *Iliad* 23, in which there are two distinct contests. That between Antilochus and Menelaus is one, and we have just seen that Nestor's speech foreshadows it briefly but significantly. The main contest is that between Diomedes, who wins first prize, and Eumelos, who has the fastest horses, but who crashes and finishes last. We will consider both of these contests, because Nestor is deeply involved in both. We will begin with the contest between Diomedes, who wins first prize, and Eumelos, for it is the race of Eumelos, who crashes, that has primary relevance to the race of the youthful Nestor as I have reconstructed it. It is Eumelos's last-place prize, we recall, that will instead be awarded to Nestor.

§2.28 In the narrative of the race, when all have rounded the turning post, Eumelos shoots out ahead of the rest and Diomedes follows him closely. Diomedes is about to challenge for the lead when Apollo, out of spite, knocks the whip from Diomedes' hands, and Diomedes' chariot falls further behind. Athena, Diomedes' protectress, has seen all this, and she now intervenes in the race. She gives Diomedes back his whip and puts strength in his horses, and, in her own show of spite, she breaks Eumelos's yoke. With no yoke to restrain them, Eumelos's horses run in different directions and the chariot pole falls to the ground. Eumelos himself tumbles from the chariot, scraping elbows, mouth, and nose, and bruising his forehead. His eyes fill with tears and his voice is stopped. Diomedes turns his horses to one side and passes Eumelos, leaving the rest of the field far behind, for Athena has put strength into Diomedes' horses and she has given glory to Diomedes himself (*Iliad* 23.373–400).

§2.29 The race of Eumelos, which is manipulated by two jealous gods, hardly resembles the race that we have reconstructed for Nestor against the Epeian twins, except for the fact that Eumelos too crashes. But there is more to Eumelos's race in *Iliad* 23 than the race itself. He also has, as it were, a virtual race, which is presented to us in the form of a dispute that breaks out between two of the spectators, Idomeneus and Ajax. This is narrated following the description of the other contest in the race, that between Antilochus and Menelaus. The spectators are seated together, but they are too far away to see any of the action that has taken place after the rounding of the turning post. This includes all the decisive action in both contests. Idomeneus, who sits apart from the others on higher ground, is the first to hear the voice of the charioteer in the lead, which he recognizes, and to identify the markings of his horse as it comes into view. He rises and calls to the other spectators, asking if they can also see that the leader is no longer who it was when the racers disappeared from view, but someone else. Idomeneus then immediately surmises what has actually befallen the early leader Eumelos, namely that his chariot came to grief on the plain, for he is nowhere in sight now (*Iliad* 23.460–464):

αἲ δέ που αὐτοῦ
ἔβλαβεν ἐν πεδίῳ, αἳ κεῖσέ γε φέρτεραι ἦσαν·
ἤτοι γὰρ τὰς πρῶτα ἴδον περὶ τέρμα βαλούσας,
νῦν δ' οὔ πῃ δύναμαι ἰδέειν· πάντῃ δέ μοι ὄσσε
Τρωϊκὸν ἂμ πεδίον παπταίνετον εἰσορόωντι.

I suppose his mares,
which were ahead to that point, were undone on the plain;
indeed the mares that I saw rounding the turn first
I cannot see anywhere now; and my eyes search everywhere
as I look out along the Trojan plain.

Having surmised the truth of the matter, however, Idomeneus does not leave it at that, but proceeds to speculate that alternatively the earlier leader crashed not in the open plain, but at the turning post (*Iliad* 23.465–468):

ἦε τὸν ἡνίοχον φύγον ἡνία, οὐδὲ δυνάσθη
εὖ σχεθέειν περὶ τέρμα καὶ οὐκ ἐτύχησεν ἑλίξας·
ἔνθά μιν ἐκπεσέειν ὀΐω σύν θ' ἅρματα ἆξαι,
αἳ δ' ἐξηρώησαν, ἐπεὶ μένος ἔλλαβε θυμόν.

Or the reins flew from the charioteer, and he was not able
to hold on well around the post, and did not succeed in turning;
there, I think, he fell out and broke his chariot,
and his mares careened off the course when frenzy seized their
spirit.[38]

Idomeneus finishes his speech by calling on the other spectators to stand and look, for he is not sure, but he thinks that the new leader is Diomedes. A dispute breaks out when Ajax, son of Oileus, abusively contradicts Idomeneus, calling him a wild talker who is too old to see clearly when the horses are still a long way off. He ends by claiming that the same horses as before are still in the lead, and that Eumelos himself still stands in his chariot holding the reins (*Iliad* 23.480–481):

ἵπποι δ' αὐταὶ ἔασι παροίτεραι, αἳ τὸ πάρος περ,
Εὐμήλου, ἐν δ' αὐτὸς ἔχων εὔληρα βέβηκε.

The same mares are in the lead as before,
Eumelus's, and he himself stands in his chariot holding the reins.

The dispute escalates when Idomeneus abuses Ajax in return, calling him quarrelsome and inferior to the other Argives, and challenges him to a bet. Ajax is about to make a heated reply when Achilles puts a stop to the unseemly wrangling, calling on both to sit and watch, for they will soon see for themselves how the racers finish. As soon as Achilles ends his speech, Diomedes drives his chariot in, finishing the race in triumph and ending all dispute.

§2.30 In the race that Idomeneus imagines Eumelos to have run, which we may call Eumelos's virtual race, the gods do not interfere, and his crash takes

---

38 With the verb *exērōēsan* Idomeneus suggests that Eumelos's horses may have swerved off the course and so disappeared from the race.

place where it would naturally do so, at the turning post. Eumelos's virtual crash is, I think, meant specifically to describe Nestor's actual crash in his youthful race against the Epeian twins. Precisely because Eumelos's crash is distanced from Nestor in the narrative, it is allowed in its virtual form to describe Nestor's crash exactly. Nestor's own speech to Antilochus, as we have seen, alludes in a fragmentary way to his crash, but does not present a complete picture. The main purpose of the dispute between spectators is, I think, to present just such a complete picture. An important part of this picture has to do with the reins. Idomeneus speculates that the reins flew from Eumelos's hands *(ẽe tòn hēníokhon phúgon hēnía)* and that he therefore could not hold onto his horses around the turning post. When Ajax contradicts him, saying that Eumelos's horses are still in the lead, and that Eumelos himself still stands in the chariot "holding the reins" *(ékhōn eúlēra)*, attention is again drawn to the reins, and this attention, I think, has to do with Nestor's race. We recall that when Nestor, in accepting the prize that should have gone to Eumelos, tells of his own loss to the Epeian twins, the key to understanding his loss is the repeated phrase used to describe just one of the twins, *émpedon hēniókheuen, / émpedon hēniókheu',* "he steadfastly held the reins, steadfastly held the reins." It is now clear from Eumelos's virtual race that this phrase must be turned around and applied to Nestor in order to interpret his loss: Nestor did *not* hold onto the reins, and it was this that caused his crash at the turning post. The phrase that Idomeneus uses of Eumelos, *phúgon hēnía,* "the reins flew (from him)," is vivid, and would seem to imply that Eumelos, in the mind of Idomeneus, was flailing with the reins to make his horses go faster—that he was using the reins as a whip—and that they slipped from his grasp as a result. This is what we should also imagine for Nestor. His crash was not like the one that he warns Antilochus against in his speech, where the charioteer reins in too hard and turns too tightly. In his own race, Nestor, like the unskilled charioteer that he describes to Antilochus, did not restrain his horses at all, but used the reins to incite his horses, and then let the reins fly from his hands at the turning post, with all the disastrous consequences that Idomeneus imagines for Eumelos: the charioteer prostrate on the ground, his chariot broken, and his horses carried off the end of the course by their own speed.[39]

---

39 See n2.38 above on the verb *exēróēsan* in *Iliad* 23.468. A charioteer would of course natu-
rally give his horses freer rein when urging them on; cf., for example, the phrase *rhutà
khalaínontes,* "slackening the reins," used of racers who "incite" *(ephíesan)* their horses in
Hesiod *Shield of Heracles* 306–309:

> εὐπλεκέων δ' ἐπὶ δίφρων
> ἡνίοχοι βεβαῶτες ἐφίεσαν ὠκέας ἵππους

§2.31 If the purpose of Eumelos's virtual race in *Iliad* 23 is to make explicit the nature of Nestor's race against the twins, what of Eumelos's actual race against Diomedes? Does this race too have something to do with Nestor's race? Everything in this race is distorted, as we have seen, by the interference of the gods Apollo and Athena. But if we allow for this distortion, connections with Nestor's race begin to emerge. In the dynamics of Nestor's race, it was the fact that he lacked "restraint" to balance his "incitement" that led to his crash. Restraint in Nestor's race was represented by the reins, which one of his twin opponents held steadily, but which Nestor himself let fly. Eumelos too is undone by a lack of restraint in that his yoke, which Athena breaks, represents restraint no less than Nestor's reins. But Eumelos's "lack of restraint" is less his own characteristic trait than the result of the goddess's action, and it is thus of a purely symbolic nature.[40] This is entirely apt if Eumelos's race is a deliberate transformation of Nestor's race. The "lack of restraint," resulting from the broken yoke, is vividly portrayed in Eumelos's race, as the two horses run in different directions, and the consequences for Eumelos are also vividly portrayed. Everything in this picture is relevant to Nestor's crash except the breaking of Eumelos's yoke, and this, as we have seen, is relevant indirectly (*Iliad* 23.392–397):

ἵππειον δέ οἱ ἦξε θεὰ ζυγόν· αἳ δέ οἱ ἵπποι
ἀμφὶς ὁδοῦ δραμέτην, ῥυμὸς δ' ἐπὶ γαῖαν ἐλύσθη.

ῥυτὰ χαλαίνοντες, τὰ δ' ἐπικροτέοντα πέτοντο
ἅρματα κολλήεντ'.

Standing on the well-plaited chariots
the charioteers incited their swift horses,
slackening the reins, and the tightly-joined chariots
flew rattling on.

But Nestor did more than give his horses free rein; he lashed his horses until the reins flew from his hands. See §2.78 below for the phrase *phúgon hēnía* used of Nestor himself in *Iliad* 8.137.

40 Eumelos is eager, as when he is "much the first" to step forward for the race, but he is also "the best at horsemanship" (*Iliad* 23.287–289):

ὣς φάτο Πηλεΐδης, ταχέες δ' ἱππῆες ἄγερθεν.
ὦρτο πολὺ πρῶτος μὲν ἄναξ ἀνδρῶν Εὔμηλος
Ἀδμήτου φίλος υἱός, ὃς ἱπποσύνῃ ἐκέκαστο.

So Peleus's son spoke, and the swift horsemen gathered.
The lord of men Eumelus stood up much the first,
Admetus's dear son, who was the best at horsemanship.

Eumelos's "eagerness" is not the same fault as in Nestor's case.

αὐτὸς δ' ἐκ δίφροιο παρὰ τροχὸν ἐξεκυλίσθη,
ἀγκῶνάς τε περιδρύφθη στόμα τε ῥῖνάς τε,
θρυλίχθη δὲ μέτωπον ἐπ' ὀφρύσι· τὼ δέ οἱ ὄσσε
δακρυόφι πλῆσθεν, θαλερὴ δέ οἱ ἔσχετο φωνή.

The goddess broke his horses' yoke; the mares
ran apart on the road and the pole slipped to the ground.
He himself rolled from the chariot alongside the wheel,
and his elbows, mouth, and nose were skinned,
and above his brows his forehead was bruised; his eyes
filled with tears, and his vibrant voice was stilled.

§2.32 If the symbol of restraint is shifted from the reins in Nestor's race to the yoke in Eumelos's race, the symbol of incitement in both races is the same, namely the whip. In Nestor's race against the twins, just one of the twins had the function of urging the horses on with the whip (*hò d' ára mástigi kéleuen*). In Diomedes' race against Eumelos, Apollo knocks the whip from Diomedes' hands and Athena returns it to him. As she does so, she herself performs the function of the whip by putting strength into Diomedes' horses (*Iliad* 23.388–390):

οὐδ' ἄρ' Ἀθηναίην ἐλεφηράμενος λάθ' Ἀπόλλων
Τυδεΐδην, μάλα δ' ὦκα μετέσσυτο ποιμένα λαῶν,
δῶκε δέ οἱ μάστιγα, μένος δ' ἵπποισιν ἐνῆκεν.

But Athena did not fail to notice Apollo when he tricked
the son of Tydeus, but hurried quickly after the shepherd of the
    warriors
and gave him his whip, and put incitement into his horses.

In terms of the basic opposition between Indo-European twins, the whip belongs to the immortal twin, whose function is to "bring back to life." This is precisely the function that the goddess Athena plays in the race of Diomedes, when his horses are slowed by loss of the whip. When we consider Athena's action in the race, Diomedes' victory over Eumelos is the victory of two against one, just as the twins' victory over Nestor was.

§2.33 In the transformation of the twins' race into Diomedes' race the essence of that race is preserved by Athena's action in giving Diomedes back his whip and putting strength into his horses. There are also of course significant differences between Athena in Diomedes' race and the twin who plied the whip in the race against Nestor. It is two against one in Diomedes' race, but Athena does not ride in Diomedes' chariot. And yet Athena's help for Diomedes in the chariot race recalls an earlier occasion when she did mount his chariot and ride with him, namely when he wounded the war god Ares in *Iliad* 5.[41] That famous battle of two against one provides just the right image if we want to compare Athena and Diomedes, as a pair, to the Epeian twins.[42] But let us focus rather on the differences between these two pairs. When the twins won, each of them—one holding the reins and the other plying the whip—was indispensable to the victory. In Diomedes' race against Eumelos, he might have won anyway if neither Apollo nor Athena had interfered. He was about to pass Eumelos, or at least draw even with him, when Apollo knocked the whip from his hands (*Iliad* 23.382–384):

καί νύ κεν ἢ παρέλασσ' ἢ ἀμφήριστον ἔθηκεν,

εἰ μὴ Τυδέος υἷϊ κοτέσσατο Φοῖβος Ἀπόλλων,

ὅς ῥά οἱ ἐκ χειρῶν ἔβαλεν μάστιγα φαεινήν.

Tydeus's son would either have passed him or made a close race
    of it
if Phoebus Apollo had not held a grudge at his expense
and knocked the shining whip from his hands.[43]

And the final difference between this race and Nestor's race is the negative role that both gods play, as Apollo's anger with Diomedes is outdone by Athena's anger with Eumelos, at least in terms of its results. This is jealous anger, for Apollo himself bred Eumelos's horses (*Iliad* 2.766), and his anger with Diomedes

41 *Iliad* 5.835–863.
42 Note that Athena takes both whip and reins in *Iliad* 5.840, unlike the distribution of functions between the Epeian twins in *Iliad* 23.641–642. Athena puts *ménos* into Diomedes at the start of *Iliad* 5, well before she enters his chariot, as she herself says (*Iliad* 5.125–126):

ἐν γάρ τοι στήθεσσι μένος πατρώϊον ἧκα
ἄτρομον, οἷον ἔχεσκε σακέσπαλος ἱππότα Τυδεύς.

I have put your ancestors' unflinching *ménos* into your breast,
such as the shield-brandishing horseman Tydeus used to have.

She goes on to say that she has taken the mist from his eyes so that he can tell gods from men, and tells him to wound only Aphrodite among the gods.
43 Diomedes is called the best charioteer in *Iliad* 23.357; Eumelos is called the best in *Iliad* 23.536. We do not know which of the two would have won if the gods had not interfered; we know only that, with Athena's help, Diomedes did win.

thus derives in some large measure from his support for Eumelos.[44] Diomedes is likewise Athena's favorite, and the depth of her anger with Eumelos, in causing his crash, is really just the measure of her love for Diomedes.

§2.34 In the transformation of the twins' race against Nestor into Diomedes' race against Eumelos, the whip that Athena gives back to Diomedes and the strength that she puts into his horses are the essential points: Athena provides "incitement." We are not allowed to lose sight of either motif in the rest of Diomedes' race. When Diomedes turns to avoid Eumelos's crashed chariot and shoots out far in front of the other racers, Athena provides the horses with *ménos* (*Iliad* 23.398–400):

Τυδεΐδης δὲ παρατρέψας ἔχε μώνυχας ἵππους,
πολλὸν τῶν ἄλλων ἐξάλμενος· ἐν γὰρ Ἀθήνη
ἵπποις ἧκε <u>μένος</u> καὶ ἐπ' αὐτῷ κῦδος ἔθηκε.

The son of Tydeus turned aside and kept his solid-hoofed horses
    on course,
jumping far out in front of the others; for Athena
put <u>incitement</u> into the horses and set glory on him.

Attention at this point shifts to Antilochus and his race against Menelaus, and here too Antilochus recognizes that Diomedes has Athena's help; when he calls on his horses to challenge those of Menelaus, he knows that he cannot

44 Eumelos is the son of Admetos (*Iliad* 2.714), whom Apollo served as herdsman for a year ("Apollodorus" 1.9.15, 3.10.4). This explains how Apollo came to breed Eumelos's horses, and support him in the race. But there is also more to Apollo's opposition to Diomedes insofar as this too continues the episode in *Iliad* 5: in *Iliad* 5 Diomedes wounds Aeneas and then Aphrodite as she tries to rescue Aeneas; when the wounded Aphrodite lets go of Aeneas Apollo protects him (5.344–346), and Diomedes attacks Apollo four times before he is finally warned off (5.436–442). In the end Diomedes retreats "avoiding the wrath (*mênis*) of Apollo" (5.443–444), and Apollo rescues Aeneas from the battlefield. Athena had told Diomedes to attack only Aphrodite among the gods (5.129–132), and Apollo warns Diomedes to know his place as a mortal (*Iliad* 5.440–442):

φράζεο Τυδεΐδη καὶ χάζεο, μηδὲ θεοῖσιν
ἶσ' ἔθελε φρονέειν, ἐπεὶ οὔ ποτε φῦλον ὁμοῖον
ἀθανάτων τε θεῶν χαμαὶ ἐρχομένων τ' ἀνθρώπων.

Take thought, son of Tydeus, and yield, and do not wish
to think thoughts equal to the gods, since the race
of immortal gods and of men who walk on the earth is never the same.

Diomedes avoids Apollo's wrath in *Iliad* 5, but a reminder of his wrath returns in *Iliad* 23 when he knocks the whip from Diomedes' hands.

challenge those of Diomedes, for Athena has given them speed and Diomedes himself glory (*Iliad* 23.403–406):

> ἔμβητον καὶ σφῶϊ· τιταίνετον ὅττι τάχιστα.
> ἤτοι μὲν κείνοισιν ἐριζέμεν οὔ τι κελεύω
> Τυδεΐδεω ἵπποισι δαΐφρονος, οἷσιν Ἀθήνη
> νῦν ὤρεξε <u>τάχος</u> καὶ ἐπ' αὐτῷ κῦδος ἔθηκεν.

> You two push forward too; stretch out to full speed.
> I do not command you to compete with those horses,
> the ones of keen-spirited Diomedes, to whom Athena
> has now granted <u>speed</u>, and put glory on Diomedes himself.

Near the end of the race, when Diomedes comes into view, it is the whip, which he repeatedly lashes "from the shoulder," that dominates the scene (*Iliad* 23.499–500):

> Τυδεΐδης δὲ μάλα σχεδὸν ἦλθε διώκων,
> <u>μάστι</u> δ' αἰὲν ἔλαυνε κατωμαδόν.

> The son of Tydeus came racing in, close to them,
> and with the <u>whip</u> kept driving, swinging it from his shoulder.

When Diomedes comes to a halt and leaps from his chariot, he leans his whip against the yoke of his chariot in what seems to be a deliberately symbolic act, and Sthenelos meanwhile collects first prize for him (*Iliad* 23.507–511):

> στῆ δὲ μέσῳ ἐν ἀγῶνι, πολὺς δ' ἀνεκήκιεν ἱδρὼς
> ἵππων ἔκ τε λόφων καὶ ἀπὸ στέρνοιο χαμᾶζε.
> αὐτὸς δ' ἐκ δίφροιο χαμαὶ θόρε παμφανόωντος,
> <u>κλῖνε δ' ἄρα μάστιγα ποτὶ ζυγόν</u>· οὐδὲ μάτησεν
> ἴφθιμος Σθένελος, ἀλλ' ἐσσυμένως λάβ' ἄεθλον.

> He stood in the middle of the assembly, and much sweat poured
> from the horses' necks and chests to the ground.
> He himself jumped from the all-shining chariot to the ground,
> <u>and leaned the whip against the yoke</u>. Not a moment was lost
> by steadfast Sthenelos, who immediately seized the prize.

What Diomedes does as his prize is claimed for him sums up his race. In leaning the whip against the yoke he draws attention to the the token of his victory, the whip, and, equally important, the token of Eumelos's defeat, the yoke. Diomedes' yoke remained intact, and he thus maintained the "restraint" that was one of the two elements necessary for victory. The other element, "incitement," was provided by Diomedes' immortal partner, Athena, for without Athena Diomedes would have had no whip to put down at the end of the race. These two symbols, the whip and the yoke, also sum up Diomedes' race against Eumelos as a transformation of Nestor's race against the twins, for it was from Nestor's race against the twins that the qualities of "incitement" and "restraint" as the determinants of victory—and defeat—came in the first place.

§2.35 On the surface of the poem Nestor has no connection with the race between Diomedes and Eumelos in *Iliad* 23. The elaborate network of connections that does exist is all below the surface. In this respect, the race between Antilochus and Menelaus is different, for Nestor is his son's advisor, and his connection with his son's race is on the surface of the poem. But the underlying issue throughout the chariot race of *Iliad* 23, including the race between Antilochus and Menelaus, is the youthful Nestor's crash in his race against the Epeian twins. With regard to the crash itself there is no connection on the surface in the race between Antilochus and Menelaus, for there is no crash in this race. There is, however, a connection between the quality in the young Nestor that led to his crash, namely his unrestrained "incitement," and the race that his son runs. For Antilochus passes Menelaus by means of a dangerous—indeed reckless—maneuver that forces Menelaus to give way in order to avoid a crash. Antilochus executes this maneuver at a narrowing of the road, where part of the roadbed has been washed away and there is room for only one chariot at a time. As Antilochus begins to pass, Menelaus calls on him to restrain his horses lest he cause both their chariots to crash, and to wait for a wider road in order to pass (*Iliad* 23.426–428):

Ἀντίλοχ' ἀφραδέως ἱππάζεαι, ἀλλ' ἄνεχ' ἵππους·
στεινωπὸς γὰρ ὁδός, τάχα δ' εὐρυτέρη παρελάσσαι·
μή πως ἀμφοτέρους δηλήσεαι ἅρματι κύρσας.

Antilochus, you are driving recklessly, hold back your horses;
the road is narrow but will soon be wider to pass;
you will hurt us both if you hit my chariot.

But Antilochus, far from showing restraint, as Menelaus has called on him to do, surges ahead all the more, urging his horses on with the whip as if he did not even hear Menelaus (*Iliad* 23.429–430):

ὣς ἔφατ', Ἀντίλοχος δ' ἔτι καὶ πολὺ μᾶλλον ἔλαυνε

κέντρῳ ἐπισπέρχων ὡς οὐκ ἀΐοντι ἐοικώς.

So he spoke, but Antilochus still drove on, much more even than
    before,
laying on with his goad, like one not hearing.

At this moment Antilochus, paying no heed to the call to restrain his horses, but lashing them all the more with his whip, is the reembodiment of his father as he once was in his race against the Epeian twins. Whereas Nestor crashed, however, Menelaus gives way to Antilochus, who thus takes the lead. A crash is avoided, but it is not Antilochus's doing that avoids it. For his part, the crash would have occurred, and this virtual crash is described when Menelaus gives way to avoid it, and his horses drop behind those of Antilochus (*Iliad* 23.433–437):

αἳ δ' ἠρώησαν ὀπίσσω

Ἀτρεΐδεω· αὐτὸς γὰρ ἑκὼν μεθέηκεν ἐλαύνειν

μή πως συγκύρσειαν ὁδῷ ἔνι μώνυχες ἵπποι,

δίφρους τ' ἀνατρέψειαν ἐϋπλεκέας, κατὰ δ' αὐτοὶ

ἐν κονίῃσι πέσοιεν ἐπειγόμενοι περὶ νίκης.

But behind him fell the horses
of Atreus's son; for he himself deliberately let up from driving
so the solid-hoofed horses would not run into each other on the
    road
and overturn the well-plaited chariots, and they themselves
fall in the dust as they pressed for victory.

§2.36 In Eumelos's race against Diomedes, as we earlier saw, the young Nestor's race is reenacted insofar as there is an actual crash, but the crash is brought on by Athena, not by Eumelos himself. Unlike the young Nestor, Eumelos does not embody incitement without restraint, and he therefore does not crash at the turning post, as Nestor did, but in the open plain through no fault of his own. Only in the speculation of Idomeneus does Eumelos crash at the turning post, and thus provide an explicit picture of the youthful

Nestor's crash. In this involved way Eumelos reenacts Nestor's crash, but he lacks the attitude that caused it. With Antilochus it is just the opposite, for he has the attitude that caused Nestor's crash, but he is spared the actual crash that his father suffered by the restraint of Menelaus. The two races, that of Eumelos, in both its actual and virtual forms, and that of Antilochus, complement each other in providing a complete picture of the race of the youthful Nestor. While Nestor's connection with his son's race is on the surface of the poem in one way (he is his son's advisor), in another way it is as hidden as his connection with Eumelos's race. It is the aged Nestor, in his speech of advice, who has an overt connection with Antilochus's race. The young Nestor, on the other hand, is completely hidden in Antilochus's race, just as he was in Eumelos's. There are thus two Nestors to deal with in his son's race, the old and the young, and we need to look more carefully at his son's relationship with each of them.

§2.37 We saw earlier in analyzing Nestor's speech of advice that Antilochus is characterized in very different terms from the youthful Nestor who crashed at the turning post. Whereas Nestor was not yet a horseman, Antilochus has been taught horsemanship by Zeus and Poseidon, and, in particular, he knows well how to round the turning post. With teachers like Zeus and Poseidon, Antilochus already knows most of what his father has to tell him, and Nestor says as much early in his speech: τῶ καί σε διδασκέμεν οὔ τι μάλα χρεώ, "therefore there is no great need to instruct you" (*Iliad* 23.308). Antilochus thus resembles the old Nestor, not the young, in terms of his knowledge and skill. He is further brought into relation to the aged Nestor, and distanced from the youthful Nestor, by the fact that his horses are slow. These horses are in fact his father's, and their lack of speed reflects Nestor's own aged condition.[45] It is because his horses are slow that Antilochus must employ shrewd tactics, particularly around the turning post. These are tactics that Nestor knows now, with his years of experience, but did not know, or at least did not use, when he raced against the twins. On the surface of the poem, then, everything in Nestor's speech seems calculated to make Antilochus resemble the aged Nestor rather than the youthful Nestor. But the fact is, of course, that Antilochus is a young man, and in his race against Menelaus he acts like one, with all the impetuosity and recklessness of youth. If we look closely, furthermore, the aged Nestor, in his speech, prepares the way for his son's dangerous maneuver without quite seeming to do so. We have already seen that when Nestor contrasts the unskilled and the skillful

45 See n2.36 above.

charioteer in his speech, he really contrasts himself as a young man with his
son.[46] Let us look again at his description of the skillful charioteer, whom
Antilochus resembles (*Iliad* 23.322–325):

ὃς δέ κε κέρδεα εἰδῇ ἐλαύνων ἥσσονας ἵππους,
αἰεὶ τέρμ' ὁρόων στρέφει ἐγγύθεν, οὐδέ ἑ λήθει
ὅππως τὸ πρῶτον τανύσῃ βοέοισιν ἱμᾶσιν,
ἀλλ' ἔχει ἀσφαλέως καὶ τὸν προὔχοντα δοκεύει.

But the one who, driving worse horses, knows all the tricks,
he, keeping his eye on the turning post, turns close to it, and it
     does not escape his notice
how he may first bring his horses to full speed with the oxhide
     reins,
but he drives steadily and keeps his eye on the leader.

It is clear that Nestor intends Antilochus to take these words to heart for they
pertain to his situation. His horses are inferior, and he will need to round the
turning post tightly to stay in the race. But Antilochus already knows how
to do this, and the turning post plays no part in his race. What pertains to
Antilochus's actual race is what follows. This is very clear in the final phrase
of the description of the skillful charioteer, who "keeps his eye on the leader"
after rounding the turning post. This is what Antilochus in fact does in his
race, and Nestor's description of the skillful charioteer breaks off with a
phrase that seems intended to connect with the actual race when the narra-
tive finally reaches it, and Antilochus calls on his horses to overtake those
in front of them. But Antilochus also takes to heart what Nestor says in the
previous line, and this is made clear by the last words of his speech to his
horses as he fastens on his dangerous plan to pass Menelaus on the narrow
stretch of road (*Iliad* 23.415–416):

ταῦτα δ' ἐγὼν αὐτὸς τεχνήσομαι ἠδὲ νοήσω
στεινωπῷ ἐν ὁδῷ παραδύμεναι, οὐδέ με λήσει.

But I myself will contrive this and perceive the right moment for
     it,
how to pass on the narrow road, and it will not escape my
     notice.

46 See §2.26 above.

§2.38 With the final words of his speech, *oudé me lései*, Antilochus repeats Nestor's phrase *oudé he léthei* in his description of the skillful charioteer. When Antilochus says, "and it will not escape my notice," he refers to perceiving the right moment to execute his dangerous plan. If we look closely at Nestor's speech, we see that Antilochus remembers not only his father's words, but what he meant by them. Nestor says of the skillful charioteer that, after rounding the turning post tightly, "it does not escape his notice how first to stretch with the oxhide reins." There is no object for the verb "stretch," but "horses" is easily understood, and the phrase "stretch his horses" must mean "bring them to full speed."[47] Nestor says that the skillful charioteer perceives when "first" (*tò prôton*) to bring his horses to full speed, and Antilochus hears this advice and acts on it, for he recognizes his opportunity when it comes and he seizes it. There is thus a connection between Nestor's speech and Antilochus's race, but it is a slender one, and it is deliberately so. It is up to Antilochus to enact the real meaning of Nestor's advice, which relates to Nestor's own youthful recklessness.[48] This is an issue that is carefully kept hidden from view throughout the chariot race in *Iliad* 23. Thus Nestor in his speech, after effectively advocating that Antilochus look for his opportunity and seize it, does not go on to sanction dangerous tactics. Far from it. Nestor changes course abruptly and says that the skillful charioteer "drives steadily" (*all' ékhei asphaléōs*).[49] Nestor's speech thus returns safely to its theme, and attention is diverted from the implication of his words. This part of Nestor's speech then ends with the phrase *kaì tòn proúkhonta dokeúei*, "he keeps his eye on the leader," which looks ahead to Antilochus's race, where Antilochus will do exactly what he has been told. It is significant that the phrase that connects Nestor's speech and Antilochus's race means "does not escape notice," for the connection itself is a deliberately subtle one. When Antilochus says that it will not escape his notice when to pass Menelaus on the narrow road, it should also not escape our notice that it is his father who has put him up to this dangerous tactic without quite seeming to do so.

§2.39 If there is irony in the fact that Nestor puts Antilochus up to his dangerous tactic, there is further irony in the fact that Antilochus gets away

---

47 Compare *Iliad* 16.375, *tanúonto dè mónukhes híppoi*, "the solid-hoofed horses went full speed," where the verb *tanúonto* means literally "were stretched."

48 When Nestor says that the skillful charioteer knows "when first to press (the horses) with the ox-hide reins" he comes close to evoking his own disastrous race against the twins, and the role of the reins in that race. The reference to the reins, instead of the whip, is at least consistent with such an evocation.

49 The implication in *asphaléōs* of "not stumbling" is to the point here. The verb *ékhei* often means to "drive" horses (Cunliffe 1924 s.v. no. 39).

with it, and takes second prize from Menelaus, whereas Nestor himself, when he was young, paid for his unrestrained incitement with an inglorious defeat. A necessary balance between incitement and restraint has been upset in Antilochus's race, and this balance must be restored at the end of his race before he is allowed to keep his victory. It was Menelaus who saved Antilochus from catastrophe by giving way to him on the narrow road. But Menelaus was angered by Antilochus's failure to heed him and wait for a wider road to pass, and although he gave way, he warned Antilochus as he drove past that he would challenge his right to second prize (*Iliad* 23.439–441):

Ἀντίλοχ' οὔ τις σεῖο βροτῶν ὀλοώτερος ἄλλος·

ἔρρ', ἐπεὶ οὔ σ' ἔτυμόν γε φάμεν πεπνῦσθαι Ἀχαιοί.

ἀλλ' οὐ μὰν οὐδ' ὣς ἄτερ ὅρκου οἴσῃ ἄεθλον.

Antilochus, no other mortal is more destructive than you;
down with you, since we Achaeans wrongly say you are wise.
But I swear you will not win a prize this way without taking an
    oath.

At the end of the race the awarding of second prize occasions a whole new contest, which begins when Achilles takes pity on Eumelos, who comes in last of all the racers, on foot, and Achilles proposes to give him second prize. But Antilochus shows the same determination in claiming second prize that he did in winning it, telling Achilles that he will be angry with him if he is deprived of what he has won (*Iliad* 23.543–544):

ὦ Ἀχιλεῦ μάλα τοι κεχολώσομαι αἴ κε τελέσσῃς

τοῦτο ἔπος· μέλλεις γὰρ ἀφαιρήσεσθαι ἄεθλον....

Achilles, I will be very angry with you if you carry out
this word of yours; for you are about to take away my prize....

Antilochus says that Eumelos has only himself to blame for his misfortune, and that he should have prayed to the gods who foiled him, and he tells Achilles to award Eumelos a special prize if he pities him.[50] At the end of his speech, Antilochus is defiant, saying that he will not give up the mare, his

---

50 Note the irony of the situation when Antilochus, who succeeded with his rash tactic, refuses to yield his prize to the reembodiment of his father, who failed with a similar tactic when he was young. For a different interpretation of the dispute for second prize, see Hammer 2002:134–143, who focuses on Achilles' role in the dispute in political terms.

prize, and that he will fight with anyone who tries to take it from him (*Iliad* 23.553–554):

τὴν δ᾽ ἐγὼ οὐ δώσω· περὶ δ᾽ αὐτῆς πειρηθήτω
ἀνδρῶν ὅς κ᾽ ἐθέλησιν ἐμοὶ χείρεσσι μάχεσθαι.

But I will not give her up; let any man try for her
who wishes to fight me with fists.

This sets the stage for Menelaus to rise up once Achilles has given in to Antilochus by awarding Eumelos a special prize. Menelaus is exceedingly angry, and he in effect accepts the challenge that Antilochus has just thrown down. Menelaus at first calls on the other Achaeans to judge between them, but then says that he will judge the matter himself in a way that no one can fault: he calls on Antilochus to take his whip in his hand and swear by Poseidon that he did not use it unfairly to defeat him in the race (*Iliad* 23.581–585):

Ἀντίλοχ᾽ εἰ δ᾽ ἄγε δεῦρο διοτρεφές, ἧ θέμις ἐστί,
στὰς ἵππων προπάροιθε καὶ ἄρματος, αὐτὰρ ἱμάσθλην
χερσὶν ἔχε ῥαδινήν, ᾗ περ τὸ πρόσθεν ἔλαυνες,
ἵππων ἁψάμενος γαιήοχον ἐννοσίγαιον
ὄμνυθι μὴ μὲν ἑκὼν τὸ ἐμὸν δόλῳ ἄρμα πεδῆσαι.

Zeus-fostered Antilochus, come here and, as is customary and
    right,
standing in front of your horses and chariot hold in your hands
the slender whip with which you drove ahead of me,
and taking hold of your horses swear by the earthholder, the
    earthshaker,
that you did not deliberately bind my chariot with deceit.

These words of Menelaus, in the dispute over second prize, put the contest for this prize back to where it was in the race itself when Menelaus called on Antilochus to give way and wait for a wider road in order to pass. In the race Antilochus paid no attention, but rushed impetuously ahead. Now, however, he defers to Menelaus, giving up the prize mare to him and offering to make further restitution in order not to fall from his favor. Antilochus admits his mistake and he recognizes that Menelaus is both older and better than he. This change of attitude on the part of Antilochus changes Menelaus's attitude as well, and when Antilochus hands over the prize mare to him, Menelaus graciously allows him to keep it, saying that Antilochus had never been so heedless and thoughtless in the past (οὔ τι παρήορος οὐδ' ἀεσίφρων / ἦσθα πάρος, *Iliad* 23.603–604), and had contributed much to his own cause at Troy.

§2.40 In his race against Menelaus, Antilochus won by his unrestrained incitement, but he is not allowed to keep his prize at the end of the race until he shows the restraint that was lacking in his race itself. Thus he restores the balance that he lost when, acting on his father's advice, he reenacted his father's own youthful lack of restraint in his race against the Epeian twins. And since Antilochus restores this balance, his race, unlike his father's, is allowed to have a successful outcome.

§2.41 Nestor's youthful race against the twins underlies both contests in the chariot race of *Iliad* 23. The two contests come together, briefly, in the dispute over second prize, when Antilochus, who has courted disaster in carrying out his aged father's advice, refuses to relinquish his prize to Eumelos, who has met with disaster in reenacting the youthful Nestor's race. Moreover, it is as a result of his son's refusal to give up his prize to Eumelos that Nestor himself is awarded Eumelos's prize when Eumelos is awarded a special prize. There is thus a double irony in Antilochus's action as it relates to his father, in that it is his father's substitute to whom he refuses the undue honor of being awarded second prize, and it is his father himself who, indirectly through his son's action, is awarded precisely the honor that is due him, that of last prize.

§2.42 The awarding of last prize to Nestor, which draws forth from him the story of his race against the Epeian twins, is the culmination of the chariot race in *Iliad* 23. This scene, like the rest of the chariot race, is played out on two levels. On the surface, Achilles awards Nestor a vacant prize in honor of Patroclus because Nestor is too old to compete and win prizes for himself. When Achilles says that Nestor will not box, wrestle, throw the spear, or race on foot in the games for Patroclus, this leads seamlessly to Nestor's story of the games for Amarynkeus at Bouprasion, for these were the four contests that he won on that day. The contest that he lost, the chariot race, is left until last, and his loss is not explained, at least on the surface. Instead, Nestor tells why the twins won, namely that they outnumbered him, and that one held the reins while the other used the whip. His story ends there, as he goes on to urge that younger men participate in the games for Patroclus, for he must bow to grievous old age. He then bids Achilles to honor his dead companion with funeral games, and he finishes by accepting the prize that Achilles has given him and thanking him for the honor that he has thus shown him (*Iliad* 23.647–650):

τοῦτο δ' ἐγὼ πρόφρων δέχομαι, χαίρει δέ μοι ἦτορ,
ὥς μευ ἀεὶ μέμνησαι ἐνηέος, οὐδέ σε λήθω,
τιμῆς ἧς τέ μ' ἔοικε τετιμῆσθαι μετ' Ἀχαιοῖς.
σοὶ δὲ θεοὶ τῶνδ' ἀντὶ χάριν μενοεικέα δοῖεν.

I gladly receive this, and my heart rejoices
that you always remember me, well-intentioned as I am, and I do
not escape your notice
as to the honor that it befits me to receive among the Achaeans.
In return for these things may the gods give you heart-warming
thanks.

These are the final lines of the episode, and on the surface all is straightforward. Nestor accepts his prize gladly (*próphrōn*), and, when he rejoices that Achilles always remembers him, he draws attention to his own being "kindly-disposed" (*enēéos*). The final line, in which Nestor calls on the gods to repay Achilles for his kindness, is wholly without ambiguity regarding the harmony between the two heroes with which the episode ends.

§2.43 But the scene is also the culmination of what has been going on beneath the surface throughout the episode. The climax at this level is the description of Nestor's chariot race against the twins, in which the reason for the twins' victory, the fact that one held the reins while the other used the whip, also contains the reason for Nestor's loss if one understands (or knows) Nestor's tradition and can thus turn the reason around and view it from Nestor's perspective. The reason for Nestor's loss is not given, but it will not escape the notice of those who have understood what has gone on beneath the surface of the chariot race from the very start. They will know that Nestor crashed, and that this is the real reason that he receives last prize from Achilles. There is thus a double meaning when Nestor says to Achilles at the end of the episode that his heart rejoices, not only because Achilles always remembers him, but specifically because "I do not escape your notice—*oudé se léthō*—as to the honor that it befits me to receive among the Achaeans." The honor that it befits Nestor to receive is, from the point of view of his youthful crash, last prize, and that is what he has in fact just been given by Achilles. The irony of the phrase that calls attention to the unspoken meaning of Nestor's prize, *oudé se léthō*, "nor do I escape your notice," must be intentional. We have seen that variants of the same phrase are used twice earlier in the chariot race to connect Nestor's speech of advice

to his son to the dangerous tactics that his son employs in his race: speaking
of the skillful charioteer Nestor says *oudé he léthei / hóppōs tò prôton tanúsēi
boéoisin himâsin*, and when Antilochus prepares to look for the moment to
seize his opportunity, he repeats his father's words in the form *oudé me lései*.
The phrase connects Antilochus's rash tactic to his father's advice. But there
is yet another occurrence of this phrase in the chariot race, although we have
not yet taken notice of it. This occurrence is also in Nestor's speech of advice
to Antilochus, shortly after its first occurrence in Nestor's characterization
of the skillful charioteer. At the end of this characterization, Nestor goes on
immediately to draw his son's attention to the actual turning post which he
must round in his race (*Iliad* 23.326):

σῆμα δέ τοι ἐρέω μάλ' ἀριφραδές, οὐδέ σε λήσει.
I will tell you a very clear sign, and it will not escape your
notice.

The repetition *oudé he léthei / oudé se lései* in the space of four lines is striking
in itself, and the second occurrence is as significant as the first. Whereas the
first occurrence connects Nestor's speech with the actual race of Antilochus,
the second occurrence introduces the long, ironic description of the turning
post, which has nothing to do with the actual race of Antilochus, but has
everything to do with the as yet unspoken race of Nestor against the twins.
It is Nestor's emphasis on the turning post in his speech to Antilochus that
serves to put his youthful race firmly in the mind of alert listeners right from
the start of the episode.[51] It is thus the second occurrence of the phrase,
to introduce the turning post, that establishes it as a leitmotif, not just in
Antilochus's race, but in the entire chariot race of *Iliad* 23. When this occur-
rence of the phrase, evoking the role of the turning post in Nestor's youthful
race, is added to the others, it is clear that the final occurrence of the phrase
in the form *oudé se léthō* is an intentional climax. With this phrase, Nestor in
effect says to Achilles: "You know that I crashed at the turning post; that is
why you have given me last prize."[52]

51 At the end of the passage on the turning post comes Nestor's warning about a crash.
52 In *Iliad* 23.652 Achilles proceeds from the chariot race to the next contest "when he had
heard the whole tale of Neleus's son," ἐπεὶ πάντ' αἶνον ἐπέκλυε Νηλεΐδαο; the view that
aînos, "tale," has the connotation "coded message" in Homer is strongly supported by its
occurrence in this line (for *aînos* as "coded message" see Nagy 1979:235–241, who points
to the related forms *ainíssomai*, "utter an oracular response," and *aínigma*, "riddle"); *aînos*,
"coded message," would seem to be the precise term for the speech that Nestor has just
delivered (cf. Meuli 1975 [1954] 752, who also sees a hidden meaning in Nestor's *aînos*,
but identifies it as Nestor's veiled hint that he should receive the remaining prize; Alden

§2.44 The intentional irony of Nestor's role in the chariot race, which reaches a peak in his use of the phrase *oudé se léthō* at the end of the episode, must be kept in mind when we widen the focus and consider the relevance of Nestor's

---

2000:102–110 offers another solution to the riddle posed by the word *aînos* in *Iliad* 23.652, namely that Nestor once accepted with restraint an unfair defeat by the Molione and that he thus contrasts favorably with Menelaus when tricked by Antilochus). In terms of seeing what is hidden from view, the spectators in the chariot race of *Iliad* 23 are put in the same position as the Homeric audience, and they thus represent the Homeric audience in this episode: the race becomes invisible to the spectators at the turning post, and thus an object of dispute, and it is in relation to the turning post that the Homeric audience must also see what is hidden from view. For the spectators the dispute about the leader in the race is resolved at the the end of the race; for the Homeric audience the issue of the turning post's relevance in the race is resolved by Nestor's acceptance of last prize at the end of the episode as a whole. It is worth emphasizing that the phrase deployed to such meaningful effect in the chariot race is itself formulaic: cf. *oudé se léthō*, "I do not escape your notice," *Iliad* 1.561, 10.279; *oudé me léseis*, "you will not escape my notice," *Odyssey* 13.393; *oudé se lései*, "it will not escape your notice," *Odyssey* 11.126 (cf. n2.64 below for this occurrence). The deployment of the phrase in the chariot race is simply a matter of the oral poet's artistry in the use of his conventional medium. In *Iliad* 2 there is a different form of the phrase that seems related to its occurrences in *Iliad* 23. The "baneful dream" (*oûlos óneiros*) sent by Zeus to Agamemnon to tell him that he can now take Troy comes in the form of Nestor; before the dream departs the phantom Nestor tells Agamemnon not to forget the dream when he awakens, and the phrase that this Nestor uses is *mēdé se léthē / haireítō*, "may forgetfulness not seize you" (*Iliad* 2.33–34). The real Nestor, when Agamemnon repeats his dream in council, appears to reject it, saying that if anyone but Agamemnon had had this dream the Achaean leaders would not believe it; but Nestor in fact accepts the dream and all the other leaders are persuaded by him. The irony is obvious: it is Nestor—both the phantom Nestor and the real Nestor—who persuade the Achaeans to pursue a disastrous course, but the real Nestor escapes all responsibility for the plan. This is like the situation in the chariot race for Patroclus, where there are again two Nestors, the old Nestor of the present and the young Nestor who once raced at Bouprasion, and the old Nestor of the present bears no responsibility for the calamitous actions of the young Nestor, who remains largely hidden from view. In configuring a double Nestor in *Iliad* 2 the Homeric poets seem to have had in mind Nestor's role later in the poem. The phantom Nestor of *Iliad* 2 anticipates the hidden Nestor of *Iliad* 23 especially in terms of the "incitement" that each represents: in *Iliad* 2 it is the phantom Nestor that sets Agamemnon in motion. The connection between the two episodes is, I think, borne out by the phrase *mēdé se léthē* in *Iliad* 2 and its four-fold echo in *Iliad* 23. There are of course differences between the two episodes both in the situation (phantom self versus former self) and in the formulaic phrase (noun *léthē* versus verbs *léthō/léthei/lései*), but there is also a remarkable similarity. Nestor's ironic role in *Iliad* 2 raises a final point. Nestor in the *Iliad* is typically seen as a conventional supporter of established authority, and of Agamemnon in particular (see e.g. Wilson 2002:63, 73, 141–142 on Nestor's role in the quarrel between Achilles and Agamemnon in *Iliad* 1). The point is not wrong, but it takes Nestor's actions on the surface of the poem too much at face value; there is also an unconventional Nestor beneath the surface of the poem. In the balance between "incitement" and "restraint," the surface Nestor is mainly "restraint," the hidden Nestor is wholly "incitement." For the irony of Nestor's appearance in Agamemnon's dream in *Iliad* 2 cf. Dickson 1995:147–148, who points out that Aristarchus athetized the real Nestor's speech (Dickson 1995:147, 155n28; cf. 159).

youthful crash to Patroclus. Achilles awards last prize to Nestor as a memorial of the funeral of Patroclus, whom he will see no more (*Iliad* 23.615–621):

πέμπτον δ' ὑπελείπετ' ἄεθλον,
ἀμφίθετος φιάλη· τὴν Νέστορι δῶκεν Ἀχιλλεὺς
Ἀργείων ἀν' ἀγῶνα φέρων, καὶ ἔειπε παραστάς·
"τῆ νῦν, καὶ σοὶ τοῦτο γέρον κειμήλιον ἔστω
Πατρόκλοιο τάφου μνῆμ' ἔμμεναι· οὐ γὰρ ἔτ' αὐτὸν
ὄψῃ ἐν Ἀργείοισι· δίδωμι δέ τοι τόδ' ἄεθλον
αὔτως."

But fifth prize was left,
a two-handled bowl. Achilles gave it to Nestor,
carrying it through the assembly of the Argives; standing next
to him he said:
"Take this now, old man, and let it be your possession
to serve as a memorial of Patroclus's burial; for you will see him
no more among the Argives; I give you this prize like that,
freely."

Nestor has of course been deeply involved in Patroclus's fate since he first instigated his entry into battle in Achilles' place. We have seen that Nestor gave Patroclus a paradigm to follow in his own story in *Iliad* 11, telling how he once took his brother's place as a warrior horseman, but that the point of his story was deliberately withheld. Patroclus then followed not only Nestor's advice, but also his example in taking Achilles' place and becoming a "warrior horseman," but he paid for this with his life. It is thus entirely appropriate that the first and most important contest in Patroclus's funeral games should be the chariot race, that this race should be dominated from start to finish by Nestor, and that the unspoken point of Nestor's presence should be his own youthful catastrophe. It is a second paradigm for Patroclus, not to follow, but to explain, after the fact, what has befallen him. The point of Nestor's example is as unspoken in *Iliad* 23 as it was in *Iliad* 11, and this is important. The consistent irony of Nestor's role in relation to Patroclus shows that his role is truly of one piece.

§2.45 What is left unspoken in Nestor's story in *Iliad* 11, namely that the story concerns how he first became a horseman, becomes overt in the case of Patroclus, who is called "horseman Patroclus" when he takes Achilles' place in battle. Something similar occurs in the case of Nestor's second story. The unspoken point of this story is that Nestor crashed because he could not round the turning post. This unspoken point is relevant to Patroclus not only in general terms, but also in specific terms, for Patroclus dies when he fails to do as Achilles told him to do, to turn back from battle before it is too late. The need to do this is clearly established in Achilles' speech, when he agrees to let Patroclus go into battle but imposes a condition to protect his own honor and his companion's safety. Achilles tells Patroclus to "come back" when he has driven the Trojans from the ships (ἐκ νηῶν ἐλάσας ἰέναι πάλιν, *Iliad* 16.87), and not to wish to fight without his companion, for this would bring Achilles dishonor. Achilles then warns Patroclus against getting caught up in the heat of battle and leading an attack on Troy itself, lest Apollo enter the battle in Troy's defense. Everything that Achilles warns against is of course destined to take place, including Apollo's hand in Patroclus's death. What Patroclus for his part fails to do is what Achilles expressly commands, and that is to "turn back" as soon as he has brought the light of salvation to the Achaean ships (*Iliad* 16.95–96):

ἀλλὰ πάλιν τρωπᾶσθαι, ἐπὴν φάος ἐν νήεσσι
θήῃς, τοὺς δ' ἔτ' ἐᾶν πεδίον κάτα δηριάασθαι.

But turn back once you have put the light of salvation
among the ships, and let the others go on fighting along the
    plain.

§2.46 The failure to "turn back" is the cause of Patroclus's death as surely as it was the cause of Nestor's crash. If after slaying Sarpedon Patroclus had heeded Achilles' words, he would have lived, but instead he went after the enemy in his chariot (*Iliad* 16.684–687):

Πάτροκλος δ' ἵπποισι καὶ Αὐτομέδοντι κελεύσας
Τρῶας καὶ Λυκίους μετεκίαθε, καὶ μέγ' ἀάσθη
νήπιος· εἰ δὲ ἔπος Πηληϊάδαο φύλαξεν
ἦ τ' ἂν ὑπέκφυγε κῆρα κακὴν μέλανος θανάτοιο.

Patroclus, calling out to his horses and to Automedon,
went after the Trojans and Lycians, but he was greatly deluded,
the fool; if he had heeded the word of the son of Peleus
he would have escaped the evil doom of black death.

Patroclus's heedlessness—his failure to obey Achilles' command to turn
back—reminds us of the chariot race, and Antilochus's failure to heed
Menelaus's command to restrain himself. Antilochus, urging his chariot on
with his whip, is like a man who does not even hear: κέντρῳ ἐπισπέρχων ὡς
οὐκ ἀΐοντι ἐοικώς (Iliad 23.430). Antilochus's heedless incitement, we have
seen, reenacts the youthful Nestor's state of mind when he crashed at the
turning post. Patroclus, we now see, also reenacts this state of mind when the
gods call him to death (Iliad 16.693).[53]

§2.47 Now that we have considered the chariot race in Iliad 23 in its
own right and in relation to the fate of Patroclus, let us also consider it more
closely from the standpoint of the Indo-European twin myth. The basic
myth is that the mortal twin dies and the immortal twin brings him back
to life. This myth seems to have been transposed directly into the terms of
the chariot race that the Epeian twins won against Nestor, if we interpret
the function of holding the reins and restraining the horses as equivalent
to death, and the function of using the whip and stirring the horses up as
equivalent to bringing back to life. I have already argued that it makes sense
to interpret the inciting of the horses as a matter of bringing back to life. It is
perhaps less intuitive to see the restraining of the horses as a matter of dying,
but there is an element in the chariot race for Patroclus that suggests that
this symbolism was inherent in the twins' race and it concerns the turning
post. When Nestor points out the turning post to Antilochus, describing it
in detail, he speculates that it was either made into a turning post by earlier
generations, or that it is a grave. The latter alternative, the grave, occurs first,
and it is the significant one (Iliad 23.326–333):

> σῆμα δέ τοι ἐρέω μάλ' ἀριφραδές, οὐδέ σε λήσει.
>
> ἕστηκε ξύλον αὖον ὅσον τ' ὄργυι' ὑπὲρ αἴης
>
> ἢ δρυὸς ἢ πεύκης· τὸ μὲν οὐ καταπύθεται ὄμβρῳ,
>
> λᾶε δὲ τοῦ ἑκάτερθεν ἐρηρέδαται δύο λευκὼ
>
> ἐν ξυνοχῇσιν ὁδοῦ, λεῖος δ' ἱππόδρομος ἀμφὶς

---

53 Achilles describes the state of mind which Patroclus is to avoid—and which he instead
enters into completely—as "exulting in warfare and battle" (ἐπαγαλλόμενος πολέμῳ καὶ
δηϊοτῆτι, Iliad 16.91). It is victory over Sarpedon that brings Patroclus to this state of mind;
before encountering Sarpedon he in fact heeds Achilles' warning. When Patroclus's horses
jump the ditch (Iliad 16.380), Hector escapes (Iliad 16.383) and the Trojans flee for the city;
Patroclus does not pursue them, but turns back on the Trojans left behind and forces them
back toward the ships (ἂψ ἐπὶ νῆας ἔεργε παλιμπετές, Iliad 16.395). This action soon leads
to his fateful encounter with Sarpedon (Iliad 16.419).

ἤ τευ σῆμα βροτοῖο πάλαι κατατεθνηῶτος,
ἤ τό γε νύσσα τέτυκτο ἐπὶ προτέρων ἀνθρώπων,
καὶ νῦν τέρματ' ἔθηκε ποδάρκης δῖος Ἀχιλλεύς.

I will tell you a very clear sign, and it will not escape your notice.
A dried stump stands about an arm-span above the ground,
of oak or pine; it does not rot with the rain,
and two white stones lean against it on either side
at the juncture of the roads, and the horse-track around it is
    smooth;
either it is the grave of some mortal who died long ago,
or it was made into a racing marker among earlier men,
and swift-footed shining Achilles has made it the turning point
    now.

Since the turning post plays no part in the race to honor Patroclus, but was central to Nestor's race, we may wonder whether Nestor, with this elaborate description, does not describe the turning post in his own race against the twins, including the fact that the turning post was a grave—perhaps the grave of king Amarynkeus, whose funeral was being celebrated.[54] If so, the reason for the symbolism of death and a return to life would be clear, for the death being celebrated by the race would itself be part of the race's symbolism. It is at the turning post that the twin holding the reins—let us call him the mortal twin—exercised his function of restraining the horses in order to change directions. Nestor's hint that the turning post is a grave allows us to equate this function with dying. The grave is the actual point of death, and when this point was reached, the twin with the whip—let us call him the immortal twin—stood ready to initiate the return to life.[55]

54 Note that if the *sēma* described by Nestor was a grave it belonged to a man long dead (βροτοῖο πάλαι κατατεθνηῶτος); is this meant to connect the *sēma* with the bygone era of Nestor's own race? This would be entirely appropriate given the real purpose of the description of the *sēma* in Nestor's speech. In the Archaic period, perhaps in imitation of Nestor's description, columns seem to have been used as combined tomb markers and turning posts (see McGowan 1995).

55 In Rome, before the Circus Maximus was built in Julius Caesar's time, a place was simply "marked out" (*designatus*) in the valley between the Palatine and the Aventine for use in games (Livy 1.35.8); the starting point and the turning point for chariot races were associated with sanctuaries of two goddesses, *Stimula*, the "whip" personified, and *Murcia*, a goddess of restraint (see below). Wiseman 1995:137 makes the case that Romulus and Remus, in the augury that determined the site of the future Rome, took their stands above the two ends of the racecourse: "In Ennius' narrative of the augury contest, Romulus is on the Aventine

§2.48 We next need to consider from another perspective the immortal twin's function in the race, which is symbolized by the whip and which can be defined as "incitement." In the Indo-European twin myth, as we have seen, "bringing back to life and light," the function that the immortal twin exercised on behalf of his mortal brother, described a mental as well as a physical function. We found indirect evidence for this in both the Vedic and the Greek versions of the Indo-European twin myth, and we pointed to its significance for Nestor. For the etymology of his name, like that of the Vedic name Nā́satyā, seems to be closely related to the etymology of Greek nóos, "mind." Whereas Néstōr and Nā́satya- mean "he who brings back to life," nóos means (I argue) a "bringing back to life," and therefore Néstōr, like the Indo-European immortal twin, should personify the mental function designated by this noun.

§2.49 The chariot race in *Iliad* 23 gives good reason to equate "incitement," which characterized the youthful Nestor in his race against the Epeian twins, with nóos, and we will come to this matter shortly. But it is not immediately obvious that Nestor himself is to be connected with nóos in *Iliad* 23, for nóos belongs to his youthful race, and its role is therefore hidden, just as is his race itself. The speech of advice that the aged Nestor gives to his son is full of talk about "intelligence," and the need for it in his son's race, but it is *mē̂tis*, "shrewdness," that Nestor commends to Antilochus, not nóos: it is *mē̂tis* that will enable Antilochus to prevail in spite of slow horses. Nestor introduces this theme with the verb *mētísasthai*, saying that the other racers have faster horses than Antilochus, but they do not know how to "employ more shrewdness" (*pleíona...mētísasthai*). A virtual paean to *mē̂tis* follows, in which Antilochus is exhorted to use *mē̂tis* in every form and the advantage of *mē̂tis* is extolled in a list of pursuits, ending with that of the charioteer (*Iliad* 23.311–318):

τῶν δ' ἵπποι μὲν ἔασιν ἀφάρτεροι, οὐδὲ μὲν αὐτοὶ
πλείονα ἴσασιν σέθεν αὐτοῦ μητίσασθαι.

---

proper, and Remus on the *mons Murcus*. That means, I think, that Romulus the hasty was above the starting line of the Circus and the grove of Stimula, and Remus the slow was above the turning point of the Circus and the shrine of Murcia." If Wiseman is right, the roles of the Roman twins in relation to the chariot race are virtually the same as in Greek; this is a fascinating correspondence, but it is unclear to me whether it is due to common inheritance or borrowing (common innovation is also theoretically possible). For the two goddesses, cf. Augustine *City of God* 4.16: *vocaverunt...deam Stimulam quae ad agendum ultra modum stimularet, deam Murciam quae praeter modum non moveret ac faceret hominem...murcidam, id est nimis desidiosum et inactuosum*, "They called a goddess Stimula who *stimulated* to greater than normal activity, and a goddess Murcia who did not move a man more than normal and made him *murcidus...*, that is, excessively lazy and inactive." In the chariot race, it seems clear, the goddesses Stimula and Murcia represented "incitement" and "restraint."

ἀλλ' ἄγε δὴ σὺ φίλος <u>μῆτιν</u> ἐμβάλλεο θυμῷ
παντοίην, ἵνα μή σε παρεκπροφύγῃσιν ἄεθλα.
<u>μῆτι</u> τοι δρυτόμος μέγ' ἀμείνων ἠὲ βίηφι·
<u>μῆτι</u> δ' αὖτε κυβερνήτης ἐνὶ οἴνοπι πόντῳ
νῆα θοὴν ἰθύνει ἐρεχθομένην ἀνέμοισι·
<u>μῆτι</u> δ' ἡνίοχος περιγίγνεται ἡνιόχοιο.

The others have faster horses, but they themselves do not
know more than you how to <u>devise intelligent schemes</u>.
But come, dear son, and put into your spirit <u>intelligent schemes</u>
of all sorts so that the prizes do not escape you.
<u>By intelligence</u> the woodcutter is much better than by strength;
<u>by intelligence</u>, moreover, a helmsman on the wine-dark sea
holds his swift ship on course when it is battered by the winds;
and <u>by intelligence</u> charioteer surpasses charioteer.

The quality of *mêtis* has an undeniable relevance to Antilochus's race. His horses are slow, and he needs skill and shrewdness to win.[56] But skill and shrewdness do not really define the bold act that brings him victory. That is a matter of *nóos* if we look to the dispute for second prize, and consider how Antilochus himself characterizes his transgression when he apologizes to Menelaus. He tells Menelaus to forbear, for he, Antilochus, is young, whereas Menelaus is older and better, and the transgression that he has committed is characteristic of his youth (*Iliad* 23.587–590):

ἄνσχεο νῦν· πολλὸν γὰρ ἔγωγε νεώτερός εἰμι
σεῖο ἄναξ Μενέλαε, σὺ δὲ πρότερος καὶ ἀρείων.
οἶσθ' οἷαι νέου ἀνδρὸς ὑπερβασίαι τελέθουσι·
<u>κραιπνότερος μὲν γάρ τε νόος, λεπτὴ δέ τε μῆτις</u>.

Have patience with me now, for I am much younger
than you, lord Menelaos; you are older and better.
You know what the transgressions of a young man are like:
<u>his *nóos* is swifter, but his *mêtis* is slight</u>.

56 Note what the poet says of Antilochus when he finishes the race in second place ahead of Menelaus (*Iliad* 23.515): κέρδεσιν, οὔ τι τάχει γε, παραφθάμενος Μενέλαον, "overtaking Menelaus not by speed, but by tricks." The word *kérdesin* here is to be compared with *kérdea* in Nestor's characterization of the skillful charioteer (*Iliad* 23.322): ὃς δέ κε <u>κέρδεα</u> εἰδῇ ἐλαύνων ἥσσονας ἵππους, "but the one who, driving worse horses, knows all the <u>tricks</u>."

The phrase *leptḕ dé te mḗtis* is clear. "Slight" *mḗtis* means too little *mḗtis*, and that is what Antilochus has displayed by his reckless act.[57] But the phrase *kraipnóteros mèn gár te nóos*, "his *nóos* is swifter," or "his *nóos* is too swift," requires comment. If *nóos* is associated with speed in the first place—if, that is, *nóos* is a matter of "incitement," and is symbolized by the whip—then a *nóos* that is "too swift" may in some sense be said to be too much itself rather than too little.[58] This amounts to saying that Antilochus's bold act was indeed an act of *nóos*, but of *nóos* unbalanced by its opposite, restraint.

§2.50 Menelaus, who during the race calls out to Antilochus that he is driving "foolishly" (*aphradéōs hippázeai*, Iliad 23.426), after the race, when he accepts Antilochus's apology, uses words that imply that Antilochus's mind was uncharacteristically unbalanced in this race (*Iliad* 23.602–604):

Ἀντίλοχε νῦν μέν τοι ἐγὼν ὑποείξομαι αὐτὸς
χωόμενος, ἐπεὶ οὔ τι παρήορος οὐδ' ἀεσίφρων
ἦσθα πάρος.

Antilochus, I yield to you now myself
although I am angry, since you were not at all loose-witted or
      deluded in your mind
before this.[59]

---

57 This is so despite his father's earlier statement that the other contestants do not surpass Antilochus in *mḗtis*. The notion that a young man lacks *mḗtis* implies that *mḗtis* comes with age, and this too fits with the aged Nestor's ringing endorsement of the quality in his speech of advice to his son (Nestor's age similarly associates him with "restraint"; cf. §2.77 below and EN2.1 [end] to n2. 62 below). Another factor in Nestor's focus on *mḗtis* in this speech is that *mḗtis* implies deception, and Nestor's very use of the word, as suggested above, is itself a disguise, masking the quality that marked his own youthful crash. As Sfyroeras (unpublished) points out, the phrase *huphaínein érkheto mētin*, "began to weave *mḗtis*," which is twice used of Nestor in the *Iliad* to introduce plans of his own devising (the Achaean wall in *Iliad* 7.324 and the embassy to Achilles in *Iliad* 9.93), implies deception (cf. *Odyssey* 9.422, where *dólous*, "wiles," is added as a second object to *mētin*; cf. also *Odyssey* 4.678, 4.739, 5.356, 13.303, 13.386, *Iliad* 6.187). Nestor's role in the *Iliad* is marked by irony not only in the chariot race, but throughout (cf. n2.52 above), and this pervasive irony gives him a wily aspect close to *mḗtis*. For another perspective on the role of *mḗtis* in Antilochus's race, cf. Detienne and Vernant 1974, chapter 1.

58 For the connection of *nóos* with speed, cf. also *Odyssey* 7.36: ὠκεῖαι ὡς εἰ πτερὸν ἠὲ νόημα "fast as an arrow or a thought (*nóēma*)," a comparison for the speed of the Phaeacian ships, and *Iliad* 15.80: ὡς δ' ὅτ' ἂν ἀΐξῃ νόος ἀνέρος, "as when a man's *nóos* darts," a comparison for Hera's speed; cf. Frame 1978:79 with n72. A different pairing of *nóos* and *mḗtis* occurs in *Iliad* 10. 226: ἀλλά τέ οἱ βράσσων τε νόος, λεπτὴ δέ τε μῆτις, "but his *nóos* is too short and his *mḗtis* slight"; as opposed to *nóos* that is too swift, *nóos* that is "too short" (*brássōn*) is *nóos* that is too little rather than too much.

59 The adjective *paréoros*, which means "loosely attached (mentally)," may in this instance also contain a suggestion of loose control over horses; note that the noun *paréoros* means

He concludes this line of thought with the ringing alliterative phrase νῦν αὖτε νόον νίκησε νεοίη, "but now youth has overcome your *nóos.*"[60] The sense of imbalance and of the recklessness of youth in Menelaus's characterization hits the mark, but he is wrong when he says that Antilochus's *nóos* has been defeated. That could have been said of the youthful Nestor, who crashed, but in Antilochus's race it is *nóos* that has triumphed. We see this in the race itself, when Antilochus calls out to his horses to pass Menelaus, and he says that he himself will contrive and "perceive" (*noḗsō*) when to pass on the narrow road (*Iliad* 23.415–416):

> ταῦτα δ᾽ ἐγὼν αὐτὸς τεχνήσομαι ἠδὲ <u>νοήσω</u>
> στεινωπῷ ἐν ὁδῷ παραδύμεναι, οὐδέ με λήσει.

> But I myself will contrive this and <u>perceive the right moment for it,</u>
> how to pass on the narrow road, and it will not escape my notice.

The verb *noḗō* also occurs in the introduction to Nestor's speech of advice, when, standing by his son's side, about to offer counsel for his benefit, he is said to direct his words to "one who already has *nóos* himself" (*Iliad* 23.304–305):

> πατὴρ δέ οἱ ἄγχι παραστὰς
> μυθεῖτ᾽ εἰς ἀγαθὰ φρονέων <u>νοέοντι καὶ αὐτῷ.</u>

> Standing near him his father
> spoke to him with good intentions, <u>and he himself already understood.</u>

If the phrase *noéonti kaì autôi* is a signal before the race starts of the role that *nóos* will play in Antilochus's victory, then the final statement concerning his race, when second prize is at last awarded, also concerns *nóos*, and it underscores the crucial role that *nóos* has played in this race. Menelaus, who refuses to allow second prize to go to Antilochus, and who pointedly says to him "youth has overcome your *nóos,*" is, so to speak, corrected on both points

---

the (loosely attached) "trace horse."

60 νεοίη, "youth," is a *hapax legomenon*; see Matthews 1996:385–386 for the possibility that Antimachus in the fifth century BC read νόον νίκησε <u>νόημα</u> in this line, whatever such an unlikely phrase would have meant.

when, bowing to Antilochus's own renewed sense of restraint, he hands over second prize to Antilochus's companion, who is named, significantly, *Noḗmōn* (*Iliad* 23.609–613):

"τώ τοι λισσομένῳ ἐπιπείσομαι, ἠδὲ καὶ ἵππον
δώσω ἐμήν περ ἐοῦσαν, ἵνα γνώωσι καὶ οἵδε
ὡς ἐμὸς οὔ ποτε θυμὸς ὑπερφίαλος καὶ ἀπηνής."
Ἦ ῥα, καὶ Ἀντιλόχοιο <u>Νοήμονι</u> δῶκεν ἑταίρῳ
ἵππον ἄγειν· ὃ δ' ἔπειτα λέβηθ' ἔλε παμφανόωντα.

"Therefore I will be persuaded by you since you appease me so,
    and I will give up
the mare, even though it is mine, so that these men may know
how my spirit is never arrogant or harsh."
So he spoke, and he gave the horse to <u>Noemon</u>, Antilochus's
    companion,
to lead away; then he took the all-shining cauldron.

The name *Noḗmōn*, derived from *nóēma*, "thought," and thus indirectly from *noéō* and *nóos*, is a good name for a servant of Nestor, which is what this figure seems intended to be.[61] But he is heard of nowhere else, and he has every appearance of having been created for the occasion so that his name, and his action in taking second prize from Menelaus, may say all that needs to be said to sum up Antilochus's victory: this was a victory of *nóos*—overly swift *nóos* to be sure, but *nóos* all the more for that.[62]

---

61 The name of Nestor's maidservant in *Iliad* 11, *Hekamḗdē*, daughter of *Arsínoos*, similarly reflects Nestor's own characterization (see §2.12 above).

62 Two other minor figures in Homer are named *Noḗmōn*: one lends Telemachus his ship for the journey to Pylos (*Odyssey* 4.630–657); the other is a Lycian slain by Odysseus (*Iliad* 5.678; Odysseus slays six other Lycians in the same passage, two of whom, Alastor and Chromios, also have names connected with Nestor; see n1.8 above). It perhaps seems counterintuitive that *nóos* is aligned with "incitement" rather than "restraint" in an opposition between the two qualities; in Plato, where *nóos* represents reason as opposed to both warlike spirit (*thumós*) and the lower appetites (*epithumíai*), *nóos* would seem to be on the side of "restraint" rather than "incitement" (although the role of *éros* in causing the soul's upward movement toward the "noetic" realm suggests a more complicated picture). In Homer too one can make the case that words for mental activity (*mêtis, boulḗ, nóos*) all tend to be used in opposition to the word or the concept of *bíē*, "force," and thus to represent "restraint" as opposed to a "lack of restraint" characteristic of a warrior's *bíē* (cf. Wilson 2005:9–10). But the opposition in the twin myth operates along a different axis from this; the warrior quality at issue in the twin myth, insofar as it is aligned with "restraint," is that of the defensive warrior, for which the proper word is *alkḗ* rather than *bíē* (see Benveniste

§2.51 What we have found in the race of Antilochus with respect to *nóos* really pertains to Nestor himself. For, as we saw earlier, Antilochus reembodies the unrestrained incitement of his father in his father's race against the Epeian twins.[63] We can now say that a sense of unrestrained incitement is as intrinsic to the noun *nóos* as it is to the name *Néstōr*. The noun and the name are indistinguishable in the analysis of Nestor's race against the twins. The symbol of both is the whip. The danger of unrestrained *nóos* suggests that the word itself, and what it denoted, originated in the context of a larger duality, in which "incitement" was balanced by restraint. This amounts to saying that the noun *nóos* originated in the context of the Indo-European twin myth. What is most striking is that this context was still very much alive, and well understood, in the Homeric period, as we can see from *Iliad* 23.

§2.52 There is a further aspect of the chariot race in *Iliad* 23 that seems relevant to *nóos* and its etymological meaning "bringing back to life/bringing back to the light," and that is the whole issue of deliberate concealment and the need by the Homeric audience to "perceive" what is intentionally left unsaid. The phrase *oudé se lései* (and its variants) is used four times to draw attention to what is deliberately hidden, and what is hidden in the episode can be reduced to a single issue, namely the youthful Nestor's unrestrained "incitement." This is the missing link that connects Nestor's speech with Antilochus's race, and this is what is left out when the aged Nestor dwells on the care to be exercised in rounding the turning post, and when he later receives the prize that should have gone to the charioteer who crashed. The Homeric audience itself is called on to "bring back to light" the youthful Nestor's unrestrained "incitement," which is to say his *nóos*, the quality with which his name identifies him. Nestor's role in the chariot race, one might say, is so constructed as to involve the audience in a process of *nóos* over the very meaning of the word.[64]

1969:2.72–74 for *alkḗ*). As for *nóos*, significant as the etymology may be in a context like the chariot race of *Iliad* 23, etymology does not restrict the word's range of use in other Homeric contexts; cf. the remarks in n1.105 above. Other questions with respect to the opposition between "incitement" and "restraint," including how a different opposition between *mêtis* and *bíē* compares with it, are discussed in EN2.1.

63 I earlier raised the question why Nestor, if his name associates him with *nóos*, should extol *mêtis* in his speech of advice to Antilochus (§1.39 above). I think the answer is now clear: Antilochus's characterization of the transgressions of a young man—that his *nóos* is too swift and his *mêtis* slight—is really meant to characterize the young Nestor. Thus the aged Nestor's paean to *mêtis*, while not out of character (cf. n2.57 above), is nevertheless highly ironic. It is part of the intentional concealment of the young Nestor's role in *Iliad* 23.

64 Nagy 1983 analyzes the relationship between the verb *noéō*, "perceive," and the noun *sêma*, "sign," in various epic contexts, including the chariot race of *Iliad* 23. He draws attention to

§2.53 If Greek *nóos*, as derived from the root **nes-*, originated in the context of the Indo-European twin myth, a question arises about Greek *nóstos*, "return home." Did this noun, in its earlier meaning "return to life," also originate in the context of the Indo-European twin myth? The key to this question is Nestor's role in the *Odyssey*, to which we now turn. Before we do, however, we must touch on one last issue in *Iliad* 23, namely the relationship between the funeral games for Patroclus and the *nóstoi* of the Achaeans from Troy.

§2.54 A connection between the funeral games of *Iliad* 23 and the *nóstoi* of the Achaeans has been noticed before.[65] The clearest example is the footrace, in which the contest between Odysseus and the lesser Ajax seems to foreshadow the *nóstoi* of both heroes. Near the end of the footrace Odysseus prays to Athena, and she makes his limbs light and gives him victory, just as she will one day help him to return home; Ajax, on the other hand, she trips in cow dung, just as she will one day send a storm and wreck his ships.[66] There is nothing surprising in this connection between a footrace—a *díaulos*, with two legs and a turn between—and a return home. In Aeschylus's *Agamemnon* Clytemnestra uses this very image when she says of her husband, who has not yet completed his *nóstos*, that he must "*turn* the other leg of the double racecourse back again" (*Agamemnon* 343–344):

δεῖ γὰρ πρὸς οἴκους <u>νοστίμου</u> σωτηρίας

<u>κάμψαι</u> διαύλου θάτερον κῶλον πάλιν.

---

the phrase *oudé se lései*, "it will not escape your notice," which Nestor uses in relation to the turning post, and to the variations of this phrase throughout the chariot race of *Iliad* 23. He points out that in *Odyssey* 11, when Teiresias tells Odysseus the *sêma* by which he will know where to plant his oar after his return home, he uses the same line as Nestor in his reference to the turning post (*Odyssey* 11.126 = *Iliad* 23.326): <u>σῆμα</u> δέ τοι ἐρέω μάλ᾽ ἀριφραδές, <u>οὐδέ σε λήσει</u>, "I will tell you a very clear <u>sign, and it will not escape your notice</u>." A *sêma*, "sign," is something to be understood as well as perceived, as Nagy points out. The turning post is the key to the chariot race and to Nestor's role in it, the word *sêma*, as illuminated by Nagy, seems especially apt when Nestor himself first draws attention to it. The special importance of the word in the context of the turning post is indicated by the fact that it occurs again five lines later in Nestor's speech, here in the meaning "grave" (text in §2.47 above). The repetition of the word is like the repetition of the phrase *oudé he léthei*, "and it does not escape his notice," in the form *oudé se lései*, "and it will not escape your notice," within four lines in the very same context.

65 Cf. Whitman 1958:263–264 on connections between contests in *Iliad* 23 and the later fates of heroes.

66 Athena's role in the footrace (*Iliad* 23.768–783) is after the turn: ἀλλ᾽ ὅτε δὴ πύματον τέλεον δρόμον, "but when they were completing the end of the course," *Iliad* 23.768. For the storm sent against Ajax see *Odyssey* 4.499–502, and cf. *Odyssey* 5.108–111, and 3.135 and 166. With Odysseus's prayer to Athena in the footrace (*Iliad* 23.770) one might compare his prayer to Athena near the end of his *nóstos*, in which he asks that he win favor with the Phaeacians, his ultimate homebringers (*Odyssey* 6.324–327).

For there is need of the salvation of a <u>return</u> home,
to <u>turn</u> the other leg of the double racecourse back again.[67]

It is also clear from a general perspective why there should be a connection between funeral games and the *nóstoi* of the competitors, given the context of death of the funeral games and the underlying context of death and a return to life of the *nóstoi*. It would seem that the chariot race above all, in which the symbolism of a death and return to life is inherent in the grave that serves as a turning post, should foreshadow the competitors' *nóstoi*, and indeed a connection between Diomedes' blazing victory in the chariot race and his easy *nóstos* has been noticed.[68] There is more to say about Diomedes in this regard, and there is also something to be said about Menelaus, who eventually reaches home, and Antilochus as well, who dies in Troy. We will return to the races of all three of these heroes in relation to their *nóstoi* once we have considered Nestor's role in the *Odyssey* and the Achaeans' *nóstoi* on their own terms. But it must be recognized from the outset that the chariot race is connected with the *nóstoi* only secondarily. This is clear when we consider Eumelos. The reason that he crashes has nothing to do with his *nóstos* as far as we know. Eumelos crashes, as we have seen, in order to reenact, in transposed form, the crash of the youthful Nestor. Eumelos was chosen for this role because he had the fastest horses, and was considered, with Diomedes, the best charioteer.[69] The primary function of the chariot race in *Iliad* 23 is to reenact Nestor's race in all its dimensions. Therefore the primary connection with the *nóstoi* is shifted to the footrace, where maximum point and contrast are achieved through the participation of Odysseus and Ajax. We should also note that the chariot race is linked to the footrace, and is illuminated by it,

---

67 The phrase νοστίμου σωτηρίας, "salvation of a return home," is repeated from Aeschylus's *Persians* 797, where the ghost of Dareios says that the defeated Persian army will not meet with νοστίμου σωτηρίας (i.e. will not return from Greece).

68 Whitman 1958:264.

69 According to "Apollodorus" *Epitome* 5.5 Eumelos wins the chariot race in the funeral games of Achilles. If this is an old tradition it would explain why Achilles calls Eumelos "best" and awards him a special prize despite his loss. For further discussion, see n2.117 below. In Quintus of Smyrna the chariot race for Achilles (4.500–544) has a long gap in it (after 4.524) and it is not clear who the victor is: Eumelos takes the early lead, as in the games for Patroclus, but Menelaus rejoices in his "victory" at the end of the episode (4.522 and 541). It is not clear that Menelaus's "victory" means first prize (consider his contest with Antilochus for second prize in *Iliad* 23), and it is not clear why Eumelos, with the fastest horses, should have failed to win first prize; we may infer that he did not crash from the fact that two other competitors, Thoas and Eurypylos, fell from their chariots and are treated for wounds after the race (4.538–540). In what remains of the episode there is no indication how Eumelos finished the race after taking the early lead.

in the dispute between spectators. For it is the same Ajax, who will soon be tripped in cow dung by Athena, who abusively contradicts Idomeneus, saying that Eumelos is still in first place in the chariot race. Ajax does not know that Athena has shattered Eumelos's yoke and sent him to the ground, just as he does not foresee that she will soon do the same thing to him in the footrace, and much worse later in his *nóstos*. Thus the crash of Eumelos is indirectly connected with Ajax's *nóstos*, but not his own. The footrace and the chariot race must be considered together to see the connection between the games of *Iliad* 23 and the *nóstoi*. It is both races that make this connection.[70]

§2.55 Something else is missing in the relationship between the chariot race and the *nóstoi*, and that is Nestor's own role in the *nóstoi*, to which we now turn. Nestor is not a competitor in the chariot race, so he cannot be part of any transfer from one event to the other in the same way as, say, Diomedes. But Nestor is in fact far from being absent altogether from the picture. I noted earlier that Nestor is twice featured as a horseman in the action at Troy, in *Iliad* 8 and in *Iliad* 11. We have dealt with *Iliad* 11, where Nestor rescues the wounded Makhaon on his chariot and brings him to his tent. We have yet to deal with *Iliad* 8, where "the horseman Nestor" first appears as such in the poem. This episode works with the chariot race in *Iliad* 23 to complete the picture of Nestor's part in the *nóstoi*, which is crucial, and which affects three others who compete in the two races of *Iliad* 23, namely Diomedes, Antilochus, and Odysseus. After we consider Nestor's account of the *nóstoi* in *Odyssey* 3 we will consider his role in *Iliad* 8 and then return for a final look at *Iliad* 23.

---

70 Antilochus, who comes in last behind both Odysseus and Ajax in the footrace (*Iliad* 23.785–792), is another link with the chariot race, in which he is an apparent victor. In terms of his *nóstos*—Antilochus dies at Troy—it is the footrace that counts; his role in the chariot race has primarily to do with his father's former race, and not his own later fate.

Chapter 6.

ODYSSEY 3 AND ILIAD 8

§2.56 In the *Odyssey* Nestor is the same figure as in the *Iliad* except that he is now at home in Pylos ten years after the war. In the *Iliad* he is said to have outlived two generations of men and to rule in yet a third; in the *Odyssey* much the same is said of him.[71] In the *Iliad*, as we have seen, Nestor plays a large role of an unusual sort in the story of Patroclus. His role is based upon his own epic traditions concerning his youth, as he retells them in his advanced old age. In the *Odyssey* he is called on to tell another story, but not about his youth. Telemachus visits him to ask about his father, Odysseus, who has not returned to Ithaca in the ten years since the war ended, but whose death has also not been reported. Telemachus wants to hear what Nestor knows, either from direct observation or from hearsay. Nestor tells him, but his story is all about what he himself saw and experienced at first hand soon after the fall of Troy, when the Achaeans left for home. He then parted company with Odysseus, and he has heard nothing about him since. Telemachus thus learns little to encourage him, and he must wait until he visits Menelaus in Sparta to learn what Menelaus heard from Proteus, the old man of the sea, that Odysseus is still alive on Calypso's island.[72]

§2.57 In the *Iliad* the stories about Nestor's youth that relate to Patroclus are told in such a way as to conceal their true purpose and point. Their relevance is not on the surface of the poem, but just below the surface. Something similar is at work in Nestor's account of the departure from Troy. In the *Iliad* what is deliberately withheld is Nestor's myth, in which he does not save his warrior brother, but takes his place. In the *Odyssey* the same myth remains

---

71 See n1.2 above for a comparison of *Iliad* 1.250–252 with *Odyssey* 3.245–246.
72 *Odyssey* 4.555–560.

the essence of the figure Nestor, and it explains what really took place when Nestor last saw Odysseus. What must also be kept in mind, however, is the meaning of Nestor's name, for this is central to his role in the *Odyssey*. *Néstōr* is "he who brings home," and when he parts company from Odysseus at the very moment of the Achaeans' homecoming from Troy, he reenacts his own myth, for just as he did not save his brother, he does not bring Odysseus home. What the consequences of this are for Odysseus remain to be considered, but they do involve a kind of death, just as in the case of Nestor's brother Periklymenos. Although Odysseus will return from this death it will not be by Nestor's agency, but through others. In and of itself, Nestor's role in the homecoming of Odysseus is a negative one based on his own myth, and this is the unspoken point of *Odyssey* 3.

§2.58 The key point in this, and the point with which we begin, is that a *nóstos* has an essential connection with the Indo-European twin myth. This is not an obvious point when we think of the return home from Troy of an entire army or its various contingents. Nestor too knows from hearsay how various contingents fared once they departed from Troy, and he passes this information on to Telemachus, mentioning the safe return of the Myrmidons under Achilles' son, of Philoktetes, and of the Cretans under Idomeneus (*Odyssey* 3.186–192). But this is not the heart of his story. Phemios also sings of the "return of the Achaeans" to the suitors in *Odyssey* 1, and in the brief description of his song this return is characterized as a "grim" one (*Odyssey* 1.326–327):

ὁ δ' Ἀχαιῶν νόστον ἄειδε
λυγρόν, ὃν ἐκ Τροίης ἐπετείλατο Παλλὰς Ἀθήνη.

He sang of the Achaeans' grim return,
which Pallas Athena ordained for them from Troy.

It is this grim return, brought on by Pallas Athena, that Nestor recounts first, and from firsthand experience, to Telemachus. If we follow his account in detail, we will find not only how the entire Achaean *nóstos* is conceived of in terms of the twin myth, but also how this myth relates to Nestor and Odysseus.

§2.59 When Telemachus begs Nestor to tell him the truth, if ever Odysseus carried out a promised word or deed for him at Troy, Nestor thinks first of the grief that the Achaeans suffered at Troy, which he recalls as the place of death for all the best of the Achaeans, and he names Ajax, Achilles,

Patroclus, and his own son Antilochus, who all perished there (*Odyssey* 3.103–112). As for the many other evils that they suffered at Troy, he could not tell them all if Telemachus stayed five or six years to ask about them (*Odyssey* 3.113–117). When Nestor goes on to mention the evils that for nine years the Achaeans devised against the Trojans "with all kinds of wiles" (*pantoíoisi dóloisi*, *Odyssey* 3.119), and that Zeus barely brought to completion, the way is prepared to introduce the subject of Odysseus, and of Nestor's own relationship with Odysseus. No one, he says, wished to compete with Odysseus in *mêtis* (*Odyssey* 3.120), for he was by far the best "in all kinds of wiles" (*pantoíoisi dóloisi*, *Odyssey* 3.122).[73] After paying Telemachus a compliment for his own "seemly" speech, which is so like his father's (*Odyssey* 3.122–125), Nestor says that during the war he and Odysseus never disagreed with each other in an assembly or a council, but "having one mind" (*héna thumòn ékhonte*) they counseled what was best for the Argives (*Odyssey* 3.126–129):

> ἔνθ' ἦ τοι εἷος μὲν ἐγὼ καὶ δῖος Ὀδυσσεὺς
> οὔτε ποτ' εἰν ἀγορῇ δίχ' ἐβάζομεν οὔτ' ἐνὶ βουλῇ,
> ἀλλ' ἕνα θυμὸν ἔχοντε νόῳ καὶ ἐπίφρονι βουλῇ
> φραζόμεθ' Ἀργείοισιν ὅπως ὄχ' ἄριστα γένοιτο.

> During the time there shining Odysseus and I
> never spoke on opposite sides in assembly or council,
> but with one spirit, by intelligence and wise counsel,
> we advised the Argives how what was best might come about.

§2.60 But things changed after Troy was captured, as is signaled by the word, *autár*, "however," as Nestor's story continues; what happened "during the war, on the one hand" (*heîos mén*, *Odyssey* 3.126) was not the same as what happened after the war (*autàr epeí*, "however, when," *Odyssey* 3.130). But the significance of the word *autár* for the relationship between Nestor and Odysseus after the war had ended will not be brought out for another twenty-nine lines. First we will hear what befell the Achaeans as a whole after Troy was sacked. This is the story of the "grim return" of the Achaeans that Phemios began to tell in Book 1. In Nestor's account, it was first of all Zeus who devised this "grim return" for the Argives, because of the wrongs committed by some of them. But, as in Phemios's song, it was Athena, who,

---

73 Cf. Odysseus's characterization of himself in *Odyssey* 9.19–20: *hòs pâsi dóloisin / anthrópoisi mélō*, "(I) who am a concern to (am known to) all men for my wiles."

because of her own anger, caused the actual destruction of many of the Achaeans (*Odyssey* 3.130–135):

αὐτὰρ ἐπεὶ Πριάμοιο πόλιν διεπέρσαμεν αἰπήν,

[βῆμεν δ᾽ ἐν νήεσσι, θεὸς δ᾽ ἐκέδασσεν Ἀχαιούς,]

καὶ τότε δὴ Ζεὺς λυγρὸν ἐνὶ φρεσὶ μήδετο νόστον

Ἀργείοισ᾽, ἐπεὶ οὔ τι νοήμονες οὐδὲ δίκαιοι

πάντες ἔσαν. τῶ σφεων πολέες κακὸν οἶτον ἐπέσπον

μήνιος ἐξ ὀλοῆς γλαυκώπιδος ὀβριμοπάτρης.

But when we had sacked the steep city of Priam,
[and we went in our ships and the god scattered the Achaeans,]
then indeed Zeus plotted in his mind a grim return
for the Argives, since not all were prudent or just;
thus many of them met an evil fate
because of the anger of the destructive grey-eyed one, daughter
of a mighty father.

What Athena did first to set this "grim return" in motion was to cause a quarrel (*éris*) between the two Atreidai, the commanders-in-chief of the Achaeans: ἥ τ᾽ ἔριν Ἀτρεΐδῃσι μετ᾽ ἀμφοτέροισιν ἔθηκε (*Odyssey* 3.136). The scene of the quarrel was a drunken and disorderly assembly of the entire army which the Atreidai called at nightfall (*Odyssey* 3.137–140):

τὼ δὲ καλεσσαμένω ἀγορὴν ἐς πάντας Ἀχαιούς,

μάψ, ἀτὰρ οὐ κατὰ κόσμον, ἐς ἠέλιον καταδύντα,

οἱ δ᾽ ἦλθον οἴνῳ βεβαρηότες υἷες Ἀχαιῶν,

μῦθον μυθείσθην, τοῦ εἵνεκα λαὸν ἄγειραν.

Those two called an assembly for all the Achaeans,
carelessly and without proper order, as the sun was setting,
and the sons of the Achaeans came, heavy with wine;
both made speeches telling why they had gathered the warriors.

The Atreidai had called the assembly to consider the army's return, but they disagreed over what should be done. Menelaus spoke first, and he urged the Achaeans "to remember their *nóstos*," but this did not please Agamemnon, who foolishly wished "to restrain the army," and to try to appease the angry Athena with sacrifices (*Odyssey* 3.141–147):

ἔνθ' ἦ τοι Μενέλαος ἀνώγει πάντας Ἀχαιοὺς
νόστου μιμνήσκεσθαι ἐπ' εὐρέα νῶτα θαλάσσης·
οὐδ' Ἀγαμέμνονι πάμπαν ἑήνδανε· βούλετο γάρ ῥα
λαὸν ἐρυκακέειν ῥέξαι θ' ἱερὰς ἑκατόμβας,
ὡς τὸν Ἀθηναίης δεινὸν χόλον ἐξακέσαιτο,
νήπιος, οὐδὲ τὸ ἤδη, ὃ οὐ πείσεσθαι ἔμελλεν·
οὐ γάρ τ' αἶψα θεῶν τρέπεται νόος αἰὲν ἐόντων.

Then Menelaus urged all the Achaeans
to remember their return across the wide back of the sea;
but this did not please Agamemnon at all; for he wanted
to restrain the warriors and offer sacred hecatombs
to appease the dread anger of Athena—
the fool, he did not know that she was not to be persuaded,
for the mind of the gods who are forever is not quickly changed.

§2.61 Athena sets the "grim return" of the Achaeans in motion by causing a split between the two Atreidai. As we have noted earlier, the Atreidai, in their association with Helen, are twin figures.[74] What finally divides them is the very issue of their *nóstos*, and their opposition to each other in the Achaean assembly strikingly resembles, in what each brother wants to do separately, the different functions that the Epeian twins performed between them in their chariot race against Nestor: to "incite" on the one hand, and to "restrain" on the other hand. Menelaus, who "urged all the Achaeans to remember their return," has the function of the immortal twin, which is to "incite" and to "bring back to life"; these two ideas are in fact intertwined, since the context of Menelaus's incitement is a *nóstos*, with its underlying sense of a "return to life." Agamemnon, who "wished to restrain the army," has the mortal twin's function. The context is again significant, for Troy, as Nestor emphasizes at the beginning of his speech, was a place of death, and to "restrain" the army there was in effect to deny it a *nóstos* in both senses of the word, not only a "return home," but also a "return to life." Thus the Atreidai exercised the functions of the twins of the Indo-European myth, but they did not work together, as the Epeian twins did in the chariot race, but split apart. For the Atreidai themselves the consequence of this split was a sharp contrast in their fates. Whereas Menelaus, despite delays on the way,

74 See n1.156 above.

would eventually reach home in Sparta, and beyond that was fated not to die, but to be sent to live in bliss in the Elysian fields because of his marriage to Helen, the daughter of Zeus (*Odyssey* 4.561–569), Agamemnon would perish *en nóstōi*, "in his *nóstos*" (*Odyssey* 4.497) at the hands of his wife Clytemnestra. In other words, Agamemnon, despite the fact that he would again set foot on his native soil, would not have a *nóstos* in the sense of a "safe return."[75]

§2.62 The division between the Atreidai had consequences not only for themselves, but for the Achaean army as a whole. When the Atreidai quarreled in the assembly about their *nóstos*, the army was split in two (*Odyssey* 3.148–150):

ὣς τὼ μὲν χαλεποῖσιν ἀμειβομένω ἐπέεσσιν
ἕστασαν· οἱ δ' ἀνόρουσαν ἐϋκνήμιδες Ἀχαιοὶ
ἠχῇ θεσπεσίῃ, δίχα δέ σφισιν ἥνδανε βουλή.

So those two stood there exchanging harsh words;
the well-greaved Achaeans rose
with a deafening roar, and were split in the counsel that they
favored.

The two factions passed the night harboring harsh thoughts toward each other in their minds, and when dawn came one part of the army, including Nestor, prepared to set sail (*Odyssey* 3.151–154):

νύκτα μὲν ἀέσαμεν χαλεπὰ φρεσὶν ὁρμαίνοντες
ἀλλήλοισ'· ἐπὶ γὰρ Ζεὺς ἤρτυε πῆμα κακοῖο·
ἠῶθεν δ' οἱ μὲν νέας ἕλκομεν εἰς ἅλα δῖαν
κτήματά τ' ἐντιθέμεσθα βαθυζώνους τε γυναῖκας.

---

75 Ajax too died *en nóstōi*; Proteus, the old man of the sea, refers to Ajax and Agamemnon in one breath as the two leaders of the Achaeans to suffer this fate (*Odyssey* 4.496–497): ἀρχοὶ δ' αὖ δύο μοῦνοι Ἀχαιῶν χαλκοχιτώνων / ἐν νόστῳ ἀπόλοντο, "two leaders only of the bronze-clad Achaeans / perished in their return." Whereas Ajax perished in the middle of the sea, Agamemnon perished at home, but neither one achieved a *nóstos* (cf. *Odyssey* 24.96, where Agamemnon's shade refers to his own death *en nóstōi*, "in my return"). The reason that Ajax and Agamemnon are paired in Proteus's speech is, I think, that they are examples of the two great dangers that Odysseus must face to achieve his *nóstos*: surviving Poseidon's attack on him at sea when he nears Scheria (Ajax was destroyed at sea by Poseidon), and overcoming the rivals for his wife (Agamemnon was destroyed by the rival for his wife). A successful *nóstos*, in the sense that Odysseus will achieve it, is contrasted with the failed *nóstos* of both heroes.

We spent the night harboring harsh thoughts in our minds
against each other; for Zeus prepared pain of evil for us;
at dawn some of us dragged our ships into the shining sea
and put aboard our possessions and deeply girdled women.

But the half of the army remaining with Agamemnon was "restrained" as the others put out to sea (*Odyssey* 3.155–158):

ἡμίσεες δ' ἄρα λαοὶ ἐρητύοντο μένοντες
αὖθι παρ' Ἀτρεΐδῃ Ἀγαμέμνονι, ποιμένι λαῶν·
ἡμίσεες δ' ἀναβάντες ἐλαύνομεν· αἱ δὲ μάλ' ὦκα
ἔπλεον, ἐστόρεσεν δὲ θεὸς μεγακήτεα πόντον.

But half of the warriors were held back there waiting
with the son of Atreus, Agamemnon, shepherd of the warriors;
the other half of us went aboard and rowed away; the ships
      quickly
set sail, and the god smoothed the sea teeming with great
      creatures.

In these lines, with the division of the army into two halves, one of which is "restrained" while the other half begins its return, it is clear that the twin myth enacted by the Atreidai sets the basic terms for the whole "grim return" of the Achaeans. It is hard not to equate the two halves of the army with those who would achieve a safe *nóstos* and those who would not. This does not mean that we need to catalogue every contingent at Troy on one side or the other, or that even the poet could have done so. The division is, I think, intended to be schematic rather than comprehensive. For Agamemnon and those whom he "restrained," the outlook was not good. At best they were guilty of "foolishness" in thinking an angered Athena could be appeased (cf. *népios*, "foolish," of Agamemnon in *Odyssey* 3.146).[76] Presumably this half of the army also coincided with the evildoers who caused Athena's wrath in the first place, although we can name only a few of these, and perhaps the poet could not have named many more.[77] Again the categories seem to

---

76 The immortal twin was marked by "intelligence," and the "foolishness" of Agamemnon, the mortal twin in this situation, should be viewed from this perspective.
77 Ajax is the only real evildoer. Agamemnon himself is treated as an undeserving victim by the *Odyssey*. It has been argued that Odysseus too merited Athena's wrath, but that the tradition for this is naturally minimized in the *Odyssey*; Jenny Clay, for example, argues that Athena's long absence during Odysseus's *nóstos* is explained by his culpability (Clay

be suggestive rather than all inclusive. The basic categories, however, are those that emerge from the twin myth as reenacted by the Atreidai. Like the Atreidai, the army was divided into those who would achieve a safe *nóstos* and those who would not.

§2.63 Nestor's account, having made clear that the basic terms of the Achaeans' *nóstos* are those of the twin myth, next focuses on his own role in this *nóstos*. As we have seen, Nestor was with the half of the army that set sail on the morning after the army was split by the quarrel. His account is about to come back to the point from which he began, and which has been left hanging in the meantime, namely his relationship with Odysseus. During the war, he said, he and Odysseus never disagreed with one another in an assembly or council, but "with one mind" they devised what was best for the Argives by their wits and shrewd council; but when Troy was sacked, things (we infer) changed. We have heard how Zeus devised an evil homecoming for the Achaeans, and how Athena split the army in two. Now, twenty-nine lines later, we learn that the unanimity between Nestor and Odysseus during the war did indeed change after the war, just as the word *autár* in *Odyssey* 3.130 implies. For when those with Menelaus reached the nearby island of Tenedos, and stopped to offer sacrifices, another quarrel (*éris*) broke out. Nestor does not say who the parties to the quarrel were but Odysseus was clearly one of the parties, for he turned back and returned with his ships and men to Agamemnon. Who the other party was Nestor does not say, but he makes clear that he himself was no longer of one mind with Odysseus as he had been hitherto. For when Odysseus turned back to Agamemnon, Nestor fled in the opposite direction (*Odyssey* 3.159–166):

ἐς Τένεδον δ' ἐλθόντες ἐρέξαμεν ἱρὰ θεοῖσιν,

οἴκαδε ἱέμενοι· Ζεὺς δ' οὔ πω μήδετο νόστον,

σχέτλιος, ὅς ῥ' ἔριν ὦρσε κακὴν ἔπι δεύτερον αὖτις.

1983:50–51, with references to similar views held by others). The case against Odysseus depends primarily on *Odyssey* 5.105–111, where Hermes gives Calypso an account of how Odysseus came to her island which differs from Odysseus's own account: in Hermes' account, when Troy was sacked and those who fought at Troy left for home, they sinned against Athena in their return (ἀτὰρ ἐν νόστῳ Ἀθηναίην ἀλίτοντο, *Odyssey* 5.108); Athena sent a storm against them in which all Odysseus's companions were destroyed, but Odysseus himself escaped to Calypso's island. This is certainly an abbreviated account, which leaves out (among much else) the cattle of Helios and the role of Zeus in destroying Odysseus's last ship and remaining companions, and some would explain the discrepancy as due to abbreviation alone; but Odysseus too claims the authority of Hermes, through Calypso, for his version of events (in particular, the role of Zeus in dashing his ship, *Odyssey* 12.389–390), and this looks like a genuine conflict of traditions.

οἱ μὲν ἀποστρέψαντες ἔβαν νέας ἀμφιελίσσας
ἀμφ' Ὀδυσῆα ἄνακτα δαΐφρονα ποικιλομήτην,
αὖτις ἐπ' Ἀτρεΐδῃ Ἀγαμέμνονι ἦρα φέροντες·
αὐτὰρ ἐγὼ σὺν νηυσὶν ἀολλέσιν, αἵ μοι ἔποντο,
φεῦγον, ἐπεὶ γίνωσκον, ὃ δὴ κακὰ μήδετο δαίμων.

Coming to Tenedos we made sacrifices to the gods,
eager to reach home; but Zeus did not yet plot our return,
hard-hearted god, but caused strife to break out again a second
    time.
Some turned their oared ships and went back,
those with Odysseus, the keen-spirited king with inventive
    mind,
bowing again to Agamemnon, the son of Atreus.
But I, with all the ships that followed me,
fled, because I recognized that the god plotted evil.

§2.64 Nestor does not say that it was he who quarreled with Odysseus on the island of Tenedos, but it is clear from his account that this is what happened. When Nestor says that he "realized that the god intended evil," he shows that he had a clear view about the situation that confronted them on Tenedos, and when he says that he fled with his ships, he shows that he had a firm conviction about what to do and acted on it. No more need be said to show that Nestor and Odysseus, who had always been of one mind during the war, quarreled bitterly and split from each other after the war on the issue of their *nóstos*. This is what the subtle design of Nestor's whole account is intended to show. Nestor is giving this account to Odysseus's son, who has come to him to find out about his father, and it is thus more than fitting that he suppress an explicit statement of the quarrel that constituted their final leave-taking from one another. This suppression is also wholly consistent with Nestor's role in the *Iliad*, as we have examined it in the story of Patroclus in *Iliad* 11 and 23. In the way that Nestor's role is handled poetically there is no difference between the *Iliad* and the *Odyssey*, and this as an important point in its own right. It means that we may continue to expect the kind of subtlety that marked his role in the *Iliad* in the *Odyssey* as well.

§2.65 What is the significance of Nestor's account for the story of Odysseus? The first thing to note is that Odysseus left Troy after the first quarrel, with the part of the army that remembered its *nóstos*, and that, in my view, was destined to return home safely. If the first quarrel made the basic division between the saved and the damned, so to speak, then Odysseus was among the saved, although he might not reach home safely for a long time. And what took place on Tenedos ensured that he would not return for a long time, for not only did he mistakenly return to Agamemnon and the half of the army being "restrained" by him; he also separated himself from *Néstōr*, "the homebringer." The weight of this fact in the story of course depends heavily on the meaning of the name *Néstōr*, which I believe was still crystal clear to the Homeric audience.[78]

§2.66 For Nestor's own story his name is of equal significance. Nestor's myth is not to bring his brother back to life, and the same negative fact is repeated in his failure to bring Odysseus home. But Nestor, "the home-bringer," does more than simply return home in his story in *Odyssey* 3. Others did that, and the simple fact of returning does not bring out what is special about Nestor. Nestor, if we follow his story closely, brought another hero home. When Nestor fled from Tenedos in the opposite direction from Odysseus, he was not alone; Diomedes fled with him (*Odyssey* 3.165–167):

αὐτὰρ ἐγὼ σὺν νηυσὶν ἀολλέσιν, αἵ μοι ἕποντο,

φεῦγον, ἐπεὶ γίνωσκον, ὃ δὴ κακὰ μήδετο δαίμων.

φεῦγε δὲ Τυδέος υἱὸς ἀρήϊος, ὦρσε δ' ἑταίρους.

But I, with all the ships that followed me,
fled, because I recognized that the god plotted evil.
And the warlike son of Tydeus fled, rousing his companions.

Nestor and Diomedes are a pair on their *nóstos*, as is made clear by the next lines, which concern Menelaus, the leader of the half of the army that had left Troy for home after the first quarrel. Nestor and Diomedes leave Tenedos together, and Menelaus only overtakes them when they stop on the island of Lesbos to ponder a major decision about the rest of their journey home (*Odyssey* 3.168–172):

---

78 The reconstructed verb *nései* in *Odyssey* 18.265, if its occurrence in this traditional line had not yet been changed to the form *anései* of our manuscripts by the Homeric era, implies that the name *Néstōr* was still understood in the Homeric era. Conversely, if the name *Néstōr* was still understood, so too must the verb *nései* have been. Nestor's role in *Odyssey* 3 is the key to both issues (cf. §1.23–§1.24 above). I use the term "homebringer" of Nestor (and "homebringing" of his function) for the sake of convenience; I have in mind the terms "homecomer" and "homecoming," with which these terms contrast.

ὀψὲ δὲ δὴ μετὰ νῶϊ κίε ξανθὸς Μενέλαος,
ἐν Λέσβῳ δ' ἔκιχεν δολιχὸν πλόον ὁρμαίνοντας,
ἢ καθύπερθε Χίοιο νεοίμεθα παιπαλοέσσης,
νήσου ἔπι Ψυρίης, αὐτὴν ἐπ' ἀριστέρ' ἔχοντες,
ἢ ὑπένερθε Χίοιο παρ' ἠνεμόεντα Μίμαντα.

Late indeed after us came fair-haired Menelaus,
and found us at Lesbos pondering our long voyage,
whether we should return above rocky Chios,
past the island of Psyria, keeping Chios on our left,
or beneath Chios past windy Mimas.

The issue was whether to cut straight across the Aegean for home, with all the risks that the open sea entailed, or to take a safer course to the south by way of Mount Mimas on the mainland and the Cyclades islands, and risk being caught by the divine wrath through this delay. A divine sign was asked for and given, to cross the sea directly to Euboea, which they did, landing on the southern tip of the island in Geraistos, where they offered a sacrifice of thanks to Poseidon (*Odyssey* 3.173–179):

ἠτέομεν δὲ θεὸν φῆναι τέρας· αὐτὰρ ὅ γ' ἥμιν
δεῖξε, καὶ ἠνώγει πέλαγος μέσον εἰς Εὔβοιαν
τέμνειν, ὄφρα τάχιστα ὑπὲκ κακότητα φύγοιμεν.
ὦρτο δ' ἐπὶ λιγὺς οὖρος ἀήμεναι· αἱ δὲ μάλ' ὦκα
ἰχθυόεντα κέλευθα διέδραμον, ἐς δὲ Γεραιστὸν
ἐννύχιαι κατάγοντο· Ποσειδάωνι δὲ ταύρων
πόλλ' ἐπὶ μῆρ' ἔθεμεν, πέλαγος μέγα μετρήσαντες.

We asked the god to show us a sign, and he showed us one;
he urged us to cut across the middle of the sea to Euboea
so that we might escape the evil as quickly as possible.
A shrill wind began to blow; our ships swiftly
crossed the fishy paths of the sea to Geraistos,
putting in at night; we offered Poseidon
many bulls' thighs, having crossed the great sea.

Menelaus is not heard of again in this account, but we learn later in *Odyssey* 3, when Telemachus asks Nestor where Menelaus was when Agamemnon was murdered, that Menelaus accompanied them from Geraistos as far as Cape Sounion in Attica, where his helmsman Phrontis, the son of Onetor, died and was buried (*Odyssey* 3.276–285). Menelaus later departed from Sounion on his own and was blown off course when he rounded Cape Maleia, but that has nothing to do with Nestor and his return, which is the subject of Nestor's first account. This account mentions only Diomedes, who, after sacrifices were made at Geraistos, safely reached home in Argos on the fourth day (*Odyssey* 3.180–182):

τέτρατον ἦμαρ ἔην, ὅτ' ἐν Ἄργεϊ νῆας ἐΐσας
Τυδεΐδεω ἕταροι Διομήδεος ἱπποδάμοιο
ἵστασαν.

It was the fourth day when the companions of horse-breaking Diomedes,
Tydeus's son, brought their well-balanced ships to rest in Argos.

Nestor was with Diomedes from the beginning of his *nóstos* to the end, and having left him safely in Argos, he completed his own *nóstos* effortlessly with a godsent wind that never abated (*Odyssey* 3.182–183):

αὐτὰρ ἐγώ γε Πύλονδ' ἔχον, οὐδέ ποτ' ἔσβη
οὖρος, ἐπεὶ δὴ πρῶτα θεὸς προέηκεν ἀῆναι.

But I kept on for Pylos, and the wind never let up after the god first sent it to blow.[79]

---

79 To reach Pylos from Argos he had to round Cape Maleia; this he did without incident, in contrast to Menelaus, whom a storm blew off course all the way to Egypt. The *Nostoi* followed the same tradition as the *Odyssey* for the return of Nestor and Diomedes on the one hand and of Menelaus on the other hand; Proclus's summary begins as follows (*Chrestomathy* lines 279–287 [Allen 1912:108 lines 16–22]): Ἀθηνᾶ Ἀγαμέμνονα καὶ Μενέλαον εἰς ἔριν καθίστησι περὶ τοῦ ἔκπλου. Ἀγαμέμνων μὲν οὖν τὸν τῆς Ἀθηνᾶς ἐξιλασόμενος χόλον ἐπιμένει. Διομήδης δὲ καὶ Νέστωρ ἀναχθέντες εἰς τὴν οἰκείαν διασῴζονται. μεθ' οὓς ἐκπλεύσας ὁ Μενέλαος μετὰ πέντε νεῶν εἰς Αἴγυπτον παραγίνεται, τῶν λοιπῶν διαφθαρεισῶν νεῶν ἐν τῷ πελάγει, "Athena puts Agamemnon and Menelaus into a quarrel about the departure. Agamemnon remains to propitiate Athena's anger. Diomedes and Nestor set sail and arrive home safely. Menelaus leaves after them and arrives in Egypt with five ships, the rest of his ships having been destroyed in the sea." Homer seems to know nothing of the tradition, attested first for Mimnermus (fr. 22 West = scholia to Lycophron 610), that Diomedes' wife Aigialeia was unfaithful and plotted against him, and that Diomedes had to flee Argos for Italy, where he was killed; this, according to Mimnermus, was Aphrodite's punishment of Diomedes for his wounding her at Troy;

This completes Nestor's account of what he saw and experienced at first hand during the *nóstos Akhaiôn*. He reached home with great speed, and learned nothing of the fate of the other Achaeans; about them he can only tell Telemachus what he has learned from hearsay (*Odyssey* 3.184–187):

ὣς ἦλθον, φίλε τέκνον, ἀπευθής, οὐδέ τι οἶδα
κείνων, οἵ τ' ἐσάωθεν Ἀχαιῶν οἵ τ' ἀπόλοντο.
ὅσσα δ' ἐνὶ μεγάροισι καθήμενος ἡμετέροισι
πεύθομαι, ἣ θέμις ἐστί, δαήσεαι, οὐδέ σε κεύσω.

Thus I came, dear child, ignorant, and I know nothing
of those Achaeans who were saved and those who perished.
But what I find out sitting in my halls,
that you will learn, as is right, and I will not hide it from you.

§2.67 Nestor does not say that he brought Diomedes safely home to Argos, just as he does not say that he quarreled with Odysseus and left him behind in Troy. But there can be no mistaking the fact that when Nestor and Diomedes left Tenedos together, Nestor was the leader if it was he who quarreled with Odysseus. For in this quarrel Nestor must have argued for an immediate *nóstos*, and departed at once when Odysseus returned in the opposite direction to Agamemnon. Diomedes, then, must simply have followed Nestor, not only in leaving Tenedos, but through his entire *nóstos*. This again is not stated, but is to be understood nonetheless. After leaving Tenedos, the next point of decision was Lesbos, where Nestor and Diomedes were still pondering their course, whether to cross the open sea or not, when Menelaus caught up with them. The question was decided for them, and for Menelaus as well, who now joined them, by a sign from the god urging them to make straight for Euboea across the open sea. Nestor says that "we asked the god for a sign, and he showed one to us," but signs from the gods must be both perceived and interpreted before they can be followed, and of the three heroes on Lesbos the likeliest to have noticed and interpreted correctly the god's sign is Nestor, at least to judge by his own words on two occasions in the *Iliad*. The first is in *Iliad* 2, where there is an interesting contrast to be

---

but in the Homeric episode itself Aigialeia is called *períphrōn*, "prudent," a characteristic epithet of Penelope, the paragon of faithfulness (*Iliad* 5.412; cf. Matthews 1996:250–253). Marks 2008, ch. 5, argues that Nestor's account of the Achaeans' *nóstoi* deliberately suppresses stories of further wanderings in the case of Diomedes and others (Neoptolemos, Philoctetes, Idomeneus), and that these traditions were therefore already in existence; this may well be the case.

noticed between Nestor and Odysseus with regard to signs and in other respects as well. These two both play a role when Agamemnon tests the army, and the army unexpectedly breaks for the ships. In line with the contrast between Nestor and Odysseus on their *nóstos*, where Odysseus plays the mortal twin to Nestor's immortal twin, Odysseus "restrains" the army's headlong flight, most dramatically in the case of Thersites whom he smites with the staff, whereupon Nestor "incites" them, particularly Agamemnon, to return to the business of war.[80] Each of them in his speech to the army recalls an omen that occurred on their departure for Troy ten years earlier, but whereas Odysseus recalls the portent that the prophet Calchas interpreted for all,[81] Nestor tells of a sign that he saw for himself. After telling Agamemnon to rule steadfastly, and to let those few go to ruin who wish to return home on their own before they learn whether "Zeus's promise was a lie or not" (*Iliad* 2.348–349), he vouches for the favorable sign that he saw from Zeus (lightning on the right) with the emphatic first person verb *phēmí*, "I declare" (*Iliad* 2.350–353):

φημὶ γὰρ οὖν κατανεῦσαι ὑπερμενέα Κρονίωνα
ἤματι τῷ ὅτε νηυσὶν ἐν ὠκυπόροισιν ἔβαινον
Ἀργεῖοι Τρώεσσι φόνον καὶ κῆρα φέροντες
ἀστράπτων ἐπιδέξι' ἐναίσιμα σήματα φαίνων.

For on my word the mighty son of Kronos nodded assent
the day the Argives boarded their swift-traveling ships
carrying death and destruction to the Trojans;
he flashed lightning on the right and showed a favorable sign.

---

80 In this scene Hera first tells Athena to "restrain" each man with gentle words (*erḗtue, Iliad* 2.164), and Athena repeats the command to Odysseus (*erḗtue, Iliad* 2.180), who carries it out (*erētúsaske, Iliad* 2.189). On the *dêmos* he uses the staff (*Iliad* 2.198–206), until finally all but Thersites are "restrained in their seats" (*erḗtuthen dè kath' hédras, Iliad* 2.211). He then smites Thersites after his outburst (*Iliad* 2.265–269). Nestor then chides the army and tells Agamemnon to keep steady counsel and to rule the Argives as before (*Iliad* 2.344–345), ending his speech with a piece of tactical advice for the commander-in-chief. For Odysseus's role in restraining others as typical of him, in this scene and elsewhere, cf. Lentini 2006:121n3 and 140n1.

81 Odysseus speaks as follows (*Iliad* 2.299–300):

τλῆτε φίλοι, καὶ μείνατ' ἐπὶ χρόνον ὄφρα δαῶμεν
ἢ ἐτεὸν Κάλχας μαντεύεται ἦε καὶ οὐκί.

Hold out, friends, and wait for a time until we know
whether Calchas prophesies truly or not.

He then recounts the portent of the serpent that ate nine sparrows and Calchas's interpretation that the Argives would fight for nine years and capture Troy in the tenth.

The second passage is in *Iliad* 15, when Apollo destroys the Achaean wall and the Achaeans themselves are hemmed in by their ships. All pray to the gods, but Nestor most of all, and in his prayer he seems to refer to the same sign from Zeus that he recalls in *Iliad* 2 when he calls on Zeus to remember if he ever promised a safe return to "anyone" (*Iliad* 15.367–376):

ὣς οἳ μὲν παρὰ νηυσὶν ἐρητύοντο μένοντες,
ἀλλήλοισί τε κεκλόμενοι καὶ πᾶσι θεοῖσι
χεῖρας ἀνίσχοντες μεγάλ' εὐχετόωντο ἕκαστος·
Νέστωρ αὖτε μάλιστα Γερήνιος οὖρος Ἀχαιῶν
εὔχετο χεῖρ' ὀρέγων εἰς οὐρανὸν ἀστερόεντα·
"Ζεῦ πάτερ εἴ ποτέ <u>τίς</u> τοι ἐν Ἄργεῖ περ πολυπύρῳ
ἢ βοὸς ἢ οἰὸς κατὰ πίονα μηρία καίων
εὔχετο νοστῆσαι, σὺ δ' <u>ὑπέσχεο</u> καὶ <u>κατένευσας</u>,
τῶν μνῆσαι καὶ ἄμυνον Ὀλύμπιε νηλεὲς ἦμαρ,
μηδ' οὕτω Τρώεσσιν ἔα δάμνασθαι Ἀχαιούς."

Thus they were pinned down waiting by their ships;
and shouting to each other and raising their hands
they each prayed loudly to all the gods;
but most of all Nestor, guardian of the Achaeans,
prayed stretching his hands toward the starry sky:
"Father Zeus, if ever <u>anyone</u> in Argos rich in wheat,
burning the fat thighs of an ox or sheep,
prayed to return home safely, and you <u>promised</u> and <u>nodded
assent</u>,
remember those things, god of Olympus, and ward off the piti-
less day,
and do not let the Achaeans be conquered like this by the
Trojans."

Nestor does not limit the prayers that Zeus may have heard to his own,[82] but surely his own prayer is included, for how else did he know that Zeus had

---

82 The alternative sacrifices (ἢ βοὸς ἢ οἰὸς, "either of an ox or a sheep"), as well as the pronoun τις, "someone," generalize the situation. Note too that in *Iliad* 2, when Nestor affirms the positive sign that he once saw, he responds to Agamemnon, who in his "trial" of the army denies the positive sign that he once saw (*Iliad* 2.111–115; cf. Christensen 2007:168–169).

"promised" a safe return to anyone, except by noticing a sign in answer to his own prayer?[83] It is significant that the prayers of which he reminds Zeus in *Iliad* 15 concern a *nóstos* from Troy: the reason that *Néstōr*, the "homebringer," prays more than the others in *Iliad* 15 is precisely that the Achaeans' *nóstos* is at issue now that the Achaean wall has been broken. And in answer to Nestor's prayer, Zeus reaffirms the promise that he made to him before. The sign of Zeus's earlier promise to Nestor was a lightning bolt sent on the right (*Iliad* 2.353). Zeus reconfirms his promise to Nestor by thundering when he hears his prayer in the desperate situation of *Iliad* 15 (*Iliad* 15.377–378):

ὣς ἔφατ' εὐχόμενος, μέγα δ' ἔκτυπε μητίετα Ζεύς,
ἀράων ἀΐων Νηληϊάδαο γέροντος.

So he spoke praying, and the deviser Zeus thundered
hearing the prayers of the aged son of Neleus.

---

83 Nestor's prayer in *Iliad* 15 and his speech in *Iliad* 2 have a formal similarity in that both refer to Zeus's "promise" and his "nod of assent." The pattern is formulaic. In *Iliad* 15.374 the phrase ὑπέσχεο καὶ κατένευσας, "you promised and nodded assent," is used (essentially the same formula occurs in Agamemnon's "trial" of the army: ὑπέσχετο καὶ κατένευσεν, "he promised and nodded assent," *Iliad* 2.112; see previous note). Nestor's speech in *Iliad* 2 differs slightly in that the phrase Διὸς...ὑπόσχεσις is used instead of a verb "to promise" to suit the more complex context (*Iliad* 2.344–350):

Ἀτρεΐδη σὺ δ' ἔθ' ὡς πρὶν ἔχων ἀστεμφέα βουλὴν
ἄρχευ' Ἀργείοισι κατὰ κρατερὰς ὑσμίνας,
τούσδε δ' ἔα φθινύθειν ἕνα καὶ δύο, τοί κεν Ἀχαιῶν
νόσφιν βουλεύωσ'· ἄνυσις δ' οὐκ ἔσσεται αὐτῶν·
πρὶν Ἄργος δ' ἰέναι πρὶν καὶ Διὸς αἰγιόχοιο
γνώμεναι εἴ τε ψεῦδος ὑπόσχεσις εἴ τε καὶ οὐκί.
φημὶ γὰρ οὖν κατανεῦσαι ὑπερμενέα Κρονίωνα....

Son of Atreus, keep firm counsel now as before
and command the Argives in the fierce fighting,
and let these one or two who take counsel apart from the Achaeans
perish; they will have no effect;
before returning to Argos find out first
whether the promise of the aegis-holder Zeus is a lie or not.
For I say that the mighty son of Kronos nodded in assent....

Zeus's promise is different in the two passages (a safe return in *Iliad* 15 versus the capture of Troy in *Iliad* 2) but the occasion seems to be the same; note that if Nestor's words τούσδε δ' ἔα φθινύθειν, "let these men perish," in *Iliad* 2 are taken literally he implies that the "one or two" who leave Troy prematurely will not have a safe return: the promise of a safe return, it seems, depends on staying to take Troy.

We do not know who heard and understood this sign, since the text does not say, but we may be sure that Nestor himself did, since it was he who prayed for it. The only reaction to the sign that is mentioned is on the part of the Trojans, who misunderstand it, taking it as favorable to their attack (*Iliad* 15.379–380):[84]

Τρῶες δ' ὡς ἐπύθοντο Διὸς κτύπον αἰγιόχοιο,
μᾶλλον ἐπ' Ἀργείοισι θόρον, μνήσαντο δὲ χάρμης.

But when the Trojans heard the thunderclap of the aegis-holder Zeus,
they assaulted the Argives all the more and were minded for battle.

§2.68 Keeping in mind the two passages in the *Iliad* that bear on Nestor's ability to interpret signs from the gods when a *nóstos* is at issue, I return to the sign that was given on Lesbos when Nestor, Diomedes, and Menelaus hesitated there, and I think that there is every reason to believe that it was Nestor who both solicited and correctly interpreted this sign.[85] This is an important point, for the only occasion on which *Néstōr*, "the homebringer," truly acts out his name in the Homeric poems is when he escorts Diomedes from Tenedos to Argos, and the decision to cross the sea directly from Lesbos to Euboea was a critical moment in this journey. Nestor's apparent action in perceiving and interpreting a sign from the god reveals something important about the function of "homebringer" itself, as designated by Nestor's name. If we consider the entire journey, it is really a series of decisions between two alternatives, and the journey is successful because Nestor unfailingly chooses the right alternative in each case. The first correct decision was to leave Troy with Menelaus, and not to stay behind with Agamemnon. The second was to flee onward from Tenedos, and not to return to Agamemnon with Odysseus. The final correct decision, for which a divine sign was sought, was to cross the open sea as quickly as possible from Lesbos to Euboea, and not to take the slower, apparently less dangerous route to the south through the Cyclades. The accurate perception and correct interpretation of divine signs, which

84 For the purposes of the plot the Trojans must press their attack at this point so that Patroclus, who is in Eurypylos's tent, will hear them and return to Achilles.
85 There is a further passage in the *Iliad* where Nestor correctly interprets a sign from Zeus: *Iliad* 8.130–144. This passage, which is discussed §2.76 below, is also very much to the point here in that the episode containing it features both Nestor and Diomedes and evokes their *nóstos* together.

is emphasized in the case of the decision made at Lesbos, also characterized Nestor's earlier decisions. When he fled from Tenedos with Diomedes, it was because he "recognized" that the god planned evil things (*Odyssey* 3.166):

φεῦγον, ἐπεὶ <u>γίνωσκον</u>, ὃ δὴ κακὰ μήδετο δαίμων.

I fled, because I <u>recognized</u> that the god plotted evil.

Presumably Nestor had as clear an idea of what the gods intended when he first left Troy with Menelaus, for he calls Agamemnon "foolish" to think that by staying he could pacify Athena's wrath with sacrifices, since the mind of the gods is not easily changed (*Odyssey* 3.146–147):

<u>νήπιος</u>, οὐδὲ τὸ ἤδη, ὃ οὐ πείσεσθαι ἔμελλεν·
οὐ γάρ τ᾽ αἶψα θεῶν τρέπεται νόος αἰὲν ἐόντων.

<u>The fool</u>, he did not know that she was not to be persuaded, for the mind of the gods who are forever is not quickly changed.

§2.69 The essence of Nestor's action as the "homebringer," then, is to make the right choice between two alternatives at each stage of the journey on the basis of an accurate perception of what the gods intend. The splitting of the issue into two alternatives at each new turn, the forging ahead quickly on the basis of an accurate perception of the right choice, and the simultaneous discarding of the wrong choice—all this describes a basic mental process. This is to say that the action of *Néstōr*, "he who brings home," in negotiating each new turn on his *nóstos*, at the same time describes the process of *nóos*, "mind," which is equivalent to *Néstōr* in derivation and meaning. We know from the chariot race in *Iliad* 23 that *nóos* is "incitement" as opposed to "restraint," and that both qualities are necessary to round the turning post and complete the race successfully. A successful *nóstos* also involves turns, but a series of them instead of the single turn of the chariot race. Each new turn requires deliberation, and a choice must be made between two alternatives because there is doubt as to the correct course.[86] *Néstōr* and *nóos* represent the right choice in

86 The notion of "doubt" itself offers a useful parallel. Latin *dubium* and *dubitare*, "doubt," contain the root of *duo*, "two"; "to be in doubt" (*in dubio esse*) is etymologically "to be in two" (cf. German *zweifeln* from *zwei*). The Greek phrase *en doiêi*, "in doubt," is the equivalent of Latin *in dubio*; the root of *doiê* is **dwei-*, which is also found in Greek *déos* and *deídō*, "fear, be afraid." Benveniste 1954:254–255 (= 1966:294–295) points out a striking collocation of the phrase *en doiêi*, "in doubt," and the verb *deídimen*, "we are afraid," in *Iliad* 9.229–231 (addressed to Achilles by Odysseus):

each case, moving forward rapidly from one deliberation to the next, and to another after that, until finally the entire *nóstos* is successfully completed. The other half of the duality is the wrong choice, which is discarded at every new turn. In this process the "incitement" that defines *nóos* is at the same time a matter of "accurate perception," for a successful *nóstos* depends on a perception of the correct choice at each new turn. Nestor, who accurately perceives signs from the gods, is again the embodiment of *nóos*, and of the verb *noéō* that is derived from *nóos*, inasmuch as the essential idea in both is "clear perception." If *nóos* is both "incitement" and "clear perception," the other half of the dual mental process is more complex. In the chariot race the Epeian twins are successful because one twin slows the chariot to make the turn, while the other incites it to win the race. The two twins stay together, and their inseparability is their strength. In the *nóstos* of *Odyssey* 3, however, there is a split between the right choice and the wrong choice, and the wrong choice is discarded. At two points the wrong choice is represented by an individual who is left behind. Agamemnon is left behind by Menelaus in Troy, and Odysseus is left behind by Nestor when he flees from Tenedos. Agamemnon and Odysseus are both in the position of the mortal twin, who dies and is not brought back to life, as in Nestor's own variant of the twin myth. It thus appears that Nestor's myth represents a further development of the Indo-European twin myth from the standpoint of the mental process that this myth describes. The same may also be said of *nóos*, which is depicted through *Néstōr* in the *nóstos* of *Odyssey* 3.[87] But in spite of this development, *Néstōr* and *nóos* remain involved in a duality. In the case of *Néstōr*, he brings Diomedes home, and Diomedes is thus in the position of the mortal twin of the Indo-European myth. He is inseparable from

---

ἀλλὰ λίην μέγα πῆμα διοτρεφὲς εἰσορόωντες
<u>δείδιμεν</u>· <u>ἐν δοιῇ</u> δὲ σαωσέμεν ἢ ἀπολέσθαι
νῆας ἐϋσσέλμους, εἰ μὴ σύ γε δύσεαι ἀλκήν.

But seeing a very great woe, Zeus-nourished one,
<u>we are afraid</u>; it is <u>in doubt</u> whether we will save our well-benched ships
or they will be destroyed if you do not put on your might.

For the dynamics of Nestor's return from Troy cf. Dickson 1995:80–81.

87 I suggested in §1.69 above that the mental process at issue in the Indo-European twin myth was an alternation between consciousness and unconsciousness. In the Greek myth the mental process is more developed that that, and perhaps it was more developed than that in the Indo-European myth as well, but the evidence is lacking: the Sanskrit evidence for the "intelligence" of the immortal twin (the epic figure Sahadeva and the Vedic collocation *dasrā́ bhiṣájā*) no longer relates to the basic dynamic of the twin myth, an alternation between life and death. Hence there is nothing in Indic to compare with the Greek Nestor in order to determine the mental process of the Indo-European myth.

Nestor, who is in the position of the Indo-European immortal twin, until his *nóstos* is completed. Thus at Lesbos, unlike what happened at Tenedos and Troy, no one is left behind.[88]

§2.70 The word *nóos* is not present in Nestor's description of his *nóstos*, but the word does have an interesting occurrence earlier in his account, when he describes the harmony that existed between himself and Odysseus as counselors for the Argives during the war. He says that he and Odysseus never disagreed in assembly or council, "but having one mind we counseled what was best for the Argives with nóos and shrewd counsel" (*Odyssey* 3.126–129):

ἔνθ' ἦ τοι εἷος μὲν ἐγὼ καὶ δῖος Ὀδυσσεὺς
οὔτε ποτ' εἰν ἀγορῇ δίχ' ἐβάζομεν οὔτ' ἐνὶ βουλῇ,
ἀλλ' ἕνα θυμὸν ἔχοντε νόῳ καὶ ἐπίφρονι βουλῇ
φραζόμεθ' Ἀργείοισιν ὅπως ὄχ' ἄριστα γένοιτο.

During the time there shining Odysseus and I
never spoke on opposite sides in assembly or council,
but with one spirit, by intelligence and wise counsel,
we advised the Argives how what was best might come about.[89]

Nestor of course stresses the like-mindedness of Odysseus and himself with the phrase *héna thumòn ékhonte*, and the harmony between them at this stage

88 Did Diomedes "restrain" Nestor at Lesbos before Nestor received a sign from the god to proceed with the dangerous crossing of the open sea? This does not seem altogether likely when we consider the relationship between Nestor and Diomedes in the *Iliad* (see below on *Iliad* 8.130–171, where Nestor restrains an impetuous Diomedes). But roles in the *Iliad* may have been reversed in the *Odyssey*. From the standpoint of the underlying twin myth it would be interesting if Diomedes advocated the slower, safer course through the Cyclades, Nestor the faster, more dangerous course through the open sea, and if Nestor then sought and got the sign to take the bolder course and persuaded Diomedes to follow.

89 The underlined phrase has only one parallel in Homer, and there *boulé* is replaced by *mêtis*: it occurs in a speech of Penelope to Odysseus regarding her reputation, which troubles her because of her inability to show him proper hospitality (*Odyssey* 19.325–328):

πῶς γὰρ ἐμεῦ σύ, ξεῖνε, δαήσεαι, εἴ τι γυναικῶν
ἀλλάων περίειμι νόον καὶ ἐπίφρονα μῆτιν,
εἴ κεν ἀϋσταλέος, κακὰ εἱμένος ἐν μεγάροισι
δαινύῃ;

How will you learn about me, stranger, whether I surpass
other women at all in mind and shrewd intelligence,
if you dine in my halls unbathed,
dressed in rags?

is the point. The phrase *epíphroni boulêi*, "with shrewd counsel," nevertheless suggests Odysseus more than it does Nestor: the phrase occurs only one other time in Homer, namely in *Odyssey 16*, when Odysseus reveals himself to his son, and Telemachus repeats what he has always heard about his father, that he is both a warrior and "shrewd in counsel" (*Odyssey 16*.241–242):

ὦ πάτερ, ἦ τοι σεῖο μέγα κλέος αἰὲν ἄκουον,

χεῖράς τ' αἰχμητὴν ἔμεναι καὶ <u>ἐπίφρονα βουλήν</u>.

Father, I always heard your great fame,
that you are a spearman with your hands and that you are
<u>shrewd</u> in <u>counsel</u>.[90]

If *epíphroni boulêi*, "with shrewd counsel," characterizes Odysseus more particularly than it does Nestor, then *nóōi*, "with mind," characterizes Nestor more particularly than it does Odysseus, and there thus seems to be a subtle division between them even in the context of their like-mindedness. The subtle distinction in the phrase *nóōi kaì epíphroni boulêi*, moreover, is reinforced by the fact that it echoes, by its wording and placement in the line, the phrase *egṑ kaì dîos Odusseús* two lines before. The echo of *egó* in *nóōi* is particularly strong, and I think that it is intentional. The intent is to draw attention to *Néstōr*, not only as the "homebringer," but as the embodiment of *nóos*. We have already examined passages in the *Iliad* that equate *nóos* with *Néstōr* in an apparently deliberate way.[91] This example in *Odyssey 3* belongs with them, for while it is perhaps more subtle, it is also more significant. Nestor, as the embodiment of *nóos*, is about to reveal what this really means by his account of his *nóstos*. At the same time, the subtle distinction drawn between himself and Odysseus in terms of *nóos* and "shrewd counsel," even during the war, points ahead to the time when each would go his own way—Nestor to bring Diomedes home through his *nóos*, Odysseus to pursue his own fate through his "shrewd counsel."

§2.71 There is another hero besides Odysseus whom Nestor fails to bring home from Troy, and this is his own son Antilochus, who dies in the war. The loss of Antilochus is a matter of close personal grief to Nestor, who in *Odyssey*

---

90 The phrase ἐπίφρονα βουλήν/ ἐπίφρονι βουλῇ occurs in Homer only in the two passages discussed; there is another example in Hesiod *Theogony* 896 with reference to Athena: ἴσον ἔχουσαν πατρὶ μένος καὶ <u>ἐπίφρονα βουλήν</u>, "having strength and <u>shrewd counsel</u> equal to her father."

91 §1.35–§1.36 above.

3, in recalling all the grief that the Achaeans suffered at Troy (ὀϊζύος, *Odyssey* 3.103), remembers the death of his own son most of all (*Odyssey* 3.108–112):

> ἔνθα δ' ἔπειτα κατέκταθεν ὅσσοι ἄριστοι·
> ἔνθα μὲν Αἴας κεῖται ἀρήϊος, ἔνθα δ' Ἀχιλλεύς,
> ἔνθα δὲ Πάτροκλος, θεόφιν μήστωρ ἀτάλαντος,
> ἔνθα δ' ἐμὸς φίλος υἱός, ἅμα κρατερὸς καὶ ἀταρβής,
> Ἀντίλοχος, περὶ μὲν θείειν ταχὺς ἠδὲ μαχητής.

> There all our best men in the end were killed;
> there lies warlike Ajax, there Achilles,
> there Patroclus, a counselor equal to the gods,
> there my own dear son, strong and unflinching,
> Antilochus, fast beyond others at running and a fighter.

Antilochus's death is also a matter of grief to Peisistratos, Nestor's youngest son, when he accompanies Telemachus to Sparta, and Menelaus's warm speech of regret for the missing Odysseus turns the minds of all to grief. Peisistratos grieves for his brother Antilochus, whom Memnon, son of the dawn goddess Eos, slew (*Odyssey* 4.186–188):

> οὐδ' ἄρα Νέστορος υἱὸς ἀδακρύτω ἔχεν ὄσσε·
> μνήσατο γὰρ κατὰ θυμὸν ἀμύμονος Ἀντιλόχοιο,
> τόν ῥ' Ἠοῦς ἔκτεινε φαεινῆς ἀγλαὸς υἱός.

> Nor did Nestor's son keep his eyes dry from tears,
> for he remembered in his heart faultless Antilochus,
> whom the shining son of the radiant dawn goddess slew.[92]

For Nestor there is perhaps a special pathos in the fact that, whereas he brings Diomedes safely home, he cannot bring his own son home. The pathos is deepened by the fact that Diomedes is close in age to Antilochus, or even younger. In the council at the beginning of *Iliad* 9, when Diomedes defiantly rejects Agamemnon's defeatism and says that he and his companion Sthenelos will remain to take Troy alone if necessary, Nestor gently rebukes him, as a father would his youngest son, for not reaching the "goal" (*télos*) of his words. Nestor himself then takes over for Diomedes, and remedies the

---

92 In his speech to Menelaus Peisistratos says that he grieves for Antilochus although he never met or saw him (*Odyssey* 4.199–202).

deficiencies in his advice by going through everything at length and in detail (*Iliad* 9.53–62):

Τυδεΐδη περὶ μὲν πολέμῳ ἔνι καρτερός ἐσσι,
καὶ βουλῇ μετὰ πάντας ὁμήλικας ἔπλευ ἄριστος.
οὔ τίς τοι τὸν μῦθον ὀνόσσεται ὅσσοι Ἀχαιοί,
οὐδὲ πάλιν ἐρέει· ἀτὰρ οὐ τέλος ἵκεο μύθων.
ἦ μὲν καὶ νέος ἐσσί, ἐμὸς δέ κε καὶ πάϊς εἴης
ὁπλότατος γενεῆφιν· ἀτὰρ πεπνυμένα βάζεις
Ἀργείων βασιλῆας, ἐπεὶ κατὰ μοῖραν ἔειπες.
ἀλλ' ἄγ' ἐγών, ὃς σεῖο γεραίτερος εὔχομαι εἶναι,
ἐξείπω καὶ πάντα διίξομαι· οὐδέ κέ τίς μοι
μῦθον ἀτιμήσει', οὐδὲ κρείων Ἀγαμέμνων.

Son of Tydeus, you are strong beyond others in battle
and you are best in counsel among all your age-mates.
No one among the Achaeans will find fault with your speech
or contradict it. But you have not reached the goal of your
    words.
Indeed you are young, and might even be my son,
the youngest born; still you say wise things
to the kings of the Argives, since you have spoken fitly.
But come, I, who claim to be older than you,
will speak out and go through everything, and no one
will disrespect my speech, not even the ruler Agamemnon.[93]

§2.72 The relationship between Nestor and Diomedes, which is compared to that between a father and son in this passage, should be kept in mind in *Odyssey* 3. Indeed Nestor's claim that Diomedes has not reached the "goal" of his words (*ou télos híkeo múthōn*) and that he himself, by contrast, "will go through everything" (*pánta diíxomai*), should be seen in close relation to their eventual *nóstos* together, when it will be Nestor who will guide them through each new turn, at Tenedos and Lesbos, to the "goal" of their journey. The relationship between Nestor and Diomedes that is depicted in the *Iliad* is thus consistent with, and serves to flesh out, what is implied in the *Odyssey*.

---

93 In the rest of his speech Nestor orders the young men to guard the Greek camp and he calls on Agamemnon to summon a council of elders (*Iliad* 9.63–78); at the council of elders he suggests his plan to send an embassy to Achilles.

§2.73 Book 9 is not the only context in which the *Iliad* depicts the rela-
tionship between Nestor and Diomedes. The passage in Book 9 actually
follows on and develops an episode in Book 8, in which Nestor's trace horse is
shot by Paris, and Nestor himself is rescued by Diomedes. The episode begins
when Zeus weighs the fates of the Achaeans and Trojans at midday, and the
fate of the Achaeans sinks. Zeus sends a lightning bolt which the Achaeans
see and all then begin to flee (*Iliad* 8.66–79). Only Nestor remains, because his
trace horse is wounded and throws his other two horses into confusion.[94] As
Nestor struggles to cut the trace horse free, Hector bears down on him, and
only Diomedes sees the old man's plight (*Iliad* 8.80–91):

Νέστωρ οἶος ἔμιμνε Γερήνιος οὖρος Ἀχαιῶν
οὔ τι ἑκών, ἀλλ' ἵππος ἐτείρετο, τὸν βάλεν ἰῷ
δῖος Ἀλέξανδρος Ἑλένης πόσις ἠϋκόμοιο
ἄκρην κὰκ κορυφήν, ὅθι τε πρῶται τρίχες ἵππων
κρανίῳ ἐμπεφύασι, μάλιστα δὲ καίριόν ἐστιν.
ἀλγήσας δ' ἀνέπαλτο, βέλος δ' εἰς ἐγκέφαλον δῦ,
σὺν δ' ἵππους ἐτάραξε κυλινδόμενος περὶ χαλκῷ.
ὄφρ' ὁ γέρων ἵπποιο παρηορίας ἀπέταμνε
φασγάνῳ ἀΐσσων, τόφρ' Ἕκτορος ὠκέες ἵπποι
ἦλθον ἀν' ἰωχμὸν θρασὺν ἡνίοχον φορέοντες
Ἕκτορα· καί νύ κεν ἔνθ' ὁ γέρων ἀπὸ θυμὸν ὄλεσσεν
εἰ μὴ ἄρ' ὀξὺ νόησε βοὴν ἀγαθὸς Διομήδης.

Gerenian Nestor, guardian of the Achaeans, alone remained,
not willingly, but his horse was in trouble, hit by an arrow
from shining Alexander, husband of beautiful-haired Helen,
at his topmost point, where hairs first
grow on horses' heads and the most vulnerable spot is.
He reared up in pain, but the shaft sank into his brain,
and he threw the other horses into confusion, rolling about the
    bronze weapon.
While the old man cut the horse's traces,
jumping in with his sword, Hector's swift horses
came through the tumult carrying a bold driver,

94 It is ironic that only Nestor, the best at perceiving signs, cannot obey this one.

Hector himself; there the old man would have lost his life
if Diomedes had not sharply perceived him.

The suggestion in *Iliad* 9 that the relationship between Nestor and Diomedes
is like that between a father and son grows out of this episode in *Iliad* 8, for
this episode evokes the later death of Antilochus, which it closely resembles.[95]
When Diomedes comes to Nestor's aid, and saves him, he anticipates an event
that is similar in all respects except one. Antilochus saves his father's life as
does Diomedes, but he does so at the cost of his own life. Diomedes, on the
other hand, lives to be brought home by Nestor at the end of the war. The
death of Antilochus occurs after the death of Hector, when the Aethiopian
Memnon has become the Trojans' champion, and it is thus Memnon who
imperils Nestor and slays Antilochus. The episode lies outside the time span
of the *Iliad*, but is recreated in virtual form by the episode in *Iliad* 8. The actual
episode, which was known to the *Odyssey* and formed part of the *Aethiopis*,[96] is
told in full in Pindar, *Pythian* 6, where the story of Antilochus's death is used
to illustrate the general precept to honor one's parents. The similarities to
the episode in *Iliad* 8 are that it is again the wounding of Nestor's trace horse
by Paris's arrow that puts the old man in danger, and that he is rescued by
a young man from the onrush of the Trojans' chief hero, Hector in the case
of Diomedes, Memnon in the case of Antilochus. Pindar tells the story of
Antilochus as follows (*Pythian* 6.28–42):[97]

> ἔγεντο καὶ πρότερον Ἀντίλοχος βιατὰς
>
> νόημα τοῦτο φέρων,
>
> ὃς ὑπερέφθιτο πατρός, ἐναρίμβροτον
>
> ἀναμείναις στράταρχον Αἰθιόπων
>
> Μέμνονα. Νεστόρειον γὰρ ἵππος ἄρμ᾽ ἐπέδα

95 The Homeric poets, who knew that Antilochus died at Troy at Memnon's hands (*Odyssey*
   4.186–188; see §2.71 above), do not tell the story, which appears first in Pindar (see below
   in text). For M. L. West's view that the Memnon tradition was unknown to the *Iliad*, see
   EN4.7 below. In my view Kakridis 1949:75–83 all but proves that the Memnon tradition was
   known to the *Iliad* (again see EN4.7 below).

96 In the *Aithiopis* (Proclus *Chrestomathy* lines 188–189, Allen 1912:106 lines 4–6) "Antilochus
   is slain by Memnon, Achilles kills Memnon." The inscription on the *Tabula Iliaca Capitolina*
   (*IG* XIV 1284), which lists the *Aithiopis* of Arctinus among the sculptor's sources, identi-
   fies one of the scenes as "Achilles, Memnon, Antilochus" (cf. Sadurska 1964:29–30; Allen
   1912:126). Nestor's complaint at Antilochus's death that he had lived too long (Propertius
   2.13.46–50, Juvenal 10.246–255) is a presumed feature of the story in the *Aithiopis* (see Allen
   1912:126–127).

97 The *Aithiopis* is presumably Pindar's source.

Πάριος ἐκ βελέων δαϊχθείς· ὁ δ' ἔφεπεν
κραταιὸν ἔγχος·
Μεσσανίου δὲ γέροντος
δονηθεῖσα φρὴν βόασε παῖδα ὅν,

χαμαιπετὲς δ' ἄρ' ἔπος οὐκ ἀπέριψεν· αὐτοῦ
μένων δ' ὁ θεῖος ἀνήρ
πρίατο μὲν θανάτοιο κομιδὰν πατρός,
ἐδόκησέν τε τῶν πάλαι γενεᾷ
ὁπλοτέροισιν ἔργον πελώριον τελέσαις
ὕπατος ἀμφὶ τοκεῦσιν ἔμμεν πρὸς ἀρετάν.

Long ago the warrior Antilochus
was one to bear this in his mind,
who died for his father
standing up to man-slaying Memnon,
leader of the Aethiopian horde. Nestor's horse,
slain by Paris's arrows, had tied his chariot down; his foe
was coming at him with his powerful spear.
The aged Messenian,
his mind shaken, shouted to his son,

and the word he hurled did not fall to the ground.
Staying there the godlike man
bought his father's safety at the price of his own death;
accomplishing a prodigious feat
he seemed to those who came later
to be the highest of those born in ancient times
for courage on behalf of a parent.

§2.74 The connection of the episode in *Iliad* 8 with Antilochus's death is well understood and appreciated, but the episode has a further connection that has not been realized, namely with *Odyssey* 3. For when Diomedes saves Nestor, he simultaneously saves his own *nóstos* inasmuch as Nestor is his "homebringer." The connection of the episode in *Iliad* 8 with Antilochus's death is deepened by its further connection with *Odyssey* 3 through the contrast that is thereby evoked between Diomedes, who will return home in Nestor's care, and Antilochus, who will perish saving his father's life. The connection between *Iliad* 8 and *Odyssey* 3 involves a deliberate reversal of roles in that Nestor, who will bring Diomedes safely home, must first be saved himself. In *Iliad* 8 Diomedes is the savior. The role reversal is extended by the fact that Nestor must be rescued, not when he functions as *Néstōr*, "he who brings home," but when he functions as a "horseman"—as *hippóta Néstōr*. This is Diomedes' domain, and if Nestor and Diomedes reenact the twin myth in their *nóstos*, with Nestor playing the role of the immortal twin, then the same myth is also at play in *Iliad* 8, where Diomedes dominates in the role of the "warrior horseman." There is still a role reversal in that Diomedes saves Nestor, but he does so as a warrior.[98]

§2.75 The connection between *Iliad* 8 and *Odyssey* 3 goes beyond Diomedes. The real point of Nestor's account in *Odyssey* 3 is not that he brought Diomedes home, but that he did not bring Odysseus home. This point is also alluded to in *Iliad* 8, with a role reversal paralleling that in the case of Nestor and Diomedes. For just as Nestor does not save Odysseus in *Odyssey* 3 in the context of their *nóstos*, Odysseus very pointedly does not save Nestor in *Iliad* 8. When Diomedes sees the old man in trouble, he shouts to Odysseus to halt his shameful flight and help drive Hector back, but Odysseus *pays no heed*, and dashes on to the ships (*Iliad* 8.90–98):

καί νύ κεν ἔνθ' ὁ γέρων ἀπὸ θυμὸν ὄλεσσεν
εἰ μὴ ἄρ' ὀξὺ νόησε βοὴν ἀγαθὸς Διομήδης·
σμερδαλέον δ' ἐβόησεν ἐποτρύνων 'Οδυσῆα·
"διογενὲς Λαερτιάδη πολυμήχαν' 'Οδυσσεῦ
πῇ φεύγεις μετὰ νῶτα βαλὼν κακὸς ὣς ἐν ὁμίλῳ;
μή τίς τοι φεύγοντι μεταφρένῳ ἐν δόρυ πήξῃ·
ἀλλὰ μέν' ὄφρα γέροντος ἀπώσομεν ἄγριον ἄνδρα."
ὣς ἔφατ', <u>οὐδ' ἐσάκουσε</u> πολύτλας δῖος 'Οδυσσεύς,
ἀλλὰ παρήϊξεν κοίλας ἐπὶ νῆας 'Αχαιῶν.

There the old man would have lost his life
if Diomedes had not sharply perceived him;

---

98 There is a difference between Pindar's *Pythian* 6 and *Iliad* 8 in that Nestor calls to Antilochus for help in Pindar, but Diomedes "sharply perceives" (*oxù nóēse, Iliad* 8.91) Nestor's peril. Is this act of *nóos* also part of the role reversal in which Diomedes is the savior instead of Nestor?

he bellowed out a shout, rousing Odysseus:
"Zeus-born son of Laertes, Odysseus of many devices,
where are you fleeing, turning your back like a coward in the
    crowd?
May no one plant his spear in your back as you run away;
but stay until we drive this wild warrior away from the old man."
So he spoke, but much-suffering shining Odysseus <u>did not listen</u>
    to him,
but darted back to the hollow ships of the Achaeans.

This is all that is said about Odysseus, in a brief episode that seems to go
nowhere, and to amount to nothing more than a gratuitous slander on this
hero's reputation.[99] But the point of this little episode is to evoke the *nóstoi* of

---

99 Ovid gives the episode this slant when, in the judgment of arms, Ajax describes Odysseus's
    shameful behavior in abandoning Nestor (*Metamorphoses* 13.63–69):

    qui licet eloquio fidum quoque Nestora vincat,
    haud tamen efficiet, <u>desertum</u> ut <u>Nestora crimen</u>
    esse rear nullum; qui cum plorasset Ulixen
    vulnere tardus equi fessusque senilibus annis,
    <u>proditus a socio est</u>; non haec mihi crimina fingi
    scit bene Tydides, qui nomine saepe vocatum
    corripuit trepidoque fugam exprobravit amico.

    Even if he surpasses faithful Nestor in eloquence,
    he still will not convince me that his <u>desertion of Nestor</u>
    was no <u>reproach</u>; when Nestor, slowed by his horse's wound
    and worn out by his own old years, begged Ulysses for help,
    <u>he was betrayed by his companion</u>; that these charges are not made up by me
    the son of Tydeus knows well, who called him repeatedly by name
    and rebuked him, and reproached his frightened friend for his flight.

    The *Iliad* itself seems to recognize the danger that Odysseus has been seriously dimin-
    ished as a hero by his retreat in *Iliad* 8, for he is given a counterbalancing scene in *Iliad*
    11.404–410, where he resolves to stand alone against the entire Trojan army:

    ὤ μοι ἐγὼ τί πάθω; μέγα μὲν κακὸν αἴ κε φέβωμαι
    πληθὺν ταρβήσας· τὸ δὲ ῥίγιον αἴ κεν ἁλώω
    μοῦνος· τοὺς δ' ἄλλους Δαναοὺς ἐφόβησε Κρονίων.
    ἀλλὰ τί ἤ μοι ταῦτα φίλος διελέξατο θυμός;
    οἶδα γὰρ ὅττι κακοὶ μὲν ἀποίχονται πολέμοιο,
    ὃς δέ κ' ἀριστεύῃσι μάχῃ ἔνι τὸν δὲ μάλα χρεὼ
    ἐστάμεναι κρατερῶς, ἤ τ' ἔβλητ' ἤ τ' ἔβαλ' ἄλλον.

    Oh what am I to suffer? It is a great evil if I flee,
    fearing the crowd of warriors; but it is more horrible if I am caught
    alone; Kronos's son has frightened the others away.
    But why does my dear heart ponder this?

Odyssey 3, for just as Diomedes needs Nestor to complete his *nóstos*, Odysseus does not. Morever, the suggestion of Odysseus's cool indifference towards Nestor makes more sense when we realize that the situation is meant to call to mind the way Nestor and Odysseus would one day part from each other on the island of Tenedos in bitter disagreement—neither heeding the other.[100]

§2.76 The episode in *Iliad* 8 thus alludes to the *nóstoi* of *Odyssey* 3 and to the death of Antilochus simultaneously. As the episode proceeds, the relationship between Nestor and Diomedes, which is destined to culminate in their *nóstos* together, is of primary interest. We have already seen that this relationship is depicted in *Iliad* 9, when Nestor reminds Diomedes that he is young enough to be his son, and therefore has not reached the "goal" of his words in addressing the Achaean leaders, as Nestor himself then goes on to do. This episode in *Iliad* 9 depends on the episode in *Iliad* 8 in that the contrast in ages, which Nestor turns to his advantage in the meeting of the leaders, was first brought up by Diomedes on the battlefield, when he chided Nestor for his old age, his weak attendant, and his slow horses. In such terms does he greet Nestor when, without the help of Odysseus, he comes to Nestor's rescue by himself (*Iliad* 8.99–104):

Τυδεΐδης δ' αὐτός περ ἐὼν προμάχοισιν ἐμίχθη,

στῆ δὲ πρόσθ' ἵππων Νηληϊάδαο γέροντος,

καί μιν φωνήσας ἔπεα πτερόεντα προσηύδα·

"ὦ γέρον ἦ μάλα δή σε νέοι τείρουσι μαχηταί,

σὴ δὲ βίη λέλυται, χαλεπὸν δέ σε γῆρας ὀπάζει,

ἠπεδανὸς δέ νύ τοι θεράπων, βραδέες δέ τοι ἵπποι."

I know that cowards shrink from war,
and that whoever is best in battle
must stand firm, and is either struck or strikes another.

In a perceptive study of Odysseus's role in the *Iliad* Pache 2000:21 explains Odysseus's behavior in *Iliad* 8 as a desire to survive the war, but this alone does not free him from the charge of cowardice; Odysseus is indeed a survivor, but not at the price of cowardice, as the episode in *Iliad* 11 seems meant to reestablish.

100 The verb *esakoúō* occurs only in *Iliad* 8.97 in Homer; it properly means "heed" (cf. Herodotus 4.133.2, etc.) but can also mean "hear." Is it possible that Odysseus simply does not hear Diomedes? If that is what is meant, it is inexplicable that the poet should have chosen a verb that properly means "heed," as if the distinction does not matter here. The distinction does matter, and the phrase *oud' esákouse* must mean "did not heed." At this point in the poem all the Greeks are forced to retreat as part of Zeus's plan; at the end of *Iliad* 8 the Trojans will camp outside their walls for the first time. Diomedes is the last to yield to Zeus's will (see below), but Odysseus has already made his decision, and the thought of losing Nestor does not stop him.

The son of Tydeus, although he was alone, mixed with the
    fighters in front
and stood before the horses of the aged son of Neleus,
and speaking winged words he addressed him:
"Old man, younger warriors wear you out completely,
and your strength is undone, and hard old age accompanies you,
and your attendant is weak, and your horses are slow."

Diomedes then calls Nestor onto his own chariot to see the speed of his
horses, which he took from the Trojan Aeneas in battle.[101] At Diomedes'
bidding, Nestor takes the reins and drives straight at Hector, who likewise
drives straight at them. Diomedes misses Hector with his spear but he kills
Hector's driver, and Hector must then find another. Before their encounter
can resume, which would have had dire consequences for the Trojans, Zeus
intervenes by hurling a thunderbolt in front of Diomedes' chariot, and his
horses are brought up short, cowering in fear (*Iliad* 8.130–136):

ἐνθά κε λοιγὸς ἔην καὶ ἀμήχανα ἔργα γένοντο,
καί νύ κε σήκασθεν κατὰ Ἴλιον ἠΰτε ἄρνες,
εἰ μὴ ἄρ' ὀξὺ νόησε πατὴρ ἀνδρῶν τε θεῶν τε·
βροντήσας δ' ἄρα δεινὸν ἀφῆκ' ἀργῆτα κεραυνόν,
κὰδ δὲ πρόσθ' ἵππων Διομήδεος ἧκε χαμᾶζε·
δεινὴ δὲ φλὸξ ὦρτο θεείου καιομένοιο,
τὼ δ' ἵππω δείσαντε καταπτήτην ὑπ' ὄχεσφι.

Then there would have been disaster and deeds beyond repair
    would have taken place,
and the Trojans would have been penned up in Ilion like sheep,
if the father of men and gods had not sharply perceived them;
thundering dreadfully he shot out a shining lightning bolt,
and sent it down to the ground in front of Diomedes' horses;
a dreadful flame rose from the burning sulphur,
and the team of horses cowered in fear under the chariot.

The sign from Zeus is unambiguous. It is in fact a direct warning. Nestor,
who is able to perceive subtle signs from the gods that others miss, does not

101 Diomedes captured Aeneas's horses after wounding him in *Iliad* 5.318-327 (cf. *Iliad* 5.260–273).

miss the intent of this one, and he tells Diomedes to turn back and flee: Zeus intends to give glory to Hector today, but some other day, perhaps, he will give glory to them. Diomedes, too, knows what the sign means, for he does not disagree with Nestor's words. But still he is greatly pained that he must flee, for Hector will boast about it among the Trojans, and Diomedes would rather be swallowed up by the earth than endure that. Diomedes is impassioned, but Nestor prevails by chiding him, saying that the Trojan women whose husbands Diomedes has killed will not believe Hector if he calls him a coward, and with that Nestor turns the horses and retreats (*Iliad* 8.152–158):

> "ὦ μοι Τυδέος υἱὲ δαΐφρονος, οἷον ἔειπες.
>
> εἴ περ γάρ σ' Ἕκτωρ γε κακὸν καὶ ἀνάλκιδα φήσει,
>
> ἀλλ' οὐ πείσονται Τρῶες καὶ Δαρδανίωνες
>
> καὶ Τρώων ἄλοχοι μεγαθύμων ἀσπιστάων,
>
> τάων ἐν κονίῃσι βάλες θαλεροὺς παρακοίτας."
>
> ὣς ἄρα φωνήσας φύγαδε τράπε μώνυχας ἵππους
>
> αὖτις ἀν' ἰωχμόν.

> "Son of keen-spirited Tydeus, what a thing you have said.
> For if ever Hector says that you are cowardly and weak,
> the Trojans and Dardanians will not believe him,
> nor will the wives of the great-hearted Trojan spearmen,
> whose lusty bedpartners you have thrown in the dust."
> Having spoken thus he turned the solid-hoofed horses to flight
> back through the tumult.

As they flee, Hector taunts Diomedes, just as he feared, and he must listen to himself called a woman who will never take away the wives of the Trojans. Diomedes debates in his heart three times whether to turn back again and fight, but three times Zeus thunders from Mount Ida, giving a sign of victory to the Trojans.

§2.77 When Nestor gets onto Diomedes' chariot in *Iliad* 8, and the two of them are paired as horsemen, the episode moves into the domain of Nestor's oldest traditions, his chariot race against the Epeian twins at Bouprasion. In that race the youthful Nestor, who raced alone, lacked all "restraint," and he was thus unable to make the turn around the turning post, and he crashed as a result. In *Iliad* 8 the aged Nestor, with Diomedes at his side, does turn back, and he thus avoids catastrophe. In this reversal there is a balanced pair of twins, as it were, and not a single charioteer, but Diomedes represents "incitement" and Nestor, who is far now from his youthful self, represents "restraint." His "restraint," however, is not the physical act of holding the reins, although he does that too, but an act of moral persuasion. Nestor calms Diomedes with his words, and this act of "restraining" is what turns them back toward safety.

§2.78 When the youthful Nestor lost control of his chariot, the reins flew from his hands, and the horses careened off the end of the course. This is of course not described directly in *Iliad* 23, when Nestor speaks of his loss to the twins, but indirectly, when Idomeneus speculates among the spectators about the reason for Eumelos's disappearance from the race (*Iliad* 23.465–468):

> ἦε τὸν ἡνίοχον <u>φύγον ἡνία</u>, οὐδὲ δυνάσθη
> εὖ σχεθέειν περὶ τέρμα καὶ οὐκ ἐτύχησεν ἑλίξας·
> ἔνθά μιν ἐκπεσέειν ὀΐω σύν θ' ἅρματα ἆξαι,
> αἳ δ' ἐξηρώησαν, ἐπεὶ μένος ἔλλαβε θυμόν.

> Or the <u>reins flew</u> from the charioteer, and he was not able
> to hold on well around the post, and did not succeed in turning;
> there, I think, he fell out and broke his chariot,
> and his mares careened off the course when frenzy seized their
>   spirit.

We have seen that this description, which does not apply to what actually happened to Eumelos, in fact describes what once happened to the youthful Nestor. In *Iliad* 8, in an episode that is meant to bring Nestor's youthful race to mind, the aged Nestor again lets the reins fly from his hands when Zeus hurls the thunderbolt in front of Diomedes' horses (*Iliad* 8.135–138):

> δεινὴ δὲ φλὸξ ὦρτο θεείου καιομένοιο,
> τὼ δ' ἵππω δείσαντε καταπτήτην ὑπ' ὄχεσφι·
> Νέστορα δ' ἐκ χειρῶν <u>φύγον ἡνία</u> σιγαλόεντα,
> δεῖσε δ' ὅ γ' ἐν θυμῷ, Διομήδεα δὲ προσέειπε.

> A dreadful flame rose from the burning sulphur,
> and the team of horses cowered in fear under the chariot.
> The shining <u>reins flew</u> from Nestor's hands,
> and he was afraid in his heart, and he spoke to Diomedes.

The act of dropping the reins is the same for the youthful and for the aged Nestor, but the cause and result of this act are completely changed in the second case. The youthful Nestor let the reins fly from his hands by flailing with them to gain speed, and the horses careened off the end of the course and crashed once he lost control of them. When the aged Nestor drops the reins the horses have already stopped short, frightened by Zeus's thunderbolt, and Nestor, with fear in his own heart, addresses Diomedes in order to restrain him and turn him back. The dropped reins are a signal to recall Nestor's youthful race, and to draw attention to the changes rung on that race in the present episode.[102] Knowing when and how to turn back is the point.

§2.79 *Iliad* 8, with its allusions to the *nóstoi* of Nestor and Diomedes (and to that of Odysseus) on the one hand, and to the chariot race of Nestor against the Epeian twins on the other hand, serves as a bridge between *Iliad* 23, with its chariot race, and *Odyssey* 3, with its account of the Achaeans' *nóstoi*.[103] At the end of my discussion of the chariot race in *Iliad* 23 I raised the issue of connections between this race and the *nóstoi* of the Achaeans. I return to this issue now, and begin with Diomedes, the winner of the race. Diomedes wins the race in the games for Patroclus because he has Athena's help, for she gives him back his whip when it is knocked from his hands by Apollo, and she puts *ménos* into his horses.[104] In considering Diomedes' victory over Eumelos, which is really a victory of two against one when Athena's help is taken into account, I argued that his race is a transformation of the race that the Epeian twins won against Nestor. Athena plays the part of the immortal twin in Diomedes' victory by providing "incitement" to him and to his horses. But this scheme is also relevant to Diomedes himself and to his *nóstos* from Troy, for he will not return on his own: he will need the help of Néstōr, the "homebringer." Thus his race is a deliberate foreshadowing of his *nóstos* if we are willing to view Athena's role in the race as a transformation of Nestor's role in his *nóstos*. If this is the case, it has the interesting consequence that Nestor figures on both sides in the race for first prize: the youthful Nestor

---

102 Nestor's explicitly dropped reins in *Iliad* 8 add an important confirmation that he did in fact drop the reins in his youthful race at Bouprasion; this feature of his race is of course kept out of direct view in *Iliad* 23.

103 It is worth stepping back for a moment to appreciate the unusual concentration of allusions in *Iliad* 8 to Nestor's past and future all in the same episode: his race against the Epeian twins in the past; his *nóstos* with Diomedes in the future; the death of his son Antilochus before the end of the war; his split with Odysseus on Tenedos after the war. All these different moments are present in the episode.

104 She also disables the chariot of Eumelos, who has the fastest horses and is called the best driver.

lies behind Eumelos, who crashes, and the aged Nestor, whose *nóstos* is still in the future, lies behind Diomedes' helper Athena, who plays the immortal twin to Diomedes' mortal twin in the victory over Eumelos. In this sense the aged Nestor triumphs over the youthful Nestor in the same race.[105]

§2.80 While Nestor is human and Athena is a god, and this difference is never forgotten in the Homeric poems, the two figures do have similar functions to a certain extent. We see this again in the case of Diomedes when Athena mounts his chariot in *Iliad* 5 and Nestor mounts his chariot in *Iliad* 8. This parallel, I think, is not an accident. Nor, I think, is the contrast between the two figures, for Athena mounts Diomedes' chariot to urge him on to attack and wound the god Ares, but Nestor mounts his chariot to prevent him from challenging the clearly demonstrated will of the god Zeus, much as Diomedes is tempted to do so. Behind both figures who ride beside Diomedes on his chariot is the immortal twin, whose role is to provide "incitement." But in Nestor's case, although the role of the immortal twin is, so to speak, his by birthright, he has also acquired the role of the mortal twin, and in this episode he provides "restraint." The contrast with Athena's role in *Iliad* 5 has to do with the difference between human and divine, for as Nestor tells Diomedes, a man cannot force Zeus to change his mind, since Zeus is much stronger (*Iliad* 8.143–144):

ἀνὴρ δέ κεν οὔ τι Διὸς νόον εἰρύσσαιτο
οὐδὲ μάλ' ἴφθιμος, ἐπεὶ ἦ πολὺ φέρτερός ἐστι.

A man would not change Zeus's mind,
not even a very strong one, since he is much more powerful.

§2.81 There is a link between Diomedes' victory in the chariot race in *Iliad* 23 and his easy *nóstos* in *Odyssey* 3. In both cases he is not alone. But the link is indirect since it involves the transformation of Nestor's future role as "homebringer" into a role played by the goddess Athena in the race. The link between Diomedes' *nóstos* and *Iliad* 8, on the other hand, is direct. When Nestor turns the horses back to flee, he saves Diomedes from divine wrath, just as he does later, when he flees from Tenedos with Diomedes because he "realized that the god planned evil things." Since the direct link with

---

105 This would not be the only time that Athena plays the part of the immortal twin and imitates Nestor in so doing. She does this when she disguises herself as the aged *Méntōr* and accompanies Telemachus to visit the equally aged *Néstōr* in *Odyssey* 3: the very name that she adopts when she pairs herself with Odysseus's son seems to be patterned on Nestor's name (see §2.92–§2.98 below).

Diomedes' *nóstos* is made in *Iliad* 8, it does not need to be made again in *Iliad* 23, when Diomedes wins the race driving the same team of Trojan horses that carried him safely out of battle in *Iliad* 8. In *Iliad* 23, instead of having Nestor at his side to help him, Diomedes has the help of Athena from a distance, and this too is not unrelated to his *nóstos*. For if Nestor, and not Athena, helped him in his *nóstos*, it was Athena's wrath that had to be escaped, and Athena's favor for him, again from a distance, is implied by the fact that he did escape.

§2.82 There is a link between Diomedes' race in *Iliad* 23 and his *nóstos*, but the direct link with his *nóstos* is provided by *Iliad* 8, and this must be taken into account first: *Iliad* 23 does not repeat what *Iliad* 8 has already laid out, but assumes it. What of the race of Antilochus in *Iliad* 23? His death is directly alluded to in *Iliad* 8, just as the *nóstos* of Diomedes is. In the chariot race, however, he is a victor. Is there a sense in which his failure to return home is implied in his chariot race, victory though it is? Perhaps so, if we bear in mind that Nestor himself is at the center of the events that cause his son's death—Antilochus dies trying to save his father—and that Nestor is equally involved in his son's chariot race without quite seeming to be. In analyzing Antilochus's race I traced the connection from Nestor's speech of advice to his son's dangerous maneuver by way of the repeated phrase *oudé he léthei*, which Nestor uses of the skillful charioteer who knows when to press his horses and seize the lead, and *oudé me lései*, which Antilochus utters when he sees his opportunity to do exactly what Nestor has implicitly advised him to do. Nestor's responsibility for his son's fate is the issue here, however muted it remains. Antilochus wins the race, but in a sense he does not, for he must first give up his prize to Menelaus before he is allowed to keep it.[106] The doubt that this casts on Antilochus's victory is the key point if his race indirectly alludes to his death and failure to return from Troy. We should also perhaps consider the fact that it is Achilles who first proposes to deny Antilochus second prize, though his motivation is not to dishonor Antilochus, but to honor Eumelos. I have already suggested that when Achilles singles Eumelos out for a special prize, his action resonates against the tradition, if it is old, that Eumelos won the chariot race in the games held at Achilles' own funeral.[107] There is the further question, however, whether Achilles' action

---

106 Antilochus's "victory" is a very qualified one in another sense as well: it was only the action of Menelaus in giving way that prevented catastrophe; for his own part, Antilochus deserved to crash. He will display the same reckless bravery on behalf of his father, but then no one will be able to compensate for his behavior and save him. Certainly Nestor will be powerless to do so.
107 See n2.69 above.

also relates to Antilochus. There is both relevance and pathos if Achilles'
proposal to deny Antilochus his victory is taken as an allusion to his death
in Troy, for Antilochus is Achilles' favorite, second only to Patroclus, and the
prize in question is in honor of Patroclus's death. In the "second Nekyia" in
Odyssey 24, Agamemnon tells Achilles in the underworld how the Achaeans
buried Achilles at his death with the remains of Patroclus, mixing their ashes
in the same vessel, while the ashes of Antilochus, whom Achilles honored
most after Patroclus died, remained apart (*Odyssey* 24.76–79):

> ἐν τῷ τοι κεῖται λεύκ' ὀστέα, φαίδιμ' Ἀχιλλεῦ,
>
> μίγδα δὲ Πατρόκλοιο Μενοιτιάδαο θανόντος,
>
> χωρὶς δ' Ἀντιλόχοιο, τὸν ἔξοχα τῖες ἁπάντων
>
> τῶν ἄλλων ἑτάρων μετὰ Πάτροκλόν γε θανόντα.

> In it lie your white bones, shining Achilles,
> mixed with those of Menoitios's son Patroclus who had died,
> but apart from those of Antilochus, whom you honored above all
> other companions after Patroclus died.

Because of the parallel between Patroclus and Antilochus in their closeness
to Achilles, it is right that there be a suggestion of Antilochus's fate, which
parallels Patroclus's fate, when Achilles awards the prizes to honor Patroclus's
death.[108] Even more fitting is this suggestion from the standpoint of Nestor,
who will involuntarily cause the death of his son, just as he has involuntarily
caused the death of Patroclus. But the primary unspoken point in the chariot
race concerns Nestor's connection with the death of Patroclus—these are his
funeral games—and not with the death of Antilochus. Hence, for the time
being, Antilochus is an apparent victor.[109]

§2.83 Whereas allusions to Antilochus's fate are indirect in *Iliad* 23, the
allusion to his fate in *Iliad* 8 is direct. The situation is in this respect much

---

108 Achilles, Patroclus, and Antilochus are together again in the underworld (*Odyssey*
11.467–468, 24.15–16): in both passages (which are nearly identical) Achilles occurs in the
first line, Patroclus and Antilochus in the second line.

109 Antilochus comes in last in the footrace, and this race, as already noted, has directly to
do with the Achaeans' *nóstoi*: the successful return of Odysseus on the one hand, and the
destruction of the lesser Ajax on the other hand (cf. §2.54 above). It is not a good sign for
Antilochus's *nóstos* that even Ajax, whom Athena trips, finishes ahead of him. In accepting
last prize Antilochus is respectful of his two older competitors, who have both defeated
him (*Iliad* 23.787–792), and this too connects with the chariot race, where Antilochus's
respect for Menelaus becomes the issue in the contest for second prize. That prize, which
Antilochus was barely allowed to keep, is put deeper in doubt by the footrace.

the same for Antilochus as for Diomedes. Significantly it is these two who are closest to Nestor and who mean most to him in terms of their return, in the case of Diomedes, or failure to return, in the case of Antilochus. In *Iliad* 8 the contrast between the death of Antilochus and the return of Diomedes is of primary concern in the episode's rich interplay of allusions. We thus begin to see that from Nestor's standpoint there was a need for the episode in *Iliad* 8. In *Iliad* 23 it is Nestor's relation to Patroclus, and to Patroclus's fate, that is of primary concern in terms of the episode's hidden poetic agenda. Nestor's relation to the contrasting fates of Diomedes and Antilochus is thus necessarily of secondary concern. But the fates of Diomedes and Antilochus were not of secondary concern to Nestor himself.

§2.84 Of the four main contestants in the chariot race of *Iliad* 23, we must still consider the race of Menelaus in relation to his *nóstos*. Menelaus finishes the race in third place, ahead of only Meriones, who is the worst driver and has the slowest horses (*Iliad* 23.530–531), and Eumelos, who would have finished first if he had not crashed. Menelaus finishes in the middle of the field of contestants, but his race is regarded as a loss rather than a victory because he is defeated for second prize by Antilochus. The reason for his defeat is that he deliberately holds back when Antilochus passes him on the narrow road. Antilochus's act, which is one of "incitement," is couched in terms of *nóos* in various ways, including his own statement in his apology to Menelaus that the *nóos* of a young man is "too swift." Menelaus, who holds back when Antilochus surges ahead, hesitates in other contexts as well. On his *nóstos*, after leading half the army away from Troy to Tenedos, he falls behind Nestor and Diomedes when they flee from Tenedos. He overtakes them on Lesbos when they pause to seek a sign from the god, and he accompanies them to Geraistos in Euboea, and from there to Cape Sounion. If we compare his *nóstos* up to this point with his race in *Iliad* 23, we may say that he is still in the "race," and if he has no chance of arriving home in Sparta before Diomedes reaches Argos, he has every chance of reaching home in second place after Diomedes. But then the same thing happens that happens in his race, namely he is forced to fall behind. His helmsman dies at Cape Sounion and, eager though he is to pursue his journey, he is detained in order to bury his companion and perform funeral rites; Nestor tells the story in *Odyssey* 3.284–285:

ὣς ὁ μὲν ἔνθα κατέσχετ', ἐπειγόμενός περ ὁδοῖο,
ὄφρ' ἕταρον θάπτοι καὶ ἐπὶ κτέρεα κτερίσειεν.

So he stopped there, eager though he was for the journey,
until he buried his companion and performed funeral rites.

If the rapid progress of Nestor and Diomedes on their *nóstos* is due to Nestor's
accurate perception of the correct course and his incitement in pursuing that
course through each successive turn along the way, Menelaus falls behind just
when further incitement is needed to complete the journey. Menelaus lacks
Nestor's quality of *nóos* at a critical moment, and this is symbolized by his loss
of his helmsman at Cape Sounion, for the helmsman is his ship's guide, and
the helmsman's name, significantly, is *Phróntis* (*Odyssey* 3.282). Menelaus's loss
of *Phróntis*, whose name in later Greek means "thought, meditation, delibera-
tion," represents a deficiency in himself as well.[110] Without *Phróntis*, Menelaus
is blown off course by a storm as he rounds Cape Malea. Had he stayed with
Nestor, he would have rounded this dangerous cape without incident. In the
chariot race it is Nestor's son Antilochus whose act of *nóos* Menelaus cannot
match and who leaves him behind.

§2.85 Menelaus is blown all the way to Egypt, and he wanders there
and in Phoenicia for eight years (*Odyssey* 4.82) before he is finally able to
return home, the last of the Achaeans to do so according to Athena/Mentes
(*Odyssey* 1.286). Menelaus's *nóstos* is exceedingly slow in comparison with that
of Nestor and Diomedes, and yet he does return home in the end. But if his
nóstos is ultimately successful, why is his chariot race regarded as a defeat?
The answer to this may lie in the fact that Menelaus races not just for himself,
but for himself and Agamemnon at the same time. The two of them cannot of
course actually compete together in the same chariot, but both of them are
represented in the team of horses that Menelaus drives, one of which is his,
the other Agamemnon's. This curious team is described when Menelaus rises
next after Diomedes to enter the race (*Iliad* 23.293–295):

τῷ δ' ἄρ' ἐπ' Ἀτρεΐδης ὦρτο ξανθὸς Μενέλαος
διογενής, ὑπὸ δὲ ζυγὸν ἤγαγεν ὠκέας ἵππους
Αἴθην τὴν Ἀγαμεμνονέην τὸν ἑόν τε Πόδαργον.

After him the Zeus-born son of Atreus, fair-haired Menelaus,
rose

---

110 Phrontis's patronymic *Onētorídēs* means son of "helper": the quality of "helper" belongs
to Phrontis himself in that he "helps" Menelaus on his *nóstos*, as is made clear by his loss,
after which Menelaus wanders for years (cf. Calchas, son of *Thestorídēs*, as discussed §1.14
above).

and led the swift horses under the yoke,
Aithe, Agamemnon's mare, and Podargos, his own horse.

Whereas Menelaus's horse is a male, Agamemnon's is a female, and this fact plays a part in the race. For when Antilochus calls on his horses to overtake Menelaus's he shames them with the thought of losing to a female (*Iliad* 23.407–409):

ἵππους δ' Ἀτρεΐδαο κιχάνετε, μὴ δὲ λίπησθον,
καρπαλίμως, μὴ σφῶϊν ἐλεγχείην καταχεύῃ
Αἴθη θῆλυς ἐοῦσα· τίη λείπεσθε φέριστοι;

Catch Atreus's son's horses quickly, do not lag behind,
so that Aithe, being <u>female</u>, may not heap reproach on the two
    of you;
why do you lag behind, brave ones?

Antilochus singles out Agamemnon's mare to motivate his own team, and to this extent the mare is a liability in the race, and we may ask whether this fact relates to the *nóstoi* of the two Atreidai.[111] As far as Agamemnon's *nóstos* is concerned, it is a female, his own wife Clytemnestra, who turns his *nóstos*

---

111 The point of Antilochus's phrase *Aíthē thêlus eoûsa*, "Aithe being female," seems to have more to do with an attitude, namely the shame of losing to a female, than with a reality, for mares were not necessarily the weaker sex in chariot races. Eumelos's horses, which are called the best horses of the Greeks in *Iliad* 2.763, are both mares; they are contrasted with Diomedes' Trojan horses, which are both males, when the contest between them develops after the turning post and Eumelos takes an immediate lead (*Iliad* 23.375–378):

ἄφαρ δ' ἵπποισι τάθη δρόμος· ὦκα δ' ἔπειτα
<u>αἳ</u> Φηρητιάδαο ποδώκεες ἔκφερον ἵπποι.
<u>τὰς</u> δὲ μετ' ἐξέφερον Διομήδεος <u>ἄρσενες</u> ἵπποι
Τρώϊοι, οὐδέ τι πολλὸν ἄνευθ' ἔσαν, ἀλλὰ μάλ' ἐγγύς.

At once the horses strained their hardest. Then quickly
Pheres' son's swift-footed <u>mares</u> took the lead.
After them Diomedes' Trojan <u>male</u> horses broke out,
and they weren't far behind, but very close.

In the race between Menelaus and Antilochus, furthermore, Menelaus gains quickly on his opponent near the end of the race, which he would have won if the race had been longer, and the credit for this goes to the mare (*Iliad* 23.524–527):

ἀλλά μιν αἶψα κίχανεν· ὀφέλλετο γὰρ μένος ἠΰ
ἵππου τῆς Ἀγαμεμνονέης καλλίτριχος Αἴθης·
εἰ δέ κ' ἔτι προτέρω γένετο δρόμος ἀμφοτέροισι,
τώ κέν μιν παρέλασσ' οὐδ' ἀμφήριστον ἔθηκεν.

into his destruction. It is the death of Agamemnon that turns Menelaus's own *nóstos*, successful though it is in itself, into a failure. The link between Menelaus's late return and Agamemnon's death is first established in *Odyssey* 3, when Telemachus asks Nestor how Agamemnon died, for linked to this question is another question—where was Menelaus? (*Odyssey* 3.248–249):

πῶς ἔθαν' Ἀτρεΐδης εὐρὺ κρείων Ἀγαμέμνων;
ποῦ Μενέλαος ἔην;

How did the son of Atreus, wide-ruling Agamemnon, die?
Where was Menelaus?

In his reply Nestor defends Menelaus's reputation valiantly, saying that Telemachus himself knows that Aigisthos would have received no burial, funeral rites, or lamentation if Menelaus on his return home had encountered Aigisthos alive (*Odyssey* 3.254–261). The truth is, however, that Menelaus returned too late not only to defend his brother, but even to avenge him, for Orestes had already slain Aigisthos when Menelaus returned home in the eighth year. He arrived on the very day that Orestes celebrated a funeral for his mother and Aigisthos. For Menelaus himself there is little joy in his own *nóstos* because of his brother's murder. In *Odyssey* 4, when Telemachus admires the splendor of Menelaus's palace, and Menelaus tells how he gained his possessions during his eight years of travel, he ends by saying that these possessions bring him no joy because while he wandered abroad gathering them his brother was slain (*Odyssey* 4.90–92):

εἷος ἐγὼ περὶ κεῖνα πολὺν βίοτον ξυναγείρων
ἠλώμην, τεῖός μοι ἀδελφεὸν ἄλλος ἔπεφνε
λάθρῃ, ἀνωϊστί, δόλῳ οὐλομένης ἀλόχοιο.

While I wandered in those parts gathering much livelihood,
another man slew my brother
stealthily, unawares, by the guile of his ruinous wife.

But he was gaining on him quickly; for the strength
of Agamemnon's mare, beautiful-maned Aithe, was increasing.
If both had had further to run
he would have passed him and not made it a close contest.

Guichard Romero 2004:79 notes that "popular wisdom attributed to mares special virtues, different from those of horses, and mares were sometimes considered better than males in chariot competitions"; see his n. 15 for references.

Menelaus's *nóstos* is a failure in his own eyes because of his brother's untimely death at the hands of his wife; Menelaus's race seems to foreshadow this failure in the team that he drives, which represents his brother as well as himself, and which in his brother's case draws attention to what may be called the female factor.[112]

§2.86 The hesitancy that cost Menelaus second prize in the chariot race, and that led to his long return home, continues to characterize him in his domestic life in Sparta. Compared to his wife Helen, who recognizes Telemachus as soon as she lays eyes on him from his similarity to Odysseus, Menelaus is slow to recognize him. Telemachus weeps when Menelaus says that he misses Odysseus most of those who fought at Troy, and Menelaus ponders whether to ask him who his father is or wait for him to say on his own (*Odyssey* 4.118–119). When Helen enters the room and surmises at once that this is Telemachus, Menelaus also perceives the likeness: οὕτω νῦν καὶ ἐγὼ νοέω, γύναι, ὡς σὺ ἐΐσκεις (*Odyssey* 4.148). Once Helen has pointed out the likeness, everything falls into place for Menelaus. He now sees many points of similarity to Odysseus, and he understands why mention of Odysseus made Telemachus weep (*Odyssey* 4.149–154). On his own, however, Menelaus perceived none of this. Helen takes the lead in other ways as well in *Odyssey* 4, as when she puts a drug in the wine to dull the pain of remembrance and tells a story in praise of Odysseus. Menelaus follows her lead with his own story in Odysseus's praise (*Odyssey* 4.219–289). The contrast between Helen and Menelaus is still more sharply drawn in *Odyssey* 15, when a bird omen appears at the end of a speech of Telemachus; Peisistratos calls on Menelaus to interpret the omen, Menelaus hesitates, and Helen interprets it instead (*Odyssey* 15.160–173).

§2.87 Menelaus is a follower rather than a leader in the *Iliad* too in his relationship with Agamemnon. This is perhaps the origin of his characteristic

112 The phrase *thêlus eoûsa*, "being female," used of Agamemnon's mare in *Iliad* 23 occurs only one other time in Homer. In *Iliad* 19 Agamemnon, likening himself to Zeus as a victim of *átē*, "delusion," uses the phrase of Hera in her deception of Zeus (*Iliad* 19.95–97):

καὶ γὰρ δή νύ ποτε Ζεὺς ἄσατο, τόν περ ἄριστον
ἀνδρῶν ἠδὲ θεῶν φασ' ἔμμεναι· ἀλλ' ἄρα καὶ τὸν
Ἥρη θῆλυς ἐοῦσα δολοφροσύνης ἀπάτησεν.

For indeed Zeus deluded me, who they say
is the best of men and gods; but Hera, being female,
tricked even him by her deceit.

Clytemnestra, without being directly at issue, comes to mind in this passage; she does so in the passage of the chariot race as well.

hesitancy, for Agamemnon is the commander-in-chief, and Menelaus neces-
sarily follows his brother's lead. In *Iliad* 10, with the Trojans camped nearby,
Agamemnon and Menelaus both cannot sleep, and each rises from his bed to
seek counsel. Agamemnon, who is described first, decides to seek out Nestor's
advice. Menelaus, on the other hand, goes to awaken his brother, whom he
finds already up and arming himself (*Iliad* 10.32–34):

βῆ δ' ἴμεν ἀνστήσων ὃν ἀδελφεόν, ὃς μέγα πάντων
Ἀργείων ἤνασσε, θεὸς δ' ὣς τίετο δήμῳ.
τὸν δ' εὖρ' ἀμφ' ὤμοισι τιθήμενον ἔντεα καλά.

He went to rouse his brother, who ruled greatly over all
the Argives and was honored like a god by the people.
He found him putting beautiful weapons on his shoulders.

In this situation calling for wise counsel the direction of dependency is
clear, with Menelaus seeking out Agamemnon, and Agamemnon seeking out
Nestor. Nevertheless it is Menelaus who immediately suggests to Agamemnon
the plan that is set in motion in *Iliad* 10, namely sending a spy against the
Trojans (*Iliad* 10.37–38). The brothers then part to awaken different heroes
and call them to council. When Agamemnon awakens Nestor, Nestor
prepares to follow him and call others. But first he finds fault with Menelaus
for sleeping and letting Agamemnon exert himself at this dangerous pass.
When Agamemnon corrects Nestor's misconception, he says that he is right
to blame Menelaus at other times, for he often holds back and does not wish
to exert himself, not out of hesitancy or dull-wittedness, but because he waits
for Agamemnon's lead (*Iliad* 10.120–123):

ὦ γέρον ἄλλοτε μέν σε καὶ αἰτιάασθαι ἄνωγα·
πολλάκι γὰρ μεθιεῖ τε καὶ οὐκ ἐθέλει πονέεσθαι
οὔτ' ὄκνῳ εἴκων οὔτ' ἀφραδίῃσι νόοιο,
ἀλλ' ἐμέ τ' εἰσορόων καὶ ἐμὴν ποτιδέγμενος ὁρμήν.

Old man, I urge you at other times to find fault with him,
for he often gives way and does not want to exert himself,
not because he yields to fear or helplessness of mind,
but because he looks to me and awaits my lead.[113]

---

113 Note how Agamemnon's explanation is illustrated in *Iliad* 10.61–63, where Menelaus asks
his brother for instructions:

Menelaus "gives way," not out of hesitancy or dull-wittedness, but because he needs his brother's lead. The verb *methieî*, "gives way," in *Iliad* 10.121 brings us back to Menelaus's chariot race, in which he "willingly gave way" to Telemachus to avoid a crash (*Iliad* 23.434–435):

αὐτὸς γὰρ ἑκὼν <u>μεθέηκεν</u> ἐλαύνειν
μή πως συγκύρσειαν ὁδῷ ἔνι μώνυχες ἵπποι.

For he himself deliberately <u>let up</u> driving,
so the solid-hoofed horses would not run into each other on the road.

The verb *methíēmi* used of Menelaus in these two different contexts is highly suggestive.[114] What looks like hesitancy and a lack of *nóos* in Menelaus is due to the fact that he is not used to acting on his own. Menelaus truly acts on his own for the first time at the drunken assembly after the fall of Troy, when he opposes Agamemnon and leaves him behind once and for all. This does not change his character, however, for hesitancy and a *nóos* that is not fast enough mark his *nóstos*, when he no longer has his brother's lead to follow. Menelaus's chariot race in *Iliad* 23 anticipates his *nóstos*, for he is on his own in this too, and at the crucial moment he "gives way."[115]

πῶς γάρ μοι μύθῳ ἐπιτέλλεαι ἠδὲ κελεύεις;
αὖθι μένω μετὰ τοῖσι δεδεγμένος εἰς ὅ κεν ἔλθῃς,
ἦε θέω μετὰ σ' αὖτις, ἐπὴν εὖ τοῖς ἐπιτείλω;

How do you order and command me with your word?
Shall I stay there with those men waiting until you come,
or shall I run after you again, when I have given them your orders?

114 The verb is used of Menelaus yet a third time. When he is becalmed on his *nóstos* in Egypt, on the island of Pharos, Eidothee, daughter of Proteus, pities him. She questions him as follows (*Odyssey* 4.371–373):

νήπιός εἰς, ὦ ξεῖνε, λίην τόσσον ἠδὲ χαλίφρων,
ἦε ἑκὼν <u>μεθιεῖς</u> καὶ τέρπεαι ἄλγεα πάσχων;
ὡς δὴ δήθ' ἐνὶ νήσῳ ἐρύκεαι....

Are you so exceedingly foolish and loose-witted, stranger,
or do you instead willingly <u>give way</u> and enjoy suffering woes?
For you are detained a long time on this island....

As in *Iliad* 10, *methieîs* is here distinguished from loose-wittedness. As in *Iliad* 23, the idea of *hekṓn*, "willingly, of one's own accord," is added to *methíēmi*, "give way." The verb *methíēmi* is used in a similar sense in *Iliad* 4.516, 6.523, 13.229, 15.553, 20.361, and *Odyssey* 16.377; note especially *Iliad* 6.523, where Hector chides Paris: ἀλλὰ ἑκὼν μεθιεῖς τε καὶ οὐκ ἐθέλεις, "but you give way of your own accord and are not willing."
115 Aspersions are cast on Menelaus's reputation as a warrior in *Iliad* 17.588, where Apollo, disguised as a mortal, calls him a "weak spearman" (*malthakòs aikhmētḗs*) in urging Hector

215

§2.88 This completes the comparison of the races run by the charioteers of *Iliad* 23 with their later *nóstoi*.[116] The connection is strongest for Menelaus, since his *nóstos* is not alluded to more directly elsewhere in the *Iliad*, as is the *nóstos* of Diomedes, and as is also the death of Antilochus in Troy, which denied him a *nóstos*. As we have seen, the fates of Diomedes and Antilochus are also at issue in *Iliad* 23, but they play a subordinate role to Nestor's old race against the Epeian twins, which they in different ways reenact. While Antilochus reenacts the "incitement" that characterized Nestor's race, Diomedes, with Athena's help from a distance, reenacts the successful race of the Epeian twins. The remaining contestant, Eumelos, reenacts the youthful race of Nestor himself, and this is the entire focus of Eumelos's race. We know nothing of his *nóstos*, and it is unlikely that it concerned the poet of *Iliad* 23. Eumelos's role in reenacting the youthful Nestor's race, which is the great unspoken point of the chariot race, does not compete for our attention with a secondary purpose.[117]

§2.89 Now that we have considered the relationships that connect *Iliad* 8 and *Iliad* 23 with *Odyssey* 3, we should step back briefly and consider the implications of these connections for the relationship between the *Iliad* and the *Odyssey* in general. On the one hand, *Iliad* 8, in its allusions to the *nóstoi* of Diomedes and Odysseus, seems to presuppose our *Odyssey* 3. On the other hand, the allusion in *Iliad* 8 to the death of Antilochus is not to a specific *text*, so the allusions in *Iliad* 8 to the *nóstoi* of Diomedes and Odysseus also need not

---

on against him. Plato *Symposium* 174c discusses Menelaus's character on the basis of this passage. The scholia to *Iliad* 17.588 correctly point out that the attack on Menelaus's reputation is made from an enemy's point of view, and not from the poet's (cf. also Nünlist 2002:453). This point, however, does not completely remove the stain from Menelaus.

116 About Meriones, who finishes last but for Eumelos and is the worst driver, there is nothing else to say.

117 It is the fact that Eumelos is a minor figure that suits him to his role in the chariot race of standing wholly and completely for the youthful Nestor: unless there is more to it than we know, there is no real interest in his own homecoming. The question does remain, however, whether the tradition that Eumelos won the chariot race in the funeral games of Achilles is old ("Apollodorus" *Epitome* 5.5, see n2.69 above). There seem to me to be arguments pro and con: on the one hand there is more point to Achilles' awarding Eumelos a special prize in *Iliad* 23 if it is set against such a tradition; on the other hand, if Eumelos won the chariot race in the funeral games of Achilles, his *nóstos* must also have succeeded, but in *Iliad* 23 he crashes. Does Achilles' awarding of a special prize negate the crash (and its conflict with a successful *nóstos*)? Did Apollo, who tries in vain to help Eumelos in *Iliad* 23, have a role in bringing about a successful *nóstos* for Eumelos? These are unanswerable questions. That the funeral games of Patroclus have something to do with the funeral games of Achilles (the brief account in *Odyssey* 24.85–92 is the earliest mention of the latter) can, I think, be safely assumed; for a convincing case in point see Kakridis 1949:65–83 (discussed below in n4.188 and EN4.7).

be to a specific text. I leave the issue pending for now; we will return to it in due course.[118]

§2.90 We have now considered most of Nestor's role in the *Odyssey*, which is essentially a negative one: Nestor did not bring Odysseus home; worse than that, when Nestor last saw Odysseus they had an angry dispute and parted permanently. This was the plain truth, and however unspoken it is left in *Odyssey* 3, it is in no way denied. But there are other factors that soften the harshness of what happened. In particular, Telemachus and Peisistratos, the sons of the two heroes who parted angrily, form a bond between them that heals that earlier breach. The presence of Athena, disguised as Mentor, also puts everything in a new perspective.

§2.91 Athena herself arranges for Peisistratos to take her place as Telemachus's traveling companion (*Odyssey* 3.368–370). When the two youths leave Pylos for Sparta at the end of *Odyssey* 3 they together mount the chariot that Nestor has had prepared for them (*Odyssey* 3.481–484):

ἂν δ' ἄρα Τηλέμαχος περικαλλέα βήσετο δίφρον·
πὰρ δ' ἄρα Νεστορίδης Πεισίστρατος, ὄρχαμος ἀνδρῶν,
ἐς δίφρον τ' ἀνέβαινε καὶ ἡνία λάζετο χερσί,
μάστιξεν δ' ἐλάαν.

Telemachus mounted the splendid chariot;
next to him Nestor's son Peisistratos, leader of men,
mounted the chariot and grasped the reins with his hands,
and whipped the horses up.

The quarrel that separated Nestor and Odysseus, with such dire consequences for Odysseus, is now made up by their sons, and that is the image that we are left with at the end of *Odyssey* 3, as Peisistratos takes Telemachus on his way. The role that Nestor plays in the *nóstos* of Odysseus is based on his version of the twin myth, in which he is permanently separated from his brother. So too he is permanently separated from Odysseus at the very moment of his

---

118 As the argument has made clear, Nestor's role has a hidden side to it in both the *Iliad* and the *Odyssey*, and this general similarity, I think, is itself of real importance to the relationship between the two poems. To me the correct explanation of the similarity of Nestor's role is that the *Iliad* and the *Odyssey* evolved together over a period of time. To be strictly logical, however, one could also say that the *Odyssey* simply imitates the *Iliad* with respect to Nestor. But we have not yet explored all of Nestor's role in the *Odyssey*, and it is thus too early to weigh this issue; I will return to it below in §4.23 and n4.104. For now it is enough to raise the issue.

nóstos. But the image at the end of *Odyssey* 3 is one of reintegration, and the chariot in which this reintegration takes place suggests poetically the integration of twins. The quarrel between Nestor and Odysseus has not been undone, for it cannot be, and there are echoes of this quarrel even in the very last that we hear about Nestor in the *Odyssey*. For so I would interpret *Odyssey* 15, when Telemachus returns with Peisistratos from Sparta to Pylos, but does not stop to see Nestor before embarking for Ithaca. When Telemachus asks that Peisistratos allow him to do this because of the urgency that he feels to leave, he stresses his friendship with Peisistratos himself, which is based on the earlier friendship of their fathers, and which the journey to Sparta has increased (*Odyssey* 15.195–198):

Νεστορίδη, πῶς κέν μοι ὑποσχόμενος τελέσειας
μῦθον ἐμόν; ξεῖνοι δὲ διαμπερὲς εὐχόμεθ' εἶναι
ἐκ πατέρων φιλότητος, ἀτὰρ καὶ ὁμήλικές εἰμεν·
ἥδε δ' ὁδὸς καὶ μᾶλλον ὁμοφροσύνῃσιν ἐνήσει.

Son of Nestor, I wonder if you would agree to carry out
what I say? We claim to be guest-friends without break
from the friendship of our fathers, and we are also of the same
        age;
and this journey will bring us even more to like-mindedness.

It seems significant that the word used of their increased friendship is "oneness of mind" (*homophrosúnēisin*), for that is what Nestor and Odysseus had while their friendship was intact, and what they lost at the moment of *nóstos*. That former "oneness of mind" (*héna thumòn ékhonte* is Nestor's own phrase) has now been restored in the younger generation. It also seems significant that when Peisistratos grants his companion's request, his final word should concern Nestor's anger. Telemachus is worried that Nestor will detain him in order to show him hospitality, so Peisistratos himself performs the obligations of hospitality, giving Telemachus the gifts that he himself received from Menelaus (*Odyssey* 15.206–207), and urging him to set sail before Nestor hears of his presence. For Peisistratos knows how overbearing Nestor's spirit is, and that he will come for Telemachus and not return empty-handed; in any case he will be very angry (*Odyssey* 15.211–214):

εὖ γὰρ ἐγὼ τόδε οἶδα κατὰ φρένα καὶ κατὰ θυμόν·
οἷος κείνου θυμὸς ὑπέρβιος, οὔ σε μεθήσει,

ἀλλ' αὐτὸς καλέων δεῦρ' εἴσεται, οὐδέ ἕ φημι
ἂψ ἰέναι κενεόν· μάλα γὰρ κεχολώσεται ἔμπης.

For I know this well in my mind and heart:
his spirit is so headstrong that he will not let you go,
but he will come here himself and I am sure
that he will not return empty-handed; in any case he will be
very angry.

That the last word in the *Odyssey* about Nestor should concern his anger is remarkable, but poetically it is exactly right. Overtly Nestor's imagined anger has to do with a thwarted desire to show hospitality to the son of Odysseus, but beneath the surface it brings back to mind the role that Nestor played in the return of Odysseus himself, a role that is well summarized by the allusion to his anger. In his own account of events on Tenedos there was of course no mention of Nestor's anger, and yet, if he was one party to the dispute, anger there must have been; we can judge this by the exchange of harsh words between Menelaus and Agamemnon in the first dispute on the shores of Troy: ὡς τὼ μὲν χαλεποῖσιν ἀμειβομένω ἐπέεσσιν... (*Odyssey* 3.148). The suppression of any mention of Nestor's anger in the context where it is the main point, and the resurfacing of that anger at a safe distance, and with a crucial change of context from hostility to hospitality, is in line with the poetic treatment of Nestor in the *Iliad*. In *Iliad* 23 it was Nestor's crash at the turning post in his race against the Epeian twins that was never mentioned directly, but which surfaced more than once indirectly in the chariot race for Patroclus. In the *Odyssey* the great unspoken event in Nestor's past is his quarrel with Odysseus, and the hostility that that implied. However brief the hostility, it was the final moment in the relationship between these two heroes, and therefore all important. This final moment must be kept firmly in mind throughout *Odyssey* 3, and elsewhere in the *Odyssey*, to appreciate the full dramatic effect of Nestor's presence in the poem, just as his crash at the turning post must be kept in mind throughout the chariot race of *Iliad* 23. At the beginning of *Odyssey* 3 the apprehension that Telemachus feels in approaching and addressing Nestor, which Athena, disguised as Mentor, helps him to overcome, has to do first of all with the coming of age of a young man with little experience of the wider world. But the drama of Telemachus's reluctance is heightened when we understand just whom he is afraid to approach, and the circumstances under which this figure parted from his father.

§2.92 Athena takes charge of Odysseus's homecoming at the very start of the *Odyssey*, at the council of gods in *Odyssey* 1, and her presence in Pylos in *Odyssey* 3 thus puts everything in a new perspective. It no longer matters that Odysseus split from Nestor the "homebringer," because a greater power, Athena herself, will bring him home: Athena has, as it were, already taken Nestor's place as Odysseus's immortal twin. In *Odyssey* 3 Athena's immediate concern is for Odysseus's son during his journey, which is a smaller version of Odysseus's own *nóstos*. Athena's disguise as the aged Mentor when she accompanies Telemachus derives directly, I think, from the figure of the aged Nestor, the principal figure in *Odyssey* 3. In order to hear first-hand how Odysseus lost the aged Nestor's help when Troy fell, Telemachus travels to Pylos with the aged Mentor at his side: what was split apart has thus already been put back together in a new form, as it will be again in the case of Peisistratos and Telemachus at the end of *Odyssey* 3. Peisistratos replaces Athena/Mentor in the role of Telemachus's companion, and it is Athena herself who arranges to have him do so. The point in Athena's case even more than in Peisistratos's case is the reversal of Nestor's myth, which is one of separation, in favor of a new and more powerful reintegration. Athena is not an Indo-European twin figure, but the dynamics of her role are those of the Indo-European twin myth, and this is because of Nestor.[119]

§2.93 The name *Méntōr* was chosen for Athena's disguise, I think, to echo the name *Néstōr*: the choice of name was meant to identify the figure from whom her role is borrowed. This idea, suggested in Part 1 above, can now be elaborated further. It is first of all striking that, in both these agent nouns with suffix *-tōr*, a normally intransitive root has a transitive meaning. The primary meaning of *Méntōr* is "inciter" (root **men-* of *mémona*, "be eager," *ménos*, "spirit"), and this meaning clearly evokes Nestor, whether we think of his role in the chariot race of *Iliad* 23 or his swift homecoming in *Odyssey* 3: *Méntōr*, who "makes eager," parallels *Néstōr*, who "brings back to life."[120] The mental aspect of *Néstōr*, which is summed up in the word *nóos*, also has a parallel in the name *Méntōr*, which in the *Odyssey* is associated with verbs of "remembering" and "reminding," and thus seems to have the secondary meaning "reminder"; it is because of *Néstōr*, I

---

119 In the chariot race of *Iliad* 23 Athena also plays the part of the immortal twin in aiding Diomedes, and this too has to do with Nestor (see §2.32 above).

120 For *Méntōr* as "inciter" see §1.15 above. The related noun *ménos* means something very close to "incitement" in the chariot race of *Iliad* 23 when Athena gives Diomedes back his whip and puts *ménos* in his horses; the whip suggests Nestor's own role as "inciter" in his race against the Molione.

suggest, that the *Odyssey* brings in these secondary associations, which are not primary in the name itself.[121]

§2.94 What the name *Méntōr* lacks altogether is the basic meaning of *Néstōr*, namely "homebringer."[122] In *Odyssey* 15 Athena, no longer disguised as Mentor, still acts as a *Méntōr* in relation to Telemachus when she visits him openly in Sparta in order "to remind him of his return and to incite him to return": νόστου ὑπομνήσουσα καὶ ὀτρυνέουσα νέεσθαι (*Odyssey* 15.3). I take this line as a virtual gloss on the name *Méntōr*, understood as both "inciter" (*otrunéousa*) and "reminder" (*hupomnḗsousa*), and I note the addition of the idea of "return" (in the words *nóstou* and *néesthai*) to both meanings to express what the name *Néstōr* contains in itself.

§2.95 There is a further piece of evidence. The name *Méntōr* forms a pair with the name *Menélaos* like such other name pairs as *Áktōr/Agélaos*, *Héktōr/Ekhélaos*, and *Néstōr/Nehelawos*.[123] The gloss of the name *Méntōr* in *Odyssey* 15 suggested above seems to be paralleled by a gloss of the name *Menélaos*, understood as "he who reminds the warfolk," in Nestor's account of the Achaeans' *nóstoi* in *Odyssey* 3. If this is the case there is an obvious implication for the name *Méntōr*, likewise at issue in *Odyssey* 3. The name *Menélaos* is usually derived, not from the root **men-* of *Méntōr*, but from the root **men-* of

---

121 See §1.15 above: the verb μέμνηται, "remembers," is used by the aged *Méntōr* when he reminds the Ithacans of Odysseus (ὡς οὔ τις μέμνηται, "because no one remembers," *Odyssey* 2.233); the verb ὑπέμνησεν, "reminded," is used of *Méntēs* when Athena, disguised as Mentes, reminds Telemachus of his father (*Odyssey* 1.321; the name *Méntēs*, as discussed in Part 1 above, amounts to a variant of *Méntōr* in Athena's essentially unitary role in relation to Telemachus). The semantic distinction in Greek between the simple root **men-*, "incite," and the enlarged root **mn-ā̆*, "remind," is not Indo-European (cf. n1.36 above on Latin *memini*, "remember," the formal equivalent of Greek *mémona*, "be eager"); from an IE standpoint *Méntōr/Méntēs* could mean "reminder," but in Greek this meaning is secondary and poetic.

122 Athena gives up her role as Telemachus's companion before he returns to Ithaca, so that as *Méntōr* she does not actually act as his "homebringer." But at a less literal level she is deeply involved in his *nóstos*, even as Mentor: note how, as Mentor, she prays to Poseidon in *Odyssey* 3.60–61:

δὸς δ᾽ ἔτι Τηλέμαχον καὶ ἐμὲ πρήξαντα νέεσθαι,
οὕνεκα δεῦρ᾽ ἱκόμεσθα θοῇ σὺν νηῒ μελαίνῃ.

Grant that Telemachus and I return safely, having done what we came here with our swift ship to do.

123 The relationship between the names in these pairs is close, but not as close as sometimes claimed: the names in *-tōr* cannot be considered mere short forms of the compounds in *-laos*, but belong to a broader category of independent agent nouns in *-tōr* (cf. Frame 1978:98). The first element of the compound names represents the third-person singular of an active verb (cf. n1.46 above).

Greek *ménō*, "await, withstand," as in such apparently similar compounds as *menedḗios*, "withstanding the enemy," *meneptólemos*, "withstanding battle," *menekhármēs*, "withstanding battle."[124] But the supposed meaning of *Menélaos*, "he who withstands the warfolk," has a problem: in Homer the word *laós*, by a wide margin, refers to one's own "warfolk," and not to the enemy's; this is also the case in such names as *Agélaos*, "he who leads the warfolk," *Ekhélaos*, "he who protects the warfolk," and *Nehelawos*, "he who brings the warfolk back," and it should be the case in the name *Menélaos* as well.[125]

§2.96 After the fall of Troy Menelaus "reminds the warfolk" of their "return home" when he quarrels with Agamemnon over the very issue of "return." As Nestor puts it, "Menelaus urged all the Achaeans to remember their *nóstos*" (*Odyssey* 3.141–144):

ἔνθ' ἦ τοι <u>Μενέλαος ἀνώγει πάντας Ἀχαιοὺς</u>
<u>νόστου μιμνήσκεσθαι</u> ἐπ' εὐρέα νῶτα θαλάσσης·
οὐδ' Ἀγαμέμνονι πάμπαν ἐήνδανε· βούλετο γάρ ῥα
λαὸν ἐρυκακέειν ῥέξαι θ' ἱερὰς ἑκατόμβας.

Then <u>Menelaus urged all the Achaeans</u>
<u>to remember their return</u> across the wide back of the sea;
but this did not please Agamemnon at all; for he wanted
to restrain the warriors and offer sacred hecatombs.

§2.97 In the phrase *anṓgei pántas Akhaioùs...mimnḗskesthai*, "he urged all the Achaeans to remember," the allusion to the meaning of Menelaus's name, "he who reminds the warfolk," is self-evident.[126] But it is also clear that *nóstou*,

---

124 So Chantraine 1999, s.v. *ménō*; Frisk 1960–1972, s.v. *ménō*; Risch 1974:191.

125 Exceptions to this usage of *laós* are rare in Homer; the evidence is discussed in EN2.2. The Homeric usage is well accounted for by Benveniste's observation (1969, vol. 2, 90) that *laós* refers to a "people" in relation to its leader, as in the Homeric formula, *poiména laôn*, "shepherd of the warriors/people"; the names *Agélaos* etc. bear out Benveniste's observation. *Menélaos* properly means "he who *incites* the warfolk," just as *Méntōr* properly means "he who *incites*"; in the *Odyssey* there is an extension of meaning from "inciter" to "reminder" in both names (see below for *Menélaos*).

126 There is a formulaic element at work in the diction of the two passages discussed above: the phrases νόστου ὑπομνήσουσα in *Odyssey* 15.3 and νόστου μιμνήσκεσθαι in *Odyssey* 3.142 are related. The pattern is seen again in *Iliad* 10.509–510, at the end of the night raid, where Odysseus bids Diomedes to "remember our return to the hollow ships" (νόστου δὴ μνῆσαι...νῆας ἔπι γλαφυράς). A related pattern can be seen in phrases meaning "forget one's return" (νόστου τε λαθέσθαι, *Odyssey* 9.97; νόστοιο λάθηται, *Odyssey* 9.102), and "be mindful of one's return" (νόστου τε μέδηαι, *Odyssey* 11.110 = 12.137; νόστοιο μεδοίατο, *Iliad* 9.622). The formulaic quality of the diction, however, does not diminish the play on

"their homecoming," must be added to "remember" to make Menelaus's name relevant to his own twin myth in the context of the Greeks' *nóstoi*. This additional element does not need to be specified in Nestor's case when he replays his twin myth with Odysseus on Tenedos, for his name by itself means "the homebringer."

§2.98 I come back to the point that the name *Néstōr* is central in *Odyssey* 3, and that the name *Méntōr* is meant to echo it: the two names are identical in shape, and the semantics of *Néstōr* are approximated in *Méntōr*, especially when the related name *Menélaos*, with its explicit connection to the idea of a *nóstos* in *Odyssey* 3, is taken into account.[127]

Menelaus's name in *Odyssey* 3; formulaic diction is the medium of Homeric epic. In the same passage in *Odyssey* 3 there seems to be a play on Agamemnon's name as well when the half of the army that does not leave Troy is restrained "waiting" with Agamemnon (*Odyssey* 3.155–156):

> ἡμίσεες δ' ἄρα λαοὶ ἐρητύοντο μένοντες
> αὖθι παρ' Ἀτρεΐδῃ Ἀγαμέμνονι, ποιμένι λαῶν.

But half of the warriors were held back there waiting
with the son of Atreus, Agamemnon, shepherd of the warriors.

The name *Agamémnōn* is an expressive reduplication of the verb *ménō*, "remain, wait, withstand" (see Chantraine 1999 s.v. *mémnōn*); since what separates Agamemnon from Menelaus is precisely the fact that he "remains" at Troy, a play on his name seems intended in this passage (the phrase *erētúonto ménontes*, "were held back waiting," in *Odyssey* 3.155 is formulaic, occurring three times in the *Iliad*; see §2.67 above for an example in *Iliad* 15.367, preceding Nestor's prayer to Zeus for a sign confirming the Achaeans' *nóstos*; the use of formulaic diction again does not preclude the play on the name). Agamemnon, who "wished to restrain" the army at Troy (*Odyssey* 3.143–144), plays the part of the Indo-European mortal twin (see §2.60–§2.61 above); "waiting" and "restraining" are related aspects of this role.

127 For my interpretation of the name *Menélaos* in *Odyssey* 3 it does not matter which etymology of the name, "he who *incites* the warfolk" or "he who *withstands* the warfolk," is correct; it matters only that the Homeric poets took the name to mean "he who *reminds* the warfolk," just as they took the name *Méntōr* to mean "he who reminds." It is possible that in other contexts the name *Menélaos* was understood differently, as for example in *Iliad* 3.52: οὐκ ἂν δὴ μείνειας ἀρηΐφιλον Μενέλαον, "you would not remain (stand your ground) against Menelaus" (see Martin 1989:135 for the suggestion of etymological word play here). But I would maintain that the Homeric poets got the name right in *Odyssey* 3, at least as regards the root. This is indicated not only by the meaning of *laós*, as discussed above; the meaning "he who *incites* the warfolk" also resonates in a figure who embodies the Indo-European immortal twin. It is Agamemnon, who embodies the Indo-European mortal twin (the warrior), whose name comes from *ménō*, "withstand" (cf. n2.126 above). In *Odyssey* 3 the names of both brothers have their meanings extended to suit the context: Menelaus is "he who *reminds* the warfolk," and Agamemnon is "he who *waits*"; but both names, I think, are understood correctly in terms of their roots.

§2.99 Mentor for Athena is just a disguise. In her own persona she is in control of events, and Nestor, a mere mortal, does not rival her superior power. In *Odyssey* 3 much attention is given to the transfer of responsibility for Odysseus from Nestor (he did not bring Odysseus home) to Athena (she will). The theme is introduced with references to Athena's care for Odysseus at Troy and the possibility that she may bring him home even now. Since Athena herself is present in disguise, all of this is highly ironic. Telemachus wishes that the gods would give him power to defeat his mother's suitors, but says that the gods have not granted this lot either to him or to his father. Nestor counters his pessimism with the thought that the suitors may yet be punished, either by a returning Odysseus, or by Telemachus himself if Athena loves him as much as she openly loved and cared for Odysseus at Troy (*Odyssey* 3.216–224):

τίς δ' οἶδ' εἴ κέ ποτέ σφι βίας ἀποτείσεται ἐλθών,

ἦ ὅ γε μοῦνος ἐὼν ἦ καὶ σύμπαντες Ἀχαιοί;

εἰ γάρ σ' ὡς ἐθέλοι φιλέειν γλαυκῶπις Ἀθήνη,

ὡς τότ' Ὀδυσσῆος περικήδετο κυδαλίμοιο

δήμῳ ἔνι Τρώων, ὅθι πάσχομεν ἄλγε' Ἀχαιοί·

οὐ γάρ πω ἴδον ὧδε θεοὺς ἀναφανδὰ φιλεῦντας,

ὡς κείνῳ ἀναφανδὰ παρίστατο Παλλὰς Ἀθήνη·

εἴ σ' οὕτως ἐθέλοι φιλέειν κήδοιτό τε θυμῷ,

τῷ κέν τις κείνων γε καὶ ἐκλελάθοιτο γάμοιο.

Who knows whether he will some day come and repay their
     violence,
either alone or with all the Achaeans?
For if grey-eyed Athena should wish to love you
as she once cared for glorious Odysseus
in the land of the Trojans, where we Achaeans suffered woes—
for never did I see gods love so openly
as when Pallas Athena openly stood by that man—
if she wished to love you and cared for you in her heart like that,
then some of them might stop thinking about marriage.

Telemachus refuses to believe that this will happen, even if the gods should wish it, and Athena/Mentor rebukes him sharply for his attitude (*Odyssey* 3.230–231):

Τηλέμαχε, ποῖόν σε ἔπος φύγεν ἕρκος ὀδόντων.
ῥεῖα θεός γ᾽ ἐθέλων καὶ τηλόθεν ἄνδρα σαώσαι.

Telemachus, what sort of word has escaped the barrier of your teeth?
A god who wished to could easily save a man however far off.

When Athena finishes her mission in Pylos and flies off in the form of a bird, Nestor recognizes her at once, and realizes that Telemachus does indeed have the same goddess to protect him that his father did at Troy (*Odyssey* 3.371–379). Athena's presence is as hopeful for Odysseus and his fate as it is for Telemachus, for she herself said shortly before that a god could easily save a man even from far away. But this implication is left unstated, for Nestor has more immediate thoughts in his mind. He prays to the goddess who has just visited him to give "good fame" to himself and his family, and he promises to sacrifice an unbroken heifer with gilded horns to her (*Odyssey* 3.380–384). Athena hears his prayer, and most of the rest of *Odyssey* 3 is devoted to the honor that Nestor pays her. When they go to bed at night, it is to Athena that Nestor makes his libation and prayer (*Odyssey* 3.393–394). When morning comes, the promised heifer is sacrificed in full ritual splendor, and the process is described in elaborate detail (*Odyssey* 3.404–474). In the course of the sacrifice Nestor "prays much to Athena" for yet a third time (*Odyssey* 3.445–446). The great honor paid to Athena at the end of *Odyssey* 3 balances the scene at the beginning of the book, when Telemachus and Athena arrive in Pylos in the middle of a sacrifice to Poseidon. The shift from Poseidon to Athena heightens the attention on Athena, without dishonoring Poseidon. There has also been another shift in *Odyssey* 3, and that is from Nestor to Athena as "homebringer" for Odysseus. This is a shift from human to divine, and the change of level is what is brought out in Nestor's worship of Athena at the end of the book. Odysseus, despite his long absence, has a greater power on his side now than Nestor, with whom he quarreled and split to initiate his long absence. The shift from Nestor to Athena does not dishonor Nestor, although that possibility is present throughout *Odyssey* 3 because of the negativity of Nestor's role in the *nóstos* of Odysseus. Perhaps it is to counter this possibility that Nestor explicitly prays for "good fame" (*kléos esthlón*) as soon as he recognizes Athena, and that she hears his prayer (*Odyssey* 3.380–381, 385).

Chapter 7.

ODYSSEY 11 AND THE PHAEACIANS

§2.100 Nestor is mentioned twice more in the *Odyssey*, in *Odyssey* 11 and *Odyssey* 24.[128] In *Odyssey* 11, as discussed already, only his name occurs: when Odysseus meets the ghost of Nestor's mother Chloris in the underworld, Nestor is named as one of three sons she bore to Neleus (*Odyssey* 11.281–286):

καὶ Χλῶριν εἶδον περικαλλέα, τήν ποτε Νηλεὺς
γῆμεν ἑὸν διὰ κάλλος, ἐπεὶ πόρε μυρία ἕδνα,
ὁπλοτάτην κούρην Ἀμφίονος Ἰασίδαο,
ὅς ποτ᾽ ἐν Ὀρχομενῷ Μινυηΐῳ ἶφι ἄνασσεν·
ἡ δὲ Πύλου βασίλευε, τέκεν δέ οἱ ἀγλαὰ τέκνα,
Νέστορά τε Χρομίον τε Περικλύμενόν τ᾽ ἀγέρωχον.

And I saw beautiful Chloris, whom Neleus once
married for her beauty after he gave countless wedding gifts,
the youngest daughter of Amphion, Iasus's son,
who once ruled with might over Minyan Orchomenus;
but she reigned in Pylos and bore him splendid children,
Nestor and Chromios and proud Periklymenos.

---

128 The final mention of Nestor in the poem is in *Odyssey* 24 in Agamemnon's account of Achilles' funeral: Nestor restrained the Achaeans from fleeing to the ships in panic when Thetis and the Nereids came to mourn Achilles' death (*Odyssey* 24.50–52). The scene resembles Agamemnon's testing of the army in *Iliad* 2, except that there Odysseus restrains the Achaeans from fleeing to the ships and Nestor incites them to war; see §2.67 above. The same motif in *Odyssey* 24 looks like a conscious variation of *Iliad* 2. In the main story of the *Odyssey* Nestor's final appearance (or rather non-appearance) is in *Odyssey* 15, when Telemachus bypasses him on the way to Ithaca (see §2.91 above).

This is the passage to which the *khōrízontes* drew attention because of its discrepancy with *Iliad* 11, where Neleus is said to have had twelve sons in contrast to the three sons named here. The point of interest now, however, is that Nestor, given his role in the *nóstos* of Odysseus in *Odyssey* 3, should be named at all in *Odyssey* 11. Was his name intended to slip by unnoticed in the sea of other names in the catalogue of heroines? The reason that Odysseus is in the underworld in the first place has everything to do with Nestor and his failure to give him a *nóstos*. It does not seem likely that Odysseus would mention Nestor's name at this point with no thought given to Nestor's role in *Odyssey* 3. The truth is, I think, that this passage is very much aware of Nestor's role in *Odyssey* 3. The passage, which alone in Homer names Nestor's brother Periklymenos, has to do with *Nestor's* twin myth; together with Nestor's story in *Iliad* 11 the catalogue of *Odyssey* 11 is in fact the basic text for that myth. At the literal level the passage in *Odyssey* 11 of course does not acknowledge Nestor's twin myth, but disguises it: Nestor is not one of two brothers, but one of three brothers because Chromios is named in addition to Nestor and Periklymenos. We know Chromios's story already, and it is a very short one.[129] Chromios is in the catalogue for the purpose of disguising Nestor's twin myth at the most literal level, as is consistent with the way in which this myth is treated elsewhere in the *Iliad* and the *Odyssey*. To discern Nestor's twin myth in *Odyssey* 11 we must consider its wider context in the entire catalogue of heroines.

§2.101 The heroine who follows Chloris in the catalogue is Leda, who gave birth to the Dioskouroi. In contrast to Nestor, who separated from his brother Periklymenos, the Dioskouroi remained together in life and in death; even beneath the earth they continue to share equally in life and death from one day to the next (*Odyssey* 11.298–304):

καὶ Λήδην εἶδον, τὴν Τυνδαρέου παράκοιτιν,
ἥ ῥ᾽ ὑπὸ Τυνδαρέῳ κρατερόφρονε γείνατο παῖδε,
Κάστορά θ᾽ ἱππόδαμον καὶ πὺξ ἀγαθὸν Πολυδεύκεα,
τοὺς ἄμφω ζωοὺς κατέχει φυσίζοος αἶα·
οἳ καὶ νέρθεν γῆς τιμὴν πρὸς Ζηνὸς ἔχοντες
ἄλλοτε μὲν ζώουσ᾽ ἑτερήμεροι, ἄλλοτε δ᾽ αὖτε
τεθνᾶσιν· τιμὴν δὲ λελόγχασιν ἶσα θεοῖσι.

129 See above §1.4 and n1.8.

228

And I saw Leda, the wife of Tyndareus,
who under Tyndareus gave birth to two strong-minded sons,
horse-breaking Castor and Polydeuces, good with his fists,
both of whom the life-giving earth holds alive;
and they, having honor from Zeus even under the ground,
are alive on alternate days, and then in turn
they are dead; and they receive honor equal to the gods.

The contrast between Nestor and the Dioskouroi could not be sharper: Polydeuces brought Castor back to life by sharing his immortality with his brother; Nestor, on the other hand, did not bring Periklymenos back to life, but instead took his brother's place.

§2.102 Nestor's sister Pero is a crucial bridge between the two entries in the catalogue, those of Chloris and Leda, because she is the analogue of Helen, the sister of the Dioskouroi. The wooing of Helen was a celebrated event in Greek myth, and the wooing of Nestor's sister Pero has everything in common with it. The main similarity is that in both cases the successful suitors were a pair of brothers, one of whom wooed for the other. In Helen's case the successful suitors were the two Atreidai, of whom Agamemnon wooed for Menelaus; a Hesiodic fragment tells how Castor and Polydeuces, who oversaw their sister's wooing, would have chosen Agamemnon himself had he not wooed for his brother (Hesiod fr. 197.3–5 MW):

καί νύ κε δὴ Κάστωρ τε καὶ ὁ κρατερὸς Πολυδεύκης
γαμβρὸν ποιήσαντο κατὰ κράτος, ἀλλ' Ἀγαμέμνων
γαμβρὸς ἐὼν ἐμνᾶτο κασιγνήτωι Μενελάωι.

Now Castor and strong Polydeuces
would have made him their brother-in-law by force, but Agamemnon,
being their brother-in-law, wooed for his brother Menelaus.[130]

130 Agamemnon in this passage is called the brother-in-law of the Dioskouroi (γαμβρὸς ἐών, line 5); this must mean that he had already wed Clytemnestra and was no longer himself an eligible suitor of Helen. The precise point of lines 3–4 then—that Castor and Polydeuces "would have made him (Agamemnon) their brother-in-law by force"—is not quite clear; this apparently means that they would have made him their brother-in-law if he had not already been their brother-in-law. It is not likely that γαμβρός in line 5 means "wooer" rather than "brother-in-law"—an Aeolic and Doric usage attested by Pindar and Theocritus—in view of the meaning "brother-in-law" in the previous line. At any rate Agamemnon woos not for himself but for his brother. Hesiod fr. 198.2–8 MW says that Odysseus, who wooed from Ithaca, kept promising gifts to Castor and Polydeuces but

In Pero's case the successful suitors were the brothers Melampus and Bias, Nestor's cousins. The story of how Melampus wooed Pero for his brother Bias is told twice in the Odyssey, first in Chloris's entry in Odyssey 11. After she bore Nestor, Chromios, and Periklymenos, Chloris gave birth to a daughter Pero, whom all her neighbors wooed; as Pero's bride-price Neleus demanded the cattle of Iphiklos (Odyssey 11.287–290):

τοῖσι δ' ἐπ' ἰφθίμην Πηρὼ τέκε, θαῦμα βροτοῖσι,
τὴν πάντες μνώοντο περικτίται· οὐδέ τι Νηλεὺς
τῷ ἐδίδου, ὃς μὴ ἕλικας βόας εὐρυμετώπους
ἐκ Φυλάκης ἐλάσειε βίης Ἰφικληείης....

After them she bore steadfast Pero, a wonder to mortals,
whom all her neighbors wooed; but Neleus did not
give her to anyone who did not drive the wide-browed spiral-
        horned cattle
of mighty Iphiklos from Phylake....

Only the prophet Melampus undertook to drive off the cattle of Iphiklos for his brother Bias. But Melampus was caught in the act and imprisoned for a year before he gained his own release and the release of the cattle by revealing certain prophecies. The concluding lines of Chloris's entry in the catalogue allude to these events without naming Melampus (he is here called "the fault-less prophet") and without referring to Bias at all (Odyssey 11.291–297):

...ἀργαλέας. τὰς δ' οἶος ὑπέσχετο μάντις ἀμύμων
ἐξελάαν· χαλεπὴ δὲ θεοῦ κατὰ μοῖρα πέδησε
δεσμοί τ' ἀργαλέοι καὶ βουκόλοι ἀγροιῶται.
ἀλλ' ὅτε δὴ μῆνές τε καὶ ἡμέραι ἐξετελεῦντο
ἂψ περιτελλομένου ἔτεος καὶ ἐπήλυθον ὧραι,
καὶ τότε δή μιν ἔλυσε βίη Ἰφικληείη
θέσφατα πάντ' εἰπόντα· Διὸς δ' ἐτελείετο βουλή.

...hard (to drive). Those (cattle) only the faultless prophet promised
to drive away; but he was bound by the god's harsh fate,
painful bonds, and rustic cowherds.

---

never sent them, because he knew that Menelaus, as the richest of the Achaeans, would win Helen.

But when the months and days were completed
as the year came around, and the seasons returned,
then mighty Iphiklos freed him,
after he spoke all the prophecies; and the will of Zeus was
accomplished.

More informative is the story in *Odyssey* 15, which is told in connection with a descendant of Melampus, the prophet Theoklymenos. This version of the story concerns Melampus's move from Pylos to Argos, where his descendants remained thereafter.[131] During the year that Melampus was imprisoned in Phylake Neleus seized his property, and Melampus, when he returned to Pylos, somehow paid Neleus back for this ill deed and then fled from Pylos to Argos. In this passage we hear explicitly how Melampus brought the cattle back from Phylake to Pylos and thus won a wife for his brother (*Odyssey* 15.228–239):

δὴ τότε γ᾽ ἄλλων δῆμον ἀφίκετο, πατρίδα φεύγων
Νηλέα τε μεγάθυμον, ἀγαυότατον ζωόντων,
ὅς οἱ χρήματα πολλὰ τελεσφόρον εἰς ἐνιαυτὸν
εἶχε βίῃ. ὁ δὲ τεῖος ἐνὶ μεγάροις Φυλάκοιο
δεσμῷ ἐν ἀργαλέῳ δέδετο, κρατέρ᾽ ἄλγεα πάσχων
εἵνεκα Νηλῆος κούρης ἄτης τε βαρείης,
τήν οἱ ἐπὶ φρεσὶ θῆκε θεὰ δασπλῆτις Ἐρινύς.
ἀλλ᾽ ὁ μὲν ἔκφυγε κῆρα καὶ <u>ἤλασε βοῦς ἐριμύκους</u>
<u>ἐς Πύλον ἐκ Φυλάκης</u> καὶ ἐτείσατο ἔργον ἀεικὲς
ἀντίθεον Νηλῆα, <u>κασιγνήτῳ δὲ γυναῖκα</u>
<u>ἠγάγετο πρὸς δώμαθ᾽·</u> ὁ δ᾽ ἄλλων ἵκετο δῆμον,
Ἄργος ἐς ἱππόβοτον.

Then indeed he came to the land of other people, fleeing his
own fatherland
and great-hearted Neleus, noblest of living men,
who held his many possessions for a year until its end
by force. Meanwhile he was bound in painful bonds
in the halls of Phylakos, suffering powerful woes

---

131 Melampus and Bias fled to Argos together, but this passage is interested only in Melampus, the ancestor of Theoklymenos; cf. "Apollodorus" 1.9.12 and 2.2.2 (see also above §1.11 and n1.26).

because of Neleus's daughter and heavy deception,
which the avenging fury, destructive goddess, put in his mind.
But he escaped death and <u>drove the loud-bellowing cattle</u>
<u>to Pylos from Phylake</u>, and repaid the cruel deed
of godlike Neleus, and <u>brought a wife</u>
<u>home to his brother</u>; but he went to the land of other people,
to horse-pasturing Argos.

Melampus and Bias fit the categories of the Indo-European twin myth extraordinarily well.[132] Melampus is associated with both "cattle" (he must win them) and "intelligence" (he is both a prophet and a physician). The two themes are connected in the myth insofar as Melampus must use his prophetic skill to win the cattle.[133] *Phulákē*, "prison," is the name of the place where he is held for a year (*Odyssey* 11.290, 15.236);[134] Melampus's return from this mythic place of imprisonment with the prize of cattle is a variation on the function of the Indo-European immortal twin.[135] Bias, on the other hand, is associated with both "horses" and "war," the attributes of the Indo-European mortal twin. Hesiod, who tells of the brothers' dealings with Proitos in Argos, calls Bias *hippódamos*, "horsebreaking," the same epithet that characterizes the mortal twin Castor.[136]

132 They are not called twins, but they are twin figures; see n1.24 above.
133 "Apollodorus" 1.9.12 offers a detailed account: Melampus, who understood the language of animals, heard worms talking in his prison and escaped before they ate through the beam over his head; this impressed his captor, who agreed to give him the cattle in return for curing his son (cf. n2.134 below). "Apollodorus" 1.9.11 tells how Melampus first became a prophet when snakes cleaned his ears and this enabled him to understand the language of birds.
134 In *Odyssey* 15.231 Melampus is held in the halls of *Phúlakos*, whose name, "imprisoner," matches the name of the place, *Phulákē*. In *Odyssey* 11.290 it is Iphiklos, not Phylakos, whose cattle are set as Pero's bride price; the two names are reconciled in "Apollodorus," where Phylakos is the father of Iphiklos: Melampus wins the cattle and his own freedom through his medical skill, telling Phylakos how to cure his son Iphiklos of childlessness. Melampus's medical skill is featured again in the myth of Proitos's daughters, whom he cures of madness (cf. n1.26 above); in his function as a physician Melampus corresponds to the Vedic twin gods and the Greek twins Podaleirios and Makhaon (for the latter pair see above §2.8 with n2.19).
135 Compare the Vedic name *Nā́satyā* in its association with cattle in Vedic diction, and in its association with a return from darkness in the Vedic twins' myths and rituals; compare also the cattle raid in the myth of the Dioskouroi (see above §1.66 and n1.205). In the myth of Castor's death the variant to the driving off of cattle is the carrying off of brides, the Leukippides; in the case of Melampus and Bias the winning of a bride is not a variant for the winning of cattle, but connected to it: cattle are Pero's bride price.
136 Hesiod fr. 37.10–14 MW:

οἳ δὲ καὶ εἰς Ἄργος Προῖ[το]ν πά[ρα δῖον ἵκοντο,
ἔνθά σφιν μετέδωκ[ε
ἰφθ[ι]μος Προίτου κλῆρον.[

Bias does not get the same attention as Melampus in their myths, but his name, which is formed from the noun *bíē*, "strength," is proof enough that he is a "warrior" in contrast to his brother the prophet/physician.

§2.103 I return to the wooing of Pero as the analogue to the wooing of Helen, and as the bridge between Nestor and the Dioskouroi in the catalogue of heroines. Helen is not mentioned in Leda's entry to the catalogue; only Leda's two sons, Castor and Polydeuces, are named, and their myth, which is meant to contrast with Nestor's myth (about which nothing is said explicitly) is given in full. Among Chloris's offspring Pero gets all the attention, and the reason for this is that in the next entry Helen is omitted, and Pero is meant to evoke her as soon as the entry begins with Helen's mother Leda. Pero's wooing by all her neighbors brings to mind the wooing of Helen by the entire heroic world; in particular the successful suit of the brothers Melampus and Bias brings to mind the successful suit of the brothers Agamemnon and Menelaus.[137] With Pero as the bridge from Nestor to the Dioskouroi, Nestor's unspoken myth emerges by its contrast with the Dioskouroi, whose myth is explictly given. There is a balance in what is left out from each passage (an explicit twin myth in the case of Nestor and a much-wooed sister in the case of the Dioskouroi) and this balance of omissions itself tightens the link between the two passages.[138]

ἱπποδάμωι τε [Βί]αντι [Μελάμποδί θ'
μαντοσύνηις ἰήσατ', ἐπεὶ ϝϙ[

They [went] to Argos and to Proitos [
there [he] gave them [
steadfast Proitos a share [
both to horse-breaking Bias [and to Melampus
cured with his prophetic skill, when [

137 The birth of Pero after her brothers in *Odyssey* 11 is uncannily echoed by the birth of Helen after her brothers in *Cypria* fr. 7.1 Allen: τοὺς δὲ μέτα τριτάτην Ἑλένην τέκε θαῦμα βροτοῖσι, "after them she bore a third, Helen, a wonder to mortals"; compare *Odyssey* 11.287: τοῖσι δ' ἐπ' ἰφθίμην Πηρὼ τέκε, θαῦμα βροτοῖσι, "after them she bore steadfast Pero, a wonder to mortals." The phrase *thaûma brotoîsi*, "a wonder to mortals," occurs in only these two lines in Greek epic: Pero and Helen were both "a wonder to mortals" because of their beauty, which attracted many suitors. The *Cypria* fragment, which is found in Athenaeus 8.334b-d, continues with a passage naming Nemesis as Helen's mother. From this it would appear that the *Cypria* considered Nemesis the mother of the Dioskouroi as well, but this is not certain (the first line of the fragment and the lines about Nemesis are not clearly connected; Allen indicates a lacuna between them). "Apollodorus" 3.10.7 says that according to some Nemesis rather than Leda was Helen's mother; he does not say that this pertained to the Dioskouroi as well as to Helen.

138 See n1.156 above for the female figure associated with the twins in the Indo-European myth; she is called the "daughter of the sun," and she is both the sister and common wife

§2.104 Chloris and Leda are the heart of the catalogue of heroines in *Odyssey* 11: their two entries, between them, lay bare Nestor's twin myth. The next entry is also about twins: Iphimedeia is the mother of Otos and Ephialtes by the god Poseidon. Unlike the Dioskouroi, who go on sharing life and death beneath the earth forever, these twins both died young (*Odyssey* 11.305–308):

τὴν δὲ μέτ' Ἰφιμέδειαν, Ἀλωῆος παράκοιτιν,
εἴσιδον, ἣ δὴ φάσκε Ποσειδάωνι μιγῆναι,
καί ῥ' ἔτεκεν δύο παῖδε, μινυνθαδίω δὲ γενέσθην,
Ὠτόν τ' ἀντίθεον τηλεκλειτόν τ' Ἐφιάλτην....

And after her I saw Iphimedeia, the wife of Aloeus,
who said that she made love with Poseidon
and bore two sons, but they were short-lived,
godlike Otos and far-famed Ephialtes....

The rest of this entry, after describing the size and beauty of the Aloadai, tells how they tried to storm heaven by piling Ossa on Olympus and Pelion on Ossa; but Apollo laid them low before beards covered their chins (*Odyssey* 11.309–320):

...οὓς δὴ μηκίστους θρέψε ζείδωρος ἄρουρα
καὶ πολὺ καλλίστους μετά γε κλυτὸν Ὠρίωνα·
ἐννέωροι γὰρ τοί γε καὶ ἐννεαπήχεες ἦσαν
εὖρος, ἀτὰρ μῆκός γε γενέσθην ἐννεόργυιοι.
οἵ ῥα καὶ ἀθανάτοισιν ἀπειλήτην ἐν Ὀλύμπῳ
φυλόπιδα στήσειν πολυάϊκος πολέμοιο.
Ὄσσαν ἐπ' Οὐλύμπῳ μέμασαν θέμεν, αὐτὰρ ἐπ' Ὄσσῃ
Πήλιον εἰνοσίφυλλον, ἵν' οὐρανὸς ἀμβατὸς εἴη.
καί νύ κεν ἐξετέλεσσαν, εἰ ἥβης μέτρον ἵκοντο·
ἀλλ' ὄλεσεν Διὸς υἱός, ὃν ἠύκομος τέκε Λητώ,
ἀμφοτέρω, πρὶν σφῶϊν ὑπὸ κροτάφοισιν ἰούλους
ἀνθῆσαι πυκάσαι τε γένυς εὐανθέϊ λάχνῃ.

---

of the twins. In the Greek myth Helen is the sister of the Dioskouroi but her suitors are a different pair of brothers; Pero follows the same pattern as Helen.

...whom indeed the grain-giving earth raised to be the biggest
and much the most beautiful after famous Orion;
for they were nine years old and nine cubits
wide, and they were nine fathoms tall.
Against the immortals they threatened
to set the strife of violent war on Olympus.
They strove to put Ossa on top of Olympus, and on top of Ossa
Pelion, with its fluttering leaves, so that the sky could be
ascended.
And they would have accomplished this if they had reached
young manhood;
but the son of Zeus, whom beautiful-haired Leto bore, destroyed
them
both before the hair blossomed on their cheeks beneath their
temples
and covered their chins with beautifully-flowering down.

The main point of this passage is that it, like the passage about the Dioskouroi, is explictly about twins: what is explicit in these two passages can then be read back into the passage about Nestor, where the point is implicit (in fact disguised). The early death of both twins reinforces the idea that in all three passages the issue is the life and death of twins; here is a third possible outcome: Nestor may have failed to bring Periklymenos back to life as Polydeuces did Castor, but there were worse outcomes, as the two Aloadai, who both died young, show.

§2.105 We have yet to address the most basic structural point about the catalogue, which is that it is really not one catalogue, but two catalogues insofar as it falls into two equal parts. There is a careful balance between the two parts of the catalogue both in the number of entries (five in each part) and in the total number of lines (46 in the first part and 47 in the second part). Nestor and his entry begin the second part of the catalogue; Nestor's father Neleus and his entry begin the first part of the catalogue. We have considered the first three entries in the second part of the catalogue, which all concern twins, either explicitly or implicitly. Let us now consider the first part of the catalogue, starting with the first entry. Just as Nestor is the real point of the first entry in the second part of the catalogue, Neleus is the real point of the first entry in the first part of the catalogue. Like Nestor, Neleus is a twin who separated from his brother. The story of his and his brother's birth is the main focus of Tyro's entry, which begins the catalogue as a whole. After hearing of

Tyro's father and husband, Salmoneus and Kretheus, we learn that Tyro fell
in love with the river god Enipeus (*Odyssey* 11.235–239):

ἔνθ' ἦ τοι πρώτην Τυρὼ ἴδον εὐπατέρειαν,
ἣ φάτο Σαλμωνῆος ἀμύμονος ἔκγονος εἶναι,
φῆ δὲ Κρηθῆος γυνὴ ἔμμεναι Αἰολίδαο·
ἣ ποταμοῦ ἠράσσατ' Ἐνιπῆος θείοιο,
ὃς πολὺ κάλλιστος ποταμῶν ἐπὶ γαῖαν ἵησι....

Then I saw Tyro first, born of a noble father,
who said that she was the offspring of faultless Salmoneus,
and said too that she was the wife of Kretheus, descended from
   Aeolus.
She fell in love with a river, the divine Enipeus,
who is much the most beautiful of rivers to pour forth on the
   earth....

When Tyro visited the streams of Enipeus Poseidon took on the likeness
of the river god and made love to her; he then revealed himself to her in a
speech and promised her that splendid children would be born from their
union (*Odyssey* 11.240–253):

...καί ῥ' ἐπ' Ἐνιπῆος πωλέσκετο καλὰ ῥέεθρα.
τῷ δ' ἄρα εἰσάμενος γαιήοχος ἐννοσίγαιος
ἐν προχοῇς ποταμοῦ παρελέξατο δινήεντος·
πορφύρεον δ' ἄρα κῦμα περιστάθη οὔρεϊ ἶσον,
κυρτωθέν, κρύψεν δὲ θεὸν θνητήν τε γυναῖκα.
λῦσε δὲ παρθενίην ζώνην, κατὰ δ' ὕπνον ἔχευεν.
αὐτὰρ ἐπεί ῥ' ἐτέλεσσε θεὸς φιλοτήσια ἔργα,
ἔν τ' ἄρα οἱ φῦ χειρὶ ἔπος τ' ἔφατ' ἔκ τ' ὀνόμαζε·
"χαῖρε, γύναι, φιλότητι· περιπλομένου δ' ἐνιαυτοῦ
τέξεαι ἀγλαὰ τέκνα, ἐπεὶ οὐκ ἀποφώλιοι εὐναὶ
ἀθανάτων· σὺ δὲ τοὺς κομέειν ἀτιταλλέμεναί τε.
νῦν δ' ἔρχευ πρὸς δῶμα καὶ ἴσχεο μηδ' ὀνομήνῃς·
αὐτὰρ ἐγώ τοί εἰμι Ποσειδάων ἐνοσίχθων."
ὣς εἰπὼν ὑπὸ πόντον ἐδύσετο κυμαίνοντα.

...and she wandered along the Enipeus's beautiful streams.
Taking his shape the earthholder, the earthshaker,
lay with her in the mouth of the eddying river;
a dark wave as big as a mountain rose up around them,
curved, and hid the god and the mortal woman.
He loosened her maiden's girdle and poured sleep over her.
And when the god finished the deeds of love,
he took her by the hand and spoke a word and called her by
    name:
"Rejoice, woman, in this act of love; as the year returns
you will bear splendid children, since the beds of the immortals
    are not in vain;
but you, take care of them and raise them.
Now go home and restrain yourself and do not say my name;
I am indeed Poseidon the earthshaker."
So saying he sank beneath the wavy sea.

Tyro then gave birth to the twins Pelias and Neleus, who did not remain together: Neleus left Pelias behind in Iolkos and founded Pylos by himself (*Odyssey* 11.254–257):

ἡ δ' ὑποκυσαμένη Πελίην τέκε καὶ Νηλῆα,
τὼ κρατερὼ θεράποντε Διὸς μεγάλοιο γενέσθην
ἀμφοτέρω· Πελίης μὲν ἐν εὐρυχόρῳ Ἰαολκῷ
ναῖε πολύρρηνος, ὁ δ' ἄρ' ἐν Πύλῳ ἠμαθόεντι.

And she conceived and bore Pelias and Neleus,
who became strong servants of great Zeus,
both of them; Pelias in wide Iolkos
had his home, owning many sheep, the other one in sandy Pylos.

In the final two lines of the passage Tyro's three other sons by her husband Kretheus are named (*Odyssey* 11.258–259):

τοὺς δ' ἑτέρους Κρηθῆϊ τέκεν βασίλεια γυναικῶν,
Αἴσονά τ' ἠδὲ Φέρητ' Ἀμυθάονά θ' ἱππιοχάρμην.

The queen among women bore her other sons to Kretheus,
Aison and Pheres and the chariot-fighter Amythaon.

§2.106 Just as Nestor contrasts with the Dioskouroi in the second part of the catalogue, Neleus contrasts with another pair of twins in the first part of the catalogue. The second entry in the first part of the catalogue belongs to Antiope, who bore the twins Amphion and Zethos to Zeus. Like Neleus, these twins were city founders: they founded the city of Thebes in Boeotia. Unlike Neleus, who founded Pylos by himself, these twins founded Thebes together (*Odyssey* 11.260–265):

τὴν δὲ μέτ' Ἀντιόπην ἴδον, Ἀσωποῖο θύγατρα,
ἣ δὴ καὶ Διὸς εὔχετ' ἐν ἀγκοίνησιν ἰαῦσαι,
καί ῥ' ἔτεκεν δύο παῖδ', Ἀμφίονά τε Ζῆθόν τε,
οἳ πρῶτοι Θήβης ἕδος ἔκτισαν ἑπταπύλοιο
πύργωσάν τ', ἐπεὶ οὐ μὲν ἀπύργωτόν γ' ἐδύναντο
ναιέμεν εὐρύχορον Θήβην, κρατερώ περ ἐόντε.

And after her I saw Antiope, the daughter of Asopos,
who claimed to have slept in the arms of Zeus himself,
and she bore two sons, Amphion and Zethos,
who first founded the seat of seven-gated Thebes
and walled it, since they could not inhabit wide Thebes
without walls, strong though they were.

The relationship between the first two passages in the first half of the catalogue is exactly what it is in the second half of the catalogue: twins who separate are contrasted with twins who stay together; the focus in each case is on Neleus and Nestor, the twins who separated from their brothers.[139]

139 For the city-founding function of Greek twins cf. also n2.20 above on Podaleirios, who acts separately from his brother Makhaon in this role, just as Neleus acts separately from Pelias. The city-founding function of twins has correspondences elsewhere in the Indo-European domain: Romulus and Remus, the founders of Rome, and Hengist and Horsa, the leaders of the Anglo-Saxon invasion of Britain, are examples; the Anglo-Saxon twins, both of whose names mean "horse" (for Hengist cf. German Hengst, "stallion"), are a reflex of the twin horsemen of the Indo-European myth. Other Germanic peoples (the Vandals, Langobards, and Asdingi) are also said to have been led by pairs of twins during the period of migrations; see Ward 1968:50–56 and 1970:199–200 with n30. The Theban city founders have the basic features of Indo-European twins: they are associated with horses (see EN1.3 end), and they are contrasted with each other like other Indo-European twins. In Euripides' fragmentary *Antiope* the contrast between them is cast as a debate between Zethos, the proponent of an active life, and Amphion, a contemplative musician (see Kambitsis 1972:xxii–xxx). In this debate music is equated with *sophía*, "wisdom": cf. *sophísmata*, fr. 188.5, *sophós*, frs. 186.1, 200.3, 202.2 Kannicht 2004; according to Cicero *On Invention* 1.50.94 and the *Rhetorica ad Herennium*

§2.107 The third passage in the first half of the catalogue features another twin, Heracles, but his twin Iphicles is not mentioned. Iphicles is implied, however: Alcmena, who had Heracles by Zeus, is introduced as the wife of the mortal Amphitryon, who was the father of Iphicles (*Odyssey* 11.266–268):

τὴν δὲ μετ᾽ Ἀλκμήνην ἴδον, Ἀμφιτρύωνος ἄκοιτιν,
ἥ ῥ᾽ Ἡρακλῆα θρασυμέμνονα θυμολέοντα
γείνατ᾽ ἐν ἀγκοίνῃσι Διὸς μεγάλοιο μιγεῖσα.

And after her I saw Alcmena, Amphitryon's wife,
who bore bold-battling lion-hearted Heracles
after making love in the arms of great Zeus.

According to the myth Alcmena conceived the two twins by different fathers on the same night. Zeus visited her first, and on that very night Amphitryon

---

2.27.43 Amphion's defense of music in the play is rather a defense of *sapientia*; cf. Kambitsis xxii n2 and xxviii–xxix. The active life advocated by Zethos, on the other hand, includes the duties of a citizen soldier (cf. *aspídos kútei*, "the hollow of the shield," fr. 185.5 Kannicht). Euripides seems to have recast in contemporary terms an old contrast between the twins ("intelligence" in the one, "war" in the other). "Apollodorus" 3.5.5 tells how the Theban twins were exposed by their mother and raised by a cowherd, and how Amphion practiced music whereas Zethos practiced cowherding. From the standpoint of the Indo-European myth Zethos's association with cattle is secondary; it perhaps has to do with Euripides' distinction between an *aprágmōn* Amphion, who busies himself with music, and a *poluprágmōn* Zethos, who busies himself from childhood with active pursuits (the word *aprágmōn*, "free from business, staying away from politics," and the idea of a *poluprágmōn*, "restless, meddlesome man," are found in *Antiope* fr. 193 Kannicht). Plato's *Gorgias* bears witness to the contemporary resonance of the Euripidean debate between Amphion and Zethos (the debate is alluded to in *Gorgias* 484e, 485e, 486bc, 489e). The tradition that Amphion and Zethos walled Thebes by means of the kithara, attested for Hesiod (fr. 182 MW), is ignored by Homer. At the end of Euripides' *Antiope* Hermes assigns the two twins different roles in the task of building walls for Thebes: Amphion is to play the lyre, which stones and trees will obey (fr. 223.119–126 Kannicht); in the lines addressed to Zethos there is a lacuna, but the full line that remains, while itself corrupt, has a warlike sound to it that fits the characterization of this twin: σὺ μὲν .[.]...τον ἔρυμα πολεμίων λαβών, "you, on the one hand...taking the enemies' defense," Kannicht fr. 223.118 (cf. Kambitsis ad loc. [fr. 48.89] for the uncertain text). Apollonius of Rhodes 1.735–741 pictures the twins in the act of building the Theban walls; Zethos lifts a mountain peak on his shoulders with great effort, while Amphion plays his lyre and a rock twice as large as his brother's follows him. As a parallel for Amphion the musician, the Dioskouroi are called musicians in Theocritus 22.24 (ἱππῆες κιθαρισταὶ ἀεθλητῆρες ἀοιδοί, "horsemen, kithara-players, athletes, singers"; music presumably characterized Polydeuces in contrast to Castor, but this is not attested. For a discussion of early and late sources attesting the building of the walls of Thebes by Amphion and Zethos see Hurst 2000. The double foundation of Thebes, by Cadmus on the one hand, and by Amphion and Zethos on the other hand, is studied with a focus on archaeological evidence by Berman 2004.

returned home from war and made love to her. The tale, which became the subject of comedy in Plautus, is told in the epic *Shield of Heracles*.[140] The dual paternity of Heracles and his brother, and the dichotomy between an immortal and a mortal father, reflect the categories of the Indo-European twin myth; the Dioskouroi are the model. Heracles is not called a twin in *Odyssey* 11, but he is one. In both respects this gives him something important in common with Nestor.

§2.108 The first half of the catalogue matches the second half of the catalogue in featuring twins, either explicitly or implicitly, in the first three entries, the first two of which contrast twins who separate with twins who remain together: the chief interest in each case focuses on the first entry, the twins who separate from their brothers, Neleus in the first half of the

140 Hesiod *Shield of Heracles* 35–38 (Zeus is the subject in the first two lines):

αὐτῇ μὲν γὰρ νυκτὶ τανισφύρου Ἠλεκτρυώνης
εὐνῇ καὶ φιλότητι μίγη, τέλεσεν δ' ἄρ' ἐέλδωρ·
αὐτὴ δ' Ἀμφιτρύων λαοσσόος, ἀγλαὸς ἥρως,
ἐκτελέσας μέγα ἔργον ἀφίκετο ὅνδε δόμονδε.

On one night he made love
with Electryon's slender-ankled daughter in her bed and fulfilled his desire;
on the same night warrior-rousing Amphitryon, the splendid hero,
returned to his house after accomplishing a great deed.

After the lovemaking of husband and wife (lines 39–47) the poem concludes with the birth of Alcmena's twin sons (lines 48–56); the latter passage elaborately contrasts both the fathers, one immortal and the other mortal, and the sons, one better and the other worse (Hesiod *Shield of Heracles* 48–56):

ἣ δὲ θεῷ δμηθεῖσα καὶ ἀνέρι πολλὸν ἀρίστῳ
Θήβῃ ἐν ἑπταπύλῳ διδυμάονε γείνατο παῖδε,
οὐκέθ' ὁμὰ φρονέοντε· κασιγνήτω γε μὲν ἤστην·
τὸν μὲν χειρότερον, τὸν δ' αὖ μέγ' ἀμείνονα φῶτα,
δεινόν τε κρατερόν τε, βίην Ἡρακληείην·
τὸν μὲν ὑποδμηθεῖσα κελαινεφέϊ Κρονίωνι,
αὐτὰρ Ἰφικλῆα δορυσσόῳ Ἀμφιτρύωνι,
κεκριμένην γενεήν· τὸν μὲν βροτῷ ἀνδρὶ μιγεῖσα,
τὸν δὲ Διὶ Κρονίωνι θεῶν σημάντορι πάντων.

Having submitted to the god and to much the best man
she bore twin sons in seven-gated Thebes,
one the worse, the other greatly the better man,
terrible and strong, the mighty Heracles;
him (she bore) submitting to the dark-clouded son of Kronos,
but Iphicles (she bore) to spear-shaking Amphitryon,
illustrious offspring; the one (she bore) having made love to a mortal man,
the other to Kronos's son Zeus, ruler of all the gods.

catalogue (explicitly), and Nestor in the second half of the catalogue (implicitly). The other two entries of the five total entries in each part of the catalogue, which complete the catalogue's overall structure, are the concluding passage in each part and the passage immediately preceding the concluding passage in each part. A group of three heroines finishes the second half of the catalogue, ending the entire catalogue; Epikaste and her son Oedipus finish the first half of the catalogue.[141] The two passages that precede the concluding passages are a group of three Attic heroines in the second half of the catalogue and Heracles' wife Megara in the first half of the catalogue. We will consider these passages more closely when we return to the structure of the catalogue as a whole and examine its component parts more critically.

§2.109 For now the case is clear enough: when Odysseus meets the group of ghostly heroines in the underworld, he comes face to face with Nestor's myth, which is what has put Odysseus in the underworld in the first place: Nestor did not bring Odysseus home, just as he did not bring Periklymenos back to life; if Odysseus depended on Nestor's help for his *nóstos*, there would be no hope for him. As if to make this point Odysseus interrupts his story at

---

141 A brief comment on Epikaste is in order. The catalogue of heroines in *Odyssey* 11 presents the "wives and daughters" of heroes: Odysseus says so in his introduction to the catalogue (*Odyssey* 11.225–227):

νῶϊ μὲν ὣς ἐπέεσσιν ἀμειβόμεθ', αἱ δὲ γυναῖκες
ἤλυθον, ὤτρυνεν γὰρ ἀγαυὴ Περσεφόνεια,
ὅσσαι ἀριστήων <u>ἄλοχοι</u> ἔσαν <u>ἠδὲ θύγατρες</u>.

Thus the two of us exchanged words, and the women
came, for revered Persephone roused them,
all who were <u>wives and daughters</u> of the best men.

He uses the same formulation in his epilogue at the end of the catalogue proper (*Odyssey* 11.328–329):

πάσας δ' οὐκ ἂν ἐγὼ μυθήσομαι οὐδ' ὀνομήνω,
ὅσσας ἡρώων <u>ἀλόχους</u> ἴδον <u>ἠδὲ θύγατρας</u>.

I could not say or name all
the <u>wives and daughters</u> of heroes that I saw.

Husbands and fathers of the heroines are duly named in each entry, but not very consistently, and it does not take long to emerge that the heroines are actually significant as mothers rather than as wives and daughters: it is the heroines' sons (and one daughter, Pero) who matter in this catalogue. In Epikaste, who is both wife and mother to Oedipus, the announced intention of the catalogue and its real purpose coincide, and this obviously happens in her case alone. The real purpose of the catalogue, which is to present the mothers of heroes and their sons, pertains to the entire catalogue; the clearest articulation of this purpose, in the shocking case of Epikaste, is well placed at the midpoint of the catalogue as a whole.

the end of the catalogue and proposes to his Phaeacian hosts that he end his story right there, in the underworld; he says that he saw too many ghostly heroines to go on naming them all, and that it is now time for sleep. He ends by specifying the Phaeacians themselves (along with the gods) as his hope for a *nóstos* (*Odyssey* 11.328–332):

πάσας δ' οὐκ ἂν ἐγὼ μυθήσομαι οὐδ' ὀνομήνω,

ὅσσας ἡρώων ἀλόχους ἴδον ἠδὲ θύγατρας·

πρὶν γάρ κεν καὶ νὺξ φθῖτ' ἄμβροτος. ἀλλὰ καὶ ὥρη

εὕδειν, ἢ ἐπὶ νῆα θοὴν ἐλθόντ' ἐς ἑταίρους

ἢ αὐτοῦ· πομπὴ δὲ θεοῖσ' ὑμῖν τε μελήσει.

I could not say or name all
the wives and daughters of heroes that I saw;
immortal night would pass away first. But it is time
to sleep, either going to the swift ship and crew
or here; but my voyage will be up to the gods and to you.

At this point the story of Odysseus's return has itself stopped. In order to start it up again the Phaeacians must intervene and encourage him to continue. The burden is here shifted from Nestor, who did not bring Odysseus home, to the Phaeacians, who (along with the gods) will. The interruption dramatizes this shift. Arete, the queen, is the first to speak. So far she has been rather reserved about Odysseus, but here, for the first time, she expresses complete admiration for him, and she tells the other Phaeacians not to stint on their gifts to him (*Odyssey* 11.333–341):

ὣς ἔφαθ', οἱ δ' ἄρα πάντες ἀκὴν ἐγένοντο σιωπῇ,

κηληθμῷ δ' ἔσχοντο κατὰ μέγαρα σκιόεντα.

τοῖσιν δ' Ἀρήτη λευκώλενος ἤρχετο μύθων·

"Φαίηκες, πῶς ὕμμιν ἀνὴρ ὅδε φαίνεται εἶναι

εἶδός τε μέγεθός τε ἰδὲ φρένας ἔνδον ἐΐσας;

ξεῖνος δ' αὖτ' ἐμός ἐστιν, ἕκαστος δ' ἔμμορε τιμῆς.

τῶ μὴ ἐπειγόμενοι ἀποπέμπετε μηδὲ τὰ δῶρα

οὕτω χρηΐζοντι κολούετε· πολλὰ γὰρ ὑμῖν

κτήματ' ἐνὶ μεγάροισι θεῶν ἰότητι κέονται."

So he spoke, and they all fell into a hushed silence
and were held by a spell in the dusky hall.
White-armed Arete spoke to them first:
"Phaeacians, how does this man strike you
in form and size and well-balanced mind within?
He is my guest, but each of you has a share in the honor.
So do not rush to send him away, and do not cut short
your gifts when he has such need; for many possessions
lie in your halls by the will of the gods."

The aged retainer Ekheneos speaks next; he praises the queen's speech, but he says that putting it into effect depends on Alcinous, the king (*Odyssey* 11.344–346):

ὦ φίλοι, οὐ μὰν ἦμιν ἀπὸ σκοποῦ οὐδ' ἀπὸ δόξης
μυθεῖται βασίλεια περίφρων· ἀλλὰ πίθεσθε.
Ἀλκινόου δ' ἐκ τοῦδ' ἔχεται ἔργον τε ἔπος τε.

Dear people, not at all beside the point or short of expectation
does our wise queen speak; be persuaded by her.
But on Alcinous here both word and deed depend.

Alcinous immediately ratifies the queen's proposal, bidding Odysseus wait until tomorrow for his return so that there will be time for the Phaeacians to bring him additional gifts;[142] he then says that Odysseus's journey home will be the concern of the Phaeacian men, himself in particular (*Odyssey* 11.348–353):

τοῦτο μὲν οὕτω δὴ ἔσται ἔπος, αἴ κεν ἐγώ γε
ζωὸς Φαιήκεσσι φιληρέτμοισιν ἀνάσσω·
ξεῖνος δὲ τλήτω, μάλα περ νόστοιο χατίζων,

142 Analysts have long regarded the "intermezzo" (as the interruption in Odysseus's story is sometimes called) as a secondary intrusion into the poem; see e.g. Page 1955:32–35, whose argument focuses on the addition of an extra day to Odysseus's stay (τλήτω...ἐπιμεῖναι ἐς αὔριον, "let him bear...to remain until tomorrow," *Odyssey* 11.350–351), when his departure seemed to be firmly fixed for a day earlier (αὔριον ἔς, "for tomorrow," *Odyssey* 7.318, spoken the day before). Fenik 1974:108 comments on the phrase αὔριον ἔς in *Odyssey* 7.318 that "probably no other single phrase in the Odyssey has served as the basis for more elaborate or more confident analyst criticism and reconstruction." Brian Hainsworth (Heubeck et al. 1988, vol. 1, 317) defends the phrase from such analyst criticism, arguing that "its use in the circumstances is perfectly natural and it is corrected at 11.350–351 when circumstances had changed."

ἔμπης οὖν ἐπιμεῖναι ἐς αὔριον, εἰς ὅ κε πᾶσαν
δωτίνην τελέσω. πομπὴ δ' ἄνδρεσσι μελήσει
πᾶσι, μάλιστα δ' ἐμοί· τοῦ γὰρ κράτος ἔστ' ἐνὶ δήμῳ.

This will be my word, exactly so,
if I live and rule over the oar-loving Phaeacians.
But let the stranger be patient, though he longs for his return,
and wait until tomorrow, until I make good
his whole gift. His voyage will be up to all the men,
but most of all to me; for I hold the power in the land.

When Alcinous says that Odysseus's journey home will be his concern in particular, he picks up Odysseus's final words before the interruption of his story: πομπὴ δὲ θεοῖσ' ὑμῖν τε μελήσει. With those words Odysseus shifted responsibility for his *nóstos* from Nestor to the Phaeacians. We now see that that responsibility has been shifted to Alcinous in particular, who accepts it: Alcinous has replaced Nestor as Odysseus's homebringer. To dramatize this shift Alcinous gets Odysseus to restart his story by asking him if he saw any of his companions from Troy in the underworld (*Odyssey* 11.370–372). Odysseus, in answering him, resumes his story, which in due course will take him back out of the underworld and up to the present. Alcinous has taken over for Nestor symbolically in the underworld, and as Odysseus moves forward from this point he now has Alcinous on his side.[143]

§2.110 There are strong parallels between Nestor, king of Pylos, and Alcinous, king of the Phaeacians, not only in their function as "homebringers," but also in their names, which both designate this function. Both names, as previously discussed, contain the transitive root **nes-*. The name *Alkí-noos* means "he who brings back by his strength," and its second element, like the name *Néstōr*, is closely associated with the noun *nóos* "mind," with which it

---

143 The role of the Phaeacian queen is also crucial for Odysseus's homecoming; he is told twice before he meets her that if she is well disposed toward him there is hope that he will reach home (*Odyssey* 6.313–315, 7.75–77). It is in the interruption of Odysseus's story that Arete first gives him her full endorsement. Her speech is well placed because it immediately follows Odysseus's encounters with other female figures in the underworld, his mother first, followed by the group of heroines. As has often been noted, the shift in Odysseus's story from the encounters with these female figures to encounters with his male companions from Troy is dramatized by having the queen speak first after Odysseus interrupts his story, and having the king speak next, before he resumes his story (see e.g. Pache 1999:30). The shift from a female to a male perspective is signaled especially in Alcinous's words πομπὴ δ' ἄνδρεσσι μελήσει / πᾶσι, μάλιστα δ' ἐμοί, "his voyage will be up to all the men, but to me most of all."

is identical in form. The first element, *Alki-*, which suggests a warrior's attribute, is parallel to Nestor's warrior epithet *hippóta*, "horseman." Beyond their common function and comparable names, there are also striking parallels between their families, starting with their fathers. Just as Nestor is the son of the founder of his city, so too is Alcinous. We learn this at the very outset of the Phaeacian episode, when Athena enters the Phaeacian city to appear in a dream to Nausicaa. The Phaeacians are here introduced as having formerly lived near the Cyclopes, who were stronger than they and brought them harm. Hence godlike Nausithoos moved his people to Scheria, their present home, and built a city for them. Nausithoos was now dead, and Alcinous ruled in his place (*Odyssey* 6.4–12):

οἳ πρὶν μέν ποτ' ἔναιον ἐν εὐρυχόρῳ Ὑπερείῃ,

ἀγχοῦ Κυκλώπων ἀνδρῶν ὑπερηνορεόντων,

οἵ σφεας σινέσκοντο, βίηφι δὲ φέρτεροι ἦσαν.

ἔνθεν ἀναστήσας ἄγε Ναυσίθοος θεοειδής,

εἷσεν δὲ Σχερίῃ, ἑκὰς ἀνδρῶν ἀλφηστάων,

ἀμφὶ δὲ τεῖχος ἔλασσε πόλει καὶ ἐδείματο οἴκους

καὶ νηοὺς ποίησε θεῶν καὶ ἐδάσσατ' ἀρούρας.

ἀλλ' ὁ μὲν ἤδη κηρὶ δαμεὶς Ἄϊδόσδε βεβήκει,

Ἀλκίνοος δὲ τότ' ἦρχε, θεῶν ἄπο μήδεα εἰδώς.

They once lived in wide Hypereia
near the Cyclopes, overbearing men
who harmed them, for they were greater in strength.
Uprooting his people godlike Nausithoos led them away
and settled them in Scheria, far from laboring men,
and drove a wall around the city and built dwellings,
and made temples of the gods and apportioned fields.
But he had already succumbed to death and gone to Hades,
and Alcinoos, knowing counsels from the gods, now ruled.

In this passage Nausithoos is called the founder of Scheria, and his role as founder is emphasized by a detailed description of his act: he built walls, houses, and temples, and he apportioned fields. Nestor's father Neleus was the founder of Pylos, and the parallel with Nausithoos is very striking; it is made more so by the last two lines in the passage above. These lines, saying that Nausithoos was dead and that Alcinous now ruled in his place, are

paralleled in only one place in Homer, and that is in *Odyssey* 3, when Nestor
gets up on the morning after Telemachus's arrival, and sits on the shining
stones on which Neleus once sat: Neleus too was now dead, and Nestor ruled
in his place (*Odyssey* 3.404–412):

ἦμος δ' ἠριγένεια φάνη ῥοδοδάκτυλος Ἠώς,
ὤρνυτ' ἄρ' ἐξ εὐνῆφι Γερήνιος ἱππότα Νέστωρ,
ἐκ δ' ἐλθὼν κατ' ἄρ' ἕζετ' ἐπὶ ξεστοῖσι λίθοισιν,
οἵ οἱ ἔσαν προπάροιθε θυράων ὑψηλάων
λευκοί, ἀποστίλβοντες ἀλείφατος· οἷσ' ἔπι μὲν πρὶν
Νηλεὺς ἵζεσκεν, θεόφιν μήστωρ ἀτάλαντος·
ἀλλ' ὁ μὲν ἤδη κηρὶ δαμεὶς Ἄϊδόσδε βεβήκει,
Νέστωρ αὖ τότ' ἐφῖζε Γερήνιος, οὖρος Ἀχαιῶν,
σκῆπτρον ἔχων.

But when early-born rosy-fingered dawn appeared,
the Gerenian horseman Nestor rose from bed,
and went out and sat on polished stones
that were in front of his high doors,
white and glistening with oil, on which formerly
Neleus would sit, a counselor equal to the gods;
but he had already succumbed to death and gone to Hades,
and Gerenian Nestor, guardian of the Achaeans, now sat on them
holding his scepter.

The repeated line, used first of Neleus, then of Nausithoos, occurs nowhere
else. The parallel in diction strongly reinforces the parallel in content, and it
begins to appear that the parallel in content is deliberate—that we are meant
to be reminded of Neleus and Nestor when we first hear about Nausithoos
and Alcinous.[144]

---

144 Note that Nestor's "smooth stones" to sit on (*epì xestoîsi líthoisin*, *Odyssey* 3.406) are paral-
leled in the Phaeacians' place of council when Alcinous gathers the elders to arrange
Odysseus's return (*Odyssey* 8.4–7):

τοῖσιν δ' ἡγεμόνευ' ἱερὸν μένος Ἀλκινόοιο
Φαιήκων ἀγορήνδ', ἥ σφιν παρὰ νηυσὶ τέτυκτο.
ἐλθόντες δὲ καθῖζον ἐπὶ ξεστοῖσι λίθοισι
πλησίον.

§2.111 The impression that the parallel between Nausithoos and Neleus as city founders is deliberate is confirmed by a second passage; this passage, like the passage that first introduces the Phaeacians, occurs in the context of an entrance by Athena into the Phaeacian city to help Odysseus. On her first entrance she appeared to Nausicaa in a dream. Now, on her second entrance, she disguises herself as a young maiden, and she encounters Odysseus himself in order to lead him to the Phaeacian palace. Odysseus has already learned from Nausicaa that her parents are Alcinous and Arete, the king and queen. Athena, who like Nausicaa stresses the need to make a favorable impression on the queen, goes on to give Odysseus a genealogy of the royal family, which is the same for the king and queen, since they are not only husband and wife, but also uncle and niece. Nausithoos, Athena says, was the son of Poseidon and the youngest daughter of a king of the giants named Eurymedon. This otherwise unknown figure destroyed both himself and his reckless people, but his daughter, whose name was Periboia, was apparently spared, for she bore Nausithoos to Poseidon, and Nausithoos became the king of the Phaeacians (*Odyssey* 7.56–62):

Ναυσίθοον μὲν πρῶτα Ποσειδάων ἐνοσίχθων
γείνατο καὶ Περίβοια, γυναικῶν εἶδος ἀρίστη,
ὁπλοτάτη θυγάτηρ μεγαλήτορος Εὐρυμέδοντος,
ὅς ποθ' ὑπερθύμοισι Γιγάντεσσιν βασίλευεν.
ἀλλ' ὁ μὲν ὤλεσε λαὸν ἀτάσθαλον, ὤλετο δ' αὐτός·
τῇ δὲ Ποσειδάων ἐμίγη καὶ ἐγείνατο παῖδα
Ναυσίθοον μεγάθυμον, ὃς ἐν Φαίηξιν ἄνασσε.

First Nausithoos was fathered by earthshaker Poseidon
and borne by Periboea, most beautiful of women,
the youngest daughter of great-hearted Eurymedon,

Alcinous, having sacred power, led them
to the assembly of the Phaeacians, which was built for them next to the ships.
They went and sat on polished stones,
near each other.

These are the phrases's only two occurrences in the *Odyssey*; there is a third occurrence in the *Iliad* in the litigation scene on the shield of Achilles (*Iliad* 18.504). There are variations of the phrase at *Iliad* 6.244 and 248 (θάλαμοι ξεστοῖο λίθοιο, "bedchambers of polished stone") and *Odyssey* 16.408 (ἐλθόντες δὲ καθῖζον ἐπὶ ξεστοῖσι θρόνοισιν, "they went and sat on polished thrones"); cf. also ξεστοῖσιν λάεσσι, "polished stones," in *Odyssey* 10.211 and 253 (Circe's palace).

who once ruled over the arrogant Giants.
But he destroyed his reckless people and was himself destroyed.
Poseidon made love with her and fathered a child,
great-hearted Nausithoos, who ruled among the Phaeacians.

How Eurymedon destroyed himself and his people is not told, but the answer is implied in their designation as overbearing giants. For giants in Greek myth notoriously fought against the Olympian gods and were destroyed by them. We are doubtless meant to understand that Eurymedon and his people likewise rivaled the gods and were destroyed by them. Although when and where this may have happened is left out of the account, the occasion was apparently not that of the later myth, for in that the giants' leaders are Porphyrion and Alkyoneus and there is no giant named Eurymedon.[145]

§2.112 Nausithoos's ancestry, which cannot be traced to any otherwise known myth of the giants, has a profound similarity to something else, namely the ancestry of Neleus. As we are explicitly told in the first passage of the catalogue of heroines in *Odyssey* 11, the god Poseidon made love to Tyro, the mother of Neleus, just as he did to Periboia, the mother of Nausithoos. Tyro's father, moreover, corresponds strikingly to Periboia's father. Tyro's father was Salmoneus, and Salmoneus, though not a giant, did precisely what Eurymedon did, namely destroy himself and his people through his foolish challenge of the gods. The only one of his race who was spared destruction, furthermore, was his daughter Tyro, who mated with Poseidon and gave birth to the city founder Neleus. Periboia, who gave birth to the city founder Nausithoos, likewise seems to be the sole survivor of her race.

§2.113 *Odyssey* 11 does not tell the story of Salmoneus, but seems rather to divert attention from it when it first introduces Tyro, giving her the epithet *eupatéreian*, "born of a noble father," and in the next line calling Salmoneus himself *amúmonos*, "faultless" (*Odyssey* 11.235–236):

ἔνθ' ἥ τοι πρώτην Τυρὼ ἴδον εὐπατέρειαν,
ἣ φάτο Σαλμωνῆος ἀμύμονος ἔκγονος εἶναι.

---

145 "Apollodorus" 1.6.1–2 names thirteen giants who took part in the battle at Phlegrai and Eurymedon is not among them, much less their king. There may also have been local myths of giants, and it is possible that Eurymedon represents one such. See West 1966:419 (on *Theogony* 954) for the possibility that Heracles, besides his participation in the battle at Phlegrai, slew other giants by himself on a different occasion. For further discussion of the giants in Greek tradition see EN2.3 and, from an Athenian perspective, n3.105 and n3.108 and EN3.7 below.

Then I saw Tyro first, <u>born of a noble father</u>,
who said that she was the offspring of <u>faultless</u> Salmoneus.

But if *Odyssey* 11 chooses to ignore[146] Salmoneus's myth, his myth nonetheless is well known from later sources, beginning with Hesiod.[147] Salmoneus had the temerity to rival Zeus himself, ordering his people to offer sacrifices to himself rather than to Zeus. To show that like Zeus he wielded thunder and lightning, he dragged bronze cauldrons behind his chariot to imitate thunder and threw torches into the sky to imitate lightning. We do not have the full text of the Hesiodic treatment of the myth, but a papyrus fragment (Hesiod fr. 30 MW) reveals many significant details: the harnessing of Salmoneus's horses (...ὡ]πλίζετο μ[ών]υχας ἵππου[ς, line 4), his chariot (ἅρμα [καὶ] ἵππους, line 6), the bronze cauldrons (χάλκεοί τε λ[έβ]ητες, line 7, cf. line 5), and the brightness of burning fire (σέ]λας πυρὸς αἰθ[ο]μένοιο, line 10). More fully preserved by this fragment is the reaction of Zeus, who destroys the entire people of Salmoneus because of his transgression (Hesiod fr. 30.12–19 MW):

ὁ δ᾽ ἀγᾶτ[ο πατ]ὴρ ἀνδρῶν τε θεῶν τ[ε,
σκληρὸν δ᾽] ἐβρόντ[ησεν ἀπ᾽] οὐρανοῦ ἀστερόεντος
[ ]ον δή· ἐτ[ί]ναξε δὲ γαῖαν ἅπασαν.
βῆ δὲ κατ᾽ Ο]ὐλύμποιο [χο]λούμενος, αἶψα δ᾽ ἵκανεν
λαοὺς Σαλμ]ωνῆος ἀτ[ασ]θάλου, οἳ τάχ᾽ ἔμελλον
πείσεσθ᾽ ἔρ]γ᾽ ἀΐδηλα δι᾽ ὑβ[ρ]ιστὴν βασιλῆα·
τοὺς δ᾽ ἔβα]λεν βροντῆι [τε κ]αὶ αἰθαλόεντι κεραυνῶι.
ὣς λαοὺς ἀπε]τίνεθ᾽ ὑπερβ[ασίην] βασιλῆος.

The father of men and gods was offended,
and he thundered [harshly] from the starry sky,
[ ] ; he shook the whole earth.
[He descended from] Olympus in anger, and came at once
to the people] of reckless Salmoneus, who were soon to
[suffer] ruthless deeds because of their king's outrages.
[He struck them] with a thunderbolt and flashing lightning.
[Thus he punished the people] for the transgression of the king.

---

146 Conceal would be more accurate; see below.
147 Hesiod fr. 30 MW; also "Apollodorus" 1.9.7; cf. Vergil *Aeneid* 6.585–594.

In the next lines Salmoneus's children, wife, servants, city, and palace are destroyed by Zeus's anger one after another, and Salmoneus himself is hurled into the underworld as a warning to other mortals (Hesiod fr. 30.20–23 MW):

] ς παῖδάς τε γ[υν]αῖκά τε οἰκῆάς τε,
πό]λιν καὶ δώμα[τ' ..]ίρρυτα θῆκεν ἀίστως,
τὸν δὲ λα]βὼν ἔρριψ' ἐς Τ[ά]ρταρον ἠερόεντα,
ὡς μή τις] βροτὸς ἄλλος [ἐ]ρίζοι Ζηνὶ ἄνακτι.

] his children and wife and servants
] city and house he destroyed,
and seizing him] he threw him into gloomy Tartarus,
so that no] other mortal would challenge lord Zeus.

Then we learn about Tyro, who was spared the fate of the rest of her people because she tried to stop her father from committing his act of hubris (Hesiod fr. 30.24–28 MW):

τοῦ δ' ἄρα] παῖς ἐλέλειπτο φίλη μακάρεσσι θεοῖσι
Τυρὼ ἐυπ]λόκαμος ἰκέλη χ[ρ]υσῆι Ἀφρο[δ]ίτ[ηι,
οὕνεκα νε]ικείεσκε καὶ ἤρ[ισε] Σαλμωνῆϊ
συνεχές, οὐ]δ' εἴασκε θεοῖς [βροτὸν ἰσ]οφαρίζειν·
τούνεκά] μιν ἐσάωσε πατὴρ ἀνδρῶν τε θεῶν τε.

But his] child was left, dear to the blessed gods,
Tyro with the beautiful] hair, like golden Aphrodite,
because] she quarreled and fought with Salmoneus
always,] and would not allow a mortal to act like the gods' equal;
because of that] the father of men and gods spared her.

In the next lines of the fragment Zeus leads Tyro to the house of "faultless Kretheus," who rears her, and this prepares the way for her union with Poseidon, the account of which begins just before the fragment breaks off (Hesiod fr. 30.29–35 MW).

§2.114 The resemblance between the earliest stages of the Phaeacian genealogy and the same stages of the Neleid genealogy fits an already large pattern of correspondences and can hardly be fortuitous. It would seem in fact that when we hear the first line of the catalogue of heroines and the name Tyro in *Odyssey* 11 we are meant to recall the Phaeacian genealogy and the figure Periboia in *Odyssey* 7. If attention is diverted from the correspondence by giving Salmoneus a generic epithet of approbation, *amúmonos*, "faultless,"[148] this is only what we have come to expect in contexts that involve Nestor. In the case of the Phaeacian progenitor Eurymedon his hubris has been made explicit so that his correspondence to Salmoneus may be perceived. In the case of Salmoneus we do not need to hear about his crime because it is already well known.

§2.115 We return now from the correspondence between the city founders, Neleus and Nausithoos, and their respective parentages, involving Poseidon and the daughter of a sinner in each case, to the "homebringers" themselves, Nestor and Alcinous. For it is the correspondence between these two that is central to the story of the *Odyssey*. We have so far dealt only with the first part of the Phaeacian genealogy that Athena tells to Odysseus in Book 7. What she tells him next concerns Alcinous. As in the correspondence between Eurymedon the "sinner" in *Odyssey* 7 and the "faultless" Salmoneus in *Odyssey* 11, something is made explicit in the case of the Phaeacian king Alcinous in *Odyssey* 7 that is suppressed in the case of Nestor in *Odyssey* 11. As we have seen, *Odyssey* 11 does not call Nestor a twin whose warrior brother Periklymenos died. Nor does it say that Nestor took his warrior brother's place. These are things that we have had to reconstruct painstakingly, and that we can now say are implied by the structure of the catalogue in *Odyssey* 11, but that the surface of the text deliberately disguises. In the case of Alcinous, on the other hand, what is implied for Nestor is made explicit: Alcinous had a brother named *Rhēxēnōr*, "breaker of men," who died young: Apollo shot him when he was just a bridegroom, and he left just a single daughter, Arete, whom Alcinous married (*Odyssey* 7.63–66):

Ναυσίθοος δ' ἔτεκεν Ῥηξήνορά τ' Ἀλκίνοόν τε.
τὸν μὲν ἄκουρον ἐόντα βάλ' ἀργυρότοξος Ἀπόλλων
νυμφίον, ἐν μεγάρῳ μίαν οἴην παῖδα λιπόντα,
Ἀρήτην· τὴν δ' Ἀλκίνοος ποιήσατ' ἄκοιτιν.

Nausithoos fathered Rhexenor and Alcinous.
The one silver-bowed Apollo shot while he was a bridegroom
Without any sons, leaving only a daughter in his hall,
Arete, whom Alcinous made his wife.

---

148 It is also famously given to the sinner Aigisthos (*Odyssey* 1.29).

To analyze this passage it is best to proceed backwards, beginning with what does not correspond to Nestor at all, namely Alcinous's marriage to Arete, for Nestor did not marry his own niece. Queen Arete, who is fully as important among the Phaeacians as king Alcinous is, has her own story to be uncovered, and we will devote full attention to it later. But her story has nothing to do with Nestor, and we must simply leave her out of account for now. On the other hand Arete's marriage to her father's brother does serve to give her a convenient origin,[149] which we will later see that she needs, and it also allows Alcinous to do something that is significant for his correspondence to Nestor, namely to take his brother's place by raising his brother's orphaned daughter and marrying her.[150] This of course is not the way in which Nestor took his brother's place, which he did by becoming a warrior in his own right. But the warrior nature of the brother who died has already been fully brought out in the case of Rhexenor by his name, "breaker of men," which could not be more significant, both in itself and in what it says about Nestor's myth. In itself Rhexenor is otherwise an epithet in the Homeric poems, and it is used of only one hero, namely Achilles himself (there are four occurrences in the *Iliad* and one in the *Odyssey*).[151] We should note just how unusual the name "breaker of men" is among the seafaring and peace-loving Phaeacians.[152] Unlike Achilles, who died young in battle where

---

149 And a typical one for ancient Greek society (see n2.150 below). There are two examples in Nestor's own family: Tyro was Kretheus's niece (cf. Hesiod fr. 10 MW) whom he raised and married after her father Salmoneus was destroyed (Hesiod fr. 30.25–30 MW); Amythaon married the daughter of his brother Pheres and had the sons Melampus and Bias by her ("Apollodorus" 1.9.11).

150 In Attic legal terminology Arete has the status of an *epíklēros*, "heiress," a daughter whose father had no male heirs; the *epíklēros* was required to produce a male heir for her father's line through marriage to a close relation (a father's brother or a cousin); see Cox 1998:94–99. In Athens, according to Aristotle, the father could give such a daughter to whomever he chose, and if he died intestate, the guardian of his inheritance (his *klēronómos*) could give her to whomever he chose (*Politics* 1270a26–29); the *klēronómos* was "the nearest adult male relative, or if there should be more than one equally near, the eldest of them" (Newman 1887:329; cf. also Schütrumpf 1991:312–313 for more recent discussion). For bibliography on Homeric and Attic marriage and differences between them see Foley 1994:147–148 and n208. In Sparta, if a father had not chosen a husband for an heiress, the kings did so (Herodotus 6.57.4). In Sparta, as in Athens, an heiress would no doubt be married to her nearest relation on the father's side, an uncle or cousin, so that the property would remain in the clan.

151 *Iliad* 7.228, 13.324, 16.146, 16.575; *Odyssey* 4.5. All occurrences of the epithet are in the same metrical position as the name Rhexenor in *Odyssey* 7.63. The name occurs once more, in *Odyssey* 7.146, where Arete is called "daughter of Rhexenor." The noun ῥηξηνορίη, "man-breaking might," occurs once, in *Odyssey* 14.217, in Odysseus's tale to Eumaios.

152 For the Phaeacians' names, see Welcker 1832/1845:3–4 (discussed further in n4.179 below): Alcinous has three sons and a daughter, three of whose names relate to the sea; the exception is *Laodámas*, whose name expresses "kingliness" ("das Königliche") in Welcker's term (for this figure, the Phaeacian heir apparent, see §4.49–§4.53 below; for his name see EN2.2 to

all had witnessed his preeminent right to this epithet, Nestor's brother was shot by Apollo, which is a vague form of death, but might suggest disease.[153] Rhexenor was a Phaeacian, living far from other men, and he therefore had no enemies to break. This is to say that he owes his name not to any real tradition of his own, but to his correspondence to Periklymenos, Nestor's warrior brother.

§2.116 It is remarkable how the Phaeacian genealogy in Book 7, from beginning to end, selects significant details to create an unmistakable correspondence to Nestor and his family. The most significant of these details (and the least overt correspondence) is the one that we considered last, the warrior brother who died young. In schematic form the correspondences, which constitute a virtual fingerprint for the Phaeacians' identity, are as follows:

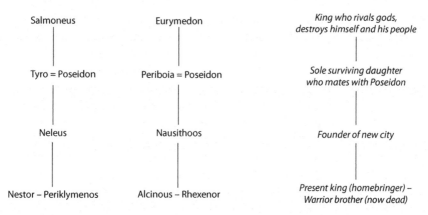

It is also worth noting how what is not essential to the purpose of the Phaeacian genealogy is left out. There is, for example, no figure corresponding to Nestor's mother Chloris, the wife of Neleus. Only Nausithoos, the father, is mentioned in telling of the birth of Rhexenor and Alcinous. And while the fact that Alcinous had a warrior brother (that they were in effect a pair of twins) is fully brought out and emphasized, Nausithoos is not given a twin to match Neleus's twin brother Pelias. The narrative does not exclude

n2.125 above and cf. n2.125 above). Among the rest of the Phaeacians eighteen have names that relate to the sea and only two do not: Polybos, who made a purple ball used for a dance (*Odyssey* 8.373) and Dymas, "famous for ships" (ναυσικλειτοῖο Δύμαντος, *Odyssey* 6.22).

153 Compare the arrows that Apollo shoots against the Achaean army in *Iliad* 1.43–52, which suggest plague, especially in the deaths of animals (dogs and asses) as well as humans. In *Odyssey* 15.407–411, on the other hand, Eumaeus tells Odysseus that on the island of Syrie, where he was born, there was no hunger or disease, but when people grew old Apollo and Artemis shot them with gentle arrows; in this case the gods' arrows seem to represent a natural death by old age, which would not apply to Rhexenor.

that Nausithoos may have had a twin brother, but the point is irrelevant to the genealogy's express purpose, which is to sketch a direct line of descent from the earliest progenitor, the giant Eurymedon, to Alcinous and Arete; it does not matter whether or not Nausithoos was a twin as far as his place in this direct line of descent is concerned. The point is also not necessary to the genealogy's unexpressed purpose, since the correspondence to Nestor's genealogy is made plain by other means.

§2.117 It has become clear at this point, I think, that the Phaeacians had no independent existence of their own, but existed by virtue of their correspondence to other figures. This is very clear in the case of Alcinous's brother Rhexenor, who owes his name to his correspondence to Nestor's warrior brother, Periklymenos. It is as true of Alcinous, whose correspondence to Nestor is the point of all the other correspondences in the genealogy. His name, "he who brings home by his might," as suggested earlier, is a recasting of the name-and-epithet combination *hippóta Néstōr*. With the name goes the function of "homebringing," and we may say that this too has come to Alcinous secondarily from Nestor. But this amounts to saying that the Phaeacians themselves have Nestor as their origin, for there is no distinction to be drawn between the king *Alkínoos*, "he who brings home by his might," and his people, for their only mythic function is to do what his name means. I am suggesting that the Phaeacians as a whole were created by the *Odyssey*, to establish the correspondence to Nestor that we have seen, and that they had no independent existence apart from this.[154] Within the *Odyssey* the Phaeacians of course claim to be the "harmless escorts of all" (πομποὶ ἀπήμονές εἰμεν ἀπάντων, *Odyssey* 8.566 = 13.174), as if their beneficiaries were legion, and when Alcinous arranges Odysseus's homecoming in his council, he alludes to others who have received an escort from them without having to endure any long wait (*Odyssey* 8.31–33):

ἡμεῖς δ', ὡς τὸ πάρος περ, ἐποτρυνώμεθα πομπήν·

οὐδὲ γὰρ οὐδέ τις ἄλλος, ὅτις κ' ἐμὰ δώμαθ' ἵκηται,

ἐνθάδ' ὀδυρόμενος δηρὸν μένει εἵνεκα πομπῆς.

154 More than a century and a half ago G. W. Nitzsch wrote to the point of the Phaeacians that "they are there only for Odysseus and the course of the *Odyssey*" ("sie nur für Odysseus und den Verlauf der Odyssee da sind," Nitzsch 1831:165; cf. Welcker 1832/1845:14, who quotes Nitzsch's statement, and also Nitzsch's related discussion, p. 78). Brian Hainsworth regards the Phaeacian genealogy as an invention, noting that "at least twelve Periboeas and eight Eurymedons are known to the mythographers," but he misses the point that the Phaeacians themselves are an invention of the *Odyssey* (Hainsworth in Heubeck et al. 1988 on *Odyssey* 7.54–66).

But, as in the past, let us press on with his conveyance;
for no one else who comes to my house
ever waits here long pleading for conveyance.[155]

Concretely, however, the *Odyssey* offers only one example, besides Odysseus himself, of a figure who was taken anywhere by the Phaeacians in their fabulous ship, and this was the hoary Rhadamanthys, whom the Phaeacians once took to see Tityos, the son of earth. Alcinous refers to this in Book 7, when he promises Odysseus that on the next day he will be carried home fast asleep on a Phaeacian ship no matter how far off he lives, even if it is farther than Euboea, where the Phaeacians once took Rhadamanthys (*Odyssey* 7.321–324):

εἴ περ καὶ μάλα πολλὸν ἑκαστέρω ἔστ᾽ Εὐβοίης·
τὴν γὰρ τηλοτάτω φάσ᾽ ἔμμεναι οἵ μιν ἴδοντο
λαῶν ἡμετέρων, ὅτε τε ξανθὸν Ῥαδάμανθυν
ἦγον ἐποψόμενον Τιτυόν, Γαιήϊον υἱόν.

Even if it is farther away than Euboea,
which is said to be farthest off by those of our people who saw it
when they took fair-haired Rhadamanthys
to see Tityos, Earth's son.

This meeting between Rhadamanthys and Tityos is otherwise unknown, but a narrative thrust is clearly suggested, for Rhadamanthys was the paradigm of justice (hence he became a judge in the underworld when he died), whereas Tityos was one of the great sinners (hence he was punished in the underworld when he was slain by Apollo). His sin was that he tried to rape the goddess Leto, and it was perhaps to warn him against his sin that Rhadamanthys visited him in Euboea.[156] But really we are free to make up whatever narrative we like

---

155 The pretense is maintained at *Odyssey* 16.227–228, where Odysseus tells Telemachus that the Phaeacians brought him home, "who also convey other men, whoever comes to them":

Φαίηκές μ᾽ ἄγαγον ναυσικλυτοί, οἵ τε καὶ ἄλλους
ἀνθρώπους πέμπουσιν, ὅτίς σφεας εἰσαφίκηται.

156 The scholia to *Odyssey* 7.324 say that Rhadamanthys came "to bring Tityos to his senses" about his evil deed (ὡς δὴ σωφρονίσων αὐτὸν) or that "Rhadamanthys, the most just judge among the Greeks, punished him earlier," i.e. before Apollo did (τοῦτον οὖν ὁ Ῥαδάμανθος ὁ δικαιότατος παρ᾽ Ἕλλησι κριτὴς ἐτιμώρησε πρότερον). These alternatives are clearly guesses based on nothing more than the text of the *Odyssey*. Welcker 1832/1845:28, 71 supposes that the *Odyssey* alludes to a real tradition for Tityos and Rhadamanthys which was known to Homer but did not survive later. He makes much of the statement of the scholia to *Odyssey*

for this meeting between sinner and judge, for Tityos, the giant, belongs with Eurymedon, the giant, who, as we have seen, was invented for the Phaeacian genealogy. Tityos was not invented for the *Odyssey*, but he is a primeval figure, and the episode conjured up for him is just that, an episode that was conjured up to give the Phaeacians one other passenger besides Odysseus.[157]

§2.118 Outside the *Odyssey* the Phaeacians have no existence at all, if one excepts the late Argonautic tradition (Apollonius of Rhodes) that Jason and Medea stopped in the land of the Phaeacians on their flight from Colchis and got married there.[158] There is a reason, of course, that the Phaeacians have

---

7.324 that the Phaeacians seem to live near the isles of the blest (φαίνονται γοῦν οἱ Φαίακες πλησίον τῶν μακάρων νήσων κατοικοῦντες), and this leads him to connect the Phaeacians with a Germanic tradition for islands of the dead in the Atlantic Ocean. He follows another of the scholiast's leads in comparing Rhadamanthys's final abode in Elysion, which is "at the ends of the earth" according to *Odyssey* 4.563, with the apparent home of the Phaeacians. The upshot is that the Phaeacians and Rhadamanthys lived near each other "at the ends of the earth," and this is the reason that they took him on his obscure mission to Euboea. I would agree that this seems entirely consistent with what the *Odyssey* says about the Phaeacians.

157 It is worth noting the quaintness of Euboea's being the farthest point that the Phaeacians ever reached if indeed they took many on their way (so also Stanford 1959 ad loc.). The conveyance of Rhadamanthys, if examined closely, is different from what the Phaeacians otherwise claim to do, which is to provide conveyance to anyone who comes to them needing it (*Odyssey* 8.31–33; see §2.117 above). Rhadamanthys cannot be imagined as simply wandering into the Phaeacians' kingdom in desperate straits like Odysseus; the Phaeacians must have picked him up where he dwelt (cf. n2.156 above). After taking him to Euboea, moreover, they must have taken him back home again, even though this detail is left out of Alcinous's brief description of the round trip: καὶ μὲν οἱ ἔνθ' ἦλθον καὶ ἄτερ καμάτοιο τέλεσσαν / ἤματι τῷ αὐτῷ καὶ ἀπήνυσαν οἴκαδ' ὀπίσσω, "They went there and they finished the voyage without toil / and came back home again on the same day" (*Odyssey* 7.325–326); this return trip is also more than what the Phaeacians claim to do routinely. The Rhadamanthys episode is meant to be vague and suggestive, as said; a further point that is suggested is worth making explicit. If Rhadamanthys indeed inhabited the Elysian fields (cf. n2.156 above), he was already "dead" when he visited Tityos. This is relevant to the "return to life" of Odysseus, the Phaeacians' only other passenger. The death-like state of Odysseus in his final return aboard the Phaeacian ship (*Odyssey* 13.80; cf. §2.120 below) goes well with the Rhadamanthys episode, so interpreted, and vice versa.

158 To be sure the Corcyreans claimed to be the Phaeacians' descendants, a claim that was well established by the fifth century BC (Thucydides 1.25.4). Welcker 1832/1845:40–41 speculates that Hesiod was the first to associate the Phaeacians with Corcyra, since Hesiod associated Odysseus's other travels with locations in Italy (cf. Welcker 1832/1845:47n103). The first attested mention of Corcyra is in the probably sixth-century *Naupaktia Epe*, which according to Pausanias 2.3.9 represented Jason and Medea as moving to Corcyra from Iolkos after the death of Pelias. How the Phaeacians figured in this epic is not known, but the story seems different from the wedding of Jason and Medea under the protection of Alcinous and Arete known from later Argonautic tradition (cf. Welcker 1832/1845:39). A major accomplishment of Welcker's essay is to show that the Homeric Phaeacians had nothing to do with Corcyra, despite the fact that this identification was taken seriously in the time of Thucydides, and probably well before Thucydides. In the Hellenistic era Eratosthenes and others distinguished

no tradition outside the *Odyssey*, and that is that the *Odyssey*, which brought the Phaeacians into existence and gave them the function of "homebringers," also takes this function away from them. After delivering Odysseus to Ithaca, the Phaeacian ship is turned to stone by Poseidon on its return trip, just as it approaches land. When the Phaeacians see this, Alcinous recalls an old prophecy that his father had told him, that Poseidon would one day strike a Phaeacian ship on its return and wall their city in with a mountain, for he begrudged their serving as harmless escorts to all (*Odyssey* 13.172–177).[159] Alcinous orders the Phaeacians to cease giving escort to mortals: πομπῆς μὲν παύεσθε βροτῶν, ὅτε κέν τις ἵκηται / ἡμέτερον προτὶ ἄστυ (*Odyssey* 13.180–181). Thus the Phaeacians' function as escorts ends with Odysseus, and this is the surest sign that it also began with Odysseus (i.e. that the *Odyssey* created the Phaeacians in the first place), for the *Odyssey* could not alter the Phaeacians' essential nature if they had an independent existence outside the tradition of this poem. The last that we hear of the Phaeacians, they pray to Poseidon not to fulfill the rest of his ancient threat, to wall the Phaeacians in behind a mountain (*Odyssey* 13.181–187). The outcome is left in doubt, as the scene shifts in mid-verse from the Phaeacians praying to Poseidon to Odysseus awakening after his journey on the shores of Ithaca (*Odyssey* 13.187). The *Odyssey* thus returns the Phaeacians to the same doubtful existence from which they came.[160]

Scheria from Corcyra, but the indentification was revived in modern times (see Welcker 1832/1845:47–60, who gives an interesting example on p. 54: Isaac Newton calculated thirty-four years between Medea's marriage on Corcyra and the fall of Troy, and on this basis calculated that the bride Nausicaa was fifty years old when she married Telemachus; as Welcker points out, Newton did not allow for the possibility that Arete was childless at the time of Medea's marriage). Many have supposed (rightly, in my view) that the Argonautic use of the Phaeacians merely imitates the *Odyssey* (cf. Welcker 1832/1845:53; for a summary of views before Welcker, either attacking or defending the identification of the Phaeacians with the Corcyreans, see Welcker 1832/1845:57–59). For the wedding of Jason and Medea among the Phaeacians as a Corcyrean invention, see Welcker 1832/1845:39–40; the Corcyreans commemorated the wedding in a festival attested by Timaeus (scholia to Apollonius of Rhodes 4.1217, 1153). Welcker 1832/1845:40 argues that Corinthian colonists brought Medea together with Hera and other divinities to Corcyra (for Hera's important place in Corcyra, cf. Thucydides 1.24.7, 3.75.5, 3.79.1; 734 BC is the traditional date for the founding of Corcyra by Corinth). The features of the Homeric Phaeacians that may have led Hesiod and later Greeks to identify them with the Corcyreans are discussed by Welcker 1832/1845:41: Thesprotians, who figure prominently in Odysseus's lying tales, are in the same geographic region as Corcyra; the place of origin of the Phaeacians' servant woman, called a γρηῦς Ἀπειραίη, "an old woman from Apeira," in *Odyssey* 7.8 (cf. Ἀπείρηθεν, "from Apeira," in *Odyssey* 7.9) was taken to be Epirus, which again is in the same geographic region as Corcyra.

159 Alcinous recalls this prophecy on an earlier occasion as well (*Odyssey* 8.564–569).

160 Note also that they live "far from grain-eating men" (ἑκὰς ἀνδρῶν ἀλφηστάων, *Odyssey* 6.8); hence no one can have any intercourse with them, or indeed any knowledge of them.

§2.119 We have seen that the Phaeacians, insofar as they are "home-bringers," derive from Nestor. It is to the Phaeacian men that the function of "homebringing" pertains, and to their king in particular, as Alcinous himself says in *Odyssey* 11.352–353: πομπὴ δ' ἄνδρεσσι μελήσει / πᾶσι, μάλιστα δ' ἐμοί. Thus it is the Phaeacian men, and Alcinous in particular, and not the Phaeacian queen, who have to do with Nestor. We have seen that this is true of the Phaeacian genealogy, in which Alcinous corresponds to Nestor but Arete has nothing to do with Nestor or his family.[161]

§2.120 Nestor's role in the *nóstos* of Odysseus, as we have seen in our analysis of *Odyssey* 3, was to leave Odysseus behind on the island of Tenedos after an angry dispute concerning the very issue of the Achaeans' *nóstos*. And given who Nestor is by his very name, and his underlying function of "bringing back

---

Analogous to the Phaeacians with respect to their non-existence outside the *Odyssey* is the Achaean wall in the *Iliad*, about which Aristotle, as quoted by Strabo 13.1.36, says: "the poet who made it also destroyed it" (ὁ δὲ πλάσας ποιητὴς ἠφάνισεν).

161 Another sign that Arete's place in the Phaeacian genealogy is, so to speak, arbitrary, is the discrepancy between Homer and Hesiod as to what her place in fact is. In the *Odyssey* Athena tells Odysseus that Arete is from the same "parents" (*tokêes*) as Alcinous before she proceeds with the rest of the Phaeacian genealogy (*Odyssey* 7.53–55):

δέσποιναν μὲν πρῶτα κιχήσεαι ἐν μεγάροισιν·
Ἀρήτη δ' ὄνομ' ἐστὶν ἐπώνυμον, ἐκ δὲ τοκήων
τῶν αὐτῶν, οἵ περ τέκον Ἀλκίνοον βασιλῆα.

You will come upon the mistress first in the halls;
Arete is her well-chosen name; she is from the same
parents who gave birth to Alcinous the king.

As the continuation of the passage shows, *tokêon* here means "parents" in an extended sense that also includes an earlier generation in the bloodline (Nausithoos is Alcinous's father but Arete's grandfather); this usage is unusual, but no more so than in *Odyssey* 4.596, when Telemachus says that he could stay in Sparta and listen to Menelaus for a year and not miss his *tokêes* (only his mother and his paternal grandfather are in Ithaca; Telemachus can hardly be including Odysseus in his statement). According to the scholia to *Odyssey* 7.54 Hesiod took Arete to be the sister of Alcinous (Hesiod fr. 222 MW). It is clear that for this Hesiod depends on *Odyssey* 7.54–55, where Arete is said to be from the same "parents" as Alcinous, but it is hard to explain why Hesiod ignores the *Odyssey*'s explanation of this statement. Perhaps it was a "learned" disagreement showing Hesiodic independence from the Homeric *Odyssey* on this point; the Hesiodic variant of a brother-sister marriage would thus be an invention, and one that could not be disputed with anything beyond the uncle-niece marriage of *Odyssey* 7, for no one knew any more about the Phaeacians than what the *Odyssey* said. In other words, the Hesiodic poets pretended to know more than the Homeric poets in this instance. If this explanation is right, it is consistent with the view that the Phaeacians really belong solely to the *Odyssey*. For further evidence that Hesiod knew nothing about the Phaeacians, but simply drew inferences from the *Odyssey*, see Welcker 1832/1845:40–41and 47n103; I note in particular his suggestion that Hesiod, who first assigned Italian locations to Odysseus's travels, also first equated Scheria with Corcyra (cf. n2.158 above).

to life," his action in effect condemns Odysseus to death. Alcinous, on the other hand, reverses all of this, simultaneously bringing Odysseus home and bringing him back to life. The fabulous nature of the Phaeacians, which derives from their being a fiction of the *Odyssey*, allows the underlying nature of Nestor's function as "homebringer" to come to the surface. The Phaeacians' very ships, in contrast to Nestor's, have a fabulous nature, for "they have no helmsman or rudders, as other ships do, but they know themselves the thoughts and minds of men, and they know the cities and rich fields of all, and they swiftly cross the gulf of the sea covered in mist and cloud" (*Odyssey* 8.557–562). The relation between "mind" and "return" is suggested by these ships, which "take aim" with "minds" of their own (τιτυσκόμεναι φρεσὶ νῆες, *Odyssey* 8.556), and which themselves "know the thoughts and minds of men" (αὐταὶ ἴσασι νοήματα καὶ φρένας ἀνδρῶν, *Odyssey* 8.559). The word *nóēma*, "thought," characterizes the ships themselves in a comparison for their speed when Athena, disguised as a Phaeacian maiden, tells Odysseus that the Phaeacian ships "are as swift as an arrow or a thought" (τῶν νέες ὠκεῖαι ὡς εἰ πτερὸν ἠὲ νόημα, *Odyssey* 7.36). The emphasis on *nóos*, "mind," through its derivative *nóēma*, comes from Nestor, for we saw that his *nóstos* with Diomedes gave ample scope to the role of *nóos* as identified with the process of *nóstos* itself. But in the Phaeacian ships this identification is given a fabulous coloration as opposed to the literal identification in Nestor's return. Likewise when Nestor brings Diomedes home to Argos, he does not bring him back to life in any literal sense, but the Phaeacians come close to doing so when they bring Odysseus home.[162] For one of the elements of the Phaeacians' conveyance is that their passengers lie overcome by sleep as the sailors drive the ship across the calm sea (*Odyssey* 7.318). In the case of Odysseus, the sleep that falls upon his brows when the Phaeacian sailors begin to row is "most like death" (*Odyssey* 13.78–80):

εὖθ' οἳ ἀνακλινθέντες ἀνερρίπτουν ἅλα πηδῷ,
καὶ τῷ νήδυμος ὕπνος ἐπὶ βλεφάροισιν ἔπιπτε,
νήγρετος ἥδιστος, θανάτῳ ἄγχιστα ἐοικώς.

When they bent back and churned the sea with oars
there fell on his brows a grateful sleep
not to be awakened from, most sweet, most nearly like death.

Odysseus does not awaken from this profound sleep until he is home on the shores of Ithaca (*Odyssey* 13.187), so that when he does so his *nóstos* is simul-

---

162 For the following cf. above §1.37, also n2.154.

taneously a "return home" and, in the terms of the simile, a "return from death." The simile makes all but explicit in the case of the Phaeacians what cannot be made explicit in Nestor's case, that his "homebringing" is at the same time a "bringing back to life."[163]

§2.121 The differences between Nestor and the Phaeacians thus have to do with the Phaeacians' fabulous nature, but their fabulous nature also allows mythic traits to come to the surface that pertain equally to Nestor but cannot be made explicit in his case. The differences, when viewed in this way, actually establish a stronger identification. Nestor and king Alcinous are, as it were, mirror images of one another in the *Odyssey*, balancing and offsetting one another on the level of the story. We need to bear this in mind when we examine the role of Alcinous in more detail on the level of the story. If Alcinous is, so to speak, a counter-Nestor on the level of the story, then the relationship that Odysseus had with Nestor, as revealed in *Odyssey* 3, should be picked up and countered in the new relationship that Odysseus has with Alcinous. The key point for Odysseus's relationship to Nestor, despite the harmony between them all through the Trojan war, was the bitter dispute that divided them when they last saw each other. If Alcinous is to take the place of Nestor in Odysseus's *nóstos*, the tension of this dispute should be present from the start when Odysseus and Alcinous meet, and then be gradually set aside. This would dramatically reverse the process of harmony ending in dispute that characterized Odysseus in his relationship to Nestor. The process must be reversed if Alcinous is indeed a mirror image of Nestor.

§2.122 There is in fact tension between Odysseus and the Phaeacians right from the start. Odysseus is told twice before he meets the Phaeacian king and queen that he must win favor with the queen.[164] Nausicaa tells him to go straight to her mother once inside the palace; she will be seated by the fire spinning wool, and her father will be there too, drinking wine. Odysseus should pass by her father and supplicate her mother, for if her mother is well

---

163 The Phaeacian ship reaches Ithaca with the sleeping Odysseus just at dawn (*Odyssey* 13.93–95):

εὖτ' ἀστὴρ ὑπερέσχε φαάντατος, ὅς τε μάλιστα
ἔρχεται ἀγγέλλων φάος Ἠοῦς ἠριγενείης,
τῆμος δὴ νήσῳ προσεπίλνατο ποντοπόρος νηῦς.

When the brightest star rose, which especially
comes and announces the light of early-born Dawn,
the sea-crossing ship approached the island.

Odysseus's *nóstos* is thus a "return to light" as well as a "return to life."
164 Nausicaa tells him this in *Odyssey* 6.313–315; Athena tells him again in *Odyssey* 7.75–77.

disposed toward him there is hope that he will return home (*Odyssey* 6.303–315). Odysseus follows this advice when he enters the palace covered in a mist. When the mist disappears Odysseus has already clasped Arete's knees, and calling her by name, he supplicates her with the words, "I have come to your husband and to your knees" (*Odyssey* 7.146–147):

> Ἀρήτη, θύγατερ Ῥηξήνορος ἀντιθέοιο,
> σόν τε πόσιν σά τε γούναθ' ἱκάνω.

> Arete, daughter of godlike Rhexenor,
> I come to your husband and to your knees.

Odysseus has come to both king and queen, but he has bypassed the king in order to supplicate the queen. When Odysseus finishes his appeal for a passage home (*Odyssey* 7.146–152), no one replies until the aged retainer Ekheneos breaks the awkward silence with a rebuke to Alcinous for letting the stranger sit on the ground in the ashes of the hearth, for everyone else waits to hear from Alcinous before speaking (*Odyssey* 7.159–161):

> Ἀλκίνο', οὐ μέν τοι τόδε κάλλιον οὐδὲ ἔοικε
> ξεῖνον μὲν χαμαὶ ἧσθαι ἐπ' ἐσχάρῃ ἐν κονίῃσιν·
> οἵδε δὲ σὸν μῦθον ποτιδέγμενοι ἰσχανόωνται.

> Alcinous, this is not decent and it is not seemly,
> that a stranger sits on the ground by the hearth in the dust;
> the others are holding back waiting for your word.

Odysseus has thus been accorded a very cool reception by the Phaeacians, and it is Alcinous, in the speech of his aged retainer, who is blamed for it. Ekheneos proceeds to tell Alcinous to raise the stranger from the ground and seat him on a chair, to order a libation to Zeus, the god of suppliants, and to offer the stranger food. All this Alcinous does, without, however, addressing Odysseus directly. He orders the herald Pontonoos to prepare the libation (*Odyssey* 7.179–181), and he tells the Phaeacians that more of the elders will be called the next day to meet and grant the stranger's request for passage home (*Odyssey* 7.189–198). All the while he refers to Odysseus in the third person, wondering aloud at the end of his speech who the stranger may be: perhaps he is a god, although before this the gods have always showed themselves openly to the Phaeacians (*Odyssey* 7.199–206). Odysseus then addresses Alcinous for the first time, proclaiming that he is a mortal who has suffered much by the will of the gods, and that he is hungry and wants to eat. He ends by asking Alcinous to give him passage home the next day. The Phaeacians all approve Odysseus's speech but still there is no direct response from Alcinous and the guests leave for the night. Now Odysseus is alone with the king and queen, and the queen speaks first, for she recognizes the garments that Nausicaa gave to Odysseus. She asks him who he is, and who gave him the garments. Did he not say that he came to their land over the sea? Odysseus tells how he came from Calypso's island and was shipwrecked near Scheria, and how Nausicaa gave him clothing when he supplicated her. Alcinous now addresses Odysseus for the first time, finding fault with his daughter for not bringing him to the palace herself. Odysseus tells him not to blame his daughter, for it was he, Odysseus, who did not want to accompany her despite her invitation. He feared that Alcinous would be angry, "for we tribes of men on earth are a jealous lot" (*Odyssey* 7.303–307):

ἥρως, μή μοι τοὔνεκ' ἀμύμονα νείκεε κούρην·
ἡ μὲν γάρ μ' ἐκέλευε σὺν ἀμφιπόλοισιν ἔπεσθαι,
ἀλλ' ἐγὼ οὐκ ἔθελον δείσας αἰσχυνόμενός τε,
μή πως καὶ σοὶ θυμὸς ἐπισκύσσαιτο ἰδόντι·
δύσζηλοι γάρ τ' εἰμὲν ἐπὶ χθονὶ φῦλ' ἀνθρώπων.

Hero, do not scold your faultless daughter for my sake,
for she urged me to follow her handmaidens,
but I was unwilling out of fear and shame
lest your heart somehow be offended when you saw it;
for we tribes of men on earth are jealous.

Alcinous answers Odysseus that his heart is not prone to wanton anger and that due measure in all things is best (*Odyssey* 7.309–310):

ξεῖν', οὔ μοι τοιοῦτον ἐνὶ στήθεσσι φίλον κῆρ
μαψιδίως κεχολῶσθαι· ἀμείνω δ' αἴσιμα πάντα.

Stranger, the heart in my breast is not such
as to become angry for no reason; all things are better in due
measure.

As if to show how far anger is from his heart at the present moment, Alcinous spontaneously prays to Zeus, Athena, and Apollo that the stranger, being such as he is and being like-minded with himself, might stay and become his son-in-law (*Odyssey* 7.311–315):

αἲ γάρ, Ζεῦ τε πάτερ καὶ Ἀθηναίη καὶ Ἄπολλον,
τοῖος ἐών, οἷός ἐσσι, τά τε φρονέων ἅ τ' ἐγώ περ,
παῖδά τ' ἐμὴν ἐχέμεν καὶ ἐμὸς γαμβρὸς καλέεσθαι,
αὖθι μένων· οἶκον δέ κ' ἐγὼ καὶ κτήματα δοίην,
εἴ κ' ἐθέλων γε μένοις.

I wish, father Zeus and Athena and Apollo,
that someone who is as you are, and thinks as I do,
would have my daughter and be called my son-in-law,
staying here; I would give a house and possessions
if you willingly remained.

But Alcinous immediately proceeds to say that no one will force the stranger to stay against his will, and as proof of this, he ordains his passage home for the next day, describing the ease and speed with which the voyage will be made, no matter how long. Odysseus responds with his own prayer to Zeus that Alcinous may carry out his promise: he would win inextinguishable fame for himself by doing so and Odysseus, for his part, would reach home (*Odyssey* 7.331–333):[165]

Ζεῦ πάτερ, αἴθ', ὅσα εἶπε, τελευτήσειεν ἅπαντα
Ἀλκίνοος· τοῦ μέν κεν ἐπὶ ζείδωρον ἄρουραν
ἄσβεστον κλέος εἴη, ἐγὼ δέ κε πατρίδ' ἱκοίμην.

Father Zeus, I wish that Alcinous might bring about all that he
    has said;
his fame on the grain-giving earth
would be inextinguishable, and I would reach my fatherland.

With this the day comes to a close, and at the end of Book 7 Odysseus goes to sleep in a bed prepared for him at Arete's direction, and the king and queen likewise go to bed.

§2.123 In this scene there is never any real doubt that Odysseus will receive passage home from the Phaeacians, for Alcinous, after being rebuked by the aged retainer Ekheneos, promises as much virtually from the start (*Odyssey* 7.189–198). But this is simply because it is his and his people's

---

165 Note that in this passage Alcinous's fame (*kléos*) is tied to Odysseus's homecoming; this is another sign (not a proof) that Alcinous is limited to the *Odyssey* tradition.

function to do so: they give passage to any stranger who comes their way, as
Alcinous says in council the next day (*Odyssey* 8.31–33):

ἡμεῖς δ', ὡς τὸ πάρος περ, ἐποτρυνώμεθα πομπήν·
οὐδὲ γὰρ οὐδέ τις ἄλλος, ὅτις κ' ἐμὰ δώμαθ' ἵκηται,
ἐνθάδ' ὀδυρόμενος δηρὸν μένει εἵνεκα πομπῆς.

But, as in the past, let us press on with his conveyance;
for no one else who comes to my house
ever waits here long pleading for conveyance.

What is significant is not that Alcinous grants Odysseus's request, but that
he must be prompted by Ekheneos to receive the stranger at all. Tension is
created when Odysseus, after making his appeal to Arete, is left sitting in the
ashes. This tension is then progressively removed, to the point that Alcinous
in the end asks Odysseus, if he wants, to stay and become his son-in-law. In the
process of defusing the tension between Odysseus and Alcinous, Arete is the
first to address Odysseus directly. When Alcinous addresses him for the first
time, the subject is Nausicaa, but the real issue is anger. In his first words to
Odysseus, we hear of Alcinous's displeasure, although his displeasure is point-
edly not with Odysseus but with his own daughter. This leads to Odysseus's
response that he acted as he did because he wished to avoid Alcinous's anger,
and to a general statement about the jealous nature of men. The culmination,
however, comes when Alcinous disavows any anger on his own part, and invites
the stranger, whom he finds like-minded with himself, to stay and become his
son-in-law. The issue of anger has been deftly raised in this scene, and just as
deftly disposed of. It is there from the start, not because there is any previous
history between Odysseus and Alcinous (there is not), but because there is a
previous history between Odysseus and Nestor, who underlies Alcinous. Being
of one mind during the war (*héna thumòn ékhonte*, *Odyssey* 3.128), Nestor and
Odysseus split in anger from each other after the war, and the consequences
for Odysseus were calamitous. Now Alcinous enters the story to reverse that
chain of events, in particular the anger with which it started. Odysseus tells
Alcinous that he did not accompany his daughter to the palace because he did
not wish to anger him. Alcinous sees the respect that the stranger has shown
him in this, and this prompts him not only to disavow any anger on his own
part, but to declare the stranger to be like-minded with himself. The issue is
Odysseus's sense of tact toward the father of an unmarried girl when Alcinous
wishes for a son-in-law like Odysseus, who thinks like himself: τοῖος ἐών, οἷός

ἐσσι, τά τε φρονέων ἅ τ' ἐγώ περ (*Odyssey* 7.312). But the underlying issue is the like-mindedness of Odysseus and Nestor, which came apart after the war, and which has now been restored in a new form.[166]

§2.124 There is more to say about Arete in this scene. She too is slow to respond to Odysseus's appeal, and his appeal, after all, is to her. Her reticence, however, seems designed to let the tension with Alcinous come to the surface. That at least is the effect of Ekheneos's speech, for he clearly makes the inhospitable treatment of the stranger the king's responsibility (everyone waits for the king to take the lead in welcoming the stranger) and thus responsibility seems to be removed from the queen. There is also the important point, which is twice impressed upon Odysseus, that his return home depends on Arete's good will. We cannot really explain Arete's importance for Odysseus's return without understanding more about her nature, and this must wait until Part 3 below. But we have already seen that she acts as a kind of buffer between Alcinous and Odysseus at their first meeting when the anger inherent in their relationship has yet to play itself out. We may even go so far as to say that part of the reason that Arete is so important to Odysseus's return is precisely the fact that Alcinous, the "homebringer," begins his relationship with Odysseus in a state of vicarious hostility, and Arete is necessary as a buffer between them. This is the dramatic effect of Odysseus's passing by Alcinous when he enters the palace and clasping Arete's knees, especially when Odysseus's first words after addressing the queen by name are "having suffered much, I come to your husband and to your knees" (σόν τε πόσιν σά τε γούναθ' ἱκάνω πολλὰ μογήσας, *Odyssey* 7.147). The implication is that Arete, as intermediary between Odysseus and Alcinous, can resolve their underlying dispute. This point is in fact anticipated earlier in Book 7, when Athena, disguised as a Phaeacian maiden, encounters Odysseus and tells him about the royal couple. This passage, which includes the Phaeacian genealogy, starts and ends with Arete, whom Odysseus is to meet first in the royal hall (*Odyssey* 7.53). After the genealogy, the great honor in which Arete is held by her husband, children, and people is described. Her people look on her as a god when they greet her as she walks through the city, "for she too does not lack good *nóos*, and she resolves quarrels even for men toward whom she is well disposed" (*Odyssey* 7.73–74):

166 The transference of anger from one context to another is also found in *Odyssey* 15, where Peisistratos warns Telemachus that Nestor will be angry if Telemachus simply bypasses him on his return to Ithaca (μάλα γὰρ κεχολώσεται ἔμπης, "in any case he will be very angry," *Odyssey* 15.214); this anger too is a transference from the quarrel between Nestor and Odysseus on Tenedos (see §2.91 above).

οὐ μὲν γάρ τι νόου γε καὶ αὐτὴ δεύεται ἐσθλοῦ,
οἷσίν τ' <u>ἐῢ φρονέῃσι</u>, καὶ ἀνδράσι νείκεα λύει.

For she too does not lack fine intelligence,
and for those to whom <u>she is well disposed</u>, even for men, she
   reconciles quarrels.

The statement that "she also" does not lack good *nóos* seems to allude to
Alcinous, whose very name indicates his possession of good *nóos*, as well as
his function as "homebringer." But Alcinous, whose genealogy in the imme-
diately preceding passage has just revealed him to be a second Nestor, has
an inherited conflict with Odysseus, and this is the point of the next line,
for Arete "resolves quarrels even between men toward whom she is well
disposed." Odysseus's homecoming depends on his resolving his former
conflict with Nestor in his new relationship with Alcinous, and this resolution
depends on Arete. This connection of ideas is strongly suggested by the end
of Athena's speech, where the statement that Arete resolves quarrels even
among men is followed by the statement that there is hope for Odysseus's
return if Arete is well disposed toward him (*Odyssey* 7.75–77):

εἴ κέν τοι κείνη γε <u>φίλα φρονέῃσ'</u> ἐνὶ θυμῷ,
ἐλπωρή τοι ἔπειτα φίλους ἰδέειν καὶ ἱκέσθαι
οἶκον ἐς ὑψόροφον καὶ σὴν ἐς πατρίδα γαῖαν.

If <u>she should be kindly disposed</u> to you in her heart,
then there is hope for you to see your dear ones and to reach
your high-roofed house and your fatherland.

The connection between resolving a conflict "for those to whom she is well-
disposed" (*hoîsín t' eù phronéēisi*) and helping Odysseus to achieve his return
"if she is kindly disposed to you" (*toi...phíla phronéēis'*) is suggested by the close
similarity of the phrases indicating Arete's attitude. The difference between
the two occurrences of the verb *phronéēisi* is that the second occurrence
applies explicitly to Odysseus whereas the first does so implicitly. Arete's
favor is necessary to undo Odysseus's underlying conflict with Alcinous, his
"homebringer."

§2.125 For Alcinous the underlying conflict with Odysseus is finished
when he wishes that the stranger would stay and marry his daughter. But it
takes two to make a quarrel, and there is anger to be resolved on Odysseus's

side as well as Alcinous's. For Alcinous it was enough to leave Odysseus sitting in the ashes for too long a time and to find fault with his own daughter for what appeared to be a similar lack of hospitality in order to raise the issue and to resolve it. For Odysseus, whose quarrel with Nestor was real, anger is more of an issue, and it takes longer to resolve. Anger is also a basic part of Odysseus's nature, as is indicated by his name and by the epic verb to which it gave rise, *odússomai*, "be angry." Among the Phaeacians Odysseus's anger exhibits itself in Book 8, when he is provoked to take part in athletic contests. His underlying quarrel with Alcinous, which recasts his quarrel with Nestor, provides the overall context for Odysseus's show of anger, but Alcinous himself is kept well away from any direct confrontation. His son Laodamas is more directly involved, but even he is too close to Alcinous to be the primary target of Odysseus's anger. This role is reserved for Euryalos, a Phaeacian youth with no direct connection to the king.

§2.126 Although Alcinous does not participate in the athletic contests of Book 8, he has a stake in them, and thus Odysseus's display of anger, while kept at a safe distance from the king, ultimately pertains to him as well. Alcinous's stake is established when he first calls for the games so that the stranger may tell those at home how much the Phaeacians surpass others in boxing, wrestling, jumping, and racing (*Odyssey* 8.100–103):

> νῦν δ' ἐξέλθωμεν καὶ ἀέθλων πειρηθῶμεν
> πάντων, ὥς χ' ὁ ξεῖνος ἐνίσπῃ οἷσι φίλοισιν
> οἴκαδε νοστήσας, ὅσσον περιγινόμεθ' ἄλλων
> πύξ τε παλαιμοσύνῃ τε καὶ ἅλμασιν ἠδὲ πόδεσσιν.

> Now let us go out and try our skill in all the contests,
> so that the stranger may tell his dear ones
> when he returns home how much we excel others
> in boxing and wrestling and jumping and running.

When Laodamas, Alcinous's son, challenges Odysseus to compete, he does so graciously, but Odysseus is clearly provoked (*Odyssey* 8.153–157):

> Λαοδάμα, τί με ταῦτα κελεύετε κερτομέοντες;
> κήδεά μοι καὶ μᾶλλον ἐνὶ φρεσὶν ἤ περ ἄεθλοι,
> ὃς πρὶν μὲν μάλα πολλὰ πάθον καὶ πολλὰ μόγησα,
> νῦν δὲ μεθ' ὑμετέρῃ ἀγορῇ νόστοιο χατίζων
> ἦμαι, λισσόμενος βασιλῆά τε πάντα τε δῆμον.

Laodamas, why do you exhort me to do these things, ridiculing me?
There are greater cares than contests in my heart,
who before now suffered much and toiled much,
and now sit in your assembly longing for a return,
begging the king and all the people.

In the final line Odysseus displays a rather surprising lack of gratitude toward Alcinous and his people, who just that morning had met in council and ordained a homecoming for him. Odysseus makes it sound as though the council reached no conclusion and he must continue to make his appeal. It is significant that Alcinous is evoked in such an ungenerous spirit precisely now, for Odysseus's only open conflict with the Phaeacians is about to burst forth. Euryalos, one of the young Phaeacian contestants, abuses Odysseus roundly, calling him a lowly sailor who has no skill in athletics. Odysseus answers Euryalos with equal abuse, calling him heedless and lacking in sense, with no grace of speech to match the grace of his youthful looks. Angered by Euryalos, Odysseus leaps to his feet and hurls the discus far beyond all the other marks (*Odyssey* 8.158–200). He then challenges the Phaeacians to compete with him in any other contest, showing that his anger is not limited to Euryalos. But his anger, which has so far been safely confined to Euryalos, must not proceed too far toward its real target, Alcinous. Thus when he challenges all the young Phaeacians to compete, he is careful to exclude Alcinous's son Laodamas from his challenge, for he is his host, and only a worthless fool would injure his own interests by competing with his host (*Odyssey* 8.208–211):

ξεῖνος γάρ μοι ὅδ᾽ ἐστί· τίς ἂν φιλέοντι μάχοιτο;
ἄφρων δὴ κεῖνός γε καὶ οὐτιδανὸς πέλει ἀνήρ,
ὅς τις ξεινοδόκῳ ἔριδα προφέρηται ἀέθλων
δήμῳ ἐν ἀλλοδαπῷ· ἕο δ᾽ αὐτοῦ πάντα κολούει.

For he is my host; who would fight with a man who loves him?
That one is indeed a witless and worthless man
who offers the strife of contests to his host
in a foreign land; he cuts short everything of his own.

Odysseus, who had a disastrous quarrel with Nestor on the island of Tenedos, is not about to make the same mistake with his host Alcinous, or with anyone close to him. Alcinous was not directly involved in the conflict with Euryalos, and after Odysseus challenges all the other Phaeacians except Laodamas to compete, Alcinous says that the stranger's words are "not unpleasing" (οὐκ ἀχάριστα, *Odyssey* 8.236), for he naturally wants to display his prowess after being provoked to anger by Euryalos. But then, to show that Alcinous himself is involved in the carefully managed conflict of the athletic contests, he no longer claims as he did before that the Phaeacians excel in all such contests (Odysseus has just proved him wrong on that point), but only in footracing, the one contest that Odysseus said he might not win because his sea voyage has sapped his strength (*Odyssey* 8.230–233). Alcinous now removes boxing and wrestling from the list of games in which the Phaeacians excel, saying that their real excellence lies not there, but in footracing and seafaring, and that what is dear to them are banquets, music, and dancing, clean clothes, warm baths, and beds (*Odyssey* 8.246–249):

> οὐ γὰρ πυγμάχοι εἰμὲν ἀμύμονες οὐδὲ παλαισταί,
> ἀλλὰ ποσὶ κραιπνῶς θέομεν καὶ νηυσὶν ἄριστοι,
> αἰεὶ δ' ἡμῖν δαίς τε φίλη κίθαρίς τε χοροί τε
> εἵματά τ' ἐξημοιβὰ λοετρά τε θερμὰ καὶ εὐναί.

> For we are not faultless boxers or wrestlers,
> but we run fast on foot and we are the best in ships,
> and always dear to us is the banquet and the lyre and dances
> and changes of clothes and warm baths and beds.

§2.127 Odysseus's display of anger has, so to speak, put the Phaeacians in their place. They are not rugged competitors, but refined practitioners of a softer life. Forced by Odysseus to modify his earlier claim, Alcinous still maintains to his guest that the Phaeacians are best at some things. His claim to Phaeacian superiority in seamanship of course goes unchallenged, for that is their particular virtue. It is also the domain to which Alcinous lays claim first, at the end of Book 7, when he describes the speed of the Phaeacian ships that will take Odysseus home (*Odyssey* 7.327–328):

> εἰδήσεις δὲ καὶ αὐτὸς ἐνὶ φρεσίν, ὅσσον ἄρισται
> νῆες ἐμαὶ καὶ κοῦροι ἀναρρίπτειν ἅλα πηδῷ.

> And you yourself will know in your mind how much the best
> my ships and youths are at churning up the sea with oars.

Alcinous also does not relinquish the Phaeacians' claim to superior speed of foot, which Odysseus has conceded to them anyway. But in addition to these two claims, for seamanship and speed of foot, Alcinous also wants to prove to his guest that the Phaeacians are better than others at singing and dancing, and so he calls out dancers to put on a display (*Odyssey* 8.250–253):

ἀλλ' ἄγε, Φαιήκων βητάρμονες ὅσσοι ἄριστοι,
παίσατε, ὥς χ' ὁ ξεῖνος ἐνίσπῃ οἷσι φίλοισιν,
οἴκαδε νοστήσας, ὅσσον περιγινόμεθ' ἄλλων
ναυτιλίῃ καὶ ποσσὶ καὶ ὀρχηστυῖ καὶ ἀοιδῇ.

But come, all the best dancers of the Phaeacians,
Show your skill, so that the stranger may tell his loved ones
When he returns home how much better we are than others
In sailing and footracing and dancing and singing.

Framed in the same language as his earlier claim to superiority in athletics, Alcinous's new claim draws no opposition from Odysseus, but complete agreement when he has witnessed the skill of the Phaeacian dancers (*Odyssey* 8.382–384):[167]

Ἀλκίνοε κρεῖον, πάντων ἀριδείκετε λαῶν,
ἠμὲν ἀπείλησας βητάρμονας εἶναι ἀρίστους,
ἠδ' ἄρ' ἑτοῖμα τέτυκτο· σέβας μ' ἔχει εἰσορόωντα.

King Alcinous, most exalted of all your people,
You boasted that your dancers are the best,
And your words have proved true; awe holds me as I watch.

As far as Odysseus's underlying conflict with Alcinous is concerned, it is over and done with, from his standpoint as well as Alcinous's, with these lines. His acceptance of Alcinous, now that he has forced him to modify (and reduce) his claims to superiority, is wholehearted and enthusiastic. To resolve the issue of Odysseus's anger completely, it only remains for Alcinous to order Euryalos, his scapegoat, to make personal amends to Odysseus, which Euryalos does with the gift of a sword and a graceful speech of apology

---

167 There are actually two dance performances (*Odyssey* 8.261–265 and 8.370–380), and Odysseus comments approvingly after the second one, in which Laodamas and Halios (another son of Alcinous) show unusual skill. Between the two dances Demodokos sings the song of Ares and Aphrodite. According to Alcinous the Phaeacians excel in singing as well as dancing (*Odyssey* 8.253), and Demodokos's song bears him out.

(*Odyssey* 8.406–411). Odysseus accepts both the sword and the apology (*Odyssey* 8.413–415), and from now on all is harmonious between Odysseus and his hosts.[168]

§2.128 In the rest of Book 8 Odysseus receives gifts from the Phaeacians and they honor him with a banquet. When they have eaten, Odysseus asks the bard Demodokos to sing the tale of the wooden horse at Troy, and he weeps as he did earlier, when Demodokos sang the tale of his own dispute with Achilles. In both tales, Odysseus is the central figure, and the two tales also relate to one another. Although the point is not made in Demodokos's first song, Odysseus prevailed in his dispute with Achilles, in which he championed "guile" over "might" as the means to take Troy;[169] for it was he who thought of the trick of the wooden horse, and the wooden horse is the subject of the second song. The second instance of Odysseus's weeping focuses attention on the question of his identity, which he has so far not revealed. Alcinous, who alone has noticed his weeping, is the one to ask Odysseus who he is, and he does so in a long speech that concludes Book 8, and prepares for Odysseus's revealing of his identity in Book 9, and the tale of his wandering in Books 9-12. In this speech Alcinous calls on Demodokos to stop his song, for the stranger has not ceased weeping since it began. It is for his sake that gifts and passage have been provided, and his enjoy-

---

168 The tone of latent hostility between Odysseus and his hosts is generalized to all the Phaeacians before he has even met his hosts, when Athena covers him in a mist on his way into the town so that none of the Phaeacians will taunt him (*Odyssey* 7.14–17):

καὶ τότ' Ὀδυσσεὺς ὦρτο πόλινδ' ἴμεν· ἀμφὶ δ' Ἀθήνη
πολλὴν ἠέρα χεῦε φίλα φρονέουσ' Ὀδυσῆϊ,
μή τις Φαιήκων μεγαθύμων ἀντιβολήσας
κερτομέοι τ' ἐπέεσσι καὶ ἐξερέοιθ' ὅτις εἴη.

And then Odysseus got up to go into the city; Athena poured
much mist around, being kindly minded toward Odysseus,
so that none of the great-hearted Phaeacians, meeting him,
would taunt him with words and ask who he was.

Disguised as a maiden, Athena then warns Odysseus directly about the Phaeacians' unfriendly attitude to strangers (*Odyssey* 7.32–33):

οὐ γὰρ ξείνους οἵ γε μάλ' ἀνθρώπους ἀνέχονται
οὐδ' ἀγαπαζόμενοι φιλέουσ', ὅς κ' ἄλλοθεν ἔλθη.

For they do not gladly suffer foreign men,
and they do not welcome and love anyone who comes from somewhere else.

Odysseus's chilly reception in the palace is well prepared for; so too is the taunt that he receives from Euryalos.

169 For the quarrel between Achilles and Odysseus (the first song of Demodokos) see Nagy 1979:23–25, 45–46.

ment is thus paramount. Therefore let him not hide his name, but speak it, and tell what land he is from so that the Phaeacian ships may take aim for it in their minds. He goes on to describe the wondrous nature of the Phaeacian ships, and he recalls Poseidon's ancient threat to end their seafaring and the safe passage that they give to mortals. Then he returns to his questions of Odysseus, asking next about his wanderings and where they have taken him. Finally he asks why he weeps when he hears of the Argives and Troy. Did Odysseus lose a kinsman at Troy, a son-in-law or a father-in-law, who are closest to one after blood relations? Or did he perhaps lose a close companion? With these questions the way is prepared for Odysseus to reveal that he not only knew Achaeans who fought at Troy, but that he was there himself, the very sacker of the city.

§2.129 In his long speech that concludes Book 8, in which he probes Odysseus for his identity, Alcinous makes a pair of statements that can be interpreted in two ways, and which, when interpreted in the second way, strike to the very heart of Odysseus's relationship with Alcinous, on the one hand, and with Nestor, on the other hand. Both relationships are based on Nestor's variant of the twin myth, the essence of which is a separation between brothers. When Odysseus is left behind by Nestor at Tenedos, he is in the position of Nestor's brother who died, and when Alcinous undertakes to bring Odysseus not only home, but back to life, he is likewise in the position of a brother—of the immortal twin in relation to the mortal twin. Alcinous's first statement pertains to himself, for when he calls on Demodokos to stop his song so that all may enjoy themselves equally, guest as well as hosts, and then reminds the Phaeacians that gifts and escort have all been prepared for the stranger's sake, he concludes his thought on the honor due a guest by saying that, for a man who has even a little sense, a guest and suppliant is "equal to a brother" (*Odyssey* 8.546–547):

ἀντὶ <u>κασιγνήτου</u> ξεῖνός θ' ἱκέτης τε τέτυκται
ἀνέρι, ὅς τ' ὀλίγον περ ἐπιψαύῃ πραπίδεσσι.

A stranger and a suppliant is equal to a <u>brother</u>
for a man who has even a little wit.

On the surface Alcinous means only that the honor due a suppliant is as great as that due a close blood relation, and there is nothing strange about that thought in an ancient Greek context. But two factors draw particular attention to Alcinous's statement at this point. First, Alcinous has himself lost his only brother, Rhexenor, and his statement that Odysseus is equal to a brother is precise in terms of Alcinous's myth, which is itself a copy of Nestor's myth. In relation to both figures Odysseus is in the position of the lost mortal twin, but whereas he was left for dead by Nestor, he will be brought back to life by Alcinous. Odysseus is truly equal to a brother in relation to Alcinous. The second factor that draws attention to Alcinous's statement is the fact that he says something strikingly similar, yet different, at the very end of his speech. In the final lines of Book 8, wanting to know why Odysseus weeps when he hears songs of Troy, he asks whether he lost a son-in-law or a father-in-law at Troy—or, he concludes, did he perhaps lose a dear companion there, "for a wise companion is in no way less than a brother" (*Odyssey* 8.581–586):

ἦ τίς τοι καὶ πηὸς ἀπέφθιτο Ἰλιόθι πρό,
ἐσθλὸς ἐών, γαμβρὸς ἢ πενθερός; οἵ τε μάλιστα
κήδιστοι τελέθουσι μεθ᾽ αἷμά τε καὶ γένος αὐτῶν.
ἦ τίς που καὶ ἑταῖρος ἀνὴρ κεχαρισμένα εἰδώς,
ἐσθλός; ἐπεὶ οὐ μέν τι <u>κασιγνήτοιο</u> χερείων
γίνεται, ὅς κεν ἑταῖρος ἐὼν πεπνυμένα εἰδῇ.

> Did some kinsman by marriage die at Troy,
> one who was a good man, a son-in-law or father-in-law? These
> are the closest ties after one's own blood and family.
> Or was it some companion who knew pleasing things,
> a good man? Since in no way inferior to a <u>brother</u>
> is one who, being a companion, knows wise things.

Alcinous asks only if Odysseus had a close companion who died at Troy, but his words can be taken another way. Odysseus did lose a companion at Troy, although not in the sense that Alcinous means. He lost Nestor, whose help he needed to return, when he quarreled with him on Tenedos. Nestor was the companion who was truly "no less than a brother" to Odysseus, first of all in the ironic sense that he failed to bring Odysseus home just as he failed to bring his brother Periklymenos back to life. But before they split on Tenedos, Nestor and Odysseus were also close companions, agreeing so completely with one another in their counsels for the Argives that, in Nestor's words, they had one mind (*héna thumòn ékhonte, Odyssey* 3.128). It is the wise Nestor, with whom Odysseus shared one mind, that seems indicated by Alcinous's words, when he first asks if a "dear companion" was lost at Troy (ἑταῖρος ἀνὴρ κεχαρισμένα εἰδώς), and says then that a "wise companion" (ὅς κεν ἑταῖρος ἐὼν πεπνυμένα εἰδῇ) is no less than a brother. With the subtle change of expression from κεχαρισμένα εἰδώς to πεπνυμένα εἰδῇ, who else but Nestor comes to mind?

§2.130 As with the phrase *antì kasignḗtou*, "equal to a brother," that Alcinous uses for Odysseus, the phrase *ou...ti kasignḗtoio khereíōn*, "in no way less than a brother," that he uses of a companion who may have died at Troy would not demand a secondary interpretation if it occurred alone. It is the fact that the word *kasígnētos*, "brother," occurs twice in Alcinous's speech that gives it a secondary meaning both times. When the secondary interpretations are grouped there is a close relation between the two uses of the word "brother," for they equate Alcinous with Nestor in relation to Odysseus, and that equation has been at issue since the beginning of the Phaeacian episode. The two uses of *kasígnētos* provide a climax to this part of the episode, just before Odysseus reveals his identity to his hosts. It is appropriate that Alcinous's final words in asking Odysseus to reveal his identity should evoke Nestor, for Nestor is the answer to the question of Alcinous's own identity, and this question has been every bit as much a part of the Phaeacian episode as Odysseus's long delay in revealing his identity.

§2.131 If the Phaeacians must wait to find out who Odysseus is, there is a reciprocal, but deeper, problem for Odysseus to solve: does he know who the Phaeacians are? There is high drama at the beginning of Book 9 when Odysseus does finally reveal his identity to the Phaeacians, and then begins his tale. But the full drama of the situation does not play itself out until Odysseus interrupts his tale in Book 11 and again converses with the Phaeacians. We have already seen that Odysseus proposes to end his tale when he is in the underworld because he has just highlighted the negative role of Nestor in his homecoming by giving Nestor's whole genealogy, with full attention to his twin myth, in the catalogue of heroines whom he met there. We have also already discussed the idea that Odysseus converses with the Phaeacians at this point because it is the Phaeacian men, and in particular king Alcinous, who will take the failed Nestor's place in providing Odysseus a *nóstos*. We now see that there is more to it than that. When Odysseus gives Nestor's genealogy, and simultaneously reveals Nestor's twin myth, he shows that in a deep sense he knows who the Phaeacians are, for Nestor's genealogy is also the core of their genealogy. When the Phaeacians respond to him at this point, it is a virtual acknowledgment that he has penetrated their identity to its core, at least as regards the king. The queen is a different matter, which we have yet to address. But we do know that her acceptance of Odysseus has twice been presented as the key to his return, and it therefore seems significant that she is the first to speak. For the first time Arete, on whose good will

Odysseus's return depends, praises him, and calls on her people to redouble their gifts to him (*Odyssey* 11.336–341).[170] It is hard not to understand Arete's one and only expression of acceptance of Odysseus as meaning that, in the same way that Odysseus knows who Alcinous and the Phaeacians are, Arete knows that he knows.

§2.132 At the end of Book 8 Alcinous asked Odysseus if he had lost a wise companion at Troy. Odysseus in effect answers that question in its secondary meaning when he presents Nestor's twin myth in the context of the catalogue of heroines. It was Nestor that he lost at Troy, and it was that loss that led him to the underworld in the first place. The two passages, in Book 8 and in Book 11, work together. The passage that ends Book 8 is not idle—it has an answer, and is in fact answered in Book 11, but both question and answer are at a secondary level. The primary meaning of Alcinous's question in Book 8—did a dear companion of Odysseus die at Troy?—is also taken up again in Book 11, but at a primary level, when Alcinous asks Odysseus whether he saw any companions who died in Troy in the underworld (*Odyssey* 11.370–372), and so motivates him to continue and complete his tale.

§2.133 It is important to see the connection between the secondary level of Alcinous's question at the end of Book 8 on the one hand, and the catalogue of heroines in Book 11 as the answer to that question on the other hand. The first point to establish is that the real question at the end of Book 8 is the secondary one, and not the primary one. The six lines of Alcinous's question are carefully framed to end with the idea of the loss of a companion who was in no way less than a brother. This is a very particular, and a very complex idea. It is not nearly as straightforward as what is not asked—did you lose a blood relative at Troy? But the idea that it was not a blood relative is crucial, and this idea is therefore anticipated in the form that Alcinous's question first takes—did you lose a kinsman by marriage, perhaps a son-in-law or father-in-law, who are closest to one after one's blood and race? The form that Alcinous's question first takes establishes that he does not have in mind blood relatives, but those who are close to blood relatives in one's affection. Having set these as the terms for his real question, Alcinous can then ask about a companion—one who was not a blood relative, but who was still no less than a brother. Taken as a whole, Alcinous's question has a thrust to it, which is carefully articulated. If it is just an idle question that he asks—one with no answer—it is hard to understand why it is given such a particular and such a

---

170 The passage is quoted §2.109 above.

complex form. If, on the other hand, the question has an answer, the form of the question makes perfect sense. The question does in fact have an answer but only at a secondary level, and this is the reason that the real question is the secondary one, and not the primary one. The secondary question determines the question's form.[171]

§2.134 I turn now from Alcinous's real question in *Odyssey* 8—who was the wise companion that you lost at Troy?—to Odysseus's implied answer in *Odyssey* 11—it was Nestor, the son of Neleus, who, in accord with his ancient twin myth, left me behind in Troy, and I as a result failed to return home. My interpretation of the catalogue of heroines in Book 11 requires that Nestor be seen as the catalogue's focus, and it is time to confront the issue of whether this is really one's experience when reading the catalogue, or whether, in spite of arguments presented so far, Nestor still seems to get lost in the catalogue's complexity. While the presence of both Nestor and Neleus in the catalogue has seemed significant to others,[172] no one seems to have noticed that the two passages containing them divide the catalogue into two virtually equal parts, and that this is the catalogue's main organizing principle. To see the reason for the bipartite structure of course requires that one know in advance Nestor's variant of the twin myth, and Nestor's myth has hitherto escaped notice. It should also be added that the Phaeacian genealogy in Book 7, with its great attention to the city founder Nausithoos, the father of Alcinous, prepares the way for the bipartite structure of the catalogue in Book 11, with the city founder Neleus beginning its first part, and with Nestor, the real point of the catalogue, beginning its second part. But however true these arguments are, the fact remains that the catalogue's structure, which I see as the key to its interpretation, has impressed itself on no one, and this is very remarkable. The reason for this is neither that the structure is not as fundamental as I argue, nor that it has simply been missed by generations of readers, but that it has been obscured by interpolations in the text. While these interpolations have not destroyed the catalogue's original bipartite structure—indeed this structure has been preserved, as I have tried to show—

171 The form of the question, with a set of alternatives, the second of which is valid, is reminiscent of the technique used in the chariot race of *Iliad* 23 when Idomeneus speculates about what befell Eumelos at the turning post: first he surmises what actually happened, a crash on the plain, then he suggests what is the real point of the scene—a crash at the turning post.
172 See Stanford 1959 on *Odyssey* 3.4; Stanford's view that Homer's Ionian audience venerated Neleus as the ancestor of the kings of Miletus and Colophon is, I think, substantially right, with a qualification in the case of Colophon (Colophon is secondary to Miletus in this affiliation; see Part 4 below).

they have still obscured it almost beyond recognition. My argument thus is that a single interpolator, who was well aware of the catalogue's bipartite structure, made additions to the catalogue in a number of places, but sought to preserve the catalogue's original structure in the process.[173]

§2.135 I do not make the suggestion of interpolations in the Homeric text lightly, and I therefore wish to begin this analysis with a passage that has drawn the attention of many scholars, namely the first passage in the catalogue, devoted to Neleus's mother Tyro. She fell in love with the river god Enipeus, and as she wandered by his riverbanks, Poseidon took on Enipeus's likeness and lay with her. From this union Pelias and Neleus were born, who were kings in separate cities, Iolkos and Pylos, and Tyro herself bore three other sons to the mortal Kretheus. Most of this passage is devoted to Tyro's dramatic union with Poseidon, who addresses her when they have made love, telling her that she will bear splendid children and revealing that he is the god Poseidon, and who then disappears beneath the waters. It has long been suspected by students of mythology that this version of the myth, in which Poseidon is the father of the twins Neleus and Pelias, is the transformation of an earlier version, in which the river god Enipeus himself was the father.[174]

---

173 For what I mean (and, more important, what I do not mean) by "interpolations," see n2.16 above regarding Cantieni's argument that Nestor's story in *Iliad* 11 contains "spurious" passages. What I mean by "interpolation" is anything that entered the Homeric poems after the Ionic phase of development. As I noted earlier, I reserve the term "Homeric" for the Ionic phase, but I by no means wish to impose this usage on those who have a different perspective. The unfortunate part of the term "interpolation" is that it automatically suggests a written text. When I use the term I prefer not to prejudge the question of the medium, whether oral or written, but to consider this issue with others on a case by case basis. There have been those who consider the catalogue of heroines as a whole an interpolation (references in Stenger 2006:231n57), and this, to say the least, is an overreaction. Those who defend the catalogue from the charge of irrelevance to Odysseus's mission in the underworld (references in Stenger 2006:231n58) often point to the role of Arete, who seems to accept Odysseus for the first time immediately after the catalogue. I agree with this point (cf. n2.143 above), and I cite Stenger 2006:230–232, who makes a good case in these terms; in the end, however, this defense of the catalogue still seems to me to fall short.

174 Preller 1894:573n1: "Indeed the narrative of *Odyssey* 11.235ff. still allows one without difficulty to guess an older form of the myth, according to which not Poseidon, but the river god Enipeus...was the original ancestor. Cf. Poseidon Ἐνιπεύς in Miletus" ("Doch lässt die Erzählung der Odyssee 11.235ff. noch unschwer eine ältere Sagenform errathen, wonach nicht Poseidon, sondern der Flussgott Enipeus...der Stammvater war. Vgl. den Poseidon Ἐνιπεύς in Milet"). For the cult of Poseidon Ἐνιπεύς in Miletus see n2.178 below. Similarly Robert 1920:39: "There Poseidon approaches her in the form of Enipeus. This is probably already a transformation of the oldest form of the myth, according to which Enipeus himself was the father of Pelias and Neleus" ("Da naht sich ihr Poseidon in der Gestalt des Enipeus. Wahrscheinlich ist das bereits eine Umgestaltung der ältesten Sagenform, nach der Enipeus selbst der Vater des Pelias und Neleus war"). Weizsäcker, Roscher's *Lexikon*

More recently, the actual language of the passage in which Poseidon appears has been found to be very closely paralleled by the Hesiodic treatment of the same myth, fragments of which have survived on papyrus. We have already seen the first part of the Hesiodic version, following on the story of Tyro's father Salmoneus, which we considered in connection with the Phaeacian genealogy. When Salmoneus was cast into Tartaros for his sin, and all his people were destroyed, Tyro alone was spared by Zeus, who gave her to her uncle Kretheus to raise. At the end of the fragment in which these events are told, the story of her union with the god Poseidon begins. When she grew up, Poseidon fell in love with her because of her beauty (Hesiod fr. 30.31–34 MW):

αὐτὰρ ἐπεί] ῥ᾽ ἥβης πολυηράτου ἐς τέλος ἦλθεν

τῆ]ς γ᾽ ἐράεσκε Ποσειδάων ἐνοσίχθων

] φιλότητι θεὸς βροτῶι, οὕνεκ᾽ ἄρ᾽ εἶδος

πασάων προύχεσκε γυναι]κῶν θηλυτεράων.

But when] she reached the completion of her much-desired
        youth
    ] Poseidon the earthshaker desired her
    ] in love a god for a mortal, because in beauty
she exceeded all] female women.

The last letters of eight more lines end this fragment, including two whole words, καλὰ ῥέεθρα, "beautiful streams," at the end of the first of these lines (Hesiod fr. 30.35 MW). In *Odyssey* 11 the line that immediately sets the scene for Tyro's affair with Poseidon (*Odyssey* 11.240) contains the same two words. Here is the description of their affair from the start (*Odyssey* 11.238–242):

ἢ ποταμοῦ ἠράσσατ᾽ Ἐνιπῆος θείοιο,

ὃς πολὺ κάλλιστος ποταμῶν ἐπὶ γαῖαν ἵησι,

καί ῥ᾽ ἐπ᾽ Ἐνιπῆος πωλέσκετο <u>καλὰ ῥέεθρα</u>.

τῷ δ᾽ ἄρα εἰσάμενος γαιήοχος ἐννοσίγαιος

ἐν προχοῇς ποταμοῦ παρελέξατο δινήεντος.

'Neleus' 112: "For that he [Neleus] was originally thought to be the son of the river god follows of itself from the narrative of the *Odyssey*" ("Denn dass er [Neleus] ursprünglich für einen Sohn des Flussgottes galt, geht aus der Erzählung der *Odyssee* selbst hervor…"). Cf. also West 1985:142.

She fell in love with a river, the divine Enipeus,
who is much the most beautiful of rivers to pour forth on the
    earth,
and she wandered along the Enipeus's <u>beautiful streams</u>.
Taking his shape the earthholder, the earthshaker,
lay with her in the mouth of the eddying river.

On the basis of *Odyssey* 11.240, the next line of the Hesiodic fragment (Hesiod fr. 30.35 MW) was restored by Merkelbach and West as: ἣ δ' ἐπ' Ἐνιπῆος πωλέσκετο] καλὰ ῥέεθρα. In the remaining seven lines of this fragment nothing but the word κούρη, "maiden," can be made out. What led Merkelbach and West to assume the same line in Hesiod as in *Odyssey* 11 has to do with two further pieces of evidence. First, the story of the union between Tyro and Poseidon in the *Odyssey* continues with the description of a curved wave, as big as a mountain, which surrounded them and hid their act of love (*Odyssey* 11.243–244):

πορφύρεον δ' ἄρα κῦμα περιστάθη οὔρεϊ ἶσον,

κυρτωθέν, κρύψεν δὲ θεὸν θνητήν τε γυναῖκα.

A dark wave as big as a mountain rose up around them,
curved, and hid the god and the mortal woman.

Vergil has a similar description of a wave in the fourth book of the *Georgics*,[175] and a scholiast tells us that this line was taken, not from *Odyssey* 11, as we would expect, but from Hesiod's *Catalogue of Women*.[176] Although there is no indication as to the Hesiodic context in which the curved wave occurred, the occurrence of what seems to be an identical wave in the story of Tyro in *Odyssey* 11 strongly suggests that in Hesiod too her story was the wave's context. The last, and most compelling, piece of evidence concerns the speech that Poseidon addresses to Tyro after they have made love, when he tells her that she will bear splendid children and then reveals his identity to her before disappearing beneath the water (*Odyssey* 11.246–253):

αὐτὰρ ἐπεί ῥ' ἐτέλεσσε θεὸς φιλοτήσια ἔργα,

ἔν τ' ἄρα οἱ φῦ χειρὶ ἔπος τ' ἔφατ' ἔκ τ' ὀνόμαζε·

---

175 Vergil *Georgics* 4.360–361: *at illum / curvata in montis faciem circumstetit unda*, "but a curved wave that looked like a mountain surrounded him"; the context is the Aristaeus epyllion.

176 Scholia to Vergil *Georgics* 4.361: *hunc versum ex Hesiodi gynecon <catalogo> transtulit* (Hesiod fr. 32 MW). For the source cf. Schwartz 1960:116–117.

"χαῖρε, γύναι, φιλότητι· περιπλομένου δ' ἐνιαυτοῦ
τέξεαι ἀγλαὰ <u>τέκνα, ἐπεὶ οὐκ ἀποφώλιοι</u> εὐναὶ
ἀθανάτων· σὺ δὲ <u>τοὺς κομέειν ἀτιταλλέμεναί τε</u>.
νῦν δ' ἔρχευ πρὸς δῶμα καὶ ἴσχεο μηδ' ὀνομήνης·
αὐτὰρ ἐγώ τοί εἰμι Ποσειδάων ἐνοσίχθων."
ὣς εἰπὼν ὑπὸ πόντον ἐδύσετο κυμαίνοντα.

And when the god finished the deeds of love,
He took her by the hand and spoke a word and called her by
     name:
"Rejoice, woman, in this act of love; as the year returns
you will bear splendid <u>children, since</u> the beds of the immortals
     are <u>not in vain</u>;
but you, <u>take care of them and raise them</u>.
Now go home and restrain yourself and do not say my name;
I am indeed Poseidon the earthshaker."
So saying he sank beneath the wavy sea.

There is another papyrus fragment of the Hesiodic version, which is only six
lines long, and in which both the beginnings and the ends of the lines have
been lost, but enough of the fragment has been preserved to show that lines
2–3 were close to or identical with Odyssey 11.249–250 (Hesiod fr. 31.1–7 MW):

```
            ]. Ποσειδάων λ[
  τέξεις δ' ἀγλαὰ τέκ]να, ἐπεὶ οὐκ ἀποφώ[λιοι εὐναὶ
  ἀθανάτων· σὺ δὲ τ]οὺς κομέειν ἀτιτα[λλέμεναί τε.
         ] ἵν' ἀγλαὰ τέκνα τ[εκ-
         ]. τανεμεσσητοι τε[
  ὣς εἰπὼν ὃ μὲν αὖτις] ἀγαστόγωι εμ[
             ]η ἔβη οἰκόνδε [νέεσθαι
                 ]. ον. [
```

      ] Poseidon [
you will bear splendid child]<u>ren since not in vai</u>[n the beds]
of immortals; but you,] <u>take care of them and raise them</u> [
         ] so that splendid children [

]   ?   [
so saying he again] (in?) the resounding [
] (she) went home [returning
] ? [

With Poseidon named in the fragment's first line, and with the resemblance of the next two lines to Poseidon's speech in *Odyssey* 11, there is every reason to believe that this Hesiodic fragment likewise concerns Tyro, and that the relationship between the two passages is one of direct imitation on the part of the passage in *Odyssey* 11.[177]

§2.136 I think that an interpolator who knew the Hesiodic version of the tale added the passage with Poseidon to *Odyssey* 11, and that the version of the tale in *Odyssey* 11 originally had the river god Enipeus rather than Poseidon as the father of Neleus and Pelias. If we remove lines 240–253 from the story, we are left with Tyro who first falls in love with the river god Enipeus, and then becomes pregnant and bears his children. The passage about Tyro would then be eleven lines long in all, as follows:

ἔνθ᾽ ἦ τοι πρώτην Τυρὼ ἴδον εὐπατέρειαν,

ἣ φάτο Σαλμωνῆος ἀμύμονος ἔκγονος εἶναι,

φῆ δὲ Κρηθῆος γυνὴ ἔμμεναι Αἰολίδαο·

ἣ ποταμοῦ ἠράσσατ᾽ Ἐνιπῆος θείοιο,

ὃς πολὺ κάλλιστος ποταμῶν ἐπὶ γαῖαν ἵησι.

ἡ δ᾽ ὑποκυσαμένη Πελίην τέκε καὶ Νηλῆα,

τὼ κρατερὼ θεράποντε Διὸς μεγάλοιο γενέσθην

---

177 There are further similarities between the two texts: in line 7 of the Hesiodic fragment Tyro returns home after Poseidon disappears beneath the water, and in *Odyssey* 11.251 Poseidon commands Tyro to return home and disappears beneath the water. I do not agree with the suggestion that the close similarity in wording and situation between the two passages can be explained by a common epic tradition underlying both (Crane 1988:97–98, Tsagarakis 2000:83–84) or that the Hesiodic fragment imitates the *Odyssey* rather than the reverse (Tsagarakis 2000:84); the point that fragments of the Hesiodic *Catalogue of Women* contain no speeches apart from this one in my view does not indicate the direction of borrowing since there is an anomaly in either case. Theoretically Hesiod could be imitating Homer (as defined n2.16 above) verbatim, but to my knowledge there are no other examples of this. Cf. Page 1955:37–38: "The second and third lines are identical with 11.249–250. They are not conventional or formular phrases; it is therefore probable that the relation between the Hesiodic poem and the *Odyssey* is one of direct imitation. In both versions Poseidon is speaking to the lady of his love; the outline of the story was identical in the two poems, and so was a good deal of the detail." Whereas Page believes that the whole catalogue is a post-Hesiodic interpolation into the *Odyssey*, I think that only limited parts are.

ἀμφοτέρω· Πελίης μὲν ἐν εὐρυχόρῳ Ἰαολκῷ
ναῖε πολύρρηνος, ὁ δ' ἄρ' ἐν Πύλῳ ἠμαθόεντι.
τοὺς δ' ἑτέρους Κρηθῆϊ τέκεν βασίλεια γυναικῶν,
Αἴσονά τ' ἠδὲ Φέρητ' Ἀμυθάονά θ' ἱπποχάρμην.

Then I saw Tyro first, born of a noble father,
who said that she was the offspring of faultless Salmoneus,
and said too that she was the wife of Kretheus, descended from
    Aeolus.
She fell in love with a river, the divine Enipeus,
who is much the most beautiful of rivers to pour forth on the
    earth.
She conceived and bore Pelias and Neleus,
who became strong servants of great Zeus,
both of them; Pelias in wide Iolkos
had his home, owning many sheep, the other one in sandy Pylos.
The queen among women bore her other sons to Kretheus,
Aison and Pheres and the chariot-fighter Amythaon.

Since we are used to a version more than twice as long as this, and one in
which Poseidon and his act of love with Tyro provide the memorable images,
it requires a considerable mental effort even to consider a version in which
Poseidon has no part—or, rather, a version in which Poseidon's part is implied
rather than explicit. For even in the shortened version Poseidon would still
be present by implication. In Miletus, the city of the historical Neleids, the
appearance of the river god Enipeus in the story would have automatically
implied Poseidon, for Ἐνιπεύς was a cult title of Poseidon in Miletus.[178] Thus
if the river god Enipeus is made Neleus's father in *Odyssey* 11, Poseidon is not
thereby excluded, but only withdrawn from direct view.[179]

§2.137 To assess the shortened version of the passage we need next to look
closely at the flow of the narrative from the line before the interpolation to the

---

178 Scholia to Lycophron 722: Ἐνιπεὺς ὁ Ποσειδῶν τιμᾶται παρὰ Μιλησίοις. The identification
     of this cult with an altar of Poseidon that the city founder Neileos was said to have estab-
     lished on Cape Poseidion (Strabo 14.1.2, 3, 5) is implied by Lycophron 722 and the scholia to
     this line: Lycophron 722 locates the cult on a "projecting headland" (ἀκτήν...προὔχουσαν),
     and the scholia specify Cape Poseidion; cf. Herda 1998:15. See Map 2 below.
179 In the Phaeacian genealogy, which is based on the Neleid genealogy, the role of Poseidon is
     explicit: he is the father of Nausithoos. This imitates his role as the father of Neleus in the
     Panhellenic myth (as opposed to the Milesian version).

line after it, and to make a judgment on its merits. With Poseidon gone, there is no longer an explicit act of love preceding Tyro's conceiving and giving birth, and this is somewhat unusual if we survey other instances in Greek epic of the feminine participle ὑποκυσαμένη (or κυσαμένη), "having conceived," and a verb meaning "gave birth" (τέκε, τέκετο, γείνατο). There are twelve such occurrences of ὑποκυσαμένη (including two of κυσαμένη) in addition to the example in *Odyssey* 11: two in the *Iliad*, four in Hesiod's *Theogony*, four in Hesiodic fragments, and two in the *Homeric Hymns*. In six of the twelve instances, an explicit act of love is mentioned first.[180] But then there are also occurrences of ὑποκυσαμένη where there is no explicit mention of an act of love.[181] In two of these a heroine is merely called the wife (*ákoitis*, "bed partner") of someone before being said to conceive and give birth. Hesiod *Theogony* 409–412 tells how the Titan Perses led Asteria to his home to be called his wife, and how she conceived and gave birth to Hekate:

> Ἀστερίην εὐώνυμον, ἥν ποτε Πέρσης
> ἠγάγετ' ἐς μέγα δῶμα φίλην κεκλῆσθαι ἄκοιτιν.

180 These include both examples in the *Iliad*, three of the four examples in the *Theogony*, one of the two examples in the *Homeric Hymns*, and none of the four examples in the Hesiodic fragments. In four of the six total examples the act of love is specified by a form of the verb μιγῆναι, "mingled": *Iliad* 6.26, Hesiod *Theogony* 125 and 308, *Homeric Hymn* 32.15; in *Iliad* 20.225 the verb is παρελέξατο, "lay next to"; in Hesiod *Theogony* 404–406 the verbal phrase ἦλθεν ἐς εὐνήν, "went to bed," occurs, and the phrase ἐν φιλότητι, "in love," follows loosely with the act of becoming pregnant and giving birth. The example with παρελέξατο in *Iliad* 20.225, in which the north wind Boreas takes on the likeness of a horse and impregnates mares, provides a useful contrast with the proposed reading of *Odyssey* 11 (*Iliad* 20.223–225):

> τάων καὶ Βορέης ἠράσσατο βοσκομενάων,
> ἵππῳ δ' εἰσάμενος παρελέξατο κυανοχαίτῃ·
> αἳ δ' ὑποκυσάμεναι ἔτεκον δυοκαίδεκα πώλους.

Boreas desired them as they grazed,
and he took on the appearance of a dark-maned horse and lay with them;
and they conceived and bore twelve colts.

In the *Odyssey*, Tyro "desires" Enipeus (same verb ἠράσσατο as in *Iliad* 20.223), she conceives and gives birth (ὑποκυσαμένη...τέκε, corresponding to ὑποκυσάμεναι ἔτεκον in *Iliad* 20.225), but there is nothing in the Tyro passage corresponding to the verb παρελέξατο, "lay with," used of Boreas.

181 These six examples include one from the *Theogony*, one from the *Homeric Hymns*, and four from the Hesiodic fragments; two of the four Hesiodic fragments (Hesiod fr. 7 and fr. 205 MW) contain ὑποκυσαμένη in the first line of the fragment, hence we do not know what preceded it. This leaves us with four valid examples, one each in the *Theogony* and the *Homeric Hymns*, and two in Hesiodic fragments.

ἡ δ' ὑποκυσαμένη Ἑκάτην τέκε, τὴν περὶ πάντων
Ζεὺς Κρονίδης τίμησε.

Asteria of good name, whom Perses once
led to his great home to be called his dear wife.
She conceived and bore Hekate, whom above all
Zeus the son of Kronos honored.

Here the connection between an act of love and the birth of a child is left as
unspoken as it is in the case of Tyro and Enipeus. Noteworthy in this passage
also is the mention of Zeus, who "honored" Hekate greatly, for in later tradi-
tion Zeus, not the Titan Perses, was frequently regarded as Hekate's father.[182]
If Hesiod knew of a rival tradition, in which Zeus rather than Perses was the
father, his reticence in depicting an act of love between Hekate's mother
and Perses may be significant, and comparable to the situation of Tyro and
Enipeus. Not to depict the act of love in explicit terms was perhaps to leave
open the question of paternity in both cases.

§2.138 A second instance involving the word *ákoitis*, Hesiod fr. 26 MW,
is less clear because the fragment is damaged in the lines before the occur-
rence of ὑποκυσαμένη in line 27. The fragment concerns Stratonike, who
bore Eurytos to Melaneus (Hesiod fr. 26.27–28 MW):[183]

τῶι δ' ὑπ[οκυσαμένη καλλίζωνος Στρατονίκη
Εὔρυτον [ἐν μεγάροισιν ἐγείνατο φίλτατον υἱόν.

To him, con[ceiving, beautifully-girdled Stratonike]
[bore in her halls a dearest son] Eurytos.

These two lines of the fragment are confidently restored because they are
preserved in the scholia to Sophocles *Women of Trachis* 266; they begin a five-
line passage concerning the offspring of Eurytos, who are the reason that the
scholiast quotes the passage. The previous five lines are preserved only on
the badly damaged papyrus fragment (Hesiod fr. 26.22–26 MW):

182 West 1966 on *Theogony* 409 notes that a fragment of Musaeus gives the same parentage for
Hecate as Hesiod "but with Perses cuckolded by Zeus" (scholia to Apollonius of Rhodes
3.1035 = Musaeus fr. 16 Diels-Kranz; the scholia to Apollonius of Rhodes 3.467 say that
"some" make Zeus rather than Perses the father). For Hekate's various fathers, including
others besides Zeus, see Steuding, Roscher's *Lexikon* 'Hekate' 1899.
183 Eurytos was the famous archer, whose son Iphitos later gave his bow to Odysseus (*Odyssey*
21.13–38; for Eurytos cf. also *Odyssey* 8.223–228). Eurytos's father Melaneus, a son of Apollo,
was also a famous archer.

] Φοῖβος Ἀπόλλων,
βῆ δὲ φέ[ρ]ων ἀνάε[δ]ν[ον εὔζωνον]Στ[ρ]α̣[τ]ονίκην·
δῶκε δὲ π[αι]δὶ [φί]λωι θαλ[ερ]ὴν [κ]ε̣κλῆσθα̣ι ἄκοιτιν
ἀ]ντιθέωι Μελ[αν]ῆϊ, [τὸν οὔρ]ε̣[σι] πότνια νύμφη
Ο]ἰ̣ίτη[ϊ]ς Προ[ν]ό[η   ]ωματ[.]ο̣υ̣.[

] Phoebus Apollo,
And he went off taking [well-girdled] Stratonike without a bride-
   price;
he gave her to his dear son to be called his flourishing wife,
to godlike Melaneus, [whom on the mount]ains the revered
   nymph
Pronoe from Mount Oeta [   ] ? [   ] ? [

Enough of this passage is preserved to see that Apollo, the father of Melaneus, brought Stratonike to Melaneus and gave her to him to be called his wife (ἄκοιτιν in line 24); the final line and a half, though the last line is especially badly damaged, seem to have concerned the nymph who bore Melaneus to Apollo; her name was apparently contained in the first part of the last line. Though the condition of the fragment makes certainty impossible, there seems to be no room for the explicit mention of an act of love between Stratonike and Melaneus before Stratonike is described as conceiving and bearing Eurytos.[184]

§2.139 For our comparison with Tyro and Enipeus, the Hesiodic fragment contains another detail of some relevance. The scholiast to Sophocles who quoted part of the passage was concerned with Stratonike, her son Eurytos, and, in particular, the children of Eurytos. He was not concerned with Melaneus, the subject of the preceding lines. He therefore seems to have slightly misquoted the first line of the passage, which he begins with the subject pronoun ἥ, referring to Stratonike; the papyrus fragment quoted above, on the other hand, begins this line with the dative pronoun τῷ, "to him," referring to Melaneus.[185] This is clearly right. In the previous lines

---

184 Is it possible that the paternity of Eurytos was disputed, being attributed to Apollo himself as well as to Apollo's son Melaneus? Then there would be the same reason as in the birth of Hekate not to make the act of love explicit (the same phrase κεκλῆσθαι ἄκοιτιν, "to be called his wife," is used in both cases). Against this is the pronoun τῷ, "to him," in line 27, which must refer to Melaneus.

185 The beginning of the line has been preserved, and enough of the next four lines has also been preserved to ensure that the papyrus contains the same passage as in the scholia.

the subject has strayed from the marriage of Stratonike to Melaneus to Melaneus's birth from Apollo and a nymph, and when Stratonike is described as giving birth without any mention of an act of love, a reference to Melaneus as the father is required, and this is what the dative pronoun τῷ provides: Stratonike bore a son Eurytos "to him." I strongly suspect that the same dative pronoun τῷ originally stood in the passage in *Odyssey* 11 concerning Tyro and Enipeus, so that the narrative flow from the passage before the interpolation to the passage after it was as follows:

ἣ ποταμοῦ ἠράσσατ᾽ Ἐνιπῆος θείοιο,

ὃς πολὺ κάλλιστος ποταμῶν ἐπὶ γαῖαν ἵησι.

<u>τῷ</u> δ᾽ ὑποκυσαμένη Πελίην τέκε καὶ Νηλῆα,

τὼ κρατερὼ θεράποντε Διὸς μεγάλοιο γενέσθην

ἀμφοτέρω.

She fell in love with a river, the divine Enipeus,
who is much the most beautiful of rivers to pour forth on the
earth.
<u>To him</u> she conceived and bore Pelias and Neleus,
who became strong servants of great Zeus,
both of them.

Since there is no explicit mention of an act of love in this passage, it tightens the narrative flow considerably to have the father to whom the children were born referred to in the dative case.[186]

§2.140 The epic examples of (ὑπο)κυσαμένη that we have surveyed so far reveal that the narrative flow of the passage proposed for Tyro and Enipeus is somewhat unusual in its non-mention of an act of love, but hardly unparalleled when we consider the two Hesiodic examples. If ἣ δ᾽ ὑποκυσαμένη was the original reading in the Tyro and Enipeus passage, Hesiod's description

Note, however, that the passage in the scholia contains a sixth line that does not match the corresponding line in the papyrus; see Merkelbach and West 1967 ad loc. for the conjecture that this line in the scholia is not Hesiodic, but perhaps from the *Oikhalias Halosis* of Kreophylos, and has simply been added to the Hesiodic passage by the scholiast.

186 *Homeric Hymn* 1 to Dionysus, which contains the third of our four instances of (ὑπο)κυσαμένη without the explicit mention of an act of love (for the fourth see n2.187 below), has only the name of the father, Zeus, in the dative case: οἱ δέ [sc. φάσ᾽, line 2] σ᾽ ἐπ᾽ Ἀλφειῷ ποταμῷ βαθυδινήεντι / κυσαμένην Σεμέλην τεκέειν Διὶ τερπικεραύνῳ, "some (say) that Semele, becoming pregnant, bore you on the deep-swirling Alpheios River to Zeus who delights in thunder" (*Homeric Hymn* 1.3–4).

of the birth of Hekate, which seems to leave the question of paternity open, would provide a parallel, for the same ambiguity may have been aimed at regarding the paternity of Neleus and Pelias. If, as I prefer, the original reading was τῷ δ' ὑποκυσαμένη, then the Hesiodic fragment concerning Stratonike and Melaneus provides a wholly satisfactory parallel. In addition, the scholiast's change of τῷ to ἥ in quoting this passage shows the ease with which the same change could have been made by the interpolator in *Odyssey* 11, once τῷ no longer fit the new context. The sequence ἥ δ' ὑποκυσαμένη is in fact the normal formulaic sequence, and there is no need to wonder how the change might have taken place.[187]

187 There is a third Hesiodic passage to discuss in which an explicit act of love is omitted, but it is another fragment, and its condition is worse than the other fragments that we have considered. This is Hesiod fr. 145 MW concerning the birth of the Minotaur from Pasiphae and a bull. The three lines concerning the birth are relatively clear (Hesiod fr. 145.15-17). As far as can be told, the act of love of Pasiphae and the bull was passed over in silence in the preceding lines, and in line 15 Pasiphae is said to have borne her offspring, not to the bull, but to Minos: ἥ δ' ὑποκ[υσα]μένη Μίνωι τέκε κα[ρτερὸν υἱόν, / θαῦμα ἰ[δεῖν, "she conceived and bore a st[rong son] to Minos, a wonder to s[ee]" (Hesiod fr. 145.15-16). In the preceding lines the version of the story is perhaps that in which Poseidon sends a bull to Minos in answer to his prayer (cf. "Apollodorus" 3.1.3-4: Minos wants to impress his subjects and so prays for the bull; Poseidon complies, but demands that the bull be sacrificed; when Minos fails to sacrifice the bull, Poseidon makes Pasiphae fall in love with it). In the two lines preceding the line with ὑποκυσαμένη, "conceiving," we can clearly make out in the first line that the bull "desired" Pasiphae; what the second line contained is only conjecture, but it is probably correct that it gave further description of Pasiphae, the object of the bull's desire: τῆς δ' ἄρ' [ἐν ὀ]φθαλμοῖσιν ἰδὼν ἠράσ[σατο... / †ταύρωι [...]ριμ ενηϙϙαμερμιδαοτα[†, "seeing her with his eyes he desired her / † bull ?? †" (Hesiod fr. 145.13-14). West, by way of example ("*sic lusit* West"), restores the second line as: Ταυρων (?)...Ηριγενης Υπεριονιδαο τε κουρης. If this is at least pointed in the right direction, there is only the verb ἠράσσατο, used of the bull's "desire" for Pasiphae, followed by Pasiphae's conceiving and bearing of the Minotaur, and no explicit mention of their act of love (a bestial act about which the less said the better?). There is a close parallel here to the passage about Tyro and Enipeus in that the verb ἠράσσατο, indicating sexual desire, suffices by itself to imply an act of love, after which the heroine conceives and gives birth. The only difference is that in one case it is the male's desire (that of the bull) and in the other case the female's desire (that of Tyro) that is indicated by the verb. There is another famous example (or rather series of examples) in which the male's desire, as expressed by the same verb ἠράσσατο, leads immediately to the birth of children with no mention of an act of love. This is in *Iliad* 14, where Zeus bids Hera to lie with him, for never before has desire of a goddess or a woman so overpowered him, not even when—and he continues with a list of seven of his conquests and their offspring. The first of these is the wife of Ixion, and she sets the pattern for the rest (*Iliad* 14.315-318):

οὐ γάρ πώ ποτέ μ' ὧδε θεᾶς ἔρος οὐδὲ γυναικὸς
θυμὸν ἐνὶ στήθεσσι περιπροχυθεὶς ἐδάμασσεν,
οὐδ' ὁπότ' ἠρασάμην Ἰξιονίης ἀλόχοιο,
ἥ τέκε Πειρίθοον θεόφιν μήστωρ' ἀτάλαντον.

§2.141 The interpolation in the passage about Tyro is but the first of several such interpolations in the catalogue of heroines. Before we proceed to consider the rest of these there are certain general points to be made, the first of which is that the interpolator knew the Hesiodic *Catalogue of Women*. The story of Poseidon and Tyro is taken directly from Hesiod, as the verbal similarity of Poseidon's speech to Tyro in particular shows. But while the interpolator appears to have taken a few lines verbatim from Hesiod, his procedure was for the most part to fashion a somewhat looser imitation, and to adapt it to its new context in the catalogue of *Odyssey* 11. The second point concerns the nature of the original passage about Tyro as I have reconstructed it. This passage invited interpolation because it deliberately suppressed what may be called the Panhellenic version of Neleus's origin in favor of an older, local variant. Why it did so doubtless had to do with the Phaeacian genealogy, to which it corresponds. While the overall correspondence is unmistakable, correspondences of detail are intentionally disguised. Thus we have seen that the Neleid progenitor Salmoneus is called "faultless," and his daughter is called "born of a noble father," whereas the corresponding figure in the Phaeacian genealogy has attributed to him all that we know really characterized the sinner Salmoneus. It is consistent with this that in the Phaeacian genealogy the father of the city founder Nausithoos should be the same as the father of the city founder Neleus in the Panhellenic version of his myth, namely the god Poseidon, but that in the passage about Neleus himself his father should instead be the river god Enipeus. By choosing the local, more obscure variant of the myth, attention is again diverted from a direct correspondence of detail. As far as the interpolator is concerned, however, the

---

The desire of a goddess or woman has never before
so poured around my heart in my breast and overcome it,
not even when I desired Ixion's wife,
who bore Peirithoos, a counselor equal to the gods.

Although this example does not contain the participle ὑποκυσαμένη, "having conceived," it is still comparable with the Tyro and Enipeus passage (as I propose to read it) for the essential point. The point of comparison is that Zeus's passion, as expressed by the verb ἠρασάμην, is followed immediately by the birth of a child. Is this the same as in the Tyro and Enipeus passage? One difference, as in the previous example, is male versus female as the subject of desire. There is also a reason that explicit acts of love are not described in Zeus's case: that would push a passage that is already close to the edge (it has been called Zeus's "Leporello catalogue") past the bounds of decency. There is, moreover, an explicit reference to an act of love at the beginning of the passage, when Zeus invites Hera to bed: νῶϊ δ' ἄγ' ἐν φιλότητι τραπείομεν εὐνηθέντε, "but come let us turn to love and go to bed" (*Iliad* 14.314). Perhaps the main conclusion to be derived from this and the other examples is that there was variety in the way that this situation was handled.

only point that matters is that the passage about Tyro in the *Odyssey* did not contain the well-known version of her myth, and thus clearly invited his response, which was to provide it.

§2.142 The interpolator's knowledge of Hesiod, which is well established by what he added to the story of Tyro, can perhaps be detected in a second passage as well, namely that concerning Chloris, the mother of Nestor. After telling of the birth of Nestor and his brothers, the passage continues with the birth of Pero, Nestor's sister, who, as we have seen, is a counterpart to Helen, and thus a crucial link to the following passage concerning the Dioskouroi. Pero's parallel with Helen is her wooing by all her neighbors, and the story of this is told starting with the condition that Neleus put on Pero's suitors, that none should have his daughter who did not drive off the cattle of Iphiklos from Phylake (*Odyssey* 11.287–290):

τοῖσι δ' ἐπ' ἰφθίμην Πηρὼ τέκε, θαῦμα βροτοῖσι,
τὴν πάντες μνώοντο περικτίται· οὐδέ τι Νηλεὺς
τῷ ἐδίδου, ὃς μὴ ἕλικας βόας εὐρυμετώπους
ἐκ Φυλάκης ἐλάσειε βίης Ἰφικληείης.

After them she bore steadfast Pero, a wonder to mortals,
whom all her neighbors wooed; but Neleus did not
give her to anyone who did not drive the wide-browed spiral-
    horned cattle
of mighty Iphiklos from Phylake.

The passage then proceeds to tell how only the "faultless seer" undertook to drive the cattle off, but he was bound for a full year before he "told all the prophecies" and Iphiklos released him (*Odyssey* 11.291–297). Although he is not named, the faultless seer is of course Melampus, who successfully wooed Pero for his brother Bias. What is very striking is that his story is joined to the preceding narrative by a highly unusual enjambment. The first word of his story is *argaléas*, "difficult," modifying *bóas*, "cattle," not in the line before, but two lines before (*Odyssey* 11.289). The rest of the passage is as follows (*Odyssey* 11.291–297):

ἀργαλέας. τὰς δ' οἶος ὑπέσχετο μάντις ἀμύμων
ἐξελάαν· χαλεπὴ δὲ θεοῦ κατὰ μοῖρα πέδησε
δεσμοί τ' ἀργαλέοι καὶ βουκόλοι ἀγροιῶται.
ἀλλ' ὅτε δὴ μῆνές τε καὶ ἡμέραι ἐξετελεῦντο

ἂψ περιτελλομένου ἔτεος καὶ ἐπήλυθον ὧραι,
καὶ τότε δή μιν ἔλυσε βίη Ἰφικληείη
θέσφατα πάντ' εἰπόντα· Διὸς δ' ἐτελείετο βουλή.

hard (to drive). Those (cattle) only the faultless prophet prom-
   ised
to drive away; but he was bound by the god's harsh fate,
painful bonds, and rustic cowherds.
But when the months and days were completed
as the year came around, and the seasons returned,
then mighty Iphiklos freed him,
after he spoke all the prophecies; and the will of Zeus was
   accomplished.

This entire passage, I believe, is the work of the same interpolator who added
the passage about Poseidon to the story of Tyro. What suggests this first is the
unusual enjambment of *argaléas* with *bóas*, two lines earlier. This would not be
unduly suspicious in itself, were it not for the fact that the Hesiodic version of
this story appears to have contained the same highly unusual enjambment. A
papyrus fragment of the Hesiodic *Catalogue of Women* tells the story in what
remains of its first seven lines.[188] The first line of this fragment contains only
two intelligible words, οὗ κλέος, "whose fame," but this is enough to establish
a hero as the line's subject, and this was very likely Iphiklos. It is the next line
that begins with an enjambed *argaléa*[s], and then continues with an apparent
reference to Melampus. The reading suggested by Merkelbach and West is
in fact close to the wording of *Odyssey* 11.291, to which they refer (Hesiod fr.
37.1–2 MW):

]νου, οὗ κλέος εσ[
ἀργαλέα[ς]· μοῦνος δ' ὑπ[εδέξατο μάντις ἀμύμων.

] whose fame [
hard (to drive); he alone pro[mised, the faultless prophet.

---

188 Hesiod fr. 37.1–7 MW. The rest of the fragment continues as follows: lines 8–9 tell how
     Pero bore a son Talaos to Bias; lines 10–15 tell how Melampus and Bias then went to Argos,
     where Melampus cured the madness of the daughters of Proitos; lines 16–23 (the last lines
     of the fragment) concern Neleus's brother Pelias. Lines 10–14 are quoted in n2.136 above.

If the first line does refer to Iphiklos, as Merkelbach and West suggest,[189] and if *argaléa[s]* in the second line does modify a previous mention of Iphiklos's cattle, the enjambment must extend over more than one line, just as in *Odyssey* 11.

§2.143 The word *argaléa[s]* in the Hesiodic fragment is thus a highly suggestive piece of evidence, but it is also true that there are no further verbal resemblances between the two passages in what remains of the Hesiodic passage. Lines 3–4 contain phrases for "he accomplished it," apparently referring to Melampus's "undertaking" (cf. ὑπ[εδέξατο, line 2), and "having a cruel bond," referring to Melampus's imprisonment for a year (Hesiod fr. 37.3–4 MW):

καὶ τὸ μὲ[ν] ἐξε[τ]έλεσσε, β[
δεσμὸν ἀεικὲς ἔχων [

In the last three lines of the story are found the phrases "he wooed for his brother" and "he brought about a delightful marriage," and there is also an explicit reference to the "spiral-horned cattle" that play such a prominent part in the story (Hesiod fr. 37.5–7 MW):

μνᾶτο γὰρ αὐτοκασιγν[ήτωι, ἥρωι Βίαντι,
ἤνυέ θ['] ἱμερόεντα γάμ[ον
βοῦς ἕλικας, καὶ ἄεθλον ἀμ[ύμονα δέξατο κούρην.

For he wooed for his broth[er, the hero Bias,
and brought about the longed-for marria[ge
the spiral-horned cattle, and [he received] the prize of the
    bla[meless girl.

§2.144 It does not matter, however, that the interpolator, apart from the striking enjambment of *argaléas*, does not seem to have had this Hesiodic passage particularly in mind when he created the passage for *Odyssey* 11. We already know from the Tyro passage that the interpolator, while he knew Hesiod, and borrowed some of Hesiod's diction, was well able to create and adapt on his own. He also borrowed diction from sources other than Hesiod. In the Pero passage we see this in the phrase that he chose to end his addition to the passage, Διὸς δ' ἐτελείετο βουλή, "and the plan of Zeus was fulfilled" (*Odyssey* 11.297). This phrase has great point in its only two other occurrences

189 Pfeiffer suggests κοίρανος, "ruler," as the line's first word.

in Greek epic, namely in the proem of the *Iliad* and in *Cypria* fr. 1, but here it
seems to be little more than a filler, suggested most likely by the proem of
the *Iliad*.[190] It is interesting that the only trace of Hesiod, the enjambment of
argaléas, occurs just where the new passage is joined to the preceding context.
I surmise that the enjambment caught the interpolator's attention as a device
well suited to his purpose of adding the story of Melampus to what had been
the bare mention of Iphiklos's cattle.

§2.145 In addition to the trace of Hesiod in the passage, there is another
reason for thinking that *Odyssey* 11 did not tell the story of Melampus, but only
implied it: as mentioned earlier, *Odyssey* 15 tells Melampus's story in detail, and
the economy of the Homeric poems does not usually allow such a repetition.
In *Odyssey* 15 Telemachus meets the seer Theoklymenos and takes him aboard
his ship on his return voyage from Pylos to Ithaca. Theoklymenos was the great
grandson of the seer Melampus, and at Theoklymenos's first appearance in the
poem the descendants of Melampus are set out in full, including both branches
of the family, and not just the branch to which Theoklymenos belongs. The
passage, which is thirty lines long (*Odyssey* 15.226–255) is about Melampus and
the Melampids, and appropriate attention is paid to the family founder at the
beginning. The catalogue of his descendants does not begin until he moves
from Pylos to Argos, marries there, and has two sons. His own story anticipates
this at the beginning by saying that he fled from Pylos to another land (*Odyssey*
15.226–228), but epic ring composition allows the whole story of the wooing
of Pero to be told before we continue with his move to Argos (*Odyssey* 15.228–
239).[191] The ring composition begins in line 228, where we learn that Melampus
fled from Pylos, where he lived in wealth (line 227), to escape from Neleus, who
forcibly held his property for a year (*Odyssey* 15.228–231):

δὴ τότε γ' ἄλλων δῆμον ἀφίκετο, πατρίδα φεύγων
Νηλέα τε μεγάθυμον, ἀγαυότατον ζωόντων,
ὅς οἱ χρήματα πολλὰ τελεσφόρον εἰς ἐνιαυτὸν
εἶχε βίῃ.

Then indeed he came to the land of other people, fleeing his
fatherland
And great-hearted Neleus, noblest of living men,

190 *Iliad* 1.5. In the *Cypria* the "plan of Zeus" is to relieve the earth of overpopulation by means
of the Trojan war (οἱ δ' ἐνὶ Τροίῃ / ἥρωες κτείνοντο, Διὸς δ' ἐτελείετο βουλή, "the heroes
were killed in Troy, and the plan of Zeus was fulfilled," *Cypria* fr. 1.6–7 Allen).
191 This passage is quoted in §2.102 above.

Who held his many possessions for a year until its end
by force.

This was the year-long period that he was imprisoned in Phylake. He was
bound there in the halls of Phylakos, who is not otherwise identified, but who
is called the father of Iphiklos in later tradition.[192] Melampus suffered these
woes because of Neleus's daughter and the *átē*, "delusion," that an avenging
fury put in his mind (*Odyssey* 15.231–234):

> ὁ δὲ τεῖος ἐνὶ μεγάροις Φυλάκοιο
> δεσμῷ ἐν ἀργαλέῳ δέδετο, κρατέρ' ἄλγεα πάσχων
> εἵνεκα Νηλῆος κούρης ἄτης τε βαρείης,
> τήν οἱ ἐπὶ φρεσὶ θῆκε θεὰ δασπλῆτις Ἐρινύς.

> Meanwhile he was bound in painful bonds
> in the halls of Phylakos, suffering powerful woes
> because of Neleus's daughter and heavy delusion,
> which the avenging fury, destructive goddess, put in his mind.

What precisely the *átē* was that an Erinys put in his mind we do not know,
but the mention of Neleus's daughter is clear. In the remaining lines of the
story we hear that Melampus, escaping death, drove the cattle back to Pylos,
that he repaid Neleus for his wicked deed, and that he thus got a wife for his
brother; he then went on to Argos (*Odyssey* 15.235–239):[193]

> ἀλλ' ὁ μὲν ἔκφυγε κῆρα καὶ ἤλασε βοῦς ἐριμύκους
> ἐς Πύλον ἐκ Φυλάκης καὶ ἐτείσατο ἔργον ἀεικὲς
> ἀντίθεον Νηλῆα, κασιγνήτῳ δὲ γυναῖκα
> ἠγάγετο πρὸς δώμαθ'· ὁ δ' ἄλλων ἵκετο δῆμον,
> Ἄργος ἐς ἱππόβοτον.

> But he escaped death and drove the loud-bellowing cattle
> to Pylos from Phylake, and repaid the cruel deed
> of godlike Neleus, and brought a wife
> home to his brother; and he went to the land of other people,
> to horse-pasturing Argos.

192 Cf. n2.134 above.
193 What he did to repay Neleus for his wicked deed is not known.

§2.146 The version of Melampus's story told in *Odyssey* 11 overlaps with this version to a very large extent. The version in *Odyssey* 11 is less complete in that it leaves out the basic detail that Melampus wooed Pero for the sake of his brother, but it adds a detail in saying that Melampus was freed by Iphiklos when he told all the prophecies. It is clear, I think, that one of the two passages is superfluous to the overall scheme of the *Odyssey*, and that one of the passages was added to the text of the poem at a later point than the other. There is, I think, no question that the passage in *Odyssey* 15 belongs to the poem, but there is good reason to doubt the genuineness of the passage in *Odyssey* 11. We may conclude therefore that the interpolator had another source besides Hesiod for the passage that he added to the story of Pero in *Odyssey* 11, namely the passage in *Odyssey* 15. In *Odyssey* 15 there is an unusual juxtaposition of the concrete and the abstract when Melampus is said to have suffered woes εἵνεκα Νηλῆος κούρης ἄτης τε βαρείης, "because of Neleus's daughter and heavy delusion." The passage in *Odyssey* 11 contains a similar juxtaposition of the abstract and the concrete when, referring to the "fault-less prophet," it says that "the harsh fate of god, strong bonds, and rustic cowherds bound him" (*Odyssey* 11.292–293):

χαλεπὴ δὲ θεοῦ κατὰ μοῖρα πέδησε
δεσμοί τ' ἀργαλέοι καὶ βουκόλοι ἀγροιῶται.

But he was bound by the god's harsh fate,
painful bonds, and rustic cowherds.

I would like to think that the interpolator of the passage in *Odyssey* 11, who was clearly a craftsman, was inspired by the rather extravagant tone of the passage in *Odyssey* 15 to create something similar in *Odyssey* 11. The first term of his tripartite subject, χαλεπὴ...θεοῦ...μοῖρα, "the harsh fate of god," looks like it may owe something to the ἄτη, "delusion," brought on by the δασπλῆτις Ἐρινύς, "avenging fury," in *Odyssey* 15. His very concrete middle term, δεσμοί τ' ἀργαλέοι, "harsh bonds," may be a transformation of the similar phrase in *Odyssey* 15.232, δεσμῷ ἐν ἀργαλέῳ δέδετο, "he was bound in a harsh bond."[194]

§2.147 In the catalogue of heroines as originally conceived, then, the passage devoted to Chloris ended with the condition that Neleus laid down for his daughter's suitors, that he would give her to no one who did not drive off

---

194 There is one other Homeric occurrence of δεσμῷ ἐν ἀργαλέῳ, "in a harsh bond," in *Odyssey* 15.444 (one of Odysseus's lying tales); *Homeric Hymn* 7.12 (to Dionysus) has δεσμοῖς... ἀργαλέοισι, "harsh bonds."

the cattle of Iphiklos. The rest of the story, which was well known, and would be told in another context later in the poem, was simply not told here. This allusive quality, whereby certain things are left unsaid, is consistent with what is found in the passage about Tyro, where knowledge of Salmoneus's hubris is assumed[195] but nothing is said about it, and it is even contradicted by his epithet "faultless." In this passage, however, the story is allusive for a different reason. Pero is the link between Nestor and the Dioskouroi in the catalogue of women, as we have seen. She is the analogue to Helen, the Dioskouroi's sister, and her function in the catalogue is fulfilled as soon as she is seen in Helen's defining role, as the prize sought by many suitors. This is the place to suggest her story with a significant detail, the cattle of Iphiklos, but not to tell the story in full. For the full story really does not concern Pero, or even her successful suitor Bias, but her suitor's brother Melampus, and this is simply not the place to tell his story. The only relevant detail in his story is that he wooed for his brother, because this is how Helen also was wooed, by Agamemnon for the sake of Menelaus. But this important detail comes to mind of itself when Pero's myth is simply alluded to. The interpolated passage, by contrast, despite the fact that it makes the story of Melampus explicit, omits this significant detail, and it thus misses the essential point of the passage as a whole.

§2.148 The two most important passages in the catalogue of heroines in *Odyssey* 11 are those devoted to Tyro and Chloris, the mothers of Neleus and Nestor, and we have now seen that both of these passages were expanded by interpolations. The next passage that we will consider was not an expansion of an existing passage, as in the case of Tyro and Chloris, but an outright addition to the catalogue. Near the end of the catalogue, there is a passage that contains a group of three heroines of Attic mythology, Phaedra, Prokris, and Ariadne. For the first two of these heroines only their names are given and nothing is said of their myths.[196] For the last named, Ariadne, there is a short account of her death, when Theseus was bringing her from Crete to Athens (*Odyssey* 11.321–325):

Φαίδρην τε Πρόκριν τε ἴδον καλήν τ' Ἀριάδνην,
κούρην Μίνωος ὀλοόφρονος, ἥν ποτε Θησεὺς
ἐκ Κρήτης ἐς γουνὸν Ἀθηνάων ἱεράων

---

195 The sin of the giant Eurymedon in the Phaeacian genealogy shows that.
196 Phaedra, daughter of Minos and wife of the Athenian Theseus, is well known. Prokris was daughter of Erechtheus, king of Athens, and unfaithful wife of Kephalos, who killed her unintentionally.

ἦγε μέν, οὐδ' ἀπόνητο· πάρος δέ μιν Ἄρτεμις ἔκτα
Δίῃ ἐν ἀμφιρύτῃ Διονύσου μαρτυρίῃσι.

I saw Phaedra and Prokris and beautiful Ariadne,
the daughter of destructive-minded Minos, whom Theseus once
brought from Crete to the hill of sacred Athens,
but he did not enjoy her; Artemis killed her first
on sea-swept Dia on the evidence of Dionysus.

In general, the Homeric poems do not make use of Attic mythology;[197] this passage is therefore anomalous and subject to doubt. While there is no hard and fast rule about this,[198] there are additional reasons to think that this passage was the work of an interpolator. The first is Dionysus's name in the phrase Διονύσου μαρτυρίῃσι, "by the evidence of Dionysus." Διόνυσος, with omicron, is the Attic form of the god's name. The Homeric form is Διώνυσος, with omega.[199] The use of the Attic form of Dionysus's name in *Odyssey* 11.325, added to the Attic context, indicates clearly that the author of the passage was not a Homeric poet, but an Athenian interpolator. We may also note an Athenian bias in the version of Ariadne's myth told here, at least as compared with the later version of her myth, in which Theseus deserts her and Dionysus rescues and weds her. Here Dionysus indicts her and Artemis kills her, and the Athenian Theseus is blameless.

§2.149 The passage with the three Athenian heroines amounts to the interpolator's signature at the end of his work. We have not yet identified all of his work in the catalogue, but this passage was his last, and it proclaims quite proudly the name of "holy Athens," Ἀθηνάων ἱεράων (*Odyssey* 11.323). It is almost as if the interpolator wished to give himself away at the end, especially in his very last phrase, Διονύσου μαρτυρίῃσι, "on the evidence of Διόνυσος." The use of the un-Homeric form, far from being an attempt to conceal anything, seems rather to be a deliberate and meaningful choice—a purposely dropped hint.

197 See Allen 1924:242–245, who cites Scott 1911, 1914, and 1921:47–72. For instances in which Homer ignores Attic myth see Scott 1911:427–428.

198 A counterexample is the reference to Erechtheus's palace in *Odyssey* 7.80–81; this passage, which Martin Nilsson recognized as highly archaic in content (Nilsson 1921:12–13, 1967:348, 1950:488), is, I think, integral to the story of the *Odyssey*; see Part 3 below (for Nilsson's view see n3.115).

199 There are three examples of Διώνυσος in the *Iliad* (6.132, 135, 14.325) and one in the *Odyssey* (24.74). The *Homeric Hymns* use both forms (omicron in 7.56, 19.46, 26.1 and 11; omega in 7.1 and 1.20; note that *Homeric Hymn* 7 uses both forms, lines 1 and 56).

§2.150 The final passage of the original catalogue is another group of three heroines, Maira, Klymene, and Eriphyle. In this passage, as in the Athenian interpolation that immediately precedes it, the first two heroines are only named, whereas the third, Eriphyle, has a comment added after her name, giving the essence of her myth (*Odyssey* 11.326–327):

Μαῖράν τε Κλυμένην τε ἴδον στυγερήν τ' Ἐριφύλην,
ἣ χρυσὸν φίλου ἀνδρὸς ἐδέξατο τιμήεντα.

I saw Maira and Klymene and hateful Eriphyle,
who took precious gold in exchange for her dear husband.

Eriphyle, the last heroine named in the catalogue, has the epithet στυγερήν, "hateful," added to her name because she was a famous sinner. She accepted a bribe from Polyneices to persuade her husband, the Argive seer Amphiaraos, to join the expedition against Thebes, although he had foreseen that this would cause his death. Finishing his catalogue on this note, Odysseus goes on to say that he could not name or tell of all the other heroines that he saw in the underworld, for the immortal night would end first (*Odyssey* 11.328–330):

πάσας δ' οὐκ ἂν ἐγὼ μυθήσομαι οὐδ' ὀνομήνω,
ὅσσας ἡρώων ἀλόχους ἴδον ἠδὲ θύγατρας·
πρὶν γάρ κεν καὶ νὺξ φθῖτ' ἄμβροτος.

But I could not say or name all
the wives and daughters of heroes that I saw;
immortal night would pass away first.

§2.151 The two-line passage with Maira, Klymene, and Eriphyle is a fitting end to the catalogue. It names three heroines at once, without identifying two of them, as a way of generalizing the situation at the end of the catalogue, and in order to convey the idea of an indefinite multitude that is to be pursued no further.[200] After Odysseus ends his account with this group

---

200 We do not know for sure who Maira and Klymene are since more than one heroine had these names. Maira is probably the daughter of Proitos, the son of Thersander, who in the *Nostoi* was said to have died a virgin (fr. 5 Allen in Pausanias 10.30.5); the same Maira (the daughter of Proitos, the son of Thersander) was said by Pherekyces to be a nymph of Artemis who was killed by the goddess after Zeus made love to her (Pherekydes *FGrHist* 3 F 170). In Tegea Maira was identified as the daughter of Atlas and wife of the local hero Tegeates (Pausanias 8.48.6). Klymene may be the figure so named in *Nostoi* fr. 4 Allen (Pausanias 10.29.6); she was a daughter of Minyas who married Kephalos (not Phylakos, as Stanford 1959 ad loc. says) and had a child Iphiklos.

of three heroines he interrupts his tale with the suggestion that all now go
to bed. The flow of the narrative is natural and the reason for the two-line
concluding passage is clear. It is likewise clear that the passage with the three
Attic heroines is a deliberate imitation of the catalogue's concluding passage
and its three Panhellenic heroines.[201] This was the interpolator's concluding
addition, as we have seen, and in it he has imitated the idea of suggesting a
multitude by only naming two of the heroines, and then telling something
about the third.[202] But the idea of multitude is out of place here, because the
catalogue needs and can accommodate only one concluding passage, and this
it already has. Before the concluding passage as the catalogue originally stood
each heroine had her own passage, and this scheme has now been altered.
Once again the interpolator has understood something of what he set out to
imitate, but in carrying out his imitation he has fundamentally changed the
nature of the original.[203]

§2.152 Let us return now to the structure of the catalogue of heroines,
including interpolations, as we have received it in the text of the *Odyssey*.
The two parts of the catalogue, headed by the passages containing Neleus
and Nestor respectively, are of roughly equal length, and each part of the
catalogue contains five entries. We will come back to the overall length of
each part when we have found all the interpolated passages. For now it is
the number of entries in each part that matters, for we have just found that
the interpolator added a completely new entry to the second part, namely
the passage of Attic heroines, which occurs second to last. The passage that
occurs second to last in the first part of the catalogue, Heracles' wife Megara,
was also, I believe, added by the interpolator. The immediately preceding

---

201 Eriphyle was from Argos; Klymene was probably Thessalian (see n2.200 above for the
daughter of Minyas); Maira is uncertain, but later at least was claimed by Tegea (see n2.200
above).

202 Compare καλήν τ' Ἀριάδνην, "and beautiful Ariadne," with στυγερήν τ' Ἐριφύλην, "and
hateful Eriphyle": the third heroine gets the epithet, as well as the story, and in the case
of Ariadne the interpolator has changed the epithet from one of blame ("hateful") to one
of praise ("beautiful"). Using an epithet of just the third person named is of course normal
Homeric practice: cf. Νέστορά τε Χρομίον τε Περικλύμενόν τ' ἀγέρωχον, "Nestor and
Chromios and proud Periklymenos."

203 Another point of comparison between the two passages is their length. The interpolator's
passage is longer, which is fitting, since it is not the last in the catalogue, and we want to
have more than a line on Ariadne in this position. But the length of the passage makes the
mention of the other two heroines, Phaedra and Prokris, inappropriate, because we want
to hear their stories too. In the genuine conclusion to the catalogue, the names of the two
heroines whose stories are not told seem more generic. There are no specific stories that
we want to hear, and in any case these heroines are soon swept away with the rest of the
multitude that Odysseus does not wish even to name.

passage is devoted to Heracles' mother, Alcmena, and Megara is simply tacked on at the end of this passage, without even a new main verb to connect her. The two passages, consisting of three lines and two lines respectively, are as follows (*Odyssey* 11.266–270):

τὴν δὲ μετ' Ἀλκμήνην ἴδον, Ἀμφιτρύωνος ἄκοιτιν,
ἥ ῥ' Ἡρακλῆα θρασυμέμνονα θυμολέοντα
γείνατ' ἐν ἀγκοίνῃσι Διὸς μεγάλοιο μιγεῖσα·

καὶ Μεγάρην, Κρείοντος ὑπερθύμοιο θύγατρα,
τὴν ἔχεν Ἀμφιτρύωνος υἱὸς μένος αἰὲν ἀτειρής.

And after her I saw Alcmena, Amphitryon's wife,
who bore bold-battling lion-hearted Heracles
after making love in the arms of great Zeus;

and Megara, bold Kreion's daughter,
whom Amphitryon's son never tiring in his strength had.

In this sequence of heroines Heracles becomes, so to speak, the principle of selection: since his mother has been chosen for inclusion in the catalogue, his wife will be too. In the genuine catalogue of heroines there was only one hero who had both his mother and his wife named, and in his case the one was not simply tacked onto the other. This was Neleus, whose mother Tyro heads the first part of the catalogue, and whose wife Chloris heads the second part. The interpolator has clearly done something very different from this, and something unparalleled in the rest of the catalogue, by juxtaposing one hero's mother and wife. On the other hand, he has followed literally the catalogue's announced intention of presenting the "wives and daughters" of heroes,[204] for Megara is very neatly presented as both a wife (of Heracles) and a daughter (of Kreon) in the two lines that the interpolator has devoted to her. Once again the interpolator has been faithful to a certain aspect of the catalogue's structure, while violating it in a more basic way. Even the catalogue's announced intention of presenting the wives and daughters of heroes he has taken more literally than does most of the rest of the catalogue. In the rest of the catalogue it is again only Tyro and Chloris who have both a father and a husband named.[205] The catalogue's real intention is in any case

---

204 Cf. n2.141 above.
205 This does not count the interpolated Ariadne (Theseus is in any case not called Ariadne's

not what it announces, for the heroines who are included have really been chosen neither as wives nor as daughters, but as mothers.[206]

§2.153 There are two passages now left for us to consider. Each of these passages, I think, explicitly narrates a story that in the original catalogue was merely alluded to. The phenomenon is thus the same as in the passage devoted to Chloris, where the story of Melampus was originally left untold, although enough was said, concerning the cattle of Iphiklos, to bring that story to mind. In the case of the passage about Melampus there were external pieces of evidence, including the enjambed word *argaléas* found in apparently the same context in Hesiod, and the repetition of the same story in *Odyssey* 15, to indicate that the passage had been interpolated. There is no such external evidence in the case of the two remaining passages, so we will have to rely on strictly internal evidence. But at this point we also know more about the interpolator's procedure, which was precisely to fill out what was originally only alluded to.[207] And we have also come to see that the original catalogue was allusive in just this way.[208] The passage devoted to Iphimedeia, the mother of the twin giants, Otos and Ephialtes, who piled Ossa on Olympus and Pelion on Ossa in their vain attempt to overthrow the gods, is sixteen lines long in the catalogue as we have received it. This passage, I believe, was originally but four lines long. The story that is narrated in the last twelve lines of the passage (the hubris of Otos and Ephialtes and their destruction at the hands of Apollo as still very young men, before their beards had matured) was all indicated, I believe, by a three-word parenthesis—μινυνθαδίω δὲ γενέσθην,

---

husband). Only Antiope (besides Tyro and Chloris) has her father named. Four heroines (besides Tyro and Chloris, and not counting the interpolated Megara) have a husband named: Alcmena, Epikaste, Leda, and Iphimedeia.

206 See n2.141 above. Megara too is a mother, but this is left out of account in *Odyssey* 11 for an obvious reason: Heracles kills Megara's children when he goes mad. This is the subject of Euripides' *Heracles*, in which Heracles kills Megara as well. The story of Heracles' madness occurred in the *Cypria*: according to Proclus *Chrestomathy* line 116 (Allen 1912:103 line 23) Nestor told the story of "Heracles' madness" (τὴν Ἡρακλέους μανίαν) to Menelaus, but the details of his account are unknown; it must have contained at least the death of Heracles' children. Megara's murder by Heracles is apparently Euripides' invention; in the more common tradition, as attested by e.g. Pausanias 10.29.7, Heracles divorces Megara because the marriage has proved unlucky; see Wilamowitz 1895:82–85. Wilamowitz (p. 83) is surely right that the brief account in *Odyssey* 11 is incompatible with Megara's murder, but at least the infanticide must have been known to the interpolator. Whereas the other heroines in the catalogue have children who collectively convey the catalogue's hidden meaning, Megara had children who cannot even be mentioned. Cf. n2.219 below.

207 This also holds for the expansion of the Tyro passage.

208 The final line of the catalogue (Eriphyle "accepted gold for her husband") is as good an example as any of the catalogue's overall allusive quality.

"but they were short-lived"—in the second last line of the original passage (*Odyssey* 11.305–308):

τὴν δὲ μέτ' Ἰφιμέδειαν, Ἀλωῆος παράκοιτιν,
εἴσιδον, ἣ δὴ φάσκε Ποσειδάωνι μιγῆναι,
καί ῥ' ἔτεκεν δύο παῖδε, μινυνθαδίω δὲ γενέσθην,
Ὠτόν τ' ἀντίθεον τηλεκλειτόν τ' Ἐφιάλτην.

And after her I saw Iphimedeia, the wife of Aloeus,
who said that she made love with Poseidon
and bore two sons, but they were short-lived,
godlike Otos and far-famed Ephialtes.

The whole story of the two Aloadai is implied in the words μινυνθαδίω δὲ γενέσθην, as a comparison with the expanded version shows.[209] The key point, however, is that their story should not be told in full here, for the sequence of passages itself follows a pattern, both in their order and in their length. In the second part of the catalogue the sequence of passages is Chloris (the mother of Nestor), Leda (the mother of the Dioskouroi), Iphimedeia (the mother of the twins Otos and Ephialtes), followed by a two-line conclusion to the catalogue as a whole (Maira, Klymene, and Eriphyle). The passage devoted to Iphimedeia achieves its purpose as soon as she is said to have been the mother of twins.[210] As for the length of passages in the second part of the catalogue, they decrease steadily from first to last, with the greatest number of lines given to Chloris (10), followed in rank order by Leda (7), Iphimedeia (4), and the concluding passage (2); the effect is to emphasize Chloris at the head of the list. The total number of lines in the second part of the catalogue is thus 23, which is 24 lines shorter than in the catalogue as it now stands. This brings us to the final interpolated passage in the catalogue, for what we

209 The expansion of the Otos and Ephialtes story was again perhaps based on Hesiod; the scholia to Apollonius of Rhodes 1.482 comment as follows on the name Ἀλωϊάδας (Hesiod fr. 19 MW): "Hesiod says that they were in name the offspring of Aloeus and Iphimedeia, but in truth of Poseidon and Iphimedeia, and that the city Alos in Aetolia was founded by their father." Unfortunately none of the Hesiodic text has survived to compare with *Odyssey* 11.

210 The fact that both twins die contrasts with the Dioskouroi (both live) and Nestor (he lives, his brother dies); see §2.104 above. But the fact that both Aloadai die is well conveyed in the first four lines of the passage through the phrase μινυνθαδίω δὲ γενέσθην, "but they were short-lived"; the full story of how they were undone by their own hubris is not needed to establish both the parallel and the contrast with the two preceding entries of the catalogue.

have now found in the second part of the catalogue applies equally to the first part. This is to say that the four entries in the first part decrease in length just as in the second part, and that the interpolator has added the same number of passages (two expansions of existing passages and one new passage) and the same number of lines (24) to the first part as to the second part. All of this is true when we realize that the passage devoted to Epikaste, the mother of Oedipus, was originally but two lines long (*Odyssey* 11.271–272):

μητέρα τ' Οἰδιπόδαο ἴδον, καλὴν Ἐπικάστην,
ἣ μέγα ἔργον ἔρεξεν ἀϊδρείῃσι νόοιο.

And I saw the mother of Oedipus, beautiful Epikaste,
who did a monstrous deed in the ignorance of her mind.

The story of Epikaste's unwitting incest with Oedipus, her son, is clearly evoked by these two lines alone, without the explicit detail of the eight lines that follow. The unwitting aspect of her deed is indicated by the phrase ἀϊδρείῃσι νόοιο, "in the ignorance of her mind," and its enormity by the phrase μέγα ἔργον, "a monstrous deed."[211] While the fact that she committed incest with her own son is deliberately withheld, it is powerfully evoked by the phrase μητέρα τ' Οἰδιπόδαο, "the mother of Oedipus," which is used to introduce her. No other heroine in the catalogue is introduced in this way— indeed they are all said to be the "daughters and wives" of heroes (*Odyssey* 11.227 and 329). Not until Epikaste, at the end of the first part of the catalogue, is the pretense that the catalogue is interested primarily in fathers and husbands dropped, and it is dropped immediately with the word μητέρα, "mother," implying "son."[212] The true purpose of the catalogue is about to be revealed in the first passage of the second part of the catalogue, where Chloris is of course important as a wife (Neleus is her husband), but, from the standpoint of the catalogue's real purpose, she is more important as a mother

211 The phrase μέγα ἔργον, "great deed" or "great misdeed," has a negative connotation in all ten of its occurrences in the *Odyssey* (on the other hand it is morally neutral in eight of nine occurrences in the *Iliad*). The closest parallel to *Odyssey* 11.272 is *Odyssey* 24.458, where the seer Halitherses characterizes as a μέγα ἔργον the conduct of the suitors in consuming Odysseus's property and dishonoring his wife: οἳ μέγα ἔργον ἔρεζον ἀτασθαλίῃσι κακῇσι, "who did a great misdeed in their evil recklessness." The phrase is also used twice of Aigisthos's corrupting of Agamemnon's wife in his absence (*Odyssey* 3.261 and 275). Cf. Jebb's comment on Sophocles *Women of Trachis* 1276f. that "μέγας, ['great'], is often nearly equivalent to δεινός, ['terrible'], as in μέγα τι παθεῖν, ['suffer something great'] (Xenophon *Anabasis* 5.8.17), etc."
212 Cf. n2.141 above.

(Nestor is her son). Epikaste, who is simultaneously a wife and a mother, and whose motherhood is emphasized, prepares the way for Chloris. The details of Epikaste's story in the rest of the passage as we have received it do not sharpen the transition to Chloris, but blunt it; to be effective the transition must be short. The two-line passage devoted to Epikaste not only prepares for the opening of the second part of the catalogue, it also balances the two-line passage at the end of the second part. In both parts of the catalogue the passages decrease steadily in length from first to last, emphasizing the first passage in each part.[213]

---

213 The eight-line addition to the Oedipus passage contains nothing that is *per se* un-Homeric. Contrary to the later legend, in which Oedipus is expelled from Thebes, these lines say that Oedipus remained and ruled in Thebes after his incest was discovered (*Odyssey* 11.274–276):

> ἄφαρ δ' ἀνάπυστα θεοὶ θέσαν ἀνθρώποισιν.
> ἀλλ' ὁ μὲν ἐν Θήβῃ πολυηράτῳ ἄλγεα πάσχων
> Καδμείων ἤνασσε θεῶν ὀλοὰς διὰ βουλάς.

> The gods at once made this known to men.
> But he suffering sorrows in lovely Thebes
> ruled over the Cadmeians by the destructive counsels of the gods.

Iliad 23.679–680, referring to a competitor at the funeral games of Oedipus in Thebes (ὅς ποτε Θήβας δ' ἦλθε δεδουπότος Οἰδιπόδαο / ἐς τάφον, "who once went to Thebes to the funeral of the fallen Oedipus"), agrees with *Odyssey* 11 in having Oedipus remain in Thebes until his death. So do other early sources. According to Hesiod when Oedipus died in Thebes, Argeia, the daughter of Adrastos (and the wife of Polyneices) went to his funeral; the scholia to *Iliad* 23.679 (Hesiod fr. 192 MW) contain this account: (ἡ διπλῆ) ὅτι βασιλεύοντα ἐν Θήβαις φησὶν ἀπολέσθαι, οὐχ ὡς οἱ νεώτεροι. καὶ Ἡσίοδος δέ φησιν ἐν Θήβαις αὐτοῦ ἀποθανόντος Ἀργείαν τὴν Ἀδράστου σὺν ἄλλοις ἐλθεῖν ἐπὶ τὴν κηδείαν Οἰδίποδος, "(This verse is marked with the *diplē*) because it says that he died while he ruled in Thebes, and not as later poets say. Hesiod too says that when he died in Thebes Argeia, Adrastos's daughter, went with others to his funeral." In a fragment of the *Thebaid*, when Oedipus curses his two sons, the scene is Thebes to judge by the "table of Kadmos" mentioned there (*Thebaid* fr. 2.2–3 Allen). For the *Oedipodia* our evidence is Pausanias 9.5.10–11 (*Oedipodia* fr. 1 Allen), who argues that Epikaste could not have borne Oedipus four children if the gods revealed their incest "immediately" (ἄφαρ), as in *Odyssey* 11.274, and who goes on to say that in the *Oedipodia* the mother was Euryganeia, not Epikaste; thus Oedipus in this poem would seem to have continued to rule in Thebes after marrying a second wife. This was perhaps the version that the author of the interpolated passage in *Odyssey* 11 followed. In this passage, where the gods immediately reveal the incest of Oedipus and Epikaste and Oedipus remains and rules, Epikaste hangs herself and visits unnamed woes on Oedipus from the grave (*Odyssey* 11.277–280):

> ἡ δ' ἔβη εἰς Ἀΐδαο πυλάρταο κρατεροῖο,
> ἀψαμένη βρόχον αἰπὺν ἀφ' ὑψηλοῖο μελάθρου
> ᾧ ἄχεϊ σχομένη· τῷ δ' ἄλγεα κάλλιπ' ὀπίσσω
> πολλὰ μάλ', ὅσσα τε μητρὸς ἐρινύες ἐκτελέουσι.

303

§2.154 When the 48 interpolated lines are removed from the catalogue
of heroines (24 from each part), the catalogue's bipartite structure stands
out starkly. In order to show this structure visually, I print the entire cata-
logue, minus interpolations, in two columns on the following facing pages
(Catalogue A): the introduction to the catalogue precedes the first column
and the conclusion to the catalogue follows the second column, and in
between the two columns themselves mirror each other perfectly. With the
text at hand let us recapitulate. The two parts of the catalogue each consist
of four passages, which decrease in length from first to last. The most impor-
tant passage in each column is now clearly the first and longest: Tyro (and
her son Neleus) in the first part; Chloris (and her son Nestor) in the second
part. The second passage in each part is shorter than the first passage, and
is directly related to it. In contrast to the fullness of detail in the Tyro and
Chloris passages which come first in each part, the passages that follow
them focus all but exclusively on the twin sons of the heroines in question:
the city founders Amphion and Zethos in the first part of the catalogue; the
twins Castor and Polydeuces in the second part. In both parts of the cata-
logue the second passage presents twins who remained together, and who
therefore contrast with Neleus, on the one hand, and Nestor on the other
hand, each of whom split from his twin brother. In the case of Nestor and
Periklymenos, the split meant the death of the warrior twin, Periklymenos.
This point is not made directly in the catalogue, but indirectly, in the contrast
presented by the Dioskouroi, both of whom remain alive beneath the earth,
even as they alternate between life and death on successive days. This is
the central message of the catalogue—the revelation of Nestor's twin myth
through the contrasting myth of the Dioskouroi—and there is no mistaking
this message once the structure of the catalogue is clear; it is worth noting
that the passages conveying this central message are further bound together
by the distinctive pattern with which they alone open (Καὶ Χλῶριν εἶδον/Καὶ
Λήδην εἶδον). The third passage in each part, which is again shorter than the

---

She went to the house of Hades, the strong gate-closer,
hanging a steep noose from the high roof-beam,
possessed by her grief; she left many sorrows behind for him,
as many as a mother's avenging spirits bring to pass.

The woes (*álgea*) that Oedipus suffers presumably refer to the war between his two sons,
but where did these children come from if the gods revealed the incest of Oedipus and
Epikaste immediately? A second wife would seem to be implied in *Odyssey* 11, as in the
Oedipodia, hence I regard the latter as a likely source for the interpolation in *Odyssey* 11.
What, if anything, the other sources (Hesiod and the *Thebaid*) had to say about this matter
is unknown.

passage that precedes it in each case, continues and reinforces the central theme of twins. In the second part of the catalogue the monstrous twins Otos and Ephialtes, who challenged the gods and were destroyed by them before reaching manhood, contrast pointedly with the Dioskouroi and their attainment of immortality and honor equal to the gods. This contrast between the Dioskouroi and the twins who follow them reinforces the contrast between the Dioskouroi and Nestor, in the passage that precedes them. The main purpose of the Dioskouroi's presence is to contrast their situation with Nestor's, and the idea of contrast with another pair of twins thus becomes a theme in itself, which is repeated in the short passage given to Otos and Ephialtes. In the first part of the catalogue the situation is similar, but also different. The third passage, which is again shorter than the passage that precedes it, concerns a twin, Heracles, but Heracles' twin brother, Iphicles, is not mentioned. Instead the different fathers of the two twins are both mentioned, for Alcmena is called the wife of the mortal Amphitryon, but she is said to have borne Heracles to the immortal Zeus. It was to the mortal Amphitryon that she bore the mortal Iphicles, and the different fates of the two brothers, with the son of Zeus alone achieving immortality, is thus suggested by leaving the son of Amphitryon out of account. The theme is thus the separation between twins, and this theme has been at issue in the first two passages of the first part of the catalogue. These passages both concern city-founding twins, but in the first passage Neleus splits from his brother Pelias to found Pylos, whereas in the second passage the twins Amphion and Zethos found Thebes together. The Heracles passage, while discontinuing the theme of city-founding twins, picks up the more important theme of the separation between twins, in the case of Neleus and Pelias, and their inseparability, in the case of Amphion and Zethos. The Heracles passage reinforces this theme rather than that of city-founding because separation versus inseparability is the crucial theme in the second part of the catalogue where the separation between Nestor and Periklymenos is realized only through the contrast with Castor and Polydeuces. Thus it is that the solitary Heracles, who was a twin but is not called one in the catalogue, prepares the way for Nestor, who likewise was a twin, but is instead presented as one of three brothers.[214]

214 Tyro's two sets of offspring (twins by a divine father, three sons by a mortal father) in a certain sense parallel Nestor's case, allowing him to be either one of two sons or one of three sons; a certain freedom of choice between two sons and three sons has been prepared for from the start of the catalogue. The catalogue thus exploits established tradition (Tyro's two sets of sons) to mark Nestor's ambiguous status as one of three sons but also a twin.

<table>
<tr><td>Introduction</td><td colspan="2">

Νῶϊ μὲν ὣς ἐπέεσσιν ἀμειβόμεθ', αἱ δὲ γυναῖκες
ἤλυθον, ὤτρυνεν γὰρ ἀγαυὴ Περσεφόνεια,
ὅσσαι ἀριστήων ἄλοχοι ἔσαν ἠδὲ θύγατρες.
αἱ δ' ἀμφ' αἷμα κελαινὸν ἀολλέες ἠγερέθοντο,
αὐτὰρ ἐγὼ βούλευον, ὅπως ἐρέοιμι ἑκάστην.
ἥδε δέ μοι κατὰ θυμὸν ἀρίστη φαίνετο βουλή·
σπασσάμενος τανύηκες ἄορ παχέος παρὰ μηροῦ
οὐκ εἴων πίνειν ἅμα πάσας αἷμα κελαινόν.
αἱ δὲ προμνηστῖναι ἐπήϊσαν, ἠδὲ ἑκάστη
ὃν γόνον ἐξαγόρευεν· ἐγὼ δ' ἐρέεινον ἁπάσας.
</td></tr>
</table>

I	(11)	Ἔνθ' ἦ τοι πρώτην Τυρὼ ἴδον εὐπατέρειαν, ἣ φάτο Σαλμωνῆος ἀμύμονος ἔκγονος εἶναι, φῆ δὲ Κρηθῆος γυνὴ ἔμμεναι Αἰολίδαο· ἣ ποταμοῦ ἠράσσατ' Ἐνιπῆος θείοιο, ὃς πολὺ κάλλιστος ποταμῶν ἐπὶ γαῖαν ἵησι· τῷ δ' ὑποκυσαμένη Πελίην τέκε καὶ Νηλῆα, τὼ κρατερὼ θεράποντε Διὸς μεγάλοιο γενέσθην· ἀμφοτέρω· Πελίης μὲν ἐν εὐρυχόρῳ Ἰαολκῷ ναῖε πολύρρηνος, ὁ δ' ἄρ' ἐν Πύλῳ ἠμαθόεντι. τοὺς δ' ἑτέρους Κρηθῆϊ τέκεν βασίλεια γυναικῶν, Αἴσονά τ' ἠδὲ Φέρητ' Ἀμυθάονά θ' ἱππιοχάρμην.
	14>	
II	(6)	Τὴν δὲ μέτ' Ἀντιόπην ἴδον, Ἀσωποῖο θύγατρα, ἣ δὴ καὶ Διὸς εὔχετ' ἐν ἀγκοίνησιν ἰαῦσαι, καί ῥ' ἔτεκεν δύο παῖδ', Ἀμφίονά τε Ζῆθόν τε, οἳ πρῶτοι Θήβης ἕδος ἔκτισαν ἑπταπύλοιο πύργωσάν τ', ἐπεὶ οὐ μὲν ἀπύργωτόν γ' ἐδύναντο ναιέμεν εὐρύχορον Θήβην, κρατερώ περ ἐόντε.
III	(3)	Τὴν δὲ μετ' Ἀλκμήνην ἴδον, Ἀμφιτρύωνος ἄκοιτιν, ἥ ῥ' Ἡρακλῆα θρασυμέμνονα θυμολέοντα γείνατ' ἐν ἀγκοίνησι Διὸς μεγάλοιο μιγεῖσα.
	2>	
IV	(2)	Μητέρα τ' Οἰδιπόδαο ἴδον, καλὴν Ἐπικάστην, ἣ μέγα ἔργον ἔρεξεν ἀϊδρείῃσι νόοιο.
	8>	
(22)	24	

Catalogue A: text.

I   (10)   Καὶ Χλῶριν εἶδον περικαλλέα, τήν ποτε Νηλεὺς
γῆμεν ἑὸν διὰ κάλλος, ἐπεὶ πόρε μυρία ἕδνα,
ὁπλοτάτην κούρην Ἀμφίονος Ἰασίδαο,
ὅς ποτ' ἐν Ὀρχομενῷ Μινυηΐῳ ἶφι ἄνασσεν·
ἡ δὲ Πύλου βασίλευε, τέκεν δέ οἱ ἀγλαὰ τέκνα,
Νέστορά τε Χρομίον τε Περικλύμενόν τ' ἀγέρωχον.
τοῖσι δ' ἐπ' ἰφθίμην Πηρὼ τέκε, θαῦμα βροτοῖσι,
τὴν πάντες μνώοντο περικτίται· οὐδέ τι Νηλεὺς
τῷ ἐδίδου, ὃς μὴ ἕλικας βόας εὐρυμετώπους
ἐκ Φυλάκης ἐλάσειε βίης Ἰφικληείης.

        7>

II   (7)   Καὶ Λήδην εἶδον, τὴν Τυνδαρέου παράκοιτιν,
ἥ ῥ' ὑπὸ Τυνδαρέῳ κρατερόφρονε γείνατο παῖδε,
Κάστορά θ' ἱππόδαμον καὶ πὺξ ἀγαθὸν Πολυδεύκεα,
τοὺς ἄμφω ζωοὺς κατέχει φυσίζοος αἶα·
οἳ καὶ νέρθεν γῆς τιμὴν πρὸς Ζηνὸς ἔχοντες
ἄλλοτε μὲν ζώουσ' ἑτερήμεροι, ἄλλοτε δ' αὖτε
τεθνᾶσιν· τιμὴν δὲ λελόγχασιν ἶσα θεοῖσι.

III   (4)   Τὴν δὲ μέτ' Ἰφιμέδειαν, Ἀλωῆος παράκοιτιν,
εἴσιδον, ἣ δὴ φάσκε Ποσειδάωνι μιγῆναι,
καί ῥ' ἔτεκεν δύο παῖδε, μινυνθαδίω δὲ γενέσθην,
Ὦτόν τ' ἀντίθεον τηλεκλειτόν τ' Ἐφιάλτην.

        12>
        5>

IV   (2)   Μαῖράν τε Κλυμένην τε ἴδον στυγερήν τ' Ἐριφύλην,
ἣ χρυσὸν φίλου ἀνδρὸς ἐδέξατο τιμήεντα.

    (23)   24

Conclusion   Πάσας δ' οὐκ ἂν ἐγὼ μυθήσομαι οὐδ' ὀνομήνω,
ὅσσας ἡρώων ἀλόχους ἴδον ἠδὲ θύγατρας·
πρὶν γάρ κεν καὶ νὺξ φθῖτ' ἄμβροτος. ἀλλὰ καὶ ὥρη
εὕδειν, ἢ ἐπὶ νῆα θοὴν ἐλθόντ' ἐς ἑταίρους
ἢ αὐτοῦ· πομπὴ δὲ θεοῖσ' ὑμῖν τε μελήσει.

Introduction		Thus the two of us exchanged words, and the women came, for revered Persephone roused them, all who were wives and daughters of noble men. They gathered in a crowd around the black blood, and I thought to myself how I might question each one. This seemed in my mind to be the best plan: drawing the sharp sword from my sturdy thigh, I did not let them all drink the black blood at once. But they came up one after the other, and each one told her birth, and I questioned them all.
I (11)		Then I saw Tyro first, born of a noble father, who said that she was the offspring of faultless Salmoneus, and said too that she was the wife of Kretheus, descended from Aeolus. She fell in love with a river, the divine Enipeus, who is much the most beautiful of rivers to pour forth on the earth.
	14>	To him she conceived and bore Pelias and Neleus, who became strong servants of great Zeus, both of them; Pelias in wide Iolkos had his home, owning many sheep, the other one in sandy Pylos. The queen among women bore her other sons to Kretheus, Aison and Pheres and the chariot-fighter Amythaon.
II (6)		And after her I saw Antiope, the daughter of Asopos, who claimed to have slept in the arms of Zeus himself, and she bore two sons, Amphion and Zethos, who first founded the seat of seven-gated Thebes and walled it, since they couldn't inhabit wide Thebes without walls, strong though they were.
III (3)		And after her I saw Alcmena, Amphitryon's wife, who bore bold-battling lion-hearted Heracles after making love in the arms of great Zeus.
	2>	
IV (2)		And I saw the mother of Oedipus, beautiful Epikaste, who did a monstrous deed in the ignorance of her mind.
	8>	
(22)	24	

Catalogue A: translation.

308

I (10)	And I saw beautiful Chloris, whom Neleus once married for her beauty after he gave countless wedding gifts, the youngest daughter of Amphion, Iasus's son, who once ruled with might over Minyan Orchomenus; but she reigned in Pylos and bore him splendid children, Nestor and Chromios and proud Periklymenos. After them she bore steadfast Pero, a wonder to mortals, whom all her neighbors wooed; but Neleus did not give her to anyone who did not drive the wide-browed spiral- horned cattle of mighty Iphiklos from Phylake.
7>	
II (7)	And I saw Leda, the wife of Tyndareus, who under Tyndareus gave birth to two strong-minded sons, horse-breaking Castor and Polydeuces, good with his fists, both of whom the life-giving earth holds alive; and they, having honor from Zeus even under the ground, are alive on alternate days, and then in turn they are dead; and they receive honor equal to the gods.
III (4)	And after her I saw Iphimedeia, the wife of Aloeus, who said that she made love with Poseidon and bore two sons, but they were short-lived, godlike Otos and far-famed Ephialtes.
12> 5>	
IV (2)	I saw Maira and Klymene and hateful Eriphyle, who took precious gold in exchange for her dear husband.

(23) 24

Conclusion   I could not say or name all
the wives and daughters of heroes that I saw;
immortal night would pass away first. But it is time
to sleep, either going to the swift ship and crew
or here; but my voyage will be up to the gods and to you.

§2.155 The last passage in each part of the catalogue is in each case the shortest, only two lines long. The function of these short passages no longer has to do with the theme of twins, which is fully worked out in the other six passages of the catalogue, the first three in each part. We have already seen that the function of the catalogue's very last passage, with the mention of three heroines in a single line, is simply to indicate a further indefinite multitude by way of conclusion: more heroines presented themselves in the underworld than Odysseus could name or tell of, just as he goes on to say. The only heroine among the final three to receive a brief elaboration is the sinner Eriphyle, who took a bribe of gold for the life of her husband, the seer Amphiaraos. We may now note the close parallel of the two-line passage that concludes the first part of the catalogue, for this too concerns a sinner, Epikaste, the mother and wife of Oedipus.[215] This parallel of course does not present itself until the catalogue concludes and the theme of the sinning woman has repeated itself in the case of Eriphyle. At that point, the entire bipartite structure of the catalogue has also become clear through the decreasing length of the passages in the two parts. The two-line passage devoted to Epikaste at the end of the first part is pivotal in this bipartite structure because of its eloquent brevity. This passage, which could hardly have been briefer, or more pointed in its brevity, is clearly perceived as a conclusion to the series of three passages that has just preceded it, in which each passage was shorter than the one before. Thus when the catalogue does not end at this point, but begins anew with a long and complex passage devoted to Nestor's mother Chloris, the catalogue's bipartite structure immediately manifests itself, and continues to work itself out through the repetition of an identical structure of four passages of decreasing length, the last of which is a two-line coda, just as in the first part.[216] There is no missing the bipartite structure in the catalogue's original form, and it is highly significant that this structure reveals itself first in the passage on Nestor. We have already seen that Nestor's deliberately unstated twin myth is the focus of the catalogue's structure in the arrangement of the five other passages that concern twins, most pointedly in the immediate juxtaposition of the passage with the Dioskouroi, but hardly less so in the case of the other four passages. While Nestor's own passage deliberately does not say that he was a twin, the

---

215 There is a contrast as well as a parallel in that Eriphyle was a conscious sinner, Epikaste an unconscious one.

216 The two-line Epikaste passage, by not stating its main point, but leaving it unstated, prepares for the same thing in Nestor's passage, which is the focus of the entire catalogue, and in which his twin myth is deliberately disguised.

focus of the other five passages on his passage just as deliberately says that he was. We may now go a step further and ask why the catalogue's highly unusual arrangement in two parallel parts was chosen. This double structure must have something to do with the catalogue's unstated point, namely Nestor's twin myth. This myth, which is the catalogue's central message, is realized only through indirect means, and the ultimate among these means is the catalogue's very bipartite structure. This structure denotes duality, and duality is the essence of Nestor's myth. Thus its own bipartite structure is the ultimate indirection by which the catalogue establishes Nestor's myth.

§2.156 The next point to note about the original form of the catalogue is that the parallelism between its two parts, while it is very close in terms of the overall length of each part—22 lines in the first part and 23 lines in the second part—is not rigid. The same is true of the individual passages when we compare their lengths, for only the two final passages are of exactly the same length, namely two lines each. The three initial passages in each part are all close in length when we compare the first part of the catalogue with the second part, but in every case there is a one-line difference: the passages that come first in each part are eleven and ten lines long, respectively; the passages that come second are six and seven lines long, respectively; and those that come third are three and four lines long, respectively. The reason for this indifference to an exact line count is that the catalogue's bipartite structure does not depend on an exact identity in terms of length for the two parts, but only on a close approximation. The only point at which an identical number of lines is easily perceptible, and has therefore been rendered, is in the final passage in each part because these passages are the shortest—two lines each. In the earlier passages the ear and the mind cannot detect the difference of a single line between corresponding passages in each part, and a rigid equivalence would thus serve no purpose. To the ear and the mind the parallelism between the two parts of the catalogue as it originally stood is completely clear from the relative lengths of the four passages in each part, which decrease from first to last, and from the approximate equivalence in length of the corresponding passages in each part.

§2.157 Although the catalogue's bipartite structure can be appreciated by the eye (I earlier arranged the catalogue on facing pages for just this purpose) it is clear that this structure was not created for the eye, but for the ear. I emphasize the oral nature of the original form of the catalogue in order to contrast it with the work of the interpolator, who added exactly 24 lines to each of the catalogue's two parts. To the interpolator an exact line count evidently did matter, and we are bound to ask why. The answer that immediately suggests itself is that the interpolator, who could not help but notice the catalogue's bipartite structure, used the medium of writing when he sought to preserve this bipartite structure by adding exactly the same number of lines (24) and the same number of passages (two expansions of existing passages and one outright addition) to each of the catalogue's two parts. While the catalogue that resulted from his efforts, which is the catalogue that has come down to us in the text of the *Odyssey*, is not readily perceived as a bipartite structure by either the ear or the eye, it was clearly the work of a literate poet, who used his eye as much as his ear in making his additions to a written text.[217]

§2.158 To look more closely into the nature of the interpolator's work, I begin by printing again the entire catalogue on the following two facing pages (Catalogue B), this time including the interpolated passages, which I indent to set them off from the catalogue in its original form. As we survey the interpolator's work, it is clear that he has preserved the careful balance between the two parts of the original catalogue in only two respects: the total number of lines is still one less in the first part, with 46, than in the second part, with 47, just as it was in the original catalogue, where the numbers were 22 and 23, respectively, and the two parts still correspond to one another in having the same number of passages, now five each instead of the original four each. These are the two basic aspects of the catalogue's original balance, hence it was these that the interpolator contrived to preserve. In doing so, however, he destroyed the original balance between the catalogue's two parts in nearly every other respect. The most disruptive addition was to Epikaste's passage, for in its original two-line form this passage signaled the transition from the first part of the catalogue to the second. Gone too, as a result of the interpolation, is the parallelism with the catalogue's two-line conclusion, for no comparable addition was made to this passage. On the other hand, the interpolator did expand both of the passages that stand first in the two parts of the catalogue, namely those containing Neleus and Nestor respectively, but even here he has destroyed the symmetry between the two passages by adding a much longer interpolation to Neleus's passage (fourteen lines) than to Nestor's (seven lines). Likewise there is no real balance between the two passages that the interpolator added outright to each part of the catalogue, except for the fact that they are the fourth passage in each part. In the first part the passage on Megara, the wife of Heracles, is only two lines long, and

---

217 I by no means wish to prejudge the relation between oral and written texts of the Homeric poems since too much is still unknown about this very issue. I believe that the observations offered above are correct, but I am aware that unconscious anachronisms may affect one's judgment in such a case. Cf. n2.173 above.

it concerns a single heroine. In the second part we have three Athenian hero-
ines grouped together in a longer five-line addition. The balance between
these two passages is purely formal, based on the count of items in a list, and
not on any more poetic consideration. The expansion of the story of Otos
and Ephialtes, the third passage in the catalogue's second part, is both very
long (twelve lines) and unbalanced by any addition to the third passage in
the catalogue's first part, which is devoted to Alcmena and her son Heracles.
There is thus the same imbalance between these two passages as between the
final two passages in each part. In effect, the expansion of Epikaste's story,
the last passage in the first part, has been "balanced" by the expansion of the
Aloadai's story, which, coming third in the second part, does not correspond
to it at all in terms of its placement. The effect of this "balancing," as of the
rest of the interpolator's work, has been to unbalance the two parts of the
catalogue all but completely.

§2.159 What was the interpolator's purpose in adding the passages
that he did to the catalogue? The first point to note is that all four of the
passages that the interpolator expanded were told so briefly in the original
catalogue as to omit in each case most of the actual story, which was alluded
to only briefly or suppressed altogether. These passages rather cried out to
have their stories told, and thus offered an interpolator both the tempta-
tion to ply his craft and a purchase on which to do so. The two-line passage
devoted to Epikaste is the clearest example of a brief allusion to a well-known
story that was simply left at that. The lack of specific detail in these two lines
invited the interpolator to add the rest of the story, or at least the heart of it,
as he did immediately with the phrase γημαμένη ᾧ υἷι, "marrying her own
son," from which he went on to Oedipus's murder of his father (ὁ δ' ὃν πατέρ'
ἐξεναρίξας) and his marrying of his mother (again the verb γῆμεν, starting
the second line of the interpolation, and matching the participle γημαμένη
used of Epikaste at the start of the first line). Similarly, in the story of the
Aloadai, the brief allusion to their fate—μινυνθαδίω δὲ γενέσθην, "but they
were short-lived"—invited the expansion that it duly received from the
interpolator. As for the wooing of Nestor's sister Pero, the original catalogue
told the story only in a negative form, that Neleus did not give his daughter
to anyone who did not drive off the cattle of Iphiklos, and the interpolator
seized on this to tell the story in a positive form, with mention of the "fault-
less seer" (Melampus) and his imprisonment and release by Iphiklos. Rather
different, however, is the expansion of the story of Tyro, for in the original
catalogue the story of her union with Poseidon was suppressed in favor of
an older version of the myth, in which she bore the twins Neleus and Pelias

ἔνθ' ἦ τοι πρώτην Τυρὼ ἴδον εὐπατέρειαν,   235
ἣ φάτο Σαλμωνῆος ἀμύμονος ἔκγονος εἶναι,
φῆ δὲ Κρηθῆος γυνὴ ἔμμεναι Αἰολίδαο·
ἣ ποταμοῦ ἠράσσατ' Ἐνιπῆος θείοιο,
ὃς πολὺ κάλλιστος ποταμῶν ἐπὶ γαῖαν ἵησι,

     καί ῥ' ἐπ' Ἐνιπῆος πωλέσκετο καλὰ ῥέεθρα.   240
τῷ δ' ἄρα εἰσάμενος γαιήοχος ἐννοσίγαιος
ἐν προχοῇς ποταμοῦ παρελέξατο δινήεντος·
πορφύρεον δ' ἄρα κῦμα περιστάθη οὔρεϊ ἶσον,
κυρτωθέν, κρύψεν δὲ θεὸν θνητήν τε γυναῖκα.

I   λῦσε δὲ παρθενίην ζώνην, κατὰ δ' ὕπνον ἔχευεν.   245
αὐτὰρ ἐπεί ῥ' ἐτέλεσσε θεὸς φιλοτήσια ἔργα,   14
ἔν τ' ἄρα οἱ φῦ χειρὶ ἔπος τ' ἔφατ' ἔκ τ' ὀνόμαζε·
"χαῖρε, γύναι, φιλότητι· περιπλομένου δ' ἐνιαυτοῦ
τέξεαι ἀγλαὰ τέκνα, ἐπεὶ οὐκ ἀποφώλιοι εὐναὶ
ἀθανάτων· σὺ δὲ τοὺς κομέειν ἀτιταλλέμεναί τε.   250
νῦν δ' ἔρχευ πρὸς δῶμα καὶ ἴσχεο μηδ' ὀνομήνης·
αὐτὰρ ἐγώ τοί εἰμι Ποσειδάων ἐνοσίχθων."
ὣς εἰπὼν ὑπὸ πόντον ἐδύσετο κυμαίνοντα.

ἡ δ' ὑποκυσαμένη Πελίην τέκε καὶ Νηλῆα,
τὼ κρατερὼ θεράποντε Διὸς μεγάλοιο γενέσθην   255
ἀμφοτέρω· Πελίης μὲν ἐν εὐρυχώρῳ Ἰαολκῷ
ναῖε πολύρρηνος, ὁ δ' ἄρ' ἐν Πύλῳ ἠμαθόεντι.
τοὺς δ' ἑτέρους Κρηθῆϊ τέκεν βασίλεια γυναικῶν,
Αἴσονά τ' ἠδὲ Φέρητ' Ἀμυθάονά θ' ἱππιοχάρμην.

II τὴν δὲ μέτ' Ἀντιόπην ἴδον, Ἀσωποῖο θύγατρα,   260
ἣ δὴ καὶ Διὸς εὔχετ' ἐν ἀγκοίνῃσιν ἰαῦσαι,
καί ῥ' ἔτεκεν δύο παῖδ', Ἀμφίονά τε Ζῆθόν τε,
οἳ πρῶτοι Θήβης ἕδος ἔκτισαν ἑπταπύλοιο
πύργωσάν τ', ἐπεὶ οὐ μὲν ἀπύργωτόν γ' ἐδύναντο
ναιέμεν εὐρύχορον Θήβην, κρατερώ περ ἐόντε.   265

III τὴν δὲ μετ' Ἀλκμήνην ἴδον, Ἀμφιτρύωνος ἄκοιτιν,
ἥ ῥ' Ἡρακλῆα θρασυμέμνονα θυμολέοντα
γείνατ' ἐν ἀγκοίνῃσι Διὸς μεγάλοιο μιγεῖσα·

IV   καὶ Μεγάρην, Κρείοντος ὑπερθύμοιο θύγατρα,
    τὴν ἔχεν Ἀμφιτρύωνος υἱὸς μένος αἰὲν ἀτειρής.   270   2

μητέρα τ' Οἰδιπόδαο ἴδον, καλὴν Ἐπικάστην,
ἣ μέγα ἔργον ἔρεξεν ἀϊδρείῃσι νόοιο

    γημαμένη ᾧ υἷϊ· ὁ δ' ὃν πατέρ' ἐξεναρίξας
    γῆμεν· ἄφαρ δ' ἀνάπυστα θεοὶ θέσαν ἀνθρώποισιν.
    ἀλλ' ὁ μὲν ἐν Θήβῃ πολυηράτῳ ἄλγεα πάσχων   275
V   Καδμείων ἤνασσε θεῶν ὀλοὰς διὰ βουλάς·
    ἡ δ' ἔβη εἰς Ἀΐδαο πυλάρταο κρατεροῖο,   8
    ἁψαμένη βρόχον αἰπὺν ἀφ' ὑψηλοῖο μελάθρου
    ᾧ ἄχεϊ σχομένη· τῷ δ' ἄλγεα κάλλιπ' ὀπίσσω
    πολλὰ μάλ', ὅσσα τε μητρὸς ἐρινύες ἐκτελέουσι.   280

Catalogue B: text.

καὶ Χλῶριν εἶδον περικαλλέα, τήν ποτε Νηλεὺς
γῆμεν ἑὸν διὰ κάλλος, ἐπεὶ πόρε μυρία ἕδνα,
ὁπλοτάτην κούρην Ἀμφίονος Ἰασίδαο,
ὅς ποτ᾽ ἐν Ὀρχομενῷ Μινυηΐῳ ἶφι ἄνασσεν·
ἡ δὲ Πύλου βασίλευε, τέκεν δέ οἱ ἀγλαὰ τέκνα,   285
Νέστορά τε Χρομίον τε Περικλύμενόν τ᾽ ἀγέρωχον.

    τοῖσι δ᾽ ἐπ᾽ ἰφθίμην Πηρὼ τέκε, θαῦμα βροτοῖσι,
    τὴν πάντες μνώοντο περικτίται· οὐδέ τι Νηλεὺς

I   τῷ ἐδίδου, ὃς μὴ ἕλικας βόας εὐρυμετώπους
    ἐκ Φυλάκης ἐλάσειε βίης Ἰφικληείης   290

    ἀργαλέας. τὰς δ᾽ οἶος ὑπέσχετο μάντις ἀμύμων
    ἐξελάαν· χαλεπὴ δὲ θεοῦ κατὰ μοῖρα πέδησε
    δεσμοί τ᾽ ἀργαλέοι καὶ βουκόλοι ἀγροιῶται.
    ἀλλ᾽ ὅτε δὴ μῆνές τε καὶ ἡμέραι ἐξετελεῦντο   7
    ἂψ περιτελλομένου ἔτεος καὶ ἐπήλυθον ὧραι,   295
    καὶ τότε δή μιν ἔλυσε βίη Ἰφικληείη
    θέσφατα πάντ᾽ εἰπόντα· Διὸς δ᾽ ἐτελείετο βουλή.

    καὶ Λήδην εἶδον, τὴν Τυνδαρέου παράκοιτιν,
    ἥ ῥ᾽ ὑπὸ Τυνδαρέῳ κρατερόφρονε γείνατο παῖδε,
    Κάστορά θ᾽ ἱππόδαμον καὶ πὺξ ἀγαθὸν Πολυδεύκεα,   300
II   τοὺς ἄμφω ζωοὺς κατέχει φυσίζοος αἶα·
    οἳ καὶ νέρθεν γῆς τιμὴν πρὸς Ζηνὸς ἔχοντες
    ἄλλοτε μὲν ζώουσ᾽ ἑτερήμεροι, ἄλλοτε δ᾽ αὖτε
    τεθνᾶσιν· τιμὴν δὲ λελόγχασιν ἶσα θεοῖσι.

    τὴν δὲ μέτ᾽ Ἰφιμέδειαν, Ἀλωῆος παράκοιτιν,   305
    εἴσιδον, ἣ δὴ φάσκε Ποσειδάωνι μιγῆναι,
    καί ῥ᾽ ἔτεκεν δύο παῖδε, μινυνθαδίω δὲ γενέσθην,
    Ὦτόν τ᾽ ἀντίθεον τηλεκλειτόν τ᾽ Ἐφιάλτην,

    οὓς δὴ μηκίστους θρέψε ζείδωρος ἄρουρα
    καὶ πολὺ καλλίστους μετά γε κλυτὸν Ὠρίωνα·   310
    ἐννέωροι γὰρ τοί γε καὶ ἐννεαπήχεες ἦσαν
III   εὖρος, ἀτὰρ μῆκός γε γενέσθην ἐννεόργυιοι.
    οἵ ῥα καὶ ἀθανάτοισιν ἀπειλήτην ἐν Ὀλύμπῳ
    φυλόπιδα στήσειν πολυάϊκος πολέμοιο.   12
    Ὄσσαν ἐπ᾽ Οὐλύμπῳ μέμασαν θέμεν, αὐτὰρ ἐπ᾽ Ὄσσῃ   315
    Πήλιον εἰνοσίφυλλον, ἵν᾽ οὐρανὸς ἀμβατὸς εἴη.
    καί νύ κεν ἐξετέλεσσαν, εἰ ἥβης μέτρον ἵκοντο·
    ἀλλ᾽ ὄλεσεν Διὸς υἱός, ὃν ἠΰκομος τέκε Λητώ,
    ἀμφοτέρω, πρίν σφωϊν ὑπὸ κροτάφοισιν ἰούλους
    ἀνθῆσαι πυκάσαι τε γένυς εὐανθέϊ λάχνῃ.   320

    Φαίδρην τε Πρόκριν τε ἴδον καλήν τ᾽ Ἀριάδνην,
    κούρην Μίνωος ὀλοόφρονος, ἥν ποτε Θησεὺς
IV   ἐκ Κρήτης ἐς γουνὸν Ἀθηνάων ἱεράων
    ἦγε μέν, οὐδ᾽ ἀπόνητο· πάρος δέ μιν Ἄρτεμις ἔκτα   5
    Δίῃ ἐν ἀμφιρύτῃ Διονύσου μαρτυρίῃσι.   325

V   Μαῖράν τε Κλυμένην τε ἴδον στυγερήν τ᾽ Ἐριφύλην,
    ἣ χρυσὸν φίλου ἀνδρὸς ἐδέξατο τιμήεντα.

Then I saw Tyro first, born of a noble father,   235
who said that she was the offspring of faultless Salmoneus,
and said too that she was the wife of Kretheus, descended from Aeolus.
She fell in love with a river, the divine Enipeus,
who is much the most beautiful of rivers to pour forth on the earth,

I

and she wandered along the Enipeus's beautiful streams.   240
Taking his shape the earthholder, the earthshaker,
lay with her in the mouth of the eddying river;
a dark wave as big as a mountain rose up around them,
curved, and hid the god and the mortal woman.
He loosened her maiden's girdle and poured sleep over her.   245
And when the god finished the deeds of love,   14
he took her by the hand and spoke a word and called her by name:
"Rejoice, woman, in this act of love; as the year returns
you will bear splendid children, since the beds of the immortals are not in vain;
but you, take care of them and raise them.   250
Now go home and restrain yourself and don't say my name;
I am indeed Poseidon the earthshaker."
So saying he sank beneath the wavy sea.

And she conceived and bore Pelias and Neleus,
who became strong servants of great Zeus,   255
both of them; Pelias in wide Iolkos
had his home, owning many sheep, the other one in sandy Pylos.
The queen among women bore her other sons to Kretheus,
Aison and Pheres and the chariot-fighter Amythaon.

II

And after her I saw Antiope, the daughter of Asopos,   260
who claimed to have slept in the arms of Zeus himself,
and she bore two sons, Amphion and Zethos,
who first founded the seat of seven-gated Thebes
and walled it, since they couldn't inhabit wide Thebes
without walls, even though they were strong.   265

III

And after her I saw Alcmena, Amphitryon's wife,
who bore bold-fighting lion-hearted Heracles
after making love in the arms of great Zeus;

IV

and Megara, bold Kreion's daughter,   2
whom Amphitryon's son never tiring in his strength had.   270

And I saw the mother of Oedipus, beautiful Epikaste,
who did a monstrous deed in the ignorance of her mind

V

marrying her own son; and he, killing his own father,
married her; the gods at once made this known to men.
But he suffering sorrows in lovely Thebes   275
ruled over the Cadmeians by the destructive counsels of the gods;   8
she went to the house of Hades, the strong gate-closer,
fastening a steep noose from the high roof-beam,
possessed by her grief; she left many sorrows behind for him,
as many as a mother's avenging spirits bring to pass.   280

Catalogue B: translation.

And I saw beautiful Chloris, whom Neleus once
married for her beauty after he gave countless wedding gifts,
the youngest daughter of Amphion, Iasus's son,
who once ruled with might over Minyan Orchomenus;
but she reigned in Pylos and bore him splendid children,   285
Nestor and Chromios and proud Periklymenos.
After them she bore steadfast Pero, a wonder to mortals,
whom all her neighbors wooed; but Neleus did not
I   give her to anyone who did not drive the wide-browed spiral-horned cattle
of mighty Iphiklos from Phylake,   290

> hard (to drive). Those (cattle) only the faultless prophet promised
> to drive away; but he was bound by the god's harsh fate,
> painful bonds, and rustic cowherds.
> But when the months and days were completed   7
> as the year came around, and the seasons returned,   295
> then mighty Iphiklos freed him,
> after he spoke all the prophecies; and the will of Zeus was accomplished.

And I saw Leda, the wife of Tyndareus,
who under Tyndareus gave birth to two strong-minded sons,
horse-breaking Castor and Polydeuces, good with his fists,   300
II   both of whom the life-giving earth holds alive;
and they, having honor from Zeus even under the ground,
are alive on alternate days, and then in turn
they are dead; and they receive honor equal to the gods.

And after her I saw Iphimedeia, the wife of Aloeus,   305
who said that she made love with Poseidon
and bore two sons, but they were short-lived,
godlike Otos and far-famed Ephialtes,

> whom indeed the grain-giving earth raised to be the biggest
> and much the most beautiful after famous Orion;   310
> for they were nine years old and nine cubits
> wide, and they were nine fathoms tall.
III Against the immortals they threatened
> to set the strife of violent war on Olympus.   12
> They strove to put Ossa on top of Olympus, and on top of Ossa   315
> Pelion, with its fluttering leaves, so that the sky could be ascended.
> And they would have accomplished this if they had reached young manhood;
> but the son of Zeus, whom beautiful-haired Leto bore, destroyed them
> both before the hair blossomed on their cheeks beneath their temples
> and covered their chins with beautifully-flowering down.   320

> I saw Phaedra and Prokris and beautiful Ariadne,
> the daughter of destructive-minded Minos, whom Theseus once
IV brought from Crete to the hill of sacred Athens,   5
> but he did not enjoy her; Artemis killed her first
> on sea-swept Dia on the evidence of Dionysus.   325

V   I saw Maira and Klymene and hateful Eriphyle,
> who took precious gold in exchange for her dear husband.

317

to the river god Enipeus. The passage that the interpolator has inserted into the middle of the original version brings Poseidon back into the story by having him take on the likeness of Enipeus and thus lie with Tyro. To the Ionians for whom the original catalogue was composed, and for the Milesians in particular, Poseidon's role in the story was always implied, even though Enipeus alone was present in it.[218] Non-Ionians, however, may not have been as attuned to the close connection between Enipeus and Poseidon. There was thus perhaps an element of correction in the interpolator's addition to the story, or at least the desire to bring the story back into line with what was more commonly known.

§2.160 The interpolator's motivation, then, certainly included the desire to fill in stories that were only alluded to or implied in the original catalogue. But there must have been more, for the desire to tell omitted stories, even the desire to modernize one of the stories on a basic point, does not explain the profound change that the interpolator has worked on the catalogue while trying to preserve its structure. We know that the interpolator was an Athenian from the three Attic heroines that he added to the catalogue in his final passage. As noted previously, this passage was the interpolator's signature, which, far from being disguised, seems to exhibit itself rather proudly as an Athenian product. As for the date of the interpolations, the first point to note is that two of the passages (that on Epikaste and Oedipus and that on Ariadne and Theseus) contain preclassical versions of the myths of the figures that they feature, and the interpolations are thus likely to belong to the sixth century BC at the latest. We have seen that the Hesiodic catalogues were used by the interpolator in at least two of his expansions of existing passages (Tyro and Chloris), and may have been used in his other two expansions as well (Epikaste and Iphimedeia). The use of the Hesiodic catalogues also seems consistent with a sixth century BC date.[219] The evidence of time and place makes it highly likely that the inter-

218 For the cult of Poseidon Enipeus in Miletus see n2.178 above.
219 Martin West dates the Hesiodic catalogues to sixth-century Athens (West 1985:130–137, 169–171; but cf. Janko 1982:85–87, 221–225, who argues for an earlier date and disputes an Attic origin). Although the poems of the epic cycle cannot be specifically detected in the interpolations of *Odyssey* 11, they were probably another source (cf. n2.213 above on the possible use of the *Oedipodia* in the Epikaste passage). The poems of the epic cycle are generally dated to the seventh and sixth centuries, and in their final form (as far as fragments show) they have been dated as late as the late sixth century (see Davies 1989, and for *Cypria* fr. 1 in particular, pp. 98–100). As discussed in n2.206 above the tradition that Heracles killed Megara's children can be inferred for the *Cypria*; it is also directly attested for Stesichorus in the mid-sixth century (Pausanias 9.11.2, who cites Panyassis as well). Is the omission of Megara's children in *Odyssey* 11 a silent correction of the tradition for their murder? For the likelihood that the interpolator took an interest in Heracles' reputation,

polations were created for that elusive artifact of sixth-century Athens, the Peisistratean recension of the Homeric poems. If so, we have found not only the occasion, but also the reason for the interpolations. For the Athenian tyrant Peisistratos, the alleged prime mover of the "recension" that bears his name, claimed descent from Nestor and Neleus through Nestor's son Peisistratos, his supposed namesake. To Peisistratos the tyrant, with his pretensions to descent from Neleus and Nestor (and thus ultimately from Poseidon), the catalogue of heroines in *Odyssey* 11, in which pride of place goes to precisely Neleus and Nestor, must have been an important part of the poems themselves. That his pretensions were in all likelihood no more than that would only increase his interest in the passage that concerned his pedigree.[220] But to make the passage apply to his pedigree the catalogue needed an Athenian dimension to it, and

see §2.164 below. In the fifth century Pindar *Isthmian* 4.67–70 sought to correct the tradition for Heracles' murder of his children (cf. Wilamowitz 1895:81–82). The motivation of Pindar as a Theban is clear; did a sixth-century Athenian intend a similar correction?

220 See Shapiro 1989 Chapter 6 ("Poseidon, *Stammvater* of the Tyrants") for the importance of Poseidon to Peisistratos and his pedigree; cf. also Shapiro 1983. Shapiro thinks that Peisistratos's claim to Neleid descent was based on fact. He addresses an interesting point, but one that does not bear directly on the actual question, when he notes that there was a cult of Poseidon Helikonios in the Attic village of Agrai (Shapiro 1989:102; reference to Eustathius *ad Iliadem* 361.36 should instead be to Kleidemos *FGrHist* 323 F 1). There was an associated cult of Demeter Thesmophoros in the same location (Kleidemos *FGrHist* 323 F 1). Shapiro proposes to date the cult of Poseidon Helikonios to the end of the Bronze Age, and to see it as the origin of the same cult in Ionia. Peisistratos's birth in the same region of Attica would then associate him with the colonists of Neleid descent who founded a new cult of Poseidon Helikonios in Ionia. Perhaps a stronger argument for the genuineness of Peisistratos's claim is the existence of an archon in 669/8 BC named Peisistratos: "An earlier namesake, surely an ancestor of the tyrant, was Archon in 669/8 BC [Cadoux 1948:90]. The family's claim to descent from the Neleids was thus no invention of the tyrant, but reached back well into the Eupatrid period" (Shapiro 1989:103; cf. Shapiro 1983:89). I think that the family probably did claim this Pylian connection as early as the archon Peisistratos, but that they did so in imitation of the Neleids of Miletus and the Medontids of Athens. The archons succeeded the Medontids as rulers in Athens. The archon Peisistratos was among the first yearly archons, the list of whom begins in 683/2 BC. The last Medontid ruler was Hippomenes, whose cruelty led to the end of his family's rule. It makes sense that an early archon (669/8 BC) claimed descent from a different branch of the same family that had now been removed from power, but only, I think, if the prestige of the Homeric poems was a factor. We must bear in mind that the Medontids and Neleids saw themselves as each others' cousins; if the Homeric poems were important to the Milesian Neleids, these poems were probably not unknown to their Athenian cousins the Medontids. If a family named a child after a son of Nestor at about 700 BC in order to claim a pedigree rivaling the pedigree of the Medontids, now removed from office (or perhaps about to be removed), this, in my opinion, says a great deal about the degree to which the Homeric poems were already known in Athens. Peisistratos the tyrant was hardly the first to introduce these poems to Athens; Solon knew them, and I surmise that other Athenians before Solon did as well. See below §3.90 and §4.43–§4.44 for further discussion.

this is exactly what it received from the interpolator. The reworked version of the catalogue still gives pride of place to Neleus and Nestor—and to Neleus in particular—but the relevance of these figures has been shifted to an Athenian perspective, so as to embrace their supposed Athenian descendant. The other change that needed to be made to the catalogue was in the passage on the birth of Neleus. It would not do to have Neleus, at the beginning of the Athenian tyrant's pedigree, called the son of a minor river god in Thessaly, when Poseidon was known to be the father. The indignity was all the greater in that the catalogue makes Poseidon or Zeus the father of all the other twin figures, including Amphion and Zethos (Zeus is the father), Heracles (Zeus is the father), Castor and Polydeuces (Tyndareus is called the father, but Zeus, the divine father, is also present in the passage), and the Aloadai (Poseidon is the father).[221] The longest passage that the interpolator inserted into the catalogue, at fourteen lines, is the one that occurs first, and now we see why. This passage reestablishes Poseidon as progenitor of the Neleids and their supposed Athenian descendant and it does so with full dramatic flourish, including a speech by the god to the heroine whom he has just deceived with his disguise about the splendid children that she will bear him.[222] Earlier, when we first considered the interpolation of this passage, I remarked that it is difficult at first to read this passage without the interpolation because it is that very passage that is most vivid and memorable. That, we may now say, is exactly what it is meant to be. The passage on Tyro, with its eleven original and fourteen interpolated lines, is by far the longest passage in the catalogue (Nestor's passage is seven lines shorter, the Aloadai's passage is eight lines shorter). This passage now dominates the catalogue as well as simply heading it. Thus the interpolator has not only corrected the out-of-date version of Neleus's birth in the original catalogue; he has made an indelible impression with his own correction. Surely this was his primary object in making over the catalogue of heroines in *Odyssey* 11.

§2.161 If we have correctly identified the origin of the interpolations in *Odyssey* 11 as the "Peisistratean recension," we can use these interpolations as primary evidence for what this "recension" actually was.[223] As the anal-

---

221 Note that after the birth of twins to the local god Enipeus in the first passage, the second passage features Antiope "who *indeed* (*dḗ*) claimed that she lay in the arms *even* (*kaí*) of Zeus" (ἣ δὴ καὶ Διὸς εὔχετ᾽ ἐν ἀγκοίνῃσιν ἰαῦσαι). A contrast with the preceding passage seems intended by the word "even," and I take this as a highlighting of the (relative) lack of pretension in Tyro's giving birth to twins by Enipeus. Otherwise I do not see the point of the word *kaí*.

222 When Poseidon says to Tyro that "the beds of the immortals are not in vain" (*Odyssey* 11.249–250), we may well imagine Peisistratos as the ultimate object of these words.

223 We can also go a long way in saying what it was not, namely the origin of the Homeric poems

ysis above has shown, there was in Athens, in all likelihood, a written text to which a literate interpolator could and did make additions.[224] Whatever the merits of other aspects of the ancient tradition for a Peisistratean recension (and the merits vary with the aspect) there is thus reason to believe the tradition of interpolations made to the Homeric text.[225]

§2.162 Chief among the interpolations alleged in antiquity is *Iliad* 2.558, in the Catalogue of Ships, which says that Ajax stationed his twelve ships from Salamis where the Athenian battle lines stood: Peisistratos or Solon is supposed to have inserted this line into the text of the *Iliad* to justify the Athenian capture of Salamis from the Megarians in the time of Solon in a campaign in which the young Peisistratos is also said to have played a part.[226]

---

themselves. Pade 1983:13–14, having detected the influence of Peisistratos in the catalogue of heroines, draws the conclusion that the Homeric poems as a whole were composed at the request of the Athenian tyrant or his sons (cf. also Larson 2000). Murray 1934:312–314 and Jensen 1980:167, whom Pade cites, hold similar views regarding a Peisistratean recension, and for them as well the role of Nestor and his family in the poems is one reason. As far as the catalogue of heroines is concerned, once we distinguish between an earlier Ionian version and a later Athenian version, the Athenian claim to authorship of the poems on the basis of the catalogue disappears. It then remains to show only that Nestor's role in the poems belongs with the Ionian version of the catalogue, i.e. that it too is Ionian, not Athenian.

224 As stated earlier (n2.217 above) I do not wish to minimize the part played by oral transmission of the Homeric text, which in some environments may have continued for a long time. While there must have been a written text to regulate the oral performance of the Homeric poems at the Panathenaia, too little is known to rule out an oral aspect to the process of interpolation even in this context. For an evolutionary model of Homeric transmission, including the Athenian phase, see Nagy 1992 and 1996:29–112.

225 Allen 1924:226–238 distinguishes four areas of ancient evidence bearing on the question of a Peisistratean recension: 1) passages dealing with the performance of the poems at the Panathenaia (this tradition is generally credible); 2) evidence for the transport of the poems to Athens (the claim in "Plato" *Hipparchus* 228b that Peisistratos's son Hipparchus was the first to bring the poems to Athens is not credible; cf. n2.220 above and, for what may explain the claim, Ritoók 1993:48); 3) passages asserting the collection of the lays (this cannot refer to the actual genesis of the Homeric poems, nor is the inclusion of anything as major as *Iliad* 10 at all likely at this stage; cf. the following point); 4) passages attesting interpolations: Allen 234–238 lists five alleged interpolations, which vary in length from a single letter (Γονόεσσαν for Δονόεσσαν, *Iliad* 2.573) to the whole of *Iliad* 10 (according to the scholia at the beginning of *Iliad* 10 this book was composed as a separate poem by Homer and added to the text of the *Iliad* by Peisistratos); the other three alleged interpolations are each a single line (*Iliad* 2.558, *Odyssey* 11.604, and *Odyssey* 11.631). The difference in scale between *Iliad* 10 and the other four instances speaks for itself.

226 Much is uncertain in the conflict between Athens and Megara over Salamis. Legon 1981:101, 122–131, 136–139 reconstructs events as follows: Megara captured Salamis from Athens in the seventh century to protect its own shipping; Solon, at the beginning of his career in the early sixth century, instigated a war to recapture it; Peisistratos, who is said to have played a part in this war but almost certainly did not, came to power thirty years later and by capturing Nisaea forced Megara to accept arbitration of the continuing dispute over

So the Megarians claimed, who had an alternative version of *Iliad* 2.557–558 that made no mention of Athens, and which they claimed was genuine. There has never been consensus on the merits of the Megarians' charge of an Athenian forgery, but there is I think more reason to credit the charge with the evidence of the catalogue of heroines to compare.[227]

§2.163 The same may be said of Plutarch's report (*Theseus* 20) of what the Megarian historian Hereas claimed in the fourth or third century BC, namely that Peisistratos inserted into *Odyssey* 11 a line that names Theseus and Peirithoos as heroes whom Odysseus wished to see in the underworld had he been allowed to stay there longer (*Odyssey* 11.631); Peisistratos inserted this line, Hereas charged, to please the Athenians. In the same passage Plutarch repeats a second charge of Hereas which concerns the works of Hesiod but is directly relevant to the catalogue of heroines in *Odyssey* 11. Hereas claimed that Peisistratos removed from the works of Hesiod a line concerning Theseus's desertion of Ariadne; according to this line (Hesiod fr. 298 MW) Theseus deserted Ariadne because he had fallen in love with another woman, namely Aigle: δεινὸς γάρ μιν ἔτειρεν ἔρως Πανοπηΐδος Αἴγλης, "for a terrible passion for Aigle, the daughter of Panopeus, afflicted him."[228] The report that Peisistratos removed this line

---

Salamis; the Spartans arbitrated the dispute and the aged Solon put the case for Athens, which included the allegedly interpolated line *Iliad* 2.558; because of his age Solon could not have done this later than the 560s or early 550s, in the early years of Peisistratos's rule (Legon 1981:138–139). Legon suggests that the Megarians were willing to give up all claims to Salamis at this time so long as they got back their port of Nisaea. In any case the Spartans awarded Salamis to Athens. The fullest source for Solon's role in the arbitration is Plutarch *Solon* 10; cf. also Strabo 9.1.10; Diogenes Laertius 1.46–48; Aristotle *Rhetoric* 1375b29–30.

227 Allen, who disbelieves the tradition for a Peisistratean recension, thinks that the Megarians forged their own version of *Iliad* 2.557–558 and invented the story that the Athenians forged their version (Allen 1924:245–246); Legon's assessment, that "neither the Athenian nor Megarian couplet inspires confidence," seems closer to the truth to me (Legon 1981:138n8).

228 The line removed by Peisistratos has been preserved for us (Hesiod fr. 298 MW), but not the context from which it was taken. Plutarch *Theseus* 20.1 makes it clear that the word γάρ, "for," in this line relates to Theseus's desertion of Ariadne. Before quoting the line Plutarch says that many stories are still told about Ariadne: some say that she hung herself when she was deserted by Theseus, others say that she was brought by sailors to Naxos to live with a priest of Dionysos, and that she had been abandoned because Theseus had fallen in love with another woman. Here Plutarch cites the verse of Hesiod, and he states Hereas's charge about it, and he repeats Hereas's further charge that Peisistratos interpolated line 11.631 into the text of the *Odyssey*: ἀπολειφθῆναι δὲ [sc. Ἀριάδνην] τοῦ Θησέως ἐρῶντος ἑτέρας· "δεινὸς γάρ μιν ἔτειρεν ἔρως Πανοπηΐδος Αἴγλης." τοῦτο γὰρ τὸ ἔπος ἐκ τῶν Ἡσιόδου Πεισίστρατον ἐξελεῖν φησιν Ἡρέας ὁ Μεγαρεύς, ὥσπερ αὖ πάλιν ἐμβαλεῖν εἰς τὴν Ὁμήρου νέκυιαν τὸ "Θησέα Πειρίθοόν τε θεῶν ἀριδείκετα τέκνα" χαριζόμενον Ἀθηναίοις. "[Others say that] she was left by Theseus who desired another woman: 'for a

from Hesiod in order to defend the reputation of the Athenian hero Theseus
offers striking support to the argument that it was likewise Peisistratos who
was responsible for the interpolations in the catalogue of *Odyssey* 11. The last of
the interpolated passages in the catalogue, as we have seen, similarly defends
the reputation of Theseus from the charge of deserting Ariadne by saying that
Artemis killed her on the evidence of Dionysus. Theseus, "who was bringing
her to the hill of holy Athens," clearly did not desert her, or have anything to
do with her death. The evidence at this point is mutually reinforcing, for the
interpolated passage of the catalogue, with its defense of Theseus, in turn lends
greater credibility to the claims of Hereas, at least regarding the removal of an
offending line of Hesiod on the part of the Athenian tyrant Peisistratos.[229]

§2.164 The final example of alleged interpolation in the Peisistratean
recension is *Odyssey* 11.604. This line concludes a passage about Heracles,
whose ghost Odysseus sees in the underworld, but who "himself" dwells
among the gods and has Hebe for a wife (*Odyssey* 11.602–604):

εἴδωλον· αὐτὸς δὲ μετ' ἀθανάτοισι θεοῖσι

τέρπεται ἐν θαλίῃς καὶ ἔχει καλλίσφυρον Ἥβην,

παῖδα Διὸς μεγάλοιο καὶ Ἥρης χρυσοπεδίλου.

...his likeness; but he himself among the immortal gods
delights in abundance and possesses beautiful-ankled Hebe,
the child of great Zeus and golden-sandaled Hera.

---

terrible passion for Aigle, the daughter of Panopeus, afflicted him." Hereas the Megarian
says that Peisistratos removed this verse from the poems of Hesiod, just as he inserted
into Homer's Nekyia the verse 'Theseus and Peirithoos, illustrious children of the gods'
to gratify the Athenians" (*Theseus* 20.1–2). Plutarch implies that in his day the Hesiodic
line was no longer part of the text of Hesiod, and this is borne out by Athenaeus 13.557b,
who cites Hesiod for the fact that Theseus wed Hippe and Aigle, but who then cites
Kerkops (not Hesiod) for Aigle as the reason that Theseus broke his oath to Ariadne; the
passage follows and enlarges a list of Theseus's wives (carried off or legally wed) found in
the Atthidographer Istros: Ἡσίοδος δέ φησιν καὶ Ἵππην καὶ Αἴγλην, δι' ἣν καὶ τοὺς πρὸς
Ἀριάδνην ὅρκους παρέβη, ὥς φησι Κέρκωψ, "Hesiod says also Hippe and Aigle, because of
whom he broke his oath to Ariadne, as Kerkops says." Athenaeus would have cited Hesiod
for Theseus's treachery if the line in question had still been part of the Hesiodic text.
229 It is noteworthy that the interpolator, who made use of the Hesiodic catalogues to expand
other passages in *Odyssey* 11, rejected the Hesiodic version of Ariadne's fate as attested by
fr. 298 MW (see n2.228 above). For the different traditions regarding Ariadne see Barrett
1964 on Euripides *Hippolytus* 339 and West 1966 on Hesiod *Theogony* 949. West comments
as follows: "Her union with Dionysus is sometimes put in Crete..., though much more
often in Naxos, where Theseus left her (first in fr. 298). A different version, perhaps older,
is preserved in *Odyssey* 11.321–325: Theseus was taking her to Athens, but Dionysus drew
attention to the elopement, and Artemis killed Ariadne on Dia."

All three of these lines have been considered spurious, and line 604 in partic-
ular was athetized according to the Homeric scholia.[230] This very line is found
three times in Hesiod, where in each case it also describes Hebe as the wife of
Heracles.[231] The scholiast says not only that this line of the *Odyssey* was athe-
tized, but that it was inserted into the *Odyssey* by Onomakritos, the poet who
was later exiled from Athens by Peisistratos's son Hipparchus for forging an
oracle of Musaeus.[232] Onomakritos was exiled by Hipparchus because he was
caught in the act of forgery and exposed by a fellow poet, Lasos of Hermione.[233]

230 The scholia to *Odyssey* 11.604 refer to the athetesis of only this line: τοῦτον ὑπὸ
'Ονομακρίτου ἐμπεποιῆσθαί φασιν. ἠθέτηται δέ, "This line they say was inserted by
Onomakritos. It is athetized." The continuation of the scholium suggests that at least some
(ἔνιοι) wished to reject line 604 but to keep line 603: ἔνιοι δὲ οὐ τὴν οἰνοχόον "Ηβην, ἀλλὰ
τὴν ἑαυτοῦ ἀνδρείαν, "Some say that Hebe does not refer to the wine-pourer but to his
own manliness (i.e. to Heracles' own *hḗbē*, 'youthful prime')." Allen 1924:238 and 1928:73
quotes other scholia stating that all three lines were athetized (see the apparatus in Allen's
OCT *Odyssey* edition ad loc. for the scholia in question); Allen 1928:73 states further that
all three lines were obelized "in the lost minuscule MS. 'J' according to the collation of
Heinsius." Stanford 1959 on *Odyssey* 11.602–604 notes simply that "these lines are gener-
ally marked as spurious." Cf. Cassio 2002:116n52.
231 Hesiod *Theogony* 952 and frs. 25.29 and 229.9 MW. The passage in the *Theogony* describes
how Heracles made Hebe his wife (Hesiod *Theogony* 950–955):

'Ήβην δ' Ἀλκμήνης καλλισφύρου ἄλκιμος υἱός,
ἷς Ἡρακλῆος, τελέσας στονόεντας ἀέθλους,
<u>παῖδα Διὸς μεγάλοιο καὶ "Ηρης χρυσοπεδίλου,</u>
αἰδοίην θέτ' ἄκοιτιν ἐν Οὐλύμπῳ νιφόεντι·
ὄλβιος, ὃς μέγα ἔργον ἐν ἀθανάτοισιν ἀνύσσας
ναίει ἀπήμαντος καὶ ἀγήραος ἤματα πάντα.

Mighty Heracles, the steadfast son of beautiful-ankled Alcmena,
having completed his grievous labors, made Hebe,
<u>the child of great Zeus and golden-sandaled Hera,</u>
his revered wife on snowy Olympus;
fortunate man, who, having accomplished a great deed among the immortals,
lives free from trouble and old age forever.

Heracles won imortality from the gods by helping them to defeat the giants (the μέγα
ἔργον, "great deed," referred to in line 954; cf. n2.145 above).
232 Text quoted n2.230 above. Herodotus 7.6 tells the story of Onomakritos's forgery and exile;
he calls him an "oracle-monger" and the "arranger" of Musaeus's oracles ('Ονομάκριτον,
ἄνδρα Ἀθηναῖον χρησμολόγον τε καὶ διαθέτην χρησμῶν τῶν Μουσαίου, Herodotus 7.6.3).
Onomakritos presumably collected and arranged the oracles of Musaeus for the benefit of
Peisistratos and his sons (cf. n2.234 below).
233 Herodotus 7.6.3–4: ἐξηλάσθη γὰρ ὑπὸ 'Ιππάρχου τοῦ Πεισιστράτου ὁ 'Ονομάκριτος ἐξ
Ἀθηνέων, ἐπ' αὐτοφώρῳ ἁλοὺς ὑπὸ Λάσου τοῦ 'Ερμιονέος ἐμποιέων ἐς τὰ Μουσαίου
χρησμὸν ὡς αἱ ἐπὶ Λήμνῳ ἐπικείμεναι νῆσοι ἀφανιοίατο κατὰ τῆς θαλάσσης· διὸ ἐξήλασέ
μιν ὁ 'Ίππαρχος, πρότερον χρεώμενος τὰ μάλιστα, "For Onomakritos was exiled from
Athens by Hipparchus, the son of Peisistratos, when he was caught in the act by Lasos of

As Herodotus reports, however, Onomakritos did the Peisistratids' bidding before his exile (ἐξήλασέ μιν ὁ Ἵππαρχος, πρότερον χρεώμενος τὰ μάλιστα, Herodotus 7.6.3), and he did so again after the Peisistratids themselves were exiled from Athens in 510 BC; in 485 BC he is found with the Peisistratids at the Persian court, where he put his knowledge of oracles at their disposal to persuade Xerxes to invade Greece.[234] It seems likely that Hipparchus exiled Onomakritos, not because he did anything against the interests of his Peisistratid patrons or of Athens, but because he was caught in the act of forgery by a non-Athenian poet and, with his credibility thus destroyed among Greeks, he was of no further use to the Peisistratids until they went to Persia.[235] On the evidence of the Homeric scholia Onomakritos borrowed a line from Hesiod and inserted it into the *Odyssey* (*Odyssey* 11.604). If he did this much it seems likely that he added the entire three-line passage on Heracles as an immortal on Olympus (*Odyssey* 11.602–604), for Peisistratos himself had a great interest in Heracles; indeed he seems to have modeled himself on Heracles, who dwelt on Olympus with the gods, when he set up residence on the Athenian Acropolis among the temples of the gods.[236]

Hermione inserting into the words of Musaeus an oracle that the islands lying near Lemnos would disappear under the sea; for this Hipparchus exiled him, having earlier made the greatest use of him."

234 Onomakritos uttered oracles in Xerxes' presence that portended well for the king's invasion of Greece but suppressed any that foretold disaster (Herodotus 7.6.4). Herodotus says that the Peisistratids had reconciled their hostility with Onomakritos when they brought him with them to the Persian court in 485 BC: ἔχοντες Ὀνομάκριτον, ἄνδρα Ἀθηναῖον χρησμολόγον τε καὶ διαθέτην χρησμῶν τῶν Μουσαίου, ἀνεβεβήκεσαν, τὴν ἔχθρην προκαταλυσάμενοι, "They had traveled up country with Onomakritos, an Athenian oracle-monger and arranger of Musaeus's oracles, having first ended their enmity" (Herodotus 7.6.3). The date 485 BC can be inferred from the fact that in Herodotus the passage concerning Onomakritos (7.6.3–5) immediately precedes the passage concerning Xerxes' conquest of Egypt (7.7), which occurred in 485 BC, and from the further fact that Darius died and was succeeded by Xerxes in the autumn of 486 BC (see How and Wells 1928 on Herodotus 7.4; for the chronology of the whole ten-year period, 490–480 BC, see How and Wells on Herodotus 7.20.1).

235 The purpose of the forged oracle, which Herodotus 7.6.3 says concerned the disappearance of islands near Lemnos, must have had something to do with Athenian interests in the region; cf. Allen 1924:240: "Tradition does not give the intention of the forgery..., but it can hardly have been other than political, and connected with Athenian designs upon the Hellespont." As to the reason that Hipparchus exiled Onomakritos, Lewis 1988:293–294 argues that genuine religious scruple was the motivation; Dillery 2005:167–168, 189 and Aloni 2006a:18 argue along the lines that I have suggested above. For a somewhat different interpretation of Onomakritos's relation to the Peisistratids, cf. Nagy 1990a:172–174.

236 Ritoók 1993:41 discusses the evidence for Onomakritos as an interpolator (and redactor) of Homer but draws no firm conclusions; the Homeric scholia to *Odyssey* 11.604 can probably be taken to mean that all three lines, 602–604, were interpolated by Onomakritos (see

§2.165 Onomakritos, who was a known "interpolator" of oracles, who
was in the pay of the Peisistratids, even (perhaps) of Peisistratos himself,[237]
and who, if he interpolated 11.602–604 into the *Odyssey*, used Hesiod for one
of the three lines, has all the qualifications necessary to be considered as the
poet of the six passages interpolated into the catalogue of heroines in *Odyssey*
11.[238] If it was not Onomakritos who interpolated these passages, it must have
been someone very much like him.[239]

Ritoók 1993:41n9). For Peisistratos's occupation of the Acropolis with his "club-bearers"
(κορυνηφόροι) see Herodotus 1.59.5–6. Boardman has made the case for Peisistratos's
special interest in Heracles, especially Heracles' arrival on Olympus (see Boardman
1972:60–62; Peisistratos's club-bearers likewise suggest Heracles). Boardman 1975 develops
the argument further, addressing Heracles' initiation into Eleusinian cult, which became
part of his Cerberus adventure in the underworld; Peisistratos was much concerned with
Eleusinian cult. Cf. Irwin 2005:152n104 for a debate regarding some parts of Boardman's
argument.

237 If Onomakritos was active for Peisistratos, who died in 527 BC, he must have been quite old
when he became active again for the Peisistratids 42 years later in 485 BC. Onomakritos's
name is linked to that of Peisistratos in a passage of Tzetzes concerning the Peisistratean
recension; it is there reported that some attributed the "recension" (διόρθωσις) of Homer
to four men in the time of Peisistratos, one of whom was Onomakritos the Athenian (two
others were Orpheus of Croton and Zopyros of Heraklea; the name of the fourth is corrupt
[Tzetzes *Perì Kōmōidías, Anecdota Graeca* 1.6, ed. Cramer, quoted by Allen 1924:232–233, also
in Kaibel 1899 p. 20; cf. Nagy 1990a:174]). Whatever the value of the rest of this report
(for the editorial commission as a Hellenistic invention to make Peisistratos resemble
the Ptolemies see Ritoók 1993:41and n13), its assigning of Onomakritos to the time of
Peisistratos was perhaps not obviously wrong or easily contradicted, and may have been
based on fact.

238 See n2.231 above for the Hesiodic line that also occurs at *Odyssey* 11.604: note that two of
the three Hesiodic occurrences of this line are in the probably sixth-century Athenian
Catalogue of Women (cf. n2.219 above), and that the third, *Theogony* 952, is in "the probably
post-Hesiodic" part of that poem (line 901 to the end in the view of West 1966:397–399, who
notes that lines 929, 939, 962, and 964 have also been proposed as the start of this part); use
of the Hesiodic catalogues in particular matches the profile of the interpolator in *Odyssey*
11. The verb used by Herodotus of Onomakritos's alleged forgery of oracles of Musaeus
is ἐμποιέω (ἐμποιέων ἐς τὰ Μουσαίου χρησμόν, "inserting an oracle into the verses of
Musaeus," Herodotus 7.6.3). The same verb may occur in the scholia to *Odyssey* 11.604 with
reference to Onomakritos's alleged insertion of 11.604 into the *Odyssey* (here ἐμπεποιῆσθαι,
"inserted," is Lobeck's emendation for πεποιῆσθαι). On the basis of Herodotus's use of the
verb ἐμποιεῖν for Onomakritos's activity a more neutral term than "interpolation" from
the standpoint of the use or non-use of writing would be *"empoíēsis"* (cf. n2.173 above). As
to the implications of ἐμποιεῖν, Graziosi 2002:41–47 argues that ποιεῖν and related words
when used of poetry emphasize composition as distinct from performance. Leaving aside
the issue of what this implies about written as distinct from oral composition, I note only
that ἐμποιεῖν would have been the proper term for the work of the interpolator in the
catalogue of heroines in *Odyssey* 11, even in his own mind.

239 A statement like "Peisistratos added this line to the Nekyia" (Hereas's charge about
Odyssey 11.631 according to Plutarch *Theseus* 20.2) does not imply that Peisistratos himself

§2.166 Peisistratos's claim to descent from Neleus and Nestor explains the interpolations made by him (or possibly by his son Hipparchus) to the catalogue of heroines in *Odyssey* 11.[240] The primary purpose was to put the god Poseidon back where he belonged at the head of the Neleid genealogy, and then to give an Athenian stamp to the catalogue as a whole, so that its relevance to Peisistratos would be perceived. This is the reason that the last of the interpolated passages is, as earlier noted, blatantly Athenian. It means to draw attention to itself and to Athens, and thereby to the ancestry of the Athenian tyrant.[241]

---

composed the line; cf. Pausanias 7.26.13, who reports the view that when Peisistratos assembled the scattered parts of the Homeric poems, "either Peisistratos himself or one of his companions" (αὐτὸν Πεισίστρατον ἢ τῶν τινα ἑταίρων) made a mistake about a particular name, putting Γονόεσσαν for Δονόεσσαν (cf. n2.225 above). Onomakritos seems to have been one of Peisistratos's "companions" if Tzetzes' reference to him as one of the four compilers of the Peisistratean recension has even limited historical value (cf. n2.237 above). Pausanias several times refers to Onomakritos as the author of poems of an Orphic nature (8.31.3, 8.37.5, 9.35.5, cf. 1.22.7), but there is no consensus as to whether Onomakritos did in fact compose such poems; Pausanias, who did not believe that Orpheus was the author of such poems, may simply have attributed them to Onomakritos as a credible alternative (see Linforth 1941:350–353; Heinze *DNP* 'Onomakritos' compares Pausanias 1.22.7, where Pausanias comments that the poems of Musaeus are mostly not genuine and attributes one such to Onomakritos).

240 Hipparchus rather than his father is associated with Homeric poetry in "Plato" *Hipparchus* 228b: ὃς [sc. Ἵππαρχος] ἄλλα τε πολλὰ καὶ καλὰ ἔργα σοφίας ἀπεδείξατο, καὶ τὰ Ὁμήρου ἔπη πρῶτος ἐκόμισεν εἰς τὴν γῆν ταυτηνί, καὶ ἠνάγκασε τοὺς ῥαψῳδοὺς Παναθηναίοις ἐξ ὑπολήψεως ἐφεξῆς αὐτὰ διιέναι, ὥσπερ νῦν ἔτι οἵδε ποιοῦσιν, "Who [sc. Hipparchus] displayed many other fine deeds of wisdom, and in particular he first brought the epics of Homer to this land, and compelled the rhapsodes at the Panathenaia to go through them in order, one after another, as they still do now." While the first part of this report is not credible (cf. n2.225 above), the "Panathenaic rule" governing rhapsodes' performances may well have been due to Hipparchus (cf. n4.106 below). Onomakritos has a stronger connection with Hipparchus than with Peisistratos in the historical tradition; this, however, says little about the act of interpolating passages into the catalogue of heroines in *Odyssey* 11, for this act, which went undetected, lay outside the historical tradition. I prefer to think that it was for Peisistratos himself that the interpolations were made.

241 This is not to say that the Athenian passage wished to be recognized as an interpolation, for surely it did not. This raises the interesting question of how early the idea arose that the Homeric poems were actually Athenian, i.e. that Homer was Athenian. This idea, which is associated with Aristarchus in the Hellenistic era, seems present already in the fifth century when Gorgias traces Homer's ancestry not to Orpheus, but to Musaeus, who was so to speak the Athenian Orpheus (see Graziosi 2002:82–83 on Gorgias fr. 25 Diels-Kranz = Proclus *Chrestomathy* line 24 [Allen 1912:100 lines 5–6]; for Musaeus as Athenian, cf. Diogenes Laertius 1.3). Traditions that synchronize Homer's birth with the Ionian migration suggest a similar tendency; for the fourth century (Aristotle and probably others) see Jacoby, commentary on Philochorus *FGrHist* 328 F 209, n11, and cf. Graziosi 2002:99 with n25; for the fifth century see Graziosi 2002:120, who interprets Thucydides to this effect. How much earlier the idea of an Athenian Homer may have arisen is unknown.

§2.167 The Ionian catalogue of heroines that was originally in *Odyssey* 11 had a very different character from the Athenian catalogue of heroines that has come down to us in *Odyssey* 11. The Ionian catalogue had no interest in telling stories for their own sake; rather it arranged everything in a structure which itself conveyed a message that under no circumstances was to be expressed more directly. In and of itself this catalogue, devoid of such vivid passages as Poseidon's impersonation of Enipeus and seduction of Tyro, is dry. The whole interest of this catalogue is the place that it occupies in the larger story, which is again a matter of structure. It is the answer to Alcinous's question whether Odysseus, his nameless guest, lost a companion at Troy: he did, and the catalogue reveals through indirection the entire myth of this lost companion, and in what sense he was lost to Odysseus. But the catalogue does more than answer Alcinous's question: it confirms the hidden identity of Alcinous himself. The catalogue in *Odyssey* 11, focusing on Nestor, is the counterpart to the Phaeacian genealogy in *Odyssey* 7, which presents Alcinous as a second Nestor. For the correspondence to work over so large a span the focus of the catalogue on Nestor has to be clear, as it is in the Ionian version of the catalogue. The point is then reinforced by having the Phaeacians, and Alcinous in particular, intervene in the story exactly when the catalogue is finished. In the Athenian catalogue this identification can no longer work, for the catalogue no longer clearly focuses on Nestor. But it would be truer to say that the identification of Nestor and Alcinous had already ceased to operate by the Athenian period, and that is why the catalogue was given a new look.[242] As long as the catalogue served the structural purpose for which it was intended, it was as alive as any passage in the Homeric poems. When it ceased to serve that purpose, it had little else going for it, and was ripe for a makeover that would give it at least one striking and memorable passage. This is the catalogue that has come down to us.[243]

---

242 For more on the early phases of transmission of the Homeric poems see Part 4 below.

243 It is also the catalogue that Polygnotos knew in the mid-fifth century BC when he painted the Nekyia in the Lesche of the Cnidians at Delphi; Pausanias, who describes the painting, names some twenty female figures in it, eleven of whom are from the catalogue of heroines in *Odyssey* 11. Of these eleven seven are from the original catalogue (Chloris, 10.29.5; Tyro [referred to as "the daughter of Salmoneus"], 10.29.7; Pero, 10.31.10; Iphimedeia, 10.28.8; the three heroines at the end of the catalogue, Maira, 10.30.5, Klymene, 10.29.6, and Eriphyle, 10.29.7); four heroines are from the expanded catalogue (Megara, 10.29.7, and the three Athenian heroines, Ariadne, 10.29.3, Phaedra, 10.29.3, and Prokris, 10.29.6). The expanded catalogue had clearly replaced the older catalogue at the date of this painting (probably between 458 and 447 BC), which would have been within a century of the expansion itself. Plato *Symposium* 190b provides later but more explicit evidence for the expanded catalogue in a reference to the attempt by Otos and Ephialtes to storm heaven

§2.168 I have now completed my discussion of Nestor's role in the *Iliad* and the *Odyssey*, and to conclude Part 2 I return briefly to a question posed at the beginning of Part 1, to which the answer is now clear. In the *Iliad* Nestor is called one of the twelve sons of Neleus, whereas in the *Odyssey* he is named as one of the three sons of Neleus and Chloris, and the question is whether this discrepancy means, as the ancient *khōrízontes* maintained, that the *Iliad* and the *Odyssey* were by different poets. We have found that when Nestor is called one of the twelve sons of Neleus in *Iliad* 11 this is a screen for a much older myth in which Nestor and his brother Periklymenos are twin figures, and that this hidden myth is a paradigm for Patroclus in his relationship with Achilles; in the *Odyssey*, where Periklymenos is named together with Nestor, a third brother is also named, but the context in which this occurs, the catalogue of heroines in *Odyssey* 11, shows by its structure that the third brother is also a screen for Nestor's twin myth, which in every other respect determines the content and shape of the catalogue. The conclusion is that the *Iliad* and the *Odyssey* do not differ fundamentally insofar as both assume Nestor's twin myth and both disguise it; the difference between the two poems is in the disguises, and this is a superficial difference with its own rationale. More will be said in Part 4 about the myth of the twelve sons of Neleus, which has its own important role in the Homeric poems and could not be omitted from them. But this myth also could not be allowed to stand as the sole truth to the exclusion of Nestor's much older tradition, and this is what the discrepancy in *Odyssey* 11 clearly conveys.[244] At the deepest level the *Iliad* and the *Odyssey* are the same with respect to Nestor and his myth.

(they are a comparison for the proto-humans in the speech of Aristophanes): καὶ ὃ λέγει Ὅμηρος περὶ Ἐφιάλτου τε καὶ Ὤτου, περὶ ἐκείνων λέγεται, τὸ εἰς τὸν οὐρανὸν ἀνάβασιν ἐπιχειρεῖν ποιεῖν, ὡς ἐπιθησομένων τοῖς θεοῖς, "and what Homer says about Ephialtes and Otos is said about them, that they tried to make an ascent into the sky in order to attack the gods."
244 Cf. §1.9 above.

Endnotes, Part 2

EN2.1 (Endnote to n2.62)

The terms *mêtis* and *bíē*, denoting "intelligence" and "strength," are explicitly opposed to each other only once in Homer (μήτι τοι δρυτόμος μέγ᾽ ἀμείνων ἠὲ βίηφι, "by intelligence the woodcutter is much better than by strength," *Iliad* 23.315), but the opposition between them matches up well with a contrast between the two heroes of the *Iliad* and the *Odyssey*, Achilles and Odysseus, and this gives the opposition a particular resonance. Indeed the first song of Demodokos in *Odyssey* 8 tells of a quarrel at Troy between Achilles and Odysseus, and this quarrel, according to the scholia, was over whether Troy would be taken by strength or artifice; although the scholia do not use the words *mêtis* and *bíē*, but a variety of other synonyms, the word *mêtis* clearly suggests itself for Odysseus, and the word *bíē* follows naturally enough to complete the contrast with Achilles (cf. Nagy 1979:45–46 and 46n2 on the scholia to *Odyssey* 8.75 and 77). Wilson 2005:10, following Cook 1995, interprets the contrast between *mêtis* and *bíē* in terms of "restraint" and a "lack of restraint," and this interpretation, I think, is valid. On the other hand, I resist deriving the contrast between Achilles and Odysseus (and a more abstract opposition between *mêtis* and *bíē*) from the Indo-European twin myth as Wilson 2005:16 proposes on the basis of Wikander 1957. The opposition between "incitement" and "restraint" that I see operating in the Indo-European twin myth has at its core the notion of "bringing back to life," and this function, belonging to the immortal twin, is what translates into "incitement"; in terms of Indo-European derivation "incitement" does not go with *mêtis* (which contains the root **ma-*, having to do with "measurement"), but *nóos*. It is true that in a contrast between *mêtis* and *bíē*, *bíē* can be seen as a "lack of restraint" on the warrior's part. In the Indo-European twin myth, by contrast, the warrior twin embodies restraint, and his restraint is not moral but physical (cf. n2.62 on *alkḗ* rather than *bíē* as the appropriate term to express this twin's restraint). When translated into the dynamics of the chariot race, as in Nestor's race against the Epeian twins, restraint resides in the twin

331

controlling the horses around the turning point (ὃ μὲν ἔμπεδον ἡνιόχευεν, /
ἔμπεδον ἡνιόχευ', "the one steadfastly held the reins, / steadfastly held the
reins"). It might be objected that Nestor, who in my interpretation operates
within the framework of the twin myth when he first becomes a horseman
in his battle with the Epeians, does not appear at all restrained in this battle,
but sweeps ahead "like a dark whirlwind." This objection, however, misses
the contrast between Nestor's battle and his chariot race, as I reconstruct the
latter; in his chariot race Nestor does not keep his horses under control and
crashes at the turning point, whereas in his battle he controls his horses and
successfully returns from Bouprasion to Pylos (for the turning point as a point
of contrast between the chariot race and the battle see §5.1 below). The oppo-
sition between "incitement" and "restraint" that I reconstruct for the Indo-
European twin myth does not preclude that these categories may be inverted
along the lines of the opposition between *mêtis* and *bíē* in a particular situa-
tion for a particular reason. The twin myth itself was not a rigid construct that
could only be applied in one way. I suggest that in the case of two Homeric
heroes on the Trojan side, Hector the warrior and Polydamas the counselor,
the twin myth is in fact inverted. Hector and Polydamas are not twins, or even
brothers; Hector is the son of Priam, and Polydamas is the son of a Trojan
elder, Panthoos (see *Iliad* 3.146 for Panthoos). But the *Iliad* treats Hector and
Polydamas as virtual twins, saying that they were born on the same night, and
contrasting them as warrior to counselor (*Iliad* 18.249–252):

> τοῖσι δὲ Πουλυδάμας πεπνυμένος ἦρχ' ἀγορεύειν
> Πανθοΐδης· ὃ γὰρ οἶος ὅρα πρόσσω καὶ ὀπίσσω·
> Ἕκτορι δ' ἦεν ἑταῖρος, ἰῇ δ' ἐν νυκτὶ γένοντο,
> ἀλλ' ὃ μὲν ἄρ μύθοισιν, ὃ δ' ἔγχεϊ πολλὸν ἐνίκα.

> To them wise Polydamas, Panthoos's son, began to speak;
> for only he saw ahead and behind;
> he was Hector's companion, and they were both born in one
>   night,
> but one of them was better with words, and the other was far
>   better with the spear.

This passage occurs in the last of four episodes in which Polydamas coun-
sels caution and restraint; in these episodes Hector twice takes his advice
(*Iliad* 12.61–80 and *Iliad* 13.726–748) and twice, when Polydamas counsels
outright retreat, rejects it (*Iliad* 12.210–250 and *Iliad* 18.254–309; for the

episodes cf. Dickson 1995:133–142). In the last episode Hector is determined to face Achilles and not to retreat behind the walls of Troy, and the Trojans are persuaded by him; the poet comments pointedly on their mistake in following Hector rather than Polydamas (*Iliad* 18.310–313):

ὣς Ἕκτωρ ἀγόρευ', ἐπὶ δὲ Τρῶες κελάδησαν
νήπιοι· ἐκ γάρ σφεων φρένας εἵλετο Παλλὰς Ἀθήνη.
Ἕκτορι μὲν γὰρ ἐπήνησαν κακὰ μητιόωντι,
Πουλυδάμαντι δ' ἄρ' οὔ τις ὃς ἐσθλὴν φράζετο βουλήν.

So Hector spoke, and the Trojans shouted their approval,
foolish men, for Pallas Athena took their wits from them.
For they approved Hector, who gave them bad advice,
but no one approved Polydamas, who devised good counsel.

If we analyze the relationship between Hector and Polydamas in terms of "incitement" and "restraint," Hector, the warrior, is clearly "incitement," and Polydamas, the counselor, is clearly "restraint." What is more, Polydamas is characterized in terms of *nóos*. In *Iliad* 13, when Polydamas urges Hector to call a council, Hector heeds his advice (to no avail since his counselors have all been killed or wounded; *Iliad* 13.726–787); Polydamas prefaces his advice with the following passage in which he identifies himself as the man of *nóos* as opposed to Hector, the man of war (*Iliad* 13.726–735):

Ἕκτορ ἀμήχανός ἐσσι παραρρητοῖσι πιθέσθαι.
οὕνεκά τοι περὶ δῶκε θεὸς πολεμήϊα ἔργα
τοὔνεκα καὶ βουλῇ ἐθέλεις περιίδμεναι ἄλλων·
ἀλλ' οὔ πως ἅμα πάντα δυνήσεαι αὐτὸς ἑλέσθαι.
ἄλλῳ μὲν γὰρ ἔδωκε θεὸς πολεμήϊα ἔργα,
ἄλλῳ δ' ὀρχηστύν, ἑτέρῳ κίθαριν καὶ ἀοιδήν,
ἄλλῳ δ' ἐν στήθεσσι τιθεῖ <u>νόον</u> εὐρύοπα Ζεὺς
ἐσθλόν, τοῦ δέ τε πολλοὶ ἐπαυρίσκοντ' ἄνθρωποι,
καί τε πολέας ἐσάωσε, μάλιστα δὲ καὐτὸς ἀνέγνω.
αὐτὰρ ἐγὼν ἐρέω ὥς μοι δοκεῖ εἶναι ἄριστα.

Hector, you are intractable in not heeding words of persuasion.
Because the god has given you warlike deeds beyond others

you also wish to know more than others in council;
but you will not be able to take everything to yourself.
For to one man the god has given warlike deeds,
to another dance, to a different man the kithara and song,
and in the breast of another far-seeing Zeus puts a good <u>mind</u>,
and many men reap the benefit of it,
and he saves many, and he knows it most of all.
But I will speak as seems to me to be best.

Similarly in *Iliad* 18, when Hector refuses to retreat inside the walls of Troy, he rejects Polydamas's *noḗmata*, "thoughts," in doing so (νήπιε μηκέτι ταῦτα νοήματα φαῖν' ἐνὶ δήμῳ, "foolish man, no longer reveal these thoughts among the people," *Iliad* 18.295). In the case of Polydamas *nóos* is clearly associated with "restraint," and this can be seen as an inversion of the twin myth; Polydamas's "restraint" is a foil to Hector's "lack of restraint," which is a key element in his tragedy (cf. Redfield 1975:143–153, who calls Polydamas Hector's "alter ego"; cf. also Taplin 1992:156–160 and Parker 2000:300). Hector's "lack of restraint" is also an inversion, for Hector, the defender of Troy, is the ultimate defensive warrior, as his name, from the verb *ékhō*, may also suggest (for this verb's Homeric meaning "to hold back, hold in check, resist" see Cunliffe 1924 s.v. no.19; for the verb's meaning "hold, protect," with which the Homeric poets interpret the name, see §1.14 above). Polydamas, as the Trojan counselor, has something in common with Nestor, the Greek counselor, and from a certain point of view their relation to *nóos* is similar: both, amid reverses on the battlefield, urge calling a council with an almost symbolic use of the word *nóos* (for Polydamas, see *Iliad* 13.732, quoted above; for Nestor, see *Iliad* 14.61–62, discussed in §1.36). Nestor also provides a comparison for Polydamas's "restraint": just as Polydamas is cast in the role of restraining Hector, Nestor plays this role in relation to Agamemnon and Achilles in *Iliad* 1, and more pointedly in relation to Diomedes in *Iliad* 8 (for this episode see §2.77).

EN2.2 (Endnote to n2.125)
My interpretation of the name *Menélaos* as "he who incites the warfolk" is consistent with the fact that Homeric *laós*, by a wide margin, refers to one's own "warfolk" and not to the enemy's; the interpretation "he who withstands the warfolk" is not consistent with this fact. I count 174 examples in the *Iliad* and 42 examples in the *Odyssey* in which unmodifed *laós* (this excludes instances of *laòs Akhaiôn*, *laòs Trōïkós*, and the like) can be identified as one's

own as opposed to the enemy's *laós*; I count only nine counterexamples: seven in the *Iliad* (2.799, 7.342, 9.420=9.687, 11.309, 16.377, 18.153) and two in the *Odyssey* (11.500 and 518). Even as object of the verb *ólese*, "destroyed/lost," *laós* refers to one's own people in all five instances of the relevant phrase: Agamemnon (*Iliad* 2.115, 9.22), Hector (*Iliad* 22.104, 107), and Odysseus (*Odyssey* 24.428) are all said to destroy or lose their own *laós*; even in *Odyssey* 9.265, when Odysseus, referring to the fame of Agamemnon, says that "he destroyed many *laoí*" (*apólese laoùs / polloús*), the phrase must be regarded as highly ambiguous (see Pazdernik 1995:365 for the comparison with *Iliad* 9.22). The most striking of the counterexamples are in the *Odyssey*: in *Odyssey* 11.500 Achilles says that since he is no longer as he once was when "I slew the best *laós*" (*péphnon laòn áriston*) he cannot protect his father; later in the same passage Odysseus, telling Achilles how his son Neoptolemos distinguished himself at Troy, says that he could not name "how many *laós* he slew" (*hósson laòn épephnen, Odyssey* 11.518). In both of these examples the phrase "I slew/ he slew the *laós*" does not stand alone; the phrase "defending the Argives," *amúnōn Argeíoisin*, modifies the subject, making it clear that *laós* is the enemy. As noted in n2.125 Benveniste 1969, vol. 2, 90 argues that *laós* refers to a "people" in relation to its leader, as in the stock Homeric phrase for a leader, *poiména laôn* "shepherd of the warriors/people"; the *laós* that belongs to a leader is of course his own *laós* and not the enemy's, and this largely explains the one-sided Homeric usage. The phrase *poiména* (*poiméni*) *laôn* occurs 43 times in the *Iliad* and six times in the *Odyssey*. Including the occurrences of this phrase I count 132 examples in the *Iliad* and 23 in the *Odyssey* in which *laós* is used of a "people" in relation to its leader or leaders. I draw particular attention to 17 examples in the *Iliad* and one in the *Odyssey* in which there is a contrast between a "leader" or "leaders" on the one hand and those who "follow" on the other hand (*Iliad* 2.365, 578, 675, 708, 818; 4.91, 202, 430; 5.486; 11.796; 13.108, 492, 495, 710; 15.311; 16.551; 20.383; *Odyssey* 6.164). In ten of these examples the verb *hépomai* "follow" is used of the *laós*; in five examples the noun *hēgemṓn* or the verb *hēgemoneúō* is used of the leader(s); in *Iliad* 4.429–430 the noun *hēgemṓn* and the verb *hépomai* both occur. In line with this usage proper names containing the word *laós* express what a leader does for his own people, not what he does to an enemy's people: *Agélaos, Ekhélaos,* and *Ne(s)élaos* are clear examples (cf. also Homeric *Erúlaos,* "he who saves the warfolk"). Of other Homeric names with *laós* I note in particular *Laomédōn,* which also has to do with leading one's own people (for *médōn* as "leader" cf. the formulaic phrase *hēgétores ēdè médontes*). The name *Laodámas* is a possible counterexample in that the verb *dámnēmi* is used of "subduing" an enemy.

Indeed *Iliad* 11.309 (one of the nine counterexamples listed above) provides an example in which the passive of *dámnēmi* occurs in connection with the noun *laós*: after Hector kills ten *hēgemónes* he proceeds to kill a mass (*plēthús*) of other warriors, whose number is compared to waves driven on by the wind; the simile concludes: ὣς ἄρα πυκνὰ <u>καρήαθ'</u> ὑφ' Ἕκτορι <u>δάμνατο λαῶν</u>, "thus many <u>heads of the *laoí* were subdued</u> by Hector." But the verb *dámnēmi* is also used in the sense of "subduing" and "controlling" one's own people, as in *Odyssey* 3.305–306, telling how Aigisthos during Menelaus's long absence "devised evils at home, killing the son of Atreus, <u>and the people were subdued</u> by him," Αἴγισθος ἐμήσατο οἴκοθι λυγρά, / κτείνας Ἀτρεΐδην, <u>δέδμητο δὲ λαὸς</u> ὑπ' αὐτῷ. As in such later Greek names as *Dēmodámas* and *Astudámas* (Fick-Bechtel 1894:89), the idea in *Laodámas* is the "control" of what is one's own; the verbal element is no harsher than in e.g. *Iliad* 5.893, where Zeus says that he barely "subdues" Hera with his words: τὴν μὲν ἐγὼ σπουδῇ <u>δάμνημ'</u> ἐπέεσσι). In post-Homeric Greek Alcaeus fr. 364 LP provides an instance of the verb *dámnēmi* with the object *laós* that cuts both ways: ἀργάλεον Πενία κάκον ἄσχετον, ἀ μέγαν / <u>δάμναι λᾶον</u> Ἀμαχανίᾳ σὺν ἀδελφέᾳ, "Poverty, a hard, unbearable evil, who with her sister Helplessness <u>subdues</u> the great *laós*": on the one hand the meaning of the underlined phrase is not simply "controls the people," as I argue is the case in the name *Laodámas*; on the other hand the *laós* in question is not an enemy warfolk, but one's own people. We may judge how alive the meaning of a name like *Agélaos*, "he who leads the warfolk," is in Homer from the collocation of the verb *ágein* with the object *laós* in four passages of the *Iliad* (2.580, 4.407, 9.338, 10.79), and perhaps also from a passage of the *Odyssey* in which a suitor named *Agélaos* acts to summon the *laós* when Odysseus arms for the final battle with the suitors (cf. Haubold 2000:123–124 on *Odyssey* 22.131–134 and 22.241–254). Although I have considered only Homeric evidence for the word *laós* I think that this evidence is representative of Mycenaean Greek as well. Benveniste 1969, vol. 2, 95 cites Mycenaean *lawagetas*, "leader of the warfolk," as confirmation of his view that a *laós* is a people in relation to its leader. It is possible that Mycenaean *la-wo-qo-no* equals *Lāwoqʷʰonos/Laophónos*, "he who kills the warfolk," but the name is not in fact attested in later Greek; see Ventris and Chadwick 1956:425, and Heubeck 1969:537. Still more uncertain is the interpretation of Mycenaean *ra-wo-qo-ta* as *Lāwoqʷʰontās*, "killer of the *laós*." Ventris and Chadwick, in the first edition of *Documents*, hesitated about this interpretation because of the ambiguity of the syllables *qo-ta* in the Linear-B writing system (1956:425, cf. 94–95); in the second edition, 1973:579, they replaced uncertainty with a reference to Heubeck 1969, but Heubeck adds no new evidence. The feminine name *Laophóntē* that Ventris and Chadwick cite as a parallel to the proposed Mycenaean masculine name *Lāwoqʷhontās*, which in later Greek would have been *Laophóntēs*, has an uncertain claim to existence: in "Apollodorus" 1.7.7 the manuscript reading is *Leophóntē*, of which *Laophóntē* is an emendation; the only actual occurrence of a feminine name *Laophóntē*, in the scholia to Apollonius of Rhodes 1.146 (it belongs to Leda's mother), is emended by Wilamowitz 1926:137 to *Laophónē* for both grammatical and metrical reasons (Greek has no feminine agent suffix *-tē* to match the masculine agent suffix *-tēs* of the proposed name *Laophóntēs*, and if Pherekydes, the scholiast's source, took the name from a hexameter source, the form *Laophóntē* is impossible). It must be noted, however, that the emended form *Laophónē* would provide a feminine equivalent of the name *Laophónos* discussed above as a possible interpretation of Mycenaean *la-wo-qo-no*. The Mycenaean names are possible, and it is thus also possible that the Homeric collocations *péphnon laòn* and *laòn épephnen* in *Odyssey* 11 preserve something old, but the weight of the Homeric evidence is against this. Another explanation of the Mycenaean names, though not very likely, may be suggested. Heubeck 1954:24 (= 1984:252) explains Hermes' epithet Ἀργεϊφόντης as ἀργός, "shining, nimble," and φον- < *gʷhen-, 'flourish' (cf. εὐθενέω, "thrive"). Chantraine 1999 is skeptical of the root not only in Ἀργεϊφόντης (see s.v.), but also in the verb εὐθενέω (see s.v., where such other names as Κρεσφόντης and Πολυφόντης are mentioned and rejected for this interpretation). In compounds with *laós*, on the other hand, the positive sense of the root may perhaps recommend it. It remains to draw attention to the collocation *órnuthi laoús*, "stir up the warriors," in *Iliad* 15.475 and 19.139 (ἀλλ' ὄρσευ πόλεμόνδε καὶ ἄλλους ὄρνυθι λαούς, "but stir yourself to war and stir up the other warriors," 19.139). The collocation is the basis of a name, *Orsílaos*, which does not occur in Homer, but is attested later of a Boeotian (Collitz-Bechtel 1884–1915 no. 2565 line 57; cf. *Orsélaos*, also Boeotian, in *IG* VII 2062–2063, and see Bechtel 1917:353). The meaning of *Orsílaos*, "he who stirs up the people," is very close to what I take to be the meaning of *Menélaos*.

EN2.3 (Endnote to n2.145)

In his commentary on Hesiod *Theogony* 954 West 1966 cites Hesiod fr. 43a.65 MW, which "appears to refer to local Gigantes slain by Heracles alone." It is not clear how Heracles' role in any such local battle would relate to his role in the well-known battle at Phlegrai. Regarding the battle at Phlegrai "Apollodorus" 1.6.1 says that Zeus obtained the help of Heracles when he learned that victory could only be achieved with the help of a mortal; West cites as probable allusions to Heracles' participation in the gigantomachy Hesiod *Theogony* 954, in which Heracles is the subject: ὄλβιος, ὃς μέγα ἔργον ἐν ἀθανάτοισιν ἀνύσσας, "fortunate man, who, having accomplished a great deed among the immortals"; and Hesiod *Shield of Heracles* 27–29:

> πατὴρ δ' ἀνδρῶν τε θεῶν τε
> ἄλλην μῆτιν ὕφαινε μετὰ φρεσίν, ὥς ῥα θεοῖσιν
> ἀνδράσι τ' ἀλφηστῇσιν ἀρῆς ἀλκτῆρα φυτεῦσαι.

> The father of men and gods
> wove another scheme in his mind, to beget
> for gods and grain-eating men a defender from destruction.

West comments that "there are no other allusions to the Gigantomachy in literature before Xenophanes; in art it appears at the end of the seventh century" (West 1966 on *Theogony* 954). West comments on Theogony 50, which juxtaposes the race of men and giants in the same line, that "the Giants are themselves men in the fifth century" (in Euripides *Heracles* 853 they are called ἀνοσίων ἀνδρῶν, "unholy men"). West says further that "in Homer the Giants occupy an intermediate position between men and gods: the Laestrygonians are οὐκ ἄνδρεσσιν ἐοικότες, ἀλλὰ Γίγασιν ['not like men, but like Giants'], *Odyssey* 10.120, and like the Cyclopes and Phaeacians, the Gigantes are ἀγχίθεοι ['close to the gods'], *Odyssey* 7.206, though mortal (7.59–60). Later, mankind is said to have sprung from the blood of Giants." The giants are called "big" (*megálous*) in *Theogony* 185, but West ad loc. comments that "great size is not a prominent feature of the Giants in Greek myth"; cf. also Mayer 1887:3–6. West comments on *Theogony* 186, in which the giants are described as having long spears, that "in early literature and art the Giants are regularly represented with full armour of the human type.... Only later are they reduced to fighting with boulders and tree-trunks."

Part 3.

ATHENS

Chapter 8.

ARETE AND NAUSICAA

§3.1 *Odyssey* 3 brings together two figures, Nestor and Athena, whose functions are related in the story of Odysseus's return: Nestor is the "homebringer" who ten years earlier failed to bring Odysseus back from Troy; Athena is the goddess who has now undertaken to free Odysseus from Calypso's island and bring about his long delayed return home. The shift from Nestor to Athena in Odysseus's story is a shift from the human to the divine, and *Odyssey* 3 dramatizes this; Athena is disguised as the mortal *Mentor* when she and Telemachus meet the mortal *Nestor*, but in reality she is herself, a Goddess. The shift from human to divine dominates the story in the latter part of *Odyssey* 3, where Nestor, once he recognizes Athena, acknowledges her superior power through prayers, a wine offering, and an elaborate ox sacrifice.

§3.2 In *Odyssey* 7 Athena, disguised as a Phaeacian maiden, guides Odysseus to the Phaeacian royal palace, telling him of the Phaeacian king and queen whom he is about to meet. Her speech reveals that the king has a hidden identity beneath the surface of the poem: his genealogy makes him a second Nestor, a "homebringer" who will succeed where Nestor failed. But the king's hidden identity raises a question about the queen, who is part of the same genealogy: she alone corresponds to nothing in Nestor's genealogy. There is a striking imbalance here. Athena presents the queen as more important for Odysseus than the king: she mentions the queen first, and she says that Odysseus will meet her first when he enters the palace; she goes on to describe the great respect in which the queen is held by all, including the king; she ends by repeating what the Phaeacian princess has already told Odysseus, that his hopes for a homecoming depend on the favor of the

Phaeacian queen.¹ Given the relative importance of king and queen in this speech it does not make sense that we learn who the king is at a deeper level, but not the queen; if the king has a hidden identity, so too must the queen. The speech in fact makes the queen an enigma.²

§3.3 In Scheria Athena is fully in charge of events; she has been duly authorized by Zeus, who, before he sends Hermes to free Odysseus, foreshadows the entire Phaeacian episode, proclaiming that Odysseus will build a raft and reach Scheria in twenty days, that the Phaeacians will honor him like a god

---

1 Athena begins with the queen (δέσποιναν μὲν πρῶτα κιχήσεαι ἐν μεγάροισιν, "you will come upon the mistress first in the halls," *Odyssey* 7.54), and ends with her (*Odyssey* 7.75-77):

εἴ κέν τοι κείνη γε φίλα φρονέῃσ' ἐνὶ θυμῷ,
ἐλπωρή τοι ἔπειτα φίλους ἰδέειν καὶ ἱκέσθαι
οἶκον ἐς ὑψόροφον καὶ σὴν ἐς πατρίδα γαῖαν.

If she should be kindly disposed to you in her heart,
then there is hope for you to see your dear ones and to reach
your high-roofed house and your fatherland.

Nausicaa earlier told Odysseus to bypass the king and supplicate the queen (*Odyssey* 6.310-311): τὸν παραμειψάμενος μητρὸς περὶ γούνασι χεῖρας / βάλλειν ἡμετέρης, ἵνα νόστιμον ἦμαρ ἴδηαι, "pass by him and throw your hands around the knees of my mother so that you may see your day of return."

2 Athena introduces the Phaeacian genealogy as if to explain the queen; having told Odysseus that he will encounter the queen first in the palace Athena gives her name and says that she has the same progenitors as the king (*Odyssey* 7.54-55): Ἀρήτη δ' ὄνομ' ἐστὶν ἐπώνυμον, ἐκ δὲ τοκήων / τῶν αὐτῶν, οἵ περ τέκον Ἀλκίνοον βασιλῆα. The genealogy follows, in the course of which it becomes clearer with each new generation that this is actually Nestor's genealogy in disguise. A climax is reached in *Odyssey* 7.63, which says that Nausithoos had two sons, Rhexenor and Alcinous, for this line, as we have seen, contains the core of Nestor's twin myth, which is never presented in such overt terms of Nestor himself. It is precisely at this moment of maximum clarity that the genealogy becomes an enigma. Rhexenor, who by his name alone, "breaker of men," re-embodies the essential nature of Nestor's warrior brother Periklymenos, immediately loses all correspondence to Nestor and his family by being father to Arete, whom Alcinous marries when his brother dies. Clarity and enigma are in fact totally intertwined at the end of the genealogy, where Alcinous's warrior brother is the subject of an expansion (*Odyssey* 7.64-66):

τὸν μὲν ἄκουρον ἐόντα βάλ' ἀργυρότοξος Ἀπόλλων
νυμφίον, ἐν μεγάρῳ μίαν οἴην παῖδα λιπόντα,
Ἀρήτην. τὴν δ' Ἀλκίνοος ποιήσατ' ἄκοιτιν.

The one silver-bowed Apollo shot while he was a bridegroom
without any sons, leaving only a daughter in his hall,
Arete, whom Alcinous made his wife.

The fact that Rhexenor died reflects Nestor's twin myth, but the fact that he fathered Arete does not; the fact that Alcinous took his brother's place with respect to Arete cuts both ways (cf. §2.115 above).

and send him on his way with greater treasure than he would have brought from Troy, and that he will again reach home (*Odyssey* 5.33–42). The Phaeacians are like performers in a play of which this is the synopsis, and which Athena stage-manages. She goes to work at the beginning of Book 6, arriving in Scheria and entering the bedchamber of the princess Nausicaa, who is the first of the Phaeacians to take center stage; Athena appears to Nausicaa in a dream disguised as a friend, a maiden like herself, and Nausicaa is set in motion by this dream as soon as she awakens. Later, when Odysseus approaches the Phaeacian city, Athena appears again disguised as a Phaeacian maiden, and this time tells Odysseus about Arete and Alcinous, drawing special attention to Arete.

§3.4 Athena introduces both Nausicaa and Arete, and after each introduction she quits the stage, as it were, leaving it free for the princess and the queen. There is a close parallel between the two introductions, for in both cases when Athena departs she leaves Scheria altogether and goes to a particular destination, which is different in each case. In Book 6, having instructed the sleeping Nausicaa, Athena leaves Scheria for Olympus, the home of the gods, which is described in all its remote splendor (*Odyssey* 6.41–47):

ἡ μὲν ἄρ' ὣς εἰποῦσ' ἀπέβη γλαυκῶπις Ἀθήνη
Οὔλυμπόνδ', ὅθι φασὶ θεῶν ἕδος ἀσφαλὲς αἰεὶ
ἔμμεναι· οὔτ' ἀνέμοισι τινάσσεται οὔτε ποτ' ὄμβρῳ
δεύεται οὔτε χιὼν ἐπιπίλναται, ἀλλὰ μάλ' αἴθρη
πέπταται ἀννέφελος, λευκὴ δ' ἐπιδέδρομεν αἴγλη·
τῷ ἔνι τέρπονται μάκαρες θεοὶ ἤματα πάντα.
ἔνθ' ἀπέβη γλαυκῶπις, ἐπεὶ διεπέφραδε κούρῃ.

So speaking grey-eyed Athena departed
for Olympus, where they say the steadfast seat of the gods
is; it is not disturbed by winds and it is never made wet by rain
and snow doesn't come near it, but a clear sky
stretches out without clouds, and a white radiance is shed upon it.
In it the blessed gods live at their ease forever.
There the grey-eyed one went when she had instructed the
     maiden.

In Book 7, having drawn Odysseus's particular attention to the Phaeacian queen as he approaches the Phaeacian palace, Athena leaves Scheria and flies to Marathon and Athens and enters the strong house of Erechtheus (*Odyssey* 7.78–81):

ὣς ἄρα φωνήσασ' ἀπέβη γλαυκῶπις Ἀθήνη
πόντον ἐπ' ἀτρύγετον, λίπε δὲ Σχερίην ἐρατεινήν,
ἵκετο δ' ἐς Μαραθῶνα καὶ εὐρυάγυιαν Ἀθήνην,
δῦνε δ' Ἐρεχθῆος πυκινὸν δόμον.

So spoke grey-eyed Athena, and she departed
across the barren sea and left lovely Scheria,
and she came to Marathon and Athens with the wide ways
and entered the strong house of Erechtheus.

§3.5 Athena's two departures from Scheria work together; they correlate with the two characters that she introduces. At least her first departure does this. In her first departure Athena flies to Olympus and takes her place in her father's household; this destination is appropriate to Nausicaa, a daughter in her father's household, and a *koúrē*, "maiden" (*Odyssey* 6.47), like Athena herself.[3] Athena's second destination is the palace of the Athenian king Erechtheus on the Acropolis of Athens; why she goes there we are not told: Athena simply disappears into the palace and we are left to speculate.[4] The only certainty is that the palace of Erechtheus is the sacred site of the city goddess of Athens; on this site Athena *Poliás* had her temple from time immemorial (i.e. from the Bronze Age) and on this site her temple long remained.[5]

3 As Zeus's daughter Athena has the epithet *koúrē Diós*, which is all but exclusively hers (see n3.56 below).

4 It is striking that Athena, having traveled to Athens, simply vanishes once she arrives. Hainsworth ad loc. (Heubeck et al. 1988) comments on the contrast with Aphrodite's withdrawal to Paphos in *Odyssey* 8.362–366, where the goddess is shown reveling in her cult:

ἡ δ' ἄρα Κύπρον ἵκανε φιλομμειδὴς Ἀφροδίτη,
ἐς Πάφον, ἔνθα τέ οἱ τέμενος βωμός τε θυήεις.
ἔνθα δέ μιν Χάριτες λοῦσαν καὶ χρῖσαν ἐλαίῳ,
ἀμβρότῳ, οἷα θεοὺς ἐπενήνοθεν αἰὲν ἐόντας,
ἀμφὶ δὲ εἵματα ἕσσαν ἐπήρατα, θαῦμα ἰδέσθαι.

Smile-loving Aphrodite came to Cyprus,
to Paphos, where her precinct and fragrant altar are.
There the Graces bathed her and annointed her with ambrosial
oil, such as glistens on the skin of the gods who are forever,
and clothed her with lovely garments, a wonder to see.

5 The *pólis*, "city," to which Athena's epithet *poliás* refers is what later became known as the *akrópolis*, or "high city"; Pausanias 1.26.6 has the cult title Athena Polias in mind when he refers to Athena's old image as follows: Ἀθηνᾶς ἄγαλμα ἐν τῇ νῦν ἀκροπόλει, τότε δὲ ὀνομαζομένη πόλει, "the image of Athena on what is now the acropolis, but then was called the *pólis* (city)" (cf. n3.23 below). Other cities besides Athens had cults of Athena Polias (several in Ionia did; cf.

We know much less about who the goddess actually was who inhabited this temple in the Homeric era. The only direct evidence for her is our passage in *Odyssey* 7. Is it possible that, just as Athena's first destination is appropriate to Nausicaa, a maiden, Athena's second destination is appropriate to Arete, a married woman, and that Athena herself is a different figure in Erechtheus's palace than she is on Olympus? We are led to think so by a further striking parallelism in the text of *Odyssey* 7, for no sooner does Athena disappear into the palace of Erechtheus than Odysseus sets out for the palace of Alcinous, inside which, as he has just heard, Arete awaits; the transition from one palace to the other occurs in mid-line (*Odyssey* 7.81–82):

δῦνε δ' Ἐρεχθῆος πυκινὸν δόμον. αὐτὰρ Ὀδυσσεὺς
Ἀλκινόου πρὸς δώματ' ἴε κλυτά.

She entered the strong house of Erechtheus. But Odysseus went on to the famous house of Alcinous.

The two palaces look like they are meant to be equivalent, and so too the female figures inside them.[6]

Lenschau 1944:225), but the connection between the goddess and the city named for her (not the reverse; cf. Nilsson 1967:434) was of a special order; in *Odyssey* 7.80, where the city's name occurs in the singular form Ἀθήνην, and is therefore identical with the name of the goddess, the identification between city and goddess is particularly strong. Presumably there was once a similar relationship between the nymph named *Mukēnē* in *Odyssey* 2.120 and the city named *Mukēnē* in *Iliad* 4.52, *Odyssey* 3.304, etc.; the plurals *Mukēnai* and *Athēnai* are "elliptic" in origin, similar to the "elliptic" duals discussed in n1.119 and n1.132 above; see Nagy 1997:167–177. The exceptional position of Athena Polias in Athens has something to do with the unusual continuity of early Athenian history. Polignac 1995:86, referring to "the historical peculiarity of Athens, which the violent upheavals of the end of the Helladic period did not affect with such intensity as other regions of Greece," continues as follows: "In Athens, the palace monarchy, although possibly weakened by those upheavals, was not swept away but probably found itself caught in a general movement of recession that undermined its authority little by little. That increasingly tenuous continuity would account for the exceptional importance, in the city of Athens, of the only acropolis where a truly poliad deity really did take over from the last vestiges of a disintegrating royal house."

6 The parallel between the two palaces is noted by Nagy 1997:173. The male figures inside the two palaces are equally at issue; the worship of Athena Polias was closely connected with the worship of Erechtheus, who shared the same sacred space on the Acropolis. But what the relationship was between the goddess and the primordial king is as open to question as the nature of Athena Polias in Athens in the Homeric era; the two questions are in fact intimately related. *Odyssey* 7.81–82 is again our only primary evidence, and this passage suggests that the pairs Athena/Erechtheus and Arete/Alcinous are equivalent. The only other Homeric evidence for Athena and Erechtheus as a pair is the Athenian entry to the Catalogue of Ships (*Iliad* 2.546–551), but this passage in my view (and in the view of others) reflects later circumstances than does *Odyssey* 7.78–81 (see §3.86–§3.89 below).

§3.6 At the end of Athena's speech to Odysseus as she guides him to the Phaeacian palace Arete is an enigma. What is her hidden identity? I suggest that her hidden identity is Athena Polias, the city goddess of Athens. If this is so, Athena, who has revealed Alcinous's hidden identity by what she says, immediately goes on to reveal Arete's hidden identity by what she does.[7] The result is that Alcinous and Arete together reflect Nestor and Athena together, and this makes perfect sense from the standpoint of Odysseus's *nóstos*: as dramatized in *Odyssey* 3 Nestor and Athena are the two figures who matter in Odysseus's *nóstos*, and Athena matters more than Nestor. This configuration, I suggest, is recreated in the Phaeacian royal couple, but whereas Alcinous is changed from a negative to a positive figure, Arete simply retains the preeminent position to which her hidden identity entitles her. Recreating Athena and Nestor, who are on different planes in *Odyssey* 3, as a royal couple dwelling in the same palace is admittedly a bold stroke; what mediates between the two situations is the relationship between Erechtheus and Athena Polias in Athens, which is itself a large question, and one to which I will return.

§3.7 Athena's two departures from Scheria are parallel, and as in other cases where there is a deliberate pairing of this kind, the more significant moment is the second.[8] Attention is drawn to Athena's second departure by the mere fact of repetition, and this attention has a definite purpose if Athena's second destination answers a question that has just been raised. Athena's first departure is also significant, but more in hindsight. At the beginning of Book 6 we are learning about the Phaeacians for the first time, and we note that Athena's first destination is appropriate to the princess Nausicaa, but we do not ask why. We will come back to Nausicaa, who for now is just Nausicaa; it is enough to say that if Athena the city goddess of Athens is the hidden identity of the Phaeacian queen, there is no reason why Athena the Olympian goddess

---

7 If the purpose of her trip to Athens is this, it explains why she simply vanishes into the palace; we see inside this palace by following Odysseus into the Phaeacian palace.
8 Examples of this are the repeated word *kasígnētos*, "brother," in *Odyssey* 8 (see §2.129–§2.130 above) and the two parts of the catalogue of heroines in *Odyssey* 11. The correspondence in such cases is, figuratively speaking, a rhyme, which immediately calls attention to itself, and which thereby invites reflection and interpretation. Leonard Muellner's analysis of the succession myth in Hesiod's *Theogony* (Muellner 1996:52–93) provides an interesting comparison for this phenomenon: Muellner shows that key concepts in the succession myth such as *basileús* "king" and *mêtis* "cunning" are first exemplified in action but are named only when they recur ("a concept is namable upon its recurrence, as against its first instance," Muellner 1996:71; the concept of "king" is discussed pp. 67–68, 71, 91n93; *mêtis* is discussed pp. 71, 80; cf. also pp. 94–95). Muellner, who develops an approach to myth used by the anthropologist P.-Y. Jacopin and based on the idea of "metonymy," calls the principle defined above "metonymic nominalism" (Muellner 1996:71). I see an analogy with the cases that concern us insofar as naming implies meaning, and meaning is established by recurrence.

cannot be the hidden identity of the Phaeacian princess. If we consider Athena's two departures at a more basic level, and ask why Athena so pointedly leaves Scheria on two occasions, the answer is not just that Athena as the stage manager needs to get out of the way of the actors; it is that two of the actors are in some sense the same person as Athena, and she therefore cannot appear with them in the same place at the same time.[9]

§3.8 The harder question that confronts us is not Nausicaa, but Arete. Is it true that the Phaeacian queen reflects Athena Polias, the city goddess of Athens? If so, what became of this goddess in the post-Homeric era? These are complex questions, and they have far-reaching implications. Arete is the wife of Alcinous and the mother of his children. There has long been a debate about the nature of Athena Polias and her relationship to Erechtheus. The dominant view is that of Martin Nilsson, who rejected the idea of a marriage bond between Erechtheus and Athena Polias, and instead imagined a Mycenaean war goddess living on the Acropolis in the palace of a representative Mycenaean king, namely Erechtheus. Athena's status as a virgin, which is her essential characteristic according to this view, is thus not violated.[10]

---

9 Anthony Snodgrass, when I outlined my argument about Athena in relation to the Phaeacian queen, suggested the interesting parallel of mystery novels in which the question arises why two people are never seen together, and the answer is that they are in fact the same person. The exception in the *Odyssey* is that Athena appears together with the sleeping Nausicaa; one might say that the Phaeacian shadow-play does not begin until Nausicaa awakens. Nausicaa and Arete are themselves kept separate from each other in the *Odyssey* (Nausicaa's interaction is all with her father) and this, I think, is for a related reason (cf. also n3.19 below).

10 Nilsson 1967:443: "The juxtaposition of Athena and Erechtheus on the Acropolis is to be understood quite differently...than as a matrimonial bond. Erechtheus became the representative of the Mycenaean king, in whose house the city goddess dwells" ("Das Nebeneinander von Athena und Erechtheus auf der Akropolis ist ganz anders zu verstehen...als eheliche Verbindung. Erechtheus ist zum Vertreter des mykenischen Fürsten geworden, in dessen Haus die Burggöttin wohnt"). For the war goddess, see Nilsson 1921:16 (and elsewhere later), arguing that the Mycenaeans adopted the palace goddess of the Minoans, but changed her into a war goddess, and that this explains the strange fact that the Greeks had a war goddess in the first place. In Nilsson's view the palace goddess was the personal protectress of the king, whose protection passed from father to son. The Homeric Athena continues in this role insofar as her protection of Odysseus extends to his son Telemachus and her protection of Diomedes is inherited from his father Tydeus (*Iliad* 5.800–808). Nilsson contrasts Zeus, who protects the institution of kingship rather than the person of the king, and whose protection is therefore not inherited. Athena shows signs of her origins as a palace goddess in the second half of the *Odyssey*, where she openly supports Odysseus, his son, and his father in their homeland, and where her bird epiphany in the rafters of the palace before the battle with the suitors seems to take us back to Minoan times. There is no doubt that Athena relates to her favorites as a war goddess (as when she mounts Diomedes' chariot and rides beside him in *Iliad* 5) but this does not answer the question about Athena Polias in Athens.

But it is far from clear that Athena's nature and origins were as unified as this view presupposes. There is in fact explicit evidence that Athena was worshipped as a mother goddess in at least one city, namely Elis in the northwest Peloponnesus, which had a cult of Athena *Mḗtēr*.[11] This of course does not mean that Athena Polias in Athens was a mother goddess, only that she may have been.

§3.9 To assess what Athena Polias and Erechtheus as a pair represented in early Athens an old story in Herodotus 5.82–88 should be taken into account. Once, when their crops failed, the Epidaurians asked the Athenians for sacred olive trees to cut and make into images of the pair of goddesses Auxesia ("increase") and Damia, as Delphi had instructed them to do. Delphi had specified that the images be made from olive wood, and the Epidaurians had turned to Athens as having the most sacred or perhaps the only olive trees at that time. The Athenians agreed to this request on the condition that the Epidaurians would thereafter bring yearly sacrifices to Athena Polias and Erechtheus.[12] When we consider why the Epidaurians wanted to make the images of their two goddesses from sacred Athenian olive wood, it is surely of significance that the old image of Athena Polias herself was made from sacred Athenian olive wood.[13] This suggests that the nature of the two Epidaurian goddesses in basic ways resembled that of Athena Polias. As for the two goddesses, they were not only concerned with the success of crops, as Herodotus implies; they were also goddesses of childbirth, inasmuch as the images that the Epidaurians made of them represented them on their knees

---

11　Pausanias 5.3.2, who preserves the *aítion* for this cult title: once when Elis was bereft of young men the women prayed to Athena to conceive immediately upon having sexual relations with their husbands, and when their prayer was answered they founded a temple of Athena *Mḗtēr* (τῶν δὲ Ἠλείων αἱ γυναῖκες, ἅτε τῶν ἐν ἡλικίᾳ σφίσιν ἠρημωμένης τῆς χώρας, εὔξασθαι τῇ Ἀθηνᾷ λέγονται κυῆσαι παραυτίκα, ἐπειδὰν μιχθῶσι τοῖς ἀνδράσι· καὶ ἥ τε εὐχή σφισιν ἐτελέσθη καὶ Ἀθηνᾶς ἱερὸν ἐπίκλησιν Μητρὸς ἱδρύσαντο). Unlike Farnell, who minimizes the evidence of the Elean cult (Farnell 1896, vol. 1, 303), Nilsson insists on giving it full weight (Nilsson 1967:443); Nilsson is particularly impressed by the *aítion* for the title Μήτηρ. Nilsson's conclusion nonetheless does not differ significantly from Farnell's.

12　οἱ δὲ ἐπὶ τοῖσδε δώσειν ἔφασαν ἐπ' ᾧ ἀπάξουσι ἔτεος ἑκάστου τῇ Ἀθηναίῃ τε τῇ Πολιάδι ἱρὰ καὶ τῷ Ἐρεχθέι (Herodotus 5.82.3).

13　Scholia to Demosthenes 22.13: [ἄγαλμα] ἐξ ἀρχῆς γενόμενον ἐξ ἐλαίας, ὅπερ ἐκαλεῖτο πολιάδος Ἀθηνᾶς, "[the image] made from the beginning from an olive tree, which was called that of Athena Polias"; Athenagoras *Legatio pro Christianis* 17.4: τὸ τῆς Ἀθηνᾶς [εἴδωλον]...τὸ ἀπὸ τῆς ἐλαίας τὸ παλαιόν, "the [idol] of Athena...the one from the olive tree, the old one." Other writers confirm that the image was of wood: "Apollodorus" 3.14.6 (*xóanon*); Plutarch *Moralia* fr. 158 Sandbach (*xúlinon*); cf. Frazer 1913 on Pausanias 1.26.6.

in the act of giving birth.[14] This again does not mean that Athena was neces-sarily a mother goddess herself.[15] Nevertheless, when we consider Athena Polias and Erechtheus as the recipients of annual sacrifices in compensation for the images of two goddesses of childbirth, there is reason to think that they themselves were not unconcerned with procreation.[16]

14 Herodotus reveals this detail when he tells the subsequent history of the images, after the Aeginetans stole them from the Epidaurians. The Aeginetans, the images' new owners, refused to continue the Epidaurians' practice of sending yearly sacrifices to Athens in compensation for the sacred olive wood, and the Athenians sent an unsuccessful party to Aegina to remove the images. As the Aeginetans told the story, when the Athenians began to haul the images from their bases, the images fell to their knees as if in supplication and remained like that ever after: ἐς γούνατα γάρ σφι αὐτὰ πεσεῖν, καὶ τὸν ἀπὸ τούτου χρόνον διατελέειν οὕτω ἔχοντα (Herodotus 5.86.3). Although Herodotus seems unaware of it, these are goddesses of childbirth, as parallel examples of their pose show (cf. Dümmler *RE* 'Auxesia' 2617). In Tegea Αὔγη ἐν γόνασι, "Auge on her knees," was an eponym of Eileithyia, the goddess of childbirth (it is clear from the aetiological myth that Auge, the mother of Telephos, was the original goddess of childbirth in Tegea: it was said that, while being led away on her father's orders to be drowned, she fell to her knees and gave birth—πεσεῖν τε ἐς γόνατα καὶ οὕτω τεκεῖν—at the temple of Eileithyia in the agora, in which her cult image was still to be seen in Pausanias's day [8.48.7]). In the *Homeric Hymn to Apollo* Leto is similarly described in the act of giving birth to Apollo: ἀμφὶ δὲ φοίνικι βάλε πήχεε, γοῦνα δ' ἔρεισε / λειμῶνι μαλακῷ, "throwing her arms around the palm tree she propped her knees on the soft meadow" (*Homeric Hymn to Apollo* 117–118). In Rome goddesses of child-birth called the *Nixae* (Ovid *Metamorphoses* 9.294, cf. von Basiner 1905:619n1 for the form) or *Di Nixi* were represented on their knees (Festus 174–177: *nixi di appellantur tria signa in Capitolio ante cellam Minervae genibus nixa, velut praesidentes parientium nixibus*, "*Di Nixi* is the name given to three statues in the Capitolium in front of the temple of Minerva propped [*nixa*] on their knees, as if keeping watch over the travail [*nixūs*] of those giving birth"; they were brought to Rome after the defeat of Antiochus according to some, after the defeat of Corinth according to others).

15 We can be sure that Athena's image, little as we know of it, did not represent her in the act of giving birth (cf. §3.13 below). Like Damia and Auxesia, Athena Polias was concerned with the success of crops, as certain old festivals show, for example the Procharisteria: in this festival, which took place when the grain sprouted at the end of winter, Athena was offered a sacrifice in which all the leading magistrates took part (Suda s.v.). The old agrarian significance of Athena is particularly clear here as Deubner 1932:17 notes (the festival became associated with Kore's return from the underworld after the Athenian reception of the Eleusinian cult; cf. Deubner 1932:17 with nn2 and 3 on Lycurgus 7, fr. 1 a-b Conomis). As Herodotus tells the story of the Epidaurians, their problem was a crop failure so that no more than an interest in the success of crops is strictly implied for Athena (or for Damia and Auxesia). This, I think, is too narrow a view (see n3.16 below).

16 In Herodotus's account a crop failure motivates the Epidaurians to found a new cult to the two goddesses (Ἐπιδαυρίοισι ἡ γῆ καρπὸν οὐδένα ἀνεδίδου, Herodotus 5.82.1), and once the Epidaurians have made and set up the new images the crops return (ἀγάλματα ἐκ τῶν ἐλαιέων τουτέων ποιησάμενοι ἱδρύσαντο· καὶ ἥ τε γῆ σφι ἔφερε, Herodotus 5.82.3). But the fact that the images represented the goddesses in the act of childbirth suggests that the Epidaurians faced a more general crisis of fertility involving human reproduction too (famine and childbirth failure are in fact closely related). The omission of this aspect of

§3.10 For the nature of Athena Polias in Athens we will follow where the text of *Odyssey* 7 leads, from her temple on the Acropolis to the Phaeacian palace and the Phaeacian queen. But just as Alcinous both is and is not Nestor, so Arete both is and is not Athena Polias. She is also herself, the queen of the Phaeacians, just as Alcinous is also himself, the king of the Phaeacians. At the end of the story Arete can only be herself, for the Phaeacians, as we have seen, are left to an uncertain future, and Athena can have no part in that. In his farewell speech to Arete, as he leaves the palace for the waiting Phaeacian ship, Odysseus explicitly recognizes that the Phaeacian queen is indeed a mortal (*Odyssey* 13.59–62):

χαῖρέ μοι, ὦ βασίλεια, διαμπερές, εἰς ὅ κε γῆρας
ἔλθῃ καὶ θάνατος, τά τ᾽ ἐπ᾽ ἀνθρώποισι πέλονται.
αὐτὰρ ἐγὼ νέομαι· σὺ δὲ τέρπεο τῷδ᾽ ἐνὶ οἴκῳ
παισί τε καὶ λαοῖσι καὶ Ἀλκινόῳ βασιλῆϊ.

May you fare well always, O queen, until old age
and death come, which are the condition of men.
I will return home; but in this house may you rejoice
in your children and people and in Alcinous the king.

This is the last act in the shadow-play of Arete's identity, and it ensures that nothing of Athena is left behind with her when she and the other Phaeacians return to the doubtful existence from which they came. It is not this last act, but the first act that matters for Arete's identity as Athena Polias, and this act is played out as soon as Odysseus enters the Phaeacian palace, covered in mist, and clasps Arete's knees. Arete's role is to be supplicated, and this role is built around

---

the story in Herodotus is consistent with the fact that he no longer seems aware that these were goddesses of childbirth; this aspect of the story had simply been forgotten. The events narrated by Herodotus, while they are probably legendary in part and are difficult to date, clearly belonged to an early period. The context for the earliest events, the establishment of the cult of Damia and Auxesia in Epidaurus and the negotiation between Epidaurus and Athens for the olive trees, may have been the Calaurian Amphictyony. The war between Athens and Aegina that followed the termination of the sacrifices to Athena Polias and Erechtheus (Herodotus 5.85–88) probably took place in the seventh century BC, but in any case not later than the early sixth century BC. The chronology of the events narrated by Herodotus and the nature and extent of cults of Damia and Auxesia more generally are considered in EN3.1. The annual sacrifices to Athena Polias and Erechtheus were perhaps still offered by the Epidaurians in the Homeric era, in the late eighth and early seventh centuries BC, and this possibility puts *Odyssey* 7.80–81, the only Homeric text to feature the two Athenian figures at their old cult site (for *Iliad* 2.546–551 see n3.6 above), in an interesting light. For the festival at which Athena Polias and Erechtheus received such sacrifices (an uncertain matter for so early a period) see §3.81 below; cf. also n3.197 below.

her identification with Athena Polias. The very first moment is also the most highly charged moment, for the stranger Odysseus has appeared out of nowhere grasping Arete's knees, and we have twice been told that his appeal for a *nóstos* depends entirely on his winning favor with her. The scene is electric with anticipation, and it is nothing short of stunning that Arete makes no response. We have already noted that Alcinous also makes no immediate response, and we have found good reason for that in an inherited tension that has to do with an old quarrel between Odysseus and Nestor. But Alcinous was not appealed to directly by Odysseus, and, prodded by the aged retainer Ekheneos, he also reacts to Odysseus's presence well before Arete does. Arete's behavior has seemed inexplicable.[17] What we must realize, following clues in the text, is that Odysseus has in effect grasped the knees of Athena Polias, whose ancient image stood in the palace of Erechtheus.[18] Arete at this moment has become that image, and that is why she sits in total silence. Arete eventually breaks her silence and when she does the illusion that she is Athena Polias has already begun to dissipate. Her identification with Athena Polias is never as strong again once she speaks.[19] In the end, as we have seen, the illusion is dispelled totally.

§3.11 Arete's name is well suited to her role. A verbal adjective from *aráomai*, "to pray," the name Ἀρήτη (masculine Ἄρητος) means "prayed for," as of a late-born child long "prayed for" by its parents.[20] This meaning fits Arete, who was the only child of her father Rhexenor, who is now dead. But

17 Cf. Hainsworth in Heubeck et al. 1988, vol. 1, 316–317, who identifies and discusses two major unanswered questions regarding Arete's role: Why is the importance of her role so emphasized in advance when in the event she actually does very little? Why does she remain silent for so long after Odysseus's direct appeal to her? Both questions, I think, are answered by her hidden identity.

18 For the location of Athena's ancient image, which must never have changed, see §3.48–§3.51 below. The statement in the text above is, I think, accurate, but it is not the same as the orthodox view, namely that Athena's image (and shrine) were in the Erechtheum; in contrast to Athena's shrine and image the shrine of Erechtheus did not, I think, remain fixed in one location (see §3.52–§3.54 below).

19 When she finally breaks her silence 84 lines after Odysseus's appeal to her (*Odyssey* 7.237–239) it is to ask him pointedly who he is, for she recognizes the clothes given to him by Nausicaa. Before that Arete's only presence in the poem, apart from her introduction by the disguised Athena, is as a static figure who sits and spins, and who must be supplicated by Odysseus. In this she contrasts sharply with Alcinous, who interacts vividly with Nausicaa before her laundry expedition; Arete, on the other hand, does not come to life in the poem until she finally addresses Odysseus.

20 This sense is clear from the compound adjective πολυάρητος, "much prayed for," as in *Odyssey* 19.403–404, where Odysseus is called πολυάρητος to his grandfather Autolykos when Eurykleia bids Autolykos name Odysseus at his birth:

Αὐτόλυκ', αὐτὸς νῦν ὄνομ' εὕρεο, ὅττι κε θεῖο
παιδὸς παιδὶ φίλῳ· πολυάρητος δέ τοί ἐστι.

the name also suggests the meaning "prayed to," and this fits Arete's real role, which is to be supplicated by Odysseus.²¹ The name is a perfect combination of overt and suggested meanings, corresponding to the queen's overt and hidden roles.

§3.12 Let us pursue the idea that when Odysseus grasps Arete's knees, she has in effect become Athena Polias. This idea has implications for what the ancient image of Athena Polias, which is nowhere described for us, actually was. For at the moment of supplication Arete is represented as sitting at the hearth, holding the distaff, and spinning. Nausicaa has already told Odysseus that this is how he will find her (*Odyssey* 6.303–307):²²

> ἀλλ' ὁπότ' ἄν σε δόμοι κεκύθωσι καὶ αὐλή,
>
> ὦκα μάλα μεγάροιο διελθέμεν, ὄφρ' ἄν ἵκηαι
>
> μητέρ' ἐμήν· ἡ δ' ἧσται ἐπ' ἐσχάρη ἐν πυρὸς αὐγῇ,
>
> ἠλάκατα στρωφῶσ' ἁλιπόρφυρα, θαῦμα ἰδέσθαι,
>
> κίονι κεκλιμένη.

> But when the house and courtyard enclose you,
>
> cross the hall quickly until you reach
>
> my mother; she sits at the hearth in the light of the fire,

---

Autolykos, now you yourself find a name that you would give to your child's dear child; he is much prayed for by you.

In *Homeric Hymn to Demeter* 220 Metaneira uses the adjective of her son Demophon with an even more explicit indication of its meaning: τὸν ὀψίγονον καὶ ἄελπτον / ὤπασαν ἀθάνατοι, πολυάρητος δέ μοί ἐστιν, "whom the gods have given, late born and unexpected, and he is much prayed for by me." The masculine name Ἄρητος occurs of two figures in Homer: a Trojan (*Iliad* 17.494 and 535) and a son of Nestor (*Odyssey* 3.414 and 440). Feminine Ἀρήτη occurs in Hipponax of a figure who was apparently a courtesan (frs. 20.2, 22.2, 23.1, 24 Degani); the name is probably a conceit modeled on the Phaeacian queen (cf. Hawkins 2004:223).

21 For this suggested meaning of the name see Stanford 1959 on *Odyssey* 7.54; cf. also Hainsworth (Heubeck et al. 1988) ad loc. Another instance of the adjective πολυάρητος shows how the meanings "prayed for" and "prayed to" might be combined in the poet's mind. In *Odyssey* 6 Nausicaa tells Odysseus not to let the Phaeacians see him with her lest they say that he is her intended husband, either a wandering mortal, or else "some god has come πολυάρητος in answer to her prayers, descending from the sky": ἤ τίς οἱ εὐξαμένη πολυάρητος θεὸς ἦλθεν / οὐρανόθεν καταβάς (*Odyssey* 6.280–281). Since the reference is to a god it is not clear whether the meaning is simply "much prayed for," or there may also be a suggestion of the meaning "much prayed to." The same ambiguity seems to surround the name Arete, depending on whether she is thought of as Athena's double or simply herself. It seems significant that the ambiguous verse just quoted occurs not long before Arete, and her name, are first introduced.

22 The phrase ἠλάκατα στρωφῶσ', "spinning the distaff wool," implies holding the distaff (ἠλακάτη) in one hand and spinning with the other hand.

spinning sea-purple wool from a distaff, a wonder to see,
leaning against a column.

Arete is described in exactly these terms at her first appearance in the poem
as well: when Nausicaa awakens from the dream sent by Athena and goes to
see her father and mother, she finds her mother sitting by the hearth with
women servants, holding the distaff and spinning (*Odyssey* 6.52–53):

ἡ μὲν ἐπ᾽ ἐσχάρῃ ἧστο σὺν ἀμφιπόλοισι γυναιξίν,
ἠλάκατα στρωφῶσ᾽ ἁλιπόρφυρα.

She sat at the hearth with her serving women,
spinning sea-purple wool from a distaff.

Thus the scene has already been set twice before Odysseus enters the
Phaeacian palace, and there is no need to describe it a third time. We already
have in mind the figure whose knees Odysseus grasps when he makes his
supplication. If Arete is meant to represent Athena Polias in this scene, Arete's
pose, described twice in identical terms, must be that of Athena Polias.

§3.13 When Pausanias saw the statue of Athena Polias in the second
century AD he called it the holiest object in Athens but did not describe it. He
only repeated what was commonly said about it, that it fell from heaven.[23] In
the popular imagination the image was evidently as old as the city of Athens
itself.[24] Apart from the fact that it was made of olive wood nothing is known

---

23 Pausanias says that the image was much older than the legendary synoecism of Theseus,
in which the Attic demes were united into one state; he connects what was said about the
image's divine origin with this high antiquity: τὸ δὲ ἁγιώτατον ἐν κοινῷ πολλοῖς πρότερον
νομισθὲν ἔτεσιν ‹ἢ› συνῆλθον ἀπὸ τῶν δήμων ἐστὶν Ἀθηνᾶς ἄγαλμα ἐν τῇ νῦν ἀκροπόλει,
τότε δὲ ὀνομαζομένῃ πόλει· φήμη δὲ ἐς αὐτὸ ἔχει πεσεῖν ἐκ τοῦ οὐρανοῦ, "The object
considered holiest by all many years before they formed a union from the demes is the
image of Athena on what is now the acropolis, but then was called the *pólis* (city); a legend
regarding it has it that it fell from the sky" (Pausanias 1.26.6).
24 Plutarch *Moralia* fr. 158 Sandbach says that the image was set up "by the autochthons"; for
other references to the image's antiquity cf. Kroll 1982:72–73. From the legend that the
image fell from the sky some have inferred that it was little more than an aniconic slab of
wood (Kroll 1982:73–75; Robertson 1996:29; cf. Shapiro 1989:25). That such an inference
cannot be made is shown by traditions for the palladion of Troy, which was famously said
to have fallen from the sky when Troy was founded (*diipetés/diopetés* is the adjective regu-
larly used of it, as in Clement of Alexandria *Protrepticus* 4.47.6: τὸ διοπετὲς καλούμενον,
"the so-called 'sky-fallen' [image]"), but which was also believed to represent an armed
Athena; cf. "Apollodorus" 3.12.3, who calls the image *diipetés* and says that it held a spear
in its right hand and a distaff and spindle in its left hand. The image of Artemis in Ephesus
was also called τὸ διοπετές (*Acts of the Apostles* 19.35); the image of this exotic mother
goddess is unlikely to have been aniconic.

directly about the actual image. Inscriptions of annual temple inventories for a thirty-year period in the fourth century BC list the valuable (golden) accessories of the image; they refer to the image itself simply as *hē theós*, "the goddess." The accessories, in particular a golden aegis and a golden gorgoneion, were meant to depict a warlike goddess,[25] and it is clear that these ornaments had belonged to the goddess for a period of time, probably since the sixth century.[26] It was then that the Athena Polias seems to have been

25 The *locus classicus* for the aegis and gorgoneion (here part of the aegis) is *Iliad* 5.733–742, where Athena takes off her *péplos*, which she herself made, and puts on the *khitōn* and *aigís*, which she borrows from her father, "aegis-holder Zeus":

αὐτὰρ Ἀθηναίη κούρη Διὸς αἰγιόχοιο
πέπλον μὲν κατέχευεν ἑανὸν πατρὸς ἐπ' οὔδει
ποικίλον, ὅν ῥ' αὐτὴ ποιήσατο καὶ κάμε χερσίν·
ἡ δὲ χιτῶν' ἐνδῦσα Διὸς νεφεληγερέταο
τεύχεσιν ἐς πόλεμον θωρήσσετο δακρυόεντα.
ἀμφὶ δ' ἄρ' ὤμοισιν βάλετ' αἰγίδα θυσσανόεσσαν
δεινήν, ἣν περὶ μὲν πάντῃ Φόβος ἐστεφάνωται,
ἐν δ' Ἔρις, ἐν δ' Ἀλκή, ἐν δὲ κρυόεσσα Ἰωκή,
ἐν δέ τε Γοργείη κεφαλὴ δεινοῖο πελώρου
δεινή τε σμερδνή τε, Διὸς τέρας αἰγιόχοιο.

But Athena, daughter of aegis-holder Zeus,
let slip to her father's floor her supple robe
of many colors, which she herself had made and worked by hand;
she put on the tunic of cloud-gatherer Zeus
and armed herself with weapons for tear-bringing war.
On her shoulders she put the tasseled aegis,
terrifying, around which Panic was set on every side,
and in it was Strife, and Resistance, and chilling Pursuit,
and the dread monster's Gorgon-head,
dreadful and fearful, the emblem of aegis-holder Zeus.

26 The inventories are of the *arkhaîos neós* ("old temple") from about 370–340 BC. There is virtually no variation in the ornaments of Athena Polias over the thirty-year period, and this suggests that the items had been in place for some time already (cf. Frickenhaus 1908:20, who contrasts cult images of Artemis Brauronia on which the ornaments were frequently changed in this period). The golden aegis, which played a role in the festival of the Gamelia (the priestess of Athena visited newlyweds with it) probably did not originate later than the sixth century BC. The golden gorgoneion figures in a story about the evacuation of Athens in 480 BC (Plutarch *Themistocles* 10.4); even though the story was probably fabricated by the Atthidographer Kleidemos (Jacoby, commentary on Kleidemos *FGrHist* 323 F 21; McInerney 1994:35; cf. Frost 1980:120–121), it still perhaps indicates that the gorgoneion existed at the time. Cf. Ridgway 1992:124: "It would seem as if a relatively neutral wooden image...was gradually transformed by the Athenians through the addition of attributes into a more 'typical' Athena with war-like connotations.... Since the gorgoneion may have existed by ca. 480, so would the aegis, implying that the transformation had already taken place within the sixth century. The reorganization of the Panathenaic

turned into a war goddess. The image itself was doubtless much older, but how old we do not know. It played a central part in traditions about the Cylonian conspiracy of about 630 BC: the conspirators took refuge at Athena's image but were executed on the order of the Alcmaeonid Megacles, whose sacrilege put him and his family under a lasting curse.[27] There is no reason to think that the image of Athena in this story is not the same as the one called "the goddess" in the fourth-century inventories and seen centuries later by Pausanias. My assumption is that the image existed earlier still, during the Homeric era, and that when Athena enters the "strong house of Erechtheus" in *Odyssey* 7 the Homeric audience would imagine her as entering and animating this very image. *Iliad* 6 offers a parallel for such a full-size seated image of Athena Polias in the Homeric era: Hecabe and the other Trojan women go to Athena's temple on the citadel (ἐν πόλει ἄκρῃ, *Iliad* 6.297), and Theano, the priestess, places their offering, a *péplos*, on Athena's knees (*Iliad* 6.302–303):

ἣ δ' ἄρα πέπλον ἑλοῦσα Θεανὼ καλλιπάρῃος
θῆκεν Ἀθηναίης ἐπὶ γούνασιν ἠϋκόμοιο.

Taking the robe fair-cheeked Theano
placed it on the knees of beautiful-haired Athena.[28]

---

festival, in ca. 566, may provide a suitable date for these additions to the statue." Cf. also Casson 1921:330, 332.

27 There were conflicting stories as to whether or not the conspirators had already left Athena's protection when they were executed; in the pro-Alcmaeonid version reported by Plutarch *Solon* 12.1 the conspirators attempted to keep contact with the image by means of a thread as they left the Acropolis, but the thread broke near the temple of the Erinyes and the conspirators were thereby delivered up to their just fate. It may be noted that Thucydides, in an account that seems to correct Herodotus on a point (cf. Gomme on Thucydides 1.126.8), says that the conspirators fled to Athena's altar, not to her image (καθίζουσιν ἐπὶ τὸν βωμόν, Thucydides 1.126.10; cf. ἵζετο πρὸς τὸ ἄγαλμα, Herodotus 5.71.1). For the question of whether a temple of Athena existed at the time of the Cylonian conspiracy see Herington 1955:22n4, with a reference to Judeich 1931:262n2.

28 This episode (*Iliad* 6.264–312) also offers insight into how the relation between the goddess and her image may have been perceived, for the two are not at all distinguished: the Trojan priestess lays the robe on Athena's knees and supplicates her, but Athena shakes her head in rejection (ἀνένευε δὲ Παλλὰς Ἀθήνη, *Iliad* 6.311); cf. Donohue 1988:23–24 and 41n99. Although this episode is sometimes attributed to an Athenian poet because a *péplos* was offered to Athena at the Panathenaia (so Lorimer 1950:442–449), I think that the opposite is more likely to be the case, i.e. that the Athenian ritual was influenced by Homer (cf. n3.244 below).

§3.14 What the image of Athena Polias on the Acropolis of Athens looked like has been the subject of much speculation but has yet to be determined. One thing is clear: it was a unique object in the Greek world. It was very likely of a different order from other images, including those of Athena Polias in Troy and other cities. The question of what this image was should be approached with an open mind. The fourth-century inventories reveal one very important thing about the image itself: it held a golden libation bowl (*phiálē*) in its hand. This means that its right hand was extended.[29] But the right hand cannot originally have held a *phiálē*, for this statue-type, a god offering a libation, does not occur until the late sixth or early fifth century.[30] It is likely, therefore, that the *phiálē* was added to the Athena Polias about 500 BC.[31] Why was the right hand

29 The type has been studied by Eckstein-Wolf 1952 and Simon 1953; for the *phiálē* see Luschey *RE* Supplement 7 'Phiale' 1030; Patton 1992 is a comparative study of the phenomenon of libations by gods. The evidence for the image of Athena Polias is the phrase φιάλη χρυσῆ ἣν ἐν τῇ χειρὶ ἔχει, "a gold phiale that she holds in her hand," in the inventories (*IG* II² 1424a lines 365–366 [371/70 BC]; cf. *IG* II² 1425 line 312 [368/7 BC] and *IG* II² 1424 line 16 [374/3 BC]; cf. Harris 1995:209 no. 20).

30 Luschey *RE* Supplement 7 'Phiale' 1030 dates the type to the beginning of the fifth century; so too Eckstein-Wolf 1952 and Simon 1953. Apollo is the god most often represented with a *phiálē*: Simon discusses a particular type of the group Leto, Apollo, and Artemis, which in the sixth century focuses on Apollo's kithara, but in the early fifth century focuses on a new element in Apollo's hand, a *phiálē* (Simon 1953:19). Since the studies in the early 1950s of Luschey, Eckstein-Wolf, and Simon new finds have reopened the question of the earliest date of the Apollo type. A bronze *koûros* found in Piraeus in 1959 and identified as Apollo apparently held a bow in the left hand and a *phiálē* in the right hand: the statue has been taken as an Archaic sixth-century piece, of the decade 530–520 BC, but it is more likely to be a late archaizing piece; for a detailed analysis of this still controversial piece, see Fuchs 1999:18–21, who dates it to c. 90 BC; cf. also Mattusch 1996:138–140, Palagia 1997:180–185, and Hemingway 2004:13, 21 (for additional bibliography see Fuchs 1999:10 and Lambrinudakis et al. *LIMC* 'Apollo' no. 432). A few bronze statuettes of *koûroi* dated to the late sixth century seem to have held a bow in the left hand and a *phiálē* in the right hand, and may represent Apollo: *LIMC* 'Apollo' no. 431 (525–500 BC), no. 433 (c. 510 BC), no. 434, with bow intact (c. 500 BC). A bronze statuette dated to the first half of the sixth century is conjectured to have held a *phiálē* in the right hand (*LIMC* 'Apollo' no. 430, Settis 1971:57), but such an early date would be truly exceptional for the type (Fuchs 1999:19 argues that even in the 520s a *phiálē* in the hand of the "Piraeus Apollo" would be "exceptionell"; see Fuchs 1999:19n139 for references). The question of why gods received the *phiálē* as an attribute in the late sixth or early fifth century does not directly concern us, but I note with interest Simon's argument that Apollo functioned as a priest, and as an intermediary between his father Zeus and men (Simon 1953:25). Did Athena Polias, in her new guise, likewise mediate between her people and her father Zeus? The connection between Athena as a war goddess and Zeus as her father in sixth/fifth-century Athens is discussed §3.42–§3.47 below. With respect to the golden *phiálē* of Athena Polias, it is worth noting that it is a valuable adornment like the other golden adornments recorded in the fourth-century inventories; it is no more part of the original statue than they are.

31 Eckstein-Wolf 1952:65; so also Frickenhaus 1908:23 (end of the sixth century). Eckstein-Wolf points out that artistic representations which seem to relate to the Athena Polias are

extended originally? In representations of women spinning, the right hand is extended to spin wool drawn from a distaff, which is held at a higher level by the left hand; the pose is seen in this example:[32]

Figure 1.

---

not shown holding a *phiálē* until after the type ("spendende Götter") had already appeared on other vase paintings. See n3. 33 below for artistic representations that seem to relate directly to the Athena Polias.

32 Figure 1, a seated girl spinning, is a reconstruction of a terracotta plaque from the Athenian Acropolis, c. 500 BC. The reconstruction, after Le Lasseur 1919:104, figure 48, is based on two fragmentary copies from the same mold, Acropolis Museum nos. 1329 (new numbering 13054) and 1330 (new numbering 13055); photographs in Plates 1 and 2 below. In the first plaque (Plate 1 below) the right hand and spindle are still intact; in the second plaque (Plate 2 below) the raised position of the left arm is still evident despite loss of most of the arm, including the left hand and distaff. The same position of the two hands, with a distaff in the left hand and a spindle below the right hand, appears consistently in examples of spinning women in Greek art. Further examples are seen in Plate 3 below, a profile view of a spinner on an Attic red-figure hydria by a painter close to the Clio Painter, c. 475–425; and in Plate 4 below, a frontal view of a spinner on an Attic red-figure cup attributed to the Euaion Painter, c. 475–425 BC. Female wool workers engaged in various parts of the wool working process are depicted on a sixth-century Attic black-figure lekythos attributed to the Amasis Painter, c. 575–525 BC (New York, Metropolitan Museum, no. 31.11.10; photograph and rollout drawing in Keuls 1983:215, figure 14.11 a–c). Plate 5 below is a detail of the rollout drawing: the woman spinning (second figure from the right) is standing; three other women, one seated on the left, and two standing on the left and right, are shown "drawing a roving," the step prior to spinning in the wool working process. Note that all four figures, one spinning and three drawing a roving, have their hands in the same position. For demonstrations of the ancient wool working process see Edmunds, Jones, and Nagy 2004.

The image of Athena Polias, which held a *phiálē* in its right hand, was recognized as such by August Frickenhaus in four artistic representations of a seated goddess holding a *phiálē*; in all four representations the left hand is raised higher than the right hand as it is in the spinning woman, but instead of a distaff the left hand holds a spear or a helmet; the pose, which is virtually the same as for the spinning woman, is seen in the following example:[33]

---

33 Frickenhaus 1908. The first example, Figure 2 in the text, is a reconstruction of a terra-
cotta plaque from the Athenian Acropolis, c. 500 BC (same provenience as for Figure 1).
This reconstruction, after Le Lasseur 1919:98, figure 47, is again based on two fragmentary
copies from the same mold, Acropolis Museum nos. 1337 (new numbering 13056) and 1338
(new numbering 13057); photographs in Plates 6 and 7 below. In the first plaque (Plate
6 below) the *phiálē* in the figure's right hand is still intact; in the second plaque (Plate 7
below) the raised left hand appears to have held a spear, which must have been painted
in (cf. Hutton 1897:307, 310); in Figure 2 the spear has been added to Le Lasseur's recon-
struction. The photograph in Frickenhaus 1908 (plate following p. 20, no. 1) is a composite
of both plaques. For the identification as Athena Polias (there is no distinctive attribute
in the image itself) see Hutton 1897:310–311 and Frickenhaus 1908:21. The other three
examples adduced by Frickenhaus are the following: in Plate 8 below is a drawing of an
Attic black-figure kalpis by the Nikoxenos Painter, c. 500 BC, which was once on the art
market in Rome and is now lost. For the identification as Athena Polias with *phiálē* note
the altar, the sacrificial bull, and the priestess in front of what must be a seated goddess.
In Plate 9 are photographs of an Attic white-ground lekythos, attributed to the Athena
Painter, c. 500–450 BC (cf. Frickenhaus 1908, plate following p. 22; LIMC 'Athena' no. 579,
plate p. 761; Shapiro 1989, plate 10 d-e). For the identification as Athena Polias with *phiálē*
note the altar and the two owls flanking the seated goddess; for two other examples of
the same subject by the same painter see Shapiro 1989:31n102 and plate 11 a-b. Shapiro
points out that the owl perched on Athena's shield indicates that a cult statue rather
than an epiphany of Athena is represented. In Plates 10 and 11 below are a photograph
and a drawing of reconstructed fragments of an Attic red-figure column crater signed by
Myson, c. 500–450 BC (photograph also in LIMC 'Athena' no. 578a, plate p. 761; drawing
also in Verbanck-Piérard 1988:225, figure 1). The left arm of the seated goddess appears
slightly less elevated in this example than in the other examples. In front of the goddess is
a sacrificial scene ("Opferscene," Frickenhaus 1908:21); a separate (but related?) fragment
of the vase shows an altar (this is shown in the drawing, Plate 11 below, Verbanck-Piérard
1988:225, figure 1). In this example, and in the Attic white-ground lekythos (Plate 9), the
helmet worn by Athena is the artist's free invention, unrelated to the image of Athena
Polias; see Frickenhaus 1908:21. In three of the representations adduced by Frickenhaus
the goddess's left hand holds a spear and in one it holds a helmet, namely the drawing of
the Attic black-figure kalpis, Plate 8, in which there is also a spear, but it leans against the
goddess's shoulder).

Figure 2.

All four examples adduced by Frickenhaus belong to the end of the sixth or beginning of the fifth century.³⁴ If these are indeed representations of the Athena Polias, the position of the two hands seems exactly right for spinning wool.³⁵ There is good reason to think that this is what the Athena Polias was originally represented as doing.

§3.15 The Ionian city of Erythrai had a cult image of Athena Polias from the second half of the sixth century which held a distaff in each hand.³⁶ This

34 Frickenhaus 1908:22; cf. Eckstein-Wolf 1952:65.

35 Compare the examples cited in n3.32 and n3.33 above. The correspondence between Figures 1 and 2 in the text above is especially clear. Hutton 1897:310, who published these line drawings, drew attention to "the obvious connexion" between them, but had no reason to pursue the connection further. It is interesting that the hands are again in the same position on a series of Athenian coins which Kroll 1982:70–72 refers to the image of Athena Polias; on these coins the figure is standing (Kroll thinks that the Athena Polias also was standing) and the left hand holds an owl. The fourth-century inventories of Athena's ornaments include a golden owl, which has no other obvious place to go on the Athena Polias. But there are problems in referring the coins to Athena Polias: the fourth-century inventories include a golden crown (*stephánē*) of the goddess, whereas the coins show a helmeted figure; I, for my part, do not believe that the Athena Polias was standing. If the position of the two hands on the coins nevertheless refers to the Athena Polias, it would appear that the old distaff held in the left hand was replaced by a succession of items: first perhaps a spear (as in Figure 2 above and Plates 9 and 10/11 below); then perhaps a helmet (as in Plate 8 below); then by the time of the fourth-century inventories a golden owl.

36 It was the work of the sculptor Endoios, Pausanias 7.5.9: ἔστι δὲ ἐν Ἐρυθραῖς καὶ Ἀθηνᾶς Πολιάδος ναὸς καὶ ἄγαλμα ξύλου μεγέθει μέγα καθήμενόν τε ἐπὶ θρόνου καὶ ἡλακάτην ἐν ἑκατέρᾳ τῶν χειρῶν ἔχει καὶ ἐπὶ τῆς κεφαλῆς πόλον· τοῦτο ⟨Ἐνδοίου⟩ τέχνην καὶ ἄλλοις

evidence, unusual because of the second distaff, should remove all doubt that
a distaff could also have been held by the Athena Polias in Athens.[37] The figure
in Erythrai was seated, as I believe the figure in Athens was.[38] My reason for

ἐτεκμαιρόμεθα εἶναι καὶ ἐς τὴν ἐργασίαν ὁρῶντες ἔνδον τοῦ ἀγάλματος, κτλ., "There is also
in Erythrai a temple of Athena Polias and a wooden image of her of large size and seated
on a throne, and she has a distaff in each of her hands and a polos on her head; that this is
Endoios's craftsmanship we could tell by other things, but especially by observing the work
inside the image," etc. The working life of Endoios is dated c. 540–500 BC by Raubitschek
1949:495. Images of Athena with distaff are not common in art. On a terracotta relief in
Syracuse dated to the last quarter of the fifth century BC Athena holds a distaff in her left
hand (right arm is missing; Demargne LIMC 'Athena' no. 54; Keuls 1985:251, figure 229). On
Hellenistic coins from Asia Minor (LIMC 'Athena' no. 58) Athena Ilias (named on no. 58a)
holds a distaff in her left hand and a spear in her right hand. Other possible examples (LIMC
'Athena' nos. 43, 45, 46) are all uncertain: no. 43 is the terracotta relief of a seated young
girl spinning represented in Figure 1 in §3.14 above and discussed in n3.32 above; no. 46 is
a terracotta statuette of Athena of c. 500 BC with extended right hand (left arm, which may
have held a distaff, is missing). No certain example of Athena with distaff survives from
Attica (cf. Keuls 1985:250).

37 Relevant also are loomweights discussed by Barber 1992:106: "A tangible indicator of
the close tie between Athena and weaving comes in a number of loomweights from the
Greek colonies in Italy. On these weights Athena herself appears in the form of an owl,
her sacred bird, spinning wool from a wool basket in front of her. The owl is shown with
a pair of human arms and hands (in addition to the expected wings and feet) to do the
work, as on a late fifth-century weight from Tarentum" (photograph p. 107); as noted on
p. 151 (where a lower date of c. 300 BC is given for the object) the owl also holds a distaff.
Wuilleumier 1939:439 classes this object with various others as having a commercial
purpose; Herdejürgen 1971:73–74 identifies the objects in question as tags for goods rather
than as loomweights.

38 A seated Athena Polias is argued by Frickenhaus 1908:24 and is accepted by Nilsson
1967:436n4; cf. also Fehrle 1910:199, following Frickenhaus. In arguing for a standing
figure Kroll 1982:67 relies on two pieces of indirect literary evidence. The Christian writer
Athenagoras (Legatio pro Christianis 17.4; cf. n3.13 above) refers to a "seated" statue of
Athena on the Acropolis by the sculptor Endoios; Kroll takes the description "seated" of
this statue as meant to contrast with the Athena Polias, which Athenagoras also appar-
ently attributed to Endoios. But the reason that Athenagoras calls the first statue "seated"
is that he borrows the entire description of the statue, including the seated pose, from
Pausanias 1.26.4 (see Snodgrass 2003); no inference can therefore be drawn for the pose
of the Athena Polias. The evidence of Athenagoras is discussed further in EN3.2. The
other piece of literary evidence adduced by Kroll to show that the statue of Athena Polias
was standing is the failure of Strabo to mention the statue when, in a discussion of the
seated pose of the Athena Polias in Troy, he says that "many ancient wooden statues of
Athena are seen to be seated, such as those in Phocaea, Massilia, Rome, Chios, and several
other places" (Strabo 13.1.41). The absence of the Athena Polias in Athens from this list is
rather striking, but to explain it perhaps it is enough to note with Herington 1955:24n1
that Strabo's list is "a very haphazard one, and does not claim to be complete." But it also
seems significant that Strabo does not mention the image of Athena Polias even when he
describes Athena's old temple on the Acropolis, although he mentions a lamp known to
have been next to it (see n3.40 below); the image of Athena Polias apparently impressed

thinking this, beyond what others have argued, is Arete, who is seated by the hearth in the firelight, leaning against a column.[39]

Strabo considerably less than Pausanias, and this may account for its omission in the list of 13.1.41.

39 The text does not make clear whether she is seated on a chair or on the ground; the latter perhaps seems inconsistent with her status as queen. For Alcinous, who sits next to Arete drinking wine like a god, a *thrónos* is explicitly mentioned by Nausicaa (*Odyssey* 6.305–309):

ἡ δ᾽ ἧσται ἐπ᾽ ἐσχάρῃ ἐν πυρὸς αὐγῇ,
ἠλάκατα στρωφῶσ᾽ ἁλιπόρφυρα, θαῦμα ἰδέσθαι,
κίονι κεκλιμένη· δμῳαὶ δέ οἱ εἵατ᾽ ὄπισθεν.
ἔνθα δὲ πατρὸς ἐμοῖο θρόνος ποτικέκλιται αὐτῇ,
τῷ ὅ γε οἰνοποτάζει ἐφήμενος ἀθάνατος ὥς.

She sits at the hearth in the light of the fire,
spinning sea-purple wool from a distaff, a wonder to see,
leaning against a column; her serving-women sit behind her.
And there leaning next to her (?) is my father's throne,
on which he sits and drinks wine like an immortal.

For the translation of the phrase ποτικέκλιται αὐτῇ, in which αὐτῇ may refer to the column or to Arete, or perhaps, by brachylogy, to Arete's chair, see Stanford 1959 ad loc. and cf. Cunliffe 1924 s.v. προσκλίνω. How a seated wooden figure, if it was very old, would have been constructed, is not clear. Ridgway 1977:23–25 (= 1993:27–28) imagines that in working with wood it would have been expedient to piece a statue together from several parts, and that this explains a similar technique in later (mid-seventh century on) stone statuary (cf. Donohue 1988:213 and 230). Ridgway's speculation about early wooden statuary envisions standing rather than seated figures (Ridgway 1977:37, quoted by Donohue 1988:193): "Large-scale wooden statuary seems to have existed even in prehistoric times and was probably made during the Eighth and Seventh centuries. Presumably ill-shaped at first, it eventually became anthropomorphic but colossal in that the lower part was column-like or shown as if tightly enveloped in a garment. Since religion was probably dominated by female deities, such renderings were highly appropriate for female figures" (in Ridgway's 1993 edition, p. 41, the first two sentences are modified as follows: "Sizable wooden statuary seems to have existed even in prehistoric times and was probably made during the Eighth and Seventh centuries, especially for cult images, which could be adorned with real jewelry and clothing. Some of them may have been 'colossal' in that the lower part was columnlike or shown as if tightly enveloped in a garment"). Ancient theories of the origin of Greek statuary posited aniconic images to begin with, and this has influenced modern conceptions, but less so now than formerly. As Donohue 230 states: "It is not likely that any study undertaken today of the origin of Greek sculpture would adopt an approach modelled on that of the literary sources, treating Greek statuary as an undifferentiated production traceable to simple beginnings *ex nihilo*." Rather, aniconism and the figural representation of the gods are different phenomena, which can coexist (cf. Donohue 226; Donohue 229–230 cites among others for this view Deonna 1930, vol. 1, 53–56, who "rejected neat schemes of logical developments from primitive forms; believing instead in the completeness of Greek figural vision from the earliest times, he attempted to trace the technical progress in the rendering of the fully realized human form").

§3.16 The firelight by which Arete spins, a fixed element in her description (ἐν πυρὸς αὐγῇ, *Odyssey* 6.305), also corresponds to the Athena Polias. Next to the goddess's image on the Acropolis a perpetual fire burned, which in the classical period and later was contained in an elaborate lamp (*lúkhnos*)[40], but which earlier could have been provided by a hearth. Perpetual fire is the essential element here, and from a Greek standpoint perpetual fire could be provided by either a hearth or a lamp.[41] The temple of Apollo at Delphi also had a perpetual fire, but it was placed on a hearth.[42] Plutarch, addressing the sacred nature of fire in connection with the Roman cult of Vesta, refers to the perpetual fires in the temples of Athena in Athens and of Apollo in Delphi in exactly the same terms without distinction.[43] There were also perpetual fires

40 Strabo 9.1.16 mentions the lamp as the very hallmark of Athena's old temple: he begins his brief description of the Acropolis by saying that it (the Acropolis) is Athena's sacred space (τὸ τῆς Ἀθηνᾶς ἱερὸν), and that it comprises "both the old temple of the Polias, in which is the inextinguishable lamp (ὅ τε ἀρχαῖος νεὼς ὁ τῆς Πολιάδος ἐν ᾧ ὁ ἄσβεστος λύχνος) and the Parthenon, which Ictinus made, in which is Pheidias's ivory statue, the Athena." (As noted above, for Strabo the image of Athena Polias, in contrast to the statue by Pheidias, does not merit mention, and this makes it less surprising that he omits it from a list of seated Athenas in 13.1.41; cf. n3.38 above.) Pausanias, who calls the old wooden image the holiest object in Athens and says that according to legend it fell from heaven, mentions the lamp immediately after it; he says that he will not comment on the truth of the legend about the origin of the image, but he knows who made the lamp, namely Callimachus, and he goes on to give details about it. The lamp is dated by its maker, who was active in the last third of the fifth century (cf. Gross *Der Kleine Pauly* 'Kallimachos 5'). The lamp was lit night and day, and was fed with oil but once a year on the same day. In order to draw the smoke off from the lamp a bronze palm tree reaching to the roof was used. Although Pausanias credits Callimachus with technical innovations, he does not put him in the first rank of artists.
41 Frazer 1913 on Pausanias 8.53.9, "the Common Hearth of the Arcadians," collects the evidence.
42 There are many references to the hearth in Apollo's temple at Delphi, especially in tragedy. For the location of the hearth inside the temple, see especially Diodorus Siculus 16.56.7, an account of how the Phocians in 347/6 BC, having heard that a great treasure of gold and silver was buried inside the temple, set about digging up the ground around the tripod and hearth (ἑστία) until they were frightened off by an earthquake. It was also at this ἑστία that Neoptolemos was supposed to have been slain by the priest of Apollo (Pausanias 10.24.4). For the perpetual fire on this hearth, see e.g. Aeschylus *Libation Bearers* 1036–1037, where Orestes, haunted by furies, declares his intention to set out for Apollo's temple at Delphi (μεσόμφαλόν θ' ἵδρυμα, Λοξίου πέδον) and "the firelight called undying" (πυρός τε φέγγος ἄφθιτον κεκλημένον).
43 Plutarch *Numa* 9.5 speculates that Numa entrusted the perpetual fire in Rome to the Vestal Virgins because fire and vigins are either both pure or both barren, and to support the connection with barrenness, he notes that "wherever in Greece a perpetual fire is kept, as at Delphi and Athens, it is committed to the charge, not of virgins, but of widows past the age of marriage." To support the connection with purity, Plutarch *Numa* 9.6 notes that when perpetual fires are allowed to go out they must not be kindled again from other fire,

in Greek town halls, where a hearth would perhaps seem more natural than a lamp, and indeed the prytaneia in Athens and Olympia had their perpetual fires on a hearth.[44] But lamps also served the purpose: a lamp in the town hall of Tarentum seems always to have been lit, and Theocritus attests the expression "lamp in the prytaneion" (λύχνιον ἐν πρυτανείῳ) as proverbial for sleeplessness.[45]

§3.17 Significant changes undeniably took place with respect to the Athena Polias if what was once a figure who spun wool by a hearth became a partially armed goddess seated by a lamp. I do not suppose that the lamp made by the Athenian craftsman Callimachus in the late fifth century BC was the first such lamp to appear at Athena's side. The hearth probably became a lamp when the aegis and gorgoneion were added to the image itself, perhaps as early as the early sixth century. The change to a lamp, I think, was reflected in what may be regarded as the sixth-century Athenian version of the *Odyssey*, which featured the new lamp in one prominent passage, in which Odysseus and Telemachus remove weapons from the hall of the suitors in Odysseus's palace and Athena lights their way with a golden lamp (*Odyssey* 19.31–43):

τὼ δ᾽ ἄρ᾽ ἀναΐξαντ᾽ Ὀδυσεὺς καὶ φαίδιμος υἱὸς
ἐσφόρεον κόρυθάς τε καὶ ἀσπίδας ὀμφαλοέσσας
ἔγχεά τ᾽ ὀξυόεντα· πάροιθε δὲ Παλλὰς Ἀθήνη
χρύσεον λύχνον ἔχουσα φάος περικαλλὲς ἐποίει.

but directly from the rays of the sun, and his two examples are occasions when the same two fires, in Athens and in Delphi, went out.

44 Pollux twice refers to the hearth in Athens: εἰσὶ δ᾽ ἐν αὐτῇ [sc. the Acropolis] πρυτανεῖον καὶ ἑστία τῆς πόλεως, "there are on it [the Acropolis] the prytaneion and the hearth of the city" (Pollux 9.40); [ἑστία] ἡ ἐν πρυτανείῳ, ἐφ᾽ ἧς τὸ πῦρ τὸ ἄσβεστον ἀνάπτεται, "[the hearth] in the prytaneion, on which the inextinguishable fire is lit" (Pollux 1.7). Pausanias 5.15.9 describes the hearth in Olympia: [τῷ πρυτανείῳ] ἔνθα σφίσιν ἡ ἑστία.... ἔστι δὲ ἡ ἑστία τέφρας...πεποιημένη, καὶ ἐπ᾽ αὐτῆς πῦρ ἀνὰ πᾶσάν τε ἡμέραν καὶ ἐν πάσῃ νυκτὶ ὡσαύτως καίεται, "[the prytaneion] where their hearth is.... The hearth is made of ash, and on it a fire burns every day and likewise every night."

45 In Theocritus this is the second of two proverbial expressions for sleeplessness (21.36–37): ἀλλ᾽ ὄνος ἐν ῥάμνῳ τό τε λύχνιον ἐν πρυτανείῳ· / φαντὶ γὰρ ἀγρυπνίαν τάδ᾽ ἔχειν, "an ass in thorns and the lamp in the prytaneion; for they say that these things have sleeplessness"; λύχνιον may here be a lampstand (= λυχνεῖον, so LSJ), but this does not change the point. Dionysius II, tyrant of Syracuse, dedicated an elaborate lampstand (λυχνεῖον) in the prytaneion of Tarentum (Athenaeus 15.700d citing Euphorion), which Frazer takes to be another example of perpetual fire (Frazer 1913 on Pausanias 8.53.9). The lampstand had the capacity "to burn lamps" for every day in the year (λυχνεῖον δυνάμενον καίειν τοσούτους λύχνους ὅσος ὁ τῶν ἡμερῶν ἐστιν ἀριθμὸς εἰς τὸν ἐνιαυτόν). Frazer assumes that this contrivance could burn for a year without being fed, a more plausible interpretation than to think that 365 lamps were lit simultaneously.

δὴ τότε Τηλέμαχος προσεφώνεεν ὃν πατέρ' αἶψα·
"ὦ πάτερ, ἦ μέγα θαῦμα τόδ' ὀφθαλμοῖσιν ὁρῶμαι·
ἔμπης μοι τοῖχοι μεγάρων καλαί τε μεσόδμαι
εἰλάτιναί τε δοκοὶ καὶ κίονες ὑψόσ' ἔχοντες
φαίνοντ' ὀφθαλμοῖσ' ὡς εἰ πυρὸς αἰθομένοιο.
ἦ μάλα τις θεὸς ἔνδον, οἳ οὐρανὸν εὐρὺν ἔχουσι."
τὸν δ' ἀπαμειβόμενος προσέφη πολύμητις Ὀδυσσεύς·
"σίγα καὶ κατὰ σὸν νόον ἴσχανε μηδ' ἐρέεινε·
αὕτη τοι δίκη ἐστὶ θεῶν, οἳ Ὄλυμπον ἔχουσιν."

Springing to their feet the two of them, Odysseus and his
    shining son,
carried in the helmets and bossed shields
and sharp spears. In front of them Pallas Athena
held a golden lamp and made a beautiful light.
Right then Telemachus quickly addressed his father:
"Father, I see a great wonder here with my eyes;
the walls of the rooms and the beautiful column-bases
and the fir roof-beams and the columns reaching high overhead
appear to my eyes as if a fire were burning.
Surely some god is within, one of those inhabiting the wide sky."
Answering him very wily Odysseus said:
"Be still and keep it in your mind and do not ask about it:
this indeed is the way of the gods who live on Olympus."

This passage shows how well a lamp suits a war goddess, and this may be
the passage's real point if the goddess in it is the newly transformed Athena
Polias of the Athenian Acropolis.[46]

---

46 Cook 1995 makes this passage the cornerstone of his argument that the *Odyssey* as a whole
was first composed in sixth-century Athens. While I disagree with so broad a conclusion,
and instead place the formative phase of the Homeric poems a century and a half earlier
in Ionia, I think that Cook is right to connect this passage with the lamp of Athena in her
temple on the Acropolis. What parts of the poems originated in sixth-century Athens (I
include this passage as well as the expansion of the catalogue of heroines in *Odyssey* 11)
is an open question; another possible example is briefly considered in EN3.3. For further
discussion of Athena's lamp in Homer and on the Acropolis see Parisinou 2000: 5–8 (Homer)
and 20–31 (the Acropolis). For a date in the early sixth century BC for the transformation
of the image of Athena Polias into a warrior goddess cf. n3.26 above and n3.111 below.

§3.18 We will return to changes that were made with respect to Athena Polias after the Homeric period, but our concern now is with the Homeric period itself. When Odysseus finishes his appeal to Arete and the rest of the Phaeacians, he sits in the ashes next to the hearth and the fire (*Odyssey* 7.153–154):

ὣς εἰπὼν κατ' ἄρ' ἕζετ' ἐπ' ἐσχάρῃ ἐν κονίῃσι
πὰρ πυρί.

So speaking he sat down by the hearth in the ashes
near the fire.

The scene of a suppliant seated in the ashes was presumably a familiar one in the temple of Athena Polias. Someone had to raise such a suppliant from the ashes in what amounted to a guarantee of protection on the goddess's behalf; Alcinous does this with Odysseus when prodded by Ekheneos (*Odyssey* 7.167–169):

αὐτὰρ ἐπεὶ τό γ' ἄκουσ' ἱερὸν μένος Ἀλκινόοιο,
χειρὸς ἑλὼν Ὀδυσῆα δαΐφρονα ποικιλομήτην
ὦρσεν ἀπ' ἐσχαρόφιν καὶ ἐπὶ θρόνου εἷσε φαεινοῦ.

But when Alcinous, with sacred power, heard this,
he took the hand of wise Odysseus, with inventive mind,
and raised him from the hearth and sat him on the shining chair.

The goddess herself in her temple would of course apparently do nothing during such an act, and that is what Arete does, apparently nothing. It is precisely by doing nothing that she becomes the goddess in this tableau.

§3.19 While Arete's silence and apparent lack of reaction are the crucial elements in her identification with the image of Athena Polias, other details help to reinforce her identification with the goddess in a more general way. The real Athena, disguised as a young girl, tells Odysseus that Arete's people regard her and greet her like a goddess when she walks through the city (*Odyssey* 7.69–72):

ὣς κείνη περὶ κῆρι τετίμηταί τε καὶ ἔστιν
ἔκ τε φίλων παίδων ἔκ τ' αὐτοῦ Ἀλκινόοιο
καὶ λαῶν, οἵ μίν ῥα θεὸν ὣς εἰσορόωντες
δειδέχαται μύθοισιν, ὅτε στείχῃσ' ἀνὰ ἄστυ.

Thus is she held in honor and loved from the heart
by her dear children and by Alcinous himself
and by her people, who look on her as a god
and greet her with words whenever she walks through the city.

Being compared to a god is not unique to Arete (Alcinous himself is compared
to an immortal when he sits next to her and drinks wine, Odyssey 6.309), but the
comparison seems to have further point in this context, in which the final phrase
ὅτε στείχησ' ἀνὰ ἄστυ suggests not any god in general, but the city goddess in
particular, and thus prepares for the identification with Athena Polias.[47]

§3.20 Both times that Arete is described in terms that on my interpreta-
tion match the image of Athena Polias maidservants are also present. Their
activity is not described, only that the queen sits with them (ἡ μὲν ἐπ' ἐσχάρῃ
ἧστο σὺν ἀμφιπόλοισι γυναιξίν, Odyssey 6.52), or that they sit behind her
(δμωαὶ δέ οἱ εἴατ' ὄπισθεν, Odyssey 6.307) as she spins by the fire. But a sepa-
rate passage is devoted to these maidservants in the description of Alcinous's

---

47 The phrase θεὸν ὥς, "like a god," in Odyssey 7.71 does not identify Arete as a god, but
compares her to one, just as the phrase ἀθάνατος ὥς, "like an immortal," in Odyssey 6.309
does not identify Alcinous as an immortal, but compares him to one (cf. the phrase θεοῦ δ'
ὣς δῆμος ἄκουεν, "the people listen to him like a god," in Odyssey 7.11, also said of Alcinous).
Comparisons of mortals to immortals are not at all unusual in Homer: the accusative phrase
θεὸν ὥς occurs nine times (including Odyssey 7.71); the nominative phrase θεὸς ὥς occurs
six times (five times in the phrase θεὸς δ' ὥς τίετο δήμῳ, "he is honored like a god by the
people"); constructions with the dative θεῷ occur ten times (cf. n3.64 below); the phrase
ἰσόθεος φώς, "a man equal to a god," occurs 14 times. Two verses in particular resemble the
comparison of Arete to a god in Odyssey 7.71–72: in Odyssey 8 Odysseus says to Euryalos that
the people regard a man who commands respect in the assembly by his words as a god when
he walks through the city (ἐρχόμενον δ' ἀνὰ ἄστυ θεὸν ὥς εἰσορόωσιν, Odyssey 8.173); in Iliad
22 Hecabe, lamenting Hector, recalls what help (ὄνειαρ) he was in the city (κατὰ πτόλιν) to
the men and women of Troy, "who greeted you like a god" (οἵ σε θεὸν ὥς / δειδέχατ', Iliad
22.433–435). The comparison of Arete to a god is clearly within the limits of what can be said
about a mortal, but at the same time more seems suggested. This is like the phrase θαῦμα
ἰδέσθαι, "a wonder to behold," which follows the description of Arete as seated by the hearth
spinning wool (ἡ δ' ἧσται ἐπ' ἐσχάρῃ ἐν πυρὸς αὐγῇ, / ἠλάκατα στρωφῶσ' ἁλιπόρφυρα,
θαῦμα ἰδέσθαι, Odyssey 6.305–306). The phrase θαῦμα ἰδέσθαι focuses attention on something
extraordinary, but not necessarily godlike. The word θαῦμα is normally used of objects and
situations, rarely of people; if we exclude the Cyclops in Odyssey 9.190 (a special case), it is
used of only one person besides Arete: Neleus's daughter Pero is called a θαῦμα βροτοῖσι in
the context of her wooing by all her neighbors, Odyssey 11.287, and here the context gives the
phrase its point (cf. n2.137 above). When Arete is called a θαῦμα ἰδέσθαι in lines that describe
her in terms of the image of Athena Polias, it is worth bearing in mind other wondrous
objects that get the phrase, such as the clothes in which the Charites clothe Aphrodite after
her bath in Paphos, Odyssey 8.366 (see n3.4 above), or the tripods of Hephaistos which move
on their own into and out of divine assembly, Iliad 18.377.

palace before Odysseus enters it. There are fifty of them and their tasks include grinding corn, weaving, and spinning (*Odyssey* 7.103–107):

πεντήκοντα δέ οἱ δμῳαὶ κατὰ δῶμα γυναῖκες
αἱ μὲν ἀλετρεύουσι μύλῃσ' ἔπι μήλοπα καρπόν,
αἱ δ' ἱστοὺς ὑφόωσι καὶ ἠλάκατα στρωφῶσιν
ἥμεναι, οἷά τε φύλλα μακεδνῆς αἰγείροιο·
καιρουσσέων δ' ὀθονέων ἀπολείβεται ὑγρὸν ἔλαιον.

In his palace are fifty servant women,
some of whom grind yellow grain on millstones,
and others weave fabric and spin wool,
seated like the leaves of a tall poplar;
liquid oil runs from the close-woven cloth.

The passage continues, saying that just as the Phaeacian men excel at seafaring, the women excel at weaving, for Athena has given them, beyond others, knowledge of beautiful crafts and good wits (*Odyssey* 7.108–111):

ὅσσον Φαίηκες περὶ πάντων ἴδριες ἀνδρῶν
νῆα θοὴν ἐνὶ πόντῳ ἐλαυνέμεν, ὣς δὲ γυναῖκες
ἱστὸν τεχνῆσσαι· περὶ γάρ σφισι δῶκεν Ἀθήνη
ἔργα τ' ἐπίστασθαι περικαλλέα καὶ φρένας ἐσθλάς.

As much as the Phaeacian men are skillful beyond all others
at driving a swift ship on the sea, so the women are
skillful at weaving; for Athena granted them beyond others
understanding of beautiful works and good wits.

It is possible that this entire passage is part of a later rhapsodic expansion, as the description of Alcinous's palace has been taken to be.[48] But Athena was the

48 Hainsworth (Heubeck et al. 1988) on *Odyssey* 7.81–132: "This elaborate passage invites the suspicion of rhapsodic reworking." West 2000:485–487 proposes that the passage was shifted from a different context by one of the Homeric poets using written texts. I agree with Hainsworth that parts of the passage may be "post-Homeric" (cf. n2.16 above), but I have no specific reason for such a judgment. The description of Alcinous's palace delays Odysseus's entrance into the palace and his encounter with Athena's substitute Arete, but this does not weaken the identification of Arete with Athena; that identification is firmly established when, in the space of two lines, Athena enters the palace of Erechtheus in Athens and Odysseus heads for the palace of Alcinous in Scheria (*Odyssey* 7.81–82).

goddess of crafts, especially women's crafts, and the word *érga* in the last line is the basis of her later cult title, Athena *Ergánē*.[49] The passage makes weaving, which is the special virtue of the Phaeacian women, the gift of Athena. But it is really Arete whom they emulate in this domain, as is indicated by the two descriptions of her spinning by firelight, in which the maidservants are very much her extension. In the end, of course, this comes back to Athena herself if Arete plays the part of Athena Polias.[50] Whatever the passage's origin, the

---

We know where Odysseus is going and why, and a narrative retardation devoted to the wonders of the Phaeacian palace does not change that.

49 Athena occurs as the goddess of crafts (*érga*) in both Homer and Hesiod. In the *Odyssey* the daughters of Pandareos are said to have received gifts from Hera, Artemis, and Athena; Athena's gift was to teach them *érga*, "crafts" (ἔργα δ' Ἀθηναίη δέδαε κλυτὰ ἐργάζεσθαι, *Odyssey* 20.72). In Hesiod's *Works and Days*, when Pandora is created, Zeus instructs Athena to teach her *érga*, "crafts," particularly weaving (αὐτὰρ Ἀθήνην / ἔργα διδασκῆσαι, πολυδαίδαλον ἱστὸν ὑφαίνειν, *Works and Days* 63–64). Here and elsewhere Athena is particularly associated with the production of clothing; in Homer she is said to have made her own *péplos* (πέπλον... / ποικίλον, ὅν ῥ' αὐτὴ ποιήσατο καὶ κάμε χερσίν, *Iliad* 5.734–735; cf. n3.25 above). In Hesiod *Theogony* 573–575 her contribution to Pandora is to adorn her in "shining raiment" (κόσμησε θεὰ γλαυκῶπις Ἀθήνη / ἀργυφέῃ ἐσθῆτι), including a wondrous veil (κατὰ κρῆθεν δὲ καλύπτρην / δαιδαλέην χείρεσσι κατέσχεθε, θαῦμα ἰδέσθαι). Arete has exactly the same concern for clothing in the *Odyssey*; she first breaks her silence after Odysseus's supplication when she recognizes his clothes, which she and her maidservants made (*Odyssey* 7.233–235):

toῖσιν δ' Ἀρήτη λευκώλενος ἤρχετο μύθων·
ἔγνω γὰρ φᾶρός τε χιτῶνά τε εἵματ' ἰδοῦσα
καλά, τά ῥ' αὐτὴ τεῦξε σὺν ἀμφιπόλοισι γυναιξί.

White-armed Arete began to speak to them,
for she saw and recognized the beautiful clothes, the cloak and tunic,
which she herself had made with her serving women.

Thus Arete, whose silence has marked her out as Athena, breaks her silence in a context that maintains or is at least consistent with this hidden identity. Cf. Barber 1992 for Athena's close connection with weaving. Barber 1992:105–106 cites the Arachne myth, first told in extant sources by Ovid *Metamorphoses* 6.5–145, but pictured on a Corinthian jug of c. 600 BC; see Weinberg and Weinberg 1956.

50 Arete shows that Athena *Poliás*, the city goddess of Athens, and Athena *Ergánē* are closely related figures; for the original unity of Athena *Poliás* and Athena *Ergánē* see Hutton 1897:308, and cf. Le Lasseur 1919:102–103. It is worth noting that Pausanias 1.24.3, to prove that the Athenians paid more attention to religious matters than others, says that it was the Athenians who "first gave Athena the name *Ergánē*" (πρῶτοι μὲν γὰρ Ἀθηνᾶν ἐπωνόμασαν Ἐργάνην). Nilsson, with his understanding of Athena *Poliás* as a warrior goddess, cannot explain Athena *Ergánē* any more than he can Athena *Mḗtēr*. His explanation of both is that Athena is female, and as such she was invoked by women in connection with their typical concerns: "I would sooner believe that [in Elis] women, who in their concerns, especially their desire for children, turned to a long list of goddesses simply because they were female and they felt united with them by the bond of sex, also once turned to Athena. This is the only way to explain how Athena became the guardian of female technical skills" ("Eher würde ich glauben, dass die Frauen, die sich in ihren Angelegenheiten, und zwar

particular virtues of the Phaeacian men on the one hand and the Phaeacian women on the other hand reflect the essential natures of the Phaeacian king and queen, and, in the case of the queen, point to the source of her true identity.

§3.21 The mention of Athena in this passage, while significant for the goddess later called Athena *Ergánē*, is incidental to the story of the Phaeacian episode. Athena herself, however, is not incidental to this story; she manages the episode from beginning to end.[51] Besides her two primary interventions, when she appears to Nausicaa in a dream and to Odysseus on his way to the Phaeacian palace, she makes a minor appearance when she takes on the likeness of a youth to mark the stone hurled by Odysseus in the Phaeacians' games. Twice more Athena directs events from behind the scenes: she contrives to have the shouts of Nausicaa's companions waken Odysseus when their ball lands in the river (*Odyssey* 6.112–113), and she gives Nausicaa courage to hold her ground when Odysseus first appears and her companions all flee (*Odyssey* 6.139–140).

§3.22 Athena's central place in the Phaeacian episode is highlighted at a central point in the narrative, after Nausicaa has rescued Odysseus and brought him part way to town but before he continues on his way toward the palace to meet the king and queen. Nausicaa does not want him to go all the way into town with her, fearing the comments of the townspeople. She asks him to stop at Athena's sacred grove long enough for her to reach home (*Odyssey* 6.291–296):

δήεις ἀγλαὸν ἄλσος Ἀθήνης ἄγχι κελεύθου
αἰγείρων, ἐν δὲ κρήνη νάει, ἀμφὶ δὲ λειμών·

---

besonders in ihrem Verlangen nach Kindern, an eine lange Reihe von Göttinnen wandten, nur weil diese Frauen waren und sie sich mit ihnen durch das Band des Geschlechts vereint fühlten, sich auch einmal an die Göttin Athena wandten. Nur so kann erklärt werden, dass Athena zur Beschützerin der weiblichen Kunstfertigkeit geworden ist," Nilsson 1967:444; cf. n3.11 above).

51 Athena later says as much to Odysseus when she reveals herself openly to him in Ithaca (*Odyssey* 13.299–302):

οὐδὲ σύ γ' ἔγνως
Παλλάδ' Ἀθηναίην, κούρην Διός, ἥ τέ τοι αἰεὶ
ἐν πάντεσσι πόνοισι παρίσταμαι ἠδὲ φυλάσσω,
καὶ δέ σε Φαιήκεσσι φίλον πάντεσσιν ἔθηκα.

You did not recognize
Pallas Athena, Zeus's daughter, who always
stands by you and protects you in all your toils,
and who made you dear to all the Phaeacians.

ἔνθα δὲ πατρὸς ἐμοῦ τέμενος τεθαλυῖά τ' ἀλῳή,
τόσσον ἀπὸ πτόλιος, ὅσσον τε γέγωνε βοήσας.
ἔνθα καθεζόμενος μεῖναι χρόνον, εἰς ὅ κεν ἡμεῖς
ἄστυδε ἔλθωμεν καὶ ἱκώμεθα δώματα πατρός.

Near the path you will find Athena's splendid grove
of poplar trees, and in it a spring flows, and a meadow surrounds it;
there is my father's preserve and flourishing orchard,
as far from the city as a man can be heard by shouting.
Sit there and wait for a time, until we
come to the city and reach my father's house.

Nausicaa goes on to tell Odysseus that he need only ask for her father's palace when he reaches town, for even a child can point it out; she ends her speech by telling him to bypass her father and supplicate her mother once he is inside the palace in order to gain his return home (*Odyssey* 6.297–315). Odysseus follows behind Nausicaa's wagon with the maidservants, and he stops at Athena's grove just at sunset; as he sits in Athena's sanctuary he prays to the goddess to make him welcome to the Phaeacians (*Odyssey* 6.321–327):

δύσετό τ' ἠέλιος, καὶ τοὶ κλυτὸν ἄλσος ἵκοντο
ἱρὸν Ἀθηναίης, ἵν' ἄρ' ἕζετο δῖος Ὀδυσσεύς.
αὐτίκ' ἔπειτ' ἠρᾶτο Διὸς κούρῃ μεγάλοιο·
"κλῦθί μοι, αἰγιόχοιο Διὸς τέκος, Ἀτρυτώνη·
νῦν δή πέρ μευ ἄκουσον, ἐπεὶ πάρος οὔ ποτ' ἄκουσας
ῥαιομένου, ὅτε μ' ἔρραιε κλυτὸς ἐννοσίγαιος.
δός μ' ἐς Φαίηκας φίλον ἐλθεῖν ἠδ' ἐλεεινόν."

The sun set, and they came to the famed grove
sacred to Athena, where shining Odysseus sat down.
Then at once he prayed to the daughter of great Zeus:
"Hear me, child of aegis-holder Zeus, Atrytone;
hear me now indeed, since you never heard me earlier
when I was dashed, when the famed earthshaker dashed me.
Grant that I come dear and pitied to the Phaeacians."

In his prayer Odysseus chides Athena for not hearing his earlier prayer, when Poseidon dashed his raft. Athena did more then to save Odysseus than he knows,[52] but that is the point: Odysseus does not know what Athena is doing for him even now, because she does not appear to him openly. That aspect of her role is motivated by Poseidon's hostility toward Odysseus, for it is out of respect for Poseidon that Athena stays out of sight. Book 6 ends with this explanation of Athena's behavior (*Odyssey* 6.328–331):

> ὣς ἔφατ᾽ εὐχόμενος, τοῦ δ᾽ ἔκλυε Παλλὰς Ἀθήνη·
> αὐτῷ δ᾽ οὔ πω φαίνετ᾽ ἐναντίη· αἴδετο γάρ ῥα
> πατροκασίγνητον· ὁ δ᾽ ἐπιζαφελῶς μενέαινεν
> ἀντιθέῳ Ὀδυσῆϊ πάρος ἣν γαῖαν ἱκέσθαι.

> So he spoke praying, and Pallas Athena heard him;
> but she still did not appear to him face to face, for she respected
> her father's brother; he raged furiously
> against godlike Odysseus before he reached his land.

§3.23 Since Athena does not want to appear openly to Odysseus, she appears in disguise. Her appearance as a young maiden, which follows shortly, is thus well motivated by Odysseus's prayer and by her own wish not to offend Poseidon. But this is only part of the story. Odysseus's prayer to Athena, which she does not want to answer openly, also looks forward to his supplication of Arete, who is about to play the part of Athena. The narrative actually seems to signal Arete's impending entrance on stage when Odysseus addresses his prayer to Athena, and the verb that introduces his prayer is ἠρᾶτο, "he prayed" (*Odyssey* 6.323):

> αὐτίκ᾽ ἔπειτ᾽ <u>ἠρᾶτο</u> Διὸς κούρῃ μεγάλοιο.

> Then at once he <u>prayed</u> to the daughter of great Zeus.

After Odysseus's prayer and the passage about Athena's need to remain out of sight at the end of Book 6, Book 7 opens by repeating the verb ἠρᾶτο of Odysseus's just completed prayer (*Odyssey* 7.1):

> ὣς ὁ μὲν ἔνθ᾽ <u>ἠρᾶτο</u> πολύτλας δῖος Ὀδυσσεύς.

> So much-enduring shining Odysseus <u>prayed</u> there.

The verb ἠρᾶτο has the same root as the name Ἀρήτη, "she who is prayed to," and it is striking that the verb is used twice of Odysseus's prayer shortly

---

52 *Odyssey* 5.426–427.

before the name is revealed to him by Athena in disguise (*Odyssey* 7.54).[53] There is more than one hidden identity here. Odysseus has uttered a prayer to Athena, which she answers, but only in disguise, by introducing Arete, who is about to take Athena's place. This is a complex situation, and it is carefully managed so that the two figures, Athena and Arete, do not interfere with each other. Indeed Athena, as soon as she has told Odysseus about Arete, removes herself from the scene by flying to Athens, leaving center stage to the figure that she has just introduced. Thus it is not only respect for Poseidon that keeps Athena from appearing openly to Odysseus. The hidden identity of Arete simply would not work if it had to compete with the presence of Athena in her own persona.[54]

§3.24 Odysseus's prayer to Athena in her sacred grove comes at a central point in the story: Nausicaa has played her part and attention now shifts to Arete. I have focused first on Arete, arguing that she represents Athena as a mother goddess; but Athena is also of course a virgin goddess, and both sides of her seem to be represented by the Phaeacians.[55] We must now turn to Nausicaa, who is the first to be introduced by Athena herself. When Odysseus reaches shore in Phaeacia and falls asleep, Athena contrives to have Nausicaa find him there and bring him part way to town. In the dream in which she appears to Nausicaa she tells the princess that she must go and do her washing in the morning for her wedding is near: already the best of the Phaeacians woo her, and she will not long remain a virgin. Athena then leaves Scheria and goes to Olympus, and just as her second departure identifies her as Athena the city goddess of Athens, her first departure identifies her as Athena the Olympian. The parallel between Athena's two departures from Scheria is, as already seen, clearly marked, and the significance of the

53 The form ἠρᾶτο, which occurs a total of thirteen times in Homer, occurs seven times of prayers to Athena: four times in the *Iliad* (5.114, 6.304, 10.277, 10.283) and three times in the *Odyssey* (the two verses quoted above and *Odyssey* 4.761). The two occurrences of the verb that do not concern Athena in the *Odyssey* are ironic: Athena, in disguise, prays to Poseidon, and Telemachus, following her example, does so as well (*Odyssey* 3.62 and 64); the four occurrences that do not concern Athena in the *Iliad* follow no pattern: a prayer each to Apollo (*Iliad* 1.35), the gods (θεοῖσι, *Iliad* 9.567), Spercheios (*Iliad* 23.149), and the winds (*Iliad* 23.194). Although I have not considered other forms of this verb, I note that in *Iliad* 17.568 Athena rejoices because Menelaus "prayed," ἠρήσατο, to her first of all the gods. It is the form ἠρᾶτο that particularly echoes the name Ἀρήτη, and that therefore seems pointedly used to anticipate Arete's appearance in *Odyssey* 7. The other times that ἠρᾶτο is used of prayers to Athena in Homer reinforce this connection.

54 Cf. §3.7 above.

55 It is fitting that two figures rather than one represent Athena inasmuch as one figure would not be able to sustain the weight of the part. I think of the musical play of Igor Stravinsky called *The Flood*, in which two bass voices together sing the part of God.

second departure for the hidden identity of Arete suggests a parallel signifi-
cance for her first departure. After Athena's disappearance into the palace
of Erechtheus in Athens the focus shifts back to Scheria, and to the palace
of Alcinous, where Arete awaits; so too after Athena's departure to Olympus,
the focus shifts back to Scheria, and to Nausicaa. The description of Athena's
departure to Olympus ends with the word *koúrē* in reference to Nausicaa, and
this word equally describes Athena's status on Olympus (*Odyssey* 6.47–49):

ἔνθ᾽ ἀπέβη γλαυκῶπις, ἐπεὶ διεπέφραδε κούρῃ.
αὐτίκα δ᾽ Ἠὼς ἦλθεν ἐΰθρονος, ἥ μιν ἔγειρε
Ναυσικάαν εὔπεπλον.

There the grey-eyed one went when she had instructed the maiden.
At once beautiful-throned Dawn came, who awakened her,
beautiful-robed Nausicaa.[56]

---

56 On Olympus Athena is Zeus's daughter. The phrase *koúrē Diós*, "daughter of Zeus," is used 17 of
20 times of Athena in Homer; she is also called *Diòs thugátēr*, "daughter of Zeus," eight times
in Homer, but this phrase is used more often of Aphrodite. The one time that the word *koúrē*
is used by itself of Athena Zeus is mentioned in the same line: εὐξάμενος κούρῃ γλαυκώπιδι
καὶ Διὶ πατρί, "praying to the grey-eyed maiden and to [her] father Zeus" (*Odyssey* 24.518), and
three lines later the full phrase *Diòs koúrē* occurs: εὐξάμενος δ᾽ ἄρ᾽ ἔπειτα Διὸς κούρῃ μεγάλοιο,
"praying then to great Zeus's daughter" (*Odyssey* 24.521). Used by itself the word *koúrē* means
not "daughter," but "maiden"; this meaning too fits Athena, as in *Odyssey* 24.518, quoted
above. In the Phaeacian episode the word *koúrē* in the meaning "maiden" is repeatedly used of
Nausicaa (ten times in *Odyssey* 6, once in *Odyssey* 7, and once in *Odyssey* 8). It is in fact the first
word used of Nausicaa in the poem, when Athena enters her bed chamber (*Odyssey* 6.15–16):
βῆ δ᾽ ἴμεν ἐς θάλαμον πολυδαίδαλον, ᾧ ἔνι κούρη
κοιμᾶτ᾽ ἀθανάτῃσι φυὴν καὶ εἶδος ὁμοίη.
She went into the much decorated chamber, in which the maiden
slept, like the immortal goddesses in build and beauty.
It is also the last word used of Nausicaa in the poem, at the end of Odysseus's farewell
speech to her, after he credits her with bringing him back to life (*Odyssey* 8.464–468; cf.
§3.30 below):
Ναυσικάα, θύγατερ μεγαλήτορος Ἀλκινόοιο,
οὕτω νῦν Ζεὺς θείη, ἐρίγδουπος πόσις Ἥρης,
οἴκαδέ τ᾽ ἐλθέμεναι καὶ νόστιμον ἦμαρ ἰδέσθαι·
τῷ κέν τοι καὶ κεῖθι θεῷ ὣς εὐχετοῴμην
αἰεὶ ἤματα πάντα· σὺ γάρ μ᾽ ἐβιώσαο, κούρη.
Nausicaa, daughter of great-hearted Alcinous,
may Zeus, the loud-thundering husband of Hera, now so arrange it
that I go home and see the day of my return;
if so I would pray to you as a god even there
always and forever; for you brought me back to life, maiden.

§3.25 We have considered the parallels that link the introductions of
Nausicaa and Arete in the Phaeacian episode, namely the fact that Athena
herself introduces each of them, and the further fact that Athena flies to a
particular destination after each of them has been introduced. There is
another parallel between Arete and Nausicaa themselves, and it is, dramati-
cally, the most striking. Arete's role is to be supplicated by Odysseus, and we
have seen that the actual moment of her supplication is filled with dramatic
tension: we do not know how Odysseus's appeal will be received, but we
have been told that all depends on its success. The silence that follows his
appeal raises the level of tension higher still. Only one other moment in the
Phaeacian episode compares with this in intensity, namely when Odysseus
supplicates Nausicaa. The stakes are no less high, for Odysseus has just burst
nearly naked onto a group of maidens not long from their baths in the river.
Although he covers himself with a branch, the scene is sexually charged, and
the narrative exploits this fully; first there is a wild beast simile, and then
there is an ambiguous verb *meíxesthai*, which could refer to sexual inter-
course, but in the situation does not (*Odyssey* 6.127–136):[57]

ὣς εἰπὼν θάμνων ὑπεδύσετο δῖος Ὀδυσσεύς,
ἐκ πυκινῆς δ' ὕλης πτόρθον κλάσε χειρὶ παχείῃ
φύλλων, ὡς ῥύσαιτο περὶ χροῒ μήδεα φωτός.
βῆ δ' ἴμεν ὥς τε λέων ὀρεσίτροφος, ἀλκὶ πεποιθώς,
ὅς τ' εἶσ' ὑόμενος καὶ ἀήμενος, ἐν δέ οἱ ὄσσε
δαίεται· αὐτὰρ ὁ βουσὶ μετέρχεται ἢ οἴεσσιν
ἠὲ μετ' ἀγροτέρας ἐλάφους· κέλεται δέ ἑ γαστὴρ
μήλων πειρήσοντα καὶ ἐς πυκινὸν δόμον ἐλθεῖν·
<u>ὣς Ὀδυσεὺς κούρῃσιν ἐϋπλοκάμοισιν ἔμελλε</u>
<u>μείξεσθαι, γυμνός περ ἐών· χρειὼ γὰρ ἵκανε.</u>

57 In the phrase *meíxesthai gumnós per eón* the particle *per* is concessive ("although"), but *per*
can also be intensive ("since"). There is thus a double ambiguity: "he was about to mingle
with them although he was naked" is the intended primary meaning; "he was about to
have intercourse with them since he was naked" is a possible secondary meaning. For
the threat of sexual violence in this episode see Karakantza 2003, with bibliography; the
author explains the non-violent outcome in this case by a "strange reversal of the societal
code, that puts the man in an inferior position and the maiden in self-confident control"
(p. 10; cf. p. 20). Nausicaa's "self-confident control," which is anomalous according to this
analysis, calls for an explanation, and for this I would look behind Nausicaa to Athena. For
bridal imagery in the encounter between Nausicaa and Odysseus cf. also Segal 1994:23n13
with bibliography.

So speaking shining Odysseus came out from under the thicket,
and with his stout hand he broke a spray of leaves
from the dense wood to cover the genitals on his body.
He went like a lion bred in the mountains, trusting in its might,
which goes forth beaten by rain and wind, and the eyes in it
burn; and it goes among the cattle or sheep,
or after wild deer; and its stomach commands it,
after it has made trial of the sheep, even to enter the strong
    house;
so Odysseus was about to mix with the beautiful-haired maidens,
naked as he was; for need had come.

The threat that Odysseus poses is of course clear, given his wild appearance. The other maidens all flee, but Nausicaa holds her ground, for Athena gives her courage (*Odyssey* 6.137–141):

σμερδαλέος δ' αὐτῇσι φάνη κεκακωμένος ἅλμῃ,

τρέσσαν δ' ἄλλυδις ἄλλη ἐπ' ἠϊόνας προὐχούσας.

οἴη δ' Ἀλκινόου θυγάτηρ μένε· τῇ γὰρ Ἀθήνη

θάρσος ἐνὶ φρεσὶ θῆκε καὶ ἐκ δέος εἵλετο γυίων.

στῆ δ' ἄντα σχομένη.

Disfigured by the salt sea he was a frightful sight for them to see,
and they fled in all directions to the jutting banks.
Only the daughter of Alcinous stayed; for Athena
put courage in her heart and took fear from her limbs.
She stood face to face holding her ground.

Nausicaa's courage is decisive in resolving the situation, but Odysseus must still supplicate this young maiden, and in this sexually charged encounter it will not do to grasp her knees. Thus he decides to keep his distance while supplicating her, and his first words to her, *gounoûmaí se*, "I grasp your knees," are meant only symbolically (*Odyssey* 6.145–149):

ὡς ἄρα οἱ φρονέοντι δοάσσατο κέρδιον εἶναι,

λίσσεσθαι ἐπέεσσιν ἀποσταδὰ μειλιχίοισι,

μή οἱ γοῦνα λαβόντι χολώσαιτο φρένα κούρη.

αὐτίκα μείλιχιον καὶ κερδαλέον φάτο μῦθον·

"γουνοῦμαί σε, ἄνασσα· θεός νύ τις ἦ βροτός ἐσσι;"

> It seemed more cunning to him thus as he thought about it,
> to supplicate from a distance with gentle words,
> so that the maiden would not be angry in her heart with him for
>   grasping her knees;
> right away he spoke a gentle and cunning word:
> "I grasp your knees, my lady; tell me, are you a god or a mortal?"

§3.26 Nausicaa has the heart of a warrior in this encounter: she holds her ground in the face of the obvious danger, and there is no question that she is ready to defend her maidenhood should the need arise.[58] It would not be far different if Athena's own maidenhood were threatened. Nausicaa most takes on her hidden identity as Athena the virgin warrior when she holds her ground and Odysseus wisely decides to keep his distance and supplicate her from afar. The parallel with Arete is again complete, for it is at the moment of supplication that each of these figures most closely realizes a different aspect of the goddess Athena, one the mother goddess, the other the virgin goddess.

§3.27 Nausicaa is twice compared to Artemis, the virgin hunter goddess. How do such overt comparisons fit with a hidden identity as Athena, the virgin warrior goddess? The key point is that Nausicaa's hidden identity is after all hidden, and it therefore cannot be the subject of overt comparisons. An overt comparison, moreover, means that one thing is not another, that two things are similar but remain distinct. How is Nausicaa similar to Artemis? She is a virgin, as we know from the start about this Phaeacian princess. But the comparison with Artemis suggests that she is also more than a virgin princess, that she is also, in terms of her hidden identity, a virgin goddess.

§3.28 I repeat that when Nausicaa stands her ground while all the other maidens flee, she most realizes her hidden identity as the warrior goddess Athena. I do not think that this point is undermined by the fact that Athena herself gives Nausicaa the courage to stand her ground. On the contrary I think that Athena's action establishes the point most clearly, for Nausicaa gets what is quintessentially Athena's, her warrior's heart (*thársos*, *Odyssey* 6.140), directly from Athena herself.[59] Certainly the two figures remain

---

58 Note that Odysseus fears her anger (*mḗ...kholṓsaito, Odyssey* 6.147).

59 For Athena's own *thársos* cf. *Iliad* 21.395, where Ares calls her *thársos áeton ékhousa,* "having fierce boldness." Athena often puts *thársos* into the hearts of her favorites: Diomedes (*Iliad* 5.2), Menelaus (*Iliad* 17.570), Telemachus (*Odyssey* 1.321, 3.76); the *daímōn* who inspires *thársos* in Odysseus in the Cyclops's cave (*Odyssey* 9.381) is not named, but this too suggests Athena; in *Odyssey* 14.216 Odysseus, in his lying tale to Eumaios, says that Ares and Athena once both gave him *thársos.* When Athena puts *thársos* into her favorites this of course does not give them a hidden identity. What is different about Nausicaa is that she is female like

distinct, but this is different from the overt comparisons with Artemis. In terms of Nausicaa's hidden identity the two figures are one because they have the same warrior's courage.

§3.29 In the first line of his supplication to Nausicaa Odysseus asks whether she is a god or a mortal. This is already a half step back from the full realization of Nausicaa's hidden identity. Next Odysseus speculates that if she is a goddess she must be Artemis because of her tall stature (*Odyssey* 6.149–152):[60]

γουνοῦμαί σε, ἄνασσα· θεός νύ τις ἦ βροτός ἐσσι;

εἰ μέν τις θεός ἐσσι, τοὶ οὐρανὸν εὐρὺν ἔχουσιν,

Ἀρτέμιδί σε ἐγώ γε, Διὸς κούρῃ μεγάλοιο,

εἶδός τε μέγεθός τε φυήν τ' ἄγχιστα ἐΐσκω.

I grasp your knees, my lady; tell me, are you a god or a mortal?
If you are one of the gods who inhabit the wide sky,
I think that you most resemble Artemis, daughter of great Zeus,
in beauty and stature and build.

Nausicaa was already compared with Artemis because of her tall stature before Odysseus awoke and burst upon the scene, as Nausicaa danced and played with her companions (*Odyssey* 6.102–109):

οἵη δ' Ἄρτεμις εἶσι κατ' οὔρεα ἰοχέαιρα,

ἢ κατὰ Τηΰγετον περιμήκετον ἢ Ἐρύμανθον,

τερπομένη κάπροισι καὶ ὠκείῃσ' ἐλάφοισι·

τῇ δέ θ' ἅμα Νύμφαι, κοῦραι Διὸς αἰγιόχοιο,

ἀγρονόμοι παίζουσι· γέγηθε δέ τε φρένα Λητώ·

πασάων δ' ὑπὲρ ἥ γε κάρη ἔχει ἠδὲ μέτωπα,

Athena; traditional epic means are here used to a special end and with a special meaning (the comparison of Arete to a god is similar in this respect; cf. n3.47 above).

60 Artemis was characterized especially by her tall stature (*mễkos*); this was the gift that she gave to the daughters of Pandareos according to *Odyssey* 20.71 (μῆκος δ' ἔπορ' Ἄρτεμις ἁγνή; cf. n3.49 above). In *Homeric Hymn to Apollo* 197–199 Artemis is conspicuous among other goddesses in the dance on Olympus (τῇσι μὲν οὔτ' αἰσχρὴ μεταμέλπεται οὔτ' ἐλάχεια, / ἀλλὰ μάλα μεγάλη τε ἰδεῖν καὶ εἶδος ἀγητή, "not ugly or small she dances among them, / but very big to look on and wondrous in beauty"); scenes like this may have made Artemis a typical comparison for girls who led the dance (cf. Segal 1994:23 and Calame 1977:90–92), and this would certainly have been a factor in the comparison of Nausicaa with Artemis.

ῥεῖά τ' ἀριγνώτη πέλεται, καλαὶ δέ τε πᾶσαι·
ὡς ἥ γ' ἀμφιπόλοισι μετέπρεπε παρθένος ἀδμής.

Like arrow-shooting Artemis, who goes forth on the mountains,
either on Taygetos or soaring Erymanthos,
delighting in boars and swift deer;
and field-haunting Nymphs, daughters of aegis-holder Zeus,
play with her; and Leto rejoices in her heart;
and above all the others she holds her head and brow
and is easy to recognize, but all are beautiful;
so the untamed maiden stood out among her servants.

It is between the two comparisons with Artemis that Nausicaa's true hidden identity manifests itself when she stands her ground and hears Odysseus's appeal. Odysseus then takes us a step back from this hidden identity by asking whether she is a goddess or a mortal, and by comparing her with Artemis if she is a goddess.[61] He then takes us a further step back from the identification by naming exactly what Nausicaa is on the surface of the story, a mortal maiden, a great blessing to her parents and brothers, but especially to her future husband (*Odyssey* 6.153–159):

εἰ δέ τίς ἐσσι βροτῶν, οἳ ἐπὶ χθονὶ ναιετάουσι,
τρὶς μάκαρες μὲν σοί γε πατὴρ καὶ πότνια μήτηρ,
τρὶς μάκαρες δὲ κασίγνητοι· μάλα πού σφισι θυμὸς
αἰὲν ἐϋφροσύνῃσιν ἰαίνεται εἵνεκα σεῖο,
λευσσόντων τοιόνδε θάλος χορὸν εἰσοιχνεῦσαν.

---

61 In the two passages comparing Nausicaa to Artemis note that in one the nymphs in Artemis's retinue are called *koûrai Diós* (*Odyssey* 6.105) and in the other Artemis herself is called *Diòs koúrē* (*Odyssey* 6.151); *Diòs koúrē* is Athena's characteristic epithet (see n3.56 above), and Nausicaa's hidden identity with Athena is the real point in both passages. Nausicaa's resemblance to Artemis does not preclude her resemblance to Athena; Nausicaa is compared to "goddesses" in general for her stature and appearance when Athena first comes to her bedchamber and appears to her in a dream (*Odyssey* 6.15–16):

βῆ δ' ἴμεν ἐς θάλαμον πολυδαίδαλον, ᾧ ἔνι κούρη
κοιμᾶτ' ἀθανάτῃσι φυὴν καὶ εἶδος ὁμοίη.

She went into the much decorated chamber, in which the maiden
slept, like the immortal goddesses in build and beauty.

The plural *athanátēisi*, "immortal goddesses," opens the question, to be returned to later in the story, as to which goddess in particular Nausicaa is meant to represent.

κεῖνος δ' αὖ περὶ κῆρι μακάρτατος ἔξοχον ἄλλων,
ὅς κέ σ' ἐέδνοισι βρίσας οἶκόνδ' ἀγάγηται.

But if you are one of mortals who live on earth,
your father and revered mother are thrice-blest,
and your brothers are thrice-blest; surely their heart
is always warmed with gladness because of you
when they see such a blossoming shoot entering the dance.
But he is most blessed of all in his heart,
whoever, laden with wedding gifts, leads you home.

The process of stepping back from the full impact of Nausicaa's hidden identity after the moment of its greatest realization is comparable to the similar process that we saw in the case of Arete, except that here the process takes place more quickly. So that something of the full impact remains in the end a final grace note is added when Odysseus compares Nausicaa to the sacred palm tree of Apollo on Delos (*Odyssey* 6.160–169):[62]

οὐ γάρ πω τοιοῦτον ἴδον βροτὸν ὀφθαλμοῖσιν,
οὔτ' ἄνδρ' οὔτε γυναῖκα· σέβας μ' ἔχει εἰσορόωντα.
Δήλῳ δή ποτε τοῖον Ἀπόλλωνος παρὰ βωμῷ
φοίνικος νέον ἔρνος ἀνερχόμενον ἐνόησα·
ἦλθον γὰρ καὶ κεῖσε, πολὺς δέ μοι ἕσπετο λαός,
τὴν ὁδόν, ᾗ δὴ μέλλεν ἐμοὶ κακὰ κήδε' ἔσεσθαι·
ὣς δ' αὕτως καὶ κεῖνο ἰδὼν ἐτεθήπεα θυμῷ,
δήν, ἐπεὶ οὔ πω τοῖον ἀνήλυθεν ἐκ δόρυ γαίης,
ὡς σέ, γύναι, ἄγαμαί τε τέθηπά τε, δείδια δ' αἰνῶς
γούνων ἅψασθαι· χαλεπὸν δέ με πένθος ἱκάνει.

For I have never yet seen such a mortal with my eyes,
either man or woman; awe holds me as I look at you.
Once on Delos, by the altar of Apollo, I saw such a one,
a young sapling of a palm tree rising up;

---

62 The plant comparison is first introduced in *Odyssey* 6.157, where Nausicaa is called a *thálos*, "shoot"; the poet, speaking as Odysseus, clearly already has in mind that he is about to compare Nausicaa to an *érnos*, a "sapling," in *Odyssey* 6.163. The sacred palm tree is doubtless the one that Leto grasped when she bore Apollo on Delos (*Homeric Hymn to Apollo* 117; cf. n3.14 above).

for I went there, and many warriors followed me,
on that journey that was to be my great sorrow;
and just as, when I saw it, I was struck with wonder in my heart
for a long time, for such a shaft had never before risen from the
   earth,
so, my lady, I am now struck with wonder and awe, and I am
   terribly afraid
to grasp your knees; but hard grief has come to me.

Nausicaa's remarkable stature is again presumably the immediate point of comparison, but an association with the virgin goddess Artemis is also still present through the mention of Delos and Apollo.[63] The association, however, is now one step further removed. With this somewhat mysterious tree comparison the issue of Nausicaa's hidden identity comes to rest, having been gradually distanced from its real point.

§3.30 There is a final parallel between Nausicaa and Arete in their respective hidden identities. Both are given a farewell by Odysseus before he leaves for home. We have already considered Odysseus's farewell to Arete, in which he acknowledges her mortality and thus distinguishes her from Athena Polias, whom she has so powerfully evoked. The farewell to Nausicaa comes earlier, and it, on the other hand, reminds us that she too has played an aspect of the goddess. It is when Odysseus has finished his bath and joined the banqueters for a long night of story-telling that Nausicaa, admiring him, asks that he remember her when he returns home. With Nausicaa's admiration, and her recognition that he will soon leave, the potential sexual relationship between them, which so powerfully informed their first encounter, and remained alive when Alcinous openly wished for a husband like Odysseus for his daughter, is addressed for the last time. Nausicaa reminds Odysseus that it was she who first saved him, and Odysseus responds that, if only he

---

63 Leto gave birth to Artemis on Ortygia, which is distinguished from Delos in *Homeric Hymn to Apollo* 16, but is identified with Delos in later sources (Apollonius of Rhodes 1.419, Callimachus *Hymns* 4.40, etc.). Ortygia is mentioned in *Odyssey* 15.404, where it has been identified both with Delos and with Syracuse by modern commentators. Strabo 10.5.5 identifies Ortygia with Rheneia, suitably close to Delos to be the birthplace of Apollo's twin. Such proximity is perhaps the point of the comparison of Nausicaa to Apollo's sacred tree on Delos: the tree is related to, but separate from, the goddess Artemis and her place of birth. Palm trees are associated with Artemis herself in art, especially in scenes of erotic pursuit leading to sexual consummation; cf. Karakantza 2003:14, following Sourvinou-Inwood 1985 and 1987:141, 144–145. The comparison of Nausicaa to Apollo's palm tree thus continues to suggest Artemis even when Artemis is no longer directly at issue.

reaches home, he will forever pray to her like a goddess, for she did indeed bring him back to life (*Odyssey* 8.464–468):

Ναυσικάα, θύγατερ μεγαλήτορος Ἀλκινόοιο,
οὕτω νῦν Ζεὺς θείη, ἐρίγδουπος πόσις Ἥρης,
οἴκαδέ τ᾽ ἐλθέμεναι καὶ νόστιμον ἦμαρ ἰδέσθαι·
τῷ κέν τοι καὶ κεῖθι θεῷ ὣς εὐχετοῴμην
αἰεὶ ἤματα πάντα· σὺ γάρ μ᾽ ἐβιώσαο, κούρη.

Nausicaa, daughter of great-hearted Alcinous,
may Zeus, the loud-thundering husband of Hera, now so arrange
it
that I reach home and see the day of my return;
if so I would pray to you as a god even there
always and forever; for you brought me back to life, maiden.

The last word, *koúrē*, "maiden," is the key word. To Odysseus (and to us) Nausicaa will forever be a maiden, to whom Odysseus will always pray. Athena is again evoked, for Nausicaa's role has indeed been to play the goddess who, in the overall context of the *Odyssey*, brings Odysseus back to life. But the phrase "I will pray to you like a god (θεῷ ὥς)," also implies that Nausicaa is not a god, but a mortal. Again the parallel with Arete, whom the townspeople honor "like a god (θεὸν ὥς)" when she walks through the city (*Odyssey* 7.71), is complete. But whereas for Arete the key phrase comes first, when her part in the shadow-play of hidden identities is introduced, for Nausicaa the phrase comes last, when her part is over.[64]

---

64 Cf. n3.47 above. The line at *Odyssey* 8.467 occurs again at *Odyssey* 15.181, where Telemachus tells Helen that he will pray to her like a god if Zeus accomplishes what she has just foretold about Odysseus. There are nine other comparisons of humans to gods in Homer that entail use of the dative θεῷ: Achilles says of Hector that the Trojans prayed to him like a god (θεῷ ὣς εὐχετόωντο, *Iliad* 22.394); Odysseus is said to have been cared for like a god by Calypso (κομιδή γε θεῷ ὣς ἔμπεδος ἦεν, *Odyssey* 8.453); Odysseus calls on Athena, disguised as a mortal, to save him and his possessions, saying that he prays to her like a god (εὔχομαι ὥς τε θεῷ καί σευ φίλα γούναθ᾽ ἱκάνω, *Odyssey* 13.231). There are three examples of the phrase θεῷ ἐναλίγκιος: the herald Talthybios is called "like a god in voice" (θεῷ ἐναλίγκιος αὐδήν, *Iliad* 19.250); Telemachus and Menelaus are called "like a god in person" (θεῷ ἐναλίγκιος ἄντην, *Odyssey* 2.5 and 4.310). Finally there are two verses with ἴσος and θεῷ: Phoenix says to Achilles that the Achaeans will honor him like a god (ἶσον γάρ σε θεῷ τίσουσιν Ἀχαιοί, *Iliad* 9.603); Telemachus says that the Ithacans regard Eurymachus like a god (ἶσα θεῷ Ἰθακήσιοι εἰσορόωσι, *Odyssey* 15.520).

§3.31 The one aspect of Nausicaa that seems to conflict with her hidden identity as Athena the virgin goddess is her impending marriage. But we should note at once that there is no specific bridegroom for this marriage, and that only Odysseus, whose destiny is elsewhere, is singled out as a bridegroom whom Alcinous would have wished for his daughter. To be sure Athena tells Nausicaa in her dream that she will not long remain a virgin, for the best young men among the Phaeacians already woo her (*Odyssey* 6.33–35):

οὔ τοι ἔτι δὴν παρθένος ἔσσεαι·
ἤδη γάρ σε μνῶνται ἀριστῆες κατὰ δῆμον
πάντων Φαιήκων, ὅθι τοι γένος ἐστὶ καὶ αὐτῇ.

You will not still be a maiden for long;
for already you are wooed by the best in the land
among all the Phaeacians, where your own family is.

But the real purpose of this dream is not to prepare Nausicaa for marriage but to send her out to meet Odysseus. Elsewhere as well Nausicaa's marriage is treated ambiguously at best. Odysseus, in his supplication of Nausicaa, says that she will be a great blessing to whoever marries her (*Odyssey* 6.158–159):

κεῖνος δ' αὖ περὶ κῆρι μακάρτατος ἔξοχον ἄλλων,
ὅς κέ σ' ἐέδνοισι βρίσας οἶκόνδ' ἀγάγηται.

But he is most blessed of all in his heart,
whoever, laden with wedding gifts, leads you home.

But such a marriage will take place only if Nausicaa is in fact a mortal, and not a goddess, and Odysseus's speech has perfectly balanced the two possibilities. The subject of Nausicaa's Phaeacian suitors returns once more when she warns Odysseus not to be seen with her on the way into town. The Phaeacians' jealous reaction to Odysseus, as Nausicaa imagines it, again focuses attention on Odysseus and leaves the Phaeacians themselves rather out of account as suitors of Nausicaa (*Odyssey* 6.275–284):

καί νύ τις ὧδ' εἴπῃσι κακώτερος ἀντιβολήσας·
"τίς δ' ὅδε Ναυσικάᾳ ἕπεται καλός τε μέγας τε
ξεῖνος; ποῦ δέ μιν εὗρε; πόσις νύ οἱ ἔσσεται αὐτῇ.
ἦ τινά που πλαγχθέντα κομίσσατο ἧς ἀπὸ νηὸς
ἀνδρῶν τηλεδαπῶν, ἐπεὶ οὔ τινες ἐγγύθεν εἰσίν·

ἤ τίς οἱ εὐξαμένῃ πολυάρητος θεὸς ἦλθεν
οὐρανόθεν καταβάς, ἕξει δέ μιν ἤματα πάντα.
βέλτερον, εἰ καὐτή περ ἐποιχομένη πόσιν εὗρεν
ἄλλοθεν· ἦ γὰρ τούσδε γ' ἀτιμάζει κατὰ δῆμον
Φαίηκας, τοί μιν μνῶνται πολέες τε καὶ ἐσθλοί."

And some lowly man meeting us might speak thus:
"Who is this large handsome stranger who follows Nausicaa?
Where did she find him? Surely he will be her husband.
Either she rescued a lost wanderer from his ship,
one of men from far away, since there are none nearby;
or some god, much prayed for, came in answer to her prayer,
descending from the sky, and she will have him forever.
It is better if she herself has gone and found a husband
from elsewhere; for she indeed despises those here,
the many noble Phaeacians who woo her."

Finally Alcinous offers his daughter to Odysseus, even though he knows that
Odysseus will not stay and marry her (*Odyssey* 7.311–316):

αἲ γάρ, Ζεῦ τε πάτερ καὶ Ἀθηναίη καὶ Ἄπολλον,
τοῖος ἐών, οἷός ἐσσι, τά τε φρονέων ἅ τ' ἐγώ περ,
παῖδά τ' ἐμὴν ἐχέμεν καὶ ἐμὸς γαμβρὸς καλέεσθαι,
αὖθι μένων· οἶκον δέ κ' ἐγὼ καὶ κτήματα δοίην,
εἴ κ' ἐθέλων γε μένοις· ἀέκοντα δέ σ' οὔ τις ἐρύξει
Φαιήκων· μὴ τοῦτο φίλον Διὶ πατρὶ γένοιτο.

I wish, father Zeus and Athena and Apollo,
that someone who is as you are, and thinks as I do,
would have my daughter and be called my son-in-law,
staying here; I would give a house and possessions
if you willingly remained; but if you are unwilling no one will
      hold you back
among the Phaeacians; this would not be dear to father Zeus.

Despite talk of an impending marriage, Nausicaa is in essence the virgin to
whom Odysseus does not make love when they first meet, and whom he will
likewise not stay to marry. As far as the story of the *Odyssey* is concerned,

Nausicaa is in the end left frozen in time, always on the point of marriage, never attaining to it.

§3.32 But a problem still remains. Even if Nausicaa does not realize her marriage, she intends to realize it, and this is not the attitude that we associate with the virgin goddess Athena. Nausicaa goes out and meets Odysseus because she has been told in her dream that her marriage is near and that she must have clean clothes for herself and for her husband; this is Athena's message when, disguised as Nausicaa's friend, she first appears in her dream (*Odyssey* 6.25–28):

> Ναυσικάα, τί νύ σ' ὧδε μεθήμονα γείνατο μήτηρ;
> εἵματα μέν τοι κεῖται ἀκηδέα σιγαλόεντα,
> σοὶ δὲ γάμος σχεδόν ἐστιν, ἵνα χρὴ καλὰ μὲν αὐτὴν
> ἕννυσθαι, τὰ δὲ τοῖσι παρασχεῖν, οἵ κέ σ' ἄγωνται.

> Nausicaa, how is it your mother bore you to be so careless?
> Shining clothes lie neglected by you,
> and your wedding is near, where you will have to wear
> beautiful clothes yourself and provide them to those who take
>   you in marriage.

Nausicaa, when she awakens, acts to bring about what has been foretold to her in these lines.[65] She disguises her real purpose when she asks her father for a wagon to carry the wash, speaking only of her care to provide him and her five brothers with clean clothes (*Odyssey* 6.57–65). But after her speech the poet tells us her real motive, and her father too does not fail to perceive it, namely her impending marriage (*Odyssey* 6.66–67):

> ὣς ἔφατ'· αἴδετο γὰρ θαλερὸν γάμον ἐξονομῆναι
> πατρὶ φίλῳ· ὁ δὲ πάντα νόει....

> So she spoke; for she was ashamed to name her own ripening
>   marriage out loud
> to her dear father; but he perceived it all....

§3.33 Nausicaa's impending marriage, insofar as it is the motive for her washing expedition, is a secret imparted directly to her by Athena which

---

65 In the event Nausicaa does indeed wash clothes for herself, as the dream has instructed her, but it is Odysseus rather than a future husband who also receives clean clothes from her.

she shares with no one else. Athena herself had a widespread festival called the Plynteria, the washing festival, whose real purpose is also shrouded in mystery. In Athens, where the festival concerned the only old cult of Athena, namely that of Athena Polias, the rites themselves were termed ἀπόρρητα, "not to be spoken of."[66] We know only details of these rites, which included removing the *péplos* from the statue and returning it again, presumably washed.[67]

§3.34 For the relevance of Athena's festival, the Plynteria, to Nausicaa's washing expedition in the *Odyssey*, we should by no means limit ourselves to the Athenian version of the festival. Nausicaa herself does not relate exclusively to the Athenian city goddess (that is Arete's role), but to the Olympian daughter of Zeus. To the latter figure other local versions of the Plynteria may be relevant, and these were apparently widespread. In Attica itself distinct versions of the festival, celebrated at different times from the Athenian

66 In 408 BC Alcibiades returned to Athens on the day of the Plynteria, regarded as among the unluckiest days in the year, and two sources, Xenophon and Plutarch, give information about the festival's rites in connection with this ill-omened event. Plutarch *Alcibiades* 34.1 says that the rites, which he calls ἀπόρρητα, "not to be spoken of," were performed by the Praxiergidai, who removed the ornaments from the statue of Athena and veiled it (ἦ γὰρ ἡμέρα κατέπλευσεν, ἐδρᾶτο τὰ Πλυντήρια τῆ θεῷ. δρῶσι δὲ τὰ ὄργια Πραξιεργίδαι Θαργηλιῶνος ἕκτη φθίνοντος ἀπόρρητα, τόν τε κόσμον ἀφελόντες καὶ τὸ ἕδος κατακαλύψαντες. ὅθεν ἐν ταῖς μάλιστα τῶν ἀποφράδων τὴν ἡμέραν ταύτην ἄπρακτον Ἀθηναῖοι νομίζουσιν, "On the day on which he sailed back the Plynteria were being celebrated for the goddess; the Praxiergidai celebrate these rites on the sixth day of the end of the month of Thargelion, removing the ornaments and covering the statue. Because of this the Athenians consider this day to be among the unluckiest and unsuitable for business"). Xenophon *Hellenica* 1.4.12 also speaks of the statue's being veiled and of the care taken not to conduct important business on this day ([Alcibiades] κατέπλευσεν εἰς τὸν Πειραιᾶ ἡμέρα ἦ Πλυντήρια ἦγεν ἡ πόλις, τοῦ ἕδους κατακεκαλυμμένου τῆς Ἀθηνᾶς, ὅ τινες οἰωνίζοντο ἀνεπιτήδειον εἶναι καὶ αὐτῷ καὶ τῆ πόλει. Ἀθηναίων γὰρ οὐδεὶς ἐν ταύτη τῆ ἡμέρα οὐδενὸς σπουδαίου ἔργου τολμῆσαι ἂν ἄψασθαι, "He [Alcibiades] sailed back to the Peiraieus on the day on which the city was celebrating the Plynteria, the statue of Athena being covered, which some took as an unpropitious sign both for himself and for the city. For none of the Athenians would dare to undertake any serious work on this day").

67 For the removal and return of the *péplos*, note the following: 1) an entry in Hesychius says that the Praxiergidai (who conducted the Plynteria, cf. n3.66 above) had the task of "clothing" the old statue of Athena (Hesychius s.v. Πραξιεργίδαι· οἱ τὸ ἕδος τὸ ἀρχαῖον τῆς Ἀθηνᾶς ἀμφιεννύντες); 2) a fragmentary inscription detailing the tasks of the Praxiergidai uses the same verb "clothe" with *péplos* as object (ἀμφιεννύουσιν τὸν πέπλον, *IG* I³ 7 line 11). It is inferred that this inscription refers to the ritual of the Plynteria (cf. Deubner 1932:19n11, Robertson 1996:72n74; Herington 1955:30n2 regards the inference as very probable but not certain; for further discussion of the inscription, see Parker 1996:307–308). That the *péplos* was washed can only be inferred from the name Πλυντήρια of the festival itself, which must refer to washing a garment and not to bathing the statue. This issue is discussed in EN3.4.

festival, are attested for the demes Erchia and Thorikos.[68] In addition a month
Plynterion, named for the festival, is attested on the Ionian islands of Chios,
Paros, Ios, and Thasos.[69] Martin Nilsson pointed out that what we know of
the Athenian festival, which amounts to little more than aspects of temple
cleaning, does not account for the widespread occurrence of the festival,
which therefore probably had a wider meaning originally.[70] Nausicaa, who
does the wash in preparation for her own *marriage*, clearly points toward this
wider meaning. The verb associated with the name *Pluntéria*, namely *plúnō*,
"wash (clothes)," is the one used of Nausicaa's task, and from its first occur-
rence in this context the verb is associated with marriage and loss of virginity.
Athena, disguised as Nausicaa's friend, says in her dream that she will accom-
pany her to do the wash so that she may get herself ready as quickly as
possible, for she will not long remain a virgin (*Odyssey* 6.31–33):

> ἀλλ' ἴομεν <u>πλυνέουσαι</u> ἅμ' ἠόϊ φαινομένηφι·
> καί τοι ἐγὼ συνέριθος ἅμ' ἕψομαι, ὄφρα τάχιστα
> ἐντύνεαι, ἐπεὶ <u>οὔ τοι ἔτι δὴν παρθένος ἔσσεαι</u>.

> But let us go <u>to do the wash</u> as soon as dawn appears;
> and I will come with you as helper, so that you most quickly
> may prepare yourself, <u>since not for long will you still be a maiden</u>.[71]

---

68 See Robertson 1996:51 (Athena is partnered by Aglauros in both festivals); for a fuller
    description of the evidence for these festivals see Robertson 1983:281–282 and n113.
69 Strictly speaking, we do not know that the implied festival of the Plynteria on these islands
    belonged to Athena; thus Nilsson 1906:469 lists the festivals on the islands of Chios and
    Paros under "unknown gods" ("unbekannte Götter").
70 Nilsson 1906:469: "It is surprising that a festival, whose content in Athens seems to be only
    the purification of the temple and cult image, is found in other places as well, and this
    seems to point to an earlier wider meaning" ("Es ist auffallend, ein Fest, dessen Inhalt nur
    die Reinigung des Tempels und des Xoanon in Athen zu sein scheint, an anderen Orten
    wiederzufinden, und dieses scheint auf eine einstige weitere Bedeutung hinzuweisen").
71 When Nausicaa asks her father for a wagon, she repeats the verb "to wash" in nearly iden-
    tical form but suppresses the context of marriage (*Odyssey* 6.57–61):

    πάππα φίλ', οὐκ ἄν δή μοι ἐφοπλίσσειας ἀπήνην
    ὑψηλὴν εὔκυκλον, ἵνα κλυτὰ εἵματ' ἄγωμαι
    ἐς ποταμὸν <u>πλυνέουσα</u>, τά μοι ῥερυπωμένα κεῖται;
    καὶ δὲ σοὶ αὐτῷ ἔοικε μετὰ πρώτοισιν ἐόντα
    βουλὰς βουλεύειν καθαρὰ χροῒ εἵματ' ἔχοντα.

    Daddy dear, wouldn't you hitch a wagon for me,
    a high one with good wheels, so that I can take my famed clothes,
    which lie soiled, to the river to <u>wash</u> them?

Related to the verb *plúnō* is the noun *plunoí*, "washing places," which is also found in Athena's speech; the washing places are Nausicaa's destination, which Athena says are better reached by wagon than on foot since they are far from the city (*Odyssey* 6.39–40):

καὶ δὲ σοὶ ὧδ' αὐτῇ πολὺ κάλλιον ἠὲ πόδεσσιν
ἔρχεσθαι· πολλὸν γὰρ ἄπο <u>πλυνοί</u> εἰσι πόληος.

And that way is much better for you than to go
on foot; for the <u>washing places</u> are far from the city.[72]

§3.35 At the festival of the Plynteria Athena's *péplos*, it may be inferred, was the object "washed," and this too seems to be alluded to in Nausicaa's dream. It is not so much that Athena in the dream includes *péploi* among the items to be washed, along with girdles and bed covers.[73] More significant, because more specific, is the epithet *eúpeplos*, "having a beautiful robe," that is applied to Nausicaa herself as soon as she awakens from her dream (*Odyssey* 6.48–49):

αὐτίκα δ' Ἠὼς ἦλθεν ἐΰθρονος, ἥ μιν ἔγειρε
Ναυσικάαν <u>ἐΰπεπλον</u>.

For you too it is fitting to take counsel with the first men
wearing clean clothes on your skin.

72 The *plunoí* are mentioned again when Nausicaa and her companions reach them (*Odyssey* 6.85–87):

αἱ δ' ὅτε δὴ ποταμοῖο ῥόον περικαλλέ' ἵκοντο,
ἔνθ' ἦ τοι <u>πλυνοὶ</u> ἦσαν ἐπηετανοί, πολὺ δ' ὕδωρ
καλὸν ὑπεκπρόρεεν μάλα περ ῥυπόωντα καθῆραι....

When they came to the beautiful stream of the river,
there were ever-flowing <u>washing places</u>, and much beautiful water
flowed from them to clean even very soiled clothes....

The verb *plúnō* also occurs again when the maidens have cleaned the clothes and set them out to dry (*Odyssey* 6.93–94): αὐτὰρ ἐπεὶ <u>πλῦνάν</u> τε κάθηράν τε ῥύπα πάντα, / ἑξείης πέτασαν παρὰ θῖν' ἁλός, "but when they had <u>washed</u> and cleaned all the dirt, they spread them out side by side by the shore of the sea."

73 *Odyssey* 6.36–38:

ἀλλ' ἄγ' ἐπότρυνον πατέρα κλυτὸν ἠῶθι πρὸ
ἡμιόνους καὶ ἄμαξαν ἐφοπλίσαι, ἥ κεν ἄγῃσι
ζῶστρά τε καὶ <u>πέπλους</u> καὶ ῥήγεα σιγαλόεντα.

But come urge your famed father at dawn
to hitch the mules and the wagon, which will bring
the sashes and <u>robes</u> and shining coverlets.

At once beautiful-throned Dawn came, who awakened her,
beautiful-robed Nausicaa.[74]

We have seen that when Athena leaves Nausicaa's dream and goes to Olympus,
she thereby identifies Nausicaa with the Olympian aspect of herself. When
Nausicaa awakens from this dream and attention is immediately drawn to
her *péplos*, this would seem to allude to Athena's own widespread festival, the
Plynteria.[75]

§3.36 If the Plynteria were preliminary to a marriage and a loss of
virginity, as Nausicaa's dream suggests that they were, this must be the real
point of the sexually charged initial encounter between the naked Odysseus
and the virgin Nausicaa, who is still engaged in her own clothes-washing
expedition when they meet. The narrative, as we have seen, plays with the
possibility that this encounter could have been both sexual and violent. In
another myth having to do with the Plynteria a rape actually occurs: Auge,
the priestess of Athena Alea in Tegea, was, according to the local version
of her myth, raped by Heracles while she was engaged in washing the
goddess's robe.[76]

---

74 The Homeric epithet *eúpeplos* occurs more often in the plural of groups of women than
    in the singular: sisters-in-law (εἰνατέρων ἐϋπέπλων occurs three times in the *Iliad*) and
    Achaean women (Ἀχαιϊάδων ἐϋπέπλων occurs once each in the *Iliad* and the *Odyssey*);
    besides its use of Nausicaa in *Odyssey* 6 there is only one other use in the singular, in *Iliad*
    6.372 of a serving woman (ἀμφιπόλῳ ἐϋπέπλῳ).

75 Note that Athena wears the *péplos* on Olympus in the *Iliad*, twice shedding it on her father's
    threshold when she arms for battle (*Iliad* 5.733–735 = 8.384–386):

    αὐτὰρ Ἀθηναίη κούρη Διὸς αἰγιόχοιο
    πέπλον μὲν κατέχευεν ἑανὸν πατρὸς ἐπ' οὔδει
    ποικίλον, ὅν ῥ' αὐτὴ ποιήσατο καὶ κάμε χερσίν.

    But Athena, daughter of aegis-holder Zeus,
    let slip to her father's floor her supple robe
    of many colors, which she herself had made and worked by hand.

    The *péplos* is of course the usual female garment; the unarmed Aphrodite wears it on the
    battlefield in *Iliad* 5.315, hiding Aeneas in one of its folds. For the *péplos* as a specifically
    bridal garment see Lee 2003/2004:256–257, 269, 272, 273. For another interpretation of
    the Plynteria and the role of the *péplos* in it, see Connelly 1996:78–79, who interprets the
    festival as a funerary rite in honor of Aglauros, and the garment as a sacrificial robe.

76 See n3.14 above for Auge's myth, and for a statue of the goddess of childbirth called *Aúgē en
    gónasi*, "Auge on her knees," in the temple of Eileithyia in Tegea. Euripides wrote a tragedy
    called *Auge*, according to which the title character, as Athena's priestess, was washing the
    goddess's garment when she was seized by Heracles. We know this from a fragmentary argu-
    ment to the play and from Pompeian wall paintings inspired by the play. Ludwig Koenen first
    studied the papyrus fragment and identified it as the hypothesis to Euripides' *Auge*, and his
    restoration of the text established the argument's essential content (Koenen 1969). The text

§3.37 Nausicaa on the one hand and Auge on the other hand reveal that the Plynteria had to do with a "marriage," but what did this marriage have to do with Athena? Auge, whose "marriage" is fully realized, is not Athena herself but Athena's priestess.[77] Nausicaa, who is meant to be Athena herself, remains a virgin in her encounter with Odysseus, although she is destined to

---

was improved by Wolfgang Luppe, who recognized that the length of the lines should be shortened (Luppe 1983). From this evidence we infer, first, that Arcadian Tegea had a festival like the Attic and Ionic Plynteria, whether or not the Tegean festival had this name, and, secondly, that the washing of the goddess's robe at this festival was associated with a loss of virginity of the most violent kind. The crucial lines of the restored argument tell us that Auge was "washing the garment of Athena near the fountain" when Heracles seized her. Line 10 of the fragment has the crucial letters ητα πλυν, restored as ἐσθῆτα πλύνουσαν, describing Auge as "washing the garment" of the goddess. As Koenen (p. 18) comments, one can assume that the author of the hypothesis was not the first to make a connection with the Athenian Plynteria by using the verb *plúnō* (or a word of the same stem). In the next line the letters ησιον κρ(η), restored as πλησίον κρήνης, specify a location "near the spring." Pausanias 8.47.4 mentions this spring, which was just north of the temple, and says that according to the local version of the myth this was where Auge's rape took place: ἔστι δὲ ἐν τοῖς πρὸς ἄρκτον τοῦ ναοῦ κρήνη, καὶ ἐπὶ ταύτῃ βιασθῆναι τῇ κρήνῃ φασὶν Αὔγην ὑπὸ Ἡρακλέους, οὐχ ὁμολογοῦντες Ἑκαταίῳ τὰ ἐς αὐτήν, "In the area north of the temple there is a spring, and they say that Auge was raped by Heracles at this spring, not agreeing with Hecataeus's account of her." Euripides clearly followed the local version of the myth (as opposed to that of Hecataeus) in making the Plynteria the occasion of Auge's rape (cf. Koenen, p. 10). Excavators have found a large basin with marble sides and steps where Pausanias locates the spring, just north of the temple (Robertson 1996:50 citing Dugas et al. 1924:69–71). The Pompeian wall paintings, inspired by Euripides, depict a more natural setting. Auge and a friend sit at the water's edge dipping a garment into the pool as Heracles enters the scene and lays hands on Auge. (Koenen, p. 13, reproduces the line drawings of Reinach 1922; specific references in Koenen p. 12n4). For a vivid depiction of the rape on a Thracian gilt silver bowl see Boardman 1994:184–185, figure 6.1. For a different perspective on Auge's myth see Burkert 1966:15n3, who classes it with other stories of virgins at the well.

77 There is disagreement as to how Athena's mythic priestesses relate to Athena herself. Fehrle 1910:193–194 argues that the sexual union in Athena's temple of figures like Auge, Aithra, and Medusa must come from local cults of these figures which Athena at an early point absorbed (cf. Athena Alea in Tegea, where Auge's father is called Aleos; for temples of Alea in Arcadia and Laconia, and a town Alea in northern Arcadia, see Nilsson 1967:434); when the fertility aspect of such cults no longer harmonized with Athena's character, only the original goddesses, now demoted to the status of heroines, retained some form of their old sacred marriages. Nilsson 1967:443 rejects the implication of this argument that Athena's original character is revealed by that of her priestesses, believing that the connection of these figures to Athena may be based on external circumstances rather than internal relationships. Aglauros, who is featured as Athena's priestess in aetiological myths of the Plynteria in Athens (Photius *Lexicon* s.v. Καλλυντήρια καὶ πλυντήρια), is analogous to Auge, Athena's priestess in a similar festival in Tegea (cf. Robertson 1983:282 and n116). Nilsson, consistently with his argument, does not draw conclusions for Athena from Aglauros, who has mother goddess features. With respect to Auge's rape by Heracles, Koenen 1969, developing the evidence of the argument to Euripides' *Auge*, follows Fehrle rather than Nilsson. Koenen's argument is discussed in EN3.5.

have a marriage outside the framework of the story. Does either figure indi-
cate that it was Athena herself whose marriage was at stake in the Plynteria?
Perhaps both do, but it is Nausicaa who contributes something new to the
question. The key here is that one and the same figure, Athena, is both a
virgin and a mother insofar as she is represented by both Nausicaa and Arete:
it is the same goddess Athena who goes both to Olympus, to set the stage
for Nausicaa, and to Athens, to set the stage for Arete. These two figures, on
the other hand, can only be one thing or the other, and that is why there are
two of them: Nausicaa is the virgin and Arete the mother. Athena changes
from one figure to the other, and that change is what the Plynteria are meant
to herald. We are not privy to Athena's "marriage," but a marriage there
must be if she changes from a virgin goddess to a mother goddess. Among
the Phaeacians we see the result of the marriage in Arete, who is married
to Alcinous, and we see the preparation for the marriage in the washing of
Nausicaa's *péplos*. In Athena's case the marriage heralded by the Plynteria
may have been to different figures in different places if the festival was as
widespread as it seems. Only in Athens can we identify who this figure was,
namely Erechtheus. It is worth repeating that there was only one old cult
of Athena in Athens, that of Athena Polias, and it was to this goddess that
the festival of the Plynteria belonged. If this festival was preliminary to the
marriage of a virgin goddess, we can only conclude that the same statue that
represented the mother goddess also represented a virgin goddess.[78] The
festival of the Plynteria must have originated as the preparation for an annu-
ally repeated marriage of Athena and Erechtheus. I see no other way to inter-
pret the Phaeacian evidence if Nausicaa's washing expedition alludes to the
festival of the Plynteria.[79]

78 The image of a female figure spinning wool could represent a virgin as well as a matron;
    cf. the daughters of Pandareos, whom Athena taught *érga*, "works" (i.e. women's work,
    weaving) before Aphrodite sought a marriage for them (*Odyssey* 20.72–74; cf. n3.49 above);
    cf. also *Homeric Hymn to Aphrodite* 14–15, where Athena is said to teach *érga* to tender
    maidens: ἡ δέ τε παρθενικὰς ἁπαλόχροας ἐν μεγάροισιν / ἀγλαὰ ἔργ' ἐδίδαξεν ἐπὶ φρεσὶ
    θεῖσα ἑκάστῃ, "she also teaches soft-skinned maidens splendid works, putting them in the
    minds of each." The terracotta reliefs from the Acropolis of a girl spinning (see Figure 1 in
    §3.14 and cf. n3.32 above) provide an example of such an image.
79 Note that Nausicaa's part in the story concludes just as Arete's part begins, and that the
    division between the two parts is marked by Odysseus's prayer to Athena in her sacred
    grove; this point of transition between the two figures is exactly the right moment for
    Athena, who stands behind both figures, to be invoked in her own persona. In answer to
    Odysseus's prayer she continues herself in Nausicaa's role by appearing as a young maiden
    and directing Odysseus toward Alcinous's palace; at the same time she introduces Arete
    and takes on the role of mother goddess by departing to Athens and entering Erechtheus's

§3.38 Athena is doubly represented among the Phaeacians, as both virgin war goddess and as mother goddess. She is associated with different places, Olympus and Athens, and with different male figures, her father Zeus and her male consort Erechtheus, in the parallel passages that establish her double representation; the parallelism between these two passages is the single greatest argument for the hidden identity of the Phaeacian princess on the one hand and of the Phaeacian queen on the other hand. Our primary concern is with the queen. Athena the mother goddess did not survive in Athens after the Homeric period, and Arete's hidden identity in the *Odyssey* lost its relevance as a result: *Odyssey* 7.80–81, in which Athena enters the strong house of Erechtheus, no longer conveyed what these lines are meant to convey. The changes that took place with respect to Athena and Erechtheus in post-Homeric Athens must next be considered in detail in order to complete the historical picture here proposed.

---

palace. Athena changes from the role of maiden to the role of mother goddess just when the figures representing her do. Athena is not the only Greek goddess to move back and forth between virginity and motherhood. Hera, the wife of Zeus, was said to become a virgin again each year when she bathed in the spring Kanathos in Nauplia; according to Pausanias the account of this was among "the things not to be spoken of" (*tôn aporrḗtōn*) in the initiation rites of the Argive Hera: ἐνταῦθα τὴν Ἥραν φασὶν Ἀργεῖοι κατὰ ἔτος λουμένην παρθένον γίνεσθαι. οὗτος μὲν δή σφισιν ἐκ τελετῆς, ἣν ἄγουσι τῇ Ἥρᾳ, λόγος τῶν ἀπορρήτων ἐστίν, "The Argives say that every year Hera, being bathed here, becomes a virgin. This account, from the rite which they perform for Hera, is among the *apórrhēta*" (Pausanias 2.38.2–3); cf. Nilsson 1906:44–45 and 47–49 for a bathing of Hera's statue as the likely ritual to restore the goddess's virginity in both Argos and Samos. In the argument above I have stressed the washing of clothes performed by Nausicaa and her companions, for this is what the *Odyssey* stresses, but Nausicaa and her companions also bathe afterwards in the river (λοεσσάμεναι, *Odyssey* 6.96), and this too suits the marriage context evoked by the episode: cf. the ritual bathing of marriage-age girls in the Scamander river in the Troad and their prayer to the river to take away their virginity ("Aeschines" *Epistle* 10.3–5); cf. also Thucydides 2.15.5 on the Athenian spring used from archaic times for ritual purposes before marriages.

Chapter 9.

THE CITY GODDESS OF ATHENS

§3.39 The Phaeacian king and queen are the key to the relationship between Athena Polias and Erechtheus as it once was. Aspects of this relationship, like Athena's change from virgin goddess to mother goddess in the context of the Plynteria, can be reconstructed only indirectly from the Phaeacian parallel and must therefore remain obscure; other aspects of the relationship may be absent from the Phaeacian parallel altogether.[80] But the essential relationship is plainly there: it is a marriage. A marriage bond presumably still united Athena Polias and Erechtheus when the Epidaurians made annual sacrifices to both as a pair in return for statues of the goddesses of fertility and childbirth, Damia and Auxesia. The era of these sacrifices surely coincided with the Homeric period at least in part. After the Homeric period, however, the marriage of Athena Polias and Erechtheus came to an end.[81] It had already ended by the time of a Homeric passage that is probably to be dated to the time of Solon, namely the Athenian entry to the Catalogue of Ships. This entry, which differs so markedly from the catalogue's other entries,[82] focuses

80 Mother goddesses may take their own sons as consorts, and this dual relationship, husband and son, applies to Erechtheus/Erichthonios in the view of some (e.g. Fauth 1959:466 [82], who refers to "the relationship of the *daímōn* to the mistress of the acropolis, which shifts between son and husband," ("das zwischen Sohn- und Gattenschaft wechselnde Verhältnis des Dämons zu der Herrin des Burgfelsens"). For more on this point see below §3.79 and n3.229. There is of course no question of such a dual relationship in the case of the Phaeacian queen and her husband.

81 The sacrifices of the Epidaurians were probably also terminated in the post-Homeric period, but perhaps earlier (cf. n3.16 above).

82 Whereas the other entries list a multitude of towns, this entry names only one town, Athens; for further discussion of this anomaly and its significance see below §3.87 and n3.274, n3.275, and n3.276. The problem of the Athenian entry is well presented in Simpson and Lazenby 1970:56.

above all on Erechtheus—Athens is called his land—and on Athena's relationship to him (*Iliad* 2.546–556):

οἳ δ᾽ ἄρ᾽ Ἀθήνας εἶχον ἐϋκτίμενον πτολίεθρον
δῆμον Ἐρεχθῆος μεγαλήτορος, ὅν ποτ᾽ Ἀθήνη
θρέψε Διὸς θυγάτηρ, τέκε δὲ ζείδωρος ἄρουρα,
κὰδ δ᾽ ἐν Ἀθήνης εἷσεν ἑῷ ἐν πίονι νηῷ·
ἔνθα δέ μιν ταύροισι καὶ ἀρνειοῖς ἱλάονται
κοῦροι Ἀθηναίων περιτελλομένων ἐνιαυτῶν·
τῶν αὖθ᾽ ἡγεμόνευ᾽ υἱὸς Πετεῶο Μενεσθεύς.
τῷ δ᾽ οὔ πώ τις ὁμοῖος ἐπιχθόνιος γένετ᾽ ἀνὴρ
κοσμῆσαι ἵππους τε καὶ ἀνέρας ἀσπιδιώτας·
Νέστωρ οἶος ἔριζεν· ὃ γὰρ προγενέστερος ἦεν·
τῷ δ᾽ ἅμα πεντήκοντα μέλαιναι νῆες ἕποντο.

And the men who inhabited Athens, well-founded city,
land of great-hearted Erechtheus, whom Athena,
Zeus's daughter, once nourished after the grain-giving earth
    bore him,
and set him down in Athens in her own (his own?) rich temple.
There the youths of the Athenians propitiate him with bulls and
    rams
as the years return;
those men Menestheus, the son of Peteos, led;
never was there another man on earth to equal him
in marshaling horses and shield-bearing men;
only Nestor rivaled him, for he was older;
fifty black ships followed him.

The main feature characterizing Erechtheus in this passage is that he was born from the earth; Athena's role was to nourish him and to put him in her temple in Athens, where the youths of Athens propitiated him with annual sacrifices of bulls and rams.[83] There is no hint here of the matrimonial pair that was found to inhabit the palace of Erechtheus in *Odyssey* 7.80–81. The

---

83 The recipient of the sacrifices, designated by the pronoun μιν, could be either Erechtheus or Athena; Frazer 1969 has argued convincingly that Erechtheus is meant.

annual sacrifices offered by Athenian youths to Erechtheus, moreover, are
quite different from what would have been expected from Herodotus's story
of the statues of the goddesses Damia and Auxesia: it was not to Erechtheus
alone, but to Athena Polias and Erechtheus as a pair, that annual sacrifices
were offered by the Epidaurians in return for these statues. Even the notion
that Athena and Erechtheus inhabited the same temple is not what the
passage in *Iliad* 2 presupposes if, as has been convincingly argued, the phrase
ἑῷ ἐν πίονι νηῷ in line 549 means not "in her rich temple," but "in his own
rich temple."[84] In *Odyssey* 7.80–81 the palace of Erechtheus is at the same
time the temple of Athena: Athena enters the palace of Erechtheus in order
to animate her own image, which clearly resides there.[85] In *Iliad* 2.549–551,
on the other hand, Erechtheus has not only his own sacrifices, but his own
temple as well. Simply put, the difference between the two passages seems
to be this: whereas the passage in *Odyssey* 7 concerns the marriage of Athena
Polias and Erechtheus, the passage in *Iliad* 2 concerns their separation. It is
this separation that remains to be considered more fully, for it is this sepa-
ration that survived, consigning the pair's earlier marriage to oblivion. The
change seems to have been a deliberate one. What brought it about? We will
address this question by considering separately the two new figures that
emerged, the new Athena Polias on the one hand and the new Erechtheus on
the other hand.

§3.40 There is no mystery about Athena. In Athens the virgin goddess
predominated to the exclusion of the mother goddess and became more and
more a war goddess. The golden aegis and gorgoneion that belonged to the
statue of Athena Polias in the fifth and fourth centuries vividly show how the
virgin war goddess ultimately prevailed. I have already suggested that the
change from a mother goddess, who spun wool, to a war goddess, who was
armed, may have taken place as early as the beginning of the sixth century.
At this date the influence of Homeric epic, in which Athena had long been
a war goddess, was doubtless already a factor. Indeed the golden aegis and
gorgoneion that were added as ornaments to the statue of Athena Polias
correspond closely to the Homeric description of Athena's arming.[86]

---

84 Noel Robertson and Gloria Ferrari have both reached this conclusion; see n3.117 below.

85 For the relationship of god to image see Scheer 2000:115–123; cf. Bettinetti 2001:52–54.

86 *Iliad* 5.733–742, quoted n3.25 above. In this description the last of the fearful devices on the
   aegis is the gorgon's head; why the aegis and the gorgoneion were distinct ornaments of
   the image of Athena Polias (they are listed separately in the fourth-century inventories)
   is not clear. For a date in the early sixth century BC for the transformation of the image of
   Athena Polias into a warrior goddess cf. n3.26 and §3.17 above and n3.111 below.

§3.41 How Athena first became a war goddess is a separate question to which there is no certain answer.[87] The festival of the Plynteria, if I have understood it correctly, was celebrated for a virgin goddess in preparation for her transition to mother goddess. For the virgin goddess to develop instead into a war goddess she had to remain a virgin by being separated once and for all from the mother goddess. This process seems to have taken place at different times in different places, but in most places it happened early.[88] Thus the Homeric Athena, reflecting her essential nature throughout the Greek world, is a war goddess: this is her Panhellenic form. Only where the mother goddess was deeply rooted would this process be prevented from happening, and Athens was surely the primary case of that. In the Phaeacian episode, as we have seen, there are two Athenas corresponding to Athena's two departures from Scheria: Athena the Olympian and Athena the city goddess of Athens. Athena the Olympian is the Panhellenic goddess who is found everywhere else in Homer. Athena the city goddess of Athens is found just once in Homer, in *Odyssey* 7.80–81, and even there she becomes the city goddess only by disappearing from view into the palace of Erechtheus. Thus on the surface of the Homeric text Athena is entirely the Panhellenic goddess. The local variant is below the surface of the text, but it is important enough on its own to counterbalance the Panhellenic conception in the Phaeacian episode.

§3.42 If this analysis is right, Athens in the Homeric era was out of step with the rest of the Greek world in not worshipping Athena the war goddess,

87 Nilsson (1921:16 and elsewhere) argues that the Mycenaeans adopted the palace goddess of the Minoans, but turned her into a war goddess, and this explains the strange fact that the Greeks had a female war deity at all. Direct evidence for Bronze Age war goddesses is not abundant, but full weight must be given to a female figure on a painted stucco tablet from Mycenae (see Rodenwaldt 1912, with Plate VIII; photograph also in Nilsson 1967 Plate 24.1). This figure, formed of a large Mycenaean shield with attached arms, head, and feet, stands by an altar between two female worshippers. The neck, head, and arms are white, hence the figure is female (Rodenwaldt 1912:133). The position by an altar between worshippers indicates divinity. Rodenwaldt dates the painting to the early Mycenaean period (Rodenwaldt 1912:132) and he relates the style to Minoan miniature painting (Rodenwaldt 1912:131). In historical times there was a temple of Athena on the acropolis of Mycenae where once the Bronze Age royal palace had stood, and the question arises whether the painted figure has anything to do with Athena: this is far from certain since the figure was not found in the area of Athena's temple. This issue and Athena's possible connections with other Bronze Age war goddesses are discussed in EN3.6.
88 It could have happened in Bronze Age Mycenae, for example. Höfer, Roscher's *Lexikon* 'Polias' 2610–2614 lists numerous cities with cults of Athena *Poliás* (39 instances), Athena *Polioûkhos* (11 instances), or Athena *Poliâtis* (only in Tegea, probably identical with Athena Alea; cf. n3.77 above). See also Nilsson 1967:417–418, 433, 438.

but Athena its own deeply traditional mother goddess. This situation changed in the post-Homeric period, probably starting in the seventh century at some point, when Athens came under the influence of the Homeric poems. The Athenians were the last to adopt the Panhellenic model of their city goddess, but when they did so they made up for lost time. The Panhellenic Athena had four interrelated attributes, which may be paired for convenience: she was the virgin war goddess, and the Olympian daughter of Zeus. All these attributes are implied by the golden aegis and gorgoneion that were added to the statue of Athena Polias. I again cite the passage in *Iliad* 5 where the daughter of Zeus arms for war in her father's palace on Olympus (*Iliad* 5.733–742):

αὐτὰρ Ἀθηναίη κούρη Διὸς αἰγιόχοιο
πέπλον μὲν κατέχευεν ἑανὸν πατρὸς ἐπ' οὔδει
ποικίλον, ὅν ῥ' αὐτὴ ποιήσατο καὶ κάμε χερσίν·
ἣ δὲ χιτῶν' ἐνδῦσα Διὸς νεφεληγερέταο
τεύχεσιν ἐς πόλεμον θωρήσσετο δακρυόεντα.
ἀμφὶ δ' ἄρ' ὤμοισιν βάλετ' αἰγίδα θυσσανόεσσαν
δεινήν, ἣν περὶ μὲν πάντη Φόβος ἐστεφάνωται,
ἐν δ' Ἔρις, ἐν δ' Ἀλκή, ἐν δὲ κρυόεσσα Ἰωκή,
ἐν δέ τε Γοργείη κεφαλὴ δεινοῖο πελώρου
δεινή τε σμερδνή τε, Διὸς τέρας αἰγιόχοιο.

But Athena, daughter of aegis-holder Zeus,
dropped to her father's floor her supple robe
of many colors, which she herself had made and worked by
     hand;
she put on the tunic of cloud-gatherer Zeus
and armed herself with weapons for tear-bringing war.
On her shoulders she put the tasseled aegis,
terrifying, around which Panic was set on every side,
and in it was Strife, and Resistance, and chilling Pursuit,
and the dread monster's Gorgon-head,
dreadful and fearful, the emblem of aegis-holder Zeus.

Here is the war goddess, the Olympian daughter of Olympian Zeus. Only Athena's virginity is not emphasized, although this too seems implied by her characteristic epithet *koúrē Diós*, "daughter of Zeus."[89] But virginity was an emphatic characteristic of the new goddess meant to replace the old mother goddess in Athens, and the word *parthénos*, "virgin," which is not used of Athena in Homer, soon came to be used of her in Athens. *Homeric Hymn* 28 to Athena, often considered to be an Athenian work, uses the word *parthénos* of her for the first time in Greek, probably in the sixth century. This hymn also makes use of the myth that Athena was born fully armed from the head of Zeus, which connects as closely as possible her status as Zeus's daughter to her warrior nature (*Homeric Hymn* 28.1–9):[90]

Παλλάδ' Ἀθηναίην κυδρὴν θεὸν ἄρχομ' ἀείδειν

γλαυκῶπιν πολύμητιν ἀμείλιχον ἦτορ ἔχουσαν

89 Cf. Fehrle 1910:195–196. Athena's designation as *koúrē Diós* does not by itself imply that she is a virgin (Helen also is called *koúrē Diós* in *Iliad* 3.426). The word *koúrē* here simply means "daughter" (cf. Penelope, who is often called *koúrē Ikaríoio*, "daughter of Icarius"). Only when *koúrē* is used by itself does it necessarily mean "maiden," as in the case of Nausicaa (cf. n3.56 above). Nevertheless Athena's status as Zeus's daughter, which entails her living on Olympus with the rest of the divine household, seems to be related to her virginity. Rose 1954:140 expresses the connection somewhat baldly when he derives Athena's virginity (if it is a secondary attribute) "not from any supposed preference on the part of any Greek for virginity over motherhood (cf. Kerényi 1952:24), but simply from the fact that she is an unmarried daughter of the Olympian household and therefore expected to be chaste, as the daughters of Homeric barons regularly are." In Athena's case her virginity goes closely with her warlike nature, and her warlike nature associates her closely with her father Zeus (they share the aegis, for example). The *Homeric Hymn to Aphrodite* calls Athena *koúrē Diós* when it refers to her sexual abstinence and her preference for deeds of war; Athena is named here as the first of three goddesses (Artemis and Hestia are the other two) over whom Aphrodite has no power (*Homeric Hymn to Aphrodite* 7–11):

τρισσὰς δ' οὐ δύναται πεπιθεῖν φρένας οὐδ' ἀπατῆσαι·
κούρην τ' αἰγιόχοιο Διὸς γλαυκῶπιν Ἀθήνην·
οὐ γάρ οἱ εὔαδεν ἔργα πολυχρύσου Ἀφροδίτης,
ἀλλ' ἄρα οἱ πόλεμοί τε ἄδον καὶ ἔργον Ἄρηος,
ὑσμῖναί τε μάχαι τε καὶ ἀγλαὰ ἔργ' ἀλεγύνειν.

Three goddesses she cannot persuade in their minds or deceive:
the daughter of the aegis-holder Zeus, grey-eyed Athena,
for the deeds of golden Aphrodite do not please her,
but wars and Ares' work please her,
and fighting ranks and battles, and tending to splendid works.

Even Penelope's epithet *koúrē Ikaríoio*, addressed to her by her suitors, in a certain sense restores her to maiden status (see Higbie 1995:130; cf. also, following Higbie, Dué 2002:52: "once widowed, they [women] become girls again").

90 For *Homeric Hymn* 28 as an Athenian work, cf. Wilamowitz 1932:164, Humbert 1959:231, and Herington 1955:10. For the myth of Athena's birth see Cassimatis *LIMC* 'Athena' 985–988, 1021–1023, and cf. below n3.108 and EN3.7, and n5.83.

<u>παρθένον</u> αἰδοίην ἐρυσίπτολιν ἀλκήεσσαν
Τριτογενῆ, τὴν αὐτὸς ἐγείνατο μητίετα Ζεὺς
σεμνῆς ἐκ κεφαλῆς, πολεμήϊα τεύχε᾽ ἔχουσαν
χρύσεα παμφανόωντα· σέβας δ᾽ ἔχε πάντας ὁρῶντας
ἀθανάτους· ἡ δὲ πρόσθεν Διὸς αἰγιόχοιο
ἐσσυμένως ὤρουσεν ἀπ᾽ ἀθανάτοιο καρήνου
σείσασ᾽ ὀξὺν ἄκοντα.

I begin to sing of Pallas Athena, glorious goddess,
grey-eyed, of many wiles, having a relentless heart,
<u>virgin</u>, revered, city-guarding, valiant,
Tritogeneia, whom deviser Zeus himself bore
from his august head with her golden, all-shining
weapons of war; awe held all the watching
immortals; she sprang in a rush
in front of aegis-holder Zeus from his immortal head
shaking a sharp spear.

§3.43 It was of course this virgin war goddess who predominated in fifth-century Athens. It is doubtful whether a cult of Athena Parthenos, as distinct from the cult of Athena Polias, ever existed;[91] but whether there was such a cult or not the word *parthénos* continued to be used of Athena in ways

---

91 The traditional view is that there was no cult of Athena Parthenos; cf. Herington 1955:11: "It is quite clear that in the fifth century the Athenian state, and probably its individual citizens, formally recognised only one great goddess on the Acropolis, Athena *Polias*." This issue has been reconsidered in articles in Hoepfner 1997 by Nick, Schmaltz, and especially Lipka (for Lipka see n3.92 below). The only explicit evidence for a cult devoted to Athena Parthenos is late: in AD 375, according to Zosimus 4.18.3, the hierophant Nestorios secretly performed rites for Achilles that were usually performed for Athena Parthenos. Nick 1997, who cites this evidence, regards the Athena Parthenos of Pheidias, and any image of Athena Parthenos that may have preceded it, as a "second cult image" ("Zweitkultbild") by means of which the cult of Athena Polias was modifed or expanded (cf. Nick 2002:158–176, 209); Nick imagines that the ritual performed for the statue of Athena Parthenos in the fourth century AD (which Nestorios also performed for a small image of Achilles placed at the base of the goddess's statue in the year AD 375) consisted of prayers and small offerings such as incense. Schmaltz 1997 holds a similar view that Athena Parthenos represents an expansion of the cult of Athena Polias: he contrasts the function of the old wooden image of Athena Polias (small, mobile, involved in traditional rituals) and the new image of Athena Parthenos (large, immobile, object of awe and devotion). Schmaltz refutes Herington's view (1955:46–47) that an old (Mycenaean) cult of Athena Parthenos was absorbed into the cult of Athena Polias; he instead connects the origins of Athena Parthenos, as others have done, with the reorganization of the Panathenaia in 566/5 BC (Schmaltz 1997:25).

that show that it had special meaning for the Athenians. In the first half of
the fifth century a dedication on the Acropolis from the father and the son
of one Ekphantos, whom Athena had evidently protected in battle, refers to
her as *parthénos* in the first word.⁹² This epigram, with its reference to actual
warfare, underscores the personal meaning that the virgin goddess had for
Athenian citizens. This meaning is made explicit by a literary text not far
in date from the Acropolis dedication, a chorus of Aeschylus's *Eumenides*
which addresses the Athenians as παρθένου φίλας φίλοι, "you dear ones of
the virgin dear to you" (line 999); the wider context of this particular phrase
again shows that the *parthénos* brings with her not only her own protection,
but that of her father Zeus (*Eumenides* 997–1002):

χαίρετ᾽ ἀστικὸς λεώς,
ἴκταρ ἥμενοι Διός,
παρθένου φίλας φίλοι
σωφρονοῦντες ἐν χρόνῳ.
Παλλάδος δ᾽ ὑπὸ πτεροῖς
ὄντας ἅζεται πατήρ.

Hail people of the city,
sitting next to Zeus,

92 *IG* I³ 850 (Raubitschek 1949 no. 121), dated between c. 475 and 460 BC:

[Πα]ρθένοι Ἐκφάντο με πατὲρ ἀνέθεκε καὶ ηυιὸς
      ἐνθάδ᾽ Ἀθεναίει μνῆμα πόνον Ἄρεος
Ἐγέλοχος μεγάλε‹ς› τε φιλοχσενίες ἀρετᾶς τε
      πάσες μοῖραν ἔχον τένδε πόλιν νέμεται.

The father and the son of Ekphantos dedicated me to the virgin Athena
   here as a memorial of the toils of war;
Hegelokhos, having a share of great hospitality
   and of every virtue, dwells in this city.

There are two other Acropolis dedications, both dated c. 500 BC, in which Athena is
addressed as φαρθένε (for the initial φ- note that the correct form in *IG* I³ 850 may also
be [Φα]ρθένοι), namely *IG* I³ 728 and 745 (Raubitschek 1949 nos. 40 and 79). Lipka 1997 (cf.
n3.91 above) argues that all three dedications, taken together, show that there was a cult of
Athena Parthenos by c. 500 BC. He rejects (1997:39n19) Herington's argument (1955:9) that
the vocative φαρθένε in two of the three dedications is simply a "stately form of address
to any noble maiden"; the very context of dedication, in Lipka's view, makes this unlikely.
In the case of *IG* I³ 850, quoted above, both parts of the presumed cult title, *Athena* and
Parthenos, occur in the dedication (Lipka 1997:39n19). Herington admits that this fact,
while not enough to prove a cult, is "worth bearing in mind" (1955:11). Cf. n3.95 below.

dear ones of the virgin who is dear to you,
learning restraint in the fullness of time.
You who are under Pallas's wings
her father holds in reverence.

Another passage of the *Eumenides*, spoken by Athena herself, again connects her virginity (this time without the word *parthénos*) and her closeness to Zeus; the passage also underscores the great distance from the very idea of motherhood of this virgin goddess, who had no mother herself, and so wholly favors the male (*Eumenides* 736–738):

μήτηρ γὰρ οὔτις ἔστιν ἥ μ' ἐγείνατο,
τὸ δ' ἄρσεν αἰνῶ πάντα, πλὴν γάμου τυχεῖν,
ἅπαντι θυμῷ, κάρτα δ' εἰμὶ τοῦ πατρός.

For there is no mother who bore me,
and I praise the male in all respects, except for marriage,
with my whole heart, and I am entirely my father's.

§3.44 In concrete form it was of course the Parthenon that displayed Athena *parthénos* most impressively to the city and to the world. Paradoxically this building, constructed between 447 and 432 BC, did not begin to be called the Parthenon until a century later,[93] and it was never called that officially.[94] Parthenon seems rather to have been a nickname, the exact source of which is obscure, but which soon gained currency because of its obvious aptness to the virgin goddess.[95] Athena's temple was never officially called

93 Demosthenes 22.13 and 76 (*Against Androtion*) are the first occurrences of the name.
94 It was called simply *ho neós*, "the temple," in the fifth century. For the term *hekatómpedos neós*, "hundred-foot temple," which occurs in relation to the Parthenon from the fourth century on, see Ridgway 1992:134–135 and Herington 1955:13–14; Plutarch *Pericles* 13.4 combines the name Parthenon with the adjective "hundred-foot": *tòn...hekatómpedon Parthenôna*. For the neuter term *tò hekatómpedon* on an inscription of 485/4 BC (*IG* I³ 4) there are different views: see Herington 1955:13, Ridgway 1992:125, and Robertson 1996:34–35. Herington does not distinguish *tò hekatómpedon* from the *hekatómpedos neós*; Ridgway follows Preisshofen and others in taking the neuter term of an unidentified sacred area rather than a building (so also Lipka 1997:39–42); Robertson takes the neuter term of Athena's old temple.
95 The form of the noun *Parthenón* indicates a meaning "maidens' quarters" (cf. *andrón*, "men's quarters," *gunaikón*, "women's quarters," *hippón*, "horse stable," etc.; Chantraine 1933:164–165), not "temple of the virgin" (which would be *parthéneion* or *parthénion*: see Fehrle 1910:197–198, following Reinach 1908). In fifth- and fourth-century inventory inscriptions the name Parthenon refers to only a part of the temple later so called and it is not clear whether this part is on the west side of the temple, where the treasury was, or the

the Parthenon and she herself most likely never had the cult title *parthénos*.[96]
Nevertheless the virgin war goddess is certainly the figure who occupied the
Parthenon. This is clear not only from Pheidias's statue of the war goddess
that stood in the main sanctuary of the temple, the east-facing cella. The
sculptures on the temple's exterior, also planned by Pheidias, emphasized the
same aspect of the goddess. More that that, they emphasized the close rela-
tionship of Athena as a war goddess to her father Zeus.[97] The east end of the
temple, with its entrance to the cella and the huge cult statue, was the most
important side, and the pediment sculpture at this end depicted Athena's
birth from the head of Zeus; on the west pediment, by contrast, was pictured
the myth that most concerned Athena as the local city goddess, her contest

---

east side, where the cella and the statue of the goddess were: see Fehrle 1910:197–198 and
cf. Herington 1955:13, 14n1 for the argument that this "room of the *parthénoi*" would have
belonged to female servants of the goddess in the temple's west side; Robertson 1983:273,
noting that "the smaller rear or west room of the Parthenon was divided into three parallel
and equal chambers by two pairs of columns supporting the roof," argues on the basis of
Ovid *Metamorphoses* 2.708–832 that these three chambers belonged to the three Kekropids,
Aglauros, Pandrosos, and Herse, and that these chambers were the "maidens' quarters" from
which the temple got its name (cf. below n3.261 and EN3.13 to n3.261); Ridgway 1992:134–135
follows Roux 1984 in taking the name of the goddess's cella in the east side of the temple.

96 Athena Nike and Athena Hygieia, two specialized aspects of the goddess, had cults on the
Acropolis, but there was apparently only one priestess for all Athena's cults until c. 448 BC,
when Athena Nike received a separate priestess; the creation of this priesthood is recorded
on a surviving decree of the council and assembly (*IG* I³ 35 [Tod 1946 no. 40]; cf. also *IG* I³ 36
from c. 420 BC [Tod no. 73]). Athena Hygieia had an altar (erected by the oldest Athenians
according to Aristides *Athena* 14 [vol. 1, p. 22 Dindorff]; older than the statue of the goddess
set up by Pericles according to Plutarch *Pericles* 13.8; cf. Ridgway 1992:137–138; Croissant
LIMC 'Hygieia' 554; Jahn and Michaelis 1901:47–48 on Pausanias 1.23 line 25) but apparently
no separate priestess (cf. Herington 1955:8n3). The single priesthood of Athena before c.
448 BC weighs in favor of Herington's view that there was really only one cult of Athena on
the Acropolis, namely that of Athena Polias; cf. n3.92 above and Herington 1955:8. There
remains the question of Athena's two temples on the Acropolis and their history: for "the
old temple" of Athena Polias on the north side of the Acropolis see below §3.49–§3.51 and
n3.116, n3.117, n3.118, and n3.119; for "the temple" (the Parthenon and its predecessors)
on the south side of the Acropolis see above n3.94, and below §3.47, n3.110, n3.111, and
EN3.8 to n3.111.

97 Herington 1955:57 discusses the use on the Parthenon of Olympian mythology, which to
intellectuals of the day was already outmoded, but was still the common currency of the
Greeks: "Now within the framework of the Olympian system Athena could not be made
the supreme deity: from time immemorial that belonged to Zeus, πατὴρ ἀνδρῶν τε θεῶν
τε. On the other hand the system satisfied Athenian pride in that it made Athena the
particularly favored daughter of Zeus." In my view Herington fails to see that "Olympian"
mythology was in fact dynamic in comparison with the earlier local cult of Athena Polias,
which was truly conservative; but his point does perhaps catch a distinction between the
sixth century, when the Olympian Athena was new to Athens, and a century later, when
Olympian mythology as a whole was outmoded in intellectual circles.

with Poseidon for the city of Athens itself.[98] The same contrast between the Olympian goddess at the east end and the city goddess at the west end is also found on the metope sculptures: on the east-end metopes the gigantomachy, the battle which established the Olympian gods in power by their triumph over the giants, and in which Athena played a leading role next to her father Zeus;[99] on the west-end metopes another mythical battle, but which concerned, not control of the universe, but (most likely) the mythical victory of the Athenians over the invading Amazons.[100]

§3.45 The gigantomachy represented on the east-end metopes had special relevance to Athena's principal Athenian festival, the Panathenaia: the gigantomachy was embroidered on the *péplos* offered to the goddess at this festival.[101] From this fact, and from statements in Aristotle and other ancient sources, it appears that the entire Panathenaic festival was a celebration of the Olympian gods' victory in the gigantomachy, and of Athena's triumph over the giant Aster (or Asterios) in particular.[102] On the Parthenon

98 It is not clear how old this myth is, nor how old Poseidon's very presence on the acropolis is. In my view the myth is not earlier than the sixth century BC, for in it Athena relates to Poseidon as the virgin goddess, not the mother goddess (cf. Fehrle 1910:187–188, who interprets Athena's antagonism with Poseidon in terms of her virginity). Poseidon's cult, on the other hand, must, I think, be older than the sixth century if Erechtheus was associated with it secondarily (see below §3.52–§3.54 and n3.125 and n3.127).

99 For the east-end metopes see Berger 1986:55–76 and Schwab 1996, and cf. Ferrari 2000:120n8. Boardman 1972:69 hesitates about the identification of subject ("Gigantomachies...may figure on the Parthenon metopes").

100 For the west-end metopes, see Berger 1986:99–107; Ferrari 2000:120n9 (citing Berger) comments that "the battered state of the west metopes...makes it impossible to determine if this is the battle for the Acropolis of Athens or another Amazonomachy."

101 It is uncertain whether the gigantomachy was embroidered on the *péplos* woven each year by the arrhephoroi for the Panathenaia, or only on a larger professionally woven *péplos* offered every four years at the Great Panathenaia. Mansfield 1985 argues that the yearly *péplos* was plain and the four-yearly figured (cf. also Herington 1955:60). Barber 1992:114–117 concludes that the gigantomachy was portrayed on both; cf. also Ridgway 1992:123. Mansfield argues that professional male weavers produced the four-yearly *péplos* and amateur female weavers the yearly *péplos* (cf. Barber 1992:113). If this gender distinction is valid, two Euripidean passages suggest that the yearly *péplos*, woven by females, portrayed the gigantomachy: in *Hecuba* 466–474 captive Trojan women lament that they will have to weave the gigantomachy (see n3.105 below for text), and in *Iphigenia among the Taurians* 222–224 Iphigenia laments that she will never weave a picture of Athena and the Titans; cf. Ridgway 1992:123. For the possibility that the four-yearly festival, and with it the offering of the larger *péplos*, was instituted in 566/5 BC, see below n3.244 and n3.246, and cf. EN3.16 to n3.288 below; for the possibility of a temple as early as 566/5 BC on the site of the Parthenon see §3.47 below and cf. EN3.8 to n3.111 below.

102 According to Aristotle fr. 637 Rose (scholia to Aristides *Panathenaic Oration* 189.4 [Dindorf p. 323]) the Panathenaia were celebrated "in honor of the slaying of the giant Aster by Athena" (τὰ Παναθήναια ἐπὶ Ἀστέρι τῷ γίγαντι ὑπὸ Ἀθηνᾶς ἀναιρεθέντι); other scholia

the Panathenaic procession was represented on the frieze that ran around the entire building on the wall inside the outer colonnade. This too focused on the east entrance, for the procession faces in this direction on both sides of the temple. The presentation of the *péplos* to the goddess may have been represented at the central point of the frieze, above the east door itself.[103] If so there was a careful coordination of motifs between the metopes on the east end, with their representation of the gigantomachy, and the frieze, with its representation of the festival begun in honor of the gigantomachy, and of the *péplos* in particular, which in real life contained its own embroidered representation of the gigantomachy.

§3.46 As an Olympian goddess Athena offered to Athens not only her own protection, which she had always provided as city goddess, but also the protection of her father Zeus.[104] Presumably the powerful alliance of father and daughter was clear in the battle with the giants as depicted on the sculptures of the east-end metopes, which have not survived.[105] The role of Zeus

---

ad loc. call the giant Ἀστέριος and say that the lesser Panathenaia were founded by Erichthonios in honor of the slaying of this giant, whereas the Great Panathenaia were founded by Peisistratos (ταῦτα γὰρ ἐπὶ Ἐρεχθονίου τοῦ Ἀμφικτύονος γενόμενα ἐπὶ τῷ φόνῳ τοῦ Ἀστερίου τοῦ γίγαντος· τὰ δὲ μεγάλα Πεισίστρατος ἐποίησε). Ferrari 1988 argues that in the representation of Athena on Panathenaic prize amphoras the goddess performs a dance, the Pyrrhic, which ancient sources specify for two occasions: 1) when Athena was born from Zeus's head; 2) when she celebrated the destruction of the giants. Ferrari sees the entire Panathenaic festival as a celebration of victory in the gigantomachy; cf. also Ridgway 1992:127. Shapiro 1989:38 points out that the earliest gigantomachies on vases are all datable around 560 or slightly later, and all come from the Acropolis, "a remarkable correlation of subject matter and find-spot which has no parallel in black-figure"; cf. Ridgway 1992:127. The reorganization of the Panathenaia in 566/5 BC, and the role of Peisistratos in the reorganized Panathenaia, are discussed further in EN3.16 to n3.288 below. The name Ἀστήρ/Ἀστέριος of the giant slain by Athena perhaps derives from *Iliad* 6.295, where it is said that the *péplos* offered to Athena "shone like a star" (ἀστὴρ δ' ὣς ἀπέλαμπεν); cf. Scheid and Svenbro 1994:28n48 (1996:178n48), and n3.244 below. For another view see Nagy 2002:94, who suggests that a star pattern on Athena's Panathenaic *péplos* may lie behind the name and the Homeric simile.

103 Cf. Barber 1992:113 and figure 72. For uncertainties concerning the subject matter of the frieze, cf. also Ridgway 1992:134: "On the frieze, the procession of the festival unrolls; it is unclear whether it represents the Greater or the Lesser Panathenaia, and it should be admitted that not everything about it is explicable. Perhaps the culmination of the event would have appeared in that lost portion of the frieze that only now has been suspected... above the cella door."

104 In addition to examples cited above, note the skolion (Page *PMG* 884) addressed to Athena: ὄρθου τήνδε πόλιν...σύ τε καὶ πατήρ, "lift up this city...both you and your father."

105 The partnership of Athena and Zeus in the gigantomachy is found in a Panathenaic context in Euripides *Hecuba* 466–474. Here the chorus of captive Trojan women wonders whether it will be taken to Athens to weave the race of "Titans" (i.e. Giants) "on the saffron *péplos*" (i.e. the *péplos* offered to Athena at the Panathenaia, cf. n3.101 above). In the chorus's

was certainly clear in the birth of Athena, which dominated the east end on its pediment. Here, above all, it was Zeus who was shown to be the ultimate authority standing behind his warrior daughter.[106]

§3.47 From an Athenian standpoint the gigantomachy was the ideal myth to show the warrior goddess Athena in action because in it she fought beside her father Zeus. In the eyes of Athenians what could be more reassuring, or more potent, than an alliance of their city goddess with the father of gods and men? In Homer a close alliance between father and daughter is implied when Athena borrows the aegis from Zeus and arms for battle in Troy (*Iliad* 5.733–742).[107] But in the gigantomachy the alliance is even closer: Zeus and Athena fight side by side against the same enemy, and the stakes are the gods' very rule. The gigantomachy is at once a Panhellenic myth, in which the relationship between Zeus and Athena is based on Homer, and an Athenian myth,

---

description of the *péplos* Athena is singled out first, for her horses and chariot, and Zeus provides the climax, putting the Titans to "sleep" with his thunderbolt:

ἦ Παλλάδος ἐν πόλει
τὰς καλλιδίφρους Ἀθα-
ναίας ἐν κροκέῳ πέπλῳ
ζεύξομαι ἆρα πώ-
λους ἐν δαιδαλέαισι ποι-
κίλλουσ' ἀνθοκρόκοισι πή-
ναις ἢ Τιτάνων γενεάν,
τὰν Ζεὺς ἀμφιπύρῳ κοιμί-
ζει φλογμῷ Κρονίδας;

Or will I in the city of Pallas
yoke Athena's horses with beautiful chariots
on the saffron robe, weaving them with artful
crocus-colored threads,
or the race of Titans,
which Zeus, Kronos's son,
puts to sleep with a fiery blaze?

106 Cf. Herington 1955:62: "Yet even on her temple, the Parthenon, the highest place of honour (outside the cella itself) is taken not by her, but by Zeus: it was his great seated figure that filled the centre of the eastern pediment.... I have already tried to show how the Athenians, even if they had wished to do so, could not conceivably neglect Zeus in their reverence for Athena. If Athena's greatness was to be justified in terms of Greek religion as a whole, this could be done only by showing how close she was to the fount of greatness, Zeus. And for this reason above all, as I think, Pheidias chose to span the entrance of the Parthenon with this wonderful and difficult subject, the Birth of Athena: the perfect symbol of that relationship."

107 Cf. n3.25 above. Athena actually puts on Zeus's tunic, and the aegis, which she puts on next, is not specifically said to be his; but he is called "aegis-bearing Zeus" twice in the passage, and the aegis too must be his. Later tradition differs: here Athena slays the gorgon in the gigantomachy, and from the hide she makes the aegis, which must thus be considered hers (cf. Euripides *Ion* 987–997).

in which that relationship is heightened and extended.[108] It makes perfect sense that this myth provided the aetiology for the Panathenaia, for this festival too was both Panhellenic and specifically Athenian. The Panathenaia are known to have been reorganized in about 566/5 BC. We have no knowledge of the festival that preceded this reorganization, only of the one that followed it, but it seems likely that the myth of the gigantomachy went hand in hand with this reorganization.[109] The shrine of Athena dedicated wholly to the virgin war goddess was the Parthenon. Direct evidence for a temple on the south side of the Acropolis where the Parthenon later stood does not go back beyond the Parthenon's unfinished predecessor, begun after the Battle

108 The myth of the gigantomachy seems to have developed relatively late. In contrast to the titanomachy, which is attested in Hesiod, the gigantomachy is not certainly attested until the sixth century BC (*Theogony* 954, which alludes to the gigantomachy, is in what is most likely a post-Hesiodic part of the poem; see West 1966 on *Theogony* 186 and cf. n2.238 above). In Homer the giants are an amorphous group without any specific myth, except for the Phaeacians' ancestor Eurymedon, for whom a gigantomachy is vaguely implied (n2.145 above). Hesiod *Theogony* 185–186 says that the giants were born from the earth fully armed; this probably implies a gigantomachy, but perhaps not: the Theban Spartoi were also born from the earth fully armed, and they fought only each other. Xenophanes, in the second half of the sixth century, is the first to speak of the battle of the giants, grouping it with the battle of the titans and the battle of the centaurs as subjects unfit for civilized song (Xenophanes fr. B1.21–22 Diels-Kranz/West). How far Athens inherited a Panhellenic myth, and how far it gave this myth a new form in connection with the Panathenaia, is difficult to say; in any case the myth seems not to have been a purely Athenian invention (cf. Mayer 1887:192–193 and 283, and Vian 1952:261 and 272). The reorganized Panathenaia imitated the Olympic games in choosing the gigantomachy as its foundation myth, for the Olympic games commemorated the gods' victory in the titanomachy (cf. Vian 1952:262 and 246; Ferrari 1988:473). It stands to reason that Athena's role was emphasized in the Athenian form of the myth; it is also possible that her role originated in the Athenian myth (as argued by Robertson 1985:289 on the basis of the sudden appearance of Athena in the role of giant slayer on Attic black-figure vases in the 560s; cf. n3.102 above). The importance of the gigantomachy in the Peisistratid era is shown not only by its association with the reorganized Panathenaia, but also by the fact that it was represented on a pediment of Athena's old temple (for the date and original location of this pedimental sculpture, both somewhat uncertain, cf. n3.111 below). If it was in Athens that Athena's role in the gigantomachy first became prominent, the same is probably true of Athena's birth from Zeus's head (cf. n3.90 above); this myth did not originate in Athens, but representations of it became popular there in the sixth century. There is a striking contrast between Athena, born fully armed from the head of the sky god, and the giants, born fully armed from the earth; was Athena's extraordinary birth meant to contrast her with her adversaries, and also perhaps with her own former earthbound nature? There is further discussion of Athena's birth and her role in the gigantomachy as Athenian myths in EN3.7.

109 Athena's birth from Zeus's head also seems to have been associated with the Panathenaia: the third day of the month-end was Athena's birthday in Athens (τρίτη φθίνοντος, scholia to *Iliad* 8.39), and the Panathenaic procession, which took place on the 28th of Hekatombaion, was also the third day of a month-end (cf. Deubner 1932:23–24).

of Marathon in perhaps 488 BC, and destroyed less than a decade later by the Persians in 480 BC.[110] Indirect evidence may indicate a yet earlier temple on the site, possibly from the period of the reorganization of the Panathenaia in 566/5 BC.[111]

110 488 BC is the start date proposed by Dinsmoor 1934; Korres 1997 finds evidence for a larger temple begun a decade earlier and changed to a smaller plan at the date in question.

111 See Dinsmoor 1947:109–127 (followed by Herington 1955:40; cf. also Ridgway 1992:125 with n21, 131). Korres 1997 reconsiders the question of an earlier temple in the light of new evidence; this evidence, which bears on Athena's "old temple" as well as an "Urparthenon," is discussed in EN3.8. But whenever the first temple dedicated wholly to Athena as a war goddess was built on the south side of the Acropolis, Athena Polias had presumably already been changed into a war goddess in her old temple on the north side of the Acropolis. Here (in my view) the old statue of Athena Polias was modified from a mother goddess, who spun, into a war goddess, who was armed, as early as the beginning of the sixth century BC (a bronze figurine found in Sicily showing Athena with the aegis and dated 580–560 BC [Neils 1992:146, Catalogue no. 2] provides an artistic parallel for this key feature at an early date; as Ridgway 1992:129 notes, representations of an armed Athena are widely diffused in the Greek world). A further sign of the transformation of Athena Polias into a war goddess is to be found in the old temple of Athena. The gigantomachy, which presupposes the Olympian Athena, was represented on marble sculptures of the old temple of Athena toward the end of the sixth century (for these sculptures see Boardman 1978:155 and Ridgway 1992:124–125; the sculptures have been dated c. 525 BC, but Ridgway 1992:125 and n20 reports a trend toward a lower dating of c. 510 BC on the basis of style). The Athena of the gigantomachy had a different relationship to Zeus than did the earlier figure of Athena Polias: the earlier relationship was not that of daughter to father, but of city goddess to city god. Zeus Polieus, "Zeus of the city," had an altar on the Acropolis not far from the temple of Athena Polias, "Athena of the city." Cults of Zeus Polieus and Athena Polias occur together in several cities (eight instances, including Kos, Rhodes, and Telos, are listed by Höfer, Roscher's *Lexikon* 'Polieus' 2615–2617; there may be a suggestion of such a pair of cults in Homer; see below). In Athens the Bouphonia (part of the Dipolieia, the festival of Zeus Polieus) is called a festival of Athena by the scholia to Aristophanes *Clouds* 985; Deubner 1932:160 takes this to mean that Athena Polias was associated with Zeus Polieus in the festival. In *Iliad* 6, before the Trojan women go to supplicate Athena "on the acropolis" (ἐν πόλει ἄκρῃ, *Iliad* 6.297), Hecabe surmises that Hector is on his way to supplicate Zeus "from the acropolis" (ἐλθόντ' ἐξ ἄκρης πόλιος Διὶ χεῖρας ἀνασχεῖν, *Iliad* 6.256–257), but Hector says that he is unwilling to do so because his hands are unclean (*Iliad* 6.266–267). These look like paired cults of Athena Polias and Zeus Polieus, both on an acropolis. The Athenian ritual of the Bouphonia purportedly went back to the first ox sacrifice and was thus of great antiquity; in Aristophanes the Dipolieia and Bouphonia are proverbial for old-fashioned ways, again suggesting antiquity (*Clouds* 984–985): ἀρχαῖά γε καὶ Διπολιώδη καὶ τεττίγων ἀνάμεστα / καὶ Κηκείδου καὶ Βουφονίων, "these are old-fashioned things and Dipolieia-like, and full of cicadas and Kekeides and the Bouphonia" (cf. Nilsson 1967:152–155, 401, who sees the Bouphonia as old). But the cult of Zeus Polieus was clearly secondary to that of Athena Polias on the Acropolis, having only an altar there; in the view of Deubner 1932:172–173 the cult hardly goes back to the Bronze Age, and may not even go back beyond the Archaic period; it is attributed to Peisistratos by Fehrle, Roscher's *Lexikon* 'Zeus (Beinamen)' 655. Compared to Athena's role as a city goddess Zeus's role as a city god is of secondary importance wherever it occurs. Nilsson 1967:417 characterizes

§3.48 Athena Polias was changed into the Olympian daughter of Zeus by the addition of the aegis and gorgoneion to her cult image, but the location of this image on the Acropolis surely never changed. To protect the city Athena's image must have remained steadfastly in its place. When Erechtheus and Athena were separated, therefore, it was not Athena who moved, but Erechtheus. In *Odyssey* 7.80–81 the two are together in Erechtheus's palace, which Athena enters to animate her own image, and which must also have contained the image of Erechtheus.[112] This palace became solely the temple of Athena once Erechtheus was removed from it.

§3.49 The temple of Athena Polias has long been identified with the small Ionic temple known as the Erechtheum.[113] It is the only prominent

---

cults of Zeus Polieus collectively as "wenig ausgebend" (yielding little). The relationship of Zeus and Athena in these cults has a different origin from their relationship in the myth of the gigantomachy.

112 To this point we have not considered what the old image of Erechtheus, paired with the old image of Athena, would have looked like; it is worth noting that when Arete is described in terms of Athena Polias she is paired with Alcinous, and that Alcinous in this tableau is described as seated on a throne drinking wine "like an immortal" (cf. n3.39 above). Although there is no way to demonstrate it, this may well be how Erechtheus was still represented when the Epidaurians sent sacrifices to Athena and Erechtheus as a pair, and when Athena enters Erechtheus's palace in *Odyssey* 7.80–81. Dionysus comes to mind for the wine cup that is implied, and Erechtheus, as an agrarian deity concerned with fertility and increase, may also have been represented with a cup. Dionysus seems to have been involved in the festival of the Oschophoria, celebrated in Phaleron to honor Athena Skiras, a goddess of significance for the old relationship between Athena and Erechtheus (see below §3.69 and n3.189). As an example of a cult figure sitting on a throne and holding a wine cup consider an archaic relief from Sparta (Berlin, Staatliche Museen, Antikensammlung, no. Sk 731), a photograph of which is on Plate 12 below. The identity of the male figure, and of the female figure seated next to him, is unknown (note the smaller size of the two human worshippers approaching the seated pair). Suggestions include heroized ancestors, gods of the underworld (Hades and Persephone), Dionysus (note the outsized drinking cup), and particular heroes (cf. Knittlmayer and Heilmeyer 1998:44). If the image of Erechtheus originally looked something like this, it was doubtless modified subsequently. Ferrari 2002:21, in line with her argument that Athena was not worshipped in the Erechtheum in the fifth century (or later), takes references to an *ágalma* in *IG* 1³ 474 line 75 and *IG* 1³ 475 lines 269–270 to refer to an image of Erechtheus, and not of Athena (these inscriptions are from 409/8 BC and concern work on the Erechtheum before its completion; cf. n3.120 below); Ferrari n51 thinks that it is possible that the statue of Erechtheus by Myron in Athens, "which Pausanias 9.30.1 mentions in passing in his description of Boeotia as the sculptor's best work," may have been the cult statue in question. The representation of Erechtheus in the cult statue (and in Myron's work if not the same thing) was doubtless the same heroic figure as in the bronze group that according to Pausanias 1.27.4 stood on the terrace of Athena Polias and depicted the fight between Erechtheus and Eumolpos (see §3.55 below).

113 This building, with its irregular plan and caryatid porch, was built during the last quarter of the fifth century, perhaps 418–405 BC; Treu 1971:124–125, 131 proposes that work was started before 421 BC and finished by 407/6 BC.

building still standing on the north side of the Acropolis, and Pausanias has been understood to mean this building when he describes both the shrine of Erechtheus and the temple of Athena, one after the other, in his tour of the Acropolis.[114] The existence of both shrines in one building seemed to fit with the Homeric evidence, not only *Odyssey* 7.80–81, but also *Iliad* 2.546–551, so long as the latter passage was thought to say that Athena put the earthborn Erechtheus into her own temple.[115]

§3.50 The assumption that the small Ionic temple was Athena's became complicated when foundations of a much larger Doric temple were discovered just south of it. Sometimes called the Dörpfeld temple after its discoverer, this structure, which was burned to an unknown extent in the Persian invasion of 480 BC, has been widely accepted as Athena's old temple. But it is also widely assumed that this temple was destroyed in 480 BC, and that the small Ionic temple just to the north eventually took its place.

§3.51 Gloria Ferrari, following Dörpfeld, has challenged this view with a compelling argument that Athena's old temple, damaged as it was by the Persians, remained in use throughout antiquity.[116] The small Ionic temple to the north was thus not Athena's temple at all, but the shrine of Erechtheus, entirely separate from Athena's temple, as *Iliad* 2.546–551, correctly understood, presupposes that it was.[117] A great advantage of Ferrari's scheme is that

---

114 Pausanias 1.26.5–6. Only two ancient sources use the name *Erékhtheion* of Erechtheus's shrine: Pausanias 1.26.5 and Plutarch *Lives of the Ten Orators (Lycurgus)* 843e.

115 Nilsson took the *Odyssey* passage as reflecting the original state of affairs in the Bronze Age, when the king had a cult of his personal protectress in his own palace; he took the *Iliad* passage as reflecting what happened to this cult after the monarchy collapsed: the king's personal protectress became the city's protectress, the king's palace became her temple, and the king himself became a hero with his own hero cult in this temple (see Nilsson 1921:12–13, 1967:348, 1950:488; cf. n2.198 above).

116 Ferrari 2002. Dörpfeld thought that the old temple of Athena was repaired after the Persian Wars and remained in use throughout antiquity. Ferrari argues that the temple was not repaired but remained in use in a damaged state as a kind of war memorial. The peristyle of the old temple was clearly lost at least in part in the fire, because the stylobate is encroached upon by the caryatid porch of the south side of the Ionic temple. In Ferrari's reconstruction the old temple was effectively broken into two parts by loss of the roof: the cella to the east and the opisthodomos to the west, with an empty space between them (see her reconstruction p. 25, fig. 4; the caryatid porch of the Ionic temple would have been visible between the two parts of the old temple as one looked north from the old temple's south side).

117 See Ferrari 2002:16n29 for the interpretation of ὅν ποτ' Ἀθήνη / ...κὰδ δ' ἐν Ἀθήνης εἷσεν ἑῷ ἐν πίονι νηῷ, *Iliad* 2.547, 549, as "whom Athena...put down in Athens in his own rich temple." Noel Robertson, who also argues that Athena and Erechtheus inhabited different shrines (see n3.215 below for his scheme), proposed the same interpretation of ἑῷ as "his own" in *Iliad* 2.549 (Robertson 1996:37). The situation described in *Iliad* 2 is thus different

it makes perfect sense of Pausanias's description of the two shrines, one after the other, as his tour progresses from the shrine of Erechtheus to the temple of Athena.[118] This sequence is so awkward on the assumption that both shrines were in the small Ionic temple that serious attempts have been made in recent years to find another building for the shrine of Erechtheus and to leave the small Ionic temple to Athena alone.[119] Ferrari's solution is rather to leave the Erechtheum to Erechtheus, and to claim for Athena unbroken continuity in her own old temple. It was in the cella of this temple, which is called the *arkhaîos neõs* in the fourth-century inventories, that the old image of Athena Polias (*hē theós*) must always have resided.[120]

---

from Aphrodite's placing of Phaethon in her temple to be her temple servant in *Theogony* 990–991; Nock 1930:44, 44n2 compares the two situations on the usual assumption that in *Iliad* 2.549 Athena puts Erechtheus in "her" own temple (cf. also Nagy 1997:172). For the cult relationship between Erechtheus and Athena cf. also Frickenhaus 1908a:175.

118 Ferrari, p. 16, devotes merely a sentence to Pausanias, whose account is so problematic to the traditional view of Athena's temple, when she discusses the ancient literary evidence; none of this evidence is a serious obstacle to her argument (but cf. n3.249 below).

119 In a series of publications Kristian Jeppesen draws attention to the deep difficulties for the traditional view in Pausanias's description (Jeppesen 1979, 1983, 1987), but he has not won acceptance of his own "alternative Erechtheum" near the shrine of Pandrosos (Ridgway 1992:126–127 says only that she is inclined to agree that the two shrines, of Erechtheus and of Athena, must be separated). Noel Robertson has more recently proposed a different solution, which has many attractive features, but which is quite drastic in identifying the Erechtheum with the remains of a building on the southeast corner of the acropolis, far removed from the sphere of Athena Polias on the north side. See n3.215 below for evidence from the fourth-century AD Athenian rhetorician Himerius that seems to imply that the shrines were much closer to each other than that. Cf. also Treu 1971:124–126, who argues that Euripides *Erechtheus* fr. 65.90–94 Austin (Athena's instruction to build a temple for Erechtheus) alludes to the construction of the new Erechtheum.

120 It is assumed that the image of Athena Polias was removed from the Acropolis by the Athenians when they abandoned the city before the Persian occupation in 480 BC, and that it thus survived; there was a story that the golden gorgoneion was removed on this occasion (see n3.26 above), and it seems likely that the image was also removed then (see Ridgway 1992:122). This does not affect the idea that the image, in terms of its permanent abode, remained in the same place from time immemorial. One piece of evidence has led to the usual current view that sometime in the fifth century BC the image of Athena Polias was moved from the old temple to the Erechtheum. IG I³ 474, an inscription of 409/8 BC relating to work on the Erechtheum, contains an inventory of architectural members and stone blocks for the construction. The inscription begins by identifying the reporting officials as "overseers of the temple on the acropolis in which (is) the ancient statue" (ἐ]πιστάται τõ νεὸ τõ ἐμ πόλει ἐν ἧδι τὸ ἀρχαῖον ἄγαλμα), and goes on, after naming the overseers, to say that they "recorded as follows works of the temple in the state in which they found them to be..." ([τά]δε ἀνέγραφσαν ἔργα τõ νεὸ hὸς κατέλαβον ἔχοντα). This seems to be clear evidence that the old image resided in the Erechtheum. Ferrari, on the other hand, argues that the officials in question were overseers of the old temple of Athena Polias, which still stood, and that they had responsibility for a larger *témenos* on

§3.52 Erechtheus, on the other hand, was removed from this temple, which had once been his royal palace,[121] and was placed in a shrine just to the north. *Iliad* 2.547–549 describes this relocation in terms of Athena's own primordial act: it was she who placed Erechtheus in his own temple, just as the Athenians had apparently now done. We will consider the overall intent of the *Iliad* passage later, but in part it was to reflect the new cult relationships on the Acropolis, with Erechtheus and Athena now housed in different temples, no longer in the same temple.

§3.53 The small Ionic temple, which was constructed in the latter part of the fifth century, undoubtedly had predecessors with the same irregular plan, but little is known of such predecessors from archaeology.[122] The literary

---

the acropolis than their name suggests, and that this included the Erechtheum (Ferrari 2002:17–18 and n39); this would explain the occurrence of the word "temple" with reference to two different buildings in the inscription (Ferrari's further argument that the inscription actually records materials intended for use in the old temple of Athena as well as in the Erechtheum must be abandoned: Pakkanen 2006 shows that the specifications of the materials in the inscription suit the Erechtheum but not what is known of the old temple). Other evidence shows that the old temple of Athena did indeed survive in some form (the mid-fifth century decree of the Praxiergidai, IG I³ 7 line 6, uses the phrase "behind the old temple," ὄπισ]θεν τõ νεõ τõ ἀρχ[αίο, to indicate the placement of a stele; see Ferrari 2002:15), and as long as the old temple stood it must have continued to house the old image of Athena; I agree with Ferrari that this situation probably continued throughout antiquity. The alternative is that the Athenians razed Athena's old abode and left the space vacant, and this is not plausible, especially in the fifth century (cf. Ferrari 2002:14, 25); the Persians aimed at exactly this, and the Athenians would not have completed the sacrilege for them.

121 It was once thought that two column bases from a Bronze Age palace had been discovered within the confines of the old temple, but these are now considered to be of Geometric date. The prevailing view still remains that this was once the location of the Mycenaean palace, but there is no positive evidence of this. Cf. Snodgrass 1977:29–30: "At Athens...the location of the early Athena temple, on the site of the former Mycenaean palace, between the later Parthenon and Erechtheum, is generally agreed. The only substantial evidence comes from two column bases, which were for long thought to belong to the Mycenaean palace itself. In 1962, however, two different scholars working quite independently, Professor Iakovidis and Dr Carl Nylander, came to the conclusion that the bases were more readily comparable with bases from temples of the eighth and seventh centuries" (Iakovidis 1962, especially 62–65 [2006:65–68]; Nylander 1962). Cf. also Ridgway 1992:120. For earlier attributions of the column bases to a Mycenaean palace, see Nilsson 1921:12 and Hill 1953:13–14.

122 Casanaki and Mallouchou 1983:92 (cited by Hurwit 1999:144–145) mention remains of a temple that preceded the Erechtheum on the same site; cf. also Korres 1997:229 with n73, 242, Ferrari 2002:16n28. Robertson, taking the site to be that of Athena's temple, believes that "a similar shrine always stood here" (1996:31); he mentions "certain traces of a very early shrine" detected by Stevens 1940:42 and Iakovidis 1962:87–93 (2006:95–100), noting that "these traces must remain somewhat doubtful" (Robertson 1996:36–37).

tradition, on the other hand, reveals something very important, namely that Poseidon already inhabited a predecessor of this temple when Erechtheus was moved there. So I interpret Pausanias 1.26.5, who tells us that inside the Erechtheum there were three altars, and that on the first, which belonged to Poseidon, sacrifices were also offered to Erechtheus "as the result of an oracle."[123] Here, I believe, is the actual memory of Erechtheus's transfer from Athena's temple to a temple of Poseidon, carried out, not surprisingly, with the authorization of an oracle. As a result of the transfer Erechtheus became identified with Poseidon. The resulting cult of Poseidon Erechtheus is attested in several sources, including a fifth-century inscription and a fragment of Euripides' lost *Erechtheus*.[124] Thus Erechtheus was not given a new shrine, but a new location; he effectively took over Poseidon's shrine. This, I think, is the state of affairs in *Iliad* 2.546–551, which simply omits Poseidon when it speaks of Erechtheus and his cult.[125]

§3.54 Inside the temple of Erechtheus, according to Herodotus 8.55, were the "tokens" (*martúria*) of Poseidon's contest with Athena for the city of Athens: the "sea" created by Poseidon, and the olive tree planted by Athena.[126]

---

123 ἔστι δὲ καὶ οἴκημα Ἐρέχθειον καλούμενον.... ἐσελθοῦσι δέ εἰσι βωμοί, Ποσειδῶνος, ἐφ' οὗ καὶ Ἐρεχθεῖ θύουσιν ἔκ του μαντεύματος, καὶ ἥρωος Βούτου, τρίτος δὲ Ἡφαίστου, "There is also a building called the Erechtheion.... As you go in there are altars of Poseidon, on which they also sacrifice to Erechtheus as the result of some oracle, and of the hero Boutes, and a third of Hephaistos" (Pausanias 1.26.5).

124 *IG* I³ 873 (Raubitschek 1949 no. 384), dedication found near the Erechtheum, dated tentatively 450 BC (Jeffery 1988:125). Euripides *Erechtheus* fr. 65.92–94 Austin (fr. 370.92–94 Kannicht [2004]); see §3.55 below. Note also Hesychius, Ἐρεχθεύς· Ποσειδῶν ἐν Ἀθήναις, "Erechtheus: Poseidon in Athens," and *IG* II² 3538 (first century AD): ὁ ἱερεὺς Ποσειδῶνο[ς] Ἐρεχθέος γαιηόχου, "the priest of Poseidon Erechtheus earthholder." Other evidence in Austin 1967:59–60.

125 For Poseidon's absence from the passage see below §3.72 and n3.193. Jeffery 1988 has argued that Poseidon did not have a cult on the Acropolis until the mid-fifth century BC. This, I think, does not square with Pausanias 1.26.5, which makes it clear that the altar in the Erechtheum was Poseidon's, and that Erechtheus was attached to it secondarily. I see no other way to interpret this than that the temple was originally Poseidon's. Jeffery 1988:125 misstates the case when she says that "three Acropolis dedications indicate that ca. 475–450—not earlier—a...cult of Poseidon did appear there, brought by an oracle (Pausanias 1.26.5) and linked to that of Erechtheus." It was not the cult of Poseidon, but that of Erechtheus, that was brought by an oracle (Jeffery's translation of the Pausanias passage on p. 124 is not at all a natural reading).

126 Herodotus records the miraculous regeneration of Athena's olive tree after it was burned with the rest of the temple of Erechtheus in 480 BC by the Persians; he mentions the contest of Poseidon and Athena in this connection (Herodotus 8.55): ἔστι ἐν τῇ ἀκροπόλι ταύτῃ Ἐρεχθέος τοῦ γηγενέος λεγομένου εἶναι νηός, ἐν τῷ ἐλαίη τε καὶ θάλασσα ἔνι, τὰ λόγος παρὰ Ἀθηναίων Ποσειδέωνά τε καὶ Ἀθηναίην ἐρίσαντας περὶ τῆς χώρης μαρτύρια θέσθαι. ταύτην ὦν τὴν ἐλαίην ἅμα τῷ ἄλλῳ ἱρῷ κατέλαβε ἐμπρησθῆναι ὑπὸ τῶν βαρβάρων· δευτέρῃ δὲ

In this mythic contest Poseidon and Athena were rivals, and, if the myth is old, it suggests why Erechtheus, when he was taken from Athena's temple, was relocated in Poseidon's temple: Erechtheus's new identification with Athena's rival made very clear that his old relationship as Athena's consort was over.[127]

§3.55 We come now to Erechtheus's later myth, and the reason that it gives for his presence in Poseidon's temple: Poseidon slew him with his trident and buried him in the rock.[128] According to the myth Poseidon's son Eumolpos

---

ἡμέρῃ ἀπὸ τῆς ἐμπρήσιος Ἀθηναίων οἱ θύειν ὑπὸ βασιλέος κελευόμενοι ὡς ἀνέβησαν ἐς τὸ ἱρόν, ὥρων βλαστὸν ἐκ τοῦ στελέχεος ὅσον τε πηχυαῖον ἀναδεδραμηκότα, "On this acropolis there is a temple of Erechtheus, said to be born from the earth, in which there are an olive tree and a sea, which, according to the Athenians, Poseidon and Athena put there as tokens of their claims when they contended for the country. It befell the olive tree to be burned by the barbarians with the rest of the temple; but on the day after the fire those of the Athenians ordered by the king to make sacrifices, when they went up into the temple, saw a shoot from the trunk that had sprung up as much as a cubit." For some reason the olive tree is later found in the precinct of Pandrosos, adjacent to the Erechtheum, but separate from it (Philochorus *FGrHist* 328 F 67; cf. Robertson 1996:42–43). Pausanias saw the "sea water" inside the Erechtheum, namely a saltwater well that made the sound of waves when a south wind blew; he also saw what was said to be the mark of Poseidon's trident (1.26.5): ὕδωρ ἐστὶν ἔνδον θαλάσσιον ἐν φρέατι. τοῦτο μὲν θαῦμα οὐ μέγα...ἀλλὰ τόδε ‹τὸ› φρέαρ ἐς συγγραφὴν παρέχεται κυμάτων ἦχον ἐπὶ νότῳ πνεύσαντι. καὶ τριαίνης ἐστὶν ἐν τῇ πέτρᾳ σχῆμα ("Inside there is sea water in a well. This is not a great marvel...but this well does offer a noteworthy sound of waves when a south wind blows. There is also the mark of a trident in the rock").

127 The myth of the contest between Athena and Poseidon for Athens is attested for the first time in the sculptures of the west pediment of the Parthenon. Jeffery 1988 (n3.125 above) has argued that the myth was created not long before this sculpture was begun as a reflection of the First Peloponnesian War (ca. 460–446), with Poseidon representing Corinth, Sparta, and Boeotia on the one side, and Athena representing Athens on the other side. Just as I think that the cult of Poseidon on the acropolis was older than the fifth century, I think that the myth of Poseidon's contest with Athena is likely to have been older too. Erechtheus was the newcomer to Poseidon's temple, in which he replaced Poseidon himself to a large extent. He seems to have replaced Poseidon even in relation to the "sea" which Poseidon created, which came to be called the "Erechtheian sea" according to "Apollodorus" 3.14.1: ἧκεν οὖν πρῶτος Ποσειδῶν ἐπὶ τὴν Ἀττικήν, καὶ πλήξας τῇ τριαίνῃ κατὰ μέσην τὴν ἀκρόπολιν ἀπέφηνε θάλασσαν, ἣν νῦν Ἐρεχθηίδα καλοῦσι, "Poseidon was first to reach Attica, and striking with his trident in the middle of the acropolis he laid bare a sea, which they now call the 'Erechtheian sea'." It is difficult to say how old the myth of the contest for Athens really is (cf. n3.98 above and n3.193 below). One would like to know what relationship the myth has to the rivalry between Athena and Poseidon in the *nóstos* of Odysseus in Homer. For an illuminating interpretation of the Athenian myth as it is represented on the west pediment of the Parthenon, see Binder 1984.

128 The place where Erechtheus was buried is not specified in the sources, but Poseidon's own temple, in which the marks of Poseidon's trident were pointed out in the rock (Pausanias 1.26.5), is an obvious candidate (cf. Jeppesen 1987:87). In Pausanias these marks are associated with Poseidon's "sea," but the marks may have been given more than one explanation, just as more than one god or hero received sacrifices on Poseidon's altar; see n3.130 below. An accomodation of a similar sort of older and newer myths is suggested by the term

led a Thracian army against Athens, claiming Athens as his birthright because Poseidon had really won the contest with Athena.[129] Erechtheus, defending Athens, killed Eumolpos in battle, but Poseidon, avenging his son, killed Erechtheus. By his death at Poseidon's hands Erechtheus became Poseidon Erechtheus, taking the name of his slayer in addition to his own. Such is the account in a fragment from the end of Euripides' lost *Erechtheus*, in which Athena ordains sacrifices for the dead hero (*Erechtheus* fr. 65.92–94 Austin):

κεκλήσεται δὲ τοῦ κτανόντος οὕνεκα
σεμνὸς Ποσειδῶν ὄνομ' ἐπωνομασμένος
ἀστοῖς Ἐρεχθεὺς ἐμ φοναῖσι βουθύτοις.

Because of the one who killed him he will be called
august Poseidon surnamed
Erechtheus in the slaughter of sacrificial oxen.[130]

"Erechtheian sea" in "Apollodorus" 3.14.1 (cf. n3.127 above and Jeppesen 1987:88). Other locations have been suggested for both Erechtheus's grave and Poseidon's "sea": a hole in the rock in the north slope of the Acropolis between the cave of Pan and the cave of Apollo Hypakraios for Erechtheus's grave (see Owen 1939 on Euripides *Ion* 277–282), and a deep fissure in the north slope of the Acropolis, with stairs leading down to a Mycenaean well, for Poseidon's "sea" (Jeppesen 1987:93, 95). For the possibility that Erechtheus's grave was elsewhere than on the Acropolis see n3.156 below.

129 Isocrates 12.193: Θρᾷκες μὲν γὰρ μετ' Εὐμόλπου τοῦ Ποσειδῶνος εἰσέβαλον εἰς τὴν χώραν ἡμῶν, ὃς ἠμφισβήτησεν Ἐρεχθεῖ τῆς πόλεως, φάσκων Ποσειδῶ πρότερον Ἀθηνᾶς καταλαβεῖν αὐτήν, "The Thracians invaded our land with Eumolpos, Poseidon's son, who disputed with Erechtheus about the city, claiming that Poseidon had taken possession of it before Athena." Poseidon won the contest by performing his miracle before Athena, but the gods accepted Kekrops as Athena's witness that she had performed her miracle first; see "Apollodorus" 3.14.1, quoted n3.127 above, which continues as follows: μετὰ δὲ τοῦτον ἧκεν Ἀθηνᾶ, καὶ ποιησαμένη τῆς καταλήψεως Κέκροπα μάρτυρα ἐφύτευσεν ἐλαίαν, ἣ νῦν ἐν τῷ Πανδροσείῳ δείκνυται. γενομένης δὲ ἔριδος ἀμφοῖν περὶ τῆς χώρας, Ἀθηνᾷ καὶ Ποσειδῶνι διαλύσας Ζεὺς κριτὰς ἔδωκεν, οὐχ ὡς εἶπόν τινες, Κέκροπα καὶ Κραναόν, οὐδὲ Ἐρυσίχθονα, θεοὺς δὲ τοὺς δώδεκα. καὶ τούτων δικαζόντων ἡ χώρα τῆς Ἀθηνᾶς ἐκρίθη, Κέκροπος μαρτυρήσαντος ὅτι πρώτη τὴν ἐλαίαν ἐφύτευσεν, "After him Athena came, and making Kekrops the witness of her taking of possession she planted the olive tree which is now pointed out in the Pandrosion. When a dispute arose between the two over the land, Zeus mediated and gave Athena and Poseidon judges, not Kekrops and Kranaos, as some have said, and not Erysichthon, but the twelve gods. With these judging the matter the land was decided to be Athena's since Kekrops testified that she planted the olive tree first." See Binder 1984 for priority as the criterion by which the contest was judged in the representation on the west pediment of the Parthenon; here Athena is shown as the first to act, and so as defeating Poseidon fairly rather than through a corrupt witness.

130 With these sacrifices to Poseidon Erechtheus in Euripides compare the sacrifices to Erechtheus in *Iliad* 2.550–551; they are evidently the same sacrifices (see below §3.72 and n3.194). In the Euripides passage Athena addresses Praxithea, the wife of Erechtheus; in

§3.56 Athens was at war with its neighbor Eleusis when Eumolpos and the Thracians invaded; Eleusis called the Thracians in as allies.[131] Thucydides

the two preceding lines of this passage Athena ordains a temple for Erechtheus in the middle of the Acropolis: πόσει δὲ τῶι σῶι σηκὸν ἐμ μέσηι πόλει / τεῦξαι κελεύω περιβόλοισι λαΐνοις, "for your husband I order that a precinct in the middle of the city / be built with a stone enclosure" (*Erechtheus* fr. 65.90–91 Austin). Euripides here represents the temple of Poseidon Erechtheus, well known to his Athenian audience, as having been first established for Erechtheus; in reality, as I have argued, it was first established for Poseidon. The death of Erechtheus, as narrated in the play, has not survived, but Athena refers to it when she calls on Poseidon to turn his trident away from Athens (αὐδῶ τρίαιναν τῆσδ' ἀποστρέφειν χθονός) and not to destroy the city (*Erechtheus* fr. 65.55–57 Austin), and then asks: "Did one (victim) not satisfy you? Did you not touch my heart by burying Erechtheus beneath the earth?": οὐχ εἷς ἅδην σ' ἔπλησεν; οὐ κατὰ χθονὸς / κρύψας Ἐρεχθέα τῆς ἐμῆς ἥψω φρενός; (*Erechtheus* fr. 65.59–60 Austin). From the mention of the trident in line 55 we may assume that Poseidon used his trident to split the Acropolis rock to swallow Erechtheus up. This is made explicit in Euripides *Ion* 281–282, where Ion asks Creusa, Erechtheus's daughter, about her father's death:

Ion: πατέρα δ' ἀληθῶς χάσμα σὸν κρύπτει χθονός;
Creusa: πληγαὶ τριαίνης ποντίου σφ' ἀπώλεσαν.

Ion: Did a gaping of the earth truly hide your father?
Creusa: Blows of the sea god's trident destroyed him.

Erechtheus's death replays Poseidon's contest with Athena in that in both cases the Acropolis rock is split by Poseidon's trident beneath the later temple. The two myths are in fact closely connected; cf. n3.193 below. There is an apparent allusion to the contest of Poseidon and Athena in another fragment of the *Erechtheus*, in which Praxithea defiantly rejects the possibility that Eumolpos and his army will substitute worship of Poseidon for worship of Athena in Athens: they will not, she says, crown Poseidon's trident "standing upright in the city's foundations" instead of Athena's olive and golden gorgon (*Erechtheus* fr. 50.46–49 Austin):

οὐδ' ἀντ' ἐλαίας χρυσέας τε Γοργόνος
τρίαιναν ὀρθὴν στᾶσαν ἐν πόλεως βάθροις
Εὔμολπος οὐδὲ Θρῇξ ἀναστέψει λεὼς
στεφάνοισι, Παλλὰς δ' οὐδαμοῦ τιμήσεται.

Instead of the olive tree and the golden Gorgon
Eumolpos and the Thracian army shall not deck with crowns
the trident standing upright in the city's foundations
and Pallas nowhere be honored.

The "golden gorgon" refers to the cult statue of Athena Polias, with its golden aegis and golden gorgoneion; the same golden ornament is evoked in another two-line fragment of the play, addressed to the chorus of Athenian women: ὀλολύζετ', ὦ γυναῖκες, ὡς ἔλθη θεὰ / χρυσῆν ἔχουσα Γοργόν' ἐπίκουρος πόλει, "cry out loud, women, so that the goddess may come with the golden Gorgon to aid the city" (fr. 41 Austin). Athena won the contest with Poseidon with the olive, which symbolizes her in the myth, but in Euripides' day she was symbolized no less by the golden gorgoneion that adorned her image.

131 "Apollodorus" 3.15.4: ἐπικληθεὶς [Eumolpos] ὑπὸ Ἐλευσινίων μετὰ πολλῆς συνεμάχει Θρᾳκῶν δυνάμεως, "[Eumolpos], having been called in by the Eleusinians, fought beside them with a large force of Thracians."

mentions this war between Athens and Eleusis when he speaks about the independent existence of Attic towns before they were united into one state: he says that some even waged war against each other, "like the Eleusinians with Eumolpos against Erechtheus."[132] According to Pausanias, Eleusis was incorporated into Attica at the end of this war:[133] he says that the Eleusinians retained control of the Mysteries, but otherwise became subject to Athens.[134]

§3.57 It is impossible to know what historical basis there is for a war between Athens and Eleusis in this early period.[135] In any case the role of Eumolpos as the leader of the Thracian allies of Eleusis cannot be very old. Eumolpos was the ancestor of the Eumolpidai, the family from which the chief priests of the Eleusinian Mysteries, the hierophants, came.[136] In the

132 καί τινες καὶ ἐπολέμησάν ποτε αὐτῶν, ὥσπερ καὶ Ἐλευσίνιοι μετ' Εὐμόλπου πρὸς Ἐρεχθέα, Thucydides 2.15.1. A fragmentary scholium to this Thucydides passage seems to confirm what we would suppose anyway, that in the *Erechtheus* of Euripides Athens fought not only against Eumolpos and the Thracians, but against Eleusis as well (the scholium is *Erechtheus* fr. 63 Austin); at the end of the play, furthermore, the establishment of the Eleusinian Mysteries is ordained by Zeus through Athena (*Erechtheus* fr. 65.99–102 Austin). On the other hand Treu 1971:116, 128 and n50 argues that Euripides "corrected" the tradition by not including the Eleusinians among the attackers of Athens; this possibility cannot be excluded and there are points in its favor. Phanodemus, in whose *Atthis* Athens was invaded by an army from Boeotia rather than Thrace (Phanodemus *FGrHist* 325 F 4), probably gave a different account of the role of Eleusis in this war, perhaps omitting Eleusis entirely (cf. Jacoby, commentary on Phanodemus *FGrHist* 325 F 4, pp. 179–180).

133 Thucydides does not connect the defeat of Eleusis with its incorporation into Attica; in the sentence following his reference to the war between the two towns (n3.132 above) he goes on to speak of the synoecism under Theseus (2.15.2), and he probably thought of the incorporation of Eleusis into Attica as taking place then.

134 Pausanias 1.38.3 (Immarados, the son of Eumolpos, rather than Eumolpos himself is slain in this account): γενομένης δὲ Ἐλευσινίοις μάχης πρὸς Ἀθηναίους ἀπέθανε μὲν Ἐρεχθεὺς Ἀθηναίων βασιλεύς, ἀπέθανε δὲ Ἰμμάραδος Εὐμόλπου· καταλύονται δὲ ἐπὶ τοῖσδε τὸν πόλεμον, ὡς Ἐλευσινίους ἐς τὰ ἄλλα Ἀθηναίων κατηκόους ὄντας ἰδίᾳ τελεῖν τὴν τελετήν, "When the battle of the Eleusinians against the Athenians took place, Erechtheus, the Athenians' king, died on one side, and Immarados, the son of Eumolpos, died on the other. They settled the war on the following terms, that the Eleusianians would be dependent on the Athenians in other matters, but that they would conduct the sacred rite on their own." For Immarados, cf. Pausanias 1.27.4.

135 In Jacoby's view the war between Athens and Eleusis "is *the* great event of the period of the kings; and the explanation is that a really historical memory of it was preserved. Thukydides simply mentions it as an historical fact" (Jacoby 1949:124). Kearns 1989:114 also imagines that the war has a historical basis, but not a specific one: "the traditions of what must have been many local wars and skirmishes between the towns of Attica seem to have crystallized into this one war between Athens and Eleusis."

136 See Toepffer 1889:24–80. The Eumolpidai considered themselves "descendants of Eumolpos," but originally their name probably had to do with a cult function rather than descent (cf. Durante 1957:101). In historical times members of the *génos* of Eumolpidai had residence throughout Attica and not in Eleusis specifically (cf. Toepffer 1889:45–46; Clinton 1986:46).

Homeric Hymn to Demeter, which most likely dates from the seventh century BC,[137] Eumolpos is one of a small number of Eleusinian "kings" to whom Demeter shows the performance of her sacred rites (*Homeric Hymn to Demeter* 473–476, 478–479):

ἡ δὲ κιοῦσα θεμιστοπόλοις βασιλεῦσι
δ[εῖξε,] Τριπτολέμῳ τε Διοκλεῖ τε πληξίππῳ,
Εὐμόλπου τε βίη Κελεῷ θ' ἡγήτορι λαῶν,
δρησμοσύνην θ' ἱερῶν καὶ ἐπέφραδεν ὄργια πᾶσι,
σεμνά, τά τ' οὔ πως ἔστι παρεξ[ίμ]εν [οὔτε πυθέσθαι,]
οὔτ' ἀχέειν.

But she went and showed the justice-ministering kings,
Triptolemos and horse-driving Diokles
and mighty Eumolpos and Keleos, leader of the people,
the performance of her sacred rites, and she revealed to all of
    them the august mysteries,
which are by no means to be transgressed [or learned by inquiry]
or spoken.[138]

137 Richardson 1974:11 thinks that the hymn belongs to the seventh century. Janko 1982:183 thinks that the hymn must belong to the latter half of the seventh or the early sixth century, and considers that "the linguistic evidence strongly favours a date earlier rather than later within this range."

138 I have omitted what appears to be a variant line, 477: Τριπτολέμῳ τε Πολυξείνῳ τ', ἐπὶ τοῖς δὲ Διοκλεῖ, in which the names Triptolemos and Diocles are repeated from line 474, and a new name, Polyxeinos, is added. Eumolpos also occurs earlier in the hymn, when the daughter of Keleus names him as one of the kings who rule Eleusis (*Homeric Hymn to Demeter* 153–156):

ἡμὲν Τριπτολέμου πυκιμήδεος ἠδὲ Διόκλου
ἠδὲ Πολυξείνου καὶ ἀμύμονος Εὐμόλποιο
καὶ Δολίχου καὶ πατρὸς ἀγήνορος ἡμετέροιο
τῶν πάντων ἄλοχοι κατὰ δώματα πορσαίνουσι.

The wives of wise Triptolemos and Dioklos,
of Polyxeinos and faultless Eumolpos,
of Dolikos and my own bold father,
the wives of all these men manage affairs in the houses.

The names Dolichos and Polyxeinos in this passage do not occur in the later passage about the sacred rites (however Polyxeinos occurs in the variant line 477). As Richardson 1974:194 points out, the syntax of these lines (a succession of genitives dependent on ἄλοχοι, "wives," at the end) is awkward and non-Homeric.

In this hymn, which seems to be from Eleusis, Eumolpos is an Eleusinian, and of high rank.[139] How he then came to be considered a Thracian is a puzzle,[140] but the explanation probably concerns Athens more than Eleusis: Athens viewed itself as the target of exotic foreign foes, like the Amazons who invaded when Theseus was king, and the Thracians follow this pattern.[141] It seems unlikely that the Eleusinians themselves would have made Eumolpos, one of their illustrious ancestors, a Thracian.[142]

139 For the hymn's connection with Eleusis see Clinton 1992:28–37 and 1993, who argues that the connection is not with the Mysteries, which later became prominent, but with older rites of the Thesmophoria (cf. EN3.9 to n3.166).
140 The question is discussed by Clinton 1986:46n24. The influence of Orphism at Eleusis is probably part of the explanation; cf. Kearns 1989:114: "The suggestion that the Thracian Eumolpos was partly due to the numbering of the Eleusinian hero among the Orphic poets is probably right; this is certainly the gist of Attic genealogies which make him son or father of Musaeus, under whose name verses of Orphic tendency circulated [Hiller von Gaertringen 1886:24–25; Eumolpos and Musaeus: Androtion *FGrHist* 324 F 70, Diogenes Laertius 1.3]. We are here dealing with early syncretistic attempts to place together all rites and precepts of a 'mystical' nature as essentially teaching the same wisdom. No doubt the δρώμενα of Eleusis were already capable of an Orphic interpretation, however much violence that might do to their original nature." Nilsson 1951:37n44, while granting the possibility of a historical basis to myths about Thracians, thinks that Euripides was the first to make Eumolpos a Thracian: "This must be an innovation, and the alleged fact that the founder of the Eleusinian Mysteries was a Thracian involved the mythographers in serious difficulties. There are not a few myths of Thracians in Greece (see Hiller von Gaertringen 1886:50ff.) and it seems not impossible that there may be a kernel of truth in them. For it is only natural that Thracian hosts made their way down into Greece in the early age in which many of them settled in north western Asia Minor." Parker, who agrees with the suggestion of Orphic influence (1987:203), holds open the possibility that the tradition for Eumolpos as a Thracian is older than Euripides despite the lack of evidence and certain indications to the contrary (213n68); at the same time he views with skepticism evidence for an earlier independent tradition of a war between Erechtheus and Thracians (203 and 213n69). For the birth and early adventures of the Thracian Eumolpos see "Apollodorus" 3.15.4, and Parker 1987:212n64, who questions whether the entire elaborate account could have come from the prologue to Euripides' *Erechtheus*.
141 Cf. Kearns 1989:114–115: "But we must also take into account the depiction of the adversaries of Athens—as on other occasions—as foreign and exotic." It is striking how often the invasion of Eumolpos and the Thracians is paired with the invasion of the Amazons in the Athenian rhetorical tradition, as in e.g. Isocrates *Panegyricus* 4.68: ἔτι γὰρ ταπεινῆς οὔσης τῆς Ἑλλάδος ἦλθον εἰς τὴν χώραν ἡμῶν Θρᾷκες μὲν μετ' Εὐμόλπου τοῦ Ποσειδῶνος, Σκύθαι δὲ μετ' Ἀμαζόνων τῶν Ἄρεως θυγατέρων, οὐ κατὰ τὸν αὐτὸν χρόνον, ἀλλὰ καθ' ὃν ἑκάτεροι τῆς Εὐρώπης ἐπῆρχον, μισοῦντες μὲν ἅπαν τὸ τῶν Ἑλλήνων γένος, κτλ., "While Greece was still weak there came to our land Thracians with Eumolpos, Poseidon's son, and Scythians with the Amazons, Ares' daughters, not at the same time, but when each of these groups ruled over Europe, hating as they did the whole race of the Greeks," etc. Cf. also Isocrates 12.193, Plato *Menexenus* 239b, Demosthenes 60.8. For other ancient sources on the war between Athens and Eleusis see Frazer 1913 on Pausanias 1.38.3.
142 Kearns 1989:115 shows that barbarism figured in the traditions about the Thracian invasion; she comments that this would hardly commend itself to the Eumolpidai, and that "it

§3.58 Erechtheus, for his part, hardly seems older than Eumolpos in the tradition for a war between Athens and Eleusis in the Bronze Age.[143] This, admittedly, is to cast doubt on the war itself, for if both leaders are removed little is left.[144] But this is not the essential point. Even if Athens controlled Eleusis in the Mycenaean age, as the result of a war or other-wise, we know that Eleusis was severely depopulated at the end of the Mycenaean age.[145] Whatever unity there had been doubtless lapsed and had to be re-established in the historical period.[146] The legendary war

is presumably as a patched-up compromise solution to this problem that the two-Eumolpos theory originates." Euripides' *Erechtheus* already distinguishes Eumolpos the leader of the Thracians from a second Eumolpos born from him (*Erechtheus* fr. 65.100–101 Austin). Andron *FGrHist* 10 F 13 (scholia to Sophocles *Oedipus at Colonus* 1053) has three figures named Eumolpos in a single line of descent with one or two generations between them: Ἄνδρων μὲν οὖν γράφει οὐ ‹τοῦ›τον Εὔμολπον εὑρεῖν ‹τὴν› μύησιν, ἀλλ᾽ ἀπὸ τούτου Εὔμολπον πέμπτον γεγονότα· Εὐμόλπου γὰρ γενέσθαι Κήρυκα, τοῦ δὲ Εὔμολπον, τοῦ δὲ Ἀντίφημον, τοῦ δὲ Μουσαῖον τὸν ποιητήν, τοῦ δὲ Εὔμολπον τὸν καταδείξαντα τὴν μύησιν καὶ ἱεροφάντην γεγονότα, "Andron writes that this Eumolpos did not discover the rite of initiation, but the Eumolpos born in the fifth generation after him; for from Eumolpos was born Keryx, and from him Eumolpos, and from him Antiphemos, and from him the poet Musaeus, and from him the Eumolpos who revealed the initiation and became hierophant."

143 Cf. Kearns 1989:113: "Erechtheus...is an old figure of cult worshipped in conjunction with Athena Polias, and identified by title with Poseidon. His burial on the Acropolis is unlikely to have had much to do originally with the Eleusinian war." I would modify this statement in that I see Erechtheus's *burial* on the Acropolis, like his connection with Eleusis, as a secondary matter—the two things go together in my view. But I agree with the essential point, that Erechtheus's connection with Eleusis is secondary.

144 Note that none of the other Eleusinian heroes found in the *Homeric Hymn to Demeter* takes part in the war. Jacoby, as noted above (n3.135), called the war between Athens and Eleusis *the* great event of the period of the kings in the tradition followed by Thucydides and the Atthidographers, and he thought that the explanation for this is that the war really took place. But it is precisely the isolation of this event that makes one doubt it. Kearns 1989:110, who does not reject the war as an actual event, nevertheless shows how oddly it fits with the rest of the tradition: "Attica is poor in mythical history of the 'epic' type; wars and expeditions feature little, obviously in a last-ditch attempt to link Attica with the wider Greek mythical world. Almost the only native 'historical' tradition of this sort—an event that seems to demand a specific place in time, whenever that may be—is the war with Eleusis. Other traditions about early Attica exist in an almost timeless world. Kekrops, Erechtheus and Erichthonios, Pandion are cult figures, sacral heroes whose origins lie in the diverse religious practices of the Acropolis."

145 Desborough 1964:115: "The evidence, then, from Eleusis, though not entirely clear, seems to fall in line with that of the western part of Attica: at least a serious diminution of occu-pation by the beginning of LH. III C, and thereafter a break"; cf. also Simpson 1965:110 and Sourvinou-Inwood1973:216. For Attic unity in the Mycenaean period (a separate issue) see Stubbings 1975:169 and 1975a:347–348.

146 Stanton 1990:14n6: "Although some scholars (e.g. Padgug 1972) have vigorously defended the view that Attike was unified once for all in the Mycenaean period, many others have doubted the attribution of the unification to the legendary figure of Theseus, a king before

between Athens and Eleusis has to do with what took place in the histor-
ical period, whatever may have happened earlier: the war is a retrojection
into mythic times of a more recent event.[147] Indeed Athens did not (re)gain
control of Eleusis until after the *Homeric Hymn to Demeter* was composed if
we are to judge by the remarkable fact that Athens is not even mentioned
in the hymn.[148] There is no consensus that Eleusis remained independent
as late as the seventh (or even the sixth) century;[149] but those who believe

the Trojan war. Hignett 1958:36–37, for example, argues that there was disunion after the
Mycenaean period and that the basic unification of Attike for the classical period took
place in the eighth century. A. M. Snodgrass (1977:14–21) argues that Attike was so dras-
tically depopulated in the centuries before 800 BC that any act of unification over such
a large area (about 2,650 square kilometres) in the Bronze Age would need to be imple-
mented afresh; and that it is only in the eighth century that pottery from outlying areas
becomes indistinguishable in style and quality from that of the town. Even if one accepts
a basic unification then, it is likely that Eleusis in the west and probably the area around
Marathon in the northeast were incorporated in the Athenian *polis* at a later date. The
Homeric Hymn to Demeter suggests that Eleusis was still independent (cf. the references to
the polis [*ptoliethron*] of Eleusis in line 318 and to the *dêmos* of Eleusis in line 490, and the
complete lack of reference to Athens in the hymn) when it was composed in the seventh
century (for a discussion of the date of composition see Richardson 1974:5–11). The
incorporation of Eleusis in the Athenian state may even belong to the sixth century. In
Herodotus's story of the meeting between Solon of Athens and Croesus of Lydia (Herodotus
1.29–33), a meeting which many consider legendary, Solon tells Croesus about a certain
Tellos the Athenian who brought help to his fellow citizens 'when there was a battle
between the Athenians and their neighbours at Eleusis' (Herodotus 1.30.5). It is not clear
whether the battle was against the Megarians (but fought at the border town of Eleusis) or
against the people of Eleusis. If the latter, then the passage suggests that Eleusis was not
part of the Athenian polis in the time of Solon's contemporary Tellos—that is, at the begin-
ning of the sixth century." For Tellos, see §3.59–§3.63 below; for the absence of Athens in
the *Homeric Hymn to Demeter*, see immediately below in the text.

147 Kearns 1989:103 makes the general point, which is relevant to this specific case, that
"contemporary territorial claims, both among the Greeks and elsewhere, are expressed in
terms of the deeds and possessions of one's heroic ancestors."

148 Padgug, who does not believe that Eleusis was still independent when the hymn was
composed, puts the case fairly for those who do (1972:137): "The Hymn envisages an inde-
pendent Eleusis, with its own king, Keleos, and royal palace (lines 90ff). From Grote [1872:445]
onward scholars have argued, on the basis of this consideration, that Eleusis must have been
independent at the time the poem was composed" (references to Allen, Halliday, and Sikes
1936:111–114, Mylonas 1961:3n2 [see instead Mylonas 1942:12], and Lesky 1966:86). For
Padgug's own evaluation of the evidence of the hymn, see n3.150 below.

149 Especially noteworthy is Robin Osborne's view, based on archaeology, that "culturally
Eleusis is Athenian from as far back into the Dark Age as we can go" (Osborne 1994:154);
Foley 1994:170, summarizing a paper presented by Osborne at the annual meeting of the
Archaeological Institue of America in Chicago in 1991, adds the following detail: "Pottery
and burial practice do not significantly distinguish Eleusis from the rest of Attika either at
this period [the seventh century] or earlier.... Protoattic pottery found at both Eleusis and
Athens in the seventh century was limited to Attika in its distribution. This would place

that Eleusis already belonged to Athens when the *Homeric Hymn to Demeter* was composed have yet to square this belief with the hymn.[150] The issue of

Eleusis within a nexus of cultural exclusiveness" (Foley 1994:170 and n281). While I do not contest this much of Osborne's argument, his further suggestion that "there is no reason to believe that Eleusis was not also politically Athenian from as early a date as it makes sense to talk of a political unit" (Osborne 1994:154) requires more caution; for the point that unified material culture does not mean political unity cf. Anderson 2003:19. Regarding the archaeological connections between Athens and Eleusis I note that Boardman 1975:4 offers a less conclusive view than Osborne: "What follows is based partly on Mylonas' account of the architecture [at Eleusis], checked or corrected at various points. Through the eighth and seventh centuries the pottery found in the sanctuary and cemetery includes sufficient of Athenian manufacture to indicate a ready market for Athenian goods, which we would expect at any rate from the sheer proximity of the two towns. There is also a fairly rich import of Corinthian, the other standard Greek ware of these years. It is not yet possible to draw any useful deductions from these finds since so little has yet been published." Arguments resembling modern ones were also made in antiquity to establish the affinity of Salamis (part of the region of Eleusis) with Megara on the one side or Athens on the other: both sides cited burial practice as proof that Salamis was originally theirs (Plutarch *Solon* 10.3; cf. Legon 1981:138). In his scheme of a decentralized Attica in the sixth century BC Anderson 2003:228n51 hesitates about the place of Eleusis, arguing that the bond created by the Mysteries did not entail that Eleusinians were considered Athenian citizens.

150 Padgug's argument that traditional poetry conserves remarkable archaisms, and that the independence of Eleusis in the *Homeric Hymn to Demeter* is one such archaism, is not convincing. A present state of affairs is more likely to be projected onto the past than an earlier state of affairs is to be remembered when it ceases to have any relevance to the present. M. I. Finley, in an essay called "Myth, Memory and History" (Finley 1975:11–33), concludes that the only serious Greek historical writing was about contemporary events, beginning with the Persian Wars; Diamant 1982:44, referring to Finley, emphasizes that the past was valued not for finding out "how things really were," but for its usefulness in connecting the present with the heroic age. Walton 1952, while arguing that Eleusis was subject to Athens when the *Homeric Hymn to Demeter* was composed, gives a reason for the failure of the hymn to reflect this supposed fact, namely that Eleusis had only recently lost its independence and was in danger of having the Mysteries moved to Athens; the hymn was meant to forestall this by showing that Demeter belonged in Eleusis from the start (pp. 113–114). This argument, like the once standard view, presupposes a late date of incorporation of Eleusis into Attica. A different approach is taken by Sourvinou-Inwood 1997:143, who, citing Foley 1994:174, argues that the *Homeric Hymn to Demeter* operates in terms of myth rather than history: "It is a religious poem about a divine withdrawal and return, catastrophe averted, a divine epiphany, and the foundation of a cult by a deity at a time when in the archaic mythological landscape Eleusis was not part of Athens." Sourvinou-Inwood argues that Eleusis was part of Athens since the eighth century BC; she proposes a reinterpretation of Eleusinian archaeology to show that religious processions from Athens, usually thought to have begun in the early sixth century BC, were already possible in the Geometric period (1997:133–136). But if the religious connection between Athens and Eleusis was indeed that old, we would expect the *Homeric Hymn to Demeter* to assume it, as the way things always were. The only way out is to assume, as Sourvinou-Inwood does, that the myth of a war between Athens and Eleusis was older than the *Homeric Hymn to Demeter*; the hymn could then deliberately ignore Athens, although Athens had been a fact of life in Eleusis for generations, because the hymn set itself before the war in which Eleusis was conquered. I do not share

when Eleusis was incorporated into Attica is, and ought to remain, open;[151]

the assumption that the myth of a war was older than the hymn; cf. n3.152 below. For the archaeological question see now Palinkas 2008, who reexamines the evidence of entrances and roads at Eleusis in the Geometric period and concludes that it can be used equally to refute or support an early connection between Eleusis and Athens (Palinkas 2008:44–46).

151 The case that Nilsson 1951:36–37 states for a late date of incorporation still stands in most respects (see below for the "old walls" that he mentions, which are later than he thought): "Not very long before the conquest of Salamis Eleusis had been incorporated with Athens, at some time in the late seventh century BC. It was formerly independent. There is no hint of Athens in the Homeric hymn to Demeter which was composed in that century. Some signs of the autonomy remained. The phyle named after the Eleusinian hero Hippothoon had his sanctuary at Eleusis [Pausanias 1.38.4; decrees of the phyle, found at Eleusis, *IG* II² 1149, 1153]. The Eleusinians struck coins, showing on one side Triptolemos in his car drawn by snakes and on the other a pig, the holy animal of Demeter [Köhler 1879:250–253]. This is unique, for Salamis and Oropos, which also struck coins, were administratively not Athenian territory, and it is probably a remnant of the old sovereignty. This was not forgotten in a later age. It looks like a reminiscence that in 403 BC Eleusis was made a state independent of Athens, in which the thirty tyrants and their adherents took refuge. Old walls are found on the watershed which separates the Thriasian plain from the plain of Athens, near Epano Liosia; they were never used nor mentioned in the historical age and belong probably to an earlier time when war was waged between Athens and Eleusis [Beloch 1912 vol 1. pt. 1 207; Chandler 1926:19, figs. 13 and 14]. The memories of these wars lingered on in popular tales. Herodotus's relation of Tellos (1.30) who fell in a war between Athens and Eleusis is such a one. In myth they were projected into the early mythical history of Athens.... Many authors mention the war in which Eumolpos, the eponymous ancestor of the Eumolpidae, the priestly family which furnished the highest officials of the Mysteries, the hierophants, marched against Athens, some say, at the head of Thracian hosts [Hiller von Gaertringen 1886:11ff...], and was slain by the king of Athens, whose daughter sacrificed herself to save the city." For the distinction between Athens and Eleusis in Athenian myth cf. also Nilsson 1951:54–55. The walls separating the Thriasian plain from the plain of Athens, explained by Nilsson and others in terms of political separation between Eleusis and Athens, were studied by Dow 1942, who proposed instead that the walls were built by Athens in 506 BC to stop the invasion of the Spartans under Cleomenes. Dow countered the usual interpretation by casting doubt on the political separation of Athens and Eleusis until 700 BC or later, "a view which at the moment, so far as published works go, is almost universally held." Dow's comment on the subject continues: "But the evidence is far from being decisive in favor of the view that Eleusis was independent as late as 700 BC, and there is, I think, some reason for believing that a thorough and unbiased study would move the date of the union of Attika back indefinitely. If this is ever accomplished, then this historical argument for dating the Aigaleios-Parnes wall earlier than 700 or 600 BC will vanish" (Dow 1942:198). Padgug 1972 cites Dow at the beginning of his study, which is intended to show what Dow suggests. Regarding the wall, Padgug reports that a field survey carried out in 1955 showed the wall to be fourth century, thus eliminating it as evidence (Padgug 1972:140, citing Jones, Sackett, and Eliot 1957). In my view the result of Padgug's study is only to show what is undeniably true, that there is little positive evidence for a late incorporation of Eleusis into Attica. But there may be other reasons for this lack of positive evidence than the negative conclusion drawn by Padgug. As Padgug notes in his review of prior studies of the synoecism of Attica on p. 135, "almost all conclude that the final step was the incorporation of Eleusis into the Athenian state"; I do not think that this has yet been shown to be wrong.

but the presumption should be that this did not occur until after the *Hymn to Demeter* was composed.[152]

§3.59 I noted above that Felix Jacoby called the war between Erechtheus and Eumolpos *"the* great event of the period of the kings," and that he thought that "the explanation is that a really historical memory of it was preserved." By this he did not mean that Eleusis became a permanent part of Attica as the result of such a war.[153] His point was rather that the tradition for a war is so consistent in Thucydides and the Atthidographers that it must have actually happened. I do not agree with this conclusion, but it focuses the real issue for us: how and why was an annexation that took place perhaps only two hundred years earlier obliterated from memory even for Thucydides and replaced by a war in primordial times between two mythic figures, Eumolpos and Erechtheus? In my view it was the very success of the Erechtheus-Eumolpos myth, which cast the war between Athens and

---

152 Those who believe that Eleusis was incorporated into Athens with the rest of Attica must also explain the fact that Eleusis stands apart from the rest of Attica in a crucial respect: in Attic myth only Eleusis had to be won by war. Sourvinou-Inwood, who argues that the myth of Eleusis's incorporation into Attica cannot be separated from the rise of Athens as a polis in the eighth century BC (1997:141-142), does not explain why Eleusis should have had this myth when other parts of Attica did not. Parker 1987:204 explains the difference in terms of religion rather than history: "There is no independent evidence to suggest that Eleusis was incorporated into the Athenian state later than other of the 'cities' of Attica, or with any more difficulty. The area in which the relation of Eleusis to Attica was unique was, of course, that of religion. The myth emphasises this special relationship by a technique of contrast (since the war led to peace). Pausanias' account perhaps suggests the spirit, at least, of the original denouement: 'They settled the war on the terms that the Eleusinians should be subject to the Athenians in other respects but should conduct the ceremonies themselves (1.38.3)'." Parker's argument is that the myth is meant to account for the religious independence of Eleusis through a contrast with its political dependence, and that this is the reason for the war between the two cities in the myth. I think that the truth is simpler. There was a war, and a very recent one, which made Eleusis dependent on Athens; the myth arose, not to account for religious independence, for Athens was now in control of religion too, but to give the war and its outcome a heroic pedigree. I do not think that it makes sense to speak of religious independence as distinct from political independence in the case of Eleusis. There is a critique of Sourvinou-Inwood's case for the early incorporation of Eleusis into Attica in Kennell 1997, and a response in Sourvinou-Inwood 2003:41-45.

153 Jacoby too believed that Eleusis was incorporated into Attica in the historical period; cf. his commentary on a fragment of Philochorus attesting the tradition that Kekrops founded the twelve towns of Attica, including Eleusis (Philochorus *FGrHist* 328 F 94 [= Strabo 9.1.20], commentary p. 394): "The starting point of the Atthidographer...is without doubt the united Attic state including even Eleusis, i.e. historical conditions as they existed from the seventh century onward"; cf. also his commentary on Philochorus 328 F 107, p. 431, discussing a claim by the Megarians in historical times to the Eleusinian district "which had not long been connected with Athens."

Eleusis back into mythic times, that caused the actual historical events to
disappear from memory. The myth succeeded, moreover, because it was
part of a wholesale reorganization of the most important cult relation-
ships on the Acropolis. I have already argued that Erechtheus was relocated
from Athena's temple to Poseidon's temple, and that Erechtheus effectively
replaced Poseidon in his own precinct. In terms of myth, Erechtheus was
transformed from Athena's consort, who together with her received sacri-
fices relating to fertility and procreation, to a solitary hero who at the price
of his life won Eleusis for Athens in war. How Eleusis was really won was as
little remembered as how Erechtheus came to occupy Poseidon's temple.
In both cases only traces are left in the historical record. For Erechtheus's
transfer to Poseidon's temple we have Pausanias, who tells us that sacri-
fices to Erechtheus on Poseidon's altar were added as the result of an oracle.
For the events that led to Athens' annexation of Eleusis we have, I think, a
similar trace in Herodotus, namely the reference to a figure named Tellos,
who died at Eleusis defending Athens from her neighbors.[154] I think it is not
unlikely that these neighbors were the Megarians, as has been suggested by
others, but I do not think that this excludes that a still independent Eleusis
somehow cooperated with the Megarians in the invasion.[155] In the myth
that replaced the real event in the collective memory of Athenians, the
Eleusinians summoned foreign allies from Thrace. Does this reflect a real
event in which Eleusis allied itself with Megara, its Dorian neighbor to the
west? If we assume that Athens, having won the battle at Eleusis, took this
opportunity to end the independence of Eleusis, we do not have to believe
that Athens needed much excuse to do this: minimal culpability on the
part of some Eleusinians would have sufficed as a pretext. And if Eleusinian

154 Herodotus 1.30.5.
155 Padgug 1972:139 suggests that either Megarians or Boeotians are meant by "neighbors."
Highbarger 1927:132 argues on the basis of the Tellos story that "even before Solon's time
Athens and Megara had struggled over the boundary lines of Eleusis." Legon 1981:100–101,
who believes that Eleusis was incorporated into Attica by c. 700 BC, nevertheless argues
that only Eleusinians were involved in the battle with Athens in which Tellos died; if this
means that the Tellos battle occurred before 700 BC, I disagree: Tellos must have been
an older contemporary of Solon (see below §3.61 and n3.157; cf. also Stanton 1990:14n6,
quoted above n3.146). Van Effenterre 1977 argues that Athens had loose control of Eleusis
by 700 BC but then lost it to Megara, and then won it back again under Solon in the war
in which Tellos was killed. Note the wide scope that Xenophon gives to the mythic war
with Eleusis when he refers to Erechtheus as an example of the valor of the Athenians'
ancestors, emphasizing first his "birth and nurturing," and also "the war waged in his
time against those from the whole neighboring mainland": λέγω γάρ, καὶ τὴν Ἐρεχθέως γε
τροφὴν καὶ γένεσιν, καὶ τὸν πόλεμον τὸν ἐπ' ἐκείνου γενόμενον πρὸς τοὺς ἐκ τῆς ἐχομένης
ἠπείρου πάσης (Xenophon *Memorabilia* 3.5.10; cf. n3.236 below).

culpability was but a pretext for Athenian expansion, all the more reason to replace a shabby recent affair with a heroic tale from the past to account for Eleusis's dependent status.

§3.60 The story of Tellos parallels the myth of Erechtheus in significant ways. The key parallel is the sacrificial death of an Athenian after turning the tide of battle at Eleusis and saving his city. For Erechtheus this means that after slaying Eumolpos in battle he is in turn slain by Poseidon on the Acropolis, where he is buried and honored in Poseidon's temple. For Tellos it means a heroic death at the enemy's hands in Eleusis after turning the tide of battle and a public burial.[156] The story of Tellos is told only incidentally in Herodotus. It is part of the tradition about Solon, who in his foreign travels was asked by the wealthy Lydian king Croesus whom he judged most fortunate among the mortals that he had seen. Solon surprised Croesus, who expected to hear himself named because of his wealth, by naming an unknown Athenian because of his glorious death. Being well off by Athenian standards and seeing his family also prosper, Tellos died a hero's death, saving

---

156 The parallel between Tellos and Erechtheus is closer if Erechtheus was said to have been slain on the battlefield after setting up a *tropaîon* commemorating the enemy's defeat; a death on the battlefield is in fact what the messenger in Euripides *Erechtheus* fr. 65.11–21 Austin seems to report: in lines 11–12 (following a gap of about ten lines) the messenger says in a ὡς clause that Erechtheus set up a *tropaîon*:

μη [.. Ἐρεχθεὺς ὡς τροπαῖα[
ἔστη[σε χώρ]αι τῆιδε βαρβά[ρ.

Seven lines of dialogue follow, in which the messenger gradually reveals Erechtheus's fate to Praxithea, until at last he says that Erechtheus is dead (τέθνηκ', fr. 65.21). Since the messenger has come from the battlefield to the Acropolis (cf. fr. 65.3–4), the battlefield would seem to be where Erechtheus was killed and buried; in that case we do not know what landmark, if any, was associated with Erechtheus's burial. Cf. Treu 1971:117–118: "We hear the report that Erechtheus has put up a victory monument, Eumolpos has fallen, and that—the messenger lets this come out only hesitantly at first and then reports it—Erechtheus too is dead: here the report must surely have left a place for the nearly incomprehensible fact that the victorious king of the Athenians, after erecting the victory monument, as he walked and stood, disappeared into the earth" ("Wir hören die Mitteilung, dass Erechtheus ein Siegeszeichen errichtet hat, Eumolpos gefallen ist, allerdings—was der Bote erst nur zögernd durchblicken lässt und dann mitteilt—dass auch Erechtheus τέθνηκε: Wobei die Mitteilung doch noch Platz gelassen haben muss für das beinahe Unbegreifliche, dass der siegreiche König der Athener nach Errichtung des Siegeszeichens, wie er ging und stand, in der Erde verschwunden ist"). Perhaps there was more than one view as to where Poseidon killed and buried Erechtheus (cf. n3.128 above for the temple of Poseidon-Erechtheus on the Acropolis as one likely location). Darthou 2005 proposes a different interpretation entirely of Erechtheus's end (not a burial but the final return to the earth of Athens' series of autochthonous founders).

his city, and he was honored like a hero too, being buried at public expense (Herodotus 1.30.4–5):

Τέλλῳ τοῦτο μὲν τῆς πόλιος εὖ ἡκούσης παῖδες ἦσαν καλοί τε κἀγαθοί, καί σφι εἶδε ἅπασι τέκνα ἐκγενόμενα καὶ πάντα παραμείναντα, τοῦτο δὲ τοῦ βίου εὖ ἥκοντι, ὡς τὰ παρ' ἡμῖν, τελευτὴ τοῦ βίου λαμπροτάτη ἐπεγένετο· γενομένης γὰρ Ἀθηναίοισι μάχης πρὸς τοὺς ἀστυγείτονας ἐν Ἐλευσῖνι βοηθήσας καὶ τροπὴν ποιήσας τῶν πολεμίων ἀπέθανε κάλλιστα, καί μιν Ἀθηναῖοι δημοσίῃ τε ἔθαψαν αὐτοῦ τῇ περ ἔπεσε καὶ ἐτίμησαν μεγάλως.

To Tellos, his city prospering, fine sons were born, and he saw children born to each of them, and he saw all these children surviving; then, his life being prosperous enough by our standards, a most glorious end was added to his life. In a battle against neighbors in Eleusis he fought for his countrymen, routed the enemy, and died a most excellent death; and the Athenians buried him at public expense where he fell, and honored him greatly.

§3.61 If Tellos was the flesh-and-blood hero whose death led to the incorporation of Eleusis into Attica, his association with Solon allows us to date the events to Solon's own lifetime. In the story in Herodotus Solon is asked if he has *seen* anyone whom be would call most fortunate, and it follows from his answer that Tellos was his contemporary.[157] We do not have to believe that Solon really had the conversation with Croesus that Herodotus recounts, but there is no reason not to think that the association between Solon and Tellos that this story implies is genuine: Tellos was an obscure local figure, whose obscurity is integral to the point of his story, but the story loses

---

157 Referring to Solon's wide travels Croesus says to him (Herodotus 1.30.2): νῦν ὦν ἐπειρέσθαι σε ἵμερος ἐπῆλθέ μοι εἴ τινα ἤδη πάντων <u>εἶδες</u> ὀλβιώτατον, "Now, then, the desire has come upon me to ask you whether <u>you have seen</u> anyone by now who was most fortunate of all." When he is not named as the most fortunate, Croesus goes on to ask Solon whom he puts second, and Solon again disappoints him, naming Kleobis and Biton, youths rewarded for their piety by the gods with a splendid death. The question is again whom has Solon *seen* who deserves the second honor after Tellos: ἐπειρώτα τίνα δεύτερον μετ' ἐκεῖνον <u>ἴδοι</u>, "he asked him whom <u>he had seen</u> who was second after that man" (Herodotus 1.31.1). Solon in the story is not asked to rank famous figures from the past, only mortals that he has met, hence those named are not illustrious.

its effectiveness if he was not a real part of Solon's experience.[158] I do not think that the story would falsify this point.[159]

§3.62 If Eleusis was incorporated into Attica in the late seventh century BC, Solon would have been alive to witness it, and he could also have been directly involved in it (if so, this is what linked him with the figure Tellos, the hero of the war by which Eleusis was annexed).[160] The period following the failed Cylonian conspiracy of c. 630 BC is a plausible time for this event if it was brought on, as suggested above, by Megarian-Athenian hostilities in the first place. Cylon was the son-in-law of the Megarian tyrant Theagenes, who wanted to increase his influence over his larger neighbor to the east.[161] Relations between the two cities must have been badly strained by the event,

158 The story of Solon and Croesus is one of numerous tales of the seven wise men that originated in the sixth century BC; see Regenbogen 1961 and Martin 1993. Regenbogen 1961:117–118, 120 shows that Tellos belongs to the earliest layer of the Solon and Croesus story, before the story of Kleobis and Biton was added to it. The oldest evidence for stories of the seven wise men is from the late sixth century, Hipponax fr. 65 Degani: καὶ Μύσων, ὃν Ὠπόλλων / ἀνεῖπεν ἀνδρῶν σωφρονέστατον πάντων, "And Myson, whom Apollo / proclaimed the most self-controlled of all men"; cf. also Hipponax fr. 12 Degani, which names Bias as a proverbial strong advocate (see Regenbogen 1961:118). As Regenbogen 1961:120 reconstructs the earliest version of the story of Solon and Croesus, in which Kleobis and Biton did not occur, but only Tellos, the story's point was the contrast of Greek "poverty" and "self-control" (πενία and σωφροσύνη) with barbarian "wealth" and "violence" (πλοῦτος and ὕβρις).

159 As Plutarch explicitly tells us (*Comparison of Solon and Publicola* 1.2, Solon fr. 46 West), Tellos did not occur in Solon's poems: "Tellos, whom Solon pronounced the most blessed man he knew because of his fortunate lot, his virtue, and his goodly offspring, was not celebrated in [Solon's] poems as a good man, nor did his children or any magistracy of his achieve a reputation." Note that Solon fr. 24 West praises the modest wealth and other signs of good fortune of a humble character like Tellos.

160 See n3.155 above for van Effenterre's thesis that Solon won Eleusis back from Megara after a period of Megarian control (van Effenterre 1977); this thesis is pursued interestingly in many respects by L'Homme-Wéry 1996, but remains conjectural (cf. Mülke 2002:378–379).

161 Legon 1981:100 characterizes Theagenes' role, and the condition of Athens at the time, as follows: "No elaborate theory is needed to account for Theagenes' complicity in the Cylonian coup. He saw an opportunity to help establish a friendly and even somewhat dependent regime in a neighboring state, thereby extending his (and Megara's) influence, and, perhaps broadening his power base. Athens in the 630's was still a predominantly agrarian, inward-looking state, and despite her size, population, and future greatness, it is far from ludicrous that seventh-century Megara could have taken the leading role in their relations." Part of the tradition of the Cylonian conspiracy is the alacrity with which the Athenians responded from outlying areas in Attica to the threat on the Acropolis (Thucydides 1.126.7). The synoecism of Attica is implied by this, even if Eleusis had not yet been incorporated (Legon, on the other hand, thinks that Eleusis had been incorporated about 700 BC; see n3.155 above). Did Theagenes perceive a greater threat from an expanding neighbor than Legon's characterizations of the two sides would suggest?

and they never really improved after it, with contention soon centering on the island of Salamis. When he failed to take Athens by stealth in the Cylonian affair, Theagenes may have resorted to an open invasion of Eleusis, which was also stopped short. Perhaps his pretext for this was an "invitation" from a still independent Eleusis, caught in the middle between Megara and Athens and bound to lose its independence no matter which side won, since neither side would risk losing the territory between them to the other.[162] As it happened, Tellos and the other Athenians prevailed in the battle, and Athens, perhaps influenced by Solon, annexed Eleusis. This is a construction, but it fits with the next phase of the conflict between the two cities, the contest for Salamis, which lasted through the first half of the sixth century. It has been well observed that for Athens the conquest of Salamis became a geographical necessity once it acquired Eleusis, for without Salamis Eleusis is cut off from the sea.[163] Thus it makes sense to see the Athenian pursuit of Salamis as following soon after the acquisition of Eleusis. Solon was of course the principal figure on the Athenian side in the conquest of Salamis.[164]

162 Theagenes was eventually driven from power by an aristocratic regime, which was later replaced by the unbridled democracy against which the poet Theognis railed (cf. Legon 1981:104-135). Legon 1981:101 doubts that Theagenes survived the Cylonian "fiasco" by many years: "the failure of Cylon's coup must have badly shaken Theagenes' regime. Athenian enmity had been provoked or heightened, troops had very likely been sacrificed, and nothing had been accomplished." This argument only gains force if Theagenes' legacy included not only a failed coup, but the loss of Eleusis through an open conflict with Athens.

163 Ferguson 1938:42: "It was only on the annexation of Eleusis that the possesson of Salamis became a sort of geographical necessity for Athens. To be sure the island had formed theretofore a bridge between Megara and the basin of the Kephisos, but it had not shut off completely from the open sea a valuable part of Attica." Ferguson, p. 42, dates the struggle for Salamis to the end of the seventh century at the earliest; Guarducci 1948 dates both the incorporation of Eleusis into Attica and the possession of Salamis by Athens much earlier, to the eighth century, but she agrees with Ferguson that the two events belong together: "When this possession began we do not know with certainty; but it is logical to think, as Ferguson justly observed, that it was contemporaneous with or immediately subsequent to the annexation of Eleusis on the part of Athens, inasmuch as a stable occupation of Eleusis is not conceivable without the possession of the island of Salamis, which dominates its access by sea and almost closes off its gulf" ("Quando avesse inizio questo possesso noi non sappiamo con sicurezza; ma è logico pensare, come giustamente osservò il Ferguson, che esso fosse contemporaneo o immediatamente successivo all' annessione di Eleusi da parte di Atene, in quanto una stabile occupazione di Eleusi non è concepibile senza il possesso dell' isola di Salamina, che ne domina l'accesso per mare e quasi ne chiude il golfo"; Guarducci 1948:228-229).

164 Megara probably took possession of Salamis sometime in the seventh century to put down pirates stationed there and thus to protect its own shipping (Legon 1981:101, 122). The displaced population of Salamis seems to have gone to Attica, where it became the *génos* of the Salaminioi (see n3.184 below). It is disputed whether this population was Athenian

or not before it left Salamis (Ferguson and Nilsson both assume that it was not, Guarducci argues that it was; see n3.184 below). In either case, this dispossessed group must have pressured the Athenians to recover Salamis. Plutarch *Solon* 8.1 tells us that when Solon began his public activity the Athenians had passed a law "prohibiting anyone from urging the *polis* to renew its claim to Salamis in either written or oral form, on pain of death." Legon 1981:123 is probably right that this law was meant to contain the pressure of the Salaminioi. To get around the law, the story goes, Solon composed his poem *Salamis* and pretended insanity when he recited it in public; Plutarch says that the poem was a hundred lines long, of which he quotes the first two (Plutarch *Solon* 8.2–3; Solon fr. 1 West):

αὐτὸς κῆρυξ ἦλθον ἀφ' ἱμερτῆς Σαλαμῖνος,
κόσμον ἐπέων †ὠιδὴν ἀντ' ἀγορῆς θέμενος.

I myself have come as a herald from desired Salamis,
Composing well ordered words, a song, instead of a speech.

Six additional lines of the poem are preserved by Diogenes Laertius 1.47 (Solon frs. 2–3 West):

εἴην δὴ τότ' ἐγὼ Φολεγάνδριος ἢ Σικινήτης
ἀντί γ' Ἀθηναίου πατρίδ' ἀμειψάμενος·
αἶψα γὰρ ἂν φάτις ἥδε μετ' ἀνθρώποισι γένοιτο·
"Ἀττικὸς οὗτος ἀνήρ, τῶν Σαλαμιναφετέων."

In that case I wish I were from Pholegandros or Sikinos
instead of being an Athenian, exchanging my fatherland;
For this report would quickly spread among men:
"This man is Attic, one of those who surrendered Salamis."

And:

ἴομεν ἐς Σαλαμῖνα μαχησόμενοι περὶ νήσου
ἱμερτῆς χαλεπόν τ' αἶσχος ἀπωσόμενοι.

Let us go to Salamis to fight for the desired island
and to push away our harsh shame.

According to Plutarch the performance succeeded in rousing the Athenians to action and the law was repealed. Solon himself led five hundred volunteers who surprised the Megarians on Salamis and captured the island (this is the version of Salamis's capture given in Plutarch *Solon* 9.1–3, which is more probable than another version given in Plutarch *Solon* 8.4–6, in which Solon is also the central figure; see Legon 1981:126–127). Plutarch tells of these events near the beginning of his *Life of Solon*, and we therefore assume that they fall at the beginning of Solon's career. Solon's archonship is usually dated 594/3 BC (Legon 1981:126), and thus his career probably began in the latter years of the seventh century. Solon's role is so central in the capture of Salamis that it is possible that he was himself born in Salamis, as Diogenes Laertius 1.45 and Diodorus Siculus 9.1 state (see Legon 1981:128, who leaves the possibility open that this tradition is true although it is not in the older writers). Legon 1981:101 considers whether Salamis was what pushed the Megarian tyrant Theagenes to interfere in Athenian affairs as early as 630 BC, the approximate date of the Cylonian conspiracy. Against this is the fact, which Legon acknowledges cannot be lightly dismissed, "that there is not a single mention of Theagenes in the ample and conflicting testimony on the Salamis dispute." I prefer to think that Theagenes fell from

§3.63 Tellos was honored for what he did in turning back the attack of Athens' neighbors by being buried at public expense where he fell, in Eleusis. But this minor figure was not given credit for the wider consequence of the Athenian victory, the incorporation of Eleusis into Attica: this deed was shifted to an august figure of Athenian cult, who was himself given a new myth that closely paralleled what Tellos actually did, but was set in the distant past.[165] What Erechtheus needed for his part, given his relationship with Athena Polias, was precisely a new myth, and this he got. Changes also took place in the cult of Demeter at Eleusis, which now took its direction from Athens.[166] These changes, however, occurred under the protective cover of a

power because of Eleusis, before Solon took Salamis. That, however, may make the annexation of Eleusis too early for Solon's involvement in that event. Legon does not think that Theagenes, whose dates are not known, continued in power long after the Cylonian affair ("Theagenes' tyranny probably lasted between ten and twenty years, ending before 620," p. 102). We also do not know Solon's birthdate or how long he lived. If we assume that he became archon in his thirties, he was born before 624 BC; Davies 1971:323 gives c. 630–625 BC as his probable date of birth. Solon opposed Peisistratos's first seizure of power in 561/60 BC according to Aristotle *Constitution of the Athenians* 14.2 and other sources (see Davies 1971:323, who cites evidence for 560/59 BC as Solon's date of death). Solon is also said to have represented Athens against Megara in Sparta's arbitration of the Salamis dispute, perhaps in the 560s or early 550s (see Legon, p. 138, who gives the ancient sources in n. 6). If Solon was eighty when he died, as Diogenes Laertius 1.62 says, his birthdate could be as early as c. 640 BC, but the figure eighty was probably taken from his own poem in which he says that he hopes to attain this age (Solon fr. 20.4 West; cf. Davies 1971:324).

165 For Thucydides, who seems to have connected the incorporation of Eleusis into Attica with the synoecism of Theseus rather than with the war of Erechtheus, see n3.133 above; the connection between Erechtheus's victory over Eleusis and the incorporation of the defeated town into Attica, which seems entirely natural in itself, is made by Pausanias (see n3.134 above).

166 See Richardson 1974:6–11. Changes that took place early may be associated with Solon; more pronounced changes that took place later may be associated with Peisistratos. The first "Telesterion" (a modern name for the building in which initiation into the Mysteries took place) was dated to the Solonian era, c. 600 BC, by Mylonas 1961:63–72; this structure was rebuilt on a much larger scale, perhaps in the time of Peisistratos in the mid-sixth century (lower dates of 575–550 BC and c. 500 BC for the two structures are now favored by some; see Miles 1998:28 with nn10 and 12, and Anderson 2003:187 with nn26 and 27). The temple to which the *Homeric Hymn to Demeter* refers must be earlier than the first Telesterion. It is not known if earlier structures in the same location, one of Mycenaean date, another of Geometric date, had a religious function (Richardson 1974:7, 328; Cosmopoulos 2003 argues that Megaron B, the Mycenaean structure, had a domestic religious function, but he does not address the question of continuity through the Dark Age; this question, which was answered in the negative by Darcque 1981, has now been reopened by N. Cucuzza in Lippolis 2006:67–72 on the basis of non-archaeological considerations). The chief priests of the Mysteries, the hierophants, belonged to the *génos* of the Eumolpidai, whose ancestor Eumolpos occurs in the *Homeric Hymn to Demeter*, and who therefore seems to be Eleusinian; but the Kerykes, the *génos* from which both the

myth that said that Eleusis had been in Athenian hands since time immemo-
rial—since the time of Erechtheus, who had defeated the Thracians and won
Eleusis in the period of the kings.[167]

Keryx and the Dadouchos came, seems to have been Athenian: unlike Eumolpos, their
ancestor Keryx does not occur in the *Homeric Hymn to Demeter*, and the Kerykes themselves
regarded their ancestor as the son of Hermes and a daughter of the Athenian king Kekrops
(Pausanias 1.38.3; see Richardson 1974:8; cf. also Burkert 1983:146–147). The Iacchos
procession along the Sacred Way from Athens to Eleusis, first attested for the year 480
BC (Herodotus 8.65), had the important function of connecting the Eleusinian cult with
the city; this procession was doubtless older than the fifth century but not as old as the
hymn (cf. Richardson 1974:8–9). The Eleusinion, an Athenian branch of the Eleusinian cult
(sacred objects were brought from Eleusis to the Eleusinion for a period of days before
the Mysteries were celebrated and were then returned to Eleusis as part of the procession
on the Sacred Way; see Deubner 1932:72–73, Nilsson 1951:38–39), underwent significant
construction in the period 575–550 BC (see Miles 1998:25–26 and cf. Anderson 2003:186);
it was in this same period that the first Telesterion was built in Eleusis according to the
revised dating mentioned above (Miles 1998:28; Anderson 2003:187). Other indications of
date are vague but consistent. Inscriptions regulating sacrifices in the Eleusinion belong to
the early fifth century, but they are written *boustrophēdón* and therefore must derive from
an earlier version of the mid-sixth century or before (Jeffery 1948; cf. Richardson 1974:10).
Andocides *On the Mysteries* 111 says that the *boulē* habitually met in the Eleusinion on the
day after the Mysteries "according to the law of Solon"; this phrase may mean that the
law (and with it the Eleusinion) dates from Solon's time, but the phrase was sometimes
used loosely of more recent legislation (see Macdowell 1962:120–121 and 142, ad loc.).
Archaeology shows that from at least the seventh century BC there was a sanctuary in the
area of the Eleusinion, which presumably belonged to Demeter, and which was presumably
used for celebrations of the Thesmophoria (Miles 1998:22; cf. Anderson 2003:186); when
the sanctuary's connection with Eleusis began is the crucial question for the history of the
Mysteries, and dating this connection to the seventh century (Miles 1998:22) cannot be
confirmed. Triptolemos, who is named in the *Homeric Hymn to Demeter* as one of the kings
of Eleusis, takes on a much grander role in the period of Athenian control: he receives
the gifts of grain and agriculture from Demeter in Eleusis and carries them to the rest of
mankind. The myth of Triptolemos, which makes Athens the benefactor of all mankind,
is inconsistent with the *Homeric Hymn to Demeter* 305ff., where agriculture already exists
before Persephone's rape (cf. Richardson 1974:9; see Richardson 1974 on lines 305–333,
450, and 470–482 for the possibility that the myth of Triptolemos existed at the time of the
hymn, but was of no importance to it). I interpret all these developments in Demeter's cult
as the result of a change of control from Eleusis to Athens in the time of Solon. Additional
factors and other points of view are considered in EN3.9.

167 It is remarkable that a myth was able to replace historical reality as completely as it did
in this case. There must have been a deep interest on the part of the Athenians that the
myth become the new reality. In addition, the earlier independence of Eleusis may have
been due more to Athenian quietism than to Eleusinian self-defense; this would have made
it easier to pretend that Eleusis had always been part of Attica. The Megarians remem-
bered actual events no more than the Athenians; the Megarian writers who claimed that
Athens had taken Eleusis from Megara did not say that this happened in historical times,
but under Theseus in the royal period (Plutarch *Theseus* 10.3). The Athenian myth of the
four sons of Pandion (they inherited the four parts of Attica from their father) is traced by

§3.64 Erechtheus was chosen for this new role because he had outlived his usefulness in his old role. Athena Polias, no longer a mother goddess but a virgin war goddess, did not need a consort, and a new home and a new myth were found for Erechtheus. He was given a heroic death, which prefigured and enlarged the heroic death of Tellos, and which also conveniently removed him from Athena's side. The function that he had served with Athena, having to do with fertility and increase, was no longer centered on the Acropolis, but at the newly won Eleusis. It made sense that Erechtheus should die for such a prize.[168]

§3.65 Erechtheus remained paired with Athena in one important context: the festival of the Skira (Skirophoria).[169] The war between Athens and Eleusis, pitting Erechtheus against Eumolpos, was this festival's aetiological myth, and there is thus reason to believe that the festival itself was organized (or reorganized) after Eleusis was incorporated into Attica. The Skira was a complex festival, and the evidence for it is fragmentary, but the festival's unifying theme is the relationship of Eleusis to Athens. The festival, which defines the new relationship between the two towns, at the same

Jacoby to the contest for Salamis in the first half of the sixth century BC (Jacoby, commentary on Philochorus *FGrHist* 328 F 107, pp. 430–431); in this myth three of Attica's four parts correspond to the three-party strife following the reforms of Solon (plain, shore, and diakria), but the fourth part, Megara, is an addition reflecting the contest for Salamis. Eleusis, between Athens and Megara, was necessarily part of Pandion's kingdom in terms of this myth; Pandion was preceded by Erechtheus, who first won Eleusis for Athens, so the myths are not in conflict (for the succession Kekrops - Erechtheus - Pandion - Aegeus, see Herodotus 8.44 and 1.173 and Jacoby, commentary on Hellanicus *FGrHist* 4 F 38–49). There is a question what part, if any, Eleusis played in the three-party strife of the sixth century BC; the "plain" (*pedíon*) seems to have meant the Kephisos plain north of Athens and not to have included the Thriasian plain and Eleusis, which are geographically distinct. This issue is discussed in EN3.10.

168 One of Athens' great glories was that it shared with the world Demeter's two gifts, agriculture and the Mysteries. Isocrates *Panegyricus* 4.28–29, referring to the two gifts as τούς τε καρπούς...καὶ τὴν τελετήν, "fruits...and initiation," takes them as signs not only of the goddess's favor toward Athens, but also of Athens' philanthropy toward all mankind: οὕτως ἡ πόλις ἡμῶν οὐ μόνον θεοφιλῶς, ἀλλὰ καὶ φιλανθρώπως ἔσχεν, ὥστε κυρία γενομένη τοσούτων ἀγαθῶν οὐκ ἐφθόνησεν τοῖς ἄλλοις, ἀλλ᾽ ὧν ἔλαβεν ἅπασιν μετέδωκεν, "Our city was not only so god-loving, but also so man-loving, that having become master of so many good things it did not begrudge them to other people, but gave all a share in what it had acquired." Here "our city" (ἡ πόλις ἡμῶν) is of course Athens, not Eleusis, which had long ceased to get the credit apart from Athens (cf. Clinton 1994:161; Anderson 2003:185, 192–194). In a similar way the mythic war against Eleusis became instead, in the fourth century BC, the war against Thracian barbarians, with little thought any more of Eleusis (Demosthenes 60.8; cf. Parker 1987:203–204).

169 This festival gave its name to the month in which it was celebrated, Skirophorion, the last month of the Attic year, immediately before the summer solstice.

time redefines the old relationship between Erechtheus and Athena, who no longer shared a matrimonial bond in Athena's old temple on the Acropolis.

§3.66 In the ritual procession of the Skira, which went from the Acropolis to a place on the western outskirts of Athens called Skiron, the priest of Erechtheus and the priestess of Athena were the main participants (a priest of Helios also took part). The festival occurred shortly before the summer solstice, and the procession walked under a large parasol held by members of the same illustrious family from which both the priestess of Athena and the priest of Erechtheus came, the Eteoboutads.[170] Although the priestess of Athena in this procession can only have been the priestess of Athena Polias,[171] the festival of the Skira, according to one source, belonged to Athena Skiras. The same source says that opinion was divided as to whether

---

170 Harpokration s.v. Σκίρον (who refers to Lysimachides, a writer on festivals probably of the Augustan age) attests most of these details (except that here the priest is called Poseidon's rather than Erechtheus's): Σκίρα ἑορτὴ παρ' Ἀθηναίοις, ἀφ' ἧς καὶ ὁ μὴν Σκιροφοριών. φασὶ δὲ οἱ γράψαντες περί τε μηνῶν καὶ ἑορτῶν τῶν Ἀθήνησιν, ὧν ἐστι καὶ Λυσιμαχίδης, ὡς τὸ σκίρον σκιάδιόν ἐστι μέγα, ὑφ' ᾧ φερομένῳ ἐξ ἀκροπόλεως εἴς τινα τόπον καλούμενον Σκίρον πορεύονται ἥ τε τῆς Ἀθηνᾶς ἱέρεια καὶ ὁ τοῦ Ποσειδῶνος ἱερεὺς καὶ ὁ τοῦ Ἡλίου· κομίζουσι δὲ τοῦτο Ἐτεοβουτάδαι, "The Skira, a festival of the Athenians, from which the name of the month Skirophorion comes. Those who write about the months and festivals in Athens, among whom is Lysimachides, say that the skíron is a large parasol, under which, when it is carried from the Acropolis to a place called Skiron, the priestess of Athena and the priest of Poseidon and the priest of Helios proceed. Eteoboutads carry it." Here the festival's name Skíra is derived from a noun skíron, "parasol," which is unknown outside the context of the festival (the noun occurs again in this context in the scholia to Aristophanes Ecclesiazusae 18; see n3.172 below); a reverse process of derivation is more likely to be true: i.e. the name Skirophória probably gave rise to the noun skíron to reflect a ritual of the festival, namely the carrying of a "parasol," the proper name for which (skiádion, from skía, "shade") is vaguely similar. As this folk etymology shows, one no longer knew what the name Skíra meant, nor are we much wiser; the relevant meaning of the word group to which Skíra belongs seems to be "gypsum, lime," but the actual relevance of this meaning to the festival is not immediately apparent. For the Skíra see Brumfield 1981:156–181, with references to the older literature. Discussing the wide range of meanings of such related forms as skîros, skíra, skíron, Brumfield focuses on gê leuké, "white earth," i.e. "gypsum, lime" (ἡ σκίρα δέ ἐστι γῆ λευκή, ὥσπερ γύψος, Photius Lexicon s.v. Skíros; Suda s.v. skîros), and considers the possibility that the Greeks practiced marling to fertilize fields. Her conclusion (pp. 169–170) is that this practice cannot be proved, and that, if it lies behind the festival of the Skira, it cannot be connected with the festival's known ritual (pp. 174–175; the scholia to Aristophanes Wasps 926, which say that Athena Skiras was anointed with white earth, could preserve a relic, but this information may also be guesswork). In my view the reason for the lack of connection is that the festival, which probably had its origins at an early time outside Attica, was adapted to a later set of historical circumstances within Attica (cf. n3.188 below). For discussion of festival names in -phória, including Skirophória, see Robertson 1983:245–248.

171 See e.g. Jacoby, commentary on Philochorus FGrHist 328 F 14–16, p. 289 and n72.

the Skira belonged to Athena at all: some thought that the festival belonged to Demeter and Kore.[172] The confusion seems to have arisen because all the divinities in question, Athena and Erechtheus on the one hand and Demeter and Kore on the other hand, were apparently involved in the ritual at Skiron. Skiron was located on the Sacred Way to Eleusis, near where it crossed the Kephisos River, which is the presumed western boundary of early Athens.[173] The procession of the Skira to this former boundary point has been plausibly connected with the incorporation of Eleusis into Attica: the ritual at Skiron, if it involved both Athena and Demeter, seems to have represented a kind of "religious compromise" between Athens and Eleusis.[174]

172 Scholia to Aristophanes *Ecclesiazusae* 18 (this source refers to the priest of Erechtheus, not of Poseidon): Σκίρα ἑορτή ἐστι τῆς Σκιράδος Ἀθηνᾶς, Σκιροφοριῶνος ιβ'. οἱ δὲ Δήμητρος καὶ Κόρης. ἐν ᾗ ὁ ἱερεὺς τοῦ Ἐρεχθέως φέρει σκιάδειον λευκόν, ὃ λέγεται σκῖρον, "The Skira is a festival of Athena Skiras, on the twelfth of Skirophorion. Some say it is of Demeter and Kore. In it the priest of Erechtheus carries a white parasol, which is called a *skĩron*." Other sources as well attest uncertainty about the goddess(es) to whom the festival belonged: scholia to Aristophanes *Thesmophoriazusae* 834: Σκίρα λέγεσθαί φασί τινες τὰ γινόμενα ἱερὰ ἐν τῇ ἑορτῇ ταύτῃ <u>Δήμητρι καὶ Κόρῃ</u>. οἱ δέ, ὅτι ἐπὶ Σκίρῳ θύεται τῇ <u>Ἀθηνᾷ</u>, "Some say the sacred rites that take place <u>for Demeter and Kore</u> in this festival are called the Skira. Others say that sacrifices are made <u>to Athena</u> in Skiron"; Stephanus of Byzantium s.v. Σκίρος· Σκίρα δὲ κέκληται, τινὲς μὲν ὅτι ἐπὶ Σκίρῳ <u>Ἀθηνᾷ</u> ['Ἀθήνῃσι codd.] θύεται, ἄλλοι δὲ ἀπὸ τῶν γινομένων ἱερῶν <u>Δήμητρι καὶ Κόρῃ</u> ἐν τῇ ἑορτῇ ταύτῃ ἐπὶ Σκίρῳ κέκληται, "It is called the Skira, some say because sacrifices are made <u>to Athena</u> at Skiron, but others say that it is named from the sacrifices that take place <u>for Demeter and Kore</u> in this festival at Skiron."

173 For the Kephisos as Athens' old boundary on the road to Eleusis see Deubner 1932:48, who draws this conclusion from the fact that Theseus, when he returns to Athens after slaying various evildoers, is ritually purified on the far side of the Kephisos at the altar of Zeus Meilichios before entering the city (Pausanias 1.37.4; Plutarch *Theseus* 12.1). Zeus Meilichios is a god of atonement, and his altar, in Deubner's view, served as a kind of "sacred quarantine station" which would have seen regular use by those returning to the city who were in need of purification. That the Kephisos was a boundary point on the Sacred Way seems also to be confirmed by a fragment of the *Atakta* of Istros (*FGrHist* 334 F 17). This piece of evidence is discussed in EN3.11.

174 The idea of a "religionsgeschichtliches Compromiss" was first proposed by Robert 1885:378, and has been widely accepted; cf. Simon 1983:23–24, who argues that the role of the priest of Helios in the procession to Skiron was to witness the annual renewal of a kind of "contract" (for Helios as an oath-god cf. *Iliad* 3.277). Robert took as a further instance of such a compromise the tradition for three "sacred plowings" (*árotoi hieroí*) at Athens, Eleusis, and Skiron, attested by Plutarch *Advice to the Bride and Groom* 144ab: Ἀθηναῖοι τρεῖς ἀρότους ἱεροὺς ἄγουσι, πρῶτον ἐπὶ Σκίρῳ, τοῦ παλαιοτάτου τῶν σπόρων ὑπόμνημα, δεύτερον ἐν τῇ Ῥαρίᾳ, τρίτον ὑπὸ πόλιν τὸν καλούμενον Βουζύγιον, "The Athenians perform three sacred plowings, the first in Skiron, commemorating the oldest sowing, the second in Rharia, the third under the acropolis, called the Bouzygion (ox-yoke [plowing])." According to Robert's interpretation of this evidence, which I find convincing, Athens and Eleusis both had old traditions that they were the first to plow land for planting crops,

§3.67 Pausanias, approaching the Kephisos on the Sacred Way from Athens, mentions a shrine belonging to all four of the gods in question for the Skira: Demeter and Kore, Athena and (in place of Erechtheus) Poseidon; after this shrine only one tomb remains before the river itself is crossed. The shrine of the four gods, which seems to fit exactly the notion of religious compromise as far as the gods worshipped there are concerned, and which is very close to Athens' old boundary point, has been claimed for the celebration of the Skira at the end of the ritual procession from the Acropolis.[175] The difficulty is that the location of this shrine is not called Skiron, but Lakiadai (a deme);[176] Skiron occurs a little earlier in Pausanias's account and was there-

Athens in a field beneath the Acropolis and Eleusis in the "Rharian Plain"; when the two cities were united, Skiron, by way of compromise, was given the distinction of having carried out the first plowing, replacing (or joining) both the others in this distinction. Jacoby accepts Robert's argument that the Skira represent a compromise between Athens and Eleusis, but he follows a different interpretation of the sacred plowings (see Jacoby, commentary on Philochorus *FGrHist* 328 F 14–16, n80, pp. 204 and 206); for yet another view of the tradition for the three sacred plowings see Sourvinou-Inwood 1997:147–148. Both Toepffer and Jacoby reject Robert's attempt to prove that there was no cult of Athena Skiras at Skiron, and that the Skira thus had nothing to do with Athena Skiras (Toepffer 1889:119n2; Jacoby, commentary on Philochorus *FGrHist* 328 F 14–16, n8, pp. 194–195); both cite Rohde's arguments against Robert's thesis (Rohde 1886). A connection of the procession of the Skira with Eleusis may be further suggested by another detail: a particular kind of fleece called the *Diòs kṓidion* ("Zeus's little fleece") was used in purification rites by the organizers of the Skira procession and by the torchbearer (*dāidoûkhos*) at Eleusis, as well as by others who performed purification rites (Suda s.v. Διὸς κῴδιον· ...χρῶνται δ' αὐτοῖς οἵ τε Σκιροφορίων τὴν πομπὴν στέλλοντες καὶ ὁ δᾳδοῦχος ἐν Ἐλευσῖνι, καὶ ἄλλοι τινὲς πρὸς τοὺς καθαρμοὺς ὑποστορνύντες αὐτὰ τοῖς ποσὶ τῶν ἐναγῶν, "*Diòs kṓidion*: ...they are used by those who arrange the procession of the Skirophoria and by the torchbearer in Eleusis, and for purifications by certain others, who spread them under the feet of the polluted"; see Toepffer 1889:120n2; Jacoby, commentary on Philochorus *FGrHist* 328 F 14–16, n80, p. 206; Deubner 1932:49n4, 77–78). That the Skira festival is essentially concerned with a boundary (namely the old boundary between Athens and Eleusis) is supported by a ball game called *epískuros*. The game, which may be attested as early as the late sixth century BC, contains in its name an alternate form *skûros* of the word for "gypsum, lime" found in the name *Skíra*. As Elmer 2008 shows, the game, which takes its name from a center line made (probably) of white limestone gravel, "can be understood as a symbolization of a boundary dispute"; see Elmer for the ancient evidence and the modern studies of the game, in which two opposing teams competed to win sole possession of a playing field held "in common" at the start of the game (an alternate name of the game is *epíkoinos*, "in common"). The relevance of this anthropological evidence to the religious and political meaning of the Skira, which also has to do with a boundary, seems clear.

175 So Deubner 1932:47–48, following Pfister *RE* 'Skira' 531, who develops an "analogy" of van der Loeff 1916:329 (see Jacoby, commentary on Philochorus FGrHist 328 F 14–16, n80, pp. 204–205).

176 Pausanias 1.37.2: προελθοῦσι δὲ ὀλίγον Λακίου τέμενός ἐστιν ἥρωος καὶ δῆμος ὃν Λακιάδας ὀνομάζουσιν ἀπὸ τούτου.... ἔστι δὲ καὶ...Δήμητρος ἱερὸν καὶ τῆς παιδός· σὺν δέ σφισιν

fore farther from the river (nearer the Acropolis) than Lakiadai.[177] Thus while the temple at Lakiadai may have been the goal of the Skira procession, there is reason to think that this was not the case.[178]

Ἀθηνᾶ καὶ Ποσειδῶν ἔχουσι τιμάς, "As one proceeds a little farther there is the precinct of Lakios, a hero, and the deme which they call Lakiadai after him.... And there is also...a temple of Demeter and her daughter; with them Athena and Poseidon also receive honors." The passage goes on to tell how the hero Phytalos received Demeter here, and how she gave him the first fig tree.

177 Pausanias speaks of "a place called Skiron" (χωρίον Σκῖρον...καλούμενον, 1.36.4); he explains its connection with the war of the Eleusinians against Erechtheus (see below), but he gives no physical description of the place except that there was also a torrent there called Skiron. Before he reaches the shrine of the four gods in Lakiadai Pausanias describes three intervening tombs (1.36.5–1.37.1). This does not make clear what the distance was between Skiron and Lakiadai, but it was presumably not very great. The fact remains, however, that Pausanias treats the two places as different, and the temple of the four gods is in Lakiadai, not Skiron, in his account. Deubner's suggestion (1932:47) that Pausanias describes tombs on one side of the road and then returns on the other side of the road to Skiron, and to a previously omitted temple (the one in question), is not convincing. Judeich 1931:177 describes the location of Skiron in general terms as "to be sought near the Themistoclean circular wall north of the Sacred Way in the outer Kerameikos" ("nahe dem themistokleischen Mauerring nördlich der heiligen Strasse im äusseren Kerameikos zu suchen").

178 Jacoby, commentary on Philochorus FGrHist 328 F 14–16, n80, pp. 204–205, does not accept that this shrine was used in the Skira. Its location is his main (but not only) objection. Like others he believes that the Skira involved a religious compromise between Athena and Demeter, but he also believes that there were other contexts for this compromise: "There was a great number of stories dealing with the reconciliation between Demeter and Athena, and many different cults attesting it. We know few of these stories, but to efface distinctions would be wrong in general, and in the case of the Skira in particular." Robertson 1996:73n96 sees matters differently, commenting that Jacoby "would separate Pausanias's temple from the area of Skiron, for no good reason." Robertson considers the temple of Zephyros, which was next to the temple of the four gods in Lakiadai, to be related to the Skira, and he therefore minimizes the fact that Pausanias distinguishes Lakiadai from Skiron. Jacoby, for his part, believes strongly that there was a cult of Athena Skiras in Skiron, and for him this was the probable goal of the Skira procession. Although such a cult is not attested by Pausanias (a point minimized by Jacoby, commentary on Philochorus FGrHist 328 F 14–16, p. 291), I think that Jacoby has good reason to insist that the Skira took place in Skiron. There is an important piece of indirect evidence in Strabo 9.1.9, who mentions "a ritual in Skiron" (ἐπὶ Σκίρῳ ἱεροποιία τις) in a discussion of two earlier names of Salamis, one of which was Skiras: καὶ γὰρ Σκιρὰς καὶ Κύχρεια ἀπό τινων ἡρώων, ἀφ' οὗ μὲν Ἀθηνᾶ τε λέγεται Σκιρὰς καὶ τόπος Σκίρα ἐν τῇ Ἀττικῇ καὶ ἐπὶ Σκίρῳ ἱεροποιία τις καὶ ὁ μὴν ὁ Σκιροφοριών, "indeed [it was called] Skiras and Kykhreia after certain heroes, after [one of] whom Athena is called Skiras and a place in Attica is called Skira and a certain ritual in Skiron and the month Skirophorion" (that Strabo calls the "place in Attica" Skíra rather than Skíron seems to be a simple mistake: he has given the festival name rather than the place-name; he may also have misunderstood the under-lined phrase, on which see below). The "ritual in Skiron" of Strabo is surely the Skira; Robert, who argued that the Skira have nothing to do with Athena Skiras or Skiron, took

§3.68 The ritual of the Skira is not known in enough detail to prove the religious compromise between Athens and Eleusis that the festival is widely thought to have been. But when we consider the myth of Erechtheus, the case becomes clearer. Erechtheus defeated the Eleusinians when they and their Thracian allies brought war on Athens. Skiron played a part in this war, for it was here that a prophet named Skiros, who fought for Eleusis, died and gave his name to the place of his death and burial. Pausanias, our source for this tradition, implies that there was a tomb of Skiros near the torrent Skiron (both the torrent and the place were named for him).[179] Pausanias says that the prophet Skiros came from Dodona, but this detail appears secondary; Philochorus in the fourth century BC refers to an Eleusinian prophet Skiros, saying that Athena Skiras was named for him.[180] We seem to be dealing with one and the same

---

Strabo's phrase ἐπὶ Σκίρῳ ἱεροποιία τις to mean a "ritual *for* (the hero) *Skiros*," but Rohde refuted Robert on this point among others (cf. n3.174 above). For the meaning "in Skiron" of the phrase ἐπὶ Σκίρῳ in Strabo note the same meaning of the same phrase in three other passages quoted above: Plutarch *Advice to the Bride and Groom* 144ab (quoted in n3.174 above); scholia to Aristophanes *Thesmophoriazusae* 834; and Stephanus of Byzantium s.v. Σκίρος (both quoted in n3.172 above). To add to the complexity of the temple of the four gods in Lakiadai, Pausanias, as previously mentioned (n3.176 above), tells us that the hero Phytalos first welcomed Demeter here; Toepffer 1889:135n2, 247–254 interprets this to mean that Phytalos (whom he associates with Poseidon Phytalmios in Troizen) had a cult here first, and that Demeter was brought into this cult secondarily from Eleusis.

179 Pausanias 1.36.4: Ἐλευσινίοις πολεμοῦσι πρὸς Ἐρεχθέα ἀνὴρ μάντις ἦλθεν ἐκ Δωδώνης ὄνομα Σκίρος...· πεσόντα δὲ αὐτὸν ἐν τῇ μάχῃ θάπτουσιν Ἐλευσίνιοι πλησίον ποταμοῦ χειμάρρου, καὶ τῷ τε χωρίῳ τὸ ὄνομα ἀπὸ τοῦ ἥρωός ἐστι καὶ τῷ ποταμῷ, "When the Eleusinians fought against Erechtheus a prophet came to them from Dodona by the name of Skiros...; he fell in the battle and the Eleusinians buried him near the river torrent, and the name of both the place and the river is from this hero."

180 Harpokration s.v. Σκίρον (= Philochorus *FGrHist* 328 F 14). This source attests a dispute between the Athenians and the Megarians as to the identity of the hero for whom Athena Skiras was named: Philochorus is cited for the derivation of her name ἀπὸ Σκίρου τινὸς Ἐλευσινίου μάντεως, "from a certain Skiros, an Eleusinian prophet"; the Megarian historian Praxion is cited for a derivation ἀπὸ Σκίρωνος, "from *Skírōn*," a Megarian figure. Despite the fact that Pausanias is the first to call Skiros a prophet from Dodona, and that Philochorus in the fragment above calls him an Eleusinian prophet, Jacoby argues that Philochorus too may have called him a prophet from Dodona, and that the tradition for this may be even older than Philochorus (Jacoby, commentary on Philochorus *FGrHist* 328 F 14–16, p. 290 and n81, pp. 292–293). Jacoby's argument is that the prophet associated with the grave in Skiron was said to have come from Dodona in order to separate him from the Megarian figure *Skírōn* from whom the Megarian historian Praxion derived the name of Athena Skiras. The Megarian figure *Skírōn* was said to have held the war command (*hēgemonía polémou*) when Nisos was king of Megara (Pausanias 1.39.6), and to have been killed in Eleusis when Theseus took Eleusis from Diocles (Plutarch *Theseus* 10.3). Philochorus, according to Jacoby, commentary on Philochorus *FGrHist* 328 F 14–16, pp. 292–293, "wished...to distinguish the Eleusinian Skiros, whom united Athens had admitted to her cult,...from the Megarian Σκίρων," hence his "invention of a pious prophet who came to Eleusis from Dodona: Skiros

figure here.[181] In any event it is clear that the procession of Erechtheus's priest and Athena's priestess to Skiron in the festival of the Skira was associated with the war in which Eleusis was won for Athens; the very place was named for a prophet who took part in that war on the side of Eleusis.

§3.69 There is more to say about Athena Skiras and the male figure Skiros as a pair, and this is relevant to Athena Polias and Erechtheus as a pair. Philochorus connected Athena Skiras closely with the Eleusinian prophet Skiros by deriving her name from his. A cult of Athena Skiras is not directly attested for Skiron, but the burial there of a prophet named Skiros clearly suggests one: Philochorus must have had a reason for deriving the name of Athena Skiras from that of the Eleusinian prophet, and the reason would seem to be to connect the prophet's tomb in Skiron with a cult of the goddess in the same place.[182] Such a close association between Athena Skiras and a figure

---

could not remain a Megarian." As said, Jacoby suggests that this invention may have been older than Philochorus ("the aetiological legend that a prophet from Dodona came to the assistance of the Eleusinians bears the closest resemblance to the story of the Thracian Eumolpos, but gives the impression of being much older in its nucleus," commentary on Philochorus *FGrHist* 328 F 14–16, p. 290; cf. n81), but there is no actual evidence of this. There are allusions to Dodona in two fragments of Euripides' *Erechtheus* (frs. 58 and 59 Austin), but Jacoby, commentary on Philochorus *FGrHist* 328 F 14–16, n81, does not accept these as even probable evidence that Euripides knew of a prophet from Dodona. Treu 1971:128–129 supposes that if there was a seer from Dodona in Euripides' *Erechtheus*, his role was on behalf of Athens rather than Eleusis, namely to motivate a reluctant Erechtheus to accept Delphi's command and sacrifice his daughter for the sake of an Athenian victory.

181 Even the Megarian figure *Skírōn* (see n3.180 above) is agreed to be ultimately the same figure (see Jacoby, commentary on Philochorus *FGrHist* 328 F 14–16, p. 293 and n104). The difference in the form of the names *Skíros* and *Skírōn* is secondary, reflecting rival Athenian and Megarian traditions (cf. Jacoby, commentary on Philochorus *FGrHist* 328 F 14–16, nn84 and 81). The Megarian figure is always *Skírōn*, and Athenian tradition made of him a robber whom Theseus slew by throwing him down a precipitous cliff, the "Skironian rocks" (Σκειρωνίδες πέτραι) on the coast west of Megara (Strabo 9.1.4, etc.); the Megarian writers denied all of this with proofs of Skiron's good character (Plutarch *Theseus* 10.2–3). Jacoby, noting that the Megarian Skiron "was as closely connected with Eleusis as with the Scironian rocks," leaves open the possibility that the Megarians first introduced Skiros (and a presumed goddess Skiras) to the place Skiron west of Athens on the Kephisos River (Jacoby, commentary on Philochorus *FGrHist* 328 F 14–16, n104).

182 For indirect evidence of a cult of Athena Skiras in Skiron see n3.178 above. Jacoby is convinced that Philochorus knew of such a cult in Skiron (cf. his commentary on Philochorus *FGrHist* 328 F 14–16, p. 291: "There can be no doubt that Philochoros is the authority for the version that Athena Skiras, who derives her name from Skiros, has her residence in the χωρίον Σκίρον, which equally has its name from the mantis Skiros buried there"; cf. also Jacoby, commentary on Philochorus *FGrHist* 328 F 14–16, p. 290). Other possible evidence for the cult in Skiron includes Photius *Lexicon* s.v. Σκίρον· τόπος Ἀθήνησιν, ἐφ' οὗ οἱ μάντεις ἐκαθέζοντο· καὶ Σκιράδος Ἀθηνᾶς ἱερόν· καὶ ἡ ἑορτὴ Σκιρά· οὕτω Φερεκράτης. "Skiron: a place in Athens, where prophets sat; and a temple of Athena

named Skiros is confirmed elsewhere. In Phaleron there was a well-attested cult of Athena Skiras in which there was a male figure Skiros who received divine honors on her very altar.[183] The *génos* of the Salaminioi that administered this cult is widely thought to have brought the cult with them to Athens when they were driven from Salamis by the Megarians in the late seventh century BC.[184] The cult of Athena Skiras on Salamis, the presumed ancestor of the cult in Phaleron, is attested by Herodotus in a story concerning the Battle of Salamis in 480 BC; it is also suggested in the tradition for Solon's capture of the island about 600 BC.[185] In traditions about Salamis two male figures

Skiras; and the Skira festival; so Pherekrates." Brumfield 1981:167, 178n44 takes this as evidence that the fifth-century comic playwright Pherekrates is Photius's authority for a temple of Athena Skiras in Skiron; Jacoby, on the other hand, does "not infer more for Pherecrates than that he, like Aristophanes, mentioned the Skira" (Jacoby, commentary on Philochorus *FGrHist* 328 F 14–16, n87). The scholia to Aristophanes *Ecclesiazusae* 18 call the Skira a festival of Athena Skiras, but here Skiron is of course not mentioned (see n3.172 above).

183 The cult is mentioned by Pausanias 1.1.4: ἐνταῦθα [in Phaleron] καὶ Σκιράδος Ἀθηνᾶς ναός ἐστι, "here [in Phaleron] there is also a temple of Athena Skiras"; IG II² 1232 line 23; Pausanias 1.36.4 (cf. n3.189 below and Jacoby, commentary on Philochorus *FGrHist* 328 F 14–16, pp. 292–293). The main evidence for the cult comes from an inscription of 363/2 BC containing a covenant between the two branches of the *génos* of the Salaminioi, which together administered the cult. The inscription, *Agora Inventory* I 3244, was edited with a commentary by Ferguson 1938:1–9; cf. also Nilsson 1938. Besides detailed regulations about the cult there is a full sacrificial calendar. Athena Skiras is named in lines 52 and 93 (Skiras alone appears in line 41); in line 93 Athena Skiras and Skiros are both named as recipients of sacrifices at the goddess's altar in the month Maimakterion (cf. Ferguson, p. 18). Jacoby, commentary on Philochorus *FGrHist* 328 F 14–16, n7, drew from this the conclusion that Skiros was originally a god and was still worshipped as such in Phaleron: "The Skiros of the Salaminioi is a partner in the cult with Athena Skiras, and as such he is a god. Both (and only these two) receive a sacrifice in Maimakterion (probably on the same day), Athena Skiras an οἶς ἐγκύμων ['pregnant sheep'] for 12, Skiros an οἶς ['sheep'] for 15 drachmae (3244, 93)."

184 Ferguson and Nilsson both assume that the refugees from Salamis constituted themselves as the *génos* of the Salaminioi after they resettled in Attica; one group ("the Salaminioi from the seven tribes") had its center in Melite in Athens, another group lived in Sounion ("the Salaminioi from Sounion"). Guarducci 1948 argues that the Salaminioi originated as an Attic *génos* on Salamis itself, which was therefore Attic before they were expelled. The two branches of the *génos*, which arranged cult matters between them in the inscription of 363/2 BC, had become separate *géne* by about 230/29 BC, as evidenced by another inscription, *Agora Inventory* I 3394 (also edited by Ferguson 1938:9–12). For the Salaminioi see also Parker 1996:308–316.

185 According to a story told by Athenians, and denied by Corinthians, the Corinthians fled in their ships at the start of the Battle of Salamis and were met on their way out by another boat which uncannily already knew of the Greek victory; the Corinthians heard this news and turned back just as they passed the temple of Athena Skiras on Salamis (ὡς δὲ ἄρα φεύγοντας γίνεσθαι τῆς Σαλαμινίης κατὰ ⟨τὸ⟩ ἱρὸν Ἀθηναίης Σκιράδος, περιπίπτειν σφι κέλητα θείη πομπῇ, κτλ., Herodotus 8.94.2). According to Plutarch *Solon* 9.4, the Athenians

named Skiros are distinguishable, one a founder and the other a king of the
island city.[186] But these seem to be the result of literary speculation about a

---

had an annual ceremony reenacting Solon's capture of Salamis in which an attacker
would leap from a ship and run to the top of a cliff referred to as ἄκρον τὸ Σκιράδιον,
"Cape Skiradion," near where Solon had defeated the Megarians and founded a temple
of Enyalios: ναῦς γάρ τις Ἀττικὴ προσέπλει σιωπῇ τὸ πρῶτον, εἶτα κραυγῇ καὶ ἀλαλαγμῷ
προσφερομένων, εἰς ἀνὴρ ἔνοπλος ἐξαλλόμενος μετὰ βοῆς ἔθει πρὸς ἄκρον τὸ Σκιράδιον,
"An Attic ship would sail there silently at first, then with cries and shouts they would be
carried along and one armed man would jump out with a shout and run to Cape Skiradion";
see Ferguson, p. 18, and Jacoby, commentary on Philochorus *FGrHist* 328 F 14–16, n96,
who are surely correct in taking this to be the location of the temple of Athena Skiras
(Robertson1996:74n99 gives modern Cape Arapis as the location). Strabo 9.1.9 associates
Athena's name Skiras with Salamis (Skiras was an old name of Salamis that came from the
same hero Skiros as did Athena's name; cf. n3.186 below); from this it is clear that Salamis
was an important center of the cult, perhaps the very center of it (cf. Ferguson, p. 18).

186   Strabo 9.1.9 says that Salamis received one of its former names, Skiras, from a hero named
Skiros: ἐκαλεῖτο δ' ἑτέροις ὀνόμασι τὸ παλαιόν· καὶ γὰρ Σκιρὰς καὶ Κύχρεια ἀπό τινων
ἡρώων, "In ancient times it was called by different names: indeed [it was called] Skiras
and Kykhreia after certain heroes"; this primeval figure Skiros is elsewhere called a son of
Poseidon who married the nymph Salamis (Hesychius s.v. Σκ[ε]ιρὰς Ἀθηνᾶ) and founded
Salamis (Suda s.v. Σκῖρος). It was from a king of Salamis named Skiros that Theseus got
the helmsman and prowman for his voyage to Crete (the king also sent his grandson on
the voyage); to Philochorus, the source for this myth, hero cults (*hērôia*) next to a shrine
(*hierón*) of Skiros in Phaleron bore witness to the helmsman and prowman (Plutarch *Theseus*
17.6 = Philochorus *FGrHist* 328 F 111): Φιλόχορος δὲ παρὰ Σκίρου φησὶν ἐκ Σαλαμῖνος τὸν
Θησέα λαβεῖν κυβερνήτην μὲν Ναυσίθοον, πρῳρέα δὲ Φαίακα, μηδέπω τότε τῶν Ἀθηναίων
προσεχόντων τῇ θαλάσσῃ· καὶ γὰρ εἶναι τῶν ἠιθέων ἕνα Μενέσθην Σκίρου θυγατριδοῦν·
μαρτυρεῖν δὲ τούτοις ἡρῷα Ναυσιθόου καὶ Φαίακος εἰσαμένου Θησέως Φαληροῖ πρὸς τῷ
τοῦ Σκίρου ἱερῷ, "Philochorus says that Theseus got his helmsman Nausithoos and his
bow-commander Phaeax from Skiros in Salamis, since the Athenians did not yet pay atten-
tion to the sea, and that in fact one of the unmarried youths was Menesthes, the son of
Skiros's daughter; hero shrines of Nausithoos and Phaeax, which Theseus established in
Phaleron next to the temple of Skiros, bear witness to these figures." Jacoby, commentary
on Philochorus *FGrHist* 328 F 111, n10, associates the shrine of Skiros in this passage with
the figure Skiros who receives divine honors in Phaleron together with Athena Skiras in
Agora Inventory I 3244 "although even *Agora* I 3244 mentions the priest of Athena Skiras
only, not that of her partner Skiros." What Philochorus calls a *hierón* of Skiros was more
likely a *hērôion* within the sacred enclosure of Athena Skiras; Wilamowitz deleted the
word ἱερῷ to get this sense, but Jacoby, commentary on Philochorus *FGrHist* F 111, n10,
retains the reading of the text on the grounds that Philochorus was less concerned with
explaining the cult in Phaleron than with other matters: "when dealing with the report
of Philochorus about the expedition to Crete we actually do not move in the realm of cult
but in that of the mythos or, more correctly, the turning of mythos into history. Thus the
omission of the goddess is to be explained: Theseus has little or nothing to do with Athena
either in general or in his expedition to Crete." Jacoby is more explicit about the *hierón* of
Skiros in his commentary on Philochorus *FGrHist* 328 F 14–16, n7: "The Skiros of F 111 is
king of Salamis, but Philochorus also knows (*ib.*) a Σκίρου ἱερόν at Phaleron, and we cannot
tell at once whether the occupant of this ἱερόν is the Salaminian king or whether the
temple of Athena Skiras is meant, in which the Salaminioi worshipped their god Skiros by

figure who, as we see in Phaleron, was once closely associated with Athena Skiras in cult. The original cult pair was probably a goddess Skiras and a god Skiros, before Athena absorbed the goddess Skiras, and in so doing freed Skiros to undergo transformations of his own.[187] The loosening of the bond between the original pair is in my view the same as what happened between Athena Polias and Erechtheus. This is important for the meaning of the Skira procession, if that procession ended in what was once a cult site of Skiras and Skiros, whose bond had now been loosened: if the procession, that is, ended in a place where Skiras had become Athena Skiras, and Skiros had become a prophet who died for Eleusis.[188] In the procession from the Acropolis to this

---

the side of Athena Skiras" (cf. also Jacoby, commentary on Philochorus *FGrHist* 328 F 14–16, p. 286). In Jacoby's reconstruction the Salaminian king and the god of the Salaminioi go back to the same original figure, "the cult-fellow of the goddess, the Salaminian-Phalerian Skiros, who had become free for aitiological speculation when Skiras became Athena Skiras" (p. 299).

187 This is Jacoby's reconstruction, which is somewhat speculative, but, I think, essentially correct; cf. his commentary on Philochorus *FGrHist* 328 F 14–16, n4: "The cult of the clan was at some time acknowledged by the [Athenian] State and taken over to a certain degree, surely when the clan immigrated. At that time the goddess Skiras, whom they brought with them, became Athena Skiras, symbolizing the union. This had far-reaching consequences for the literary tradition, for her cultic companion Skiros retained his simple old name because he could not be used in the same way; he thus became free for the historical-aitiological speculations of Atthidography. The clan kept to the divine person (n. 7 [quoted previous note]), but here too he was overshadowed by his female partner (cf. n. 105, Text p. 304, 33ff.)." Cf. also Ferguson 1938:19: "One fact on which modern scholars are agreed is that Skiras was a Salaminian deity, taken over by the Athenians. Since Skiros shared her altar at Phaleron, he may have been her associate on the island also. Whether she was identified with Athena before being transplanted, or only on her arrival, we cannot say for certain. The latter is the view of Gjerstad [1929:224]. Skiras and Skiros plainly go together (cf. *IG* II² 1358, where a *hērōínē* regularly accompanies a *hērōs*)."

188 As Jacoby reconstructs the (unattested) cult of Athena Skiras in Skiron, the pair Skiras-Skiros was imported here as it was in Phaleron, although it is debatable whether the cult came from Salamis or perhaps from Megara-Eleusis (only the male *Skírōn* is found in Megara-Eleusis, not a goddess Skiras [Jacoby, commentary on Philochorus *FGrHist* 328 F 14–16, n104]). In any case Megara-Eleusis-Salamis is a "closely knit geographical area," and Skiras-Skiros belong to it, whereas in Attica they are "intruders" (Ferguson 1938:19, who speaks only of Skiros, but his statement applies equally to Skiras; cf. Jacoby, commentary on Philochorus *FGrHist* 328 F 14–16, n104). This was an agrarian pair of gods and in Skiron a cult association between Skiras and Demeter may have developed next (Jacoby, commentary on Philochorus *FGrHist* 328 F 14–16, n77, p. 203). Finally, when Eleusis was incorporated into Attica, Skiras became Athena Skiras in this old borderland site "as a symbol of the political union"; Demeter, on the other hand, was too great a goddess to be subordinated to Athena in this way (Jacoby, commentary on Philochorus *FGrHist* 328 F 14–16, n77, p. 203). The verbal root of Skiras and related names associates them with "lime, gypsum, white earth" (cf. n3.170 above) and (in one way or another) with agriculture (Jacoby, commentary on Philochorus *FGrHist* 328 F 14–16, nn15, 17, 77; Brumfield 1981:156–175).

place came the priestess of Athena Polias, who had become a solitary war goddess, and the priest of Erechtheus, who had become the hero who died for Athens and won Eleusis. The parallelism with the Skiras/Skiros pair is, I think, significant. Whatever the previous history of the Skira festival may have been, at least the procession to Skiron cannot well have been instituted before the incorporation of Eleusis into Attica. Given the correspondence of the festival name Skira with the names Skiras/Skiros and Skiron, further-more, there is some reason to think that the Skira festival itself was not insti-tuted until this relatively late event had taken place.[189]

The association with white earth and lime is relevant to geographical features in Salamis (τὸ Σκιράδιον ἄκρον, see n3.185 above) and in the vicinity of Megara (αἱ Σκειρωνίδες πέτραι, see n3.181 above), but not to imported cults of (Athena) Skiras in Attica (Jacoby, commentary on Philochorus *FGrHist* 328 F 14–16, n77, p. 202: "We need not ask whether the suburb Σκῖρον and the temple of Skiras at Phaleron were also built on calcareous soil..., for the cults of both these places are imported, not indigenous"). While Jacoby's recon-struction of the cults at Skiron is not the only possible one, the general sequence that he outlines seems to me to be right.

189 I am persuaded by Jacoby that the festival of the Skira was named for Athena Skiras, and that the goddess of this festival had a cult in Skiron. The cult of Athena Skiras in Phaleron, on the other hand, had nothing to do with the Skira so far as known. In Phaleron the chief festival in honor of Athena Skiras was the Oschophoria, which may also have honored Dionysus (see Jacoby, commentary on Philochorus *FGrHist* 328 F 14–16, p. 303 and n186, for Dionysus). A footrace in which youths carried a vine-branch loaded with grapes (an *ôskhos*) was probably part of this festival. Jacoby, commentary on Philochorus *FGrHist* 328 F 14–16, pp. 294–305, argues that the race was part of the Skira on the basis of the one source that specifies the Skira for the race, namely Aristodemos, a student of Aristarchus who wrote a commentary on Pindar (Athenaeus 11.495f = Aristodemus *FGrHist* 383 F 9, Philochorus *FGrHist* 328 F 15): Ἀριστόδημος δ' ἐν τρίτῳ περὶ Πινδάρου τοῖς Σκίροις φησὶν Ἀθήναζε (?) ἀγῶνα ἐπιτελεῖσθαι τῶν ἐφήβων δρόμου· τρέχειν δ' αὐτοὺς ἔχοντας ἀμπέλου κλάδον κατάκαρπον τὸν καλούμενον ὦσχον. τρέχουσι δ' ἐκ τοῦ ἱεροῦ τοῦ Διονύσου μέχρι τοῦ τῆς Σκιράδος Ἀθηνᾶς ἱεροῦ, καὶ ὁ νικήσας λαμβάνει κύλικα τὴν λεγομένην πενταπλόαν καὶ κωμάζει μετὰ χοροῦ, "Aristodemus in the third book of his work on Pindar says that the contest of the ephebes' race to Athens [? see below] is completed at the Skira and that they run holding a vine branch loaded with fruit called an *ôskhos*. They run from the temple of Dionysus to the temple of Athena Skiras, and the victor receives the cup called the *pentaplóa* ('having five ingredients') and revels with a chorus" [Ἀθήναζε, "to Athens," seems to be a scribal addition or error; see Jacoby, commentary on Philochorus *FGrHist* 328 F 14–16, n162 and cf. n125]. But Rutherford and Irvine 1988 have now shown that the ancient category of song called the oschophorikon, which takes its name from the festival of the Oschophoria, was epinician in nature, and that Pindar composed one such at least. It is thus best not to ignore other sources associating the Oschophoria with a race (see Rutherford and Irvine 1988:46n21) in favor of the Aristodemos fragment. This means that the temple of Athena Skiras mentioned in the Aristodemos frag-ment is not what Jacoby argued, a temple in Skiron (for which this would be the only direct evidence), but the temple in Phaleron. The two cults of Athena Skiras in Attica, while they seem to have had similar origins, contrast with each other in various ways. Jacoby's final summing up is as follows (commentary on Philochorus *FGrHist* 328 F 14–16, pp. 304–305): "The cult of Skiras...developed differently according to the different conditions at the two

§3.70 When Aristophanes mentions the Skira, he refers to rites that pertained solely to women.[190] These female rites were part of the larger festival of the Skira, and it was by a narrow use of the name that they were called Skira.[191] The female rites, which were sacred to Demeter and Kore,

---

places where it appeared in Attica. The chief difference is that at Phaleron (so far as we can see), it remained a pure cult of Athena Skiras and almost purely a cult of the *genos*, whereas at Skiron the cult entered into a connexion first with the goddesses of Eleusis, later with the deities of the Akropolis. Therefore the Oschophoria is a simple festival, the Skira a complicated one. Any inferences back to the ancient cult of Salamis must be made, if they are to have any certainty, particularly (if not only) from the cult at Phaleron." A common element between the two cults, which Jacoby brings out well (commentary on Philochorus *FGrHist* 328 F 14–16, n105), is that in both the goddess is the "symbol of the union with Athens of foreign elements: at Phaleron of the reception of the 'clan' Salaminioi, at Skiron (where she may even before have entered into a somewhat loose connexion with Demeter) of the union of Athens and Eleusis." If the two cults are basically not connected, a small puzzle remains (Jacoby has no answer for it), namely why Pausanias 1.36.4 should say of the prophet Skiros from Dodona, who died and was buried in Skiron, that he founded the temple of Athena Skiras in Phaleron (cf. Jacoby, commentary on Philochorus *FGrHist* 328 F 14–16, pp. 291–293).

190 The Skira are named with the Stenia (which belonged to the Thesmophoria; cf. Deubner 1932:46, 52–53 with 52n10) as a festival celebrated specifically by women in *Thesmophoriazusae* 832–835:

χρῆν γάρ, ἡμῶν εἰ τέκοι τις ἄνδρα χρηστὸν τῇ πόλει,
ταξίαρχον ἢ στρατηγόν, λαμβάνειν τιμήν τινα,
προεδρίαν τ' αὐτῇ δίδοσθαι Στηνίοισι καὶ Σκίροις
ἔν τε ταῖς ἄλλαις ἑορταῖς αἷσιν ἡμεῖς ἤγομεν.

If one of us should bear a useful man for the city,
a contingent commander or a general, she should receive some honor,
and a front row seat should be given to her at the Stenia and the Skira
and at the other festivals we celebrate.

In Aristophanes *Ecclesiazusae* 17–18 the Skira are specified as the occasion on which women made secret plans (the lines are addressed by a solitary speaker to her lamp): ἀνθ' ὧν συνείσει καὶ τὰ νῦν βουλεύματα / ὅσα Σκίροις ἔδοξε ταῖς ἐμαῖς φίλαις, "in return for which you will know our present resolutions, which my friends passed at the Skira."

191 Robert 1885:364–367 drew this conclusion from the scholia to Aristophanes *Thesmophoriazusae* 834 and Stephanus of Byzantium s.v. Σκίρος (cf. n3.172 above). In the common source behind these two sources the question was whether the name Skira came from the place Skiron, or from rights sacred to Demeter and Kore called Skira, which were only part of the larger festival called Skira. The two sources are somewhat garbled and their texts uncertain, but the key comparison is between the phrases for the second explanation: Stephanus: ἄλλοι δὲ ἀπὸ τῶν γινομένων ἱερῶν Δήμητρι καὶ Κόρῃ ἐν τῇ ἑορτῇ ταύτῃ, "Others say from the rights sacred to Demeter and Kore in this festival"; scholia to Aristophanes: τὰ δὲ Σκίρα λέγεσθαί φασι τινες τὰ γινόμενα ἱερὰ ἐν τῇ ἑορτῇ ταύτῃ Δήμητρι καὶ Κόρῃ, "Some say the sacred rites that take place for Demeter and Kore in this festival are called the Skira." Robert's argument for a narrower use of the name Skira is accepted by Rohde 1886:116: "It is now established that Skira in the narrower sense was the name of a sacred ritual celebrated by women in honor of Demeter and Kore, which was only one episode in

presumably represent the old core of the festival itself, going back origi-
nally to non-Attic cults of the goddess Skiras. In Attica the larger festival of
the Skira represented a religious compromise between Athens and Eleusis.
Thus it is not likely that the Skira ever belonged exclusively to Athena Polias
and Erechtheus in their function as rulers of the Acropolis. The earliest cult
context for the pair as rulers of the Acropolis is the story in Herodotus of
the yearly sacrifices that they jointly received from Epidaurus in return for
statues of Damia and Auxesia. Whatever the festival was in which these sacri-
fices were received, it is not likely to have been the Skira.[192] It was only when
Athena and Erechtheus were separated from each other on the Acropolis that
they were included in the Skira, the focus of which was not the Acropolis,
but Skiron. For Erechtheus in particular, the myth of his death associated him

----

the festival celebrated ἐπὶ Σκίρῳ [Strabo 9.1.9; cf. n3.178 above], which in a wider sense was
also named Skira or Skirophoria" ("Festgestellt ist nun, dass Σκίρα im engeren Sinne der
Name einer von Weibern zu Ehren der Demeter und Kore begangenen heiligen Handlung
war, die nur eine Episode in dem ἐπὶ Σκίρῳ gefeierten Feste war, welches in weiterer
Bedeutung ebenfalls Σκίρα oder auch Σκιροφόρια genannt wurde"). The rites called Skira in
the narrower sense, which were restricted to women, and which were dedicated to Demeter
and Kore, were more widespread than the larger Athenian festival: Robertson 1983:283
draws attention to epigraphic evidence for Skira celebrated in other Attic demes (Piraeus,
Paeania, and the Marathonian Tetrapolis) and to the month Skirophorion in Iasus in Asia
Minor (the latter, as Robertson acknowledges, could have been borrowed from Athens). It
is a question how the Skira in the narrower sense spread; in terms of Jacoby's scheme (see
n3.188 above), this could only have happened once Demeter became involved in the cult of
the goddess Skiras, presumably at Skiron. For the rites celebrated in Piraeus, cf. Brumfield
1981:164: "A fourth century decree from Piraeus [*IG* II² 1177] regulates the use of the local
Thesmophorion, and mentions, as festival days when the women traditionally gather there,
the Thesmophoria, the Plerosia, Kalamaia and Skira.... It would seem that in Piraeus the
Skira was a festival of Demeter, and that it was performed by the women within the temple."
This decree, which names the Skira separately from the Thesmophoria, is cited by Rohde
1886:116, following Robert, to disprove an older idea that the Skira (like the Stenia) were part
of the Thesmophoria. Demeter's role in the Skira, which gave rise to this mistaken idea, is the
essential fact.
192 *Pace* Robertson 1996:43. I suggest instead a clan festival later transformed into the state
festival of the Panathenaia in 566/5 BC (see §3.81and n3.242 below); by the late seventh
century BC, when (in my view) the cults of Athena Polias and Erechtheus on the acropolis
were reorganized following the incorporation of Eleusis into Attica, at least the annual
sacrifices offered by the Epidaurians to the divine pair must have ceased (for a *terminus
ante quem* of 600 BC at the latest, based on the date when Periander of Corinth crushed
Epidaurus, see EN3.1 to n3.16 above). If Athens' war with Aegina, which is connected with
the interruption of these sacrifices, is datable to the time of Solon (see How and Wells 1928
on Herodotus 5.86.4) the interruption of the sacrifices may also have occurred in Solon's
time. It is more likely, however, that the war between Athens and Aegina occurred at least
a century earlier than this (cf. EN3.1 to n3.16 above).

with Eleusis and with the borderland between Athens and Eleusis. In his new cult Erechtheus still had a place on the Acropolis, in Poseidon's temple, but his myth took him down from the Acropolis to Skiron. Athena, who accompanied him there in the ritual of the Skira, remained centered on the Acropolis.

§3.71 For Athena the Skira represented an adjustment with Demeter, whose agrarian nature in her cult at Eleusis allowed Athena's own agrarian nature in her cult on the Acropolis to recede when Athens and Eleusis were joined. For Erechtheus the Skira represented an even more basic adjustment. It marked his end as an independent god. By the myth of his death he was demoted to the status of a hero, and in cult he was associated with the god Poseidon. In the ritual procession to Skiron, moreover, cult ritual seems closely related to the meaning of his new myth, which concerns the incorporation of Eleusis into Attica.

§3.72 The Athenian entry to the Catalogue of Ships in *Iliad* 2 describes annual sacrifices of bulls and rams to Erechtheus (*Iliad* 2.546–551):

οἳ δ' ἄρ' Ἀθήνας εἶχον ἐϋκτίμενον πτολίεθρον
δῆμον Ἐρεχθῆος μεγαλήτορος, ὅν ποτ' Ἀθήνη
θρέψε Διὸς θυγάτηρ, τέκε δὲ ζείδωρος ἄρουρα,
κὰδ δ' ἐν Ἀθήνης εἷσεν ἑῷ ἐν πίονι νηῷ·
ἔνθα δέ μιν ταύροισι καὶ ἀρνειοῖς ἱλάονται
κοῦροι Ἀθηναίων περιτελλομένων ἐνιαυτῶν.

And the men who inhabited Athens, well-founded city,
land of great-hearted Erechtheus, whom Athena,
Zeus's daughter, once nourished after the grain-giving earth
    bore him,
and set him down in Athens in his own rich temple.
There the youths of the Athenians propitiate him with bulls and
    rams
as the years return.

As previously discussed, Athena in this passage does not place the earthborn Erechtheus in her temple, but in his own temple, and it is there that the youths of the Athenians propitiate him with yearly sacrifices. The passage describes the new cult relationships on the Acropolis insofar as Erechtheus has been removed from Athena's temple. The fact that Erechtheus is now associated with Poseidon, on the other hand, is left out of account, for the passage is meant to celebrate Erechtheus: Athens is called his *dêmos* in the

second line.[193] But the sacrifices described in the passage must really have
been to Poseidon Erechtheus. They are the same sacrifices that are mentioned
at the end of Euripides' *Erechtheus*, when Athena ordains that a new temple
be built for Erechtheus, who will now be known as Poseidon Erechtheus in
honor of his slayer;[194] this is the figure who will be called upon ἐμ φοναῖσι
βουθύτοις, "in the slaying of sacrificial cattle" (*Erechtheus* fr. 65.90–94 Austin):

πόσει δὲ τῶι σῶι σηκὸν ἐμ μέσηι πόλει
τεῦξαι κελεύω περιβόλοισι λαΐνοις,
κεκλήσεται δὲ τοῦ κτανόντος οὕνεκα
σεμνὸς Ποσειδῶν ὄνομ' ἐπωνομασμένος
ἀστοῖς Ἐρεχθεὺς ἐμ φοναῖσι βουθύτοις.

For your husband I order that a precinct be built
in the middle of the city with a stone enclosure;

193 As an Athenian reworking of the text of Homer (cf. §3.39 above) this passage, while radi-
cally new, had to appear old, and ambiguity serves this purpose: does the possessive adjec-
tive ἑῷ in line 549 mean "her" temple or "his" temple, and, in the same vein, does the
personal pronoun μιν in line 550 mean that Athenian youths propitiate "him" or "her"?
(For the pronoun see Frazer 1969:263–264, who concludes that Erechtheus is meant, but
not before considering seriously whether Athena is meant.) The passage has it both ways:
while describing the new cult situation between Erechtheus and Athena it does not openly
conflict with the old situation. Respect for the old situation between Erechtheus and
Athena also explains why Poseidon is left out of account, for he pertains only to their new
situation. Before Erechtheus was given a sacrifical death and a place in Poseidon's temple,
Poseidon occupied his temple alone. Whether the myth of Poseidon's contest with Athena
existed at this earlier stage is not clear (cf. n3.98, n3.127, and n3.130 above); in my view this
myth probably did not arise until Erechtheus became Poseidon Erechtheus, but perhaps it
was older. Cf. Jacoby, commentary on Hellanicus FGrHist 323a F 3, pp. 26–27, who considers
the relationship between the two myths in later tradition: "the dispute between Athena
and Poseidon was superseded by the fight between Eleusis and Athens or, as one might say,
the persons and the events were distributed over the two contests." The two myths are of
course closely connected in that Eumolpos fights to reclaim what his father Poseidon won
but was then denied in the contest with Athena; cf. n3.130 above on Euripides' *Erechtheus*
and see Spaeth 1991:342–343 for other sources. Spaeth argues that the west pediment of
the Parthenon, representing the contest between Athena and Poseidon, combines with
this contest the mythic war that resulted in the incorporation of Eleusis; Spaeth's iden-
tification of figures on the pediment includes Erechtheus and Eumolpos, the two leaders
in the war, but not the daughters of Erechtheus, who are central to the myth (see §3.73
below); this, I think, casts doubt on the scheme as a whole.
194 Robertson 1985:235 argues that the same sacrifice is meant in both passages; cf. above
n3.130.

because of the one who killed him he will be called
august Poseidon surnamed
Erechtheus in the slaughter of sacrificial oxen.

Both passages, in Homer and Euripides, clearly describe important sacrifices on an impressive scale. What was the festival in which (Poseidon) Erechtheus received such sacrifices? The Athenian sacrificial calendars contain no trace of it, and this is very puzzling. The Panathenaia have been suggested as the festival, but in what is known of both sacrifices at the Panathenaia, the large and the small, there is no mention of Erechtheus.[195] This silence is hard to explain since the sacrifices to Erechtheus were performed not only in the era when the Athenian entry in *Iliad* 2 was composed, but also in the last quarter of the fifth century, when Euripides wrote the *Erechtheus*.[196] I think that an alternative proposal must be right, that the yearly sacrifices at the temple of (Poseidon) Erechtheus were yet another part of that complex festival, the Skira.[197] This means that there was a ritual not only in Skiron, where the procession of the Skira ended, but on the Acropolis, where it began. We can hardly hope to divine the exact choreography of these events, but there is no inherent difficulty in seeing them as occurring together. It is true that we do not hear of sacrifices to (Poseidon) Erechtheus on the Acropolis as part of the Skira, but we must keep in mind that we only know that the procession to Skiron was part of the Skira because the festival's name was connected with a piece of apparatus used in this part of the ritual, namely a parasol. We do not have full descriptions of the festival for its own sake.

195 The Panathenaia are suggested by Weber 1927:148, and by Jacoby, commentary on Istros *FGrHist* 334 F 4, p. 630 and n4; they are argued at greater length by Mikalson 1976; cf. also Connelly 1996:76.

196 Mikalson does not adequately address this problem. Following Ferrari 2002 I do not accept Mikalson's premise (150n34, 153) that the location of the smaller sacrifice at the Panathenaia, namely Athena's old temple, was the center of Erechtheus's cult at the dates in question (sixth and fifth centuries BC). But this issue aside it is not enough to say that of "the religiously most important offerings" (namely those made at the smaller sacrifice) "some...were surely given to Erechtheus himself" (Mikalson 1976:153). Neither the *Iliad* nor Euripides gives the impression that the sacrifices to Erechtheus were small and could be easily overlooked. Cf. Robertson 1985:235n6: "In all the direct evidence for the Panathenaea Erechtheus is never mentioned as receiving sacrifice or other ritual honours, a stumbling block which has been skirted in different ways (Ziehen *RE* 'Panathenaia' 470–474 is the fullest) and is ignored by Mikalson."

197 Robertson 1985:235. As indicated above, I do not agree with Robertson's suggestion that of old the Epidaurians brought sacrifices to Athena and Erechtheus at the Skira, but I think that he is certainly right that the new sacrifices to Erechtheus alone, as attested by *Iliad* 2 and Euripides, belonged to the Skira.

§3.73 Part of Erechtheus's myth was that he had to sacrifice his daughter to secure victory for Athens in the war with Eleusis and Eumolpos. Delphi commanded this. The sacrifice of a daughter is a constant feature in references to the myth, and it is central to the plot of Euripides' *Erechtheus* as far as we know it. Here Praxithea, Erechtheus's wife, willingly embraces her daughter's death, and her patriotic speech to this effect is quoted in full by the fourth-century orator Lycurgus, himself a member of the family that provided the priests of Erechtheus and the priestesses of Athena Polias.[198] Erechtheus had several daughters, whose number varies.[199] In Euripides' *Erechtheus* there were three daughters, and after the sacrifice of one of them the other two also sacrificed themselves because of a pact with their sister.[200] At the end

198 Lycurgus *Against Leocrates* 100. For the Eteoboutad pedigree of Lycurgus, see Davies 1971:348–353; Thomas 1989:192–193. The priest of Erechtheus and the priestess of Athena Polias came from separate branches of the Eteoboutadai (Davies 1971:348). Plutarch *Lives of the Ten Orators* (*Lycurgus*) 843e says that the priests of Poseidon traced their ancestry to Erechtheus (who is here called the son of Earth and Hephaistos and so confused with Erichthonios). Binder 1984:21 states that "the first priest of Poseidon on the Acropolis was Lykomedes, the great grandfather of Lykourgos (Plutarch *Moralia* 843e)." This conclusion is challenged (rightly, I think) by Jeppesen 1987:33–34.

199 For the Erechtheids see Austin 1967:54–55 and Kearns 1989:202, cf. 201. Only three daughters figure in Euripides' *Erechtheus* (see below). There are four daughters (apparently) in Euripides' *Ion*, four in "Apollodorus" 3.15.1, six in Photius *Lexicon* s.v. *Parthénoi*, four in Hyginus *Fables* 46. In Euripides' *Erechtheus* the three daughters all die (their names have not survived); in the *Ion* Creusa, also a daughter, survives to become Ion's mother because she was a mere infant when the other daughters died (*Ion* 277–280). Oreithyia and Prokris, two further daughters of Erechtheus, had independent traditions and thus were not among those who died for Athens (Oreithyia was carried off by the north wind Boreas, to whom she bore Zetes and Calais; Prokris married Cephalos, whom she betrayed to Minos; see "Apollodorus" 3.15.1–2 and, for sources and variants, including Kekrops instead of Erechtheus as Oreithyia's father, Frazer 1921 on "Apollodorus" 3.15.1; for the myth of Boreas and Oreithyia as possibly arising in the early fifth century BC see Griffiths *OCD³* 'Boreas'; cf. also Parker 1987:204–205). Photius says that the two oldest daughters, Protogeneia and Pandora, both sacrificed themselves for Athens; the other four daughters include Chthonia in addition to Prokris, Creusa, and Oreithyia. Hyginus *Fables* 46 says that Chthonia was the daughter who was sacrificed and that her three sisters all leapt to their deaths. "Apollodorus" 3.15.4 says that the youngest daughter was sacrificed and the rest killed themselves; this conflicts with 3.15.1, which says that Erechtheus had four daughters, namely Prokris, Creusa, Chthonia and Oreithyia. In Euripides' *Erechtheus* it may have been the oldest daughter who was sacrificed (see Jacoby, commentary on "Demaratus" *FGrHist* 42 F 4). In Greek myth there are other instances of groups of virgins sacrificed for the safety of the city, all in Athens or Boeotia; in Athens it is always a group of three virgins, in Boeotia it is always a pair (see Kearns 1989:59–63; for the phenomenon more generally cf. Kearns 1990).

200 In *Erechtheus* fr. 65.67–70 Austin Athena gives instructions for the burial of all the deceased sisters in one tomb, where the first of them was sacrificed:

θάψον νιν οὗπερ ἐξέπνευσ' ο[ἰκτ]ρὸν βίον,
καὶ τάσδ' ἀδελφὰς ἐν τάφωι τ[αὐτ]ῶι χθονὸς

of the play all three were transformed into stars, the constellation Hyades.[201] This part of Erechtheus's myth, the sacrifice of his daughters, was connected with an already existing cult, that of the Hyakinthides. These "daughters of Hyakinthos" were said to have been sacrificed by their father, Hyakinthos, when Minos laid siege to Athens.[202] This at any rate was one myth associated with what must have been an old, even pre-Greek cult of the Hyakinthides. The cult, which was located somewhere to the west of Athens (perhaps in the deme Lousia), was identified with the daughters of Erechtheus, who were thus also called the Hyakinthides, "daughters of Hyakinthos."[203] At the end

---

γενναιότητος οὕνεχ᾽, αἵτιν[ες φί]λης
ὅρκους ἀδελφῆς οὐκ ἐτόλμησα[ν λι]π̣εῖν.

Bury her where she breathed out her pitiable life,
and bury these sisters of hers in the same earthen tomb
because of their nobility, who did not dare
to abandon their oaths to their dear sister.

See Treu 1971:121–122, n25. Cf. "Apollodorus" 3.15.4: Ἐρεχθεῖ δὲ ὑπὲρ Ἀθηναίων νίκης χρωμένῳ ἔχρησεν ὁ θεὸς κατορθώσειν τὸν πόλεμον, ἐὰν μίαν τῶν θυγατέρων σφάξῃ. καὶ σφάξαντος αὐτοῦ τὴν νεωτάτην καὶ αἱ λοιπαὶ ἑαυτὰς κατέσφαξαν· ἐπεποίηντο γάρ, ὡς ἔφασάν τινες, συνωμοσίαν ἀλλήλαις συναπολέσθαι, "To Erechtheus, when he consulted the oracle about a victory of the Athenians, the god answered that he would make the war succeed if he sacrificed one of his daughters. And when he sacrificed the youngest the others sacrificed themselves; for, as some said, they had made a joint oath to die with each other." Euripides *Ion* 277–278, a brief account, says that Erechtheus sacrificed Creusa's "sisters"; it is not clear whether this is a different account from the *Erechtheus*, or only more compressed.

201 Scholia to Aratus *Phaenomena* 172: Εὐριπίδης...ἐν Ἐρεχθεῖ τὰς Ἐρεχθέως θυγατέρας Ὑάδας φησὶ γενέσθαι τρεῖς οὔσας. The name of the constellation occurs in a fragment of the play (Ὑάσιν, fr. 65.107 Austin), part of the speech in which Athena disposes matters at the play's end; earlier in the same speech Athena announces that she has already given the souls of Erechtheus's daughters a home in the aether (fr. 65.71–72 Austin). For the number of daughters in the play, cf. also the phrase ζεῦγος τριπάρθενον, "three-virgin yoke-team" (fr. 47 Austin; the phrase is quoted by Hesychius s.v., who adds that it was parodied by Aristophanes as ζεῦγος τρίδουλον, "three-slave yoke-team").

202 "Apollodorus" 3.15.8: γενομένου δὲ τῇ πόλει λιμοῦ τε καὶ λοιμοῦ, τὸ μὲν πρῶτον κατὰ λόγιον Ἀθηναῖοι παλαιὸν τὰς Ὑακίνθου κόρας, Ἀνθηίδα Αἰγληίδα Λυταίαν (Λουσίαν Meursius, cf. n3.203 below) Ὀρθαίαν, ἐπὶ τὸν Γεραίστου τοῦ Κύκλωπος τάφον κατέσφαξαν· τούτων δὲ ὁ πατὴρ Ὑάκινθος ἐλθὼν ἐκ Λακεδαίμονος Ἀθήνας κατῴκει, "When famine and pestilence came to the city, they first, in accordance with an old oracle, sacrificed the daughters of Hyakinthos, Antheïs, Aigleïs, Lutaia [*Lousia* Meursius, cf. n3.203 below], Orthaia, on the grave of Geraistos the Cyclops; their father Hyakinthos came from Sparta and lived in Athens." This myth, featuring a Spartan, is clearly secondary to the cult (cf. Kearns 1989:61–62).

203 Photius *Lexicon* s.v. Παρθένοι cites Phanodemus (*FGrHist* 325 F 4) for the identification of the daughters of Erechtheus (who were also called Παρθένοι according to Photius's entry) with the Hyakinthides; the name varied, but only one cult was at issue (cf. Kearns

of the *Erechtheus*, when Athena ordains burial in one grave for the daughters of Erechtheus,[204] she gives them the name Hyakinthides before going on to specify their rites (*Erechtheus* fr. 65.73–74 Austin):

ὄνομα δὲ κλεινὸν θήσομαι κα[θ᾽ Ἑλλ]άδα
Ὑακινθίδας βροτοῖσι κικλή[σκε]ιν θεάς.

I will establish through Greece a famous name,
Hyakinthides, for mortals to call the goddesses.

After two more mostly lost lines, Athena specifies yearly rites for the Hyakinthides, which include cattle sacrifices and sacred maidens' choruses (*Erechtheus* fr. 65.77–80 Austin):

τοῖς ἐμοῖς ἀστο[ῖς λέγ]ω
ἐνιαυσίαις σφας μὴ λελησμ[ένους] χρόνωι
θυσίαισι τιμᾶν καὶ σφαγαῖσι [βουκ]τόνοις
κοσμοῦ[ντας ἱ]εροῖς παρθένων [χορεύ]μασιν.

1989:61n70; Parker 1987:202). Photius continues that the Hyakinthides were sacrificed "on the hill of Hyakinthos above Sphendonioi (Sphendonia?)": ἐσφαγιάσθησαν δὲ ἐν τῷ Ὑακίνθῳ καλουμένῳ πάγῳ ὑπὲρ τῶν Σφενδονίων (this information is probably also from Phanodemus according to Jacoby, commentary on Phanodemus *FGrHist* 325 F 4, p. 178). These locations are not known; for Sphendonioi Wilamowitz 1931:106n1 draws attention to a τόπος Ἀθήνησιν, "place in Athens," called Σφενδόναι in the *Lexeis Rhetorikai*, p. 202.22 Bekker, and he relates the lemma ἀφιδρύματα ἐν ταῖς Σφενδόναις, "statues in Sphendonai," to the Hyakinthides (ἀφιδρύματα = ἀγάλματα, "statues"). For the location Wilamowitz refers to Stephanus of Byzantium, who says that "Lousia was one of the daughters of Hyakinthos, from whom the deme of the tribe Oineïs (gets its name)" (Stephanus of Byzantium s.v. Λουσία· τῶν Ὑακίνθου θυγατέρων ἡ Λουσία ἦν, ἀφ᾽ ἧς ὁ δῆμος τῆς Οἰνηΐδος φυλῆς). Wilamowitz says that the deme Lousia is "not far west of the city," citing his *Aristoteles und Athen*, vol. 2, 152n18, where *IG* II² 1672 line 195 provides the evidence: here, for construction at the Eleusinion in the city, the same price per load is paid for γῆ Λουσιάς, "earth from Lousia," and γῆ Σκιράς, "earth from Skiron," which means that Lousia and Skiron were about the same distance from the Eleusinion. Traill 1975:49 gives the general location of Lousia as the Kephisos valley west of Athens, as "suggested from slight literary evidence and the findspot of the gravemarker *IG* II², 6756 [the church of Hagios Theodoros in Kato Liossia] and the reference in *IG* II², 1672, line 195." Cf. also Wrede *RE* 'Lusia,' and, on the territory of the tribe Oineïs, Judeich 1931:174. Traill on his Map 1 tentatively locates Lousia to the west of the Kephisos where it was crossed by the Sacred Way. It is of course not certain that the cult of the Hyakinthides was in the deme Lousia, as this connection in Stephanus of Byzantium is based on the name of just one of the maidens. Kearns 1989:102 does not accept Stephanus of Byzantium as evidence for the location of the cult; Jacoby, commentary on Phanodemus *FGrHist* 325 F 4, p. 180, does.
204 See n3.200 above.

> To my city's citizens I say
> to pay them honor and not forget with time,
> with yearly sacrifices and the slaughter of oxen,
> adorning the festivals with sacred maiden-dances.

Were these yearly rites for the Hyakinthides, which seem to have had a long history before they became associated with the daughters of Erechtheus, part of the Skira festival to Euripides and his audience? There is reason to think so because the Hyakinthides were now part of the aetiological myth of the Skira, namely the war with Eleusis. If so, the rites were presumably included in the festival when (in my view) it was first established about 600 BC.

§3.74 Noel Robertson has proposed a further aspect to the Skira that bears on the Hyakinthides but has a wider relevance as well. Athena Nike, whose shrine on the southwest corner of the Acropolis seems to have been founded in the sixth century BC, may have played a role in the Skira.[205] There was no priestess of Athena Nike until the mid-fifth century BC,[206] and thus whatever ritual took place at her shrine was first conducted by the priestess of Athena Polias (the situation was the same with respect to Athena Skiras in the procession to Skiron: it was the priestess of Athena Polias who took part in this ritual). Since the earliest levels of Athena Nike's shrine may be contemporary with the reorganization of the Panathenaia in 566/5 BC, there has been a presumption that the ritual conducted at the shrine had to do with the Panathenaia. Robertson, however, gives reasons for dating the shrine earlier, to about 600 BC.[207] While archaeology alone does not suggest such an early date, it also does

---

205 Robertson 1996:44–46; for the Hyakinthides' rites as part of the Skira see Robertson p. 45 and §3.76 below.
206 Robertson 1996:70n57; cf. n3.96 above.
207 Robertson 1996:44–45, 70n55. One of Robertson's arguments is based on the name *Glaukôpion* of a temple of Athena in Sigeion, an Athenian settlement of c. 600 BC: the shield of Alcaeus, according to a fragment of the poet, was hung in the *Glaukôpion* as spoil by the Athenians (Alcaeus fr. 428 LP). The temple name, which is derived from Athena's Homeric epithet *glaukôpis*, "grey-eyed," also occurs in Athens, where Robertson takes it to be a nickname of the temple of Athena Nike; the name of the temple in Sigeion would have been transferred from this temple in Athens at the time of the Athenian settlement. The evidence for the name in Athens, which is indirect, begins with a passage of Euripides' *Hippolytus* concerning a temple of Aphrodite near the Acropolis and visible from the direction of Troezen (*Hippolytus* 29–33; Aphrodite says that Phaedra founded this temple before going to Troezen). This was the shrine of Ἀφροδίτη ἐπὶ Ἱππολύτῳ, "Aphrodite next to Hippolytos," the name of which is evoked in *Hippolytus* 32–33, and the tomb of Hippolytus, with which this shrine was connected (cf. the scholia to *Hippolytus* 30), is located by Pausanias 1.22.1 on the way from the Asklepieion to the Acropolis, i.e. somewhere beneath the bastion of Athena Nike on the southwest corner of the Acropolis (see Judeich 1931:324n6). The scholia to *Hippolytus* 33 cite the *Hekale* of Callimachus for the name Glaukopion, apparently to show its location on the

not exclude it.[208] If an early date is in fact correct, Athena Nike's appearance on the Acropolis would be contemporary with the incorporation of Eleusis into Attica and the ensuing "religious compromise" of the Skira. Robertson, pursuing his own line of argument, thinks that the ritual in the shrine of Athena Nike was in fact part of the Skira. He points out that *níkē*, "victory," is an insistently repeated theme in references to the war between Athens and Eleusis, the aetiological myth of the Skira.[209] In one example in particular a

---

southwest corner of the Acropolis facing Troezen (Callimachus fr. 238.11 Pfeiffer). Pfeiffer ad loc. takes the name as designating the whole southwest corner of the Acropolis; Robertson's narrowing of this to the shrine of Athena Nike and its bastion seems very plausible.

208 See Robertson 1996:44. The top of the bastion on which the temple of Athena Nike sits had collapsed or been demolished before the date of the earliest remains on the site.

209 Erechtheus is promised "victory" by an oracle whenever the story is briefly told: Lycurgus *Against Leocrates* 99: εἰς Δελφοὺς ἰὼν [Erechtheus] ἠρώτα τὸν θεόν, τί ποιῶν ἂν νίκην λάβοι παρὰ τῶν πολεμίων, "going to Delphi [Erechtheus] asked the god what he should do to gain victory from the enemy"; "Demaratus" *FGrHist* 42 F 4: Ἐρεχθεὺς ὁ τῆς Ἀττικῆς προϊστάμενος χρησμὸν ἔλαβεν, ὅτι νικήσει τοὺς ἐχθρούς, ἐὰν τὴν πρεσβυτάτην τῶν θυγατέρων Περσεφόνῃ θύσῃ, "Erechtheus, the leader of Attica, received an oracle that he would be victorious over the enemy if he sacrificed the oldest of his daughters to Persephone"; Plutarch *Greek and Roman Parallels* 310d: Ἐρεχθεὺς πρὸς Εὔμολπον πολεμῶν ἔμαθε νικῆσαι, ἐὰν τὴν θυγατέρα προθύσῃ, καὶ συγκοινωνήσας τῇ γυναικὶ Πραξιθέᾳ προέθυσε τὴν παῖδα, "When Erechtheus was fighting against Eumolpos he learned that he would be victorious if he sacrificed his daughter first, and acting together with his wife Praxithea he did sacrifice his daughter first"; "Apollodorus" 3.15.4: Ἐρεχθεῖ δὲ ὑπὲρ Ἀθηναίων νίκης χρωμένῳ ἔχρησεν ὁ θεὸς κατορθώσειν τὸν πόλεμον, ἐὰν μίαν τῶν θυγατέρων σφάξῃ, "To Erechtheus, when he consulted the oracle about a victory of the Athenians, the god answered that he would make the war succeed if he sacrificed one of his daughters." In the fragments of Euripides' *Erechtheus* the motif occurs repeatedly, first in Praxithea's famous speech (*Erechtheus* fr. 50.50–52 Austin):

χρῆσθ', ὦ πολῖται, τοῖς ἐμοῖς λοχεύμασιν,
σῴζεσθε, νικᾶτ'· ἀντὶ γὰρ ψυχῆς μιᾶς
οὐκ ἔσθ' ὅπως οὐ τήνδ' ἐγὼ σώσω πόλιν.

Citizens, make use of my child-bearing,
save yourselves, be victorious; for it cannot be
that in return for one life I will not save this city.

In *Erechtheus* fr. 65.5–6 Austin the chorus, waiting for the messenger to enter from the battlefield with news (cf. fr. 65.11 Austin), asks:]ἦ ποτ' ἀνὰ πόλιν ἀλαλαῖς ἰὴ παιὰν / κ]αλλίνικον βοάσω μέλος;, "Will I ever shout *ié paián*, the glorious victory song, with loud cries through the city?" When Praxithea questions the reluctant messenger about Erechtheus's fate, she is told that he is blessed and fortunate, and she replies "only if he lives and brings a great victory to the city" (fr. 65.16–18 Austin):

Πρ. πόσις δ' Ἐρεχθεύς ἐστί μοι σεσ[ωσμένος;
Ἀγ. μακάριός ἐστι κεῖνος εὐδαίμων [θ' ἅμα.
Πρ. εἰ ζῆι γε πόλεώς τ' εὐτυχῆ νίκην ἄγει

The last example, fr. 65.89 Austin, is discussed in §3.76 below.

connection between the war with Eumolpos and Athena Nike is in my view very convincing. In Euripides' *Phoenician Women* the prophet Teiresias enters the stage in Thebes declaring that he has just come back from Athens and the war with Eumolpos, in which he has made the Athenians "victorious" (*Phoenician Women* 854–855):

κἀκεῖ γὰρ ἦν τις πόλεμος Εὐμόλπου δορός,
οὗ <u>καλλινίκους</u> Κεκροπίδας ἔθηκ' ἐγώ.

And there was a war there against the army of Eumolpos,
in which I made Kekrops's descendants <u>victorious</u>.[210]

Back now in his own city of Thebes Teiresias is about to tell Kreon that he too must sacrifice a child, his own son Menoikeus, in order to prevail against the invading Seven, and the evocation of Erechtheus and his daughter sets the stage for this turn of events. As Robertson has brilliantly suggested, Teiresias also evokes Athena Nike at his first entrance on stage by the golden crown that he wears; as the speech quoted above continues Teiresias himself draws attention to this crown (*Phoenician Women* 856–857):

καὶ τόνδε χρυσοῦν στέφανον, ὡς ὁρᾷς, ἔχω
λαβὼν ἀπαρχὰς πολεμίων σκυλευμάτων.

And as you see I have this golden crown,
which I took as first fruits from the enemy's spoils.

Teiresias's golden crown is the emblem of "victory," as Kreon makes clear when he addresses Teiresias in the next line (*Phoenician Women* 858):

οἰωνὸν ἐθέμην <u>καλλίνικα</u> σὰ στέφη.

Your <u>victory-adorning</u> crown I took as a sign.

A golden crown as the emblem of "victory" strongly suggests the cult of Athena Nike, for such golden crowns are her own particular dedication in the nine surviving Parthenon inventories between the years 422 and 409 BC.[211]

---

210 This version of the war with Eumolpos, with Teiresias as the prophet who tells Erechtheus that he must sacrifice his daughter for "victory," is unique. In other versions the prophet Skiros may have had a similar role; Treu 1971:128–129 suggests that the better-known Teiresias has replaced Skiros as a prophet in the Euripides play, and that the prophet's role may have been to reinforce a pronouncement from Delphi that Erechtheus sought to evade.

211 *IG* I³ 351–359. There appear to be three such dedications: the first and third are listed as

§3.75 A ritual for Athena Nike on the Acropolis in the festival of the Skira would balance the ritual for (Poseidon) Erechtheus on the Acropolis in the same festival. Both rituals would presumably have preceded the procession to Skiron. Such a ritual seems to be ordained by Athena at the end of the *Erechtheus* when, reflecting the Eteoboutad claim to have provided priestesses of Athena Polias from the start, she makes Erechtheus's wife Praxithea her priestess.[212] The emphasis in these lines, however, is not on the creation of the priesthood, which is mentioned last, but on a particular burnt sacrifice to be carried out on Athena's altar by her priestess (*Erechtheus* fr. 65.95–97 Austin):[213]

σοὶ δ᾽, ἣ πόλεως τῆσδ᾽ ἐξανώρθωσας βάθρα,
δίδωμι βωμοῖς τοῖς ἐμοῖσιν ἔμπυρα
πόλει προθύειν ἱερέαν κεκλημένην.

To you, who restored this city's foundations,
I grant to make burnt sacrifices on my altars
for the city, being called my priestess.

Robertson proposes that this sacrifice was to Athena Nike in the Skira, which the priestess of Athena Polias would have carried out at Athena Nike's shrine.[214] I accept this identification, which gives Athena a separate sacrifice to balance

---

Ἀθεναίας Νίκες στέφανος χρυσὸς, "of Athena Nike a golden crown," and the second, called only στέφανος χρυσὸς, immediately follows the first. The name Athena Nike is perhaps repeated before the third dedication because the second and third dedications have the same weight (see e.g. *IG* I³ 351 lines 21–23). These are the only mentions of Athena Nike in these inscriptions. Golden crowns are of course not unique to Athena Nike, but they are clearly characteristic of her.

212 I follow Robertson 1996:45 here.
213 See Robertson 1996:45 for the emphasis on the sacrifice in this passage.
214 The verb προθύειν in the last line of this passage means "make preliminary sacrifice" (cf. Ziehen 1904); Robertson 1996:70n57 cites Casabona 1966:104–106 for a more particular meaning "sacrifice before (an undertaking for its success)." If the sacrifice was to Athena Nike on her own altar in the context of the Skira it presumably came before the procession to Skiron and was preliminary in this sense (see further §3.77 and n3.222 below). When the Skira were (re)organized c. 600 BC the only priestess of Athena on the Acropolis was the priestess of Athena Polias, whom Praxithea in Euripides is meant to represent. The priestess of Athena Polias must have continued to conduct the "preliminary sacrifice" at the altar of Athena Nike even after Athena Nike was given her own priestess in the mid-fifth century BC (cf. n3.96 above) if Euripides' audience was meant to see the origin of contemporary practice in Athena's instructions to Praxithea. Robertson proposes an instance of the sacrifice in question in an ephebic decree of 123/2 BC: an ox is led by processioners up to the Acropolis for sacrifice at the altar of Athena Nike in a separate festival which Robertson takes to be the Skira (*IG* II² 1006 lines 14–15); see Robertson 1996:70n58 for the question of the festival.

that of Erechtheus in the Skira. Both are new sacrifices, created for the Skira, and they differ from the old sacrifices to Athena Polias and Erechtheus as a pair in that they are separate sacrifices to the separate gods.[215] The establishment of Athena Nike, a goddess of "victory," on the Acropolis underscores the transformation of Athena Polias herself into a goddess of war.

§3.76 There is another instance of the motif of "victory" in Euripides' *Erechtheus*, and it has to do with the cult rituals which Athena ordains for the Hyakinthides. We have already seen that these include yearly ox sacrifices and sacred maidens' choruses (fr. 65.77–80), but the passage continues with a further ritual. The Athenians are to offer the Hyakinthides what appear to be sacrifices before battle, in which honey and water are used instead of wine (*Erechtheus* fr. 65.83–86 Austin):[216]

πρώταισι θύειν πρότομα πολεμίου δορὸς
τῆς οἰνοποιοῦ μὴ θιγόντας ἀμπέλου
μηδ' εἰς πυρὰν σπένδοντας ἀλλὰ πολυπόνου
καρπὸν μελίσσης ποταμίαις πηγαῖς ὁμοῦ.

...to offer first to them the sacrifice before a battle,
not touching the wine-producing vine

---

215 Robertson 1996:37–44 identifies the shrine of Erechtheus with a building on the southeast corner of the Acropolis (cf. n3.117 above). One attraction of this identification is that the location would balance the location of the shrine of Athena Nike on the southwest corner of the Acropolis: the two shrines at either end of the south side would clearly have been planned as a pair, being separated from each other as widely as possible (see Robertson 1996:46, and his plan of the Acropolis, fig. 2.1, p. 30). Attracted as I once was to this scheme, I no longer think that it is correct in view of Ferrari's scheme. I continue to think that the shrines were separated from each other, but according to Ferrari's rather than Robertson's scheme. An ancient piece of evidence that weighs against Robertson's scheme is the fourth-century AD orator Himerius, who places the temple of Athena Polias "close" (πλησίον) to the sacred precinct of Poseidon, saying that the Athenians reconciled the two gods to each other after their contest for the city by this proximity of their temples: οἷος δ' ὁ τῆς Πολιάδος νεὼς καὶ τὸ πλησίον τὸ Ποσειδῶνος τέμενος· συνήψαμεν γὰρ διὰ τῶν ἀνακτόρων τοὺς θεοὺς ἀλλήλοις μετὰ τὴν ἅμιλλαν, "Such is the temple of Athena Polias and the precinct of Poseidon close to it; for through their temples we joined the gods together with each other after their contest" (Himerius *Oration* 5.30). The sacred precinct of Poseidon of course means the Erechtheum, which is indeed close to the temple of Athena Polias in Ferrari's scheme, but not in Robertson's.

216 The two previous lines, which begin this passage, are mostly lost; only the words for "battle," "shield," and "army" (or a related term) can be made out. For the wineless sacrifice, cf. Philochorus *FGrHist* 328 F 12, who says that θυσίαι νηφάλιοι, "wineless sacrifices," were offered Διονύσῳ τε καὶ ταῖς Ἐρεχθέως θυγατράσι, "both to Dionysus and to the daughters of Erechtheus."

nor pouring a libation on the altar, but with
the fruit of the industrious bee together with streams of river
water.

Athena warns that enemies must be kept out of the Hyakinthides' sacred precinct to prevent them from secretly offering sacrifices that will bring "victory" to themselves and pain to Athens (*Erechtheus* fr. 65.87–89 Austin):

ἄβατον δὲ τέμενος παισὶ ταῖσδ' εἶναι χρεών,
εἴργειν τε μή τις πολεμίων θύσηι λαθὼν
<u>νίκην</u> μὲν αὐτοῖς γῆι δὲ τῆιδε πημονήν.

The sanctuary for these maidens must be untrodden,
and any of your enemies must be prevented from offering sacri-
fice secretly,
bringing <u>victory</u> to themselves and pain to this land.

Robertson is surely right that these rites in the precinct of the Hyakinthides did not precede actual battles, but were part of the festival of the Skira.[217] The πρότομα πολεμίου δορός, "sacrifice before a battle," in the festival presumably imitated the sacrifice performed before an actual battle, in which the victim's throat was hastily stabbed as the army began to move toward the grim business of human slaughter.[218] This sacrifice was carried out to portend "victory" in the most immediate context possible, and even in the imitation of it at the festival the enemy had to be kept away and prevented from stealing "victory" by performing the ritual first.

§3.77 The same pre-battle sacrifice by stabbing through the throat has been identified in the parapet sculptures of the shrine of Athena Nike.[219] Here

217 Robertson 1996:45 and 70n61. Robertson brands as "very odd" the assumption of commentators on the *Erechtheus* that a battlefield sacrifice was performed in the *ábaton* of the Hyakinthides whenever needed. Such a practice before real battles would be highly impractical if not impossible.

218 See Jameson 1991; the sacrifice is illustrated p. 218, fig. 1. For the *hapax legomenon* πρότομα in fr. 65.83, Austin 1968 ad loc. cites Photius *Lexicon* προτομίζεσθαι· προάρχεσθαι; these were sacrifices to begin a battle. For sacrifices before battle cf. also Pritchett 1974:109–115 and Parker 2000.

219 Jameson 1994; Robertson 1996:45–46. Other views of the sacrifice in these sculptures are offered by Simon 1997, Hölscher 1997, and Kalogeropoulos 2003; Jameson's view, criticized from different perspectives by these authors (Simon 1997:139–140, Hölscher 1997:152, and Kalogeropoulos 2003:285), is, according to Kalogeropoulos, "in fact not to be rejected out of hand, given the posture of the sacrificial animal" ("aufgrund der Haltung des Opfertieres tatsächlich nicht von der Hand zu weisen").

personified Nikai perform the ritual,[220] and the victims are oxen rather than the sheep or goats that were usual in the anxious moments before a battle. Robertson again sees the ritual depicted on the parapet as belonging to the Skira, and as imitating the sacrifice performed before a real battle.[221] It is certainly possible that the sacrifice depicted on the sculptures took place at this very shrine of Athena Nike.[222] If so, there is a close correspondence between this sacrifice on the Acropolis and the sacrifice at the other end of the Skira, in the *ábaton* of the Hyakinthides. In both the main concern was "victory."

§3.78 Why was there this concern for victory in the Skira? Robertson relates it to the timeless rhythm of the agricultural year: the Skira took place in the threshing season, and a successful crop was like a military victory.[223] It is undeniable that the Attic calendar was, like other calendars, agrarian in origin, but I think that the Skira were first organized in the aftermath of a real victory which had profound consequences for the Attic state. Tellos, the hero of this victory, was to Solon the most fortunate of mortals, not only for his deed, but for the honor that followed his death: γενομένης γὰρ Ἀθηναίοισι μάχης πρὸς τοὺς ἀστυγείτονας ἐν Ἐλευσῖνι βοηθήσας καὶ τροπὴν ποιήσας τῶν πολεμίων ἀπέθανε κάλλιστα, καί μιν Ἀθηναῖοι δημοσίῃ τε ἔθαψαν αὐτοῦ τῇ περ ἔπεσε καὶ ἐτίμησαν μεγάλως (Herodotus 1.30.5). A deep change in attitude took place when Eleusis was incorporated into Attica, and the Skira were not only a celebration of that event, recast as a myth from the past, but a program for the future. The long-term results of this change were evident when Euripides wrote his *Erechtheus*, when the Athenians were engaged in a pursuit of victory against their chief rival in Greece, and would soon have

---

220 "In one version of this repeated scene, on the prominent west face of the parapet, a Nike raises a sword in her right hand, and wrenches back the animal's head with her left" (Robertson 1996:46).

221 Robertson 1996:70n62. The verb προθύειν in Euripides *Erechtheus* fr. 65.97 Austin, which in Robertson's interpretation relates to this sacrifice at the temple of Athena Nike (cf. §3.75 above), is appropriate to a ritual imitating preliminaries to battle; the battle itself was perhaps represented by the procession to Skiron if the procession followed these preliminaries (cf. n3.214 above), for it was in Skiron that Athens had defended itself in mythic times. Jameson takes the ox sacrifice on the parapet sculptures as the common military practice studied in his 1991 article (n3.218 above), but for that purpose smaller animals would have been usual.

222 Robertson 1996:70n62, citing Carpenter 1929:25 and 49, says that the representation of an altar edge has been detected beside two of the Nikai, on the north and west faces, but that both instances are very dubious. See n3.214 above for the ox sacrifice at the shrine of Athena Nike in an ephebic decree of 123/2 BC.

223 Robertson 1996:52–56, also 45.

their eye on foreign conquests as well.[224] Earlier, when the Skira were first organized, the foreign enemy was more immediate, in neighboring Megara.

§3.79 Erechtheus had a double Erichthonios, with whom he was easily confused.[225] When Erechtheus was removed from Athena's temple, his place was taken by Erichthonios, who had none of the previous history as Athena's consort that made it impossible for Erechtheus to stay.[226] Erichthonios in fact seems to have come into existence to fill the void in Athena's temple that was left there by Erechtheus.[227] Erichthonios was Athena's nursling, and, in

224 The play is dated to 422 BC on the basis of Plutarch *Nicias* 9.5, but this evidence (a fragment of the play) is not conclusive; cf. Cropp and Fick 1985:79–80, who suggest a date of 416 BC or later (cf. also Parker 1987:212n64; Connelly 1996:57n27). This was also probably when the sculptures of the temple of Athena Nike were created ("the 'teens of the fifth century," Jameson 1994:318); Jameson, having identified in these sculptures the repeated motif of sacrifice before a battle, comments on the juxtaposition of another repeated motif, the trophy erected after a victory (p. 318): "Time in these scenes is compressed. Victory is sought through sacrifice, and victory has been won. We have the powerful action at the beginning and the erection of trophies at the end. The imagery telescopes the whole process, as sometimes happens in narrative art (on the west frieze of the temple a trophy and battle are both shown). The message is blunt, even brutal: Victory and Athena guarantee the success of the Athenian people, committed to battle. Nike, under Athena's eyes, ensures by the violent act of killing that the Athenians will win." Jameson comments on the contrast between the bluntness of this message and the "sensuous elegance" of the sculptures: it may be dangerous to make comparisons between politics and art, he admits, "but I would prefer to think that the same reckless confidence and loss of a realistic sense of what they could achieve that lured the Athenians to Sicily and into refusing terms of peace when they held the advantage is seen here in the combination of insouciant mannerism and blunt celebration of power" (pp. 318–319). Note that in Euripides' *Erechtheus*, as a messenger tells it, Erechtheus erected a trophy for his victory before he was slain (Ἐρεχθ] εὺς ὡς τροπαῖα[...ἔστη[σε χώρ]ᾳ τῇδε, fr. 65.12–13 Austin).

225 As in the scholia to *Iliad* 2.547, which equate the two and then give the myth of Erichthonios's birth in reference to Erechtheus in this line. The two figures are widely recognized to be doublets (see Mikalson 1976:141n1).

226 In contrast to Erechtheus, who now had a cult in his own (i.e. Poseidon's) temple, Erichthonios was buried in Athena's temple: he was both raised and buried in Athena's precinct according to "Apollodorus" 3.14.6 and 7 (ἐν δὲ τῷ τεμένει τραφεὶς Ἐριχθόνιος ὑπ' αὐτῆς Ἀθηνᾶς... Ἐριχθονίου δὲ ἀποθανόντος καὶ ταφέντος ἐν τῷ αὐτῷ τεμένει τῆς Ἀθηνᾶς, "Erichthonios having been raised in the precinct by Athena herself.... Erichthonios having died and been buried in the same precinct of Athena"); he is buried specifically in Athena's temple according to Clement of Alexandria *Protrepticus* 3.45.1 (τί δὲ Ἐριχθόνιος; οὐχὶ ἐν τῷ νεῷ τῆς Πολιάδος κεκήδευται;, "What of Erichthonios? Is he not buried in the temple of Athena Polias?"). Later sources are Marcellus of Side (c. AD 160) *IG* XIV 1389 II.30–31 (= Kaibel 1878 no. 1046 lines 89–90) and Arnobius *Against the Heathens* 6.6; cf. Robertson 1985:256.

227 I agree with Mikalson 1976, who argues that Erichthonios arose secondarily to Erechtheus; the usual view is that Erichthonios is older (see Mikalson 1976:141n1). Mikalson follows Escher *RE* 'Erechtheus' 409–410, who points out that the Athenians called themselves Erechtheidai, not Erichthonidai. Robertson 1996:64–65, following the usual view, believes

contrast to Erechtheus, he had no real adult phase in his myth. His purpose was to replace the infant Erechtheus while ignoring the now unacceptable adult figure.[228] But who was the infant Erechtheus whom he replaced? According to the Athenian entry to the Catalogue of Ships, Erechtheus was born from the earth and nursed by Athena. This is exactly the myth that was duplicated in the case of Erichthonios, but this does not mean that it was Erechtheus's original myth; rather it may only be a further innovation on the part of the Athenian entry to the Catalogue of Ships. In Erechtheus's original myth he was most likely the son as well as the consort of Athena Polias.[229] Both parts of this myth had to change: if Athena could no longer be wife to Erechtheus, she also could not be mother to him. Both changes are carried out in the Athenian entry, where Erechtheus is worshipped in his own temple

---

that Erichthonios is older than the sixth century BC, but I doubt this. We should not be misled by the fact that Erichthonios precedes Erechtheus in the genealogies; the reason for this is different (cf. n3.228 below).

228 Cf. Burkert 1966:24: "Erechtheus is the old king, Erichthonios the young king; stories are told about the death of Erechtheus and the birth of Erichthonios" ("Erechtheus ist der alte, Erichthonios der junge König; man erzählt vom Tod des Erechtheus und von der Geburt des Erichthonios"); and 24n2: "A differentiation according to the type young king-old king is shown especially by the Berlin cup F 2537 = ARV² 1268f., which has names beside the figures...: Erichthonios is a young man, Erechtheus has a beard, even though Erichthonios comes before Erechtheus in the usual genealogies because the mystery of the starting point, Kekrops-Erichthonios, must stand at the beginning" ("Die Differenzierung nach dem Typ junger König-alter König zeigt besonders die mit Beischriften versehene Berliner Schale F 2537 = ARV² 1268f. ...: Erichthonios als Jüngling, Erechtheus mit Bart, obwohl in den üblichen Genealogien Erichthonios vor Erechtheus rangiert, weil am Anfang das Geheimnis des Ursprungs stehen muss, Kekrops-Erichthonios").

229 See n3.80 above. Fauth 1959:466 [82] calls Athena, in her function as *kourotróphos* of Erechtheus, "just a modification of the 'Mother'" ("nur...eine Brechung der 'Mutter'"); this is too facile in that the "modification" must be demonstrated and explained. Simon 1953:84 comments on the mysterious nature of the relationship between mother goddess and a consort/son in the case of Cybele and Sabazios; quoting Strabo 10.3.15, who calls Sabazios τρόπον τινὰ τῆς μητρὸς τὸ παιδίον, "in a certain way the mother's child," she comments that τρόπον τινὰ, "in a certain way," does not mean that Cybele is only a *kourotróphos*, but rather "expresses a mysterious, unanalyzable connection that does not need to be either marriage or a mother-child relationship" ("Dieses τρόπον τινὰ, 'gewissermassen,' soll wohl nicht besagen, dass Kybele nur die Pflegerin des Kindes war, sondern drückt eine geheimnisvolle, nicht weiter analysierbare mythische Verbindung aus, die weder eine Ehe noch das Verhältnis Mutter-Kind zu sein braucht"). Simon compares the pairing of Athena with a male god in the temple of Athena Itonia in Koroneia: while Pausanias 9.34.1 calls this god Zeus, Strabo 9.2.29 says that "Hades is seated with Athena for some mystic reason" (συγκαθίδρυται δὲ τῇ Ἀθηνᾷ ὁ Ἅιδης κατά τινα, ὥς φασι, μυστικὴν αἰτίαν); see Foucart 1885:433 for the conjecture that the god in this mystery cult was Ares rather than Hades. For the well-known example of the Great Goddess, whose companion Attis is both son and lover, see Burkert 1983:81–82.

once Athena, having received him from the earth and nourished him, puts him there (*Iliad* 2.547–549):

ὅν ποτ' Ἀθήνη
θρέψε Διὸς θυγάτηρ, τέκε δὲ ζείδωρος ἄρουρα,
κὰδ δ' ἐν Ἀθήνης εἷσεν ἑῷ ἐν πίονι νηῷ.

whom Athena,
Zeus's daughter, once nourished after the grain-giving earth
    bore him,
and set him down in Athens in his own rich temple.

Athena here has the function of *kourotróphos* (note θρέψε in line 548), which is perfectly compatible with her virginity.[230] This much and no more is left of her once much larger role as a mother goddess: the function of *kourotróphos* is the new limit for Athena in this sphere, and it is this passage that establishes it. Erichthonios, who remains behind in Athena's temple, duplicates and thereby reinforces the new version of Erechtheus's birth as an autochthon. His name, which otherwise occurs in Homer of an early Trojan, was chosen, first, because of its resemblance to the name Erechtheus, and secondly, because of its meaning, "he of the very earth."[231] Unlike Erechtheus, whose name has no clear meaning, Erichthonios from the start was "born from the

---

230 The passage in fact emphasizes Athena's virginity in her role as nourisher by calling her Διὸς θυγάτηρ, "daughter of Zeus": this is the Olympian goddess, not the city goddess (or, rather, the city goddess has here become the Olympian goddess). Although Athena is never called *kourotróphos*, it seems legitimate to speak of her in this function (cf. Jahn 1845:73). An independent deity *Kourotróphos* is attested for Marathon in the early fourth century BC (*IG* II² 1358b line 31; cf. Deubner 1932:44) and on the Salaminioi inscription of 363/2 BC (see below §3.83, n3.262, and EN3.14). The independent goddess seems to have become associated secondarily with other goddesses, namely Ge (Earth), Demeter, and Artemis; Pausanias 1.22.3 attests a shrine of Gê *Kourotróphos* near the entrance to the Acropolis in Athens (for this goddess cf. n3.232 below). See Prehn *RE* 'Kurotrophos.'

231 Robertson 1996:62 gives this translation of the name. "Eratosthenes" *Catasterismi* 13 alludes to the meaning of the name when he refers to the "seed that fell to the earth, from which (i.e. the earth) they say a child was born, who was called Erichthonios because of this" (φερομένης εἰς τὴν γῆν τῆς σπορᾶς· ἐξ ἧς γεγενῆσθαι λέγουσι παῖδα, ὃς ἐκ τούτου Ἐριχθόνιος ἐκλήθη). For the intensifying prefix *eri-/ari-*, see Thieme 1938:159–168 (= 1968:53–60), especially 1938:161 and 164 (= 1968:54 and 57). The name Erichthonios is transparent, whereas the name Erechtheus is not (*Erekhtheús* may be related to *erékhthō*, "rend, break" if the name is Greek and not pre-Greek). The Homeric Erichthonios was an early king of Troy (son of Dardanos and father of Tros) fabled for his horses (*Iliad* 20.219–230).

earth."[232] His name is a good indication that he was created to correct an older myth in which Erechtheus was born, not from the earth, but from Athena.[233]

§3.80 It has long been debated whether the bizarre myth of Erichthonios's conception should be taken as evidence of Athena as a mother goddess. Hephaistos, who received Athena as a bride in return for assisting with his axe at Athena's birth from Zeus's head, tried to make love to her on the spot. As she escaped from him, his seed fell on her thigh and she wiped it off with a piece of wool and threw it to the ground. From this seed the earth conceived Erichthonios, whom Athena received into her own hands when he was born.[234] As Walter Burkert puts it, Athena in this story comes "within an ace" ("um ein Haar") of being Erichthonios's mother, and it is thus tempting to think of her in some sense as such.[235] But the point of the story seems to be just the opposite, that Athena emphatically remained a virgin, and if she had ever been thought of otherwise this myth was meant to set the record

232 Besides his name (and the myth of his birth) there are other signs that Erichthonios was closely associated with the earth, in particular his affinity with snakes (see §3.82 below). It is also worth noting that the Suda s.v. Κουροτρόφος γῆ says that the sacrifice to Earth Kourotrophos that preceded sacrifices to any other god was first performed by Erichthonios, and that her altar was erected by him in thanks for his foster care: ταύτῃ δὲ θῦσαί φασι πρῶτον Ἐριχθόνιον ἐν ἀκροπόλει καὶ βωμὸν ἱδρύσασθαι, χάριν ἀποδιδόντα τῇ γῇ τῶν τροφείων· καταστῆσαι δὲ νόμιμον τοὺς θύοντάς τινι θεῷ, ταύτῃ προθύειν. Here Earth's role as mother subsumes Athena's role as nurturer, a natural extension in Κουροτρόφος γῆ.

233 The myth of a simultaneous son and husband of the mother goddess must have long been suppressed in Greece generally because of the incest tabu, which the Oedipus myth clearly demonstrates. It is interesting that the Oedipus myth resonated in late fifth-century Athens, where, as Knox 1957:53–106 shows, the Sophoclean hero symbolizes the very city. If in the not distant past Erechtheus's incest was a fact of (religious) life, which had subsequently been covered over, Oedipus's relentless pursuit of the truth about his own incest casts an interesting light on the contemporary Athenian audience.

234 This (without Athena's role as *kourotróphos* at the end) is the version of the story in the scholia to Plato *Timaeus* 23e and the *Etymologicum Magnum* s.v. Ἐρεχθεύς (which connects the name Erichthonios with the noun *érion*, "wool"). "Apollodorus" 3.14.6 has a slightly different version for the first part of the story (Athena and Hephaistos first meet in Hephaistos's workshop, where he makes weapons for her); see Frazer 1921 ad loc. for other sources. There is a useful collection of texts relating to Erichthonios in Powell 1906:56–86.

235 Burkert 1985:143: "Athena, the virgin, thus comes within an ace of being the mother of the ancestral king who enjoys continuing honour in the Erechtheion. The paradox of the identity of virgin and mother is something which the myth recoils from articulating" (the 1977 German original, p. 225: "Athena, die Jungfrau, wird so um ein Haar zur Mutter des Urkönigs, der im 'Erechtheion' fortdauernde Ehren geniesst. Das Paradox der Identität von Jungfrau und Mutter auszusprechen, scheut der Mythos zurück"). Burkert follows the traditional view that Athena's temple, where Erichthonios was buried, was in the Erechtheion (see below in text).

straight.[236] Thus both sides in the debate are right insofar as the myth itself emphatically proclaims Athena's virginity, but its reason for doing so is an older myth that said precisely the opposite.[237]

236 Note the emphatic language referring to Erichthonios's birth from the earth in the last line of the following passage of dialogue between Ion and Creusa in Euripides *Ion* (267–270):

Ion: ἐκ γῆς πατρός σου πρόγονος ἔβλαστεν πατήρ;
Creusa: Ἐριχθόνιός γε· τὸ δὲ γένος μ' οὐκ ὠφελεῖ.
Ion: ἦ καί σφ' Ἀθάνα γῆθεν ἐξανείλετο;
Creusa: ἐς παρθένους γε χεῖρας, οὐ τεκοῦσά νιν.

Ion: Your father's father once sprang from the earth?
Creusa: Yes, Erichthonios; but my ancestry does not help me.
Ion: And did Athena take him up from the earth?
Creusa: Into her virgin's hands, not having given birth to him.

In this passage Erechtheus (Creusa's father) is the son of Erichthonios, and thus no longer himself an autochthon. The Athenian king lists are responsible for this change; Erechtheus was made Erichthonios's son and successor already in Hellanicus and this version was then preferred by other Atthidographers (see Jacoby, commentary on Hellanicus *FGrHist* 323a F 27 and his Introduction to Hellanicus nn119, 121, 125). In another version of the list Pandion is inserted between Erichthonios and Erechtheus ("Apollodorus" 3.14.7, 3.15.1). In the case of Erechtheus the king lists never completely replaced the older myth that he was earthborn, which was of course a fixed part of the Athenian entry to the Catalogue of Ships. Herodotus 8.55 still refers to "Erechtheus, said to be earthborn," when he speaks of his temple on the Acropolis: ἔστι ἐν τῇ ἀκροπόλι ταύτῃ Ἐρεχθέος τοῦ γηγενέος λεγομένου εἶναι νηός. Erichthonios has the same epithet "earthborn" in Euripides *Ion* 20–21 (γηγενοῦς / Ἐριχθονίου). Xenophon too ignores the version of the king lists when he refers to Erechtheus as an example of the valor of the Athenians' ancestors, emphasizing his "<u>birth and nurturing</u>" (i.e. from the earth and by Athena respectively) as well as "the war waged in his time against those from the whole neighboring mainland": λέγω γάρ, καὶ τὴν Ἐρεχθέως γε <u>τροφὴν καὶ γένεσιν</u>, καὶ τὸν πόλεμον τὸν ἐπ' ἐκείνου γενόμενον πρὸς τοὺς ἐκ τῆς ἐχομένης ἠπείρου πάσης (Xenophon *Memorabilia* 3.5.10). Isocrates, who does not mention Erechtheus by name, follows the king lists by including him in an unbroken royal succession from father to son beginning with Erichthonios and ending with Theseus; Isocrates' point is that the Athenians alone among the Greeks had royal houses that lasted four or five generations, and he deliberately motivates the succession of a second autochthon, Erichthonios, by the failure of the original autochthon, Kekrops, to have male issue (Isocrates 12.126): Ἐριχθόνιος μὲν γὰρ ὁ φὺς ἐξ Ἡφαίστου καὶ Γῆς παρὰ Κέκροπος ἄπαιδος ὄντος ἀρρένων παίδων τὸν οἶκον καὶ τὴν βασιλείαν παρέλαβεν· ἐντεῦθεν δ' ἀρξάμενοι πάντες οἱ γενόμενοι μετ' ἐκεῖνον, ὄντες οὐκ ὀλίγοι, τὰς κτήσεις τὰς αὑτῶν καὶ τὰς δυναστείας τοῖς αὑτῶν παισὶν παρέδοσαν μέχρι Θησέως, "Erichthonios, who was born from Hephaistos and Earth, took over the house and the kingship from Kekrops, who had no male children; starting then all born after him, who were not few, passed on their own possessions and their royal power to their own sons as far as Theseus."

237 Kerényi 1952 believes that the story of the begetting and birth of Erichthonios points to a *hieròs gámos* of the goddess; Rose, in his review of Kerényi, allows this as a possibility "though not with the latecomer Hephaistos" (Rose with reason objects that Kerényi's argument "stands chronology on its head"). Even less does Nilsson 1967:443 accept the myth as evidence for Athena as a mother goddess: "One must not appeal to the repugnant myth of Hephaistos's

§3.81 The first datable evidence for Erichthonios is from the mid-sixth century BC.[238] Hephaistos, who has a central role in Erichthonios's myth, did not reach Athens until 600 BC at the earliest, after Athens became involved in the northeast Aegean, Hephaistos's homeland.[239] On this reckoning

amorous pursuit, especially since Hephaistos was added later"; in Nilsson's reconstruction "Artisans thought that their goddess was suitable as a mate for their god, but her virginity resisted this; with the addition of the old idea that Erechtheus was born from the earth, the myth was corrected" ("Auf den widerlichen Mythos von der Liebeswerbung des Hephaistos um Athena sollte man sich nicht berufen, zumal Hephaistos später hinzugekommen ist. Für den Gott der Handwerker schien ihre Göttin als Gattin geeignet zu sein; dagegen stritt ihre Jungfräulichkeit. Mit Hinzunahme der alten Vorstellung, dass Erechtheus erdgeboren war, ist der Mythos zurechtgemacht worden"). Farnell 1896, vol. 1, 303 also argues that the tradition for Athena's virginity was too deep-rooted to be undone by Hephaistos: "The legend about the birth of Erichthonios clearly shows that the primitive conception of Athena's maidenhood was too strong to allow of the Athenian imagination having its way completely in its desire to affiliate the mythical parent of the *Erekhtheîdai* to their country's goddess." Of these various formulations I can accept only Rose's.

238 The myth of his birth was represented on the Amyklai throne of about 550 BC (Pausanias 3.18.13, see below). His earliest occurrences in literature are in Pindar fr. 253 Schroeder and the epic *Danaïs* (Harpokration s.v. αὐτόχθονες). The *Danaïs* is difficult to date. Huxley 1969:37–38 says only that it must have been earlier than the mid-fifth-century prose writer Acusilaus, who made use of it. Bethe *RE* 'Danais' proposes a relatively late date for the epic, not because of its knowledge of Egypt, which in Bethe's view could be much older than the re-opening of Egypt in the seventh century, but because of the occurrence of the Attic Erichthonios. My own view is that Erichthonios did not appear until the sixth century, to which the *Danaïs* would then date. It should be noted that the story of Erichthonios's conception and birth is already present in the first evidence for Erichthonios himself, whether this evidence is the Amyklai throne (Ἀθηνᾶ διώκοντα ἀποφεύγουσά ἐστιν Ἥφαιστον, "Athena is there fleeing from Hephaistos, who chases her," Pausanias 3.18.13) or the *Danaïs* (Harpokration s.v. αὐτόχθονες· ὁ δὲ Πίνδαρος καὶ ὁ τὴν Δαναΐδα πεποιηκὼς φασιν Ἐριχθόνιον τὸν Ἡφαίστου [καὶ Ἥφαιστον MSS.] ἐκ γῆς φανῆναι, "Autochthons: Pindar and the poet of the *Danaïs* say that Erichthonios the son of Hephaistos appeared from the earth"). Robertson 1983:287 denies that the Amyklai throne concerns Erichthonios's birth, but without good reason (as Robertson's own n126 makes clear).

239 See Robertson 1996:64; Robertson dates the torch race from the Academy to the Acropolis on the night before the Panathenaia to Hephaistos's arrival in Athens, which he in turn connects with Athenian interests in the Troad and Sigeion about 600 BC: "Though Lemnos happens to be famous as Hephaistos' home, the Troad shared the native culture of the offshore islands. In Homer, Hephaistos intervenes in favor of his Trojan priest Dares (a native name), whose two sons fell foul of Diomedes (*Iliad* 5.9–24)." Robertson discusses this issue in detail in his earlier study of the Panathenaia (1985:274–278); cf. p. 276: "Lemnos and the Troad were Hephaestus' homeland.... ...in the course of the sixth century Athenians thrust themselves upon this homeland, first at Sigeum, then elsewhere along the Hellespontine coast, and finally upon Lemnos itself. The chronology of this advance is obscure and disputed.... Even if Lemnos was not occupied until the beginning of the fifth century (A. J. Graham), the island and its people and customs and resources were undoubtedly well known at Athens for many years before. And the pattern of worship on Lemnos probably obtained in the area of Sigeum as well." Hephaistos's foreign origin is widely accepted (cf. Robertson 1985:274n85),

Erichthonios may have first appeared approximately when related changes
took place in Athenian cult and myth, in particular the removal of Erechtheus
from Athena's temple, and the association of Erechtheus with the war against
Eleusis in both the myth and the ritual of the Skira. Erichthonios, for his
part, was associated with the Panathenaia, Athena's principal festival. Unlike
the Skira, which formalize the separation between Athena and Erechtheus,
the Panathenaia give Erichthonios a positive (yet subordinate) association
with Athena: he is said to have founded the festival, and he is given credit
for various innovations pertaining to it, including the invention of the char-
iot.[240] The Panathenaia were reorganized in 566/5 BC, and in all likelihood

---

but the date of his arrival in Athens is uncertain. I note a steady regression in Robertson's
dating of this event, from the end of the sixth century BC (or simply "some time before c.
450"), Robertson 1983:288, to the mid-sixth century BC, Robertson 1985:274, to the early
sixth century BC, Robertson 1996:64. In view of Hephaistos's role in the Erichthonios myth a
date near the beginning of the sixth century BC would seem to be right. But I also note that
Hephaistos and Athena are associated as gods of crafts, as they were in Athens, already in
Odyssey 6.232–235 (cf. Séchan and Lévêque 1966:259–260 and n3.237 above).

240 "Apollodorus" 3.14.6 credits Erichthonios with two things of particular importance for
Athena Polias during his kingship, namely setting up her old image and establishing the
Panathenaia: καὶ τὸ ἐν ἀκροπόλει ξόανον τῆς Ἀθηνᾶς ἱδρύσατο, καὶ τῶν Παναθηναίων τὴν
ἑορτὴν συνεστήσατο. Erichthonios's connection with Athena Polias's image may, if the tradi-
tion for it is old, have to do with the transformation of this image into a warrior goddess
in the late seventh or early sixth century BC. The tradition for Erichthonios as founder of
the Panathenaia is first attested in Hellanicus *FGrHist* 323a F 2. The source of this fragment,
Harpokration s.v. Παναθήναια, also includes the statement of Istros that before Erichthonios
the Panathenaia were called the Athenaia: ἤγαγε δὲ τὴν ἑορτὴν πρῶτος Ἐριχθόνιος ὁ
Ἡφαίστου, καθά φησιν Ἑλλάνικός τε καὶ Ἀνδροτίων, ἑκάτερος ἐν α' Ἀτθίδος. πρὸ τούτου
δὲ Ἀθήναια ἐκαλεῖτο, ὡς δεδήλωκεν Ἴστρος ἐν γ' τῶν Ἀττικῶν. Jacoby, commenting on
the Istros fragment (*FGrHist* 334 F 4 pp. 630–631), argues that the rival tradition that the
Panathenaia were founded by Theseus in connection with his *synoikismós* of the Attic demes
(first attested in Plutarch *Theseus* 24.3, but probably going back to Atthidography) may
have originated only in the fifth century since Thucydides 2.15.2 attests that in his day the
Panathenaia had not yet supplanted the Synoikia as the celebration of that event. According
to Philochorus Erichthonios instituted in the Panathenaia a procession of old men carrying
olive shoots (θαλλοφόροι, Philochorus *FGrHist* 328 F 9) and in the Panathenaia and other
festivals a procession of basket-carrying maidens (κανηφόροι, Philochorus *FGrHist* 328 F 8).
The earliest sources for Erichthonios as the inventor of the chariot are Parian Marble *FGrHist*
239 F A10 and "Eratosthenes" *Catasterismi* 13; cf. also Hyginus *Astronomica* 2.13, who cites
"Eratosthenes" (Erichthonios became the constellation *Heniochos*, Latin *Auriga*, "Charioteer,"
as a reward for his invention); cf. also Vergil *Georgics* 3.113–114:

primus Erichthonius currus et quattuor ausus
iungere equos, rapidusque rotis insistere victor.

Erichthonios first dared to yoke chariots
and four horses and stand upon wheels, racing to victory.

Burkert 1966:23n1 has an exhaustive list of sources.

Erichthonios became known as the festival's founder in connection with this event.[241] We have no information about the festival before it was reorganized, but there is reason to think that what emerged as a state festival had previously been a clan festival.[242] I suspect that the clan in question was the Eteoboutads, who of old provided the priestess of Athena Polias, and to whom the festival would therefore have naturally belonged. It was to this clan festival, in all likelihood, that the Epidaurians once brought annual sacrifices to Athena Polias and Erechtheus as a pair. Erechtheus, whose priest was also provided by the Eteoboutads, may have continued at Athena's side in the clan festival until it was reorganized as a state festival in 566/5 BC, but he could

241 Eusebius *Chronicle* provides the date of the foundation of the Panathenaia: 1451 *ab Abraham* (Olympiad 53,3 = 566/5 BC) *agon gymnicus, quem Panathenaeon vocant, actus* (see Jacoby, commentary on Istros *FGrHist* 334 F 4, n2). Pherekydes *FGrHist* 3 F 2 reports that Hippokleides, a member of the *génos* of the Philaidai, was archon when the Panathenaia were established: Ἱπποκλείδης, ἐφ' οὗ ἄρχοντος Παναθήναια ἐτέθη. Pherekydes had a personal relationship with the Philaidai, whose accomplishments he therefore highlighted (cf. Jacoby 1947:28–33). Hippokleides is known otherwise as the unsuccessful suitor of Cleisthenes' daughter in Sicyon (Herodotus 6.127.4–129).

242 Cf. Jacoby, commentary on Istros *FGrHist* 334 F 4, n2, p. 508, who imagines that there were numerous clan festivals of Athena before the organization of the Panathenaia (i.e. he is not persuaded that one particular festival was reorganized as the Panathenaia in 566/5 BC): "The development in the sixth century as touched on above makes it appear more likely that only then the main festival (or better the state festival, the ἑορτὴ πάνδημος or δημοτελής) came to stand beside the numerous festivals of Athena which may originally have been entirely in the hands of certain individual clans." (Problems with the term "clan" for *génos* have been recognized since Jacoby wrote; see Ober 1989:56n8, who cites the relevant bibliography; for my purposes the term serves well enough to indicate the "birth elite" of early Athens, as Ober 1989:55–60 refers to them.) Jacoby, commentary on Istros *FGrHist* 334 F 4, p. 630, argues that the name *Athenaia* for a festival which preceded and was replaced by the *Panathenaia* (Istros *FGrHist* 334 F 4, Pausanias 8.2.1) is an invention to reconcile the tradition that Theseus founded the Panathenaia for "all the Athenians" when he united the Attic state with the older tradition for Erichthonios as the festival's founder. Pausanias 8.2.1 is decisive on this issue: τούτῳ γὰρ τῷ ἀγῶνι Ἀθήναια ὄνομα ἦν, Παναθήναια δὲ κληθῆναί φασιν ἐπὶ Θησέως, ὅτι ὑπὸ Ἀθηναίων ἐτέθη συνειλεγμένων ἐς μίαν ἁπάντων πόλιν, "the name of this festival was the Athenaia, but they say that it was (re)named the Panathenaia in Theseus's time because it was (re)founded by all the Athenians gathered in one city." There is a negative piece of evidence that must be explained: Istros *FGrHist* 334 F 4 (cf. n3.240 above) seems to say that the festival was called the *Athenaia* before Erichthonios, not Theseus; Jacoby, commentary on Istros *FGrHist* 334 F 4, p. 631, comments: "Strictly interpreted πρὸ τούτου ['before him'] should refer to Erichthonios.... The epitomist may have done more than abridge clumsily, he may have skipped a whole sentence which contained the rival version and πρὸ τούτου may actually have referred to Theseus." See Jacoby, commentary on Istros *FGrHist* 334 F 4, n2, p. 509, for *Panathenaia* as meaning 'festival of all Athenians': "A. Mommsen's conception of 'Fest aller Athener'...is perhaps favoured by Panionia, Pamboiotia, Panaitolia (Pollux 6.163), the Πανέλληνες and the Panhellenia of Hadrian."

not remain there as a full partner in the state festival; instead Erichthonios took his place and was given the more compatible, and entirely mortal role of founder of the (new) festival.[243] He was also given credit for the one part of the festival that looks genuinely old, and was most likely inherited from an earlier clan festival.[244] This was the *apobátēs* race, a chariot race in which a fully armed rider jumped from a moving chariot, ran on foot, and perhaps remounted the chariot.[245] The contest doubtless arose in funeral games for

243 The Eteoboutads traced their origins to Boutes, who was said to be a son of Pandion (and a grandson of Erichthonios) and the brother of Erechtheus ("Apollodorus" 3.14.8). According to Plutarch *Life of the Ten Orators* (*Lycurgus*) 843e the *génos* of the orator Lycurgus (the Eteoboutads) traced its origin to "Erechtheus, the son of Earth and Hephaistos." There is confusion here between Erechtheus and Erichthonios, but descent from Erechtheus may be the genuine tradition. Was Boutes originally the son of Erechtheus and Athena? If this was how the clan originally viewed its ancestry, with Athena as its ultimate parent, it is clear why Athena and Erechtheus could not remain paired in the state festival of the Panathenaia. When Erechtheus was given a birth from Earth instead of from Athena in a state cult (as reflected in *Iliad* 2.546–551) he became the symbolic parent of all Athenians, who were also originally autochthons, rather than of just one clan. Athena, on the other hand, was now a virgin, and thus the original mother of no Athenians. How far the myth of Athenian autochthony preceded these developments and how far it grew out of them is not obvious. The Eteoboutadai, who were originally called the Boutadai, were renamed in the late sixth century to distinguish them from members of the Cleisthenic deme Boutadai (cf. Toepffer 1889:117). The two branches of the family that provided the priest of Poseidon Erechtheus and the priestess of Athena Polias were distinct, being geographically separated in different demes by 508 BC; see Davies 1971:349, who considers whether one family was divided into two parts or two families were amalgamated into one, and who leans toward the latter possibility; to me the former process is more likely, the division in the family accompanying the split between Athena Polias and Erechtheus.

244 I follow Robertson 1996:63 in thinking that the offering of Athena's *péplos* at the festival did not begin until the sixth century: "the custom cannot well be earlier than the sixth century, since the very first peplos is credited to two historical weavers (Zenobius 1.56, etc.)"; Robertson 1985: 288–289 discusses the issue in more detail: "The Athenians themselves did not take the *peplos* back to the mythical beginnings; Erichthonios, credited with the first temple, the first statue, the first bearing of boughs and baskets, the first chariot, even the first money prizes, is never said to have offered the first *peplos*. Instead the manufacture of the very first *peplos* was ascribed to Acesas and Helicon, master weavers of Patara and Carystus" (sources in Robertson 1985:288); cf. Barber 1992:114 and 209n28. Robertson 1983:277 justly states that "anyone who thinks of the offering of Athena's *peplos* as an ancient yearly custom must explain how it consorts with the washing of Athena's *peplos* as an ancient yearly custom; for this was the business of the Plynteria." Cf. also Deubner 1932:12, 30. I suspect that the *péplos* was introduced in 566/5 BC in imitation of *Iliad* 6, as Davison 1952:15 and 1965:22 suggests.

245 Erichthonios is named as not only the founder of the Panathenaia but also the inventor of the *apobátēs* race in "Eratosthenes" *Catasterismi* 13: ἤγαγε δ' ἐπιμελῶς τὰ Παναθήναια καὶ ἅρμα ἡνιόχει ἔχων παραβάτην ἀσπίδιον ἔχοντα καὶ τριλοφίαν ἐπὶ τῆς κεφαλῆς· ἀπ' ἐκείνου δὲ κατὰ μίμησιν ὁ καλούμενος ἀποβάτης, "He conducted the Panathenaia attentively, and would drive a chariot with a rider who had a small shield and a helmet on his head; from him, as an imitation, comes the so-called dismounter." The term *apobátēs*, "dismounter," does not occur in

clan chieftains, like the funeral games of Patroclus in Homer. The location of the race in the agora, and the presence beneath the agora of classical times of many tombs from the Mycenaean, Protogeometric, and Geometric periods, support this conclusion.[246]

§3.82 When Athena received Erichthonios from the earth into her own hands, she put him in a box (*kístē*) which she entrusted to the three daughters of Kekrops, instructing them not to look inside the box. But some or all of the daughters did look, and they perished as a result. In a common version of the myth Aglauros and Herse looked in the box and in their maddened fright threw themselves from the Acropolis, but Pandrosos, who had no part in the offense, survived.[247] What the guilty sisters saw was a snake or pair of snakes which

---

Homer, but the armed warrior who rides "beside" the driver (*paraibátēs*, *Iliad* 23.132) and leaps from the chariot to fight seems closely related. See Crowther 1991 for a recent discussion of the athletic event, including an important and previously overlooked source for the fourth century, Demosthenes 61.23–29; cf. also Reisch *RE* 'Apobates.' There was also an *apobátēs* race in the festival of the Anthesteria (see Kyle 1987:45–46). The race at the Panathenaia still took place in the agora as late as the second century BC; see Thompson 1961:228.

246 Thompson 1961:228–229: "Within the area have come to light two votive deposits of the 7th century BC, prominent in which are terracotta representations of chariot groups and horsemen, miniature terracotta shields and pinakes, and, in one case, a miniature bronze tripod. Such offerings are appropriate to the cult of the heroized dead, and the deposits in the Agora are in all probability to be associated with some of the early burials in this area. That chariot races were indeed included in the funeral games of early Athens is clearly indicated by their prominence on late Geometric vases found in Athenian graves (Young 1939:56–57). Since some of the most richly furnished burials of the period have come to light beneath the Agora, one may safely infer that such contests occurred in that area in the 8th and 7th centuries BC." Cf. also Kyle 1984:93: "Representations of chariots, prizes and funerals on Geometric and Proto-Attic vases, in addition to significant votive deposits, support H. A. Thompson's theory that Panathenaic athletics arose as a natural development from sporadic funeral games and more organized cults of the heroized dead in the eighth and seventh centuries." Cf. also Jacoby, commentary on Istros *FGrHist* 334 F 4, n2, p. 509: "To venture a conjecture: a main feature and a specialty of the Panathenaia is the agon of the apobatai..., the introduction of which is always ascribed to Erichthonios, the 'inventor' of the *quadriga*. This agon is excellently suited for the time of the Dipylon vases and for aristocratic, pre-Solonian, Athens. Was it meant originally not for Athena, but for her foster-son and (later) cult-fellow Erichthonios-Erechtheus? Did Hippokleides in 566/5 BC enlarge this aristocratic celebration by making it *the* State festival of Athena and of 'all Athenians' by first introducing the gymnastic agones...to which the ἀγῶνες μουσικοί were added subsequently (under the sons of Peisistratos at the latest)?" For representations of the *apobátēs* event and of Erichthonios's part in it ("a favourite subject in Athenian art of the Classical period, both vase-painting and relief sculpture," Robertson 1985:266) see Kron 1976:75–76; for Geometric vases depicting the race, of which there are several, see Kron 76n339.

247 This is the version in "Apollodorus" 3.14.6 and Pausanias 1.18.2; for other versions and sources see Frazer 1921 ad loc. and Frazer 1913 ad loc. In the Atthidographer Amelesagoras *FGrHist* 330 F 1 (cited by Antigonus of Karystos *Collection of Paradoxical Stories* 12) Aglauros and Pandrosos are the guilty sisters; in Euripides *Ion* 273–274 all the sisters are apparently

Athena put in the box to guard the infant Erichthonios, or, in another version, they saw the body of Erichthonios himself which was part or all snake.[248] The

guilty and die: after Athena lifts the newborn Erichthonios from the earth (*Ion* 267–270, see n3.236 above), she gives him to Kekrops's daughters to keep unseen, and they open the goddess's box and perish on the rocks (*Ion* 271–274):

Ion: δίδωσι δ', ὥσπερ ἐν γραφῇ νομίζεται
Creusa: Κέκροπός γε σώζειν παισὶν οὐχ ὁρώμενον.
Ion: ἤκουσα λῦσαι παρθένους τεῦχος θεᾶς.
Creusa: τοιγὰρ θανοῦσαι σκόπελον ᾕμαξαν πέτρας.

Ion: She gives it, as is often shown in paintings,
Creusa: to the daughters of Kekrops to keep unseen.
Ion: I have heard that the maidens opened the goddess's box.
Creusa: For that they bloodied the rocky summit dying.

248 Cf. Frazer 1913 on Pausanias 1.18.2 for the different versions and sources. Erichthonios is seen with one snake in e.g. "Apollodorus" 3.14.6 (see below); there is a pair of snakes beside him in e.g. Euripides *Ion* 21–26, where an Athenian custom is derived from their presence as the infant's guardians:

κείνῳ γὰρ ἡ Διὸς κόρη
φρουρὼ παραζεύξασα φύλακε σώματος
δισσὼ δράκοντε, παρθένοις Ἀγλαυρίσιν
δίδωσι σώζειν· ὅθεν Ἐρεχθείδαις ἐκεῖ
νόμος τις ἔστιν ὄφεσιν ἐν χρυσηλάτοις
τρέφειν τέκν'.

The daughter of Zeus set by his side
two guardian snakes, protectors of his body,
and gave him to the Aglaurid maidens
to safeguard; from this Erechtheus's descendants there
have the custom to raise their children
amid gold-wrought snakes.

On the other hand the *Etymologicum Magnum* s.v. Ἐρεχθεύς and the scholia to Plato *Timaeus* 23e call Erichthonios himself δρακοντόπους, "snake-footed," and yet other sources make Erichthonios entirely a snake, e.g. Hyginus *Astronomica* 2.13: *virgines cistam aperuerunt et anguem viderunt: quo facto, insania a Minerva iniecta, de arce Atheniensium se praecipitaverunt. anguis autem ad Minervae clipeum confugit et ab ea est educatus,* "The maidens opened the box and saw the snake; after which, madness having been cast into them by Minerva, they threw themselves from the citadel of the Athenians. The snake, however, fled to Minverva's shield and was raised by her." In some versions the daughters of Kekrops are driven mad by Athena and throw themselves from the Acropolis, in others they are destroyed by the snake; cf. "Apollodorus" 3.14.6: τοῦτον Ἀθηνᾶ κρύφα τῶν ἄλλων θεῶν ἔτρεφεν, ἀθάνατον θέλουσα ποιῆσαι· καὶ καταθεῖσα αὐτὸν εἰς κίστην Πανδρόσῳ τῇ Κέκροπος παρακατέθετο, ἀπειποῦσα τὴν κίστην ἀνοίγειν. αἱ δὲ ἀδελφαὶ τῆς Πανδρόσου ἀνοίγουσιν ὑπὸ περιεργίας, καὶ θεῶνται τῷ βρέφει παρεσπειραμένον δράκοντα· καὶ ὡς μὲν ἔνιοι λέγουσιν, ὑπ' αὐτοῦ διεφθάρησαν τοῦ δράκοντος, ὡς δὲ ἔνιοι, δι' ὀργὴν Ἀθηνᾶς ἐμμανεῖς γενόμεναι κατὰ τῆς ἀκροπόλεως αὐτὰς ἔρριψαν, "Athena raised him in secret from the other gods, wishing to make him immortal; she put him in a box and entrusted him to Pandrosos the daughter of Kekrops, forbidding

snake motif is consistent with Erichthonios's name and his birth from the earth. In addition he may have been associated with the *oikouròs óphis*, the "temple-guarding snake," which must have inhabited Athena's temple from time immemorial. Erichthonios, because of his name and his birth, and his location in Athena's temple, was at least a striking parallel to this guardian snake.[249]

---

her to open the box. But Pandrosos's sisters opened it out of curiosity, and saw a snake coiled next to the baby; and as some say, they were destroyed by the snake itself, or as others say they went mad because of Athena's anger and threw themselves from the acropolis."

249 Herodotus tells how the *oikouròs óphis* deserted the Acropolis before the Persian occupation of 480 BC; although he does not say so specifically it is clear from his account that the temple in which the snake lived was Athena's: the snake's departure, which was detected when the monthly honey cake offered to it remained uneaten, was interpreted as the departure of "the goddess," and it was "the priestess" (i.e. Athena's priestess) who reported this dire omen (Herodotus 8.41: λέγουσι Ἀθηναῖοι <u>ὄφιν μέγαν φύλακα τῆς ἀκροπόλιος ἐνδιαιτᾶσθαι ἐν τῷ ἱρῷ</u>· λέγουσί τε ταῦτα καὶ δὴ καὶ ὡς ἐόντι ἐπιμήνια διατελέουσι προτιθέντες· τὰ δ' ἐπιμήνια μελιτόεσσά ἐστι. αὕτη δ' ἡ μελιτόεσσα ἐν τῷ πρόσθε αἰεὶ χρόνῳ ἀναισιμουμένη τότε ἦν ἄψαυστος. σημηνάσης δὲ ταῦτα <u>τῆς ἱρηίης</u> μᾶλλόν τι οἱ Ἀθηναῖοι καὶ προθυμότερον ἐξέλιπον τὴν πόλιν ὡς καὶ <u>τῆς θεοῦ</u> ἀπολελοιπυίης τὴν ἀκρόπολιν, "The Athenians say that <u>a large snake, the guardian of the acropolis, lives in the temple</u>; they not only say this, but they also set out food every month for it as actually being there; the monthly food is a honey cake. This honey cake, which previously was always consumed, was then untouched. When <u>the priestess</u> declared this the Athenians left the city even more eagerly because even <u>the goddess</u> had left the acropolis"). Consistent with this account is Eustathius 1423.8 on *Odyssey* 1.357: οἰκουρὸς δράκων <u>φύλαξ τῆς Πολιάδος</u>. ἤγουν <u>ἐν τῷ νεῷ τῆς Πολιάδος</u> διαιτώμενος, "house-guarding snake, <u>guardian of the Polias</u>, or rather living <u>in the temple of the Polias</u>." Ferrari 2002:16 and n32, regarding (as I do) the temple of Athena as distinct from the temple of Erechtheus (cf. n3.117 above), seems to suggest that the snake did not live in the temple of Athena, but in the temple of Erechtheus. The only explicit evidence for the temple of Erechtheus as the location is Hesychius s.v. οἰκουρὸν ὄφιν· τὸν τῆς Πολιάδος φύλακα δράκοντα. καὶ οἱ μὲν ἕνα φασίν, οἱ δὲ δύο <u>ἐν τῷ ἱερῷ τοῦ Ἐρεχθέως</u>, "House-guarding snake: the snake that is the guardian of the Polias. And some say that there is one, but others say that there are two <u>in the temple of Erechtheus</u>." On the face of it this is evidence that the temple of Athena (the snake's home in the other sources) was in the Erechtheum (the usual modern view), and this is a problem. If the two temples are in fact distinct, it is worth noting that the evidence of Hesychius concerns uncertainty about there being one snake or two; I suggest that there may also have been uncertainty about there being one location or (for a second snake) two. Erichthonios in my view was a relative newcomer in Athena's temple, whereas the *oikouròs óphis* was old. We do not hear that Erichthonios was ever identified with this snake (the story in Herodotus suggests rather that it was identified with "the goddess"). In later sources we hear that the snake fashioned at the feet of Pheidias's statue of Athena in the Parthenon was taken to be Erichthonios (Pausanias 1.24.7): πρὸς τοῖς ποσὶν ἀσπίς τε κεῖται καὶ πλησίον τοῦ δόρατος δράκων ἐστίν· εἴη δ' ἂν Ἐριχθόνιος οὗτος ὁ δράκων, "Next to the feet lies the shield and near the spear is a snake; this snake would be Erichthonios"; cf. Hyginus *Astronomica* 2.13, quoted n3.248 above). The snake-footed Erichthonios (see n3.248 above) parallels Kekrops, a snake from the waist down. In Attic genealogies Kekrops is always the first king of Attica; he is "what was there before the first man" (Burkert 1966:10–11), and his snake form reflects this. Kekrops was the original snake-form ancestor; Erichthonios's snake form is, I think, largely an imitation.

§3.83 The story of the daughters of Kekrops and the infant Erichthonios provided the *aítion* for the festival of the Arrhephoria. In the nighttime ritual of this festival two daughters of aristocratic families each carried a box (*kístē*) whose contents they did not know through a subterranean passage, left what they carried underground, and then returned with another wrapped and concealed object. Pausanias describes this ritual, which he does not pretend to understand in full.[250] The ritual has been variously interpreted in modern times, as has its location.[251] These are interesting questions, but they are not

250 After mentioning the temple of Pandrosos and the tradition that she had no part in the offense of her sisters, Pausanias 1.27.3 continues as follows: ἃ δέ μοι θαυμάσαι μάλιστα παρέσχεν, ἔστι μὲν οὐκ ἐς ἅπαντα γνώριμα, γράψω δὲ οἷα συμβαίνει. παρθένοι δύο τοῦ ναοῦ τῆς Πολιάδος οἰκοῦσιν οὐ πόρρω, καλοῦσι δὲ Ἀθηναῖοι σφᾶς ἀρρηφόρους· αὗται χρόνον μέν τινα δίαιταν ἔχουσι παρὰ τῇ θεῷ, παραγενομένης δὲ τῆς ἑορτῆς δρῶσιν ἐν νυκτὶ τοιάδε. ἀναθεῖσαί σφισιν ἐπὶ τὰς κεφαλὰς ἃ ἡ τῆς Ἀθηνᾶς ἱέρεια δίδωσι φέρειν, οὔτε ἡ διδοῦσα ὁποῖόν τι δίδωσιν εἰδυῖα οὔτε ταῖς φερούσαις ἐπισταμέναις—ἔστι δὲ περίβολος ἐν τῇ πόλει τῆς καλουμένης ἐν Κήποις Ἀφροδίτης οὐ πόρρω καὶ δι' αὐτοῦ κάθοδος ὑπόγαιος αὐτομάτη—, ταύτῃ κατίασιν αἱ παρθένοι. κάτω μὲν δὴ τὰ φερόμενα λείπουσιν, λαβοῦσαι δὲ ἄλλο τι κομίζουσιν ἐγκεκαλυμμένον· καὶ τὰς μὲν ἀφιᾶσιν ἤδη τὸ ἐντεῦθεν, ἑτέρας δὲ ἐς τὴν ἀκρόπολιν παρθένους ἄγουσιν ἀντ' αὐτῶν, "What surprised me the most, while it isn't known to me in all details, I will write as it takes place. Two maidens live not far from the temple of Athena Polias, and the Athenians call them arrhephoroi; they live with the goddess for a time, and when the festival is at hand they do the following at night. They put on their heads what the priestess of Athena gives them to carry, and neither she who gives it nor they who carry it know what it is. There is on the acropolis an enclosure not far from the sanctuary of Aphrodite called Aphrodite in the Gardens and through it there is a natural path leading underground—here the maidens descend. The maidens leave below what they have brought, and they receive and bring back something wrapped up; and these maidens are then discharged, and others are brought to the acropolis in place of them." The phrase οὐκ ἐς ἅπαντα γνώριμα, "not known in all details," indicating Pausanias's ignorance of parts of the ceremony, was changed in sixteenth century manuscripts and in modern editions to οὐκ ἐς ἅπαντα⟨ς⟩ γνώριμα, "not known to all," indicating the ceremony's secrecy instead (see Burkert 1966:2n1, who argues effectively against this change); Pausanias does not use the word *kístai* of what the priestess of Athena puts on the heads of the arrhephoroi, but the word occurs elsewhere in connection with the ritual (thus the first etymology of the name *Arrhephória* in the scholia to Aristophanes *Lysistrata* 642: ἐπειδὴ τὰ ἄρρητα ἐν κίσταις ἔφερον τῇ θεῷ αἱ παρθένοι, "since the maidens carried the secret things in *kístai* for the goddess"; cf. Robertson 1983:248).

251 For the widely held interpretation of the festival as a female initiation ritual, see especially Burkert 1966; a problem for this interpretation is the fact that the ritual was performed by only two girls, so that it cannot have been an actual initiation of all Athenian girls who were about to enter womanhood (Burkert 1966:19–20 explains this difficulty in terms of the change from a small community to a polis, in which the initiation became representative rather than real). Robertson 1983 rejects this interpretation and proposes that the ritual had to do with propitiating a sacred snake with a cake (this is Robertson's interpretation of the unknown object left underground by the arrhephoroi). Related to the question of interpretation is the question of location, which is addressed in EN3.12; the question of whether or not the Arrhephoria formed part of the Panathenaia is also addressed.

what concern us here. The only question here is how old the aetiological myth for this festival is. It is generally assumed that the myth and the ritual are both old. This may well be true of the ritual, but the myth raises genuine doubts. If Erichthonios belongs to an old myth, then Hephaistos, a latecomer to Athens, cannot originally have been part of it.[252] But what reason is there for thinking that Erichthonios is any older than Hephaistos in the myth?[253] The daughters of Kekrops, to whom Erichthonios was entrusted after his birth, are an odd group: Pandrosos and Aglauros had different shrines in different places on the Acropolis, whereas Herse apparently had no shrine at all.[254] Aglauros was closely associated with Athena in the festival of the Plynteria, and her cult on the Acropolis was doubtless old.[255] She had her own priestess, attested on

252 Robertson 1983:286 assumes that he was not.
253 Robertson 1983:286 says that Erichthonios's birth from Hephaistos "was evidently prompted by circumstances outside the ritual, since Hephaestus has no part in the Arrhephoria." This is so, but Erichthonios's part in the Arrhephoria is limited to the aetiological myth, which may well be secondary to the ritual.
254 The shrine of Pandrosos, which contained Athena's sacred olive tree, was adjacent to the Erechtheum (Pausanias 1.27.2); the *témenos* of Aglauros was on the north slope of the Acropolis (Pausanias 1.18.2) "immediately under the rock slope" ("unmittelbar unter dem Steinabfall der Burg," Judeich 1931:303; cf. Jacoby, commentary on Philochorus *FGrHist* 328 F 105, n5). Whereas Aglauros and Pandrosos were native Athenian goddesses rooted in the Acropolis, Herse was not a specifically Attic figure (cf. Jacoby, commentary on Philochorus *FGrHist* 328 F 105, n3); even the form of her name is non-Attic, which shows, according to Burkert 1966:12, "that the name belongs to literature, not to Attic cult" ("dass der Name der Literatur, nicht dem attischen Kult angehört"). The originally independent figures Aglauros and Pandrosos became associated in the Kekropid myth through Athena, into whose sphere both had been drawn: there was an Ἀθηνᾶ Ἄγλαυρος (Harpokration s.v. Ἄγλαυρος) and an Ἀθηνᾶ Πάνδροσος (scholia to Aristophanes *Lysistrata* 439); see Jacoby, commentary on Philochorus *FGrHist* 328 F 105, nn3 and 5, and commentary on Istros *FGrHist* 334 F 27. It was in the shrine of Aglauros that the ephebes took the oath of loyalty to the state; cf. Jacoby, commentary on Philochorus *FGrHist* 328 F 105, n5, p. 329, citing Robert 1938:296–307; cf. also Burkert 1966:12n1. For older bibliography on the Kekropids, see Jacoby, commentary on Philochorus *FGrHist* 328 F 105, n2.
255 The Plynteria are said to be held in Aglauros's honor in Hesychius s.v. πλυντήρια· ἑορτὴ Ἀθήνησιν, ἣν ἐπὶ τῇ Ἀγλαύρου τῆς Κέκροπος θυγατρὸς τιμῇ ἄγουσιν. Her death provided an *aition* for the Plynteria: when she died her clothes were left unwashed for a year, and the washing of her clothes at the end of the year was supposed to have given the festival its name (Photius *Lexicon* s.v. Καλλυντήρια καὶ πλυντήρια· τὰ μὲν πλυντήριά φησι [φασι?] διὰ τὸν θάνατον τῆς Ἀγραύλου ἐντὸς ἐνιαυτοῦ μὴ πλυθῆναι ἐσθῆτας· εἶθ' οὕτω πλυθείσας τὴν ὀνομασίαν λαβεῖν ταύτην; cf. Burkert 1966:12n2, Robertson 1983:281). The form *Ágraulos*, found in this passage and elsewhere, is a variant (with metathesis of the liquid consonants) of *Áglauros*. According to Philochorus (FGrHist 328 F 106 = scholia to Demosthenes 19.303) Agraulos was Athena's priestess: ἱέρεια δὲ γέγονεν ἡ Ἄγραυλος Ἀθηνᾶς, ὥς φησι Φιλόχορος; originally, however, Aglauros was an independent goddess, as is shown by the fact that she had her own priestess (see n3.256 below).

471

two inscriptions from the beginning and middle of the third century BC.[256]
Pandrosos likewise had her own priestess and was worshipped in her own
right.[257] What then are we to make of the fact that there was a combined priest-
hood of Aglauros and Pandrosos which the clan of the Salaminioi possessed?
This fact came to light on the Salaminioi inscription of 363/2 BC, and it was
a great surprise to modern scholars: priesthoods were hereditary and the
Salaminioi were immigrants from Salamis who resettled in Attica when
they were driven from their old home by the Megarians.[258] How could such
newcomers get possession of the cult of two old Athenian goddesses, unless
perhaps the original priestly family had died out?[259] A better explanation, I
think, is that whereas the individual cults of Aglauros and Pandrosos were
undoubtedly old, their combined cult was new when the Salaminioi consti-
tuted themselves as an Attic *génos*, probably in the early sixth century BC.[260]
The combined cult would thus have come into existence in connection with the
Arrhephoria and the myth of Erichthonios's birth, for it was in this myth that

256 The first is IG II² 3459 (found on the Acropolis between the Propylaia and the Parthenon):
Ἀγλαύρου ἱέρεα Φειδοστράτη Ἐτεοκλέους Αἰθαλίδου θυγάτηρ; the second is an honorary
decree for a priestess of Aglauros (*Supplementum Epigraphicum Graecum* 33 [1983] no. 115).
Cf. Parker 1996:311 with n72.
257 We know particulars about the dress of the priestess of Pandrosos (Pollux 10.191:
ποδώνυχον ἡ ἐσθὴς ἡ τῆς ἱερείας τῆς Πανδρόσου, "The dress of the priestess of Pandrosos
is called *podónukhon* ['reaching the toes']"; cf. Suda s.v. προτόνιον). In an inscription of the
mid-first century BC (IG II² 1039 lines 57–58) the ephebes are said to offer sacrifices on the
Acropolis to Athena Polias, Kourotrophos, and Pandrosos.
258 For the inscription, *Agora Inventory* I 3244, see n3.183 above; the priestess of Aglauros and
Pandrosos is mentioned twice, in lines 11–12 and line 45 (see EN3.14 to n3.262 below for
text). Cf. Parker 1996:311.
259 So Nilsson 1938:390 suggests: "Aglauros and Pandrosos belong to the native stratum
of Athenian cults and myths. Their myth is connected with the old-fashioned rite of
the Arrephoria. In the hieron of Pandrosos which joined the Erechtheum grew the holy
olive tree. The ephebes took the oath of loyalty to the state in the hieron of Aglauros
(Demosthenes 19.303, and the scholia). It is really astonishing that the priestess of this old
cult was taken from the genos of the Salaminioi which had only recently immigrated and
it shows the great price set upon their allegiance. We do not know how it was possible. If
originally, as do most old cults, this cult belonged to some family, the family must have
become extinct"; cf. also Nilsson 1951:35–36. For the oath of the ephebes see n3.254 above.
260 Cf. Jacoby, commentary on Philochorus *FGrHist* 328 F 105, n5, p. 329, who recognizes a
distinction between the separate cults of Aglauros and Pandrosos on the one hand and
their combined cult on the other hand (contrast Nilsson, quoted in n3.259 above); Jacoby
regards the combined cult as being as early as the sixth century BC. For the constitution
of the *génos* of the Salaminioi in the late seventh or early sixth century BC, cf. Ferguson
1938:46 (he suggests the late seventh century; cf. also n3.184 above); the *génos* and the cult
seem roughly contemporary.

the two goddesses were closely associated.[261] What also suggests this is that the clan of the Salaminioi, in addition to the priesthood of Aglauros and Pandrosos, possessed the priesthood of Kourotrophos, whose cult is elsewhere said to have been founded by Erichthonios himself in gratitude for his foster care.[262] This cult too may well have come into existence when the Salaminioi first constituted themselves as a *génos*. It was in connection with these two new cults, of Aglauros and Pandrosos on the one hand and of Kourotrophos on the other hand, that the myth of Erichthonios's birth and foster care arose. This myth was the *aítion* for the Arrhephoria, and this festival too was perhaps not as old as is generally thought.[263] We cannot be sure about this, but at least the festi-

261 There were originally two Kekropids and two arrhephoroi. This suggests that the combined cult of the two Kekropids was created for the Arrhephoria; cf. Burkert 1966:10, who notes the difference in number between the two arrhephoroi and three Kekropids as an exception to the otherwise close correspondence between the ritual and the myth even in small details. Jacoby was right, I think, to postulate that Herse was added secondarily to the Kekropid myth (cf. n3.254 above); this issue is discussed further in EN3.13. What role the priestess of Aglauros and Pandrosos might have played in the Arrhephoria, if indeed she had a role, is not clear since it was the priestess of Athena who gave the two maidens the *kístai* to be carried underground (Pausanias 1.27.3). But it is perhaps not hard to imagine other roles in the ceremony. It would seem that from the start Aglauros and Pandrosos were contrasted as the guilty and the innocent sister (cf. Jacoby, commentary on Philochorus *FGrHist* 328 F 105 n5, pp. 328–329). Perhaps Aglauros was given the role of the guilty sister because of an older tradition for her death, which may have been connected with the location of her precinct "unmittelbar unter dem Steinabfall der Burg" (Judeich 1931:303; cf. n3.254 above; cf. also Robertson 1983:275, 275n91). Aglauros's death appears in contexts other than the *aítion* of the Arrhephoria: in a rival tradition to that of the daughters of Erechtheus she is said to have sacrificed herself voluntarily in the war with Eumolpos (Philochorus *FGrHist* 328 F 105: see Jacoby, commentary on Philochorus *FGrHist* 328 F 105, for the obvious chronological difficulty of this variant to the myth of the Hyakinthids and his proposed solution); for Aglauros's death as the *aítion* of the Plynteria see n3.255 above).
262 Suda s.v. Κουροτρόφος γῆ (see n3.232 above). Ferguson 1938:21 argues that there is one priestess for all three goddesses in the Salaminioi inscription, but Nilsson 1951:35n35 refutes this; the inscription is discussed in EN3.14.
263 If the combined cult of Aglauros and Pandrosos had to do with the Arrhephoria (as I think it very likely did), this might be taken to indicate that the festival itself belongs to the early sixth century. But there are questions regarding the ritual of the Arrhephoria that do not admit of final answers, and the origin of the ritual is one. We do not know what the arrhephoroi carried underground (or what they brought back), and we are told that even the priestess of Athena did not know (Pausanias 1.27.3). The name *arrhēphóros*, which would seem to contain an answer to the question of what was carried, has no certain meaning. Some ancient sources interpret *arrhē-* as a shortened form of *arrhēta-*, "secret objects" (scholia to Aristophanes *Lysistrata* 642; Hesychius s.v. *arrhēphoría*; Deubner 1932:9–10 accepts this interpretation). A connection with *árrhikhos*, "wicker basket," has also been proposed (cf. Deubner 1932:10n1 for references, to which may be added Robertson 1983:249–250). It does not clarify the name of the festival to know that another form was

val's *aítion* was new. The central role of the Salaminioi in the new cults is what we would have expected. The changes in myth and cult reflected a redefinition of Attica, which was still in the process of absorbing the geographical unity of Eleusis and Salamis to the west of Athens.

§3.84 Everything indicates that Erichthonios, his myth, and his place in the Arrhephoria all came into existence together in the early sixth century BC. In certain respects Erichthonios resembles the Eleusinian hero Demophoon, whose myth occupies a central place in the *Homeric Hymn to Demeter*. Here, in a hymn going back to the seventh century, is another infant nursed by a goddess. Demeter wanted to make Demophoon immortal by putting him in the fire each night, and she would have done so if his mother Metaneira had not spied on her and seen what she should not have seen. In the case of Athena's nursling Erichthonios, it is the daughters of Kekrops who succumb to curiosity and see what they are forbidden to see. The result is different in that the guilty daughters of Kekrops destroy themselves on the Acropolis, whereas in Eleusis Demophoon's immortality is lost. But the loss of immortality, while it is overshadowed by the flamboyant death of the guilty Kekropids, was also part of the Athenian myth according to "Apollodorus" 3.14.6, who says that Athena wished to make Erichthonios immortal.[264] "Apollodorus" is not likely to have invented this motif, and if it belongs to the original myth, Erichthonios too must have lost his immortality through others' curiosity.[265] This is an important parallel with the Eleusinian myth, for

---

ersēphoría (written *ersephoría* in scholia to Aristophanes *Lysistrata* 642) or *errēphoría* (probable correction of *eriphoría* in Hesychius s.v. *arrhēphoría*) and that this form occurs in cult contexts other than the Arrhephoria (*ersēphóroi* are epigraphically attested for cults of *Khlóē Thémis, Eileíthuia en Ágrais,* and Demeter and Kore; cf. Jacoby, commentary on Istros *FGrHist* 334 F 27). This form of the name (*ersēphóros*) may perhaps explain why (H)erse was added to Aglauros and Pandrosos as the third Kekropid, but in Jacoby's view (commentary on Philochorus *FGrHist* 328 F 105, n3) this came about only through a lack of understanding (and a misunderstanding) of the name (H)ersephoria itself. His point is not quite clear.

264 "Apollodorus" 3.14.6: φευγούσης δὲ αὐτῆς καὶ τῆς γονῆς εἰς γῆν πεσούσης Ἐριχθόνιος γίνεται. τοῦτον Ἀθηνᾶ κρύφα τῶν ἄλλων θεῶν ἔτρεφεν, <u>ἀθάνατον θέλουσα ποιῆσαι</u>· καὶ καταθεῖσα αὐτὸν εἰς κίστην Πανδρόσῳ τῇ Κέκροπος παρακατέθετο, ἀπειποῦσα τὴν κίστην ἀνοίγειν. αἱ δὲ ἀδελφαὶ τῆς Πανδρόσου ἀνοίγουσιν ὑπὸ περιεργίας, καὶ θεῶνται τῷ βρέφει παρεσπειραμένον δράκοντα, "When she fled and the sperm fell to the ground Erichthonios was born. Athena raised him in secret from the other gods, <u>wishing to make him immortal</u>; and she put him in a box and entrusted him to Pandrosos the daughter of Kekrops, forbidding her to open the box. But Pandrosos's sisters opened it out of curiosity, and saw a snake coiled next to the baby."

265 The starting point for the Kekropids' punishment was probably an older tradition for Aglauros's suicide by jumping from the Acropolis (cf. n3.261 above); the punishment of the Kekropids replaced the loss of Erichthonios's immortality as the focal point of the myth.

it suggests why, in the creation of Erichthonios's myth, the model followed seems to have been Demophoon's myth. It was necessary that Erichthonios, in replacing Erechtheus in Athena's temple, be mortal; Erechtheus himself, in being removed from Athena's temple, had similarly been reduced to mortal status. The Eleusinian hero Demophoon provided an example of forfeited immortality for an Athenian hero to follow at a time when Eleusis was otherwise much on the Athenians' minds.[266]

§3.85 Demophoon's loss of immortality is compensated by an annual festival in his honor, which Demeter herself announces in the hymn (*Homeric Hymn to Demeter* 259–267):[267]

ἴστω γὰρ θεῶν ὅρκος ἀμείλικτον Στυγὸς ὕδωρ
ἀθάνατόν κέν τοι καὶ ἀγήραον ἤματα πάντα
παῖδα φίλον ποίησα καὶ ἄφθιτον ὤπασα τιμήν·
νῦν δ' οὐκ ἔσθ' ὥς κεν θάνατον καὶ κῆρας ἀλύξαι.
τιμὴ δ' ἄφθιτος αἰὲν ἐπέσσεται οὕνεκα γούνων
ἡμετέρων ἐπέβη καὶ ἐν ἀγκοίνῃσιν ἴαυσεν.
ὥρῃσιν δ' ἄρα τῷ γε περιπλομένων ἐνιαυτῶν
παῖδες Ἐλευσινίων πόλεμον καὶ φύλοπιν αἰνὴν
αἰὲν ἐν ἀλλήλοισι συνάξουσ' ἤματα πάντα.

May the pitless water of Styx, by whom the gods swear, know
that I would have made the dear child ageless and deathless
    forever
and granted him undying honor;
but now it is not possible for him to escape death and destruc-
    tion.
Nevertheless undying honor will attend him because he came
onto my knees and slept in my arms.
Therefore at the proper season as the years return
the sons of the Eleusinians will in his honor
forever bring together dread war against each other.

266 For other parallels between Erichthonios and Demophoon see Richardson 1974:234–235. Burkert notes a parallel between the Arrhephoria and Eleusinian ritual (1966:5n3); cf. also Deubner 1932:11n3 and Burkert 1966:10 with references to Picard 1931.
267 What the festival was (the Eleusinia?) is not known; the *pólemos*, "battle," of line 266 is the ritual combat called *ballētús* (see Richardson 1974 on lines 265–267).

The last part of this passage, as Nicholas Richardson has noted, strikingly resembles the Athenian entry to the Catalogue of Ships; in this passage too there is an annual festival, conducted by the youths of the Athenians for Erechtheus at his temple (*Iliad* 2.550–551):

ἔνθα δέ μιν ταύροισι καὶ ἀρνειοῖς ἱλάονται
κοῦροι Ἀθηναίων περιτελλομένων ἐνιαυτῶν.

There the youths of the Athenians propitiate him with bulls and
rams
as the years return.[268]

The correspondence between the two passages goes deeper than has been appreciated if the festival for Erechtheus is the Skira, celebrating Erechtheus's heroic death in war at the very moment of his victory over the Eleusinians.[269] The ritual warfare of the Eleusinians in compensation for the mythic Demophoon's death has been paralleled by a different ritual and myth celebrating the Eleusinians' defeat by Athens and their incorporation into Attica: Athens, in other words, seems to have appropriated an Eleusinian myth together with Eleusis itself.

§3.86 In antiquity much critical attention was devoted to the Salaminian entry to the Catalogue of Ships, which was widely regarded as containing

---

268 Richardson 1974:247: "The parallel between *Il.* 2.550f. and *Dem.* 265f. is striking, since Demophon as Demeter's θρεπτός ['nursling'] is in the same position as Erechtheus in relation to Athena, and the myth of Demophon suggests comparison with that of Erichthonius/Erechtheus (cf. ad *Dem.* 235ff.)." In the two rituals evoked in the two passages note the correspondence between the παῖδες Ἐλευσινίων, "boys/young men of the Eleusinians," in the *Homeric Hymn to Demeter* and the κοῦροι Ἀθηναίων, "youths of the Athenians," in *Iliad* 2, and the further correspondence between the phrase περιπλομένων ἐνιαυτῶν in the *Homeric Hymn to Demeter* and the phrase περιτελλομένων ἐνιαυτῶν in *Iliad* 2 (the two phrases, both meaning "as the years revolve," are metrical variants in Homer: περιπλομένους ἐνιαυτούς, *Iliad* 23.833, versus περιτελλομένους ἐνιαυτούς, *Iliad* 8.404; in the *Homeric Hymn to Demeter*, besides περιπλομένων ἐνιαυτῶν in line 265, there is ἔτεος περιτελλομένοιο, "as the year revolves," in lines 445 and 463). The phrase κοῦροι Ἀθηναίων, "youths of the Athenians," in *Iliad* 2 is more Homeric than the phrase παῖδες Ἐλευσινίων, "boys/young men of the Eleusinians," in *Homeric Hymn to Demeter* 266; the only comparison for the latter seems to be the phrase παῖδες δὲ Τρώων, "boys/young men of the Trojans," in *Odyssey* 11.547 (for παῖδες Ἐλευσινίων as "young men [or boys] of the Eleusianians" see Richardson 1974 on line 266 and cf. Matthews 1996:130). Behind the phrase κοῦροι Ἀθηναίων, "youths of the Athenians," lies the phrase κοῦροι Ἀχαιῶν, "youths of the Achaeans"; cf. also the phrase κούρων ἑλκόντων, "as the youths drag it," in *Iliad* 20.405 in a context close to that of *Iliad* 2.550–551, namely the sacrifice of a bull to Poseidon Helikonios.
269 See above §3.72 and n3.197 for the Skira as the festival in *Iliad* 2.

an Athenian forgery in support of Athens' claim to Salamis;[270] Solon and Peisistratos were both accused of the forgery, by the Megarians in the first instance, but by later critics as well.[271] Much less attention was devoted to the Athenian entry, which belonged to an earlier period and left fewer traces of the conflict from which it arose. There is a suggestion in Diogenes Laertius that the Megarians called the Athenian entry into question, but this is uncertain.[272]

270 *Iliad* 2.557–558:

Αἴας δ' ἐκ Σαλαμῖνος ἄγεν δυοκαίδεκα νῆας,
στῆσε δ' ἄγων ἵν' Ἀθηναίων ἵσταντο φάλαγγες.

Ajax led twelve ships from Salamis,
and leading them he stationed them where the ranks of the Athenians stood.

The second line is the alleged forgery; it was atheitzed in antiquity and is omitted in all the main medieval manuscripts.

271 According to Strabo 9.1.10 some said that Peisistratos, others that Solon inserted the line; Strabo goes on to say that "critics" (κριτικοί) rejected the line because in the *Iliad* Ajax anchors his ships not with the Athenians, but on one end with the Thessalians of Protesilaos. Strabo says that the Megareans had a rival version of the Salaminian entry (see n3.272 below); he probably refers to fourth-century Megarian historians like Dieuchidas (see Jacoby, commentary on Dieuchidas *FGrHist* 485 F 6, p. 392 and n26) and Hereas (see Jacoby, commentary on Hereas *FGrHist* 486 F 4). Solon was said to have been the line's author by "some" according to Diogenes Laertius 1.48, and by "many" according to Plutarch *Solon* 10.1. See Allen 1924:234–237.

272 Diogenes Laertius 1.57 (Dieuchidas *FGrHist* 485 F 6). In this well-known passage Solon is said to have legislated that the Homeric poems be recited by rhapsodes one after the other (ἐξ ὑποβολῆς). The continuation of the passage seems to have a gap and it is not clear why the mid-fourth century Megarian historian Dieuchidas is cited, except that whatever Dieuchidas said had to do with the Athenian entry (ἦν δὲ μάλιστα τὰ ἔπη ταυτί· "οἳ δ' ἄρ' Ἀθήνας εἶχον" καὶ τὰ ἑξῆς). As the text stands Dieuchidas is cited to support the statement that Solon did more than Peisistratos to spread Homer's fame (μᾶλλον οὖν Σόλων Ὅμηρον ἐφώτισεν ἢ Πεισίστρατος, ὥς φησι Διευχίδας ἐν πέμπτῳ Μεγαρικῶν. ἦν δὲ μάλιστα τὰ ἔπη ταυτί, κτλ.). As Jacoby, commentary on Dieuchidas *FGrHist* 485 F 6, says, no Megarian would have weighed the relative merits of Solon and Peisistratos in spreading Homer's fame. What has dropped out most likely had to do with alleged interpolations of Peisistratos and Solon. Jacoby, however, is unwilling to take for granted that Dieuchidas included the Athenian entry with other well-known cases, like the Salaminian entry, in his allegation ("Ob Dieuchidas so weit ging dass er gleichzeitig den Abschnitt über Athen B 546/56 für interpoliert erklärte wissen wir nicht"). In any case the Megarians do not seem to have had solid ground textually for their allegations; as Jacoby, commentary on Dieuchidas *FGrHist* 485 F 6 points out, there was no Megarian *ékdosis* of Homer that we know of. The Megarians countered the Athenian version of the Salaminian entry with a version of their own, which grouped Salamis with four Megarian towns (Strabo 9.1.10):

Αἴας δ' ἐκ Σαλαμῖνος ἄγεν νέας, ἔκ τε Πολίχνης,
ἔκ τ' Αἰγειρούσσης Νισαίης τε Τριπόδων τε.

Ajax led ships from Salamis, and from Polichna,
and from Aigeiroussa and Nisaia and Tripodes.

The Athenian entry seems in fact to have achieved its purpose, which was to be accepted as Homeric.[273]

Megara has no entry of its own in the Catalogue of Ships, and these lines serve as one, but they are clearly only a reworking of the Athenian version: the number of Ajax's ships (twelve) was eliminated in the Megarian version, but such a number is indispensable. Every other entry includes the number of ships (the context after all is a catalogue of ships); cf. Weber 1927:147n2.

273 The Athenian entry aims to be as Homeric as possible, particularly with regard to Athena: the Διὸς θυγάτηρ, "daughter of Zeus," of this passage is precisely the Homeric goddess. The language is likewise unexceptionably Homeric: the phrase περιτελλομένων ἐνιαυτῶν, "as the years revolve," as noted above, is a Homeric formula; the phrase κοῦροι Ἀθηναίων, "youths of the Athenians," on the other hand, is a perfect Athenian equivalent of the Homeric formula κοῦροι Ἀχαιῶν, "youths of the Achaeans," with all the heroic overtones of that phrase. Unlike the catalogue of heroines in *Odyssey* 11, the Athenian entry does not mean to give itself away as Athenian. The earliest direct evidence of the Athenian entry is in Herodotus 7.161.3, where an Athenian envoy to Gela in 480 BC refuses to let the tyrant Gelon command the Greek naval forces against the Persians, citing Homer for the Athenians' own right to do so: τῶν καὶ Ὅμηρος ὁ ἐποποιὸς ἄνδρα ἄριστον ἔφησε ἐς Ἴλιον ἀπικέσθαι τάξαι τε καὶ διακοσμῆσαι στρατόν. οὕτω οὐκ ὄνειδος οὐδὲν ἡμῖν ἐστι λέγειν ταῦτα, "One of whom (sc. the Athenians) the epic poet Homer said was the best man who came to Troy in ordering and marshaling an army. Thus there can be no reproach of us for saying this." Similar in tone and close in time is one of the three epigrams inscribed on Athenian herms by Cimon after he defeated the Persians and captured Eion in 476/5 BC. There are slightly different versions of this inscription's three elegiac couplets in Plutarch *Cimon* 7.5 and Aeschines *Against Ctesiphon* 185; Plutarch's version is as follows:

ἔκ ποτε τῆσδε πόληος ἅμ' Ἀτρείδῃσι Μενεσθεύς
    ἡγεῖτο ζάθεον Τρωικὸν ἐς πεδίον·
ὅν ποθ' Ὅμηρος ἔφη Δαναῶν πύκα θωρηκτάων
    κοσμητῆρα μάχης ἔξοχον ὄντα μολεῖν.
οὕτως οὐδὲν ἀεικὲς Ἀθηναίοισι καλεῖσθαι
    κοσμηταῖς πολέμου τ' ἀμφὶ καὶ ἠνορέης.

From this city Menestheus was once a leader with the Atreidai
    to the holy Trojan plain;
Homer once said that of the close-armored Danaans
    he was the best marshaler of battle to go there.
Thus it is not unseemly for the Athenians to be called
    marshalers of war and valor.

Earlier the Athenians claimed the right to Sigeion in the Troad on the basis of their participation in the Trojan war, but in Herodotus 5.94 this claim is not based specifically on the Athenian entry to the catalogue (it is not clear whether the period in question was the initial capture of Sigeion c. 600 BC or its later recapture by Peisistratos, since Herodotus confuses the two events). Theopompus was a sharp critic of what he regarded as Athenian falsification and exaggeration with respect to the oath of Plataea and the Battle of Marathon καὶ ὅσα ἄλλα...ἡ Ἀθηναίων πόλις ἀλαζονεύεται καὶ παρακρούεται τοὺς Ἕλληνας (Theopompus *FGrHist* 115 F 153 = Theon *Progymnasmata* p. 67 line 28); we do not know if he suspected the Athenian entry (cf. Jacoby, commentary on Dieuchidas FGrHist 485 F 6, n27).

§3.87 What makes the Athenian entry stand out from the rest of the Catalogue of Ships, just on the face of it, is the fact that Athens appears alone and no other towns in Attica are named.[274] This is not at all the way of the rest of the catalogue, although some regions of course have fewer towns named than others.[275] It is often argued that the picture of Athens in the catalogue reflects the synoecism of Theseus, as though Attica in the eyes of the Homeric poets was so highly unified at the time of the Trojan war that only Athens could be named; but this argument, even if the early synoecism is accepted, does not explain the stark contrast between Athens and the rest of the catalogue.[276] Agamemnon's Mycenae, which is supposed to have united all Greece for the war, does not stand alone, but is one of twelve towns in its entry.[277] We would perhaps not expect Athens to have twelve towns named

274 See above §3.39 and n3.82, and cf. Simpson and Lazenby 1970:56: "The difficulty with [the Athenian] entry lies not so much in what it contains as in what it omits, for although the mention of Athens itself need excite no surprise whatever period the Catalogue is thought to reflect, we should, on the analogy of other entries, have expected at least some other places in Attica to be mentioned. Page's argument (1959:171n72) that 'we have no reason to believe that any place except the great fortress of Athens was worth mentioning in the Catalogue' is not a sufficient explanation: the Catalogue elsewhere refers to plenty of places which can hardly be regarded as more worthy of mention than, for example, Eleusis, Aphidna, Marathon, or Thorikos." Ancient critics seem not to have focused on this inconsistency or drawn conclusions from it for the Athenian entry; Strabo 9.1.5 simply regards it as a peculiarity of Homer that when he says Athenians, as in the catalogue, he means the whole population of Attica, a usage that is in fact found later as well; cf. Bölte *RE* 'Sparta (Namen und Ableitungen)' 1269.

275 Of the 29 entries in the Greek catalogue two besides Athens name only one town, of which Salamis, a special case like Athens, is one; for the other, the island of Sume, see below in the text. One entry contains just the island Doulikhion and a group of islands, the Ekhinai (2.625–630); the Magnetes have no towns named, only a river, Peneios, and a mountain, Pelion (2.756–759). Boeotia, which heads the catalogue, has the greatest number of towns named at 29 (2.494–510); Orkhomenos, although in Boeotia, has its own entry because of its onetime glory, but it too is paired with another town Aspledon and does not stand alone (2.511–516). Other entries have between three and twelve towns each. To fit this picture Athens ought to look more perhaps like its neighbor Euboea, which has seven towns named: Chalcis and Eretria head the list and five other towns follow (2.536–545).

276 Cf. Simpson Lazenby 1970:56: "Some scholars have sought an explanation in the tradition that the synoecism of Attica was effected by Theseus, and so *before* the Trojan War.... But whether or not the synoecism had taken place so early is, surely, largely irrelevant to the problem we are considering: whenever the synoecism took place, it did not result in the other settlements' in Attica ceasing to exist, and, however tightly they were controlled from Athens, we should still have expected the Catalogue to refer to some of them."

277 *Iliad* 2.569–578:

οἳ δὲ Μυκήνας εἶχον ἐϋκτίμενον πτολίεθρον
ἀφνειόν τε Κόρινθον ἐϋκτιμένας τε Κλεωνάς,
Ὀρνειάς τ' ἐνέμοντο Ἀραιθυρέην τ' ἐρατεινὴν

(the seven towns of Euboea seem a better comparison), but as it is Athens in
the Athenian entry is on a par with stand-alone Syme, which is singled out
in the catalogue for its weakness and the weakness of its leader Nireus (*Iliad*
2.671–675):

Νιρεὺς αὖ Σύμηθεν ἄγε τρεῖς νῆας ἐΐσας
Νιρεὺς Ἀγλαΐης υἱὸς Χαρόποιό τ’ ἄνακτος
Νιρεύς, ὃς κάλλιστος ἀνὴρ ὑπὸ Ἴλιον ἦλθε
τῶν ἄλλων Δαναῶν μετ’ ἀμύμονα Πηλεΐωνα·
ἀλλ’ ἀλαπαδνὸς ἔην, παῦρος δέ οἱ εἵπετο λαός.

Nireus brought three balanced ships from Sume,
Nireus, the son of Aglaia and king Charopos,
Nireus, who was the most beautiful man to come to Troy
of all the other Danaans after the faultless son of Peleus;
but he was weak, and few warriors followed him.

Clearly the limitation to one city does not have the same meaning in the
case of Athens that it does in the case of Syme. The two entries, which are
constructed on different principles, must have had different origins.

§3.88 The Athenian entry was, I think, composed in its entirety about
600 BC in Athens to take the place of an earlier Athenian entry which would
have been in line with the rest of the catalogue in containing the names of

---

καὶ Σικυῶν’, ὅθ’ ἄρ’ Ἄδρηστος πρῶτ’ ἐμβασίλευεν,
οἵ θ’ Ὑπερησίην τε καὶ αἰπεινὴν Γονόεσσαν
Πελλήνην τ’ εἶχον ἠδ’ Αἴγιον ἀμφενέμοντο
Αἰγιαλόν τ’ ἀνὰ πάντα καὶ ἀμφ’ Ἑλίκην εὐρεῖαν,
τῶν ἑκατὸν νηῶν ἦρχε κρείων Ἀγαμέμνων
Ἀτρεΐδης· ἅμα τῷ γε πολὺ πλεῖστοι καὶ ἄριστοι
λαοὶ ἕποντ’.

And those who held Mycenae, a well-founded citadel,
and wealthy Corinth and well-founded Kleonai,
and those who dwelt in Orneiai and lovely Araithyrea
and Sikyon, where Adrastos first ruled,
and those who held Hyperesia and steep Gonoessa
and Pellene and dwelt around Aigion
and all through Aigialon and around wide Helike,
of these the ruler Agamemnon led one hundred ships,
the son of Atreus; and far the most and best
warriors followed him.

several Attic towns.[278] Why would such a thing have happened? It was not so much that Athens wished to present a new image of itself and of its hero Erechtheus, although that is certainly what it did. The motive, I think, is that there was something entirely unacceptable in the original Athenian entry, namely, that Eleusis was missing from the list of Attic towns that were named in it: the more towns that were named in the original entry, the more glaring the absence of Eleusis would have been. When Athens incorporated Eleusis about 600 BC, it pretended that it had always (from the days of Erechtheus) been part of Attica. This pretense had no chance of acceptance if the Homeric Catalogue of Ships not only did not support it, but completely excluded it. The solution was not to insert the name Eleusis into the Athenian entry in bald fashion, which would certainly have been ineffective, but to recast the entire entry on a different principle, and to promote the new version as the true one. If this was the plan, it succeeded brilliantly.[279]

278 Some modern scholars have argued that just parts of the Athenian catalogue have an Athenian origin (e.g. Burr 1944:40–42, who limits the Athenian lines to 550–551, the sacrifices to Erechtheus, and 553–555, the praise of Menestheus). My own view is close to that of Weber 1927, who regards the entire passage as an Athenian creation "aus einem Guss" ("from one cast"), p. 147; see especially pp. 146–149. It is theoretically possible that Athens was omitted entirely in an earlier stage of the catalogue, but I again agree with Weber, pp. 146–147, that Athenian participation in the *Iliad*, modest as it is, is too well integrated in the poem to be eliminated. If Menestheus and the Athenians were, so to speak, there from the start, then they must have been mentioned in the catalogue. One thing that the new version of the catalogue did not wish to tamper with was the identity of the Athenian leader, which must therefore have been established by tradition. If Athens had inserted itself into the Homeric poems for the first time about 600 BC it would presumably not have chosen the obscure Menestheus as leader, but Theseus or a son of Theseus. Theopompus (and others) may have wished to imply that the Athenians inserted themselves into the *Iliad* secondarily, but they evidently had no versions of the *Iliad* without Athens to prove their point. As for the earlier version of the Athenian entry that I envision, it apparently did not survive because of the prestige of the new Athenian version. Megarian writers of the fourth century, who surely would have liked to undermine Athens' claims based on the *Iliad*, cannot have found any other version to cite.

279 One may wonder about the time needed for such a bold stroke to succeed. The traditional version cannot have disappeared everywhere at once, however strongly Athens promoted the new version. I would imagine that the traditional version continued to exist in the sixth century, but we know nothing of it because it was never used against the Athenians. In the dispute over Salamis the Spartan arbitrators seem to have been perfectly willing to accept the Salaminian entry forged by the Athenians, so there is no reason to think that questions were raised about the passage preceding it upon which it depended, and which would already have been established for a longer period of time (or perhaps, if Cassio 2002:115 is right that the Salaminian entry must have been in existence for some decades before 560 BC to be accepted as evidence at the Spartan arbitration, both passages had been established for the same period of time). So far as we know it was the Megarian writers of the fourth century who objected to the Salaminian forgery, not the sixth-century Megarians

§3.89 An essential point that the new Athenian entry was meant to convey was the warlike nature of the Athenians; this after all was the *Iliad*. The point was conveyed through Erechtheus and Athena and the new relationship between them. The Athena who nourishes the earthborn Erechtheus is the Homeric war goddess, not the old Athenian mother goddess; the use of her Homeric epithet Διὸς θυγάτηρ (*Iliad* 2.548) leaves no doubt about this.[280] Erechtheus himself is given a Homeric epithet used only of heroic warriors, namely μεγαλήτωρ, "great hearted" (*Iliad* 2.547).[281] When Athena places the earthborn Erechtheus in his own temple, this is a new location for him from the standpoint of Homeric tradition (i.e. *Odyssey* 7.80–81), and the abruptness of the change is muted by the ambiguity between "her own" and "his own" in the meaning of the adjective ἑῷ. But the new order of things on the Acropolis required the meaning "his own," and this meaning was sure to prevail in time. Erechtheus's location in his own temple automatically evoked the myth of his death by Poseidon's trident and burial in the rock after his heroic victory in battle. The yearly sacrifices performed by the κοῦροι Ἀθηναίων for Erechtheus at his temple commemorated both his heroic victory and his heroic death.[282] Thus when Athens is called the δῆμος of Erechtheus at the start of the Athenian entry, it does not matter whether δῆμος means land or people, for what is conveyed is the warlike nature of Athens.[283] This is the essential point, after which the entry continues with Menestheus and his

---

involved in the actual dispute. At any rate the sixth-century Megarians would have had nothing to gain by raising the issue of the Athenian entry; this would have been to the point if the dispute had been about Athens' right to Eleusis, but that issue was settled decisively the day that Tellos died. We do not hear that Megara ever thought that it had a right to Eleusis, and the reason is, I think, that Eleusis was autonomous before it was annexed by Athens.

280 For Athena's epithet Διὸς θυγάτηρ, cf. n3.56 above. The text of the Athenian entry is given in §3.39 above.

281 The epithet is often used of a hero's *thumós*, "spirit"; it is also used once of the Cyclops (*Odyssey* 10.200). The epithet μεγάθυμος, which seems similar, is mainly used of warriors and peoples, but twice also of Athena (*Odyssey* 8.520, 13.121).

282 For Poseidon's absence from the passage see above §3.72 and n3.193. Mikalson 1976:146n21 interprets the sacrifices as belonging to a god rather than a hero on the basis of the verb ἱλάονται, "propitiated," but this form, and the usual Homeric form ἱλάσκονται as well, could surely be used of either; the verb's usage appears one-sided in Homer because (apart from this passage) there are no hero cults in Homer (cf. Farnell 1921:11). While I do not accept Mikalson's specific arguments, I do agree with him that Erechtheus was originally a god (Mikalson follows Nilsson's view that Erechtheus was a "divine child" like Hyakinthos).

283 In Homer *dêmos* designates either land or people; the well attested Mycenaean form *damo* designates a local administrative entity concerned with agriculture (Lejeune 1965:6–7). If *dêmos* is related to *daíomai*, "divide," land rather than people is its primary etymological meaning (cf. Chantraine 1999 s.vv.).

great ability as a marshaler of troops at Troy, rivaled only by Nestor (*Iliad* 2.552–556):

τῶν αὖθ᾽ ἡγεμόνευ᾽ υἱὸς Πετεῶο Μενεσθεύς.
τῷ δ᾽ οὔ πώ τις ὁμοῖος ἐπιχθόνιος γένετ᾽ ἀνὴρ
κοσμῆσαι ἵππους τε καὶ ἀνέρας ἀσπιδιώτας·
Νέστωρ οἶος ἔριζεν· ὃ γὰρ προγενέστερος ἦεν·
τῷ δ᾽ ἅμα πεντήκοντα μέλαιναι νῆες ἕποντο.

Those men Menestheus, the son of Peteos, led;
never was there another man on earth to equal him
in marshaling horses and shield-bearing men;
only Nestor rivaled him, for he was older;
fifty black ships followed him.

§3.90 The period around 600 BC is the era of Solon, and Solon, in my view, is likely to be the poet who composed the new Athenian entry to the Catalogue of Ships. Solon in fact can be associated with all the changes that we have been considering for the period. His name is linked with that of Tellos, whose death in a real battle seems to have preceded the incorporation of Eleusis into Attica. Solon the lawgiver, who reformed Athenian society, also involved himself in the reform of cults, as Jacoby's study of the *Genésia*, a festival of the dead, demonstrates.[284] The tight hold that clans had on the

---

284 Jacoby 1944. Following Mommsen 1898:174 Jacoby argues that Solon transformed indi-
vidual clan festivals of the dead (*genésia*) into one state festival. Jacoby's general point
about Solon's reform of cults is of special interest: "One may...emphasize more than has
been done hitherto that a number of important measures taken by Solon in the domain
of political life and particularly in the sphere of cult, where he did not shrink from
profound changes, form part of a definite political programme" (p. 69). On pp. 72–73
Jacoby considers other examples in the cults of Aphrodite Pandemos and Apollo Patroos.
On pp. 73–74 he contrasts the reform activity of Cleisthenes, who did not interfere with
cults, with that of Solon ninety years earlier: "The difference between the two lawgivers
is in no way surprising. The power of the clans was founded to a great extent on their reli-
gious functions; most of the cults and feasts (and certainly the most important ones were
clan festivals) were in a manner of speaking their private possession. The fact has long ago
been inferred from the privileged position left to them even in historical times at several
festivals of great religious importance, and it does not matter much that our knowledge as
to the details is rather restricted." Cf. also Jeffery 1948:110 and 110n86: "It is clear that the
body of laws attributed to Solon did contain references to various religious matters." The
examples, however, are not plentiful; Jeffery cites Photius *Lexicon* s.v. ὀργεῶνας· Σέλευκος
δὲ ἐν τῷ ὑπομνήματι τῶν Σόλωνος ἀξόνων· ὀργεῶνας φησὶ καλεῖσθαι τοὺς συνόδους
ἔχοντας περί τινας ἥρωας ἢ θεούς, "Seleukos in his treatise on Solon's law tablets says that

city goddess herself was I think weakened by the removal from her domain of Erechtheus, the ancestral progenitor of some but not all Athenians. With respect to the Athenian entry, there is no need to prove that poetry for Solon was a tool of statesmanship, for his poetry survives in sufficient quantity to speak for itself.[285] Solon demonstrably had the craft to do the job; if he was behind the incorporation of Eleusis into Attica, as his link with Tellos suggests, he also had the motive. Leo Weber has noted that the tactics for which Menestheus is celebrated in the Athenian entry are otherwise foreign to epic but remind one of Solon's reorganization of the army.[286] Other

---

they are called *orgeônes* who have gatherings for certain heroes or gods," and Pollux 1.29: Σόλων δὲ τὰ ἔμπηρα καὶ ἀφελῆ ὠνόμασε, "Solon also called the crippled ones by the term ἀφελῆ" (the context is laws ensuring the fitness of sacrificial victims).

285 See Henderson 1982 for an analysis of how Solon's poetry would have effectively communicated the statesman's program in an oral society. Although this is not the place to examine Solon's poetry in detail, fr. 4 West, as elucidated by Henderson, calls for some comment. The first four lines, which are full of assurances about Athens' ultimate well-being, open the poem with "an accumulation of Homeric words and phrases"; after this introduction Solon turns to the city's unhealthy state, and here "Homeric echoes all but vanish to make way for the poet's own personal statement and diction" in the rest of the poem, his "personal diagnosis of the ills affecting the 'great city' (μεγάλην πόλιν, line 5) which is being destroyed by its own citizens (lines 5–6)" (Henderson 1982:26–27; cf. also Irwin 2005:164–198, who distinguishes between a Homeric opening to the poem and a Hesiodic continuation). The "Homeric" opening of the poem contains all the elements that I would attribute to Solon's reform of Athena's cult: Athena's identity as the warrior protectress of Athens, her close relationship to Zeus as his daughter, and the guarantee of Zeus's protection that this relationship brings (Solon 4.1–4 West):

ἡμετέρη δὲ πόλις κατὰ μὲν Διὸς οὔποτ' ὀλεῖται
αἶσαν καὶ μακάρων θεῶν φρένας ἀθανάτων·
τοίη γὰρ μεγάθυμος ἐπίσκοπος ὀβριμοπάτρη
Παλλὰς Ἀθηναίη χεῖρας ὕπερθεν ἔχει.

Our city will never be destroyed by the destiny of Zeus
and the will of the blessed immortals.
For such a great-hearted guardian, Pallas Athena,
the daughter of a mighty father, holds her hands over it.

These lines present a picture which would have been totally familiar to fifth-century Athenians (cf. §3.42–§3.47 above), but which I think was much newer in Solon's day: the city goddess had not always been identical with the Homeric goddess. Henderson comments that "it is impossible to be sure how the Homeric echoes [of the opening lines] struck Solon's audience" (Henderson 1982:27); for my part I do not think that the Athenians heard only the comforting ring of the familiar in these lines. There is something much bolder in them—a new vision which not all Athenians, if their privileges were affected, may readily have accepted. For the question of Solon's knowledge of what we know as the *Iliad* and the *Odyssey* see n4.149 below.

286 Weber 1927:148. Weber refers to Meyer 1893:653–654 (= 1954:605) for the further observation that the name τέλη for the divisions into which Solon divided the citizens on the basis

tantalizing connections dimly suggest themselves.[287] But the general plausibility of seeing Solon's influence and direct involvement is what matters. The Athenian entry to the Catalogue of Ships in *Iliad* 2 was a serious matter of state, and a well-placed statesman is likely to have undertaken to reshape it if that statesman was also a poet.[288]

§3.91 The Athenian entry to the Catalogue of Ships does not represent the primary Ionian stage in the development of the Homeric poems, but a

---

of a strict census had a military origin, as use of the word in epic suggests (e.g. *Iliad* 10.56 and 470 and *Iliad* 18.298).

287 Solon is said to have used the phrase λιπαρὴ κουροτρόφος, "glistening nurse-mother," of Γῆ, "Earth" (Solon fr. 43 West = Choricius *Oration* 2.6); West ad loc. compares the description of Ithaca in *Odyssey* 9.27: τρηχεῖ, ἀλλ᾽ ἀγαθὴ κουροτρόφος, "rugged, but a good nurse-mother." The cult to *Kourotróphos Gê* was founded by Erichthonios in return for his nurture according to the Suda (see n3.232 above), and one wonders whether goddess and nursling were already linked (however loosely) in Solon's time. For Γῆ in Solon as both the Athenian land and the earth more generally, cf. fr. 36. 5 West, where Γῆ μέλαινα, "black Earth," is called μήτηρ μεγίστη δαιμόνων Ὀλυμπίων, "greatest mother of the Olympian gods" (line 4), but the context is Solon's land reform in Athens: τῆς ἐγώ ποτε / ὅρους ἀνεῖλον πολλαχῇ πεπηγότας, "whose boundary markers, implanted everywhere, I once removed" (lines 5–6). For the epithet λιπαρή, "glistening, bright," used of Γῆ, "Earth," cf. the phrase λιπαρὴν πόλιν, "glistening city," in Theognis 947 (the passage in which this occurs, Theognis 945–948, is attributed to Solon by Bergk; cf. West *IEG*, vol. 2, p. 144). Solon's interest in Erichthonios, which is only speculative with respect to the phrase (Γῆ) λιπαρὴ κουροτρόφος, "glistening nurse-mother (Earth)," is supported by Plato's *Critias*, in which the myth of Athena and Hephaistos as the creators of a race of autochthonous Athenians is attributed to Solon in an unfinished poem about Atlantis. There are several things in this story that suggest what I see as Solon's reform of myth and cult in Athens, including an armed "form and image" of the goddess Athena (this is the transformed image of Athena Polias), the inclusion of both Erichthonios and Erechtheus in the list of early kings (this duplication occurred when Erechtheus was removed from Athena's temple), and the pairing of Athena and Hephaistos as the first gods of Athens, responsible for the race of autochthonous Athenians. With the pairing of Athena and Hephaistos in this story we can compare Solon's own words in a different context, namely a catalogue of human pursuits in which the craftsman is said to have learned the *érga* of Athena and Hephaistos, the two gods of crafts (Solon fr. 13.49–50 West):

ἄλλος Ἀθηναίης τε καὶ Ἡφαίστου πολυτέχνεω
ἔργα δαεὶς χειροῖν ξυλλέγεται βίοτον.

Another, learning the works of Athena and Hephaistos skilled in many arts, gathers his livelihood with his hands.

When these lines were composed the pairing of Athena and Hephaistos as gods of crafts was not new (see above n3.239 [end] on *Odyssey* 6.233), but the Homeric pairing would have had its own resonance in Athens, where Hephaistos must have been new to Athenian cult, and Athena *Ergánē* was what was left of Athena as a mother goddess (cf. n3.50 above). Plato's text is considered in more detail in EN3.15.

288 If my argument is correct, Solon's importance for the Homeric poems in Athens is undervalued in comparison with the role of Peisistratos. This point is elaborated in EN3.16.

secondary Athenian stage. This secondary stage presented a new view of Athena Polias, who now brought Athens the protection of her father Zeus in addition to her own, and a new view of Erechtheus, who now received heroic honors for his sacrificial death in the war for Eleusis. Far different was the pair that the Ionian poets had in mind in *Odyssey* 7.80–81, where Athena enters the strong house of Erechtheus. The relationship between these two figures is to be seen in what follows *Odyssey* 7.80–81, where the focus of the narrative is the Phaeacian king and queen. For Athena Polias and Erechtheus in the Homeric era Arete and Alcinous are invaluable contemporary evidence.

Endnotes, Part 3

EN3.1 (Endnote to n3.16)
Cults of Damia and Auxesia had elements in common with cults of Demeter and Kore; Pausanias, who saw and sacrificed to the images of Damia and Auxesia in Aegina, says that their sacrifice was like that in Eleusis (εἶδόν τε τὰ ἀγάλματα καὶ ἔθυσά σφισι κατὰ ‹τὰ› αὐτὰ καθὰ δὴ καὶ Ἐλευσῖνι θύειν νομίζουσιν, Pausanias 2.30.4). Herodotus too describes the cult in Aegina, and a feature that he mentions, namely that worshippers propitiated the two goddesses with abusive female choruses (χοροῖσι γυναικηίοισι κερτόμοισι ἱλάσκοντο, Herodotus 5.83.3), also corresponds to what took place at festivals of Demeter (both the Stenia and the Thesmophoria, on which see Deubner 1932:53, 57–58; the prototype for women's jokes at the Thesmophoria according to "Apollodorus" 1.5.1 is the figure Iambe in *Homeric Hymn to Demeter* 194–205). The name *Auxēsía*, "increase," would seem to stand for fertility in general, human as well as agricultural; Demeter and Kore had the same broad range in their cults. Farnell 1896, vol. 3, 319n36 gives references for cults of Damia and Auxesia in Epidaurus, Aegina, Troezen, and Sparta, and for Damia alone in Amyklai, Thera, and Tarentum (in Tarentum the name is attested in the festival name *Dámeia*, Hesychius s.v.). It was presumably from Tarentum that the Roman Bona Dea acquired the name *Damia* as well as two cult terms: *damiatrix*, the name of her priestess, and *damium*, the name of her secret sacrifice (Paulus ex Festo 60 Lindsay: *Damium sacrificium, quod fiebat in operto in honore Deae Bonae.... Dea quoque ipsa Damia et sacerdos eius damiatrix appellabatur*). The earliest events in Herodotus's story (the famine in Epidaurus, the borrowing of Athenian olive wood for statues of Damia and Auxesia, the first compensatory sacrifices to Athena Polias and Erechtheus) may have been shaped by legend (cf. Dümmler *RE* 'Auxesia' 2617), but the historical core seems old; anything later than the eighth century is unlikely. The end of the compensatory sacrifices to Athena Polias and Erechtheus may be related to events c. 600 BC. In Herodotus's account the Epidaurians ended the sacrifices when Aegina stole the images of Damia and Auxesia from them; Epidaurus at first had political

control of Aegina, but at some later time the Aeginetans revolted and became independent (Herodotus 5.83.1). Since Periander of Corinth crushed Epidaurus c. 600 BC (Herodotus 3.52.7), Aegina would surely have broken free from Epidaurus then if not earlier (cf. How and Wells 1928 on Herodotus 5.83.1). The date of Athens' war with Aegina, which followed these events (Herodotus 5.85–88), has not been established. How and Wells 1928 on Herodotus 5.86.4 date the war to the time of Solon, perhaps 590–570 BC, citing Solon's substitution of the Euboic for the Aeginetan standard in coinage and his prohibition of the export of grain; the Aeginetan embargo on Attic pottery (Herodotus 5.88.2) is also noted. But earlier dates for the war are generally preferred: the early seventh century (Dunbabin 1936/1937; Bradeen 1947:239), or even mid-eighth century (Coldstream 1968:361n10 and 2003:135). The context of the earlier part of the story involving only Athens and Epidaurus may have been the Calaurian Amphictyony of which both cities were said to be members (How and Wells on Herodotus 5.82.3). Little is known of this league, which according to Strabo 8.6.14 had seven members (Athens, Epidaurus, Aegina, Minyan Orchomenus, Nauplia, Hermione, and Prasiai). Wilamowitz 1896 argues that Strabo's account reflects a reconstituted league of the third century BC, which in its older form would have had more members but was still never really important; Wilamowitz opposes the idea of a Mycenaean origin of the league, arguing that it began only in the seventh century BC. Lenschau 1944:227–228 believes that a Mycenaean origin is probable; Harland 1925 likewise proposes an early foundation of the league, noting (164n6) that late Helladic remains have been found at the sanctuary of Poseidon on Calauria, the cult center of the amphictyony. Harland 1925:162 imagines that the league had its highpoint in the eighth century and declined thereafter. A cult of Damia and Auxesia in Troezen is attested by Pausanias 2.32.2 and a cult of the goddess Auxo in Attica seems related (cf. Dümmler *RE* 'Auxesia' 2617). The cult may have been spread by the Calaurian league, unless some members of the league had the cult from the start (cf. Harland 1925:167n9).

EN3.2 (Endnote to n3.38)
Athenagoras *Legatio pro Christianis* 17.4 seems to have attributed the image of Athena Polias to the sixth-century sculptor Endoios (see n3.36 for this historical figure); this is surprising in itself, given the view in Pausanias's day that Athena's image was as old as the very city of Athens. The attribution of the image of Athena Polias to Endoios has been discounted by most students concerned with the image's origin since (among other reasons) Athenagoras is elsewhere found to be unreliable in such matters. There is also corruption

in the text at this point of the *Legatio pro Christianis* (see Herington 1955:24n1, 69–70), but we can probably ignore this issue and accept, as Kroll 1982 does, that Athenagoras did in fact attribute the Athena Polias to Endoios. Kroll, following others, argues that Athenagoras intended a contrast between the statue of Athena Polias and another statue of Athena on the Acropolis which Athenagoras also attributed to Endoios; Athenagoras described the second statue as "seated," and from this the inference is drawn that the Athena Polias, by contrast, was standing. But Athenagoras's reason for describing the second statue as seated was, I think, simply that his information came from Pausanias 1.26.4, who also attributes a statue of Athena on the Acropolis to Endoios, and who also describes this statue as seated (this seated image, which is made of stone, has survived; see most recently Marx 2001). Here as elsewhere Pausanias calls Endoios the pupil of the mythic craftsman Daedalus; this ahistorical bit of lore also appears in Athenagoras, and the coincidence is striking. If we compare the brief phrase in Athenagoras, τὴν Καθημένην Ἔνδοιος εἰργάσατο μαθητὴς Δαιδάλου, "Endoios, a pupil of Daedalus, made the Seated (Athena)," with the more detailed passage in Pausanias, Ἔνδοιος ἦν γένος μὲν Ἀθηναῖος, Δαιδάλου δὲ μαθητής, ὃς καὶ φεύγοντι Δαιδάλῳ διὰ τὸν Κάλω θάνατον ἐπηκολούθησεν ἐς Κρήτην· τούτου καθήμενόν ἐστιν Ἀθηνᾶς ἄγαλμα, "Endoios was an Athenian by race, and a pupil of Daedalus, who followed Daedalus to Crete when he fled there on account of Kalos's death; his is the seated statue of Athena," we can see that Athenagoras has simply abbreviated what he found in Pausanias. From this it follows, I think, that Athenagoras had no firsthand knowledge of the seated statue of Athena, and that he called it "seated" simply to identify it. Snodgrass 2003 makes the case for Athenagoras's general dependence on Pausanias in references to pagan cult images in the same passage (*Legatio pro Christianis* 17.4). In addition to the instance just discussed Snodgrass draws attention to another highly particular correspondence between Athenagoras and Pausanias regarding the statue of Hera in Samos, a work by the sculptor Smilis: Pausanias 7.4.4 reports that the statue was brought to Samos from Argos by the Argonauts, and Athenagoras clearly depends on this passage of Pausanias when he refers to the statue as "the Hera in Samos and Argos." Snodgrass's treatment of the question of dependence also takes into account that a high proportion— five of eight (four of seven if the two statues of Hera are counted as one)—of the attributions cited by Athenagoras also occur in Pausanias (all are works of the Archaic period; Snodgrass is not concerned with two Classical works whose attributions Athenagoras did not take from Pausanias, the Aphrodite at Knidos by Praxiteles [not in Pausanias], and the Asklepios at Epidaurus by Thrasymedes [Pausanias 2.27.2, misattributed by Athenagoras to Pheidias]).

I suggest that two of Athenagoras's three attributions of Archaic works that do not occur in Pausanias may well be his own inventions: 1) whereas both Pausanias (2.32.5) and Athenagoras (*Legatio pro Christianis* 17.4) say that the statue of Apollo on Delos was made by Tektaios and Angelion, only Athenagoras says that the statue of Artemis on Delos was made by these two sculptors; this, I suggest, may have been an extension on Athenagoras's part from Apollo to Apollo's twin; 2) whereas Pausanias says that according to popular belief the statue of Athena Polias in Athens fell from heaven, Athenagoras attributes it to Endoios. Why does Athenagoras differ from Pausanias on this? The argument that Athenagoras intends to support with all his particular examples is that pagan cult images are of such recent origin that their very makers are known; I suggest that in order to make this formula apply to the Athena Polias, Athenagoras, on his own authority, extended what he found in Pausanias of the seated Athena (namely that Endoios made it) to the statue of Athena Polias. This brings us back to Athenagoras's general unreliability as a source. Athenagoras may have followed another authority in all three cases in which he does not follow Pausanias (the third case is the Artemis at Ephesus, which Athenagoras alone, as far as we know, attributed to the same Endoios), but it seems as likely that he followed no one but himself; in particular the attribution of the Athena Polias to Endoios looks like an autoschediasm. In any case the Athenagoras passage says nothing about the pose of the Athena Polias.

EN3.3 (Endnote to n3.46)
It is undeniable that the text of Homer was to some extent shaped by sixth-century Athens, but I am not prepared to go very far in trying to identify particular Athenian passages. I feel most confident about the expansion of the catalogue of heroines in *Odyssey* 11; another strong candidate is the Athenian entry to the Catalogue of Ships in *Iliad* 2 (discussed in Chapter 9); if these examples show the possibility of Athenian expansions, Athena's lamp in *Odyssey* 19 can be added to the list; the only larger passage that I would consider from this standpoint is the end of the *Odyssey*. As argued in Chapter 9 (cf. n3.284), the Athenian entry to the Catalogue of Ships can be seen as reflecting Solon's efforts to restrain clan behavior by a rule of law on the one hand, and to make Athena the city goddess of all Athenians on the other hand; the end of the *Odyssey*, with its forestalling of a blood feud between clans through Athena's action, should, I think, at least have drawn Solon's attention. I only pose the question as to what (if anything) this may mean for the text of the end of the *Odyssey*; the phrase στάσιν ἔμφυλον, "strife within the tribe," which Solon uses in fr. 4.19 West, is a possible point of departure

(Campbell 1967 ad loc. gives parallels to the phrase, to which add *Odyssey* 15.272–273: Theoklymenos flees from home after killing a clan member, ἄνδρα κατακτὰς / ἔμφυλον, "having killed a man within his tribe"). Athena's lamp in *Odyssey* 19, if motivated by changes in the cult of Athena Polias in Athens, should also be linked with Solon (see Chapter 9).

EN3.4 *(Endnote to n3.67)*

That the *péplos* of Athena was washed in the ritual of the *Pluntéria* can only be inferred from the name of the festival itself, which must refer to the washing of a garment and not to the bathing of Athena's image (the verb *plúnō* has this semantic restriction; cf. Burkert 1970:359n11). Both activities seem to be implied by the different names given to two maidens concerned with the statue of Athena in an entry in Photius's *Lexicon* (λουτρίδες· δύο κόραι περὶ τὸ ἕδος τῆς Ἀθηνᾶς· ἐκαλοῦντο δὲ αὗται καὶ πλυντρίδες· οὕτως Ἀριστοφάνης, "*loutrídes*: two girls attending the statue of Athena; they were also called *pluntrídes*; so Aristophanes"); Robertson 1996:72n74 convincingly interprets this entry to mean that the *loutrídes* "bathed" the statue and the *pluntrídes* "washed" its *péplos*. Bathing the statue itself, which has parallels in other cults of Athena, may long have been part of the Athenian cult too, but it is not implied by the festival's name. For these parallels, see Robertson 1996:48–52 on "bathing" rites (*loûtra* or *lôtis*) for Athena at Argos and Delphi, the former described in Callimachus *Hymns* 5 (for Delphi see Robertson 1996:51). Contrary to what is found in older textbooks (e.g. Deubner 1932:18–19) the image of Athena Polias was not bathed in the sea after a solemn procession by ephebes; this notion has been disproved (see Robertson 1996:33, and Robertson 1985 n121 for references to Ziehen, Herington, and Burkert; Herington 1955:30n2 reviews the evidence for such a procession). For another official somehow concerned with cleaning Athena's *péplos* (the *kataníptēs*, the subject of an entry in the *Lexeis Rhetorikai*, p. 269.29 Bekker), see Deubner 1932:19n14, and alternatively Robertson 1996:72n74: "Another entry in the lexica, puzzling on any view, is *kataníptēs*, 'one who washes the soiled edge of Athena's robe.' Perhaps the robe in question is the one offered at the Panathenaia, after it was displayed for a time and before it was laid away in the *peplothékē*." The *péplos* offered at the Panathenaia is a major complication in the issue of the Athenian Plynteria; see n3.244 for Robertson's view (1996:63) that this *péplos* was not offered before the sixth century BC (the first *péplos* was the work of two historical weavers according to several ancient sources). The Plynteria were a much older festival than that.

EN3.5 (Endnote to n3.77)

Koenen 1969:13-14 argues on the basis of Pompeian wall paintings that Auge's encounter with Heracles is a hieròs gámos within the context of the Plynteria, and therefore closely parallel to the "sacred marriage" inferred for Athena. The evidence concerns two figures who appear in the paintings: one is an older woman who restrains Auge's companion from trying to fend off Heracles from Auge; the other is a winged maiden with a radiant nimbus around her head and branches in her hand who stands behind the entire group (according to Koenen this figure is found in other representations of marriages). All the figures in the paintings have crowns, a further sign of the sacred nature of the events. As Koenen, p. 14, puts it, what from one perspective was a rape, from another perspective was a hieròs gámos, the issue from which was Telephos, the grandson of the Tegean king and the ancestor of the Attalid kings of Pergamum. (One wonders in fact if it was the Attalid connection, irrelevant for Euripides, that gave rise to the representation of a sacred marriage on the Pompeian wall paintings; as Koenen notes, there is a Pompeian copy of a painting from Pergamum on which Telephos, under the protection of an eagle and a lion, is suckled by a deer; were there also Pergamene originals for the Auge paintings?) Following Fehrle 1910:171-177 for the festival of the Plynteria as originally having to do with Athena's own hieròs gámos, Koenen argues that her "sacred marriage" was with Heracles, as in the Auge myth. But such a relationship between Athena and Heracles, first proposed by Otto Jahn (cf. Nilsson 1967:443n1), must still be considered unproven. The interpretation of a Peisistratean-era vase painting by the Andocides painter in which Athena hands Heracles a flower as he reclines on a couch and drinks is controversial, as Koenen says (p.15); the designation of Athena as Ἡρακλέους κόρη on a contemporaneous vase painting is equally unclear (see Boardman 1972:64–65, who cites Beazley Corpus Vasorum Antiquorum against the meaning "Heracles' girl"; the phrase should mean "Heracles' daughter," which is equally opaque). It is true that various historical figures imagined themselves as Athena's husbands: thus, according to Athenaeus 12.531f, paraphrasing Theopompus (FGrHist 115 F 31), the fourth-century Thracian king Cotys had dinner prepared for himself as if Athena was about to become his bride and awaited her in his bedchamber drunk (ὅτι δεῖπνον κατεσκεύασεν ὁ Κότυς ὡς γαμουμένης αὐτῷ τῆς Ἀθηνᾶς καὶ θάλαμον κατασκευάσας ἀνέμενεν μεθύων τὴν θεόν); Demetrius Poliorcetes seems to have played a similar part in Athena's temple in Athens if Clement of Alexandria can be believed regarding his behavior with a courtesan and the image of Athena: "A marriage with Athena was prepared for him by the Athenians; but he treated the goddess disdainfully, not being able to marry her statue; he went up to the Acropolis with his courtesan Lamia and had intercourse with her (? ἐνεφυρᾶτο) in the goddess's bridal chamber, displaying to the ancient virgin the positions of the young courtesan" (καὶ γάμος ὑπὸ Ἀθηναίων αὐτῷ ὁ τῆς Ἀθηνᾶς ηὐτρεπίζετο· ὁ δὲ τὴν μὲν θεὸν ὑπερηφάνει, τὸ ἄγαλμα γῆμαι μὴ δυνάμενος· Λάμιαν δὲ τὴν ἑταίραν ἔχων εἰς ἀκρόπολιν ἀνῄει καὶ τῷ τῆς Ἀθηνᾶς ἐνεφυρᾶτο παστῷ, τῇ παλαιᾷ παρθένῳ τὰ τῆς νέας ἐπιδεικνὺς ἑταίρας σχήματα, *Protrepticus* 4.54.6). But these examples do not establish a sacred marriage between Athena and Heracles; they only show that some thought that sexual union with the virgin war goddess Athena conferred invincibility; cf. the recently discovered epigram *P. Mil. Vogl.* VIII 309 col. V 32–39 (one in a collection of epigrams attributed to the Hellenistic poet Poseidippus): an Arcadian, Aristoxeinos, dreamt that he slept with Athena and went into battle the next day as if invincible, whereupon Ares laid him low. Why such an idea occurred to some individuals may say more about these individuals than the goddess. Finally Koenen (p. 16) draws attention to Peisistratos and the story of Phye, the statuesque young woman whom Peisistratos passed off as Athena when she accompanied him in his chariot on his return to Athens, and whom he later gave to his son Hipparchus to marry; it is again not clear what bearing this marriage has on Athena herself. Boardman 1972:60–65 argues that Peisistratos saw himself as a second Heracles, and that Phye's role in his return to Athens was patterned on that of Athena in leading Heracles to Olympus for deification. Does there need to be any more to Phye's role than that?

EN3.6 (Endnote to n3.87)

The Mycenaean war goddess found in "Tsountas's House" on the acropolis of Mycenae and studied by Rodenwaldt 1912 cannot be directly connected with Athena. Rodenwaldt 1912:136 (citing Tsountas 1888, Kuruniotis 1901, *IG* IV 492) states that we know that the early Archaic temple on the acropolis, whose sculptures attest its importance, was a temple of Athena, and a good case has been made that this temple continues the cult of a Bronze Age palace goddess in roughly the same place (see Nilsson 1950:473–474, with figure 202 on p. 474). "Tsountas's House" seems to have been an independent sanctuary with attached priest's house (see Wace 1951:254–255 and, for the structure's location, Wace 1949:66–67 and figs. 19 and 25). Rodenwaldt 1912:136 and Nilsson 1967:347 both suggest that the goddess found in "Tsountas's House" is Athena's predecessor, but the distinct locations of the two sanctuaries cannot be wholly discounted. It should be noted that Nilsson is more careful

than others in claiming Bronze Age antecedents to the war goddess Athena;
he rejects, for example, the evidence of a series of so-called Palladia (Nilsson
1967:435). We do not know how widespread Athena's cults were in the Bronze
Age. Such cults are documented for the historical period and can be inferred
for an earlier period, but how much earlier is not clear. Athena's name may
occur on a Linear-B tablet from Knossos (KN V 52): *atanapotnija* is interpreted
as dative *Athanai potniai*, "Athena mistress," by Ventris and Chadwick 1973:126,
311–312, 410, but is taken by Palmer 1957:567 as the genitive of a place-
name, also having to do with Athena. In the early Archaic period Athena was
presumably the city goddess at Mycenae insofar as her temple is located on
the acropolis (cf. Nilsson 1967:433n3). She had probably replaced a local city
goddess who survives as the heroine named *Mukḗnē* with whom Penelope is
compared in *Odyssey* 2.120 (see n3.5). If *Mukḗnē* was once the city goddess of
Mycenae, who was then replaced and demoted to heroine status by Athena,
it is possible that this process had already taken place in the Bronze Age; cf.
Schachermeyr 1955:232–233, who believes that Athena was first worshipped
in Athens, but that already in Mycenaean times she was the "guardian goddess
of the city kingdoms of Mycenae, Thebes, Athens, etc." ("Schutzgöttin der
Dynastenburgen von Mykenai, Theben, Athen usw."). This is possible, but,
again, it cannot be demonstrated. The war goddess *Enuṓ*, who occurs twice
in Homer, looks old. From feminine *Enuṓ* a masculine war god *Enuálios* was
derived, who is closely identified with Ares (*enuálios* is an epithet of Ares in
Iliad 17.211; in *Iliad* 18.309, where the name *Enuálios* occurs by itself, Ares is
probably meant). The goddess *Enuṓ* is clearly older than the god *Enuálios*; is she
perhaps the Bronze Age war goddess found in "Tsountas's House"? Enyo's two
appearances in Homer are: *Iliad* 5.330–333, where Diomedes hunts the unwar-
like Aphrodite, who is contrasted with Athena and "city-sacking" Enyo:

ὃ δὲ Κύπριν ἐπῴχετο νηλέϊ χαλκῷ
γιγνώσκων ὅ τ' ἄναλκις ἔην θεός, οὐδὲ θεάων
τάων αἵ τ' ἀνδρῶν πόλεμον κάτα κοιρανέουσιν,
οὔτ' ἄρ' Ἀθηναίη οὔτε πτολίπορθος Ἐνυώ.

He attacked the Cyprian goddess with his pitiless spear
knowing that she was a weak goddess, and not one of those
          goddesses
who are masters in the warfare of men,
either Athena or city-sacking Enyo.

and *Iliad* 5.592–595, where Enyo and Ares accompany the advancing Trojans:

ἦρχε δ' ἄρα σφιν Ἄρης καὶ πότνι' Ἐνυώ,
ἣ μὲν ἔχουσα Κυδοιμὸν ἀναιδέα δηϊοτῆτος,
Ἄρης δ' ἐν παλάμῃσι πελώριον ἔγχος ἐνώμα,
φοίτα δ' ἄλλοτε μὲν πρόσθ' Ἕκτορος, ἄλλοτ' ὄπισθε.

Ares and the goddess <u>Enyo</u> led them,
she having the shameless Turmoil of war,
but Ares plied a huge spear in his hands
and walked now in front of Hector, now behind him.

EN3.7 (Endnote to n3.108)

It is a question to what extent the gigantomachy, especially Athena's role in it, was an Athenian as opposed to a Panhellenic myth. The temple of Apollo at Delphi is described by Euripides *Ion* 205–218 as having sculptural representations of the gigantomachy; in these sculptures Athena slays not Asterios, as in the Athenian myth, but Enkelados (cf. "Apollodorus" 1.6.2, where Athena is said to slay two giants, Enkelados and Pallas; cf. also Vergil *Aeneid* 3.578–582, where "Enceladus" is said to lie buried under Mount Aetna). The temple at Delphi was rebuilt after a fire in the mid-sixth century BC by the Alcmaeonids exiled from Athens (cf. n5.87). Did the Alcmaeonids perhaps adapt a Panathenaic myth to this Panhellenic setting? The description in Euripides focuses on Athena and Zeus. Although other gods take part in the battle (Dionysus is mentioned in *Ion* 216–218, others are named in "Apollodorus" 1.6.2), the Athenian chorus focuses on Athena, calling her "my own goddess" (Παλλάδ', ἐμὰν θεόν), and Zeus follows her in the description, providing a climax of power and authority. Addressing each other the chorus identify first the mythical battle itself, carved on the temple's stone walls, then Athena, brandishing her gorgon-headed shield at Enkelados, and finally Zeus, thunderbolting the giant Mimas (*Ion* 205–215):

– πάντᾳ τοι βλέφαρον διώ-
   κω. σκέψαι κλόνον ἐν τείχεσ-
σι λαΐνοισι Γιγάντων.
– ὦ φίλαι, ὧδε δερκόμεσθα.
– λεύσσεις οὖν ἐπ' Ἐγκελάδῳ
   γοργωπὸν πάλλουσαν ἴτυν...;

– λεύσσω Παλλάδ', ἐμὰν θεόν.
– τί γάρ; κεραυνὸν ἀμφίπυρον
  ὄβριμον ἐν Διὸς
  ἐκηβόλοισι χερσίν;
– ὁρῶ· τὸν δάιον
  Μίμαντα πυρὶ καταιθαλοῖ.

– I am running my eye everywhere. Look at the Battle of the
  Giants on the stone walls.
– We are looking there, friends.
– Do you see her shaking the gorgon-faced shield at Enkelados...?
– I see Pallas, my goddess.
– Of course. And the powerful fiery thunderbolt in the far-
  hurling hands of Zeus?
– I see it; he burns his enemy Mimas to ashes with the fire.

If it was in Athens that Athena's role in the gigantomachy first became prom-
inent, the same can probably be said of Athena's birth from Zeus's head; this
myth did not originate in Athens, but representations of it became popular
there in the sixth century. The myth is not explicitly mentioned in the
earliest literary sources, but it seems to be implied: in *Iliad* 5.875–880 Ares
says that Zeus fathered/bore Athena <u>himself</u> (σὺ γὰρ τέκες ἄφρονα κούρην,
Iliad 5.875; <u>αὐτὸς</u> ἐγείναο παῖδ' ἀΐδηλον, *Iliad* 5.880), and while the verbs are
ambiguous, the implication of *autós* in line 880 is clear (cf. Allen, Halliday, and
Sikes 1936 on *Homeric Hymn to Apollo* 309); in Hesiod *Theogony* 886–900 Zeus
swallows Metis so that Metis will not give birth to Athena or to a son stronger
than Zeus, and the implication is again clear: Athena will be borne by Zeus
himself. The myth of Athena's birth is made explicit in Hesiod *Theogony* 924
(αὐτὸς δ' <u>ἐκ κεφαλῆς</u> γλαυκώπιδα γείνατ' Ἀθήνην, "he himself bore grey-
eyed Athena <u>from his head</u>") and *Homeric Hymn to Apollo* 308–309 (Κρονίδης
ἐρικυδέα γείνατ' Ἀθήνην / <u>ἐν κορυφῇ</u>, "Kronos's son bore glorious Athena
<u>in his head</u>"), both of which (like *Homeric Hymn* 28) may be sixth-century
Athenian (for West's view that *Theogony* 901–1022 is a sixth-century Athenian
product see n2.238; for *Homeric Hymn to Apollo* 308–309 see §5.23 and n5.83). In
art the earliest representation of Athena's birth from Zeus's head is a terra-
cotta relief from Tenos dated c. 680 BC (Cassimatis *LIMC* 'Athena' no. 360);
other examples from outside Attica include two bronze reliefs from Olympia

(*LIMC* 'Athena' no. 361, last third of the seventh century, and no. 362, first half of the sixth century), a Corinthian pinax (*LIMC* 'Athena' no. 343, second quarter of the sixth century), and a sixth-century Spartan relief mentioned by Pausanias 3.17.3 (*LIMC* 'Athena' no. 364). But most of the examples are sixth-century Attic vase paintings, the earliest dated c. 575–570 BC (*LIMC* 'Athena' no. 334): fourteen are of Athena's actual birth (*LIMC* 'Athena' nos. 345–358, the last three dated early to mid fifth century); eight are of Zeus in labor, all dated to the sixth century (*LIMC* 'Athena' nos. 334, 335, 337–342). All together there are 24 Attic examples of the subject (including no. 363, an Acropolis relief of Athena's birth mentioned by Pausanias 1.24.2, and no. 359, a painting described by the elder Philostratus, *Imagines* 2.27) and seven non-Attic examples, including a mid-sixth century Rhodian vase painting of Zeus in labor (no. 336) and a lost (sixth-century?) painting in Elis by the Corinthian Kleanthes (no. 344).

EN3.8 (Endnote to n3.111)

In reconstructing the history of the Parthenon, Korres 1997 dates the "Urparthenon" to the early sixth century BC (chronological chart pp. 242–243) and to the rule of Peisistratos (p. 239 bottom); a date in the 560s seems indicated by these somewhat contradictory statements. The chronological chart and the site plan (p. 226, figure 2) summarize the arguments for the Parthenon's earlier history; the chronological chart also takes into account the history of Athena's "old temple" and the Erechtheum. Korres's location of the "Urparthenon," although based on limited evidence, is precise. Of great significance is a statue base and a small shrine (*naiskos*) surrounding the statue base which came to light in the 1980s in the north pteron of the Parthenon (Catling 1989:8–9; reconstruction in Ridgeway 1992:125, figure 76). This *naiskos* seems to have flanked the Urparthenon on its north side such that the front of the *naiskos* was flush with the front of the temple at its east end; in front of the *naiskos* (i.e. east of it) was an altar. In the later Parthenon both the *naiskos* and the altar were incorporated into the temple's north pteron (i.e. between the cella wall and the outer colonnade). Korres suggests that this *naiskos* was a shrine of Athena Ergane (so it is designated on his site plan and chronological chart), and he points out that the same north-south line marks the east limit not only of the Urparthenon and *naiskos*, but also of Athena's "old temple" and a precursor of the east cella of the Erechtheum (Korres 1997:229 and n73). If Korres is right that the *naiskos* was a shrine of Athena Ergane, it is tempting to think that this goddess was placed by design between the "old temple," where Athena Polias had, in my view, been transformed from a spinning goddess to a warrior goddess, and another temple devoted wholly to the warrior goddess: the spinning goddess would thus have been divorced from the city goddess and given a new (and minor) place between two temples of the warrior goddess. Korres (chart, p. 242) suggests that the "old temple" and the *naiskos* were both built later than the Urparthenon. This takes into account Dinsmoor's argument (1947:109, 117n33) that the "old temple" was built by the Peisistratids after c. 529 BC to replace a smaller structure that had been in place since Homeric times and earlier. It thus appears that the Peisistratid "old temple" was built in alignment at the east end with an already existing Urparthenon; in Korres's reconstruction the "old temple" and the Urparthenon also have similar dimensions, and in this respect as well the "old temple" seems to be patterned on the Urparthenon. On this reading of the evidence the *naiskos*, which flanked the Urparthenon, was actually contemporary with the later temple of the Peisistratids (Athena's "old temple"). The *naiskos* and the "old temple" would thus be connected by both their time of construction and (if Korres is right about Athena Ergane) their ties (present in one case, past in the other) to the spinning goddess. As for the predecessor of the Peisistratid "old temple," the image of Athena Polias had already, in my view, been transformed into a warrior goddess there; how Athena Ergane first emerged in this situation is open to speculation.

EN3.9 (Endnote to n3.166)
I interpret the developments in Demeter's cult in Eleusis discussed in n3.166 as the result of a change of control from Eleusis to Athens in the time of Solon. Those who date Athenian control of Eleusis and the Mysteries earlier see matters differently, notably Kevin Clinton (see Clinton 1993, with references to his earlier studies). One of Clinton's arguments for dating Athenian control of the Mysteries earlier than Solon is the phrase "law of Solon" in Andocides *On the Mysteries* 111 (Clinton 1993:112), but, as mentioned in n3.166, no real conclusion as to date can be drawn from this phrase; if the law concerning a meeting of the *boulē* in the Eleusinion was in fact Solon's, I would prefer to see it as regulating a new political and religious relationship between Athens and Eleusis and not a pre-existing one. Clinton's other main argument for an early date of Athenian control is based on statements in Aristotle's *Constitution of the Athenians* about the *árkhōn basileús*, who inherited the religious functions of the old king of Athens; this official, who administered "all ancestral sacrifices" (57.1), was specifically in charge of the administration of the Mysteries (57.1). The same work states earlier (3.3) that the eponymous

árkhōn administered "none of the ancestral matters, as do the *basileús* and *polémarkhos*, but merely those matters added later." If this statement is taken strictly, it implies that the *basileús* administered only matters older than the creation of the first eponymous *árkhōn* in 683/2 BC, but was that really the case? Clinton himself allows the possibility that responsibility for the Mysteries was not given to the *basileús* until after 683/2 BC (Clinton 1993:112), and others as well have not concluded from Aristotle's statement that Athenian administration of the Mysteries began so early (Allen, Halliday, and Sikes 1936:112n1; Richardson 1974:7; Anderson 2003:274n30). If new responsibilities were in fact added to the office of the *basileús* in the course of time, it is simply a question of when responsibility for the Mysteries was added, and the age of Solon seems perfectly possible; Solon, in my view, would have wished the new arrangement between Athens and Eleusis to seem "ancestral" in line with the new myth given to Erechtheus, and the administration of the Mysteries by the *árkhōn basileús* would have given this impression, just as administration by the eponymous *árkhōn* would have undermined it. The question of when the Mysteries began in Eleusis is a difficult one. The idea of a Mycenaean origin, which was once in favor, was dispelled by Darcque 1981, but has now started to reappear (Cosmopoulos 2003 and Cucuzza in Lippolis 2006:67–72 are discussed in n3.166). At the lower extreme the *Homeric Hymn to Demeter* alludes to the Mysteries, and this in my view means that the Mysteries began while Eleusis was still independent, but perhaps only at the end of this period. Clinton has argued that overall the *Homeric Hymn to Demeter* does not reflect the Mysteries, but the Thesmophoria, an earlier festival out of which the Mysteries perhaps developed (Clinton 1992:28–37 and 1993; cf. Hamilton 1993, who finds Clinton's arguments against the Mysteries "quite persuasive," but his arguments for the Thesmophoria less persuasive). The Mysteries figure at the end of the hymn (lines 473–482) as a "new foundation" (Clinton 1992:36). If the Mysteries did develop from the widespread old festival of the Thesmophoria, it is in areas where the two festivals contrast that the Mysteries presumably innovated. The great contrast between the two festivals is that the Mysteries were open to initiates of both sexes, whereas the Thesmophoria, which also had secret rites, were restricted to women (cf. Burkert 1985:242). Similarly the Mysteries were open to initiates from all cities, whereas the Thesmophoria were a local festival. Athens certainly took pride in sharing the Mysteries, the gift of Demeter, with the world (cf. n3.168). The question is how far Athens itself caused the development of the Mysteries in this direction. On the evidence of the *Homeric Hymn to Demeter* the Mysteries seem to have been open from the start to initiates from all cities (this is the natural interpretation of line 480 concerning the new rites which Demeter showed to the Eleusinian kings: ὄλβιος ὃς τάδ' ὄπωπεν ἐπιχθονίων ἀνθρώπων, "of men on earth he who has seen these things is fortunate"; cf. Walton 1952:110 and n19; Richardson 1974:311); whether the Mysteries were also open to both sexes, as in the historical period, is not known (cf. Richardson 1974:17) but may have been the case. On this reading Athens, in making the Mysteries a Panhellenic attraction, continued and expanded a movement already begun by an independent Eleusis. But it must be admitted that there is no archaeological support for a celebration of the Mysteries by an independent Eleusis; as Sourvinou-Inwood 1997:139–141 stresses, there is no archaeological evidence before the first Telesterion to support the existence of the Mysteries as we understand them. Anderson 2003:188–189, who follows Miles 1998 in downdating the first Telesterion to 575–550 BC (see n3.166), presses this lack of archaeological evidence to reach the conclusion that the *Homeric Hymn to Demeter*, which presupposes the Mysteries, dates to the middle of the sixth century BC (Sourvinou-Inwood 1997:153, whom Anderson in the main follows, assumes an early sixth-century date for the first Telesterion). For Anderson the absence of Athens from the *Homeric Hymn to Demeter* is simply consistent with the near absence of the Mysteries from the hymn: the hymn concerns the period of Eleusis's cultic independence from Athens, whatever the political relationship was during that period (Anderson 2003:274n31; cf. n3.152). If it is in fact the case that the Mysteries began only with the first Telesterion, I would come to a different conclusion about the *Homeric Hymn to Demeter*. The Pythian *Hymn to Apollo*, as will be discussed in Part 5 below, shows clear signs of successive versions: an older version was modified in response to a later event, namely the First Sacred War. If the passage concerning the Mysteries at the end of the *Homeric Hymn to Demeter* in fact dates to sometime after 600 BC, I would argue that the *Hymn to Demeter* too had successive versions: an older version dating to an independent Eleusis in the seventh century BC, and a newer version taking account of a new festival in the sixth century BC.

EN3.10 (Endnote to n3.167)
The Athenian myth of the four sons of Pandion (they each inherited from Pandion different parts of Attica, which was said to include not only Eleusis, but also Megara) is traced by Jacoby to the first half of the sixth century and the bitter contest for Salamis (Jacoby, commentary on Philochorus *FGrHist* 328 F 107, pp. 430–431). The myth corresponds to the three-party strife following the reforms of Solon (men of the plain, shore, and mountains)

with Megara added as a fourth part. It is worth considering how Eleusis fits into this picture. In an Athenian myth Eleusis is of course not part of Megara (the landmark that separates Megara from the rest of Attica in the myth is a *Púthion*, a shrine of Apollo, according to Philochorus *FGrHist* 328 F 107; for the location of this landmark, which must have been on the border between Megara and Eleusis, see Jacoby, commentary on Philochorus *FGrHist* 328 F 107, pp. 428–429). But Eleusis also does not seem to be part of the "plain" as that term was used of the strife in the sixties of the sixth century. Philochorus, who uses two of the sixth-century terms (*paralía*, "seashore," and *diakría*, "mountain district" [cf. *huperákrioi*, Herodotus 1.59.3]) does not use the third term, *pedíon*, "plain," but the phrase *hē* [*moîra*] *parà* (*perì*) *tò ástu mékhri toû Puthíou* "the [part] by (around) the city as far as the Pythion," in order to include Eleusis and the Thriasian plain with Athens in the same part of Attica. Did the term *pedíon* in its sixth century political context mean just the plain of the Kephisos valley, which is quite distinct from the Thriasian plain, separated as it is by Mount Aigaleos and Mount Parnes? If *pedíon* had this restricted meaning, Eleusis cannot have been part of the three-party conflict of the sixth century. Did its relatively recent incorporation into Attica set Eleusis apart from the rest of Attica in this way? While there can be no certainty about this point, it is still worth illustrating that the term "plain" would not naturally have included Eleusis (in Cleisthenes' different three-fold division of Attica Eleusis is part of the *paralía*, "shore," as distinct from the *ástu*, "city," of Athens, and the *mesógeia*, "interior," of Attica; cf. Jacoby, commentary on Philochorus *FGrHist* 328 F 107, p. 431). A passage of Thucydides about the Spartan invasion of Attica in the first year of the Peloponnesian War illustrates the point about the term "plain." Thucydides is at pains to explain why Archidamos stopped first at Eleusis and then at Acharnae and did not descend into the Kephisos plain (Thucydides 2.19.2–20): καὶ καθεζόμενοι ἔτεμνον πρῶτον μὲν Ἐλευσῖνα καὶ τὸ Θριάσιον πεδίον καὶ τροπήν τινα τῶν Ἀθηναίων ἱππέων περὶ τοὺς Ῥείτους καλουμένους ἐποιήσαντο· ἔπειτα προυχώρουν ἐν δεξιᾷ ἔχοντες τὸ Αἰγάλεων ὄρος διὰ Κρωπιᾶς, ἕως ἀφίκοντο ἐς Ἀχαρνάς, χωρίον μέγιστον τῆς Ἀττικῆς τῶν δήμων καλουμένων, καὶ καθεζόμενοι ἐς αὐτὸ στρατόπεδόν τε ἐποιήσαντο χρόνον τε πολὺν ἐμμείναντες ἔτεμνον. γνώμῃ δὲ τοιᾷδε λέγεται τὸν Ἀρχίδαμον περί τε τὰς Ἀχαρνὰς ὡς ἐς μάχην ταξάμενον μεῖναι καὶ ἐς τὸ πεδίον ἐκείνῃ τῇ ἐσβολῇ οὐ καταβῆναι· τοὺς γὰρ Ἀθηναίους ἤλπιζεν, ἀκμάζοντάς τε νεότητι πολλῇ καὶ παρεσκευασμένους ἐς πόλεμον ὡς οὔπω πρότερον, ἴσως ἂν ἐπεξελθεῖν καὶ τὴν γῆν οὐκ ἂν περιιδεῖν τμηθῆναι. ἐπειδὴ οὖν αὐτῷ ἐς Ἐλευσῖνα καὶ τὸ Θριάσιον πεδίον οὐκ ἀπήντησαν, πεῖραν ἐποιεῖτο περὶ τὰς Ἀχαρνὰς καθήμενος εἰ ἐπεξίασιν· ἅμα μὲν γὰρ αὐτῷ ὁ χῶρος ἐπιτήδειος ἐφαίνετο ἐνστρατοπεδεῦσαι, ἅμα δὲ καὶ οἱ Ἀχαρνῆς μέγα μέρος ὄντες τῆς πόλεως (τρισχίλιοι γὰρ ὁπλῖται ἐγένοντο) οὐ περιόψεσθαι ἐδόκουν τὰ σφέτερα διαφθαρέντα, ἀλλ᾽ ὁρμήσειν καὶ τοὺς πάντας ἐς μάχην. εἴ τε καὶ μὴ ἐπεξέλθοιεν ἐκείνῃ τῇ ἐσβολῇ οἱ Ἀθηναῖοι, ἀδεέστερον ἤδη ἐς τὸ ὕστερον τό τε πεδίον τεμεῖν καὶ πρὸς αὐτὴν τὴν πόλιν χωρήσεσθαι· τοὺς γὰρ Ἀχαρνέας ἐστερημένους τῶν σφετέρων οὐχ ὁμοίως προθύμους ἔσεσθαι ὑπὲρ τῆς τῶν ἄλλων κινδυνεύειν, στάσιν δ᾽ ἐνέσεσθαι τῇ γνώμῃ. τοιαύτῃ μὲν διανοίᾳ ὁ Ἀρχίδαμος περὶ τὰς Ἀχαρνὰς ἦν, "They stopped and began ravaging <u>Eleusis and the Thriasian plain</u> and routed some Athenian cavalry around the Rheitoi streams. Then, keeping <u>Mount Aigaleon</u> to the right, they advanced through Kropia until they came to Acharnae, the largest place in Attica among the so-called demes, and stopping there they made camp, and they stayed there for a considerable time and ravaged the land. It is said that Archidamos stayed at Acharnae, drawn up as if for battle, and did not descend into <u>the plain</u> in this invasion because of the following judgment on his part: he expected the Athenians, at the height of their power in terms of the great number of their youth, and equipped as never before for war, would perhaps come out for battle and not disregard their land being ravaged. Then, when they did not confront him at <u>Eleusis and the Thriasian plain</u>, he stopped at Acharnae and tested whether they would come out. The place seemed to him suitable to camp in, and at the same time the Acharnians, being a large part of the city (three thousand hoplites came from there) would probably not disregard their property being destroyed, but would all rush into battle. And further, if the Athenians did not come out to confront him during this invasion, there would be less to fear in the future in ravaging <u>the plain</u> and advancing against the city itself; for the Acharnians, deprived of their own property, would not be as eager to risk themselves for the others' land, and civil strife would enter their attitude. This was Archidamos's purpose in being at Acharnae."

EN3.11 (Endnote to n3.173)

A fragment of the *Atakta* of Istros (*FGrHist* 334 F 17) confirms that at some time the Kephisos River, where the Sacred Way crosses it, was an Athenian boundary, but it is not clear when. The *Atakta* (a work of "unordered" grammatical/lexicographical problems by this student of Callimachus) describes the boundary in a fragment quoted by the scholia to Sophocles *Oedipus at Colonus* 1059 to elucidate a topographical reference in the line; unfortunately the Istros fragment lacks an identifiable context of its own. Wilamowitz

1880:111n23 suggests that the boundary described in the fragment pertained to the realm of Aegeus or to some other mythological realm; Deubner 1932:48 concurs that the reference seems to be to former times; Jacoby, commentary on Istros *FGrHist* 334 F 17, agrees that the fragment seems to enumerate points belonging to a boundary, but he leaves open the question of what is bounded. The quotation from Istros is contained in the following passage of the scholia: "ἀπὸ δὲ τῆς χαράδρας ἐπὶ μὲν λείαν πέτραν." καὶ μετ' ὀλίγα, "ἀπὸ τούτου δὲ ἕως Κολωνοῦ παρὰ τὸν χαλκοῦν προσαγορευόμενον ‹ὁδὸν›, ὅθεν πρὸς τὸν Κηφισὸν ἕως τῆς μυστικῆς ὁδοῦ εἰς Ἐλευσῖνα· ἀπὸ ταύτης δὲ βαδιζόντων εἰς Ἐλευσῖνα τὰ ἐπ' ἀριστερὰ μέχρι τοῦ λόφου τοῦ πρὸς ἀνατολὰς τοῦ Αἰγάλεω," " 'From the ravine to the smooth rock.' And a little further on, 'from this (?) as far as Kolonos past the so-called bronze threshold, from there to the Kephisos as far as the mystic road to Eleusis; to the left from this road, as one walks toward Eleusis, as far as the crest to the east of Aigaleon'." The underlined phrase suggests that the Kephisos River, from where the boundary in question reached the river to where the Sacred Way crossed the river, formed part of this boundary.

EN3.12 (Endnote to n3.251)

The interpretation of the ritual of the Arrhephoria is related to the question of its location. The shrine of Aphrodite in the Gardens, near which (or in which: cf. Robertson 1983:254 and 254n42) Pausanias locates the underground passage in the ritual, is known to be southeast of the Acropolis near the Ilissos River; most interpreters accept a suggestion of Broneer 1932:53–54 that Pausanias really meant to say the precinct of Aphrodite and Eros on the north slope of the Acropolis, and they reconstruct the route of the Arrhephoroi accordingly; Robertson, on the other hand, takes the location southeast of the Acropolis at face value and understands the Arrhephoroi to be leaving and returning to the Acropolis in the course of the ceremony. In a subsequent study Robertson ties this route in with a change in the route of the Panathenaic procession to the Acropolis: this procession came from the northwest in historical times, but Robertson proposes that earlier it came from the southeast (Robertson 1983:50–54, 1996:58–65). This interpretation assumes that the Arrhephoria were part of the Panathenaia (Burkert, whose 1966 study of the Arrhephoria is subtitled "Vom Initiationsritus zum Panathenäenfest," also assumes this), but it is not clear to me that this was in fact the case (Deubner, who treats the two festivals separately, 1932:9–17, 22–35, is criticized by Burkert 1966:7–10 for his treatment of the Arrhephoria, but not on this point). The Arrhephoria were celebrated in the month of Skirophorion on an unknown day (cf. Burkert 1966:5n2, 8, Robertson 1983:283); the Panathenaia were celebrated at the end of the following month, Hekatombaion (Deubner 1932:23–24). The Arrhephoroi themselves are indirectly connected with the Panathenaia in that two of them are said to begin the weaving of the *péplos* months before its presentation to Athena at the Panathenaia (the sources speak of four Arrhephoroi, but only two conducted the annual night ritual of the Arrhephoria; Robertson 1983:276–277 argues that two others were chosen only every fourth year to begin Athena's *péplos* for the Great Panathenaia; Burkert 1966:3–5 argues that there were only two Arrhephoroi, who performed both functions; for sources see Burkert 1966:4n1). If the *péplos* ceremony itself only goes back to the sixth-century reorganization of the Panathenaia (as Robertson 1983:277 believes; cf. n3.244), the historical connection between the Arrhephoria and the Panathenaia seems to me to become very tenuous beyond that.

EN3.13 (Endnote to n3.261)
The three Kekropids (Aglauros, Pandrosos, Herse) are the central figures in the myth of the Arrhephoria, but the grouping of these three figures does not look old. As discussed in n3.254, Aglauros and Pandrosos both had old cults on the Acropolis which linked them with Athena, and this common link seems to have associated the two figures in the myth of the Arrhephoria; Herse, whose name is not specifically Attic, and who had no cult on the Acropolis, was added to complete a triad of sisters, apparently because her name, like that of Pandrosos, means "dew." Jacoby, commentary on Philochorus *FGrHist* 328 F 105, n3, points out that the name Aglauros does not mean "dew," and he takes this asymmetry as another indication that the three figures did not originally belong together: "elsewhere individual names (which are mostly late) for grouped figures either express one concept threefold or form a series: Auxo Thallo Karpo; Klotho Lachesis Atropos; Eunomia Dike Eirene; Aglaia Euphrosyne Thalia; etc."); as an example of the variation between two and three figures in a group Jacoby cites the Athenian Charites. Robertson's interesting speculation (1983:273–274; cf. n3.95) that to the three Kekropids belonged three parallel chambers in the Parthenon's west room (from which the name *Parthenõn*, "maidens' quarters," was accordingly derived) implies the inclusion of Herse in the Kekropid myth when the Parthenon was built, and also, presumably, when the Parthenon's earliest predecessor was built. The Parthenon does not seem to go back before 566/5 BC in its earlier forms (cf. §3.47, n3.111, and EN3.8); the chronology is thus not inconsistent with a sixth-century origin of the Kekropid myth.

EN3.14 (Endnote to n3.262)

Lines 8–14 of the Salaminioi inscription arrange for the two branches of the clan to have joint possession of several priesthoods; the priesthood of Aglauros and Pandrosos appears to include that of Kourotrophos: τὰς ἱερεωσύνας κοινὰς εἶναι ἀμφοτέρων εἰς τὸν αἰεὶ χρόνον τῆς Ἀθηνάας τῆς Σκιράδος, καὶ τὴν τοῦ Ἡρακλέου τõ ἐπὶ Πορθμῶι, καὶ τὴν τõ Εὐρυσάκος, καὶ τὴν τῆς Ἀγλαύρο καὶ Πανδρόσο καὶ τῆς Κορατρόφο· καὶ κληρõσθαι κοινῆι ἐξ ἀμφοτέρων ἐπειδὰν τελευτήσει τις τῶν ἱερειῶν ἢ ἱερέων, "The priesthoods shall be in common to both for all time, namely those of Athena Skiras, Herakles at Porthmos, Eurysakes, Aglauros and Pandrosos and Kourotophos. When one of the priestesses or priests dies a successor shall be elected by lot from both groups taken together" (Ferguson's translation, 1938:6). Lines 43–46 of the inscription specify the distribution of bread to cult officials; here the priestess is of Aglauros and Pandrosos only, and from this priestess a "basket-bearer" of Kourotrophos is distinguished: κήρυκι ἄρτον, Ἀθηνᾶς ἱερείαι ἄρτον, Ἡρακλέος ἱερεῖ ἄρτον, Πανδρόσο καὶ Ἀγλαύρο ἱερείαι ἄρτον, Κορατρόφο καὶ καλαθηφόρωι ἄρτον, κώπαις ἄρτον, "To the herald a loaf, to the priestess of Athena a loaf, to the priest of Herakles a loaf, to the priestess of Aglauros and Pandrosos a loaf, to the *kalathephoros* of Kourotrophos also a loaf, to the millers a loaf" (Ferguson's translation, 1938:6). Ferguson 1938:21, relying on the first passage, takes the priestess to be of all three goddesses: "The priestess of Aglauros and Pandrosos was at the same time priestess τῆς Κουροτρόφο. She was thus a pluralist.... From *IG* II² 5152 we learn that a seat was reserved in the theatre for a [priestess] Κουροτρόφου ἐξ Ἀγλαύρου. Hence the combination of the two cults may have special justification. But the association is natural. The Kourotrophion, Pandroseion, and Aglaurion lay within the area circumscribed by the περίπατος which defined the Acropolis, and between Ge (Kourotrophos) and the daughters of Kekrops there was a close natural and mythological relation [cf. Nilsson 1950:562]." Nilsson 1951:35n35, relying on the second passage quoted above, interprets the evidence of the inscription differently: "Ferguson, p. 21, is not right saying that the priestess of Aglauros and Pandrosos was at the same time the priestess of Kourotrophos. Even if ll. 11, τὴν (ἱερωσύνην) τῆς Ἀγλαύρο καὶ Πανδρόσο καὶ τῆς Κορατρόφο ['the (priesthood) of Aglauros and Pandrosos and of the Korotrophos'], can be understood so, ll. 45, Πανδρόσο καὶ Ἀγλαύρο ἱερείαι ἄρτον, Κορατρόφο καὶ καλαθηφόρωι ἄρτον ['to the priestess of Pandrosos and Aglauros bread, to (that) of Kourotrophos and to the basket carrier bread'], prove that they were distinguished. We have to understand the word τὴν ['that'] before τῆς Κουροτρόφου ['of the Kourotrophos'] in l. 12." Nilsson seems clearly correct that the priesthood was of Aglauros and Pandrosos only; Ferguson is correct in pointing out a close mythological relation with Kourotrophos, but there seems to be no evidence of a cult connection. Jacoby, commentary on Philochorus *FGrHist* 328 F 105, n5, p. 329, who follows Ferguson (he does not cite Nilsson), says that Kourotrophos was worshipped in the Aglaurion, but I do not know what evidence he has for this statement. Kourotrophos was a cult title of Demeter, Artemis, and Aphrodite, as well as of Ge; Jacoby, commentary on Philochorus *FGrHist* 328 F 10, n9, suggests that "it may be accidental that there is no evidence for κουρότροφος as an epiclesis for Athene: *IG* II² 1039, 58 (first century BC) the epheboi sacrifice ἐν ἀκροπόλει τῆι τε Ἀθηνᾶι τῆι Πολιάδι καὶ τῆι Κουροτρόφωι καὶ τῆι Πανδρόσωι ['on the Acropolis to Athena Polias, Kourotrophos, and Pandrosos']." Note that in the Athenian entry to the Catalogue of Ships Athena plays the role of kourotrophos for Erechtheus (cf. §3.79).

EN3.15 (Endnote to n3.287)

Solon was a peacemaker in Athens' civil strife of the early sixth century BC, but in external affairs his legacy was, in my view, the opposite: Solon changed Athens from a quiescent aristocratic state into a warlike democratic (i.e. more widely based) state with territorial ambitions; Eleusis, perhaps, and Salamis, certainly, were annexed in his time. Solon's transformation of the state had a central religious component in that Athena Polias, the city's embodiment, was changed from a mother goddess, whose image was a spinner, to a virgin goddess, whose image was a warrior (the new cult image, including a *phiálē*, is first found in artistic representations in the late sixth century, but most likely originated, apart from the *phiálē*, in the early sixth century); Erechtheus, her partner, was also radically changed, becoming the prototype of the autochthonous Athenian, born from the earth (*Iliad* 2.548) and ready to die for it.

This picture of Solon conforms, I think, with how Plato presents Solon in the *Timaeus* and the *Critias*, even in details. According to the *Timaeus* Solon heard from Egyptian priests of a war between ancient Athens and the lost continent of Atlantis, and he began a poem on the subject that he never completed (*Timaeus* 21c). Ancient Athens in Solon's story is a model warrior state, which in Plato is to serve to show the ideal state (i.e. the *Republic*) in action (*Timaeus* 20b–d, 26cd). Critias, who tells Solon's story in both of Plato's dialogues, is the great grandson of one Dropides, a friend and relative of Solon who heard the story from Solon himself when he returned from Egypt (*Timaeus* 20e); Critias heard the story from his grandfather Critias, Dropides' son, many years before, when as a ten-year old he took part in the festival of the Apaturia

(*Timaeus* 21a–d); after the passage of so much time Critias has had to make an effort to remember the story's details (*Timaeus* 26a; cf. *Critias* 108d).

I would suggest that it is not at all implausible that Solon began a poem on this subject, that he attributed it to Egyptian priests as his authority, and that knowledge of the poem and its subject was confined to the circle of Critias's family, which included Plato. Solon's reason for writing the poem would have been to present the new Athens, which he in large part had fashioned, as the original Athens, long since forgotten; only the Egyptian priests still knew of it. This is like the myth of Erechtheus's death, which (in my view) gave recent events the sanction of great antiquity. I do not doubt that Plato used the family tradition remembered by his kinsman Critias as a kind of "thought experiment" which he developed and expanded freely; but I would find it odd if Plato attributed a pure invention (a lie in effect) to his kinsman Critias and his family. Plato tells us that Dropides was mentioned frequently in Solon's poems (*Timaeus* 20e); is it likely that Plato would thus establish Dropides' credentials only to make him and his descendants false witnesses to the "truth" of Plato's fiction? I prefer to believe that Plato knew something about Solon that was not widely known, and that he meant to finish what Solon had begun when he took up the story of Atlantis (for sources other than Plato that mention Solon's unfinished poem, including Plutarch, Strabo, and Diodorus, see Henderson 1982:31n14; I note that Henderson himself, p. 22, takes at face value the tradition for this poem). Whether Solon actually talked with Egyptian priests on this subject is impossible to know, but it is worth noting that Egyptians' cultural awareness of their own past underwent profound changes in the dynasty that included Solon's lifetime, the twenty-sixth (664–525 BC); three pharaohs, including Amasis II (595–526 BC), began then to use royal titulature based on models from the Old Kingdom (Moyer 2002:79). Solon's hearing the story of Atlantis in Saïs, the city of this backward-looking dynasty, does not seem entirely out of place.

In Plato the Egyptian priests tell Solon that Athens was once, before the greatest of the floods, "the city best in war," and that its laws were also best: ἦν γὰρ δή ποτε, ὦ Σόλων, ὑπὲρ τὴν μεγίστην φθορὰν ὕδασιν ἡ νῦν Ἀθηναίων οὖσα πόλις <u>ἀρίστη πρός τε τὸν πόλεμον</u> καὶ κατὰ πάντα <u>εὐνομωτάτη</u> διαφερόντως (*Timaeus* 23c); these two attributes, "warlike" and "lawful," must have been the essential message of Solon's unfinished poem about Athens before the flood if the poem provided a model for the present. The Egyptian priests in the story belong to the goddess Neith in the city of Saïs, of which Neith is called the θεὸς ἀρχηγός, "founder god"; Neith is also said to be the Egyptian form of Athena, the city goddess of Athens, and both cities thus belong to her (*Timaeus* 21e). When Solon asks to hear what the priests have to tell him about ancient Athens, they begin with the story of Athena, Hephaistos, and Ge; Erichthonios, the offspring of Hephaistos and Ge, and the nursling of Athena, is identified only as "the seed of you (Athenians)," whom Athena nurtured a thousand years before she was allotted Saïs (*Timaeus* 23de): ἀκούσας οὖν ὁ Σόλων ἔφη θαυμάσαι καὶ πᾶσαν προθυμίαν σχεῖν δεόμενος τῶν ἱερέων πάντα δι' ἀκριβείας οἱ τὰ περὶ τῶν πάλαι πολιτῶν ἐξῆς διελθεῖν. τὸν οὖν ἱερέα φάναι· ʽΦθόνος οὐδείς, ὦ Σόλων, ἀλλὰ σοῦ τε ἕνεκα ἐρῶ καὶ τῆς πόλεως ὑμῶν, μάλιστα δὲ τῆς θεοῦ χάριν, ἣ τήν τε ὑμετέραν καὶ τήνδε ἔλαχεν καὶ ἔθρεψεν καὶ ἐπαίδευσεν, προτέραν μὲν τὴν παρ' ὑμῖν ἔτεσιν χιλίοις, <u>ἐκ Γῆς τε καὶ Ἡφαίστου τὸ σπέρμα παραλαβοῦσα ὑμῶν</u>, τήνδε δὲ ὑστέραν, "Solon said that when he heard this he was amazed and with all eagerness asked the priests to tell him everything about those ancient citizens accurately and in order. The priest said: 'I do not begrudge it to you, Solon, but will tell it for your sake and for your city's sake, but most of all on behalf of the goddess, who won your city and this city by lot, and raised and educated both, yours first by a thousand years, <u>when she took over from Earth and Hephaistos your seed</u>, and this city later." Critias sketches out the rest of the story, including the training in warfare that the goddess gave to both her cities (*Timaeus* 24b), Athens' crowning achievement of victory in war over the army of Atlantis (*Timaeus* 24e–25c), and the earthquakes and floods in which both the island of Atlantis and the entire Athenian fighting force disappeared (*Timaeus* 25d). After this sketch Critias proposes to use Solon's story to show the citizens of an ideal state in action, but not until the astronomer Timaeus first speaks on the origin of the cosmos (*Timaeus* 27a). Critias finally takes up his theme in the *Critias*, in which he is the main speaker. We have only the first part of this dialogue, describing both ancient Athens and Atlantis in detail, but not the war between them (like Solon, Plato seems not to have finished his project on Atlantis). As Critias retells the story, in the beginning, when all the gods chose particular places, Athena and Hephaistos chose Athens, where they made a race of noble autochthons, whose deeds were subsequently forgotten (*Critias* 109cd): ἄλλοι μὲν οὖν κατ' ἄλλους τόπους κληρουχήσαντες θεῶν ἐκεῖνα ἐκόσμουν, Ἥφαιστος δὲ κοινὴν <u>καὶ Ἀθηνᾶ</u> φύσιν ἔχοντες, ἅμα μὲν ἀδελφὴν ἐκ ταὐτοῦ πατρός, ἅμα δὲ φιλοσοφίᾳ φιλοτεχνίᾳ τε ἐπὶ τὰ αὐτὰ ἐλθόντες, οὕτω <u>μίαν ἄμφω λῆξιν τήνδε τὴν χώραν εἰλήχατον</u> ὡς οἰκείαν καὶ πρόσφορον ἀρετῇ καὶ φρονήσει πεφυκυῖαν, ἄνδρας δὲ ἀγαθοὺς <u>ἐμποιήσαντες</u> <u>αὐτόχθονας</u> ἐπὶ νοῦν ἔθεσαν τὴν τῆς πολιτείας τάξιν· ὧν τὰ μὲν ὀνόματα σέσωται, τὰ δὲ ἔργα διὰ τὰς τῶν παραλαμβανόντων φθορὰς καὶ τὰ μήκη τῶν χρόνων ἠφανίσθη, "The other gods obtained other places by lot and began to set them in order, but Hephaistos and Athena, because they have the same nature, being a brother and sister from the same father, and because they share the same pursuits, with their love of wisdom and love of crafts, also shared one allotment, this country, which fit their character, was conducive to excellence, and was naturally adapted for thought, and they put into it good men born from the earth, and into their minds they put the arrangement of the constitution; the names of these men have been preserved, but their deeds have disappeared through the destruction of their successors and by the lengths of the times involved." Although the deeds of these early Athenians were forgotten, their names were remembered; after suggesting an analogy to make such a process plausible, Critias continues (*Critias* 110a–c): ταύτῃ δὴ τὰ τῶν παλαιῶν ὀνόματα ἄνευ τῶν ἔργων διασέσωται. λέγω δὲ αὐτὰ τεκμαιρόμενος ὅτι Κέκροπός τε καὶ Ἐρεχθέως καὶ Ἐριχθονίου καὶ Ἐρυσίχθονος τῶν τε ἄλλων τὰ πλεῖστα ὅσαπερ καὶ Θησέως τῶν ἄνω περὶ τῶν ὀνομάτων ἑκάστων ἀπομνημονεύεται, τούτων ἐκείνους τὰ πολλὰ [i.e. τὰ ὀνόματα] ἐπονομάζοντας τοὺς ἱερέας Σόλων ἔφη τὸν τότε διηγεῖσθαι πόλεμον, καὶ τὰ τῶν γυναικῶν κατὰ τὰ αὐτά. καὶ δὴ καὶ τὸ τῆς θεοῦ σχῆμα καὶ ἄγαλμα, ὡς κοινὰ τότ' ἦν τὰ ἐπιτηδεύματα ταῖς τε γυναιξὶ καὶ τοῖς ἀνδράσι τὰ περὶ τὸν πόλεμον, οὕτω κατ' ἐκεῖνον τὸν νόμον ὡπλισμένην τὴν θεὸν ἀνάθημα εἶναι τοῖς τότε, ἔνδειγμα ὅτι πάνθ' ὅσα σύννομα ζῷα θήλεα καὶ ὅσα ἄρρενα, τὴν προσήκουσαν ἀρετὴν ἑκάστῳ γένει πᾶν κοινῇ δυνατὸν ἐπιτηδεύειν πέφυκεν, "In this way the names of the ancients were preserved without their deeds. I say this on the evidence that, according to Solon, most of the names that are remembered, Kekrops, Erechtheus, Erichthonios, Erysichthon, and most of the others before Theseus, were mentioned by the priests when they narrated the war that took place then, and that this was also the case with the womens' names. Consider indeed the dress and image of the goddess; since women and men both practiced war then, the people of that time, in line with this custom, had as a temple votive an armed goddess, evidence that among all male and female animals that partner together, whatever excellence belongs to each species, each member is by nature able to do that thing."

The reference to an armed "form and image of the goddess," the inclusion of Erichthonios with Erechtheus in the list of early kings, the pairing of Athena and Hephaistos as the first gods of Athens, who plant a race of autochthons there—all of this in my view relates to the real Solon and his changes of Athenian myth and cult. When Critias calls Solon's words to witness for the antiquity of the names of the early kings, he presumably refers to his family's oral tradition; there is no indication that Solon's unfinished poem also survived. But τεκμαιρόμενος, "calling to witness," is a strong word, and I am reluctant to think that Plato puts it in Critias's mouth without any real basis for doing so.

One point must remain vague. Erichthonios's autochthonous birth in the aetiological myth of the Arrhephoria, and Erechtheus's autochthonous birth in the Athenian entry to the Catalogue of Ships, are variant forms of the myth of the origins of Athenian autochthony itself. The connection between the birth from the earth of the original ancestor and of the entire race is clear in Plato's account, where the phrase "the seed of you" (τὸ σπέρμα ὑμῶν) refers both to the original ancestor and to the subsequent race, and Athena and Hephaistos are specifically said to have implanted a race of autochthons in Athens. Solon is to be connected with both forms of the myth of the original ancestor, with both Erichthonios and Erechtheus, and this raises the question whether the myth of Athenian autochthony itself was Solon's invention. There is reason to think so. The intent of the myth of autochthony, whether of the original ancestor or of the subsequent race, is to make Athena the protectress of all Athenians and no longer the mother of only some (cf. n3.243), and this strongly suggests Solon's program of reform. It is worth noting in Plato's retelling of Solon's account that Erysichthon, whom the Egyptian priests are supposed to have mentioned side by side with Erichthonios, draws attention to the common element in the two names, namely *chthōn*, "earth" (cf. Gill 1980:55 on Critias 110a7 ff.); the Attic Erysichthon, a son of Kekrops who died young and childless (to be distinguised from a figure of the same name known from Callimachus *Hymns* 6.22–117 and Ovid *Metamorphoses* 8.738–878; cf. Shapiro 1995:43 and n47 and Kearns *DNP* 'Erysichthon'), would seem to have no reason other than his name for being mentioned. But whether Plato preserves something of Solon's in pairing the two names we of course cannot say.

To be distinguished from the question considered here, whether Solon actually began a poem about Atlantis, is the question whether Plato intended his Atlantis story to be understood as fact or fiction; for the latter question see Gill 1977, 1979, 1993:63–66; Morgan 1998; cf. also Osborne 1996; Brisson 1994.

EN3.16 (Endnote to n3.288)
Fehrle 1910:199 argues that Peisistratos, with some earlier exceptions, first introduced the war goddess Athena in Athens on a large scale; he correlates the introduction of this Homeric form of the goddess on the Acropolis with the introduction of the Homeric poems at the Panathenaia. I agree with Fehrle that Athena Polias was not a war goddess in Athens before the sixth century BC, but I think that Solon rather than Peisistratos was the key figure in the goddess's transformation. I am also unconvinced that Peisistratos

(or his sons) first introduced the performance of the Homeric poems at the Panathenaia. The reorganization of the Panathenaia is securely dated to 566/5 BC, before Peisistratos seized power in Athens for the first time c. 560 BC (cf. n3.241); it was the archon Hippokleides, and not Peisistratos, who "founded" this festival. Jacoby, deriving the Panathenaia from previous clan festivals, conjectures that in 566/5 BC Hippokleides first introduced gymnastic contests in a state festival, and that "the ἀγῶνες μουσικοί [musical contests] were added subsequently (under the sons of Peisistratos at the latest)" (commentary on Istros *FGrHist* 334 F4, n2, p. 509; cf. n3.242 and n3.246). I question whether the distinction that Jacoby makes between gymnastic and musical contests is necessary; it makes more sense, I think, to see performances of Homeric poetry as integral to the Panathenaia from the start. It was at the four-yearly festival of the Great Panathenaia that the Homeric poems were later performed, and it is likely that this four-yearly festival was first instituted in the reorganization of the Panathenaia in 566/5 BC. Just as it was later assumed that Peisistratos instituted the Great Panathenaia (scholia to Aristides *Panathenaic Oration* 189.4 [Dindorf p. 323]; see n3.102), Peisistratos was thought to have instituted the Homeric performances at this festival. The role of Peisistratos (or his sons) was, I think, only to regulate performances of Homer, but as time went on this role was exaggerated, so that in "Plato" *Hipparchus* the tyrant's son, Hipparchus, is credited with bringing the Homeric poems to Athens for the first time (cf. n2.225 above). In fact the Homeric poems were already well known in Athens in Solon's time and earlier. It is worth noting that the interpolation of *Iliad* 2.558 was attributed to Solon as well as to Peisistratos (cf. n3.271 on Strabo 9.1.10); this example, whatever its factual basis (Solon may well be right: see n3.279 above for the chronological consideration raised by Casio 2002:115), serves to suggest a more general blurring between what Solon began and Peisistratos continued. I return to Athena as a war goddess in Athens. While I do not think that Peisistratos was the first to make Athena Polias a war goddess, he was clearly devoted to the goddess in this form: the legend of Phye, whom Peisistratos is supposed to have armed like Athena to accompany him in his chariot when he claimed power for the second time in Athens, is proof of this. Peisistratos may not have been the first to make Athena Polias a war goddess, but, if the Phye story is to be believed, he made bold use of this relatively recent transformation of the city goddess.

Part 4.

IONIA

Chapter 10.

THE PANIONIC LEAGUE

§4.1 Nestor, as discussed in Part 2 above, plays an extensive role beneath the surface of the Homeric poems; this role is based on Nestor's twin myth, which is itself kept hidden from view in the poems. Nestor's brother Periklymenos, who is mentioned but once in the poems, is Nestor's partner in this old myth, which is ultimately derived from the Indo-European twin myth. Homeric epic superimposed on Nestor's old myth a more recent myth, which is also mentioned but once in the poems, namely that Nestor is one of the twelve sons of Neleus. The twelve sons of Neleus, as suggested in Part 1, have to do with the twelve cities of the Ionian dodecapolis. This league of cities already existed in Homeric times if the *Iliad*, as it seems to do, alludes to the league's common festival, the Panionia.[1] The idea that Neleus had twelve sons, and that these twelve sons represented the twelve cities of the dodecapolis, can only have come from the one city of the twelve that could actually trace itself back to Neleus. This was Miletus, whose ruling family, the Neleids, were literally "descendants of Neleus." Their motive for sharing their genealogy must have been to give the league a common origin and a common ideology, which it otherwise lacked. If this analysis is correct, it means that the Neleids of Miletus were the prime movers in the organization of the dodecapolis and its common festival, the Panionia.

§4.2 Another tradition emanating from Miletus had the same thrust as the twelve sons of Neleus, but a different dynamic. The Neleid line passed through Athens on its way from Pylos to Miletus, and in Athens, as in Pylos and Miletus,

---

1 See n1.21 above for the simile in *Iliad* 20.403–405 comparing the cry of a mortally wounded Trojan to the bellowing of a bull sacrificed to Poseidon Helikonios, the god to whom the festival of the Panionia was dedicated. Locations in Ionia, including the cities of the dodecapolis, are shown on Map 1.

the Neleids were kings: Melanthos, a fifth-generation descendant of Neleus, left Pylos and acquired the kingship in Athens, and Kodros, his son, succeeded him as king of Athens.[2] Kodros was famous for his sacrificial death, by which he saved Athens from capture by the Dorians. Kodros was also the father

2 In my view the basis of this tradition was common to Miletus and Athens, and very old; in the view of Prinz and others the basis was older than Solon (fr. 4a West calls Athens the oldest land of Ionia) but still an Athenian invention (Prinz 1979:354 dates the invention to the seventh century BC; cf. also Herda 1998:9n50, who presents a range of opinions). The main source for the Neleids' ancestry is Hellanicus *FGrHist* 323a F 23 (scholia to Plato *Symposium* 208d). Omitting the generations from Deucalion to Neleus at the start of the fragment the genealogy is as follows: Neleus, Periklymenos, Boros, Penthilos, Andropompos, Melanthos, Kodros (the origin of this overly full form of the genealogy is discussed in EN4.11 to n4.155 below); the passage goes on to tell how Melanthos, the fifth descendant of Neleus, left Pylos when the Heraclids came, and how he went to Athens and won the kingship there by killing the Boeotian king in single combat to settle a border dispute (the combat provides a very strained aetiology for the festival of the Apatouria): ...Νηλέως δὲ καὶ Χλωρίδος Περικλύμενος, Περικλυμένου δὲ καὶ Πεισιδίκης Βῶρος, Βώρου δὲ καὶ Λυσιδίκης Πένθιλος, Πενθίλου δὲ καὶ Ἀγχιρόης Ἀνδρόπομπος, Ἀνδροπόμπου δὲ καὶ Ἡνιόχης τῆς Ἀρμενίου τοῦ Ζευξίππου τοῦ Εὐμήλου τοῦ Ἀδμήτου Μέλανθος. οὗτος Ἡρακλειδῶν ἐπιόντων ἐκ Μεσσήνης εἰς Ἀθήνας ὑπεχώρησεν, καὶ αὐτῷ γίνεται παῖς Κόδρος. χρόνῳ δὲ ὕστερον γενομένης τοῖς Βοιωτοῖς ἀμφισβητήσεως πρὸς Ἀθηναίους, ὡς μέν τινες, περὶ Οἰνόης καὶ Πανάκτου, ὡς δέ τινες, περὶ Μελαινῶν, καὶ τῶν Βοιωτῶν ἀξιούντων τοὺς βασιλέας προκινδυνεῦσαι περὶ τῆς χώρας εἰς μονομαχίαν καταστάντες, Ξάνθιος μὲν ὁ τῶν Βοιωτῶν βασιλεὺς ὑποδέχεται, Θυμοίτης δὲ ὁ τῶν Ἀθηναίων ἀρνεῖται, λέγων τῷ βουλομένῳ μονομαχεῖν τῆς ἀρχῆς παραχωρεῖν. Μέλανθος δὲ ὑποστὰς τὸν κίνδυνον ἐπὶ τὸ βασιλεῦσαι τῶν Ἀθηνῶν αὐτὸν καὶ τοὺς ἐξ αὐτοῦ, ὁπλισάμενος προήει, καὶ πλησίον τοῦ Ξανθίου γενόμενος εἶπεν "ἀδικεῖς, ὦ Ξάνθιε, σὺν ἑτέρῳ ἐπ᾽ ἐμὲ ἥκων καὶ οὐ μόνος, ὡς ὡμολόγητο." Ξάνθιος δὲ ταῦτα ἀκούσας μετεστράφη, θεάσασθαι βουλόμενος εἴ τις αὐτῷ ἑπόμενος εἴη· καὶ μεταστραφέντα βαλὼν αὐτὸν ἀπέκτεινεν, καὶ βασιλεὺς τῆς Ἀττικῆς ἐγένετο. ὅθεν τοῖς Ἀθηναίοις κρατήσασι τῆς χώρας ἔδοξεν ἑορτὴν ἄγειν, ἣν πάλαι μὲν Ἀπατηνόρια ὕστερον δὲ Ἀπατούρια ἐκάλουν ὡς ἀπὸ τῆς γενομένης ἀπάτης, "...from Neleus and Chloris [was born] Periklymenos, from Periklymenos and Peisidike Boros, from Boros and Lysidike Penthilos, from Penthilos and Ankhiroe Andropompos, from Andropompos and Heniokhe (the daughter of Armenios, the son of Zeuxippos, the son of Eumelos, the son of Admetos) Melanthos. The last named withdrew from Messenia to Athens when the Herakleidai came, and he had a son Kodros. When later a dispute arose between the Boeotians and the Athenians, according to some over Oinoë and Panakton, according to others over Melainai, and the Boeotians demanded that the kings put themselves at risk over the territory by engaging in single combat, Xanthios, the Boeotians' king, accepted, but Thymoites, the Athenians' king, refused, saying that he would cede his rule to whoever wished to engage in single combat. Melanthos undertook the danger in order to secure the kingship of Athens for himself and his descendants, and having armed himself went out, and when he came close to Xanthios he said 'You cheat, Xanthios, coming against me with another man and not alone as was agreed.' Xanthios turned around when he heard this, wishing to see if someone had followed him; and while he was turned Melanthos struck and killed him, and became king of Attica. From this the Athenians who had conquered the territory decided to celebrate a festival that they originally called the Apatenoria, and later the Apatouria, from the deception (*apátē*) that had taken place."

of the pair of brothers Neileos and Medon; when Medon, the elder brother, succeeded Kodros as king of Athens, Neileos, the younger brother, left Athens and founded Miletus.[3] As argued earlier, Neileos and Medon duplicate an older pair of brothers in their direct line, Neleus and Pelias: in particular Neileos, the founder of Miletus, duplicates Neleus, the founder of Pylos, in both name and myth. The form of his name, furthermore, indicates that Neileos had acquired his myth—the Kodrid myth—already by the Homeric era.[4]

§4.3 I take Neileos and Medon to be the two original sons of Kodros: between them they are the ancestors of the Neleids, who ruled Miletus, and the Medontids, who ruled Athens, and their myth accounts for the close relationship between these two cities, which was real, and at times was keenly felt.[5] But in Ionia the Kodrid myth, which belonged properly to the founder of

3 Hellanicus *FGrHist* 323a F 23 (previous note) continues as follows (the form Neleus instead of Neileos occurs here and in other sources; cf. n1.43 above): Μελάνθου δὲ Κόδρος γενόμενος ἐκδέχεται τὴν βασιλείαν· ὃς καὶ ὑπὲρ τῆς πατρίδος ἀπέθανεν τρόπῳ τοιῷδε. πολέμου τοῖς Δωριεῦσιν ὄντος πρὸς Ἀθηναίους, ἔχρησεν ὁ θεὸς τοῖς Δωριεῦσιν αἱρήσειν τὰς Ἀθήνας, εἰ Κόδρον τὸν βασιλέα μὴ φονεύσωσιν. γνοὺς δὲ τοῦτο ὁ Κόδρος, στείλας ἑαυτὸν εὐτελεῖ σκεύει ὡς ξυλιστὴν καὶ δρέπανον λαβών, ἐπὶ τὸν χάρακα τῶν πολεμίων προῄει. δύο δὲ αὐτὸν ἀπαντησάντων πολεμίων τὸν μὲν ἕνα πατάξας κατέβαλεν, ὑπὸ δὲ τοῦ ἑτέρου ἀγνοηθεὶς ὅστις ἦν, πληγεὶς ἀπέθανεν, καταλιπὼν τὴν ἀρχὴν Μέδοντι τῷ πρεσβυτέρῳ τῶν παίδων. ὁ δὲ νεώτερος αὐτοῦ παῖς Νηλεὺς τῆς δωδεκαπόλεως Ἰωνίας κτίστης ἐγένετο, "Melanthos's son Kodros received the kingship from him, and Kodros died for his country in the following way. While a war was being waged by the Dorians against the Athenians the god prophesied that the Dorians would take Athens if they did not kill Kodros the king. Kodros having learned of this dressed himself in simple clothes like a woodsman, took an ax, and set out to the enemy's camp. When two of the enemy encountered him he struck and slew one of them, but he was struck by the other, who did not know who he was, and he died, leaving the rule to Medon, the elder of his sons; his younger son Neleus became the founder of the dodecapolis of Ionia." The tradition that Neleus (i.e. Neileos) was the founder of the entire dodecapolis is secondary to the tradition that he was the founder of Miletus; the earliest source claiming his foundation of the dodecapolis is Panyassis in the fifth century, but the tradition itself, I think, goes back at least to the sixth century (see below n4.31 and §4.14). This tradition has to do with rival claims of Miletus and Ephesus to leadership of the Ionian colonization; the earliest source for the Ephesian claim is Pherekydes, also in the fifth century (see n4.32 below).

4 This conclusion is based on the following arguments developed in Part 1 above: the name of the founder of Pylos was *Nehelawos* in Mycenaean, became *Neíleōs* by regular sound changes in Ionic, and must have had the intermediate form **Neélaos* in pre-Homeric epic; the royal family of Miletus transferred the name **Neélaos* (*Neíleōs*) from the founder of Pylos to the founder of Miletus, and in consequence the Aeolic form *Nēleús* replaced **Neélaos* as the founder of Pylos in epic; since the Homeric poems call the founder of Pylos *Nēleús* I conclude that in the Homeric era the name **Neélaos* (*Neíleōs*) already belonged to the founder of Miletus and the Kodrid myth.

5 We know very little about the Medontids. In fourth-century Atthidography democratic institutions were projected back onto the Medontid rulers, who were said to be archons for ten-year periods, and before that archons for life, but not kings; for the existence of

Miletus, was extended to other cities of the dodecapolis. This extension must
have had the same purpose as the myth of the twelve sons of Neleus, namely

---

a Medontid dynasty, including its supposed last member, the cruel Hippomenes, see
below n4.150, n4.151, and n4.152. For the question of the clan's continued existence in the
historical period, see EN4.10 to n4.150 below. Carlier 1984:360–361 considers that claims of
Kodrid ancestry in Athens originated with the Medontid dynasty and not later (cf. nn 4.154
and 4.155 below). The Neleid dynasty of Miletus is better attested than are the Medontids;
for stories of particular Neleid kings of Miletus, see §4.46–§4.51 below. The more abun-
dant evidence for Neleids as compared with Medontids has to do with the Ionian tradi-
tion of novelistic stories, in which the Neleid rulers appear; cf. Jacoby 1949:392n20:
" 'novelistic tales'…, in which Ionian chronicles abounded, do not seem to have existed in
Athens at all (the Hippomenes story is decidedly not of that species)." The close relation-
ship between Miletus and Athens is seen especially at the time of the Ionian revolt, which
ended in the destruction of Miletus by the Persians in 494 BC. In instigating the revolt
in 499 BC Aristagoras, the tyrant of Miletus, appealed to Athens for help on the grounds
that Miletus had been colonized by Athens; Herodotus 5.97.2 tells how Aristagoras made
this the final argument in his successful appeal to the Athenian assembly: ταῦτά τε δὴ
ἔλεγε καὶ πρὸς τούτοισι τάδε, ὡς οἱ Μιλήσιοι τῶν Ἀθηναίων εἰσὶ ἄποικοι, καὶ οἰκός σφεας
εἴη ῥύεσθαι δυναμένους μέγα, "He said these things, and in addition to these things the
following, that the Milesians were colonists of the Athenians, and that it was right that
the Athenians, with their great power, protect them." This evidence is particularly valu-
able since it predates the fifth-century Athenian empire, which is sometimes claimed to
account for the tradition that Athens was the metropolis of Ionian cities (a view held less
now than formerly; for current views cf. Emlyn-Jones 1980:13–14 and Moggi 1996:103–104
with n105; for bibliography of Greek settlement in Ionia see Moggi 1996:103n103). Even
M. B. Sakellariou, who espouses this general point of view, makes an exception of Miletus,
and the above passage of Herodotus weighs heavily in his judgment: "This passage is
precious to us because it shows clearly that the Milesians considered themselves as origi-
nally from Athens well before Athenian imperialism inspired the fictive thesis that all the
Ionians of Asia Minor, and of the Cyclades, had come from Attica" ("Cette mention nous est
précieuse parce qu'elle montre clairement que les Milésiens se considéraient eux-mêmes
comme originaires d'Athènes bien avant que l'impérialisme athénien inspirât la thèse
fictive selon la quelle tous les Ioniens d'Asie Mineure, ainsi que ceux des Cyclades, seraient
issus de l'Attique," Sakellariou 1958:39; the author discusses the literary evidence for the
foundation of Miletus on pp. 39–44 and the institutional evidence, which is less decisive,
on pp. 44–76; see especially pp. 44 top and 75 bottom). After the destruction of Miletus
and the forced removal of its inhabitants in 494 BC (Herodotus 6.19–20), the Athenians
demonstrated the depth of their feeling when Phrynichus produced a tragedy on the fall
of Miletus and the Athenians fined him a thousand drachmas "for reminding them of
their own woes" (Herodotus 6.21.2): Ἀθηναῖοι μὲν γὰρ δῆλον ἐποίησαν ὑπεραχθεσθέντες
τῇ Μιλήτου ἁλώσι τῇ τε ἄλλη πολλαχῇ καὶ δὴ καὶ ποιήσαντι Φρυνίχῳ δρᾶμα Μιλήτου
ἅλωσιν καὶ διδάξαντι ἐς δάκρυά τε ἔπεσε τὸ θέητρον καὶ ἐζημίωσάν μιν ὡς ἀναμνήσαντα
οἰκήια κακὰ χιλίῃσι δραχμῇσι, καὶ ἐπέταξαν μηκέτι μηδένα χρᾶσθαι τούτῳ τῷ δράματι,
"The Athenians made it clear that they were exceedingly grieved by the fall of Miletus in
many other ways, but especially when Phrynichus made a play of the fall of Miletus and
produced it and the theater fell into tears, and they fined him a thousand drachmas for
reminding them of their own woes, and ordered that no one ever use this play again"). Cf.
also Strabo 14.1.7. For Milesian survivors of the Ionian revolt, see Huxley 1966:152.

to foster Panionism in the Neleids' own image. But while the twelve sons of Neleus were a poetic conceit, which did not correspond to any reality (Ionian cities apart from Miletus did not consider themselves the actual descendants of different sons of Neleus), the Kodrid myth was a political instrument and had real effects. Not all of the twelve cities accepted the myth of having had a Kodrid founder, but most did. We do not know why particular cities did not claim a Kodrid founder, but the league of twelve cities must have achieved its final number gradually, and it was perhaps only at the end of the process that a Kodrid founder—and hence Kodrid rulers—were required for a city to achieve Panionic status.[6] Phocaea, the northernmost of the twelve cities, may well have been the last admitted to the league; to gain admission it had to accept Kodrid rulers from two other cities which had already achieved Panionic status, Erythrai and Teos.[7] Phocaea, forced to accept rulers from outside, may have been an extreme case, but it shows clearly how the Kodrid myth was used. A more usual pattern was perhaps to bring a new city into the league by working with a particular family favorable to the league's goals, and to confer on that family (or families) the distinction of Kodrid descent. If this was the process, it leads back ultimately to Miletus as the prime mover in creating the Panionic league. To be a member of the league meant not just to be the notional descendant of Neleus, the founder of Pylos, but increasingly it also meant to be the descendant of Kodros, and therefore, like Miletus, to have an Athenian origin.[8]

---

6 Cf. Cook 1975:786: "For the most part the title of 'son of Codrus' is a posthumous distinction conferred, where the tradition permitted, on the founders of those cities which had achieved Panionic status."

7 Phocaea, which obtained its territory from Aeolic Cyme, was perhaps required to accept Kodrid rulers simply to insure its true Ionic character; cf. Pausanias 7.3.10: τὴν χώραν δὲ οὐ πολέμῳ, κατὰ δὲ ὁμολογίαν [οἱ Φωκαεῖς] λαμβάνουσι παρὰ Κυμαίων· Ἰώνων δὲ οὐ δεχομένων σφᾶς ἐς Πανιώνιον πρὶν ἢ τοῦ γένους βασιλέας τοῦ Κοδριδῶν λάβωσιν, οὕτω παρὰ Ἐρυθραίων καὶ ἐκ Τέω Δεοίτην καὶ Πέρικλον λαμβάνουσι καὶ Ἄβαρτον, "They [the Phocaeans] took their land from the Cymaeans not by war, but through an agreement; the Ionians did not admit them to the Panionion before they accepted kings from the race of the Codrids, and so they took Deoites and Periklos from the Erythraeans and Abartos from Teos." A fragment of the fifth-century writer Charon of Lampsakos confirms the presence of Kodrid rulers in Phocaea: Charon's tale about a pair of brothers "from Phocaea of the family of the Kodrids" is referred to by Plutarch *Bravery of Women* 255a: ἐκ Φωκαίας τοῦ Κοδριδῶν γένους ἦσαν ἀδελφοὶ δίδυμοι Φόξος καὶ Βλέψος· ὧν ὁ Φόξος ἀπὸ τῶν Λευκάδων πετρῶν πρῶτος ἀφῆκεν ἑαυτὸν εἰς θάλασσαν, ὡς Χάρων ὁ Λαμψακηνὸς ἱστόρηκεν, "There were twin brothers from Phocaea of the family of the Kodrids, Phoxos and Blepsos, one of whom, Phoxos, threw himself from the Leukadian rocks into the sea, as Charon of Lampsacus has told"; cf. Momigliano 1932:266–267.

8 Three members of the league (besides Phocaea) apparently never had traditions of Kodrid founders, namely Chios, Samos, and Klazomenai. As islands Chios and Samos were geographically secure, and perhaps they joined the league more on their own terms than

§4.4 In the fifth century, when Athens wished to justify its empire, the Kodrid myth was no doubt useful for this purpose, for it made Athens the mother city of most of Ionia, but this cannot have been the origin of the myth itself as is sometimes claimed.[9] The tradition about Phocaea, which had to

did other cities. King Hektor of Chios, whose ancestor Amphiklos came to Chios from Histiaia in Euboea three generations before him, decided to join the league on his own initiative after he drove the Carians and Abantes from the island, and when he joined he was given a special prize by the league; so the event is portrayed by Pausanias 7.4.9-10, whose source for Chios was the fifth-century poet and local historian Ion: Ἕκτωρ δὲ ἀπὸ Ἀμφίκλου τετάρτῃ γενεᾷ βασιλείαν γὰρ ἔσχε καὶ οὗτος ἐπολέμησεν Ἀβάντων καὶ Καρῶν τοῖς οἰκοῦσιν ἐν τῇ νήσῳ, καὶ τοὺς μὲν ἀπέκτεινεν ἐν ταῖς μάχαις, τοὺς δὲ ἀπελθεῖν ἠνάγκασεν ὑποσπόνδους. γενομένης δὲ ἀπαλλαγῆς πολέμου Χίοις, ἀφικέσθαι τηνικαῦτα ἐς μνήμην Ἕκτορι ὡς σφᾶς καὶ Ἴωσι δέοι συνθύειν ἐς Πανιώνιον· τρίποδα δὲ ἄθλον λαβεῖν αὐτὸν ἐπὶ ἀνδραγαθίᾳ παρὰ τοῦ κοινοῦ φησι τοῦ Ἰώνων. τοσαῦτα εἰρηκότα ἐς Χίους Ἴωνα εὕρισκον, "Hector held the kingship in the fourth generation after Amphikos, and fought against the Abantes and Carians living on the island, and he killed some of them in battles and forced others to leave under a truce; once the Chians were relieved of the war, it occurred to Hector that they should also sacrifice with the Ionians at Panionion. He [Ion] says that he received a tripod as a prize for valor from the league of the Ionians. So much I found Ion to have said concerning the Chians." Various stories are preserved about the Kodrid founder of Erythrai, Knopos or Kleopos (cf. n4.35 below for the variation of name), and the stories are instructive: Polyaenus 8.43 recounts a novelistic tale about how Knopos, one of the race of Kodrids, gained possession of Erythrai with the help of a Thessalian priestess at the time of the Ionian colonization of Asia; Pausanias 7.3.7 says that when Cretans, Lycians, Carians, and Pamphylians inhabited Erythrai, Kleopos, the son of Kodros, gathered men from all the cities of Ionia and settled them there; Athenaeus 6.258f-259f tells how Knopos king of Erythrai was murdered by usurpers and avenged by his brother. It seems clear that the central figure in these stories became a Kodrid founder only secondarily: Polyaenus straightforwardly associates this figure with the Ionian colonization of Asia, but Pausanias assumes that the Ionian cities had already been settled when they contributed to the colonization of Erythrai, and Athenaeus takes his story of murder and revenge from the second book of the *Histories* of Hippias of Erythrai about his native city; cf. Lenschau 1944:229, who thinks that this Knopos cannot have been the founder of his city, for as founder he would have occurred in the first book of Hippias.

9 Wilamowitz 1906/1971:54/146-147 and 1906a/1971:70-71/165-166, argues that the tradition for Kodrid founders did not become established until after Herodotus and Ion in the fifth century since these authors still know nothing of the conquest of Ionia by a united Athenian expedition. But rival traditions for the leadership of a united Athenian expedition are found in Panyassis and Pherekydes, and the rivalry itself, between Miletus and Ephesus, seems to go back at least to the sixth century (see above n4.3 and below n4.31 and §4.14). Others have argued that the Kodrid myth was invented in the sixth century in Athens by Peisistratos (references in Càssola 1957:88n31, including Nilsson 1951:59-64), but Peisistratos could hardly have aspired to lead the cities of Asia Minor, which were under Persian domination by c. 540 BC (cf. n4.59 below); the focus of his attention was rather Delos, and even there his influence did not last (Delos soon came under the control of Polycrates of Samos). It was not until his final return to Athens, when the cities of Asia Minor were already under Persian domination, that Peisistratos purified Delos (Herodotus 1.64.2) and may also have renewed the old Ionian festival of the Delia (so Shapiro 1989:48, but the interpretation of Thucydides 3.104.2 is ambiguous; cf n4.97 below). Thucydides

accept Kodrid rulers to be admitted to the Panionion, shows that the myth of Kodrid founders had spread among cities of the league before the league itself reached its canonical number of twelve cities.[10] This, I think, is a strong argument that the Kodrid myth is old, but there is another argument to be considered for this, namely that the basis of the Kodrid myth is woven into the very fabric of the Homeric poems: it is embodied in the Phaeacian king and queen, who respectively represent Nestor, the king of Pylos, and Athena Polias, the city goddess of Athens. In the Kodrid myth Pylos and Athens are the two main stages before migration to Asia Minor, and Alcinous and Arete, who are not only king and queen, but also uncle and niece, represent these two successive stages. This aspect of the identity of the Phaeacian royal couple has clear implications for the Phaeacians themselves. As others have seen, the Phaeacians greatly resemble the Ionians of Asia Minor in both their refined way of life and their seafaring nature.[11] Even their city resembles

---

3.104.3–6 contrasts the festival of Homer's time, to which the Ionians of the mainland and the neighboring islanders gathered, with the festival of a later time, which no longer included the mainland Ionians; Shapiro connects the later festival with Peisistratos: "To the revived Delia came choruses from Athens and the Islands, but not from the cities of mainland Ionia, who were now under Persian (earlier Lydian) rule" (Shapiro 1989:49). Cf. also Huxley 1966:124–125; Cook 1975:784.

10 Cf. Momigliano 1932:266–267.

11 See above all Welcker 1832/1845:29–37 (who cites Zell 1826:9). Singing, dancing, and banqueting, and a love of clean clothes, warm baths, and beds, define the Phaeacian way of life; Welcker cites *Odyssey* 8.246–249, in which Alcinous speaks of the Phaeacians' weaknesses, strengths, and predilections (cf. §2.126 above for this passage):

οὐ γὰρ πυγμάχοι εἰμὲν ἀμύμονες οὐδὲ παλαισταί,
ἀλλὰ ποσὶ κραιπνῶς θέομεν καὶ νηυσὶν ἄριστοι,
αἰεὶ δ' ἡμῖν δαίς τε φίλη κίθαρίς τε χοροί τε
εἵματά τ' ἐξημοιβὰ λοετρά τε θερμὰ καὶ εὐναί.

For we are not faultless boxers or wrestlers,
but we run fast on foot and we are the best in ships,
and always dear to us are the banquet and the lyre and dances
and changes of clothes and warm baths and beds.

Welcker also cites *Odyssey* 8.252–253, where Alcinous calls on dancers to accompany Demodokos so that Odysseus can tell his own people how much the Phaeacians surpass others in seafaring, speed of foot, dancing, and singing: ὅσσον περιγινόμεθ' ἄλλων / ναυτιλίῃ καὶ ποσσὶ καὶ ὀρχηστυῖ καὶ ἀοιδῇ. Singing is especially important to the Phaeacians, as we see in the three songs of Demodokos. Clean clothes are another repeated theme (and an important one for Nausicaa's hidden identity; see §3.32–§3.37 above). Nausicaa disguises her real intention in doing the wash by saying that her father must have clean clothes for the meetings of his council (*Odyssey* 6.61), and her brothers for the dance (*Odyssey* 6.64–65): οἱ δ' αἰεὶ ἐθέλουσι νεόπλυτα εἵματ' ἔχοντες / ἐς χορὸν ἔρχεσθαι, "they always wish to go to the dance with newly washed clothes." The Ionians too were known for their dress: *Iliad* 13.685 and *Homeric Hymn to Apollo* 147 call them Ἰάονες ἑλκεχίτωνες,

the coastal cities of Asia Minor, including Miletus.[12] But this identification of
the Phaeacians with the Ionians, which is so intuitively appealing, does not,
I think, go far enough: the Phaeacians are not just Ionians, but the Ionians
of the dodecapolis. I say this because the Phaeacian royal couple embodies
the Kodrid myth, which links Pylos and Athens as the two successive stages
of migration, and because the Kodrid myth was the touchstone of Panionic
status. There is confirmation that the Phaeacians represent the Ionians of
the dodecapolis, I think, in a significant detail of the Homeric text: in addi-
tion to Alcinous, who stands apart in his role as ruler, the Phaeacians have
twelve kings; Alcinous himself, as the thirteenth king, specifies their number
when he first orders the rest of the Phaeacians to prepare gifts for Odysseus
(*Odyssey* 8.390–391):

δώδεκα γὰρ κατὰ δῆμον ἀριπρεπέες βασιλῆες
ἀρχοὶ κραίνουσι, τρεισκαιδέκατος δ᾽ ἐγὼ αὐτός.

For among the people twelve illustrious kings
rule, and I myself am the thirteenth.[13]

"tunic-trailing Ionians," and Asios, a probably sixth-century Samian poet, describes them
entering Hera's sanctuary on Samos in snow-white tunics (πεπυκασμένοι εἵμασι καλοῖς, /
χιονέοισι χιτῶσι, Athenaeaus 12.525ef).

12 The Phaeacian city is laid out on a peninsula with harbors on either side, as in many Ionian
(and Aeolic) cities of the Asia Minor coast; Cook 1962:30–31 (cf. also pp. 25 and 33) compares
Lebedos and Myonessus (between Lebedos and Teos) with the Phaeacians' city for this
geographical feature. For a longer list of such peninsular cities, see Cook 1975:796–797.
Cf. also Merkelbach 1969:234: "Poet 'A' portrays the Phaeacians for us as a living like-
ness of Ionian seafarers; the activity in their city and in the harbor (*Odyssey* 6.262–272) is
a precious picture of an Ionian city" ("Die Phäaken schildert A uns als lebendiges Abbild
der ionischen Seefahrer; das Treiben in ihrer Stadt und im Hafen (*Odyssey* 6.262–272) ist
ein köstliches Bild einer ionischen Stadt"). Miletus too was laid out on a peninsula with
harbors on either side; Kenzler 1999:88–89 and 121 with n115 compares Miletus with the
Phaeacian city for its *agorá* situated on the isthmus close to the harbors (*Odyssey* 6.263–266,
etc.; for the Phaeacian *agorá* see Martin 1951:28–31, 56–62); there are indications that the
agorá of Geometric and Archaic Miletus was similarly placed, as it later was in the city
rebuilt after the Persian destruction (Kenzler 1999:87, 89; cf. Martin 1951:58).

13 When Alcinous earlier meets with his council to decide on Odysseus's *nóstos* their number
is not mentioned (they are called only Φαιήκων ἡγήτορες ἠδὲ μέδοντες, "leaders and
counselors of the Phaeacians," in *Odyssey* 8.11 and 8.26, and σκηπτοῦχοι, "scepter-bearers,"
in *Odyssey* 8.47), but they are clearly the twelve kings referred to later. We should not
be misled by the fact that Alcinous stands above the other kings as the thirteenth king:
Alcinous does not represent one city of the dodecapolis as opposed to others, but, with
his queen Arete, he represents all twelve at once. By contast Nestor, who stands behind
Alcinous, is included among the twelve sons of Neleus, and he therefore represents, at least
notionally, a particular city—any of the twelve cities except Miletus. In reality, however, a

§4.5 My basic argument in this section is that the Phaeacians represent the Ionians of the dodecapolis, who were in fact a single people only when they came together to celebrate the Panionia.[14] The identification of the Phaeacians with the Ionians assembled for the Panionia has important consequences for the Homeric poems, but we are not yet ready to deal with those. We must first deal with the fact that apart from Homer our historical evidence is late, and we therefore no longer clearly see what the role of Miletus was in the early dodecapolis. In particular the Kodrid myth needs to be considered further to support the idea that in Ionia this myth spread from Miletus. We must also consider the difficult question of the origin of the Panionic league, especially its date, for this, I think, is of great importance for the Homeric poems.

§4.6 Although the Kodrid myth was extended to other Ionian cities, Miletus never forgot that it had the basic claim to this myth. As Herodotus attests, the Milesians of his own day believed that they had originally set out "from the prytaneion (town hall) of the Athenians," and that they were therefore "the noblest of the Ionians."[15] This surely is an allusion to Neileos, the founder of Miletus, who was said to have come from the very seat of Athenian royal power, which is what Herodotus must mean by the prytaneion of the

---

particular city cannot be specified for Nestor; as Homeric hero he is the property of all. The inherent ambiguity of Nestor's relationship to the dodecapolis—he is too large a figure to be associated with any one city, but his status as one of twelve implies that he is associated with one city—is resolved in the Phaeacian scheme, where Alcinous stands above the other twelve kings.

14 The sense of ethereal unreality about the Phaeacians has much to do, I think, with the fact that they represent a people—"Panionians"—that existed as such only at a festival.

15 Herodotus 1.146. In this chapter Herodotus details the diverse origins of the Ionians (Abantes, Minyans, Dryopes, Phocians, Molossians, Arcadians, Dorians), and he concludes his account by saying that even those who claimed to be the noblest of the Ionians (i.e., the most Athenian) arrived in Ionia without wives and married Carian women after killing their fathers, husbands, and children; at the end of this tale, he names the city where it took place, Miletus: οἱ δὲ αὐτῶν ἀπὸ τοῦ πρυτανηίου τοῦ Ἀθηναίων ὁρμηθέντες καὶ νομίζοντες γενναιότατοι εἶναι Ἰώνων, οὗτοι δὲ οὐ γυναῖκας ἠγάγοντο ἐς τὴν ἀποικίην ἀλλὰ Καείρας ἔσχον, τῶν ἐφόνευσαν τοὺς γονέας. διὰ τοῦτον δὲ τὸν φόνον αἱ γυναῖκες αὗται νόμον θέμεναι σφίσι αὐτῇσι ὅρκους ἐπήλασαν καὶ παρέδοσαν τῇσι θυγατράσι μή κοτε ὁμοσιτῆσαι τοῖσι ἀνδράσι μηδὲ οὐνόματι βῶσαι τὸν ἑωυτῆς ἄνδρα, τοῦδε εἵνεκα ὅτι ἐφόνευσαν σφέων τοὺς πατέρας καὶ ἄνδρας καὶ παῖδας καὶ ἔπειτε ταῦτα ποιήσαντες αὐτῇσι συνοίκεον. ταῦτα δὲ ἦν γινόμενα ἐν Μιλήτῳ, "Those of them who set forth from the prytaneion of the Athenians and think that they are the noblest of the Ionians did not bring wives with them to the colony, but took Carian wives, whose parents they murdered. Because of this murder these women made a law and forced themselves to swear oaths to it and passed it on to their daughters, never to eat together with their husbands or to call their own husbands by name, for this reason, that they had murdered their fathers, husbands, and children, and lived with them after they had done it. This happened in Miletus."

Athenians.[16] Herodotus dislikes the arrogance of the Milesian claim, but he does not dispute the basis of the claim, nor do we.[17]

§4.7 The Kodrid myth was meant to be believed in the cities that accepted it, and the hand of Miletus in spreading it is therefore hidden. This is true in the case of the oldest evidence for the myth, namely the tradition that Phocaea accepted Kodrid rulers from Erythrai and Teos in order to be admitted to the Panionic league: the Kodrid rulers did not come from Miletus, and it is only an inference that Miletus was responsible for the spread of the Kodrid myth to Erythrai and Teos in the first place.[18] Another piece of early evidence is instructive, although again the hand of Miletus is hidden. Smyrna, according to Herodotus, was the only city to seek admission to the Panionic league and be denied;[19] it is, I think, significant that Smyrna also did not accept the Kodrid myth. Smyrna was originally an Aeolic settlement,

---

16 There was no royal palace on the fifth-century Athenian Acropolis; the prytaneion was its contemporary equivalent. How and Wells 1928 on Herodotus 1.146 take mention of the prytaneion to be an anachronistic reference by the Milesians to the place from which colonies were sent out in historical times; this seems plausible, but I find no actual parallels for a prytaneion in such a context. See n4.172 below for the likelihood that the Neleid family still had considerable power in Miletus in the fifth century BC; I think that it is very possible that Herodotus had this family particularly in mind in speaking of the Milesians' excessive pride in their Athenian origins.

17 For the genuine historical connection between Athens and Miletus see Sakellariou 1958 as discussed above n4.5; Sakellariou gives particular weight to two passages of Herodotus: 5.97 (discussed above n4.5) and the present passage, 1.146; in both cases it is the Milesians themselves who claim an Athenian origin.

18 The name of the royal family in Erythrai (as in Ephesus) was Basilidai; this name presumably became linked secondarily to Kodros in both Ephesus and Erythrai. In Athens a female figure named Basile, who was paired with Neleus in a cult to which Kodros was later added, may also reflect the link between the name Basilidai and Kodros, especially in Ephesus (for the Basilidai see below §4.11 and n4.43 and n4.44; for Basile see §4.13 below).

19 Herodotus mentions Smyrna's failure to gain admission to the league when he discusses the undue pride of the twelve member cities in the Ionian name and the exclusive nature of the Panionion itself, which the twelve cities did not wish to share with other Ionians: in fact, Herodotus says, other Ionians did not ask to join, apart from the Smyrnaeans (Herodotus 1.143.3): αἱ δὲ δυώδεκα πόλιες αὗται τῷ τε οὐνόματι ἠγάλλοντο καὶ ἱρὸν ἱδρύσαντο ἐπὶ σφέων αὐτέων, τῷ οὔνομα ἔθεντο Πανιώνιον, ἐβουλεύσαντο δὲ αὐτοῦ μεταδοῦναι μηδαμοῖσι ἄλλοισι Ἰώνων (οὐδ' ἐδεήθησαν δὲ οὐδαμοὶ μετασχεῖν ὅτι μὴ Σμυρναῖοι), "These twelve cities gloried in the name and established a sanctuary for themselves, to which they gave the name Panionion, and they resolved not to let any other Ionians participate in it (nor did any ask to participate in it except the Smyrnaeans)." Strabo 14.1.4 reports that Smyrna was in fact later admitted to the league through the good offices of Ephesus: αὗται μὲν δώδεκα Ἰωνικαὶ πόλεις, προσελήφθη δὲ χρόνοις ὕστερον καὶ Σμύρνα εἰς τὸ Ἰωνικὸν ἐναγαγόντων Ἐφεσίων· ἦσαν γὰρ αὐτοῖς σύνοικοι τὸ παλαιόν, ἡνίκα καὶ Σμύρνα ἐκαλεῖτο ἡ Ἔφεσος, "These are the twelve Ionian cities, and in later times Smyrna was also admitted to the Ionian confederacy, when the Ephesians brought them in. For in ancient times they

which became Ionian when a group of exiles from Colophon seized it through a ruse.[20] The elegiac poet Mimnermus, who lived in the latter half of the

were fellow inhabitants of the Ephesians, when Ephesus was also called Smyrna." Pausanias 7.5.1 has a similar account, and a similar unspecific phrase for the time of Smyrna's admission to the league: Σμύρναν δὲ ἐν ταῖς δώδεκα πόλεσιν οὖσαν Αἰολέων καὶ οἰκουμένην τῆς χώρας, καθ' ἃ καὶ ἐς ἐμὲ ἔτι πόλιν [ἣν] καλοῦσιν ἀρχαίαν, Ἴωνες ἐκ Κολοφῶνος ὁρμηθέντες ἀφελόμενοι τοὺς Αἰολεῖς ἔσχον· χρόνῳ δὲ ὕστερον καὶ Ἴωνες μετέδοσαν Σμυρναίοις τοῦ ἐν Πανιωνίῳ συλλόγου, "Smyrna was one of the Aeolians' twelve cites, and it was located in that part of the country that down to my time they still call the old city; Ionians who came from Colophon took it from the Aeolians and held it; at a later time the Ionians gave the Smyrnaeans a share in the Ionian assembly at Panionion." The "later time" of Smyrna's admission to the league cannot refer to the period before Alyattes and the Lydians destroyed Smyrna c. 600 BC (as Wilamowitz 1906/1971:52/144–145 and others contend; cf. EN4.3 to n4.72 below), for Herodotus's statement plainly rules this out; the reference must be instead to the revived city of Smyrna which was admitted to the revived Panionion at the end of the fourth century or beginning of the third century BC; Smyrna remained a member of this later league through Hellenistic and Roman times (cf. Roebuck 1955:38n38). The role of Ephesus in gaining Smyrna's admission (Strabo 14.1.4) goes well with such a late date, far better than with an early date (see §4.11 and n4.45 below on Ephesus's leadership of the revived Panionia, which Strabo attests for his own day); the role of Ephesus in fact makes most sense in the early-third century BC under Lysimachus (see Ragone 1986:191–194). It is interesting that a decree of the league honoring a Milesian citizen in 289 BC, which was to be inscribed and set up in each city of the league as well as at Panionion, survives in two copies, one from Miletus and the other from Smyrna: both begin with the words ἔδοξε Ἰώνων τῶι κοινῶι, "it was decreed by the league of Ionians," but the Smyrnaean copy adds the phrase τῶν τρε[ισκαί]δεκα πόλεων, "of the thirteen cities" (Dittenberger 1915–1924 no. 368 line 1 note 1). If this reflects Smyrna's pride in having become the thirteenth city of the league, Smyrna had presumably achieved this distinction recently and not centuries earlier. Strabo 14.1.37 gives a brief history of Smyrna from the destruction of the old city by Alyattes, after which the Smyrnaeans lived in villages "for about four hundred years" until Antigonus revived the city in a new location twenty stades from the old city, and Lysimachus continued to foster the new city: ἑξῆς δὲ ἄλλος κόλπος, ἐν ᾧ ἡ παλαιὰ Σμύρνα ἀπὸ εἴκοσι σταδίων τῆς νῦν. Λυδῶν δὲ κατασπασάντων τὴν Σμύρναν περὶ τετρακόσια ἔτη διετέλεσεν οἰκουμένη κωμηδόν· εἶτα ἀνήγειρεν αὐτὴν Ἀντίγονος, καὶ μετὰ ταῦτα Λυσίμαχος, καὶ νῦν ἐστι καλλίστη τῶν πασῶν, "Next is another gulf, in which was old Smyrna, twenty stades from the present city. For about four hundred years after the Lydians destroyed Smyrna it continued to be inhabited in villages; then Antigonus brought it back to life, and after that Lysimachus, and now it is the most beautiful of all the cities" (Strabo here overstates by more than a century the time between the destruction of old Smyrna c. 600 BC and the foundation of the new city by Antigonus, who died in 301 BC). Strabo and Pausanias seem to follow a common source in saying that Smyrna was admitted to the Panionion "at a later time" (χρόνοις ὕστερον, Strabo 14.1.4; χρόνῳ δὲ ὕστερον, Pausanias 7.5.1); this source perhaps wished to qualify Herodotus's statement that Smyrna was refused admission to the Panionion by providing information pertaining to the later city of Antigonus and Lysimachus.

20 Herodotus 1.150: Σμύρνην δὲ ὧδε ἀπέβαλον Αἰολέες· Κολοφωνίους ἄνδρας στάσι ἑσσωθέντας καὶ ἐκπεσόντας ἐκ τῆς πατρίδος ὑπεδέξαντο. μετὰ δὲ οἱ φυγάδες τῶν Κολοφωνίων φυλάξαντες τοὺς Σμυρναίους ὁρτὴν ἔξω τείχεος ποιευμένους Διονύσῳ, τὰς πύλας ἀποκλήισαντες ἔσχον τὴν πόλιν. βοηθησάντων δὲ πάντων Αἰολέων ὁμολογίῃ ἐχρήσαντο τὰ ἔπιπλα ἀποδόντων τῶν Ἰώνων ἐκλιπεῖν Σμύρνην Αἰολέας. ποιησάντων δὲ

seventh century BC, was from Smyrna, and in one of his poems he speaks as a descendant of the Colophonians who seized the city.[21] His voice, presumably well after Smyrna's failed attempt to join the Panionic league, suggests why that attempt may have failed. The poem in question is the following well-known fragment of Mimnermus's *Nanno* (Mimnermus fr. 9 West):

Αἰπὺ ‹ › τε Πύλον Νηλήϊον ἄστυ λιπόντες

ἱμερτὴν Ἀσίην νηυσὶν ἀφικόμεθα,

ἐς δ' ἐρατὴν Κολοφῶνα βίην ὑπέροπλον ἔχοντες

ἑζόμεθ', ἀργαλέης ὕβριος ἡγεμόνες·

κεῖθεν †διαστήεντος ἀπορνύμενοι ποταμοῖο

θεῶν βουλῇ Σμύρνην εἵλομεν Αἰολίδα.

Leaving (steep?) Pylos, the city of Neleus,
  we came in ships to longed-for Asia
and with overwhelming might we settled in lovely Colophon,
  initiators of harsh violence.
From there setting forth from the river [   ]
  we took Aeolian Smyrna by the gods' will.

It is striking that Mimnermus, who seems to stand for all Smyrnaeans in these lines, traces his ancestry back to Pylos, "the city of Neleus" (Νηλήϊον ἄστυ). Does this mean that the ancestors of Mimnermus who settled Colophon claimed Neleid descent? I do not think so. What is meant, I think, is that the ancestors who came from Pylos were on a par with the Neleids—their equals. Mimnermus's ancestors came to Colophon not through Athens, but directly from Pylos, and therefore they did not claim to be Kodrids. It has been argued that Mimnermus gives only a compressed version of his forebears' migration

---

ταῦτα, Σμυρναίους ἐπιδιείλοντο σφίσι αἱ ἕνδεκα πόλιες καὶ ἐποιήσαντο σφέων αὐτέων πολιήτας, "The Aeolians lost Smyrna in the following way: They received men from Colophon who had been defeated in civil strife and exiled from their country. Afterwards the Colophonian exiles waited for the Smyrnaeans to celebrate a festival of Dionysus outside the city walls, and they locked the gates and took possession of the city. When all the Aeolians sent help, an agreement was reached that the Aeolians would leave Smyrna if the Ionians gave them back their moveable property. They did this, and the eleven other [Aeolian] cities divided up the Smyrnaeans and made them their own citizens."

21 Smyrna was Ionian by 688 BC according to Pausanias 5.8.7 (he says that when Onomastos of Smyrna won the boxing at the twenty-third Olympic festival Smyrna was already an Ionian city: Ὀνόμαστος...ἐκ Σμύρνης συντελούσης ἤδη τηνικαῦτα ἐς Ἴωνας). How much earlier Smyrna had became Ionian is not known. Cook 1952:104, on the basis of pottery, thinks that the change from an Aeolic to an Ionian city had already occurred by 800 BC.

from Pylos to Colophon, and that an expanded version would have included an Athenian stage;[22] but this is disproved by another fragment of the *Nanno*: Strabo 14.1.3 tells us that the founder of Colophon according to the *Nanno* was "Andraimon the Pylian": Κολοφῶνα δ' Ἀνδραίμων Πύλιος (κτίζει), ὥς φησι καὶ Μίμνερμος ἐν Ναννοῖ (Mimnermus fr. 10 West). One may quibble that the Athenian Kodros too could be called a Pylian in terms of his ancestry, but to make Andraimon an Athenian on this basis is unwarranted: the two pieces of evidence from the *Nanno* are consistent in omitting any mention of Athens and they should be taken at face value.[23]

§4.8 We do not know why the Smyrnaeans were refused admission to the Panionion, but they were originally exiles from Colophon, and it has been suggested that the Colophonians who exiled them did not want them in the league.[24] I think that this suggestion may well be right, and that the Kodrid myth is a further indication of what took place. Whereas Mimnermus claimed that his ancestor Andraimon had founded Colophon, two Kodrids, Damasichthon and Promethos, are said to have founded Colophon in Pausanias's account.[25] As for Andraimon, his tomb was still extant in Pausanias's day: it was outside

---

22 Cf. Cook 1975:784; I agree with Cook that Athens played a leading role in the Ionian migration, but as the mother city of Miletus and not of all Ionia; Colophon may well have had a non-Athenian origin. The issue is discussed further in EN4.1.

23 If Andraimon came to Colophon directly from Pylos, when did he come? It is not necessary that he left Pylos when the Bronze Age city was destroyed, for Pylians seem to have survived for centuries in other locations in Messenia until the Messenian Wars. But the Messenian Wars themselves are too late a date, for the Pylians' final emigration from the Peloponnesus was not to Ionia, but to Italy. See below n5.64 and EN5.9. Mimnermus fr. 9 West, by calling Pylos "the city of Neleus," probably means to say that his ancestors founded Colophon as early as the Neleids founded Miletus; whether they actually did so seems doubtful, but the date cannot be fixed; cf. Kiechle 1960:12–13, 12n5, and Huxley 1962:147n680.

24 Jeffery 1976:225: "We can only guess at reasons [for Smyrna's rejection]: perhaps some assenting Aiolians had remained there, or perhaps Kolophon blocked the proposal because she herself had exiled these Ionians in the first place." See further EN4.3 to n4.72 below.

25 Pausanias 7.3.3: when the Ionians under their two Kodrid leaders arrived they made terms and lived together with Greeks from Crete and Thebes who already inhabited Colophon: Ἴωνες δὲ ὅρκους ποιησάμενοι πρὸς τοὺς ἐν Κολοφῶνι Ἕλληνας συνεπολιτεύοντο, οὐδὲν ἔχοντες πλέον· βασιλείαν δὲ Ἰώνων ἡγεμόνες Δαμασίχθων λαμβάνει καὶ Πρόμηθος Κόδρου παῖδες, "The Ionians made oaths with the Greeks in Colophon and lived with them as members of one state without taking advantage of them; but the leaders of the Ionians, Damasichthon and Promethos, sons of Kodros, took the kingship." The amity between the new and old settlers of Colophon in this Kodrid tradition contrasts with what Mimnermus says of his ancestors when they arrived in Colophon and began hostilities with the inhabitants (he calls them ἀργαλέης ὕβριος ἡγεμόνες, "leaders of harsh violence [*húbris*]"); as Lenschau 1944:229 remarks, *húbris* implies an assault, not on natives (that would be expected), but on other Greeks. Again there seems to be an antithesis between the Kodrid tradition for the foundation of Colophon and Mimnermus's tradition.

Colophon on the road to Lebedos, but Andraimon himself was not said to be the founder of Colophon, but of neighboring Lebedos, and a Kodrid to boot.[26] The party that prevailed in Colophon probably accepted Kodrid founders after exiling its adversaries; when Mimnermus continued to speak of his Pylian ancestor Andraimon as the founder of Colophon, the Colophonians would already have disowned Andraimon and given his tomb over to Lebedos, where he served as the Kodrid founder of this small member of the Panionic league. This is a construction, but I think it is a plausible one.[27] The important point is that the Colophonians, who were admitted to the league, accepted Kodrid founders, whereas the Smyrnaeans, who were refused admission to the league, went on claiming a non-Kodrid ancestor as the figure who first led them to Asia Minor.[28]

§4.9 The role of Miletus as leader of the early dodecapolis would be clearer if Ephesus had not replaced Miletus as the leading city of Ionia in the historical period.[29] The Ionian revolt, because it ended in disaster for

---

26 Pausanias 7.3.5: τὸ δὲ ἐξ ἀρχῆς καὶ τὴν Λέβεδον ἐνέμοντο οἱ Κᾶρες, ἐς ὃ Ἀνδραίμων σφᾶς ὁ Κόδρου καὶ Ἴωνες ἐλαύνουσι. τῷ δὲ Ἀνδραίμονι ὁ τάφος ἐκ Κολοφῶνος ἰόντι ἐστὶν ἐν ἀριστερᾷ τῆς ὁδοῦ, διαβάντι τὸν Καλάοντα ποταμόν, "Originally Carians inhabited Lebedos, until Andraimon, Kodros's son, and the Ionians drove them out. The tomb of Andraimon is on the left side of the road as one leaves Colophon and crosses the Kalaon River." Pausanias is a reliable source for this information, based as it is on his own observation of Andraimon's tomb. See Habicht 1984:43–46 and Moggi 1996:94–95 for Pausanias's independent research on local traditions for the founding of individual Ionian cities (as opposed to traditions for a single founding of all Ionia); Pausanias's information is supported epigraphically in the case of Promethos, one of the two Kodrid founders of Colophon, by a *génos* of Προμήθειοι in Colophon on a fourth-century BC inscription (Habicht 1984:45–46).

27 Cf. Wilamowitz 1906a/1971:64n3/158n2. It is possible that the party that ultimately prevailed at Colophon had already accepted Kodrid founders before exiling its adversaries, and that joining the Panionic league was one of the points of conflict between the parties, but this seems unlikely to me: whereas Smyrna probably became Ionian c. 800 BC (see n4.21 above), I doubt that the Panionic league came into existence before the mid-eighth century BC (see below §4.67 and §4.70). There is also the fact that Smyrna sought admission to the league, and an earlier opposition to league membership, if this was a cause of exile from Colophon, would not be consistent with this.

28 For hostility between Colophon and Smyrna I simply note a late piece of evidence: the *Life of Homer* preserved in the Suda s.v. Ὅμηρος (Allen 1912:256–268) refers to a war between Colophon and Smyrna in which Homer was given as a hostage to the Colophonians and thus got his name (lines 25–26 Allen): ἐκλήθη δὲ Ὅμηρος διὰ τὸ πολέμου ἐνισταμένου Σμυρναίοις πρὸς Κολοφωνίους ὅμηρον δοθῆναι, "Homer was so called from his having been given as a hostage (*hómēros*) when a war arose for the Smyrnaeans against the Colophonians." This war does not seem to refer to the capture of Smyrna as described by Herodotus, although it may be based on that.

29 Cf. Calder *OCD²/³* s.v. 'Ephesus': "City at the mouth of the river Caÿster..., which rivalled and finally displaced Miletus, and owing to the silting up of both harbours since antiquity

Miletus, was an important factor in Ephesus's rise.[30] But the rivalry between the two cities, I think, was already well established by then. Both cities claimed to have led the entire Ionian colonization, as we hear first from two mid-fifth century authors: Neleus, the founder of Miletus, was the leader of the Ionian colonization according to the poet Panyassis of Halicarnassus;[31] Androklos, the founder of Ephesus, led the Ionian colonization according to the Athenian Pherekydes.[32] This is our earliest documentation for the rivalry between the two cities, but the rivalry itself must have been older. Miletus, at

has itself been displaced by Ismir (Smyrna) as the seaport of the Maeander valley"; for the rivalry between Ephesus and Miletus cf. also Herda 1998:19.

30 Cf. Bürchner RE 'Ephesos' 2789: "The fall of the city of Miletus (493 BC) was a cause of the flourishing of Ephesus" ("Der Fall der Stadt Miletos [493] war eine Ursache des Aufblühens von Ephesos"). Ephesus took no part in the Battle of Lade (Ephesus is absent from Herodotus's catalogue of ships before the battle, Herodotus 6.8; Colophon, Klazomenai, and Lebedos are also absent); cf. also Herodotus 6.16 and Gerhard Kleiner in Kleiner et al. 1967:11. Before the Ionian revolt a famous oracle was delivered to Carians who asked whether or not to take the Milesians as allies against the Persians; the oracle's answer: πάλαι ποτ' ἦσαν ἄλκιμοι Μιλήσιοι, "the Milesians were powerful once long ago" (Diodorus 10.25.2; the oldest source is the early-fifth century lyric poet Timocreon of Rhodes fr. 7 Page [PMG 733]; the oracle is quoted and parodied by Aristophanes Wealth 1002, Wasps 1060; cf. Hiller von Gaertringen RE 'Miletos' 1597).

31 Suda s.v. Πανύασις· ...ἔγραψε...Ἰωνικὰ ἐν πενταμέτρῳ, ἔστι δὲ τὰ περὶ Κόδρον καὶ Νηλέα καὶ τὰς Ἰωνικὰς ἀποικίας, εἰς ἔπη ,ζ΄, "Panyassis...wrote...an Ionian history in pentameters, which tells the events pertaining to Kodros and Neleus and the Ionian colonies in seven thousand verses [i.e. 3500 distichs]" (for the form Neleús rather than Neíleōs cf. n4.3 above and see n1.43). Although this brief summary does not explicitly state that Panyassis made Neleus the leader of the Ionian migration, no other conclusion can naturally be drawn from it. The tradition is next found in Hellanicus FGrHist 323a F 11, which calls Erythrai "one of the cities founded by Neleus, the son of Kodros"; for Hellanicus FGrHist F 23, see n4.3 above. The Parian Marble FGrHist 239 F A27 follows Hellanicus in saying that Neleus founded Miletus and the rest of Ionia, listing the other eleven cities by name (see Jacoby, commentary on Hellanicus FGrHist F 23, n22, citing Jacoby 1949:227n5). Panyassis belongs to the first half of the fifth century BC. He was killed by Lygdamis, the tyrant of Halicarnassus, who seems to have ruled down to c. 450 BC; see Matthews 1974:12–19. Before Panyassis Cadmus of Miletus (probably sixth century BC) seems to have followed the same tradition; only the subject of his work is known, but it is significant: κτίσις Μιλήτου καὶ τῆς ὅλης Ἰωνίας, "foundation of Miletus and all Ionia" (Suda s.v. Κάδμος Πανδίονος, FGrHist 489 T 1; cf. Moggi 1996:79).

32 Strabo 14.1.3 cites Pherekydes as a source for his general description of Ionia, and for the particular role that he assigns to Androklos as leader of the Ionian colonization: ἄρξαι δέ φησιν [sc. Φερεκύδης] Ἄνδροκλον τῆς τῶν Ἰώνων ἀποικίας, ὕστερον τῆς Αἰολικῆς, υἱὸν γνήσιον Κόδρου τοῦ Ἀθηνῶν βασιλέως, γενέσθαι δὲ τοῦτον Ἐφέσου κτίστην, "[Pherekydes] says that Androklos, legitimate son of Kodros, the king of Athens, led the colony of the Ionians, which was later than the colony of the Aeolians, and that he was the founder of Ephesus." Eusebius's date for Pherekydes is 456 BC, but a reliable dating is not possible (different suggestions in Jacoby1947:33 and Huxley 1973). For Panyassis and Pherekydes as representatives of the two different traditions of Ionian leadership cf. n1.61 above.

any rate, cannot have invented its claim to overall leadership of Ionia after being crushed by the Persians in 494 BC.[33]

§4.10 For the various Kodrid founders of Ionian cities Pausanias and Strabo are our two main sources.[34] Their accounts seem "tolerably consistent," but an important difference is that Strabo follows Pherekydes, and Pherekydes presents what may be called the Ephesian version of Ionia's foundation.[35] In this version Kodros had only one legitimate son, namely Androklos, the founder of Ephesus, who was at the same time the leader of the entire Ionian colonization.[36] Kodros had only three other sons in this version, and all three—Kydrelos, the founder of Myus, Nauklos, the founder of Teos, and Knopos, the founder of Erythrai—are called bastard sons of Kodros.[37] As for Neleus, the founder of Miletus, he is not called a son of Kodros at all. In fact he is not even said to be an Athenian, but "from Pylos by race": καὶ Μίλητον δ' ἔκτισεν Νηλεὺς ἐκ Πύλου τὸ γένος ὤν. Although Strabo is clearly puzzled by the idea and does his best to get around it, Pherekydes, his source, must have identified Neleus, the founder of Miletus, with Neleus, the founder of Pylos.[38] Pherekydes portrayed Ephesus—to him the only city

33 In my view the Kodrid myth, as already known to Homer, always implied that Miletus was the leader of the Ionian colonization, but I have in mind here the explicit claim to leadership by Ephesus and the equally explicit claim by Miletus; these claims, I think, resulted from the rivalry itself.

34 Pausanias 7.2.1–7.4.10; Strabo 14.1.3.

35 Cook 1975:783: "Apart from the rival claims of the houses of Miletus and Ephesus to the leadership and from some minor discrepancies—of which the most serious concerns the Kodrid founders of Colophon—the two accounts are tolerably consistent." For Colophon see §4.8 above. There are discrepancies in the forms of the names of three of the Kodrid founders: the founder of Erythrai is Knôpos in Strabo, Kléopos in Pausanias (cf. n4.8 above); the founder of Myus is Kudrêlos in Strabo, Kuárētos in Pausanias; the founder of Teos is Naûklos in Strabo, Náoklos in Pausanias. Pausanias also gives a second Kodrid founder of Teos, Damasos, where Strabo gives only Nauklos. For the different forms of the names, which may be the error of one or the other author or manuscript corruption, see Moggi 1996:87–88 (Strabo's form Knôpos for the founder of Erythrai is confirmed by three other sources: Hippias of Erythrai, FrGHist 421 F 1 [accent Knōpós]; Polyaenus 8.43; Stephanus of Byzantium s.v. Ερυθραί, who also gives Knōpoúpolis as another name of Erythrai).

36 Strabo 14.1.3: Ἀνδροκλον...υἱὸν γνήσιον Κόδρου...γενέσθαι...Ἐφέσου κτίστην, "Androklos, legitimate son of Kodros...was the founder of Ephesus."

37 Strabo 14.1.3: Κυδρῆλος δὲ νόθος υἱὸς Κόδρου Μυοῦντα κτίζει.... Τέω...Ναῦκλος υἱὸς Κόδρου νόθος.... Ἐρυθρὰς δὲ Κνῶπος, καὶ οὗτος υἱὸς Κόδρου νόθος, "Kydrelos, a bastard son of Kodros, founded Myus.... Nauklos, a bastard son of Kodros, [founded] Teos... Knopos, who was also a bastard son of Kodros, [founded] Erythrai."

38 Strabo, no longer following Pherekydes but on his own authority, explains that Athenian Kodrids were also Pylians by ancestry: οἵ τε Μεσσήνιοι καὶ οἱ Πύλιοι συγγένειάν τινα προσποιοῦνται, καθ' ἣν καὶ Μεσσήνιον τὸν Νέστορα οἱ νεώτεροί φασι ποιηταί, καὶ τοῖς περὶ Μέλανθον τὸν Κόδρου πατέρα πολλοὺς καὶ τῶν Πυλίων συνεξᾶραί φασιν εἰς τὰς Ἀθήνας·

with a legitimate son of Kodros as founder—as the leader of the Ionian colonization. The rival for this distinction was Miletus and its Kodrid founder Neleus, whose claim to have led the Ionian colonization is found in Panyassis. The easiest way to do away with what from an Ephesian standpoint was an unwanted rival, was to confound him with his Pylian namesake. In Strabo's account this strategy is still evident.[39]

§4.11 On this analysis Ephesus in the end arrogated to itself a tradition that originally belonged to Miletus alone: originally only Miletus had a Kodrid founder, and it then extended this distinction to other cities, including Ephesus, as the Panionic league developed; in the end Ephesus claimed that only it had a genuine Kodrid founder and excluded all others, Miletus in particular, from this distinction. So I interpret the evidence, but the opposite view has also been held, namely that the traditions of Ephesus were in fact the original ones.[40] The evidence in support of this view, however, seems to me to concern what Ephesus later became rather than

---

τοῦτον δὴ πάντα τὸν λαὸν μετὰ τῶν Ἰώνων κοινῇ στεῖλαι τὴν ἀποικίαν, "The Messenians and the Pylians claim a certain relationship, according to which the newer poets say that Nestor was Messenian, and that many of the Pylians also emigrated to Athens with the party of Melanthos, the father of Kodros; and that this entire people together with the Ionians sent out the colony" (Strabo 14.1.3). Modern scholars have taken the same way out as Strabo, saying that the phrase "from Pylos by race" can also mean Athenian in this case. They have argued further that the statement that Neleus was a Pylian by race does not come from Pherekydes but is Strabo's own. It seems to me, however, that Strabo has followed Pherekydes for all the founders, even where, as here, he had to explain what did not make sense to him. The contrast between the one genuine son of Kodros and his three bastard sons shows, I think, that as far as the founders are concerned Strabo's account is all of one piece; his statement about the one genuine son, furthermore, is attributed directly to Pherekydes.

39 Pausanias gives Kodrid founders to the same four cities as Strabo, including Androklos to Ephesus, but he makes no distinction between legitimate and illegitimate Kodrids; he gives Kodrid founders to three other cities as well: Miletus (Neleus), Colophon (Promethos and Damasichthon), and Lebedos (Andraimon); these Kodrid founders seem to me to reflect what the cities themselves claimed as members of the Panionic league, which is what might also be called the Milesian version (see §4.8 above for Colophon and Lebedos). The Ephesian version denied legitimate Kodrid founders to all but Ephesus, and it denied Kodrid founders of any kind where a rival tradition existed, as for Colophon (§4.8 above). Four cities do not have Kodrid founders in either source: the islands of Chios and Samos and the northernmost cities of Phocaea and Klazomenai. The founder of Priene in both sources is Aipytos, the son of Neleus, the founder of Miletus; this makes him a Kodrid (or the son of a Kodrid) in one source but not the other. The final tally of Kodrid founders is thus four of twelve in Strabo and eight of twelve in Pausanias. This count in itself is a strong argument that the Kodrid traditions had a Milesian, not an Ephesian, origin.

40 Momigliano 1932.

what it originally was.[41] Strabo, when he continues his account of the founda-
tion of Ephesus and all Ionia by the Kodrid Androklos, refers to "the kingship
of the Ionians" (τὸ βασίλειον τῶν Ἰώνων) that was established at Ephesus;
he goes on to say that in his day descendants of the royal family were still
called "kings" (βασιλεῖς) and that they still enjoyed special privileges: front
seats at the games, purple robes as the sign of the royal family (τοῦ βασιλικοῦ
γένους), a special staff, and sacrifices to Eleusinian Demeter.[42] The emphasis

41 Wilamowitz 1906a/1971:65–66/159–160, arguing that originally Colophon was the
    leading city of Ionia, drew attention to traditions in which the origins of Ephesus were
    much humbler than later claimed by the Ephesians; according to one such tradition
    Ephesus was founded by Samian slaves (Athenaeus 6.267ab; see n4.67 below). Wilamowitz
    comments on Ephesus's modest beginnings: "In general one should not be misled by the
    city of Lysimachus and the brilliance of the Roman provincial capital to attribute a great
    importance to the old Ephesus. It first acquired this importance from the trade routes
    into the interior, when it was a base for the Lydians and Persians.... A special connec-
    tion with Athens is altogether not credible" ("Man darf sich überhaupt durch die Stadt
    des Lysimachos und den Glanz der römischen Provinzialhauptstadt nicht verleiten lassen,
    dem alten Ephesus eine grosse Bedeutung beizulegen. Die hat es durch die Handelstrasse
    ins Innere erst erhalten, als es Stützpunkt der Lyder und Perser war.... Eine besondere
    Verbindung mit Athen ist durchaus nicht glaublich"). Cf. also Högemann 2001:61: "How
    haltingly the Greeks settled in the region of old Abasa/Ephesus is shown by the report of
    the local historian Kreophylos of Ephesus (fourth century BC?) that the Ionians settled first
    on an island in the Cayster, and only twenty years later moved to the harbor of Koressos
    on the mainland (*FGrHist* 417 F 1; Knibbe 1998:72–82)" ("Wie zaghaft die Griechen sich
    im Gebiet des alten Abasa/Ephesus einnisteten, zeigt die Nachricht des Lokalhistorikers
    Kreophylos von Ephesos (4. Jh. v. Chr.?): Die Ionier hätten sich zuerst auf einer Insel im
    Kaystros niedergelassen und seien erst 20 Jahre später zum Koressos-Hafen aufs Festland
    übergesiedelt [*FGrHist* 417 F 1; Knibbe 1998:72–82]"). The island in Kreophylos's account is
    not in fact named or located; Wilamowitz takes the island to be Samos (see n4.67 below).
42 Strabo 14.1.3: ἄρξαι δέ φησιν [sc. Pherekydes] Ἄνδροκλον τῆς τῶν Ἰώνων ἀποικίας...·
    διόπερ τὸ βασίλειον τῶν Ἰώνων ἐκεῖ συστῆναί φασι, καὶ ἔτι νῦν οἱ ἐκ τοῦ γένους
    ὀνομάζονται βασιλεῖς ἔχοντές τινας τιμάς, προεδρίαν τε ἐν ἀγῶσι καὶ πορφύραν ἐπίσημον
    τοῦ βασιλικοῦ γένους, σκίπωνα ἀντὶ σκήπτρου, καὶ τὰ ἱερὰ τῆς Ἐλευσινίας Δήμητρος,
    "[Pherekydes] says that Androklos, a legitimate son of Kodros, the king of Athens, led
    the colony of the Ionians, which was later than the colony of the Aeolians, and that he
    was the founder of Ephesus...; for that reason, they say, the royal capital of the Ionians
    arose there, and even now members of the family are called kings and have certain
    honors, the front seat and purple as the insignia of the royal family at assemblies, a staff
    representing a scepter, and the sacred rites of the Eleusinian Demeter." Strabo supports
    Pherekydes' statement that Androklos led the Ionian migration with what he then adds,
    but, as the change of verb from φησίν, "he says," to φασί, "they say," shows, the source
    is no longer Pherekydes, but later authorities. It would seem from this that Pherekydes
    did not refer to "the kingship of the Ionians" (we cannot say whether or not he knew of
    it). Cf. Jacoby, commentary on Pherekydes *FGrHist* 3 F 155: "One may not conclude from
    it [Strabo's account] that Pherekydes perhaps already regarded Androklos as the 'king of
    all the Ionians' " ("Man wird daraus nicht schliessen dürfen, dass etwa schon Pherekydes

in this passage on the word βασιλεύς and its derivatives has to do with the name of the royal family at Ephesus, which was not Androklidai, as one might expect, but Basilidai.[43] This name, which is also attested for the royal family of Erythrai,[44] and which in both cities presumably referred to the rule of the city where it occurred, conveniently served Ephesus's pretensions to the "kingship of the Ionians" as well. These pretensions were not necessarily new in Strabo's time; it is perhaps more likely that they go back to the fourth or even the fifth century BC.[45] Thucydides, when he sought a comparison for the

---

Androklos als 'Allkönig der Ionier' ansah"). Jacoby of course does not deny that Pherekydes considered Androklos the leader of the Ionian colonization, for that is a different matter from the "kingship of the Ionians" at Ephesus. According to Jacoby Strabo's immediate source, in which the references to Pherekydes were included, was the Ephesian geographer Artemidorus (*floruit* 104–101 BC); the reference to the "kingship of the Ionians," and to the prerogatives of the "kings" at Ephesus, were then due to Artemidorus.

43 The name is attested by the Suda s.v. Πυθαγόρας Ἐφέσιος, where Baton of Sinope (third century BC, *FGrHist* 268 F 3) is cited for the story of Pythagoras, the cruel tyrant of Ephesus who ended the rule of the Basilidai: Πυθαγόρας Ἐφέσιος· καταλύσας δι᾽ ἐπιβουλῆς τὴν τῶν Βασιλιδῶν καλουμένην ἀρχὴν ἀνεφάνη τε τύραννος πικρότατος, κτλ., "Pythagoras the Ephesian: having ended what is called the rule of the Basilidai through a conspiracy, he showed himself to be the bitterest tyrant," etc. If Pythagoras was immediately followed by the tyrant Melas, who is dated to the time of Alyattes, his date would be c. 600 BC; otherwise he was earlier (Huxley 1966:78).

44 Aristotle *Politics* 1305b18–19: καὶ ἐν Ἐρυθραῖς δὲ ἐπὶ τῆς τῶν Βασιλιδῶν ὀλιγαρχίας ἐν τοῖς ἀρχαίοις χρόνοις, "and in Erythrai during the oligarchy of the Basilidai in the early times."

45 A fourth-century inscription found at Panionion calls the representatives to the newly refounded Panionic league of that era "scepter-bearing kings"; the inscription refers in particular to the "king of the Ephesians," and this may suggest a privileged place for the Ephesian representative among the representatives of the other cities. The inscription, edited with commentary by P. Hommel (Kleiner et al. 1967:45–63), regulates dues and fines to be administered by the "kings"; see commentary to lines 2–4, pp. 54–55, and to lines 17–25, pp. 59–63, for the term "(scepter-bearing) kings" used of the various cities' representatives. This Homeric phrase may be as old as the Homeric era as an official term of the league, but it is not attested before this inscription (Herodotus uses the term *probouloi* of the representatives sent by the cities of the sixth- and early fifth-century league); the phrase is perhaps just a high-sounding innovation of the fourth century. For the βασιλέα τὸν Ἐφε[σίων, "king of he Ephesians" in line 22 of the inscription there is unfortunately no context; see commentary p. 62. Cf. also Jeffery 1976:222–223 and for further bibliography 235n7. The phrases "scepter-bearing kings" and "king of the Ephesians" on the fourth-century inscription do not correspond to the office of "king of the Ionians" attested later at Ephesus by Strabo; it is possible that "king and prytanis," another phrase that occurs without context in the inscription (line 21), refers to a "king of the Ionians" (so Carlier 1984:453), and in this case the office is as old as the refounded Panionic league of the fourth century. Other possible evidence for the kingship of the Ionians is cited by Momigliano 1932a and Carlier 1984:450–455: Strabo 8.7.2 refers to the priest of Poseidon Helikonios at Panionion, whom Priene provided, as a βασιλεύς, "king": καὶ δὴ πρὸς τὴν θυσίαν ταύτην βασιλέα καθιστᾶσιν ἄνδρα νέον Πριηνέα τὸν τῶν ἱερῶν ἐπιμελησόμενον,

ancient festival on Delos celebrated by the Ionians of Homer's day, named the Ephesia, to which the Ionians of his own day gathered.[46] This festival, which put Ephesus at the center of fifth-century Ionia, is one likely context in which Ephesus may already have claimed for itself a symbolic "kingship of the Ionians."[47]

§4.12 Ephesus could have begun to rival Miletus for the role of leader of the Ionians at any time in the post-Homeric period; I suspect that the rivalry began early, before the period of foreign domination. Under the Lydians the role of leader of the Ionians would have meant less than it once had, and under the Persians it would have meant less still.[48] When Cyrus over-

<hr/>

"and for this sacrifice they appoint as king a young man from Priene in order to take care of the sacred rites" (the word βασιλέα in this passage is actually omitted in most manuscripts); βασιλεύς refers to a league official on an inscription from Priene of the first or second century BC (IP [Hiller 1906] no. 536); a βασιλεὺς Ἰώνων, "king of the Ionians" (βασιλεία τῶν Ἰώνων, "kingship of the Ionians") is attested several times between the first and third centuries AD on inscriptions from Chios, Didyma, Phocaea, Samos, and Ephesus. Both Momigliano and Carlier regard the "king of the Ionians" as an early institution, going back to the Ionian migration; I agree instead with Dittenberger 1903–1905 no. 489, who is cautious about the title βασιλεὺς Ἰώνων, "king of the Ionians" in the second-century AD inscription from Phocaea, warning (n9) "that it [the term king] may have been established, like many other things in that age, through a certain pretension of antiquity," ("*ne id* [*regium nomen*] *affectatione quadam antiquitatis, ut multa alia illa aetate, institutum sit*"); cf. also Herda 2006:61 and n100, who identifies the title "king of the Ionians" with the Prienean priest of Poseidon Helikonios.

46 Thucydides 3.104.3: ἦν δέ ποτε καὶ τὸ πάλαι μεγάλη ξύνοδος ἐς τὴν Δῆλον τῶν Ἰώνων τε καὶ περικτιόνων νησιωτῶν· ξύν τε γὰρ γυναιξὶ καὶ παισὶν ἐθεώρουν, ὥσπερ νῦν ἐς τὰ Ἐφέσια Ἴωνες, "There used to be in ancient times a great assembly on Delos of the Ionians and the neighboring islanders; they attended the festival with their wives and children, as the Ionians now do the Ephesia." Some have seen the final phrase as an editor's marginal comment that was included in the text, but this is not the usual view.

47 At some time after the Ionian revolt the festival of the Panionia seems to have been transferred from Mykale to Ephesus, and it is possible that this was the festival of the Ephesia mentioned by Thucydides; such a transfer of the Panionia to Ephesus, although it may have taken place later than Thucydides and be unrelated to the Ephesia, would in either case have strengthened Ephesus's claim to "the kingship of the Ionians." What is known about the Panionia after the Ionian revolt is discussed in EN4.2.

48 Domination by the Lydians was a continual threat from the time of Gyges, whose rule began c. 680 BC, until domination became a reality under Croesus, whose rule lasted from 561 to 547 BC. Herodotus reports the successive campaigns of the Lydians against the Ionians as follows: Gyges sent an expedition against Miletus and Smyrna and captured Colophon (1.14.4); Ardys took Priene and sent an expedition against Miletus (1.15); Sadyattes made war against Miletus for six years (1.17.1, 1.18.2); Alyattes sacked Smyrna (c. 600 BC) but suffered a severe defeat when he advanced against Klazomenai (1.16.2); Alyattes continued his father's war against Miletus for five years, invading yearly to destroy crops, but failed to take the city because of its access to the sea, and finally made a treaty of friendship and alliance with Miletus (1.17–22). Croesus subdued all the

threw Croesus in the mid-sixth century BC the main energy of Miletus for the previous hundred years had gone into founding its own colonies on the Black Sea, and not into leading the Ionians in any significant way. Miletus did not even attend the first meeting of the Panionic league of which we have notice. This took place after the fall of Sardis in 547 BC, when representatives of the Ionian cities met at Panionion to consider how to deal with the unforeseen arrival of the Persians at their doorstep.[49] Cyrus had refused the appeal of both the Aeolic and the Ionian cities of Asia Minor to continue to live on the same terms under the Persians as under the Lydians. But he made an exception of Miletus, which therefore did not attend the emergency meeting at Panionion.[50] Miletus was clearly no longer interested in being the

---

Greeks of Asia, beginning with Ephesus (1.26–27.1); he forced them to pay tribute (1.27.1, cf. 1.6.2); he probably also made them participate in his military levy (see Gorman 2001:123–124 and 124n64). Herodotus does not comment specifically on Miletus's status under Croesus, and it is uncertain whether it suffered the same fate as the other mainland cities; cf. Gorman 2001:124: "Nothing in Herodotus states directly that Croesus changed the terms of the existing treaty [of Alyattes] with Miletos; the historian simply says that Croesus conquered each Ionian city in turn and forced Ionia to pay tribute. There are no exceptions mentioned, and it is unlikely that the man who conquered all of western Asia would allow a prosperous commercial center in the midst of his holdings to avoid taxation. Miletos must be considered a tribute-paying ally by that time." Cook 1962:98 thinks, to the contrary, that Croesus did not reduce Miletus with the other cities, and Herodotus seems to bear this out (see n4.50 below); so also G. Kleiner in Kleiner et al. 1967:10. If this was the case Miletus's special treatment by the Persians (see n4.50 below) simply continued its previous treatment by the Lydians. Before and perhaps still under Croesus, as is apparent from the summary above, Miletus was the prize that eluded the Lydians because it could not successfully be besieged. But, as the Lydians' main target, Miletus also became isolated from the other Ionian cities and had to fend for itself. Herodotus reports that during the eleven years of invasions carried out by Alyattes under his father's rule and in his own rule (end of the seventh century BC), none of the other Ionian cities apart from Chios came to Miletus's aid (Herodotus 1.18.3).

49 This was the league's first meeting of which we know if the tradition for the league's involvement in the Meliac War more than a century earlier is left out of account (see below §4.15–§4.18).

50 Herodotus 1.141.1: Ἴωνες δὲ καὶ Αἰολέες, ὡς οἱ Λυδοὶ τάχιστα κατεστράφατο ὑπὸ Περσέων, ἔπεμπον ἀγγέλους ἐς Σάρδις παρὰ Κῦρον, ἐθέλοντες ἐπὶ τοῖσι αὐτοῖσι εἶναι τοῖσι καὶ Κροίσῳ ἦσαν κατήκοοι, "The Ionians and Aeolians, as soon as the Lydians were overthrown by the Persians, sent messengers to Cyrus in Sardis, wishing to be subject on the same terms as they were to Croesus." Cyrus, who had offered such terms before he defeated the Lydians, now withdrew the offer; he made an exception only of Miletus, which therefore did not join the others at Panionion: Ἴωνες δὲ ὡς ἤκουσαν τούτων ἀνενειχθέντων ἐς τὰς πόλις, τείχεά τε περιεβάλοντο ἕκαστοι καὶ συνελέγοντο ἐς Πανιώνιον οἱ ἄλλοι πλὴν Μιλησίων· πρὸς μούνους γὰρ τούτους ὅρκιον Κῦρος ἐποιήσατο ἐπ' οἷσί περ ὁ Λυδός, "The Ionians, when they heard these things reported in the cities, each constructed walls and assembled at Panionion, all except for the Milesians; only for them did Cyrus make an oath on the same terms as the Lydian king."

leader of the Panionic league at this historical juncture.[51] A half century later Aristagoras, the tyrant of Miletus, instigated the Ionian revolt, and for a few years Miletus led the Ionians in this failed attempt to shake off Persian rule. Miletus survived its harsh fate after the revolt, but it never again aspired to be the leader of Ionia.

§4.13 A well-known fifth-century Athenian inscription may complement the evidence of Panyassis and Pherekydes for the rival claims of Miletus and Ephesus to leadership of the foundation of Ionia. The inscription relates to a composite shrine of Kodros, Neleus, and a female figure named Basile. The inscription records a decree of the Athenian *boulḗ* and *dêmos* for the year 418/7 BC, part of which authorizes the building of an enclosure for the shrine (*hierón*), to be paid for by the leasing of the shrine's sacred land (*témenos*). Whereas the shrine is said to be of all three figures, including Kodros, the *témenos* is said to be only of Neleus and Basile.[52] It is clear that at the time of the inscription work was undertaken at an already existing shrine, but no remains of this shrine have been found, and there is thus no way to date the original cult. The fact that Kodros has no share in the *témenos* suggests that his presence in the cult is secondary, and that originally the shrine too belonged only to Neleus and Basile.[53] Basile is a shadowy figure. Her name means "queen," and one inter-

---

51 Herodotus, after his geographical account of the Ionian cities, describes the divisions among them in dealing with the Persians; not only Miletus, but also Chios and Samos, which as islands had less to fear from the Persians, split from the others at this time of Greek and especially Ionian weakness (Herodotus 1.143.1–2): τούτων δὴ ὦν τῶν Ἰώνων οἱ Μιλήσιοι μὲν ἦσαν ἐν σκέπῃ τοῦ φόβου, ὅρκιον ποιησάμενοι, τοῖσι δὲ αὐτῶν νησιώτῃσι ἦν δεινὸν οὐδέν· οὔτε γὰρ Φοίνικες ἦσάν κω Περσέων κατήκοοι οὔτε αὐτοὶ οἱ Πέρσαι ναυβάται. ἀπεσχίσθησαν δὲ ἀπὸ τῶν ἄλλων Ἰώνων οὗτοι κατ' ἄλλο μὲν οὐδέν, ἀσθενέος δὲ ἐόντος τοῦ παντὸς τότε Ἑλληνικοῦ γένεος, πολλῷ δὴ ἦν ἀσθενέστατον τῶν ἐθνέων τὸ Ἰωνικὸν καὶ λόγου ἐλαχίστου· ὅτι γὰρ μὴ Ἀθῆναι, ἦν οὐδὲν ἄλλο πόλισμα λόγιμον, "Of these Ionians the Milesians were sheltered from the panic, having made an oath, and the islanders also had nothing to fear; for the Phoenicians were not yet subject to the Persians and the Persians themselves were not sailors. These [sc. the Milesians] were detached from the other Ionians for no other reason than that the whole Hellenic race was weak then, and the Ionian people was by far the weakest of all and of the least account; for apart from Athens there was no other important city." Cf. Cook 1982a:199: "On the mainland Miletus alone preserved the treaty rights that its inaccessible situation had conferred on it. But the offshore islands were not threatened at this time."

52 The same formulation occurs twice in the decree; for the inscription, IG I³ 84, see Wycherley 1960:60–66, who translates or summarizes the relevant provisions of the decree on p. 61. See also Shapiro 1983:94 and 1986 and Robertson 1988:225–239. The shrine was probably located near the Ilissos River, south of the Acropolis: see Robertson 1988:232n85, who is hesitant about the usual identification (for which see Travlos 1971:333 fig. 435).

53 Wycherley 1960:61n3; Càssola 1957:84; Toepffer 1889:240n2, citing Wilamowitz 1885:5: "It is evident that Codrus was inserted later into the pair Neleus and Basile" ("*Codrum intrusum demum esse in communionem Nelei et Basilae apparet*").

pretation, which found favor when the inscription was discovered in the nineteenth century, and which still persists,[54] is that she represents the queen of the underworld, and that she is paired with Neleus because he too is associated with the underworld.[55] But the presence of Kodros in the cult, even if it is secondary, indicates that the Neleus of the cult is not the Pylian figure, but the Athenian son of Kodros.[56] Neleus (either figure so named) was the ancestor of the Neleids of Miletus, and this suggests, as Johannes Toepffer first saw, that Basile may well have something to do with the royal family of Ephesus, the Basilidai, who still enjoyed privileges in Strabo's time.[57] The Athenian cult

54 Cf. n4.63 below; the inscription was found in 1884.

55 This line of interpretation starts from *Iliad* 5.397, Heracles' wounding of Hades ἐν Πύλῳ ἐν νεκύεσσι, "in Pylos among the corpses," where Pylos suggests the "gates" of the underworld; the name Neleus, interpreted as "pitiless," then suggests Hades, who is described by Hesiod *Theogony* 456 as νηλεὲς ἦτορ ἔχων, "having a pitiless (*nēleés*) heart" (cf. n1.64above). Shapiro 1983:94 argues that Heracles' wounding of Hades was originally connected with his carrying off of Cerberus: "Somewhere along the line, probably very early on, there has been a confusion of Nestor's Pylos and the πύλαι, the gates of Hades where Kerberos stands guard."

56 The form of the name, however, is *Nēleús*, not *Neíleōs*, as in τέμενος τοῦ Νηλέως καὶ τῆς Βασίλης, "precinct of Neleus and Basile," in line 3 (I use post-Euclidian spelling for the inscription's pre-Euclidian spelling). The distinction between the two names, which mattered in Miletus, was perhaps ignored in Athens, where the Homeric name would have been more familiar. For a different view of the Athenian cult see Erika Simon *LIMC* 'Neleus' 728, who argues that the cult was founded to honor the Pylian ancestor of the Peisistratids and other Athenian families.

57 Toepffer 1889:240. Toepffer, who notes that there were Basilidai in Erythrai as well as in Ephesus (240n2), associates the Athenian figure Basile with both occurrences of the name in Ionia. Like Toepffer, Robertson 1988 understands that Neleus and Basile relate to Ionia rather than Athens: "Despite the shrine the younger Neleus has nothing to do in Athens except to leave" (p. 203); "At the shrine of Neleus and Basile Athens pays tribute to Neleus as founder of Miletus, and the consort Basile is meant to evoke the Neleid dynasty abroad" (p. 238). In associating Basile specifically with the ruling family of Ephesus I am in closer agreement with Toepffer than with Robertson, but I think that both are essentially right about this goddess. There are a few other occurrences of Basile in Athens and Attica (see Shapiro 1986 for an offering to Basile on a sacrificial calendar of the deme Erchia in the mid-fourth century BC, and for a shrine of Basile in the deme Eitea, attested in a deme decree of the year 332/1 BC). The shrine of Basile mentioned in Plato *Charmides* 153a is probably part of the sanctuary at issue in *IG* I³ 84, the decree of 418/7 BC (Wycherley 1960:60; cf. Travlos 1971:332). An Attic red-figure pyxis dated to the 410s BC has Basile on the lid together with Athena, the baby Erichthonios, Kekrops, and Soteria; there is also a figure named Basileia on the body of the vase, showing that Basile is distinct from this figure (Shapiro 1986:135). To pursue the question of who the Basilidai of Erythrai were, it may be worth noting that Erythrai was founded by settlers from all the other Ionian cities (Pausanias 7.3.7). Were the Basilidai then from Ephesus? If Basilidai ruled Erythrai, the Kodrids who were sent from Erythrai to Phocaea must also have been Basilidai. Note that these events would have occurred before the period of rivalry between Ephesus and Miletus. Harpokration s.v. *Eruthraîoi* says that according to Hellanicus Erythrai was one of the cities founded by Neleus

of Neleus and Basile would thus seem to reconcile the rival claims of Miletus and Ephesus to having led the foundation of Ionia by bringing both claims, so to speak, under one roof. Since we cannot date the origin of the Athenian cult we can only speculate about the motive for such a reconciliation. From an Athenian standpoint it would always have made sense to respect both versions of Ionia's foundation, whether it was led by Neileos or Androklos, since both founders came from Athens. Perhaps the cult of Neleus and Basile was founded by Peisistratos in the mid-sixth century when he purified Delos and began to celebrate the festival of the Delia. Peisistratos himself claimed to be a descendant of Pylian Neleus, although not through Periklymenos, like the Kodrids, but through Nestor and Peisistratos, his Homeric namesake. Thus personal family interest may have been part of the motive for the Athenian cult.[58] But I do not think that Peisistratos, who clearly sought to lead the Ionian islanders, is likely to have had the same ambition with respect to mainland Ionia, which at the very time when the Delia were renewed was forced to accept Persian rule in place of Lydian rule.[59] It is more plausible, I think, that the cult of Neleus and Basile goes back to Solon's time in the early sixth century BC. It was Solon, after all, who called Athens "the oldest land of Ionia" (πρεσβυτάτην...γαῖαν Ἰαονίης), a phrase which must have implied Athens' role as the metropolis of Ionia.[60] The

---

(cf. Toepffer 1889:234n2); but according to Hellanicus *FGrHist* 323a F 23 Neleus founded all twelve cities, so there is nothing distinctive about Erythrai in this.

58 The form Neleus instead of Neileos in the cult with Basile (cf. n4.56 above) would be consistent with the supposed personal interest of Peisistratos, who claimed to be a descendant of Neleus, but not of Neileos. Proximity of the shrine to the Peisistratean Olympieion has been taken to indicate that both were Peisistratean (see van der Kolf *RE* 'Neleus' 2278; for the shrine's location see Travlos 1971:332, and for its proximity to the Olympieion, Travlos 1971:291, nos. 158 and 182 on fig. 379).

59 See n4.9 above. Cyrus overthrew Croesus in 547 BC and subjugated the mainland Greeks in the next few years; cf. Cook 1982a:199: "The Greeks of Asia had fallen under Persian rule by about 540 BC (Herodotus 1.164-9)." Peisistratos returned to Athens in 546 BC and purified Delos (Herodotus 1.64.2) and renewed the Delia festival after that.

60 Solon fr. 4a West:

γινώσκω, καί μοι φρενὸς ἔνδοθεν ἄλγεα κεῖται,
  πρεσβυτάτην ἐσορῶν γαῖαν [Ἰ]αονίης
κλινομένην.

Looking I see the oldest land of Ionia
  deviating from what is right,
and pains lie in my heart.

Those who believe that the tradition for the Athenian foundation of Ionia did not arise until the Athenian empire of the fifth century take Solon's word πρεσβυτάτην to mean "most revered" rather than "oldest," but in the end these two meanings come to the same thing (cf. *Iliad* 4.59, 6.24, 18.365); see Robertson 1988:256, who cites Prinz 1979:354-355 for

cult of Neleus and Basile, like Solon's phrase for Athens, would have had to do with Athens' sense of itself as the mother city of Ionia, and as impartial in the rivalry between Ionia's leading cities.

§4.14 Pherekydes and Panyassis in the fifth century remain the earliest attested sources for the rival claims of Ephesus and Miletus to leadership of the foundation of Ionia, but an earlier piece of evidence, dated 575–550 BC, must also be taken into account. This is the date assigned to an inscription found in Samos in which "the priest of Neileos" (ὁ ἱερεὺς τõ Νέλεω) makes a dedication to the goddess Hera.[61] Neileos, the founder of Miletus, doubtless had a cult in his own city at the site of his tomb, which according to Pausanias was outside the gates of Miletus on the road to Didyma;[62] his cult had apparently spread to Samos by the mid-sixth century BC, as the dedication of his priest attests. In Samos Neileos could not be honored as the founder of Miletus, but he may well have been honored as the founder of all Ionia.[63] Traditionally Samos and Miletus were not close, but a new bond between the cities developed in the

---

a review of previous opinion; Shapiro 1989:49 and Moggi 1996:104 also take Solon's word in its usual sense "oldest." Robertson 1988:256–257 comes to the same conclusion as I do, that the the sanctuary of Neleus and Basile should be dated to Solon's time; his arguments include the location of the sanctuary to the southeast of the Acropolis, the large size of the *témenos*, and the predominance of Miletus in Solon's time, to which I would add Ephesus's rivalry with Miletus for predominance.

61 Dunst 1972:135–137 published the inscription and established that a priest made the dedication to Hera; Lazzarini 1978 narrowed the date of the inscription from the first half of the sixth century to the second quarter of the sixth century and established that the priest was of Neileos. In the inscription secondary long-e and secondary long-o are represented respectively by epsilon (the first syllable in Νέλεω) and omicron (the genitive article τõ), as opposed to -ει- and -ου- in later Ionic alphabets (Νείλεω and τοῦ). The genitive in omega is regular; cf. Attic-Ionic λεώς, gen. λεώ, "people."

62 Pausanias 7.2.6: τοῦ δὲ Νειλέως ὁ τάφος ἰόντων ἐς Διδύμους ἐστὶν οὐ πόρρω τῶν πυλῶν ἐν ἀριστερᾷ τῆς ὁδοῦ, "The tomb of Neileus is not far from the gates on the right side of the road as one goes to Didyma." It is safe to assume that an old hero cult was connected with this tomb; cf. Lazzarini 1978:191n2, who compares a sacrifice to the dead (ἐναγισμός) made to the Neleids at Metapontion (Strabo 6.1.15). Herda 1998:18 argues that a public hero cult of the city's founder most likely developed out of a private cult of the Neleid family's ancestor (the location of the cult outside the city gates rather than in the city center is an indication of this; Herda 1998:19). For Pausanias's hybrid form Neileus see n1.43 above.

63 Lazzarini 1978:191–192 invokes the "chthonian deity" that Neleus supposedly represents to explain the spread of his cult (see n4.55 above); but even more clearly in the Samian cult of *Neíleōs* than in the Athenian cult of Neleus, Basile, and Kodros we are dealing with the Athenian son of Kodros and not the founder of Pylos; another explanation is needed. Herda 1998:20 proposes that the priest of Neileos belonged to the hero cult in Miletus, and that there was no cult of Neileos in Samos; Herda's main argument, that a hero cult should not be separated from the hero's tomb, would not apply if the hero's sphere had expanded beyond a single city (cf. Malkin 1998:107n75). The dedication's failure to identify the priest as a Milesian (as is usual in dedications by foreigners) is, according to Herda 1998:21n153, explained by the absence of the priest's name.

early sixth century, when Miletus gave crucial help to Samos in a war with Priene.[64] At that moment the conditions were right for Samos, which had never claimed a Kodrid founder, to receive a cult which made Miletus the leader of the foundation of Ionia more explicitly than the spread of the Kodrid myth had ever done. By accepting Miletus's claim to have founded all Ionia at the time of Neileos the Samians presumably rejected Ephesus's rival claim to leadership in the person of its founder Androklos. It is noteworthy that Androklos, in the traditions that survive about him, is represented as hostile to Samos. According to Pausanias Androklos, after he founded Ephesus, "also took Samos from the Samians, and for a time the Ephesians held Samos and the adjacent islands." The Samians finally recovered their island, whereas Androklos was killed in a battle against the Carians which he had undertaken for the people of Priene.[65] This Androklos, who attacks Samos but champions Priene, may well have more

64 As an example of earlier relations, Samos and Miletus took opposite sides in the Lelantine war in the later eighth century BC (Miletus was an ally of Eretria and Samos was an ally of Chalcis according to Herodotus 5.99; cf. below n4.145 and n4.174). For the new situation arising from the hostilities between Samos and Priene in the early sixth century BC, cf. Huxley 1966:84: "Each side [Samos and Priene] had been causing the other moderate damage until in one battle a thousand Samians were killed. Then followed a six-year truce, after which Samos and Miletus in alliance defeated the Prienians at a place called the Oak. After this misfortune, in which the leading Prienian citizens were killed, bereaved women in Priene used to swear by 'the Darkness at the Oak' (Plutarch *Greek Questions* 20)." Bias, the Prienian sage, went as ambassador to Samos after the war and obtained the best terms he could for his city; a boundary between Samian and Prienian territory was fixed at a watershed on Mykale (*IP* [Hiller 1906] no. 37 lines 105–107). Cf. Lazzarini 1978:186, who cites the war between Samos and Priene, and the decisive intervention of Miletus, as the probable circumstances of the acceptance of the cult of Neileos in Samos; she also refers to the the establishment in the mid-seventh century BC of Naucratis, a Milesian initiative in which Samos participated (Herodotus 2.178.3 speaks of a sanctuary of Hera, founded by the Samians, next to a sanctuary of Apollo, founded by the Milesians). The cult of Neileos could have been established in Samos at any time between 650 and 550 BC. It should be noted that in siding with Samos against Priene in the battle "at the oak," Miletus changed its traditional stance with respect to Priene as well as to Samos (cf. §4.19 below). Ivantchik 2005:121–126, reinterpreting the evidence for the early sixth-century conflict between Priene and Samos, alters certain elements of the above narrative; in particular he allows (p. 124) the possibility that Plutarch, following Aristotle, mistakenly put Milesians for Samians in his reference to the battle at the Oak. It seems more likely, as Ivantchik also allows, that Miletus and Samos acted together against Priene.

65 Pausanias 7.2.8–9: ἀφείλετο δὲ καὶ Σάμον Ἄνδροκλος Σαμίους, καὶ ἔσχον Ἐφέσιοι χρόνον τινὰ Σάμον καὶ τὰς προσεχεῖς νήσους· Σαμίων δὲ ἤδη κατεληλυθότων ἐπὶ τὰ οἰκεῖα Πριηνεῦσιν ἤμυνεν ἐπὶ τοὺς Κᾶρας ὁ Ἄνδροκλος, καὶ νικῶντος τοῦ Ἑλληνικοῦ ἔπεσεν ἐν τῇ μάχῃ, "Androklos also took Samos from the Samians, and for a time the Ephesians held Samos and the neighboring islands. After the Samians had already returned to their land Androklos defended the Prieneans against the Carians, and he fell in the battle as the Greek army was winning."

to do with alliances in the first half of the sixth century than he does with the original conquest of Ionia.[66] We do not know what the attitude of Ephesus was to the hostilities between Samos and Priene, but the Samians' acceptance of the cult of Neileos is at least consistent with a rejection of the role of Ephesus and its founder Androklos in their own foundation.[67] If this picture is right, the rivalry between Ephesus and Miletus that we find reflected in the fifth-century authors Pherecydes and Panyassis must have begun at least a century earlier.

§4.15 I turn now to the question of the foundation of the Panionic league, which, if my basic arguments are correct, must already have existed in the Homeric period. Literary evidence supports such an early date for the league, but archaeological evidence does not, and it is not clear how to resolve this discrepancy. By literary evidence I do not mean the unhistorical tradition that Ionia and the festival of the Panionia were founded together four generations after the Trojan war.[68] I refer instead to the tradition that the league already existed when a city on the Carian coast named Melia (Ionic Melie) was destroyed sometime before the middle of the seventh century BC, probably at the beginning of the seventh century BC.[69] This means that the league already existed by the late eighth century BC, which is early enough for Homer. But Panionion, the meeting place of the league and the site of the Panionia, does

---

66 Knibbe 1998:79 also thinks that the occupation of Samos and the defense of Priene, both of which are attributed to Androklos, belong to a later time than the foundation of Ephesus. A new *hērôion* built for Androklos in the first century BC (Pausanias 7.2.9; cf. Knibbe 1998:78–79) of course celebrated the supposed city founder. For a possible connection between Androkleidai in Ephesus and Messenia see Toepffer 1889:244–245 and Kiechle 1959:68.

67 Athenaeus twice refers to alternatives to the Androklos legend for the foundation of Ephesus (cf. n4.41 above). Athenaeus 6.267ab, citing the Siphnian local historian Malakos, says that Samian slaves banded together, left Samos, and founded Ephesus. Athenaeus 8.361c–e, citing the Ephesian local historian Kreophylos, tells how the settlers of Ephesus, after difficulties, discovered the right location for the city through a prophecy involving a fish and a wild boar; these settlers, who "crossed over from the island after living there for twenty years," came from Samos if Wilamowitz is correct that the two legends are variants of each other (Wilamowitz 1906a/1971:65 and n2/159 and n2). The Ephesian local historian Kreophylos naturally has nothing to say about the slave origins of the settlers; did that version perhaps originate in Samos? Knibbe 1998:72–82 in his discussion of sources takes the foundation legend of Kreophylos strictly on its own terms, proposing (pp. 76 and 78) that the island from which the settlers came was Syrie in what was once the bay of Ephesus.

68 In 1086/5 BC (or 1076/5 BC) according to the Parian Marble (*FGrHist* 239 F A27; cf. G. Kleiner in Kleiner et al. 1967:6).

69 The only specific information about the location of Melia is Stephanus of Byzantium, Μελία, πόλις Καρίας. Ἑκαταῖος γενεαλογιῶν δ'. τὸ ἐθνικὸν Μελιεύς ὡς Ὑριεύς, "Melia, a city of Caria. Hecataeus *Genealogies* Book 4. The ethnic adjective is *Melieús*, like *Hyrieús*." See below for Melia's presumed location in the immediate vicinity of Panionion.

not bear out this early date. The site of Panionion has been found, with remains of an altar assumed to be that of Poseidon Helikonios, but this altar belongs to the sixth century BC, and other remains from the site are also not earlier than the sixth century BC. This is too late for Homer, and in particular it is too late for the simile in *Iliad* 20 evoking a sacrifice to Poseidon Helikonios.[70]

§4.16 The Roman architectural historian Vitruvius is the main source for the literary tradition about Melia, but we know from a Hellenistic inscription that Greek historians, especially Ionian local historians, were also much interested in what became of Melia.[71] According to Vitruvius Melia was once the thirteenth city of the Panionic league, but because of its "arrogance" the other twelve cities declared war on it and eliminated it.[72] The Meliac War, as

---

70 The site of Panionion was identified by Wiegand in 1898 and excavated by the German team of Kleiner, Hommel, and Müller-Wiener in 1957–1960; it is near the modern town of Güzelçamlı on a hill named Otomatiktepe after a World War I gun emplacement at its top. Remains of what is presumed to be Melia were found on Kaletepe, another hill two kilometers southwest of Panionion. See Kleiner et al. 1967:5, 78–170. Locations are shown on Map 2. The approximate location of Panionion has been known since the seventeenth century from an inscription found in Güzelçamlı (*IP* [Hiller 1906] no. 139; cf. Wiegand in Wiegand and Schrader 1904:24–25): this inscription, a decree of the council of the Ionians dating from the mid-fourth century BC, was, according to the inscription itself, to be set up in Panionion, which therefore must have been near Güzelçamlı where the inscription was found. The general location of Panionion on the north coast of Cape Mykale was already known from ancient sources, including Herodotus's description of the site (Herodotus 1.148): τὸ δὲ Πανιώνιόν ἐστι τῆς Μυκάλης χῶρος ἱρός, πρὸς ἄρκτον τετραμμένος, κοινῇ ἐξαραιρημένος ὑπὸ Ἰώνων Ποσειδέωνι Ἑλικωνίῳ, "The Panionion is a sacred place on Mycale, facing north, jointly dedicated by Ionians to Poseidon Helikonios" (the continuation of this passage on the location of Cape Mykale is quoted in EN4.2 to n4.47 above). Of the remains found at the site the most important is the stone altar, enclosed on three sides by a stone wall, that sits on top of the hill and must have belonged to Poseidon Helikonios. Wolfgang Müller-Wiener in Kleiner et al. 1967:28 dates the altar to the sixth rather than the seventh century; G. Kleiner ibid. 11 is unwilling to date the enclosing wall much before the middle of the sixth century; P. Hommel ibid. 75–76 dates the sparse sherds found in the altar complex and elsewhere on the hill no earlier than 600 BC. The discovery of a fourth-century BC council chamber at the foot of the hill confirms that the site is Panionion, where the Panionic league continued to meet after its fourth-century refoundation. In recent years a different location has been proposed for the archaic Panionion 3.5 kilometers from Priene on Çatallar Tepe in the Mykale range; see Lohmann 2004 and 2005. This location, which has been presented as established fact in a number of other publications, has been effectively refuted by Herda 2006 (see Herda 2006:46nn7 and 8 for the references to these publications); Herda proposes that the site in question is instead Mykalessos, a city in Caria for which Ephorus is cited by Stephanus of Byzantium s.v.; see Herda 2006:79–93.

71 Vitruvius 4.1.4–6; *IP* (Hiller 1906) 37 lines 104–105, 107–109, 120–123 (cf. also lines 53–60).

72 Vitruvius 4.1.4 calls the town Melite (an apparent mistake, Wilamowitz 1906/1971:38/128, but cf. P. Hommel in Kleiner et al. 1967:79) and lists it after the twelve cities of the Panionic league as a thirteenth member which was removed through war at the joint instigation of the others, and whose place was later taken by Smyrna: *haec Melite propter civium adro-*

it is called, is mentioned several times in an inscription from the early second century BC concerning a land dispute on Cape Mykale.[73] Melia, which was on Cape Mykale, controlled an extensive territory on Mykale which was divided up when Melia was destroyed. Allotments of Melia's land were made to four cities after the war: Priene, Samos, Colophon, and Miletus.[74] In the second century BC Samos and Priene both claimed that two particular places had been allotted to them after the Meliac War, and to make their case each side cited historians of the war, eight of whom are named in the inscription.[75] In

---

gantiam ab his civitatibus bello indicto communi consilio est sublata, cuius loco postea regis Attali et Arsinoes beneficio Smyrnaeorum civitas inter Iones est recepta, "This Melite was destroyed because of the citizens' arrogance by these cities, a war having been declared at their joint instigation; in its place the city of the Smyrnaeans, by the good offices of king Attalus and Arsinoe, was later received among the Ionians"; Vitruvius here refers anachronistically to the refounded league of the fourth century BC, which admitted Smyrna at the behest of Lysimachus (Vitruvius says Attalus rather than Lysimachus, another mistake; see Wilamowitz 1906/1971:38/128). The relationship of early Smyrna to the Panionic league, which continues to be debated, is discussed in EN4.3. Cf. also n4.19 above.

73 IP (Hiller 1906) 37 (see n4.71 above), which refers to the Μελιακὸς πόλεμος in lines 56, 108, and 118–119. This inscription shows that Melia once controlled an extensive territory on Cape Mykale, which is inferred to be the location of Melia itself (for the lack of precise information as to Melia's location see n4.69 above). Hiller von Gaertringen, who published *Inschriften von Priene* in 1906, and Wilamowitz, whose article "Panionion" appeared in the same year, had similar ideas about Melia's possible location: Hiller, p. vi, thought that Melia lay next to Priene, whose original location, though not known, cannot have been very far from Panionion (see n4.85 below); Wilamowitz 1906/1971:45–46 and 46n1/136–137 and 137n1 argued that Panionion was in or next to Melia. Wilamowitz's view has been confirmed with reasonable certainty by the discovery of what is taken to be the site of Melia two kilometers from Panionion (see n4.70 above and §4.18 and n4.86 below). This location of Melia is widely, if not universally, accepted (Ragone 1986:179 thinks that Melia may have lain elsewhere). Wilamowitz concluded that Panionion was in Melia's vicinity primarily on the basis of his argument, p. 45/137, that the Panionic league was born out of the Meliac War, and that the league appropriated Melia's cult of Poseidon Helikonios to be its center. This goes against Vitruvius's account, in which the league preceded the war, and I do not agree with Wilamowitz on this point; but the idea that Panionion became the league's center as a result of the Meliac War has much to recommend it (see further below). Herda 2006:66 considers that the sanctuary of Poseidon Helikonios became the Panionion at the latest when Melia was destroyed; for Melia's site cf. Herda 2006:60n94 with bibliography.

74 Priene and Samos are known to have received land after the war from the fact that they are the two parties to the later dispute, which concerns the original allotments (they were also the parties to another somewhat earlier dispute concerned with a different part of the original allotment; see below in text). Original allotments of land to Miletus and Colophon that were given up in later exchanges are at issue in IP (Hiller 1906) 37 lines 57 and 59. For the complicated question of what these allotments were (Miletus's in particular), see below n4.75 and n4.76, §4.68 with n4.226 and n4.227, and EN4.13 to n4.227 below.

75 IP (Hiller 1906) 37 lines 120–122 (see §4.16 and n4.71 above). The two disputed places are *Phroúrion Kárion* and *Druoûssa*; the inscription records the decision of Rhodian arbitrators in favor of Priene. In lines 103–105 the Samians maintain that "at the time that they divided

what survives of the inscription the Panionic league is not named, but the fact that Melia's territory was "allotted" to the four other cities after the war clearly suggests the action of a league.[76] Vitruvius, with his account of the league's war on Melia, and the Hellenistic inscription, with its references to allotments of land after the war, complement each other well. Vitruvius apparently followed a well-established tradition in associating the Meliac War with the Panionic league.

§4.17 The date of the Meliac War is not known, but it must have been before the mid-seventh century BC, when Cimmerians under the leader Lygdamis invaded western Asia Minor from the east and, among other hostile acts, occupied Cape Mykale for a number of years. The Cimmerian occupation upset the division of land made after the Meliac War, for the inhabitants had to vacate Mykale until Lygdamis finally withdrew. We learn about this

---

the land of the Melians, they themselves received Karion and Dryoussa according to what is stated in the histories ascribed to Maiandrios the Milesian"; but the Rhodian arbitrators rejected this evidence because seven other historians of the Meliac War, including four from Samos itself, said that Samos was allotted Phygela (Pygela) after the war; the Rhodian arbitrators also cast doubt on the authenticity of the histories ascribed to Maiandrios (lines 118–123). The Prienians do not seem to have had a positive claim to the two disputed places on the basis of the histories, but they prevailed nonetheless. The case is discussed by Ager 1996:196–210, who cites parallels for the use of historians and other writers as legal evidence (209n16).

76 The division of land by lot after the war is referred to in *IP* (Hiller 1906) 37 lines103–105, 117, 122 (cf. also line 56). Although the term for the league (τὸ Ἰώνων κοινόν) does not occur in what has survived of the inscription, it has been restored in Hiller's revised text, *IP* p. 309 (Hiller's revised text takes account of Wilamowitz 1906). In lines 55–56 the Samians cite the historian Maiandrios as asserting that the rest of Melia's land was allotted to them [by the league of Ionians] after the Meliac War : [διότι καὶ ἁ] λοιπὰ χώρα ἁ Μελιὰς [ὑπὸ Ἰώνων κοινο]ῦ αὐτοῖς ἐ[πεκλαρώθη μ]ετὰ τὸμ πόλεμον τὸμ Με[λιακόν. A mention of the league was also restored in line 58 in Hiller's original text but in his revised text the phrase τὸ Ἰώνων κοιν]ὸν has been changed to τὸ Ἰώνων δικαστήρι]ον. The context seems to be an adjustment of the original land division at a later date; the Samians say that they got one place in Melia's former territory (A[kadamis?]) for two other places, Thebai and Marathesion, in an exchange with the Milesians, "just as [the court of the Ionians decided] about them in a meeting at the Panionia" (lines 56–60): [εἴτ᾽ ἀλλαξά]σθαι αὐτᾶ[ς Σα-] / [μίους] παρὰ μὲν Μιλησίων Ἀ[κάδαμιν ἐφ᾽ ὧι δοῦναι τοῖ]ς αὐτοῖς Θή[βας] / [καὶ Μ]αραθήσιον, καθὼ[ς καὶ τὸ Ἰώνων δικαστήρι]ον ὑπὲρ αὐ[τῶν ἔ-] / [κρινε] Πανιωνίοις [ἐν τῶι συλλόγωι, παρὰ] δὲ Κολοφωνίων / Ἄναια. The name Akadamis is restored with reasonable certainty in line 57: "Scylax" *Periplus* 98 in the fourth century BC lists Akadamis with such other places as Panionion and Mykale in a description of this coast and says that it belonged to Samos; Akadamis was thus part of the Samian *peraía* in the fourth century, and this may be because it was given to Samos by Miletus at an earlier time. For Akadamis cf. Herda 2006:79n200; for the locations of other places on the Mykale coast see Shipley 1987:266–268 and fig. 22; in order from north to south the places on this coast are Pygela, Marathesion, Anaia, Panionion, and Karion/Melia; Thebai lies further south and inland; for Anaia, which the Samians got from Colophon [*IP* 37 line 60], see Fantasia 1986:127. See Map 2.

from another Hellenistic inscription concerned with a previous land dispute between Samos and Priene. This dispute was heard by Lysimachus in 283/2 BC, whose decision in favor of Samos was recorded and set up in Samos.[77] In what survives of the inscription the Prienians make the case that the original possession of the disputed place, called Batinetis ("bramble land"), was theirs, and that after Lygdamis's occupation they recovered this land intact.[78] The basis of the Prienians' claim of original possession must have been the division of land after the Meliac War. The Meliac War is not mentioned in what survives of the inscription, but, as we learn from the later dispute between Samos and Priene, historians were cited in the earlier dispute just as they were in the later dispute.[79] The historians were undoubtedly cited for the same reason, namely to establish how land was allotted after the Meliac War.[80]

---

77 Welles 1934 no. 7; see also Ager 1996:89–93; *IP* (Hiller 1906) no. 500; Dittenberger 1903–1905 no. 13.

78 The Prienians claim original possession of the land (ἡ ἐξ ἀρχῆς κτῆσις) in Welles 1934 no. 7 lines 11–12 (cf. also lines 26–27); later, they say, Lygdamis arrived and the land was evacuated until Lygdamis, having held the land for three (or seven or ten) years, returned it (lines 14–17): [ὕστε]ρον δὲ συνωμολόγουν Λυγδάμεως ἐπελθόντος ἐπὶ τὴν Ἰω[νίαν μετὰ δ]υνάμεως τούς τε λοιποὺς ἐγλιπεῖν τὴν χώραν καὶ Σαμ[ίους εἰς τὴν ν]ῆσον ἀποχωρῆσαι· τὸν δὲ Λύγδα[μιν κ]ατασχόντα [τρί]α ([ἑπτ]ά? [δέκ]α?) [ἔτη αὐτοῖς] πάλιν ἀποδιδόναι τὰς αὐτὰς κτήσεις. The Prienians evidently argued here that the land that they held after their return to Mykale was what they had possessed originally; hence the naïve idea that Lygdamis returned "the same possessions" when he departed. For their part the Samians agreed that they evacuated Mykale with the other inhabitants, but the rest of their argument, which must have been different from the Prienians' argument, has been lost (lines 29–30): μετὰ δὲ τὴν Λυγδάμεως εἰσβολὴν ἐγλιπεῖν συνωμο]λόγουν ὥσπερ καὶ οἱ λοιποὶ καὶ αὐτοὶ [τὴν χώραν, ἀποχωρῆσαι δὲ εἰ]ς τὴν νῆσον. For the location of Batinetis, which is not precisely known, see Fantasia 1986:129n52 and Magnetto 1997:130–131: Batinetis is distinct from Phrourion Karion and Dryoussa (Priene's possession of these two places was upheld by Lysimachus when he awarded Batinetis to Samos, as emerges from the later dispute for Phrourion Karion and Dryoussa, *IP* (Hiller 1906) 37 lines 125–130; see Wilamowitz 1906/1971:39n2/129n2 and Hiller von Gaertringen in Dittenberger:1915–1924 no. 688n4), but the places, though distinct, were doubtless in the same general area between the Samian *peraía* and the Prienian *khóra*; after the Cimmerians left Mykale a thousand Samians settled Batinetis, which must therefore have been flat tillable land (Welles 1934 no. 7 line 32 with Plutarch *Greek Questions* 20, on which see Wilamowitz 1906/1971:43/134, Fantasia 1986:129n52, 130n57, Magnetto 1997:130–131, 138n32; for the Plutarch passage cf. n4.64 above); the tillable nature of the land indicates the modern Karaova Plain stretching north for several kilometers from Mount Mykale, and most likely the southeast corner of this plain, closest on a straight line to Priene.

79 *IP* (Hiller 1906) 37 lines 101–102: the Rhodian arbitrators state that the Samians cited historians in the present dispute as they had in the dispute over Batinetis, "trying to show from them that Karion and the land around it had been allotted to them" (line 103); cf. Wilamowitz 1906/1971:41–42/132.

80 In the end the issue of original possession proved to be irrelevant: Lysimachus based his decision in favor of Samos on the fact that Samos had had long continuous possession of the

§4.18 The Meliac War preceded Lygdamis's occupation of Mykale, and that is all that emerges from our sources about the war's date. We know that Lygdamis's occupation of Mykale occurred c. 640 BC, and that is thus one fixed point.[81] More can be said about the date of Melia's destruction from its site, which was identified and investigated in 1957–1960.[82] It appears that after the Meliac War the site of Melia itself was allotted to Priene, and that the place was called *Phroúrion Kárion*, "Carian fortress," or simply *Kárion*, at the time of the dispute between Priene and Samos in the second century BC.[83]

---

land (cf. lines 4–6, addressed to the Samians: "If we had known that you had had this land in possession and use for so many years we should never have undertaken to hear the case").

81 The Cimmerians, who came originally from southern Russia, invaded western Asia Minor under Lygdamis (Dugdamme in an Assyrian source; for this king of the "northmen" on an inscription of Assurbanipal see Lehmann-Haupt *RE* 'Kimmerier' 417); there the Cimmerians joined forces with the Trerians, who came originally from Thrace and who may have been related to the Cimmerians; cf. Strabo 1.3.21, 14.1.40. The Cimmerians began their war on Gyges and the Lydians in c. 668 BC and were defeated by them in c. 663 BC, but they eventually took Sardis and killed Gyges in c. 640 BC. Lygdamis was forced to retreat from the coast into the interior by Gyges' successor Ardys (Ardys, who captured Priene according to Herodotus 1.15, may have captured it from Lygdamis; see Hiller von Gaertringen 1906 vii and below here). The Cimmerians were finally driven from western Asia Minor by Alyattes (cf. Herodotus 1.16.2); Alyattes defeated the Cimmerians and killed Lygdamis in 626 or 637 BC (Sulimirski and Taylor 1991:559). Herodotus 1.6.3 characterizes the Cimmerians' invasion of the Ionian cities as a transient raid in contrast to what later occurred under Croesus, when the Greek cities of Asia Minor were permanently overthrown: τὸ γὰρ Κιμμερίων στράτευμα τὸ ἐπὶ τὴν Ἰωνίην ἀπικόμενον, Κροίσου ἐὸν πρεσβύτερον, οὐ καταστροφὴ ἐγένετο τῶν πολίων, ἀλλ᾽ ἐξ ἐπιδρομῆς ἁρπαγή, "the expedition of Cimmerians that came against Ionia, which was before Croesus's time, was not an overthrow of the cities, but a seizure from a raid." Nevertheless the Cimmerians inflicted great harm on the Ionians: they destroyed Magnesia on the Maeander, burned the Artemision at Ephesus, occupied Cape Mykale, and probably occupied Priene (see Kleiner *RE* Supplement 9 'Priene' 1185 Nr. 2, although the evidence cited, *IP* 500 [= Welles 1934 no. 7] lines 14ff., concerns Mykale, and not Priene itself). The poet Callinus of Ephesus witnessed the Cimmerian invasion (Strabo 14.1.40 = Callinus fr. 5a West): νῦν δ᾽ ἐπὶ Κιμμερίων στρατὸς ἔρχεται ὀβριμοεργῶν, "Now comes the army of Cimmerians with mighty deeds." Callinus also spoke of the Trerians: Stephanus of Byzantium s.v. Τρῆρος quotes Callinus for a trisyllabic form of their name: Τρήερας ἄνδρας ἄγων, "leading the Trerian men" (Callinus fr. 4 West). For the dates of the Cimmerian invasions cf. Herda 2006:59n92 with bibliography; while exact dates are uncertain, the general period (first half and middle of the seventh century BC) is not in doubt. Ivantchik 2005:113 dates the destruction of Sardis, in which Gyges was killed, to 644 BC, and he sees this invasion as the one that most likely reached Ionia (p. 123); Ivantchik argues that the Akkadian sources used to date the destruction of Sardis to 644 BC also date the death of Lygdamis to 641 BC, and he suggests that the Cimmerians held Mykale for the three years between these two dates (for a probable three-year occupation of Mykale by the Cimmerians see n4.78 above on Lysimachus's letter to the Samians, lines 14–17).

82 See n4.70 above; cf. Herda 2006:60n94.

83 The identification of Melia with a place later known as *Phroúrion Kárion* suggests that

The Rhodians who arbitrated the dispute were convinced by Priene's argument, based on seven historians, that *Kárion* had been allotted to Priene after the Meliac War, and Priene was thus allowed to keep it.[84] Priene provided the priests for the cult of Poseidon Helikonios at Panionion, and was probably responsible for the overall administration of the cult there as well.[85] Priene

Melia too had been at least partially Carian, and this would surely have contributed to the hostility of its Ionian neighbors (cf. G. Kleiner and P. Hommel in Kleiner et al. 1967:5, 9–10, 79–82; cf. also Wilamowitz 1906/1971:43n4/134n2; Carians preceded the Ionians on Mykale according to Pherekydes, cited by Strabo 14.1.3). But Melia, which has a Greek name ("ash tree"), can have become Carian only in the course of time. The original settlement must have been Greek. Thebans who followed Cretans in the settlement of Colophon (Pausanias 7.3.1–3; cf. n4.25 above), seem to have gone on to found Melia from Colophon (see Huxley 1960). The origins of Melia and the cult of Poseidon Helikonios, which seems originally to have belonged to Melia, are discussed further in EN4.4.

84 Priene's claim to another place, Dryoussa ("oak land"), was upheld in the same arbitration; it was perhaps at this place that Samos and Miletus defeated Priene in the sixth-century battle known thereafter among the women of Priene as "the darkness at the oak" (see n4.64 above). P. Hommel in Kleiner et al. 1967:82n234 infers that Dryoussa was near Phrourion Karion in the southern end of the Karaova Plain of Cape Mykale; Hiller von Gaertringen in Dittenberger 1915–1924 no. 688n4 takes Dryoussa to be the land surrounding Phrourion Karion (note the phrase τὸ Κάριον καὶ ἁ περὶ τοῦτο χώρα, "Karion and the country around it," in the Samians' claim, and the words τὸ φρούριον καὶ τὰς χώρας τὰς περὶ τὸ φρούριον, "the fort, and (shares) of the country around the fort," in the Prienians' claim (IP [Hiller 1906] 37 lines 103 and 127; cf. n4.79 above).

85 Cf. Ziehen *RE* 'Panionia' 604: "Since the Panionion lay in the territory of Priene, it is in itself likely that this city also had the sacral administration" ("Da das Panionion im Gebiet von Priene lag, ist an sich wahrscheinlich, dass diese Stadt auch die sakrale Leitung hatte"). Strabo attests that Priene provided the priest for the cult (8.7.2 and 14.1.20; cf. EN4.2 to n4.47 above), as do inscriptions recording the sale of the priesthood of Poseidon Helikonios (IP [Hiller 1906] 201–203); cf. also Wilamowitz 1906/1971:45, 50/137, 142, who assumes that Priene provided the priest in the archaic cult as well; this is also my assumption. How Priene may have been related to Melia before Melia was destroyed is an interesting but highly speculative question. Hiller 1906 vi suggests that old Priene, whose location is unknown, was at first united with Melia, and that Melia was destroyed when it began to act too independently. There is tantalizing support for this idea in IP (Hiller 1906) 37 lines 47–48, near the start of the case that the Samians made for original possession of Karion and Dryoussa. In what seems to be a section devoted to the origins of the Meliac War there appears the phrase "the Prienians with the Melians," followed by the phrase "but civil strife broke out" (lines 47–48):

Πριαν[εῖ]ς μετὰ Μελιέ[ων----------------------πόλιν (?)]
μίαν ἔ[χειν], στάσιος δὲ γε[νομένας------------------]

Hiller has supported his idea that stasis split one city into two by suggesting the word πόλιν before μίαν (for a different interpretation of these lines see Shipley 1987:29–30, who suggests πολεμίαν or Σαμίαν for Hiller's πόλιν μίαν). Hiller's suggestion would locate old Priene on the site now identified as Melia, namely Kaletepe, but in Hiller's day Melia's location had not been established and Hiller himself had no definite location in mind (Kaletepe was established as Melia's location by Kleiner et al. 1967; note that Wilamowitz 1906:133n3

was the closest city of the league to Panionion and it makes sense that it was
given this function. It also makes sense that Priene was allotted the site of
Melia, which was doubtless a useful outpost in tending to the nearby cult.
The remains discovered at Melia's site, now called Kaletepe, bear out this
reconstruction of Melia's end and subsequent transformation into a Prienian
fortress. The circular wall around the top of the hill and the two houses
excavated inside the wall belong to the seventh century BC, and thus to the
Prienian fortress.[86] The necropolis at the bottom of the hill contains older
remains, but it was no longer used in the seventh century BC; it must have
belonged to an earlier settlement, presumably Melia.[87] In this necropolis
were found fragments of Protogeometric and Geometric pottery, including
Late Geometric pottery; the Late Geometric fragments show that the necrop-
olis continued to be used down to c. 700 BC or a little later.[88] At this point the
necropolis ceased to be used, and this, it is thought, marks the end of Melia.[89]

---

identifies the ruins on Kaletepe as Phrourion Karion, as do also Wiegand and Schrader
1904, Karte I, but no connection with the site of ancient Melia is made by these authorities;
cf. Herda 2006:62). If Hiller is right that Priene and Melia were once one city, the Samians'
argument may have been that Melia became separated from Priene through stasis, but that
Priene was not allotted the actual land of Melia after the Meliac War. It need only be added
that if Melia was in fact split off from Priene, and if Samos could point to historians for this
fact, it seems more likely that the land was allotted to Priene and not to Samos after the
war. Whatever the Samians' argument was, there seems to have been little real doubt that
Priene rather than Samos originally possessed Karion.

86 W. Müller-Wiener in Kleiner et al. 1967:97–127; but cf. also Herda 2006:62 and n108, who
suggests that the oval house may be Late Geometric on the basis of comparative evidence
from Miletus, and that the circular wall also, in which a few Late Geometric sherds were
found, may belong to Melia rather than the later Prienian fortress. A later wall, dated
to the sixth century BC, was found at the base of the hill, and this would belong to the
Prienian fortress.

87 The occupants of the seventh-century fortress must have buried their dead elsewhere,
perhaps in Priene.

88 See the catalogue of unpainted Geometric fragments by P. Hommel in Kleiner et al.
1967:166. The evidence is discussed in EN4.5.

89 Gyges' attacks on the Ionian cities, which began c. 680 BC, constitute a lower limit for the
Meliac War, for the Ionian cities cannot well have begun a war against Melia after Gyges
began his attacks on them; cf. Lenschau 1944:236, and P. Hommel in Kleiner et al. 1967:92,
who considers an attack on Melia unthinkable ("nicht mehr denkbar") after Gyges' attacks
began. Gyges, who captured the lower city of Colophon (Herodotus 1.14.4), presumably did
so before the Cimmerians began their war on him in 668 BC. Colophon, which acquired
Anaia through the division of Melia's land, must have taken part in the Meliac War;
Hommel, p. 93, speculates that Colophon, which later gave up Anaia to Samos and appar-
ently got nothing in exchange for it, became too preoccupied with Gyges to have further
interest in Mykale (for Anaia, named in *IP* [Hiller 1906] 37 line 60, see n4.76 above). In addi-
tion to capturing Colophon Gyges attacked Smyrna, Miletus, and Magnesia.

§4.19 If we follow the literary tradition, the Panionic league was founded before c. 700 BC, when Melia was destroyed. We cannot confirm this date by the remains at Panionion, which, as noted above, barely go back to 600 BC, and this discrepancy remains a problem.[90] The Homeric poems are the reason that I have devoted attention to the Panionic league, and I return now to the poems themselves. Further insight into the league's origins can, I think, be derived from the poems, and this will be one aim of the argument to follow. I will conclude the present section by returning to what seems to me the most important factor in the origin and development of the Panionic league, namely the role of Miletus and the Neleid family in the process, whatever the process may have been. Their role, I think, is clear from the Kodrid myth, which properly belonged to Miletus, and which Miletus extended to other cities in the league in order to fashion an identity for the league in its own image. I have argued that Colophon accepted the Kodrid myth in place of an older rival myth; in doing so Colophon would have followed the lead of Miletus.[91] Priene, to judge by its version of the Kodrid myth, followed

---

90 Cf. Jeffery 1976:209 on Panionion: "The start of the cult cannot yet be dated by archaeology; there are traces of a great altar and a council chamber on the Otomatik Tepe (now definitely identified as the site of the precinct); but they are not earlier than the sixth century, although on the Ilica Tepe nearby are traces of habitation which go back apparently to the Mycenean period." For İliça Tepe, see G. Kleiner in Kleiner et al. 1967:12, who thinks that before Melia joined the league as a thirteenth member and was destroyed by it a site other than Panionion was the league's cult center: "If one wants to remain in this vicinity, Iliça Tepe, as a late second millennium site, offers itself as the oldest Panionion. Its wall does not remind one so much of Çamli's Kaletepe...as of Mycenaean fortifications" ("Will man in der Umgebung bleiben, bietet sich als Anlage des späten 2. Jts. der Iliça Tepe als ältestes Panionion an. Seine Mauer erinnert nicht so sehr an Çamlis Kaletepe...als an mykenische Befestigungen"). But an earlier center for the league at İliça Tepe, which Kleiner proposed only as a possibility to pursue through further excavations, would still not account for the lack of evidence at Panionion for more than a century after the Meliac War. For the difficulty of identifying early altars built from ephemeral materials see Herda 2005:258 (bibliography 258n76); where such altars were replaced by permanent stone altars like that at Panionion the earlier remains are more easily identified, but there may still be ambiguity (see Herda 2005:258n76). If one is guided strictly by the lack of archaeological evidence for the origin of the cult at Panionion, one is led to a date for the origin of the league that to most would seem too low. J. M. Cook, who has gone in this direction, is exceptional, revising downward his date for the Panionic league twice in light of the archaeological evidence: the date of c. 800 BC that he first proposed (Cook 1961:31) he lowered to c. 700 BC (Cook 1975:803), and he later wrote that this date too "must be lowered" (Cook 1982:750); cf. Cook's reviews of Kleiner et al. 1967 (Cook 1969:718 and Cook 1970).

91 See above §4.7–§4.8 on the distinction between the Pylian past of the Neleids, who came through Athens and became Kodrids, and of Mimnermus's ancestors, who came directly from Pylos to Colophon. Colophon chose for itself a Kodrid past, like that of Miletus, and

Miletus's lead most closely of all: Aipytos, the founder of Priene, was not a son of Kodros, but a son of Neileos, the founder of Miletus; the founder of Priene, in other words, was a second-generation Kodrid, dependent on Miletus for his Kodrid status.[92] It cannot be an accident that Priene was also given control of the cult of Poseidon Helikonios at Panionion. If Priene controlled the cult at Panionion, Miletus, I think, controlled Priene, its smaller neighbor across the Gulf of Latmos.

---

rejected a foundation by Mimnermus's ancestors. As noted earlier (EN4.4 to n4.83 above), Melia seems to have been founded from Colophon. How did Colophon then come to participate in the destruction of Melia? Shipley 1987:31 compares the destruction of a daughter city by the mother city to the hostility between Corinth and Corcyra. I note that Colophon had hostile relations not only with Melia, but also, it seems, with Smyrna. Was the issue at Melia, as at Smyrna, an unwillingness to follow the lead of Miletus? The party that prevailed at Colophon was willing to do precisely this, as its acceptance of the Kodrid myth shows.

92 Pausanias 7.2.10; Strabo 14.1.3 (cf. n4.39 above). I note that this version of the Kodrid myth, like some other versions already considered, is more likely to have arisen early, when Miletus was preeminent, than late, when Miletus had lost that status. For traditions of other founders of Priene besides Aipytos cf. Herda 2006:77n195.

Chapter 11.

THE FESTIVAL OF THE PANIONIA

AND THE HOMERIC POEMS

§4.20 The Phaeacians, as argued earlier, represent the Ionians in the one context in which they were a single people, namely the celebration of the Panionia. With their love of songs, dances, and banquets, the Phaeacians bring out the festive side of the Ionians, and this is for good reason if they are meant to evoke the Ionians at the celebration of the Panionia. The Phaeacians' seamanship also fits with the context of a festival, for the Ionians must have come to Panionion (if the festival took place there from the start) primarily by ships.

§4.21 A love of song is the most interesting attribute of the Phaeacians insofar as they represent the Ionians. Demodokos, the blind poet who three times entertains the Phaeacians while Odysseus is their guest, represents this attribute most directly. More significant, however, is Odysseus himself, to whom the Phaeacians listen with rapt attention when he sings the song of his own *nóstos*. Through four entire books of the *Odyssey* Odysseus is the poet and the Phaeacians are his audience. Odysseus here represents the Homeric poets, who did the actual singing, and the Phaeacian audience represents the Homeric audience, which did the actual listening.[93] If Odysseus's Phaeacian audience in fact represents the Homeric audience, I think that we have found the occasion on which the Homeric poems were performed during their formative Ionian phase, namely the festival of the Panionia. This, to repeat,

93 Doherty 1995:87–92 discusses the relationship between the Phaeacians and the Homeric audience; Louden 1999:50–68 also discusses this relationship but emphasizes Alcinous as Odysseus's audience over the Phaeacians as a group.

was the only occasion on which the Ionians of the dodecapolis, whom the Phaeacians represent, actually came together as one. Among the things that they did there, if the Phaeacians who listen to *Odyssey* 9–12 are a guide, was to listen to a performance of the Homeric poems.

§4.22 It is no surprise if a *panéguris* like the Panionia was the occasion for the performance of such large-scale epics as the *Iliad* and the *Odyssey*. Gilbert Murray saw clearly a century ago that these extravagant poems actually demanded a *panéguris* in order to be performed.[94] The festival of the Panionia does not emerge into the light of history until the mid-sixth century, when the twelve-city league had already become a defensive alliance faced with enemies that overmatched it.[95] We simply do not know what this league

---

94 *The Rise of the Greek Epic* 1907:170–176 (modified in later editions: see Murray 1934:187–194); cf. also Wade-Gery 1952:14; Durante 1957:106–107; Webster 1964:268; Thornton 1984:28; Ford 1997:86. According to Wade-Gery: "It is, surely, one of the few things certain in the Homeric Question, that a poem of the length and coherence of the *Iliad* presupposes a panegyris of some days' duration"; this, I would add, is no less true of the *Odyssey*. In Durante's view: "All the salient characteristics that distinguish Homeric poetry presuppose or suit the atmosphere of the *panegyris*" ("Tutti i caratteri salienti che contraddistinguono la poesia omerica presuppogono o si addicono all' atmosfera della *panegyris*"). Durante lists several such characteristics, among which the first, the choice of theme in the *Iliad*, suggests an interesting comparison with later rhetorical tradition: "If we want to find other literary manifestations in which the theme that informs every verse of the poem, that is, the alternative between Greeks and barbarians, is represented with the same clarity, we must look to the πανηγυρικοὶ λόγοι ['panegyrics'] like the *Olympicus* of Lysias and the *Panegyricus* of Isocrates" ("Se vogliamo trovare altre manifestazioni letterarie in cui si ripresenti con la stessa nettezza il motivo che informa di sé ogni verso del poema, cioè l'alternativa fra Greci e barbari, dobbiamo rifarci ai πανηγυρικοὶ λόγοι come l'*Olimpico* di Lisia e il *Panegirico* di Isocrate"). Durante cites Murray 1934:193n1 for this point, and also for a point about the Homeric gods, whom Murray 1934:265 calls "an enlightened compromise made to suit the conveniences of a federation." Durante's other points include the absence of obscenity from the Homeric poems, suitable for the presence of chaste wives and children at a *panégyris*, and the non-local nature of the artificial Homeric dialect. He summarizes as follows: "Thus the *panegyris*, not the royal banquet, is the ideal background of Homeric poetry: the agora, not the megaron; it is not for nothing that Demodocus is λαοῖσι τετιμένος ['honored by the people'], *Odyssey* 8.472 " ("Dunque è la *panegyris* lo sfondo ideale della poesia omerica, non il banchetto regio: l'agorà, non il megaron; non per nulla Demodoco è λαοῖσι τετιμένος, θ 472"). Finally he cites Pagliaro 1953:51–62, who argues that early poetic exhibitions at festivals by *aoidoí*, like later poetic exhibitions by rhapsodes, were organized as competitions; according to Pagliaro the phrase ἀνεβάλλετο ἀείδειν in the *Odyssey* ("he began to sing") properly indicates "the poet's first intervention, in relation to successive interventions" ("il primo intervento dell' aedo, correlativo agli interventi successivi") and so forms a pair with the phrase ἐξ ὑποβολῆς ῥαψῳδεῖσθαι, "to perform as a rhapsode in succession" (Diogenes Laertius 1.57), which is technical language for a rhapsodic recitation in a competition. For Pagliaro's argument see also Pagliaro 1970.

95 In the mid-sixth century power shifted from the Lydians to the Persians, but the Lydians had already changed conditions fundamentally for the Ionians more than a century

did in the latter eighth century and the beginning of the seventh century, before these enemies appeared on the scene.[96] We do know, however, that the Homeric poems were later performed at another festival, the Panathenaia, and it does not seem rash to extrapolate backward from this festival to the Panionia.[97] We also have the earlier evidence of the Delian *Hymn to Apollo*, which represents itself as the creation of a blind bard from Chios (*Homeric Hymn to Apollo* 172, τυφλὸς ἀνήρ, οἰκεῖ δὲ Χίῳ ἔνι παιπαλοέσσῃ). The blind bard from Chios is meant to be Homer himself, the supposed ancestor of the Homeridai, rhapsodes who lived on Chios and undoubtedly performed the

---

earlier. Cook 1975:800, speaking of the arrival at the start of the seventh century of the Cimmerians, who overthrew the Phrygian capital at Gordion but had no lasting effect on the Ionians, contrasts the change brought about by the Lydians at about the same time: "Altogether more momentous was the transference of political power to Sardis, which lay only two or three days' march from the Greek cities and controlled the routes to the different sectors of the coast. There could thenceforward be no common defence of the Ionic cities against attacks from the interior power."

96 Ideas about the original purpose of the league differ: based on the evidence of Herodotus for a later period Wilamowitz 1906/1971:47/138 thought that the purpose was political ("it is therefore a political union; it doesn't stand out as sacral" ["es ist also ein politischer Bund, sakral tritt er nicht hervor"]); Roebuck 1955, on the other hand, thought that the league must have originated as a religious amphictyony.

97 Wade-Gery 1952 devoted attention near the start of his study (pp. 2–6) to the Panionia as a likely context for the performance of the *Iliad*. For the relevance of later festivals, including the Panathenaia, to the question, cf. also Durante 1957:106: "For anyone who proceeds backwards from the historical stage of epic recitations, *from known to unknown*, there can be no doubt that the genesis of the epic is inseparable from the institution of the rhapsodic contest and from the context that this necessarily presupposes, the religious festival" ("Per chi proceda a ritroso da quello che è lo stadio storico delle recitazioni epiche, *from known to unknown*, non può esservi dubbio che la genesi della epos è inscindibile dall'istituto dell'agone rapsodico e dall'ambiente che questo necessariamente presuppone, la festa religiosa"); cf. also Durante 1976:197. Durante, who mentions other festivals like the Delia, thinks especially of the Panionia (1957:106): "But the greatest Ionian festival was the Panionia celebrated on Mycale; now the simile in *Iliad* 20.403–5 shows, as ancient and modern interpreters have seen, that the author of the passage knew firsthand the sacrifice to Poseidon Helikonios that was performed at this festival" ("Ma la più grande festa ionica erano i *Panionia* celebrati a Micale: orbene, il paragone Y 403–5 mostra, come videro esegeti antichi e moderni, che l'autore del passo conosceva *de visu* il sacrificio a Posidone Eliconio che si effettuava in questa festa"); Durante cites Ziehen *RE* 'Panionia' 602, with bibliography. It may be that the Peisistratids had the specific model of the Delia in mind when they instituted rhapsodic contests at the Panathenaia; it has even been suggested that when Peisistratos purified Delos he terminated the Delia and transferred the rhapsodic contests from that festival to the Panathenaia (Murray 1934:191–192; cf. Durante 1957:106n44 and 1976:197n2; for the opposite view, that Peisistratos renewed the Delia after he purified Delos, see n4.9 above; the ambiguity lies in Thucydides 3.104.2, which refers to the Athenians' first penteteric celebration of the Delia, but it is unclear whether the purification of Delos with which Thucydides connects this event was that under Peisistratos or that in 426 BC).

Homeric poems when the Delian *Hymn to Apollo* was composed.[98] The Delian *Hymn to Apollo* is thus well aware of the *Iliad* and the *Odyssey*, and it is striking how its picture of the blind bard Homer resembles the Phaeacian bard Demodokos; it is more striking still how the Ionians, who are described in the hymn as gathered for a festival on Delos, resemble the Phaeacians: the correspondences include a love of games, dancing, and singing, a godlike grace, swift ships, and great wealth (*Homeric Hymn to Apollo* 146–155):

> ἀλλὰ σὺ Δήλῳ Φοῖβε μάλιστ' ἐπιτέρπεαι ἦτορ,
> ἔνθα τοι ἑλκεχίτωνες Ἰάονες ἠγερέθονται
> αὐτοῖς σὺν παίδεσσι καὶ αἰδοίης ἀλόχοισιν.
> οἱ δέ σε πυγμαχίῃ τε καὶ ὀρχηθμῷ καὶ ἀοιδῇ
> μνησάμενοι τέρπουσιν ὅταν στήσωνται ἀγῶνα.
> φαίη κ' ἀθανάτους καὶ ἀγήρως ἔμμεναι αἰεὶ
> ὃς τότ' ἐπαντιάσει' ὅτ' Ἰάονες ἀθρόοι εἶεν·
> πάντων γάρ κεν ἴδοιτο χάριν, τέρψαιτο δὲ θυμὸν
> ἄνδρας τ' εἰσορόων καλλιζώνους τε γυναῖκας
> νῆάς τ' ὠκείας ἠδ' αὐτῶν κτήματα πολλά.

But, Phoebus, you delight your heart most of all in Delos,
where the tunic-trailing Ionians gather
with their children and revered wives.
They delight you with boxing and dancing and singing
whenever they hold contests in your memory.
He would say that they are deathless and ageless,
whoever should be present then, when the Ionians are gathered
            together.
For he would see the grace of all of them, and delight his heart
seeing the men and beautifully-girdled women
and the swift ships and their many possessions.

---

98 By the Homeric poems I mean the *Iliad* and *Odyssey*, which, whatever else came to be associated with the name Homer, the early Homeridai surely also performed; the issue of what was attributed to Homer in the course of time is discussed further in EN4.6. I date the composition of the Delian *Hymn to Apollo* to the mid-seventh century BC; this issue is also discussed in EN4.6. For the blind bard of the Delian *Hymn to Apollo* as representing the Homeridai of Chios, cf. Dyer 1975.

Friedrich Welcker emphasized this passage when he argued that the Phaeacians represent the Ionians of Homer's time.[99] The resemblance is so great, however, that one may legitimately ask whether the portrayal of Homer and the Ionians in the *Homeric Hymn to Apollo* was not directly inspired by the portrayal of Demodokos and the Phaeacians in the *Odyssey*.[100] The Delian *Hymn to Apollo*, I think, originated close enough in time to when poetry still flourished at the festival of the Panionia to be well aware that the Phaeacians represented this *panēguris*, and to use them as the poetic model for a contemporary Ionian festival on Delos.[101] If this argument is correct, the portrayal of the Delia in the *Homeric Hymn to Apollo* brings us as close in time to the early celebration of the Panionia as we are likely to come, apart from what the Phaeacians reveal about this festival in the Homeric poems themselves.

§4.23 I have already said that, in my view, the Panionia were the occasion for the performance of both the *Iliad* and the *Odyssey*. Now I wish to insist on the idea that the performance that took place there was of the two

99 Welcker 1832/1845:33–34; cf. n4.11 above.
100 I am especially struck by the comparison of the Ionians to gods in the *Homeric Hymn to Apollo* (one would say that they are ἀθανάτους καὶ ἀγήρως, "deathless and ageless," line 151), given the Phaeacians' epithet, ἀγχίθεοι, "close to the gods," in *Odyssey* 5.35 and 19.279, and the Phaeacians' role in the *Odyssey*, in which two of them (in my view) actually represent the goddess Athena. Welcker 1832/1845:34 notes that the Ionians' "wealth" (κτήματα) in *Homeric Hymn to Apollo* 155 also has a close correspondence in the *Odyssey*: the same word κτήματα occurs in a reference to the Phaeacians' great wealth in Arete's speech in *Odyssey* 11.340–341: πολλὰ γὰρ ὑμῖν / κτήματ' ἐνὶ μεγάροισι θεῶν ἰότητι κέονται, "for many possessions lie in your halls by the will of the gods." Finally I draw attention to the Ionians' "swift ships" (νῆάς τ' ὠκείας) in *Homeric Hymn to Apollo* 155, since swift ships are such an essential feature of the Phaeacians' characterization.
101 Performances of the Homeric poems at the Panionia cannot have lasted much into the seventh century BC; see §4.40 below. They would have ended before the time of the Delian *Hymn to Apollo*, but not long before. For a different view of the description of the Delian festival in the *Homeric Hymn to Apollo*, see Burkert 1987:54; going beyond the idea that he (and independently R. Janko) had reached earlier, namely that a Delian and a Pythian hymn to Apollo were combined into one hymn for Polycrates' celebration of a joint *Púthia kaì Délia* festival on Delos in 523 or 522 BC, Burkert suggests that much of the Delian hymn, including the description of the festival, was composed for Polycrates' joint festival: "Parts of the text may well be older, but the arrangement belongs to the Polykrates festival, including the description of the Delian festival itself contained in the text." Burkert proposes this late dating in particular for the hymn's description of the singing of a chorus of Delian maidens. Be this as it may, I continue to follow Janko in dating the core of the Delian hymn, including the description of the Ionians gathered for a festival on Delos, to the seventh century BC. (For the festival of Polycrates as the context for the combined *Homeric Hymn to Apollo*, see Burkert 1979:59–60, 59n29 and Janko 1982:112–114, 258n76; cf. also Aloni 1989. The ancient sources for the combined festival concern a proverb relating to the festival's name; they cite Menander and Epicurus for the proverb; see Burkert 1979:59n31.)

poems together, in sequence. I make this claim on the basis of Nestor's role in the two poems, which, as I have analyzed it, is of a single piece, bridging both poems. Nestor's role in the story of Patroclus in the *Iliad* matches his role in the story of Odysseus in the *Odyssey*, in both substance and style; his role in both cases is based on his twin myth, but in both cases the myth itself is deliberately withheld. This overall congruence cannot be accidental, but must have arisen from a single source.[102] When Nestor's role as a whole is taken into account, the narrower question of a bridge between the two poems, which I have so far been reluctant to press, takes on a new look.[103] There is in fact good reason to press it. The bridge at issue is the episode in *Iliad* 8 that seems to allude to events recounted in *Odyssey* 3: Nestor, Diomedes, and Odysseus play out a drama during the war at Troy that will, with significant role reversals, be repeated after the war has ended and the departing army reaches Tenedos. The drama as it was played out on Tenedos is the main point of Nestor's account to Telemachus in *Odyssey* 3; Odysseus broke with Nestor on Tenedos, and this, to judge by Diomedes' speedy return home, added ten years to Odysseus's *nóstos*, the ten years that constitute the *Odyssey*. We may say that if Odysseus had not broken with Nestor on Tenedos, there would be no *Odyssey*, and in this sense *Odyssey* 3 explains why there is a story to tell at all. But Nestor does not say in so many words that Odysseus broke with him; this must be inferred from his account. In *Iliad* 8 it is the opposite: Odysseus pointedly breaks with Nestor when Nestor is in mortal danger and Odysseus does not heed the call to help him but flees by himself to the ships; this action itself, however, is inexplicable except when seen in the context of *Odyssey* 3, Nestor's account of the *nóstoi*. While the explicit nature of Odysseus's action at Troy immediately brings to mind his later action on Tenedos, his later action is only implied when the time comes to recount it. The episodes complement each other in this way, and this, I think, reflects an overall design.[104] If we are

---

102 Nestor's role is extensive enough in both poems to justify conclusions for the poems in their entirety; in the *Iliad* all of Nestor's appearances contribute to one unified role, and in the *Odyssey* the Phaeacians must be taken into account together with Nestor himself. Nestor's twin myth is put directly into play in *Iliad* 11, after allusions to it earlier in the poem; it remains in play until *Odyssey* 11, where it is fixed once and for all in a constellation of other twin myths, and a final echo of it is heard in *Odyssey* 15.

103 See above §2.89 and n2.118, and cf. §2.64.

104 Cf. n1.2 above on the motif of Nestor's three-generation lifespan, which is deployed in the *Iliad* to introduce Nestor for the first time, and is redeployed in the *Odyssey* to recall that first introduction. These instances are related to "Monro's Law," which properly concerns the complementary distribution of content between the two poems. But whereas other instances of complementary distribution (including the way in which the motif of Nestor's three-generation lifespan is deployed) reflect the *Odyssey*'s awareness of the *Iliad*, and do

justified in saying that *Iliad* 8 alludes to *Odyssey* 3, this means that the two poems coexisted when *Iliad* 8 was first composed. This conclusion has important implications for the genesis of the Homeric poems, which must have developed, not sequentially, but in tandem.[105]

§4.24 At the Panathenaia in Athens teams of rhapsodes performed the Homeric poems, one rhapsode taking over from another until the performance was completed.[106] We do not know any of the details of these performances:

---

not logically require the earlier coexistence of the two poems, *Iliad* 8, in my view, alludes to *Odyssey* 3, and that is a different matter. If the principle that the *Iliad* can allude to the *Odyssey* is first established, then other possible examples suggest themselves: what Achilles says to Odysseus in *Iliad* 9.312–313 (ἐχθρὸς γάρ μοι κεῖνος ὁμῶς Ἀΐδαο πύλῃσιν / ὅς χ᾽ ἕτερον μὲν κεύθῃ ἐνὶ φρεσίν, ἄλλο δὲ εἴπῃ, "For he is hateful to me like the gates of Hades, / whoever hides one thing in his mind and says another thing") may anticipate and turn against Odysseus what Odysseus himself says in *Odyssey* 14.156–157 (ἐχθρὸς γάρ μοι κεῖνος ὁμῶς Ἀΐδαο πύλῃσι / γίνεται, ὃς πενίῃ εἴκων ἀπατήλια βάζει, "For he is hateful to me like the gates of Hades, / who succumbs to poverty and says deceitful things"; cf. Edwards 1987:222 and Wilson 2002:86); similarly the footrace in *Iliad* 23 may allude to the *nóstos* of Odysseus as told in the *Odyssey*, and more particularly to the destruction of the lesser Ajax as told in *Odyssey* 4; it may also be that in *Iliad* 19, when Odysseus urges Achilles to let the army eat, "the *Iliad* answers the *Odyssey* directly" (Pucci 1987:169); and *Iliad* 10, which to some extent resembles the *Odyssey* in language (cf. Hainsworth 1993:154) and theme (the ambush theme of *Iliad* 10, as studied by Edwards 1985, is at least suggestive of the *Odyssey*), need not be later than the rest of the *Iliad* in order to allude to the *Odyssey* and its themes (cf. n4.126 below). It remains true, of course, that the Homeric poems also allude to epic traditions that do not appear, or do not appear prominently, in either poem; the specific instance of Memnon is discussed in EN4.7. Therefore it cannot be completely excluded that *Iliad* 8 alludes, not to *Odyssey* 3, but to the epic *nóstoi* tradition in general.

105 For those who believe that both poems were traditional this idea will not be hard to accept; but it remains to say exactly what it means that both poems were traditional, for two such large-scale poems, so symmetrical with each other, obviously did not always exist side by side. We still have to confront the problem of the expansion of the epics to their present size and design at a particular time.

106 This is the so-called Panathenaic rule, which is attributed to Hipparchus in "Plato" *Hipparchus* 228b: τὰ Ὁμήρου ἔπη πρῶτος ἐκόμισεν εἰς τὴν γῆν ταυτηνί, καὶ ἠνάγκασε τοὺς ῥαψῳδοὺς Παναθηναίοις ἐξ ὑπολήψεως ἐφεξῆς αὐτὰ διιέναι, ὥσπερ νῦν ἔτι οἵδε ποιοῦσιν, "He first brought the epics of Homer to this land, and compelled the rhapsodes at the Panathenaia to go through them in order, one after another, as they still do now." Cf. Diogenes Laertius 1.57, where the rule is attributed to Solon: τά τε Ὁμήρου ἐξ ὑποβολῆς γέγραφε ῥαψῳδεῖσθαι, οἷον ὅπου ὁ πρῶτος ἔληξεν, ἐκεῖθεν ἄρχεσθαι τὸν ἐχόμενον, "He proposed the law that the poems of Homer be performed in succession, so that where the first rhapsode left off, from there the next would begin" (Diogenes' source was Dieuchidas of Megara, whose attribution of the Panathenaic rule to Solon reflects the values of democratic Athens; see Ritoók 1993:47–48, Nagy 1999:131–132). There is disagreement among scholars whether the *Iliad* and the *Odyssey* were performed in their entirety at the Panathenaia. Burkert 1987:49–50 makes the case against such a complete performance: "There never could be a question of reciting the complete text of the *Iliad* at a rhapsodic contest. To recite the whole of the *Iliad* alone, not to mention the *Odyssey* and all the other

the number of rhapsodes involved, the length of individual performances, the number of performances per day, the number of performances overall.[107] At any rate several rhapsodes took part, and we must imagine something of the kind for the Panionia as well, where both poems were, as I have argued, performed together in sequence. But here is the great difficulty. Whereas at the Panathenaia the Homeric poems already existed and had only to be performed in a prescribed order, these poems were, I believe, actually created at the Panionia as they were performed. When I say that the poems were created at the Panionia, I mean more precisely that traditional poems were expanded in repeated performances to the monumental size and complex design that they retained from then on with only relatively minor changes through future generations.[108] But how were the poems expanded in the first place? The explanation for the monumental scale of the Homeric poems to which there is an almost irresistible temptation to run is the technique of writing, which entered

---

works still attributed to Homer, would take thirty to forty hours, more than the time available for all the tragedies and comedies at the Great Dionysia, which clearly was the more important literary event in Athens. Homerids could only produce selections from the huge thesaurus that remained in the background." Burkert (60n44) cites the scholia to Aristides *Panathenaic Oration* 147.9 (Dindorf p. 196) that the Panathenaia lasted four days. But Mikalson 1975:34 (cited by Burkert) notes that on the Athenian calendar the last two days of Hekatombaion do not have the usual month-end meetings and he takes this to mean that the celebration of the Panathenaia ended on the last day of the month, Hekatombaion 30; he suggests further that the lack of all public meetings on Hekatombaion 23–30 may indicate a festival of eight days. Cf. also Stanley 1993:401n36, who, for Homeric performances, prefers the longer festival of Mikalson. Without going into the question of the festival's length West 1999:382 (cf. also 372) simply assumes "the complete performance of the poems of Homer" at the Panathenaia; Stephanie West shares this view in Jensen et al. 1999:70. The Panathenaic rule implies that before the rule was imposed episodes were performed out of order (cf. Burgess 2001:14), and this in turn suggests incomplete performance of the poems; it may be that performance in the correct order entailed complete performance as well.

107 We do not even know for certain that both the *Iliad* and the *Odyssey* were performed, although the phrases τὰ Ὁμήρου ἔπη in Plato and τά τε Ὁμήρου in Diogenes Laertius make that a fair assumption.

108 Nestor's complex role in the *Iliad* and the *Odyssey*, for example, would belong to the period of the poems' expansion at the Panionia, but modifications to the parts of the poems in which Nestor plays this role were also made in future generations: the catalogue of heroines in *Odyssey* 11, which is an integral part of Nestor's Panionic role, received a Panathenaic overlay in the sixth century (see §2.160 above); Nestor's story in *Iliad* 11, I think, received a comparable overlay in the fifth century (see Part 5 below on the passages in his story containing precise geographical description). There were other modifications of the poems as well, such as the Athenian entry to the Catalogue of Ships (see §3.87–§3.91 above). Such later modifications are not negligible, but they are minor compared with the Panionic core of the two poems.

Greek culture close to the period in question.[109] The idea is, more or less, that a single great poet saw the potential of the written word for expanding traditional poems vastly beyond their inherited limits and so created two monumental epics, which he performed piecemeal here and there as the occasion arose.[110] This model assumes that a poet, trained to compose as he performed before an audience, instead dictated his poetry to a scribe or even wrote it down himself, and was thus able to leave behind a fixed text which others continued to perform as prescribed. It is true that a written text was most likely a feature of the Panathenaic performance of Homer, although not in a simple way.[111] I do not see, however, how a written text, produced as outlined above, could have been performed at the festival of the Panionia. I continue to take as my starting point Murray's argument (as formulated by Wade-Gery) "that a poem of the length and coherence of the *Iliad presupposes* a panegyris of some days' duration," and I add that such a *panḗguris* is doubly presupposed if the performance, as I have argued, was of the *Odyssey* as well as the *Iliad*. A single poet could not have performed this combined work, and it would be fantastic to imagine one doing so. Did a single poet then train others to help him with the performance? This may be closer to the truth, but I do not think that writing played any part in the process.[112] I suggest that the crucial element was rather the

109 The earliest inscription of more than a few letters, the Dipylon vase inscription, dates from 740–730 BC and contains a dactylic hexameter. See below §4.58–§4.65 and n4.194 for the question of the relationship of this inscription, and of the somewhat later "Nestor's cup" inscription, to the Homeric poems.

110 To explain the monumental scale of the Homeric poems both Parry and Lord thought in terms of oral dictation; their experiments with living oral traditions in Yugoslavia have given the dictation theory legitimacy (Parry 1971:451; Lord 1960:124–128, 148–154). Janko 1998 is among those who have espoused the dictation theory more recently; Nagy 1999a, who rejects the theory, critiques Janko's argument. West 2000 also rejects the dictation theory, but he does so in order to assert the even more improbable theory of a completely literate Homer; cf. also West 2001:108.

111 At the Panathenaia a written text was a control on what the rhapsodes performed, and not a means enabling them to perform it; the rhapsodes were specialists in remembering their repertoire and did not need writing to achieve this; cf. Nagy 2002:15–16. Nagy's distinction between a "transcript" at this stage and a "script" two centuries or more later is to the point (for Nagy's evolutionary scheme of Homeric poetry see his 1996a:110, 2002:6). For the likelihood that writing was used to add a Panathenaic layer to the catalogue of heroines in *Odyssey* 11, see §2.157 above; control of what was henceforth to be included in Panathenaic performances was clearly the issue in this case, which directly concerned the Peisistratids. The role that writing may have played in the transmission of the Homeric poems before the Panathenaic stage is impossible to discern, but it too was probably far from a simple matter; cf. Cassio 2002:114.

112 I explain more fully my objections to the theory that writing was used to create the *Iliad* and the *Odyssey* below §4.57 and n4.191, n4.192, n4.193.

Panionic festival itself, which recurred at regular intervals, and thus provided the context for the poems to grow and develop over time: to borrow an image from another art, the regularly recurring festival provided the fixed loom on which the fabric of the two poems was woven. This, I think, was a completely oral process. The problem is to imagine how it took place.

§4.25 In historical times poets who performed at festivals competed for prizes. Poetry, like athletics, was a competition, and at some festivals there were contests in both pursuits. We take the agonistic nature of Greek culture for granted and do not consider any other model, even for the performance of the Homeric poems by rhapsodes at the Panathenaia. But does it not seem strange that the arena in which these rhapsodes competed, namely the performance of the Homeric poems, in the end produced a highly collaborative effort? I think that we must allow for the element of collaboration, however un-Greek it may seem at first, in the creation of the Homeric poems at the Panionia. The Panionic league itself was a collaboration of twelve cities, and I think that the Homeric poems served this collaboration.[113] We can hardly know how the poetic collaboration would have started, but surely a great poet was involved. This poet, I think, stood closest to Miletus, and thus knew all the traditions of the Neleids, Nestor's traditions above all. But I imagine that there was something spontaneous about the collaboration when it began, and so I think in terms of two great poets, each firing the imagination of the other. This second poet perhaps came from a different city of the league, perhaps Priene. Then too a third great poet could have been present from the start, perhaps from Colophon. What every one of these *aoidoí* could do, to judge by modern parallels, was to hear a song once and perform it as he heard it. Thus they would have listened to each other as they took turns developing and expanding traditional songs before an audience at the Panionia. Presumably the greatest poet among them was recognized as such by his peers, and this poet had the greatest influence on the development of the poems, but this too was a matter of degree: each of the poets would have been listened to as he contributed to the emerging design of the epics. And what were these epics? There had long been poems about a war at Troy, and some of these may already have been developed on a considerable scale by individual poets. I imagine that the poetic collaboration at Panionion

---

113 Greek society (especially archaic Greek society) was defined as agonistic by Burckhardt in *Griechische Kulturgeschichte* and Nietzsche in *Homer's Wettkampf*, but there is another side to the issue; for the current debate as to "competitive" versus "cooperative" values in Homer there are references in Haubold 2000:5n23. For the competitive aspect of Greek poetry see especially the work of Pagliaro (n4.94 above).

began with one such poem about Troy, namely the poem that featured the anger of the Thessalian hero Achilles. The tale of Odysseus was probably less developed when it too was incorporated into a combined performance at the Panionia. The poem about Odysseus was therefore more thoroughly shaped by the collaborative process than was the more traditional poem about the war at Troy.[114] If we ask which of the poets was responsible for making a poem about a *nóstos* the companion piece to a poem about the war at Troy, this must have been the poet from Miletus, for he knew all the epic traditions of *Néstōr*, who was the very personification of the *nóstos* tradition. This same poet would also have developed Nestor's role in the *Iliad* as we know it.

§4.26 As the poems took shape and established themselves at the center of the Panionia more poets may have been added to the effort. In the earlier stages of the poems' development the league itself may still have been in the process of development. The principle that evolved, I think, was that each city of the league should be represented in the collaborative effort, and that as new cities were added to the league the number of poets grew. In the end the league reached its canonical number of twelve cities, and at this point, I think, the number of poets who took part in the recurring performance of the Homeric poems was also, ideally, twelve.

§4.27 The number of books in the Homeric poems is a multiple of twelve, and this fact, I think, may reflect the final stage that the poetic collaboration reached.[115] It is not immediately clear how the book divisions would

---

114 The relationship between the two Sanskrit epics may be comparable: Smith 1980:73 contrasts the *Rāmāyaṇa* with the more traditional *Mahābhārata*: "It is rather as though the *Rāmāyaṇa* had been composed *in the manner of* an epic, rather than having evolved *as* an epic." Nagy 1996:45n66, referring to Smith's argument, suggests that "a similar argument could be developed about the Homeric *Odyssey* as opposed to the *Iliad*." This is my view precisely. For an illustration of the way in which the *Odyssey* may have been developed from local origins into its Panhellenic form see Marks 2003, whose argument uses the internal evidence of Homeric epic in combination with later sources.

115 Opinions as to the origin of the book divisions vary widely, from attributing them to Alexandrian librarians, to regarding them as organic and authentic. Van Sickle 1980:9–12 argues for a date between the third and first centuries BC, and Taplin 1992:285–286 thinks that the book divisions originated with Aristarchus; Mazon 1942:137–140, Broccia 1967, and Stanley 1993:249–261 are among those who regard the divisions as authentic. Stephanie West, who concludes that the book divisions are pre-Alexandrian, suggests that they go back to the fourth-century book trade (West 1967:18–25; cf. Pfeiffer 1968:115–116), and later proposes that the divisions originated in the sixth century for rhapsodes' performances at the Panathenaia (Heubeck et al. 1988–1992, vol. 1, 39–40). I would go back still further and trace the rhapsodes' practice in Athens, including the book divisions, to the Homeridai of Chios, and I see no reason why the book divisions cannot be wholly oral in origin (for the Homeridai as the likely source of the Panathenaic text, cf. Nagy 1992:48 and Graziosi 2002:205, and as the likely source of the Panathenaic rule, Nagy 2009:PI§§54,

have corresponded to performance.[116] I think that the *Odyssey*, which at
the start was probably less evolved than the *Iliad*, and which was therefore
more thoroughly shaped by the process of poetic collaboration, offers a clear
indication, especially in the first half of the poem. This half of the *Odyssey*
breaks naturally into three segments of four books each: the Telemachia
(1–4), the Phaeacian books (5–8), and the adventures of Odysseus (9–12). Now
four books multiplied by twelve, the ideal number of poets at the Panionia,
gives forty-eight books, or the complete *Iliad* and *Odyssey*. Can the rest of
the *Odyssey* and the *Iliad* also be broken into four-book segments, and were
these the basic units of performance? To consider the second question first,
a four-book unit of performance is in fact suggested by Odysseus's perfor-
mance in *Odyssey* 9–12, if this performance is regarded as the ideal epic
performance. But four books are a very long performance for one oral poet
to judge by modern parallels, where the usual performance is closer to one
book of Homer in length.[117] Even for the hero Odysseus, who can be expected
to surpass mortals of a later day in this pursuit as in others, the performance
is long, for he proposes to end it and go to sleep part way through his third
book. I suggest that four books are indeed the basic unit of performance, but
in the sense of a single sitting rather than of a single singer: I think that the
singers alternated book by book (thus it took four different singers to tell the
story told by Odysseus alone); each singer, ideally, would still have sung four
books of the combined *Iliad* and *Odyssey*, but not in sequence. As for the order
in which the poets performed, we can imagine any number of ways in which
that order might be determined, and indeed the basic principle here, I think,
was flexibility. The indispensable requirement to become one of the twelve
poets would have been the ability to perform the entire *Iliad* and *Odyssey* even
as the two poems continued to evolve; parts could thus change among singers

144–145, 166–167; for origins of the book divisions in the oral phase of the poems see below
in text). At some point the twenty-four letters of the Ionic alphabet were assigned to the
twenty-four books of both poems, and it has been suggested that this practice too goes
back to Homer (Goold 1960:289); but Ionic alphabets in the Homeric period varied from
twenty to twenty-six letters (see Taplin 1992:285), and use of the standard Ionic alphabet
to number the books doubtless began later. The primary factor in the number of books
is not the alphabet, but, as I will argue below, the number twelve and its multiples. West
1967:19n30 suggests something similar: "The use of the Ionic alphabet (instead of the deci-
mal-alphabetical system) is strange…, but intelligible if the twenty-four-fold division was
canonical."

116 There have been many attempts to correlate book divisions with performance; for a recent
treatment, see M. S. Jensen in Jensen et al. 1999:5–35, with comments by eleven other
scholars, 35–83.

117 M. S. Jensen in Jensen et al. 1999:25–26, citing Notopoulos 1964, Mazon 1942:138.

from one performance to the next, and probably would have done so. But the best poets surely kept control of the process, and if parts of the poems needed further development, the best poets would have undertaken to develop them in performance, and all would have taken note of the new state of the song. One poet was doubtless regarded as the best of all, and that poet would have exercised the greatest influence over the ongoing development of the poems. The poems would have continued to be refined further and further by this process as long as it continued.

§4.28 A performance, in the sense of a sitting, would have been devoted to a single segment of the story. Can the Homeric poems in fact be broken up into a series of four-book segments? The test is to see if we can determine a simple narrative purpose, within the overall narrative purpose of each poem, to each such four-book segment, for each individual performance (i.e. each individual sitting) must have had its own story to tell.[118] For the *Odyssey* the four-book scheme fits perfectly, for each of the poem's resulting six segments has its own rather simple story to tell.[119] Books 1–4 begin with Telemachus in Ithaca and take him as far as Sparta in search of his father. Books 5–8 begin with Odysseus on Calypso's island and take him as far as the Phaeacians, with whom he engages. In Books 9–12 Odysseus tells the Phaeacians how he once got from Troy to Calypso's island, where he stayed until his release only shortly before. In Books 13–16 Odysseus and Telemachus both return to Ithaca and are reunited; this segment ends when father and son, now reunited, go to sleep in the swineherd's hut. In Books 17–20 Odysseus, known only to his son, enters his own palace and meets with his own wife. In Books 21–24 Odysseus slays the suitors and reclaims his wife and kingdom. Each of these segments is well defined and thus well suited for a separate performance, each performance perhaps taking place on a separate day. Odysseus gives his own four-book performance after an evening feast, and we might also imagine this at the festival of the Panionia. With a performance of four books each evening the *Odyssey* would have taken six days to complete.

§4.29 A second test to decide whether the six segments can be separated from each other by intervals between performances is to look more closely at the junctures between the segments. Ideally a segment should reach the end of its own theme and prepare the way for the next segment's theme; in some cases this preparation for the next segment might involve suspense in

---

118 Episodes in serial dramas are constructed on this principle, but in these (I think of television serials) an overall structure is usually weak or lacking.

119 See n4.123 below for a similar analysis in Thornton 1970.

order to raise the audience's expectations for the next night's performance. Books 1–4 end with Telemachus in Sparta, and here there is indeed suspense, but it is long-range suspense: the narrative will not return to Telemachus in Sparta until Book 15, which is in the fourth segment of the poem and thus three days off in terms of performance. We might say that here the audience is left in suspense not for the sake of the next night's performance, but for the sake of the poem's overall development. In Books 5–8 Odysseus takes center stage, and enormous suspense is raised at the end of Book 8 when Alcinous asks Odysseus why he weeps when he hears of Troy. Alcinous's final question to Odysseus is whether he lost some companion "equal to a brother" at Troy. This, I think, was a significant question to leave not only for Odysseus to answer in the next performance, but also for the Homeric audience to ponder in the interval before the next performance.[120] The next segment begins with Odysseus's reply to Alcinous, in the course of which he reveals his identity and proceeds to tell his whole story. The opening of Book 9 is the reply to a question at the end of Book 8, and it thus follows the end of Book 8 without any break in terms of narrative time. But for this very reason a pause—a highly dramatic pause—would be effective; thus I think that the next performance, after a day's interval, could well begin: "Odysseus spoke to him in reply" (*Odyssey* 9.1–4):

---

120 See §2.129 above on the passage concluding *Odyssey* 8 (*Odyssey* 8.577–586):

εἰπὲ δ' ὅ τι κλαίεις καὶ ὀδύρεαι ἔνδοθι θυμῷ
Ἀργείων Δαναῶν ἠδ' Ἰλίου οἶτον ἀκούων.
τὸν δὲ θεοὶ μὲν τεῦξαν, ἐπεκλώσαντο δ' ὄλεθρον
ἀνθρώποισ', ἵνα ᾖσι καὶ ἐσσομένοισιν ἀοιδή.
ἤ τίς τοι καὶ πηὸς ἀπέφθιτο Ἰλιόθι πρό,
ἐσθλὸς ἐών, γαμβρὸς ἢ πενθερός; οἵ τε μάλιστα
κήδιστοι τελέθουσι μεθ' αἷμά τε καὶ γένος αὐτῶν.
ἤ τίς που καὶ ἑταῖρος ἀνὴρ κεχαρισμένα εἰδώς,
ἐσθλός; ἐπεὶ οὐ μέν τι κασιγνήτοιο χερείων
γίνεται, ὅς κεν ἑταῖρος ἐὼν πεπνυμένα εἰδῇ.

Tell me why you weep and grieve in your heart
when you hear the fate of the Argive Danaans and Troy.
The gods made that fate, and spun out destruction
for men, so that there might be a song for those to come.
Did some kinsman by marriage die at Troy,
one who was a good man, a son-in-law or father-in-law? These
are the closest ties after one's own blood and family.
Or was it some companion who knew pleasing things,
a good man? Since in no way inferior to a brother
is one who, being a companion, knows wise things.

τὸν δ' ἀπαμειβόμενος προσέφη πολύμητις Ὀδυσσεύς·
"Ἀλκίνοε κρεῖον, πάντων ἀριδείκετε λαῶν,
ἦ τοι μὲν τόδε καλὸν ἀκουέμεν ἐστὶν ἀοιδοῦ
τοιοῦδ', οἷος ὅδ' ἐστί, θεοῖσ' ἐναλίγκιος αὐδήν."

Answering him very wily Odysseus said:
"King Alcinous, most exalted of all your people,
this is a fine thing, to listen to a singer
such as this one is, like the gods in voice."

All that need be remembered from the previous performance for these lines to open the next performance is that Alcinous asked Odysseus why he weeps at the mention of Troy. The audience already knows the answer to this question; they only need to hear Odysseus himself say it—indeed they are waiting to hear him say it. The long delay in Odysseus's revelation of his identity, which has continued throughout the latter half of the second performance (Books 7 and 8), would be reinforced by the break before the beginning of the third performance, and such added suspense seems entirely appropriate.[121] Odysseus's speech is in many ways the centerpiece of the *Odyssey*, and

---

121 The reference for the demonstrative pronoun τόν in the first line of Book 9 is made clear by the vocative Ἀλκίνοε in the next line. The opening of *Odyssey* 21, which begins another four-book segment of the poem, is similar: the feminine demonstrative pronoun τῇ in the first line is made clear by the name Penelope in the next line (*Odyssey* 21.1–2):

τῇ δ' ἄρ' ἐπὶ φρεσὶ θῆκε θεὰ γλαυκῶπις Ἀθήνη,
κούρῃ Ἰκαρίοιο, περίφρονι Πηνελοπείῃ....

To her the goddess grey-eyed Athena put it in mind,
to Ikarios's daughter, wise Penelope....

The opening of Book 21 differs from the opening of Book 9 in that Penelope is not mentioned at the end of the previous book, but only in the new book. Such a transition to a new subject by way of a demonstrative pronoun is not uncommon. A similar change of subject to Penelope occurs in *Odyssey* 18.157–160 (the suitor Amphinomos is the subject in line 157):

ἂψ δ' αὖτις κατ' ἄρ' ἕζετ' ἐπὶ θρόνου ἔνθεν ἀνέστη.
τῇ δ' ἄρ' ἐπὶ φρεσὶ θῆκε θεὰ γλαυκῶπις Ἀθήνη,
κούρῃ Ἰκαρίοιο, περίφρονι Πηνελοπείῃ,
μνηστήρεσσι φανῆναι.

He sat back down on the chair from which he rose.
To her the goddess grey-eyed Athena put it in mind,
to Ikarios's daughter, wise Penelope,
to appear to the suitors.

it needs to be closely connected both with what precedes it and what follows it. This has to do with his Phaeacian audience in both cases. The power of Odysseus's story is such that after it his Phaeacian audience is spellbound (*Odyssey* 13.1–4):

ὣς ἔφαθ', οἱ δ' ἄρα πάντες ἀκὴν ἐγένοντο σιωπῇ,

κηληθμῷ δ' ἔσχοντο κατὰ μέγαρα σκιόεντα.

τὸν δ' αὖτ' Ἀλκίνοος ἀπαμείβετο φώνησέν τε·

"ὦ 'Οδυσεῦ...."

So he spoke, and they all fell into a hushed silence
and were held by a spell in the shadowy hall.
And then Alcinous anwered him and said:
"O Odysseus...."

If a pause in performance followed Odysseus's story these lines at the beginning of the next performance may at first seem to lack a point of reference. I suggest instead that the phrase ὣς ἔφαθ', "thus he spoke," was enough to evoke the entire performance of the previous evening, and that the new opening, as it continues, gives expression to the spell that must have been cast over the Homeric audience itself in the interval since the previous performance; the Homeric audience would thus find itself mirrored by the Phaeacian audience, and this effect too, I think, was by design insofar as the Phaeacian audience represented the Homeric audience. I have already commented that at the end of the next four-book segment (the fourth segment) Odysseus and Telemachus, reunited in Ithaca, fall asleep in the swineherd's hut (*Odyssey* 16.481); this brings to a fitting conclusion the reunion of father and son that is this segment's basic theme. The next segment begins with the dawn of a new day, which lasts through more than three of this segment's four books.[122] By the end of this segment, in which the disguised Odysseus enters his palace and meets with his wife, the suitors have insulted Odysseus as they insulted

---

As regards the demonstrative pronoun, then, the opening of *Odyssey* 9 is not abrupt but follows a pattern of epic composition. The point remains, of course, that Odysseus in Book 9 replies (ἀπαμειβόμενος) to something just said, and this must be regarded as striking and unusual if it is the start of a new performance.

122 The day that begins at *Odyssey* 17.1 finally ends at *Odyssey* 20.91, when a new day dawns. In this segment of the poem the action continues through day and night and then into the next day: when Odysseus finally sleeps in *Odyssey* 20.54, Penelope remains awake and prays to Artemis; when dawn then appears Odysseus reawakens and hears Penelope, who is still awake and weaping (*Odyssey* 20.91–92).

Telemachus at the beginning of the poem, and the seer Theoklymenos, foreseeing the suitors' doom, has left the palace (*Odyssey* 20.363–372). This segment ends on a note of high suspense, as the suitors prepare a feast, and the poet comments that sweet as this feast was none could have proved less pleasing for the suitors (*Odyssey* 20.390–394):

δεῖπνον μὲν γὰρ τοί γε γελώοντες τετύκοντο
ἡδύ τε καὶ μενοεικές, ἐπεὶ μάλα πόλλ' ἱέρευσαν·
δόρπου δ' οὐκ ἄν πως ἀχαρίστερον ἄλλο γένοιτο,
οἷον δὴ τάχ' ἔμελλε θεὰ καὶ καρτερὸς ἀνὴρ
θησέμεναι· πρότεροι γὰρ ἀεικέα μηχανόωντο.

They laughed as they prepared their meal,
which was sweet and satisfying to the spirit, since they had
    slaughtered many animals.
But no other meal would in any way be less pleasing than the
    one
which the goddess and the strong man were about to
make; for the suitors were first to devise unseemly deeds.

This ending prepares for the final performance, which might be entitled simply φόνος, "slaughter." At the beginning of Book 21 Penelope, through Athena's prompting, thinks of the archery contest, and this is in fact called φόνου ἀρχή, "the beginning of the slaughter" (*Odyssey* 21.1–4):

Τῇ δ' ἄρ' ἐπὶ φρεσὶ θῆκε θεὰ γλαυκῶπις Ἀθήνη,
κούρῃ Ἰκαρίοιο, περίφρονι Πηνελοπείῃ,
τόξον μνηστήρεσσι θέμεν πολιόν τε σίδηρον
ἐν μεγάροισ' Ὀδυσῆος, ἀέθλια καὶ φόνου ἀρχήν.

The goddess grey-eyed Athena put in the mind
of wise Penelope, the daughter of Ikarios,
to place for the suitors the bow and the grey iron
in the halls of Odysseus, a contest and the beginning of the
    slaughter.

After dealing with the suitors Odysseus reclaims his wife and defends his kingdom, and with this the poem ends.

§4.30 The *Odyssey*, I think, meets the tests that we have set for the division of the poem into six separate performances. As proposed earlier, these six performances may be imagined as taking place on six successive evenings of the Panionia—the last six evenings. On the first six evenings of the Panionia, I now further propose, the *Iliad* was performed. But can the *Iliad*, by the same tests that we applied to the *Odyssey*, also be broken into six four-book segments? I reiterate that the *Iliad* probably had an older and more highly developed tradition that did the *Odyssey*, but in spite of this I think that the six-segment scheme works very well for the *Iliad* too. Let us examine the six four-book segments, asking the same question that we asked of the *Odyssey*: within the overall story of the *Iliad* does each segment have its own story to tell, and would each separate story have made a good evening's entertainment? Somewhat more needs to be said of the *Iliad* than of the *Odyssey* to make the case, but the criteria are the same.[123]

§4.31 Books 1–4 are all introductory. Book 1 introduces the specific theme of the *Iliad*, the wrath of Achilles, and Books 2–4 broaden the context of the poem to the war at Troy as a whole: Book 2, the Catalogue of Ships, tells who fought in the war; Book 3, the duel between Menelaus and Paris with Helen looking on, dramatizes the cause of the war; Book 4, in which a Trojan breaks the truce of Book 3, repeats the Trojan perfidy that began the war. Book 4 ends with a return to battle: here for the first time in the poem the two armies actually clash. The stage is thus set for a full-scale battle in the second segment.

---

123 I was unaware when I wrote this analysis of the *Iliad* into four-book segments that in 1965 J. A. Davison had proposed the same thing, and that in 1970 and 1984 Agathe Thornton had substantially developed Davison's idea. Davison, arguing against the possibility of large-scale interpolation in the post-Homeric *Iliad*, proposed the six four-book segments as likely units of performance on the basis of numbers alone: unlike the individual books of the *Iliad*, which vary considerably in length, the four-book segments are more even in length (Davison 1965:23–25). Following Davison Thornton noted an indentical structural principle in the *Odyssey* on the basis of both numbers and content (Thornton 1970 xiii–xiv, 120–128); Thornton later turned her attention to the *Iliad*, which, again following Davison, she analyzed into six performance units on the basis of content (Thornton 1984:46–63). While giving all due credit to Davison for discovering the principle at issue and to Thornton for developing a case for it, I have thought it best to leave my own original analysis unchanged. Thornton's more detailed analysis of the *Iliad*'s content may be compared with my own, which is independent of it, but which is in substantial agreement with it. For the lengths of the four-book segments of both poems see n4.134 below. A point of particular interest to me in Davison's argument is his view that each segment would have been performed by four different poets, and that the individual books have to do with this division of labor. I have come to the same conclusion. The main point in which I differ from Davison is that I do not assume that writing played any part in the creation of the poem(s).

§4.32 In Books 5–8 Zeus sets in motion his plan to honor Achilles by giving the Trojans the upper hand in battle. The balance begins to shift in this segment, for the Achaeans have the upper hand at first, but at the end of the segment the Trojans fight on equal terms with the Achaeans, and are even able to camp outside their walls for the first time. The key figure in this section is Diomedes, who is most able to carry the fight to the Trojans now that Achilles is gone: if Diomedes is subdued, no other Achaean will prevail. In Book 5, teamed with the war goddess Athena, Diomedes has his way with the Trojans; but in Book 8, teamed with Nestor, Diomedes has a very different outcome: Zeus hurls a thunderbolt in front of Diomedes' horses and warns him off any attempt to take Troy by himself.[124] Zeus also warns Athena off in Book 8 when she arms with Hera to help the Achaeans. These reversals from Book 5 to Book 8 frame this segment, which ends, after further fluctuations in the battle, with the

---

124 Diomedes' central role in the second segment of the the poem is foreshadowed near the end of the first segment, when Agamemnon reviews the troops and chides Diomedes for being a lesser warrior than his father (*Iliad* 4.370–400). Unlike his companion Sthenelos, Diomedes takes Agamemnon's chiding in good part (*Iliad* 4.401–421), and this foreshadows his role in the second segment: on the one hand he will soon demonstrate his valor with deeds rather than words; on the other hand there are limits to what he can do, as the scene with Agamemnon, with its negative comparison of Diomedes to Tydeus, seems to suggest. Diomedes' role in this segment also has an intermediate stage: in Book 6 he refuses to fight with Glaukos the Lycian because they are ancestral guest friends. Broccia 1967:86 finds Diomedes' role in this episode so different from his role in Book 5 that he regards the episode as an addition ("aggiunta") rather than as part of the conception of Book 5. But if Books 5–8 feature an overall reversal in Diomedes' role, as suggested above, Book 6 fits well as the neutral stage between his onslaught in Book 5 and his retreat in Book 8 (even in Book 5 Diomedes does not have his way completely with the Trojans: Aeneas escapes him with Apollo's help, just as he later escapes Achilles). Broccia's idea of an "aggiunta" is meant to illustrate his theory that the *Iliad* was expanded to monumental proportions by rhapsodes in competition, each building on what the previous singer had sung, without any *a priori* design; but I would view any such "addition" from the standpoint of the development of Books 5–8 as a separate performance, and in this there was a design in terms of the segment's basic action. In the confrontation between Glaukos and Diomedes in Book 6, an Ionian audience would have been much interested in Glaukos's Greek descent from Sisyphos, given the statement in Herodotus 1.147 that some Ionians took Cauconian Pylians as their kings, other Ionians took Lycian descendants of Glaukos as their kings, and still others took kings of both origins. As an ancestor of some of the Ionians Glaukos was the perfect opponent for Diomedes *not* to fight. To me this speaks of an overall design in the segment. It may be noted that Herodotus 2.116.3 refers to *Iliad* 6.289–292 as ἐν Διομήδεος Ἀριστηίη, "in the Aristeia (Prowess) of Diomedes"; this name is usually applied only to Book 5, and Herodotus seems to have extended it to this part of Book 6, where the Trojan women pray to Athena to stop Diomedes, offering her a particular gift. One wonders if the name could have been used of the entire segment Books 5–8, but I think not: while the focus on Diomedes would have been appropriate for the entire segment, his *aristeía* in the first part of the segment turns into a retreat by the end of the segment.

Trojans encamped outside their city walls. The beautiful simile that ends this segment, comparing the Trojans' campfires on the plain to the multitude of stars in heaven, is an impressive end to this poetic performance, if that is what it is.[125] The other important events in Books 5–8 essentially highlight the central place of Achilles in the *Iliad*, even in his absence: the meeting of Hector and Andromache in Book 6, which foreshadows Hector's death and Troy's destruction, keeps the decisive role of Achilles present despite his absence; in Book 7 the duel between Hector and Ajax, the greatest defensive warriors on either side, ends in a draw, and this likewise bodes ill for Hector, who must ultimately face a greater warrior than Ajax in Achilles. Until Achilles returns, however, the Trojans will fight with the Achaeans on at least even terms, as Hector does in his duel with Ajax, and as the Trojan army does before it camps for the night outside the walls of Troy.

§4.33 The simile at the end of Book 8, evoking the majesty of the night sky, was a good place to pause to await the next night's performance, for the next segment, Books 9–12, begins with two episodes set in this night filled with enemy campfires: the embassy to Achilles in Book 9, which fails, and the night raid in Book 10, which succeeds.[126] This segment too has a dramatic conclusion, marking a further stage in Zeus's plan to honor Achilles: at the end of Book 12 Hector breaches the Achaean wall and the Achaeans are forced back as far as they can go, to their very ships.[127] The breach of the

---

125 The end of Book 8 is considered a major break in the performance of the *Iliad* by Heiden 1996, who divides the *Iliad* into three units for performance (the end of Book 15 is the second major break in Heiden's scheme). The end of Book 8 and the beginning of Book 9 happen to contain an instance of "Zielinski's law" in that the assembly called by the Trojans (*Iliad* 8.489–541) and the assembly called by the Achaeans (*Iliad* 9.9–78) presumably occur at the same time (cf. Cantieni 1942:36).

126 I think that Book 10 belonged to the *Iliad* from the start and that the ancient notice that it was composed separately by Homer and interpolated into the *Iliad* by Peisistratos is not to be trusted (scholia to the beginning of *Iliad* 10: φασὶ τὴν ῥαψῳδίαν ὑφ' Ὁμήρου ἰδίᾳ τετάχθαι καὶ μὴ εἶναι μέρος τῆς Ἰλιάδος, ὑπὸ δὲ Πεισιστράτου τετάχθαι εἰς τὴν ποίησιν, "They say that this rhapsody was placed on its own by Homer and was not part of the *Iliad*, but that it was placed in the poem by Peisistratos"). If Book 10 has much in common with the *Odyssey*, that, in my view, is no argument against its having been composed at the Panionia. Cf. Hainsworth 1993:151–155 and n4.104 above. In a full-scale study of the subject Dué and Ebbott 2010 attribute differences between Book 10 and other parts of the *Iliad* to differences in theme, and this, I think, is the right approach; the narrower question is to what extent Book 10 has the *Odyssey* in view.

127 The Achaean wall, which figures prominently in the battle of the third segment, is hastily constructed part way through the second segment (*Iliad* 7.436–441). The ending of Book 12, where Hector breaches the wall, is a dramatic highpoint: nowhere does Hector appear more menacing than here, as he leaps through the breach with fire in his eyes. After he smashes the gate with a huge stone, the book ends as follows (*Iliad* 12.462–471):

Achaean wall marks a definite stage in Zeus's plan to tip the balance in favor of the Trojans; unlike the end of the second segment, where the Trojans fight on equal terms with the Achaeans, they now have the upper hand. From the Achaean standpoint the episodes in this segment can all be viewed as attempts to deal with the loss of Achilles. Like the embassy of Book 9, the wall in Book 12 proves to be a vain attempt to deal with Achilles' absence. More hopeful for the Achaeans are the successful night raid of Book 10 and, in Book 11, Nestor's appeal to Patroclus to take Achilles' place in battle.

§4.34 In Books 13–16 the battle is carried to the Achaeans' ships, where a defeat will mean disaster for the Achaeans themselves. This dire point is nearly reached in Book 16, when Hector, spurred on by Zeus, sets fire to one of the ships.[128] In Book 16, however, Patroclus takes Achilles' place in battle and drives the Trojans back to the walls of Troy, where he is then slain by Apollo. This segment ends with the death of Patroclus, which will bring Achilles himself back into battle in the next segment. This segment, in its own right,

> ὃ δ' ἄρ' ἔσθορε φαίδιμος Ἕκτωρ
> νυκτὶ θοῇ ἀτάλαντος ὑπώπια· λάμπε δὲ χαλκῷ
> σμερδαλέῳ, τὸν ἕεστο περὶ χροΐ, δοιὰ δὲ χερσὶ
> δοῦρ' ἔχεν· οὔ κέν τίς μιν ἐρύκακεν ἀντιβολήσας
> νόσφι θεῶν ὅτ' ἐσᾶλτο πύλας· πυρὶ δ' ὄσσε δεδήει.
> κέκλετο δὲ Τρώεσσιν ἑλιξάμενος καθ' ὅμιλον
> τεῖχος ὑπερβαίνειν· τοὶ δ' ὀτρύνοντι πίθοντο.
> αὐτίκα δ' οἳ μὲν τεῖχος ὑπέρβασαν, οἳ δὲ κατ' αὐτὰς
> ποιητὰς ἐσέχυντο πύλας· Δαναοὶ δὲ φόβηθεν
> νῆας ἀνὰ γλαφυράς, ὅμαδος δ' ἀλίαστος ἐτύχθη.

> Shining Hector leapt in,
> his face like swift night. He shone with the terrible bronze
> that he had put on around his body, and he had
> two spears in his hands; no one meeting him but the gods would have stopped him
> when he sprang inside the gates; his eyes were ablaze with fire.
> Turning around in the throng he called out to the Trojans
> to go over the wall; and they listened as he urged them on.
> Straightaway some went over the wall, and some poured in
> through the well-built gates; the Danaans fled
> through the hollow ships, and an inescapable din arose.

This is a highly suspenseful place to leave the audience at the end of one performance, with a full day to wait for the next performance; it deserves the name cliff-hanger.

128 Zeus literally pushes Hector forward in *Iliad* 15.694–695 (τὸν δὲ Ζεὺς ὦσεν ὄπισθε / χειρὶ μάλα μεγάλῃ, "Zeus pushed him from behind with his very large hand"), and the book ends in suspense, as Ajax, beleaguered by the Trojans, does not give way but continues to ward off fire from the ships (*Iliad* 15.743–746). In Book 16 Hector finally cuts Ajax's sword in two and sets fire to a ship, and the poet invokes the Muses to tell this part of the story (*Iliad* 16.112–124). The increased intensity at this point serves the story of Patroclus, whom Achilles sends into battle when he sees the fire in the ship (*Iliad* 16.124–129).

tells a very dramatic story: at the moment of greatest danger to the Achaeans Patroclus enters battle and saves them, but he pays for this with his life. It is worth noticing how the story in this segment is developed for its own sake. The preceding segment ended with great suspense as Hector crashed through the Achaean wall with fire in his eyes. When the narrative continues the great intensity of the preceding segment is immediately diminished, for it will take more than three books before Hector actually sets fire to one of the Achaean ships. Events must develop at their own pace in this new segment, and a slower pace is brought about by having Zeus become distracted. This happens most notably in Book 14, when Hera seduces him, and Poseidon is thus able to intervene openly against Hector. But it also happens immediately at the start of the new segment. At the beginning of Book 13 Zeus shifts his attention to far-off, exotic peoples: the king of the gods, whose plan at Troy is well in hand at this point, seems to have other places on which he must keep an eye.[129] This immediate shift of focus, after the great suspense of the preceding segment, is classic narrative technique.[130] With Zeus distracted by other matters the battle can rage back and forth for three books before Hector sets fire to one of the ships and Patroclus enters the battle. The intensity builds

---

129 *Iliad* 13.1–9:

    Ζεὺς δ' ἐπεὶ οὖν Τρῶάς τε καὶ Ἕκτορα νηυσὶ πέλασσε,
    τοὺς μὲν ἔα παρὰ τῇσι πόνον τ' ἐχέμεν καὶ ὀϊζὺν
    νωλεμέως, αὐτὸς δὲ πάλιν τρέπεν ὄσσε φαεινὼ
    νόσφιν ἐφ' ἱπποπόλων Θρῃκῶν καθορώμενος αἶαν
    Μυσῶν τ' ἀγχεμάχων καὶ ἀγαυῶν Ἱππημολγῶν
    γλακτοφάγων Ἀβίων τε δικαιοτάτων ἀνθρώπων.
    ἐς Τροίην δ' οὐ πάμπαν ἔτι τρέπεν ὄσσε φαεινώ·
    οὐ γὰρ ὅ γ' ἀθανάτων τινα ἔλπετο ὃν κατὰ θυμὸν
    ἐλθόντ' ἢ Τρώεσσιν ἀρηξέμεν ἢ Δαναοῖσιν.

    When Zeus had brought the Trojans and Hector near the ships,
    he let them have hardship and toil beside them
    without pause, but he himself turned his shining eyes away,
    looking down on the land of horse-tending Thracians
    and close-fighting Mysians and proud milk-eating
    Horse-milkers and Abioi, the most just of men.
    No longer did he turn at all his shining eyes to Troy;
    for in his heart he did not expect any of the immortals
    to come and help the Trojans or Danaans.

    That this is simply a distraction is clear from the fact that Zeus is here checking up on a tribe that is called "the most just of men": clearly there can be no need of Zeus's intervention there.

130 Familiar to all is the cliff-hanger that ends "to be continued," and then resolves itself immediately in the next episode and goes off in a new direction.

gradually through the first three books of the segment and reaches a peak early in the fourth book, when fire is set to a ship, but this only sets the stage for the real climax of the segment, the *aristeía* and death of Patroclus in the rest of the fourth book.[131]

§4.35 The rest of the story of the *Iliad*, in which Achilles avenges the death of Patroclus, takes two segments to tell. The first segment, Books 17–20, ends with Achilles' re-entry into battle. But the climax of this battle, Achilles' defeat of Hector, occurs in the poem's final segment, Books 21–24. Thus the goal of Books 17–20 is an important moment in the poem, the return of Achilles to battle, but not the poem's climax.[132] The end of this segment

131 The Achaean wall, which marks a stage in the development of the story when it is breached at the end of Book 12, is put back in play in this segment: while Zeus sleeps the Trojans are driven back outside the wall, and when he awakens Apollo repeats Hector's earlier action, smashing the wall and leading the Trojans through again (*Iliad* 15.1–8, 360–366). The wall well illustrates the separate development of the story in the two segments.

132 The final confrontation between Achilles and Hector is anticipated in Book 20 only to be put off until the poem's final segment. When Achilles first enters battle (20.41–46), he wants Hector but does not yet find him (20.75–78), and Apollo sends Aeneas his way instead; this confrontation, which takes up the middle of the book (20.79–352), ends inconclusively when Poseidon saves Aeneas. When the two armies finally come to grips, Apollo warns Hector not to confront Achilles (20.375–378). Only now, toward the end of Book 20, does Achilles slay his first victims: he slays three victims (20.381–406) before Hector's brother Polydoros becomes his fourth victim, and this draws Hector himself into a confrontation with Achilles (20.407–423). The two heroes address each other and fight, but Athena renders Hector's spear-cast ineffectual, and Apollo rescues Hector from the battlefield as Achilles is about to slay him. Apollo's action pointedly contrasts with his role in the final confrontation between Hector and Achilles, when he will desert Hector. For now Achilles lets Hector go and turns to other victims, slaying ten more to end Book 20. Thus does Achilles enter battle for the first time in the *Iliad*. The final segment of the poem is closely connected with this segment, continuing virtually without break, and this, I think, is by design: Achilles is in pursuit of the fleeing Trojans at the end of Book 20, and Book 21 begins exactly there (*Iliad* 21.1–5):

Ἀλλ' ὅτε δὴ πόρον ἷξον ἐϋρρεῖος ποταμοῖο
Ξάνθου δινήεντος, ὃν ἀθάνατος τέκετο Ζεύς,
ἔνθα διατμήξας τοὺς μὲν πεδίον δὲ δίωκε
πρὸς πόλιν, ᾗ περ Ἀχαιοὶ ἀτυζόμενοι φοβέοντο
ἤματι τῷ προτέρῳ, ὅτε μαίνετο φαίδιμος Ἕκτωρ.

But when they reached the ford of the beautiful-flowing,
eddying Xanthos, whom immortal Zeus fathered,
he cut them asunder there, and he chased some to the plain
toward the city, where the Achaeans had fled in terror
the day before, when shining Hector raged.

No subjects are expressed to tell us who came to the river and who separated them from each other, pursuing some of them to the city and trapping others in the river, and this has made the division between Books 20 and 21 among the most problematic in the *Iliad*

573

raises anticipation for the final segment of the poem, and this, again, is consistent with the idea that each segment was performed separately. Let us now briefly consider Books 17–20 as a single unified piece. Following the death of Patroclus at the end of Book 16, Book 17 opens with the battle for his body: Hector and the Trojans strip his armor, but the Achaeans rescue his dead body. In Book 18 Achilles learns of his companion's death, but he cannot go into battle to avenge him until his armor, now in Hector's hands, is replaced; Book 18 ends with the fashioning of brilliant new armor for Achilles by Hephaistos. Book 19 brings Achilles back into the Achaean assembly for the first time since Book 1, and he and Agamemnon now end their quarrel; after the army eats (and Achilles abstains) all arm for battle. In Book 20 the two armies enter battle, and the gods likewise take sides for the conflict. Only toward the end of the book is first blood drawn, and Achilles draws it; by the end of the book Achilles has slain fourteen victims, and they are the only victims on either side. Book 20 is Achilles' re-entry into battle, and even the gods, whom Zeus gives permission to fight on either side at the beginning of the book, take seats and simply watch through the rest of the book. At the end of the book Achilles, who is compared to a forest fire, is in full cry. To reduce the action of the entire segment to a single theme, it is this: Achilles learns of Patroclus's death and enters battle to avenge him.

§4.36 In the poem's final segment, Books 21–24, the battle continues until Hector is slain in Book 22; in Book 23 Achilles celebrates the funeral of his now avenged companion Patroclus; in Book 24, finding his humanity again after his murderous rampage against the Trojans and his subsequent ravaging of Hector's dead body, Achilles ransoms Hector's body to his father Priam, and the *Iliad* reaches a fitting conclusion. As the last segment of the poem begins Achilles is utterly unstoppable, but he is finally contained and prevented from taking Troy against destiny by the intervention of the gods who sat by as spectators in the previous segment. The battle is cast in the most elemental terms when fire and water are pitted against each other in the persons of the river god Xanthos and the fire god Hephaistos. The intervention of the gods allows the Trojans to escape inside their walls, which Achilles cannot storm. But Achilles is allowed his last and most important victim, Hector, who does not escape inside Troy. By the end of the poem Achilles has overcome his anger against even this foe. To reduce the action of

---

(Broccia 1967:19–22 discusses this book division first, as one that in his view must have originated outside of performance); but for anyone following the poem so far there is no ambiguity, and the point, I think, is to maintain the intensity of Achilles' entry into battle: the final two segments of the poem work together in this.

this segment to a single theme, it is perhaps this: Achilles' anger, although it is fulfilled, is also contained, first by the intervention of the gods, and finally by a more internal process within Achilles himself. This is a resolution not only of the final segment of the poem, but of the poem as a whole.

§4.37 I have offered a preliminary analysis of both Homeric poems as a series of four-book segments that served as the basic units not only of performance but also of composition. To substantiate this idea I have paid attention to certain details of the poems and ignored other details. The real test of the idea will require more thorough analysis of each segment, as far as this can still be done, to see how each segment might have been developed as an individual unit of performance.[133] For my purposes, however, the results are positive enough to proceed with a scheme of twelve successive performances, each carried out by four poets, which together made up the *Iliad* and the *Odyssey*: these twelve performances, repeated periodically at the Panionia, were the only existence that the poems had when they were first created in the form that we know them.[134] To repeat my earlier metaphor, the fabric of the *Iliad* and the *Odyssey* was woven on the fixed loom of the Panionia. I am now prepared to describe this loom in somewhat more detail. I have suggested that the festival lasted twelve days. This may in fact be too long a time for participants in a *panḗguris* to be absent from home. If so the time can be reduced to six days by imagining two performances each day instead of one; just as Demodokos performs songs of Troy after two feasts on the same

133 One test case might begin with the study of Whitman and Scodel 1981. The authors have analyzed the close interrelationship of episodes in *Iliad* 13–15, some of which are repeated to convey simultaneous action (Zielinski's law). The analysis, I think, may provide an insight into how the action within this particular segment was developed. I would emphasize, however, that Book 16, to which the authors refer only tangentially, is part of the same segment. The proof of this is that the climax of the struggle in Books 13–15 does not occur until early Book 16, when Hector finally sets fire to an Achaean ship; this triggers the segment's true climax, Patroclus's entry into battle and eventual death. Given the onward thrust of the action from the end of Book 15, where a beleaguered Ajax continues to ward off fire from the ships, into Book 16, where Hector cuts Ajax's spear in two and sets fire to a ship (16.101–124), I disagree with Heiden 1996:19–22 that the end of Book 15 constitutes one of two major breaks in the performance of the *Iliad* (the other being at the end of Book 8; cf. n4.125 above); this seems to me to disregard the development of the story at the most basic level of action.

134 In the text of the Homeric poems as we have it the twelve four-book segments vary in length between 1757 lines (Books 5–8 of the *Odyssey*) and 2972 lines (Books 13–16 of the *Iliad*). Based on these figures the longest performance would have been 1.7 times as long as the shortest performance. The total lines for the six segments of the *Iliad* are as follows: Books 1–4: 2493; Books 5–8: 2485; Books 9–12: 2611; Books 13–16: 2972; Books 17–20: 2305; Books 21–24: 2827. For the *Odyssey* the totals are as follows: Books 1–4: 2222; Books 5–8: 1757; Books 9–12: 2233; Books 13–16: 2011; Books 17–20: 2032; Books 20–24:1855.

day, there could have been two performances of the *Iliad* and the *Odyssey* on
each day of the Panionia.[135] It is even possible to shorten the time to four days
by imagining three performances per day (Demodokos performs three songs
including the lay of Ares and Aphrodite in one day), but this would have
allowed time for little else given the scale of the poems; the festival must, I
think, have lasted at least six days, and this number seems acceptably short
from the standpoint of the participants' absence from home.[136] How often
the festival recurred we do not know even for the historical Panionia: for my
scheme to work the festival must have recurred at least yearly, since a four-
yearly festival could not have produced the *Iliad* and the *Odyssey*.[137] Even a
yearly festival may seem too infrequent for the creation of the poems, unless
we assume that the poets gathered before the festival and rehearsed for as
long as needed. Such a preliminary gathering of poets probably would have
been necessary even if the performances occurred more frequently than once
yearly, given the size of the poems and the number of poets involved.

135 After the daytime feast Demodokos sings the quarrel of Achilles and Odysseus (*Odyssey*
8.73–82); after the nighttime feast he sings the Trojan horse (*Odyssey* 8.499–520). On the
next day Demodokos sings an unspecified song after a daytime feast as Odysseus waits for
the sun to set and his voyage home to begin (*Odyssey* 13.27–28). Węcowski 2002 takes night-
time epic performance among the Phaeacians to be against their usual practice of retiring
with the sun; he interprets the provision made for nighttime feasting in the description
of Alcinous's palace (*Odyssey* 7.98–102) to be an intrusion from the poet's world, which
already featured the nighttime symposium, into the heroic world, in which days end at
sunset. But Odysseus's performance in Books 9–12, I suggest, has to do with contempo-
rary epic performance at a *panéguris* more than with the contemporary symposium.
Taplin 1992:29–30, 39–40 suggests that Homeric performances took place at night at the
Panathenaia and earlier festivals; cf. Ford 1997:88.
136 For the possibility that the Panathenaia lasted six days or more see n4.106 above. A six-day
celebration of the Panionia, allowing three days for the performance of the *Iliad* and three
days for the *Odyssey*, is in line with Wade-Gery's estimate that the *Iliad* took three days to
perform at a *panéguris* (Wade-Gery 1952:14–16, 69nn39–40, 70n42); the famous three-day
reading of the *Iliad* by the poet Ronsard may be an apt comparison (Wade-Gery 1952:16).
Davison 1965:23–25, who proposes that the performance of the *Iliad* was divided into
six four-book segments, imagines a three-day performance of two segments per day;
Thornton 1984:46–63, following Davison's scheme, imagines a performance either three or
six days in length, with only one segment per day in a six-day performance (1984:48, 58).
137 The Panathenaia was a yearly festival, but poetic contests occurred only at the Great
Panathenaia every fourth year (Lycurgus *Against Leocrates* 102 implies this). There is no
real parallel for the yearly poetic performances that I posit; I recognize this lack, but I add
that there is also no parallel for poems on the scale of the *Iliad* and *Odyssey*: more frequent
performances would have been necessary to create the poems at the Panionia than to recite
them at the Great Panathenaia. Quadrennial Greek festivals were mostly expanded versions
of annual festivals like the Panathenaia (see Ziehen *RE* 'Penteteris' 537–538). The Olympic
and Pythian games are exceptions; in both cases there is evidence that an eight-year cycle
preceded the four-year cycle (see Nilsson 1967:644–647; cf. Ziehen *RE* 'Penteteris' 539).

§4.38 Among the Phaeacians, who represent the Ionians, there are, in addition to feasts accompanied by song, games and dances.[138] There is no indication that games were part of the Panionia in historical times, but this would be a strange omission for the early period that concerns us. Alcinous says that the Phaeacians do not excel at games, apart from running, and it is hard to know what to conclude from this regarding the place of games at the Panionia. To me it seems likely that there were games, but that they were not the central feature of the festival; this, as among the Phaeacians, was rather banqueting and song.

§4.39 Games would of course have been competitive. Were poetic performances also competitive, as they later were at the Panathenaia and elsewhere? When poets from the twelve cities performed the *Iliad* and the *Odyssey*, they collaborated, but the situation would also have fostered competition: the audience was made up of citizens from all twelve cities, and while all were Panionians and interested in the poems' overall story, they were also citizens of individual cities with a keen interest in seeing their own city's poet perform, and perform well. There may not always have been twelve poets to perform the poems (only four were strictly necessary), but there would always have been pressure for a full twelve arising from the shame of those not represented by their own poet in the performance.

§4.40 The Homeric poems, I think, continued to evolve with each new performance at the Panionia. This process could have gone on indefinitely, with the poems reaching ever higher levels of refinement, but at some point the process stopped. Why? More than one explanation is possible for this, but among the more likely, I think, is that the Panionia continued for only a limited period of time before foreign pressure effectively destroyed it as the fixed loom on which the poems were created. Certainly when the Cimmerians under Lygdamis occupied Mykale for a period of years in the mid-seventh century BC the Panionia could not have been celebrated at all.[139] But foreign pressure may have ended the performance of the Homeric poems at the Panionia even earlier in the seventh century, when the Lydians under Gyges began to attack Ionian cities about 680 BC.[140] When the collaboration began

138 The games follow the daytime feast (*Odyssey* 8.97–255). After the games Demodokos performs the song of Ares and Aphrodite, which youths accompany with a dance (8.256–369); Alcinous's sons Halios and Laodamas then follow with a particularly athletic dance (8.370–380).
139 The Cimmerians occupied Mykale for at least three and as many as ten years; cf. n4.78 above on Welles 1934 no. 7.
140 The Homeric poems seem to be aware of the Lydians and Gyges. Achilles' first victim when he enters battle in *Iliad* 20 is from "under Mount Tmolos," an identifying feature of the later Lydian homeland (*Iliad* 20.381–385):

and how long it lasted is impossible to say without knowing more about the origins of the Panionic league, but I do not think that a long period of time was necessary to develop the poems to the state in which we know them; ten years or so was perhaps enough. But the poems may also have developed over a longer period if the Panionic league arose earlier in the eighth century BC than is now generally thought.[141]

ἐν δ' Ἀχιλεὺς Τρώεσσι θόρε φρεσὶν εἱμένος ἀλκὴν
σμερδαλέα ἰάχων, πρῶτον δ' ἕλεν Ἰφιτίωνα
ἐσθλὸν Ὀτρυντεΐδην πολέων ἡγήτορα λαῶν,
ὃν νύμφη τέκε νηῒς Ὀτρυντῆϊ πτολιπόρθῳ
<u>Τμώλῳ ὕπο νιφόεντι</u> Ὕδης ἐν πίονι δήμῳ.

Achilles leapt among the Trojans, having put on resoluteness in his heart,
shouting terribly, and he slew Iphition first,
Otryntes' noble son, the leader of many warriors,
whom a water nymph bore to city-sacking Otryntes
<u>beneath snowy Tmolos</u> in the rich land of Hyde.

Later geographers identified Hyde, Iphition's town, with the Lydian capital Sardis; cf. Leaf and Bayfield 1898 ad loc. When Achilles exults over his first victim he refers to his birth by the λίμνη Γυγαίη, the "Gygaean lake" (*Iliad* 20.389–392):

κεῖσαι Ὀτρυντεΐδη πάντων ἐκπαγλότατ' ἀνδρῶν·
ἐνθάδε τοι θάνατος, γενεὴ δέ τοί ἐστ' ἐπὶ <u>λίμνῃ</u>
<u>Γυγαίῃ</u>, ὅθι τοι τέμενος πατρώϊόν ἐστιν
Ὕλλῳ ἐπ' ἰχθυόεντι καὶ Ἕρμῳ δινήεντι.

You lie still, son of Otryntes, most violent of men;
here is your death, but your birth is by the <u>Gygaean lake,</u>
where your ancestral precinct is,
on the fish-filled Hyllos and the eddying Hermos.

The "Gygaean lake" is also mentioned in *Iliad* 2, in the Trojan catalogue, where it is in the territory of the Maeonians (*Iliad* 2.864–866):

Μῄοσιν αὖ Μέσθλης τε καὶ Ἄντιφος ἡγησάσθην
υἷε Ταλαιμένεος τὼ <u>Γυγαίη</u> τέκε <u>λίμνη</u>,
οἳ καὶ <u>Μῇονας</u> ἦγον <u>ὑπὸ Τμώλῳ</u> γεγαῶτας.

Mesthles and Antiphos led the Maeonians,
the sons of Talaimenes, whom the <u>Gygaean lake</u> bore;
they led the <u>Maeonians, born under Mount Tmolos.</u>

The Maeonians, "born under Mount Tmolos," are epic predecessors of the Lydians. The λίμνη Γυγαίη was perhaps not named for the famous king Gyges (cf. Kirk 1985 on *Iliad* 2.864–866: "The Gygaean lake...was presumably named after an ancestor of the famous Guges"), but the Homeric phrase seems at least to evoke the famous king. The Homeric phrase (which is found also in Herodotus) and the Maeonians are discussed further in EN4.8.

141 For the issue of the league's date of origin, cf. n4.90 above and §4.66–§4.71 below; it is perhaps more accurate to say that there is no current consensus as to date.

§4.41 When the regularly recurring performances at the Panionia came to an end the Homeric poems could no longer continue to evolve by the same process that had allowed their expansion on a monumental scale; in fact the poems could not continue to exist at all unless the poets who had created them continued to perform them in the final form that they had reached at the festival. But where would such performances have occurred if not at the Panionia? Although mainland Ionia came under increasing pressure from about 680 BC, the same was not true of the islands of Samos and Chios, which, protected by geography, remained free of Lydian domination even under Croesus in the mid-sixth century BC.[142] On both these islands schools of rhapsodes appeared at an early date: on Samos the Kreophyleioi, and on Chios the Homeridai. The Kreophyleioi preserved an epic about Heracles, the *Oikhalias Halosis*;[143] the Homeridai of Chios preserved the more prestigious tradition of

142 Herodotus 1.27 tells how Bias of Priene (or Pittacus of Mytilene) dissuaded Croesus from building ships and attempting to overthrow the islanders, convincing him that the islanders would welcome meeting Croesus in a sea battle, just as he would welcome meeting them in a land battle. Croesus thus gave up his plan to build a navy and instead made a pact of guest-friendship with the islanders: κάρτα τε ἡσθῆναι Κροῖσον τῷ ἐπιλόγῳ καί οἱ, προσφυέως γὰρ δόξαι λέγειν, πειθόμενον παύσασθαι τῆς ναυπηγίης. καὶ οὕτω τοῖσι τὰς νήσους οἰκημένοισι Ἴωσι ξεινίην συνεθήκατο, "Croesus was very pleased by the reasoning, and, being persuaded by him, for he seemed to speak to the point, he stopped building ships. And so he made a treaty of guest-friendship with the Ionians who inhabited the islands" (Herodotus 1.27.5).

143 See Burkert 1972:77nn13 and 15 for sources on the Kreophyleioi; particularly interesting in Burkert's study is his analysis of the debt that the *Oikhalias Halosis*, which Burkert dates to the seventh century BC (p. 82), owes to the Homeric poems in terms of themes and general style (pp. 82–85). Callimachus weighed the relative merits of the two traditions in a famous epigram on the *Oikhalias Halosis* (Callimachus *Epigrams* 6 Pfeiffer):

τοῦ Σαμίου πόνος εἰμὶ δόμῳ ποτὲ θεῖον ἀοιδόν
   δεξαμένου, κλείω δ' Εὔρυτον ὅσσ' ἔπαθεν,
καὶ ξανθὴν Ἰόλειαν, Ὁμήρειον δὲ καλεῦμαι
   γράμμα· Κρεωφύλῳ, Ζεῦ φίλε, τοῦτο μέγα.

I am the Samian's work, who once received the divine poet
   in his home; I celebrate Eurytos and all that he suffered,
and fair-haired Iole; I am called Homer's
   writing: for Kreophylos, by Zeus, this is a great thing.

Callimachus's judgment of the Samian tradition may be more negative than Burkert would have it. I note in particular the contrast in the first line between τοῦ Σαμίου, "the Samian," at the beginning of the line and θεῖον ἀοιδόν, "divine poet," at the end of the line: here, and again in the last line of the epigram, Homer is pointedly ranked above Kreophylos. Callimachus's judgment that the *Oikhalias Halosis*, although it is called Homeric, is in fact Kreophylos's work, must have to do with the poem's quality. Burkert (p. 76) thinks that the epigram hovers between appreciation and irony with respect to Kreophylos, but irony seems to me to predominate. Graziosi 2002:190 does not see irony in the epigram's tone of praise for the *Oikhalias*

the Homeric poems.[144] How did the Homeridai, on Chios, come into possession

---

Halosis, but her own discussion (Graziosi 2002:193, cf. also 193–200) is not inconsistent with such a reading. Strabo 14.1.18, who quotes the epigram to offset the story of Homeric author-ship, does not concern himself with the reasons behind Callimachus's judgment.

144 For the Homeridai as preservers of the *Iliad* and the *Odyssey* see EN4.6 to n4.98 above. For ancient sources and modern opinion concerning the Homeridai see Burkert 1972:79n20, who remarks that they are little more than a name for us, and for the ancient world as well; see also Allen 1924:42–50. Pindar *Nemean* 2.1–5 attests that the Homeridai were still rhapsodes in the fifth century; their performances, Pindar says in a comparison with his victor's achievement, often began with a hymn to Zeus:

Ὅθεν περ καὶ Ὁμηρίδαι
ῥαπτῶν ἐπέων τὰ πόλλ' ἀοιδοί
ἄρχονται, Διὸς ἐκ προοιμίου, καὶ ὅδ' ἀνήρ
καταβολὰν ἱερῶν ἀγώνων νικαφορίας δέδεκται πρῶτον, Νεμεαίου
ἐν πολυϋμνήτῳ Διὸς ἄλσει.

From the point that the Homeridai singers also
usually begin their stitched words,
from a prooimion of Zeus, this man too
has first received a foundation of victories in the holy games
in the much-hymned grove of Nemean Zeus.

The scholia to Pindar *Nemean* 2.1 say that the Homeridai were originally descendants of Homer who sang his poetry by inheritance: Ὁμηρίδας ἔλεγον τὸ μὲν ἀρχαῖον τοὺς ἀπὸ τοῦ Ὁμήρου γένους, οἳ καὶ τὴν ποίησιν αὐτοῦ ἐκ διαδοχῆς ἦδον. But later, the scholia continue, the rhapsodes no longer claimed Homer as an ancestor; one of these later rhapsodes was the Chian Kynaithos who, according to the scholia, composed the *Homeric Hymn to Apollo* about the end of the sixth century BC and attributed it to Homer: μετὰ δὲ ταῦτα καὶ οἱ ῥαψῳδοὶ οὐκέτι τὸ γένος εἰς Ὅμηρον ἀνάγοντες. ἐπιφανεῖς δὲ ἐγένοντο οἱ περὶ Κύναιθον, οὕς φασι πολλὰ τῶν ἐπῶν ποιήσαντας ἐμβαλεῖν εἰς τὴν Ὁμήρου ποίησιν. ἦν δὲ ὁ Κύναιθος τὸ γένος Χῖος, ὃς καὶ τῶν ἐπιγραφομένων Ὁμήρου ποιημάτων τὸν εἰς Ἀπόλλωνα γεγραφὼς ὕμνον ἀνατέθεικεν αὐτῷ. οὗτος οὖν ὁ Κύναιθος πρῶτος ἐν Συρακούσαις ἐραψῴδησε τὰ Ὁμήρου ἔπη κατὰ τὴν ξθ' Ὀλυμπιάδα, ὡς Ἱππόστρατός φησιν, "After this the rhapsodes no longer traced their ancestry [*génos*] to Homer. Those around Kynaithos were famous, who they say composed many verses and inserted them into the poetry of Homer. Kynaithos was a Chian by race, and of the poems claimed for Homer he wrote the hymn to Apollo and attributed it to Homer. This Kynaithos gave the first rhapsodic performance of the Homeric poems in Syracuse in the sixty-ninth Olympiad, so Hippostratos says." Whereas the scholia seem to report a reliable tradition when they say that the Homeridai of the late sixth century did not claim Homer as their ancestor, the first part of the statement, that the original Homeridai were Homer's offspring, is, I think, an erroneous inference from the name Homeridai itself (see next note). For Kynaithos see Burkert 1979 and cf. Nagy 2009:PI§§157–179, E§§84–89, 116, 118, 124; Nagy, PI§§174–176, E§86, argues that if the combined *Homeric Hymn to Apollo* was in fact commissioned by Polycrates to celebrate the *Púthia kaì Délia* (cf. n4.101 above), it was Kynaithos who performed this commission. Durante 1976:188n2 leaves open the possibility that Homeridai, though particularly associ-ated with Chios, were also found in other Ionian cities; whether or not this was the case in Colophon (see Pasquali 1913:88–92 on Nicander Ὁμήρειος), the Kreophyleioi of Samos should not be considered Homeridai (Rzach *RE* 'Homeridai' 2150 makes clear that the legendary Kreophylos is a very different creature from the Chian Homerid Kynaithos).

of the Homeric poems? I suggest that the same poets who created these poems at the Panionia remained together, in whole or in part, and continued to perform—and thus preserve—the poems in the relative tranquillity of Chios.[145] The name Homeridai, according to the interpretation of it that I accept, would have described this group of poets most aptly while they still *came together* from twelve different cities to perform at the festival of the Panionia.[146] If the poets were already called Homeridai when they performed at the Panionia, they would have brought with them to Chios not only the poems, which were part of their identity, but also their collective name, which was also distinctively theirs. But on Chios they did not have to "come together" as they had for the

145 If Chios rather than Samos became the home of the Homeric poems, Miletus perhaps had something to do with that; I note that whereas Miletus and Samos took different sides in the Lelantine war (cf. n4.64 above), Miletus and Chios remained allies throughout the early period: during Alyattes' repeated attacks on Miletus c. 600 BC none of the Ionian cities came to Miletus's aid except Chios, which did so to repay Miletus for help in Chios's earlier war with Erythrai (Herodotus 1.18.3; cf. n4.48 above). Huxley 1966:51 suggests that the war between Chios and Erythrai could have been part of the Lelantine war; this conflict between Chalcis and Eretria over the Lelantine Plain in Euboea became more widespread, with allies on both sides, and probably lasted many years, but the details are unknown (Thucydides 1.15.3 says that the rest of Greece took part in the war, but, as Huxley 1966:51 says, the problem is to find enough allies for each of the protagonists). If the Lelantine war began early enough and lasted long enough, it may have coincided with the period in which the Panionic league developed. Surely many local rivalries had to be overcome when the league came into being, and the conflict between Erythrai and Chios was perhaps one; Miletus and Samos may also have had to reconcile differences for the sake of the league. But differences doubtless remained in the long run, and these may have been a factor in the move of the Homeridai to Chios rather than Samos, where a rival guild of rhapsodes took root. For further consideration of the earliest development of the Panionic league see below n4.162 and §4.67. For the Lelantine war as possible background to this development see below §4.50–§4.51 and n4.174; Bearzot 1983:76 considers the war between Chios and Erythrai to be part of the Lelantine war, which, following Sordi 1958:42–51, she dates late (mid-seventh century BC; cf. n4.174 below for the problem of dating the Lelantine war).

146 I follow Durante 1957 (republished with modifications in Durante 1976:185–204) for the derivation and interpretation of the name. The essentials are as follows: The names Ὁμηρίδαι and Ὅμηρος, which belong to the same lexical series as e.g. the verb ὁμηρέω, "meet with" (*Odyssey* 16.468), derive from *som-, "together," and the root ar- of ἀραρίσκω, "join together, fasten" (the root vowel is lengthened in the compound forms by Wackernagel's Law, as in e.g. στρατηγός, "general" [root *ag- of ágō, "lead"], πανήγυρις, "festival" [cf. *ageíro*, "gather"]; Wackernagel 1889). A derivative form in *-ios*, Ὁμάριος, was the epithet of Zeus as god of a common festival of the Achaeans celebrated near Helike in Achaea; the neuter form Ὁμάριον designated that festival's site, literally "place of coming together." The association of the names *Homērídai* and *Hómēros* with festivals, based on Greek *Homários* and *Homárion*, is strongly supported by a Sanskrit comparison: Sanskrit *samará-*, "coming together, battle, festival reunion," is the exact cognate of Greek *Hómēros*, and the derivative form *samaryá-*, "battle, festival reunion, poetic contest," is the exact cognate of *Homários/Homárion*. Durante's proposal is discussed further in EN4.9.

Panionia, for they were now together permanently. In time, as the poems were passed from one generation of rhapsodes to the next, this guild of rhapsodes, which existed to preserve the Homeric poems, would have come to resemble a *génos*. At this stage the mythical figure of Homer, the supposed ancestor of the Homeridai and the creator of the *Iliad* and the *Odyssey*, presumably arose.[147] On Chios the poems no longer served the larger purpose for which they were created at the Panionia, but were preserved and passed on for their own sake.

§4.42 Chios, I think, was the point of diffusion for the Homeric poems; it was from there that they reached the rest of the Greek world. We do not know how soon this process began, but it was probably not long after the Homeridai established themselves on the island. Writing was not necessary to preserve the poems if the Homeridai, as rhapsodes, were dedicated to this very task; writing was also not needed to carry the poems abroad if other rhapsodes simply heard them performed by the Homeridai and remembered what they heard. Writing, I think, became important only in the next century at the Panathenaia, and not as an aid to performance even there, but as a control on the content and structure of the poems. The role that the Homeridai first played on Chios in safeguarding the tradition of the poems was later played in Athens by a written text.[148]

147 Cf. the scholia to Pindar *Nemean* 2.1, quoted n4.144 above. The earliest sources for the Homeridai as a *génos* are Acusilaus (early fifth century) and Hellanicus, both cited by Harpokration s.v. Ὁμηρίδαι· γένος ἐν Χίῳ, ὅπερ Ἀκουσίλαος ἐν γ᾽, Ἑλλάνικος ἐν τῇ Ἀτλαντιάδι ἀπὸ τοῦ ποιητοῦ φησιν ὠνομάσθαι, "Homeridai: a *génos* in Chios, which Akusilaos in the third book and Hellanicus in the *Atlantias* say was named from the poet."

148 For the Panathenaia see n4.111 above (cf. also n4.106 and n4.107 above). Albert Lord showed that a fully creative oral tradition does not maintain a song in a fixed form over time and drew the following conclusion for Homer (Lord 1970:18): "[The] dream of an Homeric *Iliad* and *Odyssey* preserved 'in oral tradition' in 'more or less' the same form over several generations is demonstrably false if the Greek tradition was in the first phase of oral tradition." In my view Homeric tradition was not still "in the first phase of oral tradition" when it fell to the Homeridai to preserve it (Powell 1991:189 quotes only the first part of Lord's statement to support his view of a written Homer; the second part of Lord's statement seems to me to be an important qualification, and one that Milman Parry also understood; cf. Parry 1971:337). It is possible that writing eventually became a factor in preserving the poems in the hands of the Homeridai on Chios, but I do not think that this is a necessary hypothesis. I should also emphasize that I do not exclude some variation in the tradition of the poems either among the early Homeridai or at the later Panathenaia, but I think that in both cases the limits of variation remained fairly narrow—how narrow is the question. Gregory Nagy has stressed the distinction between a written text and a progressively fixed text (cf. Nagy 1992:51: "There can be textuality—or better, textualization—without written text"; cf. also Nagy 1996:40). In Nagy's model the process of diffusion accounts for fixation: the more wide spread the poems became the more fixed they became. I would modify this model to allow the Homeridai a central role in the process of diffusion; it was through the Homeridai, who first fixed the poems, that the poems were spread.

§4.43 But the performance of the poems at the Panathenaia in the mid-sixth century BC was not the first that Athens had heard of the Homeric poems. Solon, as noted earlier, seems to have been well acquainted with the poems at the end of the seventh century BC, and others before him must also have known them.[149] I speculate that the poems reached Athens almost

---

149 I argued in n3.285 above that Solon fr. 4 West presents the Homeric view of Athena Polias, which differed markedly from the Athenians' traditional view of their own city goddess. But does Solon have specifically Homer in mind in his depiction of Athena Polias or epic tradition in general? Werner Jaeger argued that Solon fr. 4, in which Athena holds her protective hands over Athens but the Athenians destroy the city by their own stupidity, alludes to *Odyssey* 1.32–34, where Zeus says that men wrongly blame gods for evils brought on by themselves through their own recklessness (Jaeger 1926); a direct link here is possible but cannot be proved (cf. Mülke 2002:96). Maria Noussia (Noussia and Fantuzzi 2001:238) thinks a direct correspondence in language probable between fr. 4 and *Odyssey* 4, where Penelope's sister appears to Penelope in a dream and reassures her that Telemachus will be safe because he has Athena's protection (*Odyssey* 4.825–829):

θάρσει, μηδέ τι πάγχυ μετὰ φρεσὶ δείδιθι λίην·
<u>τοίη γάρ οἱ πομπὸς</u> ἅμ' ἔρχεται, ἥν τε καὶ ἄλλοι
ἀνέρες ἠρήσαντο παρεστάμεναι, δύναται γάρ,
<u>Παλλὰς Ἀθηναίη</u>· σὲ δ' ὀδυρομένην ἐλεαίρει·
ἥ νῦν με προέηκε τεῖν τάδε μυθήσασθαι.

Have courage, and do not at all fear overly much in your heart;
<u>for such an escort</u> goes with him, whom other men as well
have prayed to stand by their side, for she has the power,
<u>Pallas Athena</u>; she pities you in your grief;
it is she who has now sent me to tell you these things.

The resemblance to the opening of Solon fr. 4 West is striking:

ἡμετέρη δὲ πόλις κατὰ μὲν Διὸς οὔποτ' ὀλεῖται
αἶσαν καὶ μακάρων θεῶν φρένας ἀθανάτων·
<u>τοίη γὰρ</u> μεγάθυμος <u>ἐπίσκοπος</u> ὀβριμοπάτρη
<u>Παλλὰς Ἀθηναίη</u> χεῖρας ὕπερθεν ἔχει.

Our city will never be destroyed by the destiny of Zeus
and the will of the blessed immortals.
<u>For such a</u> great-hearted <u>guardian, Pallas Athena,</u>
the daughter of a mighty father, holds her hands over it.

A more general Homeric pattern is indicated by *Iliad* 4.390, where Athena's help for Tydeus in days past is expressed in similar terms (τοίη οἱ ἐπίρροθος ἦεν Ἀθήνη); the correspondence of the Solon passage can be with this passage as well. Noussia 2006:147–148 sees a similar correspondence in language and theme between Solon fr. 4a.1–2 West (Solon's *álgea*, "woes") and *Iliad* 24.522–523 and *Odyssey* 24.423 (cf. Vox 1984:53–54); Noussia 2002:496–503 attributes the phrase αἰπύν...οὐρανόν, "steep...sky," in Solon fr. 13.21–22 West to Solon's knowledge of an old variant (οὐρανὸν αἰπύν, "steep sky") reported by Zenodotus for the phrase οὐρανὸν εὐρύν, "wide sky," in *Iliad* 3.364 and 15.192. Irwin 2005:113–153 detects an "Odyssean-stance" in Solon's poetry, which she connects with his political activity, especially regarding Salamis; the case that she makes is persuasive in my view. For further discussion of Homeric reception at an early period see below n4.209 and n5.59.

immediately after they took root on Chios, and that even earlier they may
have begun to be known in Athens directly from the Panionia: Athens, after
all, was one of the two keys to Panionian identity (Pylos was the other), and
this must have given the city a special status with respect to both the festival
and the poems. The Kodrid myth, which underlies the Phaeacians' identity
in the *Odyssey*, begins with the brothers Neileos and Medon, who gave rise to
the ruling families of Miletus and Athens, the Neleids and the Medontids. We
know very little about the Medontids.[150] The only name that stands out in this
line of rulers is Hippomenes, whose cruelty toward his own daughter brought
about the end of the Medontid dynasty.[151] Hippomenes was closely associated

150 Cf. n4.5 above. For the pedigree of the Medontidai see Jacoby, commentary on Hellanicus
     FGrHist 323a F 23, pp. 43–51. Jacoby, p. 51, argues that Hellanicus first constructed a pedi-
     gree for this dynasty as part of a list to fill the gap between the Ionian migration in Medon's
     time and the first annual archon in 683/2 BC; Jacoby even regards the last Medontid ruler,
     Hippomenes, about whom there was an actual tradition (see below n4.151 and n4.152),
     as having been made a Medontid only secondarily (see n4.152 below). There was further
     manipulation of the Medontid tradition by democratic authors, who made the Medontidai
     archons rather than kings; details of the democratic scheme are discussed in EN4.10. While
     there is little actual history of the Medontidai (Hippomenes may be the exception), there
     is epigraphic evidence of a phratry named Medontidai, and a *génos* of this name may still
     have existed in the fifth century BC; the evidence is discussed in EN4.10.
151 See Jacoby, commentary on Hellanicus *FGrHist* 323a F 23, p. 45 and n29, for sources and vari-
     ants of the story. An excerpt from Aristotle's *Constitution of the Athenians* (Aristotle fr. 611.1
     Rose = Heraclides Lembus 371.1 Dilts) says that kings were no longer chosen from the Kodrids
     because the Kodrids had become weak and effeminate, but that Hippomenes tried to remove
     this charge by killing his daughter and an adulterer in gruesome fashion: ἀπὸ δὲ Κοδριδῶν
     οὐκέτι βασιλεῖς ᾑροῦντο διὰ τὸ δοκεῖν τρυφᾶν καὶ μαλακοὺς γεγονέναι. Ἱππομένης δὲ εἷς
     τῶν Κοδριδῶν βουλόμενος ἀπώσασθαι τὴν διαβολήν, λαβὼν ἐπὶ τῇ θυγατρὶ Λειμώνῃ μοιχόν,
     ἐκεῖνον μὲν ἀνεῖλεν ὑποζεύξας [μετὰ τῆς θυγατρὸς] τῷ ἅρματι, τὴν δὲ ἵππῳ συνέκλειεν ἕως
     ἀπόληται, "They no longer chose kings from the Kodrids because they seemed to indulge in
     luxury and to have become effeminate. Hippomenes, one of the Kodrids, wishing to throw off
     this slander, seized an adulterer with his daughter Leimone and killed him by hitching him
     [with his daughter] to a chariot; he locked her up with the horse until she died." This excerpt
     stops short of what should be the point, namely that the Kodrids (Medontids) permanently
     lost power because of popular hatred for Hippomenes' deed. Nikolaos of Damascus *FGrHist*
     90 F 49 makes Hippomenes' fall from power explicit in his version of the story: Ἱππομένης,
     ὁ Ἀθηναίων ἄρχων, ἐξέπεσε τῆς ἀρχῆς δι' αἰτίαν τοιάνδε. ἦν αὐτῷ θυγάτηρ, ἥντινα τῶν
     ἀστῶν τινος λάθρα αἰσχύναντος, ὑπ' ὀργῆς καθεῖρξεν εἰς οἴκημα δήσας σὺν ἵππῳ, καὶ τροφὴν
     οὐδετέρῳ εἰσέπεμπε. πιεσθεὶς οὖν λιμῷ ὁ ἵππος, ἐφορμήσας τῇ παιδὶ, ἀναλώσας τε αὐτὴν, καὶ
     αὐτὸς ὕστερον ἀπέθανε. μετὰ ταῦτα ἐπισκαφείσης αὐτοῖς τῆς οἰκήσεως, ἀπ' ἐκείνου ὁ χῶρος
     ἐκαλεῖτο Ἵππου καὶ Κόρης, "Hippomenes, the Athenians' ruler, fell from power through the
     following cause. He had a daughter, whom, when one of the citizens secretly brought shame
     on her, he angrily locked in a building, tying her to a horse, and he sent food in to neither
     one. And so the horse, pressed by hunger, attacked the girl and consumed her, and later died
     itself. After this the building was razed over them, and from that time the place was called 'of
     the Horse and the Maiden'."

with a particular place in Athens, and this topographical association seems old.[152] He was also assigned a particular place in the sequence of ten-year archons who were supposed to follow the lifelong archons and precede the annual archons, and perhaps the date that this represents is also not far from the mark. If Hippomenes spelled the end of the monarchy, he is credibly situated close to the end of the eighth century BC. All we know for sure, however, is that the Medontid dynasty had come to an end by 683/2 BC, when the list of annual archons begins.

§4.44 The Athenian tyrant Peisistratos claimed descent from Nestor's son Peisistratos.[153] This, I think, was a fiction made to rival the genuine claim

152 The name of the place is Ἵππου καὶ Κόρης, "of the Horse and the Maiden" (Nikolaos of Damascus, see previous note) or Παρ' ἵππον καὶ κόρην, "By the horse and the maiden" (*Lexeis Rhetorikai*, p. 295.12 Bekker; scholia to Aeschines 1.182 [367b Dilts]; cf. Suda s.v.). The entry in the *Lexeis Rhetorikai* (which follows the scholia to Aeschines according to Jacoby, commentary on Hellanicus *FGrHist* 323a F 23, n17) is as follows: Παρ' ἵππον καὶ κόρην· ὄνομα τόπου Ἀθήνησιν. ἐκλήθη δὲ οὕτως ἀπὸ τοῦ τὸν Ἱππομένην, ἕνα τῶν Κοδριδῶν, βασιλέα ὄντα, τῆς παιδὸς αὐτοῦ διαφθαρείσης τὴν παρθενίαν, ἀγανακτήσαντα καθεῖρξαι αὐτὴν ἐν τῷ χωρίῳ ἐκείνῳ μεθ' ἵππου μαινομένου, ὑφ' οὗ προδήλως ἔμελλεν ἀπολεῖσθαι, "By the Horse and the Maiden: the name of a place in Athens. It was called this for the following reason: Hippomenes, one of the Kodrids, who was king, bore it ill when his daughter lost her virginity, and locked her up in that place with a crazed horse, beneath which she was destined to die in full view." The "crazed horse" (ἵππου μαινομένου) in this version of the story was suggested by the name Hippomenes. In the Suda s.v. Παρίππον καὶ κόρη, where a "crazed horse" again appears, the form of the name is Hippomanes, making the connection even closer: Παρίππον καὶ κόρη· τόπος Ἀθήνησιν οὕτω καλούμενος· ἐπειδή τις τοῦ γένους τῶν Κοδριδῶν, Ἱππομάνης τοὔνομα, ὃς καὶ τελευταῖος ἐβασίλευσε, τὴν θυγατέρα καθεῖρξεν ἐν χωρίῳ τινὶ μεθ' ἵππου μαινομένου, διότι λαθραίῳ μίξει τὴν παρθενίαν αὐτῆς ἐλυμήνατο. καὶ ὁ ἵππος τὴν κόρην βίαν ἐποιήσατο· ἀφ' οὗ Πάριππος καὶ κόρη ὁ τόπος, ἐν ᾧ τὸ πάθος ὑπέστη, καλεῖται, "By the Horse and the Maiden: a place in Athens so called because one of the family of the Kodrids, Hippomanes by name, who was also the last king, locked his daughter in a place with a crazed horse for the reason that she had dishonored her virginity by secret intercourse. And the horse ravished the girl; from this the place in which she underwent the suffering is called 'By the Horse and the Maiden'." This source also makes it explicit that Hippomenes was the last king (τελευταῖος ἐβασίλευσε). Jacoby, who regards the Hippomenes story as a genuine old aition, which "surely...had originally no other purpose but to explain the name...of a locality," believes that "the *Atthis* made Hippomenes a Medontid, and made the disappearance of the second family of kings the consequence of his gruesome deed" (Jacoby 1949:145). This seems to me to imply that no tradition whatsoever survived for how Athens was governed before the start of the annual archonship. I prefer to think that there really were Medontid kings, and that Hippomenes was quite possibly the last of them. Cf. Carlier 1984:495, who argues that detailed stories of the end of kingship in Greece, like the story of Hippomenes in Athens (among others, see Carlier 1984:495n23), have a factual basis.

153 Herodotus 5.65 gives this information when he tells how the Peisistratids were driven from power in 510 BC: μετὰ δὲ ἐξεχώρησαν ἐς Σίγειον τὸ ἐπὶ τῷ Σκαμάνδρῳ, ἄρξαντες μὲν Ἀθηναίων ἐπ' ἔτεα ἕξ τε καὶ τριήκοντα, ἐόντες δὲ καὶ οὗτοι ἀνέκαθεν Πύλιοί τε καὶ Νηλεῖδαι,

to Neleid descent on the part of the Medontids of Athens on the one hand and the Neleids of Miletus on the other hand.[154] The rival claim by the tyrant's family, moreover, presupposes the existence of the Homeric poems since the *Odyssey* is the only likely source of the tradition that Nestor had a son named Peisistratos.[155] Among the early names on the list of annual Athenian archons is another figure named Peisistratos, who was the annual archon in 669 BC; this figure is thought to be the ancestor of the sixth-century tyrant, and, since he lived first, he is taken as an argument that the tyrant had a genuine claim to descent from Neleus, the founder of Pylos.[156] But in my view the basic

---

ἐκ τῶν αὐτῶν γεγονότες καὶ οἱ ἀμφὶ Κόδρον τε καὶ Μέλανθον, οἳ πρότερον ἐπήλυδες ἐόντες ἐγένοντο Ἀθηναίων βασιλέες. ἐπὶ τούτου δὲ καὶ τὠυτὸ οὔνομα ἀπεμνημόνευσε Ἱπποκράτης τῷ παιδὶ θέσθαι τὸν Πεισίστρατον, ἐπὶ τοῦ Νέστορος Πεισιστράτου ποιεύμενος τὴν ἐπωνυμίην, "Afterwards they went away to Sigeion on the Scamander, having ruled the Athenians for thirty-six years, they too being in origin Pylians and Neleids, born from the same ancestors as those around Kodros and Melanthos, who earlier as immigrants had become kings of the Athenians. In memory of this Hippocrates gave his son the same name Peisistratos, naming him after Nestor's son Peisistratos" (Herodotus 5.65.3–4). Cf. above §4.13 end.

154　The Medontids and the Neleids were Kodrids, whereas Peisistratos claimed a non-Kodrid connection with the same original ancestor, the Pylian Neleus. Rivalry with Athens' past Medontid rulers is perhaps suggested by the wording in Herodotus 5.65.3 used to describe the position claimed by Peisistratos and his family: ἐόντες δὲ <u>καὶ οὗτοι</u> ἀνέκαθεν Πύλιοί τε καὶ Νηλεῖδαι, <u>ἐκ τῶν αὐτῶν γεγονότες</u> καὶ οἱ ἀμφὶ Κόδρον τε καὶ Μέλανθον, οἳ πρότερον ἐπήλυδες ἐόντες ἐγένοντο Ἀθηναίων βασιλέες, "<u>they too</u> being in origin Pylians and Neleids, <u>born from the same ancestors</u> as those around Kodros and Melanthos, who earlier as immigrants had become kings of the Athenians." Kodrid descent was attributed to Solon (Diogenes Laertius 3.1; Plutarch *Solon* 1.1); it is not clear what the basis for this was (cf. Davies 1971:323), but it would seem to have nothing to do with Peisistratos. The mothers of Solon and Peisistratos were cousins according to Heraclides Ponticus (Plutarch *Solon* 1.2), but Solon's alleged Kodrid descent was through his father (Diogenes Laertius 3.1), and Peisistratos's claim to descent from Pylian Neleus was presumably through his father as well. Cf. Aly *RE* 'Solon' 948.

155　I view Nestor himself as an epic rather than historical figure, and so too his sons; even within epic I doubt that Nestor or his sons had wide currency outside the Homeric poems (see §4.56 below) despite the counterexample of Antilochus's death at the hands of Memnon (see EN4.7 to n4.104 above). Leaving Antilochus aside for now (see n4.189 below), I suggest that his brother Peisistratos, who did not go to Troy, had minimal existence outside the Homeric poems, or none at all. To put the genealogical claim of the Athenian tyrant Peisistratos in perspective it is significant that his political opponents, the Alcmaeonids and the Paionids, made the same claim to be descendants of Nestor through two of his other sons: the Alcmaeonids claimed to be descendants of Thrasymedes, the Paionids of Antilochus. The genealogical claims of the Alcmaeonids and the Paionids, as Toepffer 1889:225–228 argues (and as their very names show) are fictitious; in my view their claims cast doubt on Peisistratos's claim as well: if Peisistratos's claim had been seen as unassailable, it probably would not have invited rival claims from his opponents. The rival Athenian claims to descent from Nestor are discussed further in EN4.11.

156　Shapiro 1983:89: "The Peisistratos who was archon in 669/668 is almost certainly an ancestor of the Tyrant named for the same Neleid hero." The date is determined indirectly as follows: according to Pausanias 2.24.7 Peisistratos was archon in the fourth year of an

point remains that Nestor's son Peisistratos belonged to epic rather than historical tradition, and a different explanation thus suggests itself: if the two Athenian figures named Peisistratos in fact came from the same family, we may suppose that this family's pretension to Neleid descent began with the naming of the first figure, and was already well established by the time of the second.[157] The family's original pretension would have arisen from a rivalry with the traditional seat of Athenian power, namely the Medontid dynasty, which had been removed from power by the time of the archonship of the first Athenian Peisistratos, and perhaps also by the time of his birth and naming. The basis of the family's rival claim was the Homeric poems, which must already have made an impression in Athens at the time. The naming of the first Athenian Peisistratos, in other words, may be taken, provisionally at least, as evidence that the Homeric poems were already known in Athens in the early seventh century BC.[158]

Olympiad, the number of which is missing from the text; Pausanias mentions the victory of Eurybotos the Athenian in the *stádion* in the same Olympiad, and this victor, with the name Eurybates, is attested for the twenty-seventh Olympiad by both Dionysius of Halicarnassus 3.1.3 and Sextus Iulius Africanus *List of the Victors at the Olympic Games*; cf. Cadoux 1948:90. Pausanias 2.24.7 concerns the Battle of Hysiai, in which Argos defeated Sparta; this event occurred in the archonship of Peisistratos, and is thus dated to 669/8 BC as well. For the likelihood that the archon of this year was an ancestor of the tyrant cf. Davies 1971:445: "At all events, though homonymity is the only argument for supposing that Peisistratos (I), archon in 669/8, was an ancestor, this argument is nearly strong enough by itself."

157 In Herodotus 5.65.4 there is a close connection between the Pylian ancestry of past Athenian kings (passage quoted in n4.154 above) and the naming of the future tyrant Peisistratos after Nestor's son: ἐπὶ τούτου δὲ καὶ τὠυτὸ οὔνομα ἀπεμνημόνευσε Ἱπποκράτης τῷ παιδὶ θέσθαι τὸν Πεισίστρατον, ἐπὶ τοῦ Νέστορος Πεισιστράτου ποιεύμενος τὴν ἐπωνυμίην, "Hence Hippocrates remembered to give his son the same name Peisistratos, naming him after Nestor's son Peisistratos" (or perhaps "remembering [this] Hippocrates gave...," with ἀπεμνημόνευσε...θέσθαι standing for ἀπομνημονεύσας...ἔθετο by enallage; for ἐπὶ τούτου, "hence," cf. Herodotus 2.57.1; 7.40. 3; 7.83.1; 7.193.2). His family, I think, had high ambitions for the future tyrant from his birth. Another sign of the family's ambitions for the future tyrant even before his birth, if the story is not an invention after his tyranny became a fact, is the portent of the kettle that boiled without fire when Hippocrates visited Delphi (Herodotus 1.59.1); while the interpretation given to this supernatural event is negative (Chilon the Spartan advises Hippocrates not to conceive a son), there is something larger than life about the portent itself, and this could be useful to one who deliberately rivaled former kings.

158 This explanation, I think, provides an answer to a real question regarding Peisistratos and his family; cf. Davies 1971:445: "As with the Alkmeonidai, we cannot yet properly explain or explain away the tradition that the Peisistratidai were of Pylian and royal origin (Hdt. 5.65.3), but for the latter, as for the Alkmeonidai, this tradition must be taken in conjunction with demonstrable Eupatrid status" (for the family's connections and status cf. also Anderson 2003:30 and 227n43). As to how Athenians became aware of the Homeric poems at the end of the eighth or beginning of the seventh century BC, I suggest that as Ionians they may have been honored guests at the Panionia, and thus present at the creation; cf. §4.63 below.

§4.45 In Athens the Medontids had disgraced themselves and fallen from power through weakness and cruelty, but the basis of their hereditary power, descent from Neleus, did not disappear immediately, at least as a claim, if I am right about the family of Peisistratos and its pretensions. Let us assume that this is the case and consider implications for the Homeric poems. If the Homeric poems were used to support this family's pretensions, as I have suggested, there must, I think, have been an awareness that these poems had supported the position of the Neleids in the Ionian world: the Athenian family's rivalry may have been with the Medontids' pedigree, but the means chosen to pursue this rivalry, descent from Nestor's son, reflects directly on the Neleids, the Medontids' cousins in Miletus, and their relationship to the Homeric poems.

§4.46 I return now to the Panionia as the birthplace of the Homeric poems, and to the role of the Neleids at the Panionia. Although there is no direct evidence for the Neleids' role at this festival, I have used the indirect evidence of the Homeric poems, especially the Phaeacians, to argue that the Neleids were the prime movers of both the festival and the league. There may also be evidence of a different kind for this question. Stories of particular Neleids survived into the historical period, and while these stories do not touch on the point at issue, they may still offer indirect evidence. The stories are also worth considering in their own right, for they give substance to the Neleids' rule of Miletus, which I have dealt with so far only as an abstraction.

§4.47 The earliest source for a particular Neleid king of Miletus is Aristotle, and the Neleid named by him is Phobios. This king's story, which is uncertain as to date, has a romantic aspect, and to this is due its survival: Parthenius retold the story in his *Erotica Pathemata* in the first century BC.[159] Phobios, "one of the Neleids, who was then ruling the Milesians," had in his household a hostage from Halicarnassus;[160] Phobios's wife fell in love with this hostage, was rejected by him, killed him, and hung herself. Phobios, being accursed, gave up the kingship to another figure, Phrygios.[161] From this

---

159 Parthenius *Erotica Pathemata* 14 (= Aristotle fr. 556 Rose); Parthenius names Aristotle and authors of Milesian tales as his two sources (ἱστορεῖ Ἀριστοτέλης καὶ οἱ τὰ Μιλησιακά).

160 ἐκ δὲ Ἁλικαρνασσοῦ παῖς Ἀνθεὺς ἐκ βασιλείου γένους ὡμήρευσε παρὰ Φοβίῳ, ἑνὶ τῶν Νειλειδῶν, τότε κρατοῦντι Μιλησίων, "The boy Antheus was a hostage from the royal family of Halicarnassus at the house of Phobios, one of the Neileids, who then ruled the Milesians" (Parthenius 14). Aristotle was clearly the source for the statement that Phobios was one of the Neleids and that he ruled Miletus.

161 Φοβίος μέντοι διὰ ταύτην τὴν αἰτίαν ὡς ἐναγὴς παρεχώρησε Φρυγίῳ τῆς ἀρχῆς, "But Phobios gave up the rule to Phrygios for this reason, being accursed" (Parthenius 14). Phrygios too must have been a Neleid, for the story concerns a personal tragedy, not a change of dynasty.

story something can be deduced about early relations between Miletus and Halicarnassus, the Doric city to the south of Miletus that in time, through the influence of Miletus, became strongly Ionic in character.[162] The name Phrygios indicates that by the time this Neleid king was born there was already contact with the Phrygians, and this suggests eighth-century dates for him and his predecessor Phobios.[163]

§4.48 Phrygios (probably the same Phrygios, but possibly another) occurs in another story.[164] The story concerns relations between Miletus and Myus, the small city next to Miletus on the Gulf of Latmos, which, like Miletus, was a member of the dodecapolis. In this story a party in Miletus opposed to the rule of the "sons of Neleus" takes refuge in Myus, and the citizens of the two cities thereafter do not mix except during festivals.[165] During a festival of Artemis in

162 Milesian influence, as it extended south, first reached Iasos on the Gulf of Bargylia between Miletus and Myndos (see Map 1); Iasos was reputedly a colony of Argos, but according to Polybius 16.12 a "son of Neleus" (i.e. a Neleid) was brought from Miletus to Iasos to help the inhabitants in their war against the Carians (cf. Huxley 1966:49 and Hicks 1887:83–84). Further south Halicarnassus may also have felt the influence of Miletus in the early period (cf. Huxley 1966:50); by the fifth century BC, at any rate, Halicarnassus had become fully Ionic in dialect. Miletus's influence was doubtless exerted northwards as well as southwards; we should bear this in mind when we consider the early formation of the Panionic league among cities whose populations were far from uniform in origin.

163 According to the fifth-century BC Lydian historian Xanthus (*FGrHist* 765 F 14 = Strabo 14.5.29) the Phrygians came to Asia from Europe after the Trojan war; their arrival, once associated with the collapse of the Hittite empire c. 1200 BC, is now usually dated to the tenth or ninth century BC (Neumann 1988:16). Inscriptions in Old Phrygian begin in the second half of the eighth century BC in an alphabet based on Greek and Semitic models (Lejeune *OCD*³ 'Phrygian language'). For the "close interchange of goods and cultural influences" that took place between Phrygians and Greeks in the later eighth century BC see Barnett 1975:428–429; for the arrival of the Phrygian cult of the Kabeiroi in Miletus in the late eighth century BC see Barnett 1975:437 and cf. n4.177 below. The cultural exchange is dated somewhat later by Cook 1975:799 ("The excavations seem to show that there was no exchange of manufactured objects or artistic motifs between Phyrygians and Greeks before the seventh century"). Högemann 2001:62 sets Homer in relation to Phrygia: "Homer was a contemporary Anatolian witness: he had experienced the history of the Phrygian kingdom under Midas of Gordion (from c. 750 BC), his brilliant period, but also his brutal end at the hands of the Cimmerians (676 BC)" ("Homer war anatolischer Zeitzeuge: Er hat die Geschichte des Phrygerreiches unter Midas von Gordion (ab ca. 750) erlebt, seine Glanzzeit, aber auch sein brutales Ende durch die Kimmerier [676]"); Eusebius's dates for Midas are 738–696/5 BC; for Midas's death by drinking bull's blood see Strabo 1.3.21. Sources for the Phrygians are discussed by Carrington 1977. For the cult of the Kabeiroi in and near Miletus (Didyma and Assessos) see Laumonier 1958:173–174, 545, 569, 572, 585; cf. also Graf *DNP* 'Kabeiroi' 124, 125, 127.

164 Plutarch *Bravery of Women* 253f–254b; Polyaenus 8.35; Aristaenetus *Epistolai* 1.15. The story was also told by Callimachus (*Aitia* frs. 80–83 Pfeiffer).

165 Polyaenus 8.35: οἱ ἐν Μιλήτῳ Ἴωνες πρὸς τοὺς Νηλέως παῖδας στασιάσαντες ἀνεχώρησαν ἐς Μυοῦντα κἀκεῖθεν ἐπολέμουν· οὐ μὴν ὅγε πόλεμος ἄσπονδος ἦν, ἀλλὰ ἐν ταῖς ἑορταῖς

Miletus Phrygios, "one of the sons of Neleus," falls in love with a woman from Myus and grants her wish to make peace between the two cities.[166] Stripped of its romantic dress this looks like a dynastic marriage that brought Myus into Miletus's orbit; we see here a particular Neleid king extending the reach of Miletus over another Panionic city, and this suggests how, in a general way, Miletus may have dealt with other Panionic cities that were farther off and larger.[167] The festival with which the marriage was associated was called *Nēleís*, the "Neleid festival," and this suggests that the two cities became realigned on the Neleids' terms. This seems highly likely in any case.[168]

§4.49 The last Neleid king of Miletus was named Leodamas.[169] He became king when he proved himself a greater benefactor of the Milesian people than did a rival in his own family.[170] But Leodamas was undone by this rival, who slew him at a public festival and made himself tyrant.[171] Ultimately Leodamas

---

ἦν αὐτοῖς ἐπιμιξία, "The Ionians in Miletus, being at odds with the sons of Neleus, withdrew to Myus and carried on a war from there; the war indeed was not without truces, but there was mixing between them at festivals."

166 Polyaenus 8.35: Πύθου ἀνδρὸς ἐνδόξου θυγάτηρ Πιερία ἑορτῆς οὔσης παρὰ Μιλησίοις, ἣν Νηληΐδα κλήζουσιν, ἧκεν ἐς Μίλητον. τῶν Νηλέως παίδων [ὁ δυνατώτατος] ὄνομα Φρύγιος Πιερίας ἐρασθεὶς ἤρετο, τί ἂν αὐτῇ μάλιστα γίγνοιτο κεχαρισμένον, κτλ., "Pieria, the daughter of Pythos, a respected man, came to Miletus when the Milesians were celebrating a festival which they call the *Nēleís*. [The most powerful] of the sons of Neleus, Phrygios by name, fell in love with Pieria and asked her what the most pleasing thing was that could happen for her," etc. In Polyaenus (and also in Plutarch) there is an explicit connection between the exile of the Neleids' opponents to Myus and the period of hostility between Miletus and Myus that ends with a marriage; Huxley 1966:49 is misleading on this.

167 It seems reasonable to assume that Miletus's reconciliation with neighboring Myus took place before the Panionic league came into being; this is a broad indication of the league's date if Phrygios, because of his name, belongs to the eighth century BC. Cf. n4.163 above and §4.67–§4.68 below; but cf. also §4.71 below on the possibility of an earlier date for the league. For a different view of the story of Phrygios and Myus see Herda 1998:34n276, 41, who regards it as a Hellenistic invention.

168 Polyaenus and Plutarch both call the festival *Nēleís*; Plutarch and Aristaenetus both say that the festival was for Artemis. Herda 1998:25–40 argues that the festival belonged to both Neileos, the city founder, and Artemis Kithone; Sakellariou 1958:50n1 and 54n7 takes the festival to be that of an Artemis *Nēleís*.

169 Conon *FGrHist* 26 F 1 xliv (Photius *Bibliotheca* 186, Bekker pp. 139b–140a); Nikolaos of Damascus *FGrHist* 90 F 52 and 53. Both authors are of Augustan date.

170 Conon, who calls the rival Phitres, tells this part of the story; Photius's summary of Conon begins: ἡ μδ' ἱστορία φησὶν ὡς Λεωδάμας καὶ Φίτρης ἤρισαν ὑπὲρ τῆς Μιλησίων βασιλείας γένους ἄμφω ὄντε βασιλείου, "The forty-fourth narrative says that Leodamas and Phitres quarreled over the kingship of the Milesians, both being of the royal family" (Conon *FGrHist* 26 F 1 xliv).

171 Nikolaos of Damascus, who calls the rival Amphitres, tells this part of the story, beginning with the murder of Laodamas and the tyranny of Amphitres: Λεωδάμας ἐβασίλευσε Μιλησίων...εἰς ὃ φόνον αὐτῷ βουλεύσας Ἀμφιτρὴς ἐν ἑορτῇ Ἀπόλλωνος ἄγοντα ἑκατόμβην

was avenged when those responsible for his death were either killed or exiled. But the result of this series of events was that the Neleid dynasty in Miletus came to an end.[172]

τῷ θεῷ Λεωδάμαντα κατὰ τὴν ὁδὸν ἀπέκτεινεν, αὐτὸς δὲ μετὰ τῶν αὐτοῦ στασιωτῶν τὴν πόλιν κατελάβετο, καὶ τύραννος ἐγένετο, ἰσχύϊ προύχων Μιλησίων, "Leodamas was king of the Milesians...until Amphitres plotted his murder and killed him at the festival of Apollo as he drove a hecatomb for the god along the road, and he himself seized the city with his faction and became tyrant, holding the chief place among the Milesians by force" (Nikolaos of Damascus *FGrHist* 90 F 52).

172 Amphitres was killed in battle by the sons and friends of Leodamas. After Amphitres's death, the people elected an *aisumnḗtēs* who proscribed or exiled Amphitres's followers. The second of the two excerpts of Nikolaos (*FGrHist* 90 F 53) concludes: οἱ μὲν δὴ Νηλεῖδαι κατελύθησαν ὧδε, "thus were the Neleids removed from power." For the date of the Neleids' fall from power the tenth or ninth century BC (proposed by Gorman 2001:92) is too early, the late eighth or early seventh century BC likely; see Herda 2005:290, who makes the *terminus ante quem* c. 630 BC, the date at which Miletus's colony of Sinope was founded (here, and at Olbia [founded c. 575–550 BC] the two institutions that replaced the kingship at Miletus, the *aisumnḗtēs* and the Molpoi, are found in association with the cult of Apollo Delphinios as at Miletus). The Neleid family survived long after its fall on the evidence of an inscription from the first century BC recording an official "of the lineage (*patriá*) of the Neileidai" (Collitz-Bechtel 1884–1915 no. 5501; cf. n1.45 above; for *patriá* as a "gentilicial subgroup of the phratries" ["gentilizische Untergruppe der Phratrien"] see Herda 1998:19n138 with reference). The name "Neleid" does not occur on other inscriptions, but there is indirect evidence that the family was still active politically in the fifth century BC. Glotz 1906 argued this on the basis of a fifth-century banishment decree from Miletus (Tod 1946 no. 35, Meiggs and Lewis 1988 no. 43), which in Glotz's view recorded the banishment of members of the Neleid family in the mid-fifth century (and then remained in place to color the account in Nikolaos of Damascus of the earlier banishment of Neleids under Amphitres). Barron 1962 extended Glotz's idea that the inscription recorded the banishment of Neleids, arguing that in the mid-fifth century a Neleid oligarchy held power in Miletus for a few years before being banished. Against this is a more recent redating of the inscription to shortly after 479 BC when the city was reoccupied after the Persian defeat (see Robertson 1987:378–379; Herda 1998:18). Much of the case for the Neleids' activity at the time of the decree depends on names that are interpreted as belonging to Neleids: Alkimos and Cresphontes, who were banished in the decree; Kretheus and Peisistratos, names of officials in Miletus during the period. Meiggs and Lewis 1988:105–107, while not accepting that there was a full-scale Neleid oligarchy in the mid-fifth century, accept that the names in question probably belonged to Neleids. Robertson 1987:379 and n56 does not accept this, but cf. Herda 1998:18. In my view not all the names are equally convincing, in particular Cresphontes, the name of the Heraclid conqueror of Messenia (the name also occurs in Apollonia Pontica, a colony of Miletus; see Herda 1998:10n55). The name Cresphontes seems appropriate for a Neleid only if the distinction between Messenians and Pylians blurred by poets (e.g. Pindar *Pythian* 6.35; cf. Strabo 14.1.3) was also blurred by the Neleid family; but Ephorus 70 F 116 (Strabo 8.4.7) shows that still in the fourth century BC Cresphontes and the Dorians were thought to have controlled only a limited part of Messenia, which did not include Pylos (see Kiechle 1959:43, 56, 68). The name Kretheus, on the other hand, is impeccably Neleid, belonging to Neleus's step-father (it is also attested on Linear-B tablets from Pylos; Ventris and Chadwick 1973:260, 553; cf. Chadwick and

§4.50 Leodamas deserves closer scrutiny. Although we cannot date him exactly, the fact that he was the last Neleid to hold the kingship in Miletus suggests the latter part of the eighth century BC. Leodamas became king by waging a successful war for Miletus against Karystos in Euboea; his rival lost his bid to become king by failing in a campaign against another enemy of Miletus at the time, the island of Melos.[173] It has been suggested that these foreign campaigns had something to do with the Lelantine war, a generalized conflict involving much of the Greek world, probably in the late eighth century.[174]

§4.51 From the little that has survived about Leodamas he seems to have been an impressive figure. His brilliant military success made him king,[175] and as king he won great praise, being both just and "after the heart

---

Baumbach 1963 s.v.); this name by itself, I think, clearly suggests that the Neleids were still a political force in fifth-century Miletus. Herda 1998:18 and n135 adds another piece of evidence, drawing attention to a late Archaic altar dedicated by several prytaneis, one of whom is named Leodamas. When Herodotus refers to the Milesians as "those who set out from the prytaneion of the Athenians and consider themselves the noblest of the Ionians" (see n4.15 above), he may well have had contemporary Neleids especially in mind (cf. n4.16 above). Barron 1962:4n25 has suggested that Teichioussa, fifteen miles south of Miletus on an inlet of the sea (see Map 2), was the ancestral seat of the Neleids; he bases this on the fact that the first-century official "of the lineage of the Neileidai" (see above) is from the deme Teichioussai. Barron notes further that this official's phratry, Pelagonidai, also suggests the Neleids: Pelagon is the name of a Pylian leader under Nestor in *Iliad* 4.295. For the fifth-century banishment decree cf. also Rhodes 1992:58–59.

173 In Conon the two Neleids are both sent on foreign campaigns to end the civil strife caused by their rivalry: τὸ κοινὸν δὲ τῇ ἐκείνων κακούμενοι στάσει τῆς μὲν φιλονεικίας μετὰ πολλὰ πάθη ἐξίσταντο, ἔκρινον δ' ἐκεῖνον βασιλεύειν, ὃς Μιλησίους πλείω ἀγαθὰ ἐργάσοιτο, "Being harmed as a city by the strife of those men they [the Milesians] freed themselves of the rivalry after many sufferings, and decided that whichever did more good for the Milesians, he was king" (Conon *FGrHist* 26 F 1 xliv). The war with Melos requires further comment; see §4.69 below.

174 See Huxley 1966:50, Herda 1998:45–46; for the Lelantine war cf. n4.64 and n4.145 above; for the problem of dating the Lelantine war see Hall 2002:232–234, 237–238 and cf. Herda 1998:46, 42n333. With respect to Karystos and Melos Conon says only that Miletus had wars with both at the time: ἦσαν δ' αὐτοῖς τότε δύο πόλεμοι Καρυστίοις καὶ Μηλιεῦσι (Conon *FGrHist* 26 F 1 xliv). For the question of the historicity of Leodamas's war against Karystos cf. Herda 1998:45–46 and n376.

175 The campaigns of Leodamas and his rival are summarized in Conon as follows: καὶ πρὸς μὲν Μῆλον (αὐτῷ γὰρ ὁ κλῆρος τοῦτον ἐδίδου τὸν πόλεμον) Φίτρης στρατεύσας ἄπρακτος ἀναστρέφει· Λεωδάμας δὲ λαμπρῶς κατὰ Καρυστίων ἀνδραγαθήσας, καὶ κατὰ κράτος ἑλὼν τὴν πόλιν καὶ ἀνδραποδισάμενος, Μιλήτου ἐπανιὼν κατὰ τὰ συγκείμενα βασιλεύει, "And Phitres, campaigning against Melos (for the lot gave him this war), returned unsuccessful; but Leodamas, brilliantly showing his courage against the Karystians, whose city he seized by force and enslaved, ruled Miletus when he returned according to the agreement" (Conon *FGrHist* 26 F 1 xliv).

(κατᾱθύμιος)" of his city.[176] Leodamas, in short, was remembered as a great leader in war and peace who was loved by his people.[177] If we look for a particular Neleid who played the role at the Panionia that I have attributed to the Neleid family overall, Leodamas, the last Neleid king of Miletus, has much to recommend him for both his likely date and his great reputation. The development of the Homeric poems to their definitive shape at the Panionia may have taken more than one generation, but there is no reason not to associate Leodamas with at least their final stage of development.[178] If the king who was laid low by a kinsman in his own city had first brought Panionism to full flower in the Homeric poems, it is a good story, worthy of Greek tragedy. Whether it is more than that is, I think, an important question, worthy of serious consideration. My answer again has to do with the Phaeacians. We already know that the two most important figures among the Phaeacians, the king and queen, are more than they seem to be on the surface of the *Odyssey*. The same is true of the Phaeacian princess, Nausicaa. Next in importance in the royal family is Laodamas, the Phaeacian prince, and he too, I think, has a hidden identity. If the king and queen represent the Ionians' past, the prince, I suggest, represents their actual present. That present is still in the future from the standpoint of the story of the *Odyssey*, and, accordingly, Laodamas does not yet rule, but he is destined to rule one day. The name Laodamas is exceptional among the Phaeacians, whose names have overwhelmingly to do with the sea and seafaring: even in the royal family only *Laodámas* expresses, to use Friedrich Welcker's term, "das Königliche" ("kingliness").[179] I suggest

---

176 Nikolaos of Damascus *FGrHist* 90 F 52: Λεωδάμας ἐβασίλευσε Μιλησίων, καὶ ἐν τοῖς μάλιστα ἐπηνεῖτο, δίκαιός τε ὢν καὶ τῇ πόλει καταθύμιος, "Leodamas ruled the Milesians, and he was among the most praised, being both just and after the heart (according to the spirit) of the city." For the βασιλεὺς καταθύμιος as the model for Augustan rule in Nikolaos see Parmentier 1991:233–234.

177 Leodamas's reputation comes through clearly in both sources for him, although he is the primary focus in neither one. The main point of Conon's story is that Leodamas brought back a captive from Karystos named Euangelos, the ancestor of a priestly family at Branchidai (cf. n4.232 below). Nikolaos of Damascus, as his final words show (οἱ μὲν δὴ Νηλεῖδαι κατελύθησαν ὧδε, "thus were the Neleids removed from power"), narrated the end of the Neleid dynasty in Miletus, and Leodamas's role in this was only to be murdered by his rival; Nikolaos's narrative focuses on the struggle against Leodamas's murderer after he made himself tyrant, in particular the role of the Kabeiroi, new gods brought in from Phrygia to defeat him in battle.

178 For the question of the time needed for the Homeric poems to develop at the Panionia see §4.40 above and also §4.70–§4.71 below.

179 Welcker 1832:3: "Von den drei Söhnen des Alcinous (8.119) drückt nur der erste, Laodamas, das Königliche aus" ("Of the three sons of Alcinous [*Odyssey* 8.119] only the first, Laodamas, expresses kingliness"). Alcinous's other two sons, as Welcker notes, have names related to

---

that the Phaeacian prince is named for the Milesian king, who bears the same
quintessentially "kingly" name in its Ionic form.[180]

§4.52 It is perhaps a bold suggestion to see a living king represented in
Homeric epic, which, as we know, is oriented strictly toward the past. But a
living Neleid king was a genuine link to the Ionians' past as that past, in Pylos
and Athens, is represented in the Phaeacian royal couple. The link between
past and present is established in the poem when Odysseus, the embodiment
of the epic past, first appears in the Phaeacian palace grasping the knees of
the queen, and the king, prompted by his retainer, raises him from the ashes:
in an act that is at once entirely natural and deeply significant the king bids
his son, the prince Laodamas, to give his seat to Odysseus, and Laodamas, his
father's favorite, does as he is bidden (*Odyssey* 7.167–171):

αὐτὰρ ἐπεὶ τό γ' ἄκουσ' ἱερὸν μένος Ἀλκινόοιο,

χειρὸς ἑλὼν Ὀδυσῆα δαΐφρονα ποικιλομήτην

ὦρσεν ἀπ' ἐσχαρόφιν καὶ ἐπὶ θρόνου εἷσε φαεινοῦ,

υἱὸν ἀναστήσας ἀγαπήνορα Λαοδάμαντα,

ὅς οἱ πλησίον ἷζε, μάλιστα δέ μιν φιλέεσκε.

But when Alcinous, whose power is sacred, heard this,
he took the hand of wise Odysseus with the inventive mind

---

the sea and seafaring (Halios and Klytoneos), as do two others in the royal family (Nausicaa
and Nausithoos). Eighteen other Phaeacians have names related to the sea and seafaring:
Ekheneos, Pontonoos, Akroneos, Okyalos, Elatreus, Nauteus, Prymneus, Ankhialos,
Eretmeus, Ponteus, Proreus, Thoon, Anabesineos, Amphialos, Polyneos, Tektonides,
Euryalos, Naubolides. Only Polybos, who made the purple ball used in the dance (*Odyssey*
8.373), and perhaps Dymas, "famous for ships" (ναυσικλειτοῖο Δύμαντος, *Odyssey* 6.22),
do not have sea-related names. In the royal family three figures have names that are not
related to the sea, Alcinous, Arete, and Laodamas, and all three names are significant.
180 For the meaning of the name Laodamas, "he who subdues/controls the people," see above
EN2.2. There are a few bearers of the name in addition to the Neleid king of Miletus (for
two Athenian statesmen of the fifth and fourth centuries BC see Wickert *RE* 'Leodamas';
five heroes called 'Laodamas' are treated separately by Meuli *RE* s.v.). For the "kingli-
ness" of the name, cf. Herodotus 5.61.1: in Thebes Eteocles had a son Laodamas, who was
supposed to have dedicated a tripod with the following inscription in the temple of Apollo
Ismenios (note μουναρχέων, "ruling alone"):

Λαοδάμας τρίποδ' αὐτὸς ἐϋσκόπῳ Ἀπόλλωνι
μουναρχέων ἀνέθηκε τεῒν περικαλλὲς ἄγαλμα.

Laodamas himself, ruling alone, dedicated a tripod,
a very beautiful gift, to you, keen-sighted Apollo.

and raised him from the hearth and sat him on the shining chair,
removing his son from it, courteous Laodamas,
who sat close to him, and whom he loved most.

§4.53 The proper relationship between present and past is defined in this
scene: it is a unique honor for a living king to be represented in Homeric epic,
and that is the main point; but the proper epic role for this future king is simply
to give his seat to the great hero of the past.[181] There is more to the story, but
giving up the seat is the significant act, which sets the tone for the rest. The
rest is what takes place at the games, in which Odysseus is provoked to take
part and hurls the discus far beyond all the others. In this scene there is a great
contrast in behavior between Laodamas, who invites Odysseus to compete, and
Euryalos, who abuses Odysseus as a lowborn seaman when he declines the invi-
tation. After Odysseus shows his mettle for all to see, he turns on Euryalos in
an angry speech.[182] This speech is rightly seen as an example of the widespread

---

181 Compare the Archaic relief from Sparta shown in Plate 12 below (cf. n3.112 above), in which
the two seated heroes (or perhaps gods) are much bigger than the human worshippers who
approach them (see also n3.112 above); Renaissance paintings in which a miniature living
patron stands in front of the throne of a larger-than-life seated saint offer a further analogy.

182 *Odyssey* 8.166–177 (see the following note for the underlined passage):

ξεῖν', οὐ καλὸν ἔειπες· ἀτασθάλῳ ἀνδρὶ ἔοικας.
οὕτως οὐ πάντεσσι θεοὶ χαρίεντα διδοῦσιν
ἀνδράσιν, οὔτε φυὴν οὔτ' ἄρ φρένας οὔτ' ἀγορητύν.
ἄλλος μὲν γὰρ εἶδος ἀκιδνότερος πέλει ἀνήρ,
ἀλλὰ θεὸς μορφὴν ἔπεσι στέφει· οἱ δέ τ' ἐς αὐτὸν
τερπόμενοι λεύσσουσιν, ὁ δ' ἀσφαλέως ἀγορεύει
αἰδοῖ μειλιχίῃ, μετὰ δὲ πρέπει ἀγρομένοισιν,
ἐρχόμενον δ' ἀνὰ ἄστυ θεὸν ὣς εἰσορόωσιν.
ἄλλος δ' αὖ εἶδος μὲν ἀλίγκιος ἀθανάτοισιν,
ἀλλ' οὔ οἱ χάρις ἀμφὶ περιστέφεται ἐπέεσσιν,
ὡς καὶ σοὶ εἶδος μὲν ἀριπρεπές, οὐδέ κεν ἄλλως
οὐδὲ θεὸς τεύξειε, νόον δ' ἀποφώλιός ἐσσι.

You have not spoken well, stranger. You seem like a reckless man.
It is clear that the gods do not give graces to all men,
neither stature nor wit nor eloquence.
For one man is weaker in looks,
but the god crowns his words with beauty; others look at him
with delight, and he speaks unerringly
with gentle modesty, and he stands out among those gathered,
and they look on him as a god as he walks through the city.
Another man is like the immmortals in beauty,
but no grace crowns his words,
like you, who have striking beauty, and not even a god
would fashion it otherwise, but you are worthless in your mind.

literary type known as the "instruction of princes."[183] But it is easy to miss the

183 *Speculum principum*, "princes' mirror," is the medieval term sometimes used in discussions of the type. For examples in various cultures and traditions, all concerned with transmitting proper legal, religious, political, and social behavior, see West 1978:3–25; Greek examples include Hesiod's *Works and Days*, the fragmentary *Precepts of Chiron* (*Kheírōnos Hupothêkai*), and the poetry of Theognis. Martin 1984 argues that in Greek the instruction of princes had a distinct existence as a genre (*hupothêkai*), and that poets in other genres such as epic and theogonic poetry could draw on this tradition for specific purposes. The example that Martin proposes is the passage quoted above, *Odyssey* 8.166–177, in which Odysseus chastises Euryalos. As Walcot 1963:12 first noticed, this passage uses language that corresponds closely to language in a passage of Hesiod's *Theogony*; the passage, *Theogony* 79–93, concerns the muse Calliope, who bestows fair speech on kings (specific correspondences of language between the two passages are underlined; cf. the preceding note):

Καλλιόπη θ'· ἡ δὲ προφερεστάτη ἐστὶν ἁπασέων.
ἡ γὰρ καὶ βασιλεῦσιν ἅμ' αἰδοίοισιν ὀπηδεῖ.
ὅντινα τιμήσουσι Διὸς κοῦραι μεγάλοιο
γεινόμενόν τε ἴδωσι διοτρεφέων βασιλήων,
τῷ μὲν ἐπὶ γλώσσῃ γλυκερὴν χείουσιν ἐέρσην,
τοῦ δ' ἔπε' ἐκ στόματος ῥεῖ μείλιχα· οἱ δέ νυ λαοὶ
πάντες ἐς αὐτὸν ὁρῶσι διακρίνοντα θέμιστας
ἰθείῃσι δίκῃσιν· <u>ὁ δ' ἀσφαλέως ἀγορεύων</u>
αἶψά τι καὶ μέγα νεῖκος ἐπισταμένως κατέπαυσε·
τούνεκα γὰρ βασιλῆες ἐχέφρονες, οὕνεκα λαοῖς
βλαπτομένοις ἀγορῆφι μετάτροπα ἔργα τελεῦσι
ῥηιδίως, μαλακοῖσι παραιφάμενοι ἐπέεσσιν·
<u>ἐρχόμενον δ' ἀν' ἀγῶνα θεὸν ὣς ἱλάσκονται</u>
<u>αἰδοῖ μειλιχίῃ, μετὰ δὲ πρέπει ἀγρομένοισι.</u>
τοίη Μουσάων ἱερὴ δόσις ἀνθρώποισιν.

...and Kalliope; she is the foremost of all [the Muses].
For she accompanies even revered kings.
Whomever among Zeus-nourished kings
the daughters of great Zeus honor and look on when he is born,
they pour sweet dew on his tongue,
and gentle words flow from his mouth; and all the people
see him deciding laws
with straight decisions. <u>He, speaking unerringly,</u>
stops even a great quarrel at once with his understanding.
There are prudent kings because they bring about a different outcome
for the people when they are misled in assembly,
persuading them with gentle words;
<u>as he walks through the assembly they supplicate him like a god</u>
<u>with gentle reverence, and he stands out among those gathered.</u>
Such is the sacred gift of the Muses to men.

In Martin's view Hesiod does not imitate the *Odyssey* in this passage, and the *Odyssey* does not imitate Hesiod (both arguments have been maintained in the past, with no consensus reached). Both passages, Martin argues, make use of elements belonging to an independent tradition of *hupothêkai* (cf. Walcot 1963:12–13, whose argument Martin

key figure in this scene, who is in fact Laodamas. He is the royal prince, and it is for his benefit that the instruction is offered.[184] Or rather he stands for a future king of the same name, and it is for the benefit of the future king that the instruction is offered. The instruction is not offered directly, but indirectly, by way of a counterexample. All attention is focused on the example of wrong behavior, and the real object of the instruction stands by unnoticed.[185] It is

---

develops). Particularly attractive is Martin's interpretation of the poetic situation in the *Odyssey*. Odysseus has not yet revealed his identity, and Euryalos takes him for a lowborn man unskilled in athletic contests; Odysseus reveals himself to be a king not only by his throw of the discus, but by his speech to Euryalos, in which he shows that he not only knows accepted standards of behavior, but that he also knows how to instruct princes in them. The implied contrast in Odysseus's speech is between himself, a king who does not outwardly appear to be one, and Euryalos, a prince whose outward appearance is faultless, but who lacks a king's gift of fair speech. I find this interpretation persuasive, particularly with respect to Odysseus: the contrast between his appearance and his fair speech is also part of Helen's characterization of him in *Iliad* 3. Whatever the relationship between the Homeric and the Hesiodic passages (Butterworth 1986:34–36 again argues for the priority of the Homeric passage, and with some force), Martin's identification of a tradition of "instruction of princes" behind the Homeric passage is illuminating.

184 As far as outward appearance is concerned, Odysseus's statement to Euryalos could apply even more to Laodamas: Euryalos is said to be second to Laodamas in beauty and form when he rises to take part in the footrace (*Odyssey* 8.115–117):

ἂν δὲ καὶ Εὐρύαλος, βροτολοιγῷ ἶσος Ἄρηϊ,
Ναυβολίδης, ὃς ἄριστος ἔην εἶδός τε δέμας τε
πάντων Φαιήκων μετ' ἀμύμονα Λαοδάμαντα.

Up stood Naubolos's son Euryalos, equal to man-destroying Ares,
who was best in beauty and build
of all the Phaeacians after faultless Laodamas.

185 But Laodamas too is involved in this scene: Odysseus includes him and all the young Phaeacian athletes when he says that they taunt him with their challenge (*Odyssey* 8.153–157):

Λαοδάμαν, τί με ταῦτα κελεύετε κερτομέοντες;
κήδεά μοι καὶ μᾶλλον ἐνὶ φρεσὶν ἤ περ ἄεθλοι,
ὃς πρὶν μὲν μάλα πολλὰ πάθον καὶ πολλὰ μόγησα,
νῦν δὲ μεθ' ὑμετέρῃ ἀγορῇ νόστοιο χατίζων
ἧμαι, λισσόμενος βασιλῆά τε πάντα τε δῆμον.

Laodamas, why do you bid me to do this, taunting me?
There are more cares in my heart than games,
who have suffered many things and had may toils before,
and now sit in your assembly longing for my return,
supplicating the king and all the people.

The second person plural in Odysseus's reply (κελεύετε/ὑμετέρῃ) helps to redirect attention from Laodamas to Euryalos, who speaks next in answer to Odysseus; in fact, however, Laodamas alone issued the actual challenge to Odysseus (*Odyssey* 8.145–151). For Alcinous's role in this scene see §2.125–§2.127 above.

true, I think, that Odysseus describes his own inmost self, hidden at present
to outward appearance, when he characterizes the man with the gift of fair
speech (*Odyssey* 8.171–173):[186]

ὁ δ' ἀσφαλέως ἀγορεύει

αἰδοῖ μειλιχίῃ, μετὰ δὲ πρέπει ἀγρομένοισιν,

ἐρχόμενον δ' ἀνὰ ἄστυ θεὸν ὣς εἰσορόωσιν.

> He speaks unerringly
> with gentle modesty, and he stands out among those gathered,
> and they look on him as a god as he walks through the city.

But indirectly his words also set the standard for a prince who will become
king of the Phaeacians, and for a like-named future king who, in reality,
already hears these words at the festival of the Panionia. The standard for
this future king, one could say, is Odysseus himself, insofar as it is himself
that Odysseus describes in these lines.[187]

§4.54 Laodamas is the last piece in my interpretation of the Phaeacians.
The Neleids gave to some of the Ionians who celebrated the Panionia a common
past in the form of the Kodrid myth, and in Homeric epic this myth was univer-
salized in the Phaeacians, whose king and queen embody the first two stages
of the myth, Pylos and Athens. Laodamas, the future king, brings that common
past down to the present: the Ionians who celebrated the Panionia embraced
not only a collective past based on that of Miletus, but also a collective present
in which Miletus was still the leader. Laodamas, if he does indeed represent
the Neleid king Leodamas, is, as it were, the living proof of the central role
that Miletus must have played in the creation of the Panionic league on the
one hand, and in the development of the Homeric poems on the other hand.
Miletus's future role still lay hidden in the heroic age, when the city was held
by barbarian Carians (Καρῶν βαρβαροφώνων, *Iliad* 2.867–869), but the future is
nonetheless prefigured in the Phaeacian prince.

---

186 I follow Martin here (see n4.183 above).
187 It seems significant that this princely instruction is delivered at games that are most likely
meant to evoke contemporary games at the Panionia. For the attitude of Euryalos toward
an apparently lowborn participant cf. Mann 1998, who studies the aristocratic origins of
the classical gymnasium, and who argues that the Phaeacians' games, including the exclu-
sive attitude of Euryalos, are a precursor of the gymnasium (Mann 1998:15–18); Mann
dates the institutionalization of the gymnasium to the first half of the sixth century BC,
when aristocrats' traditional role had been diminished by the development of the polis
and phalanx warfare (Mann 1998:18–20).

§4.55 Leodamas has his own personal story, and it is worth asking what light his story throws on Homeric epic. This Neleid prince had to win the kingship in a contest with a rival, and his uncertain situation, at the very least, corresponds to the precarious state of kingship seen in the Homeric poems, where Odysseus must rid his palace of a host of rivals, and Agamemnon, who is unsure of his position in the *Iliad*, loses both his position and his life to a rival, as told in the *Odyssey*. Leodamas too was ultimately murdered by his rival for the kingship of Miletus, but presumably this part of the story still lay in the future when the Homeric poems were composed. The very fact that Leodamas had a rival at his back from the start of his career, however, throws a certain light on the "instruction of princes" in *Odyssey* 8, where right and wrong behavior are contrasted with each other in the persons of the courteous Laodamas and the offensive Euryalos. I do not propose that Euryalos too is based on a historical figure, but he does perhaps personify the danger that kingship faced. Euryalos is not presented as a rival for the Phaeacian kingship, but is that how he would have struck an Ionian audience, and is that why Odysseus spares nothing to put him in his proper place?

§4.56 I have made my case for the role of Miletus and the Neleids in the creation of the Homeric poems at the festival of the Panionia. The parts of the poems in which the influence of the Neleids is, to my mind, certain are Nestor's role in both poems and the Phaeacian episode of the *Odyssey* in its entirety. It is time to consider common characteristics of these parts of the poems and to draw conclusions from them. Surely the most salient characteristic of these parts of the poems is the veil of secrecy that surrounds them, or, if that is too strong a term, the extended irony that characterizes them. It is of course in the nature of traditional epic poetry, and of other poetry as well, to allude to different parts of the tradition and thereby to add meaning to whatever subject is at hand. The death and funeral of Patroclus in the *Iliad*, for example, allude to the death and funeral of Achilles outside the *Iliad*, and this deepens the significance of Patroclus's story.[188] But the irony of Nestor's role goes well beyond this in scope, and it differs in quality as well. The quality of Nestor's ironic role is perhaps best exemplified by his speech at the end of the chariot race for Patroclus, when he thanks Achilles for his special

---

188 See Kakridis 1949:65–83: the scene in *Iliad* 18 in which Thetis and the Nereids visit Achilles as he grieves at the news of Patroclus's death most likely reflects a similar scene, elsewhere in the tradition, in which Thetis and the Nereids come to lament Achilles' own death (Kakridis 65–75); in *Iliad* 23, when the winds Boreas and Zephyros do not come to help burn Patroclus's pyre and have to be called specially, there is reason to think that this motif is drawn from Achilles' funeral (Kakridis 75–83; see EN4.7 to n4.104 above).

prize, and rejoices that he does not escape Achilles' notice as to the honor that befits him (_Iliad_ 23.648–649):

> οὐδέ σε λήθω,
> τιμῆς ἧς τέ μ' ἔοικε τετιμῆσθαι μετ' Ἀχαιοῖς.

> And I do not escape your notice
> as to the honor that it befits me to receive among the Achaeans.

So much care is taken in the chariot race to mask Nestor's real role that the phrase _oudé se léthō_, "I do not escape your notice," at the episode's end can only be taken as a touchstone to separate those who know what his real role in the race has been from those who do not. Clearly there must have been those whose "notice" Nestor did escape because they did not know his traditions and therefore could not understand the irony of his role; otherwise the secrecy surrounding his role has no point, for a secret known to all is not a secret, and it is hard to see why the Homeric poems would go to such lengths to conceal what was simply common knowledge. It is for this reason that I do not think that Nestor's epic traditions were as widely known as is often assumed. Rather, I think that these traditions were the closely held possession of the Neleid family in Miletus, where they had long been the subject of song in the relatively closed world of the Neleid court. At the Panionia, where the _Iliad_ took shape, Nestor was given a new role at Troy which built on his earlier epic traditions.[189] These earlier traditions were the key to under-

---

189 In his separate epic traditions Nestor was a young man; only when Nestor was added to the saga of Troy was the figure of the old man created (cf. Cantieni 1942:87). The idea that at Troy Nestor operates among the third generation of heroes during his own lifetime is meant, I think, to establish a sharp divide between the aged Nestor (who is new) and the young Nestor (who is old); a middle-aged Nestor does not exist in epic as far as we know. It was perhaps to distinguish the old hero at Troy from the young hero in Pylos that the _hippóta Néstōr_ of ancient Pylian fame became _Gerḗnios hippóta Néstōr_ at Troy, if _Gerḗnios_, derived from _géras_, "privilege of the old," simply means "old," as forcefully argued by Bader 1980:55–56: note in particular _Iliad_ 4.325, where Nestor, referring to his role as counselor and speaker (i.e. to his Homeric role in essence) says τὸ γὰρ γέρας ἐστὶ γερόντων, "for that is the privilege of the old"; a full and convincing morphological analysis of the derivation of _Gerḗnios_ from _géras_ has now been offered by Timothy Barnes in an unpublished paper delivered at the 2008 annual meeting of the American Philological Association. The question that remains is when and how the aged figure came into existence in epic. Among those who take Nestor to be a historical figure (and even among those who do not) the assumption has been that his role at Troy goes back indefinitely far in epic tradition. I propose instead that the aged Nestor is strictly the creation of the _Iliad_ and the _Odyssey_ at the Panionia. This view may need to be modified to take account of Antilochus's death at the hands of Memnon, to which, I have argued (EN4.7 to n4.104 above), the _Iliad_ alludes in

standing Nestor's hidden role in the *Iliad* and the *Odyssey*, and a knowledge of them must have spread to the other Ionians. Knowing Nestor's traditions would have been a sign of having embraced Miletus's Panionic ideology, and there may thus have been an eagerness to acquire them; in this regard the spread of Nestor's traditions would have been like the spread of the Kodrid myth, and this was no doubt the point. The Kodrid myth is embodied in the Phaeacians, and in order to understand the Phaeacians the Ionians first had to understand Nestor's role in both poems. Homeric epic gives the Phaeacians a large place in the overall design of the two poems, and this, I think, is a measure of the extent to which Homeric epic was a tool to advance the Neleids' Panionic agenda. As knowledge of Nestor's traditions and an understanding of his Homeric role spread so too did Panionism. Thus there was a balance between those who knew Nestor's traditions and those who did not, even among the Ionians who celebrated the Panionia. We may say that in this sense Nestor's traditions were esoteric, and this allowed the key to them to be lost, except perhaps among the Homeridai, when the Homeric poems left the Panionia.[190] Nestor's traditions were never, I think, common knowledge.

Book 8: this allusion, if it is real, presupposes Nestor's role at Troy, and the question again is how old that role is. I argued earlier that Memnon, insofar as his death leads directly to Achilles' death (as it does in the *Aithiopis* of Arctinus; see Proclus *Chrestomathy* lines 188-192 [Allen 1912:106 lines 4-9]), is a variant of Hector, who has this role in the *Iliad* (or is at least said to have it in the *Iliad*). Patroclus and Antilochus are likewise variants in the same story, for their deaths precede Achilles' encounters with Hector and Memnon respectively. Patroclus, I think, is the older variant: in the *Iliad* Antilochus is brought into the story of Patroclus as a parallel, as when he tells Achilles of Patroclus's death and thus foreshadows his own death, and when he competes in the chariot race for Patroclus, where the parallel with Patroclus arises from the dangerous example set by Nestor for both young men, one of whom has already died. In *Odyssey* 24, where Agamemnon tells Achilles in the underworld about his burial at Troy, he makes the relationship between Patroclus and Antilochus clear: Achilles was buried with Patroclus in the same golden urn, but Antilochus was buried separately (*Odyssey* 24.76-78). Patroclus and Antilochus—whom Achilles "honored most after Patroclus died" (*Odyssey* 24.78-79)—are ranked here, and the ranking, I think, correlates directly with the age of their traditions. I thus do not think that the tradition for Antilochus's death need be much older than the Homeric poems, or that it necessarily arose outside the Panionia itself, where epic song probably included more than the Homeric poems. This, however, is to reach the limit of what can be said on this speculative subject. It was at the Panionia, I think, that in an even more fundamental way the *Odyssey* took shape (see n4.114 above for the idea that the *Odyssey* is, so to speak, a secondary epic as compared with the more traditional *Iliad*). I hold to the view that it was the Neleids, with their epic hero *Néstōr*, who made a *nóstos* poem the companion piece to the *Iliad*; this was the Neleids' particular epic domain (cf. above §4.25 end).

190 The Phaeacians, who represent the Ionians at the Panionia, also represent the creation of the Homeric poems at the Panionia; this is easily inferred from Odysseus's poetic performance before the Phaeacians in Books 9-12 of the *Odyssey*. It is interesting to keep this

§4.57 The level of refinement that characterizes Nestor's hidden role in the *Iliad* and the *Odyssey* could only have been attained, I think, through repeated performances before an audience that was challenged to understand what it heard, and that responded to the challenge. The refinement of Homeric poetry, especially as I see it in the deployment of Nestor's traditions, is to me a great argument that these poems were created orally. I do not think that a literate poet, or a poet who dictated to a scribe, could have produced Nestor's role, which spans the two poems, all in one step, or that an audience would have understood it if he did. A literate poet would of course have had no way to perform the two poems before one audience, and thus no reason to create Nestor's hidden role in the two poems in the first place.[191]

---

equation between the Phaeacians and the Homeric poems in mind when the Phaeacians are threatened with disappearance after Odysseus's return home: the Homeric poems too were threatened with disappearance, since their existence depended on performance at the Panionia, and such performance was not destined to last. Within the *Odyssey* we are not told whether the Phaeacians were spared by Poseidon, who had threatened to wall them off from the sea and the world beyond with a mountain. In another sense, however, they were sealed off, for their hidden identity as the Ionians at the Panionia was forgotten when the Homeric poems ceased to be performed there (only the Homeridai remembered their hidden identity, as the *Hymn to Apollo* shows; see §4.22 above). But the Homeric poems themselves were preserved, by the Homeridai on Chios, and with them the Phaeacians were also preserved, albeit behind a veil. The Phaeacians and their uncertain future within the *Odyssey* are an intriguing metaphor for the Homeric poems themselves. To what degree the Homeric poets may have been conscious of this metaphor is unknowable, but I do not think that they would have been totally unaware of it. I think that they knew that the fate of the Phaeacians, even if they survived as part of the Homeric poems, was to have their significance forgotten, for a true secret cannot easily survive as such in the long run. In Plato's *Ion* the rhapsode Ion discusses with Socrates the advice that Nestor gives Antilochus before the chariot race, and the point of the discussion is whether a poet is qualified to offer real technical advice on the subject of chariot racing (*Ion* 537a–538b). This discussion, which takes Nestor's advice for rounding the turning post wholly at face value, is, I think, the measure of what had been lost from this episode at a deeper level; the irony at this deeper level of the episode now escaped the notice of all, including professional rhapsodes like Ion.

191 One might call this the problem of the poet: What possible motive can the hypothetical literate poet have had for creating masterpieces on a monumental scale if they could never be performed before one audience? There is a related problem of audience: What audience would have wanted to hear only fragments of highly unified works? That the poems were necessarily performed piecemeal is, I think, a fatal weakness of the theory of literacy or dictation. F. A. Wolf used the image of an "inland ship" to describe the situation of a poem without an audience (cf. Ford 1997:84); it does not diminish Wolf's point that he thinks in terms of readers rather than listeners when he says: "If Homer lacked readers, then I certainly do not understand what in the world could have impelled him to conceive and plot out poems which were so long and so unified in the close interconnection of their parts" ("*si Homero lectores deerant, plane non assequor, quid tandem eum impellere potuisset in consilium et cogitationem tam longorum et continuo partium nexu consertorum carminum*") (Wolf

This is perhaps the greatest argument against the theory of the literate or dictating poet, but the refinement of Nestor's role counts little less for me. A literate poet simply did not have the means to achieve the level of refinement that was open to oral poets under the special circumstances of the Panionia. There every performance was a further refinement. For a literate poet further refinement, once he managed to get twenty-five thousand verses into written form, would have been practically impossible.[192] For a literate poet the initial form would have been the final form, and that simply does not account for the *Iliad* and the *Odyssey* as we know them.[193]

§4.58 This is not to deny that writing was available in the Homeric era. The first Greek inscription of any length dates to 740–730 BC, which, in my view, is probably when the Homeric poems began to take shape in Ionia. This would seem to be proof enough that the Homeric poems too could have been written down at the same early date. The Dipylon vase inscription, as it is called, contains a dactylic hexameter resembling a line of Homer in its formulaic technique, and this would seem to make the case for literacy all the stronger.[194] But the inscription, while showing that writing had indeed become

---

1795:112, Part 1, Chapter 26; English translation 1985:116 as adapted by Ford 1997:84); Murray 1934:187 expands on Wolf as follows: "Every work of art that was ever created was intended in some way to be used. No picture was painted for blind men; no ship built where there was no water. What was to be the use of the *Iliad*?" (cf. Ford 1997:108). Taplin 1992:22–44 posits complete performances of the *Iliad* in the eighth century BC, but by the poet Homer alone; this model, which is strained to the limit to account for performances of the *Iliad*, breaks down for performances of the *Iliad* and *Odyssey* combined. Stanley 1993:279–281 pictures complete performance of the poems for the first time at the festival of the Panathenaia in the sixth century; this is the right model but the wrong date for the poems' composition. Cf. Ford 1997:88–89.

192 It is not that a literate poet could not be subtle in what he created; it is that he would have had to create all his subtlety from the start, with only limited opportunities to improve what he had written, and a laborious process to record these improvements when he made them. For oral poets the poems existed only in performance and in the memory of past performances, and each new performance was therefore an invitation to further refinement. The audience was a partner in this process, for the audience had to approve what it heard for the process to continue. But if we imagine a single poet producing the same degree of subtlety and refinement through the use of writing, we are hard pressed to see what the audience could have contributed to the process.

193 I have this final problem with the theory of literacy or dictation: given the enormous success of the two monumental poems, why did no one else imitate the innovative new method that produced them and create something else on the same scale? Surely the method, which differed from the methods of all other poets, could not have been kept a secret for long. As far as we know, nothing like the *Iliad* and *Odyssey* was ever again produced.

194 In the post-Euclidian alphabet the hexameter reads: ὃς νῦν ὀρχηστῶν πάντων ἀταλώτατα παίζει, "whoever now performs most gracefully of all dancers." The inscription also

available for certain purposes when the Homeric poems were composed, is
a long way from a written *Iliad* and *Odyssey* in both scale and purpose, and
these differences, I think, are decisive.[195]

§4.59 Somewhat later than the Dipylon vase inscription is the "Nestor's
cup" inscription.[196] This inscription is again, and for the same reasons, not
evidence for a written *Iliad* and *Odyssey*, but it raises the question of the
spread of the Homeric poems in whatever way from their place of origin. The
Nestor's cup inscription was found in Pithekoussai (modern Ischia) among
the western Greeks, and it apparently refers to our *Iliad*. The inscription
contains three verses, the first of which, in my view, refers to Nestor's cup in
Iliad 11. While it is possible that the reference is not to *Iliad* 11 in particular,
but to epic tradition in general, I do not think that this is the case for reasons
given earlier: I do not think that Nestor's traditions, which were a well-kept
secret even within the Homeric poems, were at all widely known outside of
the Homeric poems. The Nestor's cup inscription is an ideal place to consider
this idea more closely.

§4.60 The inscription occurs on a clay cup whose fragments have been
reassembled. There are small gaps in the text that must be restored, and one
such gap causes some uncertainty of interpretation; the text and interpreta-
tion that I follow are those of Calvert Watkins:

---

contains the beginning of a second line, which may be read τοῦ τόδε, "his this" (the vase is
a prize). The vase has been definitely attributed to the Dipylon master and is thus securely
dated to 740–730 BC (Powell 1991:158 with references in n92). Powell 1991:160–161 nicely
compares the hexameter with *Odyssey* 8.382: Ἀλκίνοε κρεῖον, πάντων ἀριδείκετε λαῶν,
"King Alcinous, most exalted of all your people," which has the same juxtaposition of
πάντων, "of all," and superlative adjective (or adverb) in the same metrical position.

195 For the purpose of poetic inscriptions I quote Nagy 1992:35: "The language of the earliest
   inscribed utterances makes it clear that writing was being used as an *equivalent* to perfor-
   mance, not as a *means* for performance. It is evident from the language of the earliest
   inscriptions from the eighth century and thereafter, and the pattern holds all the way till
   550 BC or so, that the speech-act of performance was thought to be inherent in the given
   inscription itself, which normally communicates in the first person, as if it were a talking
   object." Nagy here follows Svenbro 1988:33–52 (English translation 1993:26–43).

196 *Supplementum Epigraphicum Graecum* 14 (1957) no. 604. The date of the inscription is not
   certain, but it is not later than the end of the eighth century BC. The date first proposed,
   the third quarter of the eighth century, is, I think, a little too early; see below §4.64–§4.65,
   where I argue for a date closer to the end of the century. The earlier date was proposed by
   Buchner, who discovered the inscription (Buchner and Russo 1955). The earlier date, which
   would rival the date of the Dipylon vase inscription, still has a considerable attraction; cf.
   Powell 1991:163 regarding the Nestor's cup inscription: "According to recent opinion, it is
   the second oldest complete Greek alphabetic inscription, after the Dipylon oinochoe, or
   just as old, given the uncertainty of all this."

Νέστορός ἐ[στ]ι εὔποτ[ον] ποτήριον.
ὃς δ' ἂ‹ν› τοῦδε πίησι ποτηρί[ου], αὐτίκα κεῖνον
ἵμερος αἱρήσει καλλιστε[φά]νου Ἀφροδίτης.

Nestor's cup is good to drink from.
But he who drinks from this cup, forthwith him
desire of fair-garlanded Aphrodite will seize.

Watkins has made a convincing case that the first line refers to Nestor's famous cup in *Iliad* 11, whereas the two lines that follow refer to the clay *skúphos* on which the inscription is written; the contrast between the iambic trimeter of the first line and the dactylic hexameter of the last two lines, and the contrast between the phrase Νέστορος...ποτήριον, "Nestor's...cup," in the first line and the phrase τοῦδε ποτηρίου, "this cup," in the second line, lead to this conclusion.[197] To these metrical and phraseological contrasts, which are well brought out by Watkins, I would add a contrast of meaning as well: the idea that the cup on which the inscription appears will produce erotic passion cannot be associated with the old man Nestor's cup, unless this is a joke; the purpose of the cup in *Iliad* 11 is not erotic, but medicinal. Nestor's cup is simply a foil to the cup bearing the inscription; it was chosen for the purpose because it offered a contrast, and because it was famous.

§4.61 The contrast between Nestor's cup and the cup with the inscription, however, is not essential to my argument. What is essential to my argument is a reference to *Iliad* 11, and that is not affected if the reading ε[ἰμ]ι, "I am," is preferred to ἐ[στ]ι, "is," in line 1, and if a rather ordinary clay *skúphos*, as a kind of joke, claims to be Nestor's famous cup. If it is granted that the inscription refers to the epic hero Nestor and his cup, I repeat that I do not think that the reference is to Nestor's epic tradition in general, but to *Iliad* 11 in particular, and to support this argument I turn now to the passage in *Iliad* 11.[198] I will argue that Nestor's cup is wholly a function of the story in *Iliad* 11 and that it probably had no prior existence in epic.

197 Watkins 1976. Others have thought that only one cup is referred to in the inscription: either Nestor's cup in *Iliad* 11, which the clay cup claims to be, or the cup of a local Pithekoussan who happened to be named Nestor; these interpretations both restore ε[ἰμ]ι, "I am," rather than ἐ[στ]ι in the first line of the inscription. The issue is discussed further in EN4.12.
198 Watkins 1976:38 leaves open the possibility that the inscription does not allude to *Iliad* 11 "as we know it," but to epic tradition generally. I think that the allusion is in fact quite specific.

§4.62 The question is whether the elaborate cup in which Nestor prepares a *kukeōn* to restore the wounded warrior Makhaon is a fixed attribute of the Pylian king. Nestor is said to have brought this cup with him from home (*Iliad* 11.632), and there is thus no doubt that for the story of *Iliad* 11 the cup is specifically his. The existence of an actual Bronze Age artifact resembling Nestor's cup has significantly strengthened the impression that Nestor had always had such a cup in Greek epic tradition. This famous artifact, however, is from Mycenae, and presumably kings of many Bronze Age cities had similar elaborate cups to drink from. Why would Nestor be known for his cup unless there was something truly distinctive about it? [199] What seems to distinguish Nestor's cup in *Iliad* 11, besides its elaboration, is the fact that it is very large and very heavy when full: another man would have had difficulty lifting it, but Nestor lifted it with ease (*Iliad* 11.636–637):

ἄλλος μὲν μογέων ἀποκινήσασκε τραπέζης

πλεῖον ἐόν, Νέστωρ δ' ὁ γέρων ἀμογητὶ ἄειρεν.

Another man would have lifted it from the table with effort,
since it was full, but the old man Nestor lifted it without effort.

This motif has a purpose in the episode, for Nestor is about to tell a story in which his deeds of war push the limit, to say the least, of what a single man could do. This is the point of his story, for in his battle with the Epeians he was not just one man, but, by his twin myth, the equivalent of two. Now the cup that is described in *Iliad* 11 also seems to be twice the size, or at least to have twice the elaboration, of an ordinary cup if we consider the cup from Mycenae to be an ordinary cup. Nestor's cup has twice as many handles and twice as many decorative doves per handle as does the cup from Mycenae, and it also has two bases.[200] Here is the description of Nestor's cup, which his maidservant Hekamede sets on the table next to the ingredients for a *kukeōn* (*Iliad* 11.632–635):

πὰρ δὲ δέπας περικαλλές, ὃ οἴκοθεν ἦγ' ὁ γεραιός,

χρυσείοις ἥλοισι πεπαρμένον· οὔατα δ' αὐτοῦ

---

199 In the case of Achilles' shield, and Ajax's, we know what distinguished them from other shields.

200 It is not clear exactly what is meant by two "bases" (πυθμένες), and it is thus hard to compare this feature of Nestor's cup with the Mycenaean artifact. Leaf finds an equivalent feature on the Mycenaean artifact (see following note), and he may well be right. Be this as it may, the poet does not let the opportunity slip to repeat that Nestor's cup is in every respect double, including its base.

τέσσαρ' ἔσαν, <u>δοιαὶ</u> δὲ πελειάδες ἀμφὶς ἕκαστον
χρύσειαι νεμέθοντο, <u>δύω</u> δ' ὑπὸ πυθμένες ἦσαν.

Next to these [she put] a beautiful cup which the old man
    brought from home,
pierced with gold studs; it had <u>four handles</u>,
and around each one <u>two</u> golden doves
were pecking, and there were <u>two</u> bases underneath.

Walter Leaf compares Nestor's cup with the Bronze Age artifact as follows: "This famous cup of Nestor receives an interesting illustration in the cup represented in Plate IV, which was found at Mykenai by Schliemann; it is of solid gold and stands eight or nine inches high. The poetical cup only differs in having four handles (οὔατα) instead of two, and two doves to each instead of one only."[201] Nestor's cup is distinctive, at least in relation to the Mycenaean artifact, but what makes it distinctive fits so well with the meaning of his story to Patroclus in *Iliad* 11, in which Nestor proves that he was worth two of any other man, that it is far more plausible that his cup is a poet's flight of fancy, inspired by the story to come, than that Nestor was known through the ages for having a goblet with twice the usual number of handles, doves, and perhaps even bases. To me the cup looks like an ad hoc creation—based on knowledge of real Bronze Age objects, to be sure—to enhance the meaning of a particular episode in *Iliad* 11, which involves not only Makhaon, but also Patroclus, and the whole larger story of the *Iliad*.[202] This analysis falls short of

201 Leaf and Bayfield 1908 on *Iliad* 11.632 (Plate IV is on p. 518); Leaf adds that "The four handles are to be regarded as placed in pairs, one pair at each side, not at equal intervals all round the cup." Leaf has two suggestions for the cup's two "bases," the second more plausible than the first: 1) πυθμένες may designate the supports running from the base of the cup to the two pairs of handles (the Mycenaean cup has two such supports running from the base of the cup to its two single handles), but this is a strange use of the word "base": what would the actual base then be called? 2) In addition to the base on which the whole object stands, the bottom of the actual cup represents a second base, which protrudes slightly but noticeably on the Mycenaean artifact. To say that the cup has two bases would thus be a way of identifying this kind of cup. (The gold studs on Nestor's cup have no equivalent on the Mycenaean cup unless the rivets attaching the two supports to the base count as ἧλοι; cf. Leaf and Bayfield, ibid. In any case there are no decorative studs on the Mycenaean cup.)

202 See §2.11–§2.17 above. In a number of scenes in the *Iliad* a single hero lifts a rock that two men of today could not lift (Diomedes, Hector, and Aeneas in *Iliad* 5.303, 12.447, and 20.286 are all said to do this; Ajax in *Iliad* 12.383 does something analogous). The fact that the comparison is between one man and two suggests a connection with Nestor and his cup in *Iliad* 11: the explicit comparison is different (Nestor easily lifts what another man could only lift with difficulty), but the point of the comparison is the same: Nestor in the

proof positive that Nestor's cup belongs only to the *Iliad*, but it gives support
to my contention, based on a more general argument, that the Nestor's cup
inscription in fact alludes to the *Iliad* as we know it.[203]

§4.63 But how did Euboean colonists in the west know about the *Iliad*
if, as I have argued, the Homeric poems existed only in performance at
the Panionia? In a strict sense this would have been the case, but word of
the poems may have traveled more widely. There were probably guests at
the Panionia who, if they had poetic skills, could have carried parts of the
poems away with them. I have already suggested that Athenians, who inhab-
ited (in Solon's phrase) "the oldest land of Ionia," were perhaps specially
honored guests at the Panionia and may have become aware of the Homeric
poems in this way, so to speak, from the start.[204] Euboea was also Ionian, and

---

story he is about to tell is more than a match for two heroes at once. It is possible that
the comparisons with men of today (οἷοι νῦν βροτοί εἰσ', "such as mortals are now") in
the four passages cited above derive from Nestor's comparison in *Iliad* 1.272 between the
heroes of his youth and those at Troy (οἳ νῦν βροτοί εἰσι, "who are mortals now"); cf. Kirk
1990 on *Iliad* 5.304, who also sees a relationship between the Nestor passage and the other
four passages but in rather different terms.

203 My more general argument is that Nestor's traditions were not widely known outside the
Homeric poems (see §4.56 above), but I cannot claim this as an absolute principle (see
above n4.155 and n4.189 above on Antilochus and Memnon). Achilles' shield may be an
analogous case to Nestor's cup, but I see significant differences. I would argue that Achilles'
shield was part of the story of Achilles' wrath for as long as Patroclus was part of the same
story; we do not know how long that was, but I think that Patroclus was certainly part of
the story before the development of our *Iliad* at the Panionia. Nestor's role in the *Iliad*, on
the other hand, I think actually began at the Panionia under Neleid influence. The secret
nature of Nestor's traditions in the *Iliad* has no counterpart in the case of Patroclus and
Achilles; their tradition, I think, was widely known. Cf. n4.189 above on the relative ages of
the traditions for Patroclus and Antilochus. For another view of the Nestor's cup inscrip-
tion and its relation to the *Iliad* and earlier epic tradition see S. West 1994, who argues that
both the inscription and the *Iliad* allude to an older tradition about Nestor and his cup; cf.
also Graziosi 2002:135n33. One reason for this view is the apparently puzzling statement
in the *Iliad* that Nestor more than others was able to lift his cup; this motif seems to both
West 1994:13–14 and Graziosi to point to an unknown older tradition about the cup. In my
view the motif is integral to the story as it is told in the *Iliad* (see the discussion above and
§5.4 below).

204 See above §4.44 and n4.158. It is possible that Nestor's aborted battle with the Actorione
Molione is represented on a late eighth-century Attic vase on which what appear to be
Siamese twins stand in a chariot and are attacked by a single figure; given that Nestor's
traditions were not widely known outside the Homeric poems (see §4.56 above) the vase
would be further evidence of early Athenian awareness of the *Iliad*. But the subject is
disputed; cf. King 1977:34: "The attacker of the double figure on the belly zone of the famous
Subdipylon oinochoe from the Agora (about 725 BC) is usually identified with Nestor, and
the subject is taken to be the struggle between Nestor and the twins which is described in
Iliad 11.750–752.... But it is still possible that Heracles is the attacker: the encounter in which
Iphicles was wounded has also been suggested as the subject [Fraser 1940:460n8]." Another

Pithekoussai, the earliest Greek colony in the west, was founded by the two leading cities of Euboea, Chalcis and Eretria.[205] Perhaps Pithekoussans, being Ionian, were also sometimes guests at the Panionia. They lived a long way from Ionia, but their Euboean colonizers were well known travelers, and they perhaps were intermediaries in spreading the word to their western colony.[206] Herodotus represents the Panionic league as an exclusive club, which, as Smyrna discovered, did not admit new members. But admitting new members is not the same as admitting occasional guests, and in any case we should not be overly influenced by Herodotus's experience of Ionian exclusivity in the fifth century BC. In the eighth century BC the league was expanding and the mentality would have been different.[207] This is not to say that the Ionians of

---

interpretation is offered by Fittschen 1969:74, who states "rather convincingly" (King 1977:39n29) that the theme of the vase is two chariot groups against one. See also Hampe 1950:56 and n126 with bibliography; King 1977:34, 38n27, 39nn28 and 29, with bibliography; Shapiro 1983:89, with figures 6.2a, 2b; Snodgrass 1998:30–31, who comes down against an identification with Nestor and the Molione. Cf. also below n4.209 end.

205 Strabo 5.4.9.
206 It is worth noting that Euboea is a point of reference for the Phaeacians: in *Odyssey* 7 Alcinous promises to take Odysseus home even if he lives beyond Euboea, where Phaeacians once brought Rhadamanthys to see Tityos (cf. §2.117 above); Euboea, those who went there say, is the farthest land (*Odyssey* 7.317–324):

πομπὴν δ' ἐς τόδ' ἐγὼ τεκμαίρομαι, ὄφρ' ἐΰ εἰδῇς,
αὔριον ἔς· τῆμος δὲ σὺ μὲν δεδμημένος ὕπνῳ
λέξεαι, οἱ δ' ἐλόωσι γαλήνην, ὄφρ' ἂν ἵκηαι
πατρίδα σὴν καὶ δῶμα, καὶ εἴ πού τοι φίλον ἐστίν,
εἴ περ καὶ μάλα πολλὸν ἑκαστέρω ἔστ' Εὐβοίης·
τὴν γὰρ τηλοτάτω φάσ' ἔμμεναι οἵ μιν ἴδοντο
λαῶν ἡμετέρων, ὅτε τε ξανθὸν Ῥαδάμανθυν
ἦγον ἐποψόμενον Τιτυόν, Γαιήϊον υἱόν.

I decree an escort for this time, so that you may know it well,
for tomorrow; throughout the voyage you will lie overcome by sleep,
and they will ply the placid sea until you reach
your fatherland and home, or wherever is dear to you,
even if it is farther away than Euboea,
which is said to be farthest off by those of our people who saw it
when they took fair-haired Rhadamanthys
to see Tityos, Earth's son.

There was a strong tie between Eretria and Miletus, allies in the Lelantine war (cf. n4.64 above); for the campaign of the Milesian king Leodamas against Karystos in the context of this war see Herda 1998:46 and n4.174 above.

207 We do not know when Smyrna unsuccessfully sought admission, but I suspect that it was soon after the league was formed; Smyrna, as argued earlier, may have been denied admission for particular reasons having to do with its origins from Colophon, and not from a general policy of exclusion, as one might infer from Herodotus; see my discussion §4.7–§4.8 above.

the dodecapolis were not conscious of their special identity; on the contrary,
I think that it was they who, when they heard the Homeric poems, under-
stood Nestor's hidden role, and so recognized themselves in the Phaeacians.
Perhaps the secrecy of the Homeric poems with respect to Nestor's role
and the Phaeacians' identity had to do with the presence of outsiders at the
Panionia. If not even all the Ionians of the dodecapolis knew Nestor's secrets,
surely he must have escaped the notice of outside guests at their festival
entirely. The main point to be explained in Nestor's role remains the reason
for its total secrecy, and a distinction between members and guests at the
Panionia helps with this problem.

§4.64 How an awareness of *Iliad* 11 could have penetrated to the western
Greek world while the Homeric poems were still in the process of develop-
ment is not as intractable a problem as it might seem. It is true, I think, that
the *Iliad* and the *Odyssey* existed in their entirety only in performance at the
Panionia, but parts of the poems—indeed all of the poems—could have been
performed piecemeal elsewhere. It is not surprising that what attracted atten-
tion in distant Pithekoussai was the description of an unusual object; it would
be far more surprising, I think, if an awareness of Nestor's real role in *Iliad* 11,
and elsewhere in the Homeric poems, had spread outside the Panionia. But if
this analysis is correct, the date of the Nestor's cup inscription becomes the
terminus ante quem for the full-scale development of the Homeric poems at
the Panionia. It is therefore important to date this inscription as accurately
as possible, and I think that current opinion may date it somewhat too early.
There is no agreed-on absolute date, but the comparison (and rivalry) of the
Nestor's cup inscription with the oldest Greek inscription, the Dipylon vase
inscription, causes reluctance to go lower than c. 725 BC, and some would
date the Nestor's cup inscription even earlier.[208] I do not propose to lower this
date by much, only to c. 700 BC at the latest. The *Iliad* and the *Odyssey* were, I
think, the newest songs in the air, which many heard (or heard about) for the
first time, when the inscription was written: this stage, I think, came at the
end of the eighth century BC.[209]

208 Cf. n4.196 above.
209 Accordingly the writer of the inscription had first heard of Nestor's fabulous cup not long
before the inscription was written (the fame of the newest songs had spread quickly, as in
the dictum at *Odyssey* 1.351–352). The question of when the Homeric poems became widely
known has been discussed above on the basis of texts (see EN4.6 to n4.98 above, and, with
respect to Solon's knowledge of Homer, n4.149 above), and will be pursued further below
on the basis of texts, but I have not considered another criterion by which this question
is judged: representations of Homeric episodes in vase paintings. Steven Lowenstam has
devoted attention to this problem and has reached an essentially negative conclusion: to

judge by vase paintings the Homeric poems were not known as such before the early fifth century BC, and Lowenstam calls into question their existence before that date (Lowenstam 1997, especially pp. 58–67). I do not dispute the lack of evidence for Homer in vase paintings, nor the need to explain it, but there are other criteria that must also be considered in this question. In my view Lowenstam dismisses too easily the argument of Burkert (and others) that the *Iliad* and *Odyssey* were known to Stesichorus, whose death in 556 BC is thus a (very late, but nonetheless real) *terminus ante quem* for the Homeric poems (Lowenstam 1997:58–59 and, for an earlier statement of his argument, 1993:216n88; Burkert 1987:51). Lowenstam argues that a passage of Stesichorus's *Geryoneis* cannot be shown to draw from the *Iliad* because the case for this depends too much on uncertain restorations of the text, and this may be so. But he does not equally consider the case for Stesichorus's knowledge of the *Odyssey*, and this seems to me to be unassailable: Stesichorus's *Nostoi* recreated the scene in *Odyssey* 15.168ff. where Telemachus leaves Helen and Menelaus in Sparta, and Helen interprets a bird omen favorable to Odysseus's return (Stesichorus fr. 32.1–9 Page [*PMG* 209.1–9]):

θε[ῖ]ον ἐ[ξ]αίφνας τέρας ἰδοῖσα νύμφα
ὣ̣δε ̣δε[ ] Ἑλένα φωνᾶι ποτ[ὶ] παίδ᾽ Ὀδύσειο[ν·
Τηλέμαχ[ ]τις ὅδ᾽ ἁμὶν ἄγγελ[ο]ς ὠρανόθεν
δι᾽ αἰθέρο[ς ἀτ]ρυγέτας κατέπτατο, βᾶ δ[
          ]. ̣ φοινᾶι κεκλαγ{γ}ώ[ς
]...ς ὑμετέρους δόμους προφα [   ]υς
     ]..... αν ̣υς ἀνὴρ
βο]υ̣λα̣ῖς Ἀθάνας
     ]. ̣ηις αυτα λακέρυζα κορώνα.

Suddenly seeing the divine portent the nymph
thus [ ] Helen with her voice to the son of Odysseus;
Telemachus, this messenger to us from the sky
through the barren air flew down, and went [
          ] crying with its voice
] your houses [   ]
     ] man [   ]
by the coun]sels of Athena
     ] cawing crow.

This text is too close to what takes place in the *Odyssey*, and what takes place in the *Odyssey* is too particular to the development of the story of that poem, to speculate about other versions of the same story that may have been current: if other versions were that close to the *Odyssey*, in fact they were the *Odyssey*. It is uneconomical to posit anything else. There was thus a demonstrated interest in the *Odyssey* at a date when no such interest is documented on vase paintings. The reason for the latter lack of interest according to A. M. Snodgrass is that Greek visual artists had their own independent agenda to follow: they were not primarily interested in verbal art, and they thus have no real bearing on the question considered by Lowenstam (see in particular Snodgrass 1998). The question of Solon's knowledge of Homer, discussed in n4.149 above, raises the question of other early poets' knowledge of Homer: see West 1995:206–207 for possible allusions to the *Iliad* in Alcaeus fr. 44.6–8 LP (accepted by West, rejected by Lowenstam 1997:59) and Mimnermus fr. 2.1–4 West (rejected by West); for the controversies cf. Graziosi 2002:92n10. Lentini 2000 argues that Alcaeus fr. 70 LP alludes to disparate parts of the *Iliad* as we know it. In a more general comparison Seidensticker 1978 argues that Archilochus had Odysseus and the *Odyssey* in

611

§4.65 L. H. Jeffery pointed out unusual features in the script of the Nestor's cup inscription, including the formation of letters, punctuation, and a geminated lambda in the word καλλιστεφάνου, and on the basis of these features Rhys Carpenter proposed to date the inscription more than a century later than the cup itself.[210] But such a late dating was firmly rejected by the archaeologists familiar with the find-spot.[211] Jeffery herself dated the inscription "c. 700?,"[212] but, as already said, 725 or earlier has remained the usual dating. This date was proposed by Buchner when he first reported the discovery of the cup, and the same date was supported by Metzger.[213] But while the date may well be correct for the cup, it is not necessarily correct for the inscription, for the inscription was added to the cup secondarily.[214] The date of the tomb in which the cup was buried is the key issue, for this date is the *terminus ante quem* for the inscription, whose own date really cannot

---

mind as models. In Part 5 below I argue that in the late seventh or early sixth century BC the poet of the Pythian *Hymn to Apollo* was much concerned with the exact text of both the *Iliad* and the *Odyssey* (see §5.12–§5.14 and n5.59).

210 Jeffery 1961:235–236; Carpenter 1963. Jeffery writes as follows: "I know of no other example of an archaic poem in which the lines are thus separately written. Punctuation is : , as in examples from Eretria and Leontinoi [the examples are dated '550–525?' and '525?' BC by Jeffery]; *lambda* is geminated; the lettering is not tall and spidery like that of other very early inscriptions, but small and neat, very like that on Tataie's aryballos from Kyme [dated '675–650 BC?' by Jeffery]." For features of the script and other physical aspects of the inscription, cf. Powell 1991:163–164.

211 Metzger 1965, in consultation with G. Buchner. The cup's fragments were found in the necropolis of the Valle di San Montano and belonged to tomb 282. Cf. also Graham 1971:12.

212 For the date see Jeffery 1961 Plate 47.1.

213 Buchner relied solely on the date of the cup, which he put not later than the third quarter of the eighth century (Buchner 1955:220). The *skúphos* is of Aegean manufacture, perhaps from Rhodes (cf. Powell 1991:163 with n109). The design on the cup is purely Geometric in contrast to the bird motif found on the widespread Rhodian *skúphoi* of the seventh century. Nestor's cup, which was the first such Aegean *skúphos* found in Italy, cannot be precisely dated on its own (Metzger 1965:302 says only the second half of the eighth century BC); Buchner used fragments of another pottery type from the same tomb (globular proto-Corinthian *arúballoi*) to date the cup. His assumption is that the cup had been in use for some time before it was buried, but that the *arúballoi* were purely funerary, and that their date of manufacture was thus the same as their date of burial (Buchner and Russo 1955:220).

214 Carpenter 1963:83: "These lines were engraved after the vase was fired and were not added by the potter, to judge from their disregard of the ornamental painted bands girdling the vase"; Powell 1991:163–164 adds further detail: "The cup (10 x 15 cm) is decorated in black slip with rectangular decorative panels on either side consisting of four geometrically decorated metopal panels bordered at the bottom by a broad band. The horizontal band is decorated with parallel horizontal lines above and below a central horizontal zigzag. Along these parallel lines, and down the center of the zigzag, the inscription has been scratched, as if to accord with the decoration, although all three lines of the inscription begin outside the decorative horizontal band in the black slip near one of the handles."

be further specified. Metzger, in consultation with Buchner, addressed this issue, and came to the conclusion that the Protocorinthian globular *arúballoi* found in the tomb should not be dated later than 720 BC.[215] But these *arúballoi* have also been considered to be of a later style than that by Einar Gjerstad, who proposed a date "perhaps as late as 700 BC" for them.[216] The assumption that the *arúballoi* were buried at the same date that they were manufactured may also perhaps be open to question.[217] In sum, I cannot see that a date of 725 BC for the burial is more probable than a date of 700 BC, and I therefore take 700 BC as the proper *terminus ante quem*.

§4.66 The date for the Nestor's cup inscription is 700 BC or earlier, and the date for the Meliac War is 700 BC or later. The Panionic league was already in existence before the Meliac War according to the literary tradition, and this fits with my view of the Homeric poems. By the time of the Nestor's cup inscription, with its reference to *Iliad* 11, the development of the Homeric poems must have been well along, and this development, in my view, took place at the Panionia. This means that the Panionia must have been in existence before the Meliac War.

§4.67 Wilamowitz argued that the Panionic league arose after the Meliac War, but I am driven to the opposite conclusion, that the league came first. This leaves us with a number of problems. The basic problem of course remains even if the Panionic league resulted from the Meliac War as Wilamowitz proposed: at Panionion no remains earlier than 600 BC have been found and thus the league's existence earlier than this cannot be documented by archaeology. The cult of Poseidon Helikonios at Panionion is also a problem since this cult is evoked in *Iliad* 20. What can the history of this cult have been? Wilamowitz proposed that the cult originally belonged to Melia, and that the cities that destroyed Melia, when they divided Melia's territory among them, took collective responsibility for the cult, making it the common center of a new league.[218]

---

215 So I take his statement p. 304: "In these conditions the Protocorinthian aryballoi of tomb 282 should be considered earlier than the last decades of the eighth century" ("Dans ces conditions les aryballes protocorinthiens de la tombe 282 doivent être considérés comme antérieurs aux dernières décades du VIIIe siècle").

216 Gjerstad 1965:72: "The tomb contained Late Geometric pottery among which a cup that belonged to a man called Nestor, as told by its inscription, and globular Protocorinthian aryballoi of advanced shape. The latter indicate a date for the burial at the end of the 8th cent. B.C., perhaps as late as c. 700 B.C., and if the inscribed cup is somewhat earlier, that may very well be explained, as Buchner does, by the probability that the cup had been used by the deceased during his lifetime." Coldstream 1968:358n4 dates the *arúballoi* 720–710 BC (later than Metzger and earlier than Gjerstad).

217 See n4.213 above.

218 Wilamowitz 1906/1971:45–46/137. Wilamowitz argued that Melia had grown too powerful

But if the league existed before the Meliac War the process cannot have been exactly that, and here we are simply in the dark. We may suppose that the cult of Poseidon Helikonios was like the cult of Apollo at Delphi, which was originally tended by priests from nearby Krisa. Krisa was destroyed in the First Sacred War by members of the Amphictyonic league, and the cult became the league's collective responsibility. Did Melia similarly control the cult of the Panionic league, and did the "arrogance" for which Melia was destroyed have to do with its control of the league's cult?[219] This seems possible, but not likely: we have no indication that Panionion would have been the same valuable prize that Delphi was, and, at a more basic level, there is good reason to doubt that Melia was ever in the league.[220] We may alternatively suppose that the Panionic league had its center elsewhere before the Meliac War, and that when Melia was destroyed the league's center was moved to Panionion. In this case the league only acquired the cult of Poseidon Helikonios after the Meliac War, and earlier the league must have been dedicated to another god. Vitruvius in fact says that the cities that formed the league founded a temple to *Apollo Panionios*, but this evidence, which is sometimes taken at face value, is best left out of account: if the name is not simply Vitruvius's mistake for *Poseidon Helikonios*, it is best explained as an anachronistic reference on the part of Vitruvius's late-third century BC source to the cult and oracle of Apollo Klarios near Colophon.[221]

---

for its neighbors, which therefore banded together and destroyed it (p. 43/134). To illustrate Melia's presumed strength Wilamowitz pointed to the territory, extensive for the time, that it controlled on Cape Mykale (Pygela, allotted to Samos after the war, was more that twenty kilometers north of Melia itself).

219 Cf. Hiller von Gaertringen 1906 vi. The "arrogance" of Melia may be compared with the "hybris" of Krisa: in *Homeric Hymn to Apollo* 540–544 (a passage composed *post eventum*) Apollo's priests are warned against hybris and threatened with a change of regime at Delphi. Priene, which acquired the site of Melia, provided the priests of Poseidon Helikonios for the historical league. Priene may thus have been Melia's successor not only on the site of the former city, but also in the management of the cult at Panionion; cf. n4.85 above. In an event similar to that at Delphi, and at about the same time (c. 570 BC), the Eleans destroyed Pisa near Olympia and took over the conduct of the Olympic games (see Wade-Gery 1952:64n15).

220 Only Vitruvius says that the league had thirteen members, and that Melia was the thirteenth; this likely has to do with Vitruvius's late-third century source and the status of the Hellenistic city of Smyrna as the league's thirteenth member (see EN4.3 to n4.72 above). If Melia did belong to the league, the parallel with Krisa still breaks down: Krisa was made rich and arrogant by its control of an oracle consulted by outsiders, but at Panionion there was no such oracle.

221 For the question of Vitruvius's source see Ragone 1986:183–205 (and cf. EN4.3 to n4.72 above). There were cults of Apollo Panionios at Miletus, Ephesus, and Colophon in the Roman era (Ragone 1986:185n3 and 186nn2 and 3), and a passage of Nicander (*Alexipharmaca* 9–11) suggests that the cult of Apollo Panionios existed at Colophon/Klaros

But even if we leave Vitruvius out of account it is worth considering another famous cult and oracle of Apollo as the starting point of a nascent league, namely Branchidai in the territory of Miletus; this location, speculative as it is, makes good sense as a center for the earliest form of the league if Miletus was indeed the league's prime mover.[222]

§4.68 It has been suggested that the "arrogance" of Melia, for which it was destroyed, had to do with piracy.[223] If Melia was mostly Carian, Thucydides' statement that the Carians of the Aegean islands were pirates suggests that the same may have been true of Melia.[224] Melia's position overlooking the Mykale coast and controlling the strait between Mykale and Samos would have lent itself to piracy; this strait was an important shipping route, especially for Miletus, whose colonies to the north, Abydos and Parion, were founded near the end of the eighth century BC, about the time of the Meliac War.[225] If Miletus had a particular reason to eliminate Melia, it perhaps induced other cities, in particular Samos, Priene, and Colophon, to join in the

already in the Hellenistic era; see Ragone 1986:185–186 for significant points of comparison between the passage of Nicander and Vitruvius 4.1.4–6. Vitruvius discusses the origin of the Doric architectural order, and this, according to Ragone 1986:202–203, is the reason for Vitruvius's statement that the Ionians built a temple to Apollo Panionios: the temple in question is the Doric temple of Apollo at Klaros (at Panionion, significantly, there was no temple, only an altar, of Poseidon). Lenschau 1944:228 takes Vitruvius at face value, arguing that the original colonists of Ionia founded a cult to Apollo; cf. also Bearzot 1983, who speculates that the Panionic league of the seventh century BC, under the leadership of Miletus, founded a short-lived temple and oracle of Apollo Panionios at Panionion to rival the cult of Apollo at Delphi and give support to Ionian colonization.

222 The oracle and cult of Apollo at Branchidai were older than the Ionian colonization (Pausanias 7.2.6; cf. Herodotus 1.157.3). The cult was in the territory of Miletus (cf. Herodotus 1.46.2; 1.92.2), but it was administered independently until the temple was plundered and burned after the Ionian revolt (probably by Xerxes rather than Darius; see Hammond 1998). The Persians turned the oracle over to the Carians, but it was ultimately recovered by Miletus (Hammond 1998:339). If Branchidai served as the center of a nascent Panionic league it had the obvious disadvantage of distance from the league's northern cities; even after reaching Miletus visitors would have had an overland journey of sixteen kilometers to reach the oracle. For further consideration of Branchidai as a possible league center even into the late eighth century BC see n4.232 below. See Map 2 for the location of Branchidai/Didyma.
223 G. Kleiner and P. Hommel in Kleiner et al. 1967:5 and 91–93.
224 Thucydides 1.8.1. Cf. n4.83 above for the presumed Carian population of Melia.
225 P. Hommel in Kleiner et al. 1967:92n258; cf. G. Kleiner ibid. 10. Parion was a joint colony of Miletus, Erythrai, and Paros (Strabo 10.5.7, 13.1.14; Pausanias 9.27.1; cf. Olshausen *RE* Supplement 12 'Parion' 983). Eusebius's date for the foundation of Parion is 709 BC (see Cook 1946:77). Abydos was founded by Miletus with Gyges' consent according to Strabo 13.1.22, and its foundation may thus have been after rather than before the Meliac War. Hommel also mentions Cyzicus, which was founded by Miletus in 679 BC according to Eusebius (Cook 1946:77).

war.[226] The inducement for these cities would have been Melia's land, but for Miletus itself land would have been a secondary consideration.[227]

§4.69 It is possible that when Leodamas, the last Neleid king of Miletus, won the kingship in a contest with his kinsman Phitres, Miletus was already engaged in a war with Melia. According to Conon, our only source for the events, the Milesians had two wars at the time, against the Karystians and the Melians, and Phitres failed in his attempt to win the war against Melos: ἦσαν δ' αὐτοῖς τότε δύο πόλεμοι Καρυστίοις καὶ Μηλιεῦσι. καὶ πρὸς μὲν Μῆλον (αὐτῷ γὰρ ὁ κλῆρος τοῦτον ἐδίδου τὸν πόλεμον) Φίτρης στρατεύσας ἄπρακτος ἀναστρέφει, "There were then two wars, with the Karystians and the Melians. Phitres campaigned against Melos (for the lot gave him this war) and returned in failure." [228] Now Μηλιεῦσι is not the form one would expect for the name of the Melians, which, as readers of Thucydides Book 5 will remember, is Μήλιοι.[229] It is hard to understand how the correct first and second declension form of the name in -ιος was changed to a third declension form in -εύς, and it may well be that the form in the text was originally Μελιεῦσι, the

226 In *IP* (Hiller 1906) 37 four cities are named that were allotted land on Mykale after the Meliac War: Miletus, Priene, Samos, and Colophon. These may have been the only cities that made war on Melia; cf. Hommel in Kleiner et al. 1967:91: "More likely [than an action by a twelve-city league] is an action of a few neighboring cities" ("Wahrscheinlicher ist eine Aktion weniger benachbarter Städte"). Lenschau 1944:234 and Roebuck 1955:32–33 both view the war as the work of only the four cities that divided Melia's land; Roebuck, like Wilamowitz, thinks that the league did not yet exist at the time of the Meliac War. The apparent absence from the war of Ephesus, which lay closer to Melia than Colophon, is remarkable. It is possible that Ephesus should be included in the list of cities that destroyed Melia, despite the lack of evidence that Ephesus shared in the division of Melia's land. Wilamowitz 1906/1971:43/134 suggests that Ephesus, overthrown by Lygdamis, failed to recover its allotment of land after the Cimmerians withdrew, and thus its participation in the Meliac War was forgotten; Hommel p. 91, who follows Wilamowitz, goes further than Wilamowitz when he simply includes Ephesus with the other four cities as a recipient of Melia's land. It has also been argued that the presence of two historians from Ephesus (Kreophylos and Eualkes) among the eight historians adduced in the later land disputes between Samos and Priene indicates that Ephesus too was concerned with the original land division (Ragone 1986:174n1); the presence of Theopompus from Chios among the eight historians, however, runs counter to this idea insofar as Chios had no part in the land division.

227 It is clear from *IP* (Hiller 1906) 37 that Miletus was given some part or parts of Melia's land after the war, but the text of the inscription is uncertain. The likeliest reconstruction is that Miletus received only Akadamis, a place of unknown location on the Mykale coast. The evidence is discussed in EN4.13.

228 Photius's summary of Conon *FGrHist* 26 F 1 xliv; see above §4.49–§4.51 and n4.169, n4.170, n4.173, and n4.175.

229 Μάλιοι, the equivalent Doric form, is found on coins and inscriptions (*IG* XII.3 1097; *IG* VII 2419 column 2 line 8; Dittenberger 1915–1924 no. 115 (Μάλιος); cf. Zschietzschmann *RE* 'Melos' 567).

ethnic adjective of Melia, as we know from Stephanus of Byzantium:[230] Μελία, πόλις Καρίας. Ἑκαταῖος γενεαλογιῶν δ'. τὸ ἐθνικὸν Μελιεύς ὡς Ὑριεύς, "Melia, a city of Caria. Hecataeus *Genealogies* 4. The ethnic adjective is *Melieús*, like *Hurieús*." Ignorance of a vanished place on Cape Mykale called Melia could well have led a copyist to change the reference in Conon's story to the well-known island of Melos, but the change was not carried through completely: the ending -ευσι was let stand in the ethnic adjective. The conjecture that Melos should be replaced by Melia in Conon's account belongs to Hiller von Gaertringen, and to me it seems right; the argument based on the ending of the ethnic adjective is hard to refute.[231]

§4.70 If Miletus had a war with Melia, piracy may well have been the cause. If this war went badly for Miletus at first, when Phitres failed to win it, this would have been a reason to form an alliance against Melia, as Miletus seems to have done. Leodamas, who became king of Miletus by defeating Karystos, may then have succeeded where Phitres failed by involving the Panionic league against Melia. If my reconstruction is correct Leodamas came at the end of a line of Neleid kings who had begun to foster the development of the Panionic league in Miletus's own territory.[232] It was here that

---

230 Cf. n4.69 above.

231 Hiller *RE* 'Miletus' 1588, with reference to the first appearance of his conjecture in Ziebarth *IG* XII.9 p. 146 lines 64ff. For another instance in which ignorance of the vanished city Melia apparently caused a reference to it to be eliminated from a text, see EN4.4 to n4.83 above on the likely change from Μελιάς to Μηλιάς in Theopompus 115 F 103.

232 See above §4.67 end and cf. n4.90. In line with my suggestion of the cult of Apollo at Branchidai as a possible early meeting place for the Panionic league I note that Conon, as excerpted by Photius, connects Leodamas and his victory over Karystos with Branchidai and Branchus, the oracle's eponymous priest. The details of the story seem largely fictitious, but the mere connection of Branchidai with Leodamas and his foreign conquest deserves attention. Leodamas is supposed to have brought back with him from Karystos the infant ancestor of a Milesian priestly family, the Euangelidai (unattested except in this story by Conon; cf. Herda 1998:16n114); Leodamas sent the child and his mother to Branchidai, where Branchus adopted him to announce the prophecies, giving him the name Euangelos (Conon *FGrHist* 26 F 1 xliv 3–4; cf. Huxley 1966:50): αἰχμάλωτον δὲ κατὰ χρησμὸν γυναῖκα Καρυστίαν, παῖδα φέρουσαν ὑπομάσθιον, μετὰ πολλῶν καὶ ἄλλων ἀναθημάτων, ἃ δεκάτη τῶν λαφύρων ἐτύγχανον, ἀνέπεμψεν ἐν Βραγχίδαις. αὐτὸς δὲ τότε Βράγχος προϋστήκει τοῦ τε ἱεροῦ καὶ τοῦ μαντείου, ὃς τήν τε αἰχμάλωτον γυναῖκα ἐνόμισε καὶ τὸν παῖδα αὐτῆς ἔθετο. ηὔξανε δ' ὁ παῖς οὐ κατὰ λόγον ἀλλὰ θείᾳ τινὶ τύχῃ, καὶ πλέον ἢ πρὸς τὴν ἡλικίαν ἀπήντα τὸ εὐσύνετον. ποιεῖται δ' αὐτὸν ὁ Βράγχος καὶ ἄγγελον τῶν μαντευμάτων, Εὐάγγελον ὀνομάσας· οὗτος ἡβήσας τὸ Βράγχου μαντεῖον ἐξεδέξατο, καὶ ἀρχὴ γένους Εὐαγγελιδῶν παρὰ Μιλησίοις ἐγένετο, "In accordance with a prophecy he sent a captive Karystian woman with a child at her breast to Branchidai with many other offerings amounting to a tenth of the spoils; at that time Branchus himself was at the head of the temple and the oracle, and he acknowledged the captive woman as his wife and adopted her child. The boy grew, not in the normal

the Homeric poems would have taken shape and received their strong Neleid imprint. If the Panionia took place in the Neleids' own territory, this was all the more reason not to make the Neleids' role as leaders overt and heavy-handed in the poems, and this may help to explain the nature of Nestor's Homeric role. The poems would have been well developed by the date of the Nestor's cup inscription, c. 700 BC or somewhat earlier. By the same date or somewhat later the war against Melia would have been won with the support of the Panionic league, or at least with that part of the league that stood to gain by it.[233] When Melia was destroyed the league would have received a new center, less dependent on Miletus and closer to the rest of the league's cities, a change which at least some of the cities of the league had earned. This was doubtless agreeable to Miletus too, which preferred to exert its leadership from behind the scenes. The cult of Poseidon Helikonios, which had previ-ously belonged to Melia, would now have been taken over by the league, and the administration of the cult turned over to Priene, Miletus's junior partner to judge by its Kodrid myth.[234] The Homeric poems would have continued to be performed at the Panionia in the festival's new location at Panionion, but only in the short term. By c. 680 BC Gyges had begun his attacks on Ionian cities, and the Homeridai would have abandoned the Panionia for the safety of Chios soon after these attacks began. The simile in *Iliad* 20 evoking the cult of Poseidon Helikonios at Panionion must belong to the final phase of the poems' development, shortly before the poems moved offshore to Chios. The context of the simile in *Iliad* 20 is Achilles' entry into battle, and in the

---

way, but by some divine fortune, and reached a quickness of understanding beyond his years. Branchus also made him messenger of the prophecies, calling him Euangelos ['good messenger']. When he reached his youthful prime he inherited the oracle of Branchus, and this was the beginning of the family of Euangelidai among the Milesians." It is also worth noting that according to Nikolaos of Damascus Leodamas was killed while driving a heca-tomb along the road to Apollo's feast (see n4.171 above); this too likely refers to Apollo's cult at Didyma/Branchidai.

233 Thus, contrary to the literary tradition of Vitruvius, Melia would never have been part of the Panionic league (cf. n4.220 above). Here I disagree with G. Kleiner in Kleiner et al. 1967:6, who proposes that Melia joined the Panionic league as its thirteenth member and was subsequently destroyed by its neighbors, leaving the league again with twelve members and a new league center. As Wade-Gery 1952:64n15 points out, the very idea of a thirteenth city most likely arose from Smyrna's admission to the league in Hellenistic times as its thirteenth member. On this view Smyrna's position in the later league was the model for Melia's earlier position. This is consistent with the general tenor of Vitruvius's account, which conflates the Hellenistic league with the archaic league (cf. n4.72 above).

234 For Priene's administration of the cult at Panionion, see above n4.85 and n4.219. For Priene's Kodrid myth, see §4.19 and n4.92 above.

same context there is an apparent allusion to Gyges and the Lydians.[235] The two allusions, which pertain to Achilles' first and third victims in battle in the *Iliad*, go well together in terms of time and place of composition.[236] Presumably Panionion continued to be the meeting place for the league, and the Panionia continued to be celebrated there, after Homeric poetry ceased to be part of the celebration. Within a few decades the festival itself was interrupted, when Lygdamis and the Cimmerians occupied Mykale for

235 For this passage see n4.140 above and n4.236 below.
236 There is a comparable sequence of passages near the end of *Iliad* 2, where the catalogue of Trojan allies ends with the Maeonians (*Iliad* 2.864–866) and the Carians (*Iliad* 2.867–875), before a final two-line passage devoted to Sarpedon and the Lycians (*Iliad* 2.876–877): the Maeonians, predecessors of the Lydians, whose "Gygaean lake" seems meant to evoke the future Lydian king Gyges (see n4.140 above), are juxtaposed with the Carians, who inhabit Miletus and its surrounding area; it does not seem accidental that this second passage singles out, along with the Maeander River and Mount Phthiron at the head of the Gulf of Latmos, Cape Mykale, the site of the future Panionia (*Iliad* 2:867–869):

Νάστης αὖ Καρῶν ἡγήσατο βαρβαροφώνων,
οἳ Μίλητον ἔχον Φθιρῶν τ' ὄρος ἀκριτόφυλλον
Μαιάνδρου τε ῥοὰς Μυκάλης τ' αἰπεινὰ κάρηνα.

Nastes led the Carians, speakers of a foreign tongue,
who held Miletus and the thickly-leaved mountain of Phthiron
and the streams of the Maeander and the steep peaks of Mykale.

The two passages of the Trojan catalogue, though they may be "late," are organic to the poem. The same is true of the two passages devoted to Achilles' victims, neither of which should be judged an "interpolation." Leaf and Bayfield regard *Iliad* 20.383–394, the passage which seems to allude to Gyges and the Lydians, as "probably an interpolation" (Leaf and Bayfield 1898 ad loc.); they comment further (on 20.385): "If this part really belongs to the Μῆνις, it is the only instance in the ancient poem which shows any minute knowledge of the geography of Asia Minor." I agree with this judgment to the extent that the passage belongs not to the earlier tradition of the *Iliad*, but to the final period of the poem's development at the Panionia (I also point out that *Iliad* 2.864–866 shows the same geographical awareness as this passage). Consistent with this view, I think, is a linguistic feature of the passage noted by Leaf 1900–1902 on *Iliad* 20.381 as being late (cf. also Leaf and Bayfield 1898 on *Iliad* 20.383–394), namely the initial short syllable of the names Ὀτρυντεΐδην (Ὀτρυντεΐδη) and Ὀτρυντῆϊ (*Iliad* 20.383, 389, 384), as opposed to a long first syllable in all examples of Homeric ὀτρύνω. I would compare the phrases τὸ πρῶτον and τὰ πρῶτα, which always have a long first syllable (in arsis) in Homer (18 examples), but *Odyssey* 3.320 has a short syllable (in thesis) in a comparable phrase, ὅν τινα πρῶτον. The short treatment ("Attic correption") may be relatively late, but it is not un-Homeric; cf. Janko 1982:157, also 177. Högemann 2001:63 assumes that Homer knew of Gyges' sudden rise to power and subsequent rule; Högemann also cites the tradition that Gyges kept the poet Magnes of Smyrna at his court and heard his poem of a battle between the Lydians and the Amazons (Nikolaos of Damascus *FGrHist* 90 F 62), and he speculates that Gyges, who must have understood Greek, may also have heard the *Iliad* performed. The length and subject matter of the *Iliad* are, I think, against this, but the possibility exists.

at least three (and as many as ten) years about 640 BC.[237] It remains a puzzle why there are no remains at Panionion for the century between the Meliac War and about 600 BC. Perhaps the Cimmerians, who interrupted the tenure of Melia's former land, also destroyed the cult at Panionion, but there should be evidence of this on the ground. At present nothing more can be said on the subject.[238]

§4.71 Much of the argument in this section has been conjectural given the state of our evidence. For both the Homeric poems and the Panionic league the eighth century BC is a particularly difficult period. My working assumption has been that the poems and the league developed together through the latter half of the eighth century,[239] but other scenarios are possible. Some would date the Panionic league in its final twelve-city form (i.e. after Phocaea was admitted as the league's last member) to the ninth or early eighth century BC. Smyrna, which became Ionic about the beginning of the eighth century, sought admission to the league and was refused, according to Herodotus, by a twelve-member league; if Smyrna sought admission immediately after it became Ionic, and if the league at that time really did include twelve cities, an early date for the league is indicated. In that case I would not argue that the Panionic league and the Homeric poems developed together, but that the development of the poems began only after the league was fully formed. I think that this would also have been the case if the league reached its final twelve-member form only in the middle of the eighth century, Phocaea being admitted at that time, and Smyrna, Phocaea's neighbor to the south, seeking admission unsuccessfully sometime after that. If the twelve-member league did exist before the development of the Homeric poems, then the poems would have developed within their twelve-part structure, so to speak, from the start; this scenario may have advantages over the scenario proposed earlier, wherein the poems evolved gradually into a twelve-part structure as the league developed. I do not know what the precise relationship between the league and the poems was with respect to the twelve-part structure common to both, but whatever it was, I do not doubt that a relationship existed.

---

237 Cf. above n4.78 and n4.139.
238 Before leaving the subject of Ionia I must at least mention the name Ionia itself. If, as I argue, the Ionians of Asia Minor were given a common identity by the Panionic league, surely their common name also had to do with that league: if the name did not arise there, it at least gained currency there. The issue is considered further in EN4.14.
239 Cf. §4.26 above.

Endnotes, Part 4

EN4.1 (Endnote to n4.22)
I agree with the viewpoint expressed by Cook 1975:784–785 that Athens cannot be removed from the Ionian migration, but I think that he claims too much for Athens' role, as in the case of Colophon: "Many modern scholars have contended that this claim [that Athens was the main focus of emigration] was invented by the Athenians in the sixth century, or even when Athens assumed the leadership of the Ionians after the Persian Wars; and Mimnermus is cited as declaring (as he appears to do, but in a historical narrative of unique compression) that his Colophonians sailed to their beloved Asia direct from Pylus. But this view presents great difficulties. The belief in Athens as the metropolis of the Ionians was generally conceded by fifth-century writers, and the leadership of the Codrid Neleus was accepted by Panyassis, the epic poet of Halicarnassus, in the early part of that century. It seems unlikely that an Athenian political fiction could have won such immediate and universal acceptance. Literary and epigraphical evidences combine to indicate that in historical times Athens and the cities of Ionia had in common the essentials of their calendar, a number of old festivals and cults (such as the Apaturia and the worship of Eleusinian Demeter), and, basically, the four 'Ionic' tribes (Aegicoreis Argadeis, Geleontes and Hopletes). It is true that few of these Ionic institutions were exclusively Athenian; and they cannot therefore constitute direct proof that Athens wielded the dominant influence in the migrations. But their widespread diffusion in Ionia is consistent with the tradition of Athenian leadership; and certainly, if we do not believe in a 'hard core' of Ionians among the emigrants as distinct from Pylians and others, and if at the same time we believe, for instance, that Mimnermus' Pylians sailed from their old home to Ionia without first concentrating in Athens, the strength of the common Attic-Ionic institutions in Ionia cannot easily be explained." I have a different view of this matter. What the cities of the Panionic league had in common was not necessarily due to

Athens; Miletus, the daughter city of Athens, must, I think, also have been
in large part responsible by spreading its own heritage; in my view this is
what the Homeric poems suggest. In judging Mimnermus's statement about
his ancestors the key factor is not the Ionians' common institutions, but the
diversity of their origins, which Cook acknowledges in general, but wishes to
deny in this particular case. The evidence, I think, is against this.

EN4.2 (Endnote to n4.47)

Nothing is known for sure about the Panionia after the Ionian revolt. The
Persians very likely put an end to the festival after the Battle of Lade in 494
BC: the revolt was instigated at Panionion, and Herodotus 1.148.1, describing
Panionion, refers to the festival as a thing of the past in his own day: ἡ δὲ
Μυκάλη ἐστὶ τῆς ἠπείρου ἄκρη πρὸς ζέφυρον ἄνεμον κατήκουσα Σάμῳ
‹καταντίον›, ἐς τὴν συλλεγόμενοι ἀπὸ τῶν πολίων Ἴωνες <u>ἄγεσκον</u> ὁρτήν,
τῇ ἔθεντο οὔνομα Πανιώνια, "Mykale is a promontory of the mainland
facing west opposite Samos, onto which the Ionians <u>used to</u> gather from
their cities and <u>celebrate</u> a festival, to which they gave the name Panionia";
cf. Wilamowitz 1906:49/141, Caspari 1915:181–182; Kleiner in Kleiner et al.
1967:13–14). Celebration of the Panionia was later restored on Mykale, but we
do not know when. Strabo twice refers to the celebration of the festival at
Panionion in his own time (8.7.2 and 14.1.20), and his testimony is corrob-
orated by Hellenistic inscriptions (Stylianou 1983:247n12). It is usually
assumed that the festival on Mykale was resumed in the mid-fourth century
BC when Priene, the city closest to Panionion which provided the priest of
Poseidon Helikonios to the league's common cult (Strabo 8.7.2 and 14.1.20),
seems to have been refounded in a new location (under Mount Mykale
opposite Miletus); cf. Kleiner et al. 1967:14–15, 35–37, Stylianou 1983:248; cf.
also Wilamowitz 1906:50/142. But it is also possible that the refoundation
of Priene did not take place until under Alexander in the 330s BC; the issue
is discussed by Hornblower 1982a:323–330, who prefers the later date. The
possibility that the festival was transferred to Ephesus for a certain period
of time between the end of the Ionian revolt and the resumption of the
festival on Mykale is based on Diodorus 15.49.1, who says that the festival was
transferred to Ephesus because of wars on Mykale: κατὰ τὴν Ἰωνίαν ἐννέα
πόλεις εἰώθεισαν κοινὴν ποιεῖσθαι σύνοδον τὴν τῶν Πανιωνίων, καὶ θυσίας
συνθύειν ἀρχαίας καὶ μεγάλας Ποσειδῶνι περὶ τὴν ὀνομαζομένην Μυκάλην
ἐν ἐρήμῳ τόπῳ. ὕστερον δὲ πολέμων γενομένων περὶ τούτους τοὺς τόπους οὐ
δυνάμενοι ποιεῖν τὰ Πανιώνια, μετέθεσαν τὴν πανήγυριν εἰς ἀσφαλῆ τόπον,
ὃς ἦν πλησίον τῆς Ἐφέσου, "In Ionia nine [*sic*] cities were accustomed to

hold a common assembly, that of the Panionia, and to offer together ancient large sacrifices to Poseidon in the region called Mykale in a deserted place. Later when wars arose around these places they could not hold the Panionia and transferred the *panegyris* to a safe place, which was near Ephesus" (for Diodorus's nine as opposed to twelve cities in the refounded league of the fourth century there is archaeological support; cf. Herda 2006:50 and n34). Diodorus does not date the transfer of the Panionia to Ephesus, but the context is an earthquake that destroyed Helike in Achaea in 373/2 BC; before the earthquake Ionian ambassadors came to Helike seeking sacred symbols for the refoundation of the cult of Poseidon Helikonios in Ephesus but were refused, and in return for the refusal Poseidon destroyed Helike (Diodorus 15.48–49); Strabo, who omits the reason for the Ionians' request, says that refusal of the request was followed by an earthquake the next winter (Strabo 8.7.2). If we conclude from Diodorus and Strabo that the festival was moved from Mykale to Ephesus about 373/2 BC, this must be reconciled with Herodotus, who implies that the festival was no longer celebrated on Mykale when he wrote: either the festival was resumed on Mykale after Herodotus wrote and was then moved to Ephesus about 373/2 BC (an unlikely course of events) or the festival was moved to Ephesus before Herodotus's time (this does not fit with Strabo's statement that the Ionians' made their request to Helike in the same year as the earthquake). It has been plausibly suggested that Diodorus misunderstood his source Ephorus, and that shortly before 373 BC the festival was moved, not to Ephesus, but from Ephesus back to Mykale after having been celebrated for an unknown period of time at Ephesus (Stylianou 1983:248; cf. Hornblower 1991:528); the Ionian embassy would thus have sought Helike's sanction to refound the cult of Poseidon Helikonios on Mykale after an interruption that began before Herodotus wrote. In this case the Panionia must have been resumed on Mykale after the Persian Wars and been moved to Ephesus in the course of the fifth century (Hornblower 1982:245 suggests 440/39 BC; Hornblower 1991:528 reports Andrewes' suggestion of an earlier date). The question then becomes whether the festival transferred from Mykale to Ephesus in the mid-fifth century was the Ephesia mentioned by Thucydides; Hornblower 1982 argues for this identification (cf. also Hornblower 1991:527–529), Stylianou 1983 rejects it. An argument against equating the Ephesia with the Panionia is that according to Pollux 1.37 the Ephesia were dedicated to Artemis, not to Poseidon: ἑορταὶ ἔντιμοι... Ἀρτέμιδος Ἀρτεμίσια καὶ Ἐφέσια (cf. Stylianou 1983:249n27). Stylianou 1983:249 proposes a scenario for the Panionia in which the festival lapsed for the entire period between the Ionian revolt and the end of the fifth century, was then resumed near Ephesus under Spartan influence, and was then moved to Mykale in the 370s BC; this interpretation perhaps accords best with the fact that nothing is heard of the Panionia after the Ionian revolt during the fifth century. It is perhaps also possible, Diodorus notwithstanding, that there was no celebration of the Panionia between the Persian Wars and the festival's refoundation in the fourth century (Herda 2006:55). Behind the Ionians' request in 373 BC for an image of Poseidon or a model altar (or whatever the object was: for the object see Strabo 8.7.2 and Diodorus 15.49.1–2, and for the word *aphídruma*, literally "transference to another place," see Nick 2002:24 and cf. Herda 2006:56n71) lies the tradition that the Ionians of the dodecapolis came from the twelve cities of Achaea in the Peloponnesus, and brought with them the cult of Poseidon Helikonios from the city of Helike. This version of the Ionians' origins is found already in Herodotus 1.145, and while some accept it as historical (Solmsen 1909:84 derives Poseidon's cult title Helikonios from Helike; Prinz 1979:314–376 argues that the Ionians came directly from Pylos and Achaea, and not from Athens; cf. also Knibbe 1998:78n120), there are good reasons to disbelieve it, including the obvious derivation of the title Helikonios from Mount Helikon in Boeotia; see Prandi 1989:48–49 and Herda 2006:67–72 and cf. EN4.4 and EN4.9. For the particular circumstances that may have induced the Delphic oracle in 373 BC to send the Ionians to the Peloponnesus as their place of origin, see Anderson 1954:87–89 and Prandi 1989:49–59.

EN4.3 (Endnote to n4.72)
There was a tradition, preserved in the scholia to Plato, that Smyrna, before becoming a member of the Panionic league, was on occasion represented in the league by Colophon: according to this tradition, when the twelve cities were deadlocked in a vote, Colophon would cast an extra vote on behalf of Smyrnaeans who had settled in their territory. The scholia took this account from paroemiographers (Lukillos of Tarrha, first century AD, who excerpted Didymus, first century BC; see Gudeman *RE* 'Scholien [Platon]' 690) to explain the proverb τὸν κολοφῶνα ἐπιτιθέναι/προσβιβάζειν, "put the finishing stroke to a thing." The proverb occurs in Plato *Theaetetus* 153c and *Epistle* III 318b; I quote the scholia to *Theaetetus* 153c: τὸν κολοφῶνα κτλ.· παροιμία. δώδεκα πόλεις τῆς Ἰωνίας συνῄεσαν εἰς τὸ Πανιώνιον λεγόμενον, περὶ τῶν κοινῶν βουλευσόμεναι, καὶ εἴ ποτε ἴσοι αἱ ψῆφοι ἐγένοντο, οἱ Κολοφώνιοι περιττὴν ἐτίθεντο τὴν νικῶσαν· Σμυρναίους γὰρ ἐλθόντας εἶχον συνοίκους, ὑπὲρ ὧν καὶ τήνδε τὴν ψῆφον ἐτίθεντο. ὅθεν ἐπὶ τῆς κρατούσης καὶ †βεβαιοτάτης ψήφου ἡ παροιμία ἐτίθετο, οἷον τὸν Κολοφῶνα ἐπιτίθημι ἢ τὸν Κολοφῶνα ἀναγκάζω

προσβιβάζων, " 'The Colophon,' etc.: Proverb. The twelve cities of Ionia met in what is called the Panionion in order to deliberate about common affairs, and if the votes were ever tied the Colophonians cast an odd vote to break the tie. For they had as fellow inhabitants Smyrnaeans who had come there, and it was on their behalf that they cast this vote. From this was coined the proverb for the winning and...(?) vote, namely 'I add the Colophon' or 'I compel by adding the Colophon'." Colophon's supposed double vote is attested only in this context (the Suda s.v. τὸν Κολοφῶνα ἐπέθηκεν has a similar explanation of the proverb, except that here Colophon is said to play its decisive role not at Panionion but within the city of Smyrna). This evidence, which is late, has caused confusion about the early Panionic league. The evidence is no longer used as it once was to conclude, in the face of Herodotus's clear statement to the contrary, that early Smyrna was a member of the Panionic league (Wilamowitz 1906:52 held this unsupportable view), but it continues to confuse another issue, the old relationship between Colophon and Smyrna, and I question whether the evidence has any validity. Strabo gives a different explanation of the proverb, namely that Colophon's military power on land and sea gave it a decisive advantage in battles, and that Colophon's cavalry in particular "put a secure end" to any conflict (Strabo 14.1.28): ἐκτήσαντο δέ ποτε καὶ ναυτικὴν ἀξιόλογον δύναμιν Κολοφώνιοι καὶ ἱππικήν, ἐν ᾗ τοσοῦτον διέφερον τῶν ἄλλων ὥσθ', ὅπου ποτὲ ἐν τοῖς δυσκαταλύτοις πολέμοις τὸ ἱππικὸν τῶν Κολοφωνίων ἐπικουρήσειε, λύεσθαι τὸν πόλεμον· ἀφ' οὗ καὶ τὴν παροιμίαν ἐκδοθῆναι τὴν λέγουσαν "τὸν Κολοφῶνα ἐπέθηκεν" ὅταν τέλος ἐπιτεθῇ βέβαιον τῷ πράγματι, "The Colophonians once possessed noteworthy naval and cavalry power, in which they so far exceeded the others that, whenever the Colophonians' cavalry came to help in difficult battles, the battle was ended; from this the proverb arose that says 'he added the Colophon' whenever a secure end is added to a thing." Colophon had this level of military power early in its history, but lost it steadily from the early seventh century on (cf. Fogazza 1974:29–38), and Strabo's explanation is therefore unlikely to be a late invention. Colophon's double vote, on the other hand, does not look genuine. The voting procedure in question only makes sense in the case of a member city which ceased to exist and whose population was transferred to another member city. This happened to Myus in the late third century BC, when the Maeander River silted up and Myus was abandoned; Miletus, which resettled its neighbor's population in its own territory, also acquired its neighbor's vote. In the same passage of Vitruvius that tells parenthetically how third-century BC Smyrna replaced long vanished Melia as the league's thirteenth member (Vitruvius 4.1.4, see n4.72), there is also a parenthetical comment about Myus, *quae olim ab aqua est devorata, cuius sacra et suffragium Milesiis Iones adtribuerunt,* "which was once swallowed up by water, and whose sacred rites and <u>vote</u> the Ionians assigned to the Milesians." Smyrna is parallel to Myus in that Smyrna too was once destroyed and abandoned, and it is even possible that some of Smyrna's population was resettled in Colophon, although tradition says only that the Smyrnaeans were scattered in villages after their city was destroyed by Alyattes. But whether some of the population was moved to Colophon or not, Smyrna had not previously been a member of the Panionic league, and this is the decisive difference from Myus; it is not plausible that Colophon was given a double vote to represent a non-member city upon its destruction. In my view the city of Smyrna refounded by Lysimachus in the third century BC, proud of having finally achieved Panionic status, invented precedents to mitigate its newcomer status: taking the place of Melia as the league's thirteenth city (so Vitruvius and his source) is one clear example (see Ragone 1986:196; cf. also n4.220 and n4.233); half membership in the early league, on the model of Myus, is, I think, another example. The point in both cases is the same: Smyrna's status as the thirteenth member of the league was not something new under the sun; there had been a thirteenth member of the league at the start, and Smyrna itself had become a virtual thirteenth member when it was destroyed by Alyattes. Vitruvius's account of the dodecapolis goes back to a source sympathetic to Smyrna's historical pretensions (see Ragone 1986, who dates this source to the late third century BC, when Myus was abandoned; Vitruvius's "mistake" in naming Attalus in place of Lysimachus as Smyrna's benefactor fits the same late-third century date; see Ragone 1986:205). The Plato scholia do not provide a date for Colophon's alleged representation of Smyrna, but the notion that the Smyrnaeans had returned to Colophon and settled there (ἐλθόντας εἶχον συνοίκους, "they had as fellow inhabitants [Smyrnaeans] who had come there") clearly suggests the period after Alyattes' destruction of Smyrna, and some have taken this date as the historical date of a real event (Cadoux 1938:84–85; Talamo 1973:364 n110; see Moggi 1976:42 for arguments against such a historical date). Càssola 1958:164–168 argued instead that the implied political relationship between Colophon and Smyrna belongs to the period after Colophonians first seized Smyrna, and this line of argument has been followed by others (Moggi 1976:40–43; Ragone 1986:190–194). What this argument fails to address satisfactorily is the fact that Smyrna was occupied by exiles from Colophon, and that the relationship between the two cities was thus one of enmity. This situation must have reversed itself dramatically if the Smyrnaeans, after being rejected for league membership, instead accepted represention by those who had exiled them; a mere passage of time (as suggested by Moggi 1976:42 and 43n17) seems inadequate to explain such a polar shift in attitudes. In this scheme, furthermore, there is no reason why Smyrna was turned down for full league membership; the reason suggested in Herodotus, that the league already had twelve cities and membership was thus closed, in my view reverses the likely historical process: it was rather Smyrna's rejection that sealed the league's membership at twelve (for the twelve-member league as the final result of a historical process see e.g. Ragone 1986:195–196 and Moggi 1996:99n89; I do not think that the number twelve by itself arrested the league's growth, although in hindsight that would appear to be the case). I continue to believe that what kept Smyrna out of the league, from the time of its capture by Colophonian exiles until the time of its destruction by Alyattes, was the opposition of Colophon. If this was the case, there is certainly no reason to suppose that Colophon began to represent Smyrna after Smyrna was destroyed; as Moggi 1976:42 argues, representation, if it had not started earlier, would not have started then. This brings us back to the point that the tradition for Colophon's double vote is highly dubious; it does not work well no matter when it is dated.

EN4.4 (Endnote to n4.83)

There are various indications of Melia's Boeotian origins, beginning with the name Melia, which belongs to an ash-tree nymph worshipped both in Apollo's temple in Thebes and in the Ptoion, another Boeotian shrine of Apollo (for the nymph see Keil *RE* 'Melia' 505 no. 1a and Lenschau 1944:228; Lenschau derives the city name Melia from the nymph's name; P. Hommel in Kleiner et al. 1967:80 attributes this idea to Wilamowitz, but it is not in the discussion of Melia in Wilamowitz 1906:43, 46 = 1971:133–134, 137–138). The cult of Poseidon Helikonios at Panionion, which seems to have belonged to Melia before it became the common cult of the Panionic league (see n4.73 and §4.67), also fits with a Boeotian origin of Melia (cf. EN4.2 end and EN4.9); although a historical cult of Poseidon is not known on Mount Helikon in Boeotia, Aristarchus derived Poseidon's epithet from this mountain (and not from the town of Helike in Achaea, for which a cult of Poseidon is attested in *Iliad* 8.203), remarking that all of Boeotia was Poseidon's sacred land: ἡ Βοιωτία ὅλη ἱερὰ Ποσειδῶνος (*Etymologicum Magnum* s.v. Κύπρις); Poseidon's famous cult in Boeotia was at Onkhestos. Cf. also Wilamowitz 1906/1971:46n3/138n1, who notes that *Homeric Hymn* 22 to Poseidon associates Poseidon with both Mount Helikon in Boeotia and the city of Aigai in Achaea (the latter is associated with Poseidon in *Iliad* 8.203 and 13.21 as well).

Huxley 1960 argues for the foundation of Melia by Thebans from Colophon. In a fragment of Theopompus (*FGrHist* 115 F 103) the prophet Mopsos, the founder of Colophon and a descendant of the Theban prophet Teiresias, has three daughters: two of the daughters, Rhode and Pamphylia, have names associated with places; so too does the third, Μηλιάς, if her name is changed to Μελιάς to correspond to Μελίη (for the adjectival form from Μελίη cf. ἁ Μελιάς χώρα in *IP* [Hiller 1906] 37 line 55, quoted in n4.76). If Μελιάς is this daughter's true name it associates Μελίη with an origin from Thebes by way of Colophon. Theopompus is one of the eight historians cited for the Meliac War in *IP* (Hiller 1906) 37 lines 120–122, and his knowledge of Melia and its traditions is thus assured.

EN4.5 (Endnote to n4.88)

To date the destruction of Melia the Geometric pottery fragments found in the necropolis provide clear evidence. The fragments are of Protogeometric and Geometric, including Late Geometric, date, and the Late Geometric pieces show that the necropolis continued to be used down to c. 700 BC or a little later. The fragments are catalogued by P. Hommel in Kleiner et al. 1967:166. Hommel assigns to *dînos* fragments (nos. 6–9) and *kratér* fragments (nos. 11–14) a seventh-century date, by which is meant the end of Late Geometric; he puts particular weight on the *dînos* fragments: "Above all the Late Geometric *dînos* fragments (Plate 8b; IX f–i) permit the conclusion that the city existed until the end of the Geometric period" ("Vor allem die spätgeometrischen Dinosfragmente [Taf. 8b; IX f–i] lassen auf das Bestehen der Stadt bis an das Ende der geometrischen Zeit schliessen"), p. 87; cf. also p. 93: "Decisive for the dating of Melia's destruction are the latest finds of the necropolis (Plate IX f–i), which we are justified in attributing to Melia since there are no post-Geometric sherds in it. Thus a start of the Meliac War during the Cimmerian invasions, which began under Gyges in 668 BC and lasted until Ardys's reign, is also excluded" ("Ausschlaggebend für die Datierung der Zerstörung Melies sind die spätesten Funde der Nekropole (Taf. IX f–i), die wir Melia zuzuweisen berechtigt sind, da nachgeometrische Scherben in ihr fehlen. So ist auch ein Ansatz des Melischen Krieges während der Kimmeriereinfälle, die noch unter Gyges 668 einsetzen und bis unter Ardys andauern, ausgeschlossen"). Hommel compares the Late Geometric fragments found in the necropolis with similar pottery types from the Samian Heraion and from Larisa on the Hermos; he cites Eilmann 1933:73ff. (for *kratéres*) and 106ff., 139 fig. 90 a, b (for *dînoi*), and Boehlau and Schefold 1942:61f., fig. 17a, f, 113 fig. 37e (*dînoi*) and 88f., fig. 27e, cf. also 112f., fig. 37b (*kratéres*). Hommel does not give an absolute date for Melia's destruction, but his dates for the dînos and kratḗr fragments indicate early seventh century BC. Coldstream 1968:330 dates the East Greek Late Geometric period 745–680 BC. The *terminus ante quem* for the destruction of Melia may be taken to be 680 BC.

EN4.6 (Endnote to n4.98)

Richard Janko dates the Delian section of the *Homeric Hymn to Apollo* to the first half of the seventh century BC in accord with the traditional view of this hymn's early origin (Janko 1982:114–115; cf. his chronological diagram, p. 200); he thus rejects M. L. West's proposal to redate the Delian hymn to the late sixth century BC (West 1975, discussed by Janko pp. 109–112, reasserted by West 1999). I follow Janko on this question, but I narrow the date of the Delian *Hymn to Apollo* to not long before the mid-seventh century BC, after the composition of the *Iliad* and the *Odyssey* on a monumental scale. West 1999 argues further that Homer, the supposed ancestor of the Homeridai, was not necessarily associated with the *Iliad* and the *Odyssey* before the time of the Panathenaic performances (initiated, he maintains, only by Hipparchus in 522 BC). It is true that there is no early evidence connecting the name Homer with the *Iliad* and the *Odyssey*: the earliest evidence for the name Homer connects the name with an epic about Thebes and is subject to reservations even as to that epic (according to Pausanias 9.9.5 the seventh-century poet Callinus attributed an epic about Thebes to Homer [Callinus fr. 6 West]; see Davison 1968:81–82, who questions this evidence on various grounds but does not discount it entirely: at a minimum, Davison thinks, Callinus must have attributed to Homer some phrase that was not in the *Iliad* or *Odyssey* of Pausanias or Pausanias's authority but resembled a phrase in the *Thebaid*); in a poem attributed to the seventh-century poet Semonides (fr. 29 Diehl) the famous passage in *Iliad* 6 comparing the generation of men to the generation of leaves is said to be spoken by "the man of Chios" (ἐν δὲ τὸ κάλλιστον Χῖος ἔειπεν ἀνήρ, "the one most beautiful thing that the man of Chios said"), but West is probably correct in attributing this poem instead to Simonides (fr. 8 West) at the end of the sixth century (West 1974:179–180, 1993; Burkert 1987:45 tentatively accepts West's attribution to Simonides). Thus, strictly speaking, there is no early evidence connecting the name Homer with the *Iliad* or the *Odyssey*. In my view, however, there is an indirect piece of evidence for this connection: as I argue in the text (§4.22) the Delian *Hymn to Apollo*, which claims to be by "the blind man who lives in rocky Chios" (i.e. by Homer himself, the ancestor of the Homeridai in Chios), alludes specifically to the *Odyssey* in making this claim. Since I follow Janko in dating the Delian *Hymn*

to Apollo to the first half of the seventh century, I regard this as evidence that
the Homeridai, from the beginning, were closely associated with what were
later called the Homeric poems, namely the *Iliad* and the *Odyssey*. There is
no question that other poems as well came to be considered Homeric: the
hymns, some parts of the epic cycle, the *Margites*, the *Thebaid*. This process
may have begun by the mid-seventh century BC if Callinus did in fact attri-
bute a poem about Thebes to Homer. There is also evidence for the early sixth
century BC that "Homeric epic" at that time included a Theban epic, but the
evidence is again inconclusive: according to Herodotus 5.67.1 Cleisthenes,
tyrant of Sikyon c. 570 BC, ended rhapsodic performances in Sikyon "because
of the Homeric epics" (τῶν Ὁμηρείων ἐπέων εἵνεκα), which praised his
enemy Argos. Cleisthenes also ended the cult of Adrastos in Sikyon, trans-
ferring "tragic choruses" in honor of Adrastos to Dionysus and other rites to
Melanippos, Adrastos's enemy; as Burkert 1987:45 suggests, "Adrastos would
again point to the *Thebaid*." But it is possible, as West 1999:377n40 warns,
that Herodotus, in referring to "Homeric" epics in this passage, uses a term
from his own time that would not have been used in Cleisthenes' time. It also
seems quite possible that the "Homeric" epic that offended Cleisthenes was
the *Iliad*, in which Argos is again glorified (at least by contrast with Sikyon).
The term "Homeric" was apparently limited to the *Iliad* and the *Odyssey* after
these two poems became school texts, perhaps in the early fifth century BC
(see Burkert's brief discussion, 1987:56–57). Although we are in the dark for
the early period, I see no reason to deny *a priori* that "Homer" started where
he ended, with only the *Iliad* and the *Odyssey* to his name, whatever else was
attributed to him in the meantime. Surely it was the fame of these two poems
that attracted other poems to his name. For poems attributed to Homer, cf.
also Graziosi 2002:184–186; for the question of when the Homeric poems
became widely known, cf. n4.149 and n4.209.

EN4.7 (Endnote to n4.104)

If the *Iliad* and the *Odyssey* came into being together, the *Iliad* may allude
directly to the *Odyssey* in some instances. In other instances the *Iliad* may of
course allude to epic tradition generally, without reference to the *Odyssey*.
The epic hero Memnon seems to provide examples of both kinds. I have
made the case that *Iliad* 8 alludes to *Odyssey* 3 in the roles played by Nestor,
Odysseus, and Diomedes in a particular episode in each book. The episode
in *Iliad* 8 also alludes to the death of Antilochus at the hands of Memnon.
This tradition, which was known to the *Odyssey* (*Odyssey* 4.186–188, see §2.71
above), also figures in *Odyssey* 3 insofar as Nestor's grief for Antilochus is

highlighted there (*Odyssey* 3.111–112). The connection between *Iliad* 8 and *Odyssey* 3, which focuses on Nestor, Diomedes, and Odysseus, is in a sense completed by Antilochus, whose fate is of equal interest. Antilochus's death is not narrated in Homer: it lies outside the time frame of the *Iliad*, and in the *Odyssey* we learn only that "the shining son of the radiant dawn goddess slew" him (*Odyssey* 4.188). The episode, which occurs in transposed form in *Iliad* 8, is first narrated by Pindar *Pythian* 6.28–42 (see §2.73 above), whose source was the *Aethiopis* (cf. n2.96 above). But the episode was also known to the Homeric poets, as *Iliad* 8 shows (for further discussion of the tradition for Antilochus and Memnon, see n4.155, n4.189, and n4.203). Memnon's own death provides the other kind of example, in which the *Iliad* alludes to epic tradition apart from the *Odyssey*. As Johannes Kakridis argues, when Achilles is forced to summon the winds Boreas and Zephyros to burn Patroclus's funeral pyre (*Iliad* 23.192–198), this seems to allude to Achilles' own funeral, and to the death of Memnon at Achilles' hands shortly before Achilles himself meets his end: Boreas and Zephyros are Memnon's brothers (all are sons of Eos), and they will have shunned the funeral of Achilles, their brother's killer, with more reason than they shun the funeral of Patroclus in the *Iliad* (Kakridis 1949:75–83). West 2003 argues that Memnon was unknown to the poet of the *Iliad*: when Thetis says in the *Iliad* that Achilles is to die soon after Hector's death, this, according to West's argument, allows no time for the intervention of figures like Penthesileia and Memnon; Heitsch 2006:18–23, who follows West, nevertheless recognizes that *Iliad* 8 alludes to Memnon, and explains this and other apparent allusions to the *Aithiopis* as late additions to the *Iliad*. I would argue instead that there had long been shorter and longer versions of Achilles' death, and that our *Iliad* evokes the basic version (death after killing Hector) but still alludes to an expanded version (death after killing Memnon); Herodotus 2.116 points to a similar case when he says that Homer, who follows the tradition that Helen was in Troy during the Trojan war, nevertheless alludes to the tradition that she was in Egypt and Phoenicia when he refers to the Phoenician *péplos* which the Trojan women offer to Athena in *Iliad* 6.289–292.

EN4.8 (Endnote to n4.140)

The *Iliad* twice refers to "the lake of Gyges," which would seem to be named for the well-known Lydian king (*Iliad* 2.865 and 20.390–391). In later Greek the phrase Γυγάδας χρυσός (Herodotus 1.14.3) refers to the gold that Gyges dedicated in Delphi, and the name Γύγας of a promontory in the Troad indicates to Strabo that it was once in Gyges' territory (Strabo 13.1.22). The only reason to think that the phrase λίμνη Γυγαίη does not refer to the famous king is the supposed Homeric anachronism. The phrase recurs in Herodotus 1.93.5 (the tomb of Alyattes was next to the λίμνη Γυγαίη), and if we had only this evidence to consider we would naturally assume that the lake was named for the famous founder of the Mermnad dynasty. For the meaning of the name Gyges (traceable to Lydian *xuga-*, "grandfather") cf. Hawkins 2004:304. Achilles' first victim in the *Iliad*, born next to the "Gygaean lake" (*Iliad* 20.390–391), is of course a significant figure, as are those that follow: his second victim is a son of Antenor, and his fourth victim is a son of Priam (Hector is drawn into a premature confrontation with Achilles by the death of the latter; see above n4.132). Achilles' third victim, Hippodamas, evokes the Panionia when he bellows like a bull sacrificed to Poseidon Helikonios (*Iliad* 20.401–406). Achilles' first and third victims have in common that both seem to allude to the contemporary world of the Homeric audience: Gyges and the Lydians on the one hand and the Panionia on the other. For further discussion of the apparent allusion to Gyges, and its possible implications for the dating of the Homeric poems, see §4.70 and n4.236. For the relationship between the Homeric Maeonians and the historical Lydians, cf. Hawkins 2004:298–299: "It is worth noting that Homer never uses the word Λυδός or any derivative thereof. Gyges, who overthrew Candaules, seems to have been in power from about 680 to 650. If the theory that the Heraclidae were called Maeonians is accurate, and if the name Lydian only came into use again with Gyges, this might explain why Homer mentions Maeonians but not Lydians. These considerations, then, do not allow one to come to an absolute decision on the identity of the Maeonians, but the most straightforward conclusion is that Maeonian is an earlier name for Lydian. The ancient evidence seems to indicate that Maeonian and Lydian were two designations for the same people. The geographical location of the Maeonians is identical to that of the Lydians. The burden of proof rests on those who would claim that the two groups are not identical." I would modify this account only to say that the absence of the name "Lydian" from the Homeric poems does not mean that the name was not yet known in the Homeric era.

EN4.9 (Endnote to n4.146)

Durante's derivation of Greek *Hómēros*, outlined in n4.146, requires further comment. In 1976, when Durante reproduced and modified his article of 1957, he remarked that his etymological proposal had received little attention (Durante 1976:203–204); in my view his proposal still has not received the attention that it deserves. I therefore give further details of his argument and of the evidence on which it is based. I also consider certain historical issues that his argument raises.

Durante points out that the common noun *hómēros*, "hostage," is secondary to the neuter plural form *hómēra*, "pledge" or "agreement," and that the meanings "pledge" and "agreement" of the primary noun come easily from the etymological sense of a "coming together" (cf. Latin *conventum*). In antiquity the name *Hómēros* was explained by aetiological "hostage" myths (Harpokration s.v. Ὁμηρίδαι), but the name seems instead to be a back-formation from *Homērídai*, which is not a patronymic, but the designation of a special group, like *Hermokopídai*, "herm mutilators," etc.; the *Homērídai* were poets who "came together" at a festival to compete. This meaning of *Homērídai* is supported by the Greek forms *Homários* and *Homárion*, the former an epithet of Zeus, the latter the name of this god's sacred grove in Achaea, which was the meeting place ("coming together") of the Achaean league. These forms also occur as *Hamários* and *Hamárion*, confirming that the forms' first element is from *som- (zero-grade *sm̥) "together" (for the variation in the first element cf. Homeric ὁμαρτῇ/ἁμαρτῇ and see Wackernagel 1916:230/1970:70). An inscription from Arcadian Orchomenos dated 199 BC, which records the acceptance of Orchomenos into the Achaean league, contains the names *Día Amárion* and *Athánan Amarían*, gods by whom an oath is to be sworn (Collitz-Bechtel 1884–1915 no. 1634; Schwyzer 1923 no. 428). This evidence allows the name of the meeting place of the Achaean league in a passage of Strabo to be corrected from the corrupt manuscript readings AINAPION/APNAPION to AMAPION: τὸ τοῦ Διὸς ἄλσος τὸ Ἀμάριον, ὅπου συνῄεσαν οἱ Ἀχαιοὶ βουλευσόμενοι περὶ τῶν κοινῶν, "the grove of Zeus [called] the *Hamárion*, where the Achaeans met to deliberate about common affairs" (Strabo 8.7.5). Achaea, where the forms *Homárion* etc. are found, was settled from the Argolid in the late Bronze Age and retained elements of its Mycenaean past after the Dorians arrived (see Vermeule 1960:18–21); thus the relationship between Achaean *Homárion* etc. and Ionian *Homērídai* would seem to be a common origin in Mycenaean. In Achaea the *Homárion* was the meeting place of a political league which is assumed to have developed from an earlier amphictyony; the date of the political league is put as early as the eighth century BC, but more plausibly in the sixth or fifth century BC (cf. Mylonopoulos 2003:426–427, who argues for the fifth century). There is evidence that the *Homárion* was the center of a political league in the fifth century, but the evidence has been called into question. Polybius 2.39.6 says that a common cult of *Zeùs Homários* was established by Croton, Sybaris, and Caulonia in southern Italy in the mid-fifth century BC, when these cities allied with each other and reordered their constitutions on the basis of the laws and customs of their motherland Achaea: πρῶτον μὲν ἀπέδειξαν <u>Διὸς</u> <u>Ὁμαρίου κοινὸν ἱερὸν καὶ τόπον</u>, ἐν ᾧ τάς τε συνόδους καὶ τὰ διαβούλια συνετέλουν, δεύτερον τοὺς ἐθισμοὺς καὶ νόμους ἐκλαβόντες τοὺς τῶν Ἀχαιῶν ἐπεβάλοντο χρῆσθαι καὶ διοικεῖν κατὰ τούτους τὴν πολιτείαν, "First they designated <u>a common temple of Zeus Homarios and a place</u> in which they carried out deliberations together, secondly they accepted the customs and laws of the Achaeans and undertook to use them and arrange their constitution according to them." This appears to be clear evidence for the *Homárion* as an early political center in Achaea, but Morgan and Hall 1997:195 argue that Polybius wished to show that the principles of the Achaean league of his own day were based on ancient traditions, and they regard his story of the three Italian cities as an invention: the fact that Sybaris, one of the three cities, was destroyed in the sixth century (511/10 BC) by Croton, another of the three cities, is clearly a problem for the supposed fifth-century event and does not inspire confidence in Polybius's account as a whole. Following Morgan and Hall, who question whether the sanctuary of Zeus Homarios was the center of the Achaean league as early as the fifth century, Mylonopoulos 2003:424–427 argues that the original meeting place of the Achaean league was the temple of Poseidon Helikonios in Helike, and that only after this temple was destroyed by an earthquake in 373/2 BC did the *Homárion* in the territory of neighboring Aigion become the league's center (for Helike and Poseidon's cult there see Mylonopoulos 2003:35–40). These arguments complicate the use of the Achaean evidence by Durante 1957:104–105 (1976:195–197), but in my view they do not invalidate it; the Achaean *Homárion* must have existed in some form before the relatively late date of such a transfer of the league center, and the name suggests that it was a meeting place from early times. In my view the Achaean *Homárion* remains a valid comparison for the Ionian *Homērídai*. It is unclear what bearing another tradition has on the question, namely that Ionians preceded the Achaeans in Achaea and went to Athens when the Achaeans arrived (Strabo 8.7.1; Pausanias 7.1.3–5; 7.6.1–2). At any rate the rigid scheme, first attested in Herodotus 1.145–146, that the Ionians of the dodecapolis in Asia Minor came from the twelve cities of Achaea in the Peloponnesus seems unlikely to be older than the sixth century BC, the probable date of the earliest evidence for the question, a fragment of Hesiod (cf. Herda 2006:67n142 and 70, who dates the tradition for the Ionians' origins in the Peloponnesus earlier, to the seventh century BC). Hesiod fr. 9.2 MW attests the tradition that Hellen had three sons, Doros, Xouthos, and Aiolos; Doros and Aiolos are the ancestors of the Dorians and Aeolians, and Xouthos, as known from later sources, is the father of Ion and Akhaios, the ancestors of the Ionians and Achaeans: Strabo 8.7.1 tells how the descendants of Ion and Akhaios occupied Achaea in the Peloponnesus in successive stages, and how the Ionians, when they were driven from Achaea by the Achaeans, returned to Athens and from there founded Ionia, creating a dodecapolis on the Achaean model. Hesiod fr. 9 suggests that this version of the origins of the Ionian dodecapolis was known in the sixth century. If we grant the historical reality of Ionians in Achaea in the Bronze Age, and even of their subsequent movement to Athens and Ionia, it is still not clear who in the sixth century (or perhaps the seventh century) would have derived the Ionian dodecapolis directly from Achaea. This does not look like an Athenian or an Ionian idea. Perhaps it was invented by Peloponnesians, who thereby countered Athenian claims to Ionia with a rival version of Ionia's origins in the Peloponnesus; Anderson 1954:87–89 suggests that in the fourth century BC the Spartans may have made such use of this version of Ionia's origins, and Prandi 1989:49–59 elaborates a similar argument (cf. EN4.2 end). If the tradition of Ionia's Achaean origins did arise in the sixth century, it was nevertheless built on an older tradition, already in Homer, that associated Poseidon with the town of Helike and thereby offered an alternative interpretation of Poseidon's cult title Helikonios (cf. EN4.4).

An association of the name *Homērídai* with festivals and poetic competition is strongly supported by the etymological correspondence between Greek *Hómēros/Homários* and Sanskrit *samará-/samaryá-*. To illustrate the Sanskrit terms, both meaning "festival reunion" (*samaryá-* is also glossed as "poetic competition"), I quote one Vedic example of *samará-*, "festival reunion," in which the key phrase, *samaré 'tamānāḥ*, "those who come to the *samará-*," refers to poets who are clearly rivals of the poet of the verses in question, RV 6.9.2–3. The poet of these verses refers to his own activity and that of the other poets in terms of weaving; he at first despairs of his own ability to "stretch the warp" or "weave the woof" of his own song or to understand what others "who come to the *samará-*" weave; but in the second verse he remembers, as it were, the cosmic dimension of his poetic weaving and begins to assert his own competitiveness as a poet:

> *náhám tántum ná ví jānāmy ótum / ná yám váyanti <u>samaré 'tamānāḥ</u> /*
> *kásya svit putrá ihá váktvāni / paró vadāty ávareṇa pitrá*

> I understand neither how to stretch the warp nor how to weave the woof, nor what <u>those who come to the samará-</u> weave. Whose son can here speak verses beyond his surpassed father?

sá ít tántuṃ sá ví jānāty ótuṃ / sá váktvāny ṛtuthā́ vadāti /
yá ī́ṃ cíketad amŕ̥tasya gopā́ / aváś cáran paró anyéna páśyan

He will understand how to stretch the warp and weave the woof,
he will speak verses in the proper order, who, as the herdsman of
immortality, perceives it, seeing, while walking here below, beyond
another [ī́m, "it," seems to refer to the warp of the song, which
stretches to heaven].

(For weaving as a metaphor for poetry in other Indo-European traditions
including Iranian, Germanic, and Greek see Schmitt 1967:298–301; Nagy
2002:70–98 explains the semantics of Greek *húmnos*, as applied to epic perfor-
mance, in terms of a weaving metaphor.)

Having expressed my support of Durante's interpretation of the names
Homērídai and *Hómēros*, I take note of another interpretation that starts from
the same formal derivation as Durante's (*som-* + *ar-*) but takes the meaning to
be "fit together" with a metaphor borrowed from joinery. The Indo-European
root *teks-* occurs in such a metaphor from joinery (see Schmitt 1967:296–298
for the Pindaric collocation ἐπέων τέκτονες, "carpenters of words," and
cognate phrases in Indo-Iranian), and a similar metaphor is seen in Greek
Hómēros by Nagy 1979:297–300 (cf. also Nagy 1996:89–91 and 2008:2§§41–45).
This explanation has the advantage of assuming a meaning, "join," close to
that of Greek ἀραρίσκω, "join with, fasten," of the root *ar-*. On the other hand
Durante's explanation, which I find persuasive in both its analysis of Greek
forms and its comparison with Sanskrit forms, fits closer with my notion of
who the Homeridai originally were.

EN4.10 (Endnote to n4.150)

Jacoby, commentary on Hellanicus *FGrHist* 323a F 23, argues that Hellanicus
constructed a pedigree for the Medontidai as part of a list to fill the gap
between the Ionian migration in Medon's time and the first annual archon
in 683/2 BC. In Hellanicus (and in later sources such as the Parian Marble)
the Medontidai were βασιλεῖς, "kings," but another tradition arose in which
they were, from the time of Medon, first ἄρχοντες διὰ βίου, "archons for
life," then archons for ten years each. In this scheme, which reflects demo-
cratic values (cf. e.g. Pausanias 4.5.10) but is hard to trace to its origin (see
Jacoby, commentary on Hellanicus *FGrHist* 323a F 23, p. 46), the last four
(or five) Medontidai, including Hippomenes, are ten-year archons, who
are followed by three other ten-year archons from other families before
the first annual archon takes office in 683/2 BC. Hippomenes' rule ended

in 714 or 713 BC according to this scheme (see the lists preserved by later authors in von Schoeffer *RE* 'Archontes' 584). It is worth noting that in the surviving lists Medon's (son and) successor is Akastos, who was clearly given this place of honor because of a democratic institution, namely the archons' oath: according to Aristotle *Constitution of the Athenians* 3.3 the nine archons swore to "carry out the oaths made in the time of Akastos," τὰ ἐπὶ Ἀκάστου ὅρκια ποιήσειν; cf. Jacoby 1949:127. There is no certain evidence in historical times for the Medontidai as a *génos* in Athens. On *Agora Inventory* I 5509, an inscription from 367/6 BC, the name belongs to a phratry (κοινὸν φρατέρων Μεδοντιδῶν, lines 17–18), and Crosby 1941:21–22, who published the inscription, argues that other occurrences of the name also refer to a phratry rather than a *génos*. But some names belong to both a *génos* and a phratry (Crosby 1941:21n3), and Medontidai may be one of these. Jacoby, commentary on Hellanicus *FGrHist* 323a F 23, n70, argues in favor of this possibility, or at least he leaves the possibility open. Like Toepffer, whom he quotes, Jacoby attaches particular importance to *IG* I³ 1062, a boundary stone from the fifth century BC marking the "limit of the ------ (land? agora?) of the Medontidai"; this inscription was found near the entrance to the Acropolis, a fact which for Toepffer 1889:229 "fits excellently with the tradition for the royal blood of this family" ("stimmt trefflich zur Überlieferung von dem königlichen Geblüt dieses Geschlechts"). Jacoby, taking issue with Crosby, is surely correct that a *génos* rather than a phratry is meant in such literary evidence as Pausanias 4.13.7, which dates the end of the First Messenian War by reference to Medontid rule in Athens (Ἀθήνῃσι Μεδοντιδῶν τὴν ἀρχὴν ἔτι ἐχόντων τὴν δεκέτιν καὶ ἔτους Ἱππομένει τετάρτου τῆς ἀρχῆς ἠνυσμένου, "when the Medontidai still maintained the ten-year rule in Athens and the fourth year of Hippomenes' rule had been completed"); a *génos* rather than a phratry may also be meant in Hesychius s.v. Μεδοντίδαι· οἱ ἀπὸ Μέδοντος Ἀθήνῃσι, "Medontidai: descendants of Medon in Athens." But such evidence does not prove the existence of a *génos* in Jacoby's view, for the pedigree of the Medontids, on which Pausanias and perhaps also Hesychius depend, is part of the kings list constructed by Hellanicus (Jacoby, commentary on Hellanicus *FGrHist* 323a F 23, nn70 and 71).

EN4.11 *(Endnote to n4.155)*
The claim of the Athenian Peisistratids to descent from Nestor seems to have inspired rival claims on the part of the Alcmaeonids and the Paionids, political opponents of the Peisistratids: whereas the Peisistratids claimed descent from Nestor's son Peisistratos, who did not fight at Troy, the Alcmaeonids and

Paionids outdid them by claiming descent from Thrasymedes and Antilochus, both heroes of the Trojan war. Nestor's descendants through all three sons (as well as the descendants of Periklymenos) are discussed in Pausanias 2.18.8–9; in this passage the rivalry between the tyrant Peisistratos on the one hand and the Alcmaeonids and Paionids on the other hand is evident: Pausanias's source (probably an Atthidographer, possibly Philochorus; see Jacoby, commentary on Hellanicus *FGrHist* 323a F23, nn1 and 36) was clearly hostile to the tyrant Peisistratos, for all the descendants of Neleus are said to have gone to Athens except the son of Nestor's son Peisistratos (also named Peisistratos), whose destination Pausanias simply does not know: ἐκβάλλουσιν οὖν [οἱ Ἡρακλεῖδαι]...ἐκ τῆς Μεσσηνίας τοὺς Νέστορος ἀπογόνους, Ἀλκμαίωνα Σίλλου τοῦ Θρασυμήδους καὶ Πεισίστρατον τὸν Πεισιστράτου καὶ τοὺς Παίονος τοῦ Ἀντιλόχου παῖδας, σὺν δὲ αὐτοῖς Μέλανθον τὸν Ἀνδροπόμπου τοῦ Βώρου τοῦ Πενθίλου τοῦ Περικλυμένου.... οἱ δὲ Νηλεῖδαι πλὴν Πεισιστράτου (τοῦτον γὰρ οὐκ οἶδα παρ᾽ οὕστινας ἀπεχώρησεν) ἐς Ἀθήνας ἀφίκοντο οἱ λοιποί, καὶ τὸ Παιονιδῶν γένος καὶ Ἀλκμαιωνιδῶν ἀπὸ τούτων ὠνομάσθησαν. Μέλανθος δὲ καὶ τὴν βασιλείαν ἔσχεν ἀφελόμενος Θυμοίτην τὸν Ὀξύντου· Θυμοίτης γὰρ Θησειδῶν ἔσχατος ἐβασίλευσεν Ἀθηναίων, "They [the Heraclids] expelled Nestor's descendants from Messenia: Alcmaeon, the son of Sillos, the son of Thrasymedes; Peisistratos, the son of Peisistratos; the sons of Paion, the son of Antilochus; and with them Melanthos, the son of Andropompos, the son of Boros, the son of Penthilos, the son of Periklymenos.... The Neleids, with the exception of Peisistratos (for I do not know to what people he went), all came to Athens, and the *génos* of the Paionids and that of the Alcmaeonids were named after them. Melanthos also held the kingship, taking it from Thymoites, the son of Oxyntes; for Thymoites was the last of the descendants of Theseus to rule Athens." We are well informed about the Alcmaeonids' rivalry with Peisistratos, and Toepffer 1889:227 connects the Paionids with the Alcmaeonids in this rivalry through the place-name Paionia, which was close to the Alcmaeonid stronghold of Leipsydrion: it was from this stronghold that the exiled Alcmaeonids maintained their opposition to the Peisistratids after 514 BC (cf. Anderson 2003:29 and 226n39), and the proximity of Paionia suggests that the Paionids joined the Alcmaeonids in this opposition. The fictitious ancestries of both families must have been inspired by rivalry with Peisistratos and his family: in Pausanias, who reflects the rivalry, both the allied families descend from Neleus, but the Peisistratids are excluded from this distinction. Our source for "Leipsydrion above Paionia" (which seems to have been on Mount Parnes; Aristotle fr. 394 Rose) is Herodotus 5.62.2, which tells how the Alcmaeonids and those allied with them tried but failed to oust Hippias after the murder of Hipparchus in 514 BC: Ἱππίεω τυραννεύοντος καὶ ἐμπικραινομένου Ἀθηναίοισι διὰ τὸν Ἱππάρχου θάνατον Ἀλκμεωνίδαι, γένος ἐόντες Ἀθηναῖοι καὶ φεύγοντες Πεισιστρατίδας, ἐπείτε σφι ἅμα τοῖσι ἄλλοισι Ἀθηναίων φυγάσι πειρωμένοισι κατὰ τὸ ἰσχυρὸν οὐ προεχώρεε ‹ἡ› κάτοδος, ἀλλὰ προσέπταιον μεγάλως πειρώμενοι κατιέναι τε καὶ ἐλευθεροῦν τὰς Ἀθήνας, <u>Λειψύδριον τὸ ὑπὲρ Παιονίης</u> τειχίσαντες, ἐνθαῦτα οἱ Ἀλκμεωνίδαι πᾶν ἐπὶ τοῖσι Πεισιστρατίδῃσι μηχανώμενοι παρ᾽ Ἀμφικτυόνων τὸν νηὸν μισθοῦνται τὸν ἐν Δελφοῖσι, τὸν νῦν ἐόντα, τότε δὲ οὔκω, τοῦτον ἐξοικοδομῆσαι, "When Hippias was tyrant and became embittered with the Athenians because of Hipparchus's death, the Alcmaeonids, native Athenians whom the Peisistratids had exiled, and the other Athenian exiles did not succeed in returning despite their strong efforts, but suffered a great defeat when they tried to return and free Athens; fortifying <u>Leipsydrion above Paionia</u> and thereafter trying every scheme against the Peisistratids, they contracted with the Amphictyones to finish building the temple in Delphi that is there now, but was not yet there then." The Attic Paionidai, who in the myth of their Neleid descent are named for Antilochus's son Paion, may actually have taken their name from an Attic toponym (cf. Cromey 1978:66, 68; the deme name in question was in fact Paionidai rather than Paionia; cf. Rhodes 1981:235; for Herodotus's use of the form Paionia instead, cf. Irwin 2007:51–52). Hampe 1950 pushes to an extreme the possibility that not only Neleus and Nestor were historical figures, but also the descendants attributed to them (Hampe 1950:51–70). I agree with Hampe that the Neleid line was real, in Athens as in Miletus, but this does not mean that false claims to Neleid descent were not also made. Hampe himself recognizes that all the Neleid pedigrees may be late constructions (see in particular the chronology that he presents in the appendix on pp. 67–70, which he admits can be viewed either as history or as a later reconstruction of history). In my view the Neleid pedigrees are a mixture of history and fiction. While I think that Hampe claims too much for history, his article repays close reading; his description of Nestor's Homeric role on pp. 11–18, even though it is based on a completely different understanding of the Homeric figure from my own, stands out particularly to me. Seeck 1887 also took the Neleid genealogies of Athenian families at face value, and argued on this basis that the *Odyssey* had an Athenian origin; his argument was rejected by Toepffer 1889:237–238, who saw clearly that the genealogical claims of the Alcmaeonids and Paionids at least were late inventions (Toepffer 1889:226–228; about Peisistratos's genealogical claim Toepffer was more hesitant; cf. 1889:4n4). Toepffer 1889:228 also viewed the tradition of Neleid descent for the Medontid kings as unfounded (a point on which I basically differ), but he still distinguished clearly between the Medontids on the one hand and the Alcmaeonids and Paionids on the other hand in terms of depth of tradition (1889:226). In Greek genealogies the chief interest is in a mythic ancestor at the beginning of a line and a full genealogy down to the present is rare (see Thomas 1989:155–195, who contrasts Roman genealogies in this respect, pp. 100–108). For full genealogies that do occur genealogists like Pherecydes and Hellanicus seem to be responsible; Hecataeus, who famously traced himself back through sixteen generations to a god (Herodotus 2.143.1), was himself an early genealogist (cf. Thomas 1989:160). An exception with respect to mythic ancestry is the tombstone of Heropythos of Chios, probably from the mid-fifth century BC (Collitz-Bechtel 1884–1915 no. 5656; text corrected by Wade-Gery 1952:8, fig. 1), which lists ancestors through fourteen generations but does not go back to a legendary or heroic figure (cf. Thomas 1989:156, 159). The Neleid genealogy presented by Hellanicus *FGrHist* 323a F 23 is an example of the genealogist's construction of a complete line of descent; here the interval to be filled was not between a mythic ancestor and the present, but between two mythic ancestors, Neleus and Neileos, who duplicate the myth of one family's origins; this two-stage myth, which sets Pylos, Athens, and Miletus in relation to each other, and which must already have been known to Homer, is what the genealogist began with. Hellanicus's interest was presumably in Athens rather than in Miletus; hence his attention to Kodros, who matters to both cities, and to Melanthos, who belongs to Athenian myth. Sergent 1982, following Mühlestein 1965, shows by analysis of onomastic evidence that Neleids must have constituted a noble *génos* (though not necessarily the royal *génos*) in the Pylos of the Linear-B tablets; using this evidence Sergent shows further that there is a solid historical core to traditions of Pylian ancestry among Neleids in Athens and Ionia. The evidence is clearest in the case of descendants of Periklymenos (Medontids in Athens and Neleids in Miletus), but it also pertains to the three Attic *génē* claiming descent from Nestor. Thus it is not the case that there is no factual basis to the claims of Pylian ancestry on the part of the three Attic *génē*; it is rather the case that whatever claims they had were at least reshaped by the strong influence of the Homeric poems. This is essentially the conclusion reached by Sergent 1982:19, but Sergent makes an exception in the case of Peisistratos, suggesting that the poet of the *Odyssey* gave Nestor a son named Peisistratos because an Athenian family of Pylian descent made use of this name. In my view it was just the opposite: it was not the *Odyssey* that was influenced by the Athenian family in the use of the name Peisistratos, but the Athenian family that was influenced by the *Odyssey*.

EN4.12 (Endnote to n4.197)

The original editors of the Nestor's cup inscription, Buchner and Russo, took verse 1 of the inscription to refer to Nestor's cup in *Iliad* 11, and verses 2 and 3 to refer to the clay cup (*skúphos*) on which the inscription is written. Watkins 1976 also follows this interpretation. The contrast between the two cups in the wording of the inscription (Νέστορος...ποτήριον in verse 1 and τοῦδε ποτηρίου in verse 2), is reinforced by the particle δέ marking a contrast at the beginning of verse 2 and by the change of meter at this point. The iambic trimeter of the first verse has an "Aeolic base," which Watkins takes as a sign of archaism (later trimeters occasionally have the same feature, especially when they begin as here with a proper name). Watkins is not the first to suggest ἐ[στ]ι in verse 1 (it was considered but not adopted by Buchner and Russo 1955 and by Dihle 1969), but he is the first to argue persuasively for it (on p. 39 he credits his student, Michael Taylor, for suggesting to him the the inscription's basic sense). The restoration ἐ[στ]ι is preferable to ἔ[ρρο]ι, "away with," suggested by the original editors; it is also preferable to ε[ἰμ]ι, "I am," although this word is common after a name in the genitive on objects declaring themselves to be the possession of a particular owner (e.g. Θαρίο εἰμὶ ποτέριον, "I am Tharios's cup," from the Athenian agora, dated end of the eighth century by Shear 1936:33, middle of the seventh century by Young 1939:124–126 and Jeffery 1961:69; cf. Buchner and Russo 1955:221n2). The restoration ε[ἰμ]ι on the Nestor's cup inscription has been assumed by Jeffery 1961:235 and others (see Watkins 1976:37), but there are strong arguments against it. The first is space: the only likely form of this verb in the Ionic dialect of Pithekoussai is ἐμι (see Watkins 1976:38, who notes that the diphthong in the eighth-century Attic form quoted above [Θαρίο εἰμί] is an unexplained Attic anomaly; there are two further examples of εἰμι in Attica, of the seventh or sixth century, in Jeffery 1961:70 [10f and 10h]), and the space to be filled is too large for a single letter (there must have been two or three letters). The second problem is meaning, and here there are several objections. The first is that with the reading ε[ἰμ]ι the inscription refers only to the cup on which it is written, and this runs counter to the metrical and phraseological contrasts analyzed by Watkins. In addition, the ordinary clay cup on which the inscription is written now claims to be the famous cup of Nestor in *Iliad* 11, and this is ludicrous (but cf. Powell 1991:165–166, who assumes an intentional joke); alternatively, the cup says that it is the property of a man named Nestor (Dihle 1969, accepted by West 1970:171). I would agree with Watkins 1976:37 that this is "more or less a null hypothesis," and that "it is inherently far more likely that an accomplished ἀοιδός with demonstrated familiarity with the Homeric repertoire, who begins his first line with Νεστορος (a frequent position of the same name in this and other grammatical cases in the hexameter), had the Homeric hero in mind, and would assume his audience would." I mention two other suggested readings to supply the missing word in verse 1. Margherita Guarducci's reading Νέστορος μ[ὲ]ν εὔποτ[ον] ποτήριον makes a maximal contrast between an epic cup and a real cup by means of the particles μέν and δέ (Guarducci 1961, cf. also Guarducci 1967:226–227; the resulting verse is a trochaic trimeter catalectic). To give the same sense as the verb ε[ἰμ]ι, "I am," Hansen 1988 suggests instead the pronoun τ[οδ]ί, "this (is)." This reading produces a regular glyconic in place of the irregular iambic trimeter of readings with an initial epsilon; it also restores two letters, as required by the space, whereas ἐ[μ]ι (instead of ε[ἰμ]ι, see above) restores only one letter. Hansen points out further that the inscriptions with εἰμί adduced as parallels for this inscription invariably continue in the first person, and that τοῦδε ποτηρίου in line 2 of this inscription would be an unexampled change from first person to third person. By this criterion only τοδί and ἐστι are possible readings, and whereas τοδί may be metrically preferable, ἐστι, in my view, provides a better reading of the poem (I find the joke in the other reading of the poem lame if not pointless). In support of ἐστι Watkins 1976:39n21 points out the repeated sound in Νέστορός ἐστι at the beginning of the line, and the same figure again in εὔποτον ποτήριον at the end of the line. For further bibliography see Watkins 1976:25n1, Buchner and Ridgway 1993:751–759, Graziosi 2002:135n30.

EN4.13 (Endnote to n4.227)

It is clear from *IP* (Hiller 1906) no. 37 that Miletus was given some part or parts of Melia's land after the Meliac War, but the allotment seems to have been modest. Only one place, A(kadamis?), certainly belonged to Miletus before a subsequent exchange of land between Samos and Miletus rearranged their holdings; the fragmentary text is *IP* 37.57–59. In Hiller's original restoration of the text the Samians claimed to have obtained three settlements from Miletus in the exchange: A(-------), Thebai, and Marathesion; but in Hiller's revised text (*IP* p. 309, based on Wilamowitz 1906/1971:42n4/133n2; see n4.76) the Samians claimed to have given two of these settlements, Thebai and Marathesion, to Miletus in exchange for the third, A(kadamis); on this reading only the third, A(kadamis), can have been allotted to Miletus after the Meliac War. The revised text is supported by a fragment of Theopompus, which says that Miletus got Thebai from Samos (*FGrHist* 115 F 23 = scholia to Euripides *Andromache* 1): Θεόπομπος δὲ ἐν ‹γ› Ἑλληνικῶν καὶ περὶ τὴν Μυκάλην ἄλλας [Θήβας] εἶναί φησι, ταύτας δὲ Μιλησίους ἀλλάξασθαι πρὸς Σαμίους (the verb and grammatical construction in the last clause have an exact parallel in Strabo 8.6.14, which establishes the interpretation here; cf. Hiller *IP* no. 418 following Wilamowitz). Hommel in Kleiner et al. 1967:94 follows Hiller's original text (see below), but others, including Shipley 1987:34n50, follow Hiller's revised text. Keil 1908:145 follows the revised text in saying that Miletus got Marathesion from Samos. There is a difficulty with Marathesion in that according to Strabo 14.1.20 Samos gave Marathesion to Ephesus; Keil interprets this as a later development, implying that Marathesion changed hands more than once, passing from Melia to Samos to Miletus, back to Samos, and finally to Ephesus. Pygela, the settlement allotted to Samos after the Meliac War according to the historians named in *IP* 37.120–121 (cf. n4.75 and n4.76 end), has also figured in the discussion of the subsequent land exchanges between Samos and Miletus; while Pygela is not relevant to the question of Miletus's original allotment after the Meliac war, it is worth trying to clarify its later role. Keil 1908:137–138 takes it for granted that Miletus got Pygela from Samos ("...the fact that it [Pygela] fell to the Samians already at the time of the destruction of Melia, about 700 BC, to be ceded by them [later] to Miletus in an exchange" ["...die Tatsache, dass es [Pygela] bereits zur Zeit der Zerstörung von Melia, also um 700 v. Chr. den Samiern zufiel, um von ihnen im Wege des Austausches an Milet überlassen zu werden"]). Hommel in Kleiner et al. 1967:94 follows Keil with respect to Pygela and Miletus, pointing out that Pygela would have provided two useful harbors on the route north to Miletus's colonies: "The new possessions were rounded out by an exchange in that Samos gave Phygela to Miletus, to which this place must have been useful, lying with two harbors northernmost on the coast on the way to Miletus's northern colonies. For this place Miletus gave up to Samos Marathesion, which lay further to the south, and Thebes on the south slope of Mykale, which had earlier fallen victim to its expansion" ("Durch Tausch sind die neuen Besitzungen abgerundet worden, indem Samos Phygela an Milet abgab, dem dieser nördlichste an der Küste gelegene Punkt mit zwei Häfen auf seinem Weg zu den nördlichen Tochterstädten nützlich sein mußte. Es hat dafür das südlicher gelegene Marathesion und das schon früher seiner Expansion zum Opfer gefallene Theben am Mykalesüdhang an Samos abgetreten"); for Marathesion and Thebai Hommel follows Hiller's original text of *IP* 37, and Ἀ[κάδαμις he leaves out of account. It is plausible that Miletus gained possession of Pygela, but there is no real evidence for this as far as I can see; the only evidence cited by Keil is that Miletus came to Pygela's aid in 409 BC when Pygela was attacked by Athens (Xenophon *Hellenica* 1.2.2; Miletus had revolted from Athens in 412 BC). To sum up, the only land known for sure to have gone to Miletus after the Meliac War is Akadamis, if that name, as is likely, is correctly restored in *IP* 37 (cf. Hiller *IP* p. 309 and Shipley 1987:34n50, and see n4.76). Marathesion probably went to Samos rather than Miletus after the war, but we cannot be sure of that given the uncertainty of Hiller's text. Thebai, on the south slope of Mykale and across the Gulf of Latmos from Miletus, is unlikely to have been part of Melia's territory at all (cf. Wilamowitz 1906/1971:42n4/133n2); thus, if Thebai was in fact Miletus's to give to Samos, Miletus probably did not get it through the Meliac War (cf. Hommel, quoted above, who suggests acquisition before the Meliac War). If we accept the evidence of Theopompus, that Miletus got Thebai from Samos, the likeliest series of exchanges is as Shipley 1987:34, writing about Samos, describes it: "The peraea was...too large when it was acquired to be defensible for long, and possession of several minor settlements changed hands just after the Meliac War or during the Archaic period, Marathesion, Thebai, and possibly another place being given away in return for Anaia and Akadamis." What Miletus got from the Meliac War was thus only the obscure Akadamis, of unknown location; to this we might add Marathesion. I think that Miletus's main interest after the war was not Mykale's land, but the league centered on it.

EN4.14 (Endnote to n4.238)

The history of the name "Ionian," whatever its ultimate origin, is centered in Asia Minor. The name, attested in Assyrian in the eighth century BC (730s, or perhaps 715, at the earliest, references in Luraghi, *Phoenix* 60 [2006] 31n44), came to mean "Greek" in eastern cultures, a usage that continues today: Hebrew *Yawan*, Persian *Yauna*, Sanskirt *Yavana*, Egyptian demotic *Wynn*, Turkish *Yunan* (cf. Malkin 2001:3; Sancisi-Weerdenburg 2001:323, 332). In one sense the process is clear: the Ionians of Asia Minor were East Greeks whose name became known to peoples still further to the east. But the very existence of a common name must have had to do with the Panionic league, for this is what gave the Ionians a common identity (I draw attention again to the Ionians' diversity of origins, as perceived and commented on by Herodotus; see n4.15). Högemann 2001:62 aptly calls the name "Ionia" an "artificial concept" ("Kunstbegriff"): "The origin of the name 'Ionians' is unknown, but probably arose earliest in Asia Minor. Who was designated by it in the beginning? The designation 'Ionia' in any case does not go back to a people of the same name, as for example Thessaly to the Thessalians, but should be understood as an artificial concept: it stands for the cities of a region and not for a continuous territory. Herodotus may be cited as a witness for this: all Ionian cities lie either in Lydia or in Caria" ("Der Ursprung des Namens 'Ionier' ist unbekannt, wohl am ehesten kleinasiatisch. Wer wurde anfänglich damit bezeichnet? Die Bezeichnung 'Ionien' geht jedenfalls nicht auf ein gleichnamiges Volk zurück, wie z. B. Thessalien auf die Thessaler, sondern ist als ein Kunstbegriff zu verstehen: Er meint eine Städtelandschaft und kein geschlossenes Territorium. Als Zeuge sei Herodot angeführt: Alle ionischen Städte lägen teils in Lydien, teils in Karien"). In terms of their diverse origins, the Ionians were not a single people, but became one in Asia Minor; Herodotus leaves no doubt of this; cf. Högemann 2001:61, quoted in n1.56. The name "Ionian" may be old (Linear-B *ijawone*[is "possibly" a dative singular *ijawonei*, but "unlikely" a nominative plural *ijawones*, Chadwick and Baumbach 1963 s.v. Ἴων), but it was the Panionic league that gave the name currency. Herodotus says that only the cities of the dodecapolis took pride in the Ionian name, and that the other Ionians and the Athenians shunned it down to his day (Herodotus 1.143.3):

οἱ μέν νυν ἄλλοι Ἴωνες καὶ οἱ Ἀθηναῖοι ἔφευγον τὸ οὔνομα, οὐ βουλόμενοι Ἴωνες κεκλῆσθαι, ἀλλὰ καὶ νῦν φαίνονταί μοι οἱ πολλοὶ αὐτῶν ἐπαισχύνεσθαι τῷ οὐνόματι· αἱ δὲ δυώδεκα πόλιες αὗται τῷ τε οὐνόματι ἠγάλλοντο καὶ ἱρὸν ἱδρύσαντο ἐπὶ σφέων αὐτέων, τῷ οὔνομα ἔθεντο Πανιώνιον, ἐβουλεύσαντο δὲ αὐτοῦ μεταδοῦναι μηδαμοῖσι ἄλλοισι Ἰώνων (οὐδ' ἐδεήθησαν δὲ οὐδαμοὶ μετασχεῖν ὅτι μὴ Σμυρναῖοι), "Now the other Ionians and the Athenians shunned the name, not wishing to be called Ionians, but even now most of them seem to me to be ashamed of the name. But these twelve cities gloried in the name and established a sanctuary for themselves, to which they gave the name Panionion, and they resolved not to let any other Ionians participate in it (nor did any ask to participate in it except the Smyrnaeans)." If wide use of the Ionian name grew out of the Panionic league, the Neleids of Miletus must have been instrumental in promoting it. In Homer the name Ionia occurs only once, in *Iliad* 13.685, and here it means Athenian; this is what the Neleids would have wanted it to mean in terms of their own origin (*Iliad* 13.685–691):

ἔνθα δὲ Βοιωτοὶ καὶ Ἰάονες ἑλκεχίτωνες
Λοκροὶ καὶ Φθῖοι καὶ φαιδιμόεντες Ἐπειοὶ
σπουδῇ ἐπαΐσσοντα νεῶν ἔχον, οὐδὲ δύναντο
ὦσαι ἀπὸ σφείων φλογὶ εἴκελον Ἕκτορα δῖον
οἳ μὲν Ἀθηναίων προλελεγμένοι· ἐν δ' ἄρα τοῖσιν
ἦρχ' υἱὸς Πετεῶο Μενεσθεύς, οἳ δ' ἅμ' ἕποντο
Φείδας τε Στιχίος τε Βίας τ' ἐΰς.

Then the Boeotians and the tunic-trailing Ionians,
the Locrians and the Phthians and the shining Epeians

resisted him as he eagerly assaulted the ships, but they could not
push flame-like shining Hector away from themselves,
they who were ranked first among the Athenians; among these
Peteos's son Menestheus led, and there followed with him
Pheidas and Stichios and strong Bias.

This picture of an Ionian Athens fits with the picture of a Carian Miletus in
the Trojan Catalogue of Ships (*Iliad* 2.867–869; cf. §4.54 above): already during
the Trojan war, when Neleids still ruled Pylos, Ionians, who would one day
colonize Caria, inhabited Athens. In Attica the Ionian name was especially
associated with the Marathonian tetrapolis, the oldest seat of the Ionians in
Attica ("der älteste Sitz des Ionertums...in Attika," von Schoeffer *RE* 'Demoi'
26). Two passages in Strabo attest the Ionian associations of Marathon:
Xouthos, the father of Ion and Achaios, founded the tetrapolis according to
Strabo 8.7.1: Ξοῦθος δὲ τὴν Ἐρεχθέως θυγατέρα γήμας ᾤκισε τὴν τετράπολιν
τῆς Ἀττικῆς, Οἰνόην Μαραθῶνα Προβάλινθον καὶ Τρικόρυνθον. τῶν δὲ
τούτου παίδων Ἀχαιὸς μὲν φόνον ἀκούσιον πράξας ἔφυγεν εἰς Λακεδαίμονα
καὶ Ἀχαιοὺς τοὺς ἐκεῖ κληθῆναι παρεσκεύασεν, Ἴων δὲ τοὺς μετ' Εὐμόλπου
νικήσας Θρᾷκας οὕτως ηὐδοκίμησεν ὥστ' ἐπέτρεψαν αὐτῷ τὴν πολιτείαν
Ἀθηναῖοι, "Xouthos married Erechtheus's daughter and founded the tetrap-
olis of Attica, namely Oinoe, Marathon, Probalinthos, and Trikorynthos. Of his
sons one, Akhaios, committed involuntary murder and fled to Lacedaemon
and brought it about for those there to be called Achaeans, and the other,
Ion, defeated the Thracians with Eumolpos and was so well regarded that
the Athenians turned the state over to him." Strabo 8.6.15 cites Aristotle
that Ionians from the tetrapolis followed the Heraclids in their return to the
Peloponnesus and settled in the Argolid: ἡ Ἐπίδαυρος δ' ἐκαλεῖτο Ἐπίταυρος·
φησὶ δὲ Ἀριστοτέλης κατασχεῖν αὐτὴν Κᾶρας, ὥσπερ καὶ Ἑρμιόνα, τῶν δὲ
Ἡρακλειδῶν κατελθόντων Ἴωνας αὐτοῖς συνοικῆσαι τοὺς ἐκ τῆς Ἀττικῆς
τετραπόλεως συνεπομένους εἰς Ἄργος, "Epidauros was called Epitauros;
Aristotle says that Carians occupied it, as they also did Hermion, and that
when the Heraclids returned, their fellow inhabitants were the Ionians who
followed them from the Attic tetrapolis to Argos." The Ionian associations of
the Marathonian tetrapolis throw light on *Odyssey* 7.78–80, Athena's second
departure from Scheria:

ὣς ἄρα φωνήσασ' ἀπέβη γλαυκῶπις Ἀθήνη
πόντον ἐπ' ἀτρύγετον, λίπε δὲ Σχερίην ἐρατεινήν,
ἵκετο δ' ἐς Μαραθῶνα καὶ εὐρυάγυιαν Ἀθήνην.

> So spoke grey-eyed Athena, and she departed
> across the barren sea and left lovely Scheria,
> <u>and she came to Marathon and Athens with wide ways.</u>

After introducing the Phaeacian queen to Odysseus, Athena goes not just to Athens, but first to Marathon, and then to Athens; this, I suggest, is meant to reinforce the idea that Athena's destination is (in Solon's phrase) the oldest land of Ionia, and that her journey therefore has special relevance to Ionians who celebrated the Panionia.

Part 5.

PYLOS

Chapter 12.

ILIAD 11 AND THE LOCATION
OF HOMERIC PYLOS

§5.1 In *Iliad* 11 Nestor tells how he first became a horseman when he defeated the enemy Epeians in battle: entering the battle on foot he immediately slew the leader of the Epeian horsemen, seized his chariot, and like a dark whirlwind drove it straight through the enemy, slaying the double occupants of fifty chariots before he reached Bouprasion and turned back homeward in triumph. From the very start, when the Pylians answer Athena's nighttime alarm and Nestor keeps pace with the Pylian horsemen, Nestor's account of his battle is cast in terms of a chariot race. For Nestor, starting out on foot, the real race begins when he leaps onto his newly won chariot and surges into the lead; the turning point comes when he conquers the last of his fifty chariots and turns back toward Pylos in victory (*Iliad* 11.759–761):

> ἔνθ' ἄνδρα κτείνας <u>πύματον</u> λίπ<u>ον</u>· αὐτὰρ Ἀχαιοὶ
> <u>ἂψ</u> ἀπὸ Βουπρασίοιο Πύλονδ' ἔχον <u>ὠκέας ἵππους</u>,
> πάντες δ' εὐχετόωντο θεῶν Διὶ Νέστορί τ' ἀνδρῶν.

> Then I killed the <u>last man and left him</u>. But the Achaeans
> drove their <u>swift horses back</u> from Bouprasion to Pylos,
> and all prayed to Zeus among gods and Nestor among men.

The underlined elements in these lines echo similar elements in the passage of *Iliad* 23 relating to the turn in the chariot race for Patroclus (*Iliad* 23.373–375):

> ἀλλ' ὅτε δὴ <u>πύματον</u> τέλε<u>ον</u> δρόμ<u>ου</u> <u>ὠκέες ἵπποι</u>
> <u>ἂψ</u> ἐφ' ἁλὸς πολιῆς, τότε δὴ ἀρετή γε ἑκάστου
> φαίνετ', ἄφαρ δ' ἵπποισι τάθη δρόμος.

But when the <u>swift horses</u> were completing the <u>end</u> of the
    course
<u>back</u> toward the grey sea, then indeed the strength of each
showed itself, and at once the horses strained their hardest.[1]

Later in *Iliad* 23 Nestor tells how once he lost a chariot race in funeral games
for king Amarynkeus, which likewise took place at Bouprasion: then, in
contrast to his later battle, in which the turning point marked his triumph,
the turning point had been his downfall. In the *Iliad* the contrast between
Nestor's battle in *Iliad* 11 and his chariot race in *Iliad* 23 relates to Patroclus,
for whose sake both events are evoked. When Patroclus fails to turn back
from Troy, he follows the pattern of Nestor's unsuccessful race, not of his
triumphant battle. Nestor gave Patroclus the right paradigm to follow in *Iliad*
11, but Patroclus failed to follow it in one fatal respect—the turning point.

§5.2 In the story of Patroclus in the *Iliad* Nestor's calamitous chariot race is
the foil to his victorious battle, and it is thus with good reason that his battle is
also cast in terms of a chariot race.[2] But what was once imagined in *Iliad* 11 as a
virtual racecourse stretching between Pylos and Bouprasion has been drastically
recast in the story as we have it. The Epeian horsemen, whose imminent threat
requires Athena to gather the Pylians by night, do not actually advance on Pylos,
but stop and lay siege to a town on the Alpheios River (*Iliad* 11.711–713):

ἔστι δέ τις Θρυόεσσα πόλις αἰπεῖα κολώνη
τηλοῦ ἐπ' Ἀλφειῷ, νεάτη Πύλου ἡμαθόεντος·
τὴν ἀμφεστρατόωντο διαρραῖσαι μεμαῶτες.

There is a city Thryoessa, a steep hill,
far away on the Alpheios, the last city of sandy Pylos;
they besieged it, eager to destroy it.[3]

---

1 In the first line of this passage there is marked sound symbolism in the phrase πύμα<u>τ</u>ο<u>ν</u>
τέλε<u>ον</u> δρό<u>μ</u>ο<u>ν</u>, "were completing the end of the course," the repeated syllable echoing the
beating of the horses' hooves; the same figure is adapted to Nestor's battle in the phrase
πύματον λίπ<u>ον</u>, "I left my last (man)." The relationship between the two passages and to
the turning point in a chariot race is considered further in EN5.1.

2 There is another likely connection between Nestor's chariot race and his battle, but it has
not been made explicit in the *Iliad*: Neleus tried to keep Nestor from battle because he
thought him too young for war, and one reason for his judgment would have been Nestor's
crash in the chariot race. Nestor's crash, which is kept hidden in *Iliad* 23, also cannot be
acknowledged in *Iliad* 11.

3 This passage occurs immediately after the Epeian horsemen set out for Pylos and immedi-
ately before Athena warns the Pylians. In the Catalogue of Ships (*Iliad* 2.592) the town on

And the Pylian horsemen, who set out in all haste under Athena's lead to confront the enemy, do not actually confront them. Instead they stop at another river and wait for foot soldiers to join them (apparently no one but Nestor is able to keep pace on foot with the chariots); after dawn they then advance to the Alpheios river by midday, where they make sacrifices to the gods, eat supper, and sleep the night while the Epeians continue their siege of Thryoessa. Battle is finally joined the following morning, when the Pylians interrupt the Epeian siege; the passage is as follows (*Iliad* 11.722–736):

ἔστι δέ τις ποταμὸς Μινυήϊος εἰς ἅλα βάλλων
ἐγγύθεν Ἀρήνης, ὅθι μείναμεν Ἠῶ δῖαν
ἱππῆες Πυλίων, τὰ δ' ἐπέρρεον ἔθνεα πεζῶν.
ἔνθεν πανσυδίῃ σὺν τεύχεσι θωρηχθέντες
ἔνδιοι ἱκόμεσθ' ἱερὸν ῥόον Ἀλφειοῖο.
ἔνθα Διὶ ῥέξαντες ὑπερμενεῖ ἱερὰ καλά,
ταῦρον δ' Ἀλφειῷ, ταῦρον δὲ Ποσειδάωνι,
αὐτὰρ Ἀθηναίῃ γλαυκώπιδι βοῦν ἀγελαίην,
δόρπον ἔπειθ' ἑλόμεσθα κατὰ στρατὸν ἐν τελέεσσι,
καὶ κατεκοιμήθημεν ἐν ἔντεσιν οἷσιν ἕκαστος
ἀμφὶ ῥοὰς ποταμοῖο. ἀτὰρ μεγάθυμοι Ἐπειοὶ
ἀμφέσταν δὴ ἄστυ διαρραῖσαι μεμαῶτες·
ἀλλά σφι προπάροιθε φάνη μέγα ἔργον Ἄρηος·
εὖτε γὰρ ἠέλιος φαέθων ὑπερέσχεθε γαίης,
συμφερόμεσθα μάχῃ Διί τ' εὐχόμενοι καὶ Ἀθήνῃ.

There is a river Minyeios flowing into the sea
near Arene, where we waited for the bright dawn,
the horsemen of the Pylians, and the bands of foot-soldiers kept
    streaming in.
From there, armed with weapons, we came at great speed
to the sacred stream of the Alpheios at midday.

the Alpheios is not called Θρυόεσσα ("reedy"), but Θρύον ("reed"); the description of the town in the catalogue as Ἀλφειοῖο πόρον, "ford of the Alpheios," shows that it is the same town as in *Iliad* 11. The town was identified with Epitalion on the south side of the Alpheios in historical times (see §5.10 and n5.40 below).

There, sacrificing beautiful victims to mighty Zeus,
and a bull to the Alpheios, and a bull to Poseidon,
but to grey-eyed Athena a cow of the herd,
we then took supper throughout the army in companies,
and went to sleep each with his own weapons
by the streams of the river. But the great-hearted Epeians
surrounded the town, eager to destroy it.
But before that a great deed of warfare appeared to them;
for when the shining sun rose above the earth,
we met them in battle, praying to Zeus and Athena.[4]

Nestor's aristeia, beginning with his winning of horses, follows this passage.

§5.3 Räto Cantieni argued persuasively that the two passages in Nestor's story that feature the siege of a town on the Alpheios River are later expansions of an older version of the story;[5] when these two passages are omitted

---

4 This passage immediately follows Nestor's departure on foot with the Pylian horsemen; it begins with mention of the river (the "Minyan river") at which the Pylians marshaled. The "Minyan river" is here said to be near the town of Arene, which, like the town of Thryon, occurs in the Pylian entry to the Catalogue of Ships (*Iliad* 2.591–592):

οἳ δὲ Πύλον τ᾽ ἐνέμοντο καὶ <u>Ἀρήνην</u> ἐρατεινὴν
καὶ <u>Θρύον</u> Ἀλφειοῖο πόρον...

And those who inhabited Pylos and lovely <u>Arene</u>
and <u>Thryon</u>, ford of the Alpheios...

5 Cantieni 1942. Cantieni did not include the final two lines of the second passage (*Iliad* 11.735–736) in what he considered to be the interpolation (*Iliad* 11.722–734); he thus restored the older form of the story at this point as follows (*Iliad* 11.720–721, 735–738):

ἀλλὰ καὶ ὣς ἱππεῦσι μετέπρεπον ἡμετέροισι
καὶ πεζός περ ἐών, ἐπεὶ ὣς ἄγε νεῖκος Ἀθήνη.
<u>εὖτε γὰρ ἠέλιος φαέθων ὑπερέσχεθε γαίης,</u>
<u>συμφερόμεσθα μάχῃ Διί τ᾽ εὐχόμενοι καὶ Ἀθήνῃ.</u>
ἀλλ᾽ ὅτε δὴ Πυλίων καὶ Ἐπειῶν ἔπλετο νεῖκος,
πρῶτος ἐγὼν ἕλον ἄνδρα....

But even so I stood out among our horsemen
although I was on foot, for so Athena led the battle.
<u>For when the shining sun rose above the earth,</u>
<u>we met them in battle, praying to Zeus and Athena.</u>
But when the battle began between the Pylians and the Epeians,
I was the first to slay a man....

But the two lines in question (especially the particle γάρ, "for") do not follow as naturally here as they do in the received text, where they form part of the interruption of the Epeians' siege (ἀλλά σφι προπάροιθε φάνη μέγα ἔργον Ἄρηος· / εὖτε γὰρ ἠέλιος..., "but before that a great deed of warfare appeared to them; / for when the sun..."); the lines also cause a duplication in the onset of the battle (line 736, συμφερόμεσθα μάχῃ, "we met them in battle," followed by

Nestor's story moves quickly from the cattle raid and distribution of spoil to the Epeian attack, the Pylian response, and the start of the battle (*Iliad* 11.706–710, 714–721, 737–739):

ἡμεῖς μὲν τὰ ἕκαστα διείπομεν, ἀμφί τε ἄστυ
ἔρδομεν ἱρὰ θεοῖς· οἳ δὲ τρίτῳ ἤματι πάντες
ἦλθον ὁμῶς αὐτοί τε πολεῖς καὶ μώνυχες ἵπποι
πανσυδίῃ· μετὰ δέ σφι Μολίονε θωρήσσοντο
παῖδ' ἔτ' ἐόντ', οὔ πω μάλα εἰδότε θούριδος ἀλκῆς.
ἀλλ' ὅτε <u>δὴ</u> πεδίον μετεκίαθον, ἄμμι δ' Ἀθήνη
ἄγγελος ἦλθε θέουσ' ἀπ' Ὀλύμπου θωρήσσεσθαι
ἔννυχος, οὐδ' ἀέκοντα Πύλον κάτα λαὸν ἄγειρεν
ἀλλὰ μάλ' ἐσσυμένους πολεμίζειν. οὐδέ με Νηλεὺς
εἴα θωρήσσεσθαι, ἀπέκρυψεν δέ μοι ἵππους·
οὐ γάρ πώ τί μ' ἔφη ἴδμεν πολεμήϊα ἔργα.
ἀλλὰ καὶ ὣς ἱππεῦσι μετέπρεπον ἡμετέροισι
καὶ πεζός περ ἐών, ἐπεὶ ὣς ἄγε νεῖκος Ἀθήνη.
ἀλλ' ὅτε δὴ Πυλίων καὶ Ἐπειῶν ἔπλετο νεῖκος,
πρῶτος ἐγὼν ἕλον ἄνδρα, κόμισσα δὲ μώνυχας ἵππους,
Μούλιον αἰχμητήν.

We were attending to all of this, and around the city
we were making sacrifices to the gods; on the third day they all
came, both the many men themselves and the solid-hoofed
    horses,
at great speed. And with them the two Molione armed themselves,
although they were still young, not yet knowing much of furious
    warfare.
But when they <u>reached</u> the plain, Athena came
rushing to us from Olympus by night with the message to arm,
and throughout Pylos she gathered warriors who were not
    unwilling,

---

line 737, ἀλλ' ὅτε δὴ Πυλίων καὶ Ἐπειῶν ἔπλετο νεῖκος, "but when the battle began between the Pylians and the Epeians"). When the two lines in question are omitted, there is no mention of dawn in the story, but in my view that is not a problem; dawn is simply assumed.

but eager to fight. But Neleus did not
allow me to arm myself, but hid my horses;
for he said that I did not yet know the deeds of war.
But even so I stood out among our horsemen,
although I was on foot, for so Athena led the battle.
And when the battle began between the Pylians and the Epeians,
I before all others slew a man and took his solid-hoofed horses,
the spearman Moulios.[6]

§5.4 What I take to be the real purpose of Nestor's story in *Iliad* 11 has
nothing to do with siege warfare, precise geography, and complex troop move-
ments, and Cantieni's analysis, which removes these elements from an older
version of the story, is entirely convincing to me.[7] Cantieni, who saw clearly the
very different character of the older version of the story, also approached the
question from another perspective, arguing that the detailed geography of the
expanded version of the story is incompatible with the schematic geography of
the older version of the story. The specific problem is Bouprasion, the endpoint
of Nestor's rout of the Epeians in the older version of the story. Bouprasion had
a known location in antiquity: it lay on the far side of Elis from Pylos.[8] Nestor
could not possibly have driven the Epeians all the way to Bouprasion in a single

---

6 Cantieni 1942:39 argued that when the story was expanded one word in the earlier version
   of the story was also changed: in line 714, which now reads ἀλλ' ὅτε π̱ᾶ̱ν̱ πεδίον μετεκίαθον,
   Cantieni proposed that the earlier version of the story had ἀλλ' ὅτε δ̱ὴ̱ πεδίον μετεκίαθον
   (the formula ἀλλ' ὅτε δή, "but when indeed," which is frequent in Homer, also occurs in
   Nestor's story at line 737). As Cantieni demonstrates, the verb μετεκίαθον, with the preverb
   μετά, means "came to," not "crossed," but πᾶν πεδίον, "the whole plain," requires the
   meaning "crossed." In the original story Athena sounded the alarm when the Epeians "came
   to" a plain and began to cross it toward Pylos; the Pylians set out across the same plain to
   meet the attack, and battle must have been joined in the middle of the plain. The poet who
   expanded the passage, on the other hand, has made the attacking Epeians come to a town on
   the Alpheios River, and he thus turns the plain into what they "crossed" to reach the town.
7 I was convinced by Cantieni's argument already in my earlier work on Nestor (Frame
   1978:95).
8 For the location of Bouprasion see §5.9 and n5.31 below; for actual distances between
   Bouprasion and Pylos see n5.45 below. The city of Elis, located on the Peneios River, did
   not exist until 471 BC; before that date there were only scattered villages in the country of
   Elis (Strabo 8.3.2; cf. Swoboda RE 'Elis' 2423, who believes that before the synoecism of 471
   BC the Eleians had no other political center than the sanctuary of Zeus at Olympia); Visser
   1997:560–563, on the other hand, suggests that in the *Iliad* Elis can be a city as well as a
   region (he interprets *Iliad* 11.673 in this way). I use the city of Elis only as a geographical
   reference point, not as a historical reality, for the period before 471 BC; whether the name
   refers to the city or the country of Elis will be clear from context. Bouprasion lay on the far
   side of the city of Elis from Pylos, but it was still within the northern part of the country of
   Elis. See Map 3.

day unless he started, not from Pylos, but from somewhere inside Elis. In the older story this lack of realism did not matter, for everything in that story is larger than life. Nestor signals as much before his story begins, when he easily lifts a cup that another man would have lifted with difficulty: he is about to tell his own basic myth, in which he swept to victory on a virtual racecourse stretching from Pylos to Bouprasion. Nestor first became ἱππότα Νέστωρ on this virtual racecourse, and he was not held to strict geography in doing so.

§5.5 In the expanded version of Nestor's story, on the other hand, precise geography does matter. The geography of this version of the story, moreover, has a direct bearing on the location of Pylos in the Homeric poems, a vexed question since antiquity. For while Bouprasion does not fit well with the expanded version of Nestor's story, other locations in the expanded story, as we have it, are measured in accurate, realistic distances from Pylos, provided that Pylos was in the historical region of Triphylia. Most of antiquity thought that Nestor's city lay further south, in Messenia, but in Hellenistic times a learned minority championed Triphylia, and Nestor's story in *Iliad* 11 may be regarded as the cornerstone of that learned view.[9] In modern times a Bronze Age palace was discovered at Kakovatos in Triphylia in 1907, and this seemed to confirm what the learned minority had long believed.[10] But in 1939 another palace with a far stronger claim to being Bronze Age Pylos was discovered at Ano-Englianos in Messenia, and its Linear-B records were subsequently deciphered and read.[11] Even this singular achievement, however, did not settle the question: while all, with few exceptions, now concede that the Bronze Age city of Pylos was in Messenia, some draw a distinction between the actual Bronze Age city, in Messenia, and the Homeric city, which they continue to

---

9 Strabo, who considers himself an adherent of the learned minority, calls them the *Homērikóteroi*, "more Homeric" (8.3.7); the arguments that he presents in 8.3.1ff. (especially 8.3.7 and 8.3.24–27), are essentially those of the second-century BC scholar Apollodorus in his work on the Homeric Catalogue of Ships (for Strabo's sources in these sections see Bölte 1938 and cf. Meyer *RE* 'Pisa' 1739–1742). Another of Strabo's sources, Demetrius of Scepsis in the early second century BC, was probably the first to locate Pylos in Triphylia; see Meyer *RE* 'Pylos' 2153. Demetrius's work concerned the Trojan catalogue, and the Kaukones, allies of the Trojans in the *Iliad*, probably account for Demetrius's interest in Triphylia, for a tribe of Kaukones also lived in Triphylia. The name Triphylia originated at the beginning of the fourth century BC when the Spartans, having forced Elis to give up earlier conquests south of the Alpheios River, created a political union of the region under this name; see Bölte *RE* 'Triphylia' 199; Swoboda *RE* 'Elis' 2400; Nielsen 1997; for Elis and Triphylia cf. also Maddoli 1991 and Roy 1997. Triphylia is a convenient name for the region and I therefore use it anachronistically with reference to earlier historical periods as well.

10 For the location of this palace, discovered by Wilhelm Dörpfeld, see §5.7 below.

11 This well-known palace was discovered by Carl Blegen; the place-name *pu-ro* (*Pylos*) occurs often on the tablets from this site (cf. EN5.2 to n5.12 below).

locate in Triphylia.[12] This would not be the case were it not for Nestor's story in *Iliad* 11.[13]

§5.6 To appreciate the force of the argument based on Nestor's story in *Iliad* 11 a study published by Felix Bölte in 1934 is particularly enlightening.[14] Inspired by Dörpfeld's discovery at Kakovatos, which seemed to settle the question of Nestor's Pylos in favor of Triphylia, Bölte correlated everything in Nestor's story with a Pylos located in Triphylia, and the results, based on a detailed study of actual geography and topography, are very convincing.[15] Similar observations had been made in antiquity by those whom Strabo calls "the more Homeric" (*Homērikóteroi*), except that instead of the Bronze Age site at Kakovatos a small town named Pylos in the territory of Lepreon was seen as Nestor's city.[16] To Bölte the original core of Nestor's story was an accurate and detailed account of an actual battle that took place in the Bronze Age, and he regarded the palace at Kakovatos as an integral part of the epic tradition of that battle. Cantieni's 1942 study was a direct challenge to Bölte's conception of Nestor's story: the geography in the story that was old, according to Cantieni, was schematic, featuring only two places, Pylos and Bouprasion, and a plain between them; the detailed geography was added later.[17] Cantieni has

---

12 Ernst Meyer, an expert on the western Peloponnesus, has steadfastly maintained this view; his statements on the subject, which began before the decipherment of Linear-B and continued well after it, are traced in EN5.2.

13 Apart from Nestor's story in Book 11 there is no clear evidence in the *Iliad* for the location of Pylos. In the *Odyssey* the main evidence is the journey of Telemachus and Peisistratos from Pylos to Sparta and back again to Pylos, in which the pair spends a night each way in Phērai (Φηραί). There are good reasons to believe what has been challenged in modern times but was taken for granted in antiquity, namely that Phērai is the city at the head of the Messenian Gulf, and that Pylos too is thus in Messenia; the issue, including the objection that Mount Taygetus stands in the pair's way if Phērai is in Messenia, is considered in EN5.3. Other arguments based on the *Odyssey* carry little weight; for an argument based on the time required for Telemachus's voyages from Ithaca to Pylos and from Pylos back to Ithaca see EN5.7 to n5.44 below.

14 "Ein pylisches Epos" (Bölte 1934).

15 Bölte completed an earlier version of this article in 1914, seven years after Dörpfeld's discovery of Kakovatos, but publication was prevented by World War I and its aftermath; according to the author the published article differed from the earlier version in form but was essentially the same in content (Bölte 1934:319n1).

16 See below n5.24, n5.25, and EN5.4. The distance between Kakovatos and Strabo's Pylos is not great (3–4 kilometers). See Map 4. For Strabo's term *Homērikóteroi* cf. n5.9 above.

17 For a third passage with particular geographical references (*Iliad* 11.757–758) see §5.8 and n5.28 below. As Cantieni argues, it is highly unlikely that the geographical detail of Nestor's story could have been faithfully passed down from the Bronze Age because "the poem had made its way to Ionia, and here, separated from its place of origin, such details would have been the first to be subjected to an alteration, since they must have been completely without relevance or importance for the Ionians" ("das Gedicht ja nach

not yet been given his due on this issue.[18] My basic argument in his favor, as I have already made clear, has to do with the purpose of Nestor's story in *Iliad* 11, but there are other arguments to be made, and these, I think, bear Cantieni out completely. First, however, we must appreciate the force of Bölte's demonstration that in Nestor's story, as we have it, Pylos is in Triphylia.[19]

§5.7 What gives Pylos a precise location in the expanded version of Nestor's story is the river Alpheios. After leaving Pylos by night and waiting for dawn at the "Minyan river" (ποταμὸς Μινυήϊος) near Arene, the Pylians in a half day's march reach the Alpheios at midday (ἔνδιοι). In historical times Arene was identified with Samikon, a stronghold at the Klidi pass on the coast of Triphylia, and the "Minyan river" was identified with the Anigros, which entered the sea a little south of Samikon;[20] this was a strategic location,

---

Ionien wanderte und hier, losgelöst vom Entstehungsort, solche Angaben in erster Linie einer Veränderung anheimgefallen wären, da sie ja für die Ionier völlig beziehungs- und belanglos sein mussten"; Cantieni 1942:42–43). This argument, recognizing what would and would not have mattered to an Ionian poet and audience, has great force in my view.

18 Cantieni is not primarily concerned with the question of Pylos's location, which he thinks is simply indeterminate in the older version of Nestor's story (Cantieni 1942:48n99). Meyer rejects this point of view, citing Cantieni, and dismissing his characterization of the geography ("Pylos in Homer is no longer a universal folktale land that lies everywhere and nowhere" ["Pylos ist bei Homer kein Allerweltsmärchenland mehr, das überall und nirgends liegt"], Meyer 1951:126 and n25, alluding to Cantieni 1942:48n99); but Meyer fails to confront the real issue, namely Cantieni's arguments for two distinct levels in Nestor's story in *Iliad* 11. This is also the case in Vetta 2003, who argues that in the sub-Mycenaean period Pylians from Messenia concentrated in Triphylia, reformulated the geography of Nestor's story, and preserved it as such when they emigrated to Athens and Ionia. On the other hand Kiechle 1960:16 accepts Cantieni's analysis and pursues the question of Pylos's location on the basis of it; I do not agree with Kiechle's conclusions (see n5.27 below), but his discussion, pp. 16–18, at least recognizes Cantieni's basic argument.

19 Kiechle 1960 tries to evade this conclusion, but in my view he does not succeed (see n5.18 above and n5.27 below). For places in the discussion to follow see Map 4.

20 Arene is a significant place in Messenian tradition (the name also belongs to the mother of the Messenian twins, Idas and Lynkeus; cf. Wilamowitz 2006:339), but its location is uncertain. According to Strabo 8.3.19, whose source is Demetrius of Scepsis, Samikon was the usual identification; the Minyeios River is identified with the Anigros River, near Samikon, by both Strabo 8.3.19 and Pausanias 5.6.2–3. Cf. Simpson and Lazenby 1970:83, who regard the identification of Arene with Samikon as "probably correct" (Wilamowitz 2006:326 notes a modern identification of Makistos with Samikon but gives it little weight). For the significance of Demetrius of Scepsis as the apparent source for the identification of Arene with Samikon cf. above n5.9 and below §5.59, n5.201, and EN5.23 to n5.201 below; Samikon may be the true location of Homeric Arene, but the nature (and date) of the evidence in *Iliad* 11 must be taken into account. It is that evidence that concerns us now. Bölte 1934:322 describes the relevant topography around Samikon: the Klidi pass lies between the sea and Mount Lapithos (modern Mount Kaiapha), and the Anigros River, fed by waters from Mount Lapithos and springs at this mountain's base, once flowed into the sea at the south entrance to the pass (see Map 4). Although the land and river have

controlling traffic north and south through Triphylia.[21] From the south entrance of the Klidi pass (and the Anigros River) to the Alpheios is 13–16 kilometers, depending on where the Alpheios is crossed.[22] This distance is right for a half day's march by armed men at full speed (*Iliad* 11.725), and it provides a standard with which to compare other distances in the story. Pylos, the main point to be determined in the story, lay not far south of the Anigros, for the Pylians, including the foot soldiers, reached the river during the night and waited there for dawn. Bölte thought in terms of Kakovatos, eight kilometers from the south entrance to the Klidi pass, and such a distance for the Pylians' nighttime advance, compared with their half day march to the Alpheios, is clearly on the right scale. In my view, however, the distance covered by the Pylians at night was thought of as less than eight kilometers, for I do not think that the Pylos of this story is Kakovatos, but rather the town inside the territory of Lepreon known to Strabo. This Pylos, which was absorbed by Lepreon at a date not made clear by Strabo, was immediately north of Lepreon.[23] Strabo says that this Pylos lay more than 30 stades "above the sea," which is best interpreted to mean that it lay more than thirty stades

---

changed since antiquity (see Bölte *RE* 'Triphylia' 190), what appears to have been the river's mouth was still open and discernible in the nineteenth century (Bölte 1934:322). Strabo 8.3.19 describes the Anigros as deep and sluggish, so as to form a marsh; cf. also Pausanias 5.5.7–11, who describes the river in graphic detail, including its bad odor. The name *Minueîos* used of the Anigros may be more an epithet than a name; see §5.41 and n5.139 below for the tradition of Minyans in Triphylia (cf. also n5.191 below). For a study of coastal changes in this region, and at Klidi in particular, see now Kraft et al. 2005.

21 Bölte 1934:322–323 and *RE* 'Triphylia' 189. There is a photograph of the Klidi pass in *American Journal of Archaeology* 65 (1961) Plate 76 b.

22 Meyer 1951:123–124. Bölte 1934:343, with a particular crossing point in mind, says 14 kilometers.

23 See Strabo 8.3.16 for Lepreon's location south of Pylos (τοῦ δὲ Πύλου πρὸς νότον ἐστὶ τὸ Λέπρειον). Strabo 8.3.30 (end) says that the Eleians incorporated Pylos into Lepreon to gratify the Lepreans who had been victorious in war (for the Eleians rather than the Spartans as the proper subject of this sentence, see n5.142 below). Earlier in the passage Strabo uses the phrase "after the last defeat of the Messenians" to date events, and this, as Bölte *RE* 'Triphylia' 196 shows, refers to the Messenian revolt of the fifth century (464 BC and after). The evidence of Strabo is vague at best (see §5.42 and n5.142 below), but a mid-fifth century date seems likely; possible historical contexts of the synoecism are discussed in EN5.18 to n5.145 below. What form the synoecism took, whether Pylos only lost political autonomy, or its population was moved to Lepreon, is not known; cf. Kahrstedt *RE* 'Synoikismos' 1437: "Pylos ceased to exist; whether only politically or also as an inhabited place remains obscure" ("Pylos hörte auf zu bestehen; ob nur politisch oder auch als besiedelter Platz bleibt dunkel"). Bölte *RE* 'Triphylia' 197 assumes that Pylos was abandoned: "the population of Pylos was transplanted to Lepreon and its territory, as we must infer, was united with that of Lepreon" ("die Bevölkerung von Pylos wird nach Lepreon verpflanzt und das Gebiet, wie wir ergänzen müssen, mit dem von Lepreon vereinigt").

from Samikon.[24] The distance from this Pylos to the Minyeios/Anigros would have been about five kilometers (thirty stades),[25] and this, I think, is what the poet of Nestor's expanded story, who knew this landscape well, had in mind for the Pylians' nighttime advance.

§5.8 Bölte thought that in Nestor's story the details of a real Bronze Age military campaign had been preserved by epic. I would argue instead that the poet of Nestor's expanded story set out to place Pylos precisely in Triphylia, and that his new version of the story represents an argument to this effect.[26] As seen, the Alpheios River is used to break the action up into realistic stages, and thereby to fix the location of Pylos.[27] Nestor's actual battle is also set in relation to the Alpheios, and realism is again the key concern. In the old

24 Strabo 8.3.14: κατὰ ταῦτα δέ πως τὰ ἱερὰ ὑπέρκειται τῆς θαλάττης ἐν τριάκοντα ἢ μικρῷ πλείοσι σταδίοις ὁ Τριφυλιακὸς Πύλος [ὁ] καὶ Λεπρεατικός, ὃν καλεῖ ὁ ποιητὴς ἠμαθόεντα καὶ παραδίδωσι τοῦ Νέστορος πατρίδα, "In the region of these temples, thirty or some-what more stades above the sea, lies Triphylian or Leprean Pylos, which Homer calls sandy and hands down to us as Nestor's homeland." Bölte 1934:341 explains that in antiquity the distance from the town to the sea would not have been measured on a straight line, but with reference to a fixed point on itineraries, in this case the temple of Poseidon at Samikon; Strabo describes this temple in 8.3.13 and refers to it in 8.3.14 (above) in the phrase κατὰ ταῦτα τὰ ἱερὰ (the reason for the plural, which would have been singular in Strabo's source Artemidorus, has to do with Strabo's adaptation of Artemidorus; see Bölte 1934:341n6). Other ancient measurements of distance in the region, which are all consis-tent with this distance, help to visualize Pylos in relation to Lepreon, and both places in relation to Samikon and the Messenian border; this information is discussed in EN5.4.
25 Cf. Bölte 1934:342, who suggests the neighborhood of Xerochori as the location of this Pylos; cf. also Meyer *RE* 'Pylos' 2129–2130. Meyer points out that no ancient ruins are known here.
26 The question of the time and circumstances of the new version is considered at length in Chapter 14 below (§5.39–§5.61).
27 Kiechle, who accepts Cantieni's thesis that there are two versions of Nestor's story (see n5.18 above), argues that the expanded version of the story can be reconciled with a Messenian location of Pylos; with this I disagree. Kiechle 1960:18 points to the word τηλοῦ, "far," in the first expansion, which refers to the distance of the Alpheios River from Pylos (*Iliad* 11.711–712):

ἔστι δέ τις Θρυόεσσα πόλις αἰπεῖα κολώνη
τηλοῦ ἐπ' Ἀλφειῷ, νεάτη Πύλου ἠμαθόεντος.

There is a city Thryoessa, a steep hill,
far away on the Alpheios, the last city of sandy Pylos.

The Alpheios is of course farther from Messenia than it is from Triphylia, but that proves nothing; the poet of the expanded version of the story wishes to make it clear that the Alpheios is north of Pylos by an appreciable distance, such that it takes the Pylians a two-stage march to reach it, and this is what the word τηλοῦ conveys. The contrast is with the older version of the story, where there was no appreciable distance between Pylos and Elis (the virtual racecourse of this version of the story, as I have termed it above).

version of Nestor's story the distance between Pylos and Bouprasion was impossibly large if Pylos was imagined to be in its actual Messenian location. But in the expanded story, just as at one end of the action Pylos is moved northward to a realistic distance from the Alpheios, so at the other end of the action Bouprasion is moved southward to a realistic distance from the Alpheios. This is the effect of what Cantieni identified as a third expansion of Nestor's story, namely *Iliad* 11.757–758; in these two lines Bouprasion, the end point of Nestor's rout of the Epeians, is supplemented by two further place-names, the Olenian Rock and the Hill of Alesion; here in its context is the two-line expansion (*Iliad* 11.753–761, expansion indented):

ἔνθα Ζεὺς Πυλίοισι μέγα κράτος ἐγγυάλιξε·
τόφρα γὰρ οὖν ἐπόμεσθα διὰ σπιδέος πεδίοιο
κτείνοντές τ' αὐτοὺς ἀνά τ' ἔντεα καλὰ λέγοντες,
ὄφρ' ἐπὶ Βουπρασίου πολυπύρου βήσαμεν ἵππους
    <u>πέτρης</u> τ' <u>Ὠλενίης</u>, καὶ <u>Ἀλησίου</u> ἔνθα <u>κολώνη</u>
    κέκληται· ὅθεν αὖτις ἀπέτραπε λαὸν Ἀθήνη.
ἔνθ' ἄνδρα κτείνας πύματον λίπον· αὐτὰρ Ἀχαιοὶ
ἂψ ἀπὸ Βουπρασίοιο Πύλονδ' ἔχον ὠκέας ἵππους,
πάντες δ' εὐχετόωντο θεῶν Διὶ Νέστορί τ' ἀνδρῶν.

Then Zeus bestowed great power on the Pylians;
for we followed through the flat plain,
killing them and collecting their beautiful weapons,
until we brought our horses into Bouprasion rich in wheat
    <u>and the Olenian Rock</u>, and where it is called
    <u>Hill of Alesion</u>; from there Athena turned the warriors
      back again.
Then I killed the last man and left him. But the Achaeans
drove their swift horses back from Bouprasion to Pylos,
and all praised Zeus among gods and Nestor among men.[28]

---

28 The older version of the story, as Cantieni points out, needed only one name, Bouprasion in line 756, to specify the turning point (ὄφρ' ἐπὶ Βουπρασίου..., "until into Bouprasion..."); it is significant that when the turning point returns in line 760 (ἂψ ἀπὸ Βουπρασίοιο..., "back from Bouprasion...") again only this name occurs (cf. Cantieni 1942:47n97). The duplication of names for the turning point in lines 757–758 is combined with another duplication in the story as we have it: the act of turning homeward, expressed in lines 759–760 in the older version of the story (αὐτὰρ Ἀχαιοὶ / ἂψ ἀπὸ Βουπρασίοιο..., "but the Achaeans / back from Bouprasion..."), is duplicated in line 758, where Athena turns the warfolk back

Bölte made the case that the two landmarks in *Iliad* 11.757, which also occur in the Epeian entry to the Catalogue of Ships, and whose location is not certain, are north of the Alpheios and within a reasonable distance of the river for Nestor's one day rout of the Epeians to have actually taken place;[29] Bölte placed the action in the valley of the Lestenitsa River, a small tributary of the Alpheios (most likely the ancient Enipeus), and he found there features of the landscape (a rock and a hill) to correlate with the two places in Nestor's story at a distance of some 11 kilometers from the Alpheios. This distance could well have been covered by Nestor and the Pylians in a one day rout of the Epeians.[30]

---

from the other two places as well (ὅθεν αὖτις ἀπέτραπε λαὸν Ἀθήνη, "from where Athena turned the warriors back again"); with these duplications at the end of the battle compare the similar duplication of the onset of the battle in the expanded version of the story (n5.5 above).

29 In the Epeian entry to the Catalogue of Ships the Epeians' country is divided into two districts, Bouprasion and Elis, and four place-names follow, including the two at issue in *Iliad* 11, the Olenian Rock and (the Hill of) Alesion (*Iliad* 2.615–619):

οἳ δ' ἄρα Βουπράσιόν τε καὶ Ἤλιδα δῖαν ἔναιον
ὅσσον ἐφ' Ὑρμίνη καὶ Μύρσινος ἐσχατόωσα
<u>πέτρη τ' Ὠλενίη καὶ Ἀλήσιον</u> ἐντὸς ἐέργει,
τῶν αὖ τέσσαρες ἀρχοὶ ἔσαν, δέκα δ' ἀνδρὶ ἑκάστῳ
νῆες ἕποντο θοαί, πολέες δ' ἔμβαινον Ἐπειοί.

And those who lived in Bouprasion and shining Elis
as far as Hyrmine and farthest-lying Myrsinos
<u>and the Olenian Rock and Alesion</u> contain,
four leaders of these there were, and ten swift ships
followed each man, and many Epeians boarded the ships.

The two-line expansion in *Iliad* 11 seems to be based on line 617 of the catalogue, but there is uncertainty about line 617 itself, which may be an expansion of the Epeian entry to the catalogue (see Cantieni 1942:46n96); the issue is not clear-cut. On the one hand the four place-names in *Iliad* 2.616–617 seem to correspond to the four leaders of the Epeians, each place belonging to a different leader (see Simpson and Lazenby 1970:99 for the view that the four places represent the four corners of a roughly square-shaped Elis). On the other hand the syntax of line 616 (ὅσσον ἐφ'..., "as far as") does not require the verbal phrase ἐντὸς ἐέργει, "contains/bounds within," of line 617: the construction of line 616, ὅσσον ἐφ' Ὑρμίνη καὶ Μύρσινος ἐσχατόωσα, "as far as Hyrmine and farthest-lying Myrsinos," is like that of *Iliad* 21.251: Πηλεΐδης δ' ἀπόρουσεν <u>ὅσον τ' ἐπὶ δουρὸς ἐρωή</u>, "Peleus's son sprang away as far as the cast of a spear." The combination of a construction requiring no verb in *Iliad* 2.616 (ὅσσον ἐφ' Ὑρμίνη..., "as far as Hyrmine") with a subject-verb construction in *Iliad* 2.617 (πέτρη...ἐέργει, "the rock...bounds") is suspect. Given the uncertainty of *Iliad* 2.617, its relationship to *Iliad* 11.757 must also remain uncertain. In ancient times there were two different locations of the Olenian Rock, one close to the Alpheios, as in Nestor's story, and the other in the northeast corner of Elis; see the following note.

30 According to Strabo 8.3.32 the Enipeus was what was later called the Βαρνίχιος, "lamb river" (a name defended by Wilamowitz 2006:323 against those who reject it as of Slavic origin);

§5.9 A skilled craftsman expanded Nestor's story. There are signs in the text where new was grafted onto old, but these require careful observation to detect and would have gone unnoticed in a normal telling of the story. In addition to managing these transitions smoothly there were other problems to confront, or to avoid, if the new version of the story was to replace the old. The main such problem was Bouprasion if, as Hellenistic scholars said, this name referred to the coastal region north of Elis, on the road to Dyme in Achaea. Demetrius of Scepsis is the source for the statement in Strabo that a settlement called Bouprasion, which had probably once existed in the Eleian country, no longer existed in his own time, but now only "that territory is so called which is on the road that leads from the present city

---

for the identification of the Enipeus with the Lestenitsa cf. Lienau and Olshausen *DNP* 'Enipeus.' The expansions of Nestor's story make notable use of easily identifiable features of the landscape such as rivers and hills; in this regard it is worth noting the contrast between Ἀλησίου...κολώνη, "the Hill of Alesion," in the expansion of Nestor's story (*Iliad* 11.757), and the simple Ἀλήσιον of the Catalogue of Ships (2.617). There is a similar contrast with respect to the town on the Alpheios, called Θρυόεσσα πόλις αἰπεῖα κολώνη, "a city Thryoessa, a steep hill," in the expansion of Nestor's story (*Iliad* 11.711), and Θρύον Ἀλφειοῖο πόρον, "Thryon, ford of the Alpheios," in the catalogue (*Iliad* 2.592); for the problem of this town's identity and location see §5.10 and n5.40 below. The Olenian Rock, from the name alone, must have been another prominent feature of the landscape; Bölte 1934:329 argues that the Pylians cannot well have driven chariots onto this rock, and that therefore the genitive πέτρης τ' Ὠλενίης should be in the nominative (as in Iliad 2.617), a subject (with κολώνη, "hill") of the verb κέκληται, "it is called," in *Iliad* 11.758; Cantieni 1942:47 supports this. Strabo 8.3.9 says that in the opinion of some both the Olenian Rock and Alesion lay on the (northern) border of the Pisatis; in the case of Alesion modern opinion also looks to this region in southeast Elis (see Simpson and Lazenby 1970:99). Strabo 8.3.10 (Apollodorus is the source) gives the basis for the ancient view of Alesion's location: it was identified with a place called Alesiaion in Amphidolia in what was once the Pisatis: τὸ δ' Ἀλείσιον ἔστι τὸ νῦν Ἀλεσιαῖον, χώρα περὶ τὴν Ἀμφιδολίδα, ἐν ᾗ καὶ κατὰ μῆνα ἀγορὰν συνάγουσιν οἱ περίοικοι· κεῖται δὲ ἐπὶ τῆς ὀρεινῆς ὁδοῦ τῆς ἐξ Ἤλιδος εἰς Ὀλυμπίαν· πρότερον δ' ἦν πόλις τῆς Πισάτιδος, "Aleision is what is now Alesiaion, a place in Amphidolia, in which the surrounding population holds a monthly market; it lies on the mountain road from Elis to Olympia; earlier it was a city of the Pisatis." Bölte 1934:329–331 supports a location of this ancient monthly market at modern Karatula, where several valleys meet, and he discusses a hill 2.5 kilometers northeast of Karatula as the likely Ἀλησίου...κολώνη, whether or not this hill was also the site of a town. There is more uncertainty and wider disagreement about the Olenian Rock; there are arguments for placing it in the northeast corner of Elis, on the one hand, and in northern Pisatis (i.e. far to the south of the first location) on the other hand. Bölte, arguing for northern Pisatis, identifies the Olenian Rock with an impressive geological formation some 11 kilometers north of the Alpheios River. It is just this sort of landmark, I think, that the poet of Nestor's expanded story wished to conjure up in the minds of his audience. Simpson and Lazenby 1970:98 favor a location of the Olenian Rock in northeast Elis on the basis of Hesiodic evidence, and this may also be the intended location in the Catalogue of Ships. I do not think, however, that it is the intended location in the expansion of Nestor's story. Details of the evidence for the Olenian Rock are given in EN5.5.

of Elis to Dyme."[31] According to Hellenistic mythography, when Heracles was defeated by the Molione in his war against Augeias, he fled to Bouprasion to a river called βαδὺ ὕδωρ ("sweet water").[32] The earliest source for this myth is Ekhephylidas, probably in the mid-third century BC.[33] This author knew that βαδὺ ὕδωρ, with its distinctive local name, was on the road from Elis to Dyme, and this to him was the region of Bouprasion.[34] Bölte, who was certain that the endpoint of Nestor's aristeia lay on the borders of the Pisatis not far north of the Alpheios River, argued that Bouprasion must have belonged there as well, and that the Hellenistic tradition for a location north of Elis depended entirely on this one passage of Ekhephylidas, who had been mistaken and who misled others.[35] But Cantieni showed that Demetrius of

31 Strabo 8.3.8: ἦν δ', ὡς ἔοικε, κατοικία τῆς Ἡλείας τὸ Βουπράσιον ἀξιόλογον, ἢ νῦν οὐκέτ' ἐστίν· ἡ δὲ χώρα καλεῖται μόνον οὕτως ἡ ἐπὶ τῆς ὁδοῦ τῆς ἐπὶ Δύμην ἐξ Ἡλιδος τῆς νῦν πόλεως, "Bouprasion, it seems, was a noteworthy settlement of Elis, which now no longer exists; only that territory is so called which is on the road that leads from the present city of Elis to Dyme." For Demetrius of Scepsis as Strabo's source see Bölte 1934:333; Bölte (p. 334) thinks that Demetrius inferred the existence of a town from Nestor's story in *Iliad 23*, where the Epeians bury Amarynkeus in Bouprasion and his sons hold funeral games for him there (*Iliad* 23.631).

32 βαδύ = ἡδύ. Pausanias 5.3.2 connects the river and its name with the fulfillment of the prayer of Eleian women to Athena *Mētḗr*; cf. n3.11 above.

33 Bölte 1934:337; for the date of Ekhephylidas Bölte cites Jacoby *RE* 'Echephylidas' (noting an apparent quotation of Ekhephylidas by Istros) and Jacoby *RE* 'Istros' 2270 (dating Istros to the second half of the third century BC). Pherekydes in the fifth century BC may have told a similar story (scholia to Plato *Phaedo* 89c; see next note). Cantieni 1942:44 assumes that Ekhephylidas was the first to connect the river and its name with Heracles' attack on Elis; cf. also Bölte 1934:337. Bölte points out that the Eleian womens' prayer to Athena *Mētḗr* (n3.11 above) was also connected to Heracles' attack, and suggests that this was an Alexandrian elaboration of the myth.

34 Scholia to Plato *Phaedo* 89c: Ἐχεφυλλίδας δὲ αὐτὸν [sc. Heracles] ὑπὸ Κτεάτου καὶ Εὐρύτου τῶν Μολ‹υ›ονιδῶν ἡττηθῆναι κατὰ τὴν ἐπ' Αὐγείᾳ στρατείαν. διωχθέντα δὲ ἄχρι τῆς Βουπρασίδος καὶ περιβλεψάμενον, ὡς οὐδεὶς ἐξίκετο τῶν πολεμίων, ἀναψύξαι τε καὶ ἐκ τοῦ παρρέοντος ποταμοῦ πιόντα προσαγορεῦσαι τοῦτο ἡδὺ ὕδωρ, ὃ νῦν δείκνυται ἰόντων ἐκ Δύμης εἰς Ἡλιν (ἥλιον cod.), καλούμενον ὑπὸ τῶν ἐγχωρίων βαδὺ ὕδωρ. τὰ δὲ αὐτὰ καὶ Φερεκύδης καὶ Κώμαρχος καὶ Ἴστρος ἐν τοῖς Ἡλιακοῖς ἱστοροῦσιν, "Ekhephylidas [says] that he [Heracles] was defeated by the Molionidai, Kteatos and Eurytos, in his campaign against Augeias, and when he was chased as far as Bouprasis and looked around, and none of the enemy was there, he refreshed himself; drinking from the river flowing by he called it *hēdù húdōr* ('sweet water'), which is now pointed out as one goes from Dyme to Elis, *badù húdōr* being what it is called by the local inhabitants. Pherekydes, Komarchos, and Istros in his *Eleian History* tell the same thing." The form of the name ἡ Βουπρασίς, found in this passage and elsewhere, is an alternate for τὸ Βουπράσιον.

35 Bölte 1934:333–340. Strabo, following Apollodorus (cf. Cantieni 1942:43n86), refers in several passages to the location of Bouprasion northeast of Elis: in 8.7.5 the Larisos River is said to separate Dyme from Elis in the region of Bouprasion (ἐφεξῆς δ' ἐστὶν ἡ Δύμη...· διαιρεῖ δ' αὐτὴν ἀπὸ τῆς Ἡλείας κατὰ Βουπράσιον ὁ Λάρισος ποταμός); in 8.3.17 the

Scepsis, for one, cannot have taken his information from Ekhephylidas, for there is too much divergence in what they say.[36] Bölte, for his part, made the valid point that the name Bouprasion does not occur of the coast north of Elis in historical sources, either in the context of military campaigns or otherwise.[37] I conclude from this that the name Bouprasion belonged more to myth than reality, or perhaps to an earlier reality, but that its location was in any case north of Elis. This brings us back to the problem confronted by the poet who expanded Nestor's story, who had to ignore the location of this half-forgotten, semi-mythical realm, and supplement it with other names belonging to a different location close to the Alpheios River (*Iliad* 11.757–758). This disregard of Bouprasion's traditional location was evidently not so egregious as to be rejected out of hand by the intended audience, although some must have known better.[38] In any case the location of Pylos, and not the location of

---

Kaukones are said to have lived in two locations, some in Triphylia, others near Dyme in the region of "Bouprasis" and hollow Elis (τοὺς μὲν πρὸς τῇ Μεσσηνίᾳ κατὰ τὴν Τριφυλίαν τοὺς δὲ πρὸς τῇ Δύμῃ κατὰ τὴν Βουπρασίδα καὶ τὴν κοίλην Ἦλιν; "hollow Elis" designates Elis proper in contrast to the Pisatis and Triphylia, which formed part of Elis as a political entity; cf. Wilamowitz 2006:321). In Strabo 8.3.32 Bouprasion is again located between Elis and Dyme, but the passage is problematic; it is discussed in EN5.6. Istros, according to Stephanus of Byzantium s.v. Αἰγιαλός, also referred to the location of Bouprasion northeast of Elis, putting Αἰγιαλός, the Achaean city mentioned in *Iliad* 2.575, between Sikyon and Bouprasion (μεταξὺ Σικυῶνος καὶ τοῦ Βουπρασίου). Wilamowitz 2006:321–322 rightly calls Bouprasion the country (χώρα) between Elis and Dyme.

36   See Cantieni 1942:45–46. For Demetrius as the source of Strabo 8.3.8, see n5.31 above; this passage says that it seems that a settlement (κατοικία) called Bouprasion once existed, but that it no longer exists (see n5.31 above). Bölte 1934:338 argues that Demetrius, with only one source, Ekhephylidas, to follow, drew this conclusion from the fact that no κατοικία is mentioned in Ekhephylidas; but as Cantieni points out Demetrius would not have expected Ekhephylidas to mention a settlement since the end point of Heracles' flight in his account was a river. Furthermore, it seems that Demetrius, in addition to referring to a settlement and a region (χώρα) called Bouprasion, knew of a river called Bouprasion: this can be inferred from Stephanus of Byzantium s.v. Βουπράσιον, πόλις καὶ ποταμὸς καὶ χώρα τῆς Ἤλιδος, "Bouprasion, city and river and region of Elis," in which mention of a city as well as a region indicates Demetrius as the source (see Bölte 1934:334). Thus, while Ekhephylidas and Demetrius both referred to a river in the region (cf. Bölte 1934:338), in Ekhephylidas it is called βαδὺ ὕδωρ, but in Demetrius it is called Βουπράσιον. Demetrius must have had other sources for Bouprasion besides the one passage of Ekhephylidas.

37   Bölte 1934:339: "In the wars at the end of the third century, the Cleomenes War, the Social War, and then the First Macedonian War, we hear often enough, and sometimes in considerable detail, about military events that played themselves out in the northern part of Elis—one looks in vain for the name Bouprasion" ("In den Kriegen am Ende des 3. Jahrhunderts, dem Kleomenischen, dem Bundesgenossenkrieg, dann im ersten makedonischen, hören wir oft genug und zum Teil recht eingehend von militärischen Vorgängen, die sich im nördlichen Teil von Elis abspielen,—den Namen Buprasion sucht man vergebens").

38   The strongest indication that Bouprasion was traditionally thought to be north of Elis is the solid Hellenistic tradition to this effect: Hellenistic scholars had no reason to locate

Bouprasion, was the critical issue in the expanded version of Nestor's story: for Pylos real geography mattered, but for Bouprasion a semblance of real geography sufficed.

§5.10 Another delicate point in the expanded story was the crossing of the Alpheios. The narrative does not say that the Pylians crossed the Alpheios on the morning of the battle, but this is assumed, and for the Pylian chariots it would not have been a difficult matter.[39] The town of Thryoessa, which is besieged by the Epeians, is clearly meant to be the place where the river is crossed, for Thryon in the Catalogue of Ships is called precisely "ford of the Alpheios": Θρύον Ἀλφειοῖο πόρον (*Iliad* 2.593). So far everything makes sense, but the question then is where on the Alpheios was Thryoessa, and on which side of the river. The fact that the Pylians camp when they reach the Alpheios suggests that Thryoessa is on the far side of the river, facing the Pylians' camp. Furthermore, if the battle the next morning takes place in the valley of the Lestenitsa/Enipeus, this indicates where on the Alpheios Thryoessa must be. Neither of these indications, however, agrees with the ancient identification of Thryon as Epitalion, a town on the south side of the Alpheios some 5-6 kilometers west of where the Lestenitsa joins the Alpheios.[40] Bölte thus rejected Epitalion as the correct location and

---

Bouprasion north of Elis if tradition did not put it there; indeed Nestor's expanded story would have led them to locate Bouprasion where Bölte located it, close to the Alpheios, if there had been no positive reason against this. Demetrius of Scepsis and Apollodorus both thought that the distances in Nestor's story are realistic, for it was on this basis that they located Pylos in Triphylia. The fact that they nevertheless considered Bouprasion to be north of Elis is thus significant.

39 It is clear that the Alpheios had to be crossed at some time if the battle was eventually to reach Bouprasion; cf. Bölte 1934:328, who for this and other reasons rules out that the battle is set south of the river. The only question is when the Pylians cross the Alpheios. When the Pylians first reach the Alpheios, they offer sacrifices to various gods, including the Alpheios (*Iliad* 11.728); Bölte 1934:327 reasonably takes this to mean that the river is to be crossed the following morning. The crossing itself would have caused little difficulty; cf. Bölte 1934:327: "much less did the crossing present difficulties for Greek warriors; chariots could be very quickly taken apart and put back together again" ("für griechische Krieger bot der Übergang erst recht keine Schwierigkeiten; Streitwagen aber liessen sich sehr schnell auseinandernehmen und wieder zusammensetzen").

40 Strabo 8.3.24 identifies Thryon with Epitalion twice in the same passage: Apollodorus is the source of his comment that the Homeric phrase for Thryon, "ford of the Alpheios," fits Epitalion: Ἀλφειοῦ δὲ πόρον φησίν, ὅτι πεζῇ περατὸς εἶναι δοκεῖ κατὰ τοῦτον τὸν τόπον· καλεῖται δὲ νῦν Ἐπιτάλιον τῆς Μακιστίας χωρίον, "He calls it ford of the Alpheios because the river can be crossed at this place; it is now called Epitalion, a place in Makistia"; Demetrius of Scepsis is the source of a comment on the aptness of the names Thryon and Thryoessa, denoting "reeds," to the region of the lower Alpheios, including Epitalion: Θρύον δὲ καὶ Θρυόεσσαν τὸ Ἐπιτάλιόν φασιν, ὅτι πᾶσα μὲν αὕτη ἡ χώρα θρυώδης, μάλιστα δ' οἱ ποταμοί· ἐπὶ πλέον δὲ διαφαίνεται τοῦτο κατὰ τοὺς περατοὺς τοῦ ῥείθρου τόπους, "They call Epitalion Thryon and Thryoessa because this whole country is reedy, especially the

instead chose a hill in the lower Lestenitsa valley, today called Strephi, as the site of the Θρυόεσσα πόλις, αἰπεῖα κολώνη, of Nestor's story.[41] Modern opinion still favors Epitalion as the Thryon of the Catalogue of Ships, but this leaves unanswered the point that the north side of the Alpheios seems clearly indicated in Nestor's story.[42] I conclude from this that Epitalion may well have been the true site of Thryon in the Catalogue of Ships, but that, like the true location of Bouprasion, this was not a well codified piece of knowledge when Nestor's story was expanded. The expansion of the story required Thryoessa to be in a particular place, and its traditional location was sufficiently undetermined to allow this.[43] In the expanded story mention of the Alpheios is kept to a minimum, and nothing definite is said about the location of Thryoessa with respect to the river. All is left to suggestion and inference.

§5.11 Apart from the expanded version of Nestor's story in Iliad 11 the Homeric poems do not give a precise idea of Pylos's location. The poems are, however, generally consistent with a location in Messenia; this is true of the Pylian entry to the Catalogue of Ships in the Iliad, and it is also true of

---

rivers; this is more apparent at the fordable places in the stream" (Strabo 8.3.24). Strabo also mentions an alternative interpretation of Iliad 2.592 in the Pylian entry (καὶ Θρύον, Ἀλφειοῖο πόρον, καὶ εὔκτιτον Αἶπυ), according to which Epitalion was "well-built Aipu," and Thryon was the actual ford of the Alpheios rather than a town (cf. Bölte 1934:324n5).

41 Bölte 1934:328. Unlike Thryoessa, which is ἐπ' Ἀλφειῷ, "on the Alpheios" (Iliad 11.712), and the equivalent Thryon, which is called Ἀλφειοῖο πόρον, "ford of the Alpheios" (Iliad 2.592), Strephi is two kilometers from the Alpheios; Bölte's explanation for this is that the course of the Alpheios was once farther north through this part of the river (p. 328, citing Philippson 1892:314). Dörpfeld 1913:115 also looked for Thryoessa north of the Alpheios, but he identified it with steep heights south of Kukura; this location is closer to the Alpheios than Strephi, but farther from the entrance to the Lestenitsa valley than Bölte was willing to accept (one kilometer to judge from Bölte's map, p. 320). Unlike Strephi, this location has traces of a prehistoric settlement; cf. Bölte 1934:325, 328.

42 See Simpson and Lazenby 1970:83 for the usual identification with Epitalion. The Bronze Age kingdom of Pylos seems to have extended north of the Alpheios (pi-jai, which always occurs first in a list of nine cities on the Pylos tablets, may be Pheai, north of the Alpheios on the coast: Kiechle1960:58n1, citing Palmer 1956a:132; cf. also Palmer 1965:88–92; for other views of the Pylian kingdom's limits cf. Briaschi 1994:47n69 with references). Whether the Pylian kingdom in the Homeric Catalogue of Ships extends north of the Alpheios cannot be determined, but this would not have been doubted by the poet who expanded Nestor's story in view of Iliad 5.545: Ἀλφειοῦ, ὅς τ' εὐρὺ ῥέει Πυλίων διὰ γαίης, "the Alpheios, which flows wide through the land of the Pylians."

43 According to Bölte 1934:321 and 327 (who cites Dörpfeld 1913:115 and others) the Alpheios can be forded at several places between the entrance of the Lestenitsa and Olympia upstream; none of these places needs to be the Ἀλφειοῖο πόρος of Iliad 2.592 (that was probably Epitalion), but the fact that Thryon could have been at one of these places is what counted to the poet who expanded Nestor's story.

Telemachus's voyage to Pylos in the *Odyssey*.[44] On the other hand there is one episode, apart from the expanded version of Nestor's story in *Iliad* 11, that seriously calls the Messenian location of Pylos into question, and this is the old version of Nestor's story in *Iliad* 11 if it is taken literally. Epic exaggeration reaches fantastic proportions if Pylos in this story is in Messenia: Nestor covers the entire western Peloponnesus in a single day.[45] This, to repeat, is well and good in a larger-than-life story called up from the mists of time, but in the post-Homeric era the Homeric poems were taken literally in matters of geography and politics.[46] If the original version of Nestor's story was taken literally, and if Bouprasion, north of the town of Elis, was a fixed point in this story, the other point in the story, the city of Pylos, must also have lain in Eleian territory. Strangely enough there was a tradition that Nestor's city lay in the region of Elis, either in the interior of the country or on the coast.[47]

44 A particular location of Pylos cannot be demonstrated in the Catalogue of Ships, but a location in Messenia is now usually assumed; a case for Triphylia is made by Meyer *RE* 'Pylos' 2149–2150. See n5.13 above and EN5.3 to n5.13 above for the journey of Telemachus and Peisistratos from Pylos to Sparta by way of Phērai in Messenia, which implies that Pylos too was in Messenia, despite the problem of Mount Taygetos. An argument for Triphylia based on Telemachus's voyage from Ithaca to Pylos is discussed in EN5.7.

45 When Nestor finishes his story, he scarcely believes it himself: ὣς ἔον, εἴ ποτ' ἔον γε, μετ' ἀνδράσιν, "so I was, if ever I was, among men" (*Iliad* 11.762); there may be more than one reason for his disbelief: the time that has passed since his youth is certainly one reason, but the space that he covered in his story may be another (ironic) reason. The ancient measurements of the distances between Messenian Pylos (Koryphasion) and the two capes bounding the coast north of Elis that corresponds roughly to Bouprasion are 750 stades to Cape Khelonatas and 1030 stades to Cape Araxos, or 139 kilometers and 191 kilometers respectively (for the stade as equal to 185 meters in the geographical writers see Hornblower 1996:154 and Pothecary 1995); in Strabo 8.3.21, where these distances are given, the two reference points, the Alpheios River and Cape Khelonatas, must be corrected to Cape Khelonatas and Cape Araxos respectively (see Meyer *RE* 'Pylos' 2120–2121). The distance between Messenian Pylos and Triphylian Pylos (for which Samikon provided geographers with an approximation) is 400 stades (74 kilometers) according to Strabo 8.3.21; the actual distance is about 67 kilometers (Meyer *RE* 'Pylos' 2121). Shortening the distance to the coast north of Elis by this amount I make the distance from the Triphylian Pylos to Bouprasion between 72 and 124 kilometers. These distances too, like those from Messenia, are impossibly large for Nestor's story if it is taken literally; hence in the expanded version of his story, where Pylos is in Triphylia, Bouprasion has been shifted south to the vicinity of the Alpheios River (see §5.9 above). For the real distances involved in Nestor's story cf. Wilamowitz 2006:330, who calculates that they would take days to cover.

46 As, for example, in the contest between Athens and Megara for Salamis, when Solon is supposed to have supported Athens' claim with his own addition to the Catalogue of Ships; for political motives behind the Athenian entry to the Catalogue of Ships, which I also ascribe to Solon, see §3.87–§3.91 above.

47 The location in the interior of Elis was near the confluence of the Ladon and Peneios Rivers, 15 kilometers east of the town of Elis and 25 kilometers from the coast; Pausanias 6.22.5

The location in the interior seems to be what the Eleians themselves came to claim as Nestor's city, but the location on the coast was, I think, older.[48] The evidence for the location on the coast is not local historians of Elis, but the Homeric hymn to the Pythian Apollo;[49] earlier than this, furthermore,

---

gives this location, and Strabo 8.3.7 also refers to it (the Mount Skollis that Strabo mentions is just north of this location). The probable site of this inland Pylos is Armatova, excavated in 1968 and 1970; for the identification see Coleman 1986:161–165. But a location on the coast near the mouth of the Peneios (on Cape Khelonatas, west of the town of Elis) is also detectable in Strabo's confused account: he says that Pylos lay between the mouth of the Peneios and the mouth of the Seleeis: μεταξὺ δὲ τῆς τοῦ Πηνειοῦ καὶ τῆς Σελλήεντος ἐκβολῆς Πύλος ᾠκεῖτο κατὰ τὸ Σκόλλιον, "Pylos is situated between the mouth of the Peneios and that of the Selleeis by Mount Skollion." The Seleeis is a Homeric river, and what Strabo means by it is not clear: there is no other river reaching the sea near the mouth of the Peneios, and Seleeis is therefore taken as another name for the Ladon, which flows into the Peneios near the inland location of Pylos; but this interpretation, while it accounts for Strabo's mention of Mount Skollis, ignores his reference to the mouth of the Peneios (τῆς τοῦ Πηνειοῦ... ἐκβολῆς, "the outlet of the Peneios") in the location that he gives of Pylos. Even if the reference to the mouth of the Peneios is removed by omitting the article τῆς before τοῦ Πηνειοῦ (or by changing ἐκβολῆς, "outlet," to ἐμβολῆς, "inlet") in Strabo 8.3.7, this does not eliminate the problem, for another passage of Strabo makes it clear that he in fact thinks of the Eleian Pylos as lying on the coast: in 8.3.26 he argues that Homer in the *Odyssey* had the Triphylian Pylos in mind as Nestor's city because the Triphylian city is inland from the coast, whereas the other cities (i.e. the Messenian and Eleian cities) are on the sea: ἐν ταύτῃ γὰρ τῇ χώρᾳ ἐστὶν ἡ πατρὶς τοῦ Νέστορος, ἥν φαμεν Τριφυλιακὸν Πύλον καὶ Ἀρκαδικὸν καὶ Λεπρεατικόν. καὶ γὰρ δὴ οἱ μὲν ἄλλοι Πύλοι ἐπὶ θαλάττῃ δείκνυνται, οὗτος δὲ πλείους ἢ τριάκοντα σταδίους ὑπὲρ αὐτῆς, ὅπερ καὶ ἐκ τῶν ἐπῶν δῆλον, "For in this place is Nestor's fatherland, which we call the Triphylian or the Arcadian or the Leprean Pylos. Indeed the other Pyloses are located on the sea, but this one more than thirty stades from the sea, (a location) which is also clear from the poems." Cf. also n5.51 below on Strabo 8.3.27.

48 Strabo 8.3.7 says that the Eleians (presumably local historians of Elis) argued for their Pylos as Nestor's city; he goes on to say that they found tokens of the Homeric city's presence in their country: οἱ δ' οὖν ἐκ τῆς κοίλης Ἤλιδος καὶ τοιαύτην φιλοτιμίαν προσετίθεσαν τῷ παρ' αὐτοῖς Πύλῳ, καὶ γνωρίσματα δεικνύοντες Γέρηνον τόπον καὶ Γέροντα ποταμὸν καὶ ἄλλον Γεράνιον, εἶτ' ἀπὸ τούτων ἐπιθέτως Γερήνιον εἰρῆσθαι πιστούμενοι τὸν Νέστορα, "Those from hollow Elis applied this sort of ambitious rivalry toward the Pylos in their country, and they added tokens, pointing out a place Gerenos and a river Geron and another river Geranios, claiming that Nestor is called by the epithet Gerenios from these." I assume that the local historians had in mind the location of Pylos in the interior of Elis and not on the coast; in contrast to the interior location there was probably no town to point to on the coast. The earliest local histories of Elis were not written until the Hellenistic era (see Jacoby *FGrHist* nos. 408–416, commentary pp. 221–236; cf. Christesen 2005:349–350 and n73).

49 For the Pythian and Delian sections of the *Homeric Hymn to Apollo* as originally independent of each other see n4.101 above; differences in diction between the two parts are addressed by Janko 1982 (see his data on pp. 71–74 and conclusion on p. 75) and Aloni 1989:20–25, 2006:59–60. For the opposite view, that the hymn was a unity from its origin, cf. Clay 1997:501–502, 1989:87–89, and Martin 2000a; Martin argues, p. 410, that the Pythian hymn consistently expands elements of the Delian hymn, thus showing its awareness of the Delian hymn, and with this I would agree.

there is evidence that the *Odyssey* had become the focal point in a controversy regarding the supposed location of Pylos in Elis. We will consider these matters, including the likely source of such a controversy, in their own right and for their own intrinsic interest, but we should not lose sight of our ultimate object in doing so, which is the expanded version of Nestor's story in *Iliad* 11. Here the basic point is quite simple: if at the time of the Pythian *Hymn to Apollo* there was a controversy based on the Homeric poems as to whether or not Pylos lay in Elis, the expanded version of Nestor's story in *Iliad* 11 cannot yet have existed, for this version plainly rules out a location in Elis; according to this version Pylos lay south of the Alpheios River, in the historical region of Triphylia. It is thus important to show the early existence of the controversy not only for its own sake, but also for its bearing on our primary question, the date and circumstances of the expanded version of Nestor's story in *Iliad* 11.

Chapter 13.

THE *HOMERIC HYMN TO APOLLO*

AND THE TEXT OF *ILIAD* 11

§5.12 The controversy over Pylos, whether or not it was in Elis, centered on Telemachus's voyage home from Pylos to Ithaca in *Odyssey* 15. After bidding farewell to Nestor's son Peisistratos and taking on board the seer Theoklymenos, Telemachus sets sail from Pylos; as they sail north along the coast the sun sets and the ship makes for Pheai, a town on a prominent cape not far north of the mouth of the Alpheios River.[50] From here they sail past Elis, the land of the Epeians, before leaving the coast for the "fast islands" (*nêsoi thoaí*) enroute to Ithaca (*Odyssey* 15.296–300). Now Pheai is south of where Strabo's account indicates that the Eleian town of Pylos (i.e. the coastal town of Pylos) lay; thus if Telemachus began his voyage from the Eleian town of Pylos he cannot have passed Pheai on his way to Ithaca.[51] It was precisely Pheai that was the disputed point in Telemachus's journey: in fact only Aristarchus and Strabo give the name Pheai in *Odyssey* 15.297; all manuscripts of the *Odyssey* read Pherai, referring to a town well past Elis in

---

50 Pheai is about 12 kilometers north of the Alpheios mouth (see Map 3 for key locations in the following discussion). The singular form Pheia is used of the town in *Iliad* 7.135 (see §5.38 below); this form is also used of the town by Thucydides (in e.g. 2.25.4, where the name of the cape is said to be Ichthys). According to Strabo 8.3.12 Pheia was the name of the cape as well as the town; Strabo goes on to mention another cape, for which no name occurs in the text but Ichthys is conjectured. There seems to be some confusion here, for there is only one cape, and its historical name was Ichthys. It is easy (also correct?) to think of the landmark on Telemachus's voyage as the cape, and perhaps this was in Strabo's mind.

51 Strabo 8.3.27 makes the same point. The location for the Eleian Pylos suggested by Strabo 8.3.7 (Cape Khelonatas, see n5.47 above) is some 30 kilometers north of Pheai.

the historical region of Achaea.[52] This was the controversy, and in my view
Pherai was substituted for Pheai in *Odyssey* 15.297 by those who sought to put
Pylos in Elis. But this interpretation was resisted by others, and their resis-
tance, I think, is reflected in the line that follows in *Odyssey* 15: here Elis and
the Epeians are mentioned next on Telemachus's northward voyage, and the
effect of this is to preclude Pherai in the preceding line, for Pherai is already
past Elis in Achaea. I suggest that originally Telemachus made for Pheai in
his journey up the coast, and that from there he left the coast for the "swift
islands," with no mention of Elis; this geography was minimal but sufficient
for the story.[53] Elis was later added to the route, not for the sake of realism,
but to defend the name Pheai in the preceding line; the looseness with which
Elis was added is apparent in the grammatical construction following the verb
ἐπιβάλλειν, "to make for," which suits the object Φεὰς, but not the phrase
παρ' Ἤλιδα δῖαν, "along shining Elis," in the next line (*Odyssey* 15.296–300):

> δύσετό τ' ἠέλιος σκιόωντό τε πᾶσαι ἀγυιαί·
>
> ἡ δὲ Φεὰς ἐπέβαλλεν ἐπειγομένη Διὸς οὔρῳ,
>
> <u>ἠδὲ παρ' Ἤλιδα δῖαν, ὅθι κρατέουσιν Ἐπειοί.</u>
>
> ἔνθεν δ' αὖ νήσοισιν ἐπιπροέηκε θοῇσιν,
>
> ὁρμαίνων, ἤ κεν θάνατον φύγοι ἤ κεν ἁλοίη.

52 The reading *Pheás* is given by Strabo 8.3.26, the scholia to *Iliad* 7.135 (citing Aristarchus),
    and the scholia to *Odyssey* 15.297. The reading *Pherás* of the Homeric manuscripts stands
    for the Achaean city of *Pharaí*. For the location of this city see Map 3; Pausanias 7.22.1
    gives the location in terms of distance west from Patrai (150 stades) and south from the
    coast (70 stades): Φαραὶ δέ, Ἀχαιῶν πόλις, ...ὁδὸς δὲ ἐς Φαρὰς Πατρέων μὲν ἐκ τοῦ ἄστεως
    στάδιοι πεντήκοντά εἰσι καὶ ἑκατόν, ἀπὸ θαλάσσης δὲ ἄνω πρὸς ἤπειρον περὶ ἑβδομήκοντα,
    "Pharai, a city of the Achaeans, ...the road to Pharai from the city of Patrai is 150 stades,
    and inland from the sea toward the interior about 70 stades." Herodotus 1.145 names this
    city Φαρέες and locates it between Patrees (Patrai) and Olenos in his list of the twelve
    Achaean cities: Πατρέες καὶ Φαρέες καὶ Ὤλενος. Strabo 8.7.5 names the city Φάρα in the
    singular: ἡ δὲ Φάρα συνορεῖ μὲν τῇ Δυμαίᾳ. καλοῦνται δὲ οἱ μὲν ἐκ ταύτης τῆς Φάρας
    Φαριεῖς, οἱ δ' ἐκ τῆς Μεσσηνιακῆς Φαραιᾶται, "Phara borders on the territory of Dyme.
    Those from this city Phara are called *Pharieîs*, those from the Messenian city *Pharaiâtai*."
    Towns with the actual name Φεραί are found in Thessaly (e.g. *Iliad* 2.711, *Odyssey* 4.798) and
    in Aetolia (Stephanus of Byzantium s.v.). For Φηραία in Strabo 8.3.32, and its apparent rela-
    tion to Achaean Pharai, see EN5.6 to n5.35 above.
53 "Swift islands" seems to mean no more than "islands"; a specific group of islands has not
    been identified and is probably not meant (see Strabo 8.3.26 for ancient speculation about
    the Ekhinades near the entrance to the Gulf of Corinth). In the older version of *Odyssey* 15
    Telemachus left the Peloponnesian coast at Cape Pheai and headed for the "islands" (one
    of which was Ithaca), and the coast of Elis past Cape Pheai played no part in the voyage.

The sun set and all the ways grew dark;
it made for Pheai, driven by Zeus's wind,
and past shining Elis, where the Epeians have power.
From there he struck out for the fast islands,
pondering whether he would escape death or die.

§5.13 The Pythian *Hymn to Apollo*, which dates from the seventh or early sixth century BC, takes a strong stand in the controversy over Telemachus's route home in favor of the place-name Pherai. It is thus a crucial piece of evidence for the controversy itself. The hymn presents a schematic geography of the Greek world, at the center of which is Delphi. Two broad arcs, one beginning in the north, the other in the south, converge at Delphi as the hymn unfolds: first Apollo leaves Olympus in the north in search of a cult site, and his journey brings him through Thessaly, Euboea, and Boeotia to his final destination Delphi; then his future priests leave Crete in the south, and their ship, commandeered by Apollo, sails past the entire southern and western Peloponnesus before it reaches the Gulf of Krisa (Gulf of Corinth) and likewise proceeds to Delphi as its final destination. The location of Pylos is an important matter in this hymn; indeed it is a central matter. It is necessary to understand this to make sense of the hymn's geography, which is so anomalous that little attention has been paid to it on the assumption that the poet of the hymn was badly informed.[54] It is instead the case, I think, that the poet had a specific agenda with his geography, and that he carried this agenda out quite well.

§5.14 Attention is drawn to Pylos as soon as the narrative shifts from Apollo's journey southward to his future priests' voyage northward: before the Cretan sailors are hijacked and brought to Delphi, their goal is Pylos (*Homeric Hymn to Apollo* 397–399):

οἱ μὲν ἐπὶ πρῆξιν καὶ χρήματα νηῒ μελαίνῃ

ἐς Πύλον ἠμαθόεντα Πυλοιγενέας τ' ἀνθρώπους

ἔπλεον· αὐτὰρ ὁ τοῖσι συνήνετο Φοῖβος Ἀπόλλων.

They sailed in their black ship for trade and profit
to sandy Pylos and the Pylos-born men;
but Phoebus Apollo met them.

---

54 Cf. Aloni 1989:101, who develops an explanation for the hymn's geography based on the premise that the poet had no direct knowledge of the Peloponnesus; cf. also Aloni 2006:58–61.

After the dramatic appearance of Apollo on board the ship in the form of a dolphin, and the acquiescence of the Cretan sailors in Apollo's command, the ship continues on its course, which is described in significant detail: the ship rounds Cape Malea and passes the Laconian land and Cape Tainaron; the sailors try to land at Cape Tainaron, where flocks of Helios graze, but the ship no longer obeys them. It sails onward keeping the Peloponnesus at a distance until it reaches Arene and the Alpheios River. We should note in passing that nothing whatever is said about Messenia, which represents most of what the ship passes between Cape Tainaron and the Alpheios River; Messenia is a blank in this story, and Pylos is located north of the Alpheios River, in what was historically Elis (*Homeric Hymn to Apollo* 418–424):

ἀλλ' οὐ πηδαλίοισιν ἐπείθετο νηῦς εὐεργής,
ἀλλὰ παρὲκ Πελοπόννησον πίειραν ἔχουσα
ἤϊ' ὁδόν, πνοιῇ δὲ ἄναξ ἑκάεργος Ἀπόλλων
ῥηϊδίως ἴθυν'· ἡ δὲ πρήσσουσα κέλευθον
Ἀρήνην ἵκανε καὶ Ἀργυφέην ἐρατεινὴν
καὶ Θρύον Ἀλφειοῖο πόρον καὶ ἐΰκτιτον Αἶπυ
καὶ Πύλον ἠμαθόεντα Πυλοιγενέας τ' ἀνθρώπους.

But the well-built ship did not obey the rudder,
but keeping away from the fertile Peloponnesus
it went its way, and far-worker Apollo easily steered it
with the wind; plying its path
it came to Arene and lovely Argyphea
and Thryon, ford of the Alpheios, and well-built Aipy
and sandy Pylos and the Pylos-born men.

The place-names that occur here, except for otherwise unknown Argyphea (*Arguphéē*), all occur in the Pylian entry to the Catalogue of Ships, but unlike the catalogue, the *Homeric Hymn to Apollo* lines them up in order, and Pylos is placed north of Thryon and the Alpheios River. That the *Homeric Hymn to Apollo* is taking a position on the location of Pylos in the Homeric poems is clear at this point; indeed the crucial line about the Alpheios River is taken directly from the Pylian entry to the Catalogue of Ships (*Iliad* 2.591–592):

οἳ δὲ Πύλον τ' ἐνέμοντο καὶ Ἀρήνην ἐρατεινὴν
καὶ Θρύον Ἀλφειοῖο πόρον καὶ ἐΰκτιτον Αἶπυ....

And those who inhabited <u>Pylos</u> and lovely <u>Arene</u>
<u>and Thryon, ford of the Alpheios, and well-built Aipy</u>....[55]

As the voyage continues it becomes ever clearer that the location of Pylos in
the Homeric poems is the issue. In order to make room for Nestor's kingdom
north of the Alpheios, Elis itself is limited to its own northeast corner, or
just beyond this corner, in what was historically Achaea; this is achieved
by putting Elis past Dyme, the westernmost city of Achaea historically, but
once, according to Strabo, a part of the Epeian realm (*Homeric Hymn to Apollo*
425–426):

βῆ δὲ παρὰ Κρουνοὺς καὶ Χαλκίδα καὶ παρὰ <u>Δύμην</u>
ἠδὲ παρ' <u>Ἤλιδα</u> δῖαν ὅθι κρατέουσιν Ἐπειοί.

It went past Krounoi and Khalkis and past <u>Dyme</u>
and past shining <u>Elis</u>, where the Epeians have power.

The Eleians seem not yet to have reached their ultimate historical home-
land in this scheme, but to be, as it were, still enroute from their place of
origin north of the Peloponnesus.[56] The point of this idiosyncratic geography

55 The Pylian catalogue begins with Pylos because of this city's importance; the hymn
   changes this non-geographical order into a geographical order by putting Pylos after the
   Alpheios River and by substituting Argyphea for Pylos in the line with Arene.
56 Strabo 8.3.9 cites Hecataeus for Dyme as an Epeian city (φησὶ δὲ καὶ τὴν <u>Δύμην</u> Ἐπειίδα καὶ
   Ἀχαιίδα; the first part of this passage is quoted below). Castelnuovo 2002:159–163 argues
   that the name Dyme, which is not in Homer, was coined in the seventh century BC when
   the region, previously nameless, was synoecized and separated itself from Elis (Eusebius
   attests a war between Dyme and Elis in 668 BC that may have taken place in this context;
   see Castelnuovo 2002:162) and became instead the westernmost part of Achaea (various
   sources, including Strabo 8.7.5 [387], interpret the name Dyme to mean "sunset/western";
   so interpreted the name must reflect the town's position in Achaea; see Castelnuovo
   2002:160 with n7 and Wilamowitz 2006:320; Wilamowitz shows from Pausanias 7.17.7 that
   the name Dyme in the list of eighth-century BC Olympic victors [for the year 756 BC see
   2006:320n1102] is an anachronism). Hecataeus, in contrast to other sources, considers
   Epeians and Eleians different peoples in that he makes the Epeians join Heracles in
   attacking Elis: Ἑκαταῖος δ' ὁ Μιλήσιος ἑτέρους λέγει τῶν Ἠλείων τοὺς Ἐπειούς· τῷ γοῦν
   Ἡρακλεῖ συστρατεῦσαι τοὺς Ἐπειοὺς ἐπὶ Αὐγέαν καὶ συνανελεῖν αὐτῷ τόν τε Αὐγέαν καὶ τὴν
   Ἤλιν, "Hecataeus the Milesian says that the Epeians are different from the Eleians; at any
   rate he says that the Epeians campaigned with Heracles against Augeias and that together
   they destroyed Augeias and Elis" (Strabo 8.3.9). Castelnuovo 2002:168–171 argues that Elis
   and Dyme made rival claims to Epeian ancestry and that Hecataeus follows Dyme's version.
   The *Homeric Hymn to Apollo*, like other sources including Homer (cf. Wilamowitz 2006:334),
   identifies the Epeians with the Eleians (*Homeric Hymn to Apollo* 426, quoted above in text).
   Elis, which is located east of Dyme in the *Homeric Hymn to Apollo*, is apparently imagined
   as a moving entity in the migration of the Eleian people before they reached their final

reveals itself plainly in what comes next, when the Cretan ship does exactly what Telemachus's ship does in *Odyssey* 15.297, but in such a way as to end all dispute about Telemachus's route: in virtually the same language as that used of Telemachus's ship in *Odyssey* 15.297 (ἡ δὲ Φεὰς ἐπέβαλλεν ἐπειγομένη Διὸς οὔρῳ), the Cretan ship makes for Pherai, not Pheai (εὖτε Φεράς ἐπέβαλλεν ἀγαλλομένη Διὸς οὔρῳ), and Pherai is guaranteed by its location past Dyme;[57] then, to drive home the point that this all has to do with Telemachus's voyage home, Ithaca, with no regard for verisimilitude, now appears from out of the clouds (*Homeric Hymn to Apollo* 427–429):

> εὖτε Φεράς ἐπέβαλλεν ἀγαλλομένη Διὸς οὔρῳ
> καί σφιν ὑπὲκ νεφέων Ἰθάκης τ' ὄρος αἰπὺ πέφαντο,
> Δουλίχιόν τε Σάμη τε καὶ ὑλήεσσα Ζάκυνθος.

> When it made for Pherai, exulting in Zeus's wind,
> from under the clouds Ithaca's steep mountain also appeared to
>   them,
> and Doulichion and Same and wooded Zakynthos.

It does not matter that the ship has been sailing eastward, away from Ithaca and the other three islands, for more than 20 kilometers when it passes Dyme and makes for Pherai; the ship's real mission is fulfilled when Ithaca, the goal

---

destination. Here the poet archaizes on the basis of historical tradition: the Eleians came to the Peloponnesus from Aetolia according to Pausanias 5.1.3, and their dialect, which was Northwest Greek, attests to their origin outside the Peloponnesus (cf. Lafond *DNP* 'Elis' 994; Castelnuovo 2002:169 with n51). Wilamowitz 2006:322 suggests a similar archaizing view of Eleians as one time Aetolians in *Iliad* 23.633, which refers to Aetolians as competitors at Bouprasion in the distant past of Nestor's youth. In the mythic time imagined by the *Homeric Hymn to Apollo* the Eleians are established in the Peloponnesus, but they have not yet reached their ultimate homeland; they have advanced, as it were, to their penultimate homeland. On this interpretation the name Elis, which is in fact a geographical term (cf. Wilamowitz 2006:322, and, for the name's possible correspondence with Latin *valles*, see Walde-Hofmann 1938–1954 s.v. *valles* and Dräger's note at Wilamowitz 2006:290n948), represents the Eleian people before they became known as such. This picture of Eleian migration is consistent with the Dorian myth of the return of the Herakleidai, which was doubtless known to the poet of the Pythian *Hymn to Apollo* (Tyrtaeus fr. 2.12–15 West, which is roughly contemporary with the *Homeric Hymn to Apollo*, says that the Herakleidai came to Sparta from Erineos in the north; see Parker *OCD*³ 'Heraclidae'). For the archaizing view of Elis's location in the Pythian *Hymn to Apollo* cf. Frame 2006:10 and n23; there is further discussion in EN5.8 to n5.62 below.

57 Note the variation between ἐπειγομένη, "driven by," in *Odyssey* 15 and ἀγαλλομένη, "exulting in," in the *Homeric Hymn to Apollo* (Strabo 8.3.26 actually quotes *Odyssey* 15.297 with the word ἀγαλλομένη of the *Homeric Hymn to Apollo*). The variation in the hymn looks deliberate, as if to highlight the real issue in the line, the variation between Φεράς and Φεάς.

of Telemachus's voyage, manifests itself to the Cretan sailors precisely now, when their ship makes for Pherai.[58] The rest of the voyage, into the Gulf of Krisa and onward to Delphi, passes quickly and without further anomaly. But here too, significantly, there is an allusion to *Odyssey* 15; indeed there is a direct "quotation" of *Odyssey* 15, which solidifies the hymn's deliberate engagement with this Homeric text. In *Odyssey* 15 Athena sends a favorable wind as soon as Telemachus sets sail from Pylos (*Odyssey* 15.292–294):

> τοῖσιν δ' ἴκμενον οὖρον ἵει γλαυκῶπις Ἀθήνη,
> λάβρον ἐπαιγίζοντα δι' αἰθέρος, ὄφρα τάχιστα
> νηῦς ἀνύσειε θέουσα θαλάσσης ἁλμυρὸν ὕδωρ.

> Grey-eyed Athena sent them a favorable wind
> rushing briskly through the sky, so that as fast as possible
> the ship might reach its goal running across the salt water of the
> sea.

The last two verses occur virtually unchanged in the *Homeric Hymn to Apollo* when Zeus sends a west wind to speed the Cretan ship through the Gulf of Krisa (*Homeric Hymn to Apollo* 430–439):

> ἀλλ' ὅτε δὴ Πελοπόννησον παρενίσατο πᾶσαν,
> καὶ δὴ ἐπὶ Κρίσης κατεφαίνετο κόλπος ἀπείρων
> ὅς τε διὲκ Πελοπόννησον πίειραν ἐέργει,
> ἦλθ' ἄνεμος ζέφυρος μέγας αἴθριος ἐκ Διὸς αἴσης
> λάβρος ἐπαιγίζων ἐξ αἰθέρος, ὄφρα τάχιστα

58　The simultaneous appearance of the three other islands in line 429 is also meant to evoke the *Odyssey*, where the line is used repeatedly to link these islands with Ithaca. Directly relevant to the *Homeric Hymn to Apollo* is the passage in which Odysseus reveals his identity to the Phaeacians, for here Ithaca's conspicuous (ἀριπρεπές) Mount Neriton is also mentioned (*Odyssey* 9.21–24):

νναιετάω δ' Ἰθάκην εὐδείελον· ἐν δ' ὄρος αὐτῇ,
Νήριτον εἰνοσίφυλλον, ἀριπρεπές· ἀμφὶ δὲ νῆσοι
πολλαὶ ναιετάουσι μάλα σχεδὸν ἀλλήλῃσι,
Δουλίχιόν τε Σάμη τε καὶ ὑλήεσσα Ζάκυνθος.

I dwell in shining Ithaca; there is a mountain in it,
Neriton with fluttering leaves, standing out clearly; around it
many islands lie very close to each other,
Doulichion and Same and wooded Zakynthos.

Cf. also *Odyssey* 1.245–247, 16.122–124, 19.130–132.

νηῦς ἀνύσειε θέουσα θαλάσσης ἁλμυρὸν ὕδωρ.

ἄψορροι δὴ ἔπειτα πρὸς ἠῶ τ' ἠέλιόν τε
ἔπλεον, ἡγεμόνευε δ' ἄναξ Διὸς υἱὸς Ἀπόλλων·
ἷξον δ' ἐς Κρίσην εὐδείελον ἀμπελόεσσαν
ἐς λιμέν', ἡ δ' ἀμάθοισιν ἐχρίμψατο ποντοπόρος νηῦς.

But when it passed all the Peloponnesus,
and the boundless gulf toward Krisa appeared
which keeps the rich Peloponnesus separate,
a great clear west wind came by Zeus's fate
<u>rushing briskly from the sky, so that as fast as possible</u>
<u>the ship might reach its goal running across the salt water of the</u>
   <u>sea.</u>
Then they sailed back toward the dawn and the sun,
and lord Apollo, Zeus's son, led them;
they came to shining Krisa rich in vines,
to the harbor, and the seafaring ship landed on the sand.

The lines describing Athena's favorable wind, *Odyssey* 15.293–294, constitute
the third instance of direct quotation of the Homeric poems by the *Homeric
Hymn to Apollo*; the other two instances are *Homeric Hymn to Apollo* 423 = *Iliad*
2.592, naming the Alpheios River in the Pylian entry to the Catalogue of Ships,
and *Homeric Hymn to Apollo* 427 = *Odyssey* 15.297, describing the approach of
Telemachus's ship to Pheai. Together these three instances leave no doubt
that the hymn means to engage directly with the text of the Homeric poems
in general, and with the text of Telemachus's voyage home in particular.
Among the small changes in the hymn's two quotations of the *Odyssey* is
the whole point of the exercise, namely the change from the name Pheai in
Odyssey 15.297 to the name Pherai in the *Homeric Hymn to Apollo* 427.[59]

59 What the three virtual quotations imply about a largely fixed state of the Homeric text,
    regardless whether oral or written, when the Pythian *Hymn to Apollo* was composed
    is considered in Frame 2006; cf. Förstel 1979:210–211 and Janko 1982:77–78, 129–131.
    Solon's use of Homer, discussed in n4.149 above, also raises a question about the state of
    the Homeric text, which was presumably no less fixed for him than it was for the *Homeric
    Hymn to Apollo*; variation in the early stages of the Homeric text is illuminated by Rengakos
    2000, who discusses the relationship between Alcman fr. 81 Page [*PMG* 82] and Zenodotus's
    reading of *Odyssey* 6.244–245, and also between Stesichorus fr. 78 Page [*PMG* 255] and
    Zenodotus's reading of *Iliad* 21.575; cf. also Noussia 2002, discussed in n4.149 above. With
    regard to the passage of the *Homeric Hymn to Apollo* quoted above I make a further obser-
    vation: as noted earlier, the Cretan ship first turns east at Cape Araxos en route to Dyme

§5.15 Our text of *Odyssey* 15, as I have already suggested, defends itself against the place-name Pherai in *Odyssey* 15.297 by adding Elis to the route in *Odyssey* 15.298:

ἡ δὲ Φεὰς ἐπέβαλλεν ἐπειγομένη Διὸς οὔρῳ,
ἠδὲ παρ' Ἤλιδα δῖαν, ὅθι κρατέουσιν Ἐπειοί.

It made for Pheai, driven by Zeus's wind,
and past shining Elis, where the Epeians have power.

The added line, I think, was borrowed directly from the *Homeric Hymn to Apollo* in order to be used against it in this ongoing battle of the texts: in the *Homeric Hymn to Apollo* the line relocates Elis past Dyme, northeast of its historical location; in *Odyssey* 15 the line is used to reassert the known historical location of Elis, and to defend the place-name Pheai in the line before it.[60]

§5.16 In the same passage of *Odyssey* 15 there is yet another dubious line, but it seems not to concern the controversy over the location of Pylos in Elis, or at least not directly. *Odyssey* 15.295 does not occur in the manuscripts, but it is quoted twice by Strabo: βὰν δὲ παρὰ Κρουνοὺς καὶ Χαλκίδα καλλιρέεθρον, "They went past Krounoi and the beautifully flowing Khalkis." As Strabo quotes it, this line occurs after Telemachus sets sail from Pylos, when Athena sends him a fair wind, but before the sun sets and the ship makes for Pheai. Strabo quotes the line to support his argument that the Homeric Pylos lay in Triphylia: he knows of a spring called Krounoi north of Samikon in Triphylia, and Khalkis, he says, is the name of both a river and a

---

and Pheai, and it sails a considerable distance eastward before the sailors catch sight of Ithaca, which, paradoxically, is behind them, to the west, receding or disappearing from view; the hymn does not acknowledge this paradox, but makes it appear that the eastward segment of the voyage does not begin until the Gulf of Krisa is entered (ἄψορροι δὴ ἔπειτα πρὸς ἠῶ τ' ἠέλιόν τε / ἔπλεον, "they sailed back toward the dawn and the sun," lines 436–437). The geography is twisted, but consistent.

60 The line, which is the same in the two texts, follows smoothly in the *Homeric Hymn to Apollo* (the prepositional phrase ἠδὲ παρ' Ἤλιδα δῖαν, "and past shining Elis," is parallel to the two prepositional phrases that precede it: βῆ δὲ παρὰ Κρουνοὺς καὶ Χαλκίδα καὶ παρὰ Δύμην, "it went past Krounoi and Khalkis and past Dyme"), but in the *Odyssey*, as already mentioned, the line is added only loosely (ἠδὲ παρ' Ἤλιδα δῖαν is not parallel to Φεὰς, the object of the verb ἐπέβαλλεν, "made for"). The line in the *Homeric Hymn to Apollo* is itself an adaptation of two Homeric lines, which differ in the opening from the line in the *Hymn to Apollo*, and which also have a slight variation between themselves (ἢ εἰς Ἤλιδα δῖαν, ὅθι κρατέουσιν Ἐπειοί, *Odyssey* 13.275, and ἢ καὶ ἐς Ἤλιδα δῖαν, ὅθι κρατέουσιν Ἐπειοί, *Odyssey* 24.431, both lines meaning "or into shining Elis, where the Epeians have power").

town in the same region.[61] But the line, which stands alone (unenjambed) in *Odyssey* 15, clearly has a connection with the *Homeric Hymn to Apollo*, where the Cretan ship also sails παρὰ Κρουνοὺς καὶ Χαλκίδα, "past Krounoi and Khalkis," after it passes the Alpheios River and the Eleian town of Pylos, and before it passes Dyme; in the hymn these obscure place-names, Krounoi and Khalkis, are in what was historicially Elis: in fact they take the place of Elis itself, which has been shifted to the northeast from its historical location. Although we cannot say to what precisely the names Krounoi and Khalkis in the hymn refer, these names, I think, belong to the hymn first: the learned tradition followed by Strabo has availed itself of the names, which are not distinctive in themselves, to bolster the case for a Triphylian Pylos. This, I think, was a comparatively late development, and had nothing to do with the controversy in the Archaic period over the Eleian location of Pylos.[62]

§5.17 *Odyssey* 15, in my view, originally named only one location on the coast of the Peloponnesus after Telemachus's departure from Pylos, and that was Pheai, the jumping-off place to the islands; omitting line 298, which in my view was added in the Archaic period to defend the name Pheai, and line 295, which in my view was added at a later time to support an entirely different argument relating to a Triphylian Pylos, the description of Telemachus's voyage would have been as follows before the controversy over Pylos's location first arose (*Odyssey* 15.292–294, 296–297, 299–300):

61 Strabo 8.3.13, proceeding from north to south, puts these places just north of Samikon in Triphylia: εἶτα τὸ διεῖργον ὄρος τῆς Τριφυλίας τὴν Μακιστίαν ἀπὸ τῆς Πισάτιδος· εἶτ' ἄλλος ποταμὸς Χαλκὶς καὶ κρήνη Κρουνοὶ καὶ κατοικία Χαλκίς, καὶ τὸ Σαμικὸν μετὰ ταῦτα, ὅπου τὸ μάλιστα τιμώμενον τοῦ Σαμίου Ποσειδῶνος ἱερόν, "Then the mountain of Triphylia that separates Makistia from the Pisatis; then another river Chalkis and spring Krounoi and settlement Chalkis, and after these Samikon, where the most honored temple of Samian Poseidon is." In 8.3.26 Strabo quotes the line in question (*Odyssey* 15.295) with the epithet καλλιρέεθρον, "beautiful-flowing," qualifying Χαλκίδα, making Khalkis a river (cf. ποταμὸς Χαλκίς, "river Khalkis," in 8.3.13); in 10.1.9 he quotes the same line with the epithet πετρήεσσαν, "rocky," qualifying Χαλκίδα, making Khalkis a town (cf. κατοικία Χαλκίς, "settlement Khalkis," in 8.3.13).

62 Strabo's learned tradition, which goes back to Apollodorus, found two possible references for the name Khalkis in Triphylia, a river and a town, and in *Odyssey* 15.295 both possibilities were entertained with the variants καλλιρέεθρον and πετρήεσσαν (see previous note). Whether *Odyssey* 15.295 was actually interpolated by Hellenistic scholarship is a difficult question. Cf. n5.135 below on *Iliad* 7.133–135 for changes proposed by Hellenistic scholarship to a different passage; as with *Odyssey* 15.295, the changes to *Iliad* 7.133–135 are found only in Strabo, but unlike *Odyssey* 15.295, they are not part of Strabo's standard text. For the question of *Odyssey* 15.295, cf. Wilamowitz 2006:341, who attributes the line to someone's wish to put Pylos in Triphylia ("Wer den Vers zusetzte, war also einer, der Pylos nach Triphylien verlegen wollte"). Two solutions proposed by other scholars to the difficulties of *Odyssey* 15.295–300 are discussed in EN5.8.

292 τοῖσιν δ᾽ ἴκμενον οὖρον ἵει γλαυκῶπις Ἀθήνη,

293 λάβρον ἐπαιγίζοντα δι᾽ αἰθέρος, ὄφρα τάχιστα

294 νηῦς ἀνύσειε θέουσα θαλάσσης ἁλμυρὸν ὕδωρ.

296 δύσετό τ᾽ ἠέλιος σκιόωντό τε πᾶσαι ἀγυιαί·

297 ἡ δὲ Φεὰς ἐπέβαλλεν ἐπειγομένη Διὸς οὔρῳ.

299 ἔνθεν δ᾽ αὖ νήσοισιν ἐπιπροέηκε θοῇσιν,

300 ὁρμαίνων, ἤ κεν θάνατον φύγοι ἤ κεν ἁλοίη.

292 Grey-eyed Athena sent them a favorable wind

293 rushing briskly through the sky, so that as fast as possible

294 the ship might reach its goal running across the salt
water of the sea.

296 The sun set and all the ways grew dark;

297 it made for Pheai, driven by Zeus's wind.

299 From there he struck out for the fast islands,

300 pondering whether he would escape death or die.[63]

§5.18 The Pylos at the start of Telemachus's voyage home in *Odyssey* 15 is
in Messenia, but not because the narrative locates it there precisely; it is there
because, when the Homeric poems were composed, Messenia was known to
be the location of Nestor's city, and there was as yet no controversy about it.
There was also at that time a living tradition bearing witness to Pylos's true
location. After the fall of Bronze Age Pylos, the Pylians themselves did not
all leave Messenia; Pylians, still known as such, continued to live there until
the seventh century BC, when the Spartans finally drove them out in the

---

63 There are several changes of subject in this passage: as the passage stands in our texts
the ship is the subject in lines 294 and 297; "they" (the sailors) are the subject in line 295;
the setting sun and the darkening "ways" are the subjects in line 296; Telemachus is the
subject in lines 299–300. Without line 295, in which the subject is "they" (the sailors, verb
βάν), the changes of subject are fewer. There is still the change of subject from the ship to
Telemachus in the final two lines of the passage; there is also the change of subject from
the ship to the setting sun in line 296. But there is only one change of subject (the setting
sun in line 296) between two lines in which the ship is subject (294 and 297); this, I think,
makes the change of subject back to the ship in line 297 easy enough. As for the change
of subject from "it" in line 297 to "he" in line 299, it should be noted that "it" (the ship)
follows a fixed course along the shore whereas "he" (Telemachus) changes course and
heads out to sea; the different tenses of the verbs ἐπέβαλλεν, "was making for" (imper-
fect) and ἐπιπροέηκε, "struck out for" (aorist) bring out the difference between inanimate
object and human agent.

course of the Second Messenian War.[64] It appears that these Pylians, after the destruction of Bronze Age Pylos, inhabited at least two other sites in Messenia that they continued to call Pylos, the final site being at Koryphasion, at the northern end of the bay of Navarino, some 9–10 kilometers southwest of the Bronze Age city at Ano-Englianos. This site too was abandoned at the end of the Second Messenian War, but to it the name Pylos clung; most famously, this was the Pylos of the disaster that befell Spartan hoplites in 425 BC, when they were trapped on the island of Sphacteria and taken prisoner by the Athenian navy. A narrow inlet of the sea separates Sphacteria from Pylos, and Pylos is the name that Thucydides and other Athenian writers use to refer to the location of this celebrated and shocking incident of the Peloponnesian War. It was also here that a new city of Pylos was founded in the fourth century BC when the Messenians regained their independence from Sparta.[65]

64 For Messenia as the known location of Nestor's Pylos in the Homeric era cf. Wilamowitz 2006:331. The rulers of Bronze Age Pylos went to Athens when their city fell, but not the population as a whole. Although the palace at Ano-Englianos was never reoccupied, at Tragana, only 2–3 kilometers to the southwest, a Bronze Age tholos tomb continued to be used for new burials in the sub-Mycenaean and Protogeometric periods; see Kiechle 1960:7–8; Desborough 1952:281–283; Wace 1956:132–133; Webster 1964:137; Wade-Gery 1948:117. According to several passages in Pausanias Pylian survivors were still living on the Messenian coast during the Second Messenian War: when the Messenians retreated to Mount Hira after the Battle of the Great Trench, the people of Pylos and Methone (to the south of Pylos) continued to preserve the coastal districts for them (Μεσσήνιοι δὲ ὡς ἐς τὴν Εἶραν ‹ἀνῳκίσθησαν,› τῆς δὲ ἄλλης ἐξείργοντο πλὴν ὅσον σφίσιν οἱ Πύλιοι τὰ ἐπὶ θαλάσσῃ καὶ οἱ Μοθωναῖοι διέσωζον, "When the Messenians moved inland to Mount Hira, they were cut off from the rest of the country except as far as the Pylians and the Methonaians preserved the coastal regions for them," Pausanias 4.18.1); when Mount Hira was finally captured and the Messenians were enslaved, the people of Pylos and Methone took to ships and left their old homes (τῶν δὲ Μεσσηνίων ὁπόσοι περὶ τὴν Εἶραν ἢ καὶ ἑτέρωθί που τῆς Μεσσηνίας ἐγκατελήφθησαν, τούτους μὲν οἱ Λακεδαιμόνιοι προσένειμαν ἐς τὸ εἱλωτικόν· Πύλιοι δὲ καὶ Μοθωναῖοι καὶ ὅσοι τὰ παραθαλάσσια ᾤκουν, [καὶ] ναυσὶν ὑπὸ τὴν ἅλωσιν τῆς Εἴρας ἀπαίρουσιν ἐς Κυλλήνην τὸ ἐπίνειον τὸ Ἠλείων, "The Messenians who were captured around Mount Hira or elsewhere in Messenia the Spartans assigned to the helot class; but the Pylians and Methonaians and those who occupied the sea coast departed in ships for Cyllene, the seaport of the Eleians, at about the time of the capture of Mount Hira," Pausanias 4.23.1); see n5.91 for a third passage, Pausanias 3.3.4. Not all of what Pausanias says in the two passages above is reliable, but the departure of the Pylians from the Peloponnesus c. 600 BC appears to be solidly historical; the issue is discussed in EN5.9. Memories of a distinct Pylian population in Messenia seem to be preserved in fifth-century authors, but as early as Pindar Pylians are called Messenians (cf. Kiechle 1959:53–56 and n5.65 below), who are in turn distinguished from Dorians (Ephorus 70 F 116; cf. Kiechle 1959:43, 68).

65 The new city was probably founded in 365 BC (see Meyer *RE* 'Pylos' 2125). The only real proof of the existence of an earlier city of Pylos on the same site is the persistence of the name Pylos of the site down to the time of the Peloponnesian War (cf. Meyer *RE* 'Pylos' 2123). Herodotus refers to the site as Pylos at the time of the Persian Wars when he tells how the Sicilian Greeks made a show of sending aid against the Persians, but went no further than

§5.19 Significantly, however, the Spartans did not call this place Pylos, but Koryphasion, as Thucydides expressly states.[66] The name Koryphasion was doubtless old, but use of it instead of Pylos distinguishes the Spartans, and it implies, I think, a deliberate choice. The Spartans, who expelled the Pylians in the Second Messenian War, did not wish to remind themselves or others that Nestor's Homeric kingdom now lay desolate, and, more to the point, under Spartan control.[67] This suggests, I think, how the location

---

Pylos and Tainaron: περὶ Πύλον καὶ Ταίναρον γῆς τῆς Λακεδαιμονίων ἀνεκώχευον τὰς νέας, καραδοκέοντες καὶ οὗτοι τὸν πόλεμον τῇ πεσέεται, "They held up their ships around Pylos and Tainaron in the land of the Lacedaemonians, waiting to see which way the war would turn," Herodotus 7.168.2). The city at Koryphasion, abandoned after the Second Messenian War, was itself a successor to earlier places called Pylos, the first of which would have been the Bronze Age city at Ano-Englianos. There is also evidence of an intermediate location of the city before its final location at Koryphasion: Strabo is the source for a tradition that there was an "old Pylos" (παλαιὰ Πύλος) before the city at Koryphasion; this city, he says, lay under Mount Aigaleon, and when it was destroyed some of the inhabitants moved to Koryphasion (Strabo 8.4.2): ἡ μὲν οὖν παλαιὰ Πύλος ἡ Μεσσηνιακὴ ὑπὸ τῷ Αἰγαλέῳ πόλις ἦν, κατεσπασμένης δὲ ταύτης ἐπὶ τῷ Κορυφασίῳ τινὲς αὐτῶν ᾤκησαν. We do not know for sure what location Strabo had in mind for the old city, nor when the old city was abandoned for the new city at Koryphasion, but in any case the move to Koryphasion must have taken place before the Pylians left the Peloponnesus at the end of the Second Messenian War; the probable location of Strabo's "old Pylos" at modern Volimidia, five kilometers northeast of Ano-Englianos, is discussed in EN5.10. Although Messenia was regarded as Nestor's home in the classical period (Pindar *Pythian* 6.35 calls Nestor Μεσσανίου δὲ γέροντος, "the Messenian old man"), this evidence is discounted by some as relating to the Messenian resurgence of the fourth century BC, which had its roots in the fifth century BC; according to this line of thought the Messenians had to reinvent their entire past, which had been wiped clean during the period of Spartan domination, and it was only in the course of this late process that they laid claim to Nestor and Pylos (see Luraghi 2002:49n21, who follows Visser 1997:522–530 in locating the Homeric Pylos in Triphylia rather than Messenia; for Luraghi's approach, cf. Siapkas 2003:285). While there may be truth in this analysis of Messenian traditions in general, it does not explain the history of the name Pylos in Messenia.

66 Thucydides 4.3.2; the preceding passage describes the rough and desolate nature of the place, which the Athenians fortified in the spring of 425 BC: κατὰ τύχην χειμὼν ἐπιγενόμενος κατήνεγκε τὰς ναῦς ἐς τὴν Πύλον. καὶ ὁ Δημοσθένης εὐθὺς ἠξίου τειχίζεσθαι τὸ χωρίον (ἐπὶ τοῦτο γὰρ ξυνεκπλεῦσαι), καὶ ἀπέφαινε πολλὴν εὐπορίαν ξύλων τε καὶ λίθων, καὶ φύσει καρτερὸν ὂν καὶ ἐρῆμον αὐτὸ τε καὶ ἐπὶ πολὺ τῆς χώρας· ἀπέχει γὰρ σταδίους μάλιστα ἡ Πύλος τῆς Σπάρτης τετρακοσίους καὶ ἔστιν ἐν τῇ Μεσσηνίᾳ ποτὲ οὔσῃ γῇ, καλοῦσι δὲ αὐτὴν οἱ Λακεδαιμόνιοι Κορυφάσιον, "By chance a storm came up and carried the ships into Pylos. Demosthenes at once proposed to fortify the place (he had joined the expedition for this reason), and pointed out that there is an abundant supply of wood and stones, and that the place is naturally strong and, along with much of the rest of the country, uninhabited. Pylos is about four hundred stades from Sparta in what was once the Messenian land; the Spartans call it Koryphasion."

67 Kiechle 1960:8 argues that the name Pylos belonged to the location before the period of Spartan control since the Spartans, with the name Koryphasion, tried to ignore the memory of it ("...einer Erinnerung, die offensichtlich aus der Zeit vor der Errichtung der spartanischen Herrschaft stammte, da die Spartaner sie zu ignorieren versuchten...").

of Pylos first became a subject of dispute: the Spartans had no wish to claim Homeric Pylos by right of conquest, but wished rather to disclaim it, because it brought opprobrium rather than glory. But to disclaim it they had to reckon with the Homeric poems, which were at the root of their problem; without the Homeric poems, Nestor and the Pylians would not have been an issue in the first place. But given that the Homeric poems did exist there was still a way out: the Homeric poems could be reinterpreted and the location of Pylos could be shifted because Homeric geography was vague. Nestor's story in *Iliad* 11, in which he reaches Bouprasion after a one-day rout of the Epeians, invited a geographical reinterpretation: Nestor's city, on a realistic interpretation of his story, lay not in Messenia, but in Elis. The only bar to this reinterpretation was Telemachus's voyage home in the *Odyssey*, in which the town of Pheai would be passed on the way to Ithaca only if the voyage began somewhere south of the Alpheios River, namely in Messenia. Hence, I suggest, it was the Spartans who first put forth the idea that in *Odyssey* 15 the name of the town was not Pheai, but, with the addition of a single letter, Pherai.

§5.20 But what authority could the Spartans have claimed for a revised version of Telemachus's voyage in *Odyssey* 15? To this there is an answer. As Aristotle attests, the Spartans claimed a separate tradition for the Homeric poems that bypassed the Homeridai of Chios and went instead through the Kreophyleioi of Samos: Lycurgus, the legendary Spartan lawgiver, is supposed to have received the Homeric poems from descendants of Kreophylos during a visit to Samos.[68] Acccording to this tradition the Spartans were among the

---

Hornblower 1996:154–155, commenting on Thucydides 4.3.2, refers to a suggestion of Robin Osborne that the Spartans avoided the name Pylos because they did not wish to give the Messenians credit for Nestor's city; in my view it was more the case that the Spartans themselves, at least initially, wished to avoid discredit, but the two explanations are not incompatible; in the fifth century the Messenians at Naupaktos had strong feelings for Pylos as a fatherland (Thucydides 4.41.2 and 4.3.3). The name Koryphasion may be pre-Dorian, as Kiechle 1960:6 suggests, but not for the reason that Kiechle gives, namely that -σ- for -σσ- is Arcadian (that would imply an underlying -ky- or -ty-, which cannot be right in this derivative from *koruphḗ*, "top"). The name Koryphasion belonged to the cape as opposed to the city on the cape; cf. Meyer *RE* 'Pylos' 2126: "The place's double name, Koryphasion for the cape, Pylos for the city on it, easily led to mistakes" ("Der Doppelname der Örtlichkeit, Koryphasion für das Kap, Pylos für die Stadt darauf führte leicht zu Irrtümern"). Examples of the Spartans' use of the name Koryphasion are found in the document of the Peace of Nikias (Thucydides 5.18.7) and in the earlier truce document (Thucydides 4.118.4). Xenophon *Hellenica* 1.2.18 uses the name Koryphasion, perhaps showing his Spartan orientation.

68 Aristotle's evidence is from the *Constitutions* as excerpted by Heraclides Lembus (Aristotle fr. 611.10 Rose = Heraclides Lembus 372.10 Dilts): Λυκοῦργος ἐν Σάμῳ ἐγένετο. καὶ

first, if not the very first, to gain possession of the Homeric poems in mainland Greece. We may ask why it was important to the Spartans to claim not only priority of reception of the Homeric poems, but also an independent source. I suggest that the controversy over Telemachus's voyage in *Odyssey* 15 provides a sufficient reason. It is also very much to the point that the Samians, with their ships, seem to have been called in by the Spartans to expel the coastal population, including the Pylians, from the southwest Peloponnesus at the end of the Second Messenian War. The case for this is based on a passage of Herodotus, which says that the Samians sent ships to help the Spartans against the Messenians, and it is implied that this happened sometime before the tyranny of Polycrates; Herodotus does not specify the date more closely, but the Second Messenian War seems highly likely.[69] If Samos was thus useful to Sparta in

---

τὴν Ὁμήρου ποίησιν παρὰ τῶν ἀπογόνων Κρεοφύλου λαβὼν πρῶτος διεκόμισεν εἰς Πελοπόννησον, "Lycurgus came to Samos. He received Homer's poetry from the descendants of Kreophylos and was the first to bring it to the Peloponnesus." Plutarch *Lycurgus* 4.4 attests the same tradition: ἐκεῖ δὲ καὶ τοῖς Ὁμήρου ποιήμασιν ἐντυχὼν πρῶτον, ὡς ἔοικε, παρὰ τοῖς ἐκγόνοις τοῖς Κρεοφύλου διατηρουμένοις, "He also came upon the poems of Homer there for the first time, preserved, it seems, by the descendants of Kreophylos." Wilamowitz 1884:267–271 argues that this tradition was invented in the fourth century to overshadow the claim attested in "Plato" *Hipparchus* 228b that Hipparchus first brought the Homeric poems to Athens (cf. above n2.225 and n2.240). Ritoók 1993:48 reexamines the question and concludes that an independent tradition for Lycurgus cannot be excluded. Kreophylos, who was said to have entertained Homer in his home (Callimachus *Epigrams* 6 Pfeiffer; cf. Plato *Republic* 600b), was presumably thought to have received not only the *Oikhalias Halosis* from Homer (Callimachus *Epigrams* 6 Pfeifer), but also the *Iliad* and the *Odyssey*, which he would then have left to his descendants (Kreophylos is said to have received the *Iliad* from Homer by the scholia to Plato *Republic* 600b, but in this account there is contamination with other traditions; cf. Graziosi 2002:191). For a different view from mine of how Kreophylos came to be regarded as Sparta's link to the Homeric poems, cf. Graziosi 2002:205–206, who suggests that, because Kreophylos had a bad reputation in Athens, the "descendants of Kreophylos" may have been an Athenian invention intended to discredit Spartan claims to Homeric reception; Graziosi presumably thinks that these Spartan claims linked Lycurgus to Homer directly, whereas I take Kreophylos, the intermediary between the two figures, to be an old feature of the Spartan tradition. Variants of the stories linking Homer with both Kreophylos and Lycurgus are discussed in EN5.11.

69 Herodotus 3.47.1. According to what the Samians said, they once sent ships to help the Spartans against the Messenians, and in return for this good deed the Spartans sent an expedition against Polycrates when Samian exiles appealed to them for help; the Spartans maintained that besides this repayment of an earlier good deed they had their own scores to settle with Polycrates: καὶ ἔπειτα παρασκευασάμενοι ἐστρατεύοντο Λακεδαιμόνιοι ἐπὶ Σάμον, ὡς μὲν Σάμιοι λέγουσι, εὐεργεσίας ἐκτίνοντες ὅτι σφι πρότεροι αὐτοὶ νηυσὶ ἐβοήθησαν ἐπὶ Μεσσηνίους, ὡς δὲ Λακεδαιμόνιοι λέγουσι, οὐκ οὕτω τιμωρῆσαι δεομένοισι Σαμίοισι ἐστρατεύοντο ὡς τείσασθαι βουλόμενοι τοῦ κρητῆρος τῆς ἁρπαγῆς, τὸν ἦγον Κροίσῳ, κτλ., "Then the Spartans made preparations and sent an expedition against Samos, repaying, as the Samians say, a good deed, in that they themselves had earlier come with ships to the Spartans' aid against the Messenians; but the Spartans say that

removing the Pylians from Messenia, it may also have been useful in trying to expunge from Homer the very memory of their ever having been there.[70]

§5.21 If this argument is correct, the *Homeric Hymn to Apollo*, with its idiosyncratic geography, also reflects a Spartan point of view. This, I think, is the case, but there is a problem. At the end of the hymn Apollo's Cretan priests are warned against acts of hybris, for which they will be punished by being subjected to new masters.[71] The lines in question are reasonably taken as an allusion to the First Sacred War, which ended in 591 BC with the destruction of Krisa and the imposition of a new regime at Delphi.[72] The war's victors,

---

they did not make war so much to avenge the Samians at their request, but because they wished to exact punishment for the robbery of a mixing bowl which they were bringing to Croesus," etc. Kiechle 1959:33 reasonably argues that the ships once sent by Samos against the Messenians were instead (or more specifically) sent against the Pylians and the other coastal populations of Messenia during the Second Messenian War. While the episode is undated in Herodotus, it clearly preceded the tyranny of Polycrates; Kiechle's dating of it to the Second Messenian War has been accepted by others (Jeffery 1976:120; Cartledge 1982:259; cf. Huxley 1962:74). Cartledge argues that there was a centuries-long "special relationship" between Sparta and Samos, and that, to judge by the exchange of goods between them, this relationship began by c. 650 BC (Cartledge 1982:255).

70 Concerning the tradition that Lycurgus brought the Homeric poems to Sparta from Samos, Cartledge 1982:252 remarks that "this is just the sort of anecdote that would tend to become attached to a chronologically fluid wonder-worker like Lykourgos." As the date for the tradition (first found in Aristotle) linking Lycurgus with the Kreophyleioi, Janko 1992:31n50 suggests the late sixth century BC, in the time of Polycrates; I would move this back to the early sixth or late seventh century BC, i.e. to the end of the Second Messenian War: if Sparta was embarrassed by what had happened to Nestor's descendants in Messenia, so must Samos have been, after providing the naval force to drive them out. The idea that Nestor's kingdom had never been in Messenia, but in Elis, could well have been the result of Spartan-Samian connivance, especially if Samos had the Kreophyleioi to vouch for the small but necessary change to the Homeric poems (the letter rho in *Pherás*). For the Kreophyleioi and Homeric poetry, cf. n4.143 above.

71 *Homeric Hymn to Apollo* 540–544 (a lacuna seems to precede):

ἠέ τι τηΰσιον ἔπος ἔσσεται ἠέ τι ἔργον,
ὕβρις θ', ἣ θέμις ἐστὶ καταθνητῶν ἀνθρώπων,
ἄλλοι ἔπειθ' ὑμῖν σημάντορες ἄνδρες ἔσονται,
τῶν ὑπ' ἀναγκαίῃ δεδμήσεσθ' ἤματα πάντα.
εἴρηταί τοι πάντα, σὺ δὲ φρεσὶ σῇσι φύλαξαι.

There will be either some rash word or deed,
and insolence, as is the way of mortal men,
then there will be other masters over you,
under whose compulsion you will be subjected forever.
Everything has been told to you, but you guard it in your heart.

With the second person singular pronoun σύ in line 544 Apollo addresses the leader of the Cretan priests (the Κρητῶν ἀγός of line 525).

72 See Forrest 1956, especially pp. 34–35. The reality of the First Sacred War is challenged by

which included the Athenians, Sikyonians, and Thessalians, did not include the Spartans;[73] thus the *ex eventu* prophecy at the end of the *Homeric Hymn to Apollo* does not reflect a Spartan point of view. But there has long been a debate as to whether the hymn's final prophecy was added to an already existing hymn after the First Sacred War to reflect the war's outcome.[74] A strong case can in fact be made that the victors appropriated an older hymn and gave it a new twist at the hymn's end. The threat made against the priests at the end of the hymn, which had already been carried out in reality, is not only unanticipated earlier in the hymn, but it contradicts the hymn's very purpose, which is to celebrate the establishment of the Delphic oracle and its Cretan priesthood. The poem cannot well have set out from the start to undermine its own purpose at the end.[75] Particularly hard to understand in the poem is the role of Krisa, the goal of both Apollo's journey from Olympus and his future priests' voyage from Crete, if at the moment of the

Robertson 1978. Davies 1994 takes account of Robertson's argument (summarized on p. 197) and more recent work (pp. 197–200) but reaches no conclusion about the war, saying only that it (the war) remains a plausible hypothesis (p. 206); he is similarly agnostic about the final lines of the *Homeric Hymn to Apollo* (p. 193): "Allusions which may or may not be to the war have been detected in late archaic poetry in the *Homeric Hymn to Apollo*, lines 540–544 (Forrest, 1956), and in the last lines (478–480) of the Hesiodic *Aspis* (Parke and Boardman 1957)" (for the Hesiodic *Aspis/Shield* see also Guillon 1963:18–19). The city destroyed in the Sacred War is sometimes called Krisa, sometimes Kirrha; for the problem of the two names, see Daverio Rocchi *DNP* 'Krisa': Kirrha, a port on the gulf, was inhabited in the classical period and after on the evidence of archaeological remains; the sacred plain, which was perhaps the site of Homeric Krisa (there are late Mycenaean and earlier remains on a spur 1.5 kilometers north of Kirrha; for the spur cf. the phrase Κρισαῖον λόφον, "crest of Krisa," in Pindar *Pythian* 5.37) was apparently not inhabited later. In ancient tradition Kirrha and Krisa were equated. Sources for the First Sacred War (Aeschines *Against Ctesiphon* 107–113, Plutarch *Solon* 11, Pausanias 10.37.5–8; all quoted in Davies 1994:206–210) use the form Kirrha; Pausanias says that Krisa was an older name of the city.

73 See Forrest 1956:36–44 for grievances that the victors may have had against Delphi in the period before the war. These grievances are discussed in EN5.12.

74 Parke and Wormel 1956, vol. 1, 107–108 accept this interpretation.

75 Cf. Davies 1994:203: "The final lines of the *Homeric Hymn to Apollo* can hardly be read otherwise than as a warning, or more plausibly as a prophecy (presumably *post eventum*), that one regime at the shrine would be violently succeeded by another. Given that the whole poem as we have it is concerned to provide a divine charter for the oracle as Apollo's, and given that lines 388ff. are concerned to provide the Kretan sailors who had been hijacked by Apollo's epiphany with a charter as priests of the sanctuary, these final lines are disconcerting. To propose the existence of a lacuna between lines 539 and 540 does not help much, for the final lines will still explicitly cancel the charter. Unless they belong to a wholly different poem, they have to be read, I think, as an addition, tacked on to accommodate a new reality as economically as possible."

poem's composition Krisa had already been destroyed and its land withdrawn forever from human cultivation.[76]

§5.22 The hymn's final passage is the clearest evidence that an older hymn was appropriated and adapted by a new political group after the First Sacred War, but it is not the only evidence. Another expansion of the hymn is reasonably seen in lines 305–355, which describe how the goddess Hera conceived and gave birth to the monster Typhaon. The story of Typhaon's birth is set within the story of the "she-dragon" (*drákaina*) slain by Apollo near his newly founded temple at Delphi (lines 300–374). The connection between the two stories is that, among her other evil deeds, the she-dragon is said to have received the monster Typhaon from Hera's hands and raised him.[77] The story that is then told mostly concerns Hera, the monster's mother; all that we hear about the monster himself is that he did great harm to men (355, one line).[78] Nothing is said about the monster's fate, which was presumably to be

---

76 In the hymn the name Delphi does not occur, only *Krísē* (lines 269, 282, 431, 438, 445; the people are *Krísaioi*, line 446); in the hymn Krisa is Delphi.

77 The transition from the she-dragon (ἥ in line 302) to the story of Hera and Typhaon is as follows (*Homeric Hymn to Apollo* 302–307):

> ἥ κακὰ πολλὰ
> ἀνθρώπους ἔρδεσκεν ἐπὶ χθονί, πολλὰ μὲν αὐτοὺς
> πολλὰ δὲ μῆλα ταναύποδ' ἐπεὶ πέλε πῆμα δαφοινόν.
> <u>καί ποτε δεξαμένη χρυσοθρόνου ἔτρεφεν Ἥρης</u>
> <u>δεινόν τ' ἀργαλέον τε Τυφάονα πῆμα βροτοῖσιν,</u>
> <u>ὅν ποτ' ἄρ' Ἥρη ἔτικτε χολωσαμένη Διὶ πατρὶ....</u>

> <u>Who</u> did many evils
> to men on earth—many to the men themselves
> and many to thin-shanked sheep, since she was a bloody woe.
> <u>She once received from golden-throned Hera, and then raised up,</u>
> <u>terrible cruel Typhaon, a woe to mortals,</u>
> <u>whom Hera bore out of anger with father Zeus....</u>

78 The transition from the story of Hera and Typhaon back to the she-dragon (τῇ in line 356) is as follows (*Homeric Hymn to Apollo* 351–358):

> <u>ἡ δ' ἔτεκ' οὔτε θεοῖς ἐναλίγκιον οὔτε βροτοῖσι</u>
> <u>δεινόν τ' ἀργαλέον τε Τυφάονα πῆμα βροτοῖσιν.</u>
> <u>αὐτίκα τόνδε λαβοῦσα βοῶπις πότνια Ἥρη</u>
> <u>δῶκεν ἔπειτα φέρουσα κακῷ κακόν, ἡ δ' ὑπέδεκτο·</u>
> <u>ὃς κακὰ πόλλ' ἔρδεσκε κατὰ κλυτὰ φῦλ' ἀνθρώπων.</u>
> ὃς τῇ γ' ἀντιάσειε, φέρεσκέ μιν αἴσιμον ἦμαρ
> πρίν γέ οἱ ἰὸν ἐφῆκεν ἄναξ ἑκάεργος Ἀπόλλων
> καρτερόν.

> <u>She bore terrible cruel Typhaon, a woe to mortals,</u>
> <u>who was like neither gods nor mortals.</u>

slain by Zeus (as in Hesiod *Theogony* 820–868).[79] The story of Typhaon's birth adds little of relevance to the story of Apollo's slaying of the she-dragon in the *Homeric Hymn to Apollo*.[80]

Taking him revered ox-eyed Hera
brought and gave this evil one to another evil one, and she received him;
he worked many evils among the famous tribes of men.
Whoever met <u>her</u>, his day of doom would carry him off,
until the far-worker lord Apollo shot her
with a strong arrow.

79 Allen and Sikes, in the first edition of their commentary on the *Homeric Hymns* (Allen and Sikes 1904), regarded lines 305–355 of the *Hymn to Apollo* as not original in their present context; they noted, in particular, the fact that Typhaon's fate is not told in the hymn (see on lines 305–355 and on line 355). Allen and Halliday, in the second edition of the commentary (Allen, Halliday, and Sikes 1936), no longer comment on the problems of the passage's present placement, but no reason is given for the change.

80 Without the long expansion the story of Apollo and the she-dragon is as follows (*Homeric Hymn to Apollo* 300–304, 356–359):

ἀγχοῦ δὲ κρήνη καλλίρροος ἔνθα δράκαιναν
κτεῖνεν ἄναξ Διὸς υἱὸς ἀπὸ κρατεροῖο βιοῖο
ζατρεφέα μεγάλην τέρας ἄγριον, ἣ κακὰ πολλὰ
ἀνθρώπους ἔρδεσκεν ἐπὶ χθονί, πολλὰ μὲν αὐτοὺς
πολλὰ δὲ μῆλα ταναύποδ' ἐπεὶ πέλε πῆμα δαφοινόν·
ὃς τῇ γ' ἀντιάσειε, φέρεσκέ μιν αἴσιμον ἦμαρ
πρίν γέ οἱ ἰὸν ἐφῆκεν ἄναξ ἑκάεργος Ἀπόλλων
καρτερόν· ἡ δ' ὀδύνησιν ἐρεχθομένη χαλεπῇσι
κεῖτο μέγ' ἀσθμαίνουσα κυλινδομένη κατὰ χῶρον.

Nearby is the beautiful-flowing spring where the lord,
the son of Zeus, killed the she-dragon with his strong bow,
a wild monster grown to great size, <u>who</u> did many evils
to men on earth—many to the men themselves
and many to thin-shanked sheep, since she was a bloody woe.
Whoever met <u>her</u>, his day of doom would carry him off,
until the far-worker lord Apollo shot her
with a strong arrow. She, wracked with harsh pains,
lay heaving great gasps, writhing about the place.

The pronoun τῇ in line 356 (ὃς <u>τῇ</u> γ' ἀντιάσειε, "whoever met <u>her</u>") has a much clearer reference when line 356 immediately follows line 304, as above, than when it follows line 355 (see n5.78 above for text). In the hymn as we have it the transition to the expansion and the transition back to the main story both seem unnatural. Cf. Allen and Sikes 1904 on lines 305–355: "The connexion of the δράκαινα with Typhaon is very forced"; and on line 355: "Nothing more is said of Typhaon. ...the poem returns to the dragoness, by a very abrupt transition (355–356)." Aloni 2006:60 mentions differences of diction that set the Typhaon episode apart from the rest of the Pythian hymn but are in line with the Delian hymn; he does not cite examples.

§5.23 If the Typhaon episode adds little to the story of the *Homeric Hymn to Apollo*, and does so at considerable length, why is it there?[81] The political situation following the First Sacred War suggests an answer. As already noted, the episode is more about Hera than Typhaon: Hera conceived and gave birth to the monster by herself to retaliate against Zeus, who, to Hera's great discredit, had given birth to Athena without Hera's help.[82] Hera's jealous reaction casts

81 The immediate inspiration for the Typhaon episode was probably another reference to the monster later in the hymn: exulting over the dying she-dragon Apollo says that not even Typhoeus or Chimaera will ward off death from her (*Homeric Hymn to Apollo* 367–369):

οὐδέ τί τοι θάνατόν γε δυσηλεγέ᾽ οὔτε Τυφωεὺς
ἀρκέσει οὔτε Χίμαιρα δυσώνυμος, ἀλλὰ σέ γ᾽ αὐτοῦ
πύσει γαῖα μέλαινα καὶ ἠλέκτωρ Ὑπερίων.

Neither Typhoeus nor accursed Chimaera will ward off
ruthless death, but the dark earth
and the sun, shining Hyperion, will rot you here.

Typhoeus and Typhaon are alternative names of the same monster. In the *Homeric Hymn to Apollo* Typhaon is the name used throughout the passage on the monster's birth, and this too sets the passage apart from the rest of the hymn (i.e. from Typhoeus in line 367; cf. Allen and Sikes 1904 ad loc.), but not decisively (Hesiod too uses both names: Typhaon in *Theogony* 306, Typhoeus in *Theogony* 821 and 869). As to why Chimaera and Typhoeus are mentioned together in lines 367–368, it is noteworthy that Chimaera is Typhaon's daughter by Echidna in Hesiod *Theogony* 306 and 319. If that tradition is relevant to *Hymn to Apollo* 367–368 (see Allen and Sikes on line 368 for the suggestion of Gemoll that "the δράκαινα may here be identified with Echidna, Chimaera being thus the daughter of Typhoeus and the δράκαινα") the poet of the Typhaon episode makes no use of it: in this episode Typhaon is presented as the she-dragon's foster child, not as her husband or as the father of her daughter. The expansion may well have been suggested by the mention of Typhoeus in the hymn, but the intent of the expansion has more to do with the goddess Hera than with the monster that she bears (see below in text).

82 There are other traditions of Hera's giving birth on her own to retaliate against Zeus for Athena's birth: in Hesiod *Theogony* 924–929 Hera bears Hephaistos for this reason:

αὐτὸς δ᾽ ἐκ κεφαλῆς γλαυκώπιδα γείνατ᾽ Ἀθήνην,
δεινὴν ἐγρεκύδοιμον ἀγέστρατον ἀτρυτώνην,
πότνιαν, ᾗ κέλαδοί τε ἅδον πόλεμοί τε μάχαι τε·
Ἥρη δ᾽ Ἥφαιστον κλυτὸν οὐ φιλότητι μιγεῖσα
γείνατο, καὶ ζαμένησε καὶ ἤρισεν ᾧ παρακοίτῃ,
ἐκ πάντων τέχνῃσι κεκασμένον Οὐρανιώνων.

From his head he gave birth by himself to grey-eyed Athena,
terrible, panic-awakening, army-leading Atrytone,
revered, whom din and wars and battles please;
but Hera, without mingling in love, gave birth to famous Hephaistos—
she was furious and strove to best her bed partner—
Hephaistos, surpassing all the gods in arts.

The pairing of Athena and Hephaistos in this passage suggests an Athenian context (see §3.79–§3.80 above on the myth of Erichthonios's birth); West 1966:397–399 attributes this

her in the dark role of a monster's mother; as such she is presented as a foil to the glorious birth of Athena, and the latter directly concerns one of the victors in the Sacred War, namely Athens. This passage of the *Homeric Hymn to Apollo* is among the first to attest the tradition for Athena's birth from Zeus's head;[83] although the myth did not originate in Athens, representations of it became popular there in the sixth century because of what I view as profound changes to the cult of Athena Polias in the time of Solon.[84] To the time of Solon also belongs the First Sacred War, with which Solon himself was associated. The speech in which Hera announces to Zeus and the other gods her intention to bear a child by herself because Zeus bore Athena by himself really amounts

---

passage, along with the rest of the end of the *Theogony* (lines 901–1022), to the poet of the Hesiodic *Catalogue of Women*, who in West's view was a sixth-century Athenian (West 1985:130–137, 169–171; Janko 1982:85–87, 221–225 agrees with West insofar as the end of the *Theogony* and the Hesiodic *Catalogue of Women* resemble each other linguistically, but he dates both works earlier and does not see an Athenian origin; cf. n2.219 above). A fragment of the *Catalogue of Women*, in which Hera bears Hephaistos without Zeus, is consistent with this argument (Hesiod fr. 343.1–3 MW; line 3 closely resembles *Theogony* 929). For the pairing of Athena and Hephaistos in Attic cult (and only there, with the possible exception of Lemnos) see West 1966:413 on *Theogony* 927. In contrast to the above passage of the *Theogony*, Homer makes Hephaistos the son of both Hera and Zeus (*Iliad* 1.578–579, 14.338, *Odyssey* 8.312). The *Homeric Hymn to Apollo* too seems to consider Hephaistos Zeus's son when Hera speaks of him, despite the phrase ὃν τέκον αὐτὴ in line 317 (for similar phrases in Hesiod *Theogony* 924, quoted above, and *Iliad* 5.880, see EN3.7); as commentators note, Hera "would have been even with Zeus without the birth of a monster" if she were Hephaistos's sole parent; hence ὃν τέκον αὐτή should not mean "whom I bore by myself," but "who is my very own son (and not another goddess's)" (Allen, Sikes, and Halliday 1936 ad loc.). Ares too may have been considered the son of Hera alone, without any fathering by Zeus (cf. Ovid *Fasti* 5.229–258, noted by West 1966 on *Theogony* 922).

83 The motif of Athena's birth from Zeus's head appears immediately after the first mention of Typhaon's birth (*Homeric Hymn to Apollo* 307–310):

ὅν ποτ' ἄρ' Ἥρη ἔτικτε χολωσαμένη Διὶ πατρὶ
ἡνίκ' ἄρα Κρονίδης ἐρικυδέα γείνατ' Ἀθήνην
ἐν κορυφῇ· ἡ δ' αἶψα χολώσατο πότνια Ἥρη
ἠδὲ καὶ ἀγρομένοισι μετ' ἀθανάτοισιν ἔειπε....

Whom Hera once bore, being angry with father Zeus
because the son of Kronos bore glorious Athena
in his head; revered Hera suddenly became angry
and spoke among the assembled gods....

The motif of Athena's birth from Zeus's head also appears in Hesiod *Theogony* 924 (see n5.82 above) and *Homeric Hymn* 28.5, both of which, like this passage of the *Homeric Hymn to Apollo*, seem to have a sixth-century Athenian origin (for *Homeric Hymn* 28, see n3.90 above).

84 See above n3.90 and n3.108 (end) and EN3.7.

to glorification of Athena and of Athens.[85] There may be a related point when Hera, having been excluded by Zeus from the birth of Athena, sets out to give birth to a creature of equal prominence among the gods; here too Athena is the standard of comparison.[86] Cities devoted to Hera's cult can have taken

85 Note in particular lines 311–315:

> κέκλυτέ μευ πάντες τε θεοὶ πᾶσαί τε θέαιναι,
> ὡς ἔμ᾽ ἀτιμάζειν ἄρχει νεφεληγερέτα Ζεὺς
> πρῶτος, ἐπεί μ᾽ ἄλοχον ποιήσατο κέδν᾽ εἰδυῖαν·
> καὶ νῦν νόσφιν ἐμεῖο τέκε γλαυκῶπιν <u>Ἀθήνην</u>,
> <u>ἣ πᾶσιν μακάρεσσι μεταπρέπει ἀθανάτοισιν.</u>

> Hear me, all you gods and all you goddesses,
> how the cloud-gatherer Zeus was the first to dishonor me
> after he made me his devoted wife;
> now without me he has borne grey-eyed <u>Athena</u>,
> <u>who stands out among all the blessed gods.</u>

Hera says that Zeus's action has brought her dishonor, but the other side of this is the honor that would have been hers as Athena's mother. This is the point of the last line above, and it can be felt again in the following lines, where Hera addresses Zeus directly (lines 322–325):

> σχέτλιε ποικιλομῆτα τί νῦν μητίσεαι ἄλλο;
> πῶς ἔτλης οἶος τεκέειν γλαυκῶπιδ᾽ Ἀθήνην;
> οὐκ ἂν ἐγὼ τεκόμην; καὶ σὴ κεκλημένη ἔμπης
> ἦα ῥ᾽ ἐν ἀθανάτοισιν οἳ οὐρανὸν εὐρὺν ἔχουσι.

> Hard-hearted wily-minded one, what else will you devise?
> How have you dared to bear grey-eyed Athena alone?
> Could I not have borne her? At any rate I was called yours
> among the immortals who inhabit the wide sky.

These lines reflect as positively on Athena as they do negatively on Hera.

86 Note that Hera uses a similar phrase to describe the status of Athena among the gods (ἣ πᾶσιν μακάρεσσι μεταπρέπει ἀθανάτοισιν, "who stands out among all the blessed gods," line 315) and the status that she intends for her own offspring (lines 326–327):

> καὶ νῦν μέν τοι ἐγὼ τεχνήσομαι ὥς κε γένηται
> παῖς ἐμὸς <u>ὅς κε θεοῖσι μεταπρέποι ἀθανάτοισιν.</u>

> And now I will contrive that a son of mine
> may be born <u>who might stand out among all the blessed gods.</u>

Hephaistos, whom Hera bore with Zeus (see n5.82 above), lacked status among the gods, as Hera complains (lines 316–317). By the time of this passage of the *Homeric Hymn to Apollo* Hephaistos had a part in Athenian cult, although his rank was well below that of Athena (see §3.79–§3.80 above, on the arrival of Hephaistos's cult in Athens c. 600 BC, and on Athena's rejection of Hephaistos as a lover in the myth of Erichthonios's birth). Hera, as she herself says, did her best to destroy Hephaistos by throwing him into the sea, and she gives Thetis no thanks for having saved him (lines 318–321). This motif further alienates Hera from the standpoint of Athenian cult, in which Hephaistos was honored, albeit

no pride in the representation of the goddess as the mother of a monster. In mainland Greece Hera's most important cult was at Argos, and Cleisthenes of Sikyon, another victor in the First Sacred War, was a bitter enemy of Argos. Is not the Hera of the *Homeric Hymn to Apollo* the Argive goddess as viewed from Sikyon, Athens' ally in the Sacred War? The expansion of the *Homeric Hymn to Apollo*, in its positive attitude toward Athena and its negative attitude toward Hera, will thus reflect the viewpoints of these two allies in the Sacred War.[87]

§5.24 We are not primarily concerned with the *Homeric Hymn to Apollo* as it reflects the interests of the victors in the First Sacred War, but with an earlier version of the hymn, before the two expansions just considered were composed.[88] This earlier version must have come into existence before the First Sacred War, but not long before it, if the hymn, as argued above, reflects a Spartan point of view. The Spartans drove the Pylians from Messenia at the end of the Second Messenian War.[89] The dates of the Second Messenian War are a matter of debate, but for the end of the war there is a valuable piece of evidence: Epameinondas, when he defeated the Spartans at Leuctra in 371 BC, is reported to have said that he gave the Messenians back their freedom after 230 years.[90] In line with this figure the end of the Second Messenian War, and the departure of the Pylians from Messenia, can be firmly dated to c. 600 BC.

---

humbly. Hera's name is then totally blackened when she proceeds in her speech from her attempted murder of Hephaistos to her deliberate plan to give birth to a man-destroying monster.

87 The hymn's negative attitude toward Hera has precedents in the Homeric poems (e.g. *Iliad* 4.35–36, where Zeus accuses Hera of wanting to eat the Trojans raw, or *Iliad* 4.51–54, where Hera offers the destruction of three of her favorite cities, including Argos, in exchange for Troy); but the hymn carries Hera's resentfulness and vengefulness to an extreme. Sikyon had close ties especially with the Athenian family of the Alcmaeonids: Megacles, the son of Alcmaeon (the Athenian commander in the First Sacred War; Plutarch *Solon* 11.2, citing records of Delphi), won the hand of Cleisthenes' daughter Agariste in a celebrated marriage contest at Sikyon (Herodotus 6.130). The Alcmaeonids were politically aligned with Solon (cf. Forrest 1956:40 and 50), the instigator of the First Sacred War (Plutarch *Solon* 11.1, citing Aristotle; Plutarch discounts the tradition that Solon actually led the Athenians in the war; Davies 1994:201 suggests that Solon's role in the war was invented in the late fifth century; cf. also Fowler 1998:14n33). The Alcmaeonids had a personal stake in the Sacred War if they had been put under a curse by Delphi for the execution of the Cylonian conspirators; they maintained their influence with the new regime at Delphi later in the sixth century, when they lavishly rebuilt the temple of Apollo in return for Delphi's support against the Peisistratids (Herodotus 5.62.2–63.1).

88 For the likelihood of a third short expansion of the hymn, also made after the First Sacred War, see §5.33 and §5.35–§5.36 below.

89 See §5.18 and n5.64 above.

90 Plutarch *Sayings of Kings and Commanders* 194b. The figure 230 is confirmed by Aelian *Varia Historia* 13.42.

Soon after the end of the Second Messenian War, perhaps immediately after it, the earlier version of the *Hymn to Apollo* would have been composed.[91]

§5.25 As a parallel to the *Homeric Hymn to Apollo*, if it was indeed a Spartan poem, I suggest a poem of Tyrtaeus, the Spartan poet who, more than any other figure, was identified with the Second Messenian War.[92] I do not

91 Recent scholarship has lowered the dates for both the First and the Second Messenian War: the First Messenian War, which was once dated to the eighth century BC, has been redated to 700/690–680/670 BC; the Second Messenian War, which was once thought to have erupted after Sparta's loss to Argos at Hysiai in 669 BC, has been redated to 640/630–600 BC (see Meier *DNP* 'Messenische Kriege,' citing Parker 1991 and Meier 1998:91–99). Earlier dates for both wars are found in e.g. Huxley 1962; Huxley nevertheless dates the end of the second war and the departure of the Pylians from Messenia to c. 600 BC, and in this he should be followed (Huxley 1962:59). Pausanias 3.3.4 dates the Messenian revolt (Second Messenian War) to the reign of the Spartan king Anaxander and says that the coastal towns in Messenia held out and remained free after the other Messenians were expelled or enslaved by the Spartans: ἐπὶ δὲ Ἀναξάνδρου τοῦ Εὐρυκράτους—τὸ γὰρ χρεών ἤδη Μεσσηνίους ἤλαυνεν ἐκτὸς Πελοποννήσου πάσης—ἀφίστανται Λακεδαιμονίων οἱ Μεσσήνιοι. καὶ χρόνον μὲν ἀντέσχον πολεμοῦντες· ὑπόσπονδοι δὲ ὡς ἐκρατήθησαν ἀπῄεσαν ἐκ Πελοποννήσου, τὸ δὲ αὐτῶν ἐγκαταλειφθὲν τῇ γῇ Λακεδαιμονίων ἐγένοντο οἰκέται πλὴν οἱ τὰ ἐπὶ τῇ θαλάσσῃ πολίσματα ἔχοντες, "In the time of Anaxander the son of Eurykrates—for fate was already driving the Messenians from all of the Peloponnesus—the Messenians revolted from the Spartans. They held out fighting for a time, and when they were defeated they left the Peloponnesus under a truce; those left in the country became the Spartans' slaves, except for those with cities on the sea." Anaxander, as Huxley 1962:59 convincingly argues, belongs to the second half of the seventh century (for Anaxander cf. also Pausanias 3.14.4); once the rest of Messenia was subdued, the coastal towns of Pylos and Methone were presumably quickly dealt with at the war's end (cf. n5.69 above).

92 Most of what later historians knew about the Second Messenian War came from the poetry of Tyrtaeus. Tyrtaeus's date depends on the date of the Second Messenian War: formerly he was associated with a supposed first phase of the war following the Battle of Hysiai in 669 BC (so Huxley1962:57, 59; cf. n5.91 above); now that such a first phase of the war is not accepted, Tyrtaeus's war is equated with Anaxander's war in the second half of the seventh century (see n5.91 above). Lower dates for the Second Messenian War and Tyrtaeus entail a lower date for the First Messenian War, which Tyrtaeus says took place in the time of "our fathers' fathers" (Tyrtaeus fr. 5.6 West); in the same fragment he says that the first war was fought under the Spartan king Theopompos and lasted for twenty years (Tyrtaeus fr. 5 West):

ἡμετέρῳ βασιλῆϊ, θεοῖσι φίλῳ Θεοπόμπῳ,
    ὃν διὰ Μεσσήνην εἵλομεν εὐρύχορον,
Μεσσήνην ἀγαθὸν μὲν ἀροῦν, ἀγαθὸν δὲ φυτεύειν·
    ἀμφ' αὐτὴν δ' ἐμάχοντ' ἐννέα καὶ δέκ' ἔτη
νωλεμέως αἰεὶ ταλασίφρονα θυμὸν ἔχοντες
    αἰχμηταὶ πατέρων ἡμετέρων πατέρες·
εἰκοστῷ δ' οἱ μὲν κατὰ πίονα ἔργα λιπόντες
    φεῦγον Ἰθωμαίων ἐκ μεγάλων ὀρέων.

...to our king, Theopompos, dear to the gods,
    through whom we took wide Messene,

have in mind Tyrtaeus's war poems, in which Tyrtaeus exhorts the Spartans to maintain their steadfast courage, but his *Eunomia*, "Good Order," in which he invokes the authority of Delphi for the Great Rhetra, the Spartans' constitution. Plutarch has preserved an archaic prose version of this constitution, which was presumably what the Spartan assembly once enacted. Tyrtaeus gives a poetic version of the constitution, which he says was brought back from Delphi.[93] The Great Rhetra defined the political roles of the kings and elders on the one hand and of the people on the other hand. The poetic version of Tyrtaeus, which, it has been suggested, may contain the actual words of the Delphic oracle in the last four hexameter lines, interspersed with Tyrtaeus's own additions in the five pentameter lines, is as follows (Tyrtaeus fr. 4 West):

Φοίβου ἀκούσαντες Πυθωνόθεν οἴκαδ' ἔνεικαν
μαντείας τε θεοῦ καὶ τελέεντ' ἔπεα·
ἄρχειν μὲν βουλῆς θεοτιμήτους βασιλῆας,
οἷσι μέλει Σπάρτης ἱμερόεσσα πόλις,
πρεσβυγενέας τε γέροντας· ἔπειτα δὲ δημότας ἄνδρας
εὐθείαις ῥήτραις ἀνταπαμειβομένους
μυθεῖσθαί τε τὰ καλὰ καὶ ἔρδειν πάντα δίκαια,
μηδέ τι βουλεύειν τῇδε πόλει ‹σκολιόν›·
δήμου τε πλήθει νίκην καὶ κάρτος ἔπεσθαι.
Φοῖβος γὰρ περὶ τῶν ὧδ' ἀνέφηνε πόλει.

After listening to Phoebus they brought home from Pytho
the god's oracles and sure predictions.

Messene good for plowing and good for planting;
they fought for it for nineteen years
without ever ceasing, with patient hearts,
those spearmen, our fathers' fathers;
in the twentieth year they left their rich lands
and fled from the great mountain Ithome.

The dates now given for the First Messenian War (see n5. 91 above) are in line with the content of this fragment: if Tyrtaeus himself lived in the latter part of the seventh century a twenty-year war would have been waged in the first quarter of the seventh century by the generation of Tyrtaeus's grandfather.

93 The fragment (Tyrtaeus fr. 4 West) does not say who brought the oracle back from Delphi; the subject of οἴκαδ' ἔνεικαν, "[they] brought home," in the fragment's first line (see below in text) must have occurred in a preceding line. Cf. n5.94 below.

Those to initiate counsel are the divinely honored kings
in whose care is Sparta's lovely city,
and the aged elders; and then the men of the people,
responding with straight utterances,
are to speak fair words and act justly in everything,
and not give the city <crooked> counsel.
Victory and power are to accompany the mass of the people.
For such was Phoebus' revelation about these things to the city.[94]

As in the *Homeric Hymn to Apollo*, where Delphi's higher authority is claimed for a partisan view of political geography, Tyrtaeus here attributes to Delphi something controversial. This, at least, is what Plutarch, following Aristotle, says.[95] According to Plutarch the Great Rhetra, as originally brought back from Delphi, gave final authority to the people, but this authority was subsequently taken away from them by an additional clause, or rider. The additional clause said that the people had final authority only if they made no "crooked" (*skoliá*) pronouncement in response to initiatives of the kings and elders; the people's will, in other words, could effectively be set aside.[96] But what Plutarch regards as two separate items, the original Rhetra and a

94 The translation follows that of Gerber 1999:41, modified to distinguish the hexameters from the pentameters. The idea that Tyrtaeus repeats the hexameters of Delphi (the four hexameters underlined above) and adds his own pentameters as a kind of commentary was suggested by Bergk 1882:11 and is accepted by West 1970a:151, 1974:184–185. The final two couplets of the fragment are found only in Diodorus 7.12.6, one of the fragment's two sources; the other source, Plutarch *Lycurgus* 6.5, while it lacks the final two couplets, has what seems to be the older version of the first couplet (that given in West's text above), in which a nameless group brings the oracle home from Delphi; most likely meant are the Spartan *Púthioi*, whose function was to receive and report Delphi's pronouncements (see Herodotus 6.57.2 and Xenophon *Constitution of the Lacedaemonians* 15.5; Cartledge 1978:26, 30 suggests that the *Púthioi* go back to the eighth century BC; cf. Cartledge 2002:111). Diodorus's version of the first couplet, on the other hand, allows Lycurgus to be the oracle's recipient (as Diodorus says he was). The different versions are discussed in EN5.13.

95 See Van Wees 1999:21 for the likelihood that Plutarch's entire discussion goes back to Aristotle's *Spartan Constitution* (Plutarch *Lycurgus* 6.2 cites Aristotle for the interpretation of a pair of topographical references in the Great Rhetra).

96 Plutarch *Lycurgus* 6.4 (text as at West, Tyrtaeus fr. 4): ὕστερον μέντοι τῶν πολλῶν ἀφαιρέσει καὶ προσθέσει τὰς γνώμας διαστρεφόντων καὶ παραβιαζομένων, Πολύδωρος καὶ Θεόπομπος οἱ βασιλεῖς τάδε τῇ ῥήτρᾳ παρενέγραψαν· "αἰ δὲ σκολιὰν ὁ δᾶμος ἔροιτο, τοὺς πρεσβυγενέας καὶ ἀρχαγέτας ἀποστατῆρας εἶμεν," "Later, however, when the people distorted and did violence to motions by removing and adding things, the kings Polydoros and Theopompos inserted the following into the Rhetra: 'If the people should say something crooked, the elders and the kings will dissolve the assembly' " (with the adjective σκολιάν, "crooked," the noun ῥήτραν, "pronouncement," is understood; for the phrase ἀποστατῆρας εἶμεν see LSJ s.v. ἀποστατήρ); cf. Huxley 1962:44.

subsequent rider, Tyrtaeus presents as a single oracle emanating from Apollo himself: the fragment's final hexameter (line 9), which proclaims the decisive authority (νίκην καὶ κάρτος) of the people, represents the purpose of the original Rhetra; the rider, on the other hand, has been woven into the two preceding pentameters (lines 6 and 8), and here the people respond to initiatives "with *straight* pronouncements" (εὐθείαις ῥήτραις, line 6) and are forbidden to counsel anything *"crooked"* (σκολιόν, line 8). The word σκολιόν has been restored in line 8, which is corrupt; the restoration corresponds to the actual wording of the rider in Plutarch (σκολιάν), and in my view it is probably correct, but it is not certain.[97] It is also uncertain whether Aristotle, when he made a distinction between the original Rhetra and a later rider, reported a genuine tradition or arrived at this conclusion on his own; some would prefer to see the rider as part of the Rhetra from the start, as in Tyrtaeus.[98] There are also historical and chronological uncertainties pertaining to the Rhetra and the rider when they are regarded as separate.[99]

97 In Diodorus, the only source for the last four lines of the poem, line 8 is transmitted as the following unmetrical phrase: μηδέ τι ἐπιβουλεύειν τῇδε πόλει. Restoration of the word σκολιόν at the end of line 8 (and deletion of the prefix ἐπι- in ἐπιβουλεύειν) was first proposed by Bach in his 1831 edition of Callinus, Tyrtaeus, and Asius; cf. Van Wees 1999:30n31, who prefers a different emendation, and proposes a different interpretation of the fragment as a whole, having nothing to do with the Great Rhetra. Van Wees's interpretation, which is a reminder of how uncertain the whole matter of the Great Rhetra is, is discussed in EN5.14.

98 Wade-Gery, who believes that the two parts of the Rhetra were enacted together, thinks that Aristotle invented the theory of a separate rider (Wade-Gery 1944:115 [= 1958:67–68]); so also Van Wees 1999:21; Huxley, on the other hand, believes that the rider was separate (see below in text). Among German scholars Kiechle 1963:162–176 argues that there was a separate "addition" ("Zusatz") to the Rhetra, and Bringmann 1975 holds the opposite view. For further bibliography see Van Wees 1999:33n60 and 35n70.

99 Plutarch *Lycurgus* 6, following Aristotle, says that Lycurgus received the original Rhetra from the Delphic oracle, and that the rider was added later by the two Spartan kings, Theopompos and Polydoros (cf. n5.95 and n5.96 above). But if the rider was in fact added in Tyrtaeus's time, Theopompos and Polydoros were perhaps responsible for the original Rhetra itself. The political reform fits the character of the younger king, Polydoros, who was known to have been well disposed toward the people (cf. Huxley 1962:40–41); we do not know the attitude toward political reform of the older king, Theopompos, but he was perhaps less favorable to it (cf. Huxley 1962:51). How to account for Aristotle's version of events is a question. Aristotle presumably attributed the original Rhetra to Lycurgus, as in Plutarch; if so, he may have followed the variant of the first two lines of Tyrtaeus fr. 4 found in Diodorus rather than the version found in Plutarch (cf. EN5.13 to n5.94 above). As for the two kings, whose names were separated from each other in the king lists by two generations, Aristotle presumably linked them because he found them linked in Tyrtaeus (cf. Huxley 1962:20–21 and 103nn73 and 75). As seen, Tyrtaeus makes the rider part of the original Rhetra; if Tyrtaeus linked the kings' names in the context of the original Rhetra, Aristotle may have inferred that the two kings added the rider (cf. Huxley 1962:51).

Still I think it is more likely that Aristotle, in separating the rider from the Rhetra, did not invent this interpretation, but relied on a tradition.[100] I also think that the interpretation of Tyrtaeus fr. 4 as an actual hexameter oracle delivered to kings Theopompos and Polydoros, to which Tyrtaeus added his own pentameters incorporating the substance of the later rider as if it too were part of the oracle, deserves serious consideration. If this is what in fact took place, then Huxley has a point when he describes Tyrtaeus, insofar as his representation of the Great Rhetra is concerned, as "an able propagandist and a successful exponent of the despicable craft of rewriting the past";[101] presumably the urgency of the Messenian revolt had something to do with Tyrtaeus's constitutional sleight of hand, and also prevented any real opposition to it.[102]

§5.26 Rewriting the past is also the issue in the *Homeric Hymn to Apollo*, insofar as the hymn erases the Homeric city of Pylos from Messenia in mythic times to match what had happened only recently in historical time. The

---

100 I do not see what theoretical consideration would have prompted Aristotle to propose, as an actual historical development, a change from an originally democratic constitution to an aristocratic abridgement of this constitution if such a change was not in fact attested. It would seem more intuitive to proceed in the opposite direction, as Wade-Gery and others have in fact done, i.e., to disbelieve the tradition for an early democratic constitution, and to make what was reportedly a later aristocratic reaction into part of the original arrangement instead. In any case there is a real historical plausibility to an early democratic constitution in Sparta if, as seems to have been the case, it was brought to Sparta from Crete, where a similar development is detectable (Huxley 1962:46–47; cf. Raaflaub and Wallace 2007:23–24, 36–41). The tradition that the constitution came from Delphi does not conflict with such a Cretan origin, for the priesthood of Apollo at Delphi also had a Cretan origin. Van Wees 1999:14–21, believing that the idea of a separate rider to the Rhetra began with Aristotle, suggests how this idea may have suggested itself: in line with his argument that Tyrtaeus's *Eunomia* in reality had nothing to do with the Great Rhetra, Van Wees argues that the Spartan king Pausanias, exiled in 395 BC, first connected the two in his tract *Against the Laws of Lycurgus* (1999:17), and that Aristotle, following Pausanias, drew a further conclusion based on the text of the *Eunomia* (1999:21).

101 Huxley 1962:55; cf. Tarditi 1983:7, who calls Tyrtaeus "un uomo di parte" with respect to the Spartan aristocracy, i.e. biased in its favor.

102 The rider may have been prompted not only by the Messenian War, but also by the people's simultaneous demand for land redistribution. The latter was a subject of Tyrtaeus's *Eunomia* according to Aristotle *Politics* 1306b36–1307a2 (Tyrtaeus fr. 1 West), in a discussion of conditions under which factions arise in aristocracies: ἔτι ὅταν οἱ μὲν ἀπορῶσι λίαν οἱ δ' εὐπορῶσιν (καὶ μάλιστα ἐν τοῖς πολέμοις τοῦτο γίνεται· συνέβη δὲ καὶ τοῦτο ἐν Λακεδαίμονι ὑπὸ τὸν Μεσηνιακὸν πόλεμον· δῆλον δὲ [καὶ] τοῦτο ἐκ τῆς Τυρταίου ποιήσεως τῆς καλουμένης Εὐνομίας· θλιβόμενοι γάρ τινες διὰ τὸν πόλεμον ἠξίουν ἀνάδαστον ποιεῖν τὴν χώραν), "Also whenever some are excessively badly off and some are well off (this happens most often in wars; it also happened in Sparta at the time of the Messenian War; this is clear from the poem of Tyrtaeus called the *Eunomia*; for some, distressed by the war, proposed to redistribute the land").

parallel with the *Eunomia* of Tyrtaeus may be short of conclusive, but it is a basis for comparison nonetheless. The context for the hymn, however, would have been quite different from the context for the *Eunomia* of Tyrtaeus. Like other Homeric hymns, the *Homeric Hymn to Apollo* must have been composed as a *prooímion* to introduce a performance of Homeric poetry. Such *prooímia* were composed in Sparta as they were elsewhere, the practice having been introduced there by Terpander of Lesbos in the first half of the seventh century,[103] and Terpander is known to have taught his musical craft to others in Sparta as well.[104] Would Tyrtaeus, after the apparent success of his elegies in the Second Messenian War, have turned to a different kind of poetry later in life, once the war had been won? His poetry would still have served Sparta's interests, but now in a more international setting, as opposed to the domestic purpose of his elegies. We know that performances of Homeric poetry took place at Spartan festivals; Terpander gave performances of Homeric poetry, and of his own *prooímia*, in poetic contests.[105] At a festival outsiders, especially

---

103 Terpander was said to have won the first poetic competition at the festival of the Karneia, the first celebration of which was dated between 676 and 673 BC; the sources of this information are Hellanicus (*FGrHist* 4 F 85) and Sosibius (*FGrHist* 595 F 3), both cited by Athenaeus 14.635e (= Gostoli 1990 T 1). The sources do not specifically say that Terpander introduced the practice of composing *prooímia* at Sparta, but this seems to be implied. "Plutarch" *On Music* is the source for Terpander's *prooímia* as preludes to Homeric performances: most explicit is *On Music* 6.1133c (= Gostoli T 34), which says that early citharodic performers, "after discharging their duty to the gods, which they did as they pleased, passed at once to the poetry of Homer and the rest. This can be seen in Terpander's preludes (*prooímia*)"; note also *On Music* 3.1132c (= Gostoli T 27): according to Heraclides Ponticus, Terpander set his own epic verses (ἔπη) and those of Homer to music and performed them in poetic contests; and *On Music* 4.1132d (= Gostoli T 32): Terpander composed preludes (*prooímia*) which were sung to the cithara in epic verses (ἐν ἔπεσιν). A fragment of Terpander (Page *PMG* 697 = Gostoli F 2) appears to be the start of a *prooímion* to Apollo; see Gostoli 1990:129 for the question of whether the text of this fragment should be emended to yield a line of hexameter. In contrast to Homeric rhapsodes, Terpander is said to have set his own and Homer's verses to music (*On Music* 3.1132c and 4.1132d, cited above). In the history of Homeric performance Terpander is unusual in having performed epic to music; the rhapsodes, whose performances were not sung (this characteristic defines *rhapsōidía* according to Ford 1988), represent the norm. For the relationship of *kitharōidía* to *rhapsōidía* in the performance of epic, cf. Ford 1988:303n25; for a more comprehensive treatment, see Power 2010.

104 "Plutarch" *On Music* 9.1134b (= Gostoli 1990 T 18): ἡ μὲν οὖν πρώτη κατάστασις τῶν περὶ τὴν μουσικὴν ἐν τῇ Σπάρτῃ, Τερπάνδρου καταστήσαντος, γεγένηται, "The first institution for musicians, set up by Terpander, came into being in Sparta" ("La prima scuola musicale è nata a Sparta per opera di Terpandro" [Gostoli]).

105 See n5.103 above. "Plutarch" *On Music* 9.1134b, which attributes the first "institution (school) of musicians" (κατάστασις τῶν περὶ τὴν μουσικήν) to Terpander in Sparta (n5.104 above), associates the second such κατάστασις with the Gymnopaidiai at Sparta among other festivals.

other Peloponnesians, would be present, and this offered an opportunity, if not to rewrite the past, at least to present the Spartan point of view. In such a setting a performance of the *Homeric Hymn to Apollo*, as *prooímion*, could have been associated with *Odyssey* 15 as part of the Homeric performance that followed. This would have been an ideal occasion to present the corrected version of Telemachus's voyage home from Pylos, the true course of which had international significance c. 600 BC.[106]

§5.27 I do not want to push the idea of Tyrtaeus as poet of the *Homeric Hymn to Apollo* too hard.[107] I prefer to fall back on the more general idea that the *Homeric Hymn to Apollo* reflects a Spartan agenda. Victors in the Second Messenian War, the Spartans did not wish to be known as having driven Nestor's descendants from their ancestral homeland at the war's end. For this reason they called the abandoned place Koryphasion, not Pylos. The Homeric poems were reinterpreted to show that Nestor's kingdom lay not in Messenia, but in Elis; this was accomplished with the change of a single word in the *Odyssey*, from *Pheás* to *Pherás*, and this change was defended. The *Homeric Hymn to Apollo* presents a complete defense of the change, and it cunningly implies that Apollo himself endorsed the new interpretation of Telemachus's voyage: Apollo, in the form of a dolphin, was on board when the ship sailed past the Peloponnesus, town by town. When the ship passes Pylos north of the Alpheios River, blame for the expulsion of Nestor's descendants shifts

106 The three main festivals at Sparta, the Karneia, the Hyakinthia, and the Gymnopaidiai, were all dedicated to Apollo. If Homeric poetry was performed at these festivals (there is evidence only for the Karneia, cf. n5.103 above; for all three as musical festivals in general the evidence is in Herington 1985:7, 25, 162, 165–166), the performances were presumably preceded by a hymn to Apollo, the festival's god in each case; for this reason, as well as others, the *Homeric Hymn to Apollo* seems very much at home in Sparta. A perusal of Robert Parker's essay called "Spartan Religion" (Parker 1988) gives an idea of Apollo's pre-eminent place at Sparta: "The god who dominated Spartan festivals was lucid, disciplined Apollo" (p. 151); it was Apollo, "above all," who dominated Spartan religion (p. 145); the colossal Archaic statue of Apollo at Amyklai, 45 feet high, was "doubtless the most sacred object in all Laconia" (p. 146); the Spartan kings had a "special relationship with Apollo of Delphi" (p. 143); "Delphic Apollo was closely associated with the kings. The *Púthioi*, permanent officials whose job it was to consult Delphi on public business—a post known only from Sparta—were royal appointees and shared the kings' tent" (p. 154); the Spartans "loved oracles, more perhaps than did the citizens of any other Greek state, and granted them an unusual importance in political debate. Had not their own constitution been prescribed by Apollo of Delphi himself?" (p. 154).

107 I have not systematically compared the language of Tyrtaeus with the language of the Pythian *Hymn to Apollo*, but I see no great difference between them: both use essentially Homeric diction. In EN5.15 a few points of comparison in the language of the two are considered; a different proposal concerning the Pythian hymn, namely that its language is Hesiodic (Martin 2000a), is also discussed.

from the Spartans, and lands, subtly but squarely, on the Eleians instead. In the mythic time of Apollo's voyage around the Peloponnesus with his future priests, the Eleians had not yet descended to their historical homeland, but lived in what was later western Achaea. This implies something about the fate of the Pylians. By the time the *Homeric Hymn to Apollo* was composed the Eleians had long occupied their historical homeland, which included (it is implied) what once was Pylos. Where had the Pylians gone? Ask the Eleians. Who better, after all, to take the blame for the final extinction of Pylos than Pylos's ancient enemy in the Homeric poems?[108]

§5.28 The *Homeric Hymn to Apollo* does not identify itself overtly with Sparta or any city; the sole focus of the hymn is Delphi, which stands above all at the center of the hymn's world. There Apollo establishes an oracle for men who will ever after bring him sacrifices, as many as inhabit the fertile Peloponnesus and Europe and the sea-girt islands; so Apollo proclaims when he reaches his destination (*Homeric Hymn to Apollo* 287–293):

> ἐνθάδε δὴ φρονέω τεύξειν περικαλλέα νηὸν
> ἔμμεναι ἀνθρώποις χρηστήριον οἵ τέ μοι αἰεὶ
> ἐνθάδ' ἀγινήσουσι τεληέσσας ἑκατόμβας,
> ἠμὲν <u>ὅσοι Πελοπόννησον πίειραν ἔχουσιν,</u>
> <u>ἠδ' ὅσοι Εὐρώπην τε καὶ ἀμφιρύτους κατὰ νήσους,</u>
> χρησόμενοι· τοῖσιν δ' ἄρ' ἐγὼ νημερτέα βουλὴν
> πᾶσι θεμιστεύοιμι χρέων ἐνὶ πίονι νηῷ.

> Here I plan to build a beautiful temple
> to be an oracle for men who will forever
> drive perfect hecatombs here for me,
> <u>all the men that inhabit the fertile Peloponnesus</u>
> <u>and Europe and the sea-girt islands</u>
> when they seek oracles; to all of them
> I would give unerring counsel when I prophesy in my rich
>   temple.

---

108 It is possible that the Spartans also had a particular score to settle with Elis at the end of the Second Messenian War in that, according to Strabo 8.4.10 and Pausanias 4.15.7, the Eleians were allies of the Messenians in that war; this evidence, however, is regarded with skepticism. The issue is discussed in EN5.16.

Delphi is the center,[109] and among those who will consult Apollo's oracle at Delphi the Peloponnesians (ὅσοι Πελοπόννησον πίειραν ἔχουσιν) have pride of place, as before the First Sacred War they in fact did;[110] Europe (the northern Greek mainland) and the islands fill out Delphi's world. The hymn betrays no obvious Spartan bias, for this would reveal its hidden purpose. The "Laconian land" is duly recognized in the hymn, but without drawing attention to itself; it is represented by Cape Malea and Cape Tainaron, and by a cult to Helios on Cape Tainaron, about which nothing else is known.[111] It is not the

109 Delphi has only one challenger as the center in the hymn, namely the spring of Telphousa in Boeotia: Apollo first proposes to establish his oracle at Telphousa, but the nymph Telphousa persuades him to go to Delphi instead. Feeling himself tricked by Telphousa Apollo later returns from Delphi and founds a second oracle, but that is precisely the point: Telphousa is Apollo's second oracle, not his first. Delphi is supreme. The speech that Apollo gives at Delphi, announcing his intention to build an oracle there, is the same speech that he gave at Telphousa before being persuaded to move on (lines 247–253): there are minor differences at the beginning of the speech, but the lines about the Peloponnesus, Europe, and the islands are the same.

110 Corinth and Sparta had the closest relationship with the oracle: Delphi backed Corinth's colonizing efforts (Forrest 1956:51, 1982:309), and it "approved if it did not originate the Lykurgan reforms" in Sparta (Forrest 1956:52). Parke and Wormell 1956, vol. 1, 82–98 (Ch. 2: "The Oracle and Sparta in Early Times") emphasize the difficulty of determining the real extent of Sparta's relationship with Delphi: "Of all the states of the Greek mainland Sparta was the one which was regarded by later generations as the most closely linked with Delphi in its early development. There is a certain amount of original and genuine evidence on the subject, but this advantage is somewhat offset by the obscurity of the whole matter, which results partly from the mystification about their past practised by the Spartans, partly from the misguided efforts of other Greeks to illuminate the subject by conjectures and inventions" (p. 83). Forrest 1982:310–311 sees a temporary decline in Sparta's relationship with Delphi in the years following c. 670 BC.

111 The Cretans wish to disembark at Tainaron to see whether the dolphin will stay on board, but Apollo prevents them (*Homeric Hymn to Apollo* 409–415):

> πρῶτον δὲ παρημείβοντο Μάλειαν,
> πὰρ δὲ Λακωνίδα γαῖαν ἁλιστέφανον πτολίεθρον
> ἷξον καὶ χῶρον τερψιμβρότου Ἠελίοιο
> Ταίναρον, ἔνθα τε μῆλα βαθύτριχα βόσκεται αἰεὶ
> Ἠελίοιο ἄνακτος, ἔχει δ' ἐπιτερπέα χῶρον.
> οἱ μὲν ἄρ' ἔνθ' ἔθελον νῆα σχεῖν ἠδ' ἀποβάντες
> φράσσασθαι μέγα θαῦμα καὶ ὀφθαλμοῖσιν ἰδέσθαι....

> First they passed Maleia,
> then, passing by the Laconian land, a sea-girt citadel,
> they came to the land of mortal-delighting Helios,
> Tainaron, where the deep-fleeced sheep of lord Helios
> graze forever and have a delightful land.
> They wished to stop the ship and disembark
> to mark the great wonder and see with their eyes....

inland city of Sparta itself that receives attention, but an apparently old cult on the outer limits of Spartan territory. This of course is far more attention than is paid to Messenia, which is not even mentioned in the hymn, but is bypassed as if it did not exist: as far as the hymn is concerned Messenia was a deserted, empty place then as now.

§5.29 We have so far looked only at the southern half of the world centered on Delphi in the hymn, the half marked out by the voyage of Apollo and his priests. The northern half of this world is marked out by Apollo alone when he goes in search of a site for his oracle. As already said, the arc of Apollo's initial journey southward is counterbalanced by the arc of the Cretans' voyage northward, both ending in Delphi; the overall scheme is like two halves of a circle that connect at one point only. We must now examine the hymn's northern geography to see how it corresponds to its southern geography. This will provide a check on conclusions already reached for the Cretans' voyage around the Peloponnesus, especially the importance of the location of Pylos in the interpretation of the hymn as a whole.

§5.30 The hymn's northern geography is in general very good. Between Olympus and Krisa seventeen tribes and places are named: all are correctly located and put in the proper order with two apparent exceptions, which are easily explained, and one real exception, which requires a different explanation altogether. It is the exceptions, both apparent and real, that reveal most about the true intentions of the *Homeric Hymn to Apollo*.

§5.31 The journey begins when Apollo leaves Olympus and descends to Pieria (line 216): Πιερίην μὲν πρῶτον ἀπ' Οὐλύμποιο κατῆλθες. This is in fact one of the journey's apparent anomalies. In the *Iliad* Hera leaves Olympus by way of Pieria when she heads north to Thrace.[112] Because the geography of

---

It has been suggested that in line 410 ἀλιστέφανον πτολίεθρον, "sea-girt citadel," be emended to Ἕλος τ' ἔφαλον πτολίεθρον, "and Helos, a city on the sea," referring to a town between Cape Malea and Cape Tainaron at the head of the Laconian Gulf; this gives more point to πτολίεθρον, "city, citadel," but the added geographical detail seems unnecessary and out of place (cf. Allen and Sikes 1904 ad loc.).

112 *Iliad* 14.225–228:

Ἥρη δ' ἀΐξασα λίπεν ῥίον Οὐλύμποιο,
Πιερίην δ' ἐπιβᾶσα καὶ Ἠμαθίην ἐρατεινὴν
σεύατ' ἐφ' ἱπποπόλων Θρῃκῶν ὄρεα νιφόεντα
ἀκροτάτας κορυφάς.

Darting forth Hera left the peak of Olympus,
and traversing Pieria and lovely Emathia
she sped over the snowy mountains of the horse-tending Thracians,
the highest peaks.

the *Hymn to Apollo* seems aberrant and capricious at other points, it has been assumed that the poet, following Homer without due care, has Apollo set off in the wrong direction from Olympus.[113] It is true, I think, that the poet of the hymn has the Homeric model in mind, but this does not mean that he follows it carelessly. This is not his practice in the rest of the hymn, where, on the contrary, he seeks to correct the transmission of the Homeric poems in a crucial point: it is a poor start toward that goal if the poet stumbles at the very outset. In fact he does not do so. Pieria was the coastal region primarily east and north of Olympus, stretching as far north as the Haliakmon River, but it also reached south of Olympus to the Peneios River.[114] Apollo goes southeast from Olympus toward the coast,[115] and this must be where the next point on his journey is, an unknown Lektos: this place is called ἠμαθόεις, "sandy," and like "sandy Pylos" it must be on the sea (lines 217–218): Λέκτον τ' ἠμαθόεντα παρέστιχες ἠδ' Αἰνιῆνας / καὶ διὰ Περραιβούς.[116] In contrast to un-Homeric Lektos, the Ainianes (*Ainiênes/Eniênes*) and the Perrhaiboi, whom Apollo passes next, are both known from Homer: situated thus between well-known places, Olympus and Pieria, to the north and two Homeric tribes to the south, unknown Lektos makes the same impression as the otherwise unknown

---

For locations on the first half of Apollo's journey see Map 5.

113 This is suggested in Allen and Sikes 1904 ad loc.: "Pieria is strictly N. of Olympus, whereas Apollo was coming south. The poet appears to have borrowed from Ξ without due care (in Ξ the geography is right, as Hera is going to Thrace)." In Allen, Halliday, and Sikes 1936 the sentence "the poet appears to have borrowed from Ξ without due care" is omitted, but the implication remains.

114 For the lower Peneios River as Pieria's southern boundary, see Strabo 7 fr. 14: ἐπὶ μὲν δὴ ταῖς ἐκβολαῖς τοῦ Πηνειοῦ ἐν δεξιᾷ Γυρτὼν ἵδρυται, Περραιβικὴ πόλις καὶ Μαγνῆτις.... ἐπὶ δὲ θάτερα ἡ Πιερία, "Gyrton is situated at the outlet of the Peneios on the right [south] side, a Perrhaibian and Magnetan city.... On the other side is Pieria." Cf. Geyer RE 'Makedonia' 650: "The country east of Olympus from the Peneios to the Haliacmon was called Pieria according to all ancient testimony" ("Die Landschaft am Ostfuss des Olymp vom Peneios bis zum Haliakmon hiess nach allen antiken Zeugnissen Pieria"); Pape-Benseler 1911 s.v. und Forbiger 1877, vol. 3, 727 are cited for the ancient sources.

115 Consistent with this movement of Apollo is the departure of Hermes for Calypso's island in *Odyssey* 5: Hermes too starts from Olympus (this much is implied) and goes by way of Pieria to the sea (Πιερίην δ' ἐπιβὰς ἐξ αἰθέρος ἔμπεσε πόντῳ, *Odyssey* 5.50).

116 Apart from this unknown Lektos only Pylos in Greek epic has the epithet ἠμαθόεις (there are two instances in the *Homeric Hymn to Apollo*; that another town besides Pylos should have the epithet in this hymn is noteworthy). Emendations have been suggested for unknown Lektos, but these make Apollo's journey truly incoherent; Allen, Halliday, and Sikes 1936 ad loc. cite two: Baumeister changed Λέκτον to Λάκμον, a peak in the Pindos range far to the west (cf. Strabo 6.2.4 [271]); Matthiae changed the epithet ἠμαθόεντα, "sandy," to Ἠμαθίην τε in line with *Iliad* 14.226, making Apollo, like Hera, head north into Thrace (see n5.113 above). Another town named Λεκτός (or Λεκτόν) lay on the coast of Asia Minor (Thucydides 8.101.3).

Argyphea in the group of towns near the Alpheios River in the voyage of the Cretan ship (*Homeric Hymn to Apollo* 421–424):

> ἡ δὲ πρήσσουσα κέλευθον
> Ἀρήνην ἵκανε καὶ Ἀργυφέην ἐρατεινὴν
> καὶ Θρύον Ἀλφειοῖο πόρον καὶ ἐΰκτιτον Αἶπυ
> καὶ Πύλον ἠμαθόεντα Πυλοιγενέας τ᾽ ἀνθρώπους.

> Plying its path
> it came to Arene and lovely Argyphea
> and Thryon, ford of the Alpheios, and well-built Aipy
> and sandy Pylos and the Pylos-born men.

Except for Argyphea all the towns in this passage are not only Homeric, but they occur together in the Pylian entry to the Catalogue of Ships: the poet of the hymn follows Homer, but not blindly, for he knows other names, Argyphea and Lektos, in addition to what Homer furnishes.

§5.32 The Ainianes and the Perrhaiboi, who are next to each other in the *Homeric Hymn to Apollo*, are closely paired in the Homeric Catalogue of Ships, where they share one leader; but in the Catalogue of Ships two separate locations are given for these tribes, around Dodona in Epirus, and around the Titaressos River, a tributary of the Peneios River in Thessaly.[117] If the Titaressos River is indeed to be identified with the Europos River in Thessaly, as Strabo says, the two Homeric locations of the Ainianes and the Perrhaiboi

---

117   *Iliad* 2.748–755:

Γουνεὺς δ᾽ ἐκ Κύφου ἦγε δύω καὶ εἴκοσι νῆας·
τῷ δ᾽ Ἐνιῆνες ἕποντο μενεπτόλεμοί τε Περαιβοὶ
οἳ περὶ Δωδώνην δυσχείμερον οἰκί᾽ ἔθεντο,
οἵ τ᾽ ἀμφ᾽ ἱμερτὸν Τιταρησσὸν ἔργα νέμοντο
ὅς ῥ᾽ ἐς Πηνειὸν προΐει καλλίρροον ὕδωρ,
οὐδ᾽ ὅ γε Πηνειῷ συμμίσγεται ἀργυροδίνῃ,
ἀλλά τέ μιν καθύπερθεν ἐπιρρέει ἠΰτ᾽ ἔλαιον·
ὅρκου γὰρ δεινοῦ Στυγὸς ὕδατός ἐστιν ἀπορρώξ.

Gouneus led twenty-two ships from Kyphos;
the Enianes and the staunch Perrhaiboi followed him,
who made their homes around wintry Dodona,
and others inhabited the country around the lovely Titaressos,
which sends its beautiful-flowing water into the Peneios,
but it does not mix with the silver-eddying Peneios,
but flows over it like oil;
for it is a branch of the Styx's water, a dread oath to swear by.

are widely separated from each other and difficult to reconcile.[118] In historical times both the Ainianes and the Perrhaiboi lived in Thessaly,[119] and Thessaly is what the poet of the *Homeric Hymn to Apollo* also intends. Like Strabo, the poet may well have had the Europos River in mind for the Homeric Titaressos, for the Europos is on Apollo's path from Pieria to the next point on his journey after he passes the two tribes, namely Iolkos. Depending on how the poet understood the Homeric Catalogue of Ships, he probably took Thessaly to be not only the historical homeland of the Ainianes and the Perrhaiboi, but their Homeric homeland as well.[120]

118 Strabo 7 fr. 15 identifies the Titaressos with the Europos, which marked the boundary between lower Macedonia and Thessaly. Strabo 9.5.20 says that the Titaresios (as he calls it) "rises in the Titarios mountain, which connects with Olympus, and flows into the territory of Perrhaibia near Tempe, and somewhere in that neighborhood unites with the Peneios." He comments that the pure water of the Peneios and the oily water of the Titaresios do not mix, just as Homer says (*Iliad* 2.753–754, n5.117 above). The conjunction of a river in the east with Dodona in the west produces what Simpson and Lazenby 1970:149 call an insoluble problem; in the end these authors choose Dodona as the true Homeric location and reject Strabo's identification of the Titaressos with the Europos. Strabo, on the other hand, reconciles the two locations in favor of Thessaly; he says that the oracle of Dodona was originally near Skotoussa in Thessaly and was later moved to Epirus (Strabo 9.5.20; 7.7.12; 7 fr. 1, 1a, 1b).

119 In classical times the Ainianes lived in the upper Spercheios valley in southern Thessaly (Σπερχειὸς ποταμὸς ῥέων ἐξ Ἐνιήνων ἐς θάλασσαν ἐκδιδοῖ, "the Spercheios River flows out of [the country of] the Enianes and empties into the sea," Herodotus 7.198. 2); earlier they had a home farther north in Thessaly, closer to the Perrhaiboi (Strabo 9.5.22). The Perrhaiboi lived around the Peneios River in Thessaly (Strabo 7 fr. 15); in the classical era Herodotus 7.131 seems to locate them on the lower Peneios near the coast (in this passage Xerxes waits in Pieria until a division of his army clears a road through the "Macedonian mountain" into the country of the Perrhaiboi: ὁ μὲν δὴ περὶ Πιερίην διέτριβε ἡμέρας συχνάς· τὸ γὰρ δὴ ὄρος τὸ Μακεδονικὸν ἔκειρε τῆς στρατιῆς τριτημορίς, ἵνα ταύτῃ διεξίῃ ἅπασα ἡ στρατιὴ ἐς Περραιβούς, "He lingered several days in Pieria; for a third of his army was clearing the Macedonian mountain so that the entire army could come through by that route into the land of the Perrhaiboi"; Pieria was on the coast [see n5.114 above], and so presumably were the Perrhaiboi). A location near the coast for the Perrhaiboi is confirmed by Strabo 7 fr. 14 (n5.114 above), where on either side of the Peneios "near the outlets" of the river (ἐπὶ...ταῖς ἐκβολαῖς τοῦ Πηνειοῦ) are said to lie Piera to the north and the "Perrhaibic city" (Περραιβικὴ πόλις) of Gyrton to the south.

120 Strabo 9.5.22 says that the two tribes once dwelt near each other in Thessaly, the Perrhaiboi in the region later still called Perrhaibia (cf. Strabo 7 fr. 15), and the Ainianes in the Dotian Plain near Mount Ossa and Lake Boibeïs. The two tribes were then separated, as they later were historically. A few of the Ainianes remained in the north, but most were driven south to the Spercheios River and into Mount Oeta by the Lapiths (Strabo presents this compressed version of the Ainianes' migration to the region called Ainis, their historical home; longer versions, found in Plutarch *Greek Questions* 13 and 26, are discussed by Sakellariou 1984 and 1990:190–200). As for the Perrhaiboi, some drew together round the western parts of Olympus and remained there, being neighbors to the Macedonians (i.e. in the vicinity of the Titaressos), but most were driven out of their country into

§5.33 Apollo's next steps are straightforward and clear: he comes to Iolkos, and then to two places in Euboea, Cape Kenaion in the north and the Lelantine Plain further south (*Homeric Hymn to Apollo* 218–220):

> τάχα δ' εἰς Ἰαωλκὸν ἵκανες,
> Κηναίου τ' ἐπέβης ναυσικλείτης Εὐβοίης·
> στῆς δ' ἐπὶ Ληλάντῳ πεδίῳ.

> And soon you came to Iolcus,
> and set foot on Kenaion in Euboea, famous for ships,
> and stood on the Lelantine Plain.

Apollo rejects the Lelantine Plain as the site for his temple and crosses the Euripos strait from Euboea into Boeotia (lines 220–222); the first places he comes to in Boeotia, after an unnamed mountain, are Mykalessos and Teumessos, which are on a straight line to Thebes, the next point on his journey (lines 223–224).[121] Here, as elsewhere, the poet archaizes, saying that Thebes was not yet inhabited, but was still covered with forest (lines 225–228).[122] Next Apollo comes to Onkhestos, the site of a cult to Poseidon,

---

the mountains around Athamania and Pindus (i.e. in the vicinity of Dodona). The stage described in Homer, according to this scheme, is the first stage, when the two tribes lived side by side in Thessaly. It is likely that the poet of the *Homeric Hymn to Apollo* had the same scheme in mind: he pairs the two tribes because they are paired in Homer, and he puts them in Thessaly, near what seems to be the Europos/Titaressos. How this poet understood the location of Dodona in Homer we cannot say, but perhaps Strabo's tradition that the oracle was once in Thessaly before it migrated to Epirus was also known to him. The point is that this poet presents a coherent picture of the two tribes, which also squares with the Homeric picture if the latter is intepreted in a particular way. If the poet did think of the oracle of Dodona as having had an earlier location than its historical location, this would be consistent with his placement of Elis in the voyage of Apollo's priests, which is also meant to represent an earlier location than the historical location of Elis (see §5.14 and §5.15 above; cf. §5.34 below).

121 For locations on the second half of Apollo's journey see Map 6. Guillon 1963:92 points out that there is a hill (Messapios), but not a mountain, on Apollo's route inland from the Euripos; his conclusions about an earlier route past the Ptoion, to the northwest, are in my view unconvincing.

122 I again take issue with Guillon, who sees in this feature of the poem an anti-Theban bias on the part of the poet; on the contrary, Thebes, despite its not yet being in existence, is called "holy," and the epithet cannot be explained away as traditional, and thus unavoidable, as Guillon 1963:92 argues (*Homeric Hymn to Apollo* 225–228):

Θήβης δ' εἰσαφίκανες ἕδος καταειμένον ὕλῃ·
οὐ γάρ πώ τις ἔναιε βροτῶν ἱερῇ ἐνὶ Θήβῃ,
οὐδ' ἄρα πω τότε γ' ἦσαν ἀταρπιτοὶ οὐδὲ κέλευθοι
Θήβης ἂμ πεδίον πυρηφόρον, ἀλλ' ἔχεν ὕλη.

where the ritual of horses, chariots, and drivers who leap to the ground, and who dedicate their chariots if they crash, is described at length (lines 229–238). So far all is in order, but now we come to the one real exception to the hymn's geographical coherence. Before Apollo reaches the next town, Haliartos, he crosses the Kephisos River and (passes) the town of Okalea (*Homeric Hymn to Apollo* 239–243):

> ἔνθεν δὲ προτέρω ἔκιες ἑκατηβόλ᾽ Ἄπολλον·
> Κηφισὸν δ᾽ ἄρ᾽ ἔπειτα κιχήσαο καλλιρέεθρον,
> ὅς τε Λιλαίηθεν προχέει καλλίρροον ὕδωρ·
> τὸν διαβὰς Ἑκάεργε καὶ Ὠκαλέην πολύπυργον
> ἔνθεν ἄρ᾽ εἰς Ἁλίαρτον ἀφίκεο ποιήεντα.

> You went on from there, far-shooter Apollo,
> and came then to the beautiful-flowing Kephisos,
> which pours forth its beautiful-flowing water from Lilaia;
> crossing it, far-worker, and many-towered Okalea,
> you came from there to grassy Haliartos.

Here something has gone badly wrong, for the Kephisos River, which does indeed rise near the town of Lilaia, north of Delphi and Mount Parnassos in Phokis, empties into the western end of the Kopaic Lake. Onkhestos and Haliartos, on the other hand, border the south shore of the Kopaic Lake at its eastern end. Apollo, who is moving west, is nowhere near the Kephisos River as yet, nor will he ever have to cross it on his way to Delphi. If the Kephisos River is wildly out of place, the town of Okalea is less so, but it too is on the wrong side of Haliartos, some thirty stades west of that town according to Strabo.[123] Apollo, for whatever reason, approaches Haliartos from the wrong direction. For now I simply note that the problem lies in lines 239–242, and continue to follow Apollo's journey westward, first to Haliartos (line 243), and onward to Delphi from there. From Haliartos Apollo first proceeds to the spring of Telphousa, where he proposes to build his temple, but the nymph Telphousa persuades

---

You came to the seat of Thebes clothed in forest;
for no mortal yet lived in holy Thebes,
nor were there yet paths and ways
through the wheat-bearing plain of Thebes, but a forest possessed it.

123 Okalea, which occurs in the Catalogue of Ships (*Iliad* 2.501), is said by Strabo 9.2.26 to lie halfway between Haliartos and the Alalkomenion (at Alalkomenai), thirty stades from each: ἡ δ᾽ Ὠκαλέη μέση Ἁλιάρτου καὶ Ἀλαλκομενίου ἑκατέρου τριάκοντα σταδίους ἀπέχουσα. For the problem in Apollo's route see Map 6.

him to go on to Krisa instead (lines 244–276). The final point on Apollo's journey before he reaches his destination in Krisa involves another anomaly, but only an apparent one. This is the city of the hybristic Phlegyai, who dwell in a valley near the "Kephisis Lake" (*Homeric Hymn to Apollo* 277–280):

ἔνθεν δὲ προτέρω ἔκιες ἑκατηβόλ' Ἄπολλον,
ἷξες δ' ἐς Φλεγύων ἀνδρῶν πόλιν ὑβριστάων,
οἳ Διὸς οὐκ ἀλέγοντες ἐπὶ χθονὶ ναιετάασκον
ἐν καλῇ βήσσῃ Κηφισίδος ἐγγύθι λίμνης.

You went on from there, far-shooter Apollo,
and came to the city of the Phlegyai, violent men,
who, having no regard for Zeus, live upon the earth
in a beautiful valley near the Kephisis Lake.

The city of the Phlegyai, as we know from Strabo and Pausanias, was Panopeus, which lay in Phokis about halfway from Telphousa to Delphi.[124] But the "Kephisis Lake" (Κηφισὶς λίμνη), near which the city is said to lie, is another name for the Kopaic Lake,[125] and Panopeus does not lie near the Kopaic Lake, but 15 kilometers west of it. It has been suggested that by the "Kephisis Lake" is meant the Kephisos River, to which Panopeus is closer, although the town does not lie on the river either, but some distance south of it. The solution to the problem, I think, lies in another direction. According to Pausanias, before the hybristic Phlegyai moved westward to their historical home in Phokis, they lived in Orkhomenos in Boeotia;[126] unlike Panopeus, Orkhomenos lay next to the Kopaic Lake, at its western end where the Kephisos River emptied into it. Again the poet archaizes. The implication is

---

124 Strabo 9.2.42 says that the town lay above the territory of Orkhomenos in Phokis (ὑπέρκειται δ' Ὀρχομενίας ὁ Πανοπεύς, Φωκικὴ πόλις); cf. Strabo 9.3.14, Pausanias 10.3.1. Pausanias 10.4.1 comments that in his time Panopeus did not deserve to be called a city.

125 Strabo 9.2.27, commenting on different names for the lake, cites Pindar: ὕστερον δ' ἡ πᾶσα Κωπαῒς ἐλέχθη κατ' ἐπικράτειαν.... Πίνδαρος δὲ καὶ <u>Κηφισσίδα</u> καλεῖ ταύτην, "Later the whole lake was called the Kopaïs, this name predominating.... Pindar also calls it the <u>Kephissis</u>."

126 Pausanias 10.4.1: καὶ γενέσθαι μὲν τῇ πόλει τὸ ὄνομα λέγουσιν [sc. the people of Panopeus] ἀπὸ τοῦ Ἐπειοῦ πατρός, αὐτοὶ δὲ οὐ Φωκεῖς, Φλεγύαι δὲ εἶναι τὸ ἐξ ἀρχῆς καὶ ἐς τὴν γῆν διαφυγεῖν φασι τὴν Φωκίδα ἐκ τῆς Ὀρχομενίας, "They [the people of Panopeus] say that their city got its name from the father of Epeios, and that they are not Phocians, but Phlegyans originally, and they say that they fled into the Phocian country from the country of Orkhomenos"; cf. also Pausanias 9.36.2: καὶ ἀπέστησάν τε ἀνὰ χρόνον ἀπὸ τῶν ἄλλων Ὀρχομενίων ὑπὸ ἀνοίας καὶ τόλμης οἱ Φλεγύαι καὶ ἦγον καὶ ἔφερον τοὺς προσοίκους, "In the course of time the Phlegyans through their witlessness and recklessness withdrew from the other Orkhomenians, and began to plunder and rob their neighbors."

that at the time of Apollo's journey the Phlegyai still occupied the land of Orkhomenos, "near the Kephisis Lake," and that perhaps Orkhomenos itself did not yet exist.[127] But if Orkhomenos did not yet exist, neither did Thebes, the successor to Orkhomenos's glory in Boeotia; that point, as seen, was anticipated in the hymn when Apollo passed the site of future Thebes, still covered in trees.

§5.34 The location of the Phlegyai in the hymn is against expectation, and very deliberately so: the initial impression is that their "city" is Panopeus, but this impression is corrected by the phrase Κηφισίδος ἐγγύθι λίμνης, "near the Kephisis Lake," at the end of the passage. This sets the stage for a similar dislocation in the second part of the hymn, where Elis is placed not where it was known to be historically, but in western Achaea.[128] The dislocation of Elis is vital to the hymn's main purpose, which is to create a picture of Pylos and the Pylian kingdom lying north of the Alpheios River. That purpose, I think, is already served in Apollo's journey past the city of the Phlegyai. With the shift of the Phlegyai from Phokis to Boeotia, the final stages of Apollo's journey are not as evenly spaced as they would be otherwise: Phokis is now a blank apart from Krisa. This too has a counterpart in the second part of the hymn, where Messenia is a blank. The omission of Messenia is of course also an essential part of the hymn's principal objective, and it seems to be anticipated by the imbalance between the final two stages of Apollo's journey to Delphi.

§5.35 I return now to lines 239–242, where Apollo temporarily ceases to move west through Boeotia in well-measured stages, as he does both before and after these lines, and is suddenly far off to the west crossing the Kephisos River in the wrong direction and moving eastward through Okalea

---

127 If strict logic is applied an inconsistency arises from an implication in the hymn of Orkhomenos's non-existence, namely the simultaneous existence of Pylos: Chloris, the wife of Neleus, the founder of Pylos, is the daughter of Amphion, the king of Orkhomenos, according to *Odyssey* 11; if Pylos exists (as it does in the hymn), so must Orkhomenos. But this, I think, is to look more closely than the poet intended. There is another possibility to consider. In Pausanias 9.36.2 the Phlegyai separate themselves from "the other Orkhomenians" (see previous note); this could be what the poet of the *Homeric Hymn to Apollo* had in mind, and it would allow Orkhomenos to exist at the time of Apollo's journey. The Phlegyai in fact seem to be a mythic contrast to the Minyai, a name applied to the Orkhomenians (and others); the similar formation of the names Μινύαι and Φλεγύαι suggests a contrasting pair; there is also a genealogical connection that puts the two on the same level, but whereas the seafaring Minyai descend from Poseidon, the wild Phlegyai descend from Ares (cf. Buttmann 1829:222–224). This too, however, goes beyond what is intended in the hymn; in the hymn the Phlegyai sit where Orkhomenos should be and Orkhomenos is simply not there.

128 Cf. n5.120 above on the placement of the Ainianes and the Perrhaiboi.

toward Haliartos, the next point in his interrupted westward journey. Like two other passages in the *Homeric Hymn to Apollo*, namely the passage threatening a change of regime at Delphi and the passage devoted to Hera's birth of Typhaon, this passage too must be an expansion of the hymn on the part of the victors in the First Sacred War. The earlier hymn, which would have had the sanction of the former regime at Delphi, was appropriated by the victors of the Sacred War by right of conquest. The earlier hymn was politically charged insofar as it reflected Spartan propaganda following the Second Messenian War, and this propaganda would not have been acceptable to the victors in the First Sacred War: the earlier hymn pictures a Pylos north of the Alpheios River, but Athens, one of the victors in the Sacred War, never forgot that Pylos once lay in Messenia, before Sparta put an end to it there. The key to the Spartan reinterpretation of Pylian geography in the hymn is the Alpheios River, which the Cretan ship passes before it reaches Pylos on its way north. It is no accident that another river, the Kephisos, has been woven into the hymn by means of an expansion, and that this river makes nonsense of Apollo's journey west through Boeotia. The effect of this is to undermine the meaning of the voyage north of the Cretan ship: the expansion reverses the relative locations of Haliartos and the Kephisos River in order to show that the relative locations of Pylos and the Alpheios River in the hymn are also backwards. With the inclusion of lines 239–242 none of the hymn's geography can any longer be taken seriously.[129]

§5.36 If we look at lines 239–242 more closely there are clear signs that the passage represents an expansion of the earlier hymn. Line 241, describing the source of the Kephisos River, is also found in Hesiod with only a minor variation of the verb (προΐει, "sends forth," instead of προχέει, "pours forth"): ὅς τε Λιλαίηθεν προΐει καλλίρροον ὕδωρ, "which sends forth its beautiful-flowing water from Lilaia" (Hesiod fr. 70.18 MW = fr. 37 Rz.).[130] The correspondence

---

129 To the point here are the comments of George Forrest in another context (1982:315): "The world of propaganda is a topsy-turvy world.... Greeks rarely denied an opponent's story—they preferred to take it over and stand it on its head."

130 The line is attributed to Hesiod by the scholia to *Iliad* 2.522 (and by Eustathius 275.17 on *Iliad* 2.523): ὁ δὲ Κηφισσὸς ποταμός ἐστι τῆς Φωκίδος, ἔχων τὰς πηγὰς ἐκ Λιλαίας, ὥς φησιν Ἡσίοδος "ὅς—ὕδωρ," "The Kephisos River is in Phokis, having its source from Lilaia, as Hesiod says..." (Eustathius has Λιλαίηθεν, "from Lilaia," the scholia A Λιλαίῃσι, "at Lilaia"). In Hesiod fr. 70.18 MW only the end of the line]ροο[ν] ὕδωρ, "-flowing water," survives; this papyrus fragment reveals the context of the line in Hesiod, namely Athamas and his descendants (the Kephisos is the divine father of one of his descendants, Eteoklos). Lilaia, at the source of the Kephisos, occurs in Homer in the Phocian entry to the Catalogue of Ships: οἵ τε Λίλαιαν ἔχον πηγῇς ἔπι Κηφισοῖο, "and those who inhabit Lilaia at the source of the Kephisos," *Iliad* 2.523.

with Hesiod, like such correspondences elsewhere, points toward a sixth-century Athenian borrowing from the *Catalogue of Women*; there is agreement here with the hymn's other two expansions, which, as seen, also probably had an Athenian origin.[131] In line 242, "having crossed it (the Kephisos River) and Okalea," the construction with two objects of a single verb is highly compressed, and the second object, Okalea, does not really fit the verb's meaning "crossed": Okalea has been squeezed in to provide a reference for line 243, "from there you arrived at Haliartos," and to show the backwards direction of Apollo's journey at this point. Without lines 239–242 the description of the chariot ritual at Onkhestos, which ends at line 238, is not followed by the generic line 239: ἔνθεν δὲ προτέρω ἔκιες ἑκατηβόλ' Ἄπολλον, "you went on from there, far-shooter Apollo," but by the specific line 243: ἔνθεν ἄρ' εἰς Ἁλίαρτον ἀφίκεο ποιήεντα, "from there you came to grassy Haliartos." The generic line and the specific line begin the same, and, as far as the transition from line 238 is concerned, nothing is missed when lines 239–242 are omitted.[132]

§5.37 As the *Homeric Hymn to Apollo* confirms, there was a real contest in the early sixth century as to the location of Homeric Pylos. There were moves and countermoves in this contest, and no resolution was reached. As a sign that the Spartan position did not simply give way after the First Sacred War, however much the *Homeric Hymn to Apollo* was neutralized by the victors of that war, I repeat the fact that in *Odyssey* 15.297 the entire manuscript tradition follows the Spartan version of Telemachus's voyage home from Pylos: the manuscripts all read *Pherás* instead of *Pheás*. How this version of the voyage was able to establish itself I do not know, but the fact is that it did.

§5.38 *Odyssey* 15 and the *Homeric Hymn to Apollo* provide the main evidence of the Spartan attempt to shift the location of Homeric Pylos from Messenia to Elis after the Second Messenian War, but there is another important piece of evidence still to consider, from the *Iliad*. As in *Odyssey* 15 and the *Homeric Hymn to Apollo*, the point at issue is again the location of Pylos relative to the town

---

131 Hesiodic catalogue poetry was used to expand the catalogue of heroines in *Odyssey* 11 in a sixth-century Athenian context (see above §2.135, §2.142–§2.144, n2.209 and n2.213 ; cf. §2.160, §2.164). For the Athenian character of the Typhaon episode, see §5.23 above. The *post eventum* threat of regime change at the end of the hymn need not be exclusively Athenian since there were other victors in the Sacred War, but Athens is the likely exponent of their point of view.

132 The generic line also occurs before Apollo's arrival at Onkhestos and at the city of the Phlegyai, *Homeric Hymn to Apollo* 229 and 277 respectively; in both cases a passage of more than one line follows. The expansion in lines 239–242 makes use of the same pattern, namely generic line followed by short passage. When the expansion is removed there is no need for the generic line: Apollo's onward progress to Haliartos is told in one line; in the following line Apollo arrives at Telphousa.

of *Pheaí*, on the coast of Elis, but in the *Iliad* the form of the name is *Pheiá*, in the singular, and with *ei* for *e*. In *Iliad* 7, to shame the Achaeans into meeting Hector in single combat, Nestor tells how he once accepted the challenge of the club-wielding Arcadian giant Ereuthalion, and slew him. The Pylians were at war with the Arcadians, their neighbors to the east, and the battle between champions took place at the Keladon River, where the two armies fought. This, at least, is how the story begins in *Iliad* 7.133–134, but in the next line, 135, an additional location is given, and an additional river is specified, the Iardanos: this line sets the battle "by the walls of Pheia" (*Iliad* 7.133–136):

> ἡβῷμ' ὡς ὅτ' ἐπ' ὠκυρόῳ Κελάδοντι μάχοντο
> ἀγρόμενοι Πύλιοί τε καὶ Ἀρκάδες ἐγχεσίμωροι
> <u>Φειᾶς πὰρ τείχεσσιν Ἰαρδάνου ἀμφὶ ῥέεθρα.</u>
> τοῖσι δ' Ἐρευθαλίων πρόμος ἵστατο ἰσόθεος φώς.

> I wish I were young, as when, beside the swift-flowing Keladon,
> the assembled Pylians and the spear-mad Arcadians fought,
> <u>by the walls of Pheia around the streams of the Iardanos,</u>
> and Ereuthalion, a godlike man, stood as their champion.

The location of the battle beside two different rivers has long been suspected, and the presence of Pheia in the story has seemed wholly inexplicable: how can Pheia, ten miles north of the Alpheios River on the coast of Elis, have been the site of a battle between Pylos and Arcadia?[133] The answer, however, is clear:

---

133 Kirk 1990:252–253 offers this half-hearted explanation: "If the western Arcadians were in Parrhasia (vol. I, 218), then they might have interfered as far to the N-W as Pheia; though somewhere further south, around Arene indeed, might have been a more plausible area for border clashes with Pylians." Visser 1997:524 and 524n31 thinks that there must have been a different town of Pheia in Arcadia: "In the east—in line with...*Iliad* 7.133–135—the rivers Keladon and Iardanos as well as the city of Pheia seem to mark the border with Arcadia; these rivers can of course not be exactly located.... The Pheai named in *Odyssey* 15.297 is not, then, the same place as the one in *Iliad* 7, since the Pheai of the *Odyssey* is certainly, in view of the context, presented as lying on the coast, and the western boundary of Arcadia cannot, despite Ps.-Scylax 44, be displaced to the coast of the Ionian sea; otherwise Homer would not have to have Agamemnon provide the ships for the Arcadians" ("Im Osten schei-nen—entsprechend der...Ilias-Stelle H 133–135—die Flüsse Keladon und Iardanos sowie die Stadt Pheia die Grenze nach Arkadien hin zu markieren; allerdings lassen sich diese Flüsse nicht exakt lokalisieren.... Das in o 297 genannte Pheai ist dann nicht derselbe Ort wie der im H der Ilias, da das Pheai der *Odyssee* auf Grund des Kontextes mit Sicherheit an der Küste liegend vorgestellt ist und man die Westgrenze Arkadiens trotz Ps.-Skyl. 44 wohl nicht bis an die Küste des Ionischen Meeres verlegen kann; sonst müsste Homer Agamemnon nicht die Schiffe für die Arkader stellen lassen").

the Pylos envisaged by *Iliad* 7.135 lay in Elis, north of the Alpehios, and also north of Pheia, just as it does in the *Homeric Hymn to Apollo*. When the Arcadians attacked this Pylos, they first had to pass Pheia, where Nestor stopped them by slaying their champion. *Iliad* 7.135 is an expansion of Nestor's story, which is intended to change the site of his battle from Arcadia to the coast of Elis.[134] The presence of the town *Pheia* in *Iliad* 7.135 must be viewed together with the absence of the town *Pheai* in the manuscript tradition of *Odyssey* 15.297: *Pheia* is a correction of *Pheai* both as to the form of the name (singular *Pheia*, not plural *Pheai*), and as to the town's location relative to Nestor's Pylos (south of it, not north). The one-line expansion of Nestor's story in *Iliad* 7 and the one-word change in Telemachus's voyage home in *Odyssey* 15 constitute the entire reworking of Homer with respect to the location of Pylos in Elis. Everything else in the poems stayed the same because no other change was needed.[135]

---

134 This assumes that the Keladon River was in Arcadia, although such a river is not definitely known; Callimachus *Hymns* 3.107 refers to a Keladon River in Arcadia, but he may have taken the name from *Iliad* 7.133; Pausanias 8.38.9 mentions a tributary of the Alpheios called the Kelados, which could be the Keladon. The river name Keladon has a generic quality; it means "sounding," as of rushing water (cf. the phrase πὰρ ποταμὸν κελάδοντα, "along a sounding/rushing river," in *Iliad* 18.576); a mythical river in Miletus is named Kelados/Keladon (Herda 2006a:302–310, 448), and this too suggests the name's generic quality. Wilamowitz 2006:336 proposes that Keladon in *Iliad* 7.133 is not a name but a common noun, "river," referring to the Iardanos two lines later, but this is at best difficult. The name may be an invention in *Iliad* 7.133, but in any case Arcadia seems to be the intended location. For the possibility that the name Keladon is an invention, cf. Willcock 1964:146, who argues that Nestor's entire story in *Iliad* 7 is the poet's invention (a problem for this argument, as Hainsworth 1993:297 points out, is the occurrence of Ereuthalion in *Iliad* 4.319, which anticipates the story in *Iliad* 7; Willcock 1964:142–143 argues that Nestor's story in *Iliad* 1.259–274 is likewise the poet's invention). The Iardanos River near Pheia also presents a problem in that no river of any size is found near Pheia, although a stream in the vicinity could be meant (a ποτάμιον, "small river," near the town of Pheia was taken as the Iardanos by some ancient scholars, Strabo 8.3.12). Simpson and Lazenby 1970:94 comment as follows: "Pheia is presumably the same as classical Pheia, securely located at Ayios Andreas near Katakolon, while the River Iardanos is presumably the stream immediately to north of the village of Skaphidia." The phrase Ἰαρδάνου ἀμφὶ ῥέεθρα, "around the streams of the Iardanos," in *Iliad* 7.135 is also found in *Odyssey* 3.292, where it refers to a river in western Crete; see n5.135 below for further discussion of the Iardanos River in *Iliad* 7.135.

135 In the Hellenistic age there was a further development with respect to the expansion of Nestor's story in *Iliad* 7. Strabo 8.3.21 tells us of a town named *Kháa* near Lepreon in Triphylia, past which a river called the *Akídōn* flowed; there was also a tomb of Iardanos next to this river. Strabo says that in Nestor's story some read *Kháa* for *Pheiá* and *Akídōn* for *Keládōn*:

ἡβῷμ᾽, ὡς ὅτ᾽ ἐπ᾽ ὠκυρόῳ Ἀκίδοντι μάχοντο
ἀγρόμενοι Πύλιοί τε καὶ Ἀρκάδες ἐγχεσίμωροι
Χάας πὰρ τείχεσσιν.

I wish I were young, as when, beside the swift-flowing <u>Akidon</u>,
the assembled Pylians and the spear-mad Arcadians fought,
by the walls of <u>Khaa</u>.

According to Strabo this text was put forth because Khaa is closer than Pheia to Arcadia, and closer to the tomb of Iardanos as well (Strabo does not say with what wording the tomb of Iardanos was substituted for the streams of Iardanos in this version of the text, but Ἰαρδάνου ἠρίον ἀμφί is a possibility). To the reasons that Strabo gives for this version of *Iliad* 7.135 I would add that it was presumably due to the learned minority (Strabo's *Homērikóteroi*) who thought that Homeric Pylos lay in Triphylia near Lepreon; cf. n5.62 above. We can say more. The scholia to *Iliad* 4.319 give two versions of an account by Ariaithos of Tegea (fourth century BC) of Nestor's conquest of Ereuthalion, one of which puts the conflict on the Akidon River (Ariaithos *FGrHist* 316 F 7; see Jacoby's commentary ad loc. for the two versions, one of which says that Nestor's conquest of Ereuthalion was unfairly won, and both of which say that the Arcadians proceeded to defeat the Pylians in battle; cf. Wilamowitz 2006:337–338); this Arcadian tradition, which changes the outcome of Nestor's story in *Iliad* 7, may well have gone hand in hand with the variant reading in *Iliad* 7.135. Didymus read something else again in *Iliad* 7.135, namely Φηρᾶς for Φειᾶς and Δαρδάνου for Ἰαρδάνου (Δαρδάνου ἀμφὶ ῥέεθρα). What the point of this version was is unclear (perhaps it had to do with a tradition for Dardanos's birth in a cave near the Anigros River, Strabo 8.3.19), but the scholia to *Iliad* 7.135 citing Didymus also say that Pherekydes told this version of the story (see Wilamowitz 2006:337); with Pherekydes we are back in the fifth century BC, when *Iliad* 7.135 was evidently open to dispute because the idea of an Eleian Pylos had already faded. Pausanias 5.18.6 says that a scene without names on the chest of Cypselus at Olympia was interpreted by some as the battle at Pheia on the Iardanos River between the Pylians and Arcadians (but by others as a meeting between the Eleians and the Aetolians with Oxylos); if the chest of Cypselus, which probably belongs to the late seventh or sixth century BC, in fact portrayed Nestor's battle with the Arcadians it would have done so close to the time of the expansion of Nestor's story in *Iliad* 7, perhaps reflecting contemporary interest in that story.

Chapter 14.

THE TEXT OF *ILIAD* 11
IN THE FIFTH CENTURY BC

§5.39 There was a controversy in the late seventh and early sixth centuries BC as to the location of Homeric Pylos, whether north or south of the Alpheios River, and the battleground for this controversy was *Odyssey* 15, and also *Iliad* 7; this brings us back to the real question: could such a controversy have occurred if another passage in the Homeric poems plainly showed that Pylos lay south of the Alpheios River? This in turn brings us back to our real object, the passages in Nestor's story in *Iliad* 11 that do plainly show that Pylos lay south of the Alpheios River, in Triphylia. Only one conclusion is possible: these passages did not yet exist when the *Homeric Hymn to Apollo* was composed, nor did they yet exist when the *Homeric Hymn to Apollo* was appropriated and expanded by the victors of the First Sacred War. The passages in *Iliad* 11, in other words, can be no earlier than the first half of the sixth century BC, and they may well be later than that.

§5.40 The question to ask is when it would have made sense to introduce a new candidate, in Triphylia, into an old dispute concerning Pylos's location. The key to the likely circumstances, I think, is the historical expansion of Elis south into Triphylia: at some point it would have made sense to recast Nestor's fight with the Eleians as a fight between Elis, the aggressor, and Triphylia, the victim of Eleian aggression. In the long run Elis absorbed Triphylia completely, as far as Triphylia's border with Messenia.[136] This did

---

136 I note that Wilamowitz 2006:335 takes Nestor's *Iliad* 11 story as a whole to be a reflection of the Eleians' aggression against more immediate neighbors in southern Elis and the Pisatis in the period between 776 BC (the first Olympiad) and c. 600 BC; although the roots of Nestor's story are in my view much older than that (for Wilamowitz's dating of the

not happen all at once, but there are really only two periods to consider for the expansion of Nestor's story, the first half of the sixth century BC, and the second half of the fifth century BC, and of these the first half of the sixth century BC is not at all likely. When Elis overthrew and absorbed the Pisatis c. 570 BC, two allies of the Pisatans in northern Triphylia, Skillous and Makistos, were also overthrown.[137] We do not know what became of the population of these cities, but it seems to have remained in place.[138] Eleian

---

so-called "Nestoris" to c. 700 BC see Burkert in Wilamowitz 2006:13), the story's concrete form probably owes something to historical conditions during the Homeric era. But the issue for the expansion of Nestor's story is not southern Elis and the Pisatis, but Triphylia. Bölte's comment, RE 'Triphylia' 199: "The politics of the Triphylians were determined at all times by their opposition to Elis" ("Die Politik der Triphylier war zu allen Zeiten bestimmt durch den Gegensatz zu Elis"), concerns the historical period primarily. In Strabo's time the border between Triphylia and Messenia was the Neda River, south of Lepreon (Strabo 8.3.22); in a passage dealing with Homeric geography Strabo 8.4.1 refers to a cape on the border between Messenia and Triphylia, apparently indicating a boundary other than the Neda at an earlier time.

137 Skillous lay a few kilometers south of the Alpheios, to the southwest of Olympia; Makistos (or Makiston), whose location is unknown, is variously placed east of Skillous near the Alpheios, and further to the south near Samikon (see Bölte RE 'Makiston' 775–776, who supports a location near Samikon). The Pisatans' allies also included Dyspontion, a perioikic city in Elis on the road from Olympia to the later town of Elis. For the Eleians' overthrow of the Pisatans and their allies, cf. EN5.16 to n5.108 above. The main source for this event, Pausanias 6.22.4, represents the Pisatans and their allies as aggressors in the war; this probably reflects the bias of Pausanias's source and is regarded with skepticism (Swoboda RE 'Elis' 2390): Πύρρου δὲ τοῦ Πανταλέοντος μετὰ Δαμοφῶντα τὸν ἀδελφὸν βασιλεύσαντος Πισαῖοι πόλεμον ἑκούσιον ἐπανείλοντο Ἠλείοις, συναπέστησαν δέ σφισιν ἀπὸ Ἠλείων Μακίστιοι καὶ Σκιλλούντιοι, οὗτοι μὲν ἐκ τῆς Τριφυλίας, τῶν δὲ ἄλλων περιοίκων Δυσπόντιοι.... Πισαίους μὲν δὴ καὶ ὅσοι τοῦ πολέμου Πισαίοις μετέσχον, ἐπέλαβεν ἀναστάτους ὑπὸ Ἠλείων γενέσθαι, "When Pantaleon's son Pyrrhos ruled after his brother Damophon, the Pisatans entered into a voluntary war against the Eleians, and the Makistians and Skillountians in Triphylia revolted with them from the Eleians, and also the Dyspontians among the other neighboring peoples.... It befell the Pisatans and all who joined the Pisatans in war to be destroyed by the Eleians." Cf. also Pausanias 5.6.4: τῶν μὲν δὴ πόλεων ἦν τῶν ἐν τῇ Τριφυλίᾳ καὶ Σκιλλοῦς· ἐπὶ δὲ τοῦ πολέμου τοῦ Πισαίων πρὸς Ἠλείους ἐπίκουροί τε Πισαίων οἱ Σκιλλούντιοι καὶ διάφοροι τοῖς Ἠλείοις ἦσαν ἐκ τοῦ φανεροῦ, καὶ σφᾶς οἱ Ἠλεῖοι τούτων ἕνεκα ἐποίησαν ἀναστάτους, "Skillous also was one of the cities in Triphylia; during the war of the Pisatans against the Eleians the Skillountians were allies of the Pisatans and openly hostile to the Eleians, and for this the Eleians destroyed them."

138 Pausanias 6.22.4 (see previous note) says that it was the fate of the Pisatans and all their allies to be destroyed by the Eleans (ἀναστάτους ὑπὸ Ἠλείων γενέσθαι); about the fate of the Dyspontians Strabo 8.3.32 gives the futher information that they left their city and that most went to Epidamnos and Apollonia: αὐτοῦ δ' ἔστι...καὶ τὸ Δυσπόντιον κατὰ τὴν ὁδὸν τὴν ἐξ Ἤλιδος εἰς Ὀλυμπίαν ἐν πεδίῳ κείμενον· ἐξελείφθη δέ, καὶ ἀπῆραν οἱ πλείους εἰς Ἐπίδαμνον καὶ Ἀπολλωνίαν, "Here is...also Dyspontion, on the road from Elis to Olympia, lying in a plain; but it was abandoned, and most of the people went to Epidamnos and Apollonia." We hear nothing further about the fate of Makistos and Skillous, but Skillous,

aggression, at any rate, was limited to these two cities in northern Triphylia, and this is not enough to explain the expansion of Nestor's story in *Iliad* 11. The early sixth century is the wrong time for another reason as well as I interpret the evidence. It was at the beginning of this century that an Eleian Pylos was first put forth as an alternative to Messenian Pylos, and the controversy was limited to the single name Pheai in *Odyssey* 15. It is not likely that a new version of *Iliad* 11, offering a different solution to the question of Pylos, would so soon thereafter have been either composed or accepted by one or the other of the parties to the controversy. This goes in particular for Sparta, which had only recently put its case for an Eleian Pylos, and it goes for Athens as well, which never forgot that Pylos lay in Messenia. If these two parties, whose interest in Pylos's location emerges clearly from the *Homeric Hymn to Apollo*, were not involved, it is highly unlikely that anyone else was interested in the question to the extent of providing a new solution.

§5.41 Elis's primary aggression against the cities of Triphylia took place in the fifth century, as we know from Herodotus, a contemporary witness. Herodotus names six cities in Triphylia that (according to his account) were founded from Laconia by Minyans, the descendants of Argonauts who had settled in Laconia, and he comments that most of these six cities were overthrown by the Eleians during his lifetime: the cities in question are Lepreon, Makistos, Phrixai, Pyrgos, Epion, and Noudion.[139] Herodotus does not say which of the six cities were overthrown in his lifetime ("most" must mean that either four or five of them suffered this fate), but one that successfully defended itself against Elis and managed to survive at least during Herodotus's lifetime was Lepreon.[140] Lepreon, as we have seen, included in its

---

at least, was later inhabited and is unlikely to have been abandoned in the first place. Evidence for the later history of Skillous and Makistos in Triphylia, and of the Pisatis, is discussed in EN5.17.

139 Herodotus 4.148; Herodotus says that of the Minyans forced to leave Laconia some joined the Spartan colonization of Thera, but most went to the country of the Paroreatai and Kaukones (i.e. Triphylia), whom they drove out to found the six new cities: οἱ γὰρ πλέονες αὐτῶν ἐτράποντο ἐς τοὺς Παρωρεάτας καὶ Καύκωνας, τούτους δὲ ἐξελάσαντες ἐκ τῆς χώρης σφέας αὐτοὺς ἐξ μοίρας διεῖλον, καὶ ἔπειτα ἔκτισαν πόλις τάσδε ἐν αὐτοῖσι, Λέπρεον, Μάκιστον, Φρίξας, Πύργον, Ἔπιον, Νούδιον· τουτέων δὲ τὰς πλέονας ἐπ᾽ ἐμέο Ἠλεῖοι ἐπόρθησαν, "Most of them turned toward the Paroreatai and Kaukones, and driving these people out of their country, they divided themselves into six groups, and amongst them they then founded the following cities, Lepreon, Makiston, Phrixai, Pyrgon, Epion, Noudion. The Eleians destroyed most of these cities during my lifetime" (Herodotus 4.148.4).

140 We know that Lepreon still remained free of Elis in 418 BC (Thucydides 5.62), but it is unclear what happened after that (see below §5.44 end and n5.153 and n5.155). Whether Herodotus was still alive and at work on the *Histories* after 421 BC is controversial (cf. EN5.18 end to n5.145 below).

territory the Pylos that is the apparent focus of Nestor's expanded story in
Iliad 11.[141] Lepreon's resistance to Elis, which is well documented for the first
half of the Peloponnesian War, provides exactly the right motivation for the
expansion of Nestor's story in *Iliad* 11: Nestor's story could be made to evoke
Lepreon's resistance to Elis if the Pylos of this story was the city that Lepreon
contained within its borders, and this, in effect, is what the expansion of
Nestor's story is meant to show.

§5.42 To consider the question of who could have taken Lepreon's part
in this way, we need to follow the story more closely. The story begins at some
time before the Peloponnesian War, when a previously independent town of
Pylos was united with Lepreon; although the evidence is fragmentary, this
part of the story emerges reasonably clearly. Strabo, in a rather confused
account, says that Pylos was united with Lepreon after a successful war; he
implies that the Spartans brought about the synoecism, but, as the rest of his
account shows, the Eleians rather than the Spartans must have done so.[142] If
Elis united Pylos with Lepreon after a successful war, it is tempting to see a
reference to these events in Thucydides, in his account of how the hostili-
ties between Elis and Lepreon during the Peloponnesian War first began.
According to Thucydides, Elis once came to Lepreon's aid in a war against the
Arcadians; in return for their help the Eleians demanded half of Lepreon's
land, but after the war they allowed Lepreon to keep the land and pay an
annual tribute of one talent instead. The Lepreans paid the tribute until the

141 See n5.23 and n5.24 above on the location of Pylos north of Lepreon on the Leprean border,
and the question of whether the population of Pylos remained in place or was moved to
Lepreon when Lepreon absorbed Pylos.

142 Strabo 8.3.30 (end): καὶ αὐτὸν δὲ τὸν Πύλον τὸν ἠμαθόεντα εἰς τὸ Λέπρειον συνῴκισαν,
χαριζόμενοι τοῖς Λεπρεάταις κρατήσασι πολέμῳ, καὶ ἄλλας πολλὰς τῶν κατοικιῶν
κατέσπασαν, ὅσας γ' ἑώρων αὐτοπραγεῖν ἐθελούσας, καὶ φόρους ἐπράξαντο, "They joined
sandy Pylos itself with Lepreon, gratifying the Lepreans who had prevailed in a war,
and they destroyed as many of the other communities as they saw wishing to act inde-
pendently, and they exacted tribute." The subject of this sentence, which refers to the
overthrow of Triphylian cities (καὶ ἄλλας πολλὰς τῶν κατοικιῶν κατέσπασαν, "and they
destroyed many of the other settlements"), must be the Eleians, as in Herodotus 4.148.4,
which refers to the same events; by the same token the tribute mentioned (καὶ φόρους
ἐπράξαντο, "and they exacted tribute") must refer to the tribute exacted by Elis from
Lepreon as described by Thucydides. The problem is that the sentence comes at the end of
a sweeping historical account of how Sparta helped Elis gain control over Triphylia as far
as the Messenian border (this problematic passage is discussed in EN5.18 to n5.145 below).
The sentence quoted above is appended to the end of this passage with no indication of a
change of subject, and the subject thus still seems to be the Spartans. For the necessary
change of subject to the Eleians in this sentence, see Bölte *RE* 'Triphylia' 197. The war won
by Lepreon, after which Elis incorporated Pylos into Lepreon, is considered further in
EN5.18 to n5.145 below.

outbreak of the Peloponnesian War, when they stopped; Elis then tried to exact the tribute by force and Lepreon turned to Sparta for help.[143] The land that Lepreon agreed to give up, but in the end kept, was in all likelihood the town of Pylos: Thucydides' expression "half the land" (ἡμίσεια τῆς γῆς) corresponds well to Pylos, for Pylos, at least notionally, doubled Lepreon's territory when it was added to it.[144] Strabo and Thucydides probably refer to the same war in their respective accounts, but they do not necessarily do so.[145] This, however, is a secondary point. What seems clear is that the territory for which Lepreon paid Elis tribute until the outbreak of the Peloponnesian War was Pylos.

§5.43 At the outbreak of the Peloponnesian War Lepreon seized the opportunity to stop paying the tribute to Elis, which was doubtless burdensome.[146] In terms of Homeric analogy, this was like Nestor's putting an end to Elis's raids on Pylos's cattle. The analogy was all the closer inasmuch as Lepreon's payments of tribute, we can be reasonably sure, were for the sake of the Pylos that lay within its borders. This time, however, it was not Nestor who saved the day against the enemy to the north, but the Spartan army. Sparta, as much as Lepreon, had a stake in the conflict that ensued with Elis, and this is an important point in understanding the expansion of Nestor's story. With respect to Nestor's Homeric city Sparta had a history of finding an alternative to Messenian Pylos, and it makes sense that Sparta should again

---

143 Thucydides 5.31.2-3: πολέμου γὰρ γενομένου ποτὲ πρὸς Ἀρκάδων τινὰς Λεπρεάταις καὶ Ἡλείων παρακληθέντων ὑπὸ Λεπρεατῶν ἐς ξυμμαχίαν ἐπὶ τῇ ἡμισείᾳ τῆς γῆς καὶ λυσάντων τὸν πόλεμον Ἡλεῖοι τὴν γῆν νεμομένοις αὐτοῖς τοῖς Λεπρεάταις τάλαντον ἔταξαν τῷ Διὶ τῷ Ὀλυμπίῳ ἀποφέρειν. καὶ μέχρι μὲν τοῦ Ἀττικοῦ πολέμου ἀπέφερον, ἔπειτα παυσαμένων διὰ πρόφασιν τοῦ πολέμου οἱ Ἡλεῖοι ἐπηνάγκαζον, οἱ δ' ἐτράποντο πρὸς τοὺς Λακεδαιμονίους, "Once when the Lepreans were at war with certain Arcadians and the Eleians were summoned as allies by the Lepreans on the condition of <u>half their land</u>, the Eleians, when they concluded the war, fixed a tribute of one talent for the Lepreans to pay to Olympian Zeus for the land, which the Lepreans continued to inhabit. They paid the tribute until the Attic war, when they stopped on the pretext of the war; the Eleians began to compel them by force, and they turned to the Spartans."

144 Cf. Bölte 1934:341: "It is an obvious thing to see in the territory of Pylos the ἡμίσεια τῆς χώρας, 'half the land,' that according to Thucydides 5.31.2 the Lepreans offered the Eleians for their armed help against the Arcadians" ("Es liegt nahe, in dem Gebiet von Pylos die ἡμίσεια τῆς χώρας zu erblicken, welche die Lepreaten nach Thuk. 5.31.2 den Eleiern für Waffenhilfe gegen die Arkader anboten"); cf. also Bölte *RE* 'Triphylia' 197–198.

145 In Thucydides Elis demands half of Lepreon before fighting the war; in Strabo Pylos becomes part of Lepreon after the war. How these two accounts can be reconciled is considered in EN5.18.

146 Andrewes (Gomme et al. 1970) comments on Thucydides 5.31.2 that as an annual rent a talent "looks high for half the Lepreatis," although that depends on the size of the latter at the time.

somehow be involved when, at a later time and in different circumstances, a new alternative was put forth. But we need to follow the story more closely to understand Sparta's role.

§5.44 We have already seen that when Lepreon shook off its annual payment of tribute, the Eleians "brought pressure to bear" (ἐπηνάγκαζον), and Lepreon turned to Sparta for help.[147] According to Thucydides Sparta was asked to arbitrate the dispute, but the Eleians, thinking that they would lose the arbitration, did not wait for a decision and began to lay waste the Lepreans' land. The Spartans proceeded with the arbitration anyway and decided in favor of Lepreon, which they judged to be an independent state, and against Elis, which they judged to be an aggressor; when Elis did not respect their decision, the Spartans stationed a garrison in Lepreon.[148] Thucydides does not make clear how early in the Archidamian War these events occurred, only that the Lepreans stopped their payments of tribute after the war began. The peace that ended the ten-years war in 421 did not change the situation, and Elis felt grievously wronged by Sparta for having received its subject city in revolt and for not returning it at the war's end, as, in Elis's view, Sparta was bound to do. The grievance was serious enough for Elis to join the anti-Spartan alliance organized by Argos when Argos's thirty-year treaty with Sparta was about to expire in 421.[149] It is in relation to

147 Thucydides 5.31.3 (n5.143 above).
148 Thucydides 5.31.3–4: καὶ δίκης Λακεδαιμονίοις ἐπιτραπείσης ὑποτοπήσαντες οἱ Ἠλεῖοι μὴ ἴσον ἕξειν ἀνέντες τὴν ἐπιτροπὴν Λεπρεατῶν τὴν γῆν ἔτεμον. οἱ δὲ Λακεδαιμόνιοι οὐδὲν ἧσσον ἐδίκασαν αὐτονόμους εἶναι Λεπρεάτας καὶ ἀδικεῖν Ἠλείους, καὶ ὡς οὐκ ἐμμεινάντων τῇ ἐπιτροπῇ φρουρὰν ὁπλιτῶν ἐσέπεμψαν ἐς Λέπρεον, "After the matter was turned over to the Spartans for arbitration, the Eleians, suspecting that they would not get their due, gave up the arbitration and began to ravage the Lepreans' land. The Spartans nonetheless decided that the Lepreans were independent and the Eleians were in the wrong, and on the grounds that the Eleians had not remained in the arbitration they sent a garrison of hoplites to Lepreon."
149 Thucydides 5.31.5: οἱ δὲ Ἠλεῖοι νομίζοντες πόλιν σφῶν ἀφεστηκυῖαν δέξασθαι τοὺς Λακεδαιμονίους καὶ τὴν ξυνθήκην προφέροντες ἐν ᾗ εἴρητο, ἃ ἔχοντες ἐς τὸν Ἀττικὸν πόλεμον καθίσταντό τινες, ταῦτα ἔχοντας καὶ ἐξελθεῖν, ὡς οὐκ ἴσον ἔχοντες ἀφίστανται πρὸς τοὺς Ἀργείους, καὶ τὴν ξυμμαχίαν, ὥσπερ προείρητο, καὶ οὗτοι ἐποιήσαντο, "The Eleians, thinking that the Spartans had received a city that had revolted from them, and citing the treaty in which it is stated that what the various cities had going into the Attic war they should also have at the end of the war, thinking that they had been treated unfairly they revolted to the Argives, with whom they made an alliance, as has already been said." It is not clear to what treaty the Eleians referred in their charge against Sparta. Andrewes (Gomme et al. 1970) ad loc. discusses the possibility that it may have been the Peace of Nikias as originally discussed but not as finally formulated (the Peace of Nikias contained no provision regarding subject states); in that case the Eleians also extended the provision from relations between adversaries to relations between allies. Another possibility is that

Elis's action in joining this alliance that Thucydides gives the background to the dispute between Elis and Sparta over Lepreon. Later in the same summer of 421 Sparta began to settle helot soldiers returning from Thrace and new helot recruits in Lepreon.[150] In the following summer, 420, the Olympic games were celebrated, which the Eleians as usual oversaw; the festival became a scene of great alarm when the Eleians refused to admit the Spartans to the games, and it was feared that the Spartan army would appear on the scene to force an entry for the Spartans and allow them to sacrifice and compete. The ban against the Spartans had to do with their alleged violation of the Olympic truce when they attacked a fort held by the Eleians and sent a force of a thousand hoplites into Lepreon.[151] The Eleians imposed a fine on the Spartans for the violation of the truce, but the Spartans refused to pay it on the grounds that the truce had not been proclaimed in Sparta when their hoplites were sent out. It was for refusing to pay the fine that the Spartans were banned from the games, and the Spartans themselves let the matter lie, staying home to sacrifice. At the festival, however, fear of a Spartan reprisal was raised to a fever pitch when a prominent Spartan, Likhas, entered his chariot into competition together with the Theban contestants and won the race. Because he had no right to enter the race, the Boeotian state was

the Peloponnesian allies made a treaty among themselves at the outbreak of the war, but this would imply, as Andewes says, an extraordinary degree of mutual distrust.

150 Thucydides 5.34.1: καὶ τοῦ αὐτοῦ θέρους ἤδη ἡκόντων αὐτοῖς τῶν ἀπὸ Θράκης μετὰ Βρασίδου ἐξελθόντων στρατιωτῶν, οὓς ὁ Κλεαρίδας μετὰ τὰς σπονδὰς ἐκόμισεν, οἱ Λακεδαιμόνιοι ἐψηφίσαντο τοὺς μὲν μετὰ Βρασίδου Εἵλωτας μαχεσαμένους ἐλευθέρους εἶναι καὶ οἰκεῖν ὅπου ἂν βούλωνται, καὶ ὕστερον οὐ πολλῷ αὐτοὺς μετὰ τῶν νεοδαμώδων ἐς Λέπρεον κατέστησαν, κείμενον ἐπὶ τῆς Λακωνικῆς καὶ τῆς Ἠλείας, ὄντες ἤδη διάφοροι Ἠλείοις, "In the same summer the soldiers returning with Brasidas from Thrace, whom Klearidas had brought there after the treaty, arrived in Sparta; the Spartans voted that the helots who fought with Brasidas were free and could live where they wished, and not long after settled them with the new helot recruits in Lepreon, which borders on the Spartan and Eleian countries, the Spartans already being at odds with the Eleians." The helots who fought with Brasidas in Thrace received their freedom on their return; the other group mentioned in the passage, the *neodamôdai*, were also freed helots, but they seem to have received their freedom before or at their enrollment. Both groups were settled in Lepreon after the peace of 421.

151 Thucydides 5.49.1: καὶ Λακεδαιμόνιοι τοῦ ἱεροῦ ὑπὸ Ἠλείων εἴρχθησαν ὥστε μὴ θύειν μηδ' ἀγωνίζεσθαι, οὐκ ἐκτίνοντες τὴν δίκην αὐτοῖς ἣν ἐν τῷ Ὀλυμπιακῷ νόμῳ Ἠλεῖοι κατεδικάσαντο αὐτῶν φάσκοντες ‹ἐς› σφᾶς ἐπὶ Φύρκον τε τεῖχος ὅπλα ἐπενεγκεῖν καὶ ἐς Λέπρεον αὐτῶν ὁπλίτας ἐν ταῖς Ὀλυμπιακαῖς σπονδαῖς ἐσέμψαι, "The Spartans were banned from the temple so as not to sacrifice or compete because they had not paid the penalty that the Eleians decided against them according to the Olympic law; the Eleians claimed that the Spartans had carried out an armed attack against them at Phyrkos, a fort, and had sent hoplites of theirs into Lepreon during the Olympic truce." The fort, which is otherwise unknown, was presumably in the territory of Lepreon.

announced the victor. To show that he was the true victor, Likhas came onto the course and crowned the charioteer, whereupon the Eleian umpires beat him in full view and drove him off.[152] This drama, for all its intensity, changed nothing with respect to Lepreon, which like Sparta (except for Likhas) stayed away from the games. Two years later, in the summer of 418, the situation in Lepreon was still the same. Argos's anti-Spartan alliance, joined by Mantinea and Elis in 421, and by Athens in 420, took various actions against Sparta in the summer of 418 before being defeated by Sparta at Mantinea. After freeing Arcadian hostages held by Sparta in Orkhomenos, the alliance debated where to go next: the Mantineans wanted to attack Tegea, the Eleians Lepreon; when the Argives and the Athenians sided with Mantinea, the Eleians went home in anger.[153] This is the last that we hear of the standoff between Elis and Lepreon

152 Thucydides 5.50.4: δέος δ' ἐγένετο τῇ πανηγύρει μέγα μὴ ξὺν ὅπλοις ἔλθωσιν οἱ Λακεδαιμόνιοι, ἄλλως τε καὶ ἐπειδὴ καὶ Λίχας ὁ Ἀρκεσιλάου Λακεδαιμόνιος ἐν τῷ ἀγῶνι ὑπὸ τῶν ῥαβδούχων πληγὰς ἔλαβεν, ὅτι νικῶντος τοῦ ἑαυτοῦ ζεύγους καὶ ἀνακηρυχθέντος Βοιωτῶν δημοσίου κατὰ τὴν οὐκ ἐξουσίαν τῆς ἀγωνίσεως προελθὼν ἐς τὸν ἀγῶνα ἀνέδησε τὸν ἡνίοχον, βουλόμενος δηλῶσαι ὅτι ἑαυτοῦ ἦν τὸ ἅρμα· ὥστε πολλῷ δὴ μᾶλλον ἐπεφόβηντο πάντες καὶ ἐδόκει τι νέον ἔσεσθαι. οἱ μέντοι Λακεδαιμόνιοι ἡσύχασάν τε καὶ ἡ ἑορτὴ αὐτοῖς οὕτω διῆλθεν, "There was a great fear at the festival that the Spartans would come in arms, especially when the Spartan Likhas, the son of Arkesilaos, was given blows on the course by the umpires; when his chariot won and the Boeotian state was proclaimed the victor because of his ineligibility, he proceeded onto the course and tied a wreath onto the charioteer, wishing to show that the chariot was his; as a result all were in a much greater state of fear, and it seemed that something would happen. But the Spartans remained calm and thus the festival passed for them." Thucydides says that the Boeotian people was announced the victor in the race; Xenophon, who also tells of the incident, says that Likhas gave his chariot to the Thebans to race (*Hellenica* 3.2.21). Xenophon makes clear how painful the whole episode was to the Spartans: when the Spartans made war on the Eleians twenty years later, one of their grievances even then was having been barred from the games and having had one of their citizens, an old man, beaten and driven from the course: Λακεδαιμόνιοι...πάλαι ὀργιζόμενοι τοῖς Ἠλείοις καὶ ὅτι ἐποιήσαντο συμμαχίαν πρὸς Ἀθηναίους καὶ Ἀργείους καὶ Μαντινέας, καὶ ὅτι δίκην φάσκοντες καταδεδικάσθαι αὐτῶν ἐκώλυον καὶ τοῦ ἱππικοῦ καὶ τοῦ γυμνικοῦ ἀγῶνος, καὶ οὐ μόνον ταῦτ' ἦρκει, ἀλλὰ καὶ Λίχα παραδόντος Θηβαίοις τὸ ἅρμα, ἐπεὶ ἐκηρύττοντο νικῶντες, ὅτε εἰσῆλθε Λίχας στεφανώσων τὸν ἡνίοχον, μαστιγοῦντες αὐτόν, ἄνδρα γέροντα, ἐξήλασαν, "The Spartans... had long been angry with the Eleians because of the alliance that they had made with the Athenians, Argives, and Mantineans, and also because they had barred the Spartans from the chariot race and athletic competition, claiming that a fine had been levied against them; and this was not enough, but after Likhas handed over his chariot to the Thebans and they were proclaimed victors, and when he then entered the course to crown the charioteer, the Eleians beat him, an old man, and drove him off" (Xenophon *Hellenica* 3.2.21).

153 Thucydides 5.62.1–2: μετὰ δὲ τοῦτο ἔχοντες ἤδη τὸν Ὀρχομενὸν ἐβουλεύοντο οἱ ξύμμαχοι ἐφ' ὅτι χρὴ πρῶτον ἰέναι τῶν λοιπῶν. καὶ Ἠλεῖοι μὲν ἐπὶ Λέπρεον ἐκέλευον, Μαντινῆς δὲ ἐπὶ Τεγέαν· καὶ προσέθεντο οἱ Ἀργεῖοι καὶ Ἀθηναῖοι τοῖς Μαντινεῦσιν. καὶ οἱ μὲν Ἠλεῖοι ὀργισθέντες ὅτι οὐκ ἐπὶ Λέπρεον ἐψηφίσαντο ἀνεχώρησαν ἐπ' οἴκου, "After this, having Orkhomenos now in hand, the allies debated which of the remaining objectives they

until the end of the war, when Sparta set Elis's subject cities in Triphylia free. Lepreon was among the cities freed, and it follows that at some time between 418 and 404 Elis regained control of Lepreon from Sparta.[154] We do not know when or in what circumstances that occurred.[155]

§5.45 Nestor's story, in my view, was expanded while Lepreon still held out against Elis, for after Lepreon succumbed the expansion of the story would have been pointless. This leaves a fairly long period to consider for the composition of the passages, namely the twenty-seven years of the Peloponnesian War. But there is a passage in Nestor's story that has so far been left out of account, which relates, I think, to the Olympic celebration of 420 BC. The humiliation inflicted by Elis on the Spartan Likhas after the

---

should attack first. The Eleians urged Lepreon, the Mantineans Tegea, and the Argives and Athenians supported the Mantineans. The Eleians, angry that they had not voted to attack Lepreon, went home." Later in the summer the Eleians sent three thousand hoplites to the allies, but they arrived too late for the battle at Mantinea (Thucydides 5.75.5).

154 Xenophon *Hellenica* 3.2.25; the Lepreans, with the Makistians, were the first to revolt to Agis when he invaded, but others soon followed: περιόντι δὲ τῷ ἐνιαυτῷ φαίνουσι πάλιν οἱ ἔφοροι φρουρὰν ἐπὶ τὴν Ἦλιν, καὶ συνεστρατεύοντο τῷ Ἄγιδι πλὴν Βοιωτῶν καὶ Κορινθίων οἵ τε ἄλλοι πάντες σύμμαχοι καὶ οἱ Ἀθηναῖοι. ἐμβαλόντος δὲ τοῦ Ἄγιδος δι' Αὐλῶνος, εὐθὺς μὲν Λεπρεᾶται ἀποστάντες τῶν Ἠλείων προσεχώρησαν αὐτῷ, εὐθὺς δὲ Μακίστιοι, ἐχόμενοι δ' Ἐπιταλιεῖς. διαβαίνοντι δὲ τὸν ποταμὸν προσεχώρουν Λετρῖνοι καὶ Ἀμφίδολοι καὶ Μαργανεῖς. ἐκ δὲ τούτου ἐλθὼν εἰς Ὀλυμπίαν ἔθυε τῷ Διὶ τῷ Ὀλυμπίῳ· κωλύειν δὲ οὐδεὶς ἔτι ἐπειρᾶτο. θύσας δὲ πρὸς τὸ ἄστυ ἐπορεύετο, κόπτων καὶ κάων τὴν χώραν, καὶ ὑπέρπολλα μὲν κτήνη, ὑπέρπολλα δὲ ἀνδράποδα ἡλίσκετο ἐκ τῆς χώρας, "In the course of the year the ephors called up a levy against Elis, and all the allies except the Boeotians and Corinthians joined Agis in the campaign, including the Athenians. When Agis invaded the country through Aulon, the Lepreans immediately revolted from the Eleians and joined him, as did the Makistians, and next the Epitalians. When he crossed the river the Letrinians, Amphidolians, and Marganians joined him. After this he went to Olympia and sacrificed to Olympian Zeus; no one any longer tried to stop him. After he sacrificed he marched toward the city, cutting and burning the land, and a great number of beasts and a great number of slaves were captured from the country" (Xenophon *Hellenica* 3.2.25–26).

155 Aristophanes' *Birds*, produced in 414 BC, calls Lepreon "Eleian," but this is probably only to identify the city geographically (cf. Andrewes in Gomme et al. 1970 on Thucydides 5.31.2); thus it does not necessarily follow that Elis had regained Lepreon by 414. The two heroes of the play seek a new city to inhabit and the Hoopoe first suggests two Greek cities, Lepreon in Elis and Opous in Lokris, both of which are rejected with puns: Lepreon because of Melanthios, an obnoxious tragic poet said to have leprosy; Opous because of Opountios, a one-eyed informer (lines 149–154). The important point is the balance between the expressions "Lepreon in Elis" (τὸν Ἠλεῖον Λέπρεον) and "the Opountians of Lokris" (τῆς Λοκρίδος Ὀπούντιοι): geographical location seems to be the point in the one case as in the other. One might argue that the passage indicates that in 414 Lepreon was open for settlement, but the same possibility must then be admitted for Opous (cf. Andrewes). The status of Lepreon in 414 is simply not known. (For the gender of τὸν Ἠλεῖον Λέπρεον in Aristophanes see Fraenkel 1959:11–12.)

chariot race in 420, which caused such a stir at the time, and which the Spartans still remembered with anger at the end of the war, has a parallel in Nestor's story. Neleus once sent a four-horse chariot to Elis to compete in a race, and Augeias outraged the Pylian king by seizing his horses and sending his charioteer packing; the episode is narrated when Neleus takes his share of the spoil from Nestor's cattle raid (*Iliad* 11.696–702):

ἐκ δ' ὃ γέρων ἀγέλην τε βοῶν καὶ πῶϋ μέγ' οἰῶν

εἵλετο κρινάμενος τριηκόσι' ἠδὲ νομῆας.

καὶ γὰρ τῷ χρεῖος μέγ' ὀφείλετ' ἐν Ἤλιδι δίῃ

τέσσαρες ἀθλοφόροι ἵπποι αὐτοῖσιν ὄχεσφιν

ἐλθόντες μετ' ἄεθλα· περὶ τρίποδος γὰρ ἔμελλον

θεύσεσθαι· τοὺς δ' αὖθι ἄναξ ἀνδρῶν Αὐγείας

κάσχεθε, τὸν δ' ἐλατῆρ' ἀφίει ἀκαχήμενον ἵππων.

The old man took out for himself a herd of cattle and a great
        flock of sheep,
choosing three hundred and the herders.
For a great debt was owed to him in shining Elis,
four prizewinning horses together with the chariot,
which had gone there for prizes; for they were going to run
for a tripod, but Augeias, king of men, kept them there
and sent the driver away grieving for the horses.

Cantieni, in his study of Nestor's story, makes a compelling case that this passage, like the three passages containing precise geographical references, is a later expansion of the story.[156] Before the passage begins Pylians who had been robbed by the Epeians are summoned at dawn to collect their due from Nestor's cattle raid, and past events are briefly narrated to explain the low state of Pylos's fortunes at the time of Nestor's raid (*Iliad* 11.685–695):

κήρυκες δ' ἐλίγαινον ἅμ' ἠοῖ φαινομένηφι

τοὺς ἴμεν οἶσι χρεῖος ὀφείλετ' ἐν Ἤλιδι δίῃ·

οἳ δὲ συναγρόμενοι Πυλίων ἡγήτορες ἄνδρες

δαίτρευον· πολέσιν γὰρ Ἐπειοὶ χρεῖος ὄφειλον,

ὡς ἡμεῖς παῦροι κεκακωμένοι ἐν Πύλῳ ἦμεν·

---

156 Cantieni 1942:63–67.

ἐλθὼν γάρ ῥ' ἐκάκωσε βίη Ἡρακληείη
τῶν προτέρων ἐτέων, κατὰ δ' ἔκταθεν ὅσσοι ἄριστοι·
δώδεκα γὰρ Νηλῆος ἀμύμονος υἱέες ἦμεν·
τῶν οἶος λιπόμην, οἳ δ' ἄλλοι πάντες ὄλοντο.
ταῦθ' ὑπερηφανέοντες Ἐπειοὶ χαλκοχίτωνες
ἡμέας ὑβρίζοντες ἀτάσθαλα μηχανόωντο.

The heralds made a shrill cry when dawn appeared
for those to come to whom a debt was owed in shining Elis,
and the Pylians' leading men came together
and divided the spoil. For the Epeians owed a debt to many,
since few of us were left in Pylos and we were badly off,
for mighty Heracles had come and hurt us badly
in earlier years; all the best men had been killed.
Twelve sons of faultless Neleus we had been,
but of those only I was left; the others had all perished.
Emboldened by this the bronze-clad Epeians
treated us outrageously and devised reckless deeds.

In this passage the narrative moves skillfully from present to past to more distant past, and then to recent past again;[157] the passage that comes next returns to the present and continues with Neleus's share of the spoil. This is the case with or without the expansion coming next. Without the expansion the story moves forward in the present from Neleus's share of the spoil and the distribution of the rest to the Pylians' sacrifices to the gods and the sudden attack of the Epeian horsemen (*Iliad* 11.703–709):

τῶν ὃ γέρων ἐπέων κεχολωμένος ἠδὲ καὶ ἔργων
ἐξέλετ' ἄσπετα πολλά· τὰ δ' ἄλλ' ἐς δῆμον ἔδωκε
δαιτρεύειν, μή τίς οἱ ἀτεμβόμενος κίοι ἴσης.

---

157 As Cantieni 1942:64n135 points out, the two steps back in time are made with the same verbal device, namely the change of a passive expression into an active equivalent: χρεῖος ὀφείλετο in line 686 is changed into χρεῖος ὄφειλον in line 688, and the focus is thereby shifted from the distribution of Nestor's spoil in the present to the Epeians' raids in the past; κεκακωμένοι in line 689 is changed into ἐκάκωσε in line 690, and the focus is thereby shifted from the Pylians' condition in the past to Heracles' still earlier sack. After the four lines devoted to Heracles' sack (690–693) the narrative moves forward in time again through the same two stages, the first being a return to the Eleians' depredations of the Pylians (lines 694–695).

ἡμεῖς μὲν τὰ ἕκαστα διείπομεν, ἀμφί τε ἄστυ
ἔρδομεν ἱρὰ θεοῖς· οἳ δὲ τρίτῳ ἤματι πάντες
ἦλθον ὁμῶς αὐτοί τε πολεῖς καὶ μώνυχες ἵπποι
πανσυδίῃ.

Angered by their words and deeds
the old man took out an immense number; the rest he gave to
    the people
to distribute, so that no one would go away deprived of a fair
    share.
We were attending to all this, and around the city
we were making sacrifices to the gods; but on the third day they all
came, both the many men themselves and their solid-hoofed
    horses,
at great speed.

With the expansion, on the other hand, the narrative does not move forward but goes back again into the past for the story of Neleus's chariot. This doubling of the background to Nestor's cattle raid is the first sign that the story of Neleus's chariot is not integral to the older version of the story.[158] Another sign is the plural pronoun τῶν at the beginning of the passage above (line 703). This refers to the Epeians, who are the subject of the two immediately preceding lines in the older version of the story ('Επειοὶ...μηχανόωντο, lines 694–695); but when the expansion intervenes, the pronoun has no clear antecedent, for then the subject of the preceding lines is the singular Augeias. Perhaps the most telling sign of expansion has to do with the motivation for Nestor's cattle raid. Without the expansion there is only one motivation, namely cattle raids carried out by the Epeians; the Pylians, including Neleus, all suffered the same harm, and all were made whole by the cattle

---

158 Ring composition is used to give the background to Nestor's cattle raid: the point from which the narrative departs and to which it returns is the distribution of spoil. The expansion also employs ring composition in making Neleus's spoil a point of departure and return. One would have expected the story of Neleus's horses to be told in the first passage, when the narrative moves forward from the remote past, Heracles' sack, to the depredations of the Eleians, but there only vague terms are used (ταῦθ' ὑπερηφανέοντες... / ἡμέας ὑβρίζοντες ἀτάσθαλα μηχανόωντο): the important story, Heracles' sack, has been told, and the Epeians' outrage of the weakened Pylians is already known (they stole the Pylians' cattle); the narrative does not waste time repeating what is already known but returns to the present to continue with the story. Cf. Cantieni 1942:65, who compares certain aspects of the Meleager story (Iliad 9.529–599).

that Nestor brought back.[159] The story of Neleus's chariot provides a second motivation, which, like the second return to the past in the narrative, cannot be integral to the older version of the story; if the theft of Neleus's horses had motivated Nestor's raid in the older version of the story, Nestor would surely have recovered the horses as part of the story, and that does not happen in *Iliad* 11.[160] There are other details in the expanded passage that are not decisive in themselves, but nevertheless raise questions.[161] The four-horse chariot has no good parallel in Homer, where the two-horse chariot is the rule, as, for example, in the chariot race for Patroclus: there is only one other example of a four-horse chariot in the *Iliad*, when Hector calls to his four horses by name, and the fact that these names are followed by a verb in the dual underscores the anomaly;[162] in the *Odyssey* the only example of a four-horse chariot occurs in a simile, where features of the poets' contemporary world are permitted.[163] As an event at the Olympic games the four-horse chariot race was an

---

159 See Cantieni 1942:28–31, 61–63; Cantieni terms the purpose of Nestor's raid "compensation for stolen property" ("Entschädigung für Geraubtes," p. 29), and he interprets the phrase ῥύσι' ἐλαυνόμενος, "driving off cattle in reprisal," in *Iliad* 11.674 in this sense (p. 31 and n51); ῥύσια occurs only here in Homer.

160 Cf. §5.46 and n5.166 below.

161 The language of this expansion, as of the three other expansions of Nestor's story, is acceptably Homeric, but there is a weakness in the second line of the passage (697): the neuter plural adjective τριηκόσια, "three hundred," has no noun to modify; presumably three hundred head of livestock are meant, but the adjective is connected only very loosely with the phrase ἀγέλην τε βοῶν καὶ πῶϋ μέγ' οἰῶν, "a herd of cattle and a great flock of sheep" in the preceding line. The model for the phrase τριηκόσι' ἠδὲ νομῆας, "three hundred and the herders," in *Iliad* 11.697 is seen in *Odyssey* 21.18–19, where τριηκόσι', "three hundred," agrees with μῆλα, "sheep," in the preceding line: μῆλα γὰρ ἐξ Ἰθάκης Μεσσήνιοι ἄνδρες ἄειραν / νηυσὶ πολυκλήϊσι τριηκόσι' ἠδὲ νομῆας, "Messenian men with their many-benched ships took from Ithaca three hundred sheep and their herders."

162 *Iliad* 8.185–186:

Ξάνθέ τε καὶ σὺ Πόδαργε καὶ Αἴθων Λάμπέ τε δῖε
νῦν μοι τὴν κομιδὴν ἀποτίνετον.

Xanthos, and you, Podargos, and Aithon, and shining Lampos,
repay me [you two] now for your keep.

163 The Phaeacian ship that carries Odysseus home is compared to a four-horse chariot (*Odyssey* 13.81–85):

ἡ δ', ὥς τ' ἐν πεδίῳ τετράοροι ἄρσενες ἵπποι,
πάντες ἅμ' ὁρμηθέντες ὑπὸ πληγῆσιν ἱμάσθλης
ὑψόσ' ἀειρόμενοι ῥίμφα πρήσσουσι κέλευθον,
ὣς ἄρα τῆς πρύμνη μὲν ἀείρετο, κῦμα δ' ὄπισθεν
πορφύρεον μέγα θῦε πολυφλοίσβοιο θαλάσσης.

731

innovation dated to the twenty-fifth Olympiad, 680 BC.[164] It is not that a four-horse chariot race is impossible in Homer;[165] it is rather that in Nestor's story about his youth, which purports to represent a time long before, say, the chariot race for Patroclus, such a thing is very hard to credit in view of the very clear and consistent Homeric pattern.

§5.46 The expansion of Nestor's story is, I think, meant to evoke the Olympic games, but not the games of the eighth or the seventh century BC. Although the theft of Neleus's horses did not occur in the older version of Nestor's story in *Iliad* 11, the myth itself probably goes back to the sixth or early fifth century BC, for the fifth-century Athenian author Pherekydes is known to have recounted it. In Pherekydes' telling, furthermore, we find the full version of the myth: here Neleus's horses are not only stolen, they are also recovered; Nestor leads an army into Elis for this express purpose.[166] In

---

As four yoked stallions on the plain,
all surging together under the whip's blows,
rise high as they quickly traverse their course,
so the ship's stern rose, and behind it ran
a great dark wave of the much resounding sea.

164 Sextus Iulius Africanus *Olympionicarum Fasti (List of the Victors at the Olympian Games)* for 680 BC: προσετέθη τέθριππον καὶ ἐνίκα Παγώνδας Θηβαῖος, "The four-horse chariot was added and Pagondas the Theban won"; Pausanias 5.8.7 records the same victory without specifying the chariot type: πέμπτη δὲ ἐπὶ ταῖς εἴκοσι...ἀνηγορεύθη Θηβαῖος Παγώνδας κρατῶν ἅρματι, "In the twenty-fifth Olympiad...the Theban Pagondas was proclaimed victor in the chariot."

165 Cf. Lorimer 1950:328: "Homer's treatment of the chariot is strictly 'Mycenaean'; in war and racing alike only a pair of horses is used.... At what time the team of four became usual we cannot tell; it sometimes occurs on Dipylon vases of a late type. The four-horse chariot-race was introduced at Olympia only in the 25th Olympiad, but had probably been practised as a sport much earlier. At the time of their entry into the Peloponnese neither the Dorians nor the north-west Greeks can have been proficient in the use of the chariot, and the latter would not be likely to encourage it at the festival which they controlled. If the team of four was known in the rugged land of Attica before the end of the eighth century, it must have been familiar in other regions at least as early. The allusion to such a chariot therefore in *Iliad* 11.699ff. need be no later, nor yet the simile in *Odyssey* 13.81." Lorimer cites a Dipylon-vase depiction and adds that "plastic groups of four horses forming the handle of the lids of Geometric pyxides should also be noted." Three horses, also found in art, figure in *Iliad* 16.466–475 and are mentioned in *Odyssey* 4.590.

166 Pherekydes *FGrHist* 3 F 118 (= scholia to *Iliad* 11.674): Νηλεὺς ὁ Ποσειδῶνος, ἱππικώτατος τῶν καθ' αὑτὸν γενόμενος, ἔπεμψεν εἰς Ἦλιν ἵππους ἐς τὸν ὑπ' Αὐγέου συντελούμενον ἀγῶνα. νικησάντων δὲ τούτων, φθονήσας Αὐγέας, ἀπέσπασε τούτους, καὶ τοὺς ἡνιόχους ἀφῆκεν ἀπράκτους. Νηλεὺς δὲ γνούς, ἡσυχίαν ἦγε. Νέστωρ δὲ, ὁ τῶν παίδων αὐτοῦ νεώτατος, στρατὸν ἀθροίσας, ἐπῆλθεν Ἤλιδι. καὶ πολλοὺς ἀποκτείνας, ἀπέλαβε τοὺς ἵππους. καὶ οὐκ ὀλίγην τῶν πολεμίων ἀπέσυραν λείαν. ἡ ἱστορία παρὰ Φερεκύδῃ, "Neleus, the son of Poseidon, the most skillful horseman of his time, sent horses to Elis to the contest being held by Augeias. When these won Augeias was envious and seized them,

the expansion of Nestor's story in *Iliad* 11, on the other hand, the myth has been tailored to another purpose, and that purpose, in my view, is the evocation of the Olympic games of 420.[167]

§5.47 If the argument is on track so far, the expansion of Nestor's story in *Iliad* 11 was intended for a Spartan audience at some date after 420 BC. It is now time to face the obvious problem that the end of the fifth century BC is quite late for a new version of Nestor's story, not only to take root, but to replace completely the older version of the story. It is not a great exaggeration to say that by that time the Homeric poems were known everywhere and that everyone would be aware of the change. The key must be that the new version was accepted into the Athenian state text used to control Homeric performances at the Panathenaia, for it is from such a text that our tradition of the poems derives.[168] If those who had responsibility for maintaining the state text wished to change it in some way, change was theoretically possible; it would depend on whether whoever wanted a change had enough influence at the highest levels of Athenian government to bring it about.

§5.48 A strong case can be made, I think, that the poet who, on the one hand, wished to appeal to a Spartan audience, and who, on the other hand, had great influence in the Athenian government, was none other than Alcibiades, who in his public career was uniquely associated with both cities. But before we consider the activities of the public figure, we need to consider his credentials as a poet. In West's *Iambi et Elegi Graeci* Alcibiades

and sent the charioteers away in failure. When Neleus found out he remained calm. But Nestor, the youngest of his sons, gathered an army and attacked Elis. He killed many men and took back the horses. They also stripped not a little spoil from the enemy. The story is in Pherekydes."

167 Note that in Pherekydes' account Neleus's horses won the race in Elis (νικησάντων δὲ τούτων); this is a further correspondence to Likhas's situation. It is also worth noting that the expansion of Nestor's story refers to one charioteer as compared to the plural ἡνιόχους in Pherekydes' account; the singular corresponds to Likhas's situation, although the real comparison for the rude dismissal of Neleus's charioteer is the treatment of Likhas himself. If the myth of the theft of Neleus's horses originated in the sixth century, as seems likely, it was clearly meant to evoke the Olympic games, which were in Eleian hands after c. 570 BC (see EN5.16 to n5.108 above; cf. §5.40 above).

168 Cf. Davison 1962:223: "The text which, from Aristarchus's time down to that of Wolf, held the field against all comers, must, as its orthography shows, have come to Alexandria by way of Athens." Davison, citing Wackernagel 1916 and Chantraine 1958:5–16 for this point, is more cautious as to whether the Athenian text was a Panathenaic text (Davison 1962:232n37, 224). This issue is discussed in EN5.19. *Iliad* 7.334–335, which seems to be a fifth-century Athenian interpolation (the bones of fallen warriors brought home to their children: see Jacoby 1944a:44n30; cf. Cassio 2002:119–120), would be a parallel for the period but on a considerably smaller scale.

is represented by a single elegiac couplet, which seems to be genuine, and which thus bears witness to Alcibiades' ability to do what was done in *Iliad* 11. The couplet is addressed to the comic poet Eupolis, who in his play *Baptai*, "Bathers," lampooned Alcibiades and other public figures as devotees of an orgiastic Thracian cult. Alcibiades responded to the "bath" given him on stage by threatening, in the couplet in question, to give Eupolis a real "bath" in the sea, and to drown him in the bitterest waters. The couplet, which is preserved by the scholia to Aelius Aristides, has uncertain wording at the beginning of the first line, but the sense is perfectly clear; the following restoration retains the imperative form of the verb βάπτω, "plunge in water, bathe," transmitted by the scholiast in the first word:[169]

βάπτε σύ μ' ἐν θυμέλῃσιν, ἐγὼ δέ σε κύμασι πόντου
βαπτίζων ὀλέσω νάμασι πικροτάτοις.

Give me a bath on stage, but I will give you a bath in the waves of
    the sea
and destroy you in the bitterest of waters.

It was apparently these verses of Alcibiades that gave rise to an erroneous story, widely repeated in antiquity, that he threw Eupolis into the sea and drowned him on the way to Sicily in 415 BC.[170]

---

169 Scholia to Aristides *In Defence of the Four* 117.18 [Dindorf p. 444], where the first line begins
      with unmetrical βάπτε με ἐν. Tzetzes *On Comedy (Perì Kōmōidías)* Kaibel 1899 p. 20 gives (in
      a mostly prose version) βάπτ' ἐμέ σύ; the text given above (βάπτε σύ μ' ἐν) is proposed by
      Hiller; an indicative verb (βάπτές μ' ἐν) is proposed by Meineke (West ad loc.).
170 See West ad loc. (*IEG*, vol. 2, 29–30). According to the scholia to Aristides Alcibiades
      uttered the verses as he carried out the deed: ἄλλοι δὲ λέγουσιν ὅτι ἐκωμῴδουν ὀνομαστὶ
      τοὺς ἄνδρας μέχρις Εὐπόλιδος. περιεῖλε δὲ τοῦτο Ἀλκιβιάδης ὁ στρατηγὸς καὶ ῥήτωρ.
      κωμῳδηθεὶς γὰρ παρὰ Εὐπόλιδος ἔρριψεν αὐτὸν ἐν τῇ θαλάττῃ ἐν Σικελίᾳ συστρατευόμενον
      εἰπών· "βάπτε—πικροτάτοις," "Others say that the comic poets ridiculed men by name up
      until Eupolis. But Alcibiades, the general and statesman, put an end to this. After being
      ridiculed by Eupolis he threw him into the sea when he was on the same campaign in Sicily,
      saying [here the couplet is quoted]." Eratosthenes, who knew that Eupolis produced plays
      after 415, corrected the erroneous story (Eratosthenes *FGrHist* 241 F 19). Cicero, the source
      of this information, suggests how widespread the story was despite Eratosthenes (*Letters to
      Atticus* 6.1.18): *quis enim non dixit* Εὔπολιν τὸν τῆς ἀρχαίας *ab Alcibiade navigante in Siciliam
      deiectum esse in mare? Redarguit Eratosthenes; adfert enim quas ille post id tempus fabulas docu-
      erit. Num idcirco Duris Samius, homo in historia diligens, quod cum multis erravit, irridetur?*, "Who
      has not told how Eupolis, the poet of old comedy, was thrown into the sea by Alcibiades
      when he sailed to Sicily? Eratosthenes refutes this, for he cites the plays that he produced
      after that time. Surely Duris of Samos, a diligent historian, is not mocked because he has
      made the same mistake as many others?"

§5.49 Alcibiades was, among other things, a poet. He also had a keen interest in Homer, as an anecdote in Plutarch's *Life of Alcibiades* makes clear. When Alcibiades was a young man he asked two schoolteachers for texts of Homer. The first said that he had none, and Alcibiades struck him with his fist. The second said that he not only had a text of Homer, but that he had corrected it himself; Alcibiades thereupon asked why, when he was able to correct Homer, he taught letters (*grámmata*) and did not educate young men.[171] While this anecdote is unlikely to be strictly true, it doubtless contains an element of truth. The high regard for Homeric expertise exhibited by Alcibiades in the case of the second teacher is what I take to be the anecdote's element of truth. Such expertise, in my view, was something that Alcibiades himself possessed.[172]

§5.50 Alcibiades defected from Athens to Sparta in the winter of 415/4 BC, and when he did so he had a record of anti-Spartan activity for which he needed to make amends. Most recently he had been in Sicily, one of three generals leading the Athenian expedition there; he was recalled from Sicily on a charge of profaning the Mysteries, and rather than stand trial in Athens he defected. The Sicilian Expedition itself was in large part due to Alcibiades, who had opposed the peace that ended the war between Athens and Sparta in 421, and who did all in his power to subvert that peace in the years following. To win the assembly's approval for the Sicilian Expedition in 415 he overcame the opposition of Nikias, the author of the peace with Sparta in 421. Alcibiades first subverted the Peace of Nikias in 420, when he persuaded the Athenians to make an alliance with Argos, Mantinea, and Elis, the three Peloponnesian cities that had formed an anti-Spartan alliance the year before. In 419, while

---

171 Plutarch *Alcibiades* 7.1: τὴν δὲ παιδικὴν ἡλικίαν παραλλάσσων ἐπέστη γραμματοδιδασκαλείῳ καὶ βιβλίον ᾔτησεν Ὁμηρικόν. εἰπόντος δὲ τοῦ διδασκάλου μηδὲν ἔχειν Ὁμήρου, κονδύλῳ καθικόμενος αὐτοῦ παρῆλθεν. ἑτέρου δὲ φήσαντος ἔχειν Ὅμηρον ὑφ' ἑαυτοῦ διωρθωμένον, "εἶτα" ἔφη "γράμματα διδάσκεις Ὅμηρον ἐπανορθοῦν ἱκανὸς ὤν, οὐχὶ τοὺς νέους παιδεύεις;", "When he was no longer a child he presented himself at a grammar school and asked for a text of Homer. When the teacher said that he had nothing of Homer's, he struck him with his fist and went on. When another teacher said that he had a text of Homer corrected by himself, he said, 'So, then, you teach letters when you are able to correct Homer, and you do not educate young men?'"

172 If Alcibiades himself referred to a *diórthōsis*, "corrected edition," of Homer (in Plutarch's account he uses the word *diōrthōménon*, "corrected"), one wonders how far such "correction" might have gone in the fifth century BC. Did it go beyond trivial mistakes and entail decisions between variants, or even between rival versions, as in the case of Salamis's entry in the Catalogue of Ships, which was disputed by Megara (cf. n3.272 above)? If Alcibiades expanded Nestor's story in *Iliad* 11 as I propose, would he have considered that too a matter of *diórthōsis*, such that correcting Homer could also mean improving Homer?

Alcibiades was general, he led a small force of Athenian hoplites and archers through the Peloponnesus, adding contingents from the allied cities as he went, in order to solidify the opposition to Sparta.[173] The following year, in 418, the anti-Spartan strategy of Alcibiades reached a climax at the Battle of Mantinea; Alcibiades himself, for reasons unknown to us, had not been elected general that year. Sparta won the battle, but it had been forced to risk every-thing on a single day, and for this Alcibiades claimed full credit in Athens.[174] After the Battle of Mantinea Alcibiades could accomplish little more in the Peloponnesus.[175] His next real initiative was the Sicilian campaign, and this he was forced to abandon almost as soon as it started.

§5.51 As it turned out Alcibiades had put the Spartans at great risk but had caused them no great harm, and he was thus able to cross over to the Spartan side. He also had strong connections in Sparta. His family traditionally repre-sented Spartan interests in Athens, a role that his grandfather renounced in the mid-fifth century. Alcibiades, who was born c. 450, wished to reassume the role of Sparta's Athenian *próxenos* early in his career, and with this in mind he tended to the Spartans taken captive at Pylos in 425.[176] The trauma of having

173 Thucydides 5.52.2.
174 In the debate before the Sicilian Expedition Alcibiades defends his extravagant quest for glory, on account of which his private life is being attacked, and asks whether anyone else has better managed public affairs (Thucydides 6.16.6): Πελοποννήσου γὰρ τὰ δυνατώτατα ξυστήσας ἄνευ μεγάλου ὑμῖν κινδύνου καὶ δαπάνης Λακεδαιμονίους ἐς μίαν ἡμέραν κατέστησα ἐν Μαντινείᾳ περὶ τῶν ἁπάντων ἀγωνίσασθαι· ἐξ οὗ καὶ περιγενόμενοι τῇ μάχῃ οὐδέπω καὶ νῦν βεβαίως θαρσοῦσιν, "For having brought about a coalition of the most powerful states in the Peloponnesus I caused the Spartans, without great risk or expense to you, to fight for everything on one day at Mantinea. After that, even though they prevailed in the battle, they have never really been sure of themselves, even now." Alcibiades' failure to be elected general and take part in the Battle of Mantinea was probably due to "a vote for caution and against adventure" by the Athenians in 418 BC (Kagan 1981:91); generals elected that year who belonged to the peace party included, besides Nikias, both of the generals who fought at Mantinea, Laches and Nicostratus (see Kagan 1981:91n39 with references for their party affiliation).
175 With the loss at Mantineia "all of Alkibiades' fine plans for completing the humiliation of Sparta had gone astray" (Andrewes [Gomme et al. 1970] on Thucydides 5.80.3). Alcibiades continued to foster the Argive alliance after the battle but without great effect. He could not prevent the peace offered by Sparta and accepted by Argos in the winter of 418/7 BC (Thucydides 5.76.3). Political instability then followed in Argos, where the democracy was put down and an alliance with Sparta was concluded, and the democracy was then restored. In 416, when Alcibiades was again elected general (Diodorus 12.81.2), he sailed to Argos, took 300 pro-Spartan Argives prisoner, and put them on neighboring islands controlled by Athens (Thucydides 5.84.1).
176 Thucydides 5.43.2; this passage, which introduces Alcibiades for the first time in Thucydides, identifies him as the main leader of the party opposed to the peace with Sparta, and the main proponent of a treaty with Argos: ἦσαν δὲ ἄλλοι τε καὶ Ἀλκιβιάδης

its full citizens held prisoner in Athens finally induced Sparta to end the war in 421, but to negotiate a peace they dealt not with Alcibiades, who was still young, but with Nikias. Alcibiades was hostile to the Peace of Nikias, and did all he could to subvert it, because the Spartans had dealt with his personal enemies, increasing their power, and diminishing his own. This, as Alcibiades told a Spartan audience in the winter of 415/4, justified his anti-Spartan activities which culminated in the Battle of Mantinea in 418.[177]

ὁ Κλεινίου, ἀνὴρ ἡλικίᾳ μὲν ἔτι τότε ὢν νέος ὡς ἐν ἄλλῃ πόλει, ἀξιώματι δὲ προγόνων τιμώμενος· ᾧ ἐδόκει μὲν καὶ ἄμεινον εἶναι πρὸς τοὺς Ἀργείους μᾶλλον χωρεῖν, οὐ μέντοι ἀλλὰ καὶ φρονήματι φιλονικῶν ἠναντιοῦτο, ὅτι Λακεδαιμόνιοι διὰ Νικίου καὶ Λάχητος ἔπραξαν τὰς σπονδάς, ἑαυτὸν κατά τε τὴν νεότητα ὑπεριδόντες καὶ κατὰ τὴν παλαιὰν προξενίαν ποτὲ οὖσαν οὐ τιμήσαντες, ἣν τοῦ πάππου ἀπειπόντος αὐτὸς τοὺς ἐκ τῆς νήσου αὐτῶν αἰχμαλώτους θεραπεύων διενοεῖτο ἀνανεώσασθαι. πανταχόθεν τε νομίζων ἐλασσοῦσθαι τό τε πρῶτον ἀντεῖπεν, οὐ βεβαίους φάσκων εἶναι Λακεδαιμονίους, ἀλλ' ἵνα Ἀργείους σφίσι σπεισάμενοι ἐξέλωσι καὶ αὖθις ἐπ' Ἀθηναίους μόνους ἴωσι, τούτου ἕνεκα σπένδεσθαι αὐτούς, "There were others, but the main leader was Alcibiades, the son of Kleinias, a man young in years for another city, but held in honor because of his ancestors' reputation. He thought that it was the better policy to move closer to the Argives, but he was also opposed to peace out of pride and party rivalry; the Spartans had made the truce through Nikias and Laches, disregarding him because of his youth, and failing to value him for the old position that had once existed of looking after Spartan interests in Athens; his grandfather had renounced this position, but by looking after the captives from the island he intended to renew it. Thinking that he was being worsted on all sides he opposed the peace from the first, saying that the Spartans were not trustworthy, but had made the truce with them in order to destroy the Argives first and then to move against the Athenians alone" (Thucydides 5.43.2–3).

177 Alcibiades makes this case at the beginning of his speech to the Spartans (Thucydides 6.89.1–3): ἀναγκαῖον περὶ τῆς ἐμῆς διαβολῆς πρῶτον ἐς ὑμᾶς εἰπεῖν, ἵνα μὴ χεῖρον τὰ κοινὰ τῷ ὑπόπτῳ μου ἀκροάσησθε. τῶν δ' ἐμῶν προγόνων τὴν προξενίαν ὑμῶν κατά τι ἔγκλημα ἀπειπόντων αὐτὸς ἐγὼ πάλιν ἀναλαμβάνων ἐθεράπευον ὑμᾶς ἄλλα τε καὶ περὶ τὴν ἐκ Πύλου ξυμφοράν. καὶ διατελοῦντός μου προθύμου ὑμεῖς πρὸς Ἀθηναίους καταλλασσόμενοι τοῖς μὲν ἐμοῖς ἐχθροῖς δύναμιν δι' ἐκείνων πράξαντες, ἐμοὶ δὲ ἀτιμίαν περιέθετε. καὶ διὰ ταῦτα δικαίως ὑπ' ἐμοῦ πρός τε τὰ Μαντινέων καὶ Ἀργείων τραπομένου καὶ ὅσα ἄλλα ἐνηντιούμην ὑμῖν ἐβλάπτεσθε· καὶ νῦν, εἴ τις καὶ τότε ἐν τῷ πάσχειν οὐκ εἰκότως ὠργίζετό μοι, μετὰ τοῦ ἀληθοῦς σκοπῶν ἀναπειθέσθω, "It is necessary that I speak to you first about the slander against me, so that you do not, because of your suspicions against me, listen with bias to matters that concern us both. Although my ancestors, because of a disagreement, renounced the position of Sparta's official representative in Athens, I took it up again, and I especially looked after your interests in the disaster at Pylos. While I remained eager on your behalf, you, when you made peace with the Athenians, bestowed power on my enemies by dealing with them, and brought dishonor on me. Because of this you were justly harmed by me when I turned to the Mantineans and Argives, and in whatever else I did to oppose you; if anyone of you was angry with me unreasonably even then, when you were actually suffering, let him now consider the truth of the matter and be persuaded otherwise." Thucydides' own introduction of Alcibiades in 5.43.2–3 (see n5.176 above) anticipates his point that the Spartans dealt with his personal enemies to negotiate the peace.

§5.52 Alcibiades had a particular friend in Sparta named Endios. There was a strong family connection between the two, and Alcibiades worked closely with Endios to accomplish his objectives in Sparta. His main objective was to make Athens pay dearly for alienating him, and so to bring down his personal enemies at home; his larger objective, which he would have kept to himself in Sparta, was surely to return to Athens when the time was right, as he in fact did in 408. This is of course to simplify the story, which does not follow a straight path, but is full of intrigue at every step. The Spartans made use of Alcibiades' help for a time, but they distrusted him, and he was forced to change sides again and curry favor with the Persians in order to return to Athens. The initial help that Alcibiades gave the Spartans was limited to advice, namely to fortify Decelea and to send a Spartan general with a Peloponnesian force to Sicily. After the Athenian defeat in Sicily, and the annihilation of the Athenian force there, Athens' empire was in jeopardy, and Alcibiades helped the Spartans bring about revolt in Ionia. Alcibiades' friend Endios was elected ephor in 411, and Alcibiades persuaded him to act quickly in Chios, which was already on the point of revolt, in order to get the credit for Ionia. The Spartan king Agis, who was also trying to organize revolts, would get the credit if they delayed. Alcibiades had made a personal enemy of Agis by seducing his wife and fathering a child by her, and he thus had at least as much reason as Endios to get the best of Agis. With the backing of Endios Sparta sent a naval force, which Alcibiades accompanied, to Chios, and Chios revolted from Athens. Later in 411 Alcibiades again acted quickly to cause Miletus to revolt, and his motive was again to win credit for himself, and for Endios.[178] When

---

178 Alcibiades wanted to win for Endios and himself the "prize" (ἀγώνισμα) for having caused the greatest number of Ionian cities to revolt. In the case of Chios Alcibiades persuaded the ephors, including Endios, to send ships quickly, before news of a recent setback to the Spartan fleet reached Chios, saying that he himself would easily persuade the Chians to revolt (Thucydides 8.12.1); to Endios, privately, he spoke of Ionia (and alliance with Persia) as a "prize" to deny Agis and gain for Endios (Thucydides 8.12.2): Ἐνδίῳ τε αὐτῷ ἰδίᾳ ἔλεγε καλὸν εἶναι δι' ἐκείνου ἀποστῆσαί τε Ἰωνίαν καὶ βασιλέα ξύμμαχον ποιῆσαι Λακεδαιμονίοις, καὶ μὴ Ἄγιδος τὸ ἀγώνισμα τοῦτο γενέσθαι, "He said privately to Endios himself that it would be a fine thing to cause Ionia to revolt and to make the king an ally of the Spartans through him, and for this prize not to go to Agis." In the case of Miletus, where Alcibiades was on close terms with the leaders, he wanted to act quickly before a force sent from Sparta arrived, and thus to gain for his force of Chians, himself, the Spartan commander with whom he sailed, and Endios, who had sent him, and to whom he had promised it, the "prize" of having caused the greatest number of cities to revolt (Thucydides 8.17.2): ἐβούλετο γὰρ ὁ Ἀλκιβιάδης, ὧν ἐπιτήδειος τοῖς προεστῶσι τῶν Μιλησίων, φθάσαι τάς τε ἀπὸ τῆς Πελοποννήσου ναῦς προσαγαγόμενος αὐτοὺς καὶ τοῖς Χίοις καὶ ἑαυτῷ καὶ Χαλκιδεῖ καὶ τῷ ἀποστείλαντι Ἐνδίῳ, ὥσπερ ὑπέσχετο, τὸ ἀγώνισμα προσθεῖναι, ὅτι πλείστας τῶν πόλεων μετὰ τῆς Χίων δυνάμεως καὶ Χαλκιδέως ἀποστήσας, "Alcibiades, being on familiar terms with the leaders

Athens struck back at Miletus, Alcibiades helped in the defense of the city, but soon thereafter a Spartan ship arrived with orders for Alcibiades' death, and Alcibiades went over from the Spartans to the Persians.[179]

§5.53 Thucydides, who is well informed about Alcibiades and his activities, explains his relationship to Endios early in Book 8, when the Spartans, influenced by Alcibiades, first decide to concentrate their efforts on Ionia rather than the Hellespont in the campaign to break up Athens' empire.[180] Alcibiades was an ancestral guest-friend of Endios, and Thucydides emphasizes the great closeness between their families: it was because of this relationship that Alcibiades had a Laconian name, which was also Endios's father's name.[181] While Alcibiades was in Sparta he was clearly close to Endios. But

---

of the Milesians, wished to bring them over to Sparta's side before the ships arrived from the Peloponnesus, and to gain for the Chians, himself, Chalkides, and Endios, who had sent him, the prize that he had promised him, of causing, with the help of the Chian force and Chalkides, the greatest number of cities to revolt."

179 In explaining the death warrant Thucydides 8.45.1 comments that Alcibiades was generally mistrusted and that Agis was his personal enemy (the seduction of Agis's wife, which is found in Plutarch *Alcibiades* 23.7–8, is not mentioned by Thucydides): Ἀλκιβιάδης μετὰ τὸν Χαλκιδέως θάνατον καὶ τὴν ἐν Μιλήτῳ μάχην τοῖς Πελοποννησίοις ὕποπτος ὤν, καὶ ἀπ' αὐτῶν ἀφικομένης ἐπιστολῆς πρὸς Ἀστύοχον ἐκ Λακεδαίμονος ὥστ' ἀποκτεῖναι (ἦν γὰρ καὶ τῷ Ἄγιδι ἐχθρὸς καὶ ἄλλως ἄπιστος ἐφαίνετο), πρῶτον μὲν ὑποχωρεῖ δείσας παρὰ Τισσαφέρνην, ἔπειτα ἐκάκου πρὸς αὐτὸν ὅσον ἐδύνατο μάλιστα τῶν Πελοποννησίων τὰ πράγματα, "After the death of Chalkides and the battle in Miletus Alcibiades was suspect to the Spartans, and when a letter from them came from Sparta to Astyochos to kill him (he was Agis's enemy and he seemed untrustworthy otherwise), he first escaped to Tissaphernes out of fear, and then began to damage the Peloponnesians' interests with him as much as he could."

180 As argued by Brunt 1952, Thucydides seems to have obtained much of his information about Alcibiades and his activities directly from Alcibiades. This thesis was developed further by Delebecque 1965. Cf. Andrewes (Gomme et al. 1981) 3. The intrusion of Alcibiades' point of view is particularly noticeable in Thucydides 8.45–56 (Brunt 1952:72–96); Andrewes (Gomme et al. 1981) 94–95 accepts Brunt's argument but sees no overt bias in Alcibiades' favor in Book 8. This, I think, is debatable, especially in 8.45–56.

181 Thucydides 8.6.3 (explaining Alcibiades' role in promoting Ionia and Tissaphernes over the Hellespont and Pharnabazus as the Spartans' first target in the campaign to dismantle the Athenian empire): οἱ μέντοι Λακεδαιμόνιοι τὰ τῶν Χίων καὶ Τισσαφέρνους παρὰ πολὺ προσεδέξαντο μᾶλλον· ξυνέπρασσε γὰρ αὐτοῖς καὶ Ἀλκιβιάδης, Ἐνδίῳ ἐφορεύοντι πατρικὸς ἐς τὰ μάλιστα ξένος ὤν, ὅθεν καὶ τοὔνομα Λακωνικὸν ἡ οἰκία αὐτῶν κατὰ τὴν ξενίαν ἔσχεν· Ἔνδιος γὰρ Ἀλκιβιάδου ἐκαλεῖτο, "The Spartans were much more receptive to the Chians and Tissaphernes; for Alcibiades supported them, and he was an extremely close ancestral guest-friend of Endios, who was then ephor (because of this their house used a Spartan name; for Endios was called the son of Alcibiades)." The genuineness of the last part of this passage (ὅθεν–ἐκαλεῖτο) is open to question, but it is defended by Andrewes (Gomme et al. 1981) ad loc.; one must understand the plural αὐτῶν, "their," in the phrase ἡ οἰκία αὐτῶν, "their house," as referring to Alcibiades and his ancestors, who are implicit in the adjective describing Alcibiades as Endios's "ancestral" (πατρικός) guest-friend.

three years earlier in Athens he had tricked Endios and two other Spartans in front of the assembly in order to bring Athens into the anti-Spartan alliance of Argos, Mantinea, and Elis. Endios and the other Spartan envoys had been sent to prevent this alliance and to settle differences between Sparta and Athens. They had come with full powers to settle disputes, and Alcibiades feared that because of this they would persuade the assembly to reject the alliance with Argos. He therefore tricked the Spartans into not revealing their full-power status to the assembly, giving his word that he would deliver Pylos to them in exchange for this; when they kept their part of the agreement and denied having come with full powers he flatly denounced them to the assembly. The Spartan ambassadors were thus defeated and Alcibiades got the alliance with Argos that he wanted.

§5.54 If the story of Alcibiades' deception of the Spartan ambassadors is true, as Thucydides believed it to be, Alcibiades had amends to make to Endios when he defected to Sparta three years later.[182] I see in this a potential motive for the expansion of Nestor's story in *Iliad* 11. Alcibiades must have needed Endios's help to pave the way for him in Sparta. He also had time on his hands while arrangements for his arrival in Sparta were made. On the way back from Sicily Alcibiades escaped his Athenian escort at Thurii in southern Italy, and from there he made his way by merchant ship to Elis in the Peloponnesus, landing at the port of Cyllene.[183] He could not risk going to Sparta without a safe-conduct, and so he waited in Elis until the Spartans sent for him.[184] As he

---

For the custom by which Alcibiades was named see Herman 1987:19–20, 148 and Habicht 2000:119–120. Alcibiades' grandfather also had the name.

182 Thucydides 5.44–45. Kebric 1976 argues that Alcibiades and Endios colluded in this matter, both wanting the war to continue, and that the deception of Endios is only apparent; Herman 1987:148–150 makes a similar argument. I think it is more likely that Alcibiades persuaded the other two Spartans by first persuading his guest-friend, and that he did not hesitate to make use of Endios in this way; he would charm him again later when the time came. Brunt's argument that Thucydides has followed Alcibiades' own explanation of events, and that some of the explanation does not make sense, seems to me to have merit. But I would not include the fact that Endios was tricked among the misinformation to which Thucydides may have fallen victim (nor does Brunt make such an argument).

183 Thucydides 6.88.9: καὶ οἳ ἐκ τῆς Κορίνθου πρέσβεις παρῆσαν ἐς τὴν Λακεδαίμονα καὶ Ἀλκιβιάδης μετὰ τῶν ξυμφυγάδων περαιωθεὶς τότ' εὐθὺς ἐπὶ πλοίου φορτηγικοῦ ἐκ τῆς Θουρίας ἐς Κυλλήνην τῆς Ἠλείας πρῶτον, ἔπειτα ὕστερον ἐς τὴν Λακεδαίμονα αὐτῶν τῶν Λακεδαιμονίων μεταπεμψάντων ὑπόσπονδος ἐλθών· ἐφοβεῖτο γὰρ αὐτοὺς διὰ τὴν περὶ τῶν Μαντινικῶν πρᾶξιν, "The ambassadors from Corinth were present in Sparta, and so too was Alcibiades with his fellow exiles, having crossed immediately aboard a merchant ship from Thurii to Cyllene in Elis, then later, when the Spartans summoned him, having come under a safe-passage; for he feared them because of the Mantinea affair."

184 A stay of some length in Elis is implied by the phrase ἔπειτα ὕστερον, "then later," of his continuation on to Sparta (Thucydides 6.88.9; see previous note). There was a different

waited he perhaps revisited the landscape around Olympia. At the Olympic games the year before, in 416 BC, he had entered an unprecedented seven chariots in the chariot race, bringing immense glory to himself, and to Athens, by winning first, second, and fourth places.[185] At the games four years earlier the Spartan Likhas had been beaten by the Eleian umpires for entering the chariot race. That was the summer of 420, just after Alcibiades had brought Athens into the anti-Spartan alliance of Argos, Mantinea, and Elis. The treaty for that alliance had been engraved on a pillar and set up at Olympia expressly for the games of 420.[186] When it was feared that the Spartans would defy the ban on their participation and come in force, Athenian cavalry were among those held in readiness near the games.[187] Alcibiades knew this whole landscape well. In 419, when he led a force through the Peloponnesus to solidify the Argive alliance, he must have visited Elis, and he may well have ventured south toward the trouble spot of Lepreon. More likely he took the opportunity now, in 415, to visit Lepreon, and neighboring Pylos, as he waited to hear from Sparta about his safe-conduct. With this landscape in mind and with recollections of past Olympic games he had all he needed to expand Nestor's story. If he did not have a text of Homer, there was doubtless a schoolteacher in Elis to provide one.

---

tradition that Alcibiades went to Argos before defecting to Sparta (Isocrates 16.9, Plutarch *Alcibiades* 23.1). But if Alcibiades was Thucydides' direct informant for his activities in the war (see n5.180 above), it is hard to explain why Thucydides should be misinformed on this point. The issue is discussed in EN5.20.

185 For the date of Alcibiades' Olympic victory 416 BC is the only possibility; see Bowra 1960 and Andrewes [Gomme et al. 1970] on Thucydides 6.16.2.

186 Thucydides 5.47 quotes the treaty, which states that a stone copy of the treaty is to be set up by each state individually at Athens, Argos, and Mantinea, and that the allies "are to set up jointly a bronze stele at Olympia at the games now at hand" (καταθέντων δὲ καὶ Ὀλυμπίασι στήλην χαλκῆν κοινῇ Ὀλυμπίοις τοῖς νυνί, 5.47.11). The bronze stele at Olympia apparently also served as Elis's copy of the treaty (see Andrewes [Gomme et al. 1970] ad loc. for Elis's display of its decrees at Olympia).

187 All the allies had sent armed contingents out of fear of the Spartans (Thucydides 5.50.3): ὅμως δὲ οἱ Ἠλεῖοι δεδιότες μὴ βίᾳ θύσωσι, ξὺν ὅπλοις τῶν νεωτέρων φυλακὴν εἶχον· ἦλθον δὲ αὐτοῖς καὶ Ἀργεῖοι καὶ Μαντινῆς, χίλιοι ἑκατέρων, καὶ Ἀθηναίων ἱππῆς, οἳ ἐν Ἁρπίνῃ ὑπέμενον τὴν ἑορτήν, "Nevertheless the Eleians, fearing that they would use force to sacrifice, kept a guard of young men under arms; Argives and Mantineans came to their aid, a thousand of each, and Athenian cavalry, who were waiting for the festival in Harpine." If indeed the outrage committed against Likhas in 420 is evoked in the expansion of Nestor's story in *Iliad* 11, this, like the rest of the story, must have been calculated to win favor in Sparta, but it is not clear that it would have won favor with Likhas himself. Not enough is known of Alcibiades' attitude to Likhas to judge this. Thucydides 5.76 reports that after the Battle of Mantinea the Spartans sent Likhas to Argos to offer a peace, and that Alcibiades, who was present in Argos at the time, spoke against him, but the peace was accepted. It may be that Alcibiades did not mind perpetuating Likhas's humiliation among those who knew how and why Nestor's story had been expanded.

§5.55 Alcibiades knew where he was headed at this point, and he knew that he would need Endios's help. He had once tricked his friend in order to get Athens to join the anti-Spartan alliance of Argos, Mantinea, and Elis, but now he was joining the other side, of Sparta and Lepreon.[188] To correlate with Nestor's story the two sides could be represented by Elis on the one hand and Lepreon on the other. Whereas Alcibiades had once been on the side of Elis, he was now switching to the side of Lepreon, and thus of ancient Pylos as well. To work this out in Nestor's story was an interesting challenge. Sparta had long been on the defensive about the location of Nestor's Pylos, alleging that it was in Elis when the rest of the world knew that it was in Messenia. Who but Alcibiades would have thought of a third way out that shifted Sparta to the moral high ground as the latter-day defender of Nestor's beleaguered city?

§5.56 The effort was intended for Endios, I think, and through Endios perhaps for other Spartans.[189] The language of the expansions, as we have seen, contains nothing to mark it as un-Homeric. A skilled craftsman did the job. In terms of poetic technique there is also nothing remarkable, and this is again a sign of skill: the expansions succeed by drawing as little attention to themselves as possible, as if they had always been there.[190] It is interesting

---

188 This argument assumes that in 415 BC, when Alcibiades defected, Lepreon still remained independent of Elis and was still defended by Sparta; this, I think, was likely the case, but positive evidence is lacking after 418 BC (cf. above §5.44 end and n5.153 and n5.155). The argument also assumes that Elis did not return to Sparta's camp after the defeat of the Argive alliance at Mantinea, and for this there is independent evidence: in Thucydides 8.3.2 the list of cities that Sparta required to provide 100 ships after the defeat of Athens in Sicily does not contain Elis (the list includes Boeotians, Phocians, Locrians, Corinthians, Arcadians, Pellenians, Sicyonians, Megarians, Troizenians, Epidaurians, and Hermionians); at the end of the war, furthermore, Sparta was quick to turn its attention to Elis to settle old scores (see n5.152 and n5.154 above and cf. Andrewes [Gomme et al. 1970] on Thucydides 6.88.9). The only counterevidence is Thucydides 7.31.1, stating that a Corinthian fleet anchored at Pheia on the coast of Elis in 413 BC; this evidence may make it "possible that Elis had been brought back under Spartan control after the collapse of her alliance with Argos and Mantineia" (Andrewes [Gomme et al. 1970] on 6.88.9), but it does not make it likely.

189 Compare the situation later when Alcibiades, to win acceptance from the other Spartan ephors of his plan to free Chios, persuaded Endios first (Thucydides 8.12.1–2; see n5.178 above).

190 The first two expansions of Nestor's story begin with the same phrase ἔστι δέ τις, "there is a (certain)," a bona fide Homeric formula; what is more, both lines beginning with this formula resemble other lines in Homer: *Iliad* 11.711, ἔστι δέ τις Θρυόεσσα πόλις αἰπεῖα κολώνη, "There is a city Thryoessa, a steep hill," closely resembles *Iliad* 2.811, ἔστι δέ τις προπάροιθε πόλιος αἰπεῖα κολώνη, "There is before the city a steep hill"; likewise *Iliad* 11.722, ἔστι δέ τις ποταμὸς Μινυήϊος εἰς ἅλα βάλλων, "There is a river Minyeios flowing into the sea," resembles *Odyssey* 3.293, ἔστι δέ τις λισσὴ αἰπεῖά τε εἰς ἅλα πέτρη, "There is a smooth and steep rock into the sea." There is another example of the formula ἔστι δέ τις in *Odyssey* 4.844 (ἔστι δέ τις νῆσος μέσσῃ ἁλὶ πετρήεσσα, "There is a rocky island in the middle of the sea"), and there are also variations of the formulaic pattern (ἔστι δέ τι σπέος, "there

that the Anigros River, which is clearly meant as the point where Nestor and the Pylians mobilize after leaving their city by night, is called the "Minyan river." This is as much a periphrasis as it is a name, and it serves a dual purpose: it avoids the name Anigros, which would have drawn glaring attention to itself, and it suggests the ancient Minyans, who were associated with this very region in Alcibiades' day, as Herodotus attests.[191]

§5.57 There is one particular point in the language that I take to be highly significant in view of the authorship that I propose. It has to do with the Alpheios River, which is the central fixed point in the expansion of Nestor's story. For the geography of the expanded story to work, there can be no doubt about the Alpheios:[192] it is the Alpheios that identifies the "Minyan river" as the Anigros, for the two rivers are separated by a half-day's march, and the identification of the Anigros in turn tells us exactly where Pylos is. The standard of measurement for the distances in the expanded story is the half-day's march from the Anigros to the Alpheios, and I do not think that it is an accident that the word used to indicate a half-day's march, ἔνδιοι, "at noon," is the plural of the name Endios (*Iliad* 11.725–726):

ἔνθεν πανσυδίῃ σὺν τεύχεσι θωρηχθέντες

<u>ἔνδιοι</u> ἱκόμεσθ᾽ ἱερὸν ῥόον Ἀλφειοῖο.

From there, armed with weapons, we came at great speed
to the sacred stream of the Alpheios <u>at midday</u>.[193]

---

is a cave," *Iliad* 13.32; ἔστι πόλις Ἐφύρη, "there is a city Ephyre," *Iliad* 6.152; νῆσος ἔπειτά τις ἔστι, "then there is an island," *Odyssey* 4.354; Κρήτη τις γαῖ᾽ ἔστι, "there is a land Crete," *Odyssey* 19.172; cf. also ἔστι τις Ἑλλοπίη, "there is a certain *Hellopíē*," in Hesiod fr. 240.1 MW). Other points in the language of the expansions are discussed in EN5.21.

191 Herodotus 4.148 (see §5.41 and n5.139 above). In Nestor's expanded story the phrase ποταμὸς Μινυήϊος, "the Minyan river," is paralleled by the phrase Θρυόεσσα πόλις, "the reedy city"; the two periphrases are mutually reinforcing, the name Θρυόεσσα (which has good parallels, see EN5.21 to n5.190 above) in a sense preparing the way for the name Μινυήϊος; note that both names follow the ἔστι δέ τις formula within the same line as the formula (cf. n5.190 above; for the passages see §5.2 above).

192 Note that in the old controversy as to Pylos's location the natural feature used to establish a location in Elis was the Alpheios River: Pylos was put north of the Alpheios notably in *Homeric Hymn to Apollo* 418–424 (see §5.14 above); now, elegantly, the Alpheios is used to establish a new location in Triphylia, south of the river. The author who proposed a new solution was of course aware of the old controversy, whose terms he seems simply to have redefined.

193 Pape-Benseler 1911 s.v. Ἔνδιος, "Mittag" ("Midday") cite three other instances of the name besides Alcibiades' guest-friend: two on inscriptions (of an Athenian and a Delphian) and another of a better known Athenian from Lamptrai (Demosthenes 45.8; Isaeus 3.1–70, often; also on an inscription). Bechtel 1917:154 (discussing Ἔν-διος Λακεδαιμόνιος, "the Spartan Endios," Thucydides 5.44.3) compares the Homeric adjective ἔνδιος, "at noon,"

As previously mentioned, Alcibiades and Endios shared the name Alcibiades; it was Endios's patronymic. By identifying himself with Pylians who once marched against Elis, Alcibiades also, in a sense, shares with his guest-friend the name Endios. It is an elegant compliment and a sign of solidarity to Endios, who presumably would not have failed to notice it.[194] There is only one other instance of the adjective in Homer, as Alcibiades and Endios would both know, and there could be no mistaking the intent of its second appearance in Nestor's expanded story.[195]

§5.58 There remains the question of how the expanded version of Nestor's story entered the Athenian state text. Alcibiades was destined to return to Athens in 408. It was a moment of triumph for him, and he used it to maximum advantage. He had never answered the charge of profaning the Mysteries, and now he chose to answer it in his own way. In the celebration of the Mysteries the customary procession to Eleusis became impossible when the Spartans (at Alcibiades' suggestion) occupied Decelea; now the Athenians could reach Eleusis only by sea. In 408 Alcibiades personally conducted the procession to Eleusis under the protection of the army, to magnificent effect. He remained afterwards for some months in Athens, with ample opportunity to think about the Athenian state text of Homer, to which he must have had access in his hour of triumph.[196] Why would he have wanted to return to something that he had done in other circumstances and for another purpose? Perhaps he had simply grown fond of his own contribution to Homer and wished to see it perpetuated.

§5.59 In 424, the year after the Spartan hoplites were taken prisoner at Pylos, Aristophanes in the *Knights* quoted half an old riddle about the location

---

and its opposite ἐννύχιος, "at night," and cites the Spartan name Ἔννυχος, "at night" (*IG* V.1.193).

194 The adjective ἔννυχος (cf. ἐννύχιος, previous note) occurs in the older version of Nestor's story, *Iliad* 11.716, where Athena comes "at night" (ἔννυχος) to warn the Pylians of the Epeians' attack; the occurrence of ἔνδιος in the expansion of Nestor's story, apart from what I take to be its real purpose, offers a point of contrast. This perhaps did not go unnoticed by the poet of the expansion.

195 In *Odyssey* 4.450 Proteus comes out of the sea <u>at midday</u>: ἔνδιος δ' ὁ γέρων ἦλθ' ἐξ ἁλός. The meaning "at midday" of ἔνδιος is nicely demonstrated in this episode, in which line 4.400 refers to the same time of day with the words: ἦμος δ' ἠέλιος μέσον οὐρανὸν ἀμφιβεβήκῃ, "when the sun had reached the middle of the sky"; cf. Strabo 8.3.28, who glosses ἔνδιοι in *Iliad* 11.726 as κατὰ μεσημβρίαν, "at midday." Instances of ἔνδιος after Homer are rare and are mainly limited to Hellenistic poetry.

196 For Alcibiades' return to Athens in 408, see Xenophon *Hellenica* 1.4.8–21 and Plutarch *Alcibiades* 32–35.1. Xenophon 1.4.21 says that he left Athens in the fourth month after his arrival.

of Pylos that now had topical relevance, if only for the name.[197] The riddle itself was clearly well known since only half of it is quoted: ἔστι Πύλος πρὸ Πύλοιο, "there is a Pylos before Pylos"; the rest of the riddle, which the audience would have known, is quoted by the scholia to Aristophanes and by Strabo: Πύλος γε μέν ἐστι καὶ ἄλλος, "and there is yet another Pylos." We can account for the first two of these cities named Pylos, one "before" the other, within the region of Messenia, as earlier discussed;[198] the third Pylos referred to in this well-known riddle, which seems to have originated in the sixth century BC, can only have been in Elis.[199] The Pylos in Triphylia was not one of the three cities intended by the riddle when it was first composed, nor was it understood as one of the three cities at issue when the riddle was quoted by Aristophanes. The earliest that we can see Triphylia being taken as the location of Nestor's city is by Demetrius of Scepsis more than two centuries later.[200] During those two centuries the expanded version of Nestor's story in *Iliad* 11, which I would date to 415 BC, established itself as the dominant version and perhaps the only version of the story. That is a remarkable fact in itself.[201]

197 Aristophanes *Knights* 1059; see EN5.10 to n5.65 above. For the degree to which Pylos was on the minds of all after the surrender of the Spartan hoplites, cf. Thucydides 4.40: παρὰ γνώμην τε δὴ μάλιστα τῶν κατὰ τὸν πόλεμον τοῦτο τοῖς Ἕλλησιν ἐγένετο· τοὺς γὰρ Λακεδαιμονίους οὔτε λιμῷ οὔτ' ἀνάγκῃ οὐδεμιᾷ ἠξίουν τὰ ὅπλα παραδοῦναι, ἀλλὰ ἔχοντας καὶ μαχομένους ὡς ἐδύναντο ἀποθνῄσκειν. ἀπιστοῦντές τε μὴ εἶναι τοὺς παραδόντας τοῖς τεθνεῶσιν ὁμοίους, κτλ., "This was the most surprising event for the Greeks during the war. For they did not expect the Spartans to surrender their weapons out of hunger or any other necessity, but to hold on and fight as much as they could and die. Not believing that those who surrendered were like those who died," etc.

198 According to Strabo 8.4.2 there was an "old Pylos" in Messenia that preceded the Pylos at Koryphasion; see n5.65 above and EN5.10 to n5.65 above (the word πρό in the riddle is to be taken spatially rather than temporally).

199 In the sixth century the riddle would have reflected the controversy at the beginning of that century as to the location of Pylos in Messenia or Elis. The age and original sense of the riddle are discussed further in EN5.22.

200 See n5.9 above. Demetrius of Scepsis, born perhaps c. 205 BC, was a contemporary of Aristarchus, born c. 215 BC, who gave special status to an Athenian text, probably the Panathenaic text, in his edition of Homer (cf. n5.168 above and EN5.19 to n5.168 above); Demetrius, if my argument is correct, would also have used the Athenian state text. Strabo 8.3.7, who quotes the riddle of the three cities named Pylos in full, naturally understands Triphylian Pylos as one of the three cities (the other two being Messenian Pylos, at Koryphasion, and an Eleian Pylos), and this interpretation has prevailed ever since. For possible interest in a Triphylian Pylos on the part of a fourth-century BC Arcadian author (i.e. before Demetrius of Scepsis) see n5.135 above. For a different view from mine of the Triphylian city see Biraschi 1994:42–52, who argues that the idea of a Triphylian location for Nestor's Pylos goes back to the Archaic period.

201 The location of Pylos became a subject of interest among scholars (especially Strabo's *Homērikóteroi*) in Hellenistic times, and one might expect at least a mention of an

§5.60 Sparta's relationship with other Peloponnesians was the main factor causing shifts in the location of Nestor's Homeric city, first in the late seventh or early sixth century BC, when an Eleian location entered the picture, and again in the late fifth century BC, when a Triphylian location entered the picture. In the first instance, when Sparta expelled Messenia's coastal population at the end of the Second Messenian War, Sparta itself had a motive to deny that Messenia was ever Nestor's kingdom, and it succeeded in its denial insofar as the location of Pylos became a question, indeed a riddle, from that point on. In the late fifth century BC Sparta no longer had a stake in the location of Nestor's Pylos, but its protection of Lepreon against Elis nevertheless led to a new location for Nestor's city in Triphylia, and this new location put up a challenge to Messenia that has still not been put down.

§5.61 Sparta's effect on the question of Pylos's location, interesting as it is for the history of the transmission of the Homeric poems, is irrelevant to the meaning of Nestor's story in *Iliad* 11, the point of departure of my analysis. In that story Nestor tells how he first became *hippóta Néstōr* by conquering the entire western Peloponnesus, from Pylos to Bouprasion, in a single day. Only later did the interest of this story shift from its meaning for the story of Patroclus, its true object, to the question of the location of Pylos. To that question, which was not in the poet's mind as such, Nestor's story has no real answer.

---

alternative (shorter) version of Nestor's story in *Iliad* 11 if it still existed. We see no such mention, but our evidence, coming mostly from Strabo, is of course limited. The question whether texts persisted containing the old version of Nestor's story is considered further in EN5.23. From a modern standpoint the significant fact is that the expanded version of Nestor's story was accepted without question for more than two millenia until it was challenged by Cantieni in 1942. Still today the effects of that long unquestioned acceptance persist in a work like Edzard Visser's authoritative study of the Catalogue of Ships (Visser 1997), which continues to see Triphylia as the location of Pylos in the Homeric poems (Visser 1997:522–530), and Visser is followed by others in this (cf. above n5.65 end). Surely Alcibiades, if it was in fact he who altered Nestor's story, would have been pleased to know that he would go undetected so long. It was a point of pride with this chameleon-like character to appear more Spartan than the Spartans when he was in Sparta (Plutarch *Alcibiades* 23.3–6). He could also, I think, be more Homeric than Homer when he wished. There was also an element of truth, or something like the truth, to what he did: the coincidence of a Bronze Age site at Kakovatos and a later town named Pylos in the same vicinity seems not unlike the situation in Messenia, where the name Pylos migrated twice from one location to another; Alcibiades fully exploited the opportunity to introduce another worthy candidate where agreement had long been lacking.

Endnotes, Part 5

EN5.1 (Endnote to n5.1)
In Nestor's story in *Iliad* 11, when he routs the Epeians and the Pylians turn for home, the language imitates the language used of the turning point in a chariot race, as exemplified in the chariot race of Iliad 23. But there is a difference between the two passages in that the passage of *Iliad* 23 occurs after the turning point has already been passed; the phrase πύματον τέλεον δρόμον, "were completing the end of the course," in *Iliad* 23.373, which is echoed in the phrase ἄνδρα κτείνας πύματον λίπον, "I killed the last man and left him," in *Iliad* 11.759, actually refers to the second half of the race, the "home stretch" (*Iliad* 23.373–375):

> Ἀλλ' ὅτε δὴ <u>πύματον τέλεον δρόμον</u> ὠκέες ἵπποι
>
> ἂψ ἐφ' ἁλὸς πολιῆς, τότε δὴ ἀρετή γε ἑκάστου
>
> φαίνετ', ἄφαρ δ' ἵπποισι τάθη δρόμος.

> But when the swift horses <u>were completing the end of the course</u>
> back toward the grey sea, then indeed the strength of each
> showed itself, and at once the horses strained their hardest.

The same phrase, ἀλλ' ὅτε δὴ πύματον τέλεον δρόμον, is also used for the second half of the footrace, when Odysseus prays to Athena (*Iliad* 23.768). As the lines above occur in the chariot race, however, they give the initial impression that the turning point is at hand; the underlined phrase in the first line contributes, I think, to that impression. Nestor's speech of advice to Antilochus has created anticipation for the turn, and the first part of the chariot race, before the turn, has just been vividly described (lines 362–372; cf. n2.32 above); thus the phrase πύματον τέλεον δρόμον, "they were completing the end of the course," at first seems to refer to the end of the first part of the race, before the turn, and not to the second part of the race;

only in the next line, with the phrase "back toward the grey sea" (ἂψ ἐφ' ἁλὸς πολιῆς), does it become clear that the turn has already been made, and that the real contests are about to begin (τότε δή..., "then indeed..."). The passage, I think, misleads deliberately: the phrase πύματ<u>ου</u> τέλε<u>ου</u> δρό<u>μου</u>, in which the repeated final syllable echoes the beating of the horses' hooves, intensifies anticipation of the turning point, and the word ἂψ at the beginning of the next line, implying that the turn has already been made, is a surprise. This sudden shift of perspective has a purpose: immediately the relevance of Nestor's speech of advice for executing the turn disappears from the surface of the narrative and remains hidden through the rest of the race. The single word ἂψ effectively takes the place of the turning point in the race of *Iliad* 23. In *Iliad* 11 the same word ἂψ marks the turning point in Nestor's battle, when the victorious Pylians turn back from Bouprasion and head for home. The sound symbolism anticipating the turn is virtually the same in the battle as in the chariot race: ἔνθ' ἄνδρα κτείνας <u>πύματον</u> λίπ<u>ον</u>. Thus *Iliad* 11, in which the context is a battle, straightforwardly evokes the turn in a chariot race, whereas *Iliad* 23, in which the context is a chariot race, uses similar diction to dispose of the turn quickly after it has already occurred.

EN5.2 (Endnote to n5.12)
Ernst Meyer, an expert on the western Peloponnesus, has steadfastly maintained that in Homer the city of Pylos is in Tripylia, not Messenia. See his *RE* article 'Pylos,' 2143–2146 (completed in 1950, before the Linear-B decipherment, but published only in 1959); the Linear-B decipherment did not change Meyer's mind, as he states in an addendum to the article, 2520: "On the clay tablets of Ano-Englianos the name Pylos (pu-ro) occurs often, apparently designating the palace, although this is not certain; see Ventris-Chadwick, Documents 141f., Hampe, Gymnasium 63 (1956) 51f. But the fact that the name Pylos is also attested here already for the Mycenaean period changes nothing in the situation" ("In den Tontafeln von Ano-Englianos kommt der Name Pylos (pu-ro) häufig vor, anscheinend den Palast bezeichnend, obwohl das nicht sicher ist, s. Ventris-Chadwick, Documents 141f., Hampe, Gymnasium 63 (1956) 51f. Aber der Umstand, dass der Name Pylos damit auch hier schon für die mykenische Zeit belegt ist, ändert an der Sachlage gar nichts"). See also Meyer 1951:127 and 1957:81–82: in the latter he says: "I have...recently reestablished at length that the understanding won by the Hellenistic Homer interpreters, which was then revived especially by Dörpfeld, is the only correct and possible one, that we must look for the Homeric Pylos in Triphylia, and thus in the palace installation of Kakovatos. Even the most bril-

liant discoveries at Ano-Englianos change nothing in that, including the fact that the clay tablets found there now apparently attest the name Pylos already for this Mycenaean palace too..." ("Ich habe...vor kurzem ausführlich neu begründet, dass die schon von den hellenistischen Homererklärern gewonnene Erkenntnis, die dann besonders von Dörpfeld neu belebt wurde, die allein richtige und mögliche ist, das homerische Pylos in Triphylien und damit in der Palastanlage von Kakovatos zu suchen. Daran ändern auch die glänzendsten Entdeckungen in Ano-Englianos gar nichts, auch nicht der Zustand, dass die dort gefundenen Tontafeln nun offenbar den Namen Pylos auch schon für diesen mykenischen Palast belegen..."). Meyer restated his position again in 1978 in his authoritative article 'Messenien' (*RE* Supplement 15) 228: "That the discovery of the palace of Englianos and the clay tablets there have refuted the thesis of the Triphylian Pylos, as the defenders of the Messenian Pylos suppose, is altogether out of the question; on the contrary, this find has done the opposite and refuted with all clarity the location of the Homeric Pylos in Messenia" ("Davon, dass die Auffindung des Palastes von Englianos und die dortigen Tontafeln die These des triphylischen Pylos widerlegt hätten, wie die Verfechter des messenischen Pylos meinen, kann überhaupt keine Rede sein, im Gegenteil haben umgekehrt gerade diese Funde die Ansetzung des homerischen Pylos in Messenien mit aller Deutlichkeit widerlegt"). As Meyer here indicates, the debate over the location of Homeric Pylos has focused on the two palaces at Ano-Englianos and Kakovatos; Leonard Palmer, an ardent defender of Ano-Englianos as the site of the Homeric city, took Meyer to task for failing to revise his views on the subject (see Palmer 1965:50), but Meyer remained unmoved by such criticism.

EN5.3 (Endnote to n5.13)
The main evidence for the location of Pylos in the *Odyssey* is the journey of Telemachus and Peisistratos from Pylos to Sparta and back again to Pylos, in which the pair spends a night in Phērai (Φηραί) each way. In antiquity Phērai was understood to be the city so named at the head of the Messenian Gulf (modern Kalamata); this city lies on a direct line between Messenian Pylos and Sparta but is completely out of the way for a journey from Triphylia to Sparta. The defenders of a Triphylian Pylos dispute the Messenian location of Phērai in the *Odyssey* because of Mount Taygetos, which separates this Phērai from Sparta, and which is said to be impassable by chariot on the routes across the mountain assumed for antiquity (Meyer *RE* 'Pylos' 2144 citing Bölte *RE* 'Sparta [Geographie]' 1343–1347). Whether or not Taygetos was impassable (the point is disputed by Kiechle 1960:15n2, citing Valmin 1930:50–51 and McDonald

1942:542; Luraghi 2002:53n44 cites more recent work which emphasizes
the importance of direct connections between Sparta and Messenia across
Taygetos), it is certainly true that the text of the *Odyssey* takes no notice of a
very large impediment to the completion of Telemachus's journey if Phērai is
in Messenia. But what is the conclusion to be drawn from this? If we believe
that the Homeric poets had an accurate idea of Peloponnesian geography,
including the passage across Mount Taygetos, and that they were concerned
to convey such accuracy, we will look for another city named Phērai further
north, on the route between Triphylia and Sparta, and a possible candidate
has indeed been found: a town Φαραία is attested by Polybius 4.77.5 for some-
where east of Olympia (for the likely location of this town see Meyer 1957:85,
who locates it in Arcadia less than twenty kilometers northeast of Olympia on
the Erymanthos River; Meyer shows that another location proposed by Bölte
is based on a misunderstanding of Strabo 8.3.32; cf. EN5.6). But we will judge
the matter differently if we realize that it is Nestor's story in *Iliad* 11, and
nothing else, that gives the impression that the Homeric poets had measured
out the western Peloponnesus step by step; Nestor's story, with its detailed
geography, is thus the crux of the problem (cf. Wilamowitz 2006:330 for the
vagueness of Homer's Peloponnesian geography as the key to the problem
of Mount Taygetos). As for the identity of Phērai in the *Odyssey*, those who
deny that it is what it was thought to be in antiquity, namely the city on the
Messenian Gulf, must first of all deny the evidence of the *Odyssey* in an impor-
tant passage; when Penelope takes Odysseus's bow from the storeroom we
are told where Odysseus acquired it, namely in the house of Ortilokhos "in
Messene" (*Odyssey* 21.13–16):

> δῶρα τά οἱ ξεῖνος Λακεδαίμονι δῶκε τυχήσας
> Ἴφιτος Εὐρυτίδης, ἐπιείκελος ἀθανάτοισι.
> τὼ δ' <u>ἐν Μεσσήνῃ</u> ξυμβλήτην ἀλλήλοιϊν
> <u>οἴκῳ ἐν Ὀρτιλόχοιο</u> δαΐφρονος.

> ...gifts that a guest-friend gave him when he met him in
>   Lacedaemon,
> Eurytos's son Iphitos, who was like the immortals.
> The two of them met with each other <u>in Messene</u>
> <u>In the house of</u> prudent <u>Ortilokhos</u>.

Telemachus and Peisistratos, when they reach Phērai, spend the night in the same house, except that now Diokles, the son of Ortilokhos, inhabits it (*Odyssey* 3.488–489 = 15.186–187):

ἐς Φηρὰς δ' ἵκοντο Διοκλῆος ποτὶ δῶμα,
υἱέος Ὀρτιλόχοιο, τὸν Ἀλφειὸς τέκε παῖδα.

> They came to Phērai, to the house of Diokles,
> the son of Ortilokhos, whom the Alpheios had once sired.

Besides Mount Taygetos there is a further objection to the Messenian location of Phērai in the fact that the Alpheios River is called the father of Ortilokhos in the above passage of the *Odyssey* and in *Iliad* 5.544–546; it is argued that Phērai, Ortilokhos's city, should not be in Messenia but closer to the Alpheios. This argument, however, is outweighed by the passage concerning Odysseus's bow, which explictly says that Ortilokhos's house is in Messenia, which means Phērai (cf. Kiechle 1960:63). In Phērai local traditions of Ortilokhos and his family (which included by marriage the hero Makhaon) are found in Pausanias 4.30.3 (cf. Kiechle 1960:50, 61, 62–63; for Makhaon's presence in Messenia see above n2.20). In *Odyssey* 21 the additional specification Λακεδαίμονι, "in Lacedaemon," of the place of Odysseus's encounter with Iphitos presupposes the Spartan conquest of territory on the Messenian Gulf in the eighth century BC (i.e. before the First Messenian War) by the Spartan king Teleklos (Strabo 8.4.4, on which see Meyer *RE* 'Pylos' 2144; cf. also Pausanias 3.2.6); the same Spartan conquest perhaps explains Agamemnon's offer to Achilles in *Iliad* 9 of seven cities on the Messenian Gulf (ἐγγὺς ἁλός, *Iliad* 9.153 and 295), one of which is Phērai (*Iliad* 9.151 and 293; Cartledge 2002:98 speculates that Phērai, which was later regarded as a Spartan colony, was brought into the Spartan sphere by Teleklos; cf. Hammond 1982:327–328). It has been suggested that these seven cities, which are described as νέαται Πύλου, "outermost in Pylos" (*Iliad* 9.153 and 295), once belonged to Pylos in the Catalogue of Ships (Burr 1944:60–61; Kiechle 1960:63–65; for the word νέαται as properly implying inclusion of the cities within the kingdom of Pylos see Palmer 1965:86n1; against the suggestion Simpson and Lazenby 1970:89n37); a different list of seven cities occurs on the Pylos tablets as constituting the "further province" of the Pylian kingdom in the Mycenaean era (see Palmer 1965:88–91, who locates these cities on the western side of the Messenian Gulf, whereas, of the cities named in *Iliad* 9, at least Kardamyle lies on the gulf's eastern shore).

EN5.4 (Endnote to n5.24)

Strabo 8.3.14 says that Triphylian Pylos was 30 stades from the sea, but this figure apparently represents the distance of Pylos from Samikon (Bölte 1934:341). According to Strabo 8.3.16 (Apollodorus is his source) Samikon was 100 stades from the Alpheios River to the north and 100 stades from Lepreon to the south: μεταξὺ δὲ τοῦ Λεπρείου καὶ τοῦ Ἀλφειοῦ (Ἀννίου cod.) τὸ ἱερὸν τοῦ Σαμίου Ποσειδῶνος ἔστιν, ἑκατὸν σταδίους ἑκατέρου διέχον, "The temple of Samian Poseidon is between Lepreon and the Alpheios, 100 stades distant from each." The scholia to *Iliad* 11.726 combine the 100 stades from the Alpheios to Samikon with the 30 stades at issue for the location of Pylos to give the distance from the Alpheios to Pylos as 130 stades: δῆλον οὖν ὅτι [Νέστωρ] τοῦ Ἀρκαδικοῦ Πύλου ἄρχει, ὃς ἀπέχει Ἀλφειοῦ ἑκατὸν τριάκοντα σταδίους, "It is clear that [Nestor] rules the Arcadian Pylos, which is 130 stades from the Alpheios." Strabo 8.3.26 (Apollodorus is again the source) supports the view that this Pylos is the Homeric city by its substantial distance (more than thirty stades) from the sea: καὶ γὰρ δὴ οἱ μὲν ἄλλοι Πύλοι ἐπὶ θαλάττῃ δείκνυνται, οὗτος δὲ πλείους ἢ τριάκοντα σταδίους ὑπὲρ αὐτῆς, "Indeed the other Pyloses [that] are pointed out [are] on the sea, but this one [is] more than thirty stades inland from the sea." In light of Bölte's explanation of the distance "inland from the sea" Strabo's argument for the Triphylian Pylos is overstated. Strabo 8.3.16 treats it as self-evident that the location of the Pylians' sacrifice to Poseidon in *Odyssey* 3 was his temple at Samikon, indicating that for Strabo's Hellenistic sources the temple at Samikon had become an integral part of the case for a Triphylian Pylos (cf. Biraschi 1994:37–42); it is perhaps for this reason that Strabo appears to let Samikon stand for Triphylian Pylos in a measurement of the distance from Messenian Pylos to Triphylian Pylos (cf. n5.45 on Strabo 8.3.21 and Biraschi 1994:40n47). Triphylian Pylos represented the northern half of Lepreon's territory, and like the southern half (Lepreon itself) it bordered the coast. This is suggested by "Scylax" *Periplus* 44, who says that the παράπλους τῆς Λεπρεατῶν χώρας (i.e. Lepreon's whole coastline) was 100 stades, corresponding to the distance from the Neda River (the border between Lepreon and Messenia) and Samikon (Bölte *RE* 'Triphylia' 200). Pylos continued to be part of Lepreon in later antiquity, as Meyer *RE* 'Pylos' 2131 infers from this and other evidence: "That it later belonged to Lepreon is indirectly confirmed by Scylax 44, who still inserts between Elis and Messenia the territory of Lepreon with a coast-line of 100 stades. This agrees exactly with the distance from the coastal pass of Klidi to the Neda River. Strabo provides direct confirmation with the frequent designation of this Pylos as Λεπρεατικός, 'Leprean' " ("Die spätere

Zugehörigkeit zu Lepreon wird indirekt bestätigt durch Skylax cap. 44, der zwischen Elis und Messenien noch das Stadtgebiet von Lepreon einschiebt mit einer Küstenerstreckung von 100 Stadien. Das passt genau auf die Strecke vom Küstenpass von Klidi bis zur Neda. Direkt bestätigt es Strabo mit der häufigen Benennung Λεπρεατικός für dieses Pylos"). Lepreon itself became the political center of Triphylia in the mid-fourth century BC (cf. Bölte *RE* 'Triphylia' 200: "The region of Triphylia was politically united in the city of Lepreon" ["Die Landschaft Triphylia wurde in Lepreon städtisch geeinigt"]); for Triphylia's later history see Bölte *RE* 'Triphylia' 200–201; cf. EN5.18.

EN5.5 (Endnote to n5.30)
The location of the Olenian Rock (*Iliad* 2.617, 11.757) has been disputed since antiquity (see Rizakis 1995:119 for full details and bibliography; cf. also Dräger's note in Wilamowitz 2006:322n1115). If the four towns of Elis in the Catalogue of Ships are to be located in the country's four corners, as has been suggested (see n5.29), this, in addition to a similarity of names, is an argument for associating the Olenian Rock with the town of Olenos in western Achaea, and locating the Olenian Rock in the northeast corner of Elis. The country of the Epeians extended farther north and east, into Achaea, than did the historical region of Elis; Strabo 8.3.9 cites Hecataeus for the fact that Dyme, the westernmost city of historical Achaea, was once part of the Epeians' country (cf. n5.56), and Olenos lay next to Dyme. Besides its two occurrences in Homer the name Olenian Rock occurs in a fragment of Hesiod, which locates it on the river Peiros (Hesiod fr. 13 MW). Strabo 8.3.11, quoting the fragment, identifies the Peiros with the River Acheloos near Dyme: ὁ δὲ Τευθέας εἰς τὸν Ἀχελῷον ἐμβάλλει τὸν κατὰ Δύμην ῥέοντα, ὁμώνυμον τῷ κατὰ Ἀκαρνανίαν, καλούμενον καὶ Πεῖρον. τοῦ δ' Ἡσιόδου εἰπόντος, "ᾧκεε δ' Ὠλενίην πέτρην ποταμοῖο παρ' ὄχθας / εὐρεῖος Πείροιο," μεταγράφουσί τινες Πώροιο οὐκ εὖ, "The Teutheas joins the Acheloos, which flows through Dyme and has the same name as the river in Acarnania, and is also called the Peiros. Hesiod says: 'He inhabits the Olenian Rock by the banks / of the wide Peiros,' which some wrongly change to Poros." Herodotus 1.145, in his list of the twelve Achaean cities, says that the Peiros is in Olenos (Ὤλενος, ἐν τῷ Πεῖρος ποταμὸς μέγας ἐστί, "Olenos, in which is the big river Peiros"), and Strabo 8.7.4 seems to have reported the same information (the name of the river in Strabo is corrupt). Following Strabo 8.3.9, who says that some located both Alesion and the Olenian Rock on the borders of the Pisatis, Bölte 1934:331–333 rejects the location in northeast Elis (he argues that the Hesiodic poet used the Homeric name Olenian Rock arbitrarily to refer to Olenos, which had been abandoned at an early time; cf. Strabo 8.4.7, 8.7.5 end), and confidently identifies the

Olenian Rock with a striking formation to the east of Karatula, overlooking the Lestenitsa valley: "Here Partsch 5 pointed out east of Karatula and high above the valley a noteworthy natural formation, a narrow sandstone block with 50 meter high walls, from whose western end (325 meters above sea level) one's view ranges freely over the valley; at the east end remains are preserved of what is probably, at the oldest, a medieval structure. To the west beneath the block lies the village of Olena [Ωλένη]" ("Hier hat Partsch 5 östlich von Karatula und hoch über dem Tal ein merkwürdiges Naturgebilde nachgewiesen, einen schmalen Sandsteinklotz mit 50 m hohen Wänden, von dessen westlichen Ende (325 m ü. M.) der Blick frei über das Tal schweift; am östlichen Ende sind Reste eines wohl erst mittelalterlichen Baues erhalten. Nach Westen zu aber liegt unter dem Klotz das Dorf Olena [Ωλένη]"). Bölte correctly does not attribute great importance to the name of the modern village, but the striking nature of the landmark is highly suggestive, especially for *Iliad* 11.

EN5.6 (Endnote to n5.35)
Strabo 8.3.32, one of the passages in which Strabo locates Bouprasion between Elis and Dyme, refers to a city Φηραία "in Arcadia: it lies inland from [south of] Dyme, Bouprasion, and Elis" (ἡ δὲ Φηραία ἐστὶ τῆς Ἀρκαδίας· ὑπερκεῖται δὲ τῆς Δυμαίας καὶ Βουπρασίου καὶ Ἤλιδος). Bölte 1934:335 takes this city to be the Arcadian city of Φαραία referred to by Polybius 4.77.5 (for Pharaia see EN5.3), and he interprets the text of Strabo by taking Dyme to be a mistake for Tritaia, which is well to the south. Meyer, on the other hand, takes Φηραία in Strabo to refer to the Achaean city of Pharai (for Pharai see n5.52), which was south and slightly east of Dyme, and thus southeast of Bouprasion (Meyer 1957:84–85); this fits the location given in Strabo. Meineke, in his edition of Strabo, rejects the passage.

EN5.7 (Endnote to n5.44)
To support the idea that Homeric Pylos is in Triphylia Dörpfeld 1913:118–119 argues that Telemachus's voyage from Ithaca to Pylos, which began at sunset and ended sometime after dawn, had time to reach Triphylian Pylos but not Messenian Pylos, some 60 kilometers further on (cf. also Meyer *RE* 'Pylos' 2146). Palmer 1965:45–48 neatly disposes of this argument by pointing out that Nestor, on his return from Troy, sailed from Lesbos to Euboea in a day and part of a night, a journey of the same length as that considered impossible by Dörpfeld, and completed in the same time (a day and part of a night as compared with a night and part of a day). Whether or not such a journey was actually possible is thus irrelevant to the question (the point is well

illustrated by the map in Palmer 1965:46–47; cf. also Visser 1997:526n36). A refinement of the same argument claims that Telemachus, who in one day returns by chariot from Phērai to Pylos and by sunset sails as far as Pheai, past the Alpheios River, can only have done so if he did not have to sail the roughly 60 kilometers between the Messenian Pylos and the Triphylian Pylos (Meyer *RE* 'Pylos' 2146). In answer to this it is perhaps enough to say that if Mount Taygetos did not stop Telemachus on his way to Sparta, the journey from Phērai to Pheai in one day was also not impossible for him. But we can go further and compare the time spent on Telemachus's return voyage from Pylos to Ithaca with the full night and part of one day spent on his initial voyage from Ithaca to Pylos: Telemachus arrives back in Ithaca at dawn (*Odyssey* 15.495–496), so that his whole voyage from Pylos took part of one day and a full night, whereas his initial voyage took a full night and part of one day. The voyage home takes the same time as the voyage out, and the voyage out, as Palmer showed, can perfectly well have been to Messenian Pylos. If the point about the difficulty of reaching Pheai by sunset is pressed, there is an answer to that as well: when the sun sets (*Odyssey* 15.296), Telemachus's ship is on its way to Pheai (ἡ δὲ Φεὰς ἐπέβαλλεν, *Odyssey* 15.297) but has not yet reached it; the vagueness of the ship's location at this point frees the voyage from the demands of a tight schedule. Cf. Wilamowitz 2006:341.

EN5.8 (Endnote to n5.62)
In my discussion of *Odyssey* 15.295–300 (§5.15–§5.17) I argue that two lines of the passage, 295 and 298, were added to the text (so too Bolling 1925:244–245): according to my interpretation an early political controversy featuring an Eleian and a Messenian Pylos led to the addition of line 298, and a later scholarly controversy featuring a Triphylian Pylos led to the addition of line 295. Other solutions to the difficulties of this six-line passage have been proposed, two of which I consider here. In a recent discussion James Diggle (in Bittlestone 2005:517–518) proposes to omit from the original text of the *Odyssey* the entire passage 15.295–300, which he calls, aptly enough, a "magpie's nest." In Diggle's simplified version Telemachus sets sail from Pylos, Athena sends a following wind, and Telemachus is not mentioned again until he is on the shores of Ithaca in *Odyssey* 15.495. In my view, with lines 295 and 298 omitted, problems in the rest of the six-line passage are minor, if not entirely negligible. In line 299 a change of subject from the ship to Telemachus is not signaled, but is indicated at the beginning of line 300 by the masculine participle ὁρμαίνων, "pondering." In line 299 the verb ἐπιπροέηκε, "he struck out for," is used intransitively whereas it

takes a direct object elsewhere in Homer; the simple form of this verb (ἵημι, "send") is also used intransitively (of springs and rivers that "pour forth," *Odyssey* 7.130 and 11.239), whereas in *Iliad* 12.33 and 21.158 the verb has an object ὕδωρ, "water," in a similar context. Line 299, in which the compound verb occurs, is formulaically related to two lines in the *Iliad* in which νηυσίν, "ships," instead of νήσοισιν, "islands," occurs (in these lines, *Iliad* 17.708 and *Iliad* 18.58 = 18.439, someone sends someone else either "to the ships" or "by means of ships"); *Odyssey* 15.299 (ἔνθεν δ' αὖ <u>νήσοισιν ἐπιπροέηκε θοῇσιν</u>, "he struck out for the swift islands") in fact looks like a formulaic transformation of *Iliad* 17.708 (κεῖνον μὲν δὴ <u>νηυσὶν ἐπιπροέηκα θοῇσιν</u>, "I sent him to the swift ships"), but formulaic transformation is of course nothing unusual in Homer ("swift islands" for "swift ships" is admittedly a striking semantic shift). Line 296, saying that the sun set "and all the roadways became dark" (σκιόωντό τε πᾶσαι ἀγυιαί), is considered inappropriate by Diggle because there are no roadways at sea; but in *Odyssey* 11.12 the same line occurs when Odysseus's ship sails from Circe's island to the streams of Okeanos and the underworld. As far as the passage that Diggle would omit entirely is concerned the real question is whether Pheai belongs in the story. To this I say only that Pheai was part of the story when the Pythian *Hymn to Apollo* was composed; if it was not in the original text of the *Odyssey*, I do not know how or why it was added to the text of the *Odyssey* by so early a date. Matthews 1987 (cf. also 1996:129–134) proposes a solution in the opposite direction from Diggle, arguing that *Odyssey* 15.295–300 is all Homeric but that the lines are in the wrong order. Matthews starts from the idea that Homer, in *Odyssey* 15, presented detailed but faulty geography of the western Peloponnesus: he proposes that the following was the text of *Odyssey* 15 before later hands rearranged it and altered the underlined phrase and name:

296	δύσετό τ' ἠέλιος σκιόωντό τε πᾶσαι ἀγυιαί·
295	βὰν δὲ παρὰ Κρουνοὺς καὶ Χαλκίδα <u>καὶ παρὰ Δύμην</u>
298	ἠδὲ παρ' Ἤλιδα δῖαν, ὅθι κρατέουσιν Ἐπειοί.
297	ἡ δὲ <u>Φερὰς</u> ἐπέβαλλεν ἐπειγομένη Διὸς οὔρῳ.

296	The sun set and all the ways grew dark;
295	they went past Krounoi and Khalkis <u>and past Dyme</u>
298	and past shining Elis, where the Epeians have power.
297	It made for <u>Pherai</u>, driven by Zeus's wind.

In this text Homer's error (later copied by the *Homeric Hymn to Apollo*) was to put Dyme before Elis; on the other hand Homer correctly made Telemachus's ship head for *Pherai* (this again was copied by the *Homeric Hymn to Apollo*), for which *Pheai* was later substituted when further changes to the text were made. In Matthews' text everything but Dyme is geographically correct, and all problems of language are eliminated. But Dyme, which in this text must be near the Alpheios River between Triphylia and Elis, is wildly out of place. This is a serious error on Homer's part, especially in view of his assumed correct placement of Krounoi, Khalkis, Elis, and Pherai; in my view simple ignorance cannot well account for part of the picture (Dyme) when it conflicts so completely with the rest of the picture (the four other places, all correctly located). Matthews reaches his conclusions about the text of *Odyssey* 15 from his analysis of a fragment of the *Thebaid* of the late-fifth century poet Antimachus of Colophon; in Antimachus fr. 27 it is said that two participants in the war against Thebes threatened to do again what they formerly did when they led the Epeians and sacked Dyme (the dramatic situation seems to be a feast at the palace of Adrastus in Argos before the war against Thebes): ὡς ἐπαπειλήτην ὥσπερ Καυκωνίδα Δύμην / ἐπραθέτην παίδεσσιν Ἐπειῶν ἀρχεύοντες, "Thus the two threatened [to do] as [when] they had led the sons of the Epeians and sacked Cauconian Dyme." The sack of Dyme is an otherwise unknown mythological event; it is alluded to again in Antimachus fr. 28, where the situation seems to be that another former participant in the sack of Dyme, apparently on the other side, follows up the speech at issue in fr. 27 (cf. Matthews 1996:134): ἐν δέ νυ τοῖσι μάλα πρόφρων ἐπίκουρος ἀμορβέων / ὡμίλησ', εἵως διεπέρσατε Δύμιον ἄστυ, "I joined their company, following as a very willing ally, until you (pl.) sacked the Dymaean town." Matthews argues that Antimachus calls Dyme "Cauconian" in fr. 27 (Καυκωνίδα Δύμην) because Antimachus's text of *Odyssey* 15 (as reconstructed by Matthews) seemed to locate Dyme in Triphylia, which had strong associations with Cauconians; Antimachus, with such a text before him, inferred that Homer meant a city of Dyme other than the Achaean city, and he indicated as much by calling it Cauconian. Now it is true that the Cauconians are closely associated with Triphylia, and especially with the city of Lepreon; Matthews 1987:93 summarizes the evidence as follows: "The Kaukones in Triphylia near Lepreon are mentioned by Strabo himself (8.3.11), as is a tomb of Kaukon at the city (8.3.16). According to Aelian (*Varia Historia* 1.24), Kaukon was the father of Lepreus. Herodotus mentions the Triphylian Kaukones at 1.147 and 4.148. Zenodotos too (*ap.* Athen. 10.412A) puts the Kaukones near Lepreon, and the learned Kallimachos refers to 'the city of the Kaukones, which is called Lepreon' (*Hymn.*

1.39)." But the Cauconians were not limited to Triphylia. Strabo 8.3.17 says that there were two opinions as to their location, both of which include more than Triphylia: either they inhabited all of what Strabo knew as Elis, namely from the Messenian border in the south to Achaean Dyme in the northeast, or they were split into two groups, one in Triphylia and the other near Achaean Dyme. Matthews is probably correct in interpreting the second opinion as that of Hellenistic scholars who put Nestor's Pylos in Triphylia: their spokesman Strabo says that in order for Athena, disguised as Mentor, to part from Telemachus at Pylos and proceed on business to the Cauconians (*Odyssey* 3.366), the Cauconians had to be somewhere else besides Triphylia, Athena's presumed location at the outset of the trip (cf. Biraschi 1994:37–42). But this idea, however learned, did not arise out of nothing. There is considerable evidence that Cauconians once occupied a broad area, just as the first opinion outlined by Strabo maintained: Strabo 8.3.11 notes that there was a River Caucon between Achaean Dyme and Tritaia, southeast of Dyme; Strabo 8.3.17 reports that "Aristotle has knowledge of their [the Cauconians'] having been established especially at this latter place [i.e. in Bouprasis and Koile Elis near Dyme]"; the same passage, Strabo 8.3.17, associates Antimachus himself with the first of the two opinions concerning the Cauconians' location: "Some say that the whole of what is now called Eleia, from Messenia as far as Dyme, was called Cauconia. Antimachus, at any rate, calls all the inhabitants both Eleians [MSS. Epeians] and Cauconians" (on "Eleians" as the correct reading for "Epeians" see Matthews 1987:92n3/1996:131n132). Wilamowitz 2006:331–332, who cites the Antimachus fragment for the name Cauconian as belonging particularly to Dyme, cites evidence for a hero Caucon still further east in Arcadia ("Apollodorus" 3.8.1; but Pausanias 4.27.6, which Wilamowitz and Eitrem *RE* 'Kaukon 2' both cite for a cult of Caucon in Megalopolis, does not seem to me to relate to that city). While I do not think that it is possible to reconstruct *Odyssey* 15.295–298 on the basis of Antimachus as Matthews has attempted to do, the evidence of Antimachus seems to me revealing in another way. The sack of Dyme by the Epeians, though known only from Antimachus, fits well with the tradition found in Strabo 8.3.9 that Dyme was once part of the Epeian realm (cf. n5.56): the evidence of Antimachus suggests that Dyme became part of the Epeian realm through conquest. How was this thought to have happened? The conquest of Dyme could have been carried out from what was historically Elis, to the west of Dyme; in that case the expansion of the Eleian domain to include Dyme was simply nullified when Dyme became part of Achaea. It is also possible, I think, that the Elis that conquered Dyme is the Elis that we see located east of Dyme in the *Homeric Hymn to Apollo*. This Elis, which is imagined as a stage in the migration of the Eleian people before they reached their ultimate homeland (cf. n5.56), had to pass through Dyme to reach its final destination; if the sack of Dyme belonged to the tradition of an Eleian migration (the tradition presupposed by the *Homeric Hymn to Apollo*), Elis failed to keep possession of Dyme in this case too, but there was at least a geographical necessity to conquer Dyme in the first place. The question that remains is why Antimachus calls Dyme Cauconian. According to Strabo 7.7.1 the Cauconians were an aboriginal, pre-Greek population (cf. Bölte *RE* 'Kaukones' 65); they seem to have occupied a broad territory before the Eleians arrived, and this territory included Dyme, as discussed above. By referring to the sack of Cauconian Dyme Antimachus, I think, means to indicate an opposition between aboriginal Cauconians on the one hand and later invaders on the other hand. As for the invaders, Antimachus calls them by the mythic name Epeians, but he presumably means the historical Eleians, in line with other sources that equate Epeians and Eleians (cf. Ephorus *FGrHist* 70 F 115, F 122, F 144, Strabo 8.3.9, 8.3.33, Pausanias 5.1.3–8, 5.3.4–5.4.2; see Castelnuovo 2002:167–168 for discussion and 167n40 for other sources). The poet of the *Homeric Hymn to Apollo*, I suggest, may have had the same scheme as Antimachus in his mind when he put Elis east of Dyme: the Eleians in the hymn are thus in a position to take Dyme one day in battle, the battle later referred to by Antimachus as the sack of Dyme by the Epeians; the tradition for this sack probably first took shape in the seventh century BC when Dyme had already become part of Achaea (cf. n5.56). Dyme, for its part, claimed a different history as the very land of the Epeians to the exclusion of Elis (for Hecataeus, who attests this tradition, cf. n5.56). Dyme, it seems, chose not to remember that it became part of the Epeian realm when invading Eleians conquered its native Cauconian population, but instead elevated its former status as part of the legendary Epeian realm into an exaggerated counterclaim against Elis.

EN5.9 *(Endnote to n5.64)*
Pausanias's evidence for a Pylian population that survived in Messenia until the end of the Second Messenian War is contained in his overall account of the Second Messenian War, not all of which is reliable. His account of the Second Messenian War derives in part from the third-century BC poet Rhianos, whose tales of the Messenian hero Aristomenes seem to have pertained to events of the early fifth century BC rather than the seventh century BC (see Kiechle 1959:90–93 for this well understood issue). Rhianos's particular theme was the siege of Mount Hira, and it is in relation to this siege that Pausanias

4.23.1 mentions the departure of the Pylians (see n5.64). Kiechle 1959:31–33, cf. also 16, argues persuasively that the departure of the Pylians was known from a source other than Rhianos, as can be inferred from another passage of Pausanias: Pausanias 4.24.4 says that after the Second Messenian War the Spartans settled the Nauplians, who had previously been expelled by the Argives from their own city in the Argolid, in Methone, which had recently been abandoned by its people; the departure of the Methonaians, attested by this passage, entails the departure of the Pylians as well; the two are linked in Pausanias 4.23.1 (see n5.64). Kiechle argues that it was Pausanias's immediate source (probably a local historian of Messenia according to Kiechle 1959:4n2, citing Schwartz 1899:435–436) who combined the account of Pylos and Methone with Rhianos's tale of Mount Hira. Thus nothing can be learned from Pausanias about the Pylians' departure other than that they left by ship. Pausanias 4.23.5–10 says that they went with Messenian refugees to Zancle in Sicily, the name of which the Messenians changed to Messana, but these events belong to the early fifth century BC (486 BC according to Lomas *OCD³* 'Messana'; c. 489 BC according to Kiechle 1959:124) and have nothing to do with Pylians (for the events see Thucydides 6.4.6; Herodotus 6.23; Strabo 6.2.3; and cf. Kiechle 1959:90–91, 119–123). Kiechle 1959:34–45 argues that after the Second Messenian War the Pylians went to Metapontion in southern Italy, where a local cult of Neleids (τὸν τῶν Νηλειδῶν ἐναγισμόν, "the offering to the dead for the Neleids," Strabo 6.1.15) suggests that the Achaeans said to have settled Metapontion (Antiochus of Syracuse, cited by Strabo 6.1.15) were in fact (or at least included) Pylians. Kiechle 1959:48–49 assigns a date between 630 and 600 BC (depending on the date of the end of the Second Messenian War) for the departure of the Pylians from the Peloponnesus; Huxley 1962:59–60 also supports a date close to 600 BC. For c. 600 BC as the likely date of the end of the Second Messenian War see §5.24 and n5.91.

EN5.10 (Endnote to n5.65)
Strabo 8.4.1–2 says that before the city of Pylos was settled at Koryphasion there was an "old Pylos" seven stades inland from Koryphasion under Mount Aigaleon; this is a puzzle since there is no mountain seven stades from Koryphasion and Mount Aigaleon is unknown apart from this passage of Strabo. For the site of "old Pylos" Marinatos 1955:163 proposes Volimidia, five kilometers northeast of Ano-Englianos (Volimidia is roughly seventy stades from Koryphasion, and Marinatos1955:163n1 proposes seventy as a correction for seven in Strabo); Volimidia lies beneath a mountain to the north, which would be Mount Aigaleon (a photograph taken from Volimidia toward the

mountain is in Marinatos 1955:142). At Volimidia multiple Mycenaean graves have been found, some of which became cult sites in the eighth century BC. Meyer *RE* Supplement 15 'Messenien' 207–208 accepts Marinatos's identification of this site as "old Pylos": "Marinatos's conjecture...that this is what could be meant by the 'old Pylos' of Strabo 8.4.2 is very obvious. The traditional name of the Mycenaean palace at Englianos would have maintained itself here.... The inhabitants of this 'old Pylos' would then have taken the name of their place with them to the newly settled Koryphasion, and this would best explain the name change there. The distance given for Mount Aigaleon, near which this 'old Pylos' lay according to Strabo, of course does not agree, but must in any case be emended since there is no mountain near Pylos at the distance given by Strabo.... That according to the observations above the place was still inhabited in Roman times is probably no real counterargument, since not all the inhabitants need to have left" ("Marinatos' Vermutung, ...dass damit das 'Altpylos' von Strabo 8.4.2 gemeint sein könnte, ist recht einleuchtend. Die Namenstradition des mykenischen Palastes von Ano-Englianos hätte sich hier erhalten.... Die Bewohner dieses 'Altpyos' hätten dann den Namen ihres Orts nach dem neubesiedelten Koryphasion mitgenommen, womit die Namensveränderung bestens erklärt wäre. Die Entfernungsangabe für den Berg Aigaleon, an dem dieses Altpylos nach Strabo lag, stimmt zwar nicht, muss aber in jedem Fall emendiert werden, da es in der von Strabo genannten Entfernung keinen Berg bei Pylos gab.... Dass der Ort nach den obigen Bemerkungen auch noch in römischer Zeit bestand, ist wohl kein wirkliches Gegenargument, da ja nicht alle Bewohner abgewandert sein müssen"). Strabo's "old Pylos" most likely figures in an oracular verse which is quoted in part by Aristophanes *Knights* 1059, and is given in full by the scholia to Aristophanes and Strabo 8.3.7: ἔστι Πύλος πρὸ Πύλοιο, Πύλος γε μέν ἐστι καὶ ἄλλος, "there is a Pylos before Pylos, and there is yet another Pylos" (the scholia to Aristophanes have ἄλλη for ἄλλος; see Marinatos 1955:163n1). The verse, which in Aristophanes is called an oracle of Bakis, likely goes back to the sixth century BC (see EN5.22). In the first half of the verse, ἔστι Πύλος πρὸ Πύλοιο (Aristophanes quotes only this much), Marinatos correctly takes the preposition πρό, "before," in a spatial rather than temporal sense, and proposes that the "Pylos in front of Pylos" refers to Koryphasion, on the sea, in relation to a site inland from Koryphasion, namely the "old Pylos" of Strabo; if this is the meaning, a play on πύλη, "gate," is also likely part of the riddle. Kiechle 1960:8 has a similar interpretation, and uses it to argue that there was a tradition about Messenian Pylos in the Archaic period (cf. n5.65) : "The oracle verse: ἔστι Πύλος πρὸ Πύλοιο, 'there is a Pylos before Pylos,' which Aristophanes *Knights* 1059 already parodies, and which can probably only be explained by the assumption that it alludes to two places that lay not far from each other, one on the coast and the other somewhat inland, shows that a tradition may have been maintained for the Messenian Pylos from the Archaic period" ("Der Orakelvers: ἔστι Πύλος πρὸ Πύλοιο, den schon Aristophanes, Ritter 1059, parodierte und der sich wohl nur durch die Annahme erklären lässt, dass er auf zwei unweit voneinander gelegene Orte dieses Namens anspielt, ein Pylos an der Küste und eines etwas im Landesinneren, zeigt, dass sich aus archaischer Zeit eine Tradition über das messenische Pylos erhalten haben dürfte"). For the "yet another Pylos" of the riddle see EN5.22.

EN5.11 (Endnote to n5.68)

Kreophylos, who was said to have entertained Homer in his home (Callimachus *Epigrams* 6 Pfeiffer; cf. Plato *Republic* 600b), was also said to be Homer's son-in-law (scholia to Plato *Republic* 600b, which say further that he received the *Iliad* from Homer as a gift; cf. n5.68); this is a contamination with a similar tradition for the *Cypria* attested by Pindar fr. 265 Schroeder (see Burkert 1972:76n10, Graziosi 2002:186–193). There was also a tradition, followed by Ephorus (but, in Jacoby's view, doubtless older), that Lycurgus met Homer himself (Ephorus *FGrHist* 70 F 103, F 149.19; cf. Jacoby on Ephorus F 102 and F 173–F 175 [end], and Jacoby 1902:100–107, especially 101 and 105); Apollodorus, who must have followed Ephorus for the synchronism, had Lycurgus meet Homer when Lycurgus was still a young man (ὥστε ἐπιβαλεῖν αὐτῷ Λυκοῦργον τὸν νομοθέτην ἔτι νέον ὄντα, Clement of Alexandria *Stromata* 1.21.117.3, citing Apollodorus; cf. Jacoby 1902:100–101, Burkert 1972:77). Aristotle, who dated Lycurgus later than Homer (as did Eratosthenes and Aristarchus; cf. Jacoby 1902:105–106), had Lycurgus receive the poems not from Homer's contemporary, Kreophylos, but from Kreophylos's descendants; the earlier version of this tradition would have been that Lycurgus received the poems directly from Kreophylos, who received them from Homer. In this tradition Kreophylos was a mediating figure between Lycurgus and Homer. The tradition that Lycurgus received the poems directly from Homer, without Kreophylos as an intermediary, simplifies the story: it expresses more directly the idea that the Spartans were the first in mainland Greece to receive the Homeric poems. This priority is the point in Aelian *Varia Historia* 13.14, who says that Lycurgus was the first to bring Homer's poetry from Ionia to mainland Greece, before Peisistratos collected the poems in Athens; cf. also Dio of Prusa 2.45 (texts quoted by Allen 1924:228). I take the more complex tradition, with Kreophylos as an intermediary between Homer and Lycurgus, to be the older one (cf. n5.70). An aberrant tradition that deserves further investigation is that Kreophylos received Homer on the island of Ios just before Homer died (*Contest of Hesiod and Homer* line 322 [Allen 1912:237], Proclus *Chrestomathy* lines 30–31 [Allen 1912:100 lines 11–12]; in the Herodotean *Life of Homer* Homer dies on Ios, but he does not meet Kreophylos there). If the meeting between Homer and Kreophylos on Samos reflects a Spartan agenda, does the change from Samos to Ios reflect a counteragenda on the part of Athens?

EN5.12 (Endnote to n5.73)
Something is known of the grievances that Athens, Sikyon, and Thessaly, the victors in the First Sacred War, had against Delphi in the period before the war. Delphi was then associated primarily with Dorian states (cf. Forrest 1956:48, 1982:316; Davies 1994:204), and when Cleisthenes, the anti-Dorian tyrant of Sikyon, sought Delphi's support for his campaign against Argos, the oracle rebuffed him: Cleisthenes asked about expelling the Dorian hero Adrastos from Sikyon, and the oracle responded that Adrastos was king of Sikyon while Cleisthenes was a λευστήρ, a "stone-thrower," i.e. a common skirmisher (Herodotus 5.67.2). In Athens Delphi supported the Cylonian conspiracy (the conspiracy's failure was attributed to the misunderstanding of an oracle, which had clearly been meant to encourage the conspirators, and which doubtless came from Delphi). Forrest 1956:41 suggests that Delphi was also responsible for declaring the Alcmaeonids to be under a curse (ἐναγεῖς) after the archon Megacles put the Cylonian conspirators to death (cf. §3.13 above); Megacles' son Alcmaeon (his visit to Croesus is recounted in Herodotus 6.125) was perhaps the Alcmaeon who commanded the Athenian forces in the Sacred War (Plutarch *Solon* 11.2; cf. Toepffer 1889:243; cf. also n5.87). Forrest 1956:36–42 nicely connects the grievances of Sikyon and Athens with the final passage of the *Homeric Hymn to Apollo*, where the warning against a τηΰσιον ἔπος, "rash word," would apply to the response given to Cleisthenes (λευστήρ, "stone-thrower"), and the warning against a (τηΰσιον) ἔργον, "(rash) deed," would apply to the support given to the Cylonian conspirators. The motives of the Thessalians in the Sacred War are less clear but must have had to do with their desire to extend their influence southward to the Gulf of Corinth. The Pylaian (Anthelan) Amphictyony, which was centered around Thermopylai in southern Thessaly, and which the Thessalians dominated, was a related factor, for it became part of the Delphic Amphictyony, or Delphi became part of the Pylaian Amphictyony, with meetings alternating between

Delphi and the sanctuary of Demeter at Anthela; Forrest 1956:42–44 suggests a possible rivalry between Delphi and the Pylaian Amphictyony before the Sacred War. While much remains obscure, it seems probable that the Pylaian Amphictyony appropriated the sanctuary of Apollo at Delphi, possibly in the seventh century BC or earlier, but more likely as a result of the Sacred War in the early sixth century. On the question of the origins and early development of the Pylaian-Delphic Amphictyony see Tausend 1992:34–47; Lefèvre 1998:13–16; Sánchez 2001:32–37, 41–44; Hall 2002:144–154; cf. also Petrović 2004:265.

EN5.13 (Endnote to n5.94)
Tyrtaeus fr. 4 West, concerning the constitution that Sparta received from the Delphic oracle, has different opening couplets in the two sources for the fragment, Diodorus 7.12.6 and Plutarch *Lycurgus* 6.5; in Diodorus the fragment begins as follows:

⟨ὦ⟩δε γὰρ ἀργυρότοξος ἄναξ ἑκάεργος Ἀπόλλων

χρυσοκόμης ἔχρη πίονος ἐξ ἀδύτου

ἄρχειν μὲν....

For thus the silver-bowed far-working lord Apollo
  with the golden hair prophesied from his rich sanctuary:
  those to initiate....

This version conforms with the tradition found in Diodorus (but not attested by Tyrtaeus) that Lycurgus himself received the oracle at Delphi and brought it back to Sparta (ἡ Πυθία ἔχρησε τῷ Λυκούργῳ περὶ τῶν πολιτικῶν οὕτως, "The Pythia prophesied to Lycurgus about state matters as follows"); in Plutarch's version the plural subject of "they brought back" (οἴκαδ᾽ ἔνεικαν) conflicts with the Lycurgus tradition, which is presumed to be more recent. Diodorus's version thus seems to be an adaptation to the Lycurgus tradition, and Plutarch's version is to be preferred. The two openings have sometimes been combined, most recently by Van Wees 1999:7–8 and n25, who assumes a lacuna between them. Huxley 1962:41–45, 122n295 argues that a historical Lycurgus was one of the *Pythioi* who brought the oracle back to Sparta at the time of the kings Theopompos and Polydoros, and he combines the two openings as follows (Huxley 1962:55, 127n351):

Φοίβου ἀκούσαντες Πυθωνόθεν οἴκαδ᾽ ἔνεικαν

μαντείας τε θεοῦ καὶ τελέεντ᾽ ἔπεα·

"δῆ‹λα› γὰρ ἀργυρότοξος ἄναξ ἑκάεργος Ἀπόλλων
χρυσοκόμης ἔχρη πίονος ἐξ ἀδύτου·
'ἄρχειν μὲν...'."

> After listening to Phoebus they brought home from Pytho
>   the god's oracles and sure predictions:
> "For clear things has the silver-bowed far-working lord Apollo
>   with the golden hair prophesied from his rich sanctuary:
> 'those to initiate...'."

The traditional view that the two openings are alternatives is in my view to be preferred.

EN5.14 (Endnote to n5.97)

It must be acknowledged that very little is certain with respect to the Great Rhetra, the interpretation of which is notoriously disputed. Van Wees 1999 argues that Tyrtaeus fr. 4 West, contrary to what was mistakenly inferred in the classical period, has nothing to do with the Great Rhetra, but instead calls on the Spartan people to obey the kings and elders during the crisis of the Second Messenian War; the corrupt line 8 according to Van Wees 1999:11 (who follows Hammond 1950:48 for the line's first half) should be restored and enjambed with line 9 as follows:

> μηδ' ἔτι βουλεύειν. ὥσθ' ἅμα [vel sim.] τῇδε πόλει
> δήμου τε πλήθει νίκην καὶ κάρτος ἔπεσθαι.

> and counsel no further; thus victory and strength
> accompany this city and the mass of the people.

In this reading victory is promised to the city and the people if the kings and elders exercise their authority and the people obey them; the people's obedience consists in saying and doing what is just (line 7) in response to the straight proposals (of the kings and elders) (line 6), and counseling no further (line 8 as emended): the people, in other words, are consulted, but they can only agree with what is proposed and offer no further counsel. In accord with this reading Van Wees (1999:10) takes the phrase εὐθείαις ῥήτραις ἀνταπαμειβομένους, which describes the people in line 6, to mean "responding to straight proposals." Although Van Wees's interpretation involves other factors and is closely argued, I continue to think that the traditional explanation in terms of the Great Rhetra is correct. In the traditional

interpretation in terms of the Great Rhetra εὐθείαις ῥήτραις is best taken
as an instrumental dative and not as a true dative: the people respond "*with*
straight pronouncements" to what is proposed (Wade-Gery 1944:1, 6–7
[=1958:55, 62–64] discusses the two possible dative constructions but does
not decide between them; for *rhêtrai* as "pronouncements of the *dêmos*," cf.
Huxley 1962:120n283).

EN5.15 (Endnote to n5.107)
To compare the language of Tyrtaeus and the Pythian *Hymn to Apollo* would
require a systematic analysis beyond the scope of this study. Instead I make
two limited observations. The first concerns the use of unusual Homeric
compounds in -γενής, namely Πυλοιγενής, "Pylian-born," in the *Hymn to
Apollo* (Πυλοιγενέας τ' ἀνθρώπους, "Pylian-born men," lines 398 and 424;
cf. Πυλοιγενέος βασιλῆος, "Pylian-born king," *Iliad* 2.54, Πυλοιγενέες δέ οἱ
ἵπποι, "Pylian-born horses," *Iliad* 23.303) and πρεσβυγενής, "eldest-born,"
in Tyrtaeus (πρεσβυγενέας τε γέροντας, "eldest-born old men," fr. 4.5 West;
cf. πρεσβυγενὴς Ἀντηνορίδης, "eldest-born son of Antenor," *Iliad* 11.249). Of
course Tyrtaeus's use of πρεσβυγενέας does not count for much if he simply
repeats the wording of the Delphic oracle (see §5.25 and n5.94). But I note
that the rider to the Rhetra, as preserved by Plutarch *Lycurgus* 6.4 (cf. §5.25
and n5.96), contains the word πρεσβυγενέας, and one may wonder whether
Tyrtaeus had a hand in crafting the rider's language. A second possible corre-
spondence between Tyrtaeus and the *Homeric Hymn to Apollo* is equally uncer-
tain, but also intriguing. A papyrus fragment of Tyrtaeus containing only a
few scattered words (fr. 18 West) seems to have used the form ἀγαλλομένη,
"exulting," in the same place in the hexameter as *Homeric Hymn to Apollo* 427,
εὖτε Φερὰς ἐπέβαλλεν ἀγαλλομένη Διὸς οὔρῳ, "when it made for Pherai,
exulting in Zeus's wind." This line, with Φεράς for Homeric Φεάς, is, as I have
argued, crucial to the *Homeric Hymn to Apollo*; in Tyrtaeus there is unfortu-
nately no context for α]γ̣αλλομένη (first letter lost, second letter uncertain),
which is the only word preserved in the first line of the fragment (the phrase
κα̣ι κροκόεντα, "and saffron-colored," in the second line does not help, and
there is a gap of four lines before another word or two can be read). The verb
ἀγάλλομαι has a number of occurrences in various contexts in Greek epic,
but the feminine singular participle occurs only in these two instances, in
the *Homeric Hymn to Apollo* and in Tyrtaeus. In terms of content I note that
just as the *Homeric Hymn to Apollo* reworks a Homeric model in modifying
Telemachus's voyage, Tyrtaeus fr. 10.21–30 West perhaps also reworks a
Homeric model if his exhortation that young men not let old men fight in

front of them and die, but that they instead stand firm in the front ranks and die themselves, is adapted from Priam's speech to Achilles in *Iliad* 22.71–76 (so Bowra 1938:53–55); but in this case it is more likely that both passages adapt a traditional motif (cf. Richardson 1993:113). In any case Tyrtaeus and the *Homeric Hymn to Apollo* would hardly be alone in the Archaic period in adapting Homeric models, and a comparison between them on this basis does not lead far. While I do not insist on my suggestion that Tyrtaeus composed the Pythian *Hymn to Apollo*, I know of no better suggestion. Richard Martin (Martin 2000a) proposes that a tradition of competition between Homeric and Hesiodic poetry lies behind the division of the *Homeric Hymn to Apollo* into two parts; he views the hymn as a unified work whose purpose is to represent such a traditional competition. It is clear that the Delian part of the hymn, with its reference to the blind bard of Chios, qualifies as Homeric. The question is whether the Pythian part of the hymn qualifies as Hesiodic. To connect the Pythian part of the hymn with Hesiod there is nothing to match the overt allusion to Homer in the Delian part. Martin's case rests rather on indirect evidence. A Hesiodic fragment speaks of a joint hymnic celebration of Apollo by Hesiod and Homer on Delos (Hesiod fr. 357 MW):

> ἐν Δήλῳ τότε πρῶτον ἐγὼ καὶ Ὅμηρος ἀοιδοὶ
> μέλπομεν, ἐν νεαροῖς ὕμνοις ῥάψαντες ἀοιδήν,
> Φοῖβον Ἀπόλλωνα χρυσάορον, ὃν τέκε Λητώ.

> On Delos then for the first time Homer and I, singers,
> stitching together a song in new hymns, celebrated
> Phoebus Apollo with the golden sword, whom Leto bore.

Here seems to be a mythic precedent for the kind of joint composition that Martin has in mind. But the evidence does not apply directly to our *Homeric Hymn to Apollo*, which distinguishes between a Delian and a Pythian Apollo; the Hesiodic fragment surely concerns only the Delian Apollo, unless the unlikely assumption is made that the fragment was composed for Polycrates' unique celebration of *Púthia kaì Délia* on Delos (cf. Martin 2000a:419–420). To make the case that the Pythian part of the *Homeric Hymn to Apollo* is Hesiodic Martin draws attention to a particular stylistic feature having to do with Hermann's bridge, the tendency of epic hexameters to avoid a word break after a trochee in the fourth foot. Various factors mitigate violations of Hermann's bridge, as Martin fully discusses, and the feature is thus hard to define. Since estimates of the frequency with which Hermann's bridge is violated in any given text vary with the definition applied, raw numbers do not mean much. Martin focuses instead on a specific pattern that is exemplified in the first verse of the Hesiodic fragment above: the word break that occurs in the phrase καὶ | Ὅμηρος comes after a trochee in the fourth foot and thus technically violates Hermann's bridge; but Hermann himself did not include cases like this where a monosyllable joined in sense to what follows precedes the break ("These cases are not at all rare" ["*Haec minime rara sunt exempla*"], Hermann 1805:693; cf. West 1982:38n18 and Martin 2000a:425). Although violation of Hermann's bridge is not at issue, Martin points out that correpted καί in this position is relatively frequent in Hesiod (four examples in the *Theogony* and 12 examples in the *Works and Days*); it is also found five times in the Pythian part of the *Homeric Hymn to Apollo* (lines 176, 194, 350, 423, and 534), and this, Martin suggests, is an indication of the Pythian hymn's Hesiodic style. One problem with this argument is that there are 68 examples of the same thing (καί before the second short of the fourth foot) in the *Odyssey* (Martin's count, which he was able to do for the *Odyssey* but not for the *Iliad*; see Martin 2000a:417n54). Frequency of occurrence is higher in the Pythian part of the *Homeric Hymn to Apollo* (one per 74 lines) and in Hesiod (one per 116 lines) than in the *Odyssey* (one per 178 lines), but the difference hardly seems decisive as a mark of Hesiodic style. One instance of the pattern in the *Homeric Hymn to Apollo* warrants further comment; Martin draws attention to it, and I have discussed the line in question as well (n5.55). The line is among the several lines in the *Homeric Hymn to Apollo* that are directly modeled on the text of Homer; *Homeric Hymn to Apollo* 423 is in fact identical with *Iliad* 2.592 in the Pylian entry to the Catalogue of Ships: καὶ Θρύον Ἀλφειοῖο πόρον καὶ ἐΰκτιτον Αἶπυ, "and Thryon, ford of the Alpheios, and well-built Aipy." This line, which in the Catalogue of Ships indicates nothing about the location of Pylos, is deployed in the *Homeric Hymn to Apollo* to indicate that Pylos, mentioned in the hymn's next line (424), lay north of the Alpheios River in Elis. In my view this Homeric borrowing in the hymn has to be understood as a very deliberate Homeric borrowing, for the hymn's core issue is precisely the location of Pylos in the Homeric poems. Martin 2000a:418, on the other hand, suggests that the Pylian entry to the Catalogue of Ships may have been composed by the same rhapsodes who composed the *Homeric Hymn to Apollo* ("It may be that the same rhapsodes interested in stylizing a hymn-competition between Homer and Hesiod also had a hand in composing this *Iliad* scene"). For Martin the point of contact between the hymn and the Pylian entry to the Catalogue of Ships is a common interest in poetic competition: this is the situation *ex hypothesi* in the *Homeric Hymn to Apollo*, and Thamyris, who rivaled the Muses as a singer, is the subject of a brief account in the Pylian entry to the Catalogue of Ships (*Iliad* 2.594–600). If I am right that the line ending καὶ ἐΰκτιτον Αἶπυ, "and well-built Aipy," plays a pivotal role in the *Homeric Hymn to Apollo*, I would argue that it influenced the other lines in the hymn with similar endings beginning καί, "and," in the fourth foot, namely line 194 (καὶ ἐΰφρονες Ὧραι, "and the merry Seasons"), line 350 (καὶ ἐπήλυθον ὧραι, "and the seasons drew near"), line 534 (καὶ ἐπὶ φρεσὶ θήσω, "and I will put in your mind"), and line 176 (καὶ ἐτήτυμόν ἐστιν, "and it is true"). This would be an instance of a particular pattern, known from both Homer and Hesiod, being repeated with unusual frequency in a relatively short space simply because the pattern, in the borrowed phrase καὶ ἐΰκτιτον Αἶπυ, "and well-built Aipy," was fixed in the poet's mind at the time.

EN5.16 (Endnote to n5.108)

Strabo 8.4.10, whose source is taken to be Apollodorus (*FGrHist* 244 F 334), says that the Eleians helped the Messenians against Sparta in the Second Messenian War; this has been doubted on historical grounds. The passage names the Argives and the Pisatans as the Messenians' other allies in the war; the passage goes on to say that the Arcadians provided one of the generals on the Messenian side, namely Aristokrates, the king of Orkhomenos, and from this it is clear that the Arcadians have dropped out of Strabo's list of Messenian allies and must be restored. The passage says finally that the Pisatans also provided a general, namely Pantaleon. The passage in its entirety is as follows: πλεονάκις δ' ἐπολέμησαν [sc. οἱ Λακεδαιμόνιοι] διὰ τὰς ἀποστάσεις τῶν Μεσσηνίων. τὴν μὲν οὖν πρώτην κατάκτησιν αὐτῶν φησι Τυρταῖος ἐν τοῖς ποιήμασι κατὰ τοὺς τῶν πατέρων πατέρας γενέσθαι· τὴν δὲ δευτέραν, καθ' ἣν ἑλόμενοι συμμάχους Ἀργείους τε καὶ <u>Ἠλείους</u> ‹καὶ Ἀρκάδας› καὶ Πισάτας ἀπέστησαν, Ἀρκάδων μὲν Ἀριστοκράτην τὸν Ὀρχομενοῦ βασιλέα παρεχομένων στρατηγόν, Πισατῶν δὲ Πανταλέοντα τὸν Ὀμφαλίωνος, ἡνίκα φησὶν αὐτὸς στρατηγῆσαι τὸν πόλεμον τοῖς Λακεδαιμονίοις, "They [the Spartans] were often at war because of the Messenians' revolts. Tyrtaeus says in his poems that the Spartans' first acquistion of the Messenians was in their fathers' fathers' time, and that the second was after the Messenians chose as allies the Argives, <u>Eleians</u>, <Arcadians>, and Pisatans and revolted, and the Arcadians provided Aristokrates, the king of Orkhomenos, as general, and the Pisatans Pantaleon, the son of Omphalion; this was when Tyrtaeus says that he himself conducted the war for the Spartans" (Strabo 8.4.10). It is the presence of both the Pisatans and the Eleians on the same side in the war that causes doubts. The Pisatans and the Eleians vied for control of

Olympia and the Olympic games, and Pantaleon in particular is associated with Pisatan dominance at Olympia (he led an army to take over the games in 644 BC according to Pausanias 6.22.2; according to Strabo 8.3.30 [355] the Pisatans controlled the games still earlier, from 672 BC; see Swoboda *RE* 'Elis' 2388–2390, Maddoli, Nafissi, Saladino 1999:365–368, Taita 1999). The Eleians did not regain control of Olympia until the time of Pantaleon's second son Pyrrhos, who succeeded an older brother as king of Pisatis sometime after 588 BC (Pausanias 6.22.3–4); the Eleians were demonstrably in control by 580 BC, when they first began appointing two Hellanodikai to oversee the games (Pausanias 5.9.4; cf. Swoboda *RE* 'Elis' 2390). The rivalry between the Pisatans and the Eleians ended with the complete overthrow of the Pisatans by c. 570 BC; the Pisatis then became part of Elis, and the Eleians thereafter retained control of the games. While the outcome of this rivalry is clear, its earlier stages are less so; there are divergent traditions regarding the period of Pisatan dominance, and they can be harmonized only to a certain extent (see Swoboda *RE* 'Elis' 2388–2389). We should perhaps not be dogmatic about what took place during the Second Messenian War. Most scholars remove the Eleians from the list of Messenian allies in the text of Strabo 8.4.10 and substitute the Pylians (Schwartz 1899:432n2 first proposed this change; cf. also Jacoby 1902:130; Swoboda *RE* 'Elis' 2390; Bölte *RE* 'Triphylia' 196; Kiechle 1959:27). Huxley 1962:129n366, on the other hand, defends the reading of the manuscripts. In either case Schwartz 1899:432 went too far in arguing that the Eleians were not only not enemies of Sparta in the Second Messenian War, but were actually allies. This argument rests on a fragment of Ephorus (*FGrHist* 70 F 115 = Strabo 8.3.33) which says that an alliance between Elis and Sparta defeated Pheidon of Argos. Pheidon, whose date is uncertain (mid-eighth century according to Pausanias 6.22.2, but now usually lowered by an emendation of Pausanias to the time of the Battle of Hysiai, 669 BC) in any case predates the Second Messenian War, which is now dated to the latter half of the seventh century (640/630–600 BC; cf. n5.91); hence the alliance between Sparta and Elis that defeated Pheidon can no longer be referred to the Second Messenian War. Swoboda *RE* 'Elis' 2390 rejects the idea that Elis and Sparta were allies in the war, which rests "nur auf der ganz problematischen Erzählung des Ephoros"; cf. also Huxley 1962:129n366, 110n159, who notes that the fragment of Ephorus does not even mention the Messenians.

EN5.17 (Endnote to n5.138)

It is doubtful that Skillous and Makistos in Triphylia were destroyed by the Eleians in the sixth century BC, as Pausanias 6.22.4 says they were.

Inhabitation of Skillous is attested for the late fifth and early fourth century BC by Xenophon (*Hellenica* 6.5.2; *Anabasis* 5.3.9–10); it is also attested somewhat earlier in an inscription, most likely of the mid-fifth century BC (Dittenberger and Purgold 1896 no. 16; see the introduction to the inscription, coll. 42–43, and commentary on line 17, coll. 44–46, for the likely date and the possible circumstances of the inscription). It is thus doubtful whether Skillous was abandoned in the first place (cf. Swoboda *RE* 'Elis' 2391; Bölte *RE* 'Triphylia' 197). As for Makistos, Bölte *RE* 'Makiston' 775 gives little historical weight to the tradition about this city: "From all these notices little more can be gained in terms of historical content than that a certain conception of the age and importance of Makiston still existed" ("Aus all diesen Mitteilungen wird sich kaum mehr an historischem Gehalt gewinnen lassen, als dass eine gewisse Vorstellung von dem Alter und der Bedeutung von Makiston vorhanden war"). In the Pisatis cities were destroyed and the land was distributed among the eight Eleian demes established there (the grant of one deme's land to a newly made citizen of that deme is at issue in Dittenberger and Purgold 1896 no. 11; see the introduction to the inscription, colls. 29–30). The Pisatans themselves continued to live in unfortified settlements (Swoboda *RE* 'Elis' 2391). We do not hear of later organized unrest in the Pisatis, but Pausanias 5.10.2, saying that Elis paid for the temple of Zeus at Olympia from the spoils of its war with Pisa and its allies, raises a question; the temple of Zeus was built in the fifth century BC, and it is hard to imagine that the spoils from a war a century earlier were used; see Frazer 1913 ad loc.

EN5.18 (Endnote to n5.145)

Strabo 8.3.30 (end) gives a brief account of how Triphylian Pylos was annexed to Lepreon as the result of a war. In what seems to be a related account Thucydides 5.31.2 says that a war between Lepreans and Arcadians led to Lepreon's gaining permanent possession of half its land, which may have been Pylos, in return for an annual payment of tribute. If the two accounts concern the same war there are differences between them that must be reconciled. In Thucydides Elis bargains for half of Lepreon's land in exchange for help against the Arcadians and then accepts tribute in place of the land, which Lepreon is allowed to keep; this makes it appear that Pylos, if Pylos is at issue, belonged to Lepreon before the war as well as after it. In Strabo Elis rewards Lepreon with Pylos after Lepreon has been victorious in a war; here Lepreon acquires Pylos for the first time as a result of the war. I suggest that Strabo is right that Lepreon acquired Pylos after a war, and that Thucydides makes it appear otherwise by compressing events. Before considering

Thucydides, however, there are problems in Strabo that have a bearing on the question of the historical context. The relevant passage in Strabo begins by saying that Elis helped Sparta put down the Messenian revolt of 464 BC, and that in return Sparta helped Elis conquer all of Triphylia; as a result Triphylia became known only by the name Elis and continued to be called by that name down to Strabo's time: συνέπραξαν δὲ καὶ οἱ Λακεδαιμόνιοι μετὰ τὴν ἐσχάτην κατάλυσιν τῶν Μεσσηνίων συμμαχήσασιν αὐτοῖς τἀναντία τῶν Νέστορος ἀπογόνων καὶ τῶν Ἀρκάδων συμπολεμησάντων τοῖς Μεσσηνίοις· καὶ ἐπὶ τοσοῦτόν γε συνέπραξαν ὥστε τὴν χώραν ἄπασαν τὴν μέχρι Μεσσήνης Ἠλείαν ῥηθῆναι καὶ διαμεῖναι μέχρι νῦν, Πισατῶν δὲ καὶ Τριφυλίων καὶ Καυκόνων μηδ' ὄνομα λειφθῆναι, "The Spartans cooperated with the Eleians after the last defeat of the Messenians because they had been allies, as opposed to the descendants of Nestor and the Arcadians, who fought on the side of the Messenians; they cooperated to such an extent that the whole country as far as Messenia was called Elis and is still so called today, but of the Triphylians and Cauconians not even the name is left (Strabo 8.3.30)." This account of Elis's conquest of Triphylia is grossly oversimplified; it attributes Elis's successful expansion southward as much to Spartan help as to Elis itself, ignoring the fact that Sparta forced Elis to free all the cities of Triphylia at the end of the Peloponnesian War, and the further fact that these cities remained free for a century and a half until c. 245 BC (for Sparta's war against Elis in 402–400 BC see Xenophon *Hellenica* 3.2.23–31; cf. Bölte *RE* 'Triphylia' 196–197, 198–199, who attributes the confusion in this passage to Strabo, and not to his source Apollodorus; on this point Bölte corrects his own earlier view in Bölte 1934). There is probably some truth in the role ascribed to Sparta in Elis's expansion, but there is no agreement as to when Sparta may have played such a role: Swoboda *RE* 'Elis' 2391 argues that Sparta may have helped Elis against Pisa and its allies c. 570 BC in order to gain Elis's help in Arcadia and against any future trouble in Messenia; Bölte *RE* 'Triphylia' 197 thinks that Sparta cooperated with Elis in the fifth century in the overthrow of Triphylian cities at the end of the Messenian revolt of 464 BC; Swoboda *RE* 'Elis' 2393–2394 doubts that Sparta would have helped Elis in the overthrow of Triphylia, which he dates to after the start of the First Peloponnesian War (457 BC), when Sparta's attention was diverted. It is at the end of this loosely conceived passage on Elis's expansion into Tripylia that Strabo tells how Pylos was incorporated into Lepreon; as already discussed (see n5.142), there is confusion here in that the Eleians should be the subject of Strabo's sentence, but the Spartans appear to be, as they are of preceding sentences. But apart from this the sentence and its content seem sound: καὶ αὐτὸν δὲ τὸν Πύλον τὸν ἠμαθόεντα εἰς τὸ Λέπρειον συνῴκισαν, χαριζόμενοι τοῖς Λεπρεάταις κρατήσασι πολέμῳ, καὶ ἄλλας πολλὰς τῶν κατοικιῶν κατέσπασαν, ὅσας γ᾽ ἑώρων αὐτοπραγεῖν ἐθελούσας, καὶ φόρους ἐπράξαντο, "They joined sandy Pylos itself with Lepreon, gratifying the Lepreans who had prevailed in a war, and they destroyed as many of the other communities as they saw wishing to act independently, and they exacted tribute" (Strabo 8.3.30 [end]). The question of date for the incorporation of Pylos into Lepreon depends on the earlier part of the passage, where the phrase μετὰ τὴν ἐσχάτην κατάλυσιν τῶν Μεσσηνίων, "after the last defeat of the Messenians," indicates some time after the Messenian revolt of 464 BC, and the looseness of the passage as a whole makes this chronology uncertain. It is probably correct that Elis helped Sparta put down the Messenian revolt of 464, as Strabo says in the first sentence of the passage. Bölte and Meyer see this as the occasion for the synoecism of Lepreon and Pylos, arguing that Lepreon helped Elis and Sparta against Pylos and was awarded Pylos as a result: "In 459 BC, after the end of the helots' revolt, the Spartans supported the Eleians in the suppression of the Pylians, who were attacked in the rear by the Lepreans" ("459, nach dem Ende des Helotenaufstandes, unterstützen die Lakedaimonier die Eleier bei der Niederwerfung der Pylier, denen die Lepreaten in den Rücken fallen," Bölte RE 'Triphylia' 197); "After the last Messenian revolt of 464 BC Pylos was subjugated by the allied Eleians and Lepreans with Spartan help, and was incorporated into Lepreon" ("Nach dem letzten messenischen Aufstand von 464ff. wurde Pylos von den verbündeten Eleern und Lepreaten mit spartanischer Hilfe unterworfen und in Lepreon einverleibt," Meyer RE 'Pylos' 2131). This interpretation has in its favor the idea that Lepreon was rewarded with Pylos after winning a war (cf. Strabo's phrase χαριζόμενοι τοῖς Λεπρεάταις, "gratifying the Lepreans"). But the evidence of Thucydides suggests another interpretation, namely that Pylos became part of Lepreon not in connection with the Messenian revolt of 464 BC, but as the result of a war in which Elis helped Lepreon against the Arcadians. Thucydides may simplify a more complicated series of events when he says that the Lepreans pledged half their land to Elis in return for help against the Arcadians. As the outcome shows, what Elis wanted in this case was not land but tribute. After dealing with the Arcadians Elis perhaps joined a previously independent Pylos to Lepreon in return for yearly tribute; the synoecism could have been discussed in advance, but would more likely have resulted from the war. The Lepreans must have called in the Eleians because the Arcadians had invaded their land and threatened their existence; neighboring Pylos was presumably also threatened, and Elis, when it had played the decisive role against the

Arcadians, would have been in a position to settle matters as it saw fit. This scenario would accord with Strabo's statement that Pylos was added to Lepreon after a war. Dates are hard to fix. As discussed above, the synoecism may have followed the Messenian revolt of 464, but the Strabo passage leaves room for doubt, and if the Thucydides passage is a guide the war that led to the synoecism did not have to do with that revolt, but with an Arcadian attack on Lepreon. As for the date of the Arcadian attack, which led to Lepreon's subjection to Elis in the form of tribute payments, all that can be said for sure is that it occurred after the Battle of Plataea in 479 BC, when Lepreon still acted independently of Elis (Lepreon sent its own contingent of 200 to Plataea in 479, whereas the Eleians arrived too late for the battle; see Andrewes [Gomme et al. 1970] on Thucydides 5.31.2). The overthrow of the other Minyan cities of Triphylia (Herodotus 4.148.4), which Bölte *RE* 'Triphylia' 197 also dates to the years after the Messenian revolt, may not have occurred until the Archidamian War; such a late date is possible if Herodotus, who says that these cities were overthrown in his lifetime, was still at work on his *Histories* during the Archidamian War, and this was almost certainly the case (Jacoby *RE* Supplement 2 'Herodot' 229–232, followed by Cobet 1977, dates the publication of the *Histories* to the earlier part of the Archidamian War, 430–424 BC; Fornara 1971 and 1981 dates the publication of the *Histories* still later, to 421–415 BC, arguing that the work contains references to the end of the Archidamian War in 421 BC). How and Wells 1928 on Herodotus 4.148.4 report that Eduard Meyer, who originally dated Elis's overthrow of the Triphylian cities to the period after 470 BC, later changed his mind and dated it to the Archidamian War (the reference in How and Wells is Meyer [*Geschichte des Altertums*] iii 285, but the edition is not made clear). For the Arcadian attack on Lepreon, and the imposition of tribute by Elis, we must think in terms of a period of time before the Peloponnesian War, but how long before we simply do not know. I note as a final detail Bölte's suggestion (*RE* 'Triphylia' 197–198) that when the Arcadians attacked Lepreon they may also have conquered Epion, another of the six Minyan cities of Triphylia, for the Arcadians seem later to have sold Epion to the Eleians (Xenophon *Hellenica* 3.2.30); according to Xenophon Epion lay between Heraia and Makistos.

EN5.19 (Endnote to n5.168)

Davison 1962:232n37 cites Wackernagel 1916 to make the point that the Homeric text from Aristarchus on was based on an Athenian text, but he hesitates to call the Athenian text a Panathenaic text because of the latter term's associations with the Peisistratean recension: "J. Wackernagel's *Sprachliche*

Untersuchungen zu Homer made a contribution of first-class importance to the establishment of this point; but his arguments have now been superseded in some vital respects (especially by the decipherment of Linear B), and should not be used any longer to support ancient allegations and modern super-stitions about the 'Peisistratean recension'." Noting that the Homeric text seems to have been transliterated from an earlier Ionic alphabet into the late Ionic alphabet of twenty-four letters, and that this alphabet became official at Athens in 403/2 BC, Davison concludes: "Thus there is a certain degree of possibility that Aristarchus, who, we are told, believed Homer to have been an Athenian and to have lived about 140 years after the Trojan war..., based his second and final revision of the text of Homer upon the Panathenaic text, which had either not been available to or not been so highly valued by his predecessors.... But whether or not it is true that (as has been shown to be possible) the text which became current in the late second century B.C. was based upon the Panathenaic text, ...there is no doubt at all that the second-century text is the ancestor of almost all our surviving witnesses to the text of Homer since that time" (Davison 1962:224–225). For the period before Aristarchus Davison 1962:223 says: "So far as we can see Aristophanes, like Zenodotus, was still struggling to make critical sense of the many diver-gent texts in the library, and had failed to find an Ariadne's clue to guide him through the labyrinth. It seems that the finding of this clue was left to Aristarchus of Samothrace (c. 215–c. 145 BC), to whose outstanding work as a Homeric critic it is reasonable to ascribe the great change which came over the text of Homer in the latter part of the second century BC. Henceforward 'wild' papyri (*i.e.*, those which differ in length, or materially in wording, from the text on which our editions are based) are the exception rather than the rule; and though variations in wording persist, as is inevitable in a text with such a mixed ancestry as Homer's, we can at last speak with some confidence of a 'standard' text of the *Iliad* and *Odyssey*." The Alexandrian concept of a *koínē* text is connected to the Athenian state text by Nagy 1996a:187–191; see also Nagy 2004:54. For what Nagy calls the definitive period in Homeric trans-mission, from the mid-sixth century to the later part of the fourth century in Athens, see his 1996a:110, and more specifically, 1992:39–52. For the Homeric text of Aristarchus and Zenodotus cf. also EN5.23.

EN5.20 (Endnote to n5.184)
Thucydides 6.88.9 says that Alcibiades remained in Elis before he defected to Sparta; Isocrates 16 gives a different account, that after reaching the Peloponnesus Alcibiades made his way to Argos and remained there

quietly, but when he was outlawed in Athens he was forced to flee to Sparta. This version was presented by Alcibiades' son many years later at a trial concerning one of the chariots raced by Alcibiades at the Olympics of 416 BC (cf. n5.185 for the date of these Olympics). Alcibiades bought the chariot for another Athenian when he was in Argos before the Olympics of 416 BC, but he proceeded to race it as his own. His son was later sued by the rightful owner, and Isocrates 16 (what remains of this speech) is his son's defense. The speech is essentially a defense of the character of the elder Alcibiades, and the assertion that he was staying quietly in Argos when his enemies in Athens demanded his return is part of that defense (Isocrates 16.9): ἀλλ' ἐκεῖνος μὲν τοσαύτην πρόνοιαν ἔσχεν ὑπὲρ τοῦ μηδὲ φεύγων μηδὲν ἐξαμαρτεῖν εἰς τὴν πόλιν ὥστ' εἰς Ἄργος ἐλθὼν ἡσυχίαν εἶχεν, οἱ δ' εἰς τοσοῦτον ὕβρεως ἦλθον ὥστ' ἔπεισαν ὑμᾶς ἐλαύνειν αὐτὸν ἐξ ἁπάσης τῆς Ἑλλάδος καὶ στηλίτην ἀναγράφειν καὶ πρέσβεις πέμποντας ἐξαιτεῖν παρ' Ἀργείων. ἀπορῶν δ' ὅ τι χρήσαιτο τοῖς παροῦσιν κακοῖς καὶ πανταχόθεν εἰργόμενος καὶ σωτηρίας οὐδεμιᾶς ἄλλης αὐτῷ φαινομένης τελευτῶν ἐπὶ Λακεδαιμονίους ἠναγκάσθη καταφυγεῖν, "He had such great concern not to do any wrong to the city even in exile that he went to Argos and remained quietly, but they reached such a point of insolence that they persuaded you to exile him from all Greece, to have his banishment inscribed on a stele, and to send ambassadors to demand his return from the Argives. At a loss what to do in these evil circumstances, blocked on all sides, and with no other safety available to him, he was forced in the end to take refuge with the Spartans." The main problem with this version of events, which Plutarch *Alcibiades* 23.1 also follows, is that it conflicts with Thucydides; if Alcibiades was Thucydides' direct informant for his own activities in the war (see n5.180), it is hard to explain why Thucydides should be misinformed on this point (Brunt 1952:91–92, who believes the Argos story, acknowledges the problem). In the Isocrates passage, which has the task of explaining away Alcibiades' worst act of treason toward Athens, namely his defection to Sparta, the picture of a quiet Alcibiades being forced into this act is the rhetorical key. This does not mean that the Argos story is false, but that it may be; in the Isocrates passage there is an incontrovertible fact (the Athenian banishment decree set up for all to see) together with an assertion that ambassdors were sent to Argos to demand Alcibiades' return. The latter claim could have been built up over time from something less (suspicion in Athens that Alcibiades, who had escaped his escort in southern Italy, was now with his friends in Argos; official inquiries sent to Argos and elsewhere to try to find him) into something more. Isocrates' reliability as a witness is a controversial question with respect to another passage of this speech: in Isocrates 16.32–33 the younger Alcibiades says that his father disdained competition in events other than the chariot race because of low-class participants in such events; for those who do and do not accept this passage as evidence for Greek sport see Pritchard 2003:326–328 and 342n182.

EN5.21 (Endnote to n5.190)

Use of the formula ἔστι δέ τις, "there is a (certain)," to begin each of the first two expansions of Nestor's story in *Iliad* 11 (lines 711 and 722) shows a close knowledge of the poetic medium that the expansions are meant to imitate; in both cases specific Homeric lines seem to have been in the mind of the poet who used the formula (see n5.190). It is worth examining a few other points in the language of the expansions in *Iliad* 11 in relation to Homeric models. The phrase εἰς ἅλα βάλλων, "flowing into the sea," used of the Minyan river in *Iliad* 11.722 has close equivalents in *Iliad* 11.495 (εἰς ἅλα βάλλει) and in an oracle of Bakis reported by Herodotus 8.20.2 (εἰς ἅλα βάλλῃ), but in these examples the verb has the transitive meaning "throw" and there is a direct object; for the intransitive usage and meaning the only comparison in Homer is *Iliad* 23.462 of horses "racing around the turn," περὶ τέρμα βαλούσας. With εἰς ἅλα βάλλων in *Iliad* 11.722 may also be compared the intransitive use of normally transitive ἵημι, "send," in a similar context in *Odyssey* 11.239: ὃς πολὺ κάλλιστος ποταμῶν ἐπὶ γαῖαν ἵησι, "which is much the most beautiful of rivers to pour forth on the earth." The intransitive use of βάλλω is some-what unusual but it hardly draws attention to itself. The name Θρυόεσσα in *Iliad* 11 differs from the form Θρύον in *Iliad* 2 (see n5.3), and this too might be thought to draw unwanted attention as non-Homeric. But there are many place-names in Greek like Θρυόεσσα, in which the ending -εσσα signifies a feminine adjective: e.g. Δρυοῦσσα (uncontracted Δρυόεσσα), "oak-covered" (a place on Cape Mykale, cf. n4.75 and n4.84 above); Αἰγειροῦσσα, "poplar-covered" (Strabo 9.1.10); Πιτυοῦσσα, "pine-covered" (Strabo 9.1.9); Ποιήεσσα, "grassy" (a city on Keos, Strabo 10.5.6); Σκοτοῦσσα, "dark, gloomy" (a city in Thessaly, cf. n5.118). In Homer one of the Messenian cities offered by Agamemnon to Achilles, traditionally read as Ἱρὴν ποιήεσσαν, "grassy Hire," should perhaps be read as ἱρὴν Ποιήεσσαν, "sacred Poieessa" (*Iliad* 9.150 and 292; see Kiechle 1960:62n2 for this suggestion). The form Θρυόεσσα, "reedy" would thus be easily accepted as a doublet for Θρύον. In *Iliad* 11.712 Thryoessa is described as νεάτη Πύλου ἠμαθόεντος, "at the end of sandy Pylos"; the same expression is used in the plural to describe the seven cities offered by Agamemnon to Achilles in *Iliad* 9. As noted earlier (EN5.3 end), the phrase implies that the seven cities are part of Pylos, as they perhaps once were; but

in *Iliad* 9 the cities are Agamemnon's to dispose of, and the phrase is taken
to mean "below (i.e. beyond) sandy Pylos." In *Iliad* 11, on the other hand, the
phrase is used correctly inasmuch as the besieged town of Thryoessa (like
the town of Thryon in the catalogue) is part of Pylos. The poet of the expan-
sions has corrected Homer in this case: it must have been obvious from the
meaning of the word νέαται, "lowest, bottommost," that something was
wrong in *Iliad* 9. Correcting a Homeric mistake in this way surely did not
undermine the expanded story's pretense of being itself genuinely Homeric.
I note finally that the Attic/Ionic form ὀφείλω of the Aeolic/Homeric verb
ὀφέλλω, "owe," occurs three times in Nestor's story in *Iliad* 11 and nowhere
else in Homer; Palmer 1962:106 argues from this "enigmatic" fact, which
puzzled Wackernagel (1916:176n4/1970:16n4) and Chantraine (1958:314),
that Nestor's entire story was the product of the Peisistratean recension and
was first added to the Homeric text in the late fifth or early fourth century BC
(the earliest Attic inscription with the spelling ὀφείλω is from 428 BC; the old
Attic alphabet was officially replaced with the Ionic alphabet in 403/2 BC).
I suggest a less drastic explanation. One of the three instances of the Attic/
Ionic form is in an expansion of Nestor's story (line 698), the other two are in
the older version of the story (lines 686, 688). Did the text of the expansion,
composed in the Ionic alphabet in c. 415 BC, affect the spelling of the two
other instances of the verb? The context of all three instances of the verb is
the same (the "debt" owed by the Epeians to the Pylians), and the spelling of
all three would naturally have been made consistent.

EN5.22 (Endnote to n5.199)
In the riddle about three cities named Pylos (see EN5.10) the third Pylos can
only have been the city in Elis. The line in Aristophanes quoting the first half
of the riddle, namely *Knights* 1059, belongs to Paphlagon (Cleon), who says
earlier (line 1003) that he will recite oracles of Bakis. The attribution to Bakis
need not be taken at face value, but the fact that the riddle was well known
in 424 BC indicates that it was old. Oracles of Bakis quoted in Herodotus
belong to the early fifth century and pertain to the Persian Wars (Herodotus
8.20, 8.77, and 9.43); these oracles may have originated in the sixth century
(Herodotus 8.96, dating an oracle of an Athenian prophet named Lysistratos
many years before the Battle of Salamis, refers to an oracle of Musaeus and
Bakis in the same context). In any case there were certainly oracles of Bakis
in the sixth century: the name Bakis was an epithet of the tyrant Peisistratos,
who was much interested in oracular poetry, and who seems to have adopted
the epithet for that reason (scholia to Aristophanes *Peace* 1071; Suda s.v.

Βάκις; cf. Kern *RE* 'Bakis' 2802, Dillery 2005:180). The verse about Pylos, whether or not it was an oracle of Bakis, makes most sense if it refers to the sixth-century controversy about the location of the Homeric city. Marinatos 1955:163 came to a similar conclusion (cf. EN5.10): "It now becomes clear that by 'Pylos before Pylos' the coastal city (Koryphasion) and the city lying behind it (Englianos-Volimidia) are meant. The 'other Pylos' is the third city of the same name, which can only be the Eleian city, if Professor Hampe is right that the Triphylian Pylos was of a hypothetical kind and existed only in the fantasy of the *Homērikōteroi*" ("Es wird jetzt klar, dass mit 'Pylos vor Pylos' die Küstenstadt [Koryphasion] und das dahinterliegende 'alte Pylos' [Englianos-Volimidia] gemeint sind. Das 'andere Pylos' ist die dritte gleichnamige Stadt, die nur die elische sein kann, falls Prof. Hampe darin recht hat, dass das triphylische Pylos hypothetischer Art war und nur in der Phantasie der ὁμηρικώτεροι existierte").

EN5.23 (Endnote to n5.201)
Strabo gives no indication that the controversy in Hellenistic times over the location of Homeric Pylos involved two versions of Nestor's story in *Iliad* 11; had Strabo indicated as much, my argument that our version of Nestor's story goes back only to the late fifth century BC might well have suggested itself already. Since Strabo indicates nothing of the kind, I am bound to ask why. Strabo is a late witness who allies himself with the position of those whom he calls *Homērikōteroi*, and these scholars naturally would not have wanted to remove Triphylia from Nestor's story by pointing to a shorter alternative text; they would have assumed that the Athenian state text was authoritative. We can be reasonably sure that Apollodorus, who collaborated with Aristarchus in Alexandria, would have held this view, since Aristarchus very likely made the Athenian state text his base text (for Apollodorus cf. n5.9; for Aristarchus cf. n5.168 and EN5.19); I must assume that Apollodorus's predecessor Demetrius of Scepsis, in taking Triphylia to be Nestor's home, came to this view because he too believed that the Athenian state text contained the authoritative version of Nestor's story. A century earlier Zenodotus, dealing with rampant expansions of the Homeric poems in manuscripts from many sources, reduced the size of his text by omitting some verses and athetizing others. If comparison of manuscripts was one of Zenodotus's criteria for what to omit (his criteria are uncertain; see Davison 1962:222), such a comparison did not lead him to omit the expansion of Nestor's story in *Iliad* 11: not only do the Homeric scholia not say that Zenodotus omitted or athetized the passages in question; they say that Zenodotus read δεῖπνον for δόρπον in *Iliad* 11.730,

thus proving that his text included one of the expansions (*Iliad* 11.722–736; the disagreement between Aristarchus and Zenodotus as to this reading had to do with whether the Pylian army ate a noon meal or an evening meal on the banks of the Alpheios; cf. *Iliad* 7.380 and *Odyssey* 6.97 for alternative versions of the formula in *Iliad* 11.730, one with δόρπον, "evening meal," and the other with δεῖπνον, "noon meal"). In fourth-century BC Athens a basis at least for the later vulgate must have existed to judge by the degree of agreement between Plato's Homeric quotations and the later vulgate (see Lohse 1964, 1965, 1967), but expanded texts also existed (see Pasquali 1962:220–221). It is thought that Zenodotus may have had an early form of the vulgate at his disposal, but it is not permissible simply to equate his base text with the later vulgate (see Nickau 1977:32). My argument fits this picture if it is assumed that Zenodotus did in fact have an early form of the vulgate at his disposal, and that he paid particular attention to it. It should also be borne in mind that we do not know all the lines that Zenodotus athetized, and that we therefore cannot exclude the possibility that he athetized the passages in question. With so much unclear, the lack of traces in the Homeric scholia of an older version of Nestor's story does not constitute an argument against a late fifth-century expansion of the story; this is of course not to deny that such an argument may present itself as Homeric transmission becomes better understood. I note that J. A. Davison, in arguing against Denys Page's thesis that the Achaean wall in *Iliad* 7 postdates Thucydides, corrects Page's tacit assumption that there was only one text of the *Iliad* "current in Thucydides' day," but does not make what he calls "the relative fluidity of the 'Homeric' canon in the late fifth and early fourth centuries BC" an argument in its own right against Page's thesis (Davison 1965:14–15). It does not seem to me that such an argument can be made at present; in the case of Nestor's story in *Iliad* 11 the fact that we do not have certain knowledge of an older and shorter version does not rule out, or even make improbable, that such a version existed.

CONCLUSION

Starting from an Indo-European comparison the foregoing study has followed out the consequences of that comparison for the Homeric poems, including a reconstruction of the circumstances in which the poems were first composed on a monumental scale. To reach this point in the argument the role of the Homeric Phaeacians has been the bridge, and to understand the Phaeacians Nestor has been the key. Nestor's Homeric role is a large one, larger than it seems on the surface of the poems. In the *Iliad* Nestor frames the story of Patroclus in Books 11 and 23, and in the *Odyssey* he frames the story of Odysseus's return, first in his own persona in Book 3, and then through his Phaeacian surrogate, Alcinous, in Odysseus's final return. In both poems Nestor adds depth to the stories that he frames through a carefully concealed irony. In the *Iliad* this irony reaches a climax in the chariot race in Book 23 with the untold story of Nestor's youthful crash; in the *Odyssey* it reaches a climax in the catalogue of heroines in Book 11, which sets Nestor in the context of his unspoken twin myth, and adds the final piece to his relationship with the Phaeacians and to his role in the return of Odysseus. The catalogue of heroines is in fact the climax of Nestor's role in the two Homeric poems when his role is viewed as a totality. In evaluating the case that I have made for Nestor's Homeric role, and the consequences of his role for the origins of the Homeric poems, I put great weight on the catalogue of heroines, not only for the reason just given, that it is the climax of an irony sustained through two poems, but for the equally important reason that the very text of the catalogue of heroines depends on an appreciation of Nestor's role; the idea that Nestor's role has its basis in the twin myth has demonstrable consequences for this particular Homeric text, as I believe that I have shown, and in the last analysis I rest my case on this point. The catalogue of heroines, furthermore, offers genuine insight into the difference between an Ionian text of Homer and an Athenian text of Homer. A similar point can be made with regard to the text of Nestor's story in *Iliad* 11, the original form of which had already been discerned in 1942 without benefit of Nestor's twin myth, but which stands out more clearly in its original form when seen in the context of Nestor's myth and his resulting Homeric role. Here the contrast in texts is between the Ionian version of Nestor's story and a relatively late Athenian reworking. This too contributes an important chapter to the complex history of the Homeric poems.

Pursuing the consequences of Nestor's Homeric role has led to hard questions which I have done my best to address. If Nestor stands behind the Phaeacian king, it is in my view an inescapable consequence that Athena Polias, the city-goddess of Athens, stands behind the Phaeacian queen, and this has important implications for the original nature of Athena Polias, the city-goddess of Athens, as a mother-goddess. I have argued that the nature of this city-goddess underwent a change in the post-Homeric period to its known historical form, and I have made a case for the circumstances in which the change took place; if my reconstruction is correct the change in the city-goddess was at the same time a change in the city, having largely to do with the annexation of Eleusis, and implying a more warlike Athenian attitude in general. The masquerade in which the Phaeacian royal couple takes part in the *Odyssey* precedes any such historical development and points elsewhere for its meaning, namely to the city of Miletus and to the Neleid royal family, which traced its origins through Athens back to Pylos. The Phaeacians look like they are meant to reflect the Homeric audience, and Miletus must have been a key part of that audience; I have argued that the Homeric poems were created in the form that we know them at the festival of the Panionia, and that Miletus was the *primum mobile* of both the festival and the poems. Nestor's role in the Homeric poems points to this; in particular the tradition that he was one of the twelve sons of Neleus, which coexisted with the tradition for his twin myth, points clearly to the twelve cities of the Ionian dodecapolis, which alone celebrated the Panionia, and to which Miletus must have extended its own Neleid ancestry as a means of community formation—the community of Panionians.

I have raised hard questions and I do not delude myself that I have said the last word on any of them. Other perspectives must be brought to bear before we can know for certain what the nature of Athena Polias was in Athens during the Homeric era and whether her nature changed fundamentally thereafter; or when Eleusis was incorporated into Attica and how the cult of Athena Polias may have been affected by this; or what the nature of the festival of the Panionia was in the Homeric era; or whether the Pythian part of the *Homeric Hymn to Apollo* was indeed Spartan in outlook and as such provides the key to the tangled history of Pylos's location as an ancient problem. Archaeology in particular may always bring new information for some of these questions. But for each of these questions, and here I do claim the last word, the Homeric poems remain our most important early signpost, if only we can determine its direction.

BIBLIOGRAPHY

Ager, S. L. 1996. *Interstate Arbitrations in the Greek World, 337–90 B.C.* Berkeley.

Alden, M. 2000. *Homer Beside Himself: Para-Narratives in the Iliad.* Oxford.

Allen, T. W., ed. 1912. *Homeri Opera V.* Oxford.

———. 1924. *Homer: The Origins and the Transmission.* Reprint 1969. Oxford.

———. 1928. "Miscellanea." *Classical Quarterly* 22:73–76.

Allen, T. W., and Sikes, E. E., eds. 1904. *The Homeric Hymns.* London.

Allen, T. W., Halliday, W. R., and Sikes, E. E., eds. 1936. *The Homeric Hymns.* 2nd ed. Oxford. Reprints 1963 and 1980, Amsterdam.

Aloni, A. 1989. *L'aedo e i tiranni. Ricerche sull'Inno omerico a Apollo.* Rome.

———. 2006. *Da Pilo a Sigeo. Poemi, cantori e scrivani al tempo dei tiranni.* Alessandria.

———. 2006a. "Ricordare Pilo." *I luoghi e la poesia nella Grecia antica. Atti del convegno, Università 'G. d'Annunzio' di Chieti-Pescara, 20–22 aprile 2004* (eds. M. Vetta and C. Catenacci) 1–21. Alessandria.

Anderson, G. 2003. *The Athenian Experiment: Building an Imagined Political Community in Ancient Attica, 508–490 B.C.* Ann Arbor.

Anderson, J. K. 1954. "A Topographical and Historical Study of Achaea." *Annual of the British School at Athens* 49:72–92.

Arieti, J. A. 1983/1984. "Achilles' Inquiry about Machaon: The Critical Moment in the *Iliad.*" *Classical Journal* 79:125–130.

Arnold, E. V. 1905. *Vedic Metre in its Historical Development.* Cambridge. Reprint 1967, Delhi.

Austin, C. 1967. "De nouveaux fragments de l'*Erechthée* d'Euripide." *Recherches de Papyrologie* 4:11–67.

———. 1968. *Nova fragmenta Euripidea in papyris reperta.* Berlin.

Bader, F. 1965. *Les composés grecs du type de Demiourgos.* Paris.

———. 1980. "Rhapsodies homériques et irlandaises." *Recherches sur les religions de l'antiquité classique* (ed. R. Bloch) 9–83. Paris.

Barber, E. J. W. "The Peplos of Athena." In Neils 1992:103–117.

Barnett, R. D. 1975. "Phrygia and the Peoples of Anatolia in the Iron Age." *Cambridge Ancient History* II-2 (eds. I. E. S. Edwards et al.) 417–442. 3rd ed. Cambridge.

Barrett, W. S., ed. 1964. *Euripides, Hippolytos.* Oxford.

Barron, J. P. 1962. "Milesian Politics and Athenian Propaganda c.460–440 B.C." *Journal of Hellenic Studies* 82:1–6.

Basiner, O. von. 1905. "Nixi di und Verwandtes." *Rheinisches Museum* 60:614–623.

Bearzot, C. 1983. "La guerra lelantea e il κοινόν degli Ioni d'Asia." *Santuari e politica nel mondo antico* (ed. M. Sordi). *Contributi dell' Istituto di Storia antica* 9:57–81.

Bechtel, F. 1917. *Die historischen Personnennamen des Griechischen bis zur Kaiserzeit.* Halle. Reprint 1964, Hildesheim.

Beloch, J. 1912. *Griechische Geschichte.* 2nd ed. Strassberg. Reprint 1967, Berlin.

Benveniste, É. 1948. *Noms d'agent et noms d'action en indo-européen.* Paris.

———. 1954. "Problèmes sémantiques de la reconstruction." *Word* 10:251–264. Reprinted in Benveniste 1966:289–307.

———. 1966. *Problems de linguistique générale.* Paris.

———. 1969. *Le vocabulaire des institutions indo-européennes.* Paris.

Berger, E. 1986. *Der Parthenon in Basel. Dokumentation zu den Metopen.* Basel.

Bergk, T. 1882. *Poetae Lyrici Graeci.* Vol. 2, *Poetae elegiaci et iambographi.* 4th ed. Leipzig.

Berman, D. W. 2004. "The Double Foundation of Boiotian Thebes." *Transactions of the American Philological Association* 134:1–22.

Bettinetti, S. 2001. *La statua di culto nella pratica rituale greca.* Bari.

Binder, J. 1984. "The West Pediment of the Parthenon: Poseidon." *Studies Presented to Sterling Dow on His Eightieth Birthday* (eds. A. Boegehold et al.) 15–22. Durham, NC.

Biraschi, A. M. 1994. "Strabone e Omero. Aspetti della tradizione omerica nella descrizione del Peloponneso." *Strabone e la Grecia* (ed. A. M. Biraschi) 23–57. Naples.

Bittlestone, R. 2005. *Odysseus Unbound: The Search for Homer's Ithaca.* Cambridge.

Boardman, J. 1972. "Herakles, Peisistratos and Sons." *Revue archéologique* 1972:57–72.

———. 1975. "Herakles, Peisistratos and Eleusis." *Journal of Hellenic Studies* 95:1–12.

———. 1978. *Greek Sculpture: The Archaic Period. A Handbook.* London. Reprint 1991, New York.

———. 1994. *The Diffusion of Classical Art in Antiquity.* Princeton.

Boehlau, J., and Schefold, K. 1942. *Larisa am Hermos, die Ergebnisse der Ausgrabungen 1902-1934.* Vol. 3, *Die Kleinfunde.* Berlin.

Böhtlingk, O., and Roth, R. 1855-1875. *Sanskrit-Wörterbuch.* St. Petersburg. Reprint 1966, Wiesbaden; 1990, Delhi.

Bolling, G. M. 1925. *The External Evidence for Interpolation in Homer.* Reprint 1968. Oxford.

Bölte, F. 1934. "Ein pylisches Epos." *Rheinisches Museum* 83:319–347.

———. 1938. "Triphylien bei Strabo. Eine Quellenuntersuchung." *Rheinisches Museum* 87:142-160.

Bowra, C. M. 1938. *Early Greek Elegists.* Cambridge, MA. Reprint 1960, Cambridge.

———. 1960. "Euripides' Epinician for Alcibiades." *Historia* 9:68–79.

Bradeen, D. W. 1947. "The Lelantine War and Pheidon of Argos." *Transactions of the American Philological Association* 78:223–241.

Brelich, A. 1958. *Gli eroi greci. Un problema storico-religioso.* Rome.

Brereton, J. P. 1981. *The R̥gvedic Ādityas.* New Haven.

Bringmann, K. 1975. "Die Grosse Rhetra und die Entstehung des spartanischen Kosmos." *Historia* 24:513–538. Reprinted 2001, in *Ausgewählte Schriften* (eds. P. Scholz and J. Kobes) 11–34, Frankfurt.

Brisson, L. 1994. *Platon, Les mots et les mythes: Comment et pourquoi Platon nomma le mythe?* Paris. Trans. by G. Naddaf as *Plato the Myth Maker.* 1998. Chicago.

Broccia, G. 1967. *La forma poetica dell'Iliade e la genesi dell'epos omerico*. Messina.

Broneer, O. 1932. "Eros and Aphrodite on the North Slope of the Acropolis in Athens." *Hesperia* 1:31–55.

Brumfield, A. C. 1981. *The Attic Festivals of Demeter and their Relation to the Agricultural Year.* New York.

Brunnhofer, H. 1892. *Vom Aral bis zur Ganga.* Leipzig.

Brunt, P. A. 1952. "Thucydides and Alcibiades." *Revue des études grecques* 65:59–96.

Buchner, G., and Russo, C. F. 1955. "La coppa di Nestore e un' iscrizione metrica da Pitecusa dell' VIII secolo av. Cr." *Rendiconti della Classe di Scienze morali, storiche e filologiche dell' Accademia nazionale dei Lincei* 10:215–234.

Buchner, G., and Ridgway, D. 1993. *Pithekoussai I.* Rome.

Buitenen, J. A. B. van, ed. 1978. *The Mahābhārata.* Vol. 3. Chicago.

Burgess, J. S. 2001. *The Tradition of the Trojan War in Homer and the Epic Cycle.* Baltimore.

Burkert, W. 1966. "Kekropidensage und Arrhephoria: Vom Initiationsritus zum Panathenäenfest." *Hermes* 94:1–25.

———. 1970. "Buzyge und Palladion. Gewalt und Gericht im altgriechischen Ritual." *Zeitschrift für Religions- und Geistesgeschichte* 22:356–368.

———. 1972. "Die Leistung eines Kreophylos: Kreophyleer, Homeriden und die archaische Heraklesepik." *Museum Helveticum* 29:74–85.

———. 1979. "Kynaithos, Polykrates, and the Homeric Hymn to Apollo." *Arktouros: Hellenic Studies Presented to Bernard M. W. Knox* (eds. G. Bowersock et al.) 53–62. Berlin.

———. 1983. *Homo Necans: The Anthropology of Ancient Greek Sacrificial Ritual and Myth.* Trans. P. Bing. Berkeley. Originally published as *Homo necans: Interpretationen altgriechischer Opferriten und Mythen.* 1972. Berlin and New York.

———. 1985. *Greek Religion: Archaic and Classical.* Trans. J. Raffan. Oxford. Originally published as *Griechische Religion der archaischen und klassischen Epoche.* 1977. Stuttgart.

———. 1987. "The Making of Homer in the Sixth Century B.C.: Rhapsodes Versus Stesichoros." *Papers on the Amasis Painter and His World* 43–62. Malibu.

Burns, B. 2005. "The Aegean Prehistorian's Role in Classical Studies Today." *Prehistorians Round the Pond: Reflections on Aegean Prehistory as a Discipline* (eds. J. Cherry et al.) 115–131. Ann Arbor.

Burr, V. 1944. ΝΕΩΝ ΚΑΤΑΛΟΓΟΣ. *Untersuchungen zum homerischen Schiffskatalog.* Leipzig. Reprint 1961, Aalen.

Burrow, T. 1973. *The Sanskrit Language.* 3rd ed. London. Reprint 2001, Delhi.

Busolt, G. 1885. *Griechische Geschichte bis zur Schlacht bei Chaeroneia* I. Gotha.

———. 1893. *Griechische Geschichte* I. 2nd ed. Gotha. Reprint 1967, Hildesheim.

Butterworth, J. 1986. "Homer and Hesiod." *Studies in Honour of T. B. L. Webster* I (eds. J. H. Betts et al.) 33–45. Bristol.

Buttmann, P. 1829. *Mythologus, oder gesammelte Abhandlungen über die Sagen des Alterthums* II. Berlin.

Cadoux, C. J. 1938. *Ancient Smyrna: A History of the City from the Earliest Times to 324 A.D.* Oxford.

Cadoux, T. J. 1948. "The Athenian Archons from Kreon to Hypsichides." *Journal of Hellenic Studies* 68:70–123.

Calame, C. 1977. *Les choeurs de jeunes filles en Grèce archaïque* I. Rome.

Campbell, D. A. 1967. *Greek Lyric Poetry: A Selection of Early Greek Lyric, Elegiac and Iambic Poetry.* New York.

Cantieni, R. 1942. *Die Nestorerzählung im XI. Gesang der Ilias (V. 670-762).* Zurich.

Carlier, P. 1984. *La royauté en Grèce avant Alexandre.* Strasbourg.

Carpenter, R. 1929. *The Sculpture of the Nike Temple Parapet.* Cambridge, MA.

———. 1963. Review of Jeffery 1961. *American Journal of Philology* 84:76–85.

Carrington, P. 1977. "The Heroic Age of Phrygia in Ancient Literature and Art." *Anatolian Studies* 27:117–126.

Cartledge, P. 1978. "Literacy in the Spartan Oligarchy." *Journal of Hellenic Studies* 98:25–37.

———. 1982. "Sparta and Samos: A Special Relationship?" *Classical Quarterly* N.S. 32:243–265.

———. 2002. *Sparta and Lakonia: A Regional History 1300-362 BC.* 2nd ed. London.

Casabona, J. 1966. *Recherches sur le vocabulaire des sacrifices en grec, des origines à la fin de l'époque classique.* Aix-en-Provence.

Casanaki, M., and Mallouchou, F. 1983. *The Acropolis at Athens: Conservation, Restoration and Research 1975-1983.* Trans. J. Binder. Athens.

Caspari, M. O. B. 1915. "The Ionian Confederacy." *Journal of Hellenic Studies* 35:173–188.

Cassio, A. C. 2002. "Early Editions of the Greek Epics and Homeric Textual Criticism in the Sixth and Fifth Centuries BC." *Omero tremila anni dopo* (ed. F. Montanari) 105–136. Rome.

Càssola, F. 1957. *La Ionia nel mondo miceneo.* Naples.

———. 1958. "La struttura della lega ionica." *Labeo* 4:153–171.

Casson, S. 1921. *Catalogue of the Acropolis Museum.* Vol. 2, *Sculpture and Architectural Fragments.* Cambridge.

Castelnuovo, L. M. 2002. "Dyme achea ed epea." *Identità e prassi storica nel Mediterraneo greco* (ed. L. M. Castelnuovo) 159–171. Milan.

Catling, H. W. 1977. "Excavations at the Menelaion, Sparta, 1973–76." *Archaeological Reports* 23:24–42.

———. 1989. "Archaeology in Greece, 1988–89." *Archaeological Reports* 35:3–116.

Chadwick, J., and Baumbach, L. 1963. "The Mycenaean Greek Vocabulary." *Glotta* 41:157–271.

Chandler, L. 1926. "The North-West Frontier of Attica." *Journal of Hellenic Studies* 46:1–21.

Chantraine, P. 1933. *La formation des noms en grec ancien.* Reprint 1968. Paris.

———. 1958. *Grammaire homérique.* Vol. 1, *Phonétique et morphologie.* 3rd ed. Paris.

———. 1961. *Morphologie historique du grec.* 2nd ed. Paris.

———. 1999. *Dictionnaire étymologique de la langue grecque: histoire des mots.* 2nd ed. Paris.

Christensen, J. P. 2007. *The Failure of Speech: Rhetoric and Politics in the Iliad.* PhD diss., New York University.

Christesen, P. 2005. "Imagining Olympia: Hippias of Elis and the First Olympic Victor List." *A Tall Order: Writing the Social History of the Ancient World: Essays in Honour of William V. Harris* (eds. J.-J. Aubert, Z. Várhelyi) 319–356. Munich and Leipzig.

Clader, L. L. 1976. *Helen: The Evolution from Divine to Heroic in Greek Epic Tradition.* Leiden.

Clay, J. S. 1983. *The Wrath of Athena: Gods and Men in the Odyssey.* Princeton.

———. 1989. *The Politics of Olympus: Form and Meaning in the Major Homeric Hymns.* Princeton.

———. 1997. "The Homeric Hymns." *A New Companion to Homer* (eds. I. Morris and B. Powell) 489–507. Leiden.

Clinton, K. 1986. "The Author of the *Homeric Hymn to Demeter*." *Opuscula Atheniensia* 16:43–49.

———. 1992. *Myth and Cult: The Iconography of the Eleusinian Mysteries.* Stockholm.

———. 1993. "The Sanctuary of Demeter and Kore at Eleusis." *Greek Sanctuaries: New Approaches* (eds. N. Marinatos and R. Hägg) 110–124. London.

———. 1994. "The Eleusinian Mysteries and Panhellenism in Democratic Athens." *The Archaeology of Athens and Attica under the Democracy* (eds. W. Coulson et al.) 161–172. Oxford.

Cobet, J. 1977. "Wann wurde Herodots Darstellung der Perserkriege publiziert?" *Hermes* 105:2–27.

Coldstream, J. N. 1968. *Greek Geometric Pottery: A Survey of Ten Local Styles and their Chronology.* London.

———. 2003. *Geometric Greece: 900–700 BC.* 2nd ed. London.

Coleman, J. E. 1986. *Excavations at Pylos in Elis.* Hesperia Supplement 21. Princeton.

Collitz, H., and Bechtel, F. 1884–1915. *Sammlung der griechischen Dialekt-Inschriften.* Göttingen. Reprint 1973–1975, Nendeln/Liechenstein.

Connelly, J. B. 1996. "Parthenon and *Parthenoi*: A Mythological Interpretation of the Parthenon Frieze." *American Journal of Archaeology* 100:53–80.

Cook, E. F. 1995. *The Odyssey in Athens: Myths of Cultural Origins.* Ithaca.

Cook, J. M. 1952. "Archaeology in Greece, 1951." *Journal of Hellenic Studies* 72:92–112.

———. 1961. "Greek Settlement in the Eastern Aegean and Asia Minor." *Cambridge Ancient History* II-2 (eds. I. E. S. Edwards et al.). Fascicle of Chapter 38. Revised ed. Cambridge.

———. 1962. *The Greeks in Ionia and the East.* London. Reprints 1963 and 1965, New York.

———. 1969. Review of Kleiner et al. 1967. *Gnomon* 41:716–718.

———. 1970. Review of Kleiner et al. 1967. *Archaeology* 23:170.

———. 1975. "Greek Settlement in the Eastern Aegean and Asia Minor." *Cambridge Ancient History* II-2 (eds. I. E. S. Edwards et al.) 773–804. 3rd ed. Cambridge.

———. 1982. "East Greece." *Cambridge Ancient History* III-1 (eds. J. Boardman et al.) 745–753. 2nd ed. Cambridge.

———. 1982a. "The Eastern Greeks." *Cambridge Ancient History* III-3 (eds. J. Boardman and N. G. L. Hammond) 196–221. 2nd ed. Cambridge.

Cook, R. M. 1946. "Ionia and Greece in the Eighth and Seventh Centuries B.C." *Journal of Hellenic Studies* 66:67–98.

Cosmopoulos, M. B. 2003. "Mycenaean Religion at Eleusis: The Architecture and Stratigraphy of Megaron B." *Greek Mysteries: The Archaeology and Ritual of Ancient Greek Secret Cults* (ed. M. B. Cosmopoulos) 1–24. London.

Cox, C. A. 1998. *Household Interests: Property, Marriage Strategies, and Family Dynamics in Ancient Athens.* Princeton.

Crane, G. 1988. *Calypso: Backgrounds and Conventions of the Odyssey.* Frankfurt.

Cromey, R. D. 1978. "Attic Παιανία and Παιονίδαι." *Glotta* 56:62–69.

Cropp, M., and Fick, G. 1985. *Resolutions and Chronology in Euripides: The Fragmentary Tragedies.* London.

Crosby, M. 1941. "Greek Inscriptions." *Hesperia* 10:14–27.

Crowther, N. B. 1991. "The Apobates Reconsidered (Demosthenes lxi 23–9)." *Journal of Hellenic Studies* 111:174–176.

Cunliffe, R. J. 1924. *A Lexicon of the Homeric Dialect.* London. Reprint 1963, Norman, OK.

Cuypers, M. 2002/2003. "Ptoliporthos Akhilleus. The sack of Methymna in the *Lesbou Ktisis.*" *Hermathena* 173/174:117–135.

Darcque, P. 1981. "Les vestiges mycéniens découverts sous le Télestérion d'Éleusis." *Bulletin de correspondance hellénique* 105:593–605.

Darthou, S. 2005. "Retour à la terre: la fin de la Geste d'Érechthée." *Kernos* 18:69–83.

Davies, J. K. 1971. *Athenian Propertied Families, 600–300 B.C.* Oxford.

———. 1994. "The Tradition about the First Sacred War." *Greek Historiography* (ed. S. Hornblower) 193–212. Oxford.

Davies, M. 1989. "The Date of the Epic Cycle." *Glotta* 67:89–100.

Davison, J. A. 1952. "Homer and the Monuments." Review of Lorimer 1950. *Classical Review* N.S. 2:13–15.

———. 1962. "The Transmission of the Text." *A Companion to Homer* (eds. A. J. B. Wace and F. H. Stubbings) 215–233. London.

———. 1965. "Thucydides, Homer and the 'Achaean Wall'." *Greek, Roman and Byzantine Studies* 6:5–28.

———. 1968. *From Archilochus to Pindar: Papers on Greek Literature of the Archaic Period.* London.

Delebecque, E. 1965. *Thucydide et Alcibiade.* Aix-en-Provence.

Deonna, W. 1930. *Dédale, ou la statue de la Grèce archaïque* I. Paris.

Deoudi, M. 1999. *Heroenkulte in homerischer Zeit.* Oxford.

Desborough, V. R. d'A. 1952. *Protogeometric Pottery.* Oxford.

———. 1964. *The Last Mycenaeans and their Successors: An Archaeological Survey c. 1200–c. 1000 B.C.* Oxford.

Detienne, M., and Vernant, J.-P. 1974. *Les ruses de l'intelligence. La mètis des Grecs.* Paris. Trans. by J. Lloyd as *Cunning Intelligence in Greek Culture and Society.* 1978. Atlantic Highlands, NJ. Reprint 1991, Chicago.

Deubner, L. 1932. *Attische Feste.* Reprint 1956. Berlin.

Diamant, S. 1982. "Theseus and the Unification of Attica." *Studies in Attic Epigraphy, History, and Topography Presented to Eugene Vanderpool,* 38–47. *Hesperia* Supplement 19. Princeton.

Dickson, K. M. 1995. *Nestor: Poetic Memory in Greek Epic.* New York.

Dihle, A. 1969. "Die Inschrift vom Nestor-Becher aus Ischia." *Hermes* 97:257–261.

Dillery, J. 2005. "Chresmologues and *Manteis*: Independent Diviners and the Problem of Authority." *Mantikê: Studies in Ancient Divination* (eds. S. Johnston and P. Stuck) 167–231. Leiden.

Dinsmoor, W. B. 1934. "The Date of the Older Parthenon." *American Journal of Archaeology* 38:408–448.

———. 1947. "The Hekatompedon on the Athenian Acropolis." *American Journal of Archaeology* 51:109–151.

Dittenberger, W. 1903–1905. *Orientis Graeci Inscriptiones Selectae. Supplementum Sylloges Inscriptionum Graecarum.* Leipzig. Reprints 1960 and 1970, Hildesheim.

———. 1915–1924. *Sylloge Inscriptionum Graecarum* (ed. F. Hiller von Gaertringen). 3rd ed. Leipzig. Reprint (4th ed.) 1960, Hildesheim.

Dittenberger, W., and Purgold, K. 1896. *Olympia. Die Ergebnisse der von dem Deutschen Reich veranstalteten Ausgrabung.* Vol. 5, *Die Inschriften von Olympia* (eds. E. Curtius and F. Adler). Berlin. Reprint 1966, Amsterdam.

Doherty, L. E. 1995. *Siren Songs: Gender, Audiences, and Narrators in the Odyssey.* Ann Arbor.

Donohue, A. A. 1988. *Xoana and the Origins of Greek Sculpture.* Atlanta.

Dörpfeld, W. 1913. "Alt-Pylos." *Mitteilungen des Kaiserlich Deutschen Archäologischen Instituts. Athenische Abteilung* 38:97–139.

Dow, S. 1942. "The Aigaleos-Parnes Wall." *Hesperia* 11:193–211.

Dué, C. 2002. *Homeric Variations on a Lament by Briseis.* Lanham, MD.

Dué, C., and Ebbott, M. 2010. *Iliad 10 and the Poetics of Ambush: A Multitext Edition with Essays and Commentary.* Hellenic Studies 39. Washington, DC.

Dugas, C. et al. 1924. *Le Sanctuaire d'Aléa Athéna à Tégée au IVe siècle.* Paris.

Dumézil, G. 1945. *Naissance d'archanges: Essai sur la formation de la théologie zoro-astrienne.* Vol. 3 of *Jupiter Mars Quirinus.* Paris.

———. 1947. *Tarpeia: essais de philologie comparative indo-européenne.* Paris.

———. 1948. *Explication de texts indiens et latins.* Vol. 4 of *Jupiter Mars Quirinus.* Paris.

———. 1968. *Mythe et épopée. L'idéologie des trois fonctions dans les épopées des peuples indo-européens* I. Paris.

Dunbabin, T. J. 1936/1937. "Ἔχθρη παλαίη." *Annual of the British School at Athens* 37:83–91.

Dunham, A. G. 1915. *The History of Miletus: Down to the Anabasis of Alexander.* London.

Dunst, G. 1972. "Archaische Inschriften und Dokumente der Pentekontaetie aus Samos." *Mitteilungen des Deutschen Archäologischen Instituts. Athenische Abteilung* 87:99–163.

Durante, M. 1957. "Il nome di Omero." *Rendiconti della Classe di Scienze morali, storiche e filologiche dell' Accademia nazionale dei Lincei* 12:94–111. Reprinted with modifications in Durante 1976:185–204.

———. 1967. "Νείλεως e Νηλεύς." *Studi micenei ed egeo-anatolici* 3:33–46.

———. 1976. *Sulla preistoria della tradizione poetica greca.* Vol. 2, *Risultanze della comparazione indoeuropea.* Rome.

Dyer, R. 1975. "The Blind Bard of Chios (*Hymn. Hom. Ap.* 171–76)." *Classical Philology* 70:119–121.

Eckstein-Wolf, B. 1952. "Zur Darstellung spendender Götter." *Mitteilungen des Deutschen Archäologischen Instituts* 5:39–75.

Edmunds, S. et al. 2004. "Text & Textile: An Introduction to Wool-Working for Readers of Greek and Latin." DVD. Department of Classics, Rutgers University. New Brunswick.

Edwards, A. T. 1985. *Achilles in the Odyssey*. Königstein/Ts.

Edwards, M. W. 1987. *Homer: Poet of the Iliad*. Baltimore.

———, ed. 1991. *The Iliad: A Commentary*. Vol. 5, *Books 17-20*. Cambridge.

Eilmann, R. 1933. "Frühe griechische Keramik im samischen Heraion." *Mitteilungen des Deutschen Archäologischen Instituts. Athenische Abteilung* 58:47-145.

Eliade, M. 1958. *Patterns in Comparative Religion*. Trans. R Sheed. New York. Reprint 1996, Lincoln, NE. Originally published as *Traité d'histoire des religions*. 1949, Paris.

Elmer, D. 2008. "*Epikoinos*: The Ball Game *Episkuros* and *Iliad* 12.421-23." *Classical Philology* 103:414-423.

Emlyn-Jones, C. J. 1980. *The Ionians and Hellenism: A Study of the Cultural Achievement of the Early Greek Inhabitants of Asia Minor*. London.

Fantasia, U. 1986. "Samo e Anaia." *Serta historica antiqua I. Pubblicazioni dell' Istituto di storia antica e scienze ausiliarie dell' Università degli studi di Genova* 15:113-143.

Farnell, L. R. 1896. *The Cults of the Greek States*. Oxford. Reprint 1977, New Rochelle, NY.

———. 1921. *Greek Hero Cults and Ideas of Immortality*. Oxford.

Fauth, W. 1959. *Hippolytos und Phaidra: Bemerkungen zum religiösen Hintergrund eines tragischen Konflikts II. Abhandlungen der Geistes- und Sozialwissenschaftlichen Klasse* 8:387-516. Also published separately. Wiesbaden.

Fehrle, E. 1910. *Die kultische Keuschheit im Altertum*. Giessen. Reprint 1966, Berlin.

Feist, S. 1939. *Vergleichendes Wörterbuch der gotischen Sprache*. 3rd ed. Leiden.

Fenik, B. 1974. *Studies in the Odyssey*. Wiesbaden.

Ferguson, W. S. 1938. "The Salaminioi of Heptaphylai and Sounion." *Hesperia* 7:1-74.

Ferrari, G. 1988. "Pallas and Panathenaea." *Proceedings of the Third Symposium on Ancient Greek and Related Pottery* (eds. J. Christiansen and T. Melander) 465-477. Copenhagen.

———. 2000. "The Ilioupersis in Athens." *Harvard Studies in Classical Philology* 100:119–150.

———. 2002. "The Ancient Temple on the Acropolis at Athens." *American Journal of Archaeology* 106:11–35.

Fick, A., and Bechtel, F. 1894. *Die Griechischen Personennamen: Nach ihrer Bildung erklärt und systematisch geordnet.* 2nd ed. Göttingen.

Fick, A. 1897. "Altgriechische Ortsnamen VI." *Beiträge zur Kunde der indogermanischen Sprachen* 23:189–244.

———. 1911. "Homerika." *Zeitschrift für vergleichende Sprachforschung* 44:141–152.

———. 1914. "Älteste griechische Stammverbände." *Zeitschrift für vergleichende Sprachforschung* 46:67–127.

Finley, M. I. 1975. *The Use and Abuse of History.* Reprint 1990. London.

Fittschen, K. 1969. *Untersuchungen zum Beginn der Sagendarstellungen bei den Griechen.* Berlin.

Fogazza, G. 1974. "Colofone arcaica." *Quaderni urbinati di cultura classica* 18:23–38.

Foley, H. P. 1994. *The Homeric Hymn to Demeter: Translation, Commentary, and Interpretive Essays.* Princeton.

Fontenrose, J. E. 1988. *Didyma: Apollo's Oracle, Cult, and Companions.* Berkeley.

Forbiger, A. 1877. *Handbuch der alten Geographie.* 2nd ed. Leipzig. Reprint 1966, Graz.

Ford, A. L. 1988. "The Classical Definition of PAΨΩΙΔΙΑ." *Classical Philology* 83:300–307.

———. 1997. "The Inland Ship: Problems in the Performance and Reception of Homeric Epic." *Written Voices, Spoken Signs: Tradition, Performance, and the Epic Text* (eds. E. Bakker and A. Kahane) 83–109. Cambridge, MA.

Fornara, C. W. 1971. "Evidence for the Date of Herodotus' Publication." *Journal of Hellenic Studies* 91:25–34.

———. 1981. "Herodotus' Knowledge of the Archidamian War." *Hermes* 109:149–156.

Forrest, W. G. G. 1956. "The First Sacred War." *Bulletin de correspondance hellénique* 80:33–52.

———. 1982. "Central Greece and Thessaly." *Cambridge Ancient History* III-3 (eds. J. Boardman and N. G. L. Hammond) 286–320. 2nd ed. Cambridge.

Förstel, K. 1979. *Untersuchungen zum Homerischen Apollonhymnos*. Bochum.

Foucart, P. 1885. "Inscriptions de Béotie." *Bulletin de correspondance hellénique* 9:403–433.

Fowler, R. L. 1998. "Genealogical Thinking, Hesiod's *Catalogue*, and the Creation of the Hellenes." *Proceedings of the Cambridge Philological Society* 44:1–19.

Fraenkel, E. 1959. "Zum Text der Vögel des Aristophanes." *Studien zur Textgeschichte und Textkritik* (eds. H. Dahlmann and R. Merkelbach) 9–30. Cologne.

Frame, D. 1971. *The Origins of Greek* ΝΟΥΣ. PhD diss., Harvard University.

———. 1978. *The Myth of Return in Early Greek Epic*. New Haven.

———. 2006. "The Homeric Poems after Ionia: A Case in Point." *The Homerizon: Conceptual Interrogations in Homeric Studies* (eds. R. Armstrong and C. Dué). Washington, DC. http://chs.harvard.edu/publications.

Fraser, A. D. 1940. "The Geometric Oenochoe with Crossed Tubes from the Athenian Agora." *American Journal of Archaeology* 44:457–463.

Frazer, J. G. 1913. *Pausanias's Description of Greece*. 2nd ed. London. Reprint 1965, New York.

———. 1921. *Apollodorus, The Library, with an English Translation*. Cambridge, MA.

Frazer, R. M. 1969. "Some Notes on the Athenian Entry, Iliad B 546–56." *Hermes* 97:262–266.

Frei, P. 1968. "Zur Etymologie von griech. νοῦς." *Lemmata. Donum natalicium W. Ehlers*, 48–57. Munich.

Frickenhaus, A. 1908. "Das Athenabild des alten Tempels in Athen." *Mitteilungen des Kaiserlich Deutschen Archäologischen Instituts. Athenische Abteilung* 33:17–32.

———. 1908a. "Erechtheus." *Mitteilungen des Kaiserlich Deutschen Archäologischen Instituts. Athenische Abteilung* 33:171–176.

Frisk, H. 1960–1972. *Griechisches etymologisches Wörterbuch*. Heidelberg.

Fritz, K. von. 1943. "ΝΟΟΣ and NOEIN in the Homeric Poems." *Classical Philology* 38:79–93.

———. 1945. "ΝΟΥΣ, NOEIN, and their Derivatives in Pre-Socratic Philosophy (excluding Anaxagoras). Part I. From the Beginnings to Parmenides." *Classical Philology* 40:223–242.

Frost, F. J. 1980. *Plutarch's Themistocles: A Historical Commentary.* Princeton.

Fuchs, M. 1999. *In hoc etiam genere Graeciae nihil cedamus: Studien zur Romanisierung der späthellenistischen Kunst im 1. Jh. v. Chr.* Mainz.

García Ramón, J. L. 2004. "Zum Paradigma von idg. **nes-:* homerisch ἀπενάσσατο, Kausat. ἀπονάσσωσιν als Aoriste von (°)νέομαι und die Entstehung von Präs. ναίω." *Analecta homini universali dicata. Arbeiten zur Indogermanistik, Linguistik, Philologie, Politik, Musik und Dichtung: Festschrift für Oswald Panagl zum 65. Geburtstag* (eds. T. Krisch et al.) 33–47. Stuttgart.

Geldner, K. F. 1951–1957. *Der Rig-Veda: aus dem Sanskrit ins Deutsche übersetzt und mit einem laufenden Kommentar versehen.* Cambridge, MA.

Gerber, D., ed. 1999. *Greek Elegiac Poetry from the Seventh to the Fifth Centuries BC.* Cambridge, MA.

Gerhard, E. 1840–1858. *Auserlesene griechische Vasenbilder: Hauptsächlich etruskischen Fundorts.* Berlin.

Gill, C. 1977. "The Genre of the Atlantis Story." *Classical Philology* 72:287–304.

———. 1979. "Plato's Atlantis Story and the Birth of Fiction." *Philosophy and Literature* 3:64–78.

———. 1980. *Plato, The Atlantis Story: Timaeus 17-27, Critias.* Edited with introduction, notes, and vocabulary. Bristol.

——— 1993. "Plato on Falsehood—Not Fiction." *Lies and Fiction in the Ancient World* (eds. C. Gill and T. Wiseman) 38–87. Austin.

Gjerstad, E. 1929. "Das attische Fest der Skira." *Archiv für Religionswissenschaft* 27:189–240.

———. 1965. "Discussions Concerning Early Rome 2." *Opuscula Romana* 5:1–74.

Glotz, G. 1906. "Une inscription de Milet." *Comptes Rendus de l'Académie des Inscriptions et Belles-Lettres,* 511–529.

Goldman, R. P. 1977. *Gods, Priests, and Warriors: The Bhṛgus of the Mahābhārata.* New York.

Gomme, A. W., Andrewes, A., and Dover, K. J. 1970. *A Historical Commentary on Thucydides.* Vol. 4, *Books V 25-VII.* Oxford.

———. 1980. *A Historical Commentary on Thucydides.* Vol. 5, *Book VIII.* Oxford.

Gonda, J. 1959. *Epithets in the Ṛgveda.* The Hague.

Goold, G. P. 1960. "Homer and the Alphabet." *Transactions of the American Philological Association* 91:272–291.

Gorman, V. B. 2001. *Miletos, the Ornament of Ionia: A History of the City to 400 B.C.E.* Ann Arbor.

Gostoli, A. 1990. *Terpander: veterum testimonia collegit, fragmenta edidit, Antonia Gostoli.* Rome.

Goto, T. 1991. "Aśvín- and Nāsatya-" (in Japanese). *Journal of Indian and Buddhist Studies* 39:977–982.

Graham, A. J. 1971. "Dating Archaic Greek Inscriptions." *Acta of the Fifth International Congress of Greek and Latin Epigraphy: Cambridge 1967,* 9–17. Oxford.

Grassmann, H. 1873. *Wörterbuch zum Rig-Veda.* Leipzig. Reprint 1976, Wiesbaden.

Graziosi, B. 2002. *Inventing Homer: The Early Reception of Epic.* Cambridge.

Grote, G. 1872. *A History of Greece* II. 4th ed. London.

Guarducci, M. 1948. "L'origine e le vicende del γένος attico dei Salaminii." *Rivista di filologia classica* 76:223–243.

———. 1961. "Nuove osservazioni sull' epigrafe della 'coppa di Nestore'." *Rendiconti della Classe di Scienze morali, storiche e filologiche dell' Accademia nazionale dei Lincei* 16:3–7.

———. 1967. *Epigrafia greca* I. Rome.

Guichard Romero, L. A. 2004. "Notes on Posidippus 74 AB (*P. Mil. Vogl.* VIII 309, XI 33–XII 7)." *Zeitschrift für Papyrologie und Epigraphik* 148:77–80.

Guillon, P. 1963. *Études béotiennes. Le bouclier d'Héraclès et l'histoire de la Grèce centrale dans la période de la première guerre sacrée.* Aix-en-Provence.

Güntert, H. 1923. *Der Arische Weltkönig und Heiland. Bedeutungsgeschichtliche Untersuchungen zur indo-iranischen Religionsgeschichte und Altertumskunde.* Halle.

Habicht, C. 1984. "Pausanias and the Evidence of Inscriptions." *Classical Antiquity* 3:40–56.

———. 2000. "Foreign Names in Athenian Nomenclature." *Greek Personal Names: Their Value as Evidence* (eds. S. Hornblower and E. Matthews) 119–127. Oxford.

Hainsworth, B., ed. 1993. *The Iliad: A Commentary.* Vol. 3, *Books 9–12.* Cambridge.

Hall, J. M. 2002. *Hellenicity: Between Ethnicity and Culture.* Chicago.

Hamilton, R. 1993. Review of Clinton 1992. *Bryn Mawr Classical Review* 4.03.22 (1993), http://bmcr.brynmawr.edu/1993/04.03.22.html.

Hammer, D. 2002. *The Iliad as Politics: The Performance of Political Thought.* Norman.

Hammond, N. G. L. 1950. "The Lycurgean Reform at Sparta." *Journal of Hellenic Studies* 70:42–64.

———. 1982. "The Peloponnese." *Cambridge Ancient History* III-3 (eds. J. Boardman and N. G. L. Hammond) 321–359. 2nd ed. Cambridge.

———. 1998. "The Branchidai at Didyma and in Sogdiana." *Classical Quarterly* N.S. 48:339–344.

Hampe, R. 1950. "Die homerische Welt im Lichte der neuen Ausgrabungen: Nestor." *Vermächtnis der antiken Kunst: Gastvorträge zur Jahrhundertfeier der Archäologischen Sammlungen der Universität Heidelberg* (ed. R. Herbig) 11–70. Heidelberg.

Hansen, O. 1988. "Nestor's Cup: A New Suggestion for Restoration of the Lacuna in Line 1." *L'Antiquité classique* 57:280–281.

Harland, J. P. 1925. "The Calaurian Amphictyony." *American Journal of Archaeology* 29:160–171.

Harris, D. 1995. *The Treasures of the Parthenon and Erechtheion.* Oxford.

Haubold, J. 2000. *Homer's People: Epic Poetry and Social Formation.* Cambridge.

Hawkins, S. H. 2004. *Studies in the Language of Hipponax.* PhD diss., University of North Carolina at Chapel Hill.

Heiden, B. 1996. "The Three Movements of the *Iliad*." *Greek, Roman and Byzantine Studies* 37:5–22.

Heitsch, E. 2006. *Altes und Neues zur Ilias: Überlegungen zur Genese des Werkes.* Stuttgart.

Hemingway, S. A. 2004. *The Horse and Jockey from Artemision: A Bronze Equestrian Monument of the Hellenistic Period.* Berkeley.

Henderson, W. J. 1982. "The Nature and Function of Solon's Poetry: Fr. 3 Diehl, 4 West." *Acta Classica* 25:21–33.

Hercher, R., ed. 1873. *Epistolographi Graeci.* Paris.

Herda, A. 1998. "Der Kult des Gründerheroen Neileos und die Artemis Kithone in Milet." *Jahreshefte des Österreichischen Archäologischen Institutes in Wien* 67:1–48.

———. 2005. "Apollon Delphinios, das Prytaneion und die Agora von Milet. Neue Forschungen." *Archäologischer Anzeiger. Beiblatt zum Jahrbuch des Deutschen Archäologisches Instituts.* 2005.1:243–294.

———. 2006. "Panionion-Melia, Mykalessos-Mykale, Perseus und Medusa. Überlegungen zur Besiedlungsgeschichte der Mykale in der frühen Eisenzeit." *Mitteilungen des Deutschen Archäologischen Instituts. Abteilung Istanbul* 56:43–102.

———. 2006a. *Der Apollon-Delphinios-Kult in Milet und die Neujahrsprozession nach Didyma: Ein neuer Kommentar der sog. Molpoi-Satzung.* Mainz am Rhein.

Herdejürgen, H. 1971. *Die tarentinischen Terrakotten des 6. bis 4. Jahrhunderts im Antikenmuseum Basel.* Basel.

Herington, C. J. 1955. *Athena Parthenos and Athena Polias: A Study in the Religion of Periclean Athens.* Manchester.

———. 1985. *Poetry into Drama: Early Tragedy and the Greek Poetic Tradition.* Berkeley.

Herman, G. 1987. *Ritualised Friendship and the Greek City.* Cambridge.

Hermann, G. 1805. *Orphica.* Leipzig. Reprint 1971, Hildesheim.

Heubeck, A. 1954. "Argeiphontes und Verwandtes." *Beiträge zur Namenforschung* 5:19–31. Reprinted in Heubeck 1984:247–259.

———. 1957. "Bemerkungen zu einigen griechischen Personennamen auf den Linear-B Tafeln." *Beiträge zur Namenforschung* 8:28–35. Reprinted in Heubeck 1984:473–480.

———. 1969. "Gedanken zu griech. λαός." *Studi linguistici in onore di Vittore Pisani* II, 535–544. Brescia.

———. 1984. *Kleine Schriften zur griechischen Sprache und Literatur.* Erlangen.

———. 1987. "Zu den griech. Verbalwurzeln *nes- und *neu̯-." *Minos* N.S. 20–22:227–238.

Heubeck, A. et al., eds. 1988–1992. *A Commentary on Homer's Odyssey.* Oxford.

Hicks, E. L. 1887. "Iasos." *Journal of Hellenic Studies* 8:83–118.

Higbie, C. 1995. *Heroes' Names, Homeric Identities.* New York.

Highbarger, E. L. 1927. *The History and Civilization of Ancient Megara* I. Baltimore.

Hignett, C. 1952. *A History of the Athenian Constitution to the End of the Fifth Century B.C.* Corrected reprint 1958, reprint 1970. Oxford.

Hill, I. C. T. 1953. *The Ancient City of Athens: Its Topography and Monuments.* Cambridge, MA.

Hiller von Gaertringen, F. 1886. *De Graecorum fabulis ad Thraces pertinentibus.* Berlin.

————, ed. 1906. *Inschriften von Priene.* Reprint 1968. Berlin.

Hoepfner, W., ed. 1997. *Kult und Kultbauten auf der Akropolis.* Berlin.

Högemann, P. 2001. "Troias Untergang—was dann? Alte Dynastien, neue Reiche und die 'Ionische Kolonisation' (12.-6. Jh. v.Chr.)." *Troia: Traum und Wirklichkeit* (eds. J. Latacz et al.) 58–63. Stuttgart.

Hölscher, T. 1997. "Ritual und Bildsprache. Zur Deutung der Reliefs an der Brüstung um das Heiligtum der Athena Nike in Athen." *Mitteilungen des Deutschen Archäologischen Instituts. Athenische Abteilung* 112:143–166.

Hornblower, S. 1982. "Thucydides, the Panionian Festival, and the Ephesia (III 104)." *Historia* 31:241–245.

————. 1982a. *Mausolus.* Oxford.

————. 1991. *A Commentary on Thucydides.* Vol. 1, *Books I-III.* Oxford.

————. 1996. *A Commentary on Thucydides.* Vol. 2, *Books IV-V.24.* Oxford.

How, W. W., and Wells, J. 1928. *A Commentary on Herodotus.* Reprint of original 1912 edition with corrections. Oxford.

Humbert, J., ed. 1959. *Homère, Hymnes.* Paris.

Hunter, R., ed. 1999. *Theocritus: A Selection. Idylls 1, 3, 4, 6, 7, 10, 11 and 13.* Cambridge.

Hurst, A. 2000. "Bâtir les murailles de Thèbes." *Presenza e funzione della città di Tebe nella cultura greca* (ed. P. Bernardini) 63–81. Pisa.

Hurwit, J. M. 1999. *The Athenian Acropolis: History, Mythology, and Archaeology from the Neolithic Era to the Present.* Cambridge.

Hutton, C. A. 1897. "Votive Reliefs in the Acropolis Museum." *Journal of Hellenic Studies* 17:306–318.

Huxley, G. L. 1960. "Theopompos and Melia." *La Parola del passato: rivista di studi antichi* 15:57–58.

————. 1962. *Early Sparta.* London.

————. 1966. *The Early Ionians.* London.

————. 1969. *Greek Epic Poetry from Eumelos to Panyassis.* London.

————. 1973. "The Date of Pherekydes of Athens." *Greek, Roman and Byzantine Studies* 14:137–143.

Iakovidis, S. E. 1962. Ἡ Μυκηναϊκὴ Ἀκρόπολις τῶν Ἀθηνῶν. Athens. Trans. by M. Caskey and the author as *The Mycenaean Acropolis of Athens.* 2006. Athens.

Irwin, E. 2005. *Solon and Early Greek Poetry: The Politics of Exhortation.* Cambridge.

———. 2007. "'What's in a name?' and Exploring the Comparable: Onomastics, Ethnography, and *Kratos* in Thrace, (5.1-2 and 3-10)." *Reading Herodotus: A Study of the logoi in Book 5 of Herodotus' Histories* (eds. E. Irwin and E. Greenwood) 41–87. Cambridge.

Ivantchik, A. I. 2005. *Am Vorabend der Kolonisation. Das nördliche Schwarzmeergebiet und die Steppennomaden des 8.-7. Jhs. v. Chr. in der klassischen Literaturtradition: Mündliche Überlieferung, Literatur und Geschichte.* Berlin and Moscow.

Jacoby, F. 1902. *Apollodors Chronik. Eine Sammlung der Fragmente.* Berlin.

———. 1944. "ΓΕΝΕΣΙΑ. A Forgotten Festival of the Dead." *Classical Quarterly* 38:65–75.

———. 1944a. "*Patrios Nomos*: State Burial in Athens and the Public Cemetery in the Kerameikos." *Journal of Hellenic Studies* 64:37–66.

———. 1947. "The First Athenian Prose Writer." *Mnemosyne* 3rd S. 13:13–64.

———. 1949. *Atthis, The Local Chronicles of Ancient Athens.* Oxford.

Jaeger, W. W. 1926. "Solons Eunomie." *Sitzungsberichte der Preussischen Akademie der Wissenschaften. Philosophisch-historische Klasse,* 69–85. Trans. by A. Fiske in Jaeger 1966:75–99.

———. 1966. *Five Essays.* Montreal.

Jahn, O. 1845. *Archäologische Aufsätze.* Greifswald.

Jahn, O., and Michaelis, A. 1901. *Arx Athenarum a Pausania descripta.* 3rd ed. Bonn. Reprinted 1976 as *The Acropolis of Athens*, Chicago.

Jameson, M. H. 1991. "Sacrifice before Battle." *Hoplites: The Classical Greek Battle Experience* (ed. V. D. Hanson) 197–227. London.

———. 1994. "The Ritual of the Athena Nike Parapet." *Ritual, Finance, Politics: Athenian Democratic Accounts presented to David Lewis* (eds. R. Osborne and S. Hornblower) 307–324. Oxford.

Janko, R. 1982. *Homer, Hesiod and the Hymns: Diachronic Development in Epic Diction.* Cambridge.

———, ed. 1992. *The Iliad: A Commentary.* Vol. 4, *Books 13–16.* Cambridge.

———. 1998. "The Homeric Poems as Oral Dictated Texts." *Classical Quarterly* N.S. 48:1–13.

Jeffery, L. H. 1948. "The Boustrophedon Sacral Inscriptions from the Agora." *Hesperia* 17:86–111.

———. 1961. *The Local Scripts of Archaic Greece: A Study of the Origin of the Greek Alphabet and its Development from the Eighth to the Fifth Centuries B.C.* Revised edition with a supplement by A. W. Johnston. 1990. Oxford.

———. 1976. *Archaic Greece: The City-States c. 700–500 B.C.* London.

———. 1988. "Poseidon on the Acropolis." *Praktika tou XII Diethnous Synedriou Klasikēs Archaiologias: Athēna, 4–10 Septembriou 1983.* International Congress of Classical Archaeology (12th: 1983: Athens, Greece) 3:124–126. Athens.

Jenkins, T. 1999. "*Homêros ekainopoiêse*: Theseus, Aithra, and Variation in Homeric Myth-Making." *Nine Essays on Homer* (eds. M. Carlisle and O. Levaniouk) 207–226. Lanham, MD.

Jensen, M. S. 1980. *The Homeric Question and the Oral-Formulaic Theory.* Copenhagen.

Jensen, M. S. et al. 1999. "Dividing Homer: When and How Were the *Iliad* and the *Odyssey* Divided into Songs?" *Symbolae Osloenses* 74:5–91.

Jeppesen, K. 1979. "Where Was the So-called Erechtheion?" *American Journal of Archaeology* 83:381–394. Reprinted in Jeppesen 1987:85–98.

———. 1983. "Further Inquiries on the Location of the Erechtheion and its Relationship to the Temple of the Polias." *American Journal of Archaeology* 87:325–333. Reprinted in Jeppesen 1987:99–107.

———. 1987. *The Theory of the Alternative Erechtheion: Premises, Definition, and Implications.* Aarhus.

Jones, J. E. et al. 1957. "Τὸ Δέμα: A Survey of the Aigaleos-Parnes Wall." *Annual of the British School at Athens* 52:152–189.

Judeich, W. 1931. *Topographie von Athen.* 2nd ed. Munich.

Kagan, D. 1981. *The Peace of Nicias and the Sicilian Expedition.* Ithaca.

Kaibel, G. 1878. *Epigrammata Graeca ex lapidibus conlecta.* Berlin. Reprint 1965, Hildesheim.

———. 1899. *Comicorum Graecorum Fragmenta.* Berlin.

Kakridis, J. 1949. *Homeric Researches.* Lund.

Kalogeropoulos, K. 2003. "Die Botschaft der Nikebalustrade." *Mitteilungen des Deutschen Archäologischen Instituts. Athenische Abteilung* 118:281–315.

Kambitsis, J. 1972. *L'Antiope d'Euripide. Édition commentée des fragments.* Athens.

Kamptz, H. von. 1982. *Homerische Personennamen: Sprachwissenschaftliche und historische Klassifikation.* Göttingen.

Kannicht, R., ed. 2004. *Tragicorum Graecorum Fragmenta.* Vol. 5.1, *Euripides.* Göttingen.

Karakantza, E. D. 2003. "The Semiology of Rape: The Meeting of Odysseus and Nausikaa in Book 6 of the Odyssey." *Classics Ireland* 10:8–26.

Kassel, R., and Austin, C., eds. 2001. *Poetae Comici Graeci* I. Berlin.

Kearns, E. 1989. *The Heroes of Attica.* London.

———. 1990. "Saving the City." *The Greek City: From Homer to Alexander* (eds. O. Murray and S. Price) 323–344. Oxford.

———. 1992. "Between God and Man: Status and Function of Heroes and their Sanctuaries." *Le Sanctuaire grec* (ed. A. Schachter) 65–99. Geneva.

Kebric, R. B. 1976. "Implications of Alcibiades' Relationship with the Ephor Endius." *Historia* 25: 249–252.

Keil, J. 1908. "Zur Topographie der ionischen Küste südlich von Ephesos." *Jahreshefte des Österreichischen Archäologischen Institutes* 11:135–167. Beiblatt.

Kennell, N. M. 1997. Review of M. Golden and P. Toohey, eds., *Inventing Ancient Culture: Historicism, Periodization and the Ancient World.* London: Routledge, 1997. *Bryn Mawr Classical Review* 97.11.1 (1997), http://bmcr.brynmawr.edu/1997/97.11.01.html.

Kenzler, U. 1999. *Studien zur Entwicklung und Struktur der griechischen Agora in archaischer und klassischer Zeit.* Frankfurt am Main.

Kerényi, K. 1952. *Die Jungfrau und Mutter der griechischen Religion: Eine Studie über Pallas Athene.* Zurich.

Keuls, E. C. 1983. "Attic Vase-Painting and the Home Textile Industry." *Ancient Greek Art and Iconography* (ed. W. Moon) 209–230. Madison.

———. 1985. *The Reign of the Phallus: Sexual Politics in Ancient Athens.* New York.

Kiechle, F. 1959. *Messenische Studien: Untersuchungen zur Geschichte der Messenischen Kriege und der Auswanderung der Messenier.* Kallmünz-Opf.

———. 1960. "Pylos und der pylische Raum in der antiken Tradition." *Historia* 9:1–67.

———. 1963. *Lakonien und Sparta: Untersuchungen zur ethnischen Struktur und zur politischen Entwicklung Lakoniens und Spartas bis zum Ende der archaischen Zeit.* Munich.

King, C. 1977. "Another Set of Siamese Twins in Attic Geometric Art." *Archaeological News* 6:29–40.

Kirk, G. S., ed. 1985. *The Iliad: A Commentary.* Vol. 1, *Books 1-4.* Cambridge.

———, ed. 1990. *The Iliad: A Commentary.* Vol. 2, *Books 5-8.* Cambridge.

Klein, N. L. 1997. "Excavation of the Greek Temples at Mycenae by the British School at Athens." *Annual of the British School at Athens* 92:247–322.

Kleiner, G. et al. 1967. *Panionion und Melia.* Berlin.

Knecht, T. 1946. *Geschichte der griechischen Komposita vom Typ τερψίμβροτος.* Biel.

Knibbe, D. 1998. *Ephesus: Geschichte einer bedeutenden antiken Stadt und Portrait einer modernen Grossgrabung im 102. Jahr der Wiederkehr des Beginnes österreichischer Forschungen (1895-1997).* Frankfurt am Main.

Knittlmayer, B., and Heilmeyer, W.-D., eds. 1998. *Die Antikensammlung. Altes Museum—Pergamonmuseum. Staatliche Museen zu Berlin.* 2nd ed. Mainz am Rhein.

Knox, B. M. W. 1957. *Oedipus at Thebes.* Reprinted 1998, with new introduction. New Haven.

Koenen, L. 1969. "Eine Hypothesis zur Auge des Euripides und tegeatische Plynterien." *Zeitschrift für Papyrologie und Epigraphik* 4:7–18.

Köhler, U. 1879. "Die Münzen von Salamis Eleusis und Oropos." *Mitteilungen des Deutschen Archäologischen Institutes in Athen* 4:250–267.

———. 1885. "Inschrift von Samos." *Mitteilungen des Deutschen Archäologischen Institutes in Athen* 10:32–37.

Köhnken, A. 1965. *Apollonios Rhodios und Theokrit. Die Hylas- und die Amykosgeschichten beider Dichter und die Frage der Priorität.* Göttingen.

———. 2001. "Hellenistic Chronology: Theocritus, Callimachus, and Apollonius Rhodius." *A Companion to Apollonius Rhodius* (eds. T. Papanghelis and A. Rengakos) 73–92. Leiden.

Korres, M. 1997. "Die Athena-Tempel auf der Akropolis." In Hoepfner 1997:218–243.

Kraft, J. C. et al. 2005. "Coastal Change and Archaeological Settings in Elis." *Hesperia* 74:1–39.

Krischer, T. 1984. "Νόος νοεῖν, νόημα." *Glotta* 62:141–149.

Kroll, J. H. 1982. "The Ancient Image of Athena Polias." *Studies in Athenian Architecture, Sculpture, and Topography Presented to Homer A. Thompson,* 65–76. *Hesperia* Supplement 20. Princeton.

Kron, U. 1976. *Die zehn attischen Phylenheroen: Geschichte, Mythos, Kult und Darstellungen.* Berlin.

Kuruniotis, K. 1901. "Porossculpturen aus Mykene." *Jahrbuch des Kaiserlich Deutschen Archäologisches Instituts* 16:18–22.

Kyle, D. G. 1984. "Solon and Athletics." *Ancient World* 9:91–105.

———. 1987. *Athletics in Ancient Athens.* Leiden.

Laumonier, A. 1958. *Les cultes indigènes en Carie.* Paris.

Lazzarini, M. L. 1978. "Neleo a Samo." *Rivista di filologia e di istruzione classica* 106:179–191.

Leader, R. E. 1997. "In Death Not Divided: Gender, Family, and State on Classical Athenian Grave Stelae." *American Journal of Archaeology* 101:683–699.

Leaf, W., ed. 1900–1902. *The Iliad.* 2nd ed. London. Reprint 1960, Amsterdam.

Leaf, W., and Bayfield, M.A., eds. 1908. *The Iliad of Homer.* Vol. 1, *Books I–XII.* 2nd ed. Reprint 1965. London.

Leaf, W., and Bayfield, M.A., eds. 1898. *The Iliad of Homer.* Vol. 2, *Books XIII–XXIV.* Reprint 1968. London.

Lee, M. M. 2003/2004. "'Evil Wealth of Raiment': Deadly Πέπλοι in Greek Tragedy." *Classical Journal* 99:253–279.

Lefèvre, F. 1998. *L'Amphictionie pyléo-delphique: histoire et institutions.* Paris.

Legon, R. P. 1981. *Megara: The Political History of a Greek City-State to 336 B.C.* Ithaca.

Lejeune, M. 1965. "Le ΔΑΜΟΣ dans la société mycénienne." *Revue des études grecques* 78:1–22.

Le Lasseur, D. 1919. *Les déesses armées dans l'art classique grec et leurs origines orientales.* Paris.

Lenschau, T. 1944. "Die Gründung Ioniens und der Bund am Panionion." *Klio: Beiträge zur alten Geschichte* 36:201–237.

Lentini, G. 2000. "Pittaco erede degli Atridi: il fr. 70 V. di Alceo." *Studi italiani di filologia classica* 3rd S. 18:3–14.

———. 2006. *Il 'padre di Telemaco': Odisseo tra Iliade e Odissea.* Pisa.

Lesher, J. H. 1981. "Perceiving and Knowing in the *Iliad* and *Odyssey*." *Phronesis* 26:2–24.

———. 1994. "The Emergence of Philosophical Interest in Cognition." *Oxford Studies in Ancient Philosophy* 12:1–34.

Lesky, A. 1966. *A History of Greek Literature*. Trans. J. Willis and C. de Heer. New York. Originally published as *Geschichte der griechischen Literatur*. 2nd ed. 1963. Bern.

Létoublon, F. 1985. *Il allait, pareil à la nuit. Les verbes de mouvement en grec: supplétisme et aspect verbal*. Paris.

Lewis, D. M. 1988. "The Tyranny of the Pisistratidae." *Cambridge Ancient History* IV (eds. J. Boardman et al.) 287–302. 2nd ed. Cambridge.

L'Homme-Wéry, L.-M. 1996. *La perspective éleusinienne dans la politique de Solon*. Geneva.

Lincoln, B. 1976. "The Indo-European Cattle-Raiding Myth." *History of Religions* 16:42–65.

———. 1981. *Priests, Warriors, and Cattle: A Study in the Ecology of Religions*. Berkeley.

Linforth, I. M. 1941. *The Arts of Orpheus*. Berkeley.

Lipka, M. 1997. "Anmerkungen zu den Weihinschriften der Athena Parthenos und zur Hekatompedon-Inschrift." In Hoepfner 1997:37–44.

Lippolis, E. 2006. *Mysteria. Archeologia e culto del santuario di Demetra a Eleusi. Con contributi di Isabella Baldini Lippolis e Nicola Cucuzza*. Milan.

Loeff, van der, A. R. 1916. "De Sciris." *Mnemosyne* N.S. 44:322–337.

Lohmann, H. 2004. "Mélia, le Panionion et le culte de Poséidon Héliconios." *Les cultes locaux dans les mondes grec et romain* (ed. G. Labarre) 31–49. Lyon.

———. 2005. "Melia, das Panionion und der Kult des Poseidon Helikonios." *Neue Forschungen zu Ionien. F. Işık zum 60. Geburtstag gewidmet* (eds. E. Schwertheim and E. Winter). *Asia Minor Studien* 54:57–91.

Lohse, G. 1964, 1965, 1967. "Untersuchungen über Homerzitate bei Platon, I–III." *Helikon* 4:3–28, 5:248–295, 7:223–231.

Lommel, H. 1951. "Vedische Skizzen." *Beiträge zur indischen Philologie und Altertumskunde. Walther Schubring zum 70. Geburtstag dargebracht von der deutschen Indologie* 25–39. Hamburg.

Lord, A. B. 1960. *The Singer of Tales*. 2nd ed. 2000. Cambridge, MA.

———. 1970. "Tradition and the Oral Poet: Homer, Huso and Avdo Medjedović." *Atti del convegno internazionale sul tema: La poesia epica e la sua formazione. Roma, 28 marzo–3 aprile 1969.* Problemi attuali di scienza e di cultura 139:13–28. Rome.

Lorimer, H. L. 1950. *Homer and the Monuments.* London.

Louden, B. 1999. *The Odyssey: Structure, Narration, and Meaning.* Baltimore.

Lowenstam, S. 1993. "The Arming of Achilleus on Early Greek Vases." *Classical Antiquity* 12:199–218.

———. 1997. "Talking Vases: The Relationship between the Homeric Poems and Archaic Representations of Epic Myth." *Transactions of the American Philological Association* 127:21–76.

Luppe, W. 1983. "Die Hypothesis zu Euripides' 'Auge'." *Archiv für Papyrusforschung und verwandte Gebiete* 29:19–23.

Luraghi, N. 2002. "Becoming Messenian." *Journal of Hellenic Studies* 122:45–69.

Macdonell, A. A. 1897. *Vedic Mythology.* Strassburg. Reprint 1974, New York.

MacDowell, D., ed. 1962. *Andokides. On the Mysteries.* Reprint 1989. Oxford.

Maddoli, G. 1991. "L'Elide in età arcaica: il processo di formazione dell' unità regionale." *Geografia storica della Grecia antica. Tradizioni e problemi* (ed. F. Prontera) 150–173. Rome.

Maddoli, G. et al. 1999. *Pausania. Guida della Grecia. Libro VI. L'Elide e Olimpia.* Milan.

Magnetto, A. 1997. *Gli arbitrati interstatali. Introduzione, testo critico, traduzione, commento e indici.* Vol. 2, *Dal 337 al 196 a.C.* Pisa.

Malkin, I. 1998. *The Returns of Odysseus: Colonization and Ethnicity.* Berkeley.

———. 2001. "Introduction." *Ancient Perceptions of Greek Ethnicity* (ed. I. Malkin) 1–28. Center for Hellenic Studies Colloquia 5. Washington, DC.

Mallory, J. P. 1985. *In Search of the Indo-Europeans: Language, Archaeology and Myth.* London.

Mann, C. 1998, "Krieg, Sport und Adelskultur. Zur Entstehung des griechischen Gymnasions." *Klio* 80:7–21.

Mansfield, J. M. 1985. *The Robe of Athena and the Panathenaic Peplos.* PhD diss., University of California at Berkeley.

Marinatos, S. 1955. "ΠΑΛΑΙΠΥΛΟΣ." *Das Altertum* 1:140–163.

Marks, J. 2003. "Alternative Odysseys: The Case of Thoas and Odysseus." *Transactions of the American Philological Association* 133:209–226.

————. 2008. *Zeus in the Odyssey*. Hellenic Studies 31. Washington, DC.

Martin, R. 1951. *Recherches sur l'agora grecque: études d'histoire et d'architecture urbaines*. Paris.

Martin, R. P. 1984. "Hesiod, Odysseus, and the Instruction of Princes." *Transactions of the American Philological Association* 114:29–48.

————. 1989. *The Language of Heroes: Speech and Performance in the Iliad*. Ithaca.

————. 1993. "The Seven Sages as Performers of Wisdom." *Cultural Poetics in Archaic Greece: Cult, Performance, Politics* (eds. C. Dougherty and L. Kurke) 108–128. Cambridge.

————. 2000. "Wrapping Homer Up: Cohesion, Discourse, and Deviation in the *Iliad*." *Intratexuality: Greek and Roman Textual Relations* (eds. A. Sharrock and H. Morales) 43–65. Oxford.

————. 2000a. "Synchronic Aspects of Homeric Performance: The Evidence of the *Hymn to Apollo*." *Una nueva visión de la cultura griega antigua hacia el fin del milenio* (ed. A. González de Tobia) 403–432. La Plata, Argentina.

Marx, P. A. 2001. "Acropolis 625 (Endoios Athena) and the Rediscovery of its Findspot." *Hesperia* 70:221–254.

Matthews, V. J. 1974. *Panyassis of Halikarnassos: Text and Commentary*. Leiden.

————. 1987. "Kaukonian Dyme: Antimachos and the Text of Homer." *Eranos* 85:91–97.

————. 1996. *Antimachus of Colophon: Text and Commentary*. Leiden.

Mattusch, C. C. 1996. *Classical Bronzes: The Art and Craft of Greek and Roman Statuary*. Ithaca.

Mayer, M. 1887. *Die Giganten und Titanen in der antiken Sage und Kunst*. Berlin.

Mayrhofer, M. 1956–1980. *Kurzgefasstes etymologisches Wörterbuch des Altindischen; A Concise Etymological Sanskrit Dictionary*. Heidelberg.

————. 1966. *Die Indo-Arier im alten Vorderasien*. Wiesbaden.

————. 1986. *Etymologisches Wörterbuch des Altindoarischen*. Heidelberg.

Mazon, P. 1942. *Introduction à l'Iliade*. Reprint 1967. Paris.

McDonald, W. A. 1942. "Where Did Nestor Live?" *American Journal of Archaeology* 46:538–545.

McGowan, E. P. 1995. "Tomb Marker and Turning Post: Funerary Columns in the Archaic Period." *American Journal of Archaeology* 99:615–632.

McInerney, J. 1994. "Politicizing the Past: The *Atthis* of Kleidemos." *Classical Antiquity* 13:17–37.

Meier, M. 1998. *Aristokraten und Damoden: Untersuchungen zur inneren Entwicklung Spartas im 7. Jahrhundert v. Chr. und zur politischen Funktion der Dichtung des Tyrtaios.* Stuttgart.

Meiggs, R., and Lewis, D. M. 1988. *A Selection of Greek Historical Inscriptions to the End of the Fifth Century B.C.* 2nd ed. Oxford.

Merkelbach, R. 1969. *Untersuchungen zur Odysee.* 2nd ed. Munich.

Merkelbach, R., and West, M. L., eds. 1967. *Fragmenta Hesiodea.* Oxford.

Metzger, H. 1965. "Sur la date du graffite de la 'coupe de Nestor'." *Revue des études anciennes* 67:301–305.

Meuli, K. 1954. "Herkunft und Wesen der Fabel." *Schweizerisches Archiv für Volkskunde* 50:65–88. Reprinted in Meuli 1975:731–756.

———. 1975. *Gesammelte Schriften* II. Basel and Stuttgart.

Meyer, Ed. 1893. *Geschichte des Altertums.* Vol. 2, *Geschichte des Abendlandes bis auf die Perserkriege.* Stuttgart.

———. 1954. *Geschichte des Altertums.* Vol. 3, *Der Ausgang der altorientalischen Geschichte und der Aufstieg des Abendlandes bis auf die Perserkriege.* 3rd ed. Basel.

Meyer, Er. 1951. "Pylos und Navarino." *Museum Helveticum* 8:119–136.

———. 1957. "Arkadisches." *Museum Helveticum* 14:81–88.

Mikalson, J. D. 1975. *The Sacred and Civil Calendar of the Athenian Year.* Princeton.

———. 1976. "Erechtheus and the Panathenaia." *American Journal of Philology* 97:141–153.

Miles, M. M. 1998. *The City Eleusinion.* Princeton.

Minchin, E. 1990/1991. "Speaker and Listener, Text and Context: Some Notes on the Encounter of Nestor and Patroklos in *Iliad* 11." *Classical World* 84:273–285.

Moggi, M. 1976. *I sinecismi interstatali greci.* Vol. 1, *Dalle orgini al 338 a.C.* Pisa.

———. 1996. "L' *excursus* di Pausania sulla Ionia." *Pausanias historien* (ed. J. Bingen) 79–105. Geneva.

Momigliano, A. 1932. "Questioni di storia ionica arcaica." *Studi italiani di filologia classica* N.S. 10:259–297. Reprinted in Momigliano 1975:369–402.

———. 1932a. "Il re degli Ioni nella provincia romana di Asia." *Atti del III Congresso Nazionale di Studi Romani* 1:429–443. Bologna. Reprinted in Momigliano 1975:205–210.

———. 1975. *Quinto contributo alla storia degli studi classici e del mondo antico.* Rome.

Mommsen, A. 1898. *Feste der Stadt Athen im Altertum: Geordnet nach attischem Kalender.* 2nd ed. Leipzig.

Moreschini, A. Q. 1984. "Elementi micenei nella tradizione formulare: Γερήνιος ἱππότα Νέστωρ." *Studi micenei ed egeo-anatolici* 25:337–347.

Morgan, C., and Hall, J. 1996. "Achaian *Poleis* and Achaian Colonisation." *Introduction to an Inventory of Poleis: Symposium August, 2-26 1995* (ed. M. H. Hansen) 164–232. Acts of the Copenhagen Polis Centre 3: Copenhagen.

Morgan, K. A. 1998. "Designer History: Plato's Atlantis Story and Fourth-Century Ideology." *Journal of Hellenic Studies* 118:101–118.

Moyer, I. S. 2002. "Herodotus and an Egyptian Mirage: The Genealogies of the Theban Priests." *Journal of Hellenic Studies* 122:70–90.

Muellner, L. 1996. *The Anger of Achilles: Mênis in Greek Epic.* Ithaca.

Mühlestein, H. 1965. "Namen von Neleiden auf den Pylostäfelchen." *Museum Helveticum* 22:155–165.

Muir, J. 1872, 1874. *Original Sanskrit Texts* I, IV. 2nd ed. London. Reprint (I–V) 1967, Amsterdam.

———. 1874. *Original Sanskrit Texts* V. 3rd ed. London. Reprint (I–V) 1967, Amsterdam.

Mülke, C. 2002. *Solons politische Elegien und Iamben.* Munich.

Murray, G. 1934. *The Rise of the Greek Epic.* 4th ed. Reprint 1967. Oxford.

Mylonas, G. E. 1942. *The Hymn to Demeter and Her Sanctuary at Eleusis.* Saint Louis.

———. 1961. *Eleusis and the Eleusinian Mysteries.* Reprints 1969 and 1974. Princeton.

Mylonopoulos, J. 2003. *Πελοπόννησος οἰκητήριον Ποσειδῶνος: Heiligtümer und Kulte des Poseidon auf der Peloponnes.* Liège.

Nagy, G. 1970. *Greek Dialects and the Transformation of an Indo-European Process.* Cambridge, MA.

———. 1974. *Comparative Studies in Greek and Indic Meter.* Cambridge, MA.

———. 1979. *The Best of the Achaeans: Concepts of the Hero in Archaic Greek Poetry.* 2nd ed. 1999. Baltimore.

———. 1983. "*Sêma* and *Nóēsis*: Some Illustrations." *Arethusa* 16:35–55. Recast as Nagy 1990:202–222.

———. 1990. *Greek Mythology and Poetics.* Ithaca.

———. 1990a. *Pindar's Homer: The Lyric Possession of an Epic Past.* Baltimore.

———. 1992. "Homeric Questions." *Transactions of the American Philological Association* 122:17–60.

———. 1996. *Homeric Questions.* Austin.

———. 1996a. *Poetry as Performance: Homer and Beyond.* Cambridge.

———. 1997. "Ellipsis in Homer." *Written Voices, Spoken Signs: Tradition, Performance, and the Epic Text* (eds. E. Bakker and A. Kahane) 167–189. Cambridge, MA.

———. 1999. "Homer and Plato at the Panathenaia: Synchronic and Diachronic Perspectives." *Contextualizing Classics: Ideology, Performance, Dialogue. Essays in honor of John J. Peradotto* (eds. T. Falkner et al.) 123–150. Lanham, MD.

———. 1999a. "Irreversible Mistakes and Homeric Poetry." *Euphrosyne: Studies in Ancient Epic and its Legacy in honor of Dimitris N. Maronitis* (eds. J. Kazazis and A. Rengakos) 259–274. Stuttgart.

———. 2002. *Plato's Rhapsody and Homer's Music: The Poetics of the Panathenaic Festival in Classical Athens.* Cambridge, MA.

———. 2004. *Homer's Text and Language.* Urbana.

———. 2005. "The Epic Hero." *A Companion to Ancient Epic* (ed. J. Foley) 71–89. Oxford.

———. 2009. *Homer the Classic.* Hellenic Studies 36. Washington, DC.

———. 2010. *Homer the Preclassic.* Berkeley.

Neils, J., ed. 1992. *Goddess and Polis: The Panathenaic Festival in Ancient Athens.* Princeton.

Neumann, G. 1988. *Phrygisch und Griechisch.* Vienna.

Newman, W. L. 1887. *The Politics of Aristotle* II. Oxford. Reprint 1973, New York.

Nick, G. 1997. "Die Athena Parthenos—ein griechisches Kultbild." In Hoepfner 1997:22–24.

———. 2002. *Die Athena Parthenos: Studien zum griechischen Kultbild und seiner Rezeption.* Mainz.

Nickau, K. 1977. *Untersuchungen zur textkritischen Methode des Zenodotos von Ephesos.* Berlin.

Nielsen, T. H. 1997. "Triphylia. An Experiment in Ethnic Construction and Political Organisation." *Yet More Studies in the Ancient Greek Polis* (ed. T. H. Nielsen) 129–162. Stuttgart.

Niemeier, B., and Niemeier, W.-D. 1997. "Milet 1994–95." *Archäologischer Anzeiger. Beiblatt zum Jahrbuch des Deutschen Archäologisches Instituts* 1997:189–284.

Nilsson, M. P. 1906. *Griechische Feste von religiöser Bedeutung, mit Ausschluss der attischen.* Leipzig. Reprint 1975, Milan.

———. 1921. "Die Anfänge der Göttin Athene." *Det Kgl. Danske Videnskabernes Selskab. Historisk-filologiske Meddelelser* IV 7:3–20.

———. 1932. *The Mycenaean Origin of Greek Mythology.* New edition 1972. Berkeley.

———. 1938. "The New Inscription of the Salaminioi." *American Journal of Philology* 59:385–393.

———. 1950. *The Minoan-Mycenaean Religion and its Survival in Greek Religion.* 2nd ed. Lund. Reprint 1971, New York.

———. 1951. *Cults, Myths, Oracles, and Politics in Ancient Greece.* Lund. Reprint 1986, Göte.

———. 1967. *Geschichte der griechischen Religion* I. 3rd ed. Munich.

Nitzsch, G. W. 1831. *Erklärende Anmerkungen zu Homer's Odyssee* II. Hannover.

Nock, A. D. 1930. "Σύνναος Θεός." *Harvard Studies in Classical Philology* 41:1–62.

Notopoulos, J. A. 1964. "Studies in Early Greek Oral Poetry." *Harvard Studies in Classical Philology* 68:1–77.

Noussia, M. 2002. "Olympus, the Sky, and the History of the Text of Homer." *Omero tremila anni dopo* (ed. F. Montanari) 489–503. Rome.

———. 2006. "Strategies of Persuasion in Solon's Elegies." *Solon of Athens: New Historical and Philological Approaches* (eds. J. Blok and A. Lardinois) 134–156. Leiden.

Noussia, M., and Fantuzzi, M. 2001. *Solone. Frammenti dell' opera poetica.* Milan.

Nünlist, R. 2002. "Some Clarifying Remarks on 'Focalization'." *Omero tremila anni dopo* (ed. F. Montanari) 445–453. Rome.

Nylander, C. 1962. "Die sog. Mykenischen Säulenbasen auf der Akropolis in Athen." *Opuscula Atheniensia* 4:31–77.

Ober, J. 1989. *Mass and Elite in Democratic Athens: Rhetoric, Ideology, and the Power of the People*. Princeton.

O'Hara, J. J. 1996. *True Names: Vergil and the Alexandrian Tradition of Etymological Wordplay*. Ann Arbor.

Oldenberg, H. 1894. *Die Religion des Veda*. Berlin. 2nd ed. 1917, Stuttgart. Reprint 1970, Darmstadt.

———. 1909. *Ṛgveda. Textkritische und exegetische Noten I. Erstes bis sechtes Buch.* Berlin. Reprint 1979, Nendeln.

Osborne, C. 1996. "Space, Time, Shape, and Direction: Creative Discourse in the *Timaeus*." *Form and Argument in Late Plato* (eds. C. Gill and M. McCabe) 179–211. Oxford.

Osborne, R. 1994. "Archaeology, the Salaminioi, and the Politics of Sacred Space in Archaic Attica." *Placing the Gods: Sanctuaries and Sacred Space in Ancient Greece* (eds. R. Osborne and S. Alcock) 143–160. Oxford.

Owen, A. S., ed. 1939. *Euripides, Ion*. Oxford. Reprint 1986, Bristol.

Pache, C. O. 1999. "Odysseus and the Phaeacians." *Nine Essays on Homer* (eds. M. Carlisle and O. Levaniouk) 21–33. Lanham, MD.

———. 2000. "War Games: Odysseus at Troy." *Harvard Studies in Classical Philology* 100:15–23.

Pade, M. 1983. "Homer's Catalogue of Women." *Classica et Mediaevalia* 34:7–15.

Padgug, R. A. 1972. "Eleusis and the Union of Attika." *Greek, Roman and Byzantine Studies* 13:135–150.

Page, D. L. 1955. *The Homeric Odyssey*. Oxford.

———. 1959. *History and the Homeric Iliad*. Reprint 1976. Berkeley.

Pagliaro, A. 1953. *Saggi di critica semantica*. Messina.

———. 1970. "Origini liriche e formazione agonale dell'epica greca." *Atti del convegno internazionale sul tema: La poesia epica e la sua formazione. Roma, 28 marzo-3 aprile 1969*. Problemi attuali di scienza e di cultura 139:31–58. Rome.

Pakkanen, J. 2006. "The Erechtheion Construction Work Inventory (*IG* I³ 474) and the Dörpfeld Temple." *American Journal of Archaeology* 110:275–281.

Palagia, O. 1997. "Reflections on the Piraeus Bronzes." *Greek Offerings: Essays on Greek Art in Honour of John Boardman* (ed. O. Palagia) 177–195. Oxford.

Palinkas, J. L. 2008. *Eleusinian Gateways: Entrances to the Sanctuary of Demeter and Kore at Eleusis and the City Eleusinion in Athens*. PhD diss., Emory University.

Palmer, L. R. 1956. "Notes on the Personnel of the O-KA TABLETS (Pylos 1952)." *Eranos* 54:1–13.

———. 1956a. "Military Arrangements for the Defence of Pylos." *Minos* 4:120–145.

———. 1957. Review of Ventris and Chadwick 1956. *Gnomon* 29:561–581.

———. 1962. "The Language of Homer." *A Companion to Homer* (eds. A. Wace and F. Stubbings) 75–178. London.

———. 1963. *The Interpretation of Mycenaean Greek Texts*. Oxford.

———. 1965. *Mycenaeans and Minoans: Aegean Prehistory in the Light of the Linear B Tablets*. 2nd ed. London. Reprint 1980, Westport, CT.

Pape, W., and Benseler, G. 1911. *Wörterbuch der griechischen Eigennamen*. 3rd ed. Braunschweig. Reprint 1959, Graz.

Parisinou, E. 2000. *The Light of the Gods: The Role of Light in Archaic and Classical Greek Cult*. London.

Parke, H. W., and Boardman, J. 1957. "The Struggle for the Tripod and the First Sacred War." *Journal of Hellenic Studies* 77:276–282.

Parke, H. W., and Wormell, D. E. W. 1956. *The Delphic Oracle*. Oxford.

Parker, R. 1987. "Myths of Early Athens." *Interpretations of Greek Mythology* (ed. J. Bremmer) 187–214. London.

———. 1988. "Spartan Religion." *Classical Sparta: Techniques behind her Success* (ed. A. Powell) 142–172. Norman and London.

———. 1996. *Athenian Religion: A History*. Oxford.

———. 2000. "Sacrifice and Battle." *War and Violence in Ancient Greece* (ed. H. van Wees) 299–314. London.

Parker, V. 1991. "The Dates of the Messenian Wars." *Chiron* 21:25–47.

Parmentier, E. 1991. "Rois et tyrans chez Nicolas de Damas." *Ktèma* 16:229–244.

Parpola, A. 2004/2005. "The Nāsatyas, the Chariot and Proto-Aryan Religion." *Journal of Indological Studies* 16/17:1–63.

Parry, M. 1971. *The Making of Homeric Verse: The Collected Papers of Milman Parry* (ed. A. Parry). Oxford.

Pasquali, G. 1913. "I due Nicandri." *Studi italiani di filologia classica* 20:55–111.

———. 1962. *Storia della tradizione e critica del testo.* 2nd ed. Reprint 1988. Florence.

Patton, K. C. 1992. *When the High Gods Pour out Wine: A Paradox of Ancient Greek Iconography in Comparative Context.* PhD diss., Harvard University.

Pazdernik, C. F. 1995. "Odysseus and His Audience: *Odyssey* 9.39–40 and Its Formulaic Resonances." *American Journal of Philology* 116:347–369.

Pedrick, V. 1983. "The Paradigmatic Nature of Nestor's Speech in *Iliad* 11." *Transactions of the American Philological Association* 113:55–68.

Petrović, A. 2004. "ἀκοὴ ἢ αὐτοψία. Zu den Quellen Herodots für die Thermopylen-Epigramme (Hdt. 7,228)." *Studia Humanitatis ac Litterarum Trifolio Heidelbergensi dedicata: Festschrift für E. Christmann, W. Edelmaier, R. Kettemann* (eds. A. Hornung et al.) 255–273. Frankfurt am Main.

Pfeiffer, R. 1968. *History of Classical Scholarship from the Beginnings to the End of the Hellenistic Age.* Oxford.

Philippson, A. 1892. *Der Peloponnes. Versuch einer Landeskunde auf geologischer Grundlage. Nach Ergebnisssen eigener Reisen.* Berlin.

Picard, C. 1931. "Les luttes primitives d'Athènes et d'Eleusis." *Revue historique* 166:1–76.

Polignac, F. de. 1995. *Cults, Territory, and the Origins of the Greek City-State.* Trans. J. Lloyd. Chicago. Originally published as *La naissance de la cité grecque: cultes, espace et société VIIIe-VIIe siècles avant J.-C.* 1984. Paris.

Pothecary, S. 1995. "Strabo, Polybius, and the Stade." *Phoenix* 49:49–67.

Powell, B. 1906. *Erichthonius and the Three Daughters of Cecrops.* New York. Reprinted 1976, as *Athenian Mythology: Erichthonius and the Three Daughters of Cecrops*, Chicago.

Powell, B. B. 1991. *Homer and the Origin of the Greek Alphabet.* Cambridge.

Power, T. 2010. *The Culture of Kitharoidia.* Hellenic Studies 15. Washington, DC.

Prandi, L. 1989. "La rifondazione del 'Panionion' e la catastrofe di Elice (373 a.C.)." *Fenomeni naturali e avvenimenti storici nell' antichità* (ed. M. Sordi). *Contributi dell' Istituto di Storia antica* 15:43–59.

Preller, L. 1894. *Griechische Mythologie* I (ed. C. Robert). 4th ed. Reprint 1967. Berlin.

Prinz, F. 1979. *Gründungsmythen und Sagenchronologie.* Munich.

Pritchard, D. 2003. "Athletics, Education and Participation in Classical Athens." *Sport and Festival in the Ancient Greek World* (eds. D. Phillips and D. Pritchard) 293–349. Swansea.

Pritchett, W. K. 1974. *The Greek State at War* I. Berkeley. Originally published as *Ancient Greek Military Practices.* 1971. Berkeley.

Pucci, P. 1987. *Odysseus Polutropos: Intertextual Readings in the Odyssey and the Iliad.* Ithaca.

Raaflaub, K. A., and Wallace, R. W. 2007. " 'People's Power' and Egalitarian Trends in Archaic Greece." *Origins of Democracy in Ancient Greece* (eds. K. Raaflaub et al.) 22–48. Berkeley.

Radt, S., ed. 1999. *Tragicorum Graecorum Fragmenta.* Vol. 4, *Sophocles.* 2nd ed. Göttingen.

Ragone, G. 1986. "La guerra meliaca e la struttura originaria della lega ionica in Vitruvio 4, 1, 3–6." *Rivista di filologia e di istruzione classica* 114:173–205.

Raubitschek, A. E. 1949. *Dedications from the Athenian Akropolis: A Catalogue of the Inscriptions of the Sixth and Fifth Centuries B.C.* Cambridge, MA.

Redfield, J. M. 1975. *Nature and Culture in the Iliad: The Tragedy of Hector.* Chicago.

Regenbogen, O. 1961. "Die Geschichte von Solon und Krösus. Eine Studie zur Geistesgeschichte des 5. und 6. Jahrhunderts." *Kleine Schriften,* 101–124. Munich. Originally published in *Das humanistische Gymnasium* 41:1–20 (1930). Reprinted 1962, in *Herodot. Eine Auswahl aus der neueren Forschung* (ed. W. Marg) 375–403, Munich.

Reinach, S. 1922. *Répertoire de peintures grecques et romaines.* Paris.

Reinach, T. 1908. "ΠΑΡΘΕΝΩΝ." *Bulletin de correspondance hellénique* 32:499–513.

Rengakos, A. 2000. "Aristarchus and the Hellenistic Poets." *Seminari romani di cultura greca* 3:325–335.

Rhodes, P. J. 1981. *A Commentary on the Aristotelian Athenaion Politeia.* Oxford.

———. 1992. "The Delian League to 449 B.C." *Cambridge Ancient History* V (eds. D. M. Lewis et al.) 34–61. 2nd ed. Cambridge.

Richardson, N. J., ed. 1974. *The Homeric Hymn to Demeter.* Oxford.

———, ed. 1993. *The Iliad: A Commentary.* Vol. 6, *Books 21-24.* Cambridge.

Ridgway, B. S. 1977. *The Archaic Style in Greek Sculpture.* Princeton. Expanded and revised 2nd ed. 1993. Chicago.

———. 1992. "Images of Athena on the Akropolis." In Neils 1992:119–142.

Risch, E. 1954. "Der homerische Typus ἱππότα Νέστωρ und μητίετα Ζεύς." *Sprachgeschichte und Wortbedeutung. Festschrift Albert Debrunner gewidmet,* 389–397. Bern.

———. 1974. *Wortbildung der homerischen Sprache.* 2nd ed. Berlin.

Ritoók, 1993. "The Pisistratus Tradition and the Canonization of Homer." *Acta antiqua Academiae Scientiarum Hungaricae* 34:39–53.

Rizakis, A. D. 1995. *Achaïe.* Vol. 1, *Sources textuelles et histoire régionale.* Athens.

Robert, C. 1885. "Athena Skiras und die Skirophorien." *Hermes* 20:349–379.

———. 1920. *Die griechische Heldensage.* Vol. 2 of *Griechische Mythologie* (eds. L. Preller and C. Robert). 4th ed. Reprint 1967. Berlin.

Robert, L. 1938. *Études épigraphiques et philologiques.* Paris.

Robertson, N. 1978. "The Myth of the First Sacred War." *Classical Quarterly* N.S. 28:38–73.

———. 1983. "The Riddle of the Arrhephoria at Athens." *Harvard Studies in Classical Philology* 87:241–288.

———. 1985. "The Origin of the Panathenaea." *Rheinisches Museum für Philologie* N.S. 128:231–295.

———. 1987. "Government and Society at Miletus, 525–442 B.C." *Phoenix* 41:356–398.

———. 1988. "Melanthus, Codrus, Neleus, Caucon: Ritual Myth as Athenian History." *Greek, Roman and Byzantine Studies* 29:201–261.

———. 1996. "Athena's Shrines and Festivals." *Worshipping Athena* (ed. J. Neils) 27–77. Madison.

Rodenwaldt, G. 1912. "Votivpinax aus Mykenai." *Mitteilungen des Kaiserlich Deutschen Archäologischen Instituts. Athenische Abteilung* 37:129–140.

Roebuck, C. 1955. "The Early Ionian League." *Classical Philology* 50:26–40.

Rohde, E. 1886. "Σκίρα. ἐπὶ Σκίρῳ ἱεροποιία." *Hermes* 21:116–125. Reprinted 1901, in *Kleine Schriften* II, 370–380. Tübingen.

Rose, H. J. 1954. "Maiden and Mother?" Review of Kerényi 1952. *Classical Review* N.S. 4:139–140.

Roux, G. 1984. "Pourquoi le Parthénon?" *Comptes rendus de l'Académie des Inscriptions et Belles-Lettres* 128:301–317.

Roy, J. 1997. "The *Perioikoi* of Elis." *The Polis as an Urban Centre and as a Political Community* (ed. M. Hansen) 282–320. Copenhagen.

Ruijgh, C. J. 1967. *Études sur la grammaire et le vocabulaire du grec mycénien.* Amsterdam.

———. 1985. Review of A. Heubeck and S. West, *Omero, Odissea* I (Milan 1981). *Mnemosyne* 4th S. 38:170–176.

———. 1988. "Le Mycénien et Homère." *Linear B: A 1984 Survey* (eds. A. Davies and Y. Duhoux) 143–190. Louvain-la-Neuve.

Rutherford, I., and Irvine, J. 1988. "The Race in the Athenian Oschophoria and an Oschophoricon by Pindar." *Zeitschrift für Papyrologie und Epigraphik* 72:43–51.

Sadurska, A. 1964. *Les tables iliaques.* Warsaw.

Sakellariou, M. B. 1958. *La migration grecque en Ionie.* Athens.

———. 1984. "La migration des Aenianes." *Aux origines de l'hellénisme: la Crète et la Grèce. Hommage à Henri van Effenterre,* 173–180. Paris.

———. 1990. *Between Memory and Oblivion: The Transmission of Early Greek Historical Traditions.* Athens.

Sánchez, P. 2001. *L'Amphictionie des Pyles et de Delphes: recherches sur son rôle historique, des origines au IIe siècle de notre ère.* Stuttgart.

Sancisi-Weerdenburg, H. 2001. "Yaunā by the Sea and across the Sea." *Ancient Perceptions of Greek Ethnicity* (ed. I. Malkin) 323–346. Center for Hellenic Studies Colloquia 5. Washington, DC.

Schachermeyr, F. 1955. *Die ältesten Kulturen Griechenlands.* Stuttgart.

Scheer, T. S. 2000. *Die Gottheit und ihr Bild: Untersuchungen zur Funktion griechischer Kultbilder in Religion und Politik.* Munich.

Scheid, J., and Svenbro, J. 1994. *Le métier de Zeus: mythe du tissage et du tissu dans le monde gréco-romain.* Paris. Trans. by C. Volk as *The Craft of Zeus: Myths of Weaving and Fabric.* 1996. Cambridge, MA.

Schindler, H. 1972. *Das Wurzelnomen im arischen und griechischen.* PhD diss., University of Würzburg.

Schmaltz, B. 1997. "Die Parthenos des Phidias—zwischen Kult und Repräsentanz." In Hoepfner 1997:25–30.

Schmid, W. 1929. *Geschichte der griechischen Literatur* I-1. Munich.

Schmitt, R. 1967. *Dichtung und Dichtersprache in indogermanischer Zeit.* Wiesbaden.

Schütrumpf, E. 1991. *Aristoteles, Politik.* Vol. 2, *Books 2 and 3.* Berlin.

Schwab, K. A. 1996. "Parthenon East Metope XI: Heracles and the Gigantomachy." *American Journal of Archaeology* 100:81–90.

Schwartz, E. 1899. "Tyrtaeos." *Hermes* 34:428–468.

Schwartz, J. 1960. *Pseudo-Hesiodeia: Recherches sur la composition, la diffusion et la disparition ancienne d'oeuvres attribuées à Hésiode.* Leiden.

Schwyzer, E. 1923. *Dialectorum Graecarum exempla epigraphica potiora.* Leipzig. Reprint 1960, Hildesheim.

Scott, J. A. 1911. "Athenian Interpolations in Homer. Part I. Internal Evidence." *Classical Philology* 6:419–428.

———. 1914. "Athenian Interpolations in Homer. Part II. External Evidence." *Classical Philology* 9:395–409.

———. 1921. *The Unity of Homer.* Berkeley. Reprint 1965, New York.

Séchan, L., and Lévêque, P. 1966. *Les grandes divinités de la Grèce.* Paris.

Seeck, O. 1887. *Die Quellen der Odyssee.* Berlin.

Segal, C. 1994. *Singers, Heroes, and Gods in the Odyssey.* Ithaca.

Seidensticker, B. 1978. "Archilochus and Odysseus." *Greek, Roman and Byzantine Studies* 19:5–22.

Sens, A. 1997. *Theocritus, Dioscuri (Idyll 22).* Göttingen.

Sergent, B. 1982. "Les Pyliens à Athènes (XIIe siècle av. J.-C.)." *Revue des études anciennes* 84:5–28.

Settis, S. 1971. "Su un kouros da Medma." *Archeologia classica* 23:52–76.

Sfyroeras, P. n.d. "The Achaean Wall." Unpublished.

Shapiro, H. A. 1983. "Painting, Politics, and Genealogy: Peisistratus and the Neleids." *Ancient Greek Art and Iconography* (ed. W. Moon) 87–96. Madison.

———. 1986. "The Attic Deity Basile." *Zeitschrift für Papyrologie und Epigraphik* 63:134–136.

———. 1989. *Art and Cult under the Tyrants in Athens.* Mainz am Rhein.

———. 1995. "The Cult of Heroines: Kekrops' Daughters." *Pandora: Women in Classical Greece* (ed. E. Reeder) 39–48. Princeton.

Shear, T. L. 1936. "The Campaign of 1935." *Hesperia* 5:1–42.

Shipley, G. 1987. *A History of Samos, 800–188 BC.* Oxford.

Siapkas, J. 2003. *Heterological Ethnicity: Conceptualizing Identities in Ancient Greece.* Uppsala.

Simon, E. 1953. *Opfernde Götter.* Berlin.

———. 1983. *Festivals of Attica: An Archaeological Commentary.* Madison.

———. 1997. "An Interpretation of the Nike Temple Parapet." *The Interpretation of Architectural Sculpture in Greece and Rome* (ed. D. Buitron-Oliver) 127–143. Hanover, NH and London.

Simpson, R. Hope. 1965. *A Gazeteer and Atlas of Mycenaean Sites.* London.

Simpson, R. Hope, and Lazenby, J. F. 1970. *The Catalogue of the Ships in Homer's Iliad.* Oxford.

Smith, J. D. 1980. "Old Indian: The Two Sanskrit Epics." *Traditions of Heroic and Epic Poetry* I (ed. A. Hatto) 48–78. London.

Snell, B. 1931. Review of J. Böhme, *Die Seele und das Ich im homerischen Epos* (Berlin 1929). *Gnomon* 7:74–86.

Snodgrass, A. 1977. *Archaeology and the Rise of the Greek State: An Inaugural Lecture.* Cambridge.

———. 1988. "The Archaeology of the Hero." *Annali del Istituto universitario orientale di Napoli, Dipartimento di studi del mondo classico e del Mediterraneo antico, Sezione di archeologia e storia antica* 10:19–26.

———. 1998. *Homer and the Artists: Text and Picture in Early Greek Art.* Cambridge.

———. 2003. "Another Early Reader of Pausanias?" *Journal of Hellenic Studies* 123:187–189.

Solmsen, F. 1909. *Beiträge zur griechischen Wortforschung.* Strassburg.

Sordi, M. 1958. *La lega tessala fino ad Alessandro Magno.* Rome.

Sourvinou-Inwood, C. 1973. "Movements of Populations in Attica at the End of the Mycenaean Period." *Bronze Age Migrations in the Aegean: Archaeological and Linguistic Problems in Greek Prehistory* (eds. R. Crossland and A. Birchall) 215–225. London.

———. 1985. "Altars with Palm-Trees, Palm-Trees and *Parthenoi*." *Bulletin of the Institute of Classical Studies* 32:125–146.

———. 1987. "A Series of Erotic Pursuits: Images and Meanings." *Journal of Hellenic Studies* 107:131–153.

———. 1997. "Reconstructing Change: Ideology and the Eleusinian Mysteries." *Inventing Ancient Culture: Historicism, Periodization, and the Ancient World* (eds. M. Golden and P. Toohey) 132–164. London.

———. 2003. "Festival and Mysteries: Aspects of the Eleusinian Cult." *Greek Mysteries: The Archaeology and Ritual of Ancient Greek Secret Cults* (ed. M. Cosmopoulos) 25–49. London.

Spaeth, B. S. 1991. "Athenians and Eleusinians in the West Pediment of the Parthenon." *Hesperia* 60:331–362.

Stanford, W. B., ed. 1959. *The Odyssey of Homer*. 2nd ed. Reprints with corrections 1961, 1964, and 1965. London.

Stanley, K. 1993. *The Shield of Homer: Narrative Structure in the Iliad*. Princeton.

Stanton, G. R. 1990. *Athenian Politics c. 800–500 BC: A Sourcebook*. London.

Steets, C. 1993. *The Sun Maiden's Wedding: An Indo-European Sunrise/Sunset Myth*. PhD diss., University of California at Los Angeles.

Stenger, J. 2006. "Narrative Unbestimmtheit in der Odyssee. Ein Beitrag zu den Konventionen homerischer Epik." *Geschichte und Fiktion in der homerischen Odyssee* (ed. A. Luther) 217–238. Munich.

Stevens, G. P. 1940. *The Setting of the Periclean Parthenon. Hesperia* Supplement 3. Princeton.

Stubbings, F. 1975. "The Expansion of the Mycenaean Civilization." *Cambridge Ancient History* II-2 (eds. I. E. S. Edwards et al.) 165–187. 3rd ed. Cambridge.

———. 1975a. "The Recession of Mycenaean Civilization." *Cambridge Ancient History* II-2 (eds. I. E. S. Edwards et al.) 338–358. 3rd ed. Cambridge.

Stylianou, P. J. 1983. "Thucydides, the Panionian Festival, and the Ephesia (III 104), Again." *Historia* 32:245–249.

Sukthankar, V. S. 1936/1937. "The Bhṛgus and the Bhārata: A Text-Historical Study." *Annals of the Bhandarkar Oriental Research Institute* 18:1–76.

Sulimirski, T., and Taylor, T. 1991. "The Scythians." *Cambridge Ancient History* III-2 (eds. J. Boardman and N. G. L Hammond) 547–590. 2nd ed. Cambridge.

Svenbro, J. 1988. *Phrasikleia: anthropologie de la lecture en Grèce ancienne*. Paris. Trans. by J. Lloyd as *Phrasikleia: An Anthropology of Reading in Ancient Greece*. 1993. Ithaca.

Taita, J. 1999. "Un' anfizionia ad Olimpia? Un bilancio sulla questione nell' interpretazione storiografica moderna." *Storiografia ed erudizione: scritti in onore di Ida Calabi Limentani* (ed. D. Foraboschi) 149–186. Bologna.

Talamo, C. 1973. "Per la storia di Colofone in età arcaica." *La parola del passato: rivista di studi antichi* 28:343–375.

Taplin, O. 1992. *Homeric Soundings: The Shaping of the Iliad.* Oxford.

Tarditi, G. 1983. "Tirteo: momenti di una campagna di guera." *Aevum* 57:3–13.

Tarrant, D. 1960. "Greek Metaphors of Light." *Classical Quarterly* N.S. 10:181–187.

Tausend, K. 1992. *Amphiktyonie und Symmachie: Formen zwischenstaatlicher Beziehungen im archaischen Griechenland.* Stuttgart.

Thieme, P. 1938. "ἀριδείκετος, ἐρικύδης und Genossen." *Der Fremdling im R̥gveda. Eine Studie über die Bedeutung der Worte ari, arya, aryaman und ārya,* 159–168. Leipzig. Reprinted 1968, in *Indogermanische Dichtersprache* (ed. R. Schmitt), 53–60, Darmstadt.

Thomas, R. 1989. *Oral Tradition and Written Record in Classical Athens.* Cambridge.

Thompson, H. A. 1961. "The Panathenaic Festival." *Archäologischer Anzeiger. Beiblatt zum Jahrbuch des Deutschen Archäologisches Instituts* 76:224–231.

Thornton, A. 1970. *People and Themes in Homer's Odyssey.* Dunedin and London.

———. 1984. *Homer's Iliad: Its Composition and the Motif of Supplication.* Göttingen.

Tod, M. N. 1946. *A Selection of Greek Historical Inscriptions to the End of the Fifth Century B.C.* 2nd. ed. Oxford.

Toepffer, J. 1889. *Attische Genealogie.* Berlin. Reprint 1973, New York.

Traill, J. S. 1975. *The Political Organization of Attica: A Study of the Demes, Trittyes, and Phylai, and Their Representation in the Athenian Council.* Princeton.

Travlos, J. 1971. *Pictorial Dictionary of Ancient Athens.* London.

Treu, M. 1971. "Der Euripideische Erechtheus als Zeugnis seiner Zeit." *Chiron* 1:115–131.

Tsagarakis, O. 2000. *Studies in Odyssey 11.* Stuttgart.

Tsountas, C. 1888. "Ἀνασκαφαὶ Μυκηνῶν τοῦ 1886." Πρακτικὰ τῆς ἐν Ἀθήναις Ἀρχαιολογικῆς Ἑταιρείας τοῦ ἔτους 1886, 59–79.

Valmin, M. N. 1930. *Études topographiques sur la Messénie ancienne.* Lund.

Van Effenterre, H. 1977. "Solon et la terre d'Éleusis." *Revue internationale des droits de l'antiquité* 24:91–130.

Van Nooten, B. A., and Holland, G. B. 1994. *Rig Veda: A Metrically Restored Text with Introduction and Notes.* Cambridge, MA.

Vanschoonwinkel, J. V. 1991. *L'Égée et la Méditerranée orientale à la fin du deux-ième millénaire. Témoignages archéologiques et sources écrites.* Louvain-La-Neuve.

Van Sickle, J. 1980. "The Book-Roll and Some Conventions of the Poetic Book." *Arethusa* 13:5–42.

Van Wees, H. 1999. "Tyrtaeus' *Eunomia:* Nothing to Do with the Great Rhetra." *Sparta: New Perspectives* (eds. S. Hodkinson and A. Powell) 1–41. London.

Ventris, M., and Chadwick, J. 1956. *Documents in Mycenaean Greek.* Cambridge.

———. 1973. *Documents in Mycenaean Greek* (ed. J. Chadwick). 2nd ed. Cambridge.

Verbanck-Piérard, A. 1988. "Images et piété en Grèce classique: la contribu-tion de l'iconographie céramique à l'étude de la religion grecque." *Kernos* 1:223–233.

Vermeule, E. T. 1960. "The Mycenaeans in Achaea." *American Journal of Archaeology* 64:1–21.

Vetta, M. 2003. "L'epos di Pilo e Omero. Breve storia di una saga regionale." *ΡΥΣΜΟΣ. Studi di poesia, metrica e musica greca* (ed. R. Nicolai) 13–33. Rome.

Vian, F. 1952. *La guerre des Géants: le mythe avant l'époque hellénistique.* Paris.

Visser, E. 1997. *Homers Katalog der Schiffe.* Stuttgart.

Vox, O. 1984. *Solone autoritratto.* Padua.

Wace, A. J. B. 1949. *Mycenae. An Archaeological History and Guide.* Princeton. Reprint 1964, New York.

———. 1951. "Mycenae 1950." *Journal of Hellenic Studies* 71:254–257.

———. 1956. "The Last Days of Mycenae." *The Aegean and the Near East: Studies Presented to Hetty Goldman* (ed. S. Weinberg) 126–135. Locust Valley, NY.

Wackernagel, J. 1877. "Zum homerischen Dual." *Zeitschrift für vergleichende Sprachforschung* 23:302–310. Reprinted 1955, in *Kleine Schriften* I, 538–546, Göttingen.

———. 1889. *Das Dehnungsgesetz der griechischen Composita.* Basel. Reprinted 1955, in *Kleine Schriften* II, 897–961, Göttingen.

———. 1891. Review of P. Cauer, ed., *Iliad* 1–12 (Leipzig 1890). *Berliner philologische Wochenschrift* 11:5–9, 37–43, 1061–1065.

———. 1916. *Sprachliche Untersuchungen zu Homer.* Reprint 1970. Göttingen.

Wackernagel, J., and Debrunner, A. 1957. *Altindische Grammatik.* Vol. 2, pt. 2, *Die Nominalsuffixe.* Göttingen.

Wade-Gery, H. T. 1944. "The Spartan Rhetra in Plutarch, *Lycurgus VI*." *Classical Quarterly* 38:1–9, 115–126. Reprinted 1958, in *Essays in Greek History*, 54–85, Oxford.

———. 1948. "What Happened in Pylos?" *American Journal of Archaeology* 52:115–118.

———. 1952. *The Poet of the Iliad.* Cambridge.

Walcot, P. 1963. "Hesiod and the Law." *Symbolae Osloenses* 38:5–21.

———. 1979. "Cattle Raiding, Heroic Tradition, and Ritual: The Greek Evidence." *History of Religions* 18:326–351.

Walde, A., and Hofmann, J. B. 1938–1954. *Lateinisches etymologisches Wörterbuch.* 3rd ed. Heidelberg.

Walton, F. R. 1952. "Athens, Eleusis, and the Homeric Hymn to Demeter." *Harvard Theological Review* 45:105–114.

Ward, D. 1968. *The Divine Twins: An Indo-European Myth in Germanic Tradition.* Berkeley.

———. 1970. "The Separate Functions of the Indo-European Divine Twins." *Myth and Law Among the Indo-Europeans: Studies in Indo-European Comparative Mythology* (ed. J. Puhvel) 193–202. Berkeley.

Watkins, C. 1963. "Preliminaries to a Historical and Comparative Analysis of the Syntax of the Old Irish Verb." *Celtica* 6:1–49.

———. 1970. *Indogermanische Grammatik.* Vol. 3, pt. 1, *Geschichte der indogermanischen Verbalflexion.* Heidelberg.

———. 1976. "Observations on the 'Nestor's Cup' Inscription." *Harvard Studies in Classical Philology* 80:25–40.

Weber, L. 1927. "Die attische Interpolation im Schiffskatalog." *Wiener Studien. Zeitschrift für klassische Philologie* 45:137–152.

Webster, T. B. L. 1964. *From Mycenae to Homer.* 2nd ed. London.

Węcowski, M. 2002. "Homer and the Origins of the Symposion." *Omero tremila anni dopo* (ed. F. Montanari) 625–637. Rome.

Weinberg, G. D., and Weinberg, S. S. 1956. "Arachne of Lydia at Corinth." *The Aegean and the Near East: Studies Presented to Hetty Goldman* (ed. S. Weinberg) 262–267. Locust Valley, NY.

Welcker, F. 1832. "Die Homerischen Phäaken und die Inseln der Seligen." *Rheinisches Museum für Philologie* 1:219ff. Reprinted 1845, in *Kleine Schriften* II, 1–79, Bonn. Reprint 1973, Osnabrück.

Welles, C. B. 1934. *Royal Correspondence in the Hellenistic Period: A Study in Greek Epigraphy.* New Haven. Reprint 1974, Chicago.

West, M. L. 1966. *Hesiod, Theogony: Edited with Prolegomena and Commentary.* Oxford.

———. 1970. "Bemerkungen zu Versinschriften." *Zeitschrift für Papyrologie und Epigraphik* 6:171–174.

———. 1970a. "Archilochus and Tyrtaeus." Review of C. Prato, *Tyrtaeus* (Rome 1968). *Classical Review* N.S. 20:149–151.

———. 1974. *Studies in Greek Elegy and Iambus.* Berlin.

———. 1975. "Cynaethus' Hymn to Apollo." *Classical Quarterly* N.S. 25:161–170.

———. 1978. *Hesiod, Works and Days: Edited with Prolegomena and Commentary.* Oxford.

———. 1982. *Greek Metre.* Oxford.

———. 1985. *The Hesiodic Catalogue of Women: Its Nature, Structure, and Origins.* Oxford.

———. 1993. "Simonides Redivivus." *Zeitschrift für Papyrologie und Epigraphik* 98:1–14.

———. 1995. "The Date of the *Iliad*." *Museum Helveticum* 52:203–219.

———. 1999. "The Invention of Homer." *Classical Quarterly* N.S. 49:364–382.

———. 2000. "The Gardens of Alcinous and the Oral Dictated Text Theory." *Acta antiqua Academiae Scientiarum Hungaricae* 40:479–488.

———. 2001. "Homer durch Jahrtausende: Wie die Ilias zu uns gelangte." *Troia: Traum und Wirklichkeit* (eds. J. Latacz et al.) 108–111. Stuttgart.

———. 2003. "*Iliad* and *Aithiopis*." *Classical Quarterly* N.S. 53:1–14.

West, S., ed. 1967. *The Ptolemaic Papyri of Homer.* Cologne.

———. 1994. "Nestor's Bewitching Cup." *Zeitschrift für Papyrologie und Epigraphik* 101:9–15.

Whitman, C. H. 1958. *Homer and the Heroic Tradition.* Cambridge, MA.

Whitman, C. H., and Scodel, R. 1981. "Sequence and Simultaneity in Iliad N, Ξ, and O." *Harvard Studies in Classical Philology* 85:1–15.

Wiegand, T., and Schrader, H. 1904. *Priene. Ergebnisse der Ausgrabungen und Untersuchungen in den Jahren 1895–1898*. Berlin.

Wikander, S. 1947. "Pāṇḍavasagan och Mahābhāratas mytiska förutsättningar." *Religion och Bibel, Nathan Söderblom-sällskapets Årsbok* 6:27–39.

———. 1957. "Nakula et Sahadeva." *Orientalia Suecana* 6:66–96.

Wilamowitz-Moellendorff, U. von. 1880. *Aus Kydathen*. Berlin.

———. 1884. *Homerische Untersuchungen*. Berlin.

———. 1885. *Lectiones Epigraphicae*. Göttingen.

———. 1895. *Euripides, Herakles* I. 2nd ed. Berlin. Reprint 1959 and 1969, Darmstadt.

———. 1896. "Die Amphiktionie von Kalaurea." *Nachrichten von der Königlichen Gesellschaft der Wissenschaften zu Göttingen. Philologische historische Klasse*, 158–170. Reprinted 1971, in *Kleine Schriften* V-1, 100–113 (2nd ed.), Amsterdam.

———. 1906. "Panionion." *Sitzungsberichte der Königlichen Preussischen Akademie der Wissenschaften. Philosophisch-historische Klasse*, 38–57. Reprinted 1971, in *Kleine Schriften* V-1, 128–151 (2nd ed.), Amsterdam.

———. 1906a. "Über die ionische Wanderung." *Sitzungsberichte der Königlichen Preussischen Akademie der Wissenschaften. Philosophisch-historische Klasse*, 59–79. Reprinted 1971, in *Kleine Schriften* V-1, 152–176 (2nd ed.), Amsterdam.

———. 1926. "Pherekydes." *Sitzungsberichte der Preussischen Akademie der Wissenschaften. Philosophisch-historische Klasse*, 125–146. Reprinted 1971, in *Kleine Schriften* V-2, 127–156 (2nd ed.), Amsterdam.

———. 1931, 1932. *Der Glaube der Hellenen* I, II. Berlin.

———. 2006. *Homers Ilias (Vorlesung WS 1887/1888 Göttingen). Nach der Mitschrift von stud. phil. Alfred Züricher (1867–1895) aus Bern; herausgegeben und kommentiert von Paul Dräger. Mit einem Geleitwort von Walter Burkert: Der Meister in seiner Werkstatt: Homer-Vorlesung bei Wilamowitz*. Hildesheim.

Willcock, M. M. 1964. "Mythological Paradeigma in the *Iliad*." *Classical Quarterly* N.S. 14:141–154.

———. 1976. *A Companion to the Iliad*. Chicago.

Wilson, D. F. 2002. *Ransom, Revenge, and Heroic Identity in the Iliad.* Cambridge.

———. 2005. "Demodokos' '*Iliad*' and Homer's." *Approaches to Homer: Ancient and Modern* (ed. R. Rabel) 1–20. Swansea.

Wiseman, T. P. 1995. *Remus: A Roman Myth.* Cambridge.

Wolf, F. A. 1795. *Prolegomena ad Homerum.* Halle. Trans. by A. Grafton et al. as *Prolegomena to Homer, 1795.* 1985. Princeton.

Wuilleumier, P. 1939. *Tarente, des origines à la conquête romaine.* Paris.

Wycherley, R. E. 1960. "Neleion." *Annual of the British School at Athens* 55:60–66.

Young, R. S. 1939. *Late Geometric Graves and a Seventh Century Well in the Agora. Hesperia* Supplement 2. Athens.

Zell, K. 1826. *Ferienschriften* I. Freiburg im Breisgau.

Ziehen, L. 1904. "Die Bedeutung von προθύειν." *Rheinisches Museum* 59:391–406.

PLATES

Plates 1-2. Fragments of two terracotta plaques
from same mold: girl spinning, seated. c. 500 BC.
Athens, Acropolis Museum, no. 1329 (Plate 1); no.
1330 (Plate 2). [For discussion, see note 3.32.]

Plate 2.

Plate 3. Attic red-figure hydria: woman spin-
ning, seated. Clio Painter, c. 475–425 BC. London,
British Museum, E215.

[For discussion, see note 3.32.]

Plate 4. Attic red-figure cup: woman spinning, seated. Euaion Painter, c. 475–425 BC. Berlin, Staatliche Museen, Antikensammlung, 31426. [For discussion, see note 3.32.]

Plate 5. Attic black-figure lekythos: rollout drawing of figural scene, central portion. Attributed to the Amasis Painter, c. 575–525 BC. New York, Metropolitan Museum of Art, Fletcher Fund (1931), 31.11.10.

[For discussion, see note 3.32.]

Plates 6-7. Fragments of two terracotta plaques from same mold: Athena, with polos crown, holding phiale. c. 500 BC. Athens, Acropolis Museum, no. 1337 (Plate 6); no. 1338 (Plate 7).

[For discussion, see note 3.33.]

Plate 7.

Plate 8. Attic black-figure kalpis: seated Athena with phiale, helmet. Nikoxenos Painter, c. 550–500 BC. Once on art market in Rome, now lost. [For discussion, see note 3.33.]

a

b

c

Plate 9. Attic white-ground lekythos: seated Athena with phiale, spear. Athena Painter, c. 500–450 BC. Athens, National Archaeological Museum, no. 1138. (a) detail of seated Athena; (b and c) full view of scene.

[For discussion, see note 3.33.]

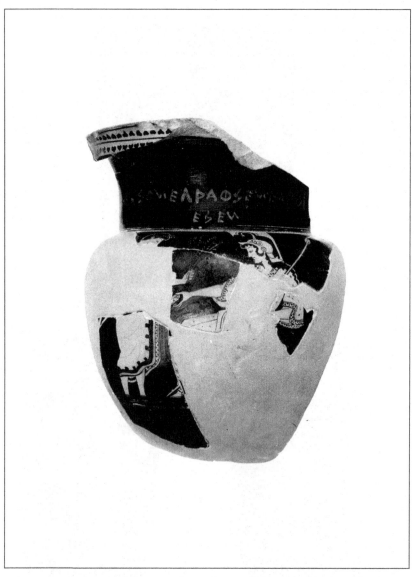

Plates 10-11. Attic red-figure column krater (fragments): seated Athena with phiale. Myson, c. 500–450 BC. Athens, National Archaeological Museum, Acropolis Collection, no. 2.806. Plate 10: Photo of reconstructed vase; Plate 11: drawing of fragments. [For discussion, see note 3.33.]

Plate 11.

839

Plate 12. Laconian hero relief from Chrysapha, near Sparta: enthroned male with kantharos and female with veil and pomegranate; at right, two figures bring votive gifts. c. 540 BC. Berlin, Staatliche Museen, Antikensammlung, no. Sk 731. [For discussion, see notes 3.112 and 4.181.]

IMAGE CREDITS

Plates 1-2 and 6-7: Hellenic Ministry of Culture / Archaeological Receipts Fund (Acropolis Museum, Athens).

Plate 3: Image © The Trustees of the British Museum.

Plate 4: Bildarchiv Preussischer Kulturbesitz / Art Resource, NY.

Plate 5: Image © The Metropolitan Museum of Art.

Plate 8: Drawing after E. Gerhard, ed., *Auserlesene griechische Vasenbilder: Hauptsächlich etruskischen Fundorts,* Vol. 4, pt. 1 (Berlin, 1840) pl. 242, no. 1.

Plates 9-10: Hellenic Ministry of Culture / Archaeological Receipts Fund (National Archaeological Museum, Athens).

Plate 11: Drawing after B. Graef and E. Langlotz, *Die antiken Vasen von der Akropolis zu Athen* II-2 (Berlin, 1909) pl. 72.

Plate 12: Bildarchiv Preussischer Kulturbesitz / Art Resource, NY.

MAPS

Map 1. By Jill Curry Robbins, after a map by Alexander Herda.

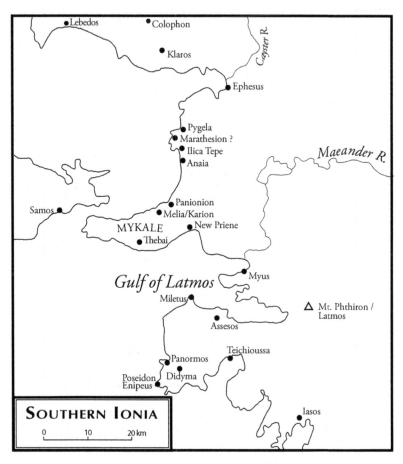

Map 2. (Detail of Map 1.) By Jill Curry Robbins, after a map by Alexander
Herda.

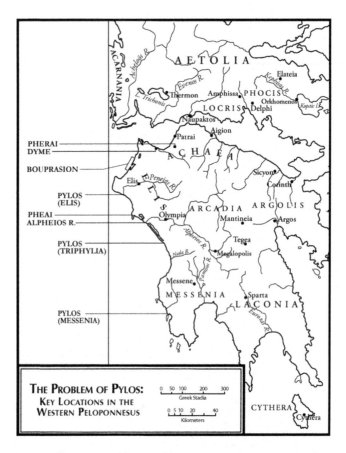

Map 3. By Jill Curry Robbins, after Pausanias, *Description of Greece.*
Loeb Classical Library. Cambridge, MA: Harvard University Press,
1918–1935, vol. 5, pl. 1.

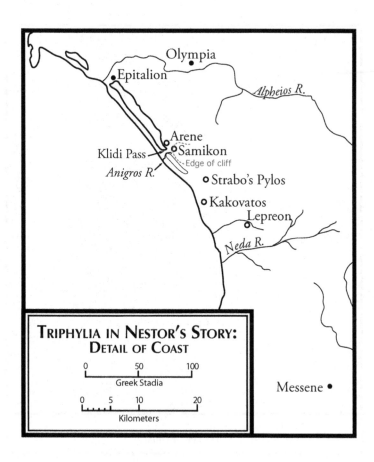

Map 4. (Detail of Map 3.) By Jill Curry Robbins.

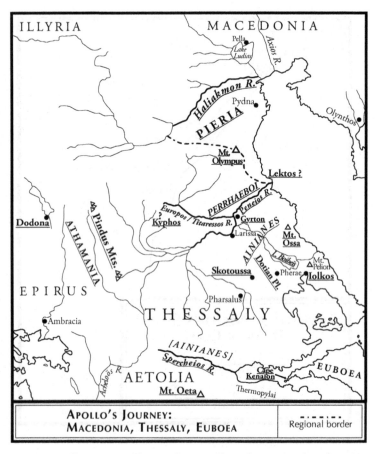

Map 5. By Jill Curry Robbins, after Strabo, *The Geography of Strabo*.
Loeb Classical Library. London: W. Heinemann, 1917, vol. 4, map 7.

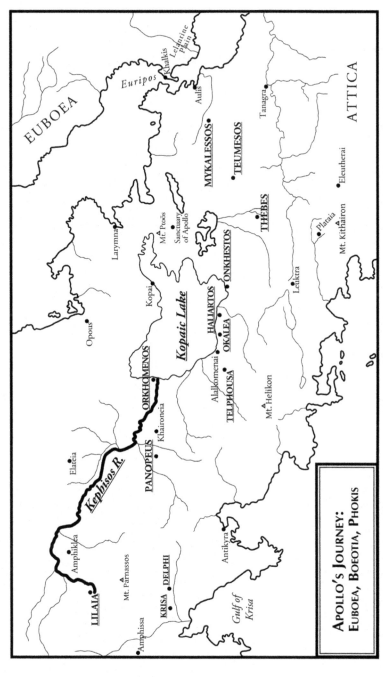

Map 6. By Jill Curry Robbins, after Pausanias, *Description of Greece.* Loeb Classical Library. Cambridge, MA: Harvard University Press, 1918–1935, vol. 5, pl. 9.

APOLLO'S JOURNEY: EUBOEA, BOEOTIA, PHOKIS

INDEX OF SOURCES

Greek Literature

A

Acts of the Apostles
19.35, 353n24

Aelian
Varia Historia, 1.24, 757; 4.5,
73n159; 13.14, 762; 13.42,
695n90

Aeschines
Against Ctesiphon, 107–113, 689n72;
185, 478n273

Ps.-Aeschines, *Epistle* 10.3–5, 391n79

Aeschylus
Agamemnon, 343–344, 170
Eumenides, 736–738, 401; 997–1002,
400; 999, 400
Libation Bearers, 1036–1037,
362n42
Persians, 797, 171n67

Alcaeus, fr. 44.6–8 LP, 611n209; fr. 70
LP, 611n209; fr. 364 LP, 336; fr.
428 LP, 451n207

Alcibiades, West *IEG* fr., 734

Alcman, fr. 2 Page, 73n158; fr. 8
Diehl, 96; fr. 21 Page, 79n180; fr.
81 Page, 680n59; fr. 148 Garzya,
79n178

Amelesagoras
FGrHist 330: F 1, 467n247

Anacreon, fr. 106 Page, 99

Andocides
On the Mysteries, 111, 431n166, 498

Andron
FGrHist 10: F 13, 419n142

Androtion
FGrHist 324: F 70, 418n140

Antigonus of Karystos
Collection of Paradoxical Stories, 12,
467n247

Antimachus, fr. 27, 757; fr. 28, 757

Apollodorus
FGrHist 244: F 334, 769

Ps.-Apollodorus, 1.5.1, 487; 1.6.1,
337; 1.6.1–2, 248n145; 1.6.2,
495; 1.7.7, 337; 1.9.7, 249n147;
1.9.9, 11n4, 13, 14, 19n23, 35n60;
1.9.11, 19n23, 232n133, 252n149;
1.9.12, 20nn25–26, 231n131,
232n133; 1.9.15, 147n44; 1.9.16,
19n23; 1.9.27, 34n57; 2.2.2,
20n26, 231n131; 2.7.2, 108n6,
112n12; 3.1.3–4, 287n187; 3.5.5,
239n139; 3.8.1, 758; 3.10.3, 96;
3.10.4, 147n44; 3.10.7, 80n180,

849

Greek Inscriptions

Sanskrit

Latin

Other Languages

INDEX OF SUBJECTS

Epikaste: occurrence of in catalogue of heroines in *Odyssey* 11, 241; place of in bipartite structure of catalogue of heroines in *Odyssey* 11, 241n141, 302, 303, 310, 312

epískuros ballgame, 435n174

Erechtheum: earlier structures on site of, 411; identification of questioned, 410, 455n215; Poseidon Erechtheus worshipped in, 412, 415n130, 445; snake in, 469n249; temple of Athena not in, 408–10, 410n120, 469n249; tokens of contest between Athena and Poseidon in, 412, 413n128

Erechtheus: Athena's nursling in Athenian entry to Catalogue of Ships, 345n6, 394, 459, 460; Athenians called people/land of in Athenian entry to Catalogue of Ships, 445, 482; autochthonous birth of in Athenian entry to Catalogue of Ships, 394, 459, 462n236; autochthonous birth secondary in myth of, 460, 466n243; cult image of, 408, 408n112; duplicated by figure of Erichthonios, 458–75, 485n287; focus of Athenian entry to Catalogue of Ships, 394, 445, 482; moved from old temple of Athena to Erechtheum in post-Homeric era, 408, 411–13, 424, 432, 445, 447n196, 458, 464, 482, 484, 485n287; name of unclear, 460; own temple inhabited by in Athenian entry to Catalogue of Ships, 395, 409, 411, 445, 482; palace of corresponds to Phaeacian palace in

Odyssey, 345, 367n48; Poseidon predecessor of in Erechtheum, 412, 424, 445; priest of in Skira, 433, 438, 442; resemblance of to Demophoon in Athenian entry to Catalogue of Ships, 475–76; sacrifices to in Athenian entry to Catalogue of Ships, 394, 414n130, 445, 446; separated from Athena by identification with Poseidon, 413; Tellos's role in annexation of Eleusis shifted to, 430, 432; temple of Athena Polias in palace of, 343, 351, 355, 395, 408, 411; worshipped as Poseidon Erechtheus in Erechtheum, 412, 446n193; worshipped in Skira, 445, 447, 454, 464, 466n243, 486. *See also* Athena Polias and Erechtheus; daughters of Erechtheus; myth of Erechtheus's heroic death; Poseidon Erechtheus

Ereuthalion, 715, 716n134, 717n135

Erichthonios: affinity with snakes of, 461n232, 468; attested first in mid-sixth century BC, 463; autochthonous birth primary in myth of, 461; buried in Athena's temple, 458n226; Erechtheus duplicated by, 458–75, 485n287; founder of Panathenaia, 464, 466; Ge Kourotrophos associated with, 461n232, 473, 485n287, 508; mortality of modeled on that of Demophoon, 474; name of, 460, 469, 510; origins of in early sixth century BC, 474, 509; parallels with Demophoon of, 474–75; said to have set

mental aspect of Indo-European twin myth: duality central to, 94n225

Méntēs, Greek: active verb **ménō*, "incite" implied by, 25n37; equivalent to Greek *Méntōr*, 25

Mentor: Athena disguised as in *Odyssey*, 28, 28n39, 217, 220–24, 341; meaning of name of as common noun in French and English, 28n39; meaning of name of in Homer, 25–28, 220; name of in relation to name Nestor, 220–24

Méntōr, Greek: active verb **ménō*, "incite", implied by, 25n37

Messenian Wars: Pylians' descendants expelled from Peloponnesus at end of, 527

Metaneira, 474

Metapontion, 760

Methone, 760

mêtis, Greek: characteristic intelligence of Odysseus, 56, 57; in relation to Antilochus in chariot race of *Iliad* 23, 165; in relation to Nestor in chariot race of *Iliad* 23, 57, 164, 169n63; in relation to Nestor in *Iliad* generally, 166n57; opposition of with *bíē*, "strength", 169n62, 331

metonymic nominalism, 346n8

Meyer, Ernst: on location of Homeric Pylos, 658n12, 748–49

Miletus: Athenian foundation of, 517, 524, 527n22, 622, 646; claim of to original Kodrid myth, 523; diminished role of as leader of Ionian dodecapolis under

Lydians and Persians, 534–36; myth of foundation of, 34; relations with Chios of, 581n145; relations with Colophon of, 549; relations with Halicarnassus of, 589; relations with Myus of, 589, 625; relations with Priene of, 540n64, 549; relations with Samos of, 539, 581n145; rivalry of Ephesus with for leadership of Ionian dodecapolis, 528–41; role of in development of Homeric poems, 598, 599; role of in formation of Ionian dodecapolis, 515, 523, 549, 598; role of in Meliac War, 616–17; ruled by Neleid kings, 17, 282, 515, 517, 537. *See also* Neleids

Mimnermus, 525–28

Minyan cities in Triphylia, 721, 743, 774

Minyan river: in Nestor's story in *Iliad* 11, 654n4, 659, 660n20, 661, 743

Minyans, 712n127

Mitanni, 59, 67, 92n214, 102

Mnāsínoos, Greek: Polydeuces' son, 86

Molione, 108; as Indo-European twins, 111, 133, 162; differentiated by use of reins and whip in chariot race with Nestor, 133, 138, 143, 145, 156, 162, 177, 191; distinctions between, 111, 133; dual paternity of, 111, 608n204; Nestor defeated by in chariot race for Amarynkeus, 131; role of in Nestor's story in *Iliad* 11, 112; Siamese twins in Hesiod, 112n14

517, 584–88; role of in devel-
opment of Homeric poems,
592–94, 599; role of in forma-
tion of Ionian dodecapolis,
18, 515, 549, 645; survival of
after royal period in Miletus,
591n172

Neleus: city founder, 19, 237, 245;
corresponds to Nausithoos
in Phaeacian genealogy, 245,
276; name of equivalent to
Ionic *Neíleōs*, 30, 33, 517; name
of explained as short-form,
31n51; name of in relation to
name *Néstōr*, 29, 36; name of
interpreted as "pitiless" by
folk etymology, 36n64; names
of sons of, 13–15; Nestor's
horses hidden by in *Iliad* 11,
108; occurrence of in catalogue
of heroines in *Odyssey* 11, 235;
patronymic forms of name
of, 33n54; Pero daughter of,
35; separation of from twin
brother Pelias, 19, 235, 237; son
of Poseidon, 19, 319, 320; twelve
sons versus three sons of in
Homer, 9, 18, 228, 329, 515. *See
also* Neleus and Pelias; Neleus
and Basile

Neleus and Basile: cult of in Athens,
524n18, 536–39

Neleus and Pelias: twin myth of
contrasted with twin myth of
Amphion and Zethos in cata-
logue of heroines in *Odyssey* 11,
238, 304

néō, Greek (reconstructed):
compared with Indo-Iranian
násati (reconstructed), 90;
contained in name *Neíleōs*,

30; etymology of Greek *Néstōr*
in relation to, 37, 38, 182n78;
etymology of Greek *nóos* in rela-
tion to, 51; Homeric occurrence
of reconstructed in *Odyssey*
18.265, 37, 38; Odysseus's return
home context of in Homer, 46,
48; original meaning "bring
back to life" of, 46

néomai, Greek, 28, 29, 30, 37, 38, 39, 90

Nestor: Alcinous in relation to,
244–54, 258, 260, 328, 341, 350;
Alcinous in relation to in *nóstos*
of Odysseus, 244, 260, 264,
272–76; anger of, 218, 265n166;
Antilochus instructed by before
chariot race of *Iliad* 23, 131,
137–40, 143, 158; appearance
of in Agamemnon's dream in
Iliad 2, 159n52; battle of with
Epeians cast in terms of chariot
race, 651, 747–48; becomes
horseman first in battle with
Epeians, 107–11, 332, 657; cattle
raid of, 48, 106; cattle raid
versus battle in central myth
of, 89n206, 105; cup of in *Iliad*
11, 606–8, 657; Diomedes savior
of in *Iliad* 8, 196–205; Diomedes'
relationship with in *Iliad*,
194–99, 201 ; epic traditions of
in relation to Neleids of Miletus,
561, 586n155, 599–601, 604,
608n203, 611; epithet *Gerénios*
of, 12n6; focal point of cata-
logue of heroines in *Odyssey* 11,
228, 241, 276, 303, 304, 310, 328;
formation of name of, 16, 23, 36;
intelligence of contrasted with
Odysseus's intelligence, 193;
irony of Homeric role of, 16, 18,

Nestor and Athena; Nestor's cup inscription; Nestor's story in *Iliad* 11

Nestor and Alcinous: comparison between in their relationship to Ionian dodecapolis, 522n13; correspondences between, 244–54; correspondences between brothers of, 251–53; correspondences between fathers of, 245–46; correspondences between genealogies of, 247–54, 266, 341

Nestor and Athena: Alcinous and Arete in relation to, 346, 521

Nestor's cup inscription, 604–13, 641–42; date of, 610–13, 618; Homeric poems fully developed before, 559n109, 610; Nestor's cup in *Iliad* 11 in relation to, 606–8

Nestor's story in *Iliad* 11: Alcibiades in relation to, 733–45; conflict between Elis and Lepreon reflected in expanded version of, 723, 742; Eleian location of Pylos in relation to older version of, 671, 686; lack of realism in older version of, 656–57, 658, 661n27, 669, 686, 746, 750; Molione in, 112; Nestor's basic myth contained in, 105-130; paradigm for Patroclus, 119, 121, 135, 160, 746; precise geography in expanded version of, 657–63, 719, 743, 750; Pylos located in Triphylia in expanded version of, 658–61, 719, 722, 743. *See also* interpolations in Nestor's story in *Iliad* 11

Nilsson, Martin: on Athena's function as mother goddess, 347n10, 368n50, 462n237; on Athena's origins as Mycenaean war goddess, 396n87; on relationship between Erechtheus and Athena in early Athenian cult, 347

noéō, Greek: Pindar's use of in central myth of Dioskouroi, 87n202; semantics of *nóos* in relation to, 51, 191

nóos, Greek: as incitement as opposed to restraint in chariot race of *Iliad* 23, 164, 168n62, 169, 190, 331; diachronic and synchronic meanings of in Homer, 52n105, 169n62, 334; etymology of, 50; origins of in Indo-European twin myth, 169, 170; relation of to Antilochus in chariot race of *Iliad* 23, 165–68; relation of to Greek *nóstos*, 56; relation of to Homeric audience, 169; relation of to name *Néstōr*, 52, 58, 94, 164, 169, 190; relation of to Nestor in chariot race of *Iliad* 23, 164, 169n63; relation of to Nestor's *nóstos*, 190–93, 259; relation of to Phaeacians' function as home-bringers, 259; semantics of in relation to faculty of vision, 51; verbal root of, 51; verbal root of active in meaning, 51, 56;

nóstos, Greek, 28, 29, 39, 58; "return to life" underlying meaning of, 171; origins of in Indo-European twin myth, 170, 174–80

otrúnō, Greek: equivalent in meaning to virtual verb **ménō*, "incite," 25n37

oudé se lései and related Homeric formulas, 153, 157, 159n52,169, 207, 600

P

Paionids, 586n155, 637–40

Panathenaia: *apobátēs* race in, 466; Arrhephoria in relation to, 503–4; Epidaurians' sacrifices to Athena Polias and Erechtheus in relation to, 444n192, 465; Erichthonios founder of, 464, 465, 466; gods' victory in gigantomachy celebrated in, 403; Homeric poems' earliest performances at, 511; Homeric poems performed at, 553, 557, 557n106, 559n111, 576n137, 582; Homeric poems' earliest performances at, 511; meaning "festival of all Athenians" of, 465n242, 467n246; origins of as clan festival, 465, 511; *péplos* offered to Athena at, 355n28, 403, 466n244, 504; reorganization of in 566/5 BC, 399n91, 404n102, 406, 406n108, 451, 464, 465, 511

Panathenaic rule, 327n240, 557n106

Pāṇḍavas: archaic religious structure represented by divine fathers of, 63, 65n141; heroes of the *Mahābhārata*, 63; Nakula and Sahadeva youngest of, 63; sons of different gods, 63; Vedic twins fathers of youngest of, 63

Pandion: myth of four sons of, 431n167, 500

Pandrosos, 402n95, 467, 470n250, 471, 471n254, 472, 504. See *also* Aglauros and Pandrosos; Kekropids

Panegyris, 552, 559, 575, 576n135

Panionia: creation of Homeric poems at, 551, 556, 557–78, 603, 618, 632; games at, 577; history of after Ionian revolt, 622–24; performance of Homeric poems at ended by foreign pressures, 577–78; predecessor of, 615, 618; represented by Homeric Phaeacians, 522, 551, 555, 601n190; role of Milesian Neleids in foundation of, 17, 515

Panionic league: date of origin of, 18n21, 523, 528n27, 578, 578n141, 590n167, 613–15, 620; defensive role of in historical period, 552; development of in relation to development of Homeric poems, 620; Ionian name in relation to, 620n238, 644; Meliac War in relation to, 613–15. See *also* Dodecapolis, Ionian

Panionion: date of foundation of, 542, 549, 549n90; meeting place of Panionic league, 535, 619; site of, 542, 549n90

Panopeus, 711, 712

Panyassis, 529, 621

Parthenon: Athena a war goddess in, 401–3, 406; Athena's relationship to Zeus featured in sculptures of, 402; name of, 401, 504; predecessors on site of, 406, 497–98

heroines in *Odyssey* 11, 9, 229; wooed by Melampus and Bias, 20, 229; wooing of in relation to wooing of Helen in catalogue of heroines in *Odyssey* 11, 229–33, 289, 295

Perpetual fire in Greek temples and prytaneia, 362. *See also* image of Athena Polias in Athens: perpetual fire next to

Perrhaiboi, 706, 707–8

Persians, 534–36, 552n95, 622

Phaeacians: catalogue of heroines in *Odyssey* 11 in relation to, 242; Corcyraeans identified with in post-Homeric tradition, 256n158, 258n161; created by *Odyssey* for *nóstos* of Odysseus, 254–57, 263n165, 350; hidden identity of penetrated by Odysseus in underworld, 274; home of near isles of blest, 256n156; homebringing function of as a "bringing back to life", 259; homebringing function of derived from Nestor, 254, 258–60; Homeric audience represented by, 551; interruption of Odysseus's tale in *Odyssey* 11 in relation to, 242, 274; Ionian dodecapolis represented by, 521, 522, 610; Kodrid myth embodied by, 521, 522, 598, 601; names of mostly sea-related, 252n152, 594n179; occurrence of in Argonautic tradition, 256; palace of corresponds to Erechtheus's palace in *Odyssey*, 345; Panionia represented by, 522, 551, 555, 601n190; portrayal of imitated

in *Hymn to Apollo*'s portrayal of Ionians, 554, 629; relation of to Nestor in *nóstos* of Odysseus, 242; stage-managed by Athena in *Odyssey*, 343, 369, 372

Phaedra: occurrence of in catalogue of heroines in *Odyssey* 11, 295

Phaleron: cult of Athena Skiras in, 439, 442n189, 443n189

Pharaia, 750, 754

Pheai: on Telemachus's route from Pylos to Ithaca, 673–75, 678, 680, 681, 686, 702, 714, 716, 721, 755, 756, 757, 766. *See also* Pheia

Pheia: alternate form of Homeric Pheai, 673n50, 716, 716n134, 742n188; interpolated in Nestor's story in *Iliad* 7, 716

Phērai, in Messenia, 658n13, 669n44, 749–51, 755

Pherai/Pharai, in Achaea, 673, 678, 675–81, 686, 702, 714, 754, 757, 766

Phēraia, 754

Pherekydes, 529, 732

phiálē, Greek: gods represented with starting in late sixth century BC, 356, 506

Phlegyai, 711–12

Phobios, 588

Phocaea, 519, 520, 524, 531n39, 537n57, 620

Phrontis, 184, 210

Phrygians, 589

Phrygios, 588, 589

Pieria, 705, 708n119,

Pisatis, 682n61, 719n136, 720, 720n137, 753, 770, 771

Priene, 615, 616n226; cult at
Panionion administered by, 547,
614n219, 618, 622; Kodrid myth
of, 531n39, 549, 618; new city of,
622; site of old city of, 547n85;
war with Samos of, 540. *See also*
Samos and Priene

Procharisteria, 349n15

Prokris: occurrence of in catalogue
of heroines in *Odyssey* 11, 295

Proteus, 178n75

Pylaian/Anthelan Amphictyony, 763

Pylians: survival of in Messenia
until Second Messenian War,
684, 746, 759–60

Pylos: location of at issue in Pythian
Hymn to Apollo, 675–80, 705, 712;
location of in Homeric poems,
657–58, 668–71, 716; location
of in Nestor's story in *Iliad* 11,
657, 746; riddle of three cities so
called, 744, 746, 761–62, 778–79

Pylos, in Elis, 657; location of,
669, 673n51; put forward as
Homeric Pylos before expan-
sion of Nestor's story in *Iliad*
11, 671; put forward as Homeric
Pylos in early textual dispute
in *Odyssey* 15, 671, 673–75, 721,
755; put forward as Homeric
Pylos in Pythian *Hymn to Apollo*,
671, 675–80, 768; referred to
in riddle of three cities called
Pylos, 745, 778; Spartan view of
as Homeric Pylos, 686, 723, 742

Pylos, in Messenia: Ano-Englianos
Bronze Age site of, 657; as
Homeric Pylos, 657, 668, 683,
721, 746, 755; Koryphasion
final location of, 684, 684n65;

located at "old Pylos" before
Koryphasion, 685n65, 745n198,
760–62; successive locations of,
684; 746n201. *See also* Pylians

Pylos, in Triphylia: absorbed by
Lepreon, 658, 660, 721–23,
741, 746n201, 752–53, 771–74;
conflict between Lepreon
and Elis in fifth century in
relation to, 723; considered
Homeric Pylos by Hellenistic
learned minority, 658, 681,
717, 745n201, 755, 779–80; in
Nestor's story in *Iliad* 11, 657,
658–61, 719; location of, 660,
752–53; not referred to in riddle
of three cities called Pylos, 745,
779

R

racecourse: *nóstos* symbolized in,
170

refrain with *ásmenoi* in *Odyssey*, 40,
42; adaptations of in *Odyssey*, 42

restraint. *See* incitement and
restraint

returns (*nóstoi*) of Greeks: fore-
shadowed in funeral games of
Patroclus, 170 (*see also* chariot
race of *Iliad* 23; footrace of *Iliad*
23)

Rhadamanthys, 255, 256n157,

Rhetra, Great, 696–700, 765–66

Rhexenor: corresponds to Nestor's
brother Periklymenos, 251–53,
254, 342n2; name of, 252; occur-
rence of in Phaeacian gene-
alogy, 251, 272, 342n2

Rhianos, 759

Thessaly: many Ionians originated from, 33; Neleids originally from, 32; Neleus born in, 34; Pylos founded from, 32

Théstōr, Greek: meaning of evoked in Homer, 24

Thrasymedes, 586n155, 638

Thriasian plain, 422n151, 432n167, 501

Thryoessa: in Nestor's story in *Iliad* 11, 652, 664n30, 667–68, 777

Thryon: in Catalogue of Ships, 653n3, 664n30, 667–68, 676, 768, 777

Titanomachy: foundation myth of Olympian Games, 406n108

Tityos, 255

tomb: as turning post in chariot race of *Iliad* 23, 138, 162, 171; in central myth of Dioskouroi, 96

Tragana, 684n64

Triptolemos, 431n166

Typhaon, role of in Pythian *Hymn to Apollo*, 690–95

Typhoeus: 692n81

Tyro: corresponds to Periboia in Phaeacian genealogy, 248–51; falls in love with river god Enipeus, 236, 277; Kretheus husband of, 19; makes love with Poseidon, 236, 277; mother of Neleus and Pelias by Poseidon, 19, 236; mother of three sons by Kretheus, 237, 305n214; occurrence of in catalogue of heroines in *Odyssey* 11, 235, 248, 304

Tyrtaeus, 696–702, 764–67

U

Uṣas, Vedic, 62

V

Vedic twins: called "thought-awakening" in *Rig-Veda*, 94; closeness to mortals of, 81, 83; connection with Uṣas of, 62; contrasted with each other in terms of cattle and horses, 65, 84, 87; contrasted with each other in terms of intelligence and war, 63, 67, 84; contrasting affinities of with priests and warriors, 81n183, 98; distinctions between two dual names of in *Rig-Veda*, 62; dual paternity of, 76; epithet *divó nápātā* of, 70, 72; explicit distinctions between in *Rig-Veda*, 62, 84; function of to "bring back to life" and "bring back to the light" designated by name *Nā́satyā*, 61; function of to "bring back to life" as a Bhārgava theme, 97; identical pair in *Rig-Veda*, 62; immortal/mortal contrast in relation to, 76; inclusion of in Soma sacrifice, 80; low status of as doctors, 84n191; morning and evening ritual of, 76; myth of no longer features one twin's salvation of other twin, 83; saviors and healers, 60, 67, 83; solar context of cult of, 62; solar context of rescue myths of, 61; two stages in career of, 81, 83; vaiśya gods, 60n121, 65n141. *See also Aśvínā*, Vedic; *Nā́satyā*, Vedic

Vitruvius, 542, 625

9 780674 032903